PEN(

VANISHED KINGDOMS

'An original and stimulating masterpiece ... an outstanding example of historical writing at its very best' Roger Morgan, *The Times Higher Education*

'This extraordinary book ... reflects the broad interests and humane vision of a scholar of prodigious learning, who believes in history as the key to a better way of thinking and living' Christopher Clark, *The Times Literary Supplement*

'A wonderful book ... There is much that lingers in the mind when this book is put down' Donald Rayfield, *Literary Review*

'All across Europe ghosts will bless him for telling their long-forgotten stories' *Economist*

'A challenging perspective on Europe's past, but also an original way of writing history ... In this brilliant, beautifully written book, Davies recovers those scattered vestiges of dead kingdoms ... *Vanished Kingdoms* is a book about memory and loss' Ben Wilson, *Daily Telegraph*

'The continent's story is turned upside down in this dazzling history ... brilliant ... a lovely eye for detail' Dominic Sandbrook, *Sunday Times*

'Always evocative ... delightfully packed with surprises to startle even the most jaded reader or traveller' Stephen Howe, *Independent*, Books of the Year

'An exuberant literary success ... written with passion and vivacity ... history par excellence' Ronald Hutton, *The Times*

Norman Davies, born in Bolton, Lancashire, is the author of the number one bestseller *Europe: A History* (1996), *Rising '44: the Battle for Warsaw* (2003), *God's Playground: A History of Poland* (1981), *The Isles* (1999) and *Europe at War* (2006). His books have been translated worldwide into a score of languages, including Chinese, Japanese and Russian. A graduate of Magdalen College, Oxford, and the University of Sussex, he worked as a schoolmaster at St Paul's School before spending a quarter of a century at SSEES, University of London, while also holding visiting posts at Columbia, McGill, Stanford, Harvard, Hokkaido, CASS Beijing, ANU Canberra, CNRS Paris, Adelaide and Cambridge. From 1997–2004 he was Supernumerary Fellow of Wolfson College, Oxford; he is now Professor at the Jagiellonian University at Kraków, an Honorary Fellow of St Antony's College, Oxford and a life member of Clare Hall and Peterhouse, Cambridge.

The recipient of numerous honorary degrees and honorary citizenships, Norman Davies was awarded the Grand Cross of Poland's Order of Merit in 1999 and, in Britain in 2001, the CMG; he is a fellow of the British Academy, and lives in Oxford and Kraków. After completing *Vanished Kingdoms* in 2011, he embarked on a round-the-world lecture tour that took in, among other stops, Abu Dhabi, Delhi, Kuala Lumpur, Singapore, Melbourne, Tasmania, New Zealand, Tahiti, California and Texas. He is now preparing a volume of essays and travel sketches.

NORMAN DAVIES

Vanished Kingdoms

The History of Half-Forgotten Europe

PENGUIN BOOKS

PENGUIN BOOKS

Published by the Penguin Group
Penguin Books Ltd, 80 Strand, London WC2R 0RL, England
Penguin Group (USA) Inc., 375 Hudson Street, New York, New York 10014, USA
Penguin Group (Canada), 90 Eglinton Avenue East, Suite 700, Toronto, Ontario, Canada M4P 2Y3
(a division of Pearson Penguin Canada Inc.)
Penguin Ireland, 25 St Stephen's Green, Dublin 2, Ireland (a division of Penguin Books Ltd)
Penguin Group (Australia), 707 Collins Street, Melbourne, Victoria 3008, Australia
(a division of Pearson Australia Group Pty Ltd)
Penguin Books India Pvt Ltd, 11 Community Centre, Panchsheel Park, New Delhi – 110 017, India
Penguin Group (NZ), 67 Apollo Drive, Rosedale, Auckland 0632, New Zealand
(a division of Pearson New Zealand Ltd)
Penguin Books (South Africa) (Pty) Ltd, Block D, Rosebank Office Park,
181 Jan Smuts Avenue, Parktown North, Gauteng 2193, South Africa

Penguin Books Ltd, Registered Offices: 80 Strand, London WC2R 0RL, England

www.penguin.com

First published by Allen Lane 2011
Published in Penguin Books 2012

008

Copyright © Norman Davies, 2011

Typeset by Jouve (UK), Milton Keynes
Printed in England by Clays Ltd, St Ives plc

ISBN: 978-0-141-04886-4

www.greenpenguin.co.uk

I'r anghofiedig

For those whom historians tend to forget

Contents

List of Illustrations   viii

List of Figures   xiv

List of Maps   xv

Introduction   1

1. Tolosa: Sojourn of the Visigoths (AD 418–507)   13
2. Alt Clud: Kingdom of the Rock (Fifth to Twelfth Centuries)   33
3. Burgundia: Five, Six or Seven Kingdoms (c. 411–1795)   85
4. Aragon: A Mediterranean Empire (1137–1714)   151
5. Litva: A Grand Duchy with Kings (1253–1795)   229
6. Byzantion: The Star-lit Golden Bough (330–1453)   309
7. Borussia: Watery Land of the Prusai (1230–1945)   325
8. Sabaudia: The House that Humbert Built (1033–1946)   395
9. Galicia: Kingdom of the Naked and Starving (1773–1918)   439
10. Etruria: French Snake in the Tuscan Grass (1801–1814)   491
11. Rosenau: The Loved and Unwanted Legacy (1826–1918)   539
12. Tsernagora: Kingdom of the Black Mountain (1910–1918)   575
13. Rusyn: The Republic of One Day (15 March 1939)   621
14. Éire: The Unconscionable Tempo of the Crown's
    Retreat since 1916   635
15. CCCP: The Ultimate Vanishing Act (1924–1991)   687

How States Die   729

Notes   740
Acknowledgements   791
Index   793

List of Illustrations

CHAPTER FRONTISPIECES

Road sign near Vouillé (Norman Davies)   14

Dumbarton Rock (Purestock/Getty Images)   34

Hammershus Castle, Bornholm (Christoph Müller)   86

Palace at Perpignan (Norman Davies)   152

Belarusian President Alexander Lukashenko
(AP Photo/Belta, Nikolai Petrov)   230

Bosphorus Bridge (Spectrum Colour Library/HIP/TopFoto)   310

Kaliningrad (STRINGER/AFP/Getty Images)   326

Republic Day Parade, Rome (AP Photo/Pier Paolo Cito)   396

Halych (Roman Zacharij)   440

Duomo in Florence (Roger Antrobus/Getty Images)   492

Schloss Rosenau in Coburg. Chalk lithograph, *c.* 1860, by Hans
A. Williard (1832–1867) (akg-images)   540

The road to Cetinje, Montenegro, 1901
(copyright © ullsteinbild/TopFoto)   576

The Prisoner of Zenda, 1952 (akg-images/album)   622

Irish Free State postage stamp (Royal Philatelic
Society, London)   636

Demonstration in Tallinn, Estonia, 1989
(AP Photo/Pekka Elomaa)   688

PLATES

1. The Burial of Alaric. Woodcut, *c.* 1855, after a drawing by Eduard
   Bendemann (1811–1899) (akg-images)

2. Clovis defeats Alaric III. Chalk lithograph by Nikolai D.
   Dmitrijeff Orenburgsky (1838–1898) after a painting
   by Friedrich Tüshaus (1832–1885), 1875 (akg-images)

3. The Book of Aneirin (National Library of Wales, Cardiff)

4. The Arms of the City of Glasgow (Public Domain)

5. Statue of William Wallace in Aberdeen, Scotland
   (Public Domain)

6. The Rhinegold. Oil painting, 1859, by Peter von Cornelius
   (ullstein bild/AKG Pressebild)

7. Dagobert Solidus (Public Domain)

8. King Gontran of Bourgogne designates his nephew Childebert II
   as his successor, miniature from the 'Chronicles of France', printed
   by A. Verard, Paris, 1493 (hand-coloured print), French School,
   fifteenth century (Biblioteca Nazionale, Turin, Italy/Index/The
   Bridgeman Art Library)

9. Frederick I Barbarossa and his sons King Henry VI and Duke
   Frederick VI. Medieval illumination from the Chronic of the
   Guelphs, 1179–1191 (Hochschul- und Landesbibliothek Fulda,
   Germany)

10. The Duke of Burgundy, Philip the Good, and his son Charles.
    From the Chronicles of Hainault. Rogier van der Weyden
    miniature, 1477 (Royal Library, Brussels)

11. Charles the Bold (1433–77), duke of Burgundy (1467–77),
    from the Rules and Ordinances of the Order of the Golden
    Fleece (vellum) (British Library, London, UK/copyright ©
    British Library Board. All Rights Reserved/The Bridgeman
    Art Library)

12. Mary of Burgundy (1457–1482), oil on wood, attributed to
    Michael Pacher, 1490 (original in a private collection)

13. Aljaferia Palace, Zaragoza (akg/Bildarchiv Monheim)

14. Naples waterfront (detail). Painting, 1465, by Francesco Pagano.
    Galleria Nazionale di Capodimonte, Naples, Italy. (akg-images/
    Erich Lessing)

15. Petronila of Aragon and Count Ramon Berenguer IV of
    Barcelona, oil on canvas 1634 (Prado Museum)

16. Ferdinand the Catholic, king of Aragon, of Sicily, and of Castile-Leon, 1452–1516. Painting, contemporary copy after late-fifteenth-century painting by Michael Sittow (1469–1525). (akg-images/Erich Lessing)

17. Isabella I, Queen of Castile, and Leon, 1451–1504. Painting, c. 1500, after Juan de Flandes, oil on wood (akg-images/Erich Lessing)

18. *The Battle of El Puig* from the St George Altarpiece (copyright © Victoria & Albert Museum, London)

19. 'The Ladder of John Klimakos', icon, twelfth century, paint and gold leaf on panel (Monastery of Saint Catherine, Mount Sinai, Egypt/Ancient Art and Architecture Collection Ltd/The Bridgeman Art Library)

20. Siege of Constantinople, 1453 (original in the Bibliotheque National, Paris)

21. Trakai Castle, Lithuania (akg-images/Volker Kreidler)

22. Mir Castle, Belarus (Alex Zalenko)

23. Barbara Radziwill (1520–51) c. 1553–56 (oil on copper), studio of Lucas Cranach the Younger (1515–86) (copyright © Czartoryski Museum, Cracow, Poland/The Bridgeman Art Library)

24. Lithuanian Statutes (National Library, Warsaw)

25. 'The Polish Plumb Cake', c. 1772 (engraving), John Lodge, (fl. 1782–d. 1796) (private collection/The Bridgeman Art Library)

26. Portrait of Stanislas II Augustus, king of Poland (pastel on paper mounted on canvas), after Marcello Bacciarelli (1731–1818) (copyright © Dulwich Picture Gallery, London, UK/The Bridgeman Art Library)

27. Summer afternoon in a 'Stetl' in Galicia. c. 1900 (ullstein bild/ Imagno)

28. A Hutsul man with horse, Poland (copyright © RIA Novosti/ TopFoto)

29. Górale men, Poland (Tatrzańskiego Parku Narodowego, Poland, with thanks to Mr Zbigniew Ładygin)

30. Lwów scene, c. 1900 (Public Domain)

31. Emperor Joseph II wearing the Order of the Golden Fleece. Oil on canvas, Georg Weickert, eighteenth century (ullstein bild/Imagno)

32. Franz Joseph (1830–1916), Austrian emperor (Mary Evans Picture Library)

33. Curonian Spit, East Prussia, wandering dune and lagoon, 1934 (copyright © ullstein bild/TopFoto)

34. Marienburg, West Prussia. Castle of the Teutonic Order, from the northwest, c. 1930 (akg-images/Paul W. John)

35. Detail from *The Battle of Grunwald* by Jan Matejko, oil on canvas, 1878 (National Museum in Warsaw)

36. Tannenberg Memorial in 1934, on the occasion of the transfer of Field Marshal Paul von Hindenburg's remains to the crypt. (ullstein bild/Imagno)

37. *The Prussian Homage* by Jan Matejko, oil on canvas, 1882 (Wawel Museum, Kraków)

38. Albrecht I von Hohenzollern, duke of Prussia, painting, 1522 (akg-images)

39. Frederick I, King of Prussia (1701–13), colour print, 1890, after a watercolour by Woldemar Friedrich (akg images)

40. Frederick William (1620–1688), the 'Great Elector', after an engraving of 1683 by Antoine Masson (TopFoto.co.uk)

41. Hautecombe monastery on the western shore of Lake Bourget, lithograph (c. 1860?) by A. Cuvillier (akg-images)

42. *Bonneville, Savoy with Mont Blanc*, by J. M. W. Turner (1775–1851) (private collection/photograph copyright © Christie's Images/The Bridgeman Art Library)

43. The citizens of Chambéry vote for annexation, summer 1860 (Mary Evans Picture Library)

44. Victor Emmanuel II of Savoy, king of Italy (copyright © 2006 Alinari/TopFoto)

45. Fiftieth anniversary of the annexation of Savoy to France, illustration, *Le Petit Journal*, 18 September 1910 (colour lithograph) (private collection/Giraudon/The Bridgeman Art Library)

46. Activists in Piazza del Quirinale before the referendum of 2 June 1946 (copyright © 2006 Alinari/TopFoto)

47. Marie Luise of Bourbon with her children. painting, 1807, by Wilhelm Titel (1784–1862) (akg-images/Rabatti/Domingie)

48. Silver florin of the Kingdom of Etruria (private collection)

49. Elisa Baciocchi, grand duchess of Tuscany, and her court, by Pietro Benvenuti, oil on canvas, 1813 (copyright © RMN/Chateau de Versailles)

50. San Miniato in Val d'Arno, Tuscany, Italy (Bruno Morandi/Robert Harding/Getty)

51. Napoleon in exile on Elba before his return to France. Aquatint, c. 1830, with later colouring (akg-images)

52. Victoria and Albert at the time of their wedding, 1840 (Mary Evans Picture Library)

53. Royal group photograph, Coburg, April 1894 (The Royal Collection, copyright © 2011 Her Majesty Queen Elizabeth II)

54. Duke Karl Eduard of Saxe-Coburg-Gotha, 1916 (bpk/Langhammer)

55. Princess Elizabeth and Prince Philip on their wedding day, 20 November 1947 (copyright © 2003 Topham Picturepoint/TopFoto.co.uk)

56. Funeral procession of George V (copyright © 2005 Topham Picturepoint/TopFoto.co.uk)

57. Hitler entering Prague, 17 March 1939 (copyright © 1999 Topham Picturepoint/TopFoto.co.uk)

58. Huszt, 1939 (Topham Picturepoint/TopFoto.co.uk)

59. Black and Tans in Dublin, 1920 (Topham Picturepoint/TopFoto.co.uk)

60. 'The Treaty Makers' (sepia photograph), English photographer (Private Collection/The Stapleton Collection/The Bridgeman Art Library)

61. Women under guard in Dublin, 1921 (copyright © Underwood & Underwood/Corbis)

62. De Valera taking the salute at an IRA parade (Topham Picturepoint/TopFoto.co.uk)

63. King George V and Queen Mary during a visit to Ireland, July 1911 (photograph by Topical Press Agency/Hulton Archive/Getty Images)

64. Participants of the Imperial Conference 1926 seated with King George V (Library and Archives Canada)

65. Queen Elizabeth II makes a speech watched by Irish *taoiseach* Enda Kenny and President Mary McAleese during a State dinner in Dublin Castle, 18 May 2011 in Dublin (photograph by Irish Governmen/Pool/Getty Images)

66, 67, 68, 69, 70. Irish postage stamps (images courtesy of the Royal Philatelic Society; with thanks to Dr Alan Huggins)

71. King Nikola of Montenegro with his family, undated (Mary Evans Picture Library)

72. King Nikola of Montenegro, *c.* 1910 (ullstein bild)

73. King Nikola in exile, France, 1921 (copyright © The Granger Collection)

74. Montenegrin postage stamps (author's collection)

75. Montenegrin postage stamps (British Library, Philatelic Collections: Supplementary Collection – Montenegro)

76. *Kalevipoeg Carrying the Boards*, 1914 (pastel on paper), by OskarKallis (1892–1917) (copyright © Art Museum of Estonia, Tallinn, Estonia/The Bridgeman Art Library)

77. Bronze Soldier monument in the Tallinn military cemetery (akg-images/RIA Nowosti)

78. Linda Monument in front of the Long Herman tower in Tallinn (copyright © RIA Novosti/TopFoto)

79. Red Army soldiers occupying Tallinn, June 1940 (private collection)

80. Volunteers of the Latvian Legion parade in Talinn, 1943 (SV-Bilderdienst)

81. The Baltic Way Protest, August 1989 (ullstein bild/Nowosti)

82. Boris Yeltsin and Mikhail Gorbachev, 1991 (copyright © RIA Novosti/TopFoto)

List of Figures

1. Carolingians and Bosonids   111
2. The Burgundian succession   129
3. Early rulers of Aragon: the House of Ramiro   164
4. The House of Trastámara   208
5. The Jagiellons   257
6. The early Radziwiłłs   263
7. Hohenzollerns and Jagiellons   357
8. The later Hohenzollerns, 1701–1918   371
9. Counts of Savoy   405
10. I Buonaparti: the Bonapartes   502
11. Bourbon – Borbón – Borbone (the Bourbons)   506
12. The Hanovers and the Wettins   550
13. The British Saxe-Coburgs and Gothas   564
14. Petrović and Karadjordjević   591

List of Maps

1 Kingdom of Tolosa, fifth–sixth centuries   19
2 Firth of Clyde   36
3 Northern Britannia, c. AD 410   47
4 The 'Old North', sixth–seventh centuries   50
5 The Viking invasions   67
6 Northern Britain, ninth–tenth centuries   71
7 Bornholm   88
8 The first Burgundian Kingdom (411–437)   92
9 The second Burgundian Kingdom (451–532/4)   95
10 Burgundy within the Frankish realms,
   mid-sixth century   101
11 The legacy of central Lotharingia   105
12 The Duchy of Burgundy, eleventh century   107
13 The Kingdom of Provence, c. 900   109
14 The Three Burgundies, c. AD 1000   113
15 The imperial Kingdom of Arles from 1032   116
16 The modern linguistic region Arpitania   121
17 The disintegration of imperial Burgundy   124
18 The Duchy and County of Burgundy
   in the fourteenth century   130
19 The States of Burgundy, fourteenth–fifteenth centuries   133
20 The Imperial Circles of the Holy Roman Empire   140
21 Pyrenees   157
22 Marches of Charlemagne's Empire, ninth century   163
23 The cradle of the Kingdom of Aragon, 1035–1137   166
24 The Iberian peninsula in 1137   172
25 The heartlands of the Crown of Aragon   178
26 Aragonese Empire   192

27 The two medieval Sicilies   194

28 The Kingdom of Mallorca   198

29 The union of Castile and Aragon, 1479   217

30 Belarus   232

31 The 'Land of the Headwaters'   241

32 The Principalities of Polatsk, *c*. twelfth century   247

33 The Grand Duchy of Lithuania under Mindaugus
    (mid-thirteenth century)   250

34 The Grand Duchy of Lithuania with the other Jagiellonian
    lands, *c*. 1500   261

35 The Polish-Lithuanian Commonwealth from 1572   273

36 The Grand Duchy of Lithuania, 1572–1795   276

37 The Partitions of Poland-Lithuania, 1772–1795   287

38 Western *gubernias* of the Russian Empire in the
    nineteenth century   292

39 Istanbul and the Bosporus   312

40 Contraction of the Byzantine Empire   318

41 Kaliningrad *oblast*   328

42 Borussia – land of the Moravia   337

43 The Teutonic State, 1410   346

44 Royal and Ducal Prussia after 1466   349

45 Brandenburg-Prussia in 1648   360

46 The growth of the Hohenzollern Kingdom, 1701–1795   369

47 The Kingdom of Prussia, 1807–1918   374

48 The Eastern frontline, 1944–1945   384

49 Rome   398

50 Savoy and Piedmont   403

51 The Kingdom of Sardinia, *c*. 1750   410

52 Italy, 1859–1861   422

53 Northern Italy, spring 1860   424

54 West Ukraine   442

55 The Kingdom of Galicia and Lodomeria, *c*. 1900   454

56 Galicia in Austria-Hungary, *c*. 1914   474

57 Florence   494

58 The Kingdom of Etruria, 1801–1807   513

59 Napoleonic Italy, 1810   526

60 Free State of Thüringia and Northern Bavaria   542

61 Saxon mini-states, c. 1900   544

62 Montenegro, 2011   578

63 The tribes of Montenegro, c. 1900   584

64 Montenegro and neighbours, 1911   593

65 Yugoslavia after 1945   615

66 Modern Zakarpattia (Carpatho-Ukraine)   624

67 Czechoslovak Republic, 1920–1938   626

68 The Republic of Carpatho-Ukraine, 1939   627

69 Ireland, 2011   639

70 Northern Ireland in the late twentieth century   670

71 Estonia   690

72 The Baltic States between the wars   707

73 Union of Soviet Socialist Republics, 1945–1991   716

74 Russia's western 'near abroad' after 1991   726

Introduction

All my life, I have been intrigued by the gap between appearances and reality. Things are never quite as they seem. I was born a subject of the British Empire, and as a child, read in my *Children's Encyclopaedia* that 'our empire' was one 'on which the sun never set'. I saw that there was more red on the map than any other colour, and was delighted. Before long, I was watching in disbelief as the imperial sunset blazed across the post-war skies amidst seas of blood and mayhem. Reality, as later revealed, belied outward appearances of unlimited power and permanence.

In my encyclopedia I also read that Mount Everest, at 29,002 feet, was the highest peak in the world and was named after the surveyor general of British India, Col. Sir George Everest. I naturally fell for the unwritten assumption, as I was supposed to, that the pinnacle of the earth was British; and I was duly impressed. It all looked very straightforward. By the time I received my copy of the Coronation Edition of Sir John Hunt's *The Ascent of Everest* as a Christmas present in 1953, of course, India had left the Empire. But I have since learned that Mount Everest had never belonged either to India or to the Empire. Since the King of Nepal did not grant Everest's men permission to enter his country, the mountain had been measured from a very great distance; 29,002 feet was not in consequence its correct height; the mountain's English name was adopted as an act of self-aggrandisement, and its most authentic names are Sagarmatha (in Nepali) and Chomolangma (in Tibetan).[1] Knowledge, I have been forced to admit, is no less fluid than the circumstances in which it is obtained.

As a boy, I was taken on several occasions to Welsh-speaking Wales. Being endowed with a very Welsh name, I immediately felt at home and gained a lasting affinity with the country. On visiting friends in a hill village near Bethesda, also Davieses, I met with people who did not normally speak English, and was given a present of my first English–Welsh dictionary, T. Gwynn Jones's *Geiriadur*;[2] it made me a lifelong collector of foreign languages, though not alas a master of Welsh. Seeing the English castles at Conwy, Harlech and Beaumaris (usually and wrongly called 'Welsh castles'), I sympathized more with the conquered than with the conquerors, and on reading somewhere that the Welsh name for 'England', *Lloegr*, meant 'the Lost Land', I fell for the fancy, imagining what a huge sense of loss and forgetting the name expresses. A learned colleague has since told me that my imagination had outrun the etymology. Yet as someone brought up in English surroundings, I never cease to be amazed that everywhere which we now call 'England' was once not English at all. This amazement underlies much of what is written in *Vanished Kingdoms*. Dover, after all, or the Avon, are pure Welsh names.

As a teenager, singing badly on the back row of the school choir, I was particularly attracted to a piece by Charles Villiers Stanford. For some reason, the stoical words and languorous melody of 'They told me Heraclitus' struck a congenial chord. So I went home and looked him up in my copy of Blakeney's *Smaller Classical Dictionary* and found he was the 'weeping Greek philosopher' from the sixth century BC. It was Heraclitus who said that 'everything is in flux' and 'You can never cross the same river twice'. He was the pioneer of the idea of transience, and he features early in my schoolboy notebook of quotations:

> They told me, Heraclitus, they told me you were dead.
> They brought me bitter news to hear and bitter tears to shed.
> I wept as I remembered how often you and I
> Had tired the sun with talking and sent him down the sky.
>
> And now that thou art lying, my dear old Carian guest,
> A handful of grey ashes, long, long ago at rest,
> Still are thy pleasant voices, thy nightingales, awake,
> For Death, he taketh all away, but them he cannot take.[3]

Heraclitus and his nightingales are not far beneath the surface of my work either.

As a school-leaver, I followed the advice of my history master to spend the summer vacation reading Edward Gibbon's *Decline and Fall of the Roman Empire*, together with his *Autobiography*. Gibbon's subject was, in his own words, 'the greatest perhaps and most awful scene in the history of mankind'.[4] I have never read anything to surpass it. Its magnificent narrative demonstrates that the lifespan even of the mightiest states is finite.

Years later, as a professional historian, I plunged into the history of Central and Eastern Europe. My first assignment as a lecturer at the University of London was to prepare a course of ninety lectures on Polish history. The centrepiece of the course was devoted to the Commonwealth or *Rzeczpospolita* of Poland-Lithuania, which at its conception in 1569 was the largest state in Europe (or at least the master of our continent's largest tract of inhabited lands). Nonetheless, in little more than two decades at the end of the eighteenth century, the Polish-Lithuanian state was destroyed so comprehensively that few people today have even heard of it. And it was not the only casualty. The Republic of Venice was laid low in the same era, as was the Holy Roman Empire.

Throughout most of my academic career, the Soviet Union was the biggest beast in my field of study, and one of the world's two superpowers. It possessed the largest territory in the world, a vast arsenal of nuclear and conventional weapons and an unparalleled array of security services. None of its guns or policemen could save it. One day in 1991 it disappeared from the map of the globe, and it has never been seen since.

Not surprisingly, therefore, when I came to write the history of *The Isles*,[5] I began to wonder if the days of the state in which I was born and live, the United Kingdom, might also be numbered. I decided that they were. My strict, Nonconformist upbringing had taught me to look askance at the trappings of power. My head still rings with the glorious, measured cadences of 'St Clement':

> So be it, Lord; Thy throne shall never,
>   Like earth's proud empires, pass away;
> Thy kingdom stands, and grows for ever,
>   Till all Thy creatures own Thy sway.[6]

To her very great credit, Queen Victoria, Empress of India, asked for this hymn to be sung at her Diamond Jubilee.

Historians and their publishers spend inordinate time and energy retailing the history of everything that they take to be powerful, prominent and impressive. They flood the bookshops, and their readers' minds, with tales of great powers, of great achievements, of great men and women, of victories, heroes and wars – especially the wars which 'we' are supposed to have won – and of the great evils which we opposed. In 2010, 380 books on the Third Reich were published in Great Britain alone.[7] If not 'Might is Right', their motto could well be 'Nothing Succeeds Like Success'.

Historians usually focus their attention on the past of countries that still exist, writing hundreds and thousands of books on British history, French history, German history, Russian history, American history, Chinese history, Indian history, Brazilian history or whatever. Whether consciously or not, they are seeking the roots of the present, thereby putting themselves in danger of reading history backwards. As soon as great powers arise, whether the United States in the twentieth century or China in the twenty-first, the call goes out for offerings on American History or Chinese History, and siren voices sing that today's important countries are also those whose past is most deserving of examination, that a more comprehensive spectrum of historical knowledge can be safely ignored. In this jungle of information about the past, the big beasts invariably win out. Smaller or weaker countries have difficulty in making their voices heard, and dead kingdoms have almost no advocates at all.

Our mental maps are thus inevitably deformed. Our brains can only form a picture from the data that circulates at any given time; and the available data is created by present-day powers, by prevailing fashions and by accepted wisdom. If we continue to neglect other areas of the past, the blank spaces in our minds are reinforced, and we pile more and more knowledge into those compartments of which we are already aware. Partial knowledge becomes ever more partial, and ignorance becomes self-perpetuating.

Matters are not improved by the trend towards ultra-specialization among professionals. The tsunami of information in today's Internet-dominated world is overwhelming; the number of journals to be read and of new sources to be consulted is multiplying geometrically, and many young historians feel compelled to restrict their efforts to tiny periods of time and minute patches of territory. They are drawn into discussing their work in arcane, academic jargon addressed to ever dwindling coteries of their like-minded peers, and the defensive cry goes up on every hand: 'That is not my period.' In consequence, since academic debate – indeed knowledge itself – progresses through newcomers challenging the methods and conclusions of their predecessors, the difficulties for historians of all ages in breaking out into unexplored territory, or of attempting to paint large-scale, inclusive panoramas, are rapidly increasing. With few exceptions – some of them of great value – the professionals stick to the well-worn ruts.

In this regard, I was pleasantly surprised to discover that one of the great names of my youth had spotted the trend long since. My own tutor at Oxford, A. J. P. Taylor, roamed widely and fearlessly over many aspects of British and European history, setting us all a good example.[8] But I did not realize until recently that Taylor's great rival, Hugh Trevor-Roper, had posed the problem in characteristically elegant fashion:

> Today most professional historians 'specialise'. They choose a period, some-times a very brief period, and within that period they strive, in desperate competition with ever-expanding evidence, to know all the facts. Thus armed, they can comfortably shoot down any amateurs who blunder . . . into their heavily fortified field . . . Theirs is a static world. They have a self-contained economy, a Maginot Line and large reserves . . . but they have no philosophy. For historical philosophy is incompatible with such narrow frontiers. It must apply to humanity in any period. To test it, a historian must dare to travel abroad, even in hostile country; to express it he must be ready to write essays on subjects on which he may be ill-equipped to write books.[9]

I wish I had read that earlier. Although Taylor apparently admired Trevor-Roper's *Essays*,[10] he did not recommend them to his students.

The above observations may be worth considering further, if only because mainstream history-making persists in its addiction to great powers, to narratives about the roots of the present and to ultra-specialized topics. The resultant image of life in the past is necessarily deficient. In reality, life is far more complex; it consists of failures, near misses and brave tries as well as triumphs and successes. Mediocrity, ungrasped opportunities and false starts, though unsensational, are commonplace. The panorama of the past is indeed studded with greatness, but it is filled in the main with lesser powers, lesser people, lesser lives and lesser emotions. Most importantly, students of history need to be constantly reminded of the transience of power, for transience is one of the fundamental characteristics both of the human condition and of the political order. Sooner or later, all things come to an end. Sooner or later, the centre cannot hold. All states and nations, however great, bloom for a season and are replaced.

Vanished Kingdoms has been conceived with such sober but not particularly pessimistic truths in mind. Several of the case studies deal with states 'that once were great'. Some deal with realms that did not aspire to greatness. Others describe entities that never had a chance. All come from Europe, and all form a part of that strange jumble of crooked timbers which we call 'European History'.

'Vanished Kingdoms' is a phrase, like 'Lost Worlds', which summons up many images. It recalls intrepid explorers trekking over the heights of the Himalayas or through the depths of the Amazonian jungle; or archaeologists, digging down through long-lost layers in the sites of Mesopotamia or ancient Egypt.[11] The myth of Atlantis is never far away.[12] Readers of the Old Testament are especially familiar with the concept. There were seven biblical kingdoms, we are told, between ancient Egypt and the Euphrates, and dedicated Old Testament scholars have laboured long and hard to establish a framework of dates and sites. Not much can be said with certainty about Ziklag, Edom, Zoboh, Moab, Gilead, Philistia and Geshur.[13] Most information about them consists of fleeting allusions, such as: 'But Absalom fled, and went to Talmai, the son of Ammihud, king of Geshur. And David mourned for his son every day.'[14] Today, after millennia of change and conflict, two of the would-be successor states to those seven kingdoms have been locked for decades in near impasse. One of them, despite overwhelming military power, has not been able to impose true peace; the other, already near-strangled, may never see the light of day.

Of course, human nature dictates that everyone is lulled into thinking that disasters only happen to others. Imperial nations, and ex-imperial nations, are particularly reluctant to recognize how quickly reality moves on. Having lived a charmed life in the mid-twentieth century, and having held out against the odds in our 'Finest Hour', the British risk falling into a state of self-delusion which tells them that their condition is still as fine, that their institutions are above compare, that their country is somehow eternal. The English in particular are blissfully unaware that the disintegration of the United Kingdom began in 1922, and will probably continue; they are less aware of complex identities than are the Welsh, the Scots or the Irish. Hence, if the end does come, it will come as a surprise. Those who seriously believe 'There'll always be an England' are whistling in the dark. And yet it was one of England's most enduring poets, writing his 'Elegy' in the tranquil shade of the churchyard at Stoke Poges, who summed up the certainty facing states and individuals alike. Thomas Gray had the measure of our essential vanity:

> The boast of heraldry, the pomp of power,
>> And all that beauty, all that wealth e'er gave,
> Awaits alike th' inevitable hour:
>> The paths of glory lead but to the grave.[15]

Sooner or later the final blow always falls. Since the defeat of the Greater German Reich in 1945, obituaries have been written for several European states. They include the German Democratic Republic (1990), the Soviet Union (1991), Czechoslovakia (1992) and the Federation of Yugoslavia (2006). There will undoubtedly be more. The difficult question is, who will be next? Judging by its current dysfunctionality, Belgium could become Europe's next Great Auk, or perhaps Italy. It is impossible to say. And no one can forecast with any certainty whether the latest infant to join Europe's family of nations, the Republic of Kosovo, will sink or swim. But anyone imagining that the law of transience does not apply to them is living in *Nephelokokkygia* (a word coined by Aristophanes to make his audience stop and think).

Modern education may have something to answer for here. In the days, not too distant, when all educated Europeans were brought up on a mixture of the Christian Gospels and the ancient classics, everyone was all too familiar with the idea of mortality, for states as well as individuals. Though Christian precepts were widely disregarded, they did teach of a kingdom 'not of this world'. The classics, propagating supposedly universal values, were the product of a revered but dead civilization. The 'Glory that was Greece' and the 'Grandeur that was Rome' had evaporated thousands of years before; they suffered the fate of Carthage and Tyre, but were still alive in people's minds.

Somehow my own education at school and university must have slipped through before the rot set in. At Bolton School I learned Latin, started Greek, and took my turn at the daily Bible readings in the Great Hall; my history and geography teachers, Bill Brown and Harold Porter, both encouraged their sixth form pupils to read books in foreign languages. During my year in France, at Grenoble, I sat in the library ploughing my way through much of Michelet and Lavisse in the hope that something would rub off. At Magdalen College, K. B. McFarlane, A. J. P. Taylor and John Stoye, a matchless trio of tutors, awaited me. In my very first tutorial, McFarlane told me, in a voice as gentle as his cats, 'not to believe everything that you read in books'; Taylor was to tell me later to forget a doctorate and write a book myself, because 'D.Phils are for second-raters'; his politics were puzzling, his pose to his pupils avuncular, his lecturing magnificent and his prose style delicious. Stoye, who was researching the Siege of Vienna at the time, helped push my horizons to the East. As a postgraduate at Sussex, I studied Russian, only to be cured of all pan-Slav illusions by a long spell in Poland. At the Jagiellonian University in Kraków, I found myself in the care of senior historians, like Henryk Batowski and Jozef Gierowski, whose careers were devoted to limiting the inroads of a totalitarian regime, and who as a result had a passionate belief in the existence of historical truth.

Back in Oxford at St Antony's, I sat at the feet of giants such as William Deakin, Max Hayward and Ronald Hingley, who rolled history, politics, literature and hair-raising wartime escapades into one; my supervisor was the late Harry Willetts, Polonist, Russicist and translator of Solzhenitsyn; his speciality seminars took place in the kitchen of his house on Church Walk, where one heard at first hand from his Polish wife, Halina, what deportation to Stalinist Siberia really involved. When I finally found an academic post at the School of Slavonic and Eastern European Studies in London, I stepped into the shadow of Hugh Seton-Watson, a polyglot of immense learning, who never forgot throughout the Cold War that Europe consisted of two halves. Hugh wrote a review of my first book, anonymously as the practice of the *TLS* then was, confessing to it some ten years later. All of us at SSEES were struggling to convey the realities of closed societies to audiences living in an open one; we were all tending slender intellectual flames that were in danger of blowing out. And that was an education in itself.

Today the barbarians have broken into the garden. Most schoolchildren have never met with Homer or Virgil; some receive no religious instruction of any sort; and the teaching of modern languages has almost ground to a halt. History itself has to fight for a reduced place in the curriculum alongside apparently more important subjects such as Economics, or IT, or Sociology or Media Studies. Materialism and consumerism are rife. Young people have to learn in a cocoon filled with false optimism. Unlike their parents and grandparents, they grow up with very little sense of the pitiless passage of time.

The task of the historian, therefore, goes beyond the duty of tending the generalized memory. When a few events in the past are remembered pervasively, to the exclusion of equally deserving subjects, there is a need for determined explorers to stray from the beaten track and to recover some of the less fashionable memory sites. It is akin to the work of the ecologists and environmentalists who care for endangered species, and of those who, by studying the fate of the dodo and the dinosaur, build up a true picture both of our planet's condition and of its prospects. The present exploration of a selection of extinct realms has been pursued with a similar sense of curiosity. The historian who sets out on the trail of The 'Kingdom of the Rock' or The 'Republic of One Day' shares the excitement of people who track down the lairs of the snow leopard or the Siberian tiger. 'I saw pale kings,' the poet recalls, 'and princes too. / Pale warriors, death-pale were they all . . .'[16]

The theme of mankind's hubris, of course, is not new. It is older than the Greeks who invented the word, and who, in the period of their greatness, discovered the statues of the Egyptian pharaohs already half-buried in the desert sands.

> 'My name is Ozymandias, king of kings:
> Look on my works, ye Mighty, and despair!'
> Nothing beside remains. Round the decay
> Of that colossal wreck, boundless and bare
> The lone and level sands stretch far away.[17]

*

From the day of this book's conception I have concentrated on two priorities: to highlight the contrast between times present and times past, and to explore the workings of historical memory. These priorities suggested that each of the studies should have a three-part structure. Part I of every chapter therefore paints a sketch of some European location as it appears today. Part II then tells the narrative of a 'vanished kingdom' that once inhabited the same location. Part III examines the extent to which the vanished kingdom has either been remembered or forgotten; usually it is poorly remembered or half-forgotten, or completely derelict.

I have also been at pains to present vanished kingdoms drawn from as many of the main periods and regions of European history as space would allow. Tolosa, for example, comes from Western Europe, Litva and Galicia from the East. Alt Clud and Éire are based in the British Isles, Borussia in the Baltic, Tsernagora in the Balkans, and Aragon in Iberia and the Mediterranean. The chapter covering the 'Five, Six or Seven Kingdoms' of Burgundia tells a medieval story that straddles modern France and Germany; Sabaudia deals mainly with the early modern period while linking France, Switzerland and Italy; and Rosenau and CCCP are confined to the nineteenth and twentieth centuries.

It goes without saying that the subject of vanished kingdoms cannot be exhausted by the limited collection of examples presented here. The 'history of half-forgotten Europe' is far more extensive than any partial selection can cover. Many earlier candidates have had to be dropped, if only for reasons of space. One such study, 'Kerno', examines King Mark's kingdom in post-Roman Cornwall, and is decorated by reflections on the theme of cultural genocide and excerpts from the work of the Cornish poet Norman Davies. Another study, 'De Grote Appel: A Short-Lived Dutch Colony', sets out the history of New Amsterdam before it was transformed into New York. A third, 'Carnaro: The Regency of the First *duce*', tells the extraordinary story of Gabriele d'Annunzio's take-over in Fiume in 1919 and concludes with his exquisite poem, '*La pioggia nel pineto*', 'Rain in the Pinewood'.

In these endeavours, I have inevitably relied heavily on the work of others. No historian can have a thorough knowledge of all parts and periods of European history, and all good generalists feast heartily on the dishes served up by their specialist confrères. Anyone setting out into unfamiliar territory needs to be armed with maps and guides and the accounts of those who went before. In the early stages of research, I gained enormously from the advice of specialist colleagues such as the late Rees Davies on the Old North, David Abulafia on Aragon, or Michał Giedroyć on Lithuania, and almost every chapter has benefited greatly from expert studies and scholarly consultations. In short, every single section of my little cathedral has been built from the bricks, stones and drawings of someone else.

I have always loved Plato's metaphor of the 'ship of state'. The idea of a great vessel, with its helmsman, crew and complement of passengers, ploughing its way across the oceans of time, is irresistible. So, too, are the many poems which celebrate it:

> *O navis, referent in mare te novi*
> *fluctus! O quid agis? Fortiter occupa*
> *portum! Nonne vides ut*
> *nudum remigio latus . . .*[18]

Or again:

> Thou, too, sail on, O Ship of State!
> Sail on, O Union, strong and great!
> Humanity with all its fears,
> With all the hopes of future years,
> Is hanging breathless on thy fate![19]

These lines from Longfellow were written out by President Roosevelt in his own hand, and sent to Winston Churchill on 20 January 1941. They were accompanied by a note which said, 'I think this verse applies to your people as it does to us.'[20]

The same thoughts come to mind when brains are racked about king-doms that have vanished. For ships of state do not sail on for ever. They sometimes ride the storms, and sometimes founder. On occasion they limp into port to be refitted; on other occasions, damaged beyond repair, they are broken up; or they sink, slipping beneath the surface to a hidden resting place among the barnacles and the fishes.

In this connection, another string of images presents itself, in which the historian becomes a beachcomber and treasure-seeker, a collector of flotsam and jetsam, a raiser of wrecks, a diver of the deep, scouring the seabed to recover what was lost. This book certainly sits comfortably in the category of historical salvage. It garners the traces of ships of state that sank, and it invites the reader, if only on the page, to watch with delight as the stricken galleons straighten their fallen masts, draw up their anchors, fill their sails and reset their course across the ocean swell.

Norman Davies
Peterhouse and St Antony's
April 2011

I

Tolosa

Sojourn of the Visigoths
(AD 418–507)

I

Vouillé, formerly Vouillé-la-Bataille, is a small country *bourg* of some three thousand souls in the French Département de la Vienne, and *chef-lieu* of a rural commune in the region of Poitou-Charente. It lies close to the Route Nationale 149, the old Roman road that runs from Poitiers to Nantes, and it is traversed by a pleasant stream, the Auzance, as it meanders towards the Atlantic. It boasts two churches, two schools, a tiny central square entered through an arch, a large *terrain de pétanques*, some fine riverside gardens, a town hall, a couple of restaurants, a modest stadium, a tall water tower, a listed chateau-hotel, Le Périgny, a Saturday market, and no special celebrity. It is also the presumed site of an early sixth-century battle. A memorial plaque, erected by the local history society in 2007 on the 1,500th anniversary, is so well hidden that the *Office de tourisme* in the square cannot always say exactly where it is.[1]

In one of those delectable adjectival flourishes which the French language adores, the inhabitants of Vouillé rejoice in the name of Vouglaisiens or Vouglaisiennes; they call the surrounding district, popular with ramblers, the Pays Vouglaisien. Not surprisingly, they take great pride in their *patrimoine*, the legacy of their forebears. A statement made in 1972 by the president of the local Syndicat d'Initiative can be found both on the municipal website and on a simple monument erected at the Carrefour de Clovis. '*L'histoire de la France*', it says with no noticeable modesty, '*commença donc a Vouillé*' ('The history of France began at Vouillé').[2]

II

On 24 August 410 Alaric the Visigoth achieved the ultimate goal of the many barbarian chiefs who invaded the crumbling Roman Empire of the West. At the third attempt, he sacked Rome:

> Having surrounded the city and once more reduced the inhabitants to the verge of starvation, he effected an entry at night through the Salarian Gate . . . This time, the king was in no humour to spare the capital of the world. The sack lasted for two or three days. Some respect was shown for churches . . . [but] the palace of Sallust . . . was burned down; and excavations on the Aventine [Hill], then a fashionable aristocratic quarter, have revealed many traces of the fires which destroyed the plundered houses. A rich booty and numerous captives, including the Emperor's sister, Galla Placidia, were taken.
>
> On the third day, Alaric led his triumphant host forth . . . and marched southward . . . His object was to cross over to Africa, probably for the purpose of establishing his people in that rich country . . . But his days were numbered. He died at Consentia [Cosenza] before the end of the year.[3]

Alaric's name meant 'the Ruler of All'.

Alaric's people, known as the Visigoths – in German, the *Westgoten* – had been the first of the Germanic hordes to break into the Roman Empire. Originating in the distant Baltic region but long settled in the abandoned province of Dacia (in modern Romania), they were semi-itinerant agriculturalists who typically stayed for long periods in one fertile vicinity before moving on to the next. They were also converts to the Arian branch of Christianity.* Displaced from their earlier districts of residence, they were seeking a new place to rest. But they never made it to Africa. Instead, being stranded in southern Italy after the sack of Rome, they bargained their way to a new accommodation with the Romans. Their success inspired their Gothic kinsfolk whom they had left far behind in Eastern Europe. Within three generations, their cousins, the Ostro- or 'Eastern' Goths, would follow them on the road to Italy.[4]

The Visigoths were not a tribe, in the usual sense of the word; and there is some doubt whether their name can be etymologically connected with

---

* Arius of Alexandria (d. 336), the principal heresiarch of the fourth century, was condemned by the Church Council of Nicaea for denying the full divinity of Christ and hence the prevailing view on the nature of the Trinity. After Nicaea, his teaching was banned by the imperial authorities.

'the West'. They had been brought together from a variety of ethnic components during Alaric's wanderings, and they only acquired the 'Western' epithet after becoming separated from the main Gothic concentration.

Alaric's exploits broke the spell that held back many of his barbarian counterparts. As a Byzantine commentator had noted, the Empire was not protected by 'rivers, lagoons or parapets, but by fear' – fear being 'an obstacle that no man has surmounted once he is convinced that he is inferior'.[5] Thanks to Alaric, the barbarians lost their sense of inferiority.

The spectacular rites of Alaric's funeral caused comment among the ancients, and have inspired much speculation among modern historians and anthropologists:

> The ferocious character of the barbarians was displayed in the funeral of a hero whose valour ... they celebrated with mournful applause ... they forcibly diverted the course of the Busentinus, a small river that washes the walls of Consentia. The royal sepulchre, adorned with the splendid spoils and trophies of Rome, was constructed in the vacant bed; the waters were then restored to their natural channel; and the secret spot where the remains of Alaric had been deposited was for ever concealed by the inhuman massacre of the prisoners who had been employed to execute the work.[6]

Despite his sensational reputation, however, 'the Ruler of All' achieved none of his long-term objectives. He was the eternal wanderer, who constantly switched his allegiance. In turn he had been Rome's ally, Rome's enemy, Rome's destroyer, a legitimate emperor's protector and a usurper's partner.[7]

In Alaric's time, the Western Empire was inundated by barbarian hordes moving across the Empire's frontiers in many directions. Britannia was succumbing to Picts from the north, to Scots from Hibernia and to Germanic raiders besieging 'the Saxon shore' to the south-east. Roman Gaul had been transfixed by 'the horde of hordes' that crossed the frozen Rhine in the winter of 406/7. War-bands of Vandals, Alans and Suevi were ransacking Gallia Aquitania in the south and spilling over the mountains into Iberia. Further hordes, including the Huns, were lining up to take the Visigoths' route through the Danubian provinces.

Alaric's successor as leader of the Visigoths, therefore, struck a deal with imperial Rome. Ataulf – the 'Noble Wolf' – agreed to leave Italy and to chase his fellow barbarians from Gaul and Spain. His one condition was that he could return to the status of an imperial *foederatus* or 'ally', which Alaric had once enjoyed. As reported by a contemporary, the historian Paulus Orosius, Ataulf's 'Declaration' makes interesting reading:

I once aspired [he said] . . . to obliterate the name of Rome; to erect on its
ruins the dominion of the Goths; and to acquire, like Augustus, the immortal fame of the founder of a new empire. By repeated experiments [however,]
I was gradually convinced that laws are essentially necessary . . . and that
the fierce untractable humour of the Goths was incapable of bearing the
salutary yoke of . . . civil government . . . it is now my sincere wish that the
gratitude of future ages should acknowledge the merit of a stranger, who
employed the sword of the Goths, not to subvert, but to restore and maintain, the prosperity of the Roman empire.[8]

The decade following Alaric's death was filled with violent conflict
not only between the Visigoths and their rivals but also among the leading Visigothic families. Ataulf marched his people from Italy to southern
Gaul and Spain, where they attacked the Vandals, Suevi and Alans. At
the same time, a simmering feud between Alaric's own dynasty and the
rival Amalfings was reignited. Ataulf, who had married the captive
Galla Placidia, was murdered in his palace at Barcelona in 415, together
with their children. So, too, was his immediate successor, Sidericus, 'the
king of five days'. The man who then emerged as leader, a brave warrior
and an astute diplomat called Vallia, is sometimes identified as Alaric's
bastard son. It was Vallia who negotiated the key treaty whereby the
Visigoths reconfirmed their status as imperial allies and received a permanent home in Roman Aquitania.

The 'Kingdom of Tolosa', therefore, started its life as a dependent but
autonomous imperial sub-state. It occupied one of the three parts into
which Gaul had traditionally been divided, and it was ruled by its tribal
chiefs operating under the standard rules of imperial *hospitalitas*. By
decree of the Emperor Honorius, the Visigoths took possession of their
new capital of Palladia Tolosa (the modern Toulouse) in 418. After
Vallia, they were to be ruled for the rest of the century by five kings:
Theodoric I, Thorismund, Theodoric II, Euric and Alaric II. Theodoric I
and Alaric II would both be killed in battle. Thorismund and Theodoric II
were both murdered. Euric, the younger brother of both Thorismund
and of the second Theodoric, brought the kingdom to the peak of its
wealth and power.[9]

The Visigoths took over Aquitania after a long period of disquiet, apparently without provoking serious opposition. The Gallo-Roman nobility,
which had once joined a rebel Gallic Empire, were not noted for their
docility. Yet the new overlords were zealous imitators of Roman ideals,

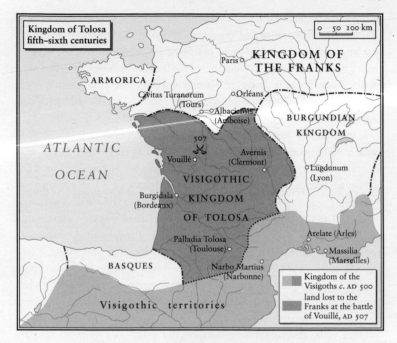

Kingdom of Tolosa
fifth–sixth centuries

0   50   100 km

KINGDOM OF
THE FRANKS

Paris

ARMORICA

Civitas Turanorum
(Tours)

Orléans

Albaciensis
(Amboise)

BURGUNDIAN
KINGDOM

ATLANTIC

OCEAN

507

Vouillé

Avernis
(Clermont)

Lugdunum
(Lyon)

VISIGOTHIC

Burgidala
(Bordeaux)

KINGDOM

OF TOLOSA

Palladia Tolosa
(Toulouse)

Arelate (Arles)

Massilia
(Marseilles)

BASQUES

Narbo Martius
(Narbonne)

Visigothic   territories

Kingdom of the
Visigoths c. AD 500
land lost to the
Franks at the battle
of Vouillé, AD 507

and the smack of strong government went unopposed. The Visigothic kings were given to taking hostages and to punishing disloyal subjects, but they did not indulge in gratuitous violence. Numerous Romans entered their service, notably the military general Nepotanius, the admiral Namatius of Saintes, and Victorius, the *dux super septem civitates*, or 'commander of Septimania'.[10] The Visigoths did not legislate separately for the Gallo-Romans, suggesting a willingness to assimilate; a new system of land tenure did not involve significant confiscations; and in religious matters, the Arian practices of the Visigothic clergy proceeded in parallel to the well-established network of Roman bishoprics and rural churches. The fact that the General Church Council of Agde could take place in Visigothic territory in 506 suggests that the non-Arians had no special fear for their safety.[11]

The Roman city of Tolosa, built on the plain beneath an ancient Celtic hill fort, had been given the epithet Palladia by the Emperor Domitian in honour of the goddess Pallas Athena, patroness of the arts. Surrounded by walls of Augustan vintage, it was fully furnished with aqueducts, theatres, baths and an elaborate sewage system, and it served the strategic Via Aquitania, which ran across southern Gaul from the Mediterranean

to the Atlantic. From the fourth century onwards, it was an active centre
of imperial Christianity and the seat of a bishop. St Saturnin, one of the
first apostles of Gaul, had been martyred in Tolosa in *c.* 257, dragged
through the streets by a wild bull. The basilica where his relics were
guarded was the main focus of Nicene worship. The chief church of the
Arians was at Nostra Domina Daurata, founded in the mid-fifth century on the site of a former temple to Apollo.

Aquitania, in fact, had a long tradition of energetic theological
debate. St Hilarius of Poitiers (*c.* 300–368) was renowned as the *Mal-
leus Arianorum*, an early 'Hammer of the Arians'. St Experius (d. 410),
bishop of Tolosa, is remembered as the recipient of a letter from Pope
Innocent I that fixed the canon of Holy Scripture. The priest Vigilantius
(*fl. c.* 400), in contrast, was regarded as a bold dissident who condemned
the superstitious cult of saints and relics. St Prosper of Aquitania (*c.*
390–455) was a historian, a disciple of St Augustine and the first con-
tinuator of Jerome's Universal Chronicle;[12] and St Rusticus of Narbonne
(d. 461), a champion of what would later emerge as 'Catholicism', battled against both the new Nestorian heresy* and the older Arianism of
his Visigoth masters.

Once Visigothic rule was established, the kingdom expanded dramatically. Acquisitions were made in almost every decade of the fifth century.
The conquest of Narbo Martius (Narbonne) in 436 provided direct
access to the Mediterranean. The whole of Septimania followed later
by gift of the imperial authorities. In the aftermath of the mid-century
irruption of the Huns, the Visigoths roamed far to the north, well
beyond the Loire, and in 470 they surged into central Gaul, incorporating both Civitas Turanorum (Tours) and Arvernis (Clermont). After
that, they took possession of Arelate (Arles) and Massilia (Marseille),
and, during a systematic campaign of conquest in Iberia, reached the
Pillars of Hercules (Gibraltar). From 474, a Roman in the Visigothic
service, Vincentius, ruled as the king's deputy in Iberia with the title of
dux hispaniarum. By the turn of the century, they controlled the largest
of all the states in the post-Roman West, and looked set to become the
principal winner among the Empire's barbarian predators.

Theodoric I, or Theodorid (r. 419–51), was blessed with numerous sons
and daughters, and used them to found an elaborate network of dynastic

---

* Nestorius, Patriarch of Constantinople in 428–31, the principal heresiarch of the fifth
century, was condemned by the Council of Ephesus for holding that Christ's nature was
equally human and divine.

alliances. But he is best remembered both by contemporary chroniclers and by later historians for his valiant part in the repulse of Attila's Huns. He perished as a faithful ally of the imperial general, Flavius Aetius, leading his warriors in June 451 into the bloody fray of the Catalaunian Fields* which preserved Gaul from the most terrible horsemen of the steppes.[13] He was succeeded in turn by three of his sons.

According to Gibbon, Thorismund (r. 451–3) had played the key role in the victory where his father perished, holding his forces in reserve on the nearby heights until he swept down and drove the Huns from the field. The victory brought him little reward. He was murdered by his brother Theodoric before his power could be consolidated, reputedly for threatening to break with the Roman alliance.

Theodoric II (r. 453–66), has enlivened the historical record partly through the colourful name of his wife, Queen Pedauco – meaning 'Goose Foot' – and partly through a rare eyewitness description of him by the Latin writer Sidonius Apollinaris. Sidonius (432–88) was bishop of Arvernis, and hence a subject of the Visigoths. One of his surviving letters answered a request from a friend to describe the king in detail:

Well, he is a man worth knowing . . . He is well set up, in height above the average man, but below the giant. His head is round, with curled hair retreating . . . His nervous neck is free from disfiguring knots. The eyebrows are bushy and arched; when the lids droop, the lashes reach almost half-way down the cheeks. The upper ears are buried under overlying locks, after the fashion of his race. The nose is finely aquiline; the lips are thin and not [unduly] enlarged . . . Every day the hair springing from his nostrils is cut back; . . . and his barber is assiduous in eradicating the rich growth on the lower part of the face. Chin, throat, and neck are full, but not fat, and all of fair complexion . . . they often flush, but from modesty, and not from anger. His shoulders are smooth, the upper- and forearms strong and hard; hands broad, breast prominent; waist receding. The spine dividing the broad expanse of back does not project, and you can see the spring of the ribs; the sides swell with salient muscle, the well-girt flanks are full of vigour. His thighs are like hard horn; the knee-joints firm and masculine; the knees themselves the comeliest and least wrinkled in the world. A full ankle supports the leg, and the foot is small to bear such mighty limbs.

. . . Before daybreak he goes with a very small suite to attend the service of his priests. He prays with assiduity, but . . . one may suspect more of habit than conviction in his piety. Administrative duties . . . take up the rest of

* An unconfirmed site usually located in the vicinity of Châlons-en-Champagne.

the morning. Armed nobles stand about the royal seat; the mass of guards in their garb of skins are ... kept at the threshold ... [F]oreign envoys are introduced. The king hears them out, and says little; ... but accelerates matters ripe for dispatch. The second hour arrives; he rises from the throne to inspect his treasure-chamber or stable.

The bishop, clearly an admirer, warms to the task:

If the chase is the order of the day, he joins it, but never carries his bow at his side, considering this derogatory to royal state. When a bird or beast is marked for him ... he puts his hand behind his back and takes the bow from a page with the string all hanging loose ... He will ask you beforehand what you would like him to transfix; you choose, and he hits. If there is a miss ... your vision will mostly be at fault, and not the archer's skill.

On ordinary days, his table resembles that of a private person. The board does not groan beneath a mass of dull and unpolished silver set on by pant-ing servitors; the weight lies rather in the conversation than in the plate; there is either sensible talk or none. The hangings and draperies ... are sometimes of purple silk, sometimes only of linen; art, not costliness, commends the fare ... Toasts are few ... In short, you will find the elegance of Greece, the good cheer of Gaul, Italian nimbleness ... and everywhere the discipline of a king's house ... The siesta after dinner is ... sometimes intermitted. When inclined for the board-game, he is quick to gather up the dice, examines them with care, shakes the box with expert hand, throws rapidly, humorously apostrophizes them, and patiently waits the issue. Silent at a good throw, he makes merry over a bad [one] ... always the philoso-pher ... Sometimes, though this is rare, supper is enlivened by sallies of mimes, but no guest is ever exposed to the wound of a biting tongue. Withal there is no noise of hydraulic organ, or choir with its conductor intoning a set piece; you will hear no players of lyre or flute, no master of the music, no girls with cithara or tabor; the king cares for no strains but those which no less charm the mind with virtue than the ear with melody. When he rises to withdraw, the treasury watch begins its vigil; armed sentries stand on guard during the first hours of slumber ... I must stay my pen; you asked for nothing more than one or two facts ... and my own aim was to write a letter, not a history. Farewell.[14]

   Theodoric II's reign came to grief through the vagaries of imperial politics. In 455, the newly appointed Roman commander in Gaul, Eparchius Avitus, visited Tolosa. News arrived during his visit that Rome had been sacked for a second time, by the Vandals; and Theodoric seized the opportunity to proclaim Avitus emperor. He then conducted the first of the Visigoths' incursions into Iberia, justifying his conquests as the recovery of imperial land. His claims did not convince the next emperor, Majorian, described by Gibbon as 'a great and heroic character', who briefly reasserted imperial authority in Gaul with energy.

Theodoric's younger brother, Euric (or Evaric or Erwig, r. 466–84), seized power in the midst of military conflicts involving not only Visigoths and imperial forces but also a number of Visigothic factions. He killed his brother, defeated a rampaging Celtic warlord, Riothamus, recrossed the Pyrenees and settled a body of Ostrogothic mercenaries from Roman service in his lands. Lawgiver as well as warrior chief, he turned out to be the most rounded personality of his House. Though familiar with Latin, he usually spoke to foreign envoys in Gothic through an interpreter. The Arian services of his royal chapel were also conducted in Gothic. He extended his realms right across Iberia. The *Codex Euricianus* of 471 was the first attempt in the post-Roman world to commit a summary of customary Germanic laws to writing.[15] It was a sign of political maturity. In 476, Euric persuaded the penultimate emperor of the West, Julius Nepos, to relinquish even nominal Roman suzerainty over the Visigoths' lands. Before he died, the Roman Empire in the West had collapsed completely. The Kingdom of Tolosa was left orphaned and sovereign.

Meticulous scholarship has tracked the progression of Visigothic kingship in the fifth century. In the first stage, the tendency was to emulate all forms of Roman legal practice and Latin titles. In the middle stage, the *Reges Gothorum* saw themselves as something better than mere *foederati*. In the last stage, as successors to the Empire, they thought themselves as good as any emperor. Over the same decades, the upper stratum of Visigothic society, the *optimates*, gradually lost their influence. Germanic tradition had stressed the equality of all warriors. Post-Roman monarchy stressed hierarchy and regal dignity.[16]

Thanks to the Frankish chronicler Gregory of Tours (534–94), Euric has been stained with the label of a persecutor of Catholics. The insinuation is unjust. A few dissaffected clerics like Bishop Quinctianus of Civitas Rutenorum (Rodez) were driven into exile. But nothing occurred to match the savage persecutions perpetrated by the Arian Vandals in North Africa.[17]

Shortly after the deaths both of Euric and of Romulus Augustulus, the last of the Western emperors, Flavius Teodoricus, alias Theodoric the Ostrogoth, accepted Byzantine instructions to march on Italy and to restore imperial fortunes. He crossed the Alps with a huge army in 488, scattered the defenders of the post-Roman order, and killed its leader, Odoacer, with his own bare hands, after a three-year siege of Ravenna. Calling on the aid of his Visigoth cousins, he overran the Italian peninsula from end to end and assumed the title of 'vice-emperor'. Bolstered by the military and cultural power of Byzantium, and by great maritime potential, his Ostrogothic kingdom based at Ravenna soon threatened to overshadow its neighbours and rivals. In addition to the Visigothic Kingdom of Tolosa, it bordered the (second) Kingdom of the Burgundians recently established in the valley of the Rhône (see pp. 94–5).[18]

Euric's son, Alaric II, who succeeded as a boy in 484, was the eighth of the royal line. He spent much energy mollifying neighbours and subjects alike. His greatest achievement lay in the preparation of the famous *Breviarum Alarici*, a highly refined compilation of Roman law. This work, which interpreted laws as well as summarizing them, was approved by a committee of nobles and clerics before being promulgated in 506. It would become a standard text throughout post-Roman Gaul until the eleventh century.[19] Furthermore, Alaric courted the Ostrogoths. He married Theodoric's daughter, and with her produced an infant son, bringing the prospect of a vast and combined pan-Gothic federation into view.

Alaric's nemesis, however, arrived in the shape of Clovis, king of the Germanic Franks, who from the 480s had begun to extend his realm into Gaul from the Rhineland and who was already busy undermining the Burgundians. Clovis was a neophyte Catholic with limitless ambitions, and the ruler most likely to feel threatened by a union of the Goths.[20] In 497 he had joined with the Bretons to mount an attack along the western coast of Aquitaine, where the port of Burdigala (Bordeaux) was briefly occupied. Sometime after that, he won a crushing victory over his eastern neighbours, the Alemanni, and felt free to pay more attention to the south. Alaric's instinct was to avoid confrontation. He had once handed back a Frankish fugitive, Syagrius, who had dared to challenge Clovis. Gregory of Tours reports how the Visigoth insisted on going to Ambaciensis (Amboise), where he engaged Clovis in face-to-face conversation on an island of the River Loire:

> *Igitur Alaricus rex Gothorum cum viderit, Chlodovechum regem gentes assiduae debellare, legatus ad eum dirigit, dicens: 'Si frater meus vellit, insederat animo, ut nos Deo propitio pariter videremus.' . . .*

When Alaric King of the Goths saw the constant conquests which Clovis was making, he sent delegates to him, saying: 'If my brother so agrees, I propose that we hold a conversation together, under God's auspices.' And when Clovis did not reply, Alaric went to meet him regardless, and they talked and ate and drank, and left each other in peace.[21]

As it turned out, Clovis could not be assuaged so easily. Recently allied both to the Burgundians, by marriage, and to the Byzantine emperor, who granted him the title of imperial consul, he aimed to steal a march on his rivals. A joint campaign against the Visigothic realm was agreed. The Byzantines were to patrol the southern coast. The Franks were to march from the north. An offer of parley from Theodoric the Ostrogoth was spurned. It was the spring of 507, and a 'flaming meteor' was lighting up the night sky:

> *Igitur Chlodovechus rex ait suis: 'Valde molestum fero, quod hi Arriani partem teneant Galliarum . . .*

> King Clovis, therefore, addressed his warriors: 'It pains me that these Arians are holding such a large part of the Gauls. Let us march with God's aid, and reduce them to our power . . .' So the army moved off [from Tours] in the direction of Poitiers . . . Reaching the River Vigenna [Vienne], which was swollen by rain, the Franks did not know how to cross until a huge hind appeared and showed them how the river could be forded . . . Pitching his tent on a hill near Poitiers, the king saw smoke rising from the Church of St Hilaire, and took it as a sign that he was to triumph over the heretics.

The scene for the fateful battle was set:

> So Clovis came to grips with Alaric, King of the Goths, in the plain of Vouillé [*in campo Vogladense*], three leagues from the city. As was their custom, the Goths feigned flight. But Clovis killed Alaric with his own hand, himself escaping [an ambush] thanks to the strength of his breastplate and the speed of his horse.[22]

The outcome, therefore, was undisputable (and the Vouglaisiens have proof positive of their name's derivation). The power of the Visigoths in Gaul was broken in a few hours. And the Franks pressed on. Some of them rode over the central mountains to garner lands as far as the Burgundian frontier. Clovis made for Burdigala, where he wintered before sacking Tolosa the following spring. A remnant of Alaric's forces made a stand at Narbonne, but most of them withdrew to the line of the Pyrenees. The Gallic heartland of their kingdom was abandoned.

Henceforth, the Visigoths would rule in Iberia alone, preserving their ascendancy there until the arrival of the Moors two centuries later.

Explanations of the Frankish victory differ widely. The victors' version conveyed by Gregory of Tours stressed the hand of a Catholic God who had aided his Catholic warriors. Even Edward Gibbon stressed the role of religion, imaginatively casting the Gallo-Roman nobility in the role of a Catholic fifth column. His arguments are now contested.[23] He is on safer ground when he writes of the fickle fortunes of war. 'Such is the empire of Fortune (if we may still disguise our ignorance under that popular name)', wrote Gibbon loftily, 'that it is almost equally difficult to foresee the events of war, or to explain their various consequences.'[24]

For a decade or more, Theodoric the Ostrogoth continued to pursue his pan-Gothic dreams. He was the designated guardian of his grandson, Alaric II's young heir, Amalric, and the nominal overlord of a supposedly nascent 'empire' stretching from the Alps to the Atlantic. Yet the pillars of his own power were crumbling. He could not maintain order in Italy, let alone challenge the Franks in Gaul or assist the Visigoths in Spain. The moment was ripe for the Roman emperors in Constantinople to launch yet another strategic offensive. Shortly after Theodoric died in 526, the Emperor Justinian prepared to lead his legions to the West in person.[25] For the rest of the sixth century, as Alaric's descendants consolidated their hold on Iberia, imperial troops remained in Italy, while the successors of Clovis the Frank put their shoulder to the long task of transforming Gallia into Francia, and Francia into France.

III

Though the Visigothic Kingdom of Tolosa lasted for eighty-nine years over a wide area, the physical evidence for its existence is minimal. Archaeological excavations have yielded almost nothing.[26] Although one gold *solidus* of Alaric II has survived, most coins from Visigothic Tolosa carry imperial inscriptions. Several hundred marble sarcophagi from the period bear no marks of identification. Almost everything that is known comes from fragmentary written sources. Even the site of the battle with Clovis is not entirely certain. One group of antiquarians equates Gregory's *campus Vogladensis* with Vouillé, another group insists on locating it at the nearby village of Voulon.[27] There is almost no mention of the Visigoths in the widespread 'Heritage' activities of

Toulouse and Aquitaine.[28] Only recently has a comprehensive bibliography been compiled to help scholars piece the jigsaw together.[29]

The church of Nostra Domina Daurata – Notre-Dame de la Daurade – whose origins were connected with the Visigoths, was totally demolished in 1761 to make way for the construction of Toulouse's riverside quays. It had housed the shrine of a Black Madonna. The original icon was stolen in the fifteenth century, and its first replacement was burned by revolutionaries in 1799. Prints survive of an early medieval octagonal chapel lined with marble columns and golden mosaics. The present-day basilica, like the cathedral of St Saturnin, is entirely modern.[30]

Fortunately, the maps and the museums are not totally bare. A cluster of place names featuring the suffix -ens, as in Douzens, Pezens and Sauzens, all in the Département de l'Aude, is judged to betray Visigothic origins. The village of Dieupentale (Tarn-et-Garonne) possesses the only name of exclusively Visigothic provenance: diup meaning 'deep', and dal, 'valley'. Certain modest types of bronzes, eagle brooches and glassware are classed in the same way, thanks to similarities with finds in Rome's former Danubian provinces. And on the road between Narbonne and Carcassonne one passes the imposing whale-back Montagne d'Alaric. Local sources explain its name by reference to fortifications dating to the reign of Ataulf, and to a persistent myth concerning the last king of Tolosa's last resting place. The mountain shelters the ruins of a medieval priory, St Pierre d'Alaric and, on its northern slopes, a registered wine region which produces vintage wines within the scope of AOC Corbières.[31]

Nowadays, some of the strongest hints of a Visigothic past in southern France emanate unexpectedly from wild legends, from historical fiction, and in particular from one small village deep in the Pyrenean foothills. Rennes-le-Château is a walled, hilltop hamlet in the Pays de Razès, containing perhaps twenty houses, a church and a medieval castle. It commands enchanting views over the Val des Couleurs, and stands beneath the 'Holy Mountain' of Bugarach, starting point of Jules Verne's *Journey to the Centre of the Earth*. Identified as the ancient city of Rhedae, it gained a reputation in the nineteenth century for having been the impregnable stronghold of the Visigoths after their expulsion from none-too-distant Tolosa. The stone pillars of the parish church were said to be of Visigothic origin, and fabulous rumours of buried treasure proliferated.[32]

In 1885, the parish was taken over by an extraordinary, not to say notorious vicar, Father Bérenger Saunière (1852–1917). Together with his neighbour and colleague, the Abbé Boudet of nearby Rennes-les-Bains, author of a bizarre volume on ancient Celtic languages,[33] Father Saunière dabbled both in history and in the occult. When renovating his church, he claimed to have discovered three parchments hidden inside a Visigothic pillar and covered in coded messages. Soon afterwards, he showed signs of ostentatious and unexplained wealth; the splendid villa and fake medieval folly which he built are still in place. When he was dying, his deathbed confession so shocked his confessor that the vicar was denied the last rites. His favourite motto, reportedly, was a quotation from Balzac: '*Il y a deux histoires: l'histoire officielle, menteuse, et l'histoire secrète, où sont les véritables causes des événements*' ('There are two sorts of history: lying official history and secret history, where the true causes of events can be found').[34]

To be fair, the Visigoths form only one of many elements in the fantastical pot-pourri of stories that have circulated since Father Saunière's death. They have been resurrected in the company of Cathars, Templars, Rosicrucians, the shadowy Priory of Sion, and the Holy Grail itself. Dan Brown's *The Da Vinci Code* is but one of a dozen books that feed off the mysterious tales.[35] According to taste, the secret Treasure of Rhedae is variously described as the 'Jewels of the Visigoths' carried off from Rome or from Tolosa, or the 'Hoard of Jerusalem', brought by the Visigoths from Byzantium. The link with the so-called 'bloodline of Christ' hangs on yet more far-fetched suppositions, namely that St Mary Magdalene travelled to southern Gaul and that her descendants married into local Visigothic families.

Nonetheless, despite the efforts of the Vouglaisiens and the Rennains – not to be confused with the Rennois of Rennes-les-Bains – the modern French nation has never really warmed to the Visigoths. Their trail is far stronger in Spain than in the country where their statehood began. This is only to be expected. After the retreat from Aquitania, the Visigoths established themselves as the dominant element in Iberia. Their second realm, the Kingdom of Toledo, lasted twice as long as the Kingdom of Tolosa, and has penetrated deeply into modern Spanish consciousness.[36] The Visigothic kings, including the monarchs of Tolosa, are honoured by statues in Madrid,* but not in Toulouse.

Some imaginative method needs to be devised, therefore, for reclaiming the lost Visigothic culture of the Aquitanian era. It might be possible, for example, to work backwards from the known realia of Visigothic Spain. After all, the religious and artistic practices which the Visigoths

---

* Next to the Royal Palace in the Plaze de Oriente.

would have taken with them from Aquitania were dominant in parts of Iberia until the late sixth century; the Gothic speech, which Sidonius heard in Tolosa, held its own in Toledo until the seventh century; and the Visigoths' political culture as first defined by Euric continued to evolve until the eighth century. Of course, great care is needed. Not everything that bears the Visigothic label, like Visigothic Chant or Visigothic Script, derives from the Visigoths. And the Iberian cultural soil into which Visigothic customs were transplanted, though similarly Romanized, was not identical to that of Gallia Aquitania.

Even so, there are several leads to work on. In ecclesiastical architecture, the exquisite simplicity of the Visigothic church of San Pedro de la Nava at Zamora could well have had parallels in post-Roman Gaul. Its surviving horseshoe arches and tunnel vaulting were clearly inspired by something that went before it. The symbolism and style of Visigothic sacred art has Byzantine roots and would also have passed through Tolosa. The influence of Gothic language on the indigenous population, though limited, would have been much the same on both sides of the Pyrenees. Words such as *suppa* (soup) or *bank* (bench) belong to the long list of Germanisms adopted by the neo-Latin idioms.[37] And, since prayers learned in childhood are the ones remembered longest, we can plausibly assume that the Gothic form of the Lord's Prayer, as recited at every stage of the Visigoths' journey from the Danube to the Douro, was also recited devoutly at Nostra Domina Daurata:

Atta unsar þu in himinam	Our Father, Thou in Heaven
weihnai namo þein	Holy be Thy name.
qimai þiudinassus þeins	Thy kingdom come
wairþai wilja þeins	Thy will be done,
swe in himina jah ana airþai.	As in Heaven so on earth.
Hlaif unsarana þana sinteinan gif uns himma daga	Give us this day our daily loaf
jah aflet uns þatei skulans sijaima	And forgive us who are in debt
swaswe jah weis afletam þaim skulam unsaraim	As we also forgive our debtors.
jah ni briggais uns in fraistubnjai	Bring us not into temptation
ak lausei uns af þamma ubilin	But free us from the evil one.
Unte þeina ist þiudangardi jah mahts	For thine is the kingdom and might
jah wulþus in aiwins.	And glory in eternity.[38]

*

The fate of the Kingdom of Tolosa naturally prompts reflections about 'alternative history'. What would have happened if Clovis had been defeated, and the Visigoths had won? It was quite possible for them to have done so. The alternative *was* a possibility, and it opens up vistas of an unrealized future. On the eve of the Battle of Vouillé, the Franks controlled perhaps one-third of post-Roman Gaul. The Visigoths, Arian Christians, were becoming overlords of Iberia as well as southern Gaul, and were linked to the Ostrogoths in Italy. The bishop of Rome enjoyed no special position among the five patriarchs of Christendom, and by far the larger part of Europe remained pagan. Had Alaric II fought off Clovis, it is entirely realistic to envisage Western Europe dominated by a pan-Gothic hegemony, while a diminished Roman Church retreated before the double advance of Arianism and Byzantine Orthodoxy. In which case, France may never have come into being, or may have developed somewhere else or in a different way. The future power of the papacy, which the Franks were destined to promote, may not have come about. Nothing is inevitable. Nothing is perfectly predictable.

Yet the endless alternative scenarios, which exist at every stage of history, do not warrant too much attention. The past is not a board game that can be played and replayed at will. What happened happened. What didn't, didn't. Clovis the Frank *did* kill Alaric the Visigoth. The Franks drove out the Visigoths, and not vice versa. It is not unreasonable to maintain, therefore, that 'The history of France began at Vouillé'.

The story of the 'post-Roman twilight' is complicated enough as it is. Historians have to take account of the sheer diversity of the 'barbarians', and hence of the richly polycultural and multi-ethnic flavour of their intermingling with settled populations. Numerous unexpected twists and turns occurred in their interactions. Above all, the timescale was enormous. The gap between the collapse of the Western Empire in 476 and the emergence of recognizable modern states like France or England spans five hundred years at least. The post-Roman twilight lasted twice as long as the Western Empire itself.

In this respect, the example of the Visigoths serves as a case study for 'Barbarian Europe' as a whole. Their sojourn in Aquitania was but one stop on a very long road. Like their cousins, the Ostrogoths and the Lombards, and their sometime neighbours the Burgundians, they belonged to an ethnic and linguistic sub-group which has totally died out. Their customs and speech were not close to Frankish, which was the progenitor of modern Dutch and Flemish and which provided the catalyst for transforming Gallo-Roman Latin into Old French. It is unlikely that Alaric II could have conversed with Clovis at Amboise without resorting either to Latin or to an interpreter. What is more, the Visigoths encountered many other 'barbarians' on the road, no doubt 'contaminating' their language, their culture and their gene pool in the process. Among them, the Vandals were East Germanic, the Suevi or 'Swabians' were Central Germanic, the Huns were Turkic, and the Alans were Iranic (like the modern Ossetians).[39]

Popular memory-making plays many tricks. One of them may be called 'the foreshortening of time'. Peering back into the past, contemporary Europeans see modern history in the foreground, medieval history in the middle distance, and the post-Roman twilight as a faint strip along the far horizon. Figures like Alaric or Clovis remain distant, faceless specks, unless plucked from their historical setting, magnified, dressed up and lionized for reasons of latter-day politics or national pride. Clovis I, king of the Franks, the victor of Vouillé, is commemorated by a magnificent tomb in the Parisian abbey of St Denis. Alaric II, whom Clovis killed, had ruled over a larger realm than that of the Franks. Yet he has no known grave, no modern monument.

Historical memory spurns even-handedness. The Visigoths must have known it. In their wisdom, they had buried their leaders in a traditional way which honoured the dead but which left no trace. The sepulchre of Alaric I, 'the Ruler of All', was washed into the sands of the sea long before his successors founded the Kingdom of Tolosa. No one but an occasional German Romantic cares to recall the moment:

> *Nächtlich am Busento lispeln*
> *Bei Cosenza dumpfe Lieder.*
> *Aus den Wassern schallt es Antwort*
> *Und in Wirbeln klingt es wieder.*

('Mournful songs whisper in the night / near Cosenza, along Busento's banks. / The waters murmur their answer, / and the whirlpools resound with singing.')[40]

2

Alt Clud

Kingdom of the Rock
(Fifth to Twelfth Centuries)

Dumbarton Rock is not one of Britain's premier historical sites. It does not figure in Britain's top fifty places to visit. It is not classed in the same league as Stonehenge or Hampton Court, or its more famous Scottish neighbours, Stirling and Edinburgh. If people know it at all, they rate it as little more than a striking local landmark.

Yet modest Dumbarton is one of those special places that have the power to conjure up the stark contrast between what is and what once was. The past is not only a foreign country that we half knew existed; it is hiding another concealed country behind it, and behind that one, another, and another – like a set of Russian *matryoshki*, in which larger dolls conceal smaller. Certainly, the surface is not a reliable guide to what lies underneath. In this case, the surface exhibits a country which we know as Scotland. Another country called England lies beyond the Borders. But Dumbarton beckons us to a world that flourished before England or Scotland had been invented.

Geologically, Dumbarton Rock is just a volcanic plug, the residual core of a prehistoric volcano whose outer cone has been washed away by erosion over aeons. Ever since the last Ice Age, it has protruded through the floodplain on the north bank of the Firth of Clyde at the point where the River Leven flows down from the Highlands. Strategically, it has had immense importance. For centuries it dominated the traffic on the Firth, guarding the gateway to the country's heartland. It deterred the invaders and intruders who sought to sail upriver from the Irish Sea, and it sheltered all those who awaited a fair wind or an ebb tide to take them downstream to the ocean. To the south, on the opposite bank, lie Paisley, Greenock and Gourock, the first of which is the site of a magnificent medieval abbey. To the east sprawls industrial Clydebank, and beyond that the great city of Glasgow. The Kilpatrick Hills and the 'Bonnie,

bonnie banks of Loch Lomond' rise to the north. To the west, as the
Firth broadens out into an imposing estuary, islands great and small
come into view, Bute, Arran and Ailsa Craig, and in the far haze the desolate Mull of Kintyre. Nothing, one might believe, could be more Scottish.

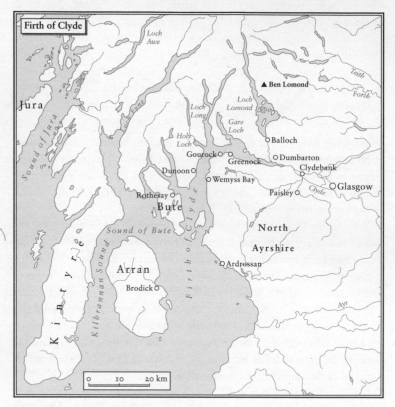

The position of Dumbarton Rock can be best appreciated from the
air as one lands at Glasgow Airport. The main flight path brings planes
in from the north, over the green and bracken-coloured braes towards
the point on the Clyde where the narrow stream ends and the Firth
begins. Looking from the right-hand window of the plane, one passes
close to the modern Clyde suspension bridge, and enjoys a grandstand
view of the shimmering waters beyond. The view is particularly dramatic on a fine summer's evening. The red glow of the sunset outlines
the distant lochs and islands. The broad expanse of the Firth shines silver, and the twin peaks of the Rock stand out against the light like a pair
of Egyptian pyramids.[1]

The Firth of Clyde is tidal. Like all the inlets and estuaries on Britain's western coasts, it is subjected to four tides in every twenty-six hours – two flood tides and two ebb tides, whose perpetual motions have not stopped since the ocean first invaded this part of Europe. An Iron Age fort once stood atop the Rock; over the millennia, sentinels have watched the processions of coracles, boats and battleships that have sailed in on the rising tide or sailed out on the ebb. In late Roman times, they would have warned of the approach of the Hibernian pirates, whom the Romans called *Scotti*.* In the ninth century they would have gasped in awe at the fearsome fleets of Viking longships. In more recent times, they would have seen the troopships and merchantmen that formed the sinews of the British Empire, and the stately Cunard liners steaming out to the Atlantic.

Not surprisingly, the town under the shadow of the Rock lived for much of its career from ship-building. The shipyard at Dumbarton was itself too small to accommodate the great ocean liners that were built at nearby Clydebank; instead, it specialized in the smaller steamships and paddleboats that have plied their trade on the Clyde for the last 200 years. Indeed, steaming 'doon the watter' from Glasgow has long been one of the most characteristic activities of the area.[2] Europe's very first commercial steamship service started up here in 1812, when the *Comet* sailed from Glasgow to Greenock. In the following decades the service was extended not only to every harbour on the Firth, but to ports as far as Oban and Stornoway. The red, white and black-tipped funnels of the steamers, mailboats and ferries of David MacBrayne's company later established a ubiquitous presence that attracted millions of trippers and travellers. The successor company of Caledonian-MacBrayne, or 'Cal-Mac', still forms an essential element of the local scene.[3] The saying persists: 'The Earth is the Lord's and all that therein is, but the Highlands and Islands belong to MacBrayne.'

Industrial development also spread up the Vale of Leven along the five riverside miles separating Dumbarton from Balloch on Loch Lomond. Dye-works, print shops and foundries were concentrated in the factories of Alexandria, Jamestown and Bonhill. Workers from the Vale of

---

* The Romans gave this name to a branch of the Gaelic-speaking people of north-eastern Ireland who raided Britannia in the late fourth century and who later settled on both sides of the North Channel. The application of the 'Scots' label, however, expanded dramatically. Originally pertaining to the Gaels from Ireland who moved to Argyll, it was later used to refer to the ninth-century kingdom created by the fusion of Gaels and Picts, and eventually to all subjects of the Kingdom of Scotland irrespective of their linguistic or ethnic origin.

Leven were known in Dumbarton as 'jeelies', because they ate their jeelies or 'jam sandwiches' in the yard while the locals went home for lunch.

There is no better way of finding one's historical and geographical bearings than by taking a steamer trip across the Firth. Even a short crossing
from Wemyss Bay to Rothesay on the Isle of Bute, or from Ardrossan to
Brodick on Arran, proves immensely stimulating, for in little more than
half an hour it takes passengers across Scotland's most important divide,
between the Lowlands and the Highlands. Wemyss Bay, in Ayrshire, 30
miles west of Glasgow, belongs to the Lallans* homeland of Robbie Burns.
Rothesay and the Isle of Bute belong to the Gaeltacht – the land of the
clans, the tartans and the Gaelic tongue. The journey should be undertaken on one of the 'bracing' days for which the Firth is famous. A stiff
breeze chops the water, blowing spray off the tips of the waves. The sturdy
ferryboat bucks and rolls confidently amid the raucous cries of the seagulls
and the pungent smell of seaweed. Charcoal-grey clouds scud overhead,
moving too fast to drop their charge of rain; patches of blue sky release
narrow torrents of sunlight that play here and there on the seawater and
on the luminous green of the opposite shore. The white bow waves dance
with the white sails of the yachts as they speed along. Holding fast to the
rail, cheeks chafed and lungs filled to overflowing, one watches transfixed
at the display of colour and movement. A rainbow glistens over the Kyles
of Bute. Then a sudden calm descends as the ferry enters the lee of the harbour, and one steps ashore, duly braced, in a different country.

This is the landscape for ever associated with the name of the Harry
Lauder (1870–1950), one of the most famous entertainers of the early
twentieth century, and reputedly the first star singer to sell a million
records. Lauder sang popular sentimental songs in a broad Scots brogue,
shattering all class barriers by his unique mixture of stoicism and tenderness. Numbers like 'I love a lassie, a bonnie Hielan' lassie' or 'Keep
right on to the end of the road' brought him a fortune from which he
built his mansion at Laudervale near Dunoon. His many tours to the
United States would invariably start with a steamer trip up the Firth
from Dunoon to the Princes Pier in Greenock.

> Roamin' in the gloamin' on the bonnie banks of Clyde,
> Roamin' in the gloamin' wi' ma lassie by ma side.
> When the sun has gone to rest, that's the time that I like best.
> O it's lovely to be roamin' in the gloamin'.[4]

*Lallans is the local name for the language of 'Lowland Scots' as spoken in the southern
part of Scotland.

A visit to Dumbarton Castle tells some of the older stories. It features in all the local guidebooks and websites:

> Dumbarton Rock stands above the River Leven where it merges with the Clyde and is the town's most famous ancient building. The castle, which stands 240 feet up on the Rock ... forms a prominent landmark on the Clyde. The Rock ... has been fortified since prehistoric times. The castle was a royal fortress long before the town became a Royal Burgh; its ownership [passed] from Scottish to English and back again. Prominent during the Wars of Independence, it was used to imprison Wallace for a short time after his capture. It was from here, too, that Mary, Queen of Scots, was conveyed to France for safety. She was trying to reach Dumbarton Castle when she suffered her final defeat at Langside.[5]

William Wallace, the 'Braveheart', and Mary Stuart are two names from Scottish history that are almost universally recognized.

On closer inspection, the twin peaks of the Rock's summit are divided by a deep chasm: at 240 feet, 'White Tower Crag' is slightly higher than the 'Beak'. The oldest surviving structure is a fourteenth-century stone arch, whence a stairway of 308 steps leads up to the top. At the bottom, the eighteenth-century Governor's House contains a small museum. Here, one learns from the pleasant young guide that the early English historian Bede wrote about a fortified city called 'Alcluith', the 'rock of the Clyde'; also that, together with Castle Dundonald in Ayrshire, Dumbarton was once the chief royal stronghold of the Kingdom of Strathclyde. 'We were invaded in 870 by the Vikings,' the guide informs us. On being asked who 'we' are, she says with a smile, 'I'm a local girl, I'm a Pict.'

The view from White Tower Crag rewards its climbers. The modern town lies immediately below, criss-crossed by ant-like people. Central Glasgow, half a dozen miles away, is veiled in mist. But the moisture-laden air to the west increases the visibility like a magnifying glass. The Firth presents itself as a giant outstretched hand, with its fingers pointing into Gareloch and Loch Long on the right, Holy Loch in the centre, and the hills of Arran and Argyll on the horizon. In the distance to the north rise the blue-grey peaks of Ben Lomond and Ben Oss. Across the river lie the pine-clad slopes of Glennifer Braes in Renfrewshire and the Hill of Stake; and in the left foreground the airport runways.

Holy Loch is a name that frequently made the headlines in the 1960s and 1970s. It is the smallest of the sea-lochs on the Firth, only two or three miles long, but it makes a perfect, sheltered harbour. For more than thirty years it was the site of a United States Navy submarine base, and the scene of concomitant demonstrations by the Campaign for Nuclear Disarmament. Officially and euphemistically labelled as Refit Site One, the base housed the SUBRON-14 submarine fleet charged with patrolling the Atlantic. There was a floating dock, a large tender ship, a flotilla of tugs and barges, and up to ten Polaris/Poseidon Class Ballistic Missile submarines. As the underwater behemoths slipped from their dock and rode into the Firth, the captain's periscope would have caught sight of the Rock some 20 miles upstream. These days the harbour is back with the Royal Navy, though one wonders for how long. The devolved government of Scotland is controlled by the Scottish Nationalist Party. If they ever win their proposed referendum for full independence, one of their first steps would be to demand the closure of the base.[6]

Dumbarton today is struggling to survive in the post-industrial age. The heyday of its ship-building came to an end in the 1960s and it has not yet found an adequate replacement. The dockside has been concreted over to form a car park, and supermarkets fill the space once used by giant warehouses. In some guidebooks to Scotland, the town is not even mentioned. Industrial decline hit the Vale of Leven earlier. Many factories there were closed down before 1939. Persistent unemployment bred radical politics, and the epithet of 'Little Moscow' was coined to match that of adjacent 'Red Clydeside'. In the 1950s the run-down district was used to locate several of Glasgow's largest projects of overspill housing. Forty and fifty years on, the massive, dilapidated estates such as the Mill of Haldane in East Balloch were the scene of equally massive campaigns of attempted urban renewal.

Yet a positive development began when one of Scotland's leading whisky distillers moved into Dumbarton to employ the laid-off dockers. 'George Ballantine's Finest' is one of the most popular and best-known brands of blended whisky in the world. Every bottle bears the proud assignations: 'Scotch Whisky, Fully Matured, Finest Quality', 'George Ballantyne & Sons, Founded in 1827 in Scotland' and 'By Appointment to the Late Queen Victoria and the Late King Edward VII'. According to the country of its destination it also carries a marker saying, 'Finest Skotská Whisky', or 'Whisky Szkocka 40%obj.' or 'Finest Skót Whisky ... Származasi Ország: Nagy Britannia (Skocia)'. At the bottom, the label reads 'Bottled in Scotland', 'Product of Scotland' and 'Allied Distillers Limited, Dumbarton G82 2SS'.[7] In whatever language, there can be no doubt: this is Scottish Scotch from Scotland.

In the early twenty-first century Dumbarton is indeed in Scotland,

and Scotland is part of the United Kingdom. But it was not always so, and it may not always be so in the future. One needs only stand atop the Rock and count the centuries. A hundred years ago, Clydeside was the lifeline of an imperial conurbation which served the Empire's manufacturing enterprises. Two hundred years ago, it was the centre of a region of the United Kingdom, often known as 'North Britain', whose Scottishness was fading, but whose Britishness was rising. Three hundred years ago it had just crossed the threshold of an unprecedented constitutional union with England. Four hundred years ago it was ruled by a king who had recently migrated to London, but who remained Scotland's sovereign. Five hundred years ago, before the Battle of Flodden, it was part of a country which regarded itself as England's equal. A thousand years ago, under King Macbeth and others, it belonged to a realm where Gaelic was still the dominant language. One thousand five hundred years ago it belonged to the 'Old North'.

Dumbarton is an English name, the Anglicized form of a Gaelic predecessor, *Dun Breteann*, meaning 'Fort of the Britons'. This, in turn, provides the clue to the people who lived on the Clyde long before the Anglophones and the Gaels arrived. Oddly enough, when the modern County Council was formed in 1889, the older spelling of the name was revived to give 'Dunbartonshire' a tinge of authenticity. (The county was abolished in 1975, since when it has been joined to the wider Strathclyde Region.)

Nonetheless, the form of the name most frequently associated with the Rock has gone round the world, carried in the memories of Scots emigrants. There is a Dumbarton in Western Australia, a second in Queensland, a third in New Zealand and a fourth in New Brunswick, Canada. In the United States, the Dumbartons are legion: in Maryland, in Virginia, in South Carolina, in Louisiana, in Wisconsin . . . One finds Dumbarton Oaks in Washington, DC; Dumbarton Village in Houston, Texas; a Dumbarton Bridge across San Francisco Bay; a Dumbarton Church in Georgetown, DC; a Dumbarton School in Baltimore; and a Dumbarton College in Illinois. In the American Civil War, the US Navy once captured a Confederate vessel called *Dumbarton*; and the Royal Navy has a fishery protection ship called HMS *Dumbarton Castle*. One finds a Dunbarton in New Hampshire.[8]

How many Dumbartonians, one wonders, know how it all started? For them at least it may be important to know that Dumbarton was not always a minor satellite of a modern metropolis. Supported by the fertile farmlands of the adjoining *Levanach* – the Vale of Leven, the original homeland of Clan Lennox – it was the centre of a powerful realm, the capital of an extensive state. Indeed, it was the seat of kings.

II

Few historians these days talk of the 'Dark Ages'. Knowing that the phrase was coined in the 1330s by the early Renaissance poet Petrarch, they feel that the implied contrast between the 'Light' of the ancient world and the alleged 'intellectual Gloom' of what followed is unjust.[9] In British history, the 'Dark Ages' is rarely employed except for the two or three centuries which started with the retreat of the Roman legions and which are notoriously short of sources. This is exactly the period that embraces the 'Kingdom of the Rock'.

Obscurity, therefore, is the period's hallmark. Coherent narratives can only be established with great difficulty, and historical investigations are a speculators' paradise. Substantiated facts form tiny islets of sure knowledge in a vast sea of blank spots and confusion. Scarce sources are often written in eccentric languages, studied only by ultra-specialists. All judgements would benefit from being classified as undisputed (very few), deductive, analogous or tentative (most).

There is also a deep-seated problem of biased advocacy. The early history of the Isles* saw a tussle for survival between the Ancient Britons, the Irish Gaels, the Scots, the Picts and a collection of immigrant Germanic 'Anglo-Saxons'. In modern times some of these parties have had enthusiastic fans. The English, who are now a dominant majority, have often taken the triumph of their forebears for granted, at least in popular history. They admire the imperialist Romans, and identify with the Anglo-Saxons, but despise the Celts. They venerate Bede, who was a Germanic Northumbrian and whom they call Venerable, and neglect his competitors. They dislike the Celtic sources, which they cannot read, routinely dismissing them as fanciful or unreliable. The Scots, whose ancestors ultimately triumphed in Scotland, can be equally self-centred. Nowadays, there are few people around to champion the cause of the 'Old North'.

This term – which the Welsh call *Yr Hen Ogledd* – requires an explanation. The Ancient Britons, dozens of territorial tribes who had dominated

---

* 'The Isles' became British by monarchical criteria in 1603 and constitutionally in 1801. They ceased to be British in 1949.

the whole of Great Britain on the eve of the Roman conquest and gave the island its name, were gradually displaced or absorbed in post-Roman times, and their former dominance in all parts of the island has largely been forgotten. Their most visible descendants, known in English as the 'Welsh', that is, the 'aliens', now inhabit only one corner of their former homeland, in a remnant that the incoming English called 'Wales', the 'Alien Land'.* Time was when things were different. After the passing of Roman Britannia and the influx of 'Anglo-Saxons', the Britons held out longest in three main regions. In one of them, modern Wales, they survived. In the other two, modern Cornwall and the 'Old North', they did not. Yet their presence there was very real, and lasted for centuries. The 'Kingdom of the Rock' was the longest-lived fragment of the Ancient Britons' stronghold in northern Britain, the region that in due course would become Scotland.

Perhaps one should start, therefore, with an undisputed fact. The kingdom *did* exist. Its story is reflected in archaeological and linguistic evidence, in the chronicles of its neighbours, in king-lists and in references from poetry and legend; it existed for six or seven hundred years. Its original name and its exact boundaries are not known. But we do know with absolute certainty that it was there. Between the dusk of Roman Britannia and the dawn of England and Scotland, several Celtic kingdoms operated in northern Britain. The 'Kingdom of the Rock' was the last of them to succumb.

The Celts of the Isles were divided in Roman times – as they still are – into two distinctive linguistic groups. On the Green Isle, *Éire*, the Gaelic or Goidelic Celts spoke a tongue categorized by linguists as 'Q-Celtic'. Their word for 'son' was *mac*. On the larger Isle of *Prydain* (Great Britain), the British Celts spoke Brythonic or 'P-Celtic'. Their word for 'son' was *map*. To the uninitiated, the Goidelic and the Brythonic branches of Celtic look and sound dissimilar, but a good teacher can quickly elucidate the processes whereby common roots were transformed by successive sound changes. The characteristic word order of verb–subject–object remained unaltered, and morphological shifts often followed parallel patterns. Both Goidelic and Brythonic Celts adopted new systems of syllabic accentuation, for example; but while Goidelic chose to place the accent on the first syllable of a word, Brythonic went for stress on the penultimate syllable. Both language groups softened

* The Old Germanic *walchaz*, 'foreign' or 'alien', is similarly reflected in the Dutch *waalsch*, meaning 'Walloon'.

the consonants between vowels. Goidelic changed *t* to *th*, Brythonic to *d*, thus changing *ciatus* (battle) into *cath* (Irish) and *cad* (Welsh). The initial *w*-sound was replaced by *f* in Goidelic and *gw* in Brythonic, giving *fir* for 'true' in Irish and *gwir* in Welsh. English ears are not accustomed to these sounds. But since Goidelic/Gaelic and Brythonic 'Old Welsh' would in time compete to be heard on the Rock, their reverberations, however imperfectly understood, form an essential part of the background.[10]

During the four centuries of Roman rule, the Romano-Britons living in the imperial province of Britannia were markedly less Latinized than their Celtic kinsfolk in Gaul or Iberia. Some of them would have been bilingual, speaking Latin for official purposes and Brythonic among themselves; others less so. When the Western Empire collapsed, they did not advance to a neo-Latin idiom parallel to French or Spanish. Instead, they largely reverted to a monolingual Brythonic, until meeting new linguistic challenges posed by Germanic invaders from the Continent, by Gaelic 'Scots' from Ireland, and later by Norse-speaking Vikings.

In modern times, everyone has become accustomed to thinking of Great Britain in terms of England, Scotland and Wales. But this modern map must be put out of mind if one wishes to understand the island's previous make-up. In the era when Britannia was collapsing, there was no England, since the Anglo-Saxon ancestors of the English were still arriving; there was no Scotland, since the Scots had not even started to arrive; and there was no clearly defined Wales. The former Romano-Britons and their P-Celtic speech were spread over most if not all of *Prydain*, and as the ethno-linguistic jigsaw changed, 'Wales' could be found in every pocket where Britons persisted.

One can observe several degrees of the persistence of Romanization in post-Roman Britain. The cities and surrounding hinterlands within the former province of Britannia remained highly Romanized. The upland tribes, including those living beyond Hadrian's Wall, had been at best partially Romanized. The 'Picts' of the further North were virtually untouched.

An important division among the post-Roman Britons resulted from the Anglo-Saxon invasions of the fifth and sixth centuries. As the 'Anglo-Saxons' pushed westwards into the Midlands, they drove a wedge between the Britons on either side of them. After the Battle of Chester in 616, Angles moving coast to coast consolidated a belt of territory from the Humber to the Mersey in the powerful state of Mercia. From then on (though contact was maintained along the western sea-lanes), the Britons of the North were cut off from the larger concentrations of their kinsfolk elsewhere. A distinction grew up between the Welsh of 'Wales', and the North Welsh, whose beleagured British community was obliged to wage a prolonged rearguard action.

Despite its shadowy outlines, however, the 'Old North' cannot be regarded as a mere footnote to the grand pageant of British history. It contained at least seven known kingdoms, whose deeds were no less derring than those of their Anglo-Saxon counterparts. It left a large body of place names and a corpus of literature – known in Welsh as *Hengerdd* or the 'Old Verse' – which makes *Beowulf* look like an upstart latecomer.[11]

The language of the Old North is usually classified in the category of Cumbric, a sub-group of P-Celtic Brythonic, and related, therefore, to Welsh, Cornish and Breton. A major problem exists for historians, of course, in that Cumbric was rarely written down and can only be reconstructed by linguists from meagre scraps of information. One such scrap is the name of Cumbria ('Land of the Welsh') itself, which once extended over a far wider area than today. Another scrap comes from the counting systems of Cumbrian shepherds. It is well attested that people faced by the decline of their native language are particularly reluctant to abandon two things: the numbers, whereby they learned to count, and the prayers through which they addressed their God. An amazing instance of this phenomenon can be found in some of the upland communities of the Borders which nowadays straddle northern England and southern Scotland. Anglicization triumphed in those parts centuries ago either in the form of northern English or of Lowland Scots, but shepherds there

Table 1. Counting in northern English,
Lowland Scots and modern Welsh

	Keswick	Ayrshire	Modern Welsh
1	yan	yinty	un
2	tyan	tinty	dau
3	tethera	tetheri	tri
4	methera	metheri	pedwar
5	pimp	bamf	pump
6	sethera	leetera	chwech
7	lethera	seetera	saith
8	hovera	over	wyth
9	dovera	dover	naw
10	dick	dik	deg

continue to count their sheep using the numerals of their Brythonic forebears. The correspondences are unmistakeable, and they were reflected
in inscriptions still visible until recently on the old sheepmarket at
Cockermouth.[12] They are the very last echoes of the Old North.

Christianity was more firmly established in late Roman Britain than
is often supposed. St Alban was put to death for his faith at Verulamium
in *c.* 304, and the Emperor Theodosius I did not give Christianity an
official monopoly until 380. It would have had little time to penetrate
into all levels of society before the departure of the legions.[13] Yet for
most of the fourth century, the Edict of Milan in 313 had granted religious toleration to Christians, and Christian practices spread patchily.
In the subsequent era, knowledge of Latin and adherence to the Roman
religion were the twin marks of the *Romanitas* that civilized Britons
savoured in the face of heathen invaders.

It was the Romans who came to use the term *Picti* for the tribes who
had clung to the old ways – to tattooing, to principled illiteracy and to
native religion – and both the Irish and the Britons were accustomed to
treat the Picts as a race apart.[14] The Irish Gaels called them *Cruithne*,
which may be what they had once called all the inhabitants of Britain.
The Welsh term *Cymry*, usually translated as 'companions' or 'compatriots', which was coming into use in late Roman times, was a form
of self-identification both for Britons of the west (modern Wales) and
for the 'Men of the Old North', but not, apparently, for the Picts. It
possessed definite overtones of *cives Romani*.

Though the Roman legions had marched north beyond their province
of Britannia on several occasions, they never conquered the whole of
the island and they only occupied the land between the Hadrianic and
the Antonine Walls, the *Intervallum*, for less than thirty years in the
mid-second century. Nonetheless they stayed long enough to forge close
ties with the more co-operative tribes and to gather basic information
from them about northern Britain. The second-century geographer
Ptolemy, who lived in Alexandria, had met soldiers and sailors returning
from Britain, and he drew a map containing many names of rivers,
towns, islands and tribes. In the far north, beyond the Antonine Wall, he
noted the *Caledonii*. In the area between the walls, he recorded four
tribes – the *Damnonii*, the *Novantae*, the *Selgovae* and the *Votadini*. In
Damnonia, he recorded six *oppida* or 'towns': Alauna, Colanica, Coria,
Lindon, Victoria and Vindogara (Colanica can also be found in another
source known as the Ravenna Cosmography). Lindon, the *Llyn Dun* or

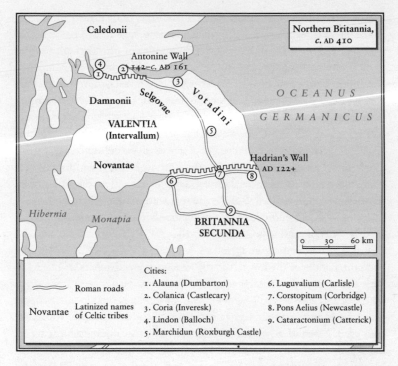

Northern Britannia,
c. AD 410

Caledonii

Antonine Wall
142–c. AD 161

Damnonii

Selgovae   Votadini

VALENTIA
(Intervallum)

Novantae

Hadrian's Wall
AD 122+

OCEANUS

GERMANICUS

Hibernia   Monapia   BRITANNIA
SECUNDA

0   30   60 km

Cities:

—— Roman roads

Novantae Latinized names
          of Celtic tribes

1. Alauna (Dumbarton)
2. Colanica (Castlecary)
3. Coria (Inveresk)
4. Lindon (Balloch)
5. Marchidun (Roxburgh Castle)

6. Luguvalium (Carlisle)
7. Corstopitum (Corbridge)
8. Pons Aelius (Newcastle)
9. Cataractonium (Catterick)

'Lake Fort', has been tentatively identified with Balloch on Loch Lomond. But Alauna is less uncertain. It means the 'headland' or 'spur', and nicely matches the locality of the Rock.[15]

The Roman names for British tribes were mainly Latin translations of Celtic originals, which English scholars rarely translate. But an attempt can be made. The *Caledonii* were possibly the 'Hard People', *Selgovae* were the 'Hunters' and the *Novantae* the 'Vigorous People'. The *Votadini* (mistranscribed by Ptolemy as *Otadini*) were the 'subjects or followers of Fothad'. The *Damnonii* were in some way connected to the Celtic word for 'deep'; 'the People of the Sea' is the most probable. It fits well with their location, and explains why other coastal tribes in Britain and Ireland, like the *Dumnonii* of the future Devon, had similar names. At all events, Damnonia was the earliest known statelet to be based on or near the Rock. Its maritime activities are hardly to be doubted: a later Irish source mentions an unidentified battleground in Ireland where Beinnie Britt killed Art, son of Conn. Beinnie was a 'Briton' from across the water. The Damnonians evidently possessed the capacity for transporting fighting men by sea.

The Rock stood only a couple of miles from the western end of the Antonine Wall on the River *Clota*, at the point where the Roman fleet would have been stationed to control the pirates of the northern sea and to facilitate the transfer of Gaulish auxiliaries helping to construct the Antonine Wall. Their presence is attested by an inscription on an altar erected at a fort on the wall only a few miles from *Brittanodunum* (Dunglass). 'CAMPES TRIBUSET BRITANI QP SETIUS IUSTUS PREF. COH IIII GAL VS LLM' (To the eternal field deities of Britain, Quintus Pisentius Justus, Prefect of the 4th Cohort of Gallic auxiliaries dedicated his willingly executed vow). The date was equivalent to AD 142. Within a couple of decades, the legions had retreated. Their plans to return never materialized. But the Emperor Caracalla (r. 209–17) established a system of forward cavalry patrols (called *areani*) north of Hadrian's Wall, and it is conceivable that the *Clota* continued to offer facilities to the Roman western fleet.[16]

In the middle of the fourth century, the northern defences of Britannia were completely overrun by what the Romans called a great *confederatio barbarica*. It is not known whether Damnonia joined in. But for two years, from 367 to 369, the government of the whole Britannic province collapsed. Marauders and deserters devastated the countryside, capturing the chief military officer and killing the commander of the fortified 'Saxon Shore' on the province's eastern and southern coasts. Order was restored by a veteran soldier, Count Theodosius, who re-garrisoned Hadrian's Wall and introduced a series of dependent buffer states both in the west and the north. In the late fourth century, a Spanish general called Magnus Maximus established himself in the west, and subsequently as 'Macsen Wledig' became the legendary founder of several Welsh dynasties. At that same time, a personage by the name of Paternus or Padarn Pesrut (Paternus of the Red Cloak) emerged as ruler of the Votadini. His red cloak signified high Roman rank; large numbers of Roman coins dated between 369 and 410 have been found on the site of his putative capital at *Marchidun* (the modern Roxburgh Castle). In 405, an entry in one of the books of Irish Annals mentions a battle fought at *strath Cluatha*, 'the Battle of the Clyde valley'. This is most likely the moment when the shadowy post-Roman states of the north were coming into existence. The buffer fiefdoms that Theodosius had put into place were turning into ready-made native 'kingdoms'.[17]

Of course, the term 'king', as used both in the sources and by historians, is something of a vanity title. These rulers were not crowned monarchs, but leaders of war-bands that enforced their will and collected tribute. Their fluctuating fortunes were defined by the number of settlements from which tribute could be extracted.

After the Roman troops withdrew from Britannia, in 410 or perhaps a little later, the *Intervallum* hosted five or possibly six or seven native kingdoms. Some are better documented than the others. 'Galwyddel' (Galloway) occupied the lands of the *Novantae*. 'Rheged', centred on Caer Ligualid (the former *Luguvalium* and modern Carlisle), straddled both sides of Hadrian's Wall. It possessed a complete late-Roman capital, including a wall, a bishop, an aqueduct and a municipal fountain that was still working 250 years later. At some point in the fifth century it was ruled by Coel Hen, the original 'Old King Cole', who spent much time campaigning in *Aeron* – the future Ayrshire – and whose name provides the starting point of the Welsh genealogical list known as 'The Descent of the Men of the North' (*Bonedd Gwyr y Gogledd*).[18] On the east coast, 'Manau' (Clackmannan) and 'Lleddiniawn' (Lothian) lined opposite shores of the Firth of Forth. They may or may not have formed separate realms, but are together regarded as the homeland of the 'Guotadin', the real Celtic name for the *Votadini*. This 'Land of Gododdin' (to use a more modern form of the name) may well have been subject to Coel Hen before breaking free. Like Rheged, it came under Christian influence at an early date. The cemetery of its capital, Dun Eidyn, contained numerous Christian graves. Neighbouring 'Bryneich' occupied the coastal strip south of Gododdin and on either side of Hadrian's Wall. Relatively speaking, the 'Kingdom of the Rock' stayed in the shadows.[19]

Fifth-century events in the *Intervallum* are illuminated to some extent by the activities of three men who attracted outside attention: Cunedda, Patrick and Ninian. Cunedda ap Edern, the 'Good Leader', was a warrior from Gododdin who *c.* 425 led a military expedition to distant Gwynedd in North Wales to eject an unwelcome colony of Irish settlers. Succeeding in his mission, he passed into history as one of the early Welsh heroes, and progenitor of Gwynedd's ruling house. His expedition, as recorded in a later historical work produced in the court of one of his successors, the *Historia Brittonum*, could have been inspired by a feeling of solidarity among the *Cymry*.[20]

Cunedda's story shows the degree to which the meagre historical sources raise as many questions as they solve. Interpretation of the king-lists continues to be as intricate as it is enigmatic. The earliest compilations for this period are to be found among the British Library's collection of

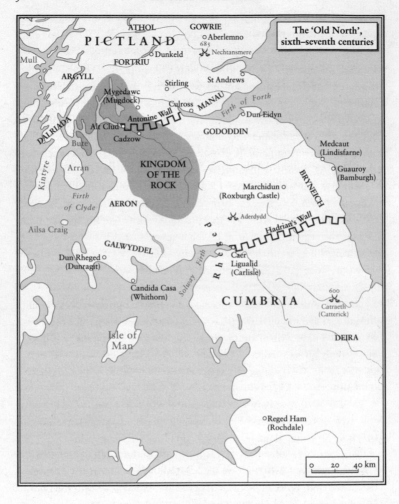

The 'Old North',
sixth–seventh centuries

ATHOL   GOWRIE
                    ○ Aberlemno
PICTLAND   685
             ○   ✕ Nechtansmere
        Dunkeld
FORTRIU
ARGYLL   Stirling   St Andrews
Mull   ○
        Mygedawc   Firth of Forth
        (Mugdock)   Culross   MANAU
DALRIADA   Antonine Wall   ○ Dun-Eidyn
        Alt Clud
        Cadzow   GODODDIN
Bute   Medcaut
Arran   (Lindisfarne)
    Firth   KINGDOM   ○ Guauroy
    of Clyde   OF THE   (Bamburgh)
        AERON   ROCK   Marchidun   BRYNEICH
Ailsa Craig   (Roxburgh Castle)
        GALWYDDEL   ✕ Aderdydd   Hadrian's Wall
Dun Rheged ○   R
(Dunragit)   Rheged
        Candida Casa   Caer
        (Whithorn)   Ligualid
                       (Carlisle)
                                    600
                       CUMBRIA   ✕ Catraeth
                                    (Catterick)
        Isle of
        Man   DEIRA

                                    ○ Reged Ham
                                      (Rochdale)

                       0   20   40 km

manuscripts known as the Harleian Genealogies, which date from an era
long after the lives of the monarchs mentioned. They mainly derive from
Wales, not from North Britain, and may be seen as attempts by the medieval Welsh to preserve the memory of their lost northern kindred. They
rarely contain reliable dates, and are full of recurring names and eccentric
spellings that cannot be pinned with certainty onto particular individuals.
Researchers have to resort to generation-counting, to detailed comparisons of sources and to endless guessing. They also have to make allowance,
in place of primogeniture, for the practice of tanistry, that is, the naming
of a successor who was not necessarily the ruler's son. One is reminded of

the task of early Egyptologists who pieced together the reigns and the dynasties of the pharaohs.

Patrick is the best documented and most studied figure of the age. He was clearly a Briton of the north who was seized by Irish pirates as a boy and sold into slavery, who escaped and studied in Gaul, and who returned to lead a mission for the conversion of Ireland. Unfortunately, the dates and locations of the British sections of his biography are hotly disputed. His birthplace, described in his writings as a *villula* or 'small estate' near a *vicus Bannevem Taberniae*, has been 'convincingly' located to a village 15 miles inland from Caer Ligualid (Carlisle).[21] An alternative location in a village that bears Patrick's name, barely a stone's throw from the Rock, is frequently overlooked,[22] as is a local story about the boy 'Succat', who was seized by pirates when fishing by the *Clota*. The fact remains, however, that one of Patrick's two surviving letters is addressed to the *milites Corotici*, whom he reprimands for allying themselves with the Picts and for warring and looting in a manner unbecoming for Romans and Christians:

> I Patrick, a sinner, very badly educated, declare myself to be a bishop in Ireland . . . I live among barbarian tribes as an exile and refugee for the love of God . . . I have written and set down with my own hand these words to be solemnly given, carried and sent to the soldiers of Coroticus. I do not say 'To my fellow citizens' . . . but 'To the fellow citizens of the devils', because of their wicked behaviour.
>
> The day after the newly baptized, still bearing the chrism, still in their white dress . . . had been ruthlessly massacred and slaughtered, I sent a letter by a holy presbyter along with other clergy. They were laughed at.
>
> Here your sheep were savaged . . . by gangsters at the behest of Coroticus. One who betrays Christians into the hands of Scots and Picts is far from the love of God. Voracious wolves have swallowed up the flock of the Lord in Ireland which had been growing nicely through hard work . . .
>
> It is the custom of the Roman Gauls who are Christians to send to the Franks . . . and to ransom baptized people who have been captured. You, on the contrary, murder them, and sell them to an outlandish people who know not God. You are virtually handing the members of Christ to a brothel . . .
>
> So I mourn for you, my dearest . . . But again I rejoice, for those baptized believers have departed this world for Paradise . . . The good will feast in confidence with Christ. They shall judge nations and rule over wicked kings for ever and ever. Amen.[23]

By general consent, this Coroticus is to be equated with Ceredig
Gueldig, otherwise Ceretic Guletic, the earliest-known ruler of 'The
Rock'. What would have been more natural then for Patrick, having
become a bishop, to address the prince of his native country? But for
their misdeeds, he would have addressed the soldiers of Coroticus as
'My fellow citizens'. *Civis*, 'citizen', was the highest form of compliment
among former Romano-Britons. At all events, to be absolutely clear, St
Patrick, like St David, was a Welshman.

So, too, was St Ninian, who, according to Bede, was sent from Carlisle to convert the southern Picts. Unfortunately, there is no indication
of a date (although the fifth century is generally preferred), and there is
no clue to the precise meaning of 'southern Picts'. If the phrase refers to
Novantae and *Selgovae*, Ninian might have been responsible for the
founding of the Christian community at *Candida Casa* (now Whithorn)
in Galloway, where the Latinus Stone dates from *c.* 450. If it meant the
Caledonians of Fortriu, he would have had to pass through the lands of
'The Rock' to reach them.[24]

Both the geography and the chronology of the links between the two
substantiated northern kings of the fifth century, Coel Hen and Ceredig
Gueldig (Coroticus), are uncertain. One possibility is that Coel Hen initially ruled over territory stretching from the Clyde to *Eboracum* (York).
However, after Coel Hen was drowned *c.* 420 in a bog at Tarbolton in
Aeron, it is not too far-fetched to assume that the 'Kingdom of the Rock'
had detached itself from Rheged, much as Gododdin might have done.
In this scenario, Ceredig becomes a successor and possibly a descendant
of Coel Hen, as well as the founder of the dynasty of 'The Rock'. Ceredig's
supposed successors – Erbin, Cinuit, Gereint, Tutagual and Caw – are
nothing but names.

The historicity of Ceredig Gueldig is based on congruent references
in the Harleian Genealogies, and is strengthened by further mention of
him in the Annals of Ulster (in the context of St Patrick's adventures), as
Coirtech regem Aloo.[25] 'Aloo', which occurs on several occasions, is
evidently a shortened form of Alauna. The early medieval *Annales Cam-
briae* (Welsh Annals), which were compiled at St David's, call him
'Ceretig Guletic map Cynlop' (Ceredig the Wealthy, son of Cynloyp).[26]
Though shadowy, he has the distinction of being more readily identifi-
able than his far more famous contemporary – King Arthur.

Up to this point, the story of 'The Rock' can be told exclusively within
the compass of the post-Roman British tribes. But in the sixth century

changes occurred that were to transform the scene radically. First, the Germanic Angles, the furthest outliers of the Anglo-Saxons, who were busy taking over southern Britannia, established a foothold on the coast of Gododdin and Bryneich. Second, Gaelic Scots from Dalriada in Ulster established a similar foothold on the north-western coast, close to, but slightly above the Rock. Henceforth, the future of the *Intervallum* would hang on the outcome of a four-sided contest between the native Britons and Picts, and the newcomer Angles and Scots. Three hundred years later, a fifth party, the Vikings, would act as a vital catalyst in the final phase of the contest.

According to Bede, 'Ida began his reign in 547.' According to the Welsh monk who lived after Bede and composed the *Historia Brittonum* in faraway Gwynedd, Ida 'added Din Guauroy to Berneich'.[27] Ida the Flamebearer was an Angle from somewhere further south. Berneich or Bryneich was the original British/Celtic name of the kingdom which he and his successors would now rule and Anglicize and which is generally known in its Latin form of *Bernicia*. Din Guauroy was the British name for the magnificent and near-impregnable coastal castle at Bamburgh.

To begin with, Ida's Angles formed a small and isolated outpost. Unlike other Anglo-Saxons, they mixed readily with the native British, creating 'the only recognisably Germano-Celtic cultural and political fusion in Britain'.[28] Their long-term strategy, dictated by their advantageous coastal position, was to link up with their kinsmen in the Kingdom of *Deur* or Deira to the south, forming a united Anglian realm in Northumbria (that is, 'North of the Humber'). At the same time, they could chip away at the surrounding British kingdoms of Rheged and Gododdin.

The Gaelic Scots on the west coast developed their activities in similar fashion. The theory that they arrived from Ireland in one mass migration is now discredited: there may well have been 'Scottish' (meaning Irish) settlements on both sides of the North Channel from much earlier times. Yet the important political fact concerns the extension of a Gaelic Kingdom of Dalriada from Ulster to the British shore of what would henceforth be known as 'Argyll' or the 'Eastern Gaels', where Aedan macGabrain began his reign in 574. The facts of the reign are known through the presence of St Columba (*c.* 521–97), who had recently planted a Christian community on the island of Iona and whose biographer, Adamnan, provides a well informed and detailed source.[29] The strategic concerns of the Gaels of Argyll are not hard to divine. On the one hand, they would have aimed to consolidate the link between Argyll and Ulster, in particular by developing their sea power. On the other, if they were not to be pushed back into the sea, they would have been tempted to expand their territory at the expense of neighbouring kingdoms – notably of the inland Picts and of the Britons of 'The Rock'.

Such is the context for one of the many strands in the unending riddle of King Arthur. The riddle is not going to be solved in a couple of pages. The literature on the subject is vast, and its conclusions are totally contradictory. Suffice it to say that there were two distinct King Arthurs, one an elusive but historical figure from the sixth century, the other a legendary medieval hero whose exploits were spun by the bards and myth-makers of a much later age. In all of this, one notes a marked tendency for Arthur-hunters from England to assume that he lived and fought in England, and for Arthur-hunters from the Borders to prove that he came from *Marchidun*, alias Roxburgh. Arthur-hunters from Glasgow place him firmly in Drumchapel, and Arthur-hunters from the Clan MacArthur display a bravado worthy of the late General Douglas MacArthur.[30] Yet Bede and Gildas are both silent on the matter, while the *Historia Brittonum* names thirteen battle sites of a 'famous *dux bellorum*' which defy identification. The historical Arthur was certainly British, since he was made famous by resisting the incursions of the Britons' enemies. After that one is looking for toponymic needles in a semi-historic haystack. Nonetheless, one is bound to be impressed by the recent surge of advocacy in favour of Arthur being a hero of northern as opposed to southern Britain. Everyone can understand the confusion between *Damnonia* and *Dumnonia*, or the misattribution by the twelfth-century Geoffrey of Monmouth of Welsh legends deriving from the 'Old North'. Beyond that, one can only say that the Rock of Dumbarton is hardly less plausible than the rock of Tintagel. The Rock of the Clyde was known to antiquaries as the *Castrum Arturi*; and both an Arthur's Stone and a King's Ridge are still to be found in the vicinity.[31]

Local historians have few qualms.[32] In his *Glasgow and Strathclyde*, James Knight waxes particularly eloquent:

> Careful research seems to show that when we trace the Arthurian legends back to their origins we arrive at a real historical person . . . the head of a British federation in Strathclyde in the century after Ninian. His enemies were the heathen Scots on the west, the Picts on the north, and the Angles on the east . . . As the result of a victory at Bowden Hill (West Lothian) in 516 he divided the conquered territories among three brothers, Urien [of Rheged], Arawn . . . and Llew or Loth, King of the Picts . . . Loth was the father of Thenaw . . . the mother of Kentigern or Mungo, the real founder

of Glasgow and its patron saint . . . In 537, a fresh pagan combination was formed under Modred, Arthur's nephew, and at Camelon near Falkirk, a great battle was fought in which both leaders fell, and which overwhelmed Christianity in Scotland for a whole generation.[33]

Whatever we might think of this, here enters St Mungo, aka Kentigern, the 'Chief Lord'. One of the most popular saints of medieval Britain, he lived through most of the sixth century, and died *c.* 613, 'a very old man'. If the *Catholic Encyclopedia* is right in putting his birth in 518, he could have reached the age of ninety-five. Historians would be on stronger ground if his Life, written by a twelfth-century monk, were not a conventional hagiography that jumbles up facts, tall tales and dubious reports of miracle-working.[34]

The saint was said to have been born on the beach at Culross in Fife. His mother, Tenew, queen of Lleddiniawn, had been cast adrift in a coracle, punished by her husband for adultery. She was somehow rescued by St Servanus, who, despite living a century later, saw the child and dubbed him in Old Welsh *Mwn gu*, 'Dear One'. Educated by the monks at Culross, Mungo made his way either to Rheged or to 'The Rock'. In one account, he is said to have walked to the Clyde, taking the body of an old man on a cart pulled by two untamed bulls and heading for the Christian cemetery at Molendinar beside the Rock, where he acquired the non-existent title of 'bishop of North Britain'.

The central years of Mungo's career were passed in Gwynedd, whither he went at the invitation of St Dewi or David, the patron of Wales and pioneer of Welsh monasticism. With David's assistance, he founded a church at Llanelwy, where the holy Asaph served as deacon; Llanelwy is now St Asaph in Flintshire. Around 580 Mungo was summoned back to Clydeside by Roderick or Rhydderch Hael, a monarch of 'The Rock' in the fifth or the sixth generation of Ceredig's dynasty. At Rhydderch's request he founded a church at Glas-gau, the 'Blue-Green Meadow', died at a ripe old age and was buried in the crypt. His tomb duly became a site of pilgrimage.

Mungo's miracles, cemented by centuries of later tradition, are best remembered by a jingle: 'Here's the bird that never flew, here's the tree that never grew. Here's the bell that never rang. Here's the fish that never swam.'[35] The four symbols of bird, tree, bell and fish appear on modern Glasgow's coat of arms. The bird stands for the pet sparrow of St Servanus that Mungo restored to life. The tree represents a dead branch which Mungo endowed with the capacity to burst into flame.

The bell was supposedly brought back from Mungo's journey to Rome. And the fish is a salmon, immortalized by the legend of 'The Salmon and the Ring':

> Once upon a time, King Rhydderch's queen, Languoreth, took a secret lover, a young soldier. As a token of her love, she foolishly gave the soldier a ring that had earlier been presented to her by her husband. When the king saw the ring on the soldier's finger, he gave him wine and disarmed him. Seizing the ring he flung it into the waters of the Clyde. He condemned the soldier to death. And he flung the queen into a dungeon.
>
> In her desperation, the queen turned to Saint Mungo for advice. The saint promptly sent his man to catch the fish in the river. The man returned with a salmon which, when cut open, contained the missing ring. The king's wrath was assuaged. The soldier was reprieved. The queen was forgiven.[36]

In some accounts Rhydderch and Languoreth are described as the 'monarchs of Cadzow', a locality to the south of Glasgow which later became the site of a royal castle and in modern times the seat of the dukes of Hamilton. Mungo also appears in some of the Arthurian legends, where textual analysts have noted similarities between the legend of 'The Salmon and the Ring' and the romance of Lancelot and Guinevere.

It is beyond doubt, however, that the greatest power in Mungo's time was wielded by Urien, king of Rheged. Urien's Latin name was *Urbigenus* or 'city-born', and it implies a conscious degree of *Romanitas*. He ruled over a domain that stretched from the southern outskirts of Glasgau to the environs of *Mancunium*, where an outpost called Reged-ham (the present Rochdale) attests his sway. The royal seat lay at Dun Rheged (Dunragit) in Galloway; the chief city was Caer Ligualid (Carlisle); the main corridor of communication the Ituna or Solway, which led to the open sea and to Ireland. Urien earned the Old Welsh epithet of *Y Eochydd*, 'Lord of the Rip-Tide', suggesting that Rheged, like 'The Rock' and Dalriada, was a significant naval power.

In the late sixth century, the Britons of the North recognized the growing threat from the Angles, and Urien mounted a grand coalition against them. His allies included Rhydderch Hael of 'The Rock', Guallauc from Lennox, Morgant of south Gododdin, Aedan macGabrain of Argyll and King Fiachna of Ulster. In 590 they set out to wipe Bernicia off the map. The Irish somehow stormed the heights of Bamburgh; and the remnants of the garrison took refuge on Medcaut, the 'Island of Tides', the Angles' name for Lindisfarne. Urien laid siege. He was on the point of total victory, when through the jealousy of Morgant, he was assassinated. The unity of the Britons was lost, and the ambitions of Rheged ended.

As in the preceding period, the king-lists of 'The Rock' from the sixth century, such as the *Bonedd Gwyr y Gogledd*, 'The Descent of the Men of the North', contain one definite name and a clutch of doubtful ones. Just as Ceredig (Coroticus) is given veracity by links with St Patrick, Rhydderch Hael is bolstered by his links to St Columba. Adamnan recalled that St Columba had visited the court of 'The Rock' and he makes Rhydderch the subject of one of the saint's prophecies:

> This same king being on friendly terms with the holy man, sent him on one occasion a secret message . . . as he was anxious to know whether he would be killed by his enemies or not. But when [the messenger] was being closely [questioned] by the saint regarding the king, his kingdom and people . . . the saint replied, 'He shall never be delivered into the hands of his enemies; he will die at home on his own pillow.' And the prophecy of the saint regarding King Roderc was fully accomplished; for, according to his word, he died quietly in his own house.[37]

Rhydderch Hael features in the *Bonedd Gwyr y Gogledd*, and in order to coincide with St Columba his regnal dates are conventionally fixed as *c*. 580–618. Adamnan describes him as *filius Tothail*, which puts Rhydderch's father, Tutagual, in the regnal time bracket of 560–80. But all further identifications are hopelessly problematic. Historians are left struggling once again in the red mist in regard to Rhydderch's successors. Dumnagual Hen, Clinoch and Cinbellin are names without dates or faces. No less than five princes called Dumnagual are referred to. One of them, who apparently had three sons, could conceivably have been the father of Gildas the chronicler.[38]

In the seventh century the Old North was shaken both by religious disputes and by shattering military battles. Interpretations inevitably vary, but all commentators agree that Catraeth, Whitby and Nechtansmere mark milestones of lasting significance.

The Battle of Catraeth occurred in *c*. 600 as a by-product of continued animosity between Britons and Angles. The conflict was exacerbated by the apprehensions of the Celtic Church, which would have heard of the Roman mission recently introduced into southern Britain by St Augustine of Canterbury.[39] It came to a head within ten years of Urien's assassination, and arose from a similar set of circumstances. This time it was Yrfai, son of Wulfsten, lord of north Gododdin, who assembled the coalition. He invited three hundred warriors to Dun Eidyn, feasted them for months on end, and then set out to do battle. Princes from Pictland and Gwynedd joined him. So, too, did Cynon, son of Clydno Eidyn, Lord of 'The Rock', whose name suggests kinship with Yrfai. The coalition deployed an elite cavalry force, and rode far to the south, beyond Bernicia, beyond Hadrian's Wall, into the eastern lands of Rheged. They called themselves *Y Bedydd* – 'The Baptized' – and claimed to be defending the old faith against the Anglian *Gynt* or 'Gentiles'. Their exploits were recorded in the greatest of the early Old Welsh epics. The opening sentence of the only surviving manuscript, known as *The Book of Aneirin*, announces the names of the poem and of its author:

> *Hwn yw e gododdin, aneirin ae cant.*[40]
> (This is the Gododdin, Aneirin sang it.)

There follows a long collection of eulogies for the fallen warriors. One of them was called Madauc or Madawg:

> *Ni forthïnt ueiri molüt nïuet,*
> *ractria riallü trin orthoret,*
> *tebïhïc tan teryd druï cïnneüet.*
> *Dïu Maurth guisgassant eü cein dühet*
> *Dïu Merchyr bü guero eü cïtunet . . .*

The chief men maintained the praise of rightful privilege
like a bright fire that has been well kindled.
On Tuesday they put on their dark covering.
On Wednesday their common purpose was bitter.
On Thursday envoys were pledged.
On Friday corpses were counted.
On Saturday their joint action was swift.
On Sunday, their red blades were redistributed.
On Monday, a stream of blood as high as the thigh was seen.
A Gododdin man tells that when they came back
before Madawg's tent after the exhaustion of battle
but one in a hundred would return.[41]

As many observers have noted, the warrior ethos, the poetic hyperbole and the tangible cult of death and slaughter has a timeless quality. These are Celts fighting Angles, but without too much variation they could well be the host of Agamemnon at Troy. The Lord of 'The Rock' was in the van:

Moch arereith ï – immetin
pan – crïssiassan cïntäränn i-mbodin . . .

He rose early in the morning
When centurions hasten in the mustering of the army,
Moving from one advanced position to another.
At the front of a hundred men he was the first to kill.
As great was his craving for corpses
As for drinking mead or wine.
It was with utter hatred
That the Lord of Dumbarton, the laughing warrior,
Would kill the enemy.[42]

Yet this time the laughing was cut short. The advance guard of the Anglian host had pulled back, and drawn their adversaries into the line of march of a second Anglian force moving up from Deira. They collided at Catraeth (the modern Catterick). The slaughter was shocking even for a society that lived from warfare, and the North British army was annihilated: only one of the three hundred chiefs returned. Yrfai and Cynon and most of their companions were slain:

E tri bet yg Kewin Kelvi . . .

The three graves on the ridge of Celvi,
Inspiration has declared them to me:
[They are] the grave of Cynon of the rugged brows,
The grave of Cynfael and the grave of Cynfeli.[43]

The road was open for the Angles to resume their inexorable progress.

The political consequences of Catraeth were worked out in the following decades. The Angles of Bernicia streamed north and overran Gododdin, so that by 631 Dun Eidyn had become Edinburgh (*burgh* meaning 'fort' was simply a calque of the Celtic *dun*). They also returned to the onslaught on Rheged which had been halted by Urien. In an earlier confrontation, the men of Deira had inflicted a Catraeth-like defeat on the Luguvalians at Aderydd (now Arthuret near Longtown in Cumbria), and had reputedly forced the bard of the city, Myrddin (Merlin), to seek refuge in the 'Forest of Cellydon' (which sounds awfully like Caledonia). Now the redoubled strength of the Angles could move into Rheged with destructive vengeance, bringing with them permanent colonists. Urien's line disappears from the record. The last king of Rheged, the exiled Llywarch Hen, is received into the Welsh court of Powys, and

Rheged itself fades away. In short, the presence of the Angles in the north is fixed from coast to coast; Bernicia's expansion is revitalized; and the British people of 'The Rock' are further isolated from their countrymen.

The religious conflict came to a head in the 660s. The issues were often those of rite or theology, like the calculation of Easter, but at their heart was a raw struggle for power. The north had been evangelized by Celtic missionaries; by St Ninian, by St Columba, by Rhun, son of Urien and bishop of Luguvalium, who claimed to have baptized Edwin of Northumbria, and by the Irishman St Aidan, who established the See of Lindisfarne *c.* 635. Yet the Roman mission, firmly allied to the expansion of Anglo-Saxon power, was unyielding. In 664 Oswy of Northumbria, far stronger than his predecessors, convened the Synod of Whitby. Despite his personal links to Celtic Christianity he ruled in favour of the Roman party, and appointed St Wilfrid as bishop of Northumbria. Henceforth, Anglian government marched hand in hand with the Roman faith. Within five years, Wilfrid was claiming to be 'bishop of Pictland'. 'It turned out that, in addition to Latin, God spoke English, not Gaelic.'[44]

It also turned out that Wilfrid had been overly optimistic. Nechtansmere, the Anglian name for a location that the Britons variously called *Llyn Garan*, the 'Heron's Pool', or *Dunnicken*, the 'Fort of Nechtan', lies well to the north of the Firth of Forth, near Forfar in modern Angus. Bede mentions it in connection with the onset of Northumbria's decline, for it was at Nechtansmere that at around three o'clock on the Saturday afternoon of 20 May 685, the army of Ecgfrith, son of Oswy, king of Northumbria, was routed by the combined forces of Pictland and 'The Rock' under a warrior with the magnificent name of Bridei map Bili. Ecgfrith and his entire royal bodyguard were cut down. 'Rashly leading his army to ravage the province of the Picts,' wrote Bede, 'and much against the advice of the Blessed Cuthbert, [Ecgfrith] was drawn into the straits of inaccessible mountains, and slain with the greatest part of his forces.'[45] The Angles were never seen in those parts again.[46]

Unusually for the 'Dark Ages', Bridei's victory left a lasting artistic monument in the so-called Aberlemno Stone. It stands in the kirkyard only six miles from the battle site, and carries the only clear battle narrative to be seen on any of the Pictish symbol-stones:

[The narrative] reads like a comic strip in a newspaper, with four scenes arranged in sequence from top to bottom. In the first, a mounted figure who may represent Bridei chases another mounted warrior. In his haste to escape the latter has thrown away his shield and sword. This man may be Ecgfrith ... turning and fleeing at the moment when he realised that an ambush had been sprung. What identifies the escaping warrior as a Northumbrian is his helmet. During excavations at the Coppergate in York a very similar design, rounded with a long nose-guard was discovered.[47]

The second scene shows Ecgfrith, or a mounted Northumbrian figure, wearing the same sort of helmet, attacking a group of Pictish infantrymen. The sculptor clearly understood military tactics because he was careful to arrange the men into the proper battle formation of three ranks. At the front stands a warrior with a sword and a round, curved shield with prominent boss. When the opposing cavalry charged he had to withstand the shock of impact. To support him another man stands immediately behind holding a long spear which projected well beyond the front rank. To the rear of the two warriors engaging the enemy, a third spearman stood in reserve. Along an extended battle line, an array of bristling spear points was designed to deter a charge, forcing cavalry horses to shy or to reel away. In a third scene, carved at the foot of the stone, the Bridei and Ecgfrith figures face each other on horseback. Ecgfrith appears to be on the point of throwing his spear while Bridei readies himself to parry it. And in a final act, tucked into the bottom right-hand corner, Ecgfrith lies dead on the battlefield. A raven, a carrion-feeder symbolizing defeat, pecks at his neck.

The Aberlemno Stone is a Pictish national manifesto. Carved a century after the great victory, its message was both simple and powerful: Pictland is different. And in 685 that 'singular identity had been preserved by force of arms'.[48]

There is no reason to query the continuity of the monarchy of 'The Rock' throughout the seventh century, but all its king-names are dubious, and several overlaps can be observed with the rulers of Pictland. Rhydderch Hael does not appear to have had sons. The succession passed to Nwython (Neithon, Nechtan), who is conceivably the same person as Nechtan, king of Pictish Fortriu (d. c. 621), after whom Nechtansmere could have been named. Nwython was father to Beli (or Bili I) and grandfather both to Ywain (Owen, Owain) and to Brude (Bridei). Owen of 'The Rock' was the victor of the Battle of Strathcarron in 642, when the king of Dalriada was killed, while his brother or half-brother, Bridei map Bili, who ruled in Fortriu, was the victor of Nechtansmere.[49] References to another run of dubious names crop up from time to time in the Annals of Ulster, showing that in their rivalry with Dalriada, the monarchs of 'The Rock' did not hesitate to take the fight across the sea to Ireland.

The consequences of Nechtansmere were never reversed. The battle had come at the end of a phase when fortunes on the Anglian-Pictish frontier had swung back and forth and the intervening territory had changed hands several times. But after Nechtansmere, both the Picts and the Britons of 'The Rock' stood their ground. The Angles put down roots to the south of the Firth of Forth, and did not venture beyond their stronghold at Stirling. They colonized Galloway and the former *Aeron* (Ayrshire) in the south-west, but they did not move on the Clyde. Within their area of settlement, they introduced their particular brand of Old English that, mixed with local idioms, led to the emergence of a language called 'Lallans' or Lowland Scots.[50] Henceforth, to the north and west of the Angles, the Gaelic Scots, the Picts and the Britons were drawn into a new, three-sided ethnic contest. Reduced to its simplest, the contest saw the Scots gaining the upper hand over the Picts, before the Picto-Scots overwhelmed the Britons. This was to take perhaps 250 years.

The eighth century and the first part of the ninth are the darkest of all. The historical record of the long decades between Nechtansmere and the irruption of the Vikings is threadbare. Despite occasional shafts of light, no continuous narrative can be constructed. As the Northumbrian Angles dug in to the south of them, and the warring Scots and Picts gradually fused together to the north, the Britons on the Clyde turned in on themselves. There are no famous monarchs; no resounding battles; no memory-cementing poems, no extant chronicles. The sources offer no clues on the subject of naval power. No expeditions by sea are recorded. No information is forthcoming on the size of armed patrols that may or may not have been maintained on the Firth of Clyde to monitor shipping and to protect the kingdom's tax-gatherers. Nothing has survived except occasional remarks among descriptions of the doings of others. Of the various peoples involved in the creation of Scotland, 'it is the Britons about whom least is known, and about whom least has been written'.[51]

For much of this time, the territorial extent of the realms of 'The Rock' can only be conjectured. Following the fall of Rheged and Godod-din, the kingdom's neighbours did not change. To the west and north-west, most of the isles and promontories were controlled by the

Dalriadan Scots. The extraordinary *Senchus* or 'Register' of Dalriada – a sort of primitive Domesday Book – shows that Kintyre was one of its most important regions.[52] It also implies that the tribute-collectors of 'The Rock' would not have ventured further afield than Bute and Arran. The main concern would have been to safeguard the seaways of the Firth. To the north, the *Clach nam Breatan* or 'British Stone', which can still be seen in Glen Falloch above the head of Loch Lomond, marked the traditional dividing line with the Picts. Beyond lay the fertile valley of Strathearn and the Pictish province of Fortriu. To the east and the south, the lands of 'The Rock' adjoined Northumbrian territory. They occupied the tributary valleys and surrounding ridges of the Clyde Basin, but not much more. One major border post would probably have been in the vicinity of modern Kelvinhead, another in the vicinity of modern Beattock. Internal communications were compact, whether by river or by sea. There was land for arable farming and livestock, and forest. The ring of upland hills facilitated a sheltered climate and sound defence lines.

Yet the kingdom's overall resources fell behind those of neighbouring states. Northumbria was at least twice as large. The merger of the Picts and the Scots was to produce another large entity. As time passed, 'The Rock' found it ever harder to compete. All the indications are that Dalriada possessed significant naval capacity.[53] One may infer that the lords of 'The Rock' would have sought to make similar provisions, but were unable to do so.

At the time of Nechtansmere, Pictland had still been pagan, and the map of Christianity in the north did not settle quickly. For a time, the Northumbrian Angles competed with the Dalriadan Scots to convert the Picts. The halting of their own territorial expansion did not stop their religious ambitions. The first two incumbents of a Northumbrian bishopric at Whithorn were Penthelm, 'Leader of the Picts', and Pentwine, 'Friend of the Picts'. Whithorn was not adjacent to Pictland, but some sort of Christian mission accompanied the bishopric. In that same era, Nechtan, king of the Picts (r. 706–24) expelled the Ionan monks and appealed to Bede's boss, the abbot of Jarrow, for advice on how to establish a church on the Roman model. In later times, he would be credited with the wholesale conversion of Pictland. In reality, he was probably just standardizing the Roman rite. His successor, Oengus I (r. 729–61), went a step further by importing the relics of St Andrew from Byzantium and building a shrine for them on the furthermost eastern shore. The people of 'The Rock', holding to the tradition of St Mungo, would not have been directly affected.

The year 731 marks the date of the most unambiguous of all references to the 'Kingdom of the Rock'. In his *Ecclesiastical History of the English People*, Bede, who died only four years later, mentions the Firth of Clyde '*ubi est civitas Brettonum munitissima usque hodie quae vocatur Alcluith*', 'where there is a city of the Britons highly fortified to the present day and called Alcluith'. Elsewhere he names '*urbem Alcluith, quod lingua eorum significavit Petram Cluit; est enim iuxta fluvium nominis illius*', 'the city of Alcluith, which in their language means Rock of the Clyde, because it lies next to the river of that name'. He also notes that the western end of the Antonine Wall is found nearby. Bede lived at Jarrow, less than 200 miles distant. The fact that he says Alcluith is fortified 'up to the present time' is ample proof that the Rock was inhabited and actively defended.[54]

Twenty years later, another short but categoric reference appears in the Welsh *Brut y Tywysogion*, the 'Chronicle of the Princes':

DCCL. *Deg mlyned a deugeint a seith cant oed oet Crist pan vu y vróydyr róg y Brytanyeit ar Picteit yg góeith Maesydaóc, ac lladaód y Brytanyeit Talargan brenhin y Picteit. Ac yna y bu uaró Teódór map Beli.*

Seven hundred and fifty was the year of Christ when the battle between the Britons and the Picts took place, [that is,] the action of Maesydog, and the Britons killed Talargan, King of the Picts. And then Tewdwr, son of Beli, died.[55]

The cryptic information is important because it tallies with other snippets of both Welsh and Irish provenance. Teudebur map Beli, son of Beli II of 'The Rock', figures in the Harleian Genealogies as a contemporary of Oengus macFerguson of Pictland, whose brother Talorgen was killed at Maesydaóc/Mygedawc – a location identified with the modern Mugdock halfway between Dumbarton and Stirling. The Irish Annals of Tigernach put the death of 'Taudar mac Bili, ri Alo Cluaide' at 752.[56]

The death of King Teudebur/Taudar initiated a period of dynastic strife in which headlines of 'Catastrophe on the Rock' could have appeared at several points. The contested throne was secured by the late king's son, Dynfwal map Teudebur, but almost immediately his kingdom was invaded by a joint army of Picts and Angles, who turned up like vultures at the feast. On 1 August 756 King Dynfwal surrendered 'The Rock' jointly to Onuist, king of the Picts, and Eadberht, king of

Northumbria; the terms of submission are not known. But ten days later, as Eadberht marched home, he and his army were suddenly wiped out 'between *Ouania* and *Niwanbrig*'. The only possible perpetrator was Onuist, whom one of Bede's continuators, without charging him with the crime directly, characterizes as 'a tyrannical butcher'. The *Ouania* or River Avon, a Welsh name, would have been the one in West Lothian, and *Niwanbrig* or 'Newbridge', which is an Anglian name, would have been somewhere beyond the Northumbrian border. The Picto-Northumbrian alliance had collapsed, and the 'Kingdom of the Rock' gained a respite.

A more persistent threat, however, came from the continuing fusion of the Picts and the Gaelic Scots in a process undoubtedly helped by the final stage of Pictland's Christianization. Three parallel operations were in play. In the cultural sphere, the Gaelic-speaking Scots, long since converted to Christianity, provided the literate clergy who drove the conversion forward. They would have had little difficulty in persuading their Pictish converts to adopt their language as well as their religious beliefs. (Their success may be compared to that of the Anglo-Saxon clergy, who in a somewhat later period simultaneously converted and Anglicized the pagan Danes of the Danelaw.) At the same time, in the geographical sphere, the Gaels were migrating eastwards, physically mingling with the Picts and forming a solid belt of Scottish settlement from Argyll to Fife. By the time that the first known list of Pictland's provinces was drawn up, two of them had Gaelic names. *Atholl*, which means 'New Ireland', lies to the east of the mountainous watershed; *Gobharaidh* or 'Gowrie' lies north of the Tay round modern Perth. In the political sphere, ever closer relations were established between the Dalriadan and Pictish ruling houses, until the distinction between them grew blurred. Since Edinburgh would long remain in Northumbrian hands, the capital of the emerging kingdom was to be located at Dunkeld. The sacred coronation stone would be housed at the nearby abbey of Scone.[57] From the standpoint of the North Britons, a new and more dangerous rival was emerging from the combination of two old enemies.

The manoeuvrings whereby Gaelic dynasts from Dalriada merged with their counterparts in Pictland cannot be reconstructed with precision. One Pictish king, Oengus I macFerguson, is known to have originated in Argyll. Another, Oengus II (r. 820–34), briefly created a joint kingdom from sea to sea a hundred years later. But a disputed succession then spawned civil war; and a decade passed before the Gaelic contender,

Cinaed mac Alpin, better known as Kenneth macAlpin (810–58), secured the throne as 'king of the Picts'. In later times, macAlpin was to be widely credited with creating the first united 'Kingdom of Scotland', yet the attribution may be premature. Under his son, Constantine I (r. 863–77, the founder of Dunkeld), Argyll and Pictland were still being governed as separate entities, and it could be that the union was only completed permanently by Constantine II (r. 900–943). The kingdom's Gaelic name of 'Alba' was not recorded in macAlpin's time; the name of 'Scotland' was not used except by outsiders.

At some point during the Picto-Gaelic fusion, St Andrew was adopted as patron of the Alban kingdom. According to legend, the relics of the saint were donated to a King Oengus; the monastery of Cennrigmonoid (the core of the modern St Andrews), which became the focus of the saint's cult, dates from the mid-eighth century. The Alban flag was designed from the blue and white saltire of St Andrew.

The union was cemented above all by the Viking invasions. Sea-raiders from Scandinavia roared onto the scene at the end of the eighth century. Pouring down the coasts, they destroyed Lindisfarne in 793 and Iona in 795, then conquered the Isle of Man and settled in Ireland, Sutherland, Orkney and Shetland. That first attack on Lindisfarne caused repercussions similar to those which followed the arrival of Ida the Flamebearer 250 years earlier. The Anglo-Saxon Chronicle trembled:

> AD 793. This year came dreadful forewarnings over the land of the North-umbrians, terrifying the people most woefully: these were great sheets of light rushing through the air, and whirlwinds, and fiery dragons flying across the firmament. These tremendous tokens were followed soon after by famine, and on the sixth day before the Ides of January . . . by the harrowing inroads of heathen men, who made lamentable havoc in the Church of God on Holy Island, by rapine and slaughter.

The Vikings, like the Scots and Angles before them, intended to stay.

The north-west of Britain was especially vulnerable. By the 830s Viking intruders were making Dalriadan Argyll unsafe for habitation, devastating coastal settlements and raiding deep into the interior. In 839 a Viking host marched into the Pictish heartland of Fortriu, and killed the two sons of Oengus II. They did not settle, but they created the vital opening for Kenneth macAlpin, then ruler of Argyll, to launch his bid for the throne.

Vikings were to cause even worse havoc in the neighbouring 'Kingdom of the Rock'. Commentators write that 'The Rock' in that era

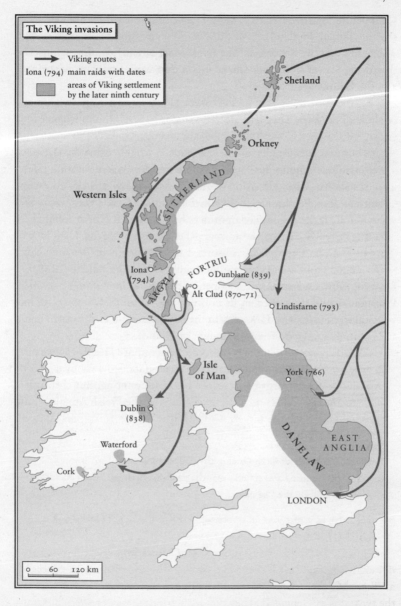

The Viking invasions

→ Viking routes
Iona (794) main raids with dates
▨ areas of Viking settlement
by the later ninth century

Shetland

Orkney

Western Isles

SUTHERLAND

Iona
(794)

ARGYLL

FORTRIU

Dunblane (839)

Alt Clud (870–71)

Lindisfarne (793)

Isle
of Man

York (766)

Dublin
(838)

DANELAW

EAST
ANGLIA

Waterford

Cork

LONDON

0   60   120 km

'seems to have remained subject to foreign control', or 'the kingdom seems to have been eclipsed'.[58] But the circumstances are nowhere clarified. The 'controllers' could have been Vikings or Picts, or 'Scots' from Dalriada, or possibly a combination of various outsiders. One solitary happening is attributed to *c.* 849: 'The Britons burned Dunblane.' Dunblane lay in Pictland, near Stirling. One possibility among several suggests that the Britons of 'The Rock' were already chafing against the growing power of a Picto-Gaelic union that would only grow stronger in the following decades.

By the late 860s the Vikings were threatening to overwhelm the whole of the Isles. They had created a major base in Dublin whence they were swarming all over Ireland and the western coasts of Britain. They held London, East Anglia and Humberside in what became the Danelaw. Wessex alone among the Anglo-Saxon kingdoms was mounting effective resistance. King Alfred of Wessex (r. 871–99) was lucky to escape their clutches. Further north, by moving up the Mersey, the Solway and the Humber, the Scandinavian raiders had created a Norse community in the Lake District of the former Rheged and a Viking Kingdom of York. They had completely absorbed the far north of Britain, which they called their 'Southland' (Sutherland). The earlier balance of power was in ruins, and the future lay open to bidders. If the Vikings prevailed, Britain would be turned in its entirety into another Norse realm like Denmark or Norway. If Wessex in the south or Alba in the north could rally, some new modus vivendi might be found.

All surviving contemporary sources agree that 'The Rock' was destroyed by Vikings in 870 or 871. The exact date can vary by a year or two, due to the hazards of retrospective year-counting. But chroniclers in Ulster, in St Davids and in three versions of the Welsh Annals all use the same name for the target, Alt Clud (the British form); and they all use verbs that imply complete destruction:

> 869. ... the battle of Cryn Onen [Ash Hill] took place.
> 870. Eight hundred and seventy was the year of Christ, and Caer Alclut was demolished by the Pagans.

> *Deg mlyned athrugeint ac wythgant oed Krist, AC Y TORRET KAER ALCLUT Y GAN Y PAGANYEIT*
>
> > (St Carodog of Llancarvan, *Brut y Tywysogion*
> > (Chronicle of the Princes))

> 869 *an Cat Brin Onnen*
> 870 *an Arx Alt Clut a gentilibus fracta est*
> 871 *an Guoccaun mersus est, rex Cereticiaun.*
>
> > (Nennius and the Welsh Annals)

870 *an Cat Brionnen annus. Cant Wrenonnen* (Ashdown)

871 *an Arx Alclut a Gentilibus fracta est. Alclut fracta est*

872 *an Guoccaun mersus est Gugan, rex Cereticiaun*
   rex Ceredigean mersus est

(Welsh Annals)

Obsesio Ailech Cluathe a Nordmannis, i.e. Amlaiph et Imhar ii regis Nord-mannorum obsederunt arcem illam et destruxerunt in fine 4 mensium arcem et predaverunt.

The siege of Ailech Cluathe by the Northmen, that is by Olaf and Ivar, two kings of the Northmen besieged the citadel, and at the end of four months destroyed and plundered it.

(Annals of Ulster)[59]

By piecing together these scattered bits of information, narratives of reasonable plausibility can be constructed:

It was in the year 870 that the Norse king of Dublin, Olaf the White ... decided on an expedition to plunder the kingdom of the Britons in Strathclyde. He set off with a large fleet from Dublin and, sailing up the Firth of Clyde, laid siege to Alclut. He was joined by another Viking ruler, Ivar Beinlaus (the 'Cripple' or 'one-legged'), who came north from York, which he had seized in 867. The garrison of Alclut held out for four months. But at length it was compelled to surrender, as the well on the Rock had dried up ... The citadel was destroyed and the kingdom of the Britons lay prostrate before the invaders, who remained in Strathclyde over the winter, [before] sailing back to Dublin with a fleet of two hundred ships laden with slaves and booty. The king of Strathclyde was killed shortly afterwards and the kingdom passed for a time under the control of neighbouring kings.[60]

The Viking fleet sailed away with its loot, heading no doubt for the Dublin slave market, though the presence of Viking-style 'hogsback' tombstones in the nearby Govan district indicates that a body of Vikings could have stayed behind.[61] But local survivors also remained; and the humbled monarchy of 'The Rock' was not eliminated. The exact fate of King Arthgal is hard to discover. One modern authority assumes that he was taken prisoner to Dublin.[62] Most accept the chronicler's statement that 'Arthgal, king of the Britons, was slain in 872 by counsel of Constantine, son of Kenneth [macAlpin]'. It is certain that the British king's son, Rhun map Arthgal, had married, or was about to marry, the sister of King Constantine I. The neatest solution, though it is uncertain, would show Constantine setting up Rhun during his father's absence and then persuading or paying the Dublin Vikings to kill Arthgal and to prevent his return.[63] One way or the other, it is clear that the Scots established their supremacy over the 'Kingdom of the Rock' in the early 870s, with Constantine I ruling as over-king and Rhun as sub-king.

As the Welsh *Brut y Tywysogion* put it, 'the men of Strathclyde who refused to unite with the English had to depart their country and go to Gwynedd'. It is likely that the Welsh chronicler was using 'English' as the English used the word 'Welsh' – to mean 'foreigners'. Yet the episode shows what really went on in the 'Dark Ages' when one native society was overrun by another. Some of the defeated population were sold into slavery. Some, probably most, stayed on to work the land and in time to integrate with the victors. But the ruling elite had to be replaced. If they were lucky, they would be given the choice of submitting to the victor's rule or of being expelled. If not, they would be killed. This explains how language and culture change in areas where the basic human gene pool remains the same. The example of post-Roman Britannia turning into Anglo-Saxon England is a prime case; the Britons of the north turning into Gaelic Strathclyders is another.

The departing elders of 'The Rock', who had chosen to reunite with their British kith and kin rather than with the incoming Gaels, could only have reached distant Gwynedd by sea. Their ships would have sailed on the tide, leaving the Rock behind, gliding past Bute and Arran (which they would have called something else), edging round the coast of *Aeron*, and out past the 'rip-tide' of the Ituna. They would have carried their bards and their scribes, who were to pass on the knowledge of the *Gwyr y Gogledd* to their Welsh hosts. As they must have known, hundreds, indeed thousands of years of history were being cut adrift with them. One cannot say for certain when this journey took place, but by 890, the exiles had appeared in the Welsh Annals, and are reported helping the king of Gwynedd to repel the 'Saxons'.[64]

From 870/871, therefore, the remaining Britons of 'The Rock' were closely subject to the rising Kingdom of 'Alba'. Formal feudal overlordship, which was slowly spreading round Europe at the time, was not yet introduced, but the shift in power was manifest. The monarchs of 'The Rock' henceforth acted in concert with their Alban superiors. The administrative centre was moved across the river from Alt Clud to Govan; and the name of Cumbria came increasingly into use for the sub-kingdom as a whole. Control over 'The Rock' and its tributary

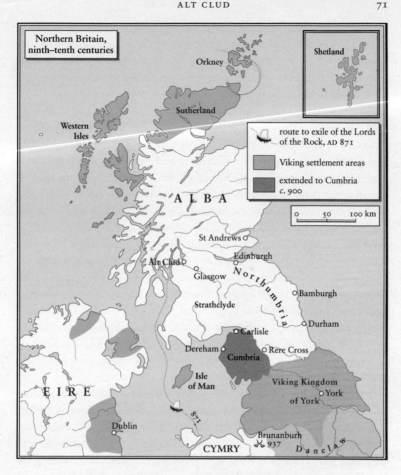

Northern Britain,
ninth–tenth centuries

Shetland

Orkney

Sutherland

Western
Isles

route to exile of the Lords
of the Rock, AD 871

Viking settlement areas

extended to Cumbria
c. 900

A L B A

0   50   100 km

St Andrews

Alt Clud   Edinburgh

Glasgow   Northumbria   Bamburgh

Strathclyde   Durham

Carlisle

Dereham   Rere Cross
Cumbria

Isle
of Man   Viking Kingdom
of York   York

E I R E

Dublin

Brunanburh
937   Danelaw

CYMRY

lands would have assisted sons and grandsons of Kenneth macAlpin to
strengthen their inheritance.

It was the Alban monarchs and their fellow Gaels who introduced
the name of Strath Cluaith or 'Strathclyde', by which Alt Clud would be
best known in later times. They had good reason to treat the people of
'The Rock' with some indulgence; from their point of view, the rulers of
Strathclyde were but a junior branch of their own family through the
maternal line. Eochaid map Rhun (*fl.* 878–9) even appears to have made
a bid for the senior, Alban throne on the strength of being Kenneth
macAlpin's grandson. One source calls him 'the first Briton to rule over
Gael'. He was dispossessed by the shadowy Giric MacRath, or 'Son of
Fortune', who held Britons, Norse and English in his house as slaves.

Yet the rift between the senior and the junior branches of the ruling family did not lead to a lasting feud. In any case, the imminent and unforeseen
collapse of Viking power beyond Hadrian's Wall was to draw the Strathclyders and the Scots into yet another set of power struggles in which
they would need to stand together.

In the tenth century, a resurgent Wessex came to the fore in southern
Britain. Within twenty years of King Alfred's death in 899 it was show-
ing signs not only of reducing the Danes and Vikings to submission but
also of creating a united 'Kingdom of all-Britain'. Athelstan (r. 924–39),
Alfred's grandson, succeeded to the Kingdom of Mercia as well as to
Wessex, and in 927 he launched a lightning northern campaign, destroy-
ing the Viking Kingdom of York, overrunning Northumbria as far as
the Forth, and obliging Constantine II, king of Scots, to sue for peace.
A meeting of five kings at Eamont Bridge in Cumbria acknowledged
Athelstan's overlordship. Apart from Athelstan and Constantine, the
participants included the king of 'West Wales', the 'king of Bamburgh'
and Ywain map Dynfwal of Strathclyde, otherwise 'Owen of Cumbria'.
The act of homage to Athelstan signalled more than the advance of
Anglo-Saxon power from the Tyne to the Forth; it marked the first step
in a long campaign by the English kings to claim hegemony over their
northern neighbours.

   Nonetheless, the humbling of Viking York and Northumbria allowed
the Strathclyders to move into part of the resultant vacuum, and to
recover many of the historic territories of the 'Old North'. In subsequent
decades, they reached southwards into the former lands of Rheged and
deep into the Pennines. Acting as a sub-state of 'Alba', they pushed the
frontier with England back beyond the zone where the Borders would
eventually settle. A boundary stone on the summit of Stainmore, variously
known as Rere Cross, Rear Cross or Rey Cross – halfway between Pen-
rith and Barnard Castle – probably marks the limit of Alban and Strathclyde
rule. A cluster of Cumbrian parish churches dedicated to St Mungo/
Kentigern, notably at Dearham near Cockermouth, attests to persistent
Clydeside influences. In this era, the customs and language of the Brythonic elements of the population, not least the Cumbric sheep-counters,
would have been strengthened, though the established dominance of the
Anglian and Norse elements was not displaced. The great majority of
Lake District place names, for example, like Bassenthwaite, Langdale or
Scafell, are self-evidently Norse in origin, while only a minority, like Der-
went, 'Oak Valley', or Helvellyn, 'Yellow Moor', are Brythonic. Dunmail

Raise on the road between Keswick and Grasmere, where in future times a cairn would mark the boundary between Cumberland and Westmorland, was named after one of the three sub-kings of Strathclyde of that name. In the early tenth century, the Dunmail cairn could have been a southern counterpart to Rere Cross on Stainmore.

Respite, however, was short. In 937, one of the most crucial, but frequently neglected battles in the history of the Isles was fought at *Brunanburh*, an unspecified location somewhere on Merseyside.[65] The Anglo-Saxon Chronicle breaks into verse for this entry. The poem, known as *The Battle of Brunanburh*, was translated by Alfred, Lord Tennyson:

> Athelstan King,
> Lord among Earls,
> Bracelet-bestower and
> Baron of Barons,
> He with his brother
> Edmund Atheling,
> Gaining a lifelong
> Glory in battle,
> Slew with the sword-edge
> There by Brunanburh,
> Brake the shield-wall,
> Hew'd the lindenwood,
> Hack'd the battleshield . . .

At Brunanburh, Athelstan of Wessex, titular 'King of All-Britain' faced a coalition of Welsh, Scots and Norse kings who were evidently alarmed by the surge of southern English power and who had brought their troops into Athelstan's territory. The king of Strathclyde, probably Ywain map Dynfwal, was among them. This was the point at which, if the fortunes of battle had favoured them, the non-English forces could have clipped the wings of Wessex. England was no more inevitable than Scotland was, and different turns could have been taken at every step of the way. As it was, Athelstan triumphed, and the anti-English coalition was broken. The Anglo-Saxon chronicler (again translated by Tennyson) proclaimed an ultimate victory over the 'Welsh':

> Never had huger
> Slaughter of heroes
> Slain by the sword-edge –
> Such as old writers

Have writ of in histories –
Hapt in this isle, since
Up from the East hither
Saxon and Angle from
Over the broad billow
Broke into Britain with
Haughty war-workers who
Harried the Welshman, when
Earls that were lured by the
Hunger of glory gat
Hold of the land.

The consequences of Brunanburh – what the English were to call the 'Great Battle' – were not immediately apparent. Indeed, Athelstan's early death inspired a temporary recovery of his enemies, and his heirs were required to fight hard to confirm his conquests. In 944–5, for example, Athelstan's half-brother and successor, Edmund the Elder, invaded the extended Kingdom of Strathclyde, defeated its sub-king, Dynfwal III – whom the Anglo-Saxon Chronicle calls 'Dunmail' – and, as part of a general settlement, insisted that Strathclyde be formally subordinated to Alba. The Alban Scots were being told to keep a tighter rein on their dependants. The sovereign life of the former 'Kingdom of the Rock' was reaching its term.

A solitary sentence in the Welsh *Brut y Tywysogion* is worthy of note. After listing the death of Bishop Emerys of St Davids in 944, it records, entirely without comment: '*Ystrat Clut adiffeithóyt y gan y Saeson*' ('Ystrat Clut was devastated by the Saxons'). This must have been at least the fourth time that 'The Rock' had been devastated, and the perpetrators can only have been the troops or allies of Edmund the Elder. But it was the first occasion that the Welsh dropped the traditional Brythonic name of Alt Clud, replacing it by Ystrad Clut, or 'Vale of Clyde' – a simple calque of the Gaelic name. The Brythonic/Cumbric character of the kingdom was slipping; Gaelicized Alban 'Strathclyde' was emerging, and the Welsh were aware of it.[66] The Britons of the Old North were not even mentioned.

In the next generation, as the Anglo-Saxon Chronicle reports, six *reguli* or 'subject kings' were required to row the barge of Edmund's successor, Edgar, along the River Dee in a ritual, Viking-style act of subordination, elsewhere called the 'Submission of Chester'. One of the later Dynfwals participated as a rower, thereby giving him a certain standing. The symbolism would not have been lost on contemporaries. Strathclyde had benefited from a temporary geographical expansion, and its political status, though diminished, was not inconsiderable. The age of independence was past. But the former Alt Clud was not yet an integral province of Alba. The descendants of Ceredig kept their separate identity, and by using old British names they clearly remained conscious of their ancestry, but their separate activities were limited. When they went to war, they and their men invariably fought alongside their Alban superiors.[67]

In the eleventh century the Britishness of Strathclyde continued to fade, even though it benefited to some extent from the new preoccupations that took centre stage both in England and in Alba. All parts of the Isles were shaken by the terminal convulsions of the Viking Age. In England, the Anglo-Saxon monarchy was overthrown by Cnut Sweynsson the Great (r. 1018–35), who briefly raised the prospect of an Anglo-Scandinavian empire. In 1066 two separate hostile expeditions landed in England. The first, led by Harald Sigurdsson 'Hardrada', sailed from Norway to the mouth of the Tyne in September and was destroyed at the Battle of Stamford Bridge. The second, led by Duke William of Normandy, the grandson of Frenchified Vikings, crossed the Channel in October and after the Battle of Hastings seized the English throne. In the years after 1066, when England was turned into a Norman colony, much of the Conqueror's time was spent in the 'Harrying of the North', in subduing Northumbria and invading Scotland. The Anglo-Scottish settlement in the Treaty of Abernethy (1072) included an act of homage which further strengthened the English argument that Scotland was by now a legal fief of England.

Northern Britain in this era was assuming the shape and character which would be recognizable throughout the Middle Ages. Though Orkney and Shetland, Sutherland and the Western Isles remained in Norse hands, the great bulk of territory was united under one ruler. Furthermore, the kings of Alba progressively adopted the title of *rex Scottorum* or 'king of the Scots', thereby cementing the concept of 'Scotland'; their conquest of northern Northumbria, which followed the capture of Edinburgh in 1020, engendered a further shift in self-identity. The absorption of the Lallans-speaking Lowlands, whose aristocracy now possessed strong English and Norman connections, challenged the previous dominance of the Gaeltacht.

Nonetheless, the House of macAlpin continued to control the monarchy of Alba/Scotland for most of the century. In 1031 Malcolm I and his associates submitted to Cnut when he came north for the purpose, and no conflict ensued. The one interval in the macAlpins' hold on the throne began in 1040, when Donnchad I (Duncan) was killed by MacBethad mac Findlaich (r. 1040–57), lord of Moray, known to contemporaries as the *Ri Deircc* or 'Red King' and to readers of Shakespeare as Macbeth. Almost all historians of the period insist that Shakespeare's play makes for great drama but for poor history.[68] No contemporary account describes him as a tyrant. He ruled right up to the eve of the Norman Conquest, and gave shelter to exiles from England. He was the last king of Alba to preside over a Gaelic-speaking court. He was killed by the forces of Malcolm III Canmore (r. 1058–93), son of the murdered Donnchad.

Such was the setting for the final span of Strathclyde's political history. The kingdom stretched deep into the zone contested between Scotland and England, and its affairs inevitably became entangled with Anglo-Scottish rivalry. At one time, it was assumed that Eogan II, otherwise known as Owain the Blind (d. 1018), was the last of his line. His presence at the Battle of Carham in 1016 or 1018 near Durham between the Scots and English is well attested. But his death there is not. In fact, the sub-monarchs of Strathclyde and their state still had decades in front of them. There are strong indications that Donnchad had ruled over Strathclyde as a royal appanage before acceding to the Alban throne; and there is little doubt that the English targeted Strathclyde during the last years of Macbeth's reign. In 1054 Siward, the mighty earl of Northumbria, who had come to Britain in Cnut's time, led a large fleet and a huge army northwards, provoking a bloody field of slaughter at the unlocated Battle of the Seven Sleepers. Macbeth was put to flight, and Siward's son killed. More to the point, according to an English chronicler, Siward 'made Mael Coluim, prince of the Cumbrians, a king'.[69] In the Scottish tradition, this prince has usually been identified as Macbeth's enemy, Malcolm Canmore; but it seems more likely that he was a Cumbrian/Strathclyder of the same name who was reinstated by Siward in the land of his forebears.[70] If this was the case, eleventh-century Strathclyde was oscillating between alternating phases of Scottish and English suzerainty.

One thing is certain: the Gaelic pressures on the Britishness of Strathclyde and on the Cumbrian language were augmented by parallel pressures from England. The steady Gaelicization which had been proceeding since the Viking destruction of 'The Rock' in 870/871, was now competing with Anglicization. The linguistic shifts have not been well documented, but would have proceeded at different speeds in different districts and in different milieux. From Rhun map Arthgal (who had a Gaelic wife) onwards, the sub-kings of Strathclyde would probably have been bilingual, with the Gaelic steadily pushing the Brythonic into the background. Thanks to the English invasion of 1054, they would have been turning increasingly to Lallans after the mid-century, just as Macbeth's court was. The sub-kings' Brythonic subjects would have accepted linguistic change less rapidly. The first of them to succumb would probably have lived in the northerly districts adjacent to Argyll, where the influx of Gaelic would have been strongest, or in the few tiny urban and ecclesiastical centres, like Glasgow. Since Church appointments were influenced by ruling circles, and education was controlled by the Church, the small educated class would have followed the fashions of the court. The farmers and pastoralists of the countryside would have been much more resistant. Centuries could have passed before the old idioms finally gave way.

In the twelfth century the passing of the dominance of the Brythonic tongue did not bring about any instant demise of the Strathclyders' sense of identity. Strathclyde would long remember its origins, and its people would long be marked by distinctive customs, by distinctive laws and no doubt by a distinctive accent. There can be little doubt, for example, that Brythonic identity endured into the era when Scotland's Highland clans were forming. Several clan names are manifestly Brythonic in origin, and a number of clan genealogies boast Brythonic ancestry. The clearest example is that of Clan Galbraith, whose Gaelic name means 'Foreign Briton' and whose ancestral fortress was built on the island of Inchgalbraith in Loch Lomond. The Galbraiths trace their origins to Gilchrist Breatnach, 'Gilchrist the Briton', who married a daughter of the earl of Lennox in the late twelfth century. Their emblem, a boar's head, is the same as that of the late kings of Strathclyde. The Colquhouns of Luss, the Kincaids, the MacArthurs and the Clan Lennox all have similar connections with the territory where Gaels and Britons once overlapped.[71]

In 1113 David, the son of Malcolm Canmore and St Margaret (1045–93), who had strong English connections, was given the title of 'prince of the Cumbrians'. The honour may have signified little more than a royal courtesy (like that of princes of Wales at the medieval English court) but it can also be taken as an indication that Strathclyde was still a discrete administrative unit, and that the kings of Scotland recognized its particularity. It was during David's years as Cumbrian prince that he built his hunting castle at Cadzow (now Hamilton), and when the first of Glasgow's permanent line of bishops was appointed the medieval bishops of Glasgow would habitually refer to their diocese as 'Cumbria'.[72] Twenty years later, after ascending the Scottish throne, King David brought Norman barons into Strathclyde , as part of the 'Davidian Revolution' and, as his late mother would have approved, adding one more layer of political and linguistic culture. Ever since the fall of 'The Rock' in 870/871, Govan and its stone-built old church had served as Strathclyde's cultural and government centre. It had been the seat of the royal residence, and it was the site of large-scale production of Celtic crosses. But it now ceded prominence to Glasgow, where David I patronized the cult of St Mungo.

Not far from Glasgow, the islands in the Firth of Clyde might plausibly be thought the most resistant strongholds of Brythonic culture. It would appear, however, that Gaelic had taken over and that Irish poets of the period were already talking of the Firth as part of their own world. In the famous *Acallam na Senórach* or 'Old Men's Colloquy', a twelfth-century Gaelic poet imagined a meeting between St Patrick, the Briton who had converted Ireland, and Caílte, a disciple of 'Fingal', the most illustrious of Ireland's legendary heroes. The meeting is entirely unhistorical; St Patrick belongs to post-Roman Britain, while Fingal is placed at a variety of points right up to the Viking Age. The latest of the Fingal legends finds him defending Glencoe against a Norse host that had sailed into Loch Leven, which would make him a contemporary to the Viking attack on Alt Clud. At all events, the two men are imagined to have exchanged views on a wide range of topics. In one sequence, St Patrick asks Caílte whether the hunting grounds are better on the Irish or the Scottish shore. The answer names an island within view of White Tower Crag:

> Arran blessed with stags, encircled by the sea,
> Island that fed hosts, where black spears turn crimson.
>
> Carefree deer on its peaks, branches of tender berries,
> Streams of icy water, dark oaks decked with mast,
>
> Greyhounds here and beagles, blackberries, fruit of sloe,
> Trees thick with blackthorns, deer spread about the oaks,

Rocks with purple lichen, meadows rich with grass,
A fine fortress of crags, the leaping of fawns and trout,

Gentle meadows and plump swine, gardens pleasant beyond belief,
Nuts on the bough of hazel, and longships sailing by.

Lovely in fair weather, trout beneath its banks,
Gulls scream from the cliffs, Arran ever lovely.[73]

When these enchanting evocations were composed, Alauna, Aloo, Alt
Clud and the Cumbrian 'Kingdom of Strathclyde' were all dissolving
into history.

'The Rock' itself drops out of sight. *Dun Breteann*, the 'Fort of the
Britons', completely disappears from the historical record between 944
and the late Middle Ages. Archaeological evidence suggests that it was
never totally abandoned, but it became, at best, a backwater. The active life
of Strathclyde had moved elsewhere. Other ports serviced the river traffic.
Ships sailed past without mooring. The city of Glasgow burgeoned further
upstream; and across the river the Barony of Renfrew served as the base of
a great Norman family, the fitzAlan-Stewarts, for whom a royal future
beckoned.[74]

Some estimates extend the terminal phase of the Cumbric language into
the thirteenth century, that is, into the age of William Wallace, Robert the
Bruce and Scotland's struggle for independence. Thanks to his exploits
in the wars against England, Wallace rose to be Scotland's national hero.
Yet his origins are extremely obscure, and historians have long contested the details of his birth and parentage. It is readily acknowledged
that Wallace's reputation is 'legend-encrusted'[75] and that 'his early life is
a mystery'.[76] Nonetheless, one faction clings to his birthdate in 1272
and to his birth in the village of Elderslie near Paisley, where an imposing monument now stands.[77] Another faction favours Kilmarnock's
Riccarton Castle in Ayrshire.[78]

One of the few hard facts in the story is that the surname of Wallace – *Uallas* in Gaelic – means 'Welshman' or 'Briton'. Like the English
name for Wales, it is a variant on the standard Germanic label for foreigner, and it was used by English-speakers both in the Welsh Marches
and in Cumbrian districts further north. As a result, there were lots of
medieval Wallaces, not only in English counties like Shropshire but also
in parts of southern Scotland. At one time, the hero's surname was
explained by the ingenious notion that his forebears migrated from

Shropshire in the retinue of the fitzAlans. But the supposition is entirely unsupported by evidence. It was the doyen of Scottish surname scholars, George Fraser Black, who first gave currency to the idea that William Wallace's paternal family were Strathclyde Britons.[79]

The geographical context is important. Wallace's traditional birthplace at Elderslie, now close to Glasgow Airport's southern runway, lies literally within sight of the Rock, and prior to the arrival of the fitzAlans in the 1130s, lay in the centre of the former British heartland. In any case, all the localities linked with the hero's early life, whether Elderslie, Riccarton or Lanark (where he killed the English sheriff in 1297), are in the same post-Brythonic vicinity. Since Gaelic had supplanted Cumbric there, they add credibility to the report that Wallace was known to his Gaelic-speaking comrades as *Uilleam Breatnach*, or 'William the Briton'. This does not prove that Wallace himself was a Cumbric-speaker. But it does hint at the slight possibility that the 'Braveheart' may have had a similar connection to Scottishness that St Patrick had to Irishness.[80]

Similar questions surround the origins of the most powerful of the Highland clans, the Campbells. Their oldest known possessions were concentrated in the district of Cowal, immediately adjacent to the Kyles of Bute; and their subsequent heartland round Loch Awe and upper Loch Fyne lies within walking distance of Loch Lomond. Their Gaelic name of MacCailinmor derives from a famous thirteenth-century warrior, 'Colin Campbell the Great', but the MacArthurs of Strachur provide a parallel line of descent. Their sobriquet of Campbell comes from the Gaelic *caim beil* or 'twisted mouth', and is usually interpreted as 'a person whose speech is unintelligible'. In other words, they were not Gaelic-speaking Scots. 'Clan Campbell', writes the latest historian of the clans, 'probably originated among the Old Welsh kindreds of the ancient kingdom of Strathclyde.'[81]

One would like to think, therefore, that somewhere in the shadow of the Rock the old ways lingered on. Perhaps, in some modest tavern or fisherman's cabin, the old-timers might have chatted in the old Cumbric-Brythonic tongue, singing the old songs, and telling the old tales about Ceredig and St Patrick, about Mungo and the Salmon, about the great battles of Catraeth, Nechtansmere and the Seven Sleepers. They would have wondered about the fate of the kinsfolk who had sailed away into exile, never to return. And they would have taught their children to count on their fingers: *yinty, tinty, tetheri, metheri, bamf . . .*

III

The history of Scotland, like the history of England, has passed through several distinct phases, in which the cultural and linguistic shifts have been no less far-reaching than the political ones. One has to put aside the popular notion that language and culture are endlessly passed on from generation to generation, rather as if 'Scottishness' or 'Englishness' were essential constituents of some national genetic code. If this were so, it would never be possible to forge new nations – like the United States of America or Australia – from diverse ethnic elements. The capacity of human societies both to absorb and to discard cultures is much underestimated. In reality, just as individuals can go abroad and merge into a foreign community, so a stationary population, if subjected to a changed linguistic and cultural environment, can quite easily be persuaded to follow suit. Dominant cultures are closely connected to dominant power groups. As the balance of power shifts, the balance of cultures shifts as well.

During the lifetime of the 'Kingdom of the Rock', the British population of the 'Old North' was repeatedly subjected to external cultural impulses. In the Roman period Latin was the challenger, together with the classical and later the Christian culture to which Latin gave access. In the 'Dark Ages' a double assault was mounted by the combination of Gaelic spreading from the north and west, and various forms of English moving in from the south. Pagan Norse culture made an impact during the Viking Age, just as Norman French did in the period following the Conquest. In the end, after a protracted struggle for survival, the Brythonic/Cumbrian language sank beneath the waves, and the 'Strathclyders' were transformed into a particular species of Scotsmen.

In medieval Scotland, the Gaelic Scots, who had founded the united kingdom in the ninth century and had given it their name, were steadily elbowed out. Their ascendancy lasted for only 200 years or so,[82] replaced by new, non-Gaelic power groups based in the southern Lowlands. They themselves were increasingly hemmed in, pushed back to their retreats in the Highlands and Islands. Having enjoyed their hour of glory by absorbing the Picts and the Britons, they were left facing the same prospect of slow annihilation that had once faced their rivals in Pictdom and the Old North. For a time, after Scotland reasserted its independence from England in the fourteenth century, a certain internal balance was maintained, but seen in the longer perspective the long rearguard action had already begun.

In the early modern era, however, the position of the Gaeltacht began to slip again. Large sections of north-eastern Scotland were being Anglicized. The Lowlanders turned Protestant while many of the Highlanders, whose clans still lived from their age-old practices of seasonal raiding and cattle-rustling, remained Catholic. Most seriously, in 1603 a Stuart king acceded to the throne of England. This gave the Scottish Lowlanders and Protestants an external power-link that the Gaels could never match. Shortly afterwards, a plantation of militant Scots Protestants was established in Ulster, cutting the Gaels off from their Irish kinsfolk. Later that century Oliver Cromwell demonstrated with fire and sword that the three kingdoms in the Isles could no longer be regarded as equals. In 1707 a Protestant Hanoverian monarchy, subservient to a distant Parliament at Westminster, was imposed. From then on, from the Gaelic viewpoint, the last stand was only a matter of time.[83]

The deep sense of injustice, and of gathering gloom, which beset the Gaels as they watched the failure of their Risings in 1715 and 1745 and the suppression of their way of life, must have echoed the feelings of the Britons of the Old North almost a thousand years before. Their warriors were no less brave. Their language was no less poetic. Their history was no less ancient. Yet they were succumbing to the bigger battalions and to political necessity. In the prelude to the decisive Battle of Culloden in 1746, the Gaelic clansmen recited their genealogies under cannonfire to give them purpose for the fight on the rain-soaked moor. The Britons at Catraeth or Nechtansmere might well have done the same. For the ill-fated Celts were imbued with a suitable spirit of fatalism. Things occurred because they had to. Nature was red in tooth and claw. Animals killed animals. Men fought men. Species became extinct, but life went on. Death was part of living.

The difference between the fate of Gaeldom and that of the Old North lies in a series of reprieves from which the Gaels have benefited. After 1746, when the Highlanders were forbidden to carry arms, to wear their tartans or to speak their native language, tens of thousands were shipped off to Canada during the Clearances, and many of the glens were left with nothing more than sheep and desolation.[84] In popular usage, 'Scotland' became near unmentionable and was replaced by 'North Britain'. After the Napoleonic Wars, however, a conscious effort was made to reintegrate the Gaelic heritage into mainstream Scottish life. When George IV visited Edinburgh in 1822, Walter Scott, whose novels had immortally romanticized Scottish history, staged a great show, where kilts and tartans could be worn again. In a symbolic gesture of reconciliation, Queen Victoria established her summer residence at Balmoral, enhancing the Highlands' romantic image. Ever since then, Scotland's identity has fed on a fascinating symbiosis between the Lowland heritage of Robbie Burns and the Highland heritage of Rob Roy MacGregor. In the twentieth century, when Gaelic was dying its second death, it received eleventh-hour resuscitation by injections of educational support, Gaelic television and radio channels, and the status of an official language.[85]

Strathclyde's modern destiny has been deeply influenced by the Highland–Lowland divide. The Firth of Clyde formed a key sector of the frontline for centuries, like the Antonine Wall before it. Yet during the Industrial Revolution the Gaels came back in force. Together with the Irish from across the sea, they poured into Victorian Clydeside, to work the mines and to build the ships. They came, not as conquering heroes, but as penniless migrants and hungry job-seekers, begging for employment in a foreign land. They, too, had to assimilate, but they gave Glasgow a large dose of its inimitable modern flavour. They made Glasgow Celtic the equal of Glasgow Rangers. They ensured that the home of Harry Lauder and St Mungo is as different from Edinburgh as *Dun Breteann* would once have been from Bernician Dunedin.[86]

Even so, the long-term prospects for the Gaelic world are precarious. Both in Ireland and in Scotland it still stands only one step from annihilation. One is reminded of the remarkable work of the Highland clergyman James Macpherson (1736–96), whose passion for the Gaels pulled off one of the great triumphs of literary fakery. His collection of poems, first published as *Ossian*, purported to be translations of works by an ancient Gaelic bard, fortuitously discovered in a dusty dungeon. They were nothing of the sort, the product, rather, of Macpherson's own fertile imagination. But they fooled most of the eminent literati of the day. They convinced Goethe, won over Scott and enchanted Napoleon. And they show that Macpherson was well aware of the precedent of 'The Rock':

> I have seen the walls of Balaclutha
> But they were desolate...
> And the voice of the people is heard no more.
> The thistle shook its lonely heard;
> The moss whistled in the wind.[87]

3

Burgundia

Five, Six or Seven Kingdoms
(c. 411–1795)

I

Bornholm, 'the Pearl of the Baltic', is a small, lonely, Danish island in the middle of the sea. It lies 100 miles east of central Denmark, and half-way between Sweden and Poland. Its area measures about 700 square miles – similar to that of the Isle of Man or of Malta, and its population, which is slowly declining, stands at the latest official count at 42,050 (2009). Administratively, since 2007 it has been tacked onto Denmark's Capital Region, and it lives from fishing, farming and mining, and in the summer from tourism. Traditional exports include granite, clinker and herrings.[1]

One usually reaches Bornholm by ferry, three and a half hours from German Sassnitz, six from Copenhagen, six and a half from Świnoujście in Poland, and two by hydrofoil from Ystad in Sweden. One can also fly to the airport at Rønne, either by SAS Scandinavian or by the local carriers, Cimber Air and until April 2010 'Wings of Bornholm'.[2]

The island's landscape is pleasantly varied. The interior presents a mixture of lush pastures and dark forests. Some of the beaches are low and sandy, others lined with steep, volcanic cliffs. Many, like the favourite Dueodde Strand, are covered in superfine, bright white sand. There are a number of small towns, such as Rønne, Nexø, Allinge, Gudhjem and Svaneke. The highest point reaches 1,082 feet. But Bornholm's most glorious feature arrives with the long summer days, which give twenty hours of bright skies, warm sun and Baltic breeze. The mild, sunny climate encourages gardens and orchards, and in sheltered spots an exotic display of flowering bushes and fig trees.

Bornholmers speak a language, *Bornholmsk*, that differs both from standard Danish and Swedish; its grammatical features such as triple genders are similar to those in Norwegian or Icelandic and its phonetic patterns similar to south-Swedish Scanian.[3] An organization called *Bevar*

Bornholmsk is devoted to the language's preservation, and several successful folk groups perform the island's music and songs.[4] Danes from Copenhagen can sometimes be seen consulting a Danish-Bornholmsk dictionary. In medical circles, the name of Bornholm is linked incongruously to a viral infection called *epidemic pleurodynia*, otherwise known as the 'Devil's Grip', the 'Grasp of the Phantom' or, more prosaically, Bornholm disease. The malady was first described in 1933.[5]

Nonetheless, tourist publicity eulogizes this 'paradise for simple souls', where all manner of open-air pursuits flourish. The brochures talk of the *Østersøens Perle* ('Pearl of the Baltic'), *Solopgangens Land* ('Sunrise Land'), *maleriske fiskelejer* ('quaint fishing hamlet'), *Pelle Erobreren* (*Pelle the Conqueror* – the title of a popular novel[6]) and, of course, *Velkommen til Bornholm*. Biking, golfing, fishing, beach-walking, kite-flying, wind-surfing and a visit to one of the nature parks are all strongly recommended. There is a Birds of Prey Show and a Butterfly Park, and, in the long June days, festivals for rock-climbers and for the enthusiasts of the modern sport of ultra-running.[7] Every year, the harbour at Tejn hosts the Bornholm Trolling Master competition, which involves sea-fishing in speedboats.[8] Since bathing or sunbathing in the nude is legal throughout Denmark, Bornholm offers infinite opportunites for naturists.[9] The area west of the lighthouse on Dueodde Strand is an old-established location. Bornholm also advertises itself as the 'Bright Green Island'. Thirty per cent of the island's energy is already generated by wind turbines in a project which aims to replace all petrol-driven cars with electric vehicles by 2011.[10]

Holiday-makers are encouraged to explore Bornholm's historical legacy, or at least parts of it. Topics not widely advertised include the lengthy refusal of the Red Army to leave after the Liberation of 1945, and the elaborate radio intercept stations which were installed by NATO during the Cold War. The main emphasis nowadays is on the enigmatic 'round churches', which the Knights Templar built in the late medieval period,[11] and on the local patriots who fought for the island's freedom from the Swedes in the mid-seventeenth century. Many visitors make for the spectacular cliff-top ruins of Hammershus Castle, the largest fortified building in northern Europe, which was built by a Danish king, Valdemar the Victorious, early in the thirteenth century and commands stunning views over the water to Sweden. An annual jousting tournament is held there, yet the view alone is sufficient reason to visit. On a fine summer's morning, the shimmering light that hovers over the waves below the battlements produces magical moments. Time and space can merge; the imagination races. Viewed from the cliff top of 'today', the cliff foot becomes 'yesterday', the advancing lines of sea horses the centuries of history, and the far shore, barely visible, the Age of the *Völkerwanderung*.

Investigations into Bornholm's earliest history are no less rewarding. Local archaeologists have established that the sequence of prehistoric graves came to a sudden end, strongly suggesting that the inhabitants had either been wiped out by a natural disaster, like the plague, or had departed en masse. Here, the Old Norse form of the island's name, *Burgundarholm*, is relevant. Alfred the Great, composing his translation of Orosius in the Viking Age, called it *Burgenda Land*.

Of course, when searching for origins, there is no need to assign one homeland to one people. Primitive tribes were mobile; they were all to some degree migrants or nomads. Even those who practised agriculture would stop for a season somewhere, and then move on. Their season might last for a couple of summers, a couple of generations, or even a couple of centuries. It came to an end when arable land was exhausted, when the climate changed, or when the next warlike tribe arrived to replace them. All in all, therefore, the traditional identification of Bornholm with the prehistoric wanderings of the Burgundians is entirely credible: by no means proven, but more than a mere possibility. Nor does it imply that Bornholm was the Burgundians' only significant stop, or that other peoples did not stop there also. But the Burgundians must have been present for long enough and in sufficient numbers for early geographers to make a lasting connection.[12]

It would be idle to suppose, however, that the average visitor worries about such matters. Only historical enthusiasts follow every turn in the fortunes of an island tossed around between successive Baltic powers. The Danes, when they think about the past, have their own priorities. They dream about Viking exploits; and they remember the time, not too long ago, when the far shore beyond Bornholm, now in Sweden, belonged to Denmark. Part of the action of the much celebrated Norse *Jomsvikingesaga*, which chronicles the wars of Vikings and Slavs, takes place on the island. Known history, the guidebook declares, began when Bornholm was the property of the medieval bishops of Lund. In modern times, the island was captured by Denmark in 1523, placed in pawn to the city of Lübeck, recovered by the Danes, occupied by the Swedes until 1648, visited by Peter the Great of Russia in 1716, seized by the Germans in 1940–45, and liberated by the Red Army.[13] Aware, perhaps, of fragments of this story, the carefree tourists paddle in the seawater or take off their clothes, ride their bikes, fly their kites and sail their boats.

In December 2010, hit by the severest of the snowstorms that paralysed much of northern Europe, Bornholm was declared a disaster area. The Danish Metereological Institute measured a minimum snowfall of 55 inches (140 centimetres) across the island, though some parts were blocked by drifts up to 20 feet (6 metres). After a week of vainly trying to dig themselves out, the inhabitants called for help. They had to rely on military vehicles to deliver supplies, and to dump mountains of snow into the sea.[14] Apart from the news that this was the coldest December since records were first kept in 1874, they had no time whatsoever to think about history.

II

Few subjects in European history have created more havoc than that summarized by the phrase 'all the Burgundies'. Conflicting information is supplied by almost every historical or reference work one cares to consult. As long ago as 1862, James Bryce, Professor of Civil Law at Oxford, was sufficiently worried to include a special note 'On the Burgundies' in his pioneering study of the Holy Roman Empire. 'It would be hard to mention any geographical name', he wrote, 'which ... has caused, and continues to cause, more confusion ... '[15]

Bryce was a man of indefatigable stamina. He was a Glaswegian, an Alpinist, a Gladstonian liberal, an ambassador to the United States, and a meticulous fact-checker. (He once climbed Mount Ararat to check where Noah's Ark had rested.) His once famous 'Note A' lists the ten entities which, by his calculation, had borne the name of Burgundy 'at different times and in different districts':

I. The *Regnum Burgundionum* (Kingdom of the Burgundians), AD 406–534.

II. The *Regnum Burgundiae* (Kingdom of Burgundy), under the Merovingians.

III. The *Regnum Provinciae seu Burgundiae* (Kingdom of Provence or of Burgundy), founded 877, 'less accurately called Cis-Jurane Burgundy'.

IV. The *Regnum Iurense, or Burgundia Transiurensis* (Kingdom of the Jura, or of 'Trans-Jurane Burgundy'), founded in 888.

V. The *Regnum Burgundiae*, or *Regnum Arelatense* (Kingdom of Burgundy or of Arles), formed in 937 by the union of III and IV.

VI. *Burgundia Minor* (the Lesser Duchy, *Klein Burgund*).

VII. The Free County or Palatinate of Burgundy (Franche-Comté, Freigrafschaft).

VIII. The *Landgrafschaft* or Landgravate of Burgundy, part of VI.

IX. The Imperial Circle of Burgundy, *Kreis Burgund*, established 1548.

X. The Duchy of Burgundy (Bourgogne), which was 'always a fief of the Crown of France'.[16]

The complexities are self-evident; one need not delve into Bryce's Note too deeply before doubts arise. Yet it is one of the few attempts to see the Burgundian problem as a whole. It naturally invites further exploration.

The Kingdom of the Burgundians (No. I on Bryce's list) was a short-lived affair. It was set up by a tribal chief or warleader, Gundahar, on the west bank of the middle Rhine in the first decade of the fifth century. He and his father Gibica had brought their people over the river into the Roman Empire, probably during the great barbarian irruption in the winter of 406–7, and then helped elevate a local usurper, Jovinus, who was proclaimed 'anti-emperor' at Moguntiacum (Mainz); Jovinus in his turn pronounced the Burgundians to be imperial 'allies'. In Rome's opinion, the whole arrangement was deeply irregular.

Where exactly the Burgundian horde had come from is the subject of much learned speculation.[17] Their presence in the late fourth century on the River Main (immediately to the east of the Roman *limes*) is documented in Roman sources, as are their wars with the Alemanni. A memorial inscription in Augusta Treverorum (Trier), attests to the Roman

service of one Hanulfus, a member of the Burgundian royal family. Earlier stages of the Burgundian itinerary are less certain. One hypothesis proposes a four-stage trek,[18] the first part of which would have taken them from Scandinavia to the lower Vistula by the first century AD. The second stage sees them moving to the Oder, the third to the middle Elbe by the third century, and the fourth to the Main.

The Burgundians spoke a Germanic language similar to that of the Goths, who also hailed from Scandinavia. Like the Goths, they had adopted the Arian form of Christianity, and may well have been familiar with the Gothic Bible (as translated by Wulfila, a converted Goth from northern Bulgaria).[19] Furthermore, through interaction with various non-Germanic tribes, they had acquired the Hunnic practice of female head-binding, which was applied to girls during infancy and elongated their skulls for life. This has had the unintended consequence of making their graves instantly recognizable to archaeologists.

Gundahar's kingdom was centred on the old Celtic capital of Borbetomagus (Worms), stretching south to Noviomagus (Speyer) and Argentoratum (Strasbourg). The newcomers, initially some 80,000 strong, were settled among a well-established Gallo-Roman population. They are mentioned in the Anglo-Saxon poem *Widsith*, in a brief recitation of fifth-century rulers. Widsith, the 'Far Traveller', was bold enough to claim that he had visited Gundahar's kingdom in person:

Mid Þyringum ic waes	I was with the Thuringians
. . . ond mid Burgendum.	. . . and with the Burgundians.
Þaer ic beag geþah.	There, they gave me a ring.
Me þaer Guðohere forgeaf	There Gunthere gave me
Glaedlicne maþþum	A shining treasure
Songes to leane.	To pay for my songs.
Naes þaet saene cyning!	He was no bad king.[20]

Gundahar's position, however, was shaky from the start. As soon as the Roman authorities regained their composure, they determined to expunge him. In 436 the Roman general Flavius Aetius, servant of the Emperor Valentinian III, called in Attila's Huns, and used them to do the bloody work. Reputedly, 20,000 Burgundians perished.

The massacre of the Burgundians passed into the annals of North European myth. Echoes of it found a place in many of the Norse sagas; and it lay at the heart of the tales of the *Nibelungen*, or as the Norsemen called them, the *Niflungar*, the descendants of Nefi and owners of a fabulous Burgundian treasure. Gundahar reappears as Gunnar; and

Gunnar's sister Gudrun gives rise to a famous lineage after her marriage to Atli (Attila). The Eddaic poem the *Atlakvida*, or 'Lay of Atli', contains many events and names characteristic of the fifth and sixth centuries, including Gunnar and Gudrun.[21] In the German tradition, by contrast, the mythical realm of *Niflheim* (Mist-Home) is inhabited by warring giants and dwarfs. Nybling is the original guardian of the hoard; Gundahar becomes Günter; Gudrun Kriemhild; and Kriemhild weds Siegfried, meaning 'Peace of Victory', son of Siegmund and Sieglind. In these later myths and sagas the Burgundians are frequently described, anachronistically, as Franks. The late-medieval *Nibelungenlied* is driven by a mix of fact and fantasy, though the basic historical underlay is rarely disputed by modern scholars:

> *Uns ist in alten maeren wunders vil geseit*
> *von helden lobebaeren, von grôzer arebeit,*
> *von freuden, hôchgezîten, von weinen und von klagen,*
> *von küener recken strîten . . .*

('We're told of wonders in the ancient tales, / of praise-worthy heroes, of great ordeals, / of joy and feasting, of weeping and wailing / and of the clash of bold warriors . . .')[22]

Following the massacre at Borbetomagus, the trail of the Burgundians briefly goes cold, but it soon resurfaces in accounts of the battles between Aetius and the Huns. There is a strong probability that one group of Burgundian warriors had been captured and conscripted by the Huns, while others under the new king, Gundioc (r. 437–74), were taken into Roman service. Burgundians in consequence fought on both sides in the great Battle of the Catalaunian Fields in June 451 (see p. 21, above), between the Roman general Aetius and the Huns, where according to Gibbon 'the whole fate of western civilisation hung in the balance'. After his victory, Aetius made Gundioc the grant of a kingdom in the province of Sabaudia (an old form of the modern Savoy: see Chapter 8). This time, the Burgundians were settling in the Empire with official approval, though a mass of survivors from Borbetomagus could have fled south spontaneously, and the imperial grant might merely have confirmed a fait accompli. Sabaudia does not figure on Bryce's list, and one has to wonder why he did not choose to count the realms of Gundahar and Gundioc as separate kingdoms. They eminently match his definition of a geographical or political name applied 'at different times to different districts'. Gundahar's parameters were 'early fifth century, Lower Rhine'; those of Gundioc 'mid-fifth century, Upper Rhône

and Saône'. There was no overlap. One meets modern descriptions of
Gundioc's realm classed either as the 'second federate kingdom' or as
'the last independent Burgundian kingdom'.[23]

The frontiers of the Burgundians' second kingdom expanded rapidly.
The initial centre was Genava (Geneva) on Lake Lemanus, where they
filled a space recently created by the displacement of the Helvetii tribe.
Soon afterwards, they turned their attention onto the district at the con-
fluence of the Rivers Arus (Saône) and Rhodanus (Rhône) in the heart
of Gaul. Within a decade, they had entered Lugdunum (Lyon), Divio
(Dijon), Vesontio (Besançon), Augustodunum (Autun), Andemantunnum (Langres) and Colonia Julia Vienna (Vienne). Frontier fortresses at
Avenio (Avignon) near the Rhône delta and at Eburodunum (Embrun)
in the mountains protected a highly compact territorial unit with first-
rate communications.

The little that is known about the Burgundians at the time of their arrival comes from a Gallo-Roman writer, who saw them enter his native Lugdunum. Sidonius Apollinaris would have been about twenty years old in 452 when he met them. He makes references in his correspondence to 'hairy giants', 'who are all seven feet tall', and who 'gabble in an incomprehensible tongue'.[24] Even less is known about the Burgundian language. A handful of words have survived in the text of legal codes (see below), and the recorded names of Burgundian rulers have decipherable meanings. Gundobad means 'bold in battle', Godomar is 'celebrated in battle'. A few modern place names can be traced to a personal name combined with the Scandinavian suffix *-ingos*. The village of Vufflens in the Vaud, for example, has been explained as 'Vaffel's Place'.[25] It is not much to go on.

In the century which separated the fall of the first kingdom from the fall of the second, five kings are recorded, all from Gibica's ancient line:

Gundioc/Gunderic (r. 437–74)
Chilperic I (r. 474–80)
Gundobad (r. 480–516)
Sigismund (r. 516–23)
Gundimar/Godomar (r. 523–34)

The foundations of a Burgundian royal palace dating from *c.* 500, including a hall and a Christian chapel, have been identified within the Roman site at Geneva,[26] and the historicity of King Godomar is affirmed by a tombstone in the old abbey cemetery of Offranges, near Evian:

IN HOC TUMOLO REQUIESCAT BONAE MEMORIAE EBROVACCUS QUI
VIXIT ANNS XIII ET MENSIS IIII ET TRANSIT X KL SEPTEMBRIS MAVUR-
TIO VIRO CLR CONSS SUB UNC CONSS BRANDOBRIGI REDIMITIONEM
A DNMO GUDOMARO REGE ACCEPERUNT.[27]

The first part of the inscription is clear. A boy, Ebrovaccus, aged thirteen years and four months, who 'lies in this mound', died during the consulship of Mavortius. The second part has inspired many guesses. 'Godomar being King', a Celtic-sounding tribe, the Brandobriges, were redeemed or ransomed. The earliest Burgundian coins were minted under imperial licence at Ravenna in the early sixth century, showing Gundobad's monogram and the head of the Roman (Byzantine) emperor. They nicely illustrate the status of a *rex* as a recognized imperial deputy.[28]

The Burgundian kings made the most of dynastic marriages. Gundioc married his sister to Ricimer (405–72), sometime assistant to

Flavius Aetius and de facto arbiter of the dying Empire. In the next generation, Chilperic's daughter Clothilda (474–545) was married to
Clovis, king of the Franks, a dozen years before he defeated the Visigoths at Vouillé (see pp. 24–6, above). As St Clothilda, she is celebrated
for persuading her powerful husband to adopt Catholic Christianity,
and is buried in the church of St Geneviève in Paris.[29]

Clothilda's uncle, Gundobad, who prided himself in the title of
Roman patrician, only gained full control of his inheritance after thirty
years of family strife, which saw the Burgundian kingdom partitioned
and ruled simultaneously from three centres, Lugdunum, Julia Vienna
and Genava. This civil war weakened the nascent state at a juncture
when it might otherwise have mounted a more active challenge to both
Franks and Visigoths.[30] Gundobad owed his Roman career to his
kinsman Ricimer, and he had the brief distinction of elevating an
emperor, Glycerius, to the throne at Ravenna. But much of his subsequent life was spent battling his own relatives, and he kept the Franks
at a distance by paying them tribute. His brother Godesigel, accompanied by Clothilda's mother, Caretana, held out in Genava until the
turn of the century. After that, he stopped the Frankish tribute, and
concentrated on Church organization and law-making. Two law codes
are attributed to him, the *Lex Romana Burgundionum* and the *Lex
Gundobada*.

The Burgundian Code (or codes), which survives in thirteen extant
manuscripts, is typical of the period when the Germanic peoples were
adopting Christianity, entering literacy and codifying law.[31] Unlike the
Codex Euricianus (see above, p. 23), it is to be regarded as supplementary to existing Roman law, consisting of a collection of customary laws
(*mores*) for the Burgundians and a number of statutes (*leges*) intended
for the ex-Roman citizens living among them. The standard modern
edition of the Burgundian Code presents 105 'constitutions', plus 4
additional enactments. Mainly promulgated at Lugdunum by Gundobad, and revised under Sigismund, they cover a huge range of subjects,
starting with Gifts, Murders and the Emancipation of Slaves and finishing with Vineyards, Asses and Oxen taken in Pledge. For almost all
offences, they set a price for restitution, and a separate sum for a fine or
punishment:

XII Of Stealing Girls

If anyone shall steal a girl, let him be compelled to pay the price set for such
a girl ninefold, and let him pay a fine to the amount of twelve *solidi*.

If a girl who has been seized returns uncorrupted to her parents, let the abductor compound six times the *wergeld* of the girl; moreover, let the fine be set at twelve *solidi*.

If indeed, the girl seeks the man of her own will and comes to his house, and he has intercourse with her, let him pay her marriage price threefold; if moreover, she returns uncorrupted to her home, let her return with all blame removed from him.[32]

One constitution lays down elaborate rules for the setting of wolf-traps with drawn bowstrings, *tensuras* (XLVI). Others provide measures for 'Jews who Presume to Raise their Hands against a Christian' (CII), or double the tariff for theft or trespass in vineyards at night (CIII).[33] Fixing the tariff was a major concern:

- A dog killed, 1 *solidus*
- A stolen pig, sheep, goat or beehive, 3 *solidi*
- A woman raped, 12 *solidi*
- A woman whose hair is cut off without cause, 12 *solidi*
- A murdered slave, 30 *solidi*
- A murdered carpenter, 40 *solidi*
- A murdered blacksmith, 50 *solidi*
- A murdered silversmith, 100 *solidi*
- A murdered goldsmith, 200 *solidi*[34]

(Women's hair would be cut off in order to enable them to fight as warriors.) Except for an occasional Burgundian phrase, such as *wergeld* or *wittimon*, the Code was written in Latin. A number of counts appended their seals to it as witnesses, thereby leaving a rare list of Burgundian personal names:

Abcar	Viliemer	Widemer	Silvan
Unnan	Hildegern	Walest	Vulfia
Sunia	Gundemund	Aunemund	Coniaric
Wadahamer	Avenahar	Hildeulf	Usgild
Aveliemer	Sigisvuld	Gundeful	Effo . . .[35]

Sigismund, son of Gundobad, a convert and a saint of the Catholic Church, is often credited with the wholesale conversion of his people. Together with his royal brothers, he campaigned none too successfully against the Franks, but was better at suppressing the Arian enclaves which had survived during the kingdom's partition. He is reputed to have strangled his infant son to exclude him from the succession, and, abducted by the Franks, he ended his life at the bottom of a well at Coulmiers, near Orléans. He was declared a martyr, and his cult spread to many parts of Europe.[36] Among his lasting achievements were a long correspondence (c. 494–523) with his chief adviser, Archbishop (later Saint) Avitus of Vienne,[37] and the foundation of the abbey at Agaunum (now St Maurice-en-Valais), a site of the *laus perennis* or 'unceasing praise' of God.[38]

The 'Catholic' ascendancy in Burgundy was systematized in 517 at the Council of Epaon (possibly Albon in the modern Dauphiné), where Avitus, whose letters constitute a very rare contemporary source, laid down guidelines for social and ecclesiastical practice. The rules whereby Arians could be reconciled to the Church were relaxed. Rules governing monasteries and convents were tightened, as were those relating to marriage and consanguinity. This last measure so enraged King Sigismund that he withdrew from communion with the Church, threatening to revert to Arianism. He relented when the bishop of Valence helped cure him when he was ill.[39]

The suppression of the (second) Kingdom of the Burgundians came about as a result of the Frankish victory in the seemingly endless Franko-Burgundian wars in the first decades of the sixth century. The key role played in those wars by Clothilda, Clovis's Burgundian widow (Clovis died in 511), was traditionally attributed to her support for Catholicism, but it was equally marked by her political engagement on behalf of her sons in their feud with her Burgundian kinsmen. The kingdom came under attack from the Franks, both from the north and, in the wake of their victory over the Visigoths at Vouillé, from the west. In 532 or 534, Gundimar, trapped between them, was proscribed, pursued and executed, and his birthright annexed.

The period during which the former Burgundian kingdom was subjected to Frankish overlordship lasted more than three hundred years, long enough for the original distinction between Franks and Burgundians to be blurred and for the Franco-Burgundian overlords to merge into the culture and society of the former Gallo-Roman population. Two dynasties were descended from the offspring of Clovis and Clothilda. The Merovingians, who ruled to 751, traced their bloodline to Merewig or Merovée, the grandfather of Clovis, and wore their hair long as a sign of royal status. The Carolingians, who ruled from 751 to 987, rose to prominence as 'mayors of the palace' of the Merovingian court at Jovis Villa (Jupille) on the River Meuse, and were descended from the famous warrior Charles Martel. Their mightiest son was Charles the Great, or Charlemagne (r. 768–814), whose dominions stretched from the Spanish March to Saxony and who raised himself to the dignity of emperor.

Those same centuries saw fundamental linguistic changes. In the days of Clovis and Gundobad, the old Frankish and Scando-Burgundian tongues had still been spoken alongside the late Latin of the Gallo-Romans. By Charlemagne's time, all these vernaculars had been replaced by a range of new idioms in the general category of *Francien* or 'Old French'. Frankish only survived in the Low Countries as the ancestor of Dutch and Flemish. Latin survived in stylized form as the language of the Church and as a written medium. Burgundian was totally submerged. The numerous variants of Old French are usually divided into two groups – the *langue d'oïl* and the *langue d'oc*. The former was characterized by the use of *hoc ille* for 'yes', hence the modern *oui*, and the latter by an unvarnished *hoc,* and in general by a closer adherence to its Latin roots. The line dividing the *oïl* and the *oc* ran right through the former Burgundian sphere, and is still very visible on today's linguistic map.[40]

Within the Frankish realms, a territorial unit known as Burgundia always existed. Many of the Merovingians styled themselves kings of '*Francia et Burgundia*' or of '*Neustria et Burgundia*'. (Neustria was the early medieval name for the north-western region round Paris.) In the late sixth century, one of the grandsons of Clovis and Clothilda, Guntram (r. 561–92), established a distinct *Regnum Burgundiae*, which functioned for a century and a half until it was reabsorbed by Charles Martel. This shadowy principality figures as No. II on Bryce's list, though it would be better described as the 'third kingdom'. Presumably on the grounds that it was not a fully sovereign state, its existence has often been ignored. Yet both of the preceding Burgundian kingdoms had similarly been subject to overlords.

Guntram or Guntramnus is an interesting figure, not just because he was declared a saint, but also because his armies fought as far afield as Brittany and Septimania in south-western Francia. For a time, as 'king of Orléans', he even shared dominion over Paris. He was the exact contemporary of the chronicler-bishop Gregory of Tours, who carefully recorded the progress of his reign, largely a non-stop series of wars,

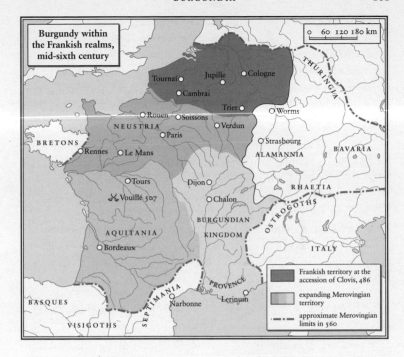

Burgundy within
the Frankish realms,
mid-sixth century

0   60 120 180 km

THURINGIA

Tournai   Jupille   Cologne

Cambrai

Trier   Worms

Rouen   Soissons

NEUSTRIA   Verdun

BRETONS   Strasbourg

Paris   ALAMANNIA   BAVARIA

Rennes   Le Mans

RHAETIA

Tours   Dijon

Vouillé 507   Chalon

OSTROGOTHS

BURGUNDIAN

AQUITANIA   KINGDOM

ITALY

Bordeaux

PROVENCE

Frankish territory at the
accession of Clovis, 486

expanding Merovingian
territory

BASQUES   Narbonne   Lerinum   approximate Merovingian
                                                   limits in 560

VISIGOTHS   SEPTIMANIA

dynastic quarrels, murders, intrigues and acts of treachery. Guntram's
marital affairs were as complex as his military campaigns:

> The good king Guntram first took a concubine Veneranda, a slave belong-
> ing to one of his people, by whom he had a son Gundobad. Later he married
> Marcatrude, daughter of Magnar, and sent his son Gundobad to Orléans.
> But when she too had a son, Marcatrude became jealous, they say ... and
> poisoned [Gundobad's] drink. Upon his death, by God's judgement ... she
> incurred the hatred of the king, and was dismissed by him. Next he took
> Austerchild, also named Bobilla. He had by her two sons, of whom the
> older was called Clothar and the younger Chlodomer.[41]

At one point, Gregory of Tours stops his narrative to present a sketch of
Divio (Dijon), which was to have a special place in Burgundian history.
He had just been talking about Gregorius, bishop of Langres:

> [Divio], where [Bishop Gregorius] was so active ... is a stronghold with
> very solid walls, built in the midst of a plain, a very pleasant place, the lands
> rich and fruitful, so that ... a great wealth of produce arrives in due season.
> On the south it has a river ... very rich in fish, and from the north comes

another little stream, which runs . . . under a bridge . . . flowing around the
whole fortified place . . . and turning the mills before the gate with wonderful speed. The four gates face the four regions of the universe, and thirty-three
towers adorn the Wall [which] is thirty feet high and fifteen feet thick . . .
On the west are hills, very fertile and full of vineyards, which produce such
a noble Falernian that [the inhabitants] disdain the wine of Ascalon. The
ancients say this place was built by the emperor Aurelian.[42]

Despite this air of plenty, if Gregory is to be believed, Guntram spent
his final years fasting, praying and weeping. His capital lay at Cabillo
(Chalon-sur-Saône), where he was buried in the church of St Marcellus.
He was declared a saint by the spontaneous acclamation of his subjects,
and became the patron of repentant murderers.

A corrective to what are sometimes thought Gregory's excessively
pro-Frankish leanings comes from Marius d'Avenches (532–96), bishop
of Lausanne (later St Marius Aventicensis), famed both for piety and
scholarship. Protector of the poor, he was said to have ploughed his
own land; as a scholar, he restarted the work of St Prosper of Aquitania,
extending Prosper's Universal Chronicle to 581.[43] The premier cleric of
the age, however, was probably St Caesarius of Arles (d. 542), a formidable preacher, theologian and prelate. Born at Cabillo, he studied at
Lerinum, and presided for nearly forty years as primate of Gaul.[44] The
Irish missionary St Columbanus (c. 540–615) would also have arrived
in Guntram's time. He lived partly as a guest at the Burgundian court
and partly as a hermit in the Vosges.[45]

At its height in 587, Guntram's *Regnum Burgundiae* briefly commanded the greater part of Gaul, including Bordeaux, Rennes and Paris,
as well as the former Burgundy of Gundobad. It was too extended for
its own good, and invited the depredations of its neighbours. Guntram's
sword-swinging successors performed numerous contorted exchanges
of thrones and territory. Several rulers' names are recorded by the
chroniclers as kings of Burgundy, of Neustria and Burgundy, or of 'all
the Franks'; as well as Guntram they include Childebert II (r. 592–5),
Theuderic II (r. 595–613), Sigebert (r. 613), Clotaire II (r. 613–29),
Dagobert (r. 629–39), Clovis II (r. 639–55) and Clotaire III (r. 655–73).

Some phases of Merovingian history are irredeemably opaque, but
the chronicler variously known as Fredegar, Fredegarius or the Pseudo-
Fredegarius (d. c. 660) throws a shaft of light on the third quarter of the
seventh century. He lived in a monastery, possibly at Chalon or Luxeuil,
and started by trying to 'improve' a number of existing chronicles. But

for eighteen years from 624 he compiled a detailed and reflective commentary on contemporary events which amply illustrates how the cult
of the blood-feud was alive and well at all social levels of Franco-
Burgundian society. A quotation from Attila is more than apt: '*Quid viro
forti suavius quam vindicta manu querere?*' ('What could be more delight-
ful for a strong man than to pursue a vendetta?') Fredegar mentions an
incident involving the emperor of Byzantium that nicely illustrates the
cheapness of human life. After two Burgundian envoys had been killed
in a brawl in Byzantine-ruled Carthage, the Emperor Maurice offered
restitution in the form of twelve men, 'to do with as you will'.[46] Fredegar's particular bugbear, not to say the object of his vilification, was the
Visigoth princess Brunechildis, who came to the Burgundian court from
Hispania and allegedly filled it with violence and hatred: '*Tanta mala et
effusione sanguinum a Brunechildis consilium in Francia factae sunt.*'[47]

Fredegar's narrative closes with the story of Flaochad, *genere Franco*
(an ethnic Frank) and mayor of the palace, who sought revenge against
a Burgundian patrician called Willebad. The two faced up with their
followers outside the walls of Augustodunum:

> Berthar, a Transjuran Frank . . . was the first to attack Willebad. And the
> Burgundian Manaulf, gnashing his teeth with fury . . . came forward with
> his men to fight. Berthar had once been a friend of his, and now said, 'Come
> under my shield and I will protect you . . .', and he lifted his shield to afford
> cover. But [Manaulf] struck at his chest with his lance . . . When Chaubedo,
> Berthar's son, saw his father in danger, he threw Manaulf to the ground,
> transfixed him with his spear, and slew all who had wounded his father.
> And thus, by God's help, the good boy saved Berthar from death. Those
> dukes who had preferred not to set their men upon Willebad now pillaged
> his tents . . . The non-fighters took a quantity of gold and silver and horses
> and other objects.[48]

As one leading scholar puts it, 'The marvel of early medieval society is
not war, but peace.'[49]

By Fredegar's time, the Merovingian monarchs were being reduced
to mere ciphers in the hands of those mayors and counts of the royal
palaces. What is more, the political centre of gravity was passing to
Frankish Austrasia (eastern Francia). Dagobert, who ruled over Neustria (the 'new western land'), was to become the butt of a lovely French
nursery rhyme: '*Le Bon Roi Dagobert / A mis sa culotte à l'envers*' ('Good
King Dagobert / put on his trousers inside out').[50] He also established

Paris as the main capital. A crucial battle at Tertry in Picardy in 687 ensured Burgundy's subordination to Austrasia.

In the early eighth century, a movement for Burgundian separatism, started by the battling Bishop Savaric of Auxerre, provoked the very outcome which it had sought to avoid. Charles Martel (688–741), founder not only of the Carolingian dynasty but also, in large part, of the Carolingian Empire, descended on Burgundy to bring it to heel. Arriving as victor of the epoch-making battle at Tours against the Saracens in 732, he proceeded to expel them equally from their footholds in Provence and Languedoc. The storming of Saracen-held Arles in 736 was one of the high points of his campaign:

> After assembling forces at Saragossa the Muslims had entered Frankish territory in 735, crossed the River Rhône and captured and looted Arles. From there they struck into the heart of Provence, ending with the capture of Avignon . . . Islamic forces [raided] Lyon, Burgundy, and Piedmont. Again Charles Martel came to the rescue, reconquering most of the lost territories in two campaigns in 736 and 739 . . . [He] put an end to any serious Muslim expedition across the Pyrenees [forever].[51]

He also put an end to hopes that the *Regnum Burgundiae* might rise again at any point soon.

In the century following Charles Martel, the Frankish Empire flourished, faltered and fell. Charlemagne spent much of his time either in the north, in Aachen, or fighting on the peripheries of his lands against Moors, Slavs and Avars, and had little direct involvement with his Burgundian domains. Yet in 773 he assembled a great army in Burgundian Geneva for his Lombard War. Emboldened by favourable messages from the Roman pope, his forces marched over the Alps in two huge columns, one crossing the pass of the Mont Cenis, the other the Great St Bernard. Having reduced Pavia, the capital of the Lombards, by a long siege, he climbed the steps of St Peter's in Rome on his knees as a penitent. Later, he created the first Papal State.[52]

In the tradition of his ancestors, Charlemagne planned to divide his empire between his sons. In the event, since only one son survived him, the empire stayed intact until it was divided in 843 between three of his grandsons. The Treaty of Verdun created divisions that would persist through much of European history. One grandson took West Francia, which was to develop into the Kingdom of France. Another took East Francia, which formed the springboard for a nascent Germany. The eldest grandson took a long strip of territory in the centre, together with the imperial title. Lothar's 'Middle Kingdom' was equally composed from three informal sections. One piece of territory in the north stretched from the North Sea to Metz, where the name of Lotharingia (Lorraine) would live on. The second section, in the centre, was an extended 'Burgundia', including Provence. The third was a long swathe running south through Italy as far as Rome. As an integrated unit, Lothar's realm proved to be a brief contrivance, yet its constituent parts long evaded permanent absorption either into France or into Germany. Burgundia was one of the most resistant.

Anyone grappling with the Carolingian legacy needs to keep the number 'three' to the fore; threefold partitions were performed three times over. Most students grasp that each of Charlemagne's grandsons received a one-third share, and it is not hard to remember that Lothar's 'Middle Kingdom' consisted of three sections. It is the third step, however, which is often forgotten. Within fifty years of the Treaty of Verdun, the former *Regnum Burgundiae*, now forming the middle section of the Middle Kingdom, was itself divided into three. (The mnemonic for the exercise is '3×3×3'.) This last tripartite division took place in three stages – in 843, 879 and 888 (contemporaneous with Alfred the Great's Anglo-Saxon England) – and it produced three new entities: the Duchy of Burgundy in the north-west, the Kingdom of Lower Burgundy in the south, and the Kingdom of Upper Burgundy in the north-east.

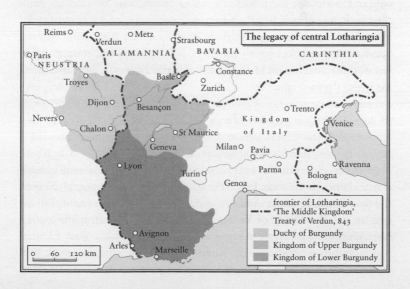

The legacy of central Lotharingia

frontier of Lotharingia,
'The Middle Kingdom'
Treaty of Verdun, 843
Duchy of Burgundy
Kingdom of Upper Burgundy
Kingdom of Lower Burgundy

The initial carving up of Charlemagne's empire in 843, therefore, was but one step in a much longer process. Although Lothar took the greater part of the sometime Burgundian kingdom, including Lyon, about one-eighth of it was awarded to West Francia. This strategically important award, consisting of the upper valley of the River Saône, including Guntram's centre at Chalon, was one of the few clauses of the Treaty of Verdun to prove permanent, and gave its new rulers a bridgehead on the southern slopes of the continental divide. Henceforth West Frankish forces, and later the armies of France, enjoyed a secure point of entry to the road to Italy.

At Verdun, West Francia's acquisition was originally given the traditional name of *Regnum Burgundiae*, but the designation proved a dead letter and for a time the area was not awarded any special status. A permanent solution was only found in the 880s, when West Francia adopted a comprehensive administrative structure made up of duchies and counties. Seven 'primitive peers' were created, each with the rank of *dux* or duke (governor), and each heading a string of dependent counts. The Duchy of Burgundy took its place alongside Aquitaine, Brittany, Gascony, Normandy, Flanders and Champagne. It represented Bryce's Burgundy No. X, although in chronological order it was the fourth.

Predictably, the duchy's affairs did not run entirely smoothly. The central figure in a long series of contorted conflicts was Richard the Justiciar (*c.* 850–921), a brother of the West Frankish queen, Richildis, wife of Charles the Bald. Richard, whose family base was Autun, travelled to Rome during Charles's imperial campaign, and was eventually rewarded with the governorship of (West Frankish) Burgundy with the title first of *marchio* (marquis, that is, border lord) and then of duke. His deathbed confession became famous: 'I die a brigand, but have saved the lives of honest men.'

From 1004, the kings of France took direct control of the duchy from the heirs of the Justiciar. Sometimes the duchy was granted in fief, sometimes held by the king in person. Until 1361, the list of dukes contained twelve names, starting with Robert le Vieux (d. 1076) and finishing with Philippe de Rouvres (r. 1346–61). The list of subordinate vassals included the counts of Chalon, of the Charolais, of Mâcon, Autun, Nevers, Avallon, Tonerre, Senlis, Auxerre, Sens, Troyes, Auxonne, Montbéliard and Bar; each of their houses would forge a long, colourful story of its own. With some delay, the duchy's administrative centre settled at Dijon, which lies on a south-flowing tributary of the Saône, appropriately called the Bourgogne, and conveniently located for easy access over the Plateau

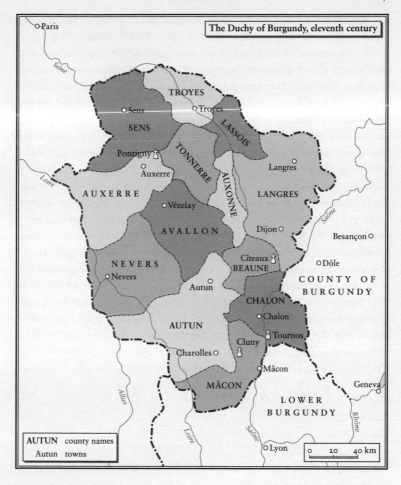

The Duchy of Burgundy, eleventh century

AUTUN county names
Autun towns

de Langres into Champagne, or upstream to the headwaters of the Seine and the road to Paris.[53]

The duchy was already the home of venerable monastic foundations, but some new names were now added. The house of Cluny, which followed the Rule of St Benedict, is often seen as the motherhouse of Western monasticism, and was founded in 910; it was the *alma mater* of three or four popes.[54] The abbey of Tournus, another tenth-century foundation, sheltered the relics of the martyred St Philibert. The abbey of Cîteaux, mother of the Cistercian Order, was founded in 1098. St Bernard (1090–1153), Church reformer and founder of the Knights Templar, arrived there as a young man,[55] and on 31 March 1146 preached the Second Crusade from the hall of the abbey of Vézelay. The abbey of Pontigny on the River Yonne dates from St Bernard's time.

The monks of these Burgundian monasteries are widely credited with the revival of the neglected art of viticulture. They were not the original pioneers, since the donation of a vineyard to the Church was recorded in the time of King Guntram. But they themselves, at the communion service, were wine consumers; and on the slopes of the Côte d'Or or of the 'Côtes de Beaune' they patiently developed vineyards of unsurpassed quality, inventing both the production methods and the time-honoured vocabulary of the *cru*, the *terroir* and the *clos*. Burgundy reds are grown from the *pinot noir* grape; most that now head the list of Grands Cru, such as the Domaine de la Romanée-Conti near Vosne, once the property of the abbey of Saint-Vivant, or Aloxe-Corton, which was launched by the cathedral chapter of Autun, or Chambertin, founded by the abbey de Bèze, started as medieval ecclesiastical enterprises. The white wines of Chablis were invented by the monks of Pontigny. The Clos de Vougeot, first planted by the monks of Cîteaux, knew just one proprietor from 1115 to the French Revolution.[56]

Chanter le vin – 'celebrating wine in song' – has formed part of the duchy's heritage ever since. Many of France's timeless drinking songs, like '*Chevalier de la Table Ronde*', or '*Boire un petit coup*', derive from Burgundy, and they celebrate a culture of good wine, good food, good company and above all good cheer:

> *Le Duc de Bordeaux ne boit qu' du Bourgogne,*
> *mais l' Duc de Bourgogne, lui, ne boit que de l'eau,*
> *ils ont aussitôt échangé sans vergogne*
> *un verr' de Bourgogne contr' le port de Bordeaux.*

'The Duke of Bordeaux drinks only Bourgogne, / but the Duke of Bourgogne he drinks water alone, / so neither felt shame when they sought to exchange / a glass of Bourgogne for the port of Bordeaux.')[57]

Meanwhile, to the east of the nascent duchy, the main part of the former Burgundian kingdom had lapsed into chaos. Lothar I's death in 855 was followed by repeated splinterings, reunifications and re-splinterings. One short-lived territorial reorganization, however, left a lasting mark. Under Lothar II (r. 835–69), the southern and south-western districts, including Lyon and Vienne, were added to a new *Regnum Provinciae*, which thereby acquired the label of 'Lower Burgundy'. In consequence, the more northerly and north-eastern districts took on the name of 'Upper Burgundy'. The frontiers soon changed, but the names stuck.

The Kingdom of Provence, created in 879, otherwise known as the Kingdom of Lower Burgundy – *le Royaume de Basse-Bourgogne* – lasted with one short break for only fifty-four years. Its territory combined the Rhône valley from Lyon to Arles, together with the original Roman province up to the foothills of the maritime Alps. Its cultural make-up was half-Burgundian and half-Provençal, thereby assisting a new form of speech called Franco-Provençal. Its main administrative centre was Arelate (Arles). It was the fifth Burgundian state and the fourth kingdom (No. III according to Bryce).

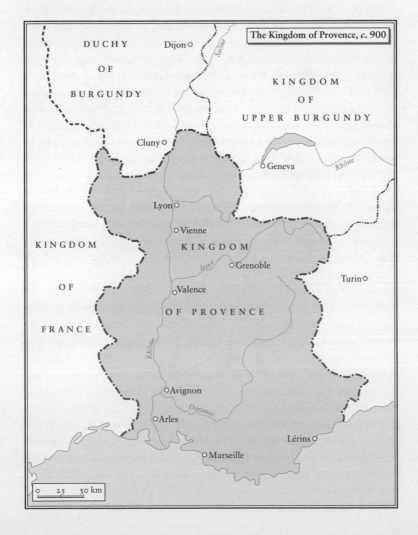

The early years of this kingdom were closely tied to the career of Count Boso (r. 879–87), who rose to power in the same way as his younger brother, Richard the Justiciar, through his links with the Frankish king and would-be emperor, Charles the Bald. His first post was as count of Lyon, but during Charles's Italian campaign of 875–7 he received the high office of *missus dominicus* (envoy or ambassador), and gained close ties with the papacy. Pope John VIII adopted him as his son, and Boso accompanied him on his journey to West Francia in 878. In the next year, however, when West Francia lost its second king in eighteen months through unexpected illnesses, Boso decided to cut loose. Returning to Provence, where he had probably already held office, he persuaded the local bishops and nobles to organize the Synod of Mantaille and to elevate him to the rank of a sovereign monarch through a 'free election'. He used the formula '*Dei Gratia id quod sum*' ('By God's Grace, this is what I am'). Boso's temerity was challenged, but the experiment survived. After he died in 887 and was buried at Vienne, his heirs, the 'Bosonids', spawned three influential lineages.[58] Two relatives ruled Provence after him: his son, Louis the Blind (r. 887–928), who was also king of Italy and nominal emperor, and his son-in-law, Hugh of Arles (r. 928–33).

Count Boso's realm commanded the rich river trade of the Rhône valley, and the main points of entry and exit between the continental interior and the Mediterranean. Its ancient cities brimmed with civilization and commerce. True, the coasts were regularly ravaged by Saracen corsairs; many prime sites on the Riviera had been infested with pirates and the sea trade to Italy was unsafe. 'Robber barons' and castle lords controlled many of the mountain valleys. Even so, any ambitious ruler like Boso would have known that he had acquired a highly promising piece of real estate. The Christian Church provided a thread of continuity and stability. Each of the main cities had its ancient bishopric, and monasticism was solidly established. The island abbey of Lerinum (Lérins), founded *c.* 410 by St Honortus, had produced many clerics who served throughout southern Gaul.[59] Much diminished, it was now subordinated to Cluny.

Parallel developments were occurring in Upper Burgundy. There, the initiative was taken by another Frankish adventurer, Rudolf of Auxerre (859–912). He and his associates, who were all connected by marriage to the Bavarian Guelphs, gave notice of rising German interest. None of the assorted overlords of central Lotharingia were strong, and opportunity beckoned. Hence, having failed in a plan to seize Alsace, Rudolf

Carolingians and Bosonids

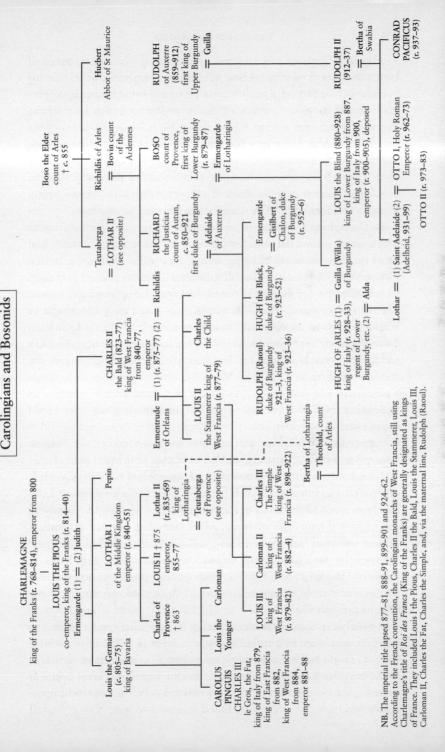

NB. The imperial title lapsed 877–81, 888–91, 899–901 and 924–62.
According to the French convention, the Carolingian monarchs of West Francia, still using
Charlemagne's title of *Roi des Francs* (King of the Franks) are generally designated as kings
of France. They included Louis I the Pious, Charles II the Bald, Louis the Stammerer, Louis III,
Carloman II, Charles the Fat, Charles the Simple, and, via the maternal line, Rudolph (Raoul).

withdrew to St Maurice (-en-Valais), which was the base of his personal lands, and conspired with leading nobles and clergymen over a different manoeuvre. In 888 an assembly was convened at St Maurice to elect him 'king of Burgundy', following the precedent set in Provence by the Synod of Mantaille. Rudolf consolidated his holdings by abandoning his claim on Alsace in return for East Francian recognition of his own sovereignty. He also made a number of prudent marriage alliances. His sister married Richard the Justiciar. One daughter married Louis the Blind and another married Boso II, count of Arles and subsequently margrave of Tuscany. The Burgundians were sticking together.

By the end of the ninth century, therefore, three separate Burgundies had appeared. One, the duchy, lay within the West Frankish orbit. The other two, the kingdoms of Upper and of Lower Burgundy, were freshly independent. The limits of Rudolf's dominion were described in the terminology of the day as lying between '*Iurum et Alpes Penninas . . . apud Sanctum Mauritium*'. For this reason, the kingdom was sometimes labelled 'Trans-Juran Burgundy' to distinguish it from the duchy in 'Cis-Juran Burgundy', but these ancient labels are confusing. In reality, Rudolf's territory covered both flanks of the Jura and stretched right across the modern Swiss cantons of Valais, Vaud, Neufchâtel and Geneva, together with Savoy and northern Dauphiné. The administrative centre was St Maurice. Here was the fifth of the Burgundian kingdoms, No. IV on Bryce's list.

'Upper Burgundy' is hard to imagine without shedding the modern concepts of 'France', 'Germany' and 'Switzerland'. One has to remind oneself constantly that the modern states of Europe had not been invented, and that the communities which preceded them were no more artificial than very many of the states of European history. The 'Upper Burgundians' practised linguistic solidarity, never spreading beyond the bounds of their old tribal foes, the German-speaking Alemanni. They were characterized by the obstinacy of highlanders, instinctively distrustful of outsiders, and they shared the memories and myths of a common past that were already half a millennium old. In the opinion of some, they were able to preserve the free spirit of old Burgundy more effectively than was possible in the French-ruled duchy or in districts more subject to external influences. As a Swiss historian has put it, '*C'est ainsi que nacquit une improbable patrie entre un marteau et une éclume*' ('It was thus, between a hammer and an anvil, that an improbable homeland was born').[60] The clear implication is that Switzerland grew from its Burgundian roots.

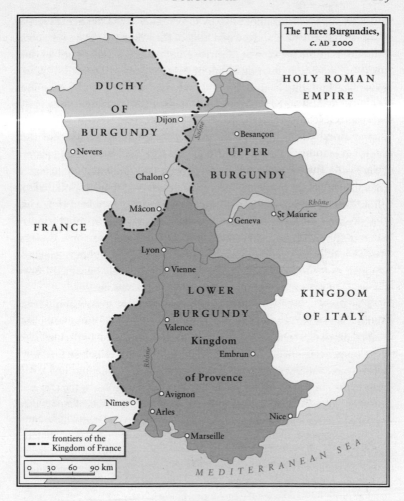

The Three Burgundies, *c.* AD 1000

DUCHY

OF

BURGUNDY

Dijon

Nevers

Chalon

Mâcon

Saône

Besançon

UPPER

BURGUNDY

Rhône

Geneva   St Maurice

FRANCE

HOLY ROMAN

EMPIRE

Lyon

Vienne

LOWER

BURGUNDY

Valence

Kingdom

of Provence

Embrun

Rhône

Avignon

Nîmes

Arles

Nice

Marseille

KINGDOM

OF ITALY

MEDITERRANEAN SEA

— · — frontiers of the
Kingdom of France

0   30   60   90 km

Few specialists would demur from the view, however, that tenth-
century Upper Burgundy was located in 'one of the most obscure periods
of mediaeval history'.* Rudolf II (d. 937), the only son of the kingdom's

---

* The author of that assessment, R. Lane Poole, sometime editor of the *English Historical
Review* and Fellow of Magdalen College, Oxford, wrestled manfully with the problem. His
Notes on Burgundy, written before the First World War, could easily be dismissed as dry-as-
dust delvings. Yet they brim with suppressed excitement as he compares ambiguous references in little-known charters and chronicles, or admires the precision with which Flodoard
of Reims distinguishes between three people, all with the same name. Two of his studies
embark on investigative detective work, trying to establish the identities of men whose full

founder, put his birthright at risk by intervening in the dangerous stakes of north Italian politics. Crowned king of the Lombards in 923, he commuted for a time between St Maurice and Pavia. The Italian nobles duly turned against him, inviting Hugh of Arles, regent of Lower Burgundy, to replace him. In 933 Rudolf and Hugh then worked out an ingenious solution. Rudolf agreed to recognize Hugh's claims in Italy, while Hugh proposed Rudolf as monarch of a joint kingdom of the Upper and Lower Burgundies. Rudolf's daughter married Hugh's son, and four years later the happy couple came into possession of their merged realms. This cardinal event, however, is surrounded with potential confusion as the kings of Upper Burgundy are variously referred to as Rudolf, Rudolphus, Ralf or Raoul. It is also odd (except for people wedded to English practice) to see that their regnal numbering continues without a break after the creation of a new kingdom. For dynastic reasons, the first Rudolph to reign over the Kingdom of the Two Burgundies is generally counted as Rudolf II, which implies that he had merely benefited from a takeover of the south, not from the creation of a new realm.[61]

The main source of confusion, though, derives from complacency about the political context of the treaty of 933. All the Burgundy-based commentaries present it as a simple bargain between two rulers. Yet developments in northern Italy were always followed closely in Germany, where the comings and goings of Rudolph and Hugh could not fail to arouse the suspicions of the Saxon Ottonian dynasty. When the two Burgundian rulers formed a close political and matrimonial alliance, their imperial German neighbours could not leave them undisturbed:

> Against the threat involved in this alliance [Emperor] Otto I's reaction was immediate. Intervening as the protector of Rudolf's fifteen year old son, Conrad, Otto invaded Burgundy, 'received king and kingdom into his possession', and thus countered the threat of a union of Italy and the Burgundian lands ... Although it was not until 1034 that Burgundy was finally united with Germany, German control was assured from 938.[62]

The German factor provided the key element in the Burgundian amalgamation. The Rudolphine dynasty was allowed to carry on, and the

---

names have not been recorded. One study deals with 'a duke near the Alps', who reportedly married a daughter of the English king, Edward the Elder (r. 899–924); the other deals with a Burgundian known only as Hugo Cisalpinus. Was it Hugh the Black, or Hugh the White, or possibly Hugh, nephew of Hugh of Italy? Neither pursuit is successful. The pleasure lies in the chase.

merger of the two Burgundian kingdoms went ahead. Yet the emperor always held the whip hand. Whenever the time was right, he or his successors could overturn the arrangement and reorder Burgundian affairs to their own advantage.

In the tenth century the future shape of Europe was slowly becoming visible. In the West, the long *Reconquista* against the Muslims was starting to turn Iberia into a peninsula of Christian states. The first ever kings of all-England mounted the throne (see p. 72, above) Under Hugues Capet (r. 987–96) and his successors, West Francia was slowly being rebranded as France;*and the three Ottonian rulers of Saxony were launching the state which in due course would become the Holy Roman Empire. As memories of the Franks faded, the old names like West Francia or Neustria, and East Francia or Austrasia, disappeared in favour of France and Germany. In Italy, the Roman pope had gained political as well as a spiritual authority. In the East, as Byzantine power and Orthodox influence receded, new states emerged. After the arrival of the Magyars in 895, centuries of deep barbarian penetration into Europe finally drew to a close. Bulgaria, Poland, Hungary and Rus', like France, England and Germany, were new polities. Despite its many transformations, Burgundy was already very old.

Despite the arbitrary manner of its creation, the Kingdom of the Two Burgundies, otherwise known from its capital as the 'Kingdom of Arles' – '*Le Royaume des Deux Bourgognes*', or in German '*Das König-reich Arelat*' – was far from being an artificial entity. It formed a natural geographical unit, made from the Rhône valley and all its tributaries from the glaciers to the sea. It was firmly based on historic Burgundia, and possessed a common post-Latin culture. In the north, via the ancient pathway of the 'Burgundian Gate' (now the Belfort Gap), it enjoyed a convenient link with the Rhineland; and in the south, via the ports of

---

* In the preceding period, the name of France had rarely been used except for the small region in the Seine valley now known as the Île de France. It was as duc de France in this limited sense that Hugues Capet first rose to prominence. When, on becoming king, he applied the name to the whole of his far larger kingdom, he was giving expression to the political claim that he and his subjects were the only true heirs to the Frankish tradition of Charlemagne and Clovis. His success may be gauged from the fact that the German name of *Frankreich*, 'Land of the Franks', became attached to the western part of Charlemagne's former empire, but not to the eastern part, which was now being subsumed into the concept of *Deutschland*. The shift in nomenclature was no doubt facilitated by the indifference of the Ottonian emperors, who as Saxons did not take offence at the loss of the Frankish label in the east.

Arles and Marseille, it was in close touch with both Italy and Iberia. Geopolitically, it lay somewhat in the lee of the tempests that were about to embroil neighbouring states. The wind blew fair for a prosperous historical voyage. This was the sixth Burgundian kingdom, James Bryce's No. V.

During the first century of its existence, the kingdom avoided the dynastic crises which blighted many similar states. The two successors

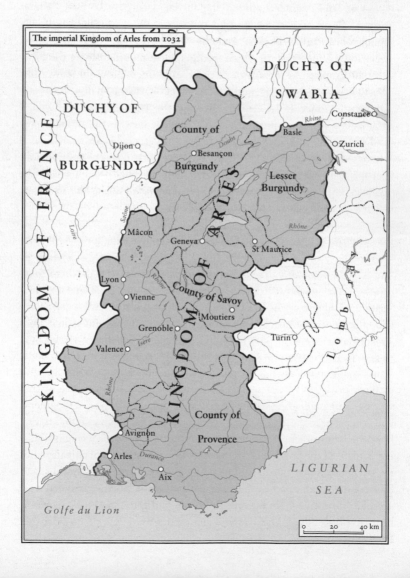

The imperial Kingdom of Arles from 1032

of Rudolf II, Conrad (r. 937–93) and Rudolf III (r. 993–1032), both
lived very long lives. Conradus Pacificus ('Konrad der Friedfertiger')
earned a sobriquet which in the medieval context, when kings were
by definition warlords, was mildly pejorative and possibly unjust. The
modern translation is usually 'the Peaceful', but it may better be rendered, if not as 'the Gutless', then at least as 'the Unwarlike'. Not that
Conrad shunned war completely. In 954 his kingdom was invaded simultaneously by a Magyar raiding party and by Saracens. He sent envoys
to the Magyars inviting them to repel the Saracens, and other envoys to
the Saracens imploring them to fight the Magyars. He then sat back,
and waited until his two enemies were cutting each other to pieces,
before ordering the Burgundian host to clear the field. In the following
decade he led expeditions against the Saracen settlements in Provence.
So he may best be characterized as a king familiar with guile as well as
gore. Surviving on the throne for fifty-six years was no mean feat in
itself.

Conrad's realm is well attested both by coinage and by ecclesiastical
charters. A bronze denier bearing the inscription CONRADUS around a
central cross, was minted in Lugdunum. The abbey of Montmajour at
Frigolet near Avignon was founded by him in 960, and, before 993,[63]
the abbey of Darentasia (Tarentaise in Savoy), whose modern name of
Moûtiers is just a corrupted form of *monasterium*. In politics, despite
Conrad's marriage to a princess from West Francia, the reign was most
clearly marked by the hostility of the Hugonids, who were minded to
renege on the agreement of 933, and by continuing German tutelage.
Conrad had been a ward at the imperial court, and his sister Adelheid
(r. 931–9) became Otto the Great's second empress. A generous benefac-
tress, she was raised to sainthood as St Adelaide. She also played a key
role as dowager-regent during the minority of her son. Conrad's later
years unfolded in the shadow of the coming Millennium, when the end
of the world was forecast. 'The tenth century was the iron age of the
world; things had gone to the worst, and now was to be the judgment
and completion.'[64] Plagues and famine foretold the cataclysm that never
happened. Some scholars present a different impression. 'The gay smiling climate of the South . . . called forth the earliest fruits of chivalry and
its attendant song,' wrote one gushing nineteenth-century enthusiast.
'During the greater part of the 10th century, while Northern France was
a prey to intestine commotions, Provence and the non-French parts of
historic Burgundy enjoyed repose under the mild rule of Conrad the
Pacific.'[65]

Conrad's son, Rudolf III, was equally dependent on German support. When the nobility rebelled, he was saved by a German force sent on the orders of the Dowager Adelheid, for the Kingdom of the Two Burgundies lacked any semblance of strong central government. The king at Arles was far removed from most of the inland regions that he hoped to control. Counts, bishops and cities asserted their sway over their localities. At the same time, decentralization had its advantages. The body politic could not be killed by a simple blow to the centre; it could only be dismantled slowly, piece by piece. Such was the fate of the 'Arelate'. It held together in ramshackle fashion long after some of its most vital members had fallen off.

To do it justice, therefore, historians would have to tell all the histories of all the petty rulers and statelets which took root alongside regal authority. In Upper Burgundy, for example, the bishop of Geneva took control of not only the city but much of the adjoining lake area too. In consequence, the *Comes*, or secular count of the Genevois, set himself up in neighbouring Eneci (Annecy), where a line of twenty-one counts ruled from the tenth century to the end of the fourteenth. Similar things happened in Lyon. The bishops of Lyon, who claimed to be primates of Gaul, had been elevated to the rank of archbishop in Frankish times and were already in firm control of the city when the Kingdom of Arles appeared. As a result, the count of the Lyonnais moved out to the neighbouring district of Forez, where, from the stronghold of Montbrison, he could orchestrate an endless duel with the archbishops.

In the northern reaches of Upper Burgundy, the 'counts-palatine of Burgundy' enjoyed special privileges in return for holding the frontier zone against the Germans of Alsace and Swabia. Their stronghold stood at Vesontio (Besançon), where Otte-Guillaume/Otto-Wilhelm of Burgundy (986–1026) founded a line of thirty-six counts that survived to the seventeenth century. In the Viennois, the counts of Albon founded a base from which Guigues d'Albon (d. 1030) created a small empire stretching all the way to the Mont Cenis. One of his descendants was to adopt a dolphin as his heraldic emblem. His successors became known as *delfini* and their domain as the Delfinat or Dauphiné.

In Lower Burgundy, a string of near-independent counties came into existence in the Rhône valley, in the Valentinois, at Orange and in the Comtat Venaissin. But the greatest power was garnered by the heirs of Count Boso. Of the three lines of Bosonids, one came to an end with Hugh of Arles (see above); a second spawned the 'counts of Provence' based at Ais (Aix-en-Provence); the third founded the mountainous

County of Fourcalquier. The ascendancy of the counts of Provence in the southern parts of the kingdom was near complete but for the rumbustious lords of Baou (Les Baux), whose impregnable fortress and indomitable will defied all comers.

Thanks to the splintering of power, the Arelate declined, and Arles sank into a capital city in name only. No coronations were held there between the tenth and the twelfth century. The magnificent Roman amphitheatre was turned into a castle, and a miserable clutch of dwellings was built for safety inside the arena. The regal church of St Trophime stood outside, waiting for better times. In such conditions, Rudolf III struggled on under ever-growing restrictions. The chroniclers gave him the label of 'der Faule' or 'le Fainéant' and 'the Pious', which together make for a 'holy loafer'. He was particularly disturbed by the depredations of the counts-palatine from the north, against whom he called in Heinrich (Henry) II, king of the Germans. Heinrich's price – like that of Duke William of Normandy in this same era – was to extract a promise to appoint him sole heir apparent. Rudolf was childless, and the succession was likely to be claimed by his cousin, Odo II of Champagne, one of the most terrifying warriors of a terrifying age. In the event, Heinrich (r. 1014–24) died before Rudolf did. But the promise was not forgotten.

The matter came to a head in 1032. As expected, Rudolf died without issue. As expected, the throne of the Two Burgundies was immediately disputed both by Odo of Champagne and by Heinrich's son, the Emperor Conrad II. The emperor won, because Odo's claim was denounced by his feudal superior, the king of France. So a measure of international recognition was granted as the 'realm of Two Burgundies' passed painlessly into the possession of the German emperors. It would stay there, in theory at least, until the very last fragment fell to the French over six centuries later.

The Holy Roman Empire of the German Nation, as it came to be called, was not a simple organism. In its later stages, it was said to contain as many princely states as there were days in the year. But after 1032, its basic threefold structure consisted of the Kingdom of Germany (*Regnum Teutonicum*), the Kingdom of Italy (*Regnum Italiae*) and the Kingdom of Burgundy (*Regnum Burgundiae*), that is the 'Kingdom of Arles' as renamed after incorporation, and commonly known in German as the *Königreich von Burgund*. Now, therefore, only two Burgundies were functioning: the dependent duchy within France and the dependent kingdom within the Empire. Should the latter be counted as a new entity or not? Bryce thought not, and treats it as a simple continuation of the Kingdom of Arles. Yet the contrary arguments are persuasive. The political context had changed radically, and the territorial base would change, too. Within a century of 1032, imperial Burgundy would experience further transformations. It is counted here as the seventh kingdom.

For the next three hundred years – a huge span of time – the imperial kingdom continued to operate as best it could. With the sole exception of Frederick Barbarossa (r. 1152–90), the distant emperors rarely took a close interest from their various residences in Germany. The essence of the kingdom's politics lay with the localities – in the ongoing feuds of the counts and the cities, on the fate of obscure battles, on the plotting of dynasts. Even so, few would have predicted that France's modest duchy might one day grow more powerful than the Empire's enormous kingdom.

The linguistic patterns which developed within the imperial kingdom are instructive. Despite German overlordship, the German language made few inroads. The main vernacular remained a Franco-Provençal idiom, the ancestor of modern Arpitan, which one can hear to this day in the streets of Lyon and in parts of western Switzerland and Savoy. To anyone with a historical ear, Arpitan carries the echoes of bygone Burgundy.[66]

The mechanism whereby imperial counts were promoted to dukedoms by the emperor seems to have been entirely haphazard. Everything depended on the power, prestige and good fortune of particular vassals at particular moments. Yet one new duchy, closely entwined with the noble German House of Zähringen, holds a special place in the story. The castle of Zähringen now lies in ruins on a hillside overlooking the town of Freiburg-im-Breisgau, but in the eleventh and twelfth centuries it was the seat of an ambitious clan of local counts, who had already won and lost two duchies, and who were now heading for the ducal ranks for a third time. The Zähringer had proved themselves efficient managers of their estates; they had exploited their legal rights over Church lands in the Black Forest, and, after founding the municipality of Freiburg, pioneered a system of consolidated local administration. They were demonstrating in miniature what the emperor longed to introduce on a larger scale. Too many Burgundian nobles had forgotten their oaths of fealty. In 1127, therefore, the emperor appointed Conrad von Zähringen *Rector* or 'governor' of the Kingdom of Burgundy,

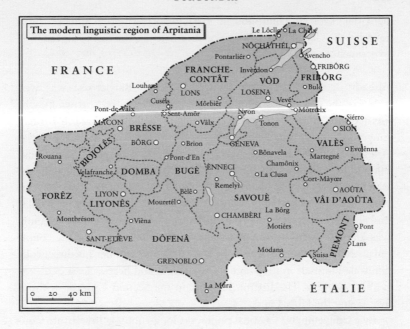

The modern linguistic region of Arpitania

rewarding him further with the lands of a newly invented Duchy of *Burgundia Minor* or 'Lesser Burgundy'. The Zähringen rectors were effectively brought in to restore discipline.[67]

The Duchy of *Burgundia Minor*, known in German as *Klein Burgund*, covered a sizeable area to the east of the Jura, coinciding quite closely with the limits of modern Francophone Switzerland. It is No. VI on Bryce's list. It contained a smaller unit within it classed as a *Landgrafschaft* or 'Landgravate', which also received the appellation of 'Burgundy' and which is No. VIII on Bryce's list. This unit consisted of the district on either side of the River Aar between Thun and Solothurn. It may or may not have reached as far as the Habichtsburg or Habsburg, the 'Hawk's Castle', which overlooks the River Aar below Solothurn, and which was to be the original seat of Central Europe's most powerful dynasty. Habsburg tradition insists that the protoplast of the family was called Guntram.[68]

As rectors and dukes, the Zähringer exercised overlordship over a large variety of nobles, counts and bishops, and over an archipelago of islands of loyal towns in the midst of a wayward countryside. They showed great energy establishing a network of incorporated towns, including Fribourg, Burgdorf, Murten (Morat), Rheinfelden and Thun. Their most active representative, Count Berthold V (*fl.* 1180–1218), built the castle of Thun, and in 1191, reportedly after killing a bear, founded the city of Berne. When he died heirless, the duchy lapsed. The experiment was not repeated.[69]

Already in the mid-twelfth century Frederick Barbarossa was well aware of the need to shore up imperial power. He was crowned king of Germany at Aachen in 1152, king of Italy at Pavia in 1154, Holy Roman Emperor in 1155 and, after considerable delay, king of Burgundy at Arles in 1173. Each of these steps was preceded by years of politicking and campaigning. In the process he made common cause with the Roman papacy, thereby giving new life to the doctrine of 'the Two Swords', whereby emperor and pope were supposed to be the dual agents, secular and ecclesiastical, of divine rule. Barbarossa's keen interest in Burgundy was kindled by his second marriage, to Beatrice, heiress of the count-palatine. Thanks to this union, he took the county under his direct rule, embroiled himself in the kingdom's quarrels, and here at least achieved nothing decisive. He died on his way to the Second Crusade without ever seeing the Holy Land.[70]

By pitting emperors against popes, the long-running 'Investiture Contest' inevitably weakened each of the supreme authorities of the medieval world. It began in the tenth century, when the Ottonian emperors first promoted their claim to control the election of popes, and it continued in fits and starts before fizzling out in the thirteenth. It centred in general round an inconclusive dispute as to whether pope or emperor was entitled to exercise jurisdiction over the other, and in particular round their rights and procedures for making appointments. It added an extra dimension to a bitter civil war in Germany, that came to an end in theory at the Concordat of Worms of 1122. But it rumbled on elsewhere, not least in England under King John. Its significance may have been exaggerated by historians, who neglect other sources of tension;[71] but in all parts of the Empire, it helped create an impasse where neither the emperor nor the pope would cede to the other's claims of supremacy, and it accelerated the fragmentation of power:

> The period of the Investiture Contest saw the establishment ... of new territorial units, and these units were the nuclei from which were created the principalities of late mediaeval Germany ... Many generations were to pass before ... the princes established full territorial control, but already at the beginning of the twelfth century the great aristocratic families were mounting the path which led to territorial sovereignty; and it was the

Investiture Contest with its revolutionary social changes which gave them the opportunity to assert and consolidate these powers.[72]

The imperial Kingdom of Burgundy was especially susceptible to this weakening of authority. One must ask why, after the interlude of the Zähringen duchy, the emperors were so reluctant to intervene and stop the rot. The best answers are geographical, political and strategic. First, thanks to imperial Burgundy's mountainous terrain, all military operations there were fraught with uncertainty. Secondly, automatic priority was given to the Kingdom of Germany. The death of every emperor was invariably followed by a campaign in which the leading candidates competed to succeed him and be crowned as king of the Germans, before proceeding towards coronation as emperor. Thirdly, having secured Germany, every monarch had to choose between attending to Italy or to Burgundy. Almost without exception, they gave precedence to Italy. Rome, the seat of the papacy, exercised a magic attraction. Papal approval carried enormous weight, and every would-be German emperor dreamed of walking in the steps of Charlemagne. So the Kingdom of Burgundy was routinely neglected. One German emperor even left Germany as well as Burgundy to fend for itself. Frederick II (r. 1220–50), half-Italian, preferred to set up his court in his mother's base in Sicily.[73]

Inexorably, therefore, the Kingdom of Burgundy was subject to a long series of secessions. Chips flew off the block at regular intervals. The original collection of territories steadily shrank. Provence went first, then the Comtat Venaissin, Lyon and the Dauphiné. The Empire frequently retained moribund claims or residual rights, but the overall effect was unmistakeable. The kingdom crumbled in slow motion. The earliest moves towards separation were taken by prelates, who in several instances assumed the status of 'prince-bishops'. Their courage was born of the emperors' need for ecclesiastical support. The bishops of Sion (in the Valais) and of Geneva broke free at a very early stage, and others simply followed.

The strongest statement of the Church's position on investiture was made in Burgundy in 1157. At the Diet of Besanz (Besançon), the papal legate ventured the opinion that the Empire was nothing more than a papal *beneficium*: that is, a voluntary gift remaining at the pope's disposal. As one historian remarked, he took the risk that one of the imperial dukes might put a battleaxe through his skull, for he was throwing doubt on to the unquestioned acceptance of the emperor's authority. He certainly put ideas into the heads of both the archbishop of Besanz and the local count.

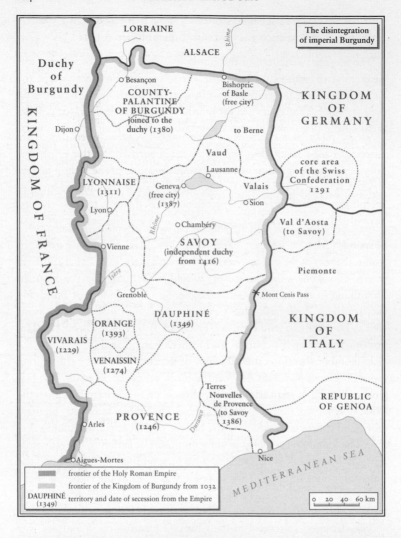

The County-Palatine of Burgundy – so called because of its location on the kingdom's northern border – was a crucial territory. Count Rainald or Renaud III (d. 1148) had already tried and failed to build his own small empire. Having inherited the County of Mâcon within the adjoining French Duchy of Burgundy, he declared himself to be a *Freigraf* or *franc comte* within the Empire. The imperial authorities showed no sympathy, confiscating most of Rainald's lands as punishment. Yet it was Rainald's daughter whom the Emperor Frederick Barbarossa married, and the memory of Rainald's 'Free County' remained.[74] In 1178, the archbishop of Besanz, a grandson of Rainald III, negotiated his way to turning his episcopal see into a *Reichsstadt* or 'imperial city', free from the feudal dues of the County-Palatine. It was a telling precedent. A couple of decades later, the bishop of Basle went one step further by creating a 'prince-bishopric', and ruling not only over his episcopal see, but also over nearby lands once confiscated from Rainald III.[75]

Large parts of the future Switzerland were also carved out of the imperial Kingdom of Burgundy. Sometime early in the thirteenth century, a peasant migration occurred from the lands of the bishop of Sion in the Valais eastward to the Grisons. The migrants took bridge-building techniques with them, opened up the Schollenen Gorge to travellers and provided access to the valuable trade route over the St Gotthard pass into Italy. In August 1291 the men of Uri, Schweiz and Unterwalden, who operated tolls on the pass, swore an oath to resist outside interference. They had performed the founding act of the Swiss Confederation.[76]

Provence, by contrast, drifted apart from Burgundy through a succession of marriages. In 1127, in stage one, the last Bosonid heiress had ceded her rights to a husband from Barcelona, thereby putting practical control of the territory beyond the Empire's reach. In 1246, the last Catalan heiress of Provence brought the same dowry to an Angevin husband, thereby launching a line of counts who were vassals of the king of France (see p. 174).[77]

And so the erosion continued. In the first quarter of the thirteenth century, the French conquered Languedoc in the course of the Albigensian Crusade, bringing them up to the right bank of the Rhône. Under St Louis, king of France (r. 1226–70), they long planned an outpost on the Mediterranean coast at Aigues-Mortes, aiming to build a crusading port and to consolidate their hold on the lower Rhône valley.[78] In 1229 agents of the king of France succeeded in ousting the bishop of Vivarium (Viviers) to create a French foothold in the Vivarais at the foot of the Cévennes.[79] The Comtat Venaissin on the opposite bank, which took its name from the small town of Venasque, was bequeathed by an heirless owner as a gift to the papacy in 1274. The enclave of Avignon, within the comtat, was sold to an exiled pope in 1348.[80] The nearby county of Aurausion (Orange) enjoyed the status of an autonomous principality under the counts of Baux, notorious for their feuding with the counts of Provence during the 'Baussenque Wars'. The legacy of the counts eventually passed to the French House of Chalon.[81]

Lugdunum – Lyon – the chief city of the Rhône valley, was growing all the time into a commercial city of the first rank. Its annual fairs, thronged by Italian merchants, provided a point of exchange between the commerce of northern and southern Europe. Yet increasingly it became an object of great strategic interest to France. Thirteenth-century Lyon was, above all, an archiepiscopal city of unusual importance. Church councils were held there. One, in 1245, excommunicated the Emperor Frederick II. Another in 1274 was attended by 500 bishops. Popes presided in person; and in 1305 Pope Clement V was crowned there. It was probably no accident that the archbishop of Lyon, Bernard de Got, was the new pope's brother.

The papal bull deposing and excommunicating Frederick II did not mince words:

> Innocent, bishop, servant of the servants of God . . . The secular prince who has been the special cause of so much discord . . . has committed four sins of the greatest gravity . . . [including] perjury . . . the arrest of our legates . . . [holding] sees, abbeys and other churches vacant . . . [and] sacrilege. Furthermore he has deservedly become suspect of heresy . . . We therefore denounce the said prince, and mark him out as an outcast who has made himself unworthy of the empire . . . Let those whose task it is . . . freely choose a successor . . . Given at Lyons on 17 July in the 3rd year of our pontificate.[82]

Such a document could never have been produced if the emperor had exercised even limited influence over what was still, in theory, an imperial city.

The Second Council of Lyon (1274) was convened to end the schism between the Catholic and Orthodox Churches. It only succeeded in confirming and defining a key item of Catholic theology, the *filioque*,* which has barred the way to reconciliation ever since. (Lyon was also the place where a long-running heretical movement was thought to have begun. Peter Valdo had preached dangerously irregular, proto-Protestant views, and was banished. But his movement persisted. Valdensian communities took to the mountains of Savoy, and would defy the authorities in the best Burgundian manner for centuries (see p. 408).[83]

Lyon, however, was riven with internal power struggles, and there-

---

* The *filioque* (literally 'and the Son') is the central element in the theological doctrine of the Double Procession of the Holy Spirit. Ever since the ninth century the Western Church has held to the view that the Holy Spirit proceeds 'from the Father and the Son'. The Eastern Church, in contrast, believes in a single fount of the divine Godhead, and in consequence holds to the formula that the Holy Spirit proceeds 'from the Father and *through* the Son'. This fine distinction caused no end of difficulties for many hundreds of years.

1. The funeral of Alaric the Visigoth, 'Ruler of All',
AD 410, in the bed of the Busento, Calabria.

2. 'The history of France began at Vouillé.'
AD 507: Clovis the Frank slays Alaric III, King of the Visigoths.

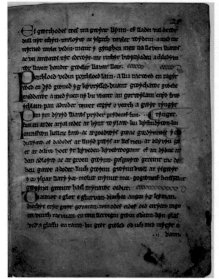

3. *Y Gododdin*: a page from the medieval Book of Aneirin, the seventh-century Old Welsh epic preserved in a thirteenth-century manuscript.

4. Bird, Tree, Fish and Ring: symbols from the legend of St Mungo (sixth century), portrayed in Glasgow's coat-of-arms.

5. William Wallace (1272–1305) – known to filmgoers as Braveheart and to his Gaelic contemporaries as *Uilleam Breatnach*, 'William the Briton'.

6. Rheingold: an episode from the legends of the *Nibelungen*, medieval tales based on echoes of the first Kingdom of the Burgundians (fifth century).

7. (*above*) A rare coin showing the head of the Merovingian King Dagobert (*c.* 603–39), 'who pulled on his trousers inside out'.

8. (*left*) Guntram or Gontran of Burgundy (*c.* 525–92), the 'Battle Crow', king and saint.

9. Frederick Barbarossa (r. 1162–90): German emperor, king of Italy and king of Burgundy, crowned at Arles in 1172.

10. Philip the Good and Charles the Bold: duke-counts of the fifteenth-century States of Burgundy.

11. Charles le Téméraire, a.k.a. Karel de Stoute (r. 1467–77): duke of Burgundy, count of Flanders, margrave of Namur, etc., etc.

12. Duchess-Countess-Margravine Mary of Burgundy (1457–82), heiress.

13. The Aljaferia Fortress: constructed in the tenth century in Iberian-Islamic style for the Muslim emirs of Zaragoza, captured in 1118 by Alfonso El Battalador, king of Aragon.

14. The Catalan galley fleet anchored off Naples (fifteenth-century miniature).

15. Queen Petronilla of Aragon and Count Rámon Berenguer IV of Barcelona, whose marriage in 1137 joined Aragon to Barcelona for nearly 600 years.

16. and 17. *Los Reyes Católicos*: Ferdinand of Aragon and Isabella of Castille, *c.* 1491.

18. Mattia Preti, *The Battle of El Puig*; Langue d'Aragon Chapel, Valletta. The battle, fought in 1238 near Valencia between Catalans and Moors, was a milestone in the *Reconquista*.

fore fell easy prey to French intrigues. The archbishop was permanently at odds both with the counts of the Lyonnais-Forez, and with the city's rich patricians. When the French won over first the count and then the patricians, the archbishop was defenceless. French troops marched in without resistance in 1311. The archbishop retained his title of 'primate of the Gauls', but power passed to a city-commune run by elected consuls subject to French approval.[84]

The Dauphiné, equally coveted by France, controlled the road to Italy over the Mont Cenis. But the counts of Albon/Vienne, who held Grenoble and the approaches to the pass, hung on until 1349, when they sold out to the king of France in a private cash deal. Henceforth, the territory would serve as a dignity for the French king's son and heir, the 'dauphin' (whether or not it still technically formed part of the Holy Roman Empire is an open question).[85]

By this stage, the imperial Kingdom of Burgundy was looking distinctly ragged. The parts that abutted Germany, like Basle and Berne, were still under the emperor's eye. But all those abutting France were being sucked beyond his reach. The emperors admitted as much. Though none of them formally renounced their claims to the kingdom, none after Conrad IV in 1264 bothered to publicize their royal Burgundian title.

Political fragmentation was obviously gaining pace, yet such a simple term hardly describes the complicated processes at work. For as the traditional units crumbled new agglomerations were growing up, often in disregard for existing state boundaries. Marriages, dowries, conquests and bequests resulted in a constant stream of mergers, de-mergers and new upstart fortunes. The typical Burgundian count was no longer the ruler of one straightforward fief dependent on one overlord. More often he was head of a complex clutch of lands, titles and claims, assembled over the generations by the combined efforts of his family's knights, wives, children and lawyers.

Examining the counts-palatine of Burgundy, for example, one sees that the original inheritance had repeatedly passed from one political sphere to another, and by marriage from one family to another: in 1156 to the German family of Hohenstaufen; in 1208 to the Bavarian House of Andechs; and in 1315 to the royal House of France. At each stage the beneficiary added his wife's titles and possessions to his own, sometimes acknowledging the former overlord, sometimes not. For the expert courtly genealogists and their clients, a significant moment loomed in 1330 when Jeanne III de France, consort of the duke of royal French Burgundy, inherited a claim to the imperial County-Palatine of Burgundy from her mother. The royal duchy and the imperial county were tantalizingly close to a permanent union. In the midst of the labyrinth of Burgundian successions (see below), Margaret, countess-palatine of Burgundy (1310–82), daughter of the French king, sought to accelerate the prospective merger. In 1366, with no particular justification, she started to promote the term of 'France-Comté' (*sic*), dropping the traditional name of 'County of Burgundy' from her charters. (She was undoubtedly playing on the precedent of Rainald III, the self-styled *franc comte*.) The established formula of 'Franche-Comté' only emerged definitively after Margaret's death. It is kingdom No. VII on Bryce's list.[86]

The mid-fourteenth century was a time of maximum distress across Europe. The Black Death struck in 1348, though it was by no means the last irruption of the bubonic plague. France was about to descend into the bear pit of the Hundred Years War with England, and the Holy Roman Empire was in uproar over the Golden Bull of 1356 and the introduction of a consolidated imperial constitution and electoral procedures. Thanks to the papal schism, there was one pope in Rome, and another in Avignon. Those few parts of the Kingdom of Burgundy which had not been lost were often disputed among neighbours. To cap it all, mind-boggling crises of succession erupted simultaneously in the Kingdom of France, in the Duchy of Burgundy and in the County-Palatine. At this point, faint-hearted readers are advised to take a break.

Studying the Burgundian succession of the 1360s, one can easily develop '*Palis-Rondon*' – as the Japanese call a squint. Three of the main players were Jean II de Valois, king of France, and two of his sons: Charles de Navarre and Philippe le Hardi. One explanation runs as follows:

> Charles II of Navarre was a grandson and heir to Margaret of Burgundy, eldest daughter of Duke Robert II of Burgundy. John II of France was a son and heir to Joan of Burgundy, second daughter of Duke Robert II of Burgundy. John was first cousin of Philip's father i.e. a cousin once removed, whereas Charles was the son of a first cousin of Philip's father i.e. a second cousin himself. Charles's mother Joan had died already in 1349. John's practical position was helped by his being the stepfather of the young duke having been married to the widowed Joan of Auvergne . . .[87]

This, one suspects, is *not* the way to explain it – even if it's correct.

Another way is to leave the finer points of the genealogical tangle to the specialists, and to probe the nomenclature and the politics. It would

The Burgundian Succession

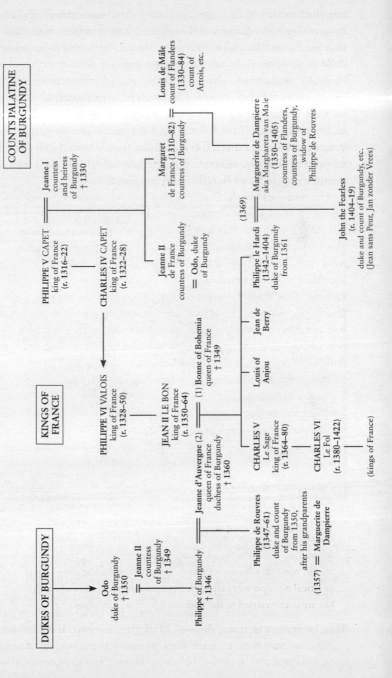

help if it were clarified at the outset that three separate women all used the same style of 'Margaret of Burgundy'; and that three individual men were all called 'Philippe de Valois'. One of them, otherwise known as Philippe de Rouvres (1347–61), thoughtlessly started the crisis in 1361 by dying prematurely during a recurrence of the plague and in an unconsummated marriage. Had he lived, he might painlessly have fused his own claims to the duchy and those of his wife to the county-palatine. Instead, all his titles were deemed to have reverted to rival claimants. What is more, the French king, Jean le Bon, decided to ignore the principle of primogeniture and, again for purely political reasons, to earmark the Duchy of Burgundy for his fourth son.

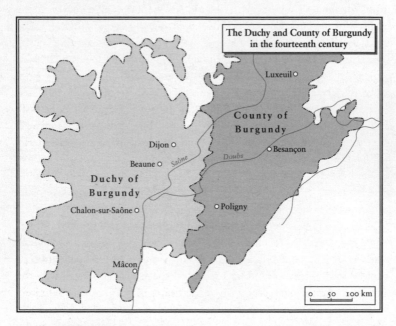

The Duchy and County of Burgundy in the fourteenth century

Luxeuil○

County of Burgundy

Dijon ○   ○Besançon

Beaune ○   *Saône*   *Doubs*

Duchy of Burgundy

Chalon-sur-Saône ○   ○Poligny

Mâcon○

0   50   100 km

The bold actions of this fourth son, Philippe de Valois, le Hardi (Philip the Bold), who had won his spurs as a teenager at the Battle of Poitiers in 1356 against England's Black Prince, provide the key to all subsequent developments. Despite his modest ranking in the French line of succession, he managed to dominate the long-running Council of Regents that ran France for decades after his father's death in 1364.[88] Also, by marrying the widow of Philippe de Rouvres, Marguerite de Dampierre, heiress to Flanders (where she was known as Marghareta van Male), he rescued a bevy of claims and titles that had earlier been dispersed. Among them was the vital claim to the County-Palatine of Burgundy, which finally reverted to Marguerite in 1384 after the death of her father. The result was a newly reunited Burgundian polity, centred on the union of duchy and county, which came together in the last two decades of Philippe le Hardi's long life. It does not figure separately on Bryce's list, but arose from a combination of Nos. X and VII.

To no one's surprise, the emergence of the duchy-county, which could only have been realized through the simultaneous weakness of France and Germany, caused severe friction. In France, it provoked a fierce and protracted civil war between two court factions, the 'Burgundians' and the 'Armagnacs', whose intrigues quickly became entangled with the politics of the Hundred Years War. The former favoured good relations both with the successors of Philippe le Hardi and with Burgundy's English allies. The latter, the French patriots, deplored the activities of their breakaway duchy and its treacherous alliance with the hereditary English enemy. From 1418 to 1436, forces from Burgundy participated in the English occupation of Paris. The imperial Germans, hopelessly divided by their own quarrels, were in no state to intervene until the Habsburg era began in the 1430s. Everyone, except perhaps the clerks of the imperial chancery, forgot that the Kingdom of Burgundy had not officially expired. In the interval, the duke-counts enjoyed a free run.

The astonishing new creation which flourished from the late fourteenth to the late fifteenth century is generally and inaccurately called the 'Duchy of Burgundy', or sometimes just 'Valois Burgundy'; it was ruled by a line of French dukes, who briefly threw off the tutelage of Paris in order to create a brilliant, wealthy and cultured civilization of their own.[89] Yet the dominant French perspective is not necessarily the best one, and the historical term of the 'States of Burgundy' is definitely to be preferred: so, too, for its rulers is the double title of 'duke-counts'. The success of the enterprise derived from the fact that the French duchy and the imperial county, having been fused at the head in a personal union, were merged into a new entity that was neither French nor German. Philippe le Hardi's family was only half-French; it was equally half-Flemish, and since Philippe's Flemish wife, Marguerite de Dampierre, had been born a subject of the emperor, at least partially imperial. Furthermore, behind the extraordinary small empire which the duke-counts assembled, from Boulogne to the Black Forest, lay the romantic idea that they were reassembling the long-lost realm of Lotharingia.

Only four duke-counts of the States of Burgundy reigned in more than a century: Philippe le Hardi/Filips de Stoute (r. 1364–1404), Jean sans Peur/Jan zonder Vrees (r. 1404–19), Philippe le Bon/Filips de Goede (r. 1419–67) and Charles le Téméraire/Karel de Stoute (r. 1467–77). Dutch and Flemish historians have their own nomenclature, of course. When they talk of rulers who were simultaneously duke (*hertog*) and count (*graaf*), they are thinking of Burgundian outsiders who were also counts of Flanders and Artois. The full list of the Burgundian States, however, cannot be limited to two Burgundies, Flanders and Artois. Charles le Téméraire, for instance, held fifteen titles: count of Artois, duke of Limburg, duke of Brabant, duke of Lothier, duke of Burgundy, duke of Luxembourg, count-palatine of Burgundy, margrave of Namur, count of Charolais, count of Zeeland, count of Flanders, count of Zutphen, duke of Guelders, count of Hainault and count of Holland.[90]

None of the duke-counts were kings. Coronations lay in the gift of the pope, and no pope would have braved the wrath of both the king of France and the German emperor in order to elevate a king of Burgundy. But in the brilliance of their courts, the wealth of their cities and the opulence of their patronage, the Burgundians outshone almost all the crowned heads of their day, and were kings in all but name.[91]

The territorial base of the new political complex differed substantially from that of all previous Burgundies. Although anchored in the duchy and the county, the greater part of the agglomeration lay in the coastal region far to the north, and did *not* include most of historic Burgundy. The personal inheritance of Marguerite de Dampierre, born at Bruges, was considerably larger and wealthier than her husband's. It stretched all the way from the ex-French counties of Vermandois and Ponthieu to the ex-imperial counties of Holland and Gelderland, and comprised all the great cities of the Low Countries: Amiens, Arras, Bruges, Ghent, Brussels and Amsterdam. Several gaps in the patchwork – at Utrecht, Cambrai, Liège and Luxeuil – were filled by dependent bishoprics. One of the fragments of imperial Burgundy that the German emperors hung on to was the county of Neuchâtel (now a canton in north-western Switzerland). This was made possible because the Emperor Rudolf I took Neuchâtel into his personal possession before handing it in fief to one of his supporters. Its proximity to Germany ensured the emperors' continuing care and attention, and it evaded the clutches both of the Valois duke-counts and of the Swiss Confederation all the way to the Treaty of Westphalia in 1648.[92] From 1707 to 1806, it belonged, eccentrically, to Prussia.

The fifteenth century saw the heyday of medieval cities. They flour-

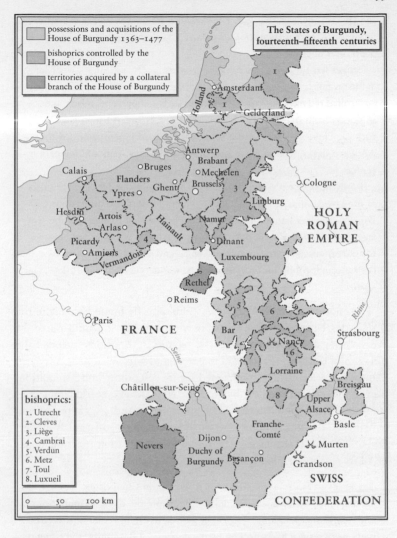

The States of Burgundy,
fourteenth–fifteenth centuries

possessions and acquisitions of the
House of Burgundy 1363–1477

bishoprics controlled by the
House of Burgundy

territories acquired by a collateral
branch of the House of Burgundy

HOLY
ROMAN
EMPIRE

FRANCE

SWISS
CONFEDERATION

bishoprics:
1. Utrecht
2. Cleves
3. Liège
4. Cambrai
5. Verdun
6. Metz
7. Toul
8. Luxueil

0   50   100 km

ished most ostentatiously in two centres, northern Italy and the Low
Countries – that is, in the States of Burgundy – and were the true habitat
of the Renaissance. Art and learning went hand in hand with commerce:

> Bruges, at this time the most international mercantile town in north-west
> Europe, was undoubtedly [Burgundy's] beating heart. Hundreds of foreign-
> ers had their residence there ... At least twelve 'nations' of foreign merchants
> enjoyed ... legal protection ... Forty or fifty Hansa merchants resided in

the city throughout the year. The northern Italians ... were even more numerous. There were also ... Catalans, Castilians, Portuguese, Basques, Scots, and English.

Bruges was the centre of a complex network ... During the six-week-long Whitsun fair ... all the foreigners left Bruges ... for Antwerp. There they controlled the trade in expensive textiles such as linen and velvet, and ... in goods from overseas like spices, wine, oil, tropical fruits, sugar, and furs ... Thus, we can imagine Bruges at the top of a pyramid, with ... Antwerp in the second place and Ghent and Ypres, regional mercantile centres.

From the thirteenth century on, Italian firms had extended credit to rulers in the Low Countries ... Duke Philip the Bold had close connections with Dino Rapondi, a banker from Lucca ... Dino settled in Flanders and lent large sums of money to the duke and to the towns ... With a bill of exchange for sixty thousand francs, payable in Venice, and a large loan, Dino provided the ransom for John the Fearless when he was captured by the Turks ... in 1396.[93]

The court of the duke-counts was itinerant. Its home base lay in the 'Palais des Ducs' in Dijon, where it wintered, but it would move off every spring for its annual progress; regular destinations included the old comtal residences at Hesdin in Artois and Mechelen near Antwerp. Contemporaries always commented on its splendour and ostentation. 'Burgundian' has become a byword for lavish dress, conspicuous consumption and making merry. The processions and pageants and the 'entries' of the duke-counts and their guests were consciously undertaken as political spectacles. The Burgundian court felt itself the equal of all its neighbours, bar none:

> The king of France ... took the road to Troyes, in Champagne ... He was accompanied by his uncles the duke of Bourbon, the duke of Touraine ... and many other knights ... [when] he arrived at Dijon ... he was received with every respect and affection by the duchess of Burgundy, and all who had come thither to do him honour. Grand entertainments were given on the occasion, and the king remained eight days at Dijon.[94]

Burgundy's ruling circles cultivated the art and the ethos of chivalry with unparalleled passion. The Order of the Golden Fleece, modelled on England's Order of the Garter, was instituted in 1430. Its rituals and ceremonies outshone all others. Its badge was mounted on a jewelled collar bearing the incongruous motto: '*Pretium Laborum Non Vile*' ('Not a Bad Reward for Working').[95] The choice of a non-Christian theme for the Order was an outward sign of interest in the ancient world. The same can be said of the manuscripts and the literary works, such as the *Épopée troyenne* or 'Trojan Epic', which graced their libraries. William Caxton, the pioneer of English printing, published a *Recuyell of the Historyes of Troye* in 1473, based on the Burgundian original.[96]

The Flemish School of painting, a centrepiece of the Northern Renaissance, was launched under Burgundian patronage. Painters such as Robert Campin (*c.* 1378–1444), Jan van Eyck (*c.* 1390–1441), who worked both for the count of Holland and for Philip the Bold, Roger van der Weyden (*c.* 1400–1464) and Hans Memling (*c.* 1430–94), a German who settled in Bruges, pioneered the secularization of European art. They moved with confidence into new genres, including portraits, still life, everyday scenes and landscape.[97] Outstanding sculptors, too, were patronized. Claus Sluter (*fl.* 1380–1405), a Dutchman, became the court sculptor at Dijon. His best-known surviving work is the *Well of Moses*, fashioned for the ducal mausoleum at the monastery of Champol.[98] Tapestries, too, were a Burgundian speciality. The costly technique of weaving gold thread into coloured designs was invented in Arras. In the fifteenth century, the *tapissiers* could produce huge, wall-hung panels depicting battles, historical scenes, ancient legends and intricate landscapes.[99]

Music blossomed alongside the visual arts. The Burgundian School started life in the ducal chapel in Dijon, where 'the Burgundian Spirit in Song' could already be heard by the century's turn.[100] But it expanded both geographically and stylistically. Guillaume Dufay (*c.* 1397–1470), a Brabanter, may have been the most famous European composer of the day. The later Franco-Flemish School produced a bevy of talent centred on the genius of Joskin van de Velde (*c.*1450–1520), better known as Josquin des Prez, who brought polyphony to its peak.[101]

Renaissance literature covered many fields from poetry to philosophy. Erasmus of Rotterdam (1466–1536), the greatest humanist of his age, was a Burgundian.[102] Both French and Dutch developed alongside Latin, and the intermingling of the vernaculars has been called 'a dialogue of two cultures'. Burgundy also provided the setting for one of the most stirring works of twentieth-century scholarship, Johan Huizinga's *Herfsttij der Middeleeuwen* (1919), known throughout the world as *The*

Waning of the Middle Ages. Huizinga (1872–1945), a professor at Leiden and a pioneer of cultural history, used detailed analysis of the rituals, art forms and spectacles at the Burgundian court to formulate his theory about the rough and vividly emotional character of late medieval life, contesting the prevailing view that it was an age full of Renaissance grace, aestheticism and enlightened debate:

> When the world was half a thousand years younger, all events had much sharper outlines than now. The distance between sadness and joy, between good and bad fortune, seemed to be much greater than for us. Every event, every deed was defined in given and expressive forms; death by virtue of the sacraments, basked in the radiance of the divine mystery. But even the lesser events – a journey, a visit, a piece of work, were accompanied by a multitude of blessings, ceremonies, sayings and conventions.[103]

Huizinga's views were hugely influential, even though they provoked hostility among some Dutch colleagues, and bewilderment in his Belgian friend Henri Pirenne.[104]

For all their extraordinary cultural patronage, politics was the prime *métier* of the duke-counts. Burgundy distinguished itself both in projects to lay the foundations of an integrated state and in the brilliance of its diplomacy. Although force could be used to suppress rebellious subjects, local particularities were respected; and it was the practice to rule by established procedure and consent. In a typical decree of 13 December 1385, Ghent felt both its lord's heavy hand and his magnanimity:

> Philip of France, duke of Burgundy, earl of Flanders and Artois, palatine of Burgundy ... to all, greeting: be it known ... our well-beloved subjects ... of our good town of Ghent, having humbly supplicated us, to have mercy, that [We] have pardoned and forgiven all misdemeanours and offences ... and have fully confirmed all the said customs, privileges, and franchises, provided they place themselves wholly under obedience [to us].[105]

The duke-counts, like the English monarchs, drew on their impossibly tangled genealogy to support their claim that they were the true kings of France, and Philip the Bold in particular was preoccupied with French affairs. When he died in 1404, his position both as a prince of the Valois blood and as an independent ruler was secure. Yet he did not neglect his 'States of Burgundy'. He was a connoisseur of fine wine, and issued detailed decrees on matters such as the banishment of the inferior gamay grape or the sacrifice of quality to quantity through excessive use of manure. Small towns like Pommard, Nuits St George and Beaune grew up in his time as centres for the *négociants*, the middlemen of the wine trade. One of his properties at the Château de Santenay on the slopes of the Côte d'Or still produces wines that bear his name.[106] He was also the principal constructor of the Palais de Ducs at Dijon.[107]

Philip's son, Jean sans Peur – John the Fearless – who had fought against the Turks as a young knight in the Crusade of Nicopolis, consolidated Burgundy's power and independence. Endlessly embroiled with his French relatives, he was murdered by the entourage of the dauphin in September 1419 on the bridge at Montereau near Paris in an encounter which he had expected to be a diplomatic parley.[108] John's son, Philippe le Bon – Philip the Good – was known in his youth as the count of Charolais, and brought 'the States' to a high degree of prestige and prosperity. He expanded them by the purchase of Namur and Luxembourg, by the conquest of Holland, Zealand and Frisia in the so-called Cold Wars, and by the inheritance of Brabant, Limburg and Antwerp. He liked to style himself, immodestly, as the 'grand duke of the West'.[109]

Philip the Good's funeral is often cited as the grandest of Burgundian spectacles. It was lavishly staged in Bruges in 1467 and was recorded in great detail by the court chronicler, Chastellain. Hundreds of mourners, dressed in black, were fitted out at official expense with cloaks reflecting their rank. The church of St Donation was filled with so many candles that the stained glass had to be broken to release the heat. Twenty thousand spectators watched the torchlight procession:

> The remains of Duke Philip . . . were placed in a closed leaden coffin weighing more than 240 pounds. A cloth of gold measuring thirty-two ells and lined with black satin covered the coffin. Twelve Archers of the Guard carried [it], [while] the pall of gold cloth . . . was held by sixteen grand barons . . . A canopy of golden cloth mounted on four large spikes was a borne aloft by four Burgundian noblemen: the counts of Joigny, Bouquan, and Blancquehain, and the seigneur de Chastelguion. Directly behind . . . walking alone was Meriadez, the Master of the Horse . . . [and] the principal director of the funeral. [He] carried the ducal sword of his late master in its richly ornate sheath, pointed down towards the ground.[110]

During the entombment, the sword was passed to the late duke's son and heir, Charles, in a gesture borrowed from French regal ceremony. It signified the continuity of princely power – but it also gave notice of Charles's intention of living by the sword.

Charles le Téméraire has variously been classed, according to translation, as 'the Bold', 'the Rash' and 'the Terrible'. He was the son of a
Portuguese princess, and through successive marriages, brother-in-law
to the kings both of France and of England. His warlike disposition had
erupted before his father's death, when in 1466, he ordered the slaughter of every man, woman and child in the rebellious town of Dinant. His
main mistake was to assume that he could offend all his neighbours
simultaneously, and in the complicated Burgundian wars of the 1470s,
his enemies eventually united against him. He soon found himself
pressed in the west by Louis XI of France, 'the Universal Spider', and in
the east by the Lorrainers, the Imperialists and the Swiss.[111]

Switzerland, which by now had absorbed large parts of the old
'Upper Burgundy', proved to be the nemesis of the 'Burgundian States'.
In three successive battles, Charles was successively humiliated, out-
manoeuvred and obliterated. At Grandson in the Vaud (2 March 1476),
where he had slaughtered the local garrison, he abandoned a vast booty,
including his solid silver bath. At the lake of Morat (Murten) in the canton of Berne (22 June 1476), his army was routed, and many of his
troops drowned. Finally, at the winter siege of Nancy (5 January 1477),
he met his death. The chronicler Philippe de Commynes recorded what
he had heard:

> The duke's . . . few troops, in bad shape, were immediately . . . either killed
> or [put to] flight . . . The Duke of Burgundy perished on the field . . . The
> manner of it was recounted to me by [prisoners] who saw him hurled to
> the ground . . . He was set upon by a crowd of soldiers, who killed him and
> despoiled his body without recognizing him. This battle was fought on . . .
> the eve of Epiphany. [Two days later], the duke's naked corpse, frozen into
> the ice of a pond, was identified: the head had been split to the chin by a
> Swiss halberd, the body many times pierced by Swiss pikes.[112]

Commynes, who had once served Charles le Téméraire, was harsh in his
judgement. 'Half of Europe', he commented, 'would not have satisfied
him.'[113]

The 'Booty of Burgundy' is a phrase most usually applied to the vast
pile of treasure which was captured by the Swiss at Grandson and which
has been appearing on the European art market ever since,[114] but it
could equally be applied to the fate of the 'States of Burgundy' as a
whole. Within a few years, the possessions of the duke-counts had been
dispersed. The duchy, swiftly occupied by French forces, reverted to
France. The County-Palatine, the 'Franche-Comté', with some delay,

reverted to the Empire. The link between the duchy and the Low Countries was severed.

The late duke-count's nineteen-year-old daughter, Mary of Burgundy
(1457–82), was now wooed by more suitors than the years of her life.
Since her duchy had been seized by the French, she fell back on her
subjects in the Low Countries. Yet they, too, were simmering with
resentment. They stopped her from choosing a husband until she granted
them a 'Great Privilege' abolishing all her father's recent impositions.
Mary was then free to make her choice, which fell on Maximilian von
Habsburg, son of the Holy Roman Emperor. The marriage was conse-
crated at Ghent on 19 August in the year that had started with the Battle
of Nancy. It was one of the great matrimonial milestones of European
history. Within five years, Mary was dead, killed by a fall from her
horse,[115] yet in the brief interval, she had given birth to three children who
would ensure the political legacy of her marriage. Her widowed husband
succeeded to the Empire; her son Philip IV was to marry the queen of
Aragon and Castile, and her grandson, Charles of Ghent, *Kezer* Karel,
better known as the Emperor Charles V, was to scoop the largest portfolio of titles and dominions ever bequeathed to a European monarch.[116]

From the geographical standpoint, the principal result of the settlement
of 1477 must be found in the permanent separation of the duchy from
the rest of the 'Burgundian Inheritance'. The duchy returned to the
Kingdom of France, where as 'Bourgogne' it became one of the provinces
of the *ancien régime*. The rest passed to the Habsburgs, who complicated
matters by adopting the title of 'duke of Burgundy' without inheriting
the duchy. In this way, the hereditary title of dukes of Burgundy, which
all Habsburg emperors used from 1477 to 1795, was associated with a
very different territory from that underlying the title of 'kings of Burgundy' which earlier emperors had once used.

The County-Palatine followed a somewhat variant course. In 1477 it
was seized by France, but only sixteen years later was restored to the
Empire by the Treaty of Senlis as the price of peace and added to
the Habsburgs' 'Burgundian Inheritance'. Its status was confirmed in
1512, at the time that the titular Duke Charles II (not yet the Emperor
Charles V) was still considering the creation of a new administrative
unit, the *Burgundischer Reichskreis* or 'Imperial Burgundian Circle'.[117]
There were a dozen such circles within the Holy Roman Empire in the
sixteenth to eighteenth centuries. The Burgundian Circle, formalized in
1548, is No. IX on Bryce's list.

Nonetheless, since the Peace of Senlis did not hold, chronic war between France and the Empire became one of the most persistent fixtures of modern European history. In the process, the territory of the 'Burgundian Circle' was gradually whittled down, exactly as the former Kingdom of Burgundy had been. In 1512, the Circle comprised twenty distinct territorial units. Over the years, it shrank and shrivelled. In 1555 a large part was transferred to the rule of Madrid as the Spanish Netherlands, but within twenty-five years half of these Spanish-ruled provinces broke free to launch themselves as the Dutch Republic. By the time the

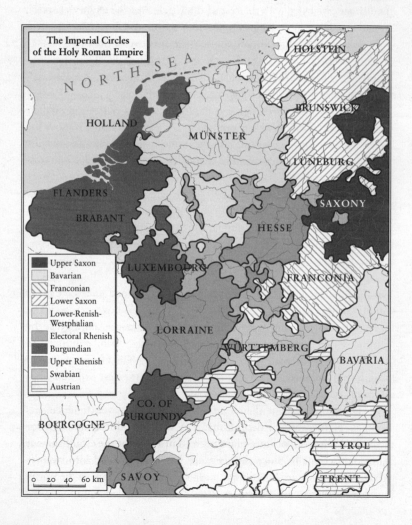

The Imperial Circles
of the Holy Roman Empire

NORTH SEA

HOLSTEIN

HOLLAND

BRUNSWICK

MÜNSTER

LÜNEBURG

FLANDERS

SAXONY

BRABANT

HESSE

Upper Saxon
Bavarian
Franconian
Lower Saxon
Lower-Renish-
  Westphalian
Electoral Rhenish
Burgundian
Upper Rhenish
Swabian
Austrian

LUXEMBOURG

FRANCONIA

LORRAINE

WÜRTTEMBERG

BAVARIA

CO. OF
BURGUNDY

BOURGOGNE

TYROL

0   20   40   60 km

SAVOY

TRENT

residue was returned by Spain to Austria in 1715, only eight of the original twenty units survived as the 'Austrian Netherlands'.[118] (The Duchy of Lorraine, incidentally, where Charles le Téméraire had died, was not incorporated into the Imperial Circle. It remained technically independent, and its last duke, *le bon roi* Stanislas (r. 1735–66), was an unemployed Polish monarch, whose daughter happened to be the queen of France.[119])

The trajectory of the County-Palatine of Burgundy, the 'Franche-Comté', was also somewhat eccentric. Most of it was handed over to Spanish rule in 1555 with the rest of the Circle. Yet the county's capital, Besanz/Besançon, remained a *Reichsstadt* within the Empire until 1651. Only then was it restored, for just one generation, as the capital of 'El Contado Franco', before being ceded to France with the rest of the county at the Treaty of Nijmegen of 1678, thus breaking the Empire's final link with its former Kingdom of Burgundy.[120]

The provinces of Bourgogne and of Franche-Comté stood side by side within the Kingdom of France from the reign of Louis XIV to the French Revolution. The former, administered from Dijon, was officially inhabited by *bourguignons* and *bourguignonnes*; the latter, administered from Besançon, by *comtois* and *comtoises*. In 1791 both were abolished, and each was replaced by republican *départements* with names of no historical significance. Everything associated with the *ancien régime* was despised. The French were deliberately cut off from their provincial identities and taught to forget the Kingdom of France, let alone the many kingdoms of Burgundy.[121]

The modern French state is famed for the centralized character of its administration. Over the last 200 years many things have changed. The revolutionary Republic was replaced by the Empire: the Empire by a restored kingdom, by a Second Republic, by a Second Empire, and by the Third, Fourth and Fifth Republics. For much of this time, one thing has not changed: Paris has proposed, and the rest of France has disposed.

In the second half of the twentieth century, however, practice was modified. A measure of decentralization was introduced in 1956 for the limited purposes of state-planning and in 1982 for the establishment of regional councils. Since then, France has been divided into twenty-two regions, which are broadly comparable in size and shape to the thirty-four pre-revolutionary provinces. One region is called Bourgogne. Its immediate neighbour is called Franche-Comté.[122] However, France's regions do not operate in the same way as the devolved countries of the United Kingdom, or the cantons of Switzerland. The powers of France's central government have not been curbed, only mildly clipped; and the appeal to historical formations has been very limited. The post-war bureaucrats who invented the regions do not appear to remember anything further back than the *ancien régime*. They ignored the Burgundian associations of Franche-Comté, and awarded the Burgundian name exclusively to the former duchy. There is no recognition that the region which they designated as 'Rhône-Alpes' is sitting on as strong a Burgundian claim as anywhere else.[123]

Nonetheless, historical memory is remarkably persistent. It may be inaccurate, confused and distorted, but it doesn't disappear easily. One hundred and eleven years passed between the abolition of Merovingian Burgundy and the founding of the Carolingian duchy; 162 years passed between the abolition of the royal French province of 'Bourgogne' and its revival as a region. Clearly, these spans are not long enough for the collective psyche to forget completely. In modern times, memories of fifteenth-century 'Burgundy' appear to have eclipsed all others, perhaps as a result of its artistic splendour. Yet one must never say 'never'. The day may yet dawn when the citizens of Geneva, Basle, Grenoble, Arles, Lyon, Dijon and Besançon will unfurl their banner and sing their anthem: 'Burgundia has not perished yet, so long as we still live!' And they might invite a representative or a delegation from Bornholm to join in the celebrations.

Bryce's Note A 'On the Burgundies' contained ten items, and it mentioned a possible eleventh. It did not concern itself with the provinces of the *ancien régime*, and for obvious reasons could not have included the present-day regions. Even so, Bryce's tally of ten or eleven 'Burgundies' is manifestly too short. According to definitions, there have been five, six or seven kingdoms, two duchies, one or two provinces, one county-palatine, one landgravate, one 'United States', one Imperial Circle, and at least one region. This brings the aggregate to a minimum of thirteen and a maximum of sixteen. At the beginning of the twenty-first century a running total of fifteen Burgundies is absolutely defensible. One is reminded of the Latin motto of Philip the Good, '*Non Aliud*' – best translated as 'Enough, but not too much'.[124]

By way of recapitulation, therefore, it may be appropriate to present a summary of Note A (Revised):

1. 410–36   The first Burgundian kingdom of Gundahar
                 (Bryce's I).

2. 451–534   The second Burgundian kingdom, founded by
                 Gundioc.

3. c. 590–734   The third (Frankish) kingdom of Burgundy
                 (Bryce's II).

4. 843–1384   The French Duchy of Burgundy (Bryce's X).

5. 879–933   The Kingdom of Lower Burgundy (Bryce's III).

6. 888–933   The Kingdom of Upper Burgundy (Bryce's IV).

7. 933–1032   The united Kingdom of the Two Burgundies
                 (Arelate) (Bryce's V).

8. c. 1000–1678 The County-Palatine of Burgundy (Franche-
                 Comté) (Bryce's VII).

9. 1032–?   The imperial Kingdom of Burgundy.

10. 1127–1218   The imperial Duchy of Lesser Burgundy
                 (Bryce's VI).

11. 1127+   The imperial Landgravate of Burgundy
                 (Bryce's VIII).

12. 1384–1477   The united 'States of Burgundy'.

13. 1477–1791   The French province of Burgundy (Bourgogne).

14. 1548–1795   The Imperial Burgundian Circle (Bryce's IX).

15. 1982+   The contemporary French region of Bourgogne.

III

Most people looking for information these days reach for their computer and the Internet. They bring up a search engine like Webcrawler, Yahoo, Google or Baidu, type in a keyword, click once, and are instantaneously rewarded with uncountable numbers of 'hits'. Traditionalists believe that new technology often produces poor results.

In the case of 'Burgundy', one click on Google (in February 2009) brought up 23,900,000 entries. The list was augmented by an option to have the keyword or keywords defined. One click on the 'Definition' offered by 'answers.com' yielded the following:

Burgundy A historical region and former province of Eastern France. The area was first organised into a kingdom by the Burgundii, a Germanic people, in the 5th century. At the height of its later power in the 14th and 15th centuries, [it] controlled vast territories in present-day Netherlands,

Belgium and north-eastern France. It was incorporated into the French
crown lands by Louis XI in 1477.[125]

No one wants to be needlessly pedantic, but seekers after precision
should be warned: every single sentence of the above definition contains
false or misleading assertions. The first area once organized into a kingdom by the Burgundii, for example, is not in eastern France.

However, one should not judge the authors of 'answers.com' too
harshly. If fifteen Burgundies is taken as a full score, they manage three
out of fifteen, or 20 per cent, which if one explores further, by no means
puts them at the bottom of the class. What is more, their faulty information derives from verifiable sources. *The Britannica Concise Encyclopedia*,
cited by 'answers.com', defines Burgundy as 'historical and governmental region, France'. The *Columbia Encyclopedia* goes for 'historic region,
E. France'. An entry from the online Wikipedia goes for 'a region historically situated in modern-day France and Switzerland ... and in the
4th century assigned by the Romans to ... the Burgundians, who settled
there in their own kingdom'.[126]

The discrepancies in these definitions are easily spotted. But it is dis-
tressing to see that their common characteristic lies in their immobility:
they are all trying to tie the concept of Burgundy to a single locality.
None grasps the key feature, namely that Burgundy was a movable feast.

The Google list on 'Burgundy' is presented in two forms. The full list,
containing over 23 million entries, is impractically long. The shortened
list contains 535 entries ranked by the frequency of their consultation.
Here, the common characteristics are a persistent focus on the present,
and again a rigid determination to locate Burgundy exclusively in France.

A new search can be conducted using two key words: 'Burgundy' plus
'History'. The resultant crop of websites looks promising. They include
'History of Burgundy', 'Burgundy – History', 'The Burgundians', and
many more. On examination, however, the drawbacks become obvious.
The text of 'The Burgundians' stops abruptly after the second kingdom,
because its remit stops in the sixth century (score 2 : 15). The home page
of the 'History of Burgundy' offers four sub-sections, the third of which
is headed 'The Glorious Age ... 1364–1477'. The purpose is to sell 'the
Glorious Duchy' and nothing else. 'Burgundy – History' reveals shameless prejudices. 'From the 10th century onward,' it opines, 'Burgundy
meant a duchy belonging to the royal family of the Capetians.' If that
were to be believed, the imperial Kingdom of Burgundy never even
existed (score 1 : 15).[127]

And so one could continue, using different keywords and different linguistic preferences. The same stunted concepts recur time and time again. A French site located via 'Bourgogne' distinguishes the early Kingdom of *Bourgondie* (the Burgundians) from 'the later [Frankish] Kingdom of *Bourgogne*', and is exceptional for mentioning the Kingdom of the Two Burgundies (score 4 : 15).

Students are frequently warned against pulling information off the Internet. Wikipedia, the self-authored, online encyclopedia, is especially suspect. 'How can anything be verified?' one hears. 'People can write whatever comes into their head.' Such fears are clearly not baseless. Yet they are widely accompanied by the assumption that the old-fashioned printed works of reference, 'the recognized authorities', are *ipso facto* more reliable. The test of this comes, therefore, when Internet sites are compared to some of the more traditional, academic products.

Burgundy, for certain, is a complex word. It carries a mass of diverse connotations. In English, for example, it has two main meanings: a place and a product. According to the *Shorter Oxford English Dictionary*, the place is defined as '1. a Kingdom, and later a duchy of the Western Empire, subsequently giving its name to a province of France'. The product is '2. ellipt. wine made in Burgundy'. Of course, one cannot expect the English to be particularly knowledgeable on continental matters, and it is not a complete surprise if the *SOED*'s entry contains flaws. What is surprising is that a mistake in word order muddies the issue unnecessarily. If the entry had read: 'Burgundy: 1. a Kingdom of the western Roman Empire, and later a duchy ...', it would have been accurate, though incomplete. As it stands, it is both inaccurate and incomplete. And as for the wine, connoisseurs would be appalled by the implication that any old plonk from the region would qualify for the 'Appellation d'Origine Contrôlée', the 'Registered Name of Origin' (score 1 : 15).[128]

The full *OED* repeats the above definitions, while adding others:

- 'shade of red of the colour of Burgundy wine'
- 'sort of head-dress for women = BOURGOIGNE (obsolete)'
- 'Burgundy hay: applied by British writers to the Lucerne plant, *Medicago sativa*, but in French originally to Sainfoin, *Onobrychis sativa* (the two were formerly confused)'
- 'Burgundy mixture, a preparation of soda and copper sulphate used for spraying potato-tops'

Under 'Burgundian', after 'belonging to Burgundy' (adj.) and 'an inhab-
itant of Burgundy' (subst.), the OED opts eccentrically for 'one of the
Teutonic nations of the Burgunds . . .' and '2. (in form of *Burgonian*) A
kind of ship . . . built in the Burgundian dominions, which in the 15th c.
included the Netherlands'. The 'Teutonic nation of Burgunds' is concep-
tually mangled, but at least the geography is not Francocentric.[129]

Webster's American Dictionary is minimalist. It offers 'a region in
France'; 'a blended red wine produced elsewhere (as California)'; and 'a
reddish purple color'. This suggests, eccentrically, that Californian burgundy is the real thing, while burgundy from Burgundy may not be.

Given the prevailing pro-French bias, one expects the French to be
better informed. *Littré* is one of the older dictionaries: '*BOUR-
GOGNE, s.m vin de Bourgogne, E de Burgundi, nom d'un peuple
germain; s.f nom vulgaire du sainfoin.*' The definitions are sparse: a
wine, a state, a people and a sort of hay, as in the OED. But there follow the headdress, the province and, unusually, 'a breakaway fragment
of pack-ice': '*nom donné par les marins aux morceaux de glace détachée
de la banquise*'. No one else has spotted the ice-floes.

Robert comes next, and again the haul is disappointing. Burgundy, as
in *Littré*, is nothing more than a province (score 1 : 15). And, despite the
list of grand crus, there is no sign of the AOC.

So one turns to Imbs, and his *Trésor de la langue française* ('Treasury
of the French Language'). This is no more fruitful. Burgundy is still a
mere province (score 1 : 15). But separate words are given for the Burgundians of old (*Burgondes*) and the Burgundians of today (*Bourguignons*).
Nonetheless, one must conclude: dictionary definitions are very inadequate, particularly on historical matters.

Encyclopedias form a large category. *The New Encyclopaedia Britannica* (1974) can draw on the phenomenal *Encyclopaedia Britannica*
(11th edition, 1911). It doesn't disappoint. After describing the ancient
Burgundians as 'Scandinavian', it gives a brief account of six kingdoms
of Burgundy plus the county, plus a duchy, plus the 'states of Burgundy',
plus the province. The seventh kingdom is at least implied. The only
items missing are the Imperial Circle, a duchy, a landgravate, and the
province (score 11 : 15).

The *Nouveau Petit Larousse*, a household name in France, starts
with an unsatisfactory definition: Burgundy, 'a region in the east of
France which is more of a historical than a geographical unity'. But the
account that follows covers six kingdoms, plus the county, duchy, 'states
of Burgundy' and province (score 10 : 15). Still no Imperial Circle. It

concludes: 'Burgundy found itself joined for a long time with Germany. The Kings of France ate into it bit by bit over the centuries.' This is tremendous news: *Larousse* is not Francocentric.[130]

The international aspect of the problem is crucial. The Burgundian question defies national frontiers. Ideally, one would draw on reference works not just from France, but from Germany, Belgium, the Netherlands and Switzerland. Each source would naturally be strong on some points and weaker on others.

A German *Brockhaus* happens to be to hand. The entry is suitably long and detailed. It distinguishes well between the Burgundy of the present, which is defined as 'a Region made up of four French departments', and five Burgundies of the past: the Koenigreich der Burgunder, from 443, the Burgundia of the Franks, from 534, the Koenigreich Burgund (Arelat), the Herzogtum Burgund, that is, the duchy, and the Freigrafschaft Burgund (Franche-Comté). In explaining the genesis of the Arelat, *Brockhaus* also mentions Boso's 'Kingdom of Lower Burgundy' (score 7 : 15). Surprisingly, no Imperial Circle.[131]

Seeking impartiality, one turns to a country with no direct links to Burgundy. An old copy of the *Wielka Encyklopedia Powszechna PWN* is also to hand. It transpires that the Poles still use the Latin form, *Burgundia*. The *EP* describes it as a 'historical land (*kraina historyczna*) in eastern France', and 'an important region for wine production'. But the long, solid, historical summary contains few deficiencies. One meets 'the 5th Century Kingdom of the Germanic Burgundians'; the kingdoms of Upper Burgundy, of Lower Burgundy, and of Arles; and from 1032 'a kingdom within the structure of Germany'. Five out of a possible seven is good. 'The name of Burgundy', it continues, 'was only preserved . . . in the Free County (Franche-Comté) which had belonged to Germany until 1382.' This statement is inaccurate, but the general narrative stays on course. 'The Duchy's period of greatness was launched by the rule of Filip Śmiały [Philip the Bold],' it says. And it does not stop, as many accounts do, with the last of the Valois duke-counts: 'After the death of Charles the Bold in 1477, his sole heiress, Marie, married the Archduke of Austria Maximilian; and a new partition of B. resulted. France recovered the Duchy of B. plus Picardy. The Habsburgs took the Netherlands plus Franche-Comté, which eventually returned to France in 1678'.[132] (Score 9 : 15.) Still no Imperial Circle.

For people without French, German or Polish, the highest hopes have to be reserved for a recently published *Gazetteer of the World*, produced by a prestigious American institution. It specializes in the descriptions of geographical places and historical territories: 'Burgundy (BUHR-ghun-dee), Fr. Bourgogne (BOORGON-yuh), historic region and former province of E central and E France. The name applies to 2 successive anc. kingdoms and to a duchy, all embracing a territory larger than the 17th–18th cent. prov. After 1790, it was divided into depts. Present-day, it forms one of France's new administrative regions'. So far, not too bad (score 5:15). Before long, however, the anachronisms creep in: 'Conquered by Caesar in his Gallic Wars, it was later settled (5th cent. A.D.) by Burgundians, a Germanic tribe, who established the First Kingdom of Burgundy.' Times and places are wrongly associated, and convoluted misconceptions proliferate:

> Partitioned during the Merovingian and Carolingian era, it was reunited (933) in the Second Kingdom comprising Cisjurane Burgundy (already known as Provence) in the S and Transjurane Burgundy (N). Soon a smaller duchy of Burgundy was created by Emperor Charles II and absorbed (1034) into the Holy Roman Empire. The duchy entered its golden age under Philip the Good and came to include most of the present Neth., Belgium, and N and E France.

The word 'soon' shows the editors trying to climb desperately from the mire. The chronology is topsy-turvy, the nomenclature scrambled, and the absorption of the duchy into the Holy Roman Empire imaginary. Fortunately, a partial recovery is staged in the final section:

> During 15th cent. Burgundy was . . . an artistic center outshining the rest of the continent. The wars of ambitious Charles the Bold, however, proved ruinous . . . His daughter, Mary of Burgundy, by marrying Emperor Maximilian I, brought most of the expanded Burgundy (but not the Fr. duchy) to the house of Hapsburg. The duchy was seized by Louis XI who made it into a Fr. Prov . . . Burgundy now lies astride the main Paris-Lyon-Marseilles RR and auto routes.[133]

(Score: hard to calculate.)

So what is the information-seeker to do? Taken together, the 'recognized authorities' are really no less imperfect than any others. The Internet, like any other library, contains works of varying value. Like all sources, it has to be used with critical vigilance, but it is not markedly inferior. Analytical studies have shown that Wikipedia, for all its faults, can sometimes match the most prestigious academic brands. It has the virtue of being constantly corrected and updated.[134]

The search, in fact, need never end. The indefatigable may wish to go on and explore the multi-authored composite historical works, often recommended for reference purposes. Unfortunately, the relevant chapter in the composite *New Cambridge Medieval History* does not open too promisingly. 'The region known as Burgundy', it begins, 'has had some of the most elastic borders of any region of France.' Once again, Burgundy is conceived in its limited French form. Medievalists, above all, should take more care.[135]

Other searchers may try their luck with the romantically titled works of yesteryear. *The Lost Kingdom of Burgundy*, for example, which hovers between fact and fiction, opens with a flourish. 'On such a night as this,' the first sentence whispers conspiratorially, 'Charles of Burgundy rode to his death. He lost an empire, monsieur, because he dare not rescue a beautiful woman.' A few pages later, it gets worse: 'The kingdom lives because its motley kings, tatterdemalion warriors, guitar-playing swashbucklers, and mace-wielding choristers have refused to remain in their moldy tombs.' Then, on page 8, one meets a sentence for which all can be forgiven. 'The ancient Burgundy was, and is, something quite apart from the France that enveloped it – a sort of Atlantis engulfed beneath seas upon seas of new people.' The author possessed the priceless gift of imaginative sympathy which so many more prestigious compilations lack. And he produced another great line. 'Moonlight', he wrote, 'is the great restorer of vanished kingdoms.'[136]

4

Aragon

A Mediterranean Empire
(1137–1714)

Perpignan is the *chef-lieu* of France's most southerly department, the Pyrénées-Orientales (dép. 64), one of five such departments within the Region of Languedoc-Roussillon. As the *corbeau* flies, it is situated 510 miles south-south-west of Paris, close to the Franco-Spanish frontier. In former times it was the provincial capital of historic Roussillon, which today borders the Spanish districts of Lleida and Gerona and the Principality of Andorra. The Côte Vermeille, the 'Scarlet Coast', lies immediately adjacent on the Golfe du Lion, 12 miles to the south, and beyond it the Costa Brava. The best way to get there is by TGV Express; fast, luxurious trains leave the Gare de Lyon four times a day for Avignon, and thence along the plain of Languedoc via Montpellier, Béziers and Narbonne. The journey takes 4 hours 45 minutes. Passengers arriving in the daytime are usually greeted by the strong southern sun, which bathes the city on average for 300 days each year.

Alternatively, one can fly to the regional airport of Perpignan-Rivesaltes, which hosts flights from domestic and international destinations including Paris-Orly, London-Stansted, Charleroi and Southampton. On entering the terminal building, the first poster one sees reads:

VISITEZ LE CHÂTEAU DES ROIS
PLACE-FORTE D'UN ROYAUME EPHÉMÈRE

('Visit the Castle of the Kings, Fortress of an Ephemeral Kingdom').[1] Few visitors could be expected to know beforehand what the 'Ephemeral Kingdom' refers to.

The old city lies on the southern bank of the River Têt, which is lined by the Boulevard de la France Libre. An inner ring road is formed by the boulevards Foch, Wilson, Briand and Poincaré which surround the imposing medieval citadel. A tangle of narrow streets filled with cafés and restaurants tumbles down towards the river, and is dominated by three squares: place de la Loge, place Verdun and the place Arago (François Arago (1786–1853) was a renowned scientific pioneer of local descent). The railway station is located at the end of the avenue Général de Gaulle.

Nonetheless, as the tourist websites emphasize, Perpignan has unmistakable foreign flavours. 'A good part of Perpignan's population is of Spanish origin,' one reads, 'refugees from the Civil War and their descendants. The southern influence is further augmented by a substantial admixture of North Africans, both Arabs and white French settlers repatriated after Algerian independence in 1962.' 'While there are few monuments to visit,' the website continues, 'Perpignan is an enjoyable city with a lively street life. Its heyday was in the 13th and 14th centuries.'[2] The most recommended sights include the medieval Loge de Mer, the cathédrale Saint-Jean, the Palais de la Députation (once the parliament of Roussillon) and, of course, the citadel.

Nowadays, Perpignan's Catalan connections are widely publicized and actively promoted. The Castilet Gate is home to a Catalan folk museum called 'Casa Pairal'. The *Office de tourisme* promotes the festivals of La Sanch at Easter, of Sant Jordi in April, when sweethearts exchange gifts, and the Festa Major at the summer solstice, which celebrates 'the spirit of Perpignan la catalane'. It invites public participation in the Catalan national dance, the *sardana*, flies the Catalan flag alongside the French tricolour, and revels in the city's sobriquet of *La Fidelissima*, once awarded to the city for resisting a French king. In short, it takes pride in *Perpigna* being '*la capitale de la Catalogne française*'. These perspectives, not recognized before the 1980s, 'have greatly enhanced our heritage'.[3]

Perpignan's local rugby club, the *Union Sportive des Arlequins Perpignanais*, or '*USA Perpignan*' for short, plays in the Catalan colours of 'blood red and gold'. Founded in 1902, it is based at the Stade Aimé Giral, and in 2008–9 won the French champions' title.[4]

As always in France, a concise academic history is on sale. A volume entitled *Histoire du Roussillon*, written by a *maître de conférences* at the University of Toulouse, starts with an eloquent invocation of the geographical setting: 'Roussillon, however, is not just the mountain range brusquely surging from the sea ... It is also the coastland of the great "Middle Sea", with all its burden of history ... Roussillon owes both its

intensity and the explosion of its destiny to the sea's presence.' The story
of the province unfolds from ancient times to the contemporary epoch.
The birth of Perpignan comes about a third of the way through:

> Originally just a simple Roman villa, it was chosen by certain counts of
> Roussillon, who established their residence there at the end of the ninth
> century, thereby supplanting the functions of the adjacent ruined city of
> Ruscino. The consecration of the parish church of St John the Baptist on
> 16 March 1025, next to the hall of the count, marks the earliest manifest-
> ation of a new political and administrative centre.[5]

The physical chessboard on which political life developed here after
the collapse of the Roman Empire evidently saw a mass of tiny lordships
struggling to exist, trapped between the rising power of the Moorish
emirs in Iberia and that of the Frankish kings in the former Gaul. Every
other mountaintop sprouted a fortified tower or castle, attesting to
a state of affairs in which every larger district had its count and every
valley its viscount. As the feudal lords battled to subordinate their
neighbours, some lordships thrived and expanded, while others shrivelled. Gradually, as the lesser fry were swallowed up, a few powerful
dynasts came to dominate. One of these was Inigo Aristra, the Basque
warlord who drove out the Carolingians from the western Pyrenees in
the early ninth century, not long after Charlemagne's campaign against
the Moors. A second, in the eleventh century, was Sancho El Mayor, originally 'King of Pamplona'.

The narrative grows infernally complicated following the disintegration of the Frankish Empire and of its outlier beyond the eastern Pyrenees,
the *Marca Hispanica* or 'Spanish March'. The historical record lists a
procession of kings, princes and counts, all with unlikely names. Who
exactly was Suniaire I, not to mention the long line of Guillaberts, Gaus-
freds and Guinards? Can Count Raymond Berenguer II (r. 1076–82)
really be a different person from Berenguer Raymond II (r. 1076–97)?
And are the Raymonds (or Raimunds) different from the Ramóns?

Seeking answers to these puzzles, one climbs the cobbled streets to
Perpignan's citadel. There, another surprise awaits in the form of an
imposing, fortress-like structure called 'Le Palais des rois'. It is not what
one expects from a palace, and looks for all the world like a desert fort
from *Beau Geste*, plucked from the sands of the Sahara. Its garden is
adorned with palm trees, and its interior displays an extraordinary mixture of ecclesiastical Gothic arches and exotic Moorish courtyards.

Cultural and historical compasses spin out of control. Who were these kings, and where was their kingdom?

In the summer of 2010 Perpignan hosted the twenty-third annual 'Estivales', a popular festival of music, dance, theatre, circus and cinema. For three weeks in July, hundreds of entertainers presented scores of performances, and tens of thousands of enthusiasts flocked to enjoy them. Large-scale open-air shows took place on the Campo Santo, a purpose-built arena constructed beside the medieval church of St Jean le Vieux; more intimate events were staged in the Cloister of the Minimes. In 2010 the main theme of Mediterranean culture was given an extra African accent. The programmes were headed by the Dunas flamenco group from Seville; the Nederland Dans Theatre, Salif Keita from Mali, Victoria Chaplin's Invisible Circus, the Africa Umoja Ensemble from South Africa, and singers such as Vanessa Paradis and Alain Souchon.[6] Yet many would say that the best of Perpignan was to be discovered on the festival's fringe by the carefree crowds sipping wine under the stars, munching tapas, applauding the street artists, listening in the park to a gypsy guitarist or an impromptu jazz band, or dreamily dancing till dawn to the scent of hibiscus.

The Pyrenees, which form a mountain range of spectacular proportions and whose dark outline stood out against the night sky of the festival, provide the permanent backdrop to Perpignan. They run for some 200 miles from sea to sea, from the picturesque painters' villages of Collioure and Banyuls on the Côte Vermeille to the elegant resorts of Biarritz and Bayonne on the Atlantic shore. In between lie a tangle of craggy ranges, deep verdant valleys, fantastic gorges, elevated plateaux, steep passes, lonely scree fields and deserts, powerful snow-driven rivers, crystal-clear lakes, flower-strewn pastures and, high above the 10,000-foot line, a world of glaciers, snowfields and rugged rock summits. The tallest peaks – the Pic de Aneto (11,168 feet), the Maladeta (10,853 feet) and the Monte Perdido (11,007 feet), to use their Spanish names – all lie in the central section. For more than 350 years, this massive natural barrier has separated France from Spain. With one small exception, in the Vall d'Aran, the Franco-Spanish frontier winds its way along the full length of the Pyrenean ridge.

   In terms of historic provinces – which were replaced during the French Revolution by the *départements* – the *montant nord* or 'northerly slope' of the Pyrenees was occupied towards its Mediterranean end by

Cerdagne as well as by Roussillon, both of which go back to the days of the *Marca Hispanica*. On the southern slopes, if one starts from the Costa Brava, the line of the March parallel to the ridge takes one today through upper Catalonia, past the Principality of Andorra, and back into the north-western corner of Catalonia. Historically, one is passing through a series of ancient counties from Perelada on the coast to Pallars in the heart of the mountains.

In some stretches, the French side of the Pyrenees is less accessible than the Spanish side. The inland valley of the Ariège, for example, which runs north from Andorra, was kept apart politically from Cerdagne and Roussillon by a near-impassable tract. As a result, the counts of Foix, who once dominated the Ariège, were drawn westwards into Béarn and Navarre. The eastern Pyrenees, in contrast, though containing some mighty summits, have always invited human movement and migration, rarely acting as the cultural and linguistic wall which political planners in Paris or Madrid might have preferred. The area of

Catalan speech, for instance, straddles the Pyrenean ridge just as Basque does in the far west.

Roussillon (Rosselló in Catalan) combines a short length of coastline with a long stretch of the Pyrenean ridge. Its 1,500 square miles are dominated by one huge mountain and two transverse rivers. Le Mont Canigou or 'Canigo' (9,137 feet), where Catalans light their traditional Midsummer Eve bonfires, is visible across the sea from the vicinity of distant Marseille. The Rivers Têt and Tech, which water the Roussillon plain, rise in the upland districts of Conflent and Vallespir respectively, once counties in their own right. The region is famed for its *vin doux naturel* from the Côte Vermeille, for its ancient Romanesque abbeys such as St Michel de Cuxa or St Martin de Canigou, and for some of 'the most beautiful villages in France' – Castelnou among them, together with Evol, Mosset, Vinca and St Laurent de Cerdans.[7] From the thirteenth century onwards, Roussillon's northernmost border, from the plateau of Caspir to the medieval fortress of Salses, formed a defence line against the growing power of France. It faces the formidable 'five sons of Carcassonne', the French castles of Aguilar, Quéribus, Peyrepertuse, Puilaurens and Termes along the Languedoc frontier. Salses was built to plug the gap between the seaside lagoons and the inland heights.

Roussillon's folklore differs markedly from that of other French regions.[8] The *sardana* is pure Catalan; men and women hold hands in a ring, and circle back and forth to measured patterns in 6/8 rhythm. The typical band is the *coble*; nine or ten wind-players blow *tenora* and *tible* (high and low oboes), *flabiol* (flute), and the goatskin *bodega* (bagpipes), usually accompanied by drum and double bass. An international folk festival is held every August at Amélie-les-Bains (Els Banys d'Arles).[9]

Unlike Roussillon, Cerdagne (Cerdanya in Catalan, Cerdaña in Spanish) is entirely landlocked, and is nowadays split into French and Spanish halves. It grew strong through its relative inaccessibility, and rich from an ancient trans-Pyrenean trade route. Its historic capital and county seat stood at Llívia. The counts of Cerdagne-Conflent, who reached their apogee during the eleventh century, founded the abbeys both of St Michel de Cuxa and of Montserrat, before bequeathing their inheritance to their descendants, the counts of Barcelona. Their legacy stayed intact until the seventeenth century. During the negotiations held at Llívia in 1659, when Cerdagne was divided, the French commissioners demanded 130 communes in northern Cerdagne; the Spanish commissioners argued that Llívia was not a commune, but a city. Llívia has remained a Spanish enclave inside French territory ever since.[10] A visit there is instructive. At the start of the local 'Historical Trail', Llívia is proclaimed to be the 'cradle of the Catalan State'.

At some 12,300 square miles, modern Catalonia or *Catalunya* is much larger than either Roussillon or Cerdagne. It is triangular in shape, and is divided into forty-one *comarques* or 'rural districts'. The top side of the triangle follows the Pyrenean frontier. The coastal side runs down at a right angle along the Costa Brava, past Barcelona and the Costa Dorada, and as far as the province of Valencia. The inland side of the triangle links the southernmost point on the coast with Catalonia's westernmost point in the mountains. Since 1978, after painful experiences under General Franco, the province has enjoyed autonomy within Spain, and has successfully reinstated the official status of the Catalan language.

The section of the eastern Pyrenees where upper Catalonia abuts the old French County of Foix reveals some of the region's geographical, historical and linguistic complexities. The Catalan district of Pallars nestles in the vicinity of three diverse neighbours. To its west lies a clutch of Spanish-speaking districts, starting with Sobrarbe and Ribagorza. To its north lies the Vall d'Aran, which can only be approached by vehicles through the Vielha tunnel and which, though located on the French side of the ridge, still belongs to Spain. The people of the Vall d'Aran speak a unique language that mixes Basque and neo-Latin elements (*aran* means 'valley' in Basque). To the east lies the Principality of Andorra, one of Europe's oldest states.

Andorra occupies a tiny mountain retreat wedged between France and Spain. For 700 years from 1278, its government was jointly supervised by the comte de Foix (or later by the préfet of the Ariège) and by the bishop of Seu d'Urgell. Since 1993, however, it has joined Monaco, Liechtenstein and San Marino as one of Europe's sovereign mini-states. The Andorrans, like the inhabitants of the '*Franja d'Aragón*' – a strip of territory immediately adjacent to Pillars – speak Catalan, but their national anthem is bilingual. Few countries can boast a national song more redolent of history:

El Gran Carlemany, mon Pare,	*Le grand Charlemagne, mon père,*
dels arabs em deslliura,	*des arabes me délivra,*
i del cel vida em dona	*et du ciel me donna la vie*
Meritxell, la Gran Mare.	*Meritxell, notre mère.*
Princesa nasqui i Pubilla,	*Je suis née princesse héritière*
entre dues nacions neutral	*neutre entre deux nations.*

sols resto l'única filla	*Seule, je reste l'unique fille*
de l'imperi Carlemany.	*de l'empire de Charlemagne,*
creient i lliure	*croyante et libre*
onze segles	*depuis onze siècles,*
creient i lliure vull ser	*pour toujours je veux l'être*
siguin els furs mos tutors	*que les Fueros soient mes tuteurs*
i mos prínceps defensors.	*et les princes mes protecteurs!*[11]

('My father, the great Charlemagne, / saved me from the Arabs, / and Meritxell, my great mother, / gave me life from Heaven. / I was born a princess, an heiress / neutral between two nations. / I remain alone, the one and only daughter / of Charlemagne's empire. /Faithful and free /for eleven centuries, / I wish to be so for ever, / may the customary laws be my tutors / and the princes my protectors.') The Andorrans still sing of Charlemagne for their country started life under his rule and was never incorporated by the great powers which succeeded him.

Nowhere can one understand the lie of the land better than standing on the high Franco-Spanish frontier south of Perpignan. The strong afternoon sun shines in one's face. The sea glistens on the horizon to the left, the last outcrop of the French coast merging into the Costa Brava. On the right, the line of the mountain ridge leads off towards Andorra and the central Pyrenees. Roussillon and Cerdagne are at one's back, and beyond them Languedoc. In front, the steep hills of Catalonia stretch out as far as the eye can see. Catalonia's chief port and city, Barcelona, is just out of sight, but it can be reached by car in little more than an hour by following the Autoroute/Autopista E-15, which snakes over the foothills below.

Thanks to the present dominance of centralized national states, it is easy to think of this Pyrenean region as peripheral, both to France and to Spain – far from Paris and far from Madrid. Rambling round the Pyrenean ridge, however, prompts doubts. Landscape, itself the product of aeons of change, evokes thoughts about the changeability of everything else. Not so very long ago, France was nowhere in sight in these parts, and Spain did not even exist. Perpignan was once a capital city. So, too, were Barcelona and Zaragoza. Then, people on both sides of the eastern Pyrenees became subjects of one king, members and beneficiaries of a political community whose furthest bounds stretched far beyond the shining horizon.

II

The origins of the kingdom can be traced to a mountain stream – the Aragon* – that flows down from the high pastures of the central Pyrenees into the broad valley of the Ebro. The river gave its name to the landlocked district, now known as the *Alto Aragón*, or 'High Aragon', whence it springs. The landscape that it traverses consists mainly of a desert plain covered by thin, chalky, salt-ridden soil. In most seasons it is characterized by dry watercourses and ash-coloured shrublands. The summers are scorchingly hot, the winters cold and snowbound. Yet the mountains which ring the plain carry oak, pine and beech forests, and the high pastures form a fine habitat for merino sheep. The Pyrenean ridge, dominated in this section by the peaks of the Aneto and the Perdido, creates a formidable barrier. A few oases of greenery nestle in the steep, upland valleys, but the only area suitable for large-scale agriculture spreads out below the mountains among the wheat fields, orchards and vineyards that line the Ebro. One of the oldest trans-Pyrenean trade routes runs across the pass of the Port de Canfranc from Zaragoza to Béarn.

Here, towards the end of the first millennium, Christian lords ruling the north-eastern perimeter of Iberia started to fight back against the Muslim Moors, who had ruled over most of the peninsula since crossing from North Africa some two centuries earlier. That gaggle of Christian lordships, large and small, had been created when Frankish power spilled over the Pyrenees to confront Islam as it advanced. Charlemagne's campaign of 778 against the Moors was recorded in the opening lines of the Old French epic poem, the *Chanson de Roland*:

> *Carles li reis, nostre emperere magnes,*
> *Set anz tuz pleins ad estet en Espaigne.*
> *Tresqu'en la mer cunquist la tere altaigne,*
> *N'i ad castel ki devant lui remaigne,*
> *Mur ne citet n'i est remés a fraindre,*
> *Fors Sarraguce, ki est en une muntaigne.*

---

* The name 'Aragon', like nearby 'Aran', is usually linked etymologically to the Basque word for 'valley'. In modern Basque it is 'Aragoa'. The territory from which the river springs was variously known in the earliest times either as Aragon after the river or as Jaca after its only sizeable settlement. In the same way, the adjacent territory to the west was variously known either as Navarra after the Basque word for 'plain' or as Pamplona after its only city. The clear implication is that Basques once lived far beyond their modern limits.

> *Li reis Marsilie la tient, ki Deu nen aimet,*
> *Mahumet sert e Apollin recleimet:*
> *Nes poet guarder que mals ne l'i ateignet.*

> Charles the King, our great Emperor,
> Advanced that year in full array into Spain.
> He conquered the high lands as far as the sea,
> No castle which stood before him,
> Nor any fortified wall was unbroken,
> Except for Zaragoza, which lies in a mountain range.
> [Zaragoza] was held by a King, Marsilie, whom God did not love.
> He served Mahomet, and worshipped Apollo:
> Poets record only the ills which he performed.[12]

Charlemagne's retreat from Zaragoza culminated in the heroic fight at the Pass of Roncevalles, where Roland and Oliver were immortalized.

Charlemagne's response to the threat from Muslim Iberia was to organize four militarized buffer zones: the March of Gascony, the March of Toulouse (to which Andorra was attached), the March of Gothia along the Mediterranean coast from Narbonne to Nîmes, and the *Marca Hispanica* from the central to the eastern Pyrenees. This fourth March consisted of no fewer than sixteen counties, each controlled by a military commissioner or *comitatus*. The first to be formed, in 760, was Roussillon; the last, in 801, Barcelona. Others on the March's eastern flank included Pallars, Urgell, Conflent, Vallespir, Cerdagne, Besalú, Perelada, Ausona, Girona and Empúries.[13] The population of these counties contained a strong admixture of Visigoths (see Chapter 1), and it is from the mingling of Frankish, Iberian and Gothic cultures that Catalonia was to assume its inimitable language and character.

In the period which followed, the overextended Franks pulled back; the power of the Moors also began to ebb and the Christian lords of the Pyrenees asserted their freedom. One of the more important lordships in the former *Marca Hispanica* centred on the County of Barcelona, which lost all semblance of subordination to the Frankish Empire once the Carolingians gave way to the Capetians. Another was the domain of Sancho El Mayor of Navarre (d. 1035), known as 'the Great', who ruled extensive lands on either side of the Pyrenees. His capital at Pamplona lay in the heart of the Basque country, which had never submitted to foreign domination. It was flanked on the west by Christian Castile and León, and to the east by the mountainous counties of Aragon, Sobrarbe and Ribagorza, all of which he came to control. For a time, he even

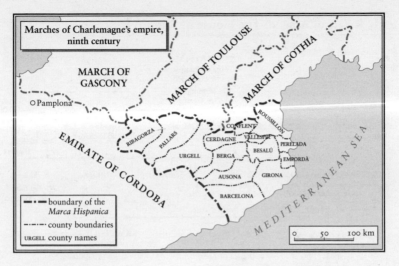

extracted recognition of his suzerainty from the count of Barcelona, Berenguer Ramón I El Corbat, 'the Crooked' (r. 1022–35).*

Sancho El Mayor was blessed with five sons, and he conceived a plan to perpetuate his family's fortunes. Taking the title of 'King of all the Spains' for himself, he designed a future whereby his Christian 'empire' would be supported by an array of tributary sub-kings. He set up his eldest legitimate son as king of Navarre; gave Castile and León to his second son; and in his will, bequeathed Sobrarbe and Ribagorza to his two youngest sons. Sancho's bastard son, Ramiro, was passed over in the will, but was left undisturbed as the *baiulus* or 'steward' of Aragon.

Needless to say, Sancho's happy scheme did not long survive its author. The four royal sons were soon embroiled in wars against their brothers. In 1050, at the Council of Coyanza, Ferdinand reaffirmed the model charter passed in León thirty years before which now provided the guidelines for all the Christian states of Iberia, including the principle of hereditary kingship. After that, he gave priority to the nascent

---

* The House of Barcelona adopted the custom of alternating the names of the counts in each generation in order to distinguish fathers from sons. Hence the son and heir of Berenguer Ramón I became Ramón Berenguer I (r. 1035–76). When the latter's countess gave birth *c.* 1053 to twin sons, therefore, the problem was solved by calling the elder twin Ramón Berenguer and the younger one Berenguer Ramón. In due course when the twins succeeded their father, Ramón Berenguer II ruled in uneasy tandem with his brother, Berenguer Ramón II El Fratricida. The sole rule of the surviving twin came about through the death of his brother in a suspicious hunting accident, very similar to that of their contemporary, William Rufus of England.

Early Rulers of Aragon: The House of Ramiro

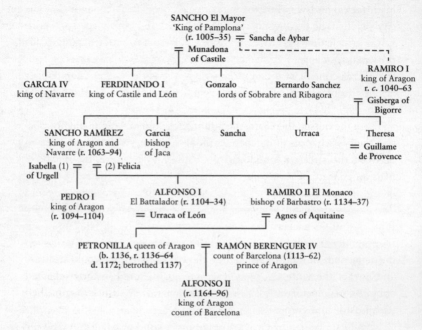

SANCHO El Mayor
'King of Pamplona'
(r. 1005–35) = Sancha de Aybar
= Munadona
of Castile

RAMIRO I
king of Aragon
r. c. 1040–63

GARCIA IV
king of Navarre

FERDINANDO I
king of Castile and León

Gonzalo   Bernardo Sanchez
lords of Sobrabre and Ribagora

= Gisberga of
Bigorre

SANCHO RAMÍREZ
king of Aragon and
Navarre (r. 1063–94)

Garcia
bishop
of Jaca

Sancha   Urraca   Theresa
= Guillame
de Provence

Isabella (1) =   = (2) Felicia
of Urgell

PEDRO I
king of Aragon
(r. 1094–1104)

ALFONSO I
El Battalador (r. 1104–34)
= Urraca of León

RAMIRO II El Monaco
bishop of Barbastro (r. 1134–37)
= Agnes of Aquitaine

PETRONILLA queen of Aragon =
(b. 1136, r. 1136–64
d. 1172; betrothed 1137)

RAMÓN BERENGUER IV
count of Barcelona (1113–62)
prince of Aragon

ALFONSO II
(r. 1164–96)
king of Aragon
count of Barcelona

Reconquista, the reconquest of the peninsula from the Moors, through which he forged a reputation that made him 'emperor of Spain'. The Christian warriors of his generation were destined to reach the gates of Seville and Toledo before being driven back. Ramiro exploited his brothers' preoccupations. Barely five years passed after their father's death before he seized Sobrarbe and Ribagorza, joined them to Aragon, and was proclaimed king. The three adjacent territories united by Ramiro formed the cradle of his kingdom's later expansion.

For the first hundred years, the House of Ramiro ruled Aragon in undisputed succession. It produced four kings, who, following a civil war among their western neighbours, came to reign in Navarre as well as in Aragon. Initially, there was no substantial Aragonese town to act as an administrative or ecclesiastical centre. Ramiro's subjects' pastoral needs were served by itinerant priests, and by the remote Benedictine monastery of San Pedro de Siresa. The city of Chaca or Jaca, previously the base for a Carolingian county, was adopted in 1063 as the seat of the first Aragonese bishopric. The larger and older city of Huesca – Roman Osca, and in the eleventh century the Moorish fortress of

Wasquah – was not conquered until forty years later. Ramiro, now King Sancho Ramírez, built the castle of Monte Aragon beside it to facilitate his attacks, and was killed by a stray arrow when reconnoitring the city's walls. The final assault was led by the late king's successor, Pedro I, Ramiro's eldest grandson, who was buried there after making it his principal residence. Regular disputes occurred with the counts of Toulouse over control of the mountain passes, but the overarching danger lay in the incessant fighting between Christians and Muslims to the south.

From the outset, therefore, the infant Kingdom of Aragon did not possess the best chances of independent long-term survival. It was squeezed between the stronger kingdoms of Castile and Navarre, the powerful Muslim emirate of Zaragoza, and, beyond Ribagorza, the eastern flank of the former March dominated by the counts of Barcelona. In those days, warlords devoured their neighbours or were devoured themselves. Ramiro and his successors could certainly benefit from their mountain retreat, but their dilemma was stark: if they tried to expand, they risked the vengeance of their rivals; if they stayed inactive, they could stagnate and attract the vultures. Their insecurity is mirrored in their repeated attempts to join forces with their neighbours, first with Navarre, then with Castile and eventually with Barcelona.

The initial historical and cultural connections of Aragon were very specific. Starting as the homeland of the pre-Roman Celtiberian tribe of the *Ilergertes*, it had never belonged to the Basque country, and had never been subject either to substantial Moorish settlement or to the heavier Frankish influences evident in Catalonia. In the continuum of the peninsula's linguistic idioms, its native speech was distinct. Aragon, above all, was small and poor. It could not raise large armies, as Castile could, and, though its society was largely free of feudal impositions, it did not possess Catalonia's commercial potential or its easy contacts with the outside world. Hence, it could only satisfy its growing circle of clients and partners by granting them wide measures of autonomy. In opposition to the traditions of Castile, 'Aragonism' favoured respect for local laws and shunned centralized authority.

The little land of Sobrarbe – one of the three constituent parts of the first Kingdom of Aragon – holds a special place in the evolution of its political traditions. According to a legend which was accepted as historical fact for centuries, the rulers were required to swear an oath embodying a formal contract with their subjects. 'We who are worth as much as you,' they were told, 'take you as our king provided that you

preserve our laws.' They were also obliged to confirm the appointment
of an elected justiciar, who was the guardian of those laws. Modern
research has shown the 'Oath of Sobrarbe' to be an invention of much
later times; even so, many commentators take it to reflect the essence of
an ancient tradition.[14]

The cradle of the Kingdom of Aragon, 1035–1137

Aragon's role in the *Reconquista* was considerable. A treacherous
game of shifting alliances developed, whereby Aragon would combine
with Castile to press the Moors, or with the Moors to restrain the Castilians. Gratuitous violence was rife. In 1064 the first campaigning season
of King Sancho Ramírez's reign had opened with a spectacular international expedition against the Muslim-held town of Barbastro. Blessed
by the pope, the Aragonese and Catalan assault force was swollen by an
army of knights from Aquitaine, Burgundy and Calabria; a siege was
mounted; and the defenders were massacred. Word spread that 50,000
souls had perished. But victory was brief. The crusaders pulled out,

laden with loot, slaves and women, leaving only a small garrison behind. In the following year, therefore, Barbastro was retaken by a Muslim relief column from Lleida, and the Christian garrison suffered the same fate as its predecessors.[15]

The first Siege of Barbastro provides the setting for a rare insight into realities of life on the Christian–Muslim frontier; it was provided by a Moorish writer, Ibn Bassam, who was familiar in turn with the account of a Jew sent into the city to ransom prominent citizens:

> When the French crusaders captured Barbastro ... in 1064, each of the principal knights received a house with all that it contained, women, children and furniture ... [The Jew] found the crusader in Moorish dress seated on a divan and surrounded by Moslem waiting girls; he ... had married the daughter of the former owner and hoped that she would give him descendants. 'Her Moslem ancestors did the same with our women when they possessed themselves of this country. Now we do likewise ...' He then turned to the girl and said in broken Arabic: 'Take your lute and sing some songs for this gentleman.' The Jew adds: 'I was pleased to see the Count show such enthusiasm as if he understood the words, though he continued drinking.'[16]

The cultural consequences of such encounters cannot have been trivial. It may be no accident that one of the leaders of the 'Crusade of Barbastro' was Guillaume VIII, duke of Aquitaine and count of Poitou, father of the first of the troubadours.[17]

Such was the world of Rodrigo Díaz (*c.* 1040–99), a Castilian knight from Vivar, who gained his early title of 'El Campeador', 'the Champion', when he slew a Navarran general in single combat. In the 1070s he was sent to collect tribute from Seville. Yet he was accused of diverting part of the king's treasure for himself, and was banished. From then on, he became a freebooter, a mercenary who sold the services of his company's lances to the highest bidder. He maintained close relations with Pedro I of Aragon, to whose son and heir he gave his daughter in marriage. But his principal employer was Moktadir, the Arab emir of Zaragoza, and it was from the Muslims that he gained the epithet of 'El Cid', 'the War Lord'. All the northern states bore the brunt of his depredations. His final exploit was to besiege Valencia at the head of an infidel army.[18]

The Cid of romance and legend, Spain's most eminent literary hero, emerged over the centuries as a knight of perfect virtue, showing little resemblance to the real Rodrigo Díaz. The first stories, written in dog Latin, began to circulate soon after his death, while the epic *Poema del Cid* dates from the late twelfth century:

> *De los sos ojos tan fuertemientre llorando,*
> *Tornava la cabeça e estrávalos catando ...*
> *Allí piensan de aguijar, allí sueltan las rriendas.*
> *A l'exida de Bivar ovieron la corneja diestra ...*
> *'¡Álbricia, Álbar Fáñez, ca echados somos de tierra?' ...*

Tears streamed from his eyes, as he turned his head and stood looking at them ... They all thought of leaving, slackened their reins. At the gate of Vivar, a crow flew on the right-hand side ... 'Good Cheer, Álva Fáñez, for we are banished from this land.

Ruy Díaz entered Burgos with his company of sixty knights. Men and women came out to see him pass, while the burghers and their wives stood at their windows, sorrowfully weeping. With one accord they all said, 'What a good vassal. If only he had a good lord!'[19]

In the wake of a raid on Aragon, Díaz once strayed further east into the domains of Raimund or Ramón Berenguer I, count of Barcelona. As usual, he plundered the countryside, and extorted tribute:

Rumours reached the ears of the Count of Barcelona that Cid Ruy Díaz was harrying the countryside; and the Count was highly incensed ... The Count was a hasty and foolish man and spoke without due reflection: 'The Cid, Rodrigo of Vivar, has done me great wrongs ... Now he is ravaging the lands under my protection. I never ... showed enmity towards him, but since he seeks me out, I shall demand redress.'

Great numbers of Moors and Christians ... went in search of the mighty Ruy Díaz of Vivar. They journeyed three days and two nights and came up with the Cid in the pine wood of Tévar. The Cid, Don Rodrigo, carrying large quantities of booty, descended from the mountains to a valley, where he received the message of Count Ramón ... [He] sent back word, saying: 'Tell the Count not to take offence. I am carrying off nothing of his ...' The Count replied: 'Not so! He shall pay for past and present injuries here and now.'

'Knights,' (said the Cid) 'make ready quickly to take up arms. Count Ramón has ... a vast host of Moors and Christians and is determined to fight ... Tighten your saddle-girths and put on your armour. Ramón

Berenguer will see the kind of man he has found today in the pine wood of Tévar . . .'

All were . . . clad in armour and mounted on their horses. They watched . . . the Franks* rode down the hill . . . [Then] the Cid, fortunate in battle, ordered the attack. His men were delighted to obey and they used their pennoned lances to good effect, striking some and overturning others. The Cid won the battle and took Count Ramón prisoner.

A great feast was prepared . . . but Count Ramón showed no relish for it. They brought the dishes and placed them in front of him, but he . . . scorned all they offered. 'I shall not eat a mouthful,' he said, 'for all the wealth of Spain. I had rather die outright since such badly shod fellows have defeated me in battle.'

To that the Cid replied in these words: 'Eat this bread, Count, and drink this wine. If you do as I say you will go free. If not, you will never see Christendom again.[20]

El Cid kept his word, and the booty. The count kept his life, and returned home to lick his wounds. As he must have realized, the future would not be decided solely by the struggle against the Moors but equally by the rivalries of Barcelona, Castile, Navarre and Aragon.

If Castile took El Cid to its heart, Aragon formally adopted St George as its patron, three centuries before the kings of England did the same. The royal standard of Aragon showed the red cross of St George on a white field, sometimes with the head of a black, crowned Moor in each of the four quarters. The cult of St George the Martyr, a fourth-century Armenian, was popular among crusaders, and was linked to Aragon's desire to become a papal protectorate. Urban II, the pope of the First Crusade, duly accepted Aragon into 'The Liberty of the Roman Church' in 1089, as he did for Barcelona a year later.[21]

Another milestone was reached in 1118. Thanks to the wars of El Cid, the emirate of Zaragoza grew weak, and Aragonese forces were emboldened to seize it. Henceforth they commanded the central valley of the Ebro. Under Alfonso I El Batallador, Zaragoza became the seat of Aragon's government, its cathedral the seat of an archbishop and the site of royal coronations and its streets the setting for elegant aristocratic palaces. The Moorish host was incorporated into the kingdom's army and the emirs' magnificent Aljaferia Castle became the residence of Christian kings.[22]

---

* The Catalans, because of their former subjection to Frankish overlordship, were still identified here as Franks.

Aragon was ceasing to be a remote backwater. Most importantly, its claim to royal status, confirmed by the pope, was now generally recognized.

Prior to the death of Alfonso I in 1134, the kingdom entered a period of dynastic panic, whose felicitous outcome could hardly have been foreseen. Alfonso, though hugely victorious as a warrior, was hugely inept as a dynast and politician. His nephew's early death, by which he himself came to the throne, failed to impress upon him the necessity of producing an heir, and his belated marriage to Urraca of León, Regent of Castile, brought none of the expected benefits. In his later years, he separated from his wife, lost his grip on Castile and remained childless. Furthermore, his brother was a celibate priest, an ex-monk who was now the bishop of Barbastro. In his will, Alfonso prepared to bequeath his realms in equal parts to three crusading orders, thereby offending all other interested parties. The nobles of Navarre promptly broke away, and severed the link with Aragon for good. The Aragonese nobility were also spurred into action, persuading the king's brother to abandon his vows and take a wife. Hence, when the monarch lay dying, the ex-monk was already committed to matrimony; a royal child would be born, and Aragon would receive a prize heiress. The short reign of Ramiro II El Monaco was deliberately designed as a temporary measure and did not avoid turbulence, but it served its purpose. As soon as he could, the dutiful king abdicated in favour of his infant daughter and returned to his monastic cell. A regency council then set about its task of finding a suitable replacement for the broken partnership with Navarre, and a suitable bridegroom for the heiress. Providentially, the neighbouring county of Barcelona had another child heir on its hands.

In 1137, therefore, the one-year-old Petronilla of Aragon – *Peyronella* in Aragonese, and *Peronela* in Catalan – was betrothed in Zaragoza to twenty-four-year-old Ramón Berenguer IV of Barcelona. The girl remained queen, while her husband adopted the style of 'prince of Aragon'. A further treaty stipulated that Aragon and Barcelona would keep their separate institutions, customs and titles, and that in the event of a premature death both states would pass to the survivor of the betrothed pair. This last precaution proved unnecessary. After fourteen years of waiting, the queen and the prince-count were formally married, and their marriage produced five children. For practical purposes, the husband ruled both in Aragon and in Barcelona, while successfully disentangling himself from involvements in Castile, where his sister, Berenguela, was now 'empress'. Ramón and Petronilla's eldest son, also

Ramón Berenguer, was appointed their joint heir. After being widowed in 1162, Petronilla renounced all her rights in favour of her son. After a quarter of a century's delay the betrothal of 1137 finally bore its full fruit; the wedding of two persons had resulted in the marriage of two states.

For his part, Ramón Berenguer dropped his Catalan name on ascending the throne, and in remembrance of El Batallador assumed the title of 'Alfonso II of Aragon and I of Barcelona'. Henceforth, a long line of monarchs would inherit the dual titles of 'kings of Aragon' and 'counts of Barcelona in Catalunya'. Monarchists, and historians paying deference to monarchy, call them 'king-counts'; Catalans and Catalanophiles call them 'count-kings'.

The union of kingdom and county had far-reaching consequences, creating an extended territorial base that combined a secure mountain stronghold with a maritime coastline of huge naval and commercial potential. It stood fair to be as wealthy as it was invincible. At the same time, like the newly emergent Portugal, Aragon-Barcelona presented a significant counterweight to Castile. It was no accident that the eldest daughter of Prince Ramón and Queen Petronilla was to be given in marriage to Sancho the Populator (r. 1185–1211), the second king of Portugal. Nonetheless, the kingdom and the county remained in some respects uncomfortable bedfellows. Each preserved its own laws, its own *Cortes* or parliament and its own language. The Aragonese language was not too dissimilar from Castilian; Catalan was more akin to Occitan, the language of Languedoc. Barcelona, founded by Hannibal's brother in the third century BC and liberated from the Moors by Charlemagne, was far more venerable than Zaragoza. The House of Berenguer, which was the successor to a line of twenty-four counts in Barcelona since the early ninth century, was undoubtedly senior to that of Ramiro. And its territorial possessions were markedly more extensive. Ever since the time of the first Count Bera (r. 801–20), son of Charlemagne's retainer William of Toulouse, those holdings had waxed and waned over the generations. But, anchored on the easternmost counties of the former *Marca Hispanica*, and especially on the maritime districts of Empordà (Ampuriés), Ausona, Girona and Barcelona, they formed a solid block of land straddling both flanks of the Pyrenees. In short, the Catalan part of the joint realm was older, larger and wealthier. Pessimists might have forecast that the two parts would never completely gel; optimists hoped each would complement the other. Both proved correct.

The Iberian Peninsula in 1137

    This 'complex monarchy' appeared on the European scene at much
the same time as the troubadours and their cult of 'courtly love'. Aragon-
Catalonia lay in the heart of the countries, including Aquitaine, Languedoc
and Provence, where the troubadours flourished. Ramón Vidal de
Besalú (c. 1196–1252), a subject of the king-count, is credited with the
first work of literary criticism in a Romance language, the *Razos de
trobar*. (His advocacy of the Occitan idiom of Limoges prompted Dante
Alighieri to write *De Vulgari Eloquentia* and to advocate the merits of
Tuscan in Italy.) Guillaume de Poitiers (1071–1126), Ponç de la Guàrdia
(*fl.* 1154–88) and Huguet de Mataplana (1173–1213) preceded Ramón
Vidal; Arnaut Catalan (*fl.* 1219–53), Amanieu de Sescars, known as *il
dieu d'amor* (*fl.* 1275–95), Jofre de Foixà (d. 1300) and others came
later.[23] Jofre was a Franciscan friar from Empordà, sent by his Order to
Sicily. His tract, *Vers e regles de trobar*, by giving examples of the works
of other songsters, became a standard compendium:

Canczon audi q'es bella 'n tresca,
Que fo de razon espanescai;
Non fo de paraulla grezesca
Ni de lengua serrazinesca.

. . .

Tota Basconn' et Aragons
E l'encontrada delz Gascons
Sabon quals es aquist canczons.[24]

('I heard a song which is beautiful in its theme, / and which was in Hispanic style, / neither Greek in its speech / nor Saracen / . . . All the Basques and the Aragonese / have heard it from the Gascons: / they know what these songs are like.') 'The art of the troubadours is the starting point of modern European literature,' wrote a British medievalist many years ago. 'And if we wish to find this mysterious element which is the quintessence of the medieval spirit, we cannot do better than to follow the example of the Romantics and look for it in the age and the country of the Troubadours.'[25]

During the early *Reconquista*, the military functions of castle lords were paramount, and favoured the growth of a powerful landed aristocracy supported by the toil of an enserfed peasantry. A score of these *rics homens* assembled small private states, establishing themselves first as counts and eventually as dukes. They included the Montcadas, the Coloma of Queralt, and the counts of Cardona, Urgell, Empúries and Pallars-Sobira. Their fortunes were to peak in the fourteenth century. The origins of the Montcada clan illustrate this development. Montcada or Moncada is a small castle/village, seven miles inland from Barcelona, close to the abbey of St Cugat des Valles. In the early twelfth century its heiress married an obscure knight called Guillem Ramón (1090–1173), who rose to be 'Great Seneschal' at the comtal court. Boosted by the gift of Tortosa-Lleida in the southern district of 'New Catalonia', their offspring thrived. In the next generation, they held some twenty to thirty castles and manors, some around Tortosa, some in the diocese of Vic, and others in the district of Girona. One of them, by marrying the heiress to Béarn, founded a trans-Pyrenean branch. From then on, their future was assured.[26] All these great families lived off the toil of the unfree, and the serfs of Aragon-Barcelona, many of them Moors, kept company with slaves. Barcelona, Valencia and later Palma all held regular slave markets. Their wares, often Moorish prisoners, were sold on either to noble and merchant households or to foreign traders.

Governmental forms were advanced for their day. Their consultative and delegatory tendencies can be traced back to the eleventh century assemblies of *pau i treva* – 'Sanctuary and Truce' – attended by the nobility; the first Catalan legal code, the *Usatges de Barcelona* (1068), was based on the decisions of those assemblies. Many authors, however, consider the joint meeting of Catalan and Aragonese nobles, convened by the king-count at Lleida in 1216, to have been the true starting point of a long parliamentary tradition. From then on, parliaments were held in all parts of the Crown lands. In Aragon, the *Cortes* held at Huesca in 1247 led to the formation of the *Fuero d'Aragon*, the 'Codex of Huesca'.[27] In Catalonia, the assembly held at Barcelona in 1283 established three 'constitutions', or fundamental laws, one making annual sessions of the assembly obligatory. These *Corts catalanes* consisted of three arms or *braços* representing the Church, the nobility and the citizens of royal towns. Their main function was legislative. With the king-count's consent, they could pass laws of their own making (*capitols de cort*), on condition that they in turn approved laws initiated by him. In due course they acted as a model for overseas territories.

Thanks to their far-reaching powers under these arrangements, the nobility acquired a strong sense of solidarity, and of equality with their rulers. For a time between 1287 and 1348 they even cultivated a theory of the right of armed resistance to oppressive monarchs. As Pedro IV later remarked, 'It is as hard as to divide the nobles of Aragon as it is to unite the nobles of Castile.'

Even before the Union, the counts of Barcelona had begun to project their power beyond Iberia. The first step was taken with the acquisition of Provence; the second, only five years later, through the bequest of Cerdanya (Cerdagne) and Besalú.

From 1032 Provence had been a margravate of the Holy Roman Empire in the imperial Kingdom of Burgundy (see p. 119). Early in the twelfth century a marriage was arranged with papal assistance between Ramón Berenguer I, count of Barcelona, and Douce de Provence, heiress to the margravate. In this way, in 1112 Provence passed under the rule of Barcelona for 134 years. When the male line failed in 1246, the marriage of Béatrice de Provence to Charles d'Anjou propelled it into the French orbit of the Angevins.[28] This was to be one of several bones of Angevin–Aragonese contention.

The marriage of 1112, celebrated in Arles on 3 February, exemplifies the complex ramifications of medieval matrimonial politics. The bride, Douce or Dulçe, an only child, had inherited Provence from her mother.

But she had also inherited the lands of her late father, Gilbert de Gévaudan, viscount of Millau. This meant that her Catalan husband took possession of both Gévaudan (in the wilds of what is now the *département* of Lozère) and Millau (where the impressive viaduct now stands on Autoroute 9). The bishop of Mende, dismayed, invited the king of France to keep the Catalans out. His initiative enabled the French to stake their very first claim to a piece of Languedoc. Eventually, Aragon sold both Gévaudan and Millau to the French in 1225.[29] But that was not the end of it. Gilbert de Gévaudan had also possessed the title to a district on the borders of the Auvergne and Rouergue, known in French as *Le Carlat* and in Catalan as *Carlades* (now in the *département* of Cantal). So Gilbert's Catalan son-in-law collected the Carlat as well, passing it on to his heirs and successors. In 1167 the Carlat was handed in fief to the counts of Rodez, who paid their feudal dues either to Barcelona or to Perpignan for 360 years.

And so the saga went on. One of the two children of Ramón Berenguer I and Douce de Provence was a girl known after her father as Berenguela de Barcelona (1116–49). She, like her mother, grew up to become a hot property, and in 1128 was married off to Alfonso VII, king of Castile. Hence, the progenitors of the royal houses both of Castile and of Aragon-Catalonia were all direct descendants of Douce de Provence.[30]

Cerdanya, in contrast, passed to Barcelona through death as opposed to marriage, after a long independent career. Its central feature is a high plateau on which the only modest town, Puigcerda, would be built. In the era of post-Carolingian fragmentation, the seat of its counts was at Ripoll, south of the Pyrenean ridge, and, like neighbouring Urgell and Rosselló, it shook off the overlordship not only of the Franks but also of all its local rivals. Its most famous count, Guifré El Pilós (Wilfred the Hairy, d. 897), sought the protection of the papacy, and had the distinction of founding the bloodline from which the House of Berenguer in Barcelona traced its origins.[31] The later counts of Cerdanya absorbed the adjacent district of Besalú, but in the early twelfth century they ran out of heirs, and in 1117 the last of them willed his inheritance to his relatives in Barcelona. From then on, for 542 years Cerdanya and Besalú furnished the central section of the natural ramparts of northern Catalonia.[32]

Prior to the Union, the flag of the County of Barcelona had consisted of four red horizontal stripes on a gold field. After the Union, this same flag often served for the whole state. The royal standard, in contrast, displayed a crowned shield quartered with the arms both of Aragon and of Catalonia. The usual regal style read '*Dei Gratia Rex Aragonensis, Comes Barchinonensis et Marchio Provinciae*' ('By God's Grace, king of Aragon, count of Barcelona and marquis of Provence'). A name for the combined realm did not at first exist. But, from the mid-thirteenth century onwards, the *Corona aragonensis*, the 'Crown of Aragon', appeared with increasing frequency, and there is every reason for modern historians to use it.

Ruling dynasties provided the threads of ownership and political control which help explain the intricate territorial jigsaw of medieval Europe. They lived by the generally accepted principles of property, inheritance and war, by feudal concepts of jurisdiction based on landownership, and by a political order run by an elaborate hierarchy of lords and vassals. They acquired their lands and titles by marriages, by legacies and bequests, by purchases, by conquest and, occasionally, by donations. They lost them by deaths in the family, by adverse legal judgments, by sale or by military defeat. They defended them with their retinues of knights, with the blessings of a deferential clergy and with whole benches of lawyers.

As suggested elsewhere, the dynastic agglomerations of the medieval period may best be understood by analogy to the international corporations of later times.[33] In a sense, the kingdom-county was a political business, and 'Aragon' was a famous brand. The business relied for protection on its military arm, but its main assets lay in land and in the money raised from fees and taxes. Each constituent territory enjoyed a large measure of self-government, where the nobles formed a local executive class running the subsidiary firms. The *Corts*, or assemblies, which the nobles dominated, formed the boards of the subsidiaries. By convention, it was the dynasty which supplied the top managerial elite – the CEOs – who were enhanced by regal status and who could move, as circumstance demanded, from firm to firm, from country to country. One should not forget that the Aragon-Barcelona 'Company' came into being in the first place through the fortuitous merger of 1137.

Contiguity is an issue. The County of Barcelona and the Kingdom of Valencia, which were joined to Aragon in the twelfth and thirteenth centuries respectively, came to be seen as constituent elements of the Crown's heartland, the main parts of the 'inner empire', which may be distinguished from the 'outer empire' overseas. Yet historians face a very real problem in categorizing Aragon's far-flung lands. In recent times, they have frequently talked of the 'Aragonese Empire' or the 'Aragon-Catalonian Empire'. Scholastic arguments which crankily complain that the Aragonese example did not resemble the ancient Roman Empire or the modern British Empire are not helpful. These unhistorical terms do serve a purpose. For, though the Crown of Aragon was dynastic in origin and decentralized in nature, it formed more than a mere ragbag of accidental possessions. It constituted a long-lasting political community with a common allegiance, common traditions, common cultural proclivities and strong economic ties.[34] How one classifies it is of secondary importance. In the opinion of a scholar whose main focus lies in the Golden Age of all-Spain, it was 'one of the most imposing states of medieval Europe'.[35]

The heirs and successors of Alfonso II and I descended in the male line for ten generations. To complicate matters, they all boasted an Aragonese-Spanish name in addition to their Catalan name, and were separately numbered according to the Aragonese and Catalan styles. Their sobriquets were written in dual Aragonese and Catalan forms:

1137–62	Petronilla of Aragon and Ramón Berenguer IV El Sant
1162–96	Alfonso II El Casto/Alfons I El Trubador
1196–1213	Pedro II El Católico/Pere I El Catolic
1213–76	Jaime I El Conquistador/Jaume I El Conquerridor
1276–85	Pedro III El Grande/Pere II El Gran
1285–91	Alfonso III El Franco/Alfons II El Liberal
1291–1327	Jaime II El Justo/Jaume II El Just
1327–36	Alfonso IV El Benigno/Alfons III El Benigne
1336–87	Pedro IV El Ceremonioso/Pere III El Ceremonioso
1387–96	Juan I El Cazador/Juan I El Cacador (the Hunter)
1396–1410	Martin I El Humano/Marti I L'Human
1410–12	Interregnum.[36]

Throughout this very long time, the royal domain never ceased to expand. Indeed, there was no period between the twelfth and the late fifteenth centuries when Aragon's 'empire' was not either swallowing new lands or busy digesting them. In the decades following the Union, several pieces of valuable real estate were obtained. While waiting to marry Queen Petronilla, Ramón Berenguer El Sant battled the Moors incessantly and in 1148 took control both of Tortosa in the south and of Lleida (Lérida) in the north-west. Rosselló fell into the hands of his son and Montpellier into the lap of his grandson.

The heartlands of the Crown of Aragon

NAVARRE

LANGUEDOC

ANDORRA   Perpignan

○ Jaca   ROUSSILLON

PALLARS   CERDANYA   PERALADA

○ Huesca   EMPORDÀ

OLD ARAGON   URGELL   Girona

○ Zaragoza   ○ Montserrat

Ebro   Lleida   ○ Barcelona

LLEIDA

EXTREMADURA   ○ Tortosa

○ Teruel   ○ Morella

○ Peñiscola

MEDITERRANEAN

SEA

COUNTY OF BARCELONA

KINGDOM OF VALENCIA

○ Burriana

○ Valencia

CASTILE

○ Alicante

Murcia ○

Kingdom of Aragon
County of Barcelona
Kingdom of Valencia

0   50   100 km

Rosselló held onto its independence for fifty years longer than Cerdanya. But it was taken over in 1172 in exactly the same way. It occupied an area of great strategic importance, commanding not only the easiest passage of the Pyrenees along the old Via Augusta, but also the transverse trade route between the Atlantic and the Mediterranean. It possessed a valuable port at Colliure (Collioure), and an important line of fortified castles including Perpinya (Perpignan), facing Languedoc. Three ancient *comarcas* or 'districts' functioned: El Conflent centred on Prada (Prades) in the valley of the Têt; Vallespir in the valley of the Tech; and, in the upper valley of the Aude, the subalpine district of Capcir.

Rosselló's five centuries in the principality of Catalonia were characterized by its role as the north-eastern bulwark of the Aragonese-Catalan heartland. It repeatedly held the line against France. During the Albigensian Crusade against the heretical Cathar sect of the early thirteenth century, which brought the French into Languedoc, it stood firm against the awesome might of Carcassonne. It also provided the usual entry point of French armies into Iberia. On one notorious occasion, it was betrayed by an abbot who personally told the French king how to penetrate the defences:

> Four monks, who were from Toulouse and were in a monastery near Argeles, went to the King of France, and one of them was the abbot. And he said to the King of France: 'Lord, I and these other monks are natives of your country and your natural subjects. If it is your pleasure, we shall show you where you can pass. Let one of your *rics homens* go at once with a thousand armed horse, and with many men afoot . . . to make roads. And, in advance of them, some thousand foot-soldiers could go . . . so that those who are making the roads need not desist from their work. And thus assuredly, Lord, you and all your followers will be able to pass over.' And the King of France said: 'Abbot, how do you know this?' 'Lord,' said he, 'because our men and our monks go to that place every day to get wood and lime. And this place, Lord, is called the Pass of Manzana. If you enquire of the count of Foix, who knows this country well, you will find it is so.' Said the King of France: 'We fully trust you; and tonight, We shall do all that is necessary . . .'[37]

This was not the first and certainly not the last time that French forces were seen in Catalonia. But they rarely prospered. On this occasion, returning to France, the French king died at Perpinya.[38]

Montpellier, a close neighbour of Nîmes and Arles, lay on the far side of the plain of Languedoc, 80 miles beyond Rosselló. It was the only major city of Languedoc-Septimania which had no Roman origins, but grew round a fortified hill whence the inhabitants sheltered from Saracen raids. It developed as a dynamic commercial centre due to the proximity of the Rhône valley and the frontier of the Holy Roman Empire; and in this respect it was not surpassed until the rise of late-medieval Marseille. Its famed schools of law and medicine were well established by the mid-twelfth century, and its reputation was boosted by the tolerance shown to Muslims, Jews and Cathars.

Montpellier's link with the Crown of Aragon was created in 1204 by the marriage of King Pedro II to the local heiress, Dame Marie de

Montpellier. The city with its large taxable wealth made up the bride's dowry. Its place in Aragonese history, however, was cemented for being the birthplace of Marie's son, Jaime El Conquistador, 'the Conqueror'. In 1208, his mother was staying in her hometown when her pregnancy was announced:

> And the notables of Montpellier disposed that [no one] should leave the palace, neither the Queen, nor they nor their wives, nor the damsels present, until nine months should be accomplished . . . And so all together, they remained with the Lady Queen very joyously. And their joy was greater still when they saw that it had pleased God . . . that the Queen grew bigger. And at the end of nine months, according to nature, she gave birth to a beautiful and fine son, who was born for the good of Christians, and more particularly for the good of his peoples . . . And with great rejoicing and satisfaction they baptised him in the church of Our Lady Saint Mary of the Tables in Montpellier, and they gave him, by the grace of God, the name of En Jaime, and he reigned many years and obtained great victories and gave great increase to the Catholic Faith and to all his vassals and subjects.
>
> And the said Infante En Jaime grew more in one year than others do in two. And it was not long before the good king, his father, died, and he was crowned King of Aragon and count of Barcelona and Urgell and Lord of Montpellier.[39]

The administration of Montpellier was not a simple matter. Prior to 1204, the predecessors of Dame Marie had shared the city's jurisdiction with the bishops of Maguelonne. But when the bishops sold their share of the city to the king of France, the Aragonese officials had to work in tandem with French officials, and separate court systems, one Aragonese and the other French, operated in parallel.

Being thus free from direct royal control and hence from restrictive legislation, Montpellier could grow rapidly. Its population at the turn of the century numbered *c*. 40,000; it possessed a thriving silk industry and it was an entrepôt between seaborne and inland trade, especially of spices, attracting a vibrant financial community. Many of the pioneering techniques of credit and banking migrated from Italy to Montpellier in its Aragonese period.

Montpellier's effective independence also made it a frequent destination for fugitives. Runaway serfs, debtors, criminals evading justice and suspected heretics all sought asylum in the city's religious houses. An inquiry into these matters ordered by the king of France in 1338 has left us a rich collection of records. The municipal courts were far from lenient; banishment and execution were common sentences. On one occasion, four foreigners who were forced to confess to assaulting a doctor of law and to leaving him for dead, were promptly executed for murder before their victim recovered.[40]

Montpellier contained a large Jewish community too, which was deeply involved in medicine, in money-lending and in controversy. Their medical and financial activities benefited all their fellow citizens; the controversies were largely theological, and were directed at fellow Jews. The correspondence between Abba Mari of Montpellier and Rabbi Ibn Adret of Barcelona reveals a concerted attack on the authority of the great Castilian scholar, Maimonides, by the prominent Talmudist Solomon of Montpellier and his circle.[41]

The presence of the Roman Church in Iberia stretched back to the days of the Roman Empire. Two martyrs to Roman persecution, St Vincent of Saragossa and St Vincent the Deacon, had both been born in Osca (Huesca). Though their veneration grew, the Church suffered deep setbacks in the centuries of Muslim dominance. The *Reconquista* gave Iberian Catholicism both its intense spirituality and its militancy. The two archdioceses of the kingdom-county – Zaragoza for Aragon and Tarragona for Catalonia – had been wrested from Muslim control in the twelfth century. Many of the churches, like the cathedral at Huesca, were established within the walls of 'purified' mosques.

A seminal role had been played by St Olegarius (Oleguer Bonestry, *c.* 1060–1137), archbishop of Tarragona, who presided over the Church Council of Barcelona in 1127, negotiated the marriage of his count to Queen Petronilla, and then consolidated ecclesiastical structures in the dioceses of Lleida, Girona, Urgell, Vic, Tortosa and Solsona. The later transfer of the bishopric of Valencia to Tarragona gave lasting offence to the Castilian archbishop of Toledo, who claimed supremacy in all reconquered lands.

Aragon-Catalonia was affected indirectly by the Church's war against the Cathar heresy in neighbouring Languedoc. The conflict inspired the creation in 1232 of a Committee of Inquisition; and it helped the rise of militarized, crusading orders, and of organizations such as the Order for the Redemption of Christian Captives. Nonetheless, many of the kingdom-county's leading clerics laid emphasis on the non-military aspects of the faith. St Raymond de Peñafort (*c.* 1175–1275), born at

Vilafranca, apart from being confessor to Jaime I, was the foremost canon lawyer of the age. St Arnau de Gurb, bishop of Barcelona from 1252 to 1284, promoted dialogue with Jews and Muslims; there was no serious bloodletting from religious causes until the pogrom against Jews in Valencia in 1391. In later periods, the Church of Aragon-Catalonia produced numerous prominent prelates. One was Cardinal Berenguer de Anglesola (d. 1408), papal legate and sometime bishop of Huesca. Another was Cardinal Joan de Casanova OP (1387–1436), Dominican bishop of Elne. Born in Barcelona and buried in Florence, he was a royal confessor, and patron of the *Psalter and Book of Hours of King Alfonso*.[42]

As in all medieval kingdoms, the coronation of the monarch was an act of supreme significance, cementing the partnership of Church and State. The ceremonies, traditionally held in the cathedral at Zaragoza, gave spectators proof positive of the monarchy's divine calling:

> It is the truth that, at vesper-time on Good Friday [1328], the Lord King [Alfonso El Benigno] sent to tell everyone that on Easter Eve all should quit the mourning they were wearing for, the Lord King, his father, and that every man should trim his beard and begin the feast . . .
>
> And so, on Saturday morning, at the time of the Alleluia and as the bells were ringing, every man was apparelled as the Lord King had commanded . . .
>
> And when the bells were ringing madly, the Lord King issued from the Aljaferia to go to the Church of San Salvador . . . First of all came, on horseback [a procession of knights carrying ceremonial swords] and after the sword of the Lord King came two carriages of the Lord King with two [lighted] wax tapers; in each wax taper there were over ten quintals of wax . . .
>
> And behind the two wax candles, came the Lord King, riding on his horse, with the most beautiful harness ever made by the hands of masters, and the sword was carried before him.

The vigil proceeded all through the night, accompanied by two holy masses:

> And when it was finished, the Lord King kissed the cross of the sword and girded it on himself, and then, drew it from the scabbard and brandished it three times. And the first time, he defied all the enemies of the Holy Catholic faith; and the second time, he engaged to defend orphans, wards and widows; and the third time, he promised to maintain justice all his life . . .

And the Lord Archbishop anointed him with chrism on the shoulder and on the right arm . . .

And . . . the Lord King himself took the crown from the altar and placed it on his own head . . . And . . . the said Lords Archbishops and Bishops and Abbots and Priors and the Lords Infantes with them, cried in a loud voice: *Te Deum laudamus*. And as they were singing, the Lord King took the golden sceptre in his right hand and put it in his left and then took the orb in his right . . .

And when . . . the Gospel had been sung, the Lord King again, with a low obeisance offered himself and his sacred crown to God, and knelt down very humbly. And . . . he went to seat himself before the altar of San Salvador, on the royal throne, and he sent for all the nobles . . . and dubbed them knights.[43]

Famously, Christianity and Islam coexisted in several parts of the Crown of Aragon. 'Nowhere was contact between the two cultures closer than on the Gulf of Lyons,' wrote Christopher Dawson; the County of Barcelona in particular 'was a kind of bridge between the two worlds'.[44] Yet the patterns were not uniform. In the lands newly occupied by the *Reconquista*, the Moors still dominated numerically. In most towns and cities of Aragon and Catalonia, they lived in closed wards, where, nonetheless, linguistic assimilation accelerated. In the countryside, they were often left to the supervision of the Knights Templar. The Jews, too, lived apart, as their own Talmudic rules required, but played a fruitful role in intellectual, medical and commercial life. Questions of tolerance and oppression, however, are almost impossible to quantify. A well-known study of the *convivencia* of Moors and Christians in fourteenth-century Aragon reports that the well-organized *mudéjar* communities experienced good times and bad, and concludes: 'the general situation of Muslims, whether desirable or undesirable', was *not* due to 'the justice or injustice of the Christian authorities'.[45]

Similar conclusions can be applied to the Jewish community. Prior to the end of the fifteenth century, apart from in Poland-Lithuania, the kingdom-county and its subject lands were one of the few parts of Europe where Jews flourished. They were particularly prominent in the reign of Jaime the Conqueror. Benveniste de Porta (*fl.* 1250–70), the king's banker, advanced loans on the security of royal taxes, and, with the Crown finances in debt to the tune of over 100,000 *sous*, became the royal tax-farmer. Moses ben Nahman Gerondi (known as Nahmanides, 1194–1270), was a famous Catalan rabbi and philosopher from

Girona. He starred in disputations both among Jews and between Jews and Christians. In the 1230s he acted as a conciliator in the conflict between Solomon of Montpellier and Maimonides, and in 1263 he took part in the heated Disputation of Barcelona with the convert, Paul the Christian. He had a lasting influence through his commentary on the Torah, which offered alternative interpretations of controversial biblical passages. Exiled through the machinations of his Dominican opponents, he founded a synagogue in Jerusalem that still survives.

Pilgrims were omnipresent among medieval travellers. There was plenty to see. The foremost pilgrimage took thousands to the Benedictine abbey of Montserrat, in the hills behind Barcelona, where one could see the miraculous *Verge negra* – the Black Madonna, *La Morenta*, the Patroness of Catalonia. The abbey of Ripoll near Girona was famous for the tomb of Count Wilfred the Hairy, for its library and for its community of learned monks, who studied Arabic manuscripts, transmitted ancient knowledge to posterity, and compiled the chronicles of the counts of Barcelona.[46] The Cistercian abbey of Poblet, in the district of Tarragona, was enthusiastically patronized by the king-counts. Its royal pantheon, surmounted by a magnificent Gothic octagon, sheltered the tombs of almost all the monarchs.

All the cities of Aragon and Catalonia boasted grand cathedral churches, while the countryside was dotted with colossal castles that proclaimed the victorious pride of the *reconquistadores*. In the heyday of castle-building, Aragon and Catalonia had manned the ramparts of Christendom; and the moving Moorish frontier had called for line after line of castles as it went forward. Some of the fortresses, like Loarre in Huesca or the mighty Aljaferia in Zaragoza, were royal foundations. Others, like Cardona, or Peratallada or the Alcañiz in Teruel, were constructed by noble warlords. All served to underline the medieval truism that the Faith went hand in hand with the sword. The Crown of Aragon was also graced by seven universities: Montpellier, Perpignan, Barcelona, Valencia, Catania and later Palermo and Naples.

Many pilgrims passed through Aragon or Catalonia on their way to Santiago di Compostela and the shrine of St James; one of the stops on the 'seashell road' was at the monastery of San Juan de la Peña near Jaca. Built in the eleventh century under an overhanging rock at the bottom of a gorge, the monastery was home to the chronicler-monks of Aragon and housed Aragon's first royal pantheon. Its tombs would certainly have challenged their visitors' knowledge of history, as they still do. One inscription reads: 'HIC REQUIESCIT FAMULUS DEI GARCIAS XIMENEZ

PRIMUS REX ARAGONUM, QUI AMPLIAVIT ECCLESIAM SANCTI IOHA-
NIS IBIQUE VITA DEFUNCTUS SEPELITUR.' It refers to a 'first king of
Aragon', probably the semi-legendary Garci Ximenez, who ruled in
Sobrarbe in the eighth century under the supremacy of Navarre long
before Ramiro's time. Another inscription is less obscure: 'HIC REQUI-
ESCIT EXIMINA, MULIER RODERICI CID' ('Here lies Eximina, the wife
of Rodriguez, El Cid').[47]

Jaime I was the king whose long reign permitted him both to extend
and to consolidate a still-vulnerable polity. Born, as we have seen, in
Montpellier during the Albigensian Crusade, he seems to have spent
time at the court of Simon de Montfort, the crusaders' commander. His
reign started badly, though, thanks to an ill-starred scheme to merge the
kingdom-county with the Kingdom of Navarre, and it was some years
before royal authority could be firmly asserted. But then, in the late
1220s, Jaime sidelined domestic problems by adventuring overseas. In
1229 he invaded the Moorish-controlled Balearic Islands, declaring
himself 'king of Mallorca'. Three years later, he entered the old stomp-
ing ground of El Cid in Valencia. After two decades of campaigning to
secure the new conglomeration, he signed the Treaty of Corbeil with the
king of France in 1258, gaining mutual recognition of the frontiers and
of all sovereign titles.

In later life, Jaime was to compose the famous Catalan *Llibre dels
Fets* or 'Book of Deeds', an autobiographical chronicle about his life
and times. The manuscript, now in the national library of Barcelona, is
written in a vernacular similar to Occitan. He made generous provision
for his ten legitimate children, and for numerous illegitimate ones. His
testament, drawn up in 1262, envisaged the division of his realms
between his two eldest sons. One of them was to inherit Aragon, Catalonia and Valencia. The other, with the title of 'king of Mallorca', was to
inherit the Balearics, Rosselló, Cerdanya and Montpellier.

Jaime I's realms presented a kaleidoscope of languages, religions and
cultures. The religious spectrum stretched from ultra-fervent Catholicism to Judaism and Islam. The urban culture of the great cities was
worlds apart from the life of Pyrenean pastoral communities, and nothing impressed so strongly as the dynamism of medieval Barcelona. The
old city, overlooking the port, was dominated by the cathedral or *seu* of
Santa Eulalia and by the densely inhabited public quarter, the Barri
Gòtic. On one side stood the ancient but none-too-imposing *Palau
Reial*, the residence of the counts, and on the other side, the *Call* or
'Jewish Quarter'. A tangle of narrow streets, where the *Ramblas* was yet

to be built, ran down to the waterfront, or rather to a sandy beach. In the time of Jaime I, the city, though already a bustling metropolis, lacked many of its later adornments. At the northern end, the *Lonja*, seat of the Consulado del Mar and resort of foreign merchants, occupied a temporary building. At the southern end, the *Drassanes* or Royal Dockyard, a spectacle of ant-like activity, was in the early stages of its expansion. The imposing palaces of the *Generalitat* and of the *Ajuntament*, where municipal assemblies would be held, were a dream of the future. Behind the docks, the church of Santa Maria del Pi served the city guilds, while the Hospital de la Santa Creu housed a medical complex. Around them, to landward, ran the unbroken line of the city walls. In front of them, a mass of merchant ships and military galleys rode at anchor, or rested on the open beach.[48]

Anyone who saw Barcelona would have understood that increasing naval power underpinned the increasing wealth and strength of the state. The *Drassanes* in Barcelona's port was but the visible base of an expanding network. The policy of constructing a permanent royal fleet is attributed to the Conqueror's father, Pedro II, who dreamed of a *regne dins el mar*, 'a kingdom in the sea'. But it demanded long-term commitment, and huge resources in money, men and materials. The chosen weapon was the seagoing galley powered by a combination of sail and oar, the latest variant on ancient Greek biremes and triremes. When the oars kicked in, these galleys could show a devastating turn of speed. The largest of them were driven by 100 or even 150 oars, each oar manned by two or three rowers. Each carried a bow-mounted battering ram, an arsenal of catapults for attack, and a strong company of crossbowmen for self-defence.[49]

Sea battles were a regular occurrence. One in particular stuck in the memory of a popular chronicler:

And when the galleys of En Conrado Lansa saw the ten galleys coming, they left the place. And the Saracens, who saw them shouted in their Saracen language 'Aur, Aur': and they came [on] with great vigour. And the galleys of En Conrado Lansa formed in a circle, and all four collected together and held council. And En Conrado Lansa said to them: 'You, my Lords, know that the favour of God is with the Lord King of Aragon and you know how many victories he has had over Saracens . . . Therefore I pray you all that you remember the power of God and of Our Lady Saint Mary, and the Holy Catholic Faith, and the honour of the Lord King and of the city of Valencia and of all the Kingdom; and that, roped together as we are, we attack resolutely, and that, on this day, we do so much that we be spoken of forever.'

And all began to shout: 'Let us attack them! Let us attack them! They will all be ours!' ... And with that he ordered trumpets and [drums] to be sounded, and with great shouts they began a vehement attack. And the four galleys, most beautifully, and without any clamour, went to the attack in the midst of the ten galleys and there the battle was most grievous and it lasted from the morning until the hour of vespers, and no one dared to eat or drink.

But Our Lord the true God and His blessed Mother, from Whom come all favours, and the good luck of the Lord King of Aragon, gave the victory to our men, in such manner that all the galleys were defeated and the men killed or taken ... [And so,] with great honour and triumph, they returned to Valencia with the galleys which they brought there, and with many Saracen captives who had hidden below deck, of whom they had much profit.[50]

In the chronicler's eyes, it was evidently a sin for Saracens to hold Christian slaves, but not for Christians to enslave Saracens.

The Balearic Islands – in Roman times, the *Gymnesiae* – have been described as 'a strategic imperative' for Aragon. Lying some 100 miles off the coast of Catalonia, they commanded the coastal trade, the approaches to the Strait of Gibraltar, and the crossing to North Africa. They provided both the stepping stones for small-scale shipping and the grand harbours which could act as naval bases. Yet they had remained in Moorish hands long after the union of Catalonia and Aragon. To Catalan sailors, this infidel stronghold must have felt like a thorn in Christian flesh. In the mind of King Jaime, it presented the most urgent of challenges.

The conquest by Jaime I, which began in 1229, absorbed formidable logistical resources. The initial attack on Mallorca (the 'Greater Island') was led by a fleet of galleys towing armoured troop-transports, whose bows opened – like those of landing-craft on the Normandy beaches – to release waves of advancing infantry. The king himself wrote a description of the operations in the *Llibre dels Fets*:

One portion of the fleet was deployed at Cambrils, but the larger part, in which we found ourselves, was in the port of Salon and on the beach, and the remainder at Tarragona ... We had 25 capital ships, 18 tarides, 12 galleys, and 100 buzas and galliots ...

Bovet's ship, in which Guillem de Montcada sailed, was to act as a guide, and had to carry a lantern as a light whilst Carro's ship had the rearguard ... I was in the galley of Montpellier towards the rear.

We set sail on Wednesday morning from Salon, with a land breeze ... It was a wonderful sight ... The whole sea appeared white with sails.

The hour of vespers came. And near the first watch, we overtook the ship of Guillem of Montcada ... and we climbed up the lantern and hailed them ... The crew responded that it was the King's ship, and that we were welcome one hundred thousand times ... And sailing by night and at the front of the fleet, we did not lower sail or change course, but let the galley run as fast as it could ... There was a beautiful moon and breeze from the south-west, and we said that we could go to Pollença ...[51]

Having ignored the bad weather forecast, and surviving a squall, during which he prayed to the Virgin Mary, the king landed safely. The troops disembarked without opposition. They then saw that they were not alone:

The Saracens were ranged before them with some five thousand footmen and two hundred horsemen. And Ramón de Montcada came and said that he would go to survey them, [adding] 'Let no one come with me.' And when he got near them, he called, [saying] 'Let us attack, for they are nothing!' And [Montcada] was the first to attack. And when the Christians came up to the Moors, at four lances' length at most, the Moors turned tail and fled. But they were pursued with such speed that more than one thousand, five hundred Saracens died, as there was no desire to take prisoners. This done, our men returned to the seashore.[52]

Thus was the voyage to Mallorca and the first engagement completed. That evening, the bishop of Barcelona delivered a sermon: 'Barons ... take heed. Those who die in this task will do so in the name of Our Lord and will receive paradise, where they will have everlasting glory. And those who live will have honour and renown for all their lives and a good end in their deaths ...'[53]

The main city of Madina was then besieged, and on its capitulation, the Almohad rulers submitted on condition that the population be spared. Madina's harbour, renamed Ciutat de Mallorca (now Palma), could henceforth act as partner for Barcelona and deny all the adjacent waters to hostile shipping.

Menorca (the 'Lesser Island') was captured in 1231 by guile. Huge fires were built on the cliffs of Cap de Formentor on Mallorca, to create the illusion of a massive armed camp. The Menorcans surrendered without a fight, buying their survival as a vassal Islamic state with the promise of annual tribute. The twin islands of Evissa (now Ibiza) and Formentera were captured in 1235 by a private crusade of the archbishop of Tarragona. According to local legend, the ruling sheikh's brother quarrelled with him over a woman in the harem, and told the besieging Catalans of a secret tunnel. The Arab mosques were torn down and replaced by Catholic churches.

Valencia, an ancient port and Roman settlement and the centre of the Moorish *tarifa* of Balansiya, now formed the focus of the king's attention. Its conquest started slightly later than that of the Balearics, and the ongoing land battles were not completed until 1304. Aragonese forces were employed almost constantly for three generations in simultaneous campaigns in the Balearics and on the Valencian coast.

The conquest of Valencia has traditionally been seen as Aragon's contribution to the religious crusade against the Moors. Yet other motives can also be identified. By fighting the Moors, the Aragonese were also rebuffing the Castilians, who had lodged an earlier stake in the area. Furthermore, by winning new royal lands King Jaime was able to strengthen the Crown against the nobles. His careful management of colonization allowed him to create new estates and new sources of revenue from which the nobles could be excluded.

The campaign advanced in spasms. Much of the fighting was defensive. In the first phase, 1232–3, Aragon captured the districts of Morella, Burriana and Peñiscola. In 1237–8 Jaime I entered the 'city of El Cid' and formally created the Kingdom of Valencia. In the third phase, in 1243–5, the Aragonese drove on into districts claimed by the Castilians, and a line of demarcation had to be established. The onset of the fourth and final phase was delayed to 1296, and lasted for eight years. The Arbitration of Torrellas (1304), as later amended, assigned Alicante to Valencia and Murcia to Castile.

The colonization of the Kingdom of Valencia, as reflected in subsequent linguistic patterns, followed twin routes. The king brought large groups of Catalan settlers into the coastal strip, thereby deciding that the future Valencian language would be a dialect of Catalan. Noble adventurers, on the other hand, set up private holdings in the inland districts, bringing settlers in from Aragon. Their descendants still employ a form of speech that is close to Aragonese.[54]

Two issues loomed large. One was the fate of the Muslim Moors, the other the form of government. The Christian population of Valencia formed a distinct minority for many years to come, but the defeated Muslims were badly needed to work the land of the new territories. There could be no question of a general expulsion. Instead, Islam was tolerated subject to the political loyalty of local leaders. In this way, the *mudéjars* of Valencia came to represent a solid Muslim enclave within Christian Iberia.[55]

The government of the Kingdom of Valencia was modelled neither on Aragon nor on Catalonia. Kingship was permanently invested in the Crown of Aragon, but the *Furs de Valencia* or 'Charters of Valencia' were produced through a lengthy process of bargaining between the Crown and the local (Christian) community. In these negotiations, occupying much of the fourteenth century, the municipality of the city of Valencia played a prominent role. Once the *Furs* were established, Valencia's power and wealth forged ahead. The wool trade supported extensive textile manufactories and underpinned the overseas commerce which made the city a worthy partner (and competitor) to Barcelona. The elegant *Lonja de la Seda* or 'Silk Exchange', which still stands, attests to the port's far-flung contacts, and the *Taula de canvis* ('table of exchange') acted both as a bank and a stock exchange.[56]

One of the side effects of the conquest of Valencia was to strengthen Aragon's hold on the inland province of Teruel that lies on the direct line between Zaragoza and Valencia. The intervening terrain is exceptionally hostile. The colonists' trail was blocked by range after range of stony mountains – including the wonderfully named Sierras Universales. The winters are notably inclement. Even today, the roads are few and far between. The remoteness of Teruel had made it a favoured place of refuge for Iberian Jews.

The fame of medieval Teruel, however, is for ever associated with a tale of star-struck lovers, Diego and Isabela, who lived there in the thirteenth century. Their tomb still stands in the parish church (no matter that Boccaccio reports an almost identical tale from Florence). The Marcillas and the Segaras of Teruel resembled the Montagues and Capulets of Verona. The Seguras were wealthy; the Marcillas impoverished. So, when Diego Marcilla asked for Isabela Segura's hand in marriage, her stern father told him that he had five years – and not a day longer! – to go away and make his fortune.

Five years passed, and Diego hadn't returned. On the day after the deadline, Isabela was ordered to wed an elderly knight. During the wedding feast, a commotion was heard. Diego had arrived, laden with riches and longing for his lady. He had counted the five years from the day of his departure, not, like the Seguras, from the day of his dismissal. That night, Diego crept into Isabela's bridal suite and begged for a kiss. '*Besame,*' he pleaded, '*que me muero*' ('Kiss me, for I'm dying'). Isabela, remembering her vows, turned away, and Diego fell dead at her feet. So the wedding was followed by a funeral. Isabela bent over Diego's bier, kissed him tenderly on the lips, and fell dead herself. The *amantes de Teruel*, separated in life, were united in death.[57]

In that same era, the heir apparent of the kingdom-county – the future Pedro III El Grande – married the heiress of Sicily, Constanza di Hohenstaufen. The fourteen-year-old bride, who arrived in Barcelona in 1262 with a fleet of galleys, laden with jewels and surrounded by an extravagant retinue, was to introduce the royal court to unaccustomed levels of opulence. The king's table, for example, abandoned its previous austerity, which had dictated a standard diet of mutton, with fish on Fridays. Detailed pantry receipts have survived to show that the royal household's culinary repertoire rapidly improved. Beef, goats' meat, poultry and salt pork with cabbage were served on ordinary days, not just at banquets, and roast pigeon figured so frequently it may have been the princess's favourite. Milk, butter, white sugar, spices, onions, spinach and other vegetables became items of daily expenditure, while large quantities of nuts and fresh fruit were consumed at breakfast. Extraordinarily intricate rules were laid down to allocate particular cuts of a carcass to particular grades of cook in lieu of salary. Soap appears on the shopping lists, indicating a dramatic step change in washing habits.[58]

Meanwhile, fifty years of royal warfare brought the nobility into a strong bargaining position. The traditional warrior caste fought the king's battles without demur, and was richly rewarded by grants of land and honours. Yet in the last years of Jaime I's reign, they increased their demands. They formed a 'Union of Liberties', calling for a charter of their rights and privileges, a definition of the powers of the justiciar, a guarantee of the rule of law, and a promise of annual parliaments. Jaime I's successor conceded their demands, issuing a General Privilege (1283), which successive kings were obliged to reconfirm. The document is rightly known as Aragon's 'Magna Carta'.[59]

The growing territorial base of the kingdom-county supplied the flow of manpower and taxes which facilitated further overseas conquests. Once the Balearic Islands had been pacified, the galleys could be sent on longer expeditions. In the two decades after 1282, they descended on Sicily, on the isles of Malta and Gozo, and even on Greece.

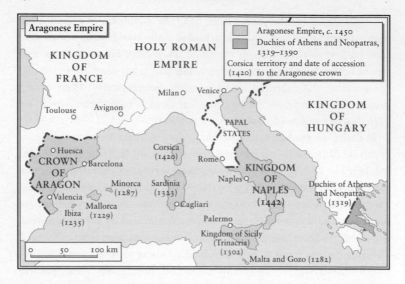

Sicily is the largest island in the Mediterranean. Because of its tri-angular shape, it had been known since Greek times as 'Trinacria', and it had lived through wave after wave of colonizations, Phoenician, Greek, Roman, Byzantine, Arab and Norman. It is dominated on the eastern side by the volcanic hulk of Mount Etna, and for the rest by rolling hills interspersed with fields of vines and olives. The easternmost port of Messina is separated by a narrow strait from southern Italy, while the westernmost port, Marsala, is equidistant to within 100 miles from Sardinia and Tunisia. In the early thirteenth century, the chief city, Palermo, had furnished the camels and the harems of the exotic and itinerant court of the Emperor Frederick II of Hohenstaufen (r. 1215–50), the so-called *Stupor Mundi*. Thanks to the rivalry between the German houses of Guelph and Ghibelline, however, the Emperor Fred-erick was drawn into a feud with the (pro-Guelph) Papal States, and he and his sons, Conrad and Manfred, were excommunicated. In 1266 the Hohenstaufens' Kingdom of Sicily, consisting of southern Italy as well as the island itself, was awarded by papal decree to the papal favourite, Charles d'Anjou.[60]

Aragon's link to Sicily came about as an unforeseen consequence of popular discontent with Angevin rule. In 1282 the citizens of Palermo turned on the Angevin-French garrison, and massacred them in a noc-turnal outrage that came to be known as the 'Sicilian Vespers'.[61] In the ensuing struggle, a group of former Hohenstaufen supporters appealed

for aid to Aragon, offering the throne to Pedro III, the husband of Manfred's daughter, Constanza. The appeal signalled confidence in Aragon's
newfound military and naval standing; the offer was a result for which
the Aragonese court had long been angling.

The War of the Sicilian Vespers, which lasted no less than twenty
years, pitted the king of France against anyone and everyone. The fighting
was concentrated on a series of naval campaigns in which the Aragonese
galley-fleet successfully denied the Angevins a safe passage for their
troops.[62] Supreme command of operations fell to Jaime II El Justo
(1267–1327), Pedro III's son, who assumed the royal claim to Sicily on
his father's death in 1285. The architect of success was, without doubt,
Admiral Ruggiero di Lauria (c. 1245–1305), a Calabrian sailor in the
Aragonese service who fought six major sea battles against preponder-
ant enemy odds and repeatedly prevailed through a mixture of daring,
guile and superior seamanship.[63]

The final outcome, in 1302, saw a compromise in which the Angevins
kept their lands on the *Continente*, while the Aragonese kept the island.
In order to confuse posterity, the reduced Angevin realm, centred on
Naples, continued to be called the Kingdom of Sicily. The new Aragonese
realm, based on Sicily, was initially called the Kingdom of Trinacria.
Charmingly, in reference to the *faro* or 'lighthouse', which stood on the
island shore of the Straits of Messina. the Angevin realm now became
known in Sicilian parlance as '*La Sicilia di qua del faro*' or 'Sicily beyond
the lighthouse'. The Aragonese realm was '*La Sicilia di qui del faro*' or
'Sicily on this side of the lighthouse'. To compound the confusion, the
Calabrians adopted the opposite perspective. For them, the tip of their
country stood at the lighthouse at Reggio, and for them Sicily became
'*di qua del faro*'.

The coronation of Jaime El Justo of Aragon-Catalonia, which took
place in Palermo on 2 February 1286, long before the war was won,
was more than a sacred and symbolic ceremony: it was the occasion
when the new king could win over his new subjects.

> Summoning, therefore, the prelates, barons and syndics of the cities and
> townships throughout the island, [the notables of the kingdom] assembled
> in parliament in Palermo . . . Thither James repaired, with the Queen and
> the Infant Don Frederic, and was crowned in the name of God and of the
> Virgin, by the Bishop of Cefalù, the Archimandrite of Messina and many
> other Sicilian prelates, as well as the Bishops of Squillaci and Nicastro.
> During the subsequent days of festivity . . . James at his own cost conferred

The two medieval Sicilies

THE KINGDOM OF NAPLES
or of Neapolitan Sicily emerged
in 1302 following the War
of the Sicilian Vespers.
Ruled by the Angevins until 1442,
it was acquired by Alfonso V of
Aragon, who separated it from
his other possessions.
It was ruled by Alfonso's descendants
until it passed to Spain in 1516.

As founded in 1130 by Roger
the Norman, inherited in 1196
by the Hohenstaufen emperors,
and donated to the Angevins
by the papacy in 1266, the original
'Kingdom of Sicily' included both
the island of Sicily and
the adjacent *Continente*.

THE KINGDOM OF TRINACRIA
or of insular Sicily was conquered
by Aragon during the War of
the Sicilian Vespers (1282–1302)
and ruled by descendants
and heirs of Pedro III
of Aragon until 1516.

PAPAL STATES · ADRIATIC SEA · Pescara · ABRUZZI · ROME · CAMPANIA · Benevento · Gaeta · Naples · Bari · TYRRHENIAN SEA · Salerno · APULIA · Brindisi · Taranto · BASILICATO · CALABRIA · IONIAN SEA · Marsala · Palermo · Messina · Reggio · SICILIA · Syracusa · 0 50 100 km

the honour of knighthood on four hundred Sicilian nobles: distributed many favours; and granted many fiefs which had lapsed to the exchequer on the expulsion of the French barons, both to do honour to this joyful occasion and to increase the number of his supporters . . .

For the same reason, during the sitting of parliament on the 5th of February, he promulgated the constitutions and immunities, as they were then called, incorporated with the laws of the Kingdom of Sicily under the head of the acts of King James, and written in the language of concession . . .[64]

For Dante Alighieri, writing in the early fourteenth century, the Sicilian Vespers and its consequences were contemporary events that he incorporated into the *Divina Commedia*. On the shores of Purgatory, for example, Dante meets the shade of Manfred, son of the Emperor Frederick II, who like his father had died excommunicate. Manfred explains that 'despite the Church's curse', repentance had given him the hope of salvation; and he begs Dante, if restored to the land of the living, to tell his 'lovely daughter' of the good news:

> ond'io ti priego che, quando tu riedi,
> vadi a mia bella figlia, genitrice
> de l'onor di Cicilia e d'Aragona,
> e dichi 'l vero a lei, s'altro si dice.

('I pray, when you return to the world, / that you go to my lovely daughter, mother / of kings in Sicily and Aragon / and tell her the truth, lest she's heard something different.')[65] As well as being the wife of Pedro III of Aragon, Manfred's daughter Constanza (still alive in 1300 as Queen Mother) was mother both of Jaime II of Aragon and of Frederico II of Sicily.

In a valley 'where nature was a painter', Dante meets the shades of negligent princes, who squandered their birthright. The setting is idyllic. The riot of flowers – '*Oro e argento fine, cocco e' biacca, indaco legno lucido sereno, fresco smeraldo*' – is mixed with a choir of souls intoning the '*Salve Regina*'. But the lesson is severe. The shades of Pedro III and Charles d'Anjou, rivals for the Sicilian throne, sing in harmony. Others receive the poet's lash. The *Nasetto*, 'the Snubnose', who 'fled and dishonoured the Lily', is Philippe III of France, who had died in Perpignan at the end of his campaign in Catalonia.[66]

Not surprisingly, the original Aragonese candidate for the thone of Sicily was long dead by the time that peace came. Pedro III's third son, Frederico, was eventually confirmed as the long-term holder of the throne. He gave rise to a new Sicilian line of the House of Aragon, ruling in parallel to their relatives in Barcelona and Majorca for more than a hundred years.[67]

The islands of Malta and Gozo passed under the Crown of Aragon in 1282, since they formed an integral part of the Kingdom of Sicily. Owing to the long wars between the Aragonese and the Angevins, however, the Maltese nobility gained a large measure of autonomy that lasted until the link with Aragon was severed centuries later. The royal government exercised control through a long series of viceroy/governors. The Arab elite was not expelled; their Muslim faith, Moorish architecture and Arabic language waned very slowly; indeed, modern Maltese is in many respects a derivative of medieval Arabic. The chief city, Mdina, retained its Arabic name while turning into a stronghold of the feudal nobility.[68]

The link with Greece also originated as an offshoot of the Crown's intervention in Sicily. At the end of the War of the Sicilian Vespers, the Aragonese army in Sicily could no longer be paid. So, with the king's approval, a powerful 'Catalan Company' was assembled and sent in 1302 as mercenaries to the Emperor of Byzantium, who was already feeling the threat from the Ottoman advance. The company's leader was an adventurer from Rosselló, Ruggier Desflors (Roger Deslaur or Roger de Flor). A Catalan soldier, who recorded their deeds for posterity, wrote that they had gone to 'Romania':

> The Emperor, in the presence of all, made Frey Roger sit down before him and gave him the baton and the cap and the banner and the seal of the Empire, and invested him with the robes belonging to the office and made him Caesar of the Empire. And a Caesar is an officer who sits in a chair near that of the Emperor, only half a palm lower, and he can do as much as the Emperor in the Empire. He can bestow gifts in perpetuity and can dispose of the treasure, impose tribute, and he can apply the question and hang and quarter ... And again, he signs himself 'Caesar of Our Empire' and the Emperor writes to him 'Caesar of Thy Empire'. What shall I tell you? There is no difference between the Emperor and the Caesar, except that ... the Emperor wears a scarlet cap and all his robes are scarlet, and the Caesar wears a blue cap and his robes are blue with a narrow gold border ...[69]

For several years the company, under Byzantine command, fought the Turks in Anatolia and gained a reputation for rapine and pillage. When its indiscipline outweighed its usefulness, it was rounded up by another regiment of Byzantine mercenaries and massacred. The survivors faced annihilation and, gathering an assortment of Balkan hirelings, deserters and desperadoes, set out on the trail of the 'Catalan Revenge'. In the process, they took possession of Athens: 'Once under Catalan control, Athens was transformed into a Catalan mini-state. Its nominal dependency on the Duchy of Achaia was renounced. Catalan was declared the official language; Catalan law replaced Byzantine law; and Catalan officials resided in the Parthenon, lords of all they surveyed.'[70] The Duchy of Neopatria (Neopatras) in central Greece was ruled in tandem with the Athenian duchy from 1319 to 1390, and outlived Aragonese rule in Athens by a decade.[71]

Aragon's elevated standing in that era can be gauged from the fact that the Angevins, having lost Sicily during the War of the Sicilian Vespers, went to great lengths to recover it by diplomatic and financial means. In 1311 Robert of Naples wrote to his Aragonese counterpart in Palermo offering to exchange the 'Kingdom of Trinacria' for the Angevin 'Kingdom of Albania' at Durazzo, together with Angevin rights in the Duchy of Achaia. He was rebuffed, but in subsequent years the offer was repeatedly increased until, in addition to Albania and Achaia, it included Sardinia, Corsica, all the former Templar possessions in southern Italy, one half of Sicily and 100,000 ounces of gold. The Aragonese were not tempted. The project lapsed.[72]

The rapid expansion of the kingdom-county and the multiplication of its dependencies inevitably generated tensions. The problems that arose can hardly be attributed to 'imperial overstretch', as might have occurred in a more centralized system.[73] Rather, they must be seen as the product of centrifugal forces that pulled the dependencies away from the heartland. Cadet branches of the ruling house snubbed their seniors, autonomous regimes adopted wayward policies and a widening gulf opened up between the centre and the peripheries.

Jaime the Conqueror had already identified the dangers when devising a scheme to divide the Crown lands into two co-equal parts. He had hoped that his two sons would co-operate in the interests of dynastic harmony, but his chosen solution produced the opposite effect. Shortly after his death in 1276, fratricidal conflict broke out between the Kingdom of Aragon and the Kingdom of Mallorca which festered for over fifty years. The Conqueror could not have foreseen two key factors, the unplanned acquisition of Sicily and the explosive growth of Mallorcan commerce, which combined to ruin the balance between the various parts of his legacy. Aragonese rule in Sicily prompted an endless feud with the Angevins, and to cap it all, large parts of the state's heartland were overrun by armed leagues of rebellious nobles. When the Black Death struck, many said that God was punishing His people justly.

The 'Kingdom of the Greater Island' came into being in 1276 following the execution of the Conqueror's testament and the partition of his possessions. Pedro, the elder son, received the dynasty's ancestral territories to the south and west of the Pyrenees, while Jaime, the younger son, received the offshore islands, the smaller provinces to the north of the mountains, and a couple of outlying possessions. The ceremonial centre of Jaime's kingdom lay on Mallorca; his mainland castle was built in Perpinya. The coat of arms of the kingdom betrayed its origins. The four

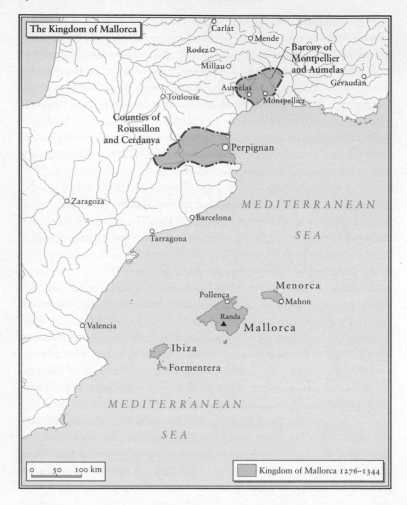

The Kingdom of Mallorca

Carlat
Mende
Rodez
Barony of
Montpellier
and Aumelas
Millau
Gévaudan
Aumelas
Toulouse
Montpellier
Counties of
Roussillon
and Cerdanya
Perpignan
Zaragoza
MEDITERRANEAN
Barcelona
SEA
Tarragona
Menorca
Pollença
Mahon
Valencia
Randa
Mallorca
Ibiza
Formentera
MEDITERRANEAN

SEA

0   50   100 km

Kingdom of Mallorca 1276–1344

vertical red stripes on a golden background – *Or, four billets gules* – the emblem of Catalonia, were superimposed by a broad, diagonal, sea-blue band – a *bend azure*. At the same time, an adjustment was made to the internal frontier between Aragon and the County of Barcelona. The border had traditionally followed the River Cinca; it was now moved eastwards to the Segre, thereby creating the *Franja*, a border strip within Aragon where most of the villages spoke (and speak) Catalan.

Pedro III, however, rejected the spirit of his father's plan and refused to accept his younger brother as an equal. Within three years, he sent his army to surround the walls of Perpinya, demanding that Jaime submit in an act of homage. It was the rule, he declared, that no king should be subject to the wishes of another. Jaime, trapped, decided to comply. Yet, notwithstanding the Treaty of Perpinya of 1279, the dispute rumbled on. Pedro's lawyers maintained that the terms of treaty, and the subsequent act of homage, had changed the Kingdom of the Greater Island into a fief of Aragon. Jaime's lawyers maintained that their father's will remained the definitive document.

In 1285 the legal arguments turned into open warfare. The king of France mounted an expedition into Catalonia, aiming to block Aragonese ambitions in Sicily. His plans backfired sensationally. Aragon rallied. The French were pushed back. And, since King Jaime was assumed to have been in collaboration with the invaders, the whole of his kingdom, including the Balearics, was taken over by Pedro's forces and effectively suspended. Papal intervention eventually assured the kingdom's restoration, but the vulnerability of the junior branch was fully exposed.

During the Aragonese occupation, Menorca was subjected to a vicious act of retribution. In 1287, aiming no doubt to refill their coffers, the Aragonese crushed the local emirate of Menorca, and rounded up the entire Muslim population; 40,000 souls were shipped off to the slave markets of North Africa. This cruel act, which had no parallel either in Mallorca or Valencia, was a milestone in the grim history of European slavery.[74] The island was resettled by Catalan colonists, and the magnificent port of Mahon was added to the growing chain of Aragonese bases.

The royal feud raged on, but despite the politics and the battles of these years, the infant kingdom's economy flourished. Agricultural methods were improved, a textile industry was launched, and ship-building developed to the point where the keels of an independent galley-fleet could be laid. Castles and palaces were built, notably the circular Bellver Castle on Mallorca, and the Palace of the Kings at Perpinya. Above all, commerce boomed. Mallorca became the entrepôt for the seaborne trade between Europe and North Africa. It was the place where the small coastal boats transferred their cargoes to larger seagoing vessels. It was equally the entry point for rare commodities – oriental spices, gold and 'porcelain' shells. New routes were exploited with Sicily and Sardinia, and even (since Jaime III had been brought up in his mother's home of Achaia) with Greece and with Mamluk Egypt. Expeditions explored ocean routes to the Canaries and to north-west Europe and independent Mallorcan consulates were set up in the Berber states of North Africa. Genoese merchants were welcomed, creating the *Lonja dels generesos* in Palma, and Mallorcans muscling in on the Atlantic trade appeared in London and Bruges. The records of Francesco Datini, 'the Merchant of Prato', reveal that he was importing Iberian wool to Italy, not from the Spanish mainland but from the islands. Naval facilities were expanded for the Aragonese fleet.[75]

As part of their strategy to maximize income from trade in their own ships, the kings of the Greater Island sought to close their ports to Barcelonan and Valencian vessels. In 1301, for example, they tried to step up the anchorage tax on Catalan ships entering Collioure, signalling their intention of treating them as foreigners. The scheme failed and was replaced by an attempt to make Barcelona pay a flat annual fee of 60,000 silver pounds. That ploy failed, too, when Barcelona argued that a similar sum should be paid to Aragon as a feudal fee for approval of the king's marriage. The cat was playing with the mouse. In due course, the Mallorcans minted their own coinage in Rosselló, and in 1342 they even launched an independent expedition to explore the Canaries. In the eyes of their Aragonese cousins, they were building an empire within the Empire.[76]

In Balearic society, the balance between Christians, Muslims and Jews was different than elsewhere. A few free Muslims remained in Mallorca, though the majority were enserfed. The Jews, in contrast, prospered mightily. They belonged to the same cultural network as their co-religionists in Barcelona, Perpinya and Montpellier; they enjoyed the right of *alyama* or self-government; and they participated energetically in the commercial boom. The *Call* or 'ghetto' in Ciutat de Mallorca was a prosperous quarter surrounding a single prominent synagogue. Apart from the solitary pogrom in 1391, generalized persecution would not set in until the fifteenth century.[77]

The kingdom's best-known subject by far was Ramón Llull (1232–1315). Philosopher, novelist, linguist and reconciler of religions, he was born in Mallorca soon after the conquest, served as a page in Jaime the Conqueror's court, studied at the University of Montpellier, and later rose to serve as seneschal of the 'Greater Island' in Perpinya. His first book, *Le Llibre de la cavalleria*, dealt with the principles of chivalry. A moment of religious ecstasy followed. The rest of his life was spent trying to harmonize the three great monotheist religions. Llull knew Arabic as well as he knew Latin, and had been trained in the work of Muslim and Jewish philosophers. He laboured for many years at the Franciscan monastery at Miramar on Mount Randa, before setting out on long tours to meet popes and princes, journeying as far afield as Georgia and Egypt and teaching in many foreign universities. At the Council of Vienne in 1311, he witnessed

the nominal acceptance of his cherished proposal for the teaching of oriental languages. He undertook repeated missions to Muslim North Africa,
where he engaged in learned disputations with the *ulemas* (religious scholars), and where his remarkable life reached its term.

Llull's works were frowned on by the Church, but never lacked admirers.
His *Ars major* and *Ars generalis* contain a mass of speculative philosophy.
His *Blaquerna* is sometimes cited as the world's first novel. His poetry, in
El Desconort or *Lo Cant de Ramon*, is beautifully simple. He even invented
a sort of cybernetic machine that claimed to unravel the mysteries of uni-
versal knowledge. Llull has rightly been called 'a great European'.[78]

Sardinia first came into Aragon's sights during the suspension of the
Kingdom of the Greater Island, when Pope Boniface VIII, seeing Aragon
as a useful ally against the troublesome Republic of Genoa, tried to
transfer both Sardinia and Corsica to Barcelona.

Medieval Sardinia was divided into four *Giudicati* or 'Judgeships',
Gallura in the north, Cagliari in the south, Logudoro in the north-west
and Arborea on the west coast. The ruling judges were military as well
as judicial officials, who passed much of their time contesting control of
the castles of the island's mountainous interior. By the turn of the fourteenth century, Gallura and Cagliari were in the pockets of the Pisans,
and Logudoro of the Genoese; Arborea was the only Judgeship to
remain fully independent.

Aragon's claim was revived by the Infante Alfonso of the Trinacrian
line. His expedition, having sailed from Mallorca, landed in the spring
of 1323:

> And the Lord Infante En Alfonso had fine weather and assembled all the
> fleet at the island of San Pietro. And they went to Palmas dels Sols and there
> all the chivalry and the almugavars landed. And, immediately, the Judge of
> Arborea came there with all his power, to receive him as lord, and a great
> number of Sardinians . . . [from] the city of Sassari surrendered to him. And
> there they made an agreement, by the Judge's advice, that the Lord Infante
> should go and besiege Iglesias . . .
>
> The Lord Infante, besieging Iglesias, attacked it every day with catapults.
> But [he] and all his host had so much sickness, that the greater part of his
> followers died . . . and he, himself, was very ill. Assuredly he would have
> been in great danger of dying, if it had not been for the great care of my
> Lady the Infanta . . .
>
> However ill the Lord Infante was, for no physician would he leave the

siege. Many times with the fever upon him he would put on his armour
and order an attack. By his good endeavour ... he reduced the town to
such a state that it surrendered. So all the host entered ... and garrisoned
the fort well. And then he came to Cagliari, and built a castle ... opposite
Cagliari and gave it the name of Bonaire.[79]

On 24 April 1326 the foundation of the Kingdom of Sardinia was proclaimed. Arborea alone offered coherent resistance.

Aragonese rule in Sardinia was not entirely even-handed. The *Coeterum*
statute of 1324 abolished Pisan law, introducing legislation that favoured
the newcomers. All public offices were reserved for Catalans, Mallorcans and Aragonese. As from 1328, a trumpet was sounded at nightfall
from the battlements of Cagliari, warning all Sardinians to leave. A parliament opened, similar to the *Corts* in Barcelona. The three estates of
feudal lords, clergy and royal officers met in separate chambers, and
exercised an advisory role. In 1354, the port of Alghero was settled by
Catalans, and their descendants speak Catalan to the present day.

The life and reign of Pedro IV (1319–87) form the centrepiece to the
whole Aragonese fourteenth century. The son of Alfonso IV and of
Teresa d'Entença, heiress of Urgell, he succeeded in 1336, inheriting a
domain that stretched right across the Mediterranean from Valencia to
Athens. He was known as El Ceremonioso from the rigid etiquette of
his court, and also as El Punyalet, 'the Poignard', after furiously cutting
up both a proposed charter of noble liberties and his own finger. His life
was filled with warfare: against his relatives, against his nobles, and
against his neighbour and namesake, Pedro the Cruel of Castile. Prior
to 1348, he prevailed against an armed insurrection of nobles, survived
the plague which killed his queen, Leonora of Portugal (the Black Death
split his reign into two clear halves), and suppressed the Kingdom of
Mallorca. Many of the events of the reign were voluminously recorded
in the chronicle which he personally commissioned.[80]

The two branches of Jaime the Conqueror's family repeatedly intermarried in the first half of the fourteenth century in the hope of reaching
reconciliation, but it never worked. The final suppression of the Kingdom of Mallorca came about through a culmination of complaints. The
commercial policy of the Mallorcans irked Barcelona. Their continuing
links to France, through Montpellier, aroused suspicions. And the last
straw was delivered by news of intrigues with the Genoese. Pedro decided
to act. In 1343 troops carried by the Catalan fleet invaded the Balearics.

In 1344 an Aragonese army stormed Perpinya. The Mallorcan court was driven into exile. In 1349 the last, desperate Mallorcan ruler, Jaime III, sold Montpellier to raise funds, then staked all on an expedition to recover Mallorca. His gamble failed. He was killed on the field of Lluc-major in southern Mallorca, and his 'Ephemeral Kingdom' died with him.[81] Though the legal claims of the Mallorcan line were kept in circulation for the lifetime of Jaime III's immediate heirs, his son the nominal Jaime IV lived in Naples as the consort of the notorious Queen Joanna I (see below, p. 211).

Pedro's decisive action completed a process of monarchical consolidation. To prevent the fragmentation of the Crown, it had been decided in his father's time that 'whoever rules in Aragon rules in Catalonia and Valencia as well'. The king now reincorporated the lands of the 'Greater Island' also.

Both in its origins and in its outcome, the noble revolt of the (second) 'Union of Liberties', which came to a head in 1347, reflected deep unrest that was no less social than political. The royal justiciar had ruled that 'a lord can maltreat his vassal whenever there is just cause', and the nobility's control over their serfs, who had no recourse beyond the mercy of their oppressor, had become near absolute. Such court records as remain of complaints against lordly malpractices are expressed in the 'tormented voices' of a virtually invisible underclass.[82] In best Aragonese fashion, the Union's leaders also added the legal right of rebellion against the king to their usual litany of petitions and demands. The rebels' sense of omnipotence was increased by the support of the king's half-brothers, who feared for the loss of their top positions in the royal line of succession.[83]

Yet the Union had picked an agile and obstinate opponent, and one who possessed ready allies, especially in Catalonia. Initially, the rebels made deep inroads into Valencia and Aragon, but they grew disunited when unexpected concessions were made. While they hesitated, the king turned to the prosperous merchant class of Barcelona, which supplied him with money and professional soldiers. The rebellion collapsed in a sea of blood at the Battle of Epila near Zaragoza in July 1348. After his victory, the king rescinded the Privilege of Union of 1287 together with all other charters making reference to the nobles' right of rebellion. At the same time, he took an oath to respect his subjects' traditional liberties, while strengthening the powers of the justiciar, whose constitutional pre-eminence dates from this time. He reached a sensible compromise, resisting the temptation to introduce a royal despotism.[84]

In the midst of these preoccupations, the Black Death struck like the Hand of God. The king was still struggling to restore order after the Union of Liberties:

The great plague began in the city of Valencia in the month of May in the year of Our Lord 1348 ... By the middle of June over 300 persons died each day. We decided to leave the city and go to Aragon ...

As soon as We arrived in Teruel We heard that the Prince En Ferrando was in Saragossa with many [others], discussing the affairs of the Union ... All that was discussed tended to Our great disgrace. But [after] some days in Teruel, the great plague began there [too], and We had to leave. And We made Our way to (Saragossa) via Tarazona, where the noble En Lop de Luna was, with an Aragonese armed company, waiting for the troops [which] the king of Castile was to send for Our assistance ...

Then We directed Our way to Our Aljaferia ... We sentenced thirteen persons to death, with confiscation of their goods, as they had committed the crime of lèse majesté. Those condemned were hanged, some at the Gate of Toledo and some in other places ...

The *jurats* [magistrates] of the city [then] begged Us that We should be pleased to discuss the state of the kingdom. Having talked with Our council, we at once agreed to hold *Cortes generals* in the city ... The first thing that We [did] was that all the acts made by the Union were judicially condemned; and, in the main building of the monastery of the Preachers, where the *Cortes* were celebrated, *all* the documents and legal processes made by the Union were burnt ... so that nothing of its acts should remain ...

We went to the Church of Sent Salvador and, standing in the pulpit ... We spoke to the people. Our discourse was, in sum, that We considered Ourselves prejudiced and injured by the Union, but that, remembering the mercy [which] the bygone kings of Aragon had been accustomed to show to their subjects, We pardoned them ... This was done in the month of August.

During the [continuing] discussions, the great plague began [again] ... and increased daily ... The *Cortes* being in agreement, We prorogued them [to] the city of Teruel ... And then the *Cortes* graciously accorded Us a *morabati* or *monedatge* [tax], which We had collected in all parts of the kingdom.

We left the city of Saragossa with the queen, Our wife, who was ill. Many days had passed since the illness started but she was better ... [So] We went to Exérica. And the illness of the queen increased so much that in a few

days she passed from this life in Exérica. As soon as she was buried and We
had dined, We mounted and went to Segorbe where the plague had come
to an end.[85]

The king was obviously too busy to tarry or to mourn. It is notable that
the *Cortes* waited until the end of the session before 'graciously' granting the king his taxes, which were payable in a seven-year cycle. (In
Castile, as in England, the king demanded his taxes *before* agreeing to
hear representations.) In the opinion of one leading scholar, this practice explains why the royal power in such a rich country suffered from
financial weakness.[86]

In the second half of his reign, Pedro IV's troubles were religious as
well as financial; he fell into a lengthy feud with the inquisitor-general
and head of the Dominican Order in Aragon, Nicolau Eymerich (1320–
99), author of *Directorium Inquisitorium* (1376), an authoritative
handbook for defining and combating witchcraft, which was defined as
a form of heresy.[87] The inquisitor was a zealot who refined the use of
torture and persecuted both the Jews of Aragon and the followers of
Ramon Llull. He was twice banished to Avignon, and twice returned.

A century after its birth, the Aragonese navy was the third biggest in
the western Mediterranean, after those of Genoa and the Moorish emir-
ates of North Africa. Its galleys were half as big again as in the thirteenth
century, carrying an average complement of 223 rowers and crewmen;
its shipyards at Barcelona, Valencia and Palma, drawing on the oak
woods of Montseny, were virtually self-sufficient except for oars. Its
increased capacity made it possible for a fleet to extend the standard
four-month tour of summer duty to twelve or even eighteen months. A
fleet of twenty-eight galleys, for example, which put to sea in 1341
under Admiral Pere de Moncada (grandson of Ruggiero di Lauria), wintered on station, only returning to Barcelona the next year.

The main threat at that time came from the North African Moors.
The Christian navies, commanded by Admiral Boccanegra of Genoa,
joined forces to isolate Muslim Granada from the Marinid rulers of
Morocco and to keep the Strait of Gibraltar open. The Castilians in particular suffered great losses, and were obliged to hire fifteen replacement
galleys from Genoa at 800 gold florins per month. For logistical reasons, however, the Aragonese were unable to fight for long without
allies, since their plans to assemble a fleet of forty heavy and twenty
light galleys were not realized. The prospect that Genoa might ally itself
with the Moors proved especially worrying. Aragon remained a major

naval force until the utility of galleys declined through the introduction of gunpowder in the late fifteenth century.

Aragon's overseas territories suffered not only from the Black Death but also from the social ills that had wracked the heartland. The most distinguished historian of Sicily, for example, has written of the rise of a 'New Feudalism'.[88] The barons rampaged with impunity; the serfs toiled without relief; the towns withered; and the monarchy was helpless. In 1377, Pedro IV of Aragon invaded Sicily in order to bring it under direct control.

Conditions in Sardinia, where Aragon waged three wars against Arborea, were no healthier. Arborea received support from Genoa, but not enough to produce a clear victory. Remarkably, despite the upheaval, one of the most talented women of the Middle Ages, Eleonora d'Arborea (1347–1404), was able to flourish both in government and in science.[89] Wife of a Genoese, and mother of successive Sardinian judges, she defended her birthright with spirit both against Aragon and against local republicans. She was an unlikely pioneer of ornithology and bird-protection – the *falco eleonora* is named in her honour – and she is remembered as the author of a famous law code, the *Carta de Logu*, which remained in force from 1395 to 1861.[90]

The death of Pedro IV in 1387 marked the culmination of a century-long period of evolution in the institutions of the Crown of Aragon. The monarchy, the administration and the political culture of the state had all been forced to respond to the growing 'empire', and all had been systematically transformed. The 'Arago-Catalan Court', as one histor-ian calls it, provided the key to 'the rise of administrative kingship'.[91] The Royal Chancery, the 'King's Memory', kept copies of all laws and letters, leaving a vast store of documentary treasures in Barcelona's *Arxiu de la Corona d'Arago*.[92] Its paper-based technology can be traced to Jaime the Conqueror's capture of Europe's first Muslim-owned paper factory at Xativa in Valencia.[93] The Royal Treasury, the 'King's Purse', kept detailed, daily records of all financial transactions. And the Royal Household, the 'King's Body', revealed 'a discreet society' of royal rela-tives, specialized bureaucrats and highly trained servants, who ran the state. One scholar's conclusion, which seems to regret the polity's ultim-ate demise, is unnecessarily pessimistic:

> The question might be asked ... whether an examination of the changes
> within the administrative system [of the Crown of Aragon] might not be

an exercise in futility. After all, [the system] left few lasting traces ... But its ultimate lack of success does not affect its value ... We have witnessed the truth that modernisation, no matter how visionary, is not enough to guarantee the survival of the state.[94]

In the 1350s Pedro IV had lined up against Castile in the so-called 'War of the Two Peters', whose causes have long since been forgotten. By the late fourteenth century, Iberia was moving towards a series of dynastic disasters which would culminate simultaneously. The ruling houses of Trastámara in Castile and of Barcelona in the kingdom-county were already intermarried, yet by the turn of the century each was eyeing up the other's uncertain prospects, as a long minority in Castile combined with a paralysing interregnum in Aragon to create a knot of problems of mind-bending complexity. The resulting convulsions continued for decades until the two houses finally united for good in the epoch-making marriage of 1469.

In Castile, the crisis began in 1406 with the premature death of King Henry III El Doliente, 'the Sufferer', whose son and heir was barely one year old. The ensuing regency was presided over by two co-regents: Henry's widow, Catherine of Lancaster, and his younger brother, Fernando d'Antequera, who had earned the sobriquet thanks to his victory over the Moors in Andalusia. The arrangement involved Aragon because Fernando and his late brother were both sons of Eleanor of Aragon, daughter of Pedro IV and Eleanour of Sicily.

In Aragon, at exactly the same time, a parallel crisis was precipitated by the death of the royal heir apparent, who had been ruling in Sicily. The king himself, Martin I El Humano, 'the Humane' – the last royal descendant of Count Wilfred the Hairy – lived on for a further four years, but the ruling house had run out of male issue. In 1410, when the king followed his son to an early grave, there was no obvious successor. No fewer than six candidates vied for the throne. They placed their claims before the assembled representatives of Aragon, Barcelona and Valencia, but no decision was reached. Then, a commission of nine notables sought to find a resolution, and an eventual winner emerged at the so-called Compromise of Caspe. The commissioners' choice was momentous, not to say adventurous, for it fell on none other than Fernando d'Antequera, infante and regent of Castile – a man who spoke no Catalan, and whose personal estates lay in southern Spain. Yet the winner proved his mettle, defeating his most recalcitrant rival, the count of Urgell, in battle at Montearagon near Huesca, and quickly restoring

The House of Trastámara

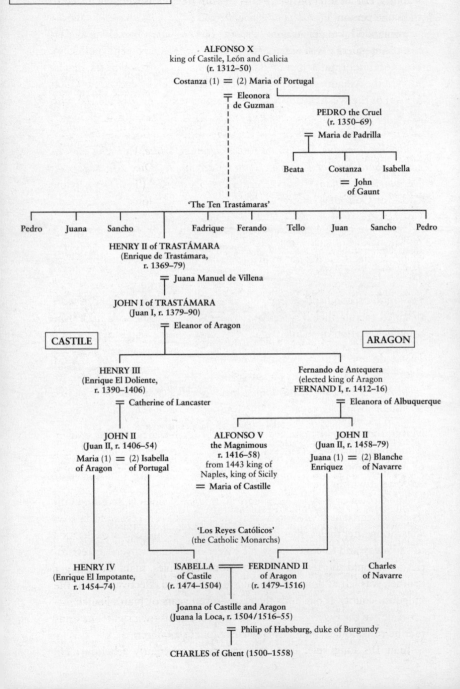

stability. For an interval, the affairs of both kingdoms were entrusted to the same person.

Fernando I, king of Aragon (r. 1412–16), known in Barcelona as 'Ferran d'Antequera', was a prudent administrator and forceful politician. His most important achievement was to press successfully for the deposition of the Aragonese antipope, Benedict XIII, thereby ending the Great Schism of the Western Church.[95] Most importantly, he was blessed with an ample supply of sons. The two older ones, Alfonso and Juan, would succeed him in turn. His regal style, as recorded in a document of 1413, reads: *'Ferdinandus, Dei Gratia Rex Aragonum, Sicilie, Valencie, Maioricarum, Sardiniae et Corsice, Comes Barchinone, Dux Athenarum et Neopatriae, ac etiam Comes Rossilonis et Ceritaniae'* ('Fernando, by the Grace of God king of Aragon, Sicily, Valencia, Majorca, Sardinia and Corsica, count of Barcelona, duke of Athens and Neopatria, and also count of Roussillon and Cerdagne').[96] Needless to say, several of the titles were redundant.

At this juncture, a clear head is necessary to disentangle the multiple coincidences of names. Fernando's nephew, the boy-king of Castile, and Fernando's second son shared the same Christian name, and both were destined to rule their respective kingdoms for long periods under the same designation of Juan II. Juan II of Castile (r. 1406–54) is generally regarded as feeble-minded. His cousin, Juan II of Aragon (r. 1458–79), was intemperate. To cap it all, in order to perpetuate the intimate relations of the courts of Toledo and Barcelona, the sister of Juan II of Castile was married off to Alfonso of Aragon, while the sister of Juan II of Aragon married Juan II of Castile. Both of these brides were called Maria; they were first cousins, and each of them married a first cousin. After their marriages, Princess Maria of Castile became Queen Maria of Aragon, and Maria of Aragon became Maria of Castile. The phrase 'keeping it within the family' gains new significance.

The Crown of Aragon escaped from this tangled web of consanguinity by an agreement of mutual convenience between Fernando I's two sons. Soon after their father died in 1416, Alfonso, his successor, decided to sail away and to concentrate his career on Aragon's overseas territories and would shortly turn his attentions to Naples. Juan, the younger brother, was left at home as lieutenant-general and effective ruler of the kingdom-county. If one adds the thirty-seven years of Juan's lieutenant-generalcy to the twenty-one years of his reign in his own right, one finds that he ruled longer than any other Aragonese monarch.

Juan II's long rule, however, was not particularly felicitous. He embroiled his subjects in a wearying saga of spats, wars and feuds that render his sobriquet of 'the Great' a mystery. Having married a Navarran princess, he spent fifty years as the effective ruler of the Kingdom of Navarre *iure uxoris*, but neglecting his other duties. In the 1450s, he was totally absorbed by a Navarrese civil war and by a vicious vendetta against his elder son, whom he had appointed viceroy in Barcelona. In the 1460s, he faced a ten-year Catalan revolt, and in the 1470s pursued an ill-judged war against Louis XI of France.

The one favourable element in his reign lay in the continuation of close ties between Aragon and Castile. The two branches of the Trastámara clan co-operated discreetly to keep the family fortunes afloat, and together, they weighed down on the dwindling power of the Moors in Granada. The culmination of their plans was achieved on 19 October 1469 at Valladolid, where Fernando, the younger son of Juan II of Aragon, was joined in wedlock to Isabella, the only daughter of Juan II of Castile. They are known to posterity as 'Ferdinand and Isabella, the Catholic Monarchs' (see below). The two principal kingdoms of Iberia were moving ever closer.

During the long, strife-filled decades of the fifteenth century, the ramshackle structures of the Crown of Aragon were undoubtedly weakened, further; the heartland increasingly lost a firm hold on its overseas dependencies. Alfonso V (r. 1416–58), king of Sicily by hereditary right and, from 1421, the designated heir to the Kingdom of Naples, emerged as one of the most resplendent princes of the early Renaissance. Surrounded by an inimitable mixture of artists, soldiers of fortune, men of letters, architects and ambitious Aragonese courtiers, he spent his time fighting, feuding, feasting and forging his reputation as 'the Magnanimous'. During his reign Corsica was captured, and Naples conquered.[97]

In theory, Corsica had formed part of the Aragonese Kingdom of Sardinia from the days of Pope Boniface. In practice, encouraged by Genoa, it had rejected Aragon's advances for more than a century. Alfonso V of Aragon personally led the expedition which conquered Corsica in 1420. Reducing the fortress of Bonifacio by siege, he briefly established a regime headed by a local viceroy. In 1453, however, unable to defend his acquisition, he handed it back to the Genoese in return for a loan from the Banco di San Giorgio. Surprisingly, the brief Aragonese presence was sufficient to introduce the symbol of the 'Moor's Head' which later emerged as Corsica's national emblem.[98]

The Kingdom of Naples – that is, the part of the original Kingdom of Sicily that had stayed in Angevin hands after 1282 – was the largest and most populous state in medieval Italy, occupying the whole of the southern half of the peninsula from the frontier of the Romagna to the heel of 'the boot'. Its territory consisted of six modern regions – Abruzzi, Molise, Campania, Puglia, Basilicata and Calabria – and coincided very closely with what Romans and northern Italians call *il Mezzogiorno*, the Midi, or 'the land of the noonday sun'. Because the Angevins were papal clients, it was also a traditional protectorate of the papacy.

For 150 years after the War of the Sicilian Vespers, the Angevin monarchs had held on to their Neapolitan inheritance. Their readiness to fight their own Angevin relatives was only exceeded by their determination to exclude their Aragonese rivals. There were two episodes of acute crisis. Both featured heirless queens – Joanna I (r. 1343–82) and Joanna II (r. 1414–35) – and both possessed a specifically Aragonese angle.

Joanna I imported four husbands, including Jaime IV, pretender to the throne of Mallorca, but none of them brought stability. Joanna II reigned over a kingdom rent by violence and scandal. Her first husband, a Habsburg, left her, and the second soon fled in fear of his life. The queen was then free to have herself crowned as sole monarch and to rule in league with successive lovers. The one that lasted longest, Giovanni Caracciolo, known as 'Sergianni', was the wealthiest of her subjects and an inveterate intriguer. Before being stabbed to death, he was a virtual dictator.

Like her earlier namesake, however, Joanna II was dogged not simply by the lack of a child and of scruples, but also by a congenital inability to stick with a decision. She designated in turn no fewer than four men as her official heir. In 1420, when the pope gave his support to an Angevin to be her successor at Naples, the queen promptly turned to Alfonso V of Aragon as counter-heir. Alfonso invaded, captured Sergianni, and was besieging the royal palace of Castel Capuano when the queen again changed her mind, repudiated him, and reverted to the pope's original candidate. *La regin' è mobile.* Later, Joanna chose another Angevin, René d'Anjou, count of Provence, to take his place.

In the two ensuing wars of the Neapolitan succession, 1420–24 and 1435–43, the fighting spread far and wide. In 1424 Alfonso's imminent victory in Naples was interrupted when he was summoned back to Barcelona to handle a crisis with Castile, sacking Marseille on his roundabout route home. In the second war, Alfonso was defeated at sea by the Genoese, taken prisoner, handed over to the Sforza family of Milan, and eventually ransomed. In the middle phase, when René d'Anjou was installed in Naples, Alfonso set up a strong naval base at Gaeta, but was repeatedly rebuffed on land. In the final phase, he successfully picked off all of the kingdom's peripheral regions, reconciled himself to the papacy, and, by making decisive use of his formidable artillery train, slowly surrounded his prize. In June 1442 René fled, and Alfonso finally entered Naples in style. He cherished it above all his other possessions. He ruled over both kingdoms of Sicily, thereby creating in personal union an early emanation of the joint *Regnum utriusque Siciliae*, the 'Kingdom of the Two Sicilies'. For the next sixty years, Naples was tightly held in the hands either of Alfonso or of his sons.

Naples in its Aragonese period ranked high in both size and opulence among Europe's port cities. Its history went back to ancient Greek times, and it served as the outlet for a region in which Greek-speaking communities survived into modern times. Its hinterland consists of the productive plain of Campagna; and its approach from the sea, with the cone of Mount Vesuvius in view, is spectacular. 'See Naples and die' is a phrase attributed to Goethe, but it is a sentiment that fits Alfonso the Magnanimous perfectly. Many of the urban landmarks were of great antiquity, but that did not prevent the incoming Aragonese from altering or embellishing them. The Greek-built fortress of Castel d'Ovo, for example, which guards the old harbour, had been strongly fortified by the Normans. The Aragonese pulled down the tall Norman towers. The cathedral of San Gennaro, patron of the city, stands on the site of a temple of Apollo; the Aragonese lavishly decorated some of the chapels. The pine-wooded promontory of Pizzofalcone (whence the breathtaking panorama across the bay to Vesuvius) had hosted the villas of the rich and powerful for nearly 2,000 years. The Aragonese simply joined the queue.

Many of the most prominent buildings dated from Angevin times. The university had been founded in the thirteenth century. The castle of St Elmo, the *Belforte*, had overlooked the city from an anterior ridge since 1343. The monastery of San Domenico Maggiore, which contains the cell of Thomas Aquinas, was completely restored in 1445. The imposing Castel Nuovo, constructed during the War of the Sicilian Vespers, protected the harbour. A triumphal arch in white marble was placed incongruously between the two round towers of the façade by the Aragonese, and dedicated to Alfonso the Magnanimous.

The city's prominence in the late fifteenth century owed much to the final phase of commericial growth prior to the long recession caused by Ottoman expansion. Naples joined Palermo, Malta, Valencia, Barcelona, Palma, Corsica and Sardinia in a naval and mercantile network which dominated the western Mediterranean.

Alfonso's coat of arms and regal style well illustrate the complexities of his position. An inscription on his triumphal arch read: 'ALFONSO REX HISPANUS SICULUS ITALICUS PIUS CLEMENS INVICTUS'. He was claiming, extravagantly, to be the 'king of Spain, Sicily and Italy'. It displays the simple arms of Aragon surmounted by a cannon and two griffins. More usually, his arms appear as Aragon quartered with Naples, in which the Neapolitan element, reflecting the city's past, contains the emblems of Hungary, Anjou and Jerusalem. In one of the last documents of his reign, dating from March 1458, his full regal style exceeded even his father's: 'Nos Alfonsus D.G. Rex Aragonum, Siciliae Citra et Ultra Farum, Valentiae, Hierusalem, Hungariae, Maioricarum, Sardiniae et Corsicae, Comes Barchinone, Dux Athenarum et Neopatriae ac etium Comes Rossilionus et Ceritaniae' ('We Alfonso, by God's Grace king of Aragon, of Sicily both before and beyond the lighthouse, of Valencia, Jerusalem, Hungary, Mallorca, Sardinia and Corsica, count of Barcelona, duke of Athens and Neopatria, and also count of Roussillon and Cerdagne').[99]

Alfonso's role as patron of the arts is the subject of differing opinions. 'No man of his day', wrote a later British consul at Barcelona, 'had a larger share of the quality called by the Italians "virtù".' He set his courtiers an example by carrying the works of Livy and Caesar on his campaigns, and by halting his army in respect for Virgil's birthplace. He was said to have been cured from illness by listening to Latin poetry, and the sycophants likened him to Seneca or to Trajan (both of whom were Iberian). On entering Naples, he set to work to turn it into a fitting rival for Florence or Venice. His sculptured portrait, attributed to Mino da Fiesole, hangs in the Louvre. Overall, however, the achievements of Naples' Quattrocentro Aragonese were relatively modest, especially under Alfonso's successors. According to Giorgio Vasari, 'the Neapolitan nobles value a horse more than a painter'.[100]

Alfonso's role as power broker was undeniably significant. Though Aragon had been an international player for two centuries, it rose in Alfonso's time to the first rank. An equal partner in the Iberian conglomerate, it also controlled a large slice of the Italian peninsula, and could exert great influence on the papacy. Possession of all the major islands of the western and central Mediterranean gave it an unrivalled hold on trade and shipping. Indeed, after Constantinople fell to the Turks in 1453, it was forced to take the lead in challenging Ottoman power. Alfonso was the chief patron of Skanderbeg, the Albanian warlord battling the Turks in the Balkans, and he even contacted distant Coptic Ethiopia with a view to forming an anti-Muslim alliance.[101]

In the opinion of Britain's leading historian of the medieval Mediterranean, Alfonso was a man of 'imperial vision' whose reign 'marks the high point of Aragonese influence', both 'within Spain and within the Mediterranean'.[102] Indeed, some of his plans which did not materialize were at least as significant as those which did. In 1448, for example, he captured the statelet of Piombino, including the island of Elba, aiming thereby to exercise greater control over Genoese shipping lanes, but he had also carved out a stepping stone into nearby Tuscany. If Alfonso had replaced the Medici in Florence at the height of the Renaissance, his name would be in every history book. As it was, all the other powers in Italy united against him and he was forced to desist. Even so, the scale of his ambition is clear. To a degree rarely admitted, he was the role model for his nephew, Fernando El Católico, who is conventionally given the sole credit for widening Aragon's horizons.

On Alfonso's death in 1458, Naples did not pass, like Sicily and the rest of the Crown of Aragon, to Alfonso's brother Juan II. In the first instance, it was bequeathed to Alfonso's bastard son, Fernando I, known as Don Ferrante (r. 1458–94). It then passed successively to Don Ferrante's son Alfonso II and grandson Fernando or Ferdinand II, and then to Don Ferrante's second son Frederico. After a brief French interlude it finally fell in 1504, like the other Crown lands, to the 'Catholic Monarchs'.

By far the longest of these Neapolitan reigns was that of the much underrated Don Ferrante, who presided over the kingdom for nearly forty years. Like his father, he possessed an inimitable mixture of courage, artistic gifts and Machiavellian ruthlessness. He also possessed a wife, Isabella of Taranto, whose dowry brought in a treasure chest of feudal claims and titles. As a result, he styled himself 'king of Jerusalem' as well as king of Naples, asserting authority over vengeful Angevins, rebellious barons and Turkish intruders alike. Don Ferrante's record bore stains and setbacks, not least the loss of Otranto to the Turks in 1480. Yet his survival during the international wars of the 1490s was proof of remarkable resilience.

*

Nothing better illustrates the international prominence of Aragon at this time than the extraordinary careers which turned an obscure Aragonese family into a household name. Borja is a small town in the province of Zaragoza, and a merchant family of that provenance was long established in Valencia. A law professor from the University of Lleida, Alfons de Borja (1378–1458), made a brilliant reputation for himself in Aragon's diplomatic service, and, thanks to his success in reconciling his master with the pope at the Council of Basle (1431–9), received a cardinal's hat. In Rome, as Cardinal 'di Borgia', he replicated the same success within the Church hierarchy, and was eventually elected pontiff as Pope Callistus III in 1455. Legend holds that he excommunicated the comet, later known as Halley's, which blazed through the skies in 1456. He quashed the judgment against Joan of Arc, and he filled Rome with Aragonese officials: his death in 1458, in the same month as Alfonso V's, sparked a riot against the hated 'Catalans'.[103]

The upward mobility of the Borgias, however, did not stop with his death. Pope Callistus had raised two of his Valencian nephews to the cardinalcy, thereby creating a powerful Borgia faction, notorious for its corruption and nepotism. One of these, Roderic Llançol de Borja (1431–1503), gained a grip on Church administration under five popes, and fathered a bevy of bastards whose interests and marriages he promoted with undivided zeal. In 1492, at a conclave swamped in gold ducats, he secured the throne of St Peter for himself, and as Alexander VI headed the papacy during its most unholy era. His pontificate was marked by the French wars in Italy, by the rise and fall of Savonarola in Florence, by zealous exploitation of the international indulgence scam (which triggered Luther's Reformation), and, in 1493, by the Bull of Donation which divided the New World between Spain and Portugal. Of his children, Giovanni, duke of Gandia, was assassinated; the much maligned Lucrezia was the source of lurid tales; and Cesare Borgia was said to be the model for Machiavelli's *Prince*.[104]

In the conventional view, the unified Kingdom of Spain was born at the end of the fifteenth century through the personal union of Ferdinand and Isabella. Thanks to that union, the ascendant Castilians are said to have exerted a dominant position over their declining Aragonese partners. This reductive interpretation ignores both the incremental steps whereby union was achieved and the very complex relationship between Castile and Aragon over many decades. From an Aragonese perspective, though the Castilians took over Aragon in 1412, the Aragonese

establishment gained ascendancy over Castile in the last quarter of the
century.

At the dynastic level, three distinct steps can be observed. In Step
One, following the installation of Fernando d'Antequera in Aragon in
1412, two branches of the Castilian House of Trastámara ruled Castile
and Aragon in parallel. In Step Two, which lasted for a quarter of a century after the marriage of Ferdinand of Aragon to Isabella of Castile in
1469 and the subsequent accession of each of the spouses to their respective kingdoms, Castile and Aragon were ruled in tandem by co-monarchs
forming a single political team. In Step Three, which began with Isabella's
death in 1504, the widowed Ferdinand added the regency of Castile to his
existing duties as the hereditary king of Aragon. (He was able to do so
because the only surviving child of the Catholic Monarchs, their daughter
Juana, had been judged insane, and incarcerated.) From that point on, he
and his successors reigned over the two kingdoms in full personal union.
But was Fernando El Católico/Ferran El Catolic Aragonese or Castilian?
The answer is that he was both. He was a prince of Aragon of Castilian
descent, who reigned for thirty-seven years in Aragon and for forty-six
years in Aragon and Castile jointly.

The prospects of the young couple had improved only gradually after
their marriage in 1469. They were both distressed by the many pains of
their parents' generation, and they set their minds on the benefits of
unification both in political and in religious affairs. They had signed a
prenuptial arrangement promising exact equality, their motto being
'*Tanto Monta, Monta Tanto, Ysabel E Fernando*' (Isabella and Ferdinand, it's all the same). Their device, drawn from their initials, was the
Y(oke) and the F(asces) – the ancient rods of authority. Following the
death of Isabella's half-brother in 1474, they became joint monarchs of
Castile, but not without their being denounced as usurpers. After the
death of Ferdinand's father in 1479, they added Aragon, Catalonia,
Valencia, Sicily and Naples to their portfolio.[105]

But for ten years, from 1462 to 1472, the kingdom-county was
wracked by civil war in which King Juan II battled against three successive pretenders: Enrique of Castile, El Impotente, Pedro V, constable of
Portugal, and René d'Anjou, count of Provence. Apart from being the
hereditary count of Provence René d'Anjou (1409–80) was duke of Lorraine, titular king of Jerusalem and the chief rival of the Aragonese in
Naples. For twenty years, after being ousted from Naples by Alfonso V,
he was a redundant royal looking for better employment. Fortune
finally smiled on him in the 1460s. The nobles of Catalonia had expelled

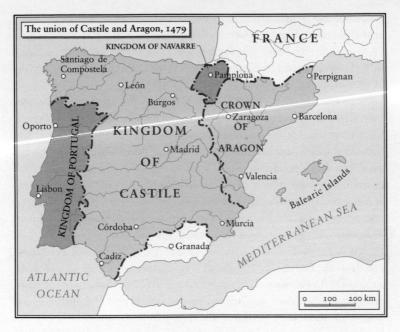

The union of Castile and Aragon, 1479

Juan II from the country, quickly followed by two hopeful 'anti-kings'. René was the third anti-king to be invited to take the throne. In practice, his 'reign' was a non-starter, and after sending his son to Barcelona to test the political climate, he sensibly stayed away. He retired to Aix-en-Provence where he devoted himself to the arts and to good works. He is known in Provençal and French history as 'Le Bon Roi René'. Memorial fountains have been erected to his name both in Aix and in Naples, but not in Barcelona. His tomb stands in the cathedral of Angers, the cradle of Angevin destiny.[106]

The troubles of the 1460s, often labelled the 'Catalan Crisis', have sometimes given rise to generalizations about 'the unexpected eclipse of the Crown of Aragon', about 'a society in retreat', and about Castile and Aragon being 'unequal partners'.[107] These judgements tell only one side of the story. There certainly was a period of vicious internal strife, and Barcelona in particular experienced steep economic decline.[108] But Castile was in uproar no less than Catalonia, and, within the Aragonese orbit, the decline of Barcelona was more than offset by the 'golden age' of Valencia and by the splendour of Naples. Commercial patterns seem to have adapted well to a fluid political environment. Catalan and Valencian merchants swarmed into Naples, and Aragonese traders protected by the Catalan Company retained an emporium as far away as the island of Aegina in Greece. The kingdom-county as a whole was by no means moribund. The leading specialist of the subject concludes, 'It was the sixteenth and not the fifteenth century that saw the decline of the Crown of Aragon.'[109]

Aragon's grip on its 'empire' started to slip after the turn of the century. Conditions in Italy had been transformed by the entry of French troops into Naples in 1495. Yet a papal coalition against the French and two royal deaths opened the way for Fernando El Católico's intervention. Based at the time in Sicily, his first thought was to partition the Neapolitan kingdom as a means of halting the French. But the victory of his general, Gonzalo de Córdoba, on the Garigliano (1502), rendered concessions unnecessary, and Naples then followed Aragon, Catalonia, Valencia, Sicily and Sardinia into united Spanish rule.

It was the Aragonese pope, Alexander VI, who dubbed Ferdinand and Isabella *Los Reyes Católicos*. The epithet was well deserved. In 1474, they had subjected their joint kingdoms to the *Santa Hermandad*, or Holy Brotherhood, a system of extra-judicial political and religious police. In 1482 they launched the all-Spanish Inquisition under the Dominican Tomás de Torquemada (1420–98). In 1492, after the fall of Granada, they expelled many Jews and Moors who refused to convert to Catholicism. Spain's religious zeal stood at the opposite end of the scale to that of the Vatican.[110] Nonetheless, the apparently wholesale expulsions of non-Christians were not unqualified. The policy aimed above all to separate converts from the unconverted, and many *conversos* continued to flourish. Having resisted conversion, many Muslim communities even stayed in place for a century and more. Luis de Santángel, a Jewish *converso* who had bankrolled Christopher Columbus, hired the Genoese ships which carried the expellees from the ports of Valencia and Catalonia. The great majority of them sailed to Naples, where they were welcomed by Don Ferrante and settled down in the Mezzogiorno, still under Aragonese rule.[111]

The early years of Ferdinand and Isabella's joint reign were marked by the last Iberian crusade against the Emirate of Granada, and by the expedition of Christopher Columbus 'to the Indies'. Both were completed in 1492–3.[112] Yet there was no move towards closer union. Indeed, the Castilians jealously guarded their monopoly on contacts with the Americas. The most important development in the kingdom-county was the establishment of a Council of Aragon to co-ordinate the affairs of the Aragonese 'empire'.[113] The Crowns of Aragon and

Castile were kept strictly apart. (One may compare Aragon's position to that of Scotland after the union of the Crowns with England in 1603; the monarch had left for greater things, but the 'auld kingdom' remained intact.)

Ferdinand, as king of Aragon, was also responsible for launching Aragonese historiography. The *Crónica de Aragón* (1499) of Gualberto Fabricio de Vagad was commissioned by him;[114] Lucio Marineo Sículo's *De Aragoniae Regibus et eorum rebus gestis libri V* (1509) provided a multi-volume tour of Aragon's past, real and imaginary, from the legendary eighth-century monarchs of Sobrarbe to the death of Alfonso V in 1458.

From 1494, Ferdinand was hard pressed to defend his dynasty. Carefully laid plans were going awry. Three of the royal couple's five children, including the crown prince, predeceased their mother. So, too, did their eldest grandson and heir. The fourth child, Juana la Loca, was mentally disturbed; and the fifth, Catalina, headed to disaster in England as 'Catharine of Aragon'. An ingenious solution was found by recognizing Juana's Habsburg husband, Philip the Fair of Burgundy, as heir apparent to the Castilian throne. But in September 1506 he died as well. In an ironical twist of fate, a few months before Isabella's death in November 1504, she and Ferdinand had been chosen to be joint emperors of the (defunct) Byzantine Empire.

Yet the worst anxieties were misplaced. The torrent of premature deaths did not carry off everyone. Despite Juana's mental illness, two of her sons, grandsons of *Los Reyes Católicos*, Carlos/Charles and Fernando/Ferdinand, grew to manhood. Both faced dazzling futures at the head of the Habsburg world. On the death of Philip the Fair, Habsburg Burgundy had passed to Carlos/Charles, his eldest son, who in 1516 also succeeded his grandfather in Castile and Aragon. Three years later he was elected Holy Roman Emperor as Charles V and became known to history as the 'emperor of the World'.[115]

Some people find the intricacies of dynastic politics tedious. To the medieval mind, they held prime importance. All the key decisions of Charles V's reign were underlain by the sheer unwieldiness of his inheritance. The first, in 1521, was to appoint his brother Ferdinand as acting emperor in Vienna; the second, in 1555, was to divide the Habsburg lands permanently and to limit the rule of his son Philip to the Spanish territories. But possession of large parts of the Americas gave the Castilian element greater weight in the conglomerate than all the other lands

put together. In 1516, when welcoming their presumptive co-king, the
Cortes of Castile made sure that Aragon was formally excluded from
the Americas. This selfish disposition was never rescinded.

In succession to Charles V, who abdicated in 1556, four kings from
the House of Habsburg mounted the throne:

Felipe II (Philip II), the Prudent (1556–98)
Felipe III (Philip III), the Pious (1598–1621)
Felipe IV (Philip IV), the Great (1621–65)
Carlos II (Charles II), the Bewitched (1665–1700)

Aragon made trouble for all of them. Philip II was the first in history to
use the title of 'king of Spain'.[116]

Old divisions persisted. Castile and Aragon were still in personal but
not constitutional union when their king was elected Holy Roman
Emperor. Yet the election did not make them a dependency of the Empire:
they remained, like Hungary, in the category of the emperor's non-imperial
territories.

After 1555, however, Aragon's predicament changed once again.
Indeed, as the Kingdom of Spain took flight, many historians talk as if
Aragon's story had finished. Such was not the case. The kingdom-county
lived on: it kept its separate laws and institutions, its languages and
traditions, and its cultural and commercial connections with its former
'empire'. And it repeatedly rebelled against Castilian presumptions.

Of Aragon's Italian possessions only Sardinia and Sicily stayed under
direct Aragonese control. Malta and Gozo were donated to the Knights
of St John in 1530.[117] Sardinia, 'the pearl of the Tyrrhenian Sea', escaped
Spain's close attention except as a naval base from which the Iberian
wool trade could be protected. Sicily stayed cut off from the rest of Italy.
Indeed, for a long time to come, Sicilians probably had more in common
with Catalans and Aragonese than with Piedmontese, Lombardi or
Tuscans.[118]

Malta, too, despite the severance of its direct link, continued to
exhibit strong Aragonese influences. From start to finish, Aragon made
a prominent contribution to the Hospitallers, whose religious ethos,
seafaring prowess and crusading traditions struck a common chord.
The Aragonese formed one of the eight *langues* or 'nations' into which
the knights were organized; the Auberge d'Aragon stands to this day as
one of the grand edifices of Valletta; and eight out of twenty-eight Grand
Masters of the Order in the Maltese period came from Aragon; the
escutcheon of Juan de Homedes (r. 1536–53) is carved into the keystone

arch of the city gate of Mdina. Most curiously, the centrepiece hanging above the altar in the chapel of the Langue d'Aragon in Valetta, a painting by Mattia Preti, shows a mounted St George slaying the Devil on the background of a medieval battle. The picture was long assumed to portray a battle-scene from the Holy Land. Recent conservation work, however, has revealed that it portrays the victory of El Puig, inflicted on the Moors in 1234 in the region south of Valencia. In other words, Preti had been commissioned to illustrate an episode in the foundation myth not of the Hospitallers, but of the Crown of Aragon.[119]

The separate identity of the Crown of Aragon was long preserved within Spain. Despite the dominance of Castile and the stream of centralizing measures flowing from the new capital in Madrid, Aragonese particularism continued to make itself felt right up to the early eighteenth century. Though the *Cortes* could only be convened by the king, the nobles maintained control over the *Diputación*, a representative body for preparing petitions, and the chief legal officer, the justiciar, could not be removed on the king's order. The *Fueros*, the corpus of Aragon's traditional laws and customs, was considered sacrosanct, and internal customs posts enforced the protective tariffs of Aragon-Catalonia's commerce. Under Philip II and his successors, the lands and people of the Crown remained proud and formally distinct until the day of its extinction.

Religion provided a source of regular trouble. The Spanish kings were eager to enforce religious uniformity, and remained dutiful supporters of the Holy Inquisition, which Ferdinand and Isabella had founded. For practical purposes, however, the Inquisition could not enforce its rulings in Aragon. The nobility was temperamentally indisposed to help; and many dissidents and suspects were able to evade investigation. At least one-third of the population of Valencia were *moriscos*, Moorish converts, whose conversion to Catholicism was barely skin-deep. In the eyes of Madrid, where central power now resided, the failure of the Inquisition to make headway against them was proof of Aragon's unreliability.

In 1582 royal troops were sent to Valencia without local agreement, and in 1589 the same thing happened in Ribagorça. But Philip II's displeasure with the Crown of Aragon came to a head through the obstinacy of a royal secretary of Catalan origin called Antonio Perez. Perez, facing a dubious charge of murder, fled prison in Madrid and on reaching Aragonese territory promptly appealed to the protection of the

Fueros. In particular, he claimed the right of a legal procedure, the *firma de manifestación*. The justiciar, Juan de Luna, ruled that Perez could not be extradited to Madrid. The viceroy was killed during violent demonstrations in Barcelona, and the king's patience snapped. An army of 12,000 men marched into Aragon. Perez was smuggled across the frontier into Béarn. The justiciar and twenty-one other officials were executed. The king then hypocritically reconfirmed the *Fueros*, and a sullen Aragon returned to the *status quo ante*.[120]

The subsequent experience of the Crown lands within the Spanish state was characterized by a long, uneasy truce punctuated by three more violent episodes. The first insurrection, known to Castilians as the 'Catalan Revolt' (1640–52) and to the Catalans either as the *Corpus de Sang* (because it broke out on the day of Corpus Christi) or as *La Guerra dels Segadors*, the 'War of the Reapers' (because the first person killed by the soldiery was an innocent reaper), was provoked by a prolonged period of oppressive taxation and by the forcible billeting of troops in the countryside. Local disturbances drew in a French army, which occupied northern Catalonia for years, and the resultant conflict cost Spain an enormous haemorrhage of blood and treasure over two decades. It was terminated by the Treaty of the Pyrenees (1659), when Rosselló and east Cerdanya were ceded to France as the price of peace.[121]

The second insurrection, between 1687 and 1697, was named the 'Revolt of the *Barretinas*' after the high-crowned berets worn by Catalan peasants. The complaints were much as before, but this time did not involve the towns and cities. Tensions rose after a peasant mob demolished the small port of Mataro, and three members of the *Diputación* were arrested in Barcelona for daring to lodge a protest against official reactions. French agents toured the villages, a rural militia was raised, military support arrived from Roussillon, and in the culminating phase Barcelona was ineffectively surrounded. Years of local raids and vicious reprisals preceded an inconclusive stalemate.[122]

The third insurrection, between 1700 and 1713, erupted in the context of the Franco-Spanish War over the Spanish Succession. Aragon, Valencia and Catalonia all declared in favour of the Austrian contender, 'Don Carlos' von Habsburg, and organized a self-governing federation. In their own eyes, they had taken to arms in defence of their ancient liberties. In the eyes of Madrid and of Versailles, they had mounted an intolerable defiance of monarchical rule. French and Spanish armies combined to reduce the rebels to obedience. Valencia was reconquered in 1707, and Aragon in 1708. Barcelona held out through two terrible sieges until September 1714.[123]

By then, further resistance was pointless, and compromise was impossible. The Treaty of Utrecht signalling the general European peace had already been signed. 'Don Carlos' had left for Vienna. The French candidate, Philippe de Bourbon, was already installed in Madrid as King Felipe V, and his officials were busy preparing the *Nueva Planta* or 'New Order', whereby uniform Castilian laws and practices would be introduced throughout Spain.[124] The Catalan separatists were totally isolated and capitulation was unavoidable. The French marshal-duke of Berwick marched in to install a military government. The pillars of the Crown's autonomy, the *Diputación* and the *Generalitat* of Catalonia, together with the mint and the university, were closed down; the system of provincial tariffs was abolished. Leaders of the 'rebellion' were executed or exiled, and a Spanish captain-general took command. The Catalan language was banned. Henceforth Castilian customs, Castilian speech and Castilian rule were to enjoy a monopoly. The name of Aragon remained as a little more than a Spanish administrative unit. The dying embers of the Crown of Aragon were extinguished for ever.

III

The 'Crown of Aragon' has not fared well on the fields of remembrance. Ultimately a loser in the competition with Castile, and a mere ghost in the nineteenth and early twentieth centuries, when most foundational historical works were compiled, it is a frequent absentee in the resultant narratives. It tends to be presented as 'a historical region of Spain', not, like its sometime counterpart, Portugal, as a sovereign state. As often as not, its legacy is treated with indifference, if not with hostility, and it is left as a codicil to the main Castilian story. Most Spaniards today have lost all sense of the Crown of Aragon's separate and extraordinary past.

The attitudes of those who might seemingly have the strongest interest in the subject give the greatest cause for reflection. For today's Aragonese and Catalans do not share a common outlook; the historic marriage of their two countries has dissolved into mental divorce. The Aragonese – inhabitants of the 'Autonomous Spanish Community' of Aragon – do not dance the *Joca Aragonese* in order to stress the historic link with Catalonia: quite the opposite. And for many Catalans, the very name of Aragon sticks in the throat. In place of the 'kingdom-county', monuments and textbooks in Catalonia refer to the 'medieval Catalan state', or to the 'Catalan Empire' or sometimes to some uniden-tified 'kingdom'. The concept of a multinational 'Crown of Aragon' is distinctly out of fashion. In academic circles, it is often replaced by the dubious neologism of the 'Catalan-Aragonese Federation'. Modern pol-itics, in fact, plagues almost all attempts to recall the Crown of Aragon with accuracy and affection. The dual kingdom-county, with its long chain of dependencies, lived and died long before the age of modern nationalism; and its ethos was ill matched to modern enthusiasms. Its memory has not been espoused by Spanish nationalism, by Catalan nationalism, nor even by provincial Aragonese particularism.

Memories of the former Crown of Aragon have in effect been carefully compartmentalized. People remember only what they want to remem-ber. They suffer from a lack of benevolent but impartial concern; and quarrels can be easily provoked. In the 1980s, for example, when the province of Aragon was seeking a new flag for the post-Franco era, it adopted a design based on the medieval standard of the Crown of Aragon,[125] where the Cross of St George is joined by the 'four carmine bars on a field of gold'. In Zaragoza, the design no doubt felt perfectly innocent and appropriate. In Barcelona, it caused outrage.[126] Protests and pamphlets proliferated. For, as every good Catalan knows, the 'car-mine and gold' belongs exclusively to the national flag of Catalonia, the *Senyera*, that was awarded to Wilfred the Hairy more than a thousand years ago. As the legend goes, the hirsute warrior was lying wounded on the battlefield. The Emperor Louis dipped his fingers in the count's own gore and drew four bloody stripes on the coverlet's cloth-of-gold. Aragon, at the time, had yet to be born![127]

Regional anthems aimed at restoring the identity of long neglected communities form another feature of post-Franco Spain. One might have expected a strong historical flavour, yet the lyrics adopted in provinces once belonging to the Crown of Aragon show little interest in the realities of the past. They may well be conditioned by animosities and inhibitions generated during the Civil War of 1936–9, and still not healed. As a result, they tend to reinforce the prevailing amnesia. In Catalonia, for example, '*Els Segadors*', 'The Reapers', has been raised from a popular song to an official hymn. Composed in the nineteenth century to recall the insurrec-tion of 1640, it breathes defiance against foreign domination, but has nothing to say about Catalonia's former Aragonese partner:

> *Catalunya triomfant*
> *Tornarà a ser rica i plena,*
> *Endarrera aquesta gent*
> *Tan ufana i tan superba.*
> > *Bon cop de falç!*
> > *Bon cop de falç,*
> > *Defensors de la terra!*
> > *Bon cop de falç!*

('Triumphant Catalonia / will return to wealth and plenty, / and will drive out those people / so mean and arrogant. / A good sickle's blow! / A good sickle's blow, / oh defenders of the land! / A good sickle's blow!')[128] One suspects that the Aragonese are now subsumed among 'those mean and arrogant' people.

In the Autonomous Community of Aragon, the official *Himno* combines an old melody with modern words, praising 'the flowers of our fields', 'the snowy peaks of our mountains', and the hopes and dreams for a future of freedom and justice. Yet its highly poetic lines contain not a single historical echo of the Crown of Aragon's ancient past:

> *Luz de Aragón, torre al viento, campana de soledad!*
> *Que tu afán propague, río sin frontera, tu razón, tu verdad!*
> *Vencedor de tanto olvido, memoria de eternidad,*
> *Pueblo del tamaño de hombres y mujeres, i Aragón, vivirás!*

('Light of Aragon, Tower in the Wind, Bell of Solitude! / Your confidence will spread, a river without bounds: so, too, your reason, your truth! / Victor over so much oblivion, memory of eternity, / a people of so many men and women, Aragon, you will live!')[129]

In Valencia, they still sing a *Himno* which has not changed since the regional Valencian Exhibition of 1909. Many consider the words to be redundant, but a recording made in 2008 by Plácido Domingo in both Castilian and Valencian has restored the anthem's fortunes:

> *Per ofrenar noves glòries a Espanya,*
> *Tots a una veu, germans, vingau.*
> *Ja en el taller i en el camp remoregen*
> *Càntics d'amor, himnes de pau!*
> > *Nostra Senyera!*
> *Glória a la Pátria! Visca Valencia!*
> > *Visca! Visca! Visca!*

('To offer up new glories to Spain / all with one voice, brothers, gather around. / In the workshops and in the fields / songs of love already resound, and hymns of peace. / Our Lady! Glory to the Fatherland, Long live Valencia! Viva! Viva! Viva!')[130]

And in Mallorca, the authorities have adopted a charming but incongrous song about a spider:

> La Balanguera misteriosa,
> Com una aranya d'art subtil,
> Buida que buida sa filiosa,
> De nostra vida treu el fil.
> Com una parca bé cavilla,
> Tixint la tela per demà.
> La balanguera fila, fila,
> La balanguera filerà.

('The mysterious Balanguera, / like a subtle and artistic spider, / empties and empties her distaff, / and draws out the thread of our lives. / Like fate she ponders well, / weaving the cloth for tomorrow. / The Balanguera spins and spins, / the Balanguera will always spin.')[131]

The musical landscape in Perpignan is necessarily rather different. The French Region of Languedoc-Roussillon has so far resisted the temptation of commissioning an official anthem. But several songs circulate as rousing examples of local patriotism. At *USA Perpignan*, they roar out the lines of '*L'Estaca*', 'The Stake'.* In the bars and in the backstreets of the festivals, the *Montanyes Regalades* or the *Montanyes de Canigou* float gently on the evening air. But the crowds predominantly speak French, and it is the French words of '*Le Hymne à la Catalogne*' that constitute the most frequent refrain:

> Perpignan, Perpignan,
> Chante, chante les catalanes.
> Perpignan, Perpignan,
> Danse, danse la Sardane!

---

* '*L'Estaca*' is a liberation song from the Franco era, composed in 1968 by the Catalan singer, Lluís Llach. It became popular in many countries, not least in Poland, where an adaptation by Jacek Kaczmarski – '*Mury*', 'The Walls' – caught on as the unofficial anthem of the Solidarity movement; anti-Fascist sentiments inspired anti-Communist lyrics. The key stanza reads: 'Wyrwij mury żeby krat, / Zerwij kajdany, połam bat. / A mury runą, runą, runą / i pogrzebią stary świat' ('Tear down the bars of the cage, / Snap the chains, and break the lash. / The walls will crumble, crumble, crumble / And hasten the old world's crash').

('Perpignan, Perpignan, / sing, sing to the Catalan girls. / Perpignan, Perpignan, / dance, dance the *sardane*!')[132]

Sometimes, it seems, history can best be invoked by dispassionate outsiders. Concluding his description of the Crown of Aragon, a foreign scholar strikes a note of serene resignation: 'The old stones are quiet now. They tell . . . of fighting and protecting and exploiting: of rural toil and herding: of praying and endowing: of trading and talking, and of links and aspirations across sunny seas.'[133]

5

Litva

A Grand Duchy with Kings
(1253–1795)

I

Belarus does not attract visitors. There are so few of them that the country fails to feature in the published International Tourism Rankings. One might be tempted to think that there is little to see, nothing of interest and no history worth mentioning. Yet Belarus, which for most of the twentieth century was known to the outside world as Byelorussia, is not boring; nor is it tiny or geographically remote. Its area of 81,000 square miles is similar to that of Scotland, Kansas or Minnesota, and prior to 1991 put it in sixth position among the fifteen republics of the Soviet Union. Its population, 10.4 million in 2007, is similar to that of Belgium, Portugal or Greece, Michigan or Pennsylvania: it is only one-third the size of its southern neighbour, Ukraine, but larger than the three Baltic States put together. Since 2004 it has been bordered by three states of the European Union, which in large part are separated by Belarus from its giant eastern neighbour, Russia. The capital Miensk, or Minsk, lies on Europe's main east–west railway line between Paris, Berlin and Moscow, or can be reached by direct flights from London Heathrow in around three hours.[1]

Low-lying and landlocked – surrounded by Lithuania, Latvia, Poland, Ukraine and Russia – Belarus has many rivers but no mountains. Its highest point at Dzyarzhynska Hara or 'Dzherzhynsky Hill' reaches a mere 1,132 feet (346 metres). Its main physical axis runs from southwest to north-east across the great European plain and along a section of the continental divide. All the rivers above the divide, the Nyoman (Nieman) and Dvina and their tributaries, flow to the Baltic; all rivers below the divide, like the Pripyat' and Berezina, flow south towards the Dniepr and the Black Sea.

The country's problems, patently severe, can best be summarized by four 'I's – Infrastructure, Image, Irradiation and, above all, *Istoriia*. As a

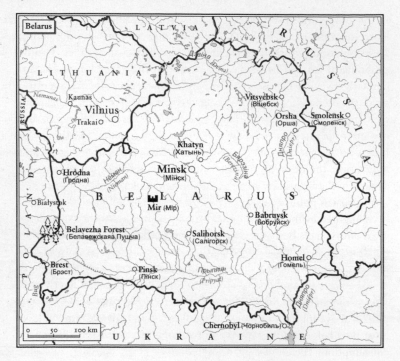

showpiece of the infrastructure, the Belarusian tourist industry can recommend no hotels in the higher international categories, no scenic routes
served by modern roads and service stations, and no holiday resorts.
Furthermore, despite some stunning tracts of primeval forest, this cannot be described as unspoiled territory.

On the surface at least, the capital Minsk is peculiarly uninteresting.
It was virtually levelled in 1944 during a frontline German–Soviet
battle, which caused horrendous loss of life, and the ruins were then
repopulated by rootless migrants, mainly Russians. Its Soviet-style urban
design emphasizes extra-large boulevards with little traffic, grandiose
public buildings for officialdom, and shoddy, decaying tower blocks for
the populace.

The overall image of Belarus, in fact, is catastrophic. It scores lower
than all other European countries in almost all fields. In the most recent
(but somewhat out-of-date) Quality of Life Index available (2005), where
Ireland came top and Zimbabwe bottom, Belarus occupied the 100th
place out of 111. In the Corruption Percentage Index (CPI, 2007), it was
150th out of 179, and in *The Economist*'s Democracy Index (2007), it

is the only entirely European country still classified as 'Not Free'.[2] Three-quarters of its Soviet-planned economy remains in state hands. Its population, which steadily rose in the post-war decades, is now declining. It is ruled by the pseudo-democratic dictatorship of Alexander Grigoryevich Lukashenko, which analysts place in the none too savoury company of other ex-Soviet regimes in Azerbaijan, Uzbekistan or Kazakhstan.[3] The official languages are Russian and Belarusian, but the latter operates at a severe disadvantage. Lukashenko, like the rest of the ex-Soviet elite, normally speaks only Russian in public. Confusion reigns over the question whether his name should not be written and spoken in the Belarusian form of 'Alyaksandr Lukashenka'.

Belarusian publicity makes no secret of the fact that the country has been blighted by the nuclear disaster at Chernobyl in April 1986. Indeed, great efforts have been made to inform the world about the damage and the costs. Chernobyl's deadly, Soviet-era reactor lies just over the border in Ukraine, but 75 per cent of the radioactive fallout drifted north, and it was Belarusian villages, Belarusian agriculture and Belarusian children which bore the brunt. The by-products of the 1986 explosion will remain active for hundreds of thousands of years. Half a century at least must pass before all fish, fungi and forest berries will be fit for human consumption. The closure of the offending reactor is nowhere in sight.[4]

The misfortunes of Belarus, however, did not begin in 1986, but recurred with painful monotony throughout the last century. The Byelorussian National Republic (BNR) of 1918, which emerged from the collapse of the Tsarist Russian Empire, was crushed by the Bolsheviks. In the 1930s up to 60 per cent of the native intelligentsia was killed in Stalin's Purges; the mass-murder site in the Kuropaty Forest near Minsk between 1937 and 1941 has still to be properly investigated.[5] In 1941–5, during the German occupation and the accompanying Holocaust, one-quarter of the entire population perished. Post-war ethnic cleansing caused the exodus of similar numbers. Soviet reconstruction was slow, and Marshall Aid was excluded.[6] Quite apart from the terrible human costs, these multiple tragedies have resulted in many Belarusians having a weak sense of their national identity.

So 'Lukashenkism' can only be rated as the country's most recent blight; it is the product of what political scientists might call 'failed transition'. The politico-socio-economic system of the USSR collapsed in the 1990s, and was not replaced by a viable alternative; Lukashenko (b. 1954) rocketed to power by filling the vacuum. In 1991 he had been a man of purely local consequence, an ex-officer of the Soviet border guard and director of a *sovkhoz* or 'state collective farm', but not a prominent member of the ruling Communist Party. He came to notice as the only deputy of the Byelorussian SSR's last assembly to vote against the abolition of the Soviet Union, and gained his foothold on power by heading a corruption commission, which promptly discredited the country's first post-Soviet leaders. Within three years, he was president.

In four terms of office – in 1994–2001, 2001–6, 2006–10 and from 2010 to the present – Lukashenko has calmly created a legal dictatorship, achieving his goals through a dubious referendum, a purpose-built constitution, and a hand-picked legislature. A police state operates, the 'president's men' enforcing obedience at all levels. The opposition is harassed. The media are shackled. Foreign protests are ignored. Western governments are courted for investment, but not for advice. In short, the president-dictator does as he likes. Fifty new 'universities' are busy training the cadres that will project Lukashenkism into the future, while several parts of the University of Minsk can only function in exile.[7] Careless talk characterizes the president as 'a would-be Putin with no missiles and no oil'; it is not a good comparison, and it underestimates his tenacity.[8] His henchmen call him '*Batka*', the 'Daddy of the Nation'. Their slogan proclaims: *Batka* Is, *Batka* Was and '*Batka* Will Be.' 'My position and the state will never allow me to become a dictator,' he says of himself, 'but an authoritarian ruling style is my characteristic.'[9]

Immediately after 1991, Belarus was taken to be a straightforward, Russian-controlled puppet state. It was (and apparently still is) the capital of the Commonwealth of Independent States (CIS), which was formed to replace the Soviet Union and to preserve Russian supremacy in a less inflexible form. In 1996, at least in theory, Belarus entered economic union with Russia, aiming to produce a customs union and a common currency within twelve years. In 2002 it even began talks on a Russian proposal for constitutional union. But none of these schemes came to fruition. Instead, they have been supplanted by a series of ever intensifying rows about 'unpaid debts', oil prices and gas supplies, and in general about Lukashenko's disinclination to dance to the Kremlin's tune. Relations deteriorated to the point of being at best ambiguous. Then in a sudden reversal, the 'Last Dictator' travelled to Moscow in 2010, in advance of a looming election, mending his fences and announcing that the oil-price dispute had been settled.[10]

The European Union was no happier with Belarus than Russia was. Lukashenko has proved resistant to all overtures for meaningful dialogue, always insisting that he will not accept 'the imposition of alien values from outside'. Protracted discussions preceded the reluctant acceptance of Belarus as a member of the EU's Eastern Partnership, inaugurated in May 2009. The Partnership complements the Union for the Mediterranean, which deals with the EU's neighbours in North Africa and the Middle East; it aims to promote good governance, energy security, environmental protection and co-operation on common issues of trade, travel and migration.[11]

The presidential election of December 2010, therefore, took place amid considerable uncertainty. In the run-up to the elections, President Dmitri Medvedyev of Russia fired off a broadside, accusing Lukashenko of repeatedly breaking his promises; among other supposed offences, he had failed to recognize the independence of Abkhazia and South Ossetia, and had granted asylum to the ousted Kirghiz president, Bakiryev. In an article entitled 'Batka Stoops To Blackmail', *Russia Today* lamented an incident in which Russia's threat to cut off oil to Belarus had apparently been countered by a Belarusian threat to cut off electricity to Kaliningrad.[12] Outside observers concluded that Russia was losing patience. Then, early in 2011, came the Wikileaks scandal. No less than 1,878 of the leaked cables related to Belarus; in a cluster dating back to 2005 American diplomats characterized Belarus as 'the last outpost of tyranny' and 'a virtual mafioso state'.[13] But Batka had little to fear. In the polls of 19 December, he had been officially declared to have received 79.7 per cent of the votes.[14] Opposition candidates, who had been allowed to stand, were beaten up afterwards by the police. Demonstration were followed by arrests. Diplomats from neighbouring countries reckoned that Lukashenko had probably lost, but he continued on his way unruffled. In an appearance on the state STV television channel, he surprised his audience by breaking into fluent Belarusian, introducing his elderly mother and courting popularity.[15]

In recent years, the thesis that dictatorships are vulnerable to the growth of new communications and technologies has gathered widespread support. The Green Revolution in Iran in 2009, the ousting of Ben Bella from Tunisia in 2010, and the revolt against President Mubarak in Egypt in 2011 have all been held up as instances where a repressed opposition mobilized itself by cellphones, Facebook and Twitter. A future-technology specialist argues the opposite case. According to Evgeny Morozov, all dictatorships control access to the Internet and possess active cyber-departments to protect their interests. The democratic character of the Net, he says, is a delusion. Morozov is Belarusian.[16]

*

Even so, the Internet offers a wealth of information about Belarus that was not available when the state came into being. Readily accessible websites list a host of attractions for hardy souls who are considering a visit, and they give a flavour of what awaits. A government-sponsored site follows six headings: Jewish History, Castles and Churches, World War II, Nature, Agro- and Eco-Tourism, and 'Healthcare Tourism'. The Jewish link informs readers that Marc Chagall, Irving Berlin and Kirk Douglas all came from Belarus, but does not suggest any places to see in connection with them. The 'World War II' link recommends the Soviet-era Belarusian National War Memorial at Khatyn (*sic*),[17] and the Soviet memory site at the fortress at Brest.[18] The 'Nature' link mentions only one of the country's six national parks, and advises people hoping to explore the Belavezha Forest to approach it via Poland. 'Do not expect a five-star service anywhere,' it warns, but 'you can swim in any lake or river without lifeguard whistling at you'. Under 'Agro-Tourism', visitors are urged to watch the harvesting of extremely unlikely local foods 'such as coconuts, pineapple, or sugar-cane'. Under 'Healthcare', one learns that 'Dentistry is lately on the rise in Belarus'. But only one spa is named, at the salt caverns of Salihorsk.[19] Most recently, winter skiing has been introduced. The National Ski Centre is at Logoisk, which has a partner at Silich Mountain. Each resort possesses one hotel.[20]

'The medieval martial castle' of Mir, some 60 miles to the south-west of Minsk, turns out to be 'the main architectural symbol' of the country.[21] It is also the seat of the national school of architectural conservation, and it well repays the journey. A splendidly illustrated English-language guidebook awaits, showing the castle in all seasons. In 2000, one learns, the castle complex was included in the UNESCO Register of World Heritage Sites.[22]

The position of the castle on a low mound and surrounded by a lake enhances the illusion of fabulously colossal proportions, as it looms over the water and the lush meadows. Its brick-and-stone battlements were constructed round a broad, interior courtyard, but the most prominent aspect is provided by tall octagonal towers that rise at the four corners, and by the central, fortified entrance gate approached over a bridge. It is the colours, however, that make the most immediate impression. The three-storey palace wing is plastered white, with red brick sills and ribbing; the entrance gate and two of the corner towers are faced with red brick interspersed with white panes and false windows, the roofs tiled in a brighter shade of orange-red that stands out magnificently against the blue sky of the summer's day or, in winter, against the deep snowdrifts. In autumn, the leaves of the park change colour to match the battlements. Sunsets at Mir are a photographer's dream.

As presented by the guidebook, however, the account of the castle's historical development needs some unscrambling. The settlement was first noted in chronicles in AD 1395, 'in connection with the unsuccessful campaign to Novogrudok of the crusaders'. For 'crusaders' read 'Teutonic Knights'. 'The Grand Lithuanian Duke Sigismund ... granted Mir to his courtier, Simeon Gedygoldovich' in 1434. So the Lithuanians ruled here. Construction of the present edifice started in the early sixteenth century. Since then, this monument to 'Gothic-Renaissance architecture' 'has remained in original form'.[23] One might expect either Gothic or Renaissance, but generally not both.

The guidebook also stresses the multi-ethnic and multi-religious character of the local community. Jews were engaged in commerce. Tartars dealt with leather-dressing. 'Belarusians' were engaged in craftsmanship. Gypsies traditionally bred horses. (The grand duke even made Jan Marcinkiewicz 'king of the gypsies'.)[24] The market square once sheltered 'Orthodox and Roman Catholic Churches, a Mosque, and a *Yeshiva* with Synagogue'. The church of 'Saint Trinity' (its walls painted in a warm shade of magnolia: the onion-domes in bright blue) became 'the Uniate Church of Basilian Monastery in 1705' and later 'an Orthodox church again', though no explanation is offered. The market square is now called '17 September Square', 17 September 1939 being the date when the Soviet Union entered the Second World War.

The guidebook states how 'the towers of Mir have withstood the rushes of the conquerors with honour', but it does not identify the onrushing conquerors by name (it could have listed the Prussians, the Poles, the Russians, the French of Napoleon, the Germans and others). The most recent private owners, from 1891 to 1939, are named as the 'Dukes Sviatopolk of Mir'. Their family mausoleum, built in 1904 by 'a well-known architect from St Petersburg', still stands in the park.[25]

One of the historic monuments not usually mentioned on the websites for foreigners is the manor of Dzyarzhynovo, formerly Oziembłów, in the Minsk region. Renovated in 2004 and opened by Lukashenko in person, this 'Historico-Cultural Centre' – a modest, timber-built, three-storey house on the edge of a forest – was the birthplace of Feliks Dzierżyński, founder of the Bolshevik secret police, the Cheka, author of Lenin's 'Red Terror', and one of the most fearsome figures in East European history. Its renovation at the start of the twenty-first century says much about Lukashenko's views and tastes.[26]

Visitors may be surprised to learn that the Lithuanian frontier is close to all these places in western Belarus. Indeed, given a free run at the customs post, a trip to Vilnius, Lithuania's capital (which the Belarusians call Vil'nya), can easily be undertaken in a day. The trip is highly recommended, if only because the culture shock is tremendous. Many Westerners were led to believe that all the countries of the Soviet bloc were grey and uniform Russian clones. Today, one sees a different reality. Lithuania is Catholic; Belarus is either Orthodox or non-religious. Lithuanians speak a Baltic language; Belarusians a Slavic tongue, somewhere between Polish and Russian. Lithuanian is written in the Latin alphabet, Belarusian in Cyrillic. Above all, Lithuania is a member of the European Union, and the material gulf between the neighbours is widening rapidly.

The mental gulf between the two countries is already next to unbridgeable. Twenty years ago, both Lithuania and Belarus formed part of the Soviet Union; each of them today looks at their past from diametrically different perspectives. Shortly after crossing the Lithuanian border, a red flag by the side of the road marks the entrance to the Isgyvenimo Drama, an attraction billed as 'Europe's Strangest Theme Park'.[27] A turning into the forest leads to a vast underground bunker built in the 1980s to house Soviet-Lithuanian television in case of nuclear war:

> Soviet anthems blare out from a creaking old radio, the few striplights that are working flicker maddeningly, and damp swarms over the walls like triffids . . . 'Forget your past! Forget your history! A colossal bullfrog of a guard in an olive-green uniform is spitting at us in Russian, while a huge Alsatian strains at the leash' . . . 'Welcome to the Soviet Union,' snarls the guard. 'Here you are nobody' . . .
>
> We are given mouldy overcoats that are so damp that they are almost liquid, and a cup of Soviet coffee with no coffee in it . . . The bullfrog gives us our orders; we will answer only in the negative or the affirmative: dissent will be punished with beatings and solitary confinement; and we will forget all thoughts other than the glory of the socialist paradise in which we now live. We stand to attention for the hoisting of the red flag, then down we go into the freezing cold. For three hours, we are humiliated, interrogated, forced to sign false confessions, shown propaganda, and taught to prepare for an attack by the imperialist pigs.
>
> Having failed to answer correctly in Russian, I get [the answer] repeated in broken, angry English. The interrogating KGB officer pushes me against a filing cabinet, and prods me in the chest, hard. 'You are English? English spy! English spy!'[28]

The aim is to make people feel what the Soviet Union was really like. 'Someone always faints,' the director explains; 'it's very easy to break people's will.' In neighbouring Belarus, where memories of the Soviet Union are still respected, this sort of exhibition is unthinkable.

Most visitors will need assistance to find their way round this geographical and historical maze. Assistance is again to hand on the Internet:

> Who are the Belarusians, anyway? What is this strange country – Belarus – which appeared on the map a few years ago, [and which] used to be called Belorussia, Byelorussia or even White Russia?
>
> Most people in the West don't even know that Belarus exists, that it has a language of its own and that it has its own history and culture. It is much more convenient to call everything between Brest and Vladivostok 'Russia'.
>
> One of the great misfortunes of the Belarusians is indeed the fact that their country's name sounds like 'Russia' ... Ukraine, for example (which is ... similar in culture and language), is in a somewhat better position. Most people probably now realise that Ukraine is an independent state and nation.
>
> Unfortunately, Belarus is still not taken seriously ... Many people believe that the Belarusians never had a state of their own ... Few people know about the existence of the Grand Duchy ... the medieval Belarusian state ... the heyday of the Belarusian nation.
>
> Belarusian history is not an easy subject to study ... One comes across several different versions which contradict each other – the Russian version, the Polish version, the Lithuanian version, the Soviet version and finally the Belarusian version. Belarus is a country [whose] history has been rewritten and falsified so many times that it is difficult to tell who can be believed ... Now, after the collapse of the Russia-dominated Soviet Union, it is finally possible to publish the Belarusian version and a number of books have appeared which deal with the contentious issues ... Unfortunately they are all in Belarusian and have not been translated ...[29]

In which case, a brief *tour d'horizon* may not be out of place. This country possesses hidden histories that rarely escape into the outside world.

II

One of the few things that can be said for certain about Europe's prehistoric peoples is that they all came from somewhere else. Northern Europe, in particular, had to be completely repopulated after the last Ice

Age, 10,000 or 12,000 years ago. Repopulation could only be effected by migrants. None of Europe's modern nations are genuinely native.

This injunction must surely be true even of the Baltic peoples – the Lithuanians, Latvians, ancient Prussians and others – who arrived in the northern parts of the European peninsula long before the historical record. By general scholarly consent, the Lithuanian language represents the oldest European branch of the Indo-European linguistic family.[30] The presence of the Balts definitely preceded the advent both of the Finnic peoples, whose ancestors drifted out of Eurasia some 2,000 years ago, and of the Slavs, who followed in the wake of the Germanics at various times during the first millennium AD.

Understanding of the processes of prehistoric settlement has latterly been considerably refined. In the nineteenth century prehistoric migration was conceived in brutal, pseudo-Darwinian terms. In the conflicts between migrant tribes and the sedentary population, the winners took all, and the losers were driven out or obliterated. Such was the conventional picture that was painted, for example, about post-Roman Britain after the arrival of the Anglo-Saxons.

Nowadays, the consensus has shifted. Migrations took place, of course, but they did not necessarily involve wholesale expulsions or mass slaughter; more usually, they caused a high degree of ethnic mixing and cultural assimilation between the incomers and their predecessors. Now that DNA can be tested, it has been discovered that the overwhelming majority of people in England are biologically descended from the pre-Anglo-Saxon and even pre-Celtic populations. One has to conclude that most of the indigenous inhabitants survived the migrations, while changing their language and culture, possibly many times.[31]

Similar issues arise in relation to the land which, to maintain an impartial air and to avoid anachronistic modernisms, may be called by the convenience label of 'MDL' (see below). The initial ethnolinguistic mix was made up of Balts, Slavs, Finnics and Germanics. All were pale-skinned, northern Europeans. All except the Finnics spoke languages of Indo-European origin. The territory was bounded in the north-west by the Baltic Sea, in the south by the vast marshland drained by the Pripyat' – the Pripet Marshes – in the west by the Vistula basin and in the east by the watershed of the upper Volga.

In ancient times, indeed until quite recently, rivers bore an importance which is often forgotten. The carriage of people and goods was far easier by water than overland, especially in spring and summer. So human settlements tended to develop on the banks of navigable rivers, and at points where access could be gained from one river system to another. The MDL was well supplied by several such interfluvial routes. The Nieman and the Dvina rivers flowed into the Baltic. The Dniepr network flowed to the Black Sea, the Volga network to the Caspian. The area where these networks converged was especially attractive for prehistoric travellers and traders.

The formation of the future state, however, needs to be considered in a slightly wider context, partly because the ethnic mix varied from district to district, and partly because three distinct habitats can be identified. The Baltic coastland was the first. It was exposed to the raids of the Vikings from the ninth to the twelfth century, and later to the seaborne inroads of Danes, Germans and Swedes. The second habitat, lying immediately behind the coast, had been formed by the last great ice cap, and contained a dense jumble of rocky, morainic ridges covered with lakes and dense forests. It was peculiarly impenetrable, and sections of it became the natural fortress of undiluted Baltic settlement. The third habitat, further inland, can be described as the 'Land of the Headwaters'. It was accessible, especially by river; it possessed attractive agricultural potential; and it became the natural meeting-place of Balts, Finnics, Germanics and Slavs. This was to be the MDL's heartland.

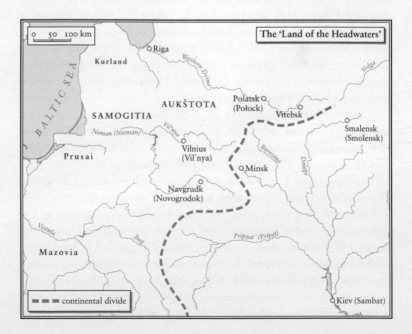

Each of the ethnolinguistic groupings consisted of numerous tribes, and the names by which they were known have generated enormous controversies. In the case of the Baltic group, for example, conventional modern nomenclature places 'Prussians' in the south-west, 'Lithuanians' in the middle and 'Latvians' in the north-east. Yet the Prussian label became attached to the Baltic Prussians' Germanized successors. The origins of the Lithuanian label is disputed by their Slavic neighbours, and the Latvian label did not emerge until the modern age. The Finnic group impinged only marginally. The Slavic group, in contrast – or at least the East Slav group – did adopt a generic name: *Rus'*. Unfortunately, debates about the roots of Rus'-Ruthenia-Rossiya-Russia have filled miles of shelving, and nomenclatural cacophony flourishes.

Chronology is vital. At the start of the second millennium, one is dealing with an age when Moscow had not even been founded, and when a Moscow-led 'Russian state' lay very far ahead. Baltic tribes inhabited much of the coastland, all of the Lakeland, and large parts of the 'Land of the Headwaters'. For the time being, the forest zone to the east, which was to become Muscovy's base, was inhabited by Finnic tribes, which called it *Siisdai*. The East Slavs were slowly expanding from an area further south, colonizing the valley of the great river which the ancient Greeks had called the Borysthenes, the Byzantines the Danapris, and the Slavs the Dniepr. They were to form the largest body of inhabitants in the region, having been left behind when their West Slavic kinsfolk moved off towards the Vistula and Elbe, perhaps in the fifth or sixth century AD, and the 'Yugo' or South Slavs began their trek towards a distant destination in post-Roman Illyria. Throughout most of the first millennium all these groups were pagan.[32]

Sometime before the end of the millenium, however, Scandinavian adventurers, known as Vikings in the West and as Varangians in the East, succeeded in establishing a regular trade route between the Baltic and Black Seas, using the 'Land of the Headwaters' as the critical point of passage. Their favourite porterage, over which Viking longships could be hauled for 15–20 miles, lay between the sources of the Dvina and the Dniepr. What is more, they built a number of forts to protect their landings and staging-posts; the forts attracted Slavic settlers, and the settlers submitted to the rule of Scandinavian overlords. They called their network of forts the *Gard – grad/grod/gorod* being the Slavic word for town or fort. In the south, beyond the Dniepr rapids, a wide area along the Black Sea coast was held by the khanate of the Khazars, a Turkic people whose lands stretched as far as the Caspian; the Varangians

would have had to pay tribute to the Khazars to reach open water and
to trade with Byzantium.

Such were the circumstances in which the East Slavs adopted the
name of *Rus'*. The derivation of the term is obscure, although it is often
related to a word for 'ruddy' or 'red-haired', as the Varangian overlords
could well have been. *Rus'*, at all events, became the name of the country. *Ruski* was the country's Slavonic language, and *Rusin* (m.) and
Rusinka (f.) were names for the inhabitants. Byzantine Greeks translated *Rus'* as *Rossiya*; *Rusin* was the derivative for the Latin terms of
Ruthenus and *Ruthenia*.

The oldest of the Varangian settlements, Holmgard, was founded
c. 860 by a chieftain called Hroerekh on the shore of Lake Ilmen, close
to the Gulf of Finland. The most northerly of the forts, Alaborg, lay on
Lake Ladoga; the most easterly at Murom near the Volga, and the most
southerly at Sambat on the Danapris, close to the existing Slavic settlement of Kiyiv (Kiev). The most westerly fort, which appears in the
Scandinavian sagas as Palteskja and entered the historical record in 862,
lay on the upper reaches of the Dvina. The Slavs, quite naturally, used
their own vocabulary and name systems. They knew Hroerekh as Rurik,
Holmgard as Novgorod, that is, 'new fort', and Palteskja as Polatsk.
Their nomenclature has obliterated all Norse forms.

In that same era, other important population shifts were taking place.
Slavic tribes, notably the *Kryvichi* and the *Dragovichi*, migrated from
the south, mingling with Balts in the fertile 'Land of the Headwaters'.
Their arrival was accompanied by agricultural advances and by linguistic
changes. Some linguists hold that a Balto-Slavic language was created;
others content themselves with the occurrence of a complex interaction
of Baltic and Slavic idioms. But none would contest the fact that the
Balto-Slavic collision created the characteristic phonological and lexical
features which gave a distinct identity to the emerging 'headwaters variant' of *ruski*.[33]

Here, one must note the contentious issue of the name of 'Litva'.
According to scholars of the Baltic persuasion, *Litva* was always and *ab
origine* the generic label used by the Baltic tribes living in their Lakeland
fastness. In its modern spelling, written as *Lietuva*, it is the modern
Lithuanian name for Lithuania. According to scholars of the Belarusian
persuasion, however, *Litva* was originally the homeland of a Slavic
tribe, and had no connection with the Balts until the Balts moved south,
absorbed the Slavic tribe and purloined its name.[34] The tribe in question
lived in a district in the upper reaches of the River Nieman, where

another fort, a 'Little Novgorod' was built. In the absence of credible information, one cannot say whether this fort began as a Varangian, a Baltic or a Ruthenian foundation. Its Slavic name appears in a variety of forms including Navahrudak, Novogrodok and Nowogródek.

Statehood reached the region before Christianity did. Three principalities emerged from the Varango–Slavic–Baltic encounters and each was connected with the same Rurikid dynasty. One was at Novgorod, where Rurik died in *c*. 879. A second was at Kiev, which was conquered by Rurik's son, Oleg. The third was at Polatsk on the River Dvina. All of them figure in the oldest of the East Slav chronicles, the *Povest' Vremennych lat* ('The Story of the Years of Time').[35] Centuries later, when the East Slavs became differentiated into separate nationalities, their foundation stories were to be fiercely contested. But at the risk of oversimplification, Kiyiv/Kiev was the main centre of the southern part of East Slavdom, in a region that would later be called Ukraine; this Kievan Rus' long exercised hegemony over the others. Novgorod, where a splendid mercantile republic was to develop, belonged to the north-eastern part of East Slavdom, that is, to 'Great Rus'. And Polatsk in the north-west planted the political seed which, with the important involvement of the Balts, would grow into the 'MDL'.

Two words of warning need to be issued. One concerns the East Slavs, and the other, the Balts. In the ninth, tenth and eleventh centuries, when Kievan Rus' was at its apogee, the area to the north-east of Kiev, the so-called *Zalesskaya Zemlya*, the 'Land beyond the Forest', had still not been absorbed. In so far as the upper valleys of the Ugra, Oka and Moskva rivers were inhabited, they were dominated by a block of Finnic settlement that for a lengthy period separated Kievan Rus' from places such as Suzdal, Yaroslavl and Rostov. Early Rus' was a world without Moscow, and, more importantly, without the self-centred theories of history which the Muscovites would later invent and impose.

The presence of Baltic tribes living west of Polatsk is well attested both from archaeology and from passing reference in their neighbours' chronicles. Yet as Slavic migration undermined their monopoly on the 'Land of the Headwaters', they retreated into their lakes and forests, shunning subsequent developments. They customarily divided their homeland into the *Zemaitis* or 'Lowland' on the coast, and the *Aukštota* or 'Upland' of the interior. The tribes of the former, known in Latin as *Samogitia*, bordered the Prussians, and the frontier zone with the Poles. They long maintained a separate identity, and one tribe, the *Sudovians* (in Polish, the *Jaćwings*), showed signs of creating their own statelet.

The Upland, in contrast, remained aloof. It was destined to stand out as Europe's last pagan stronghold.

The earliest arrival of Christianity in the region occurred in the late tenth century, and bore consequences far beyond the realm of religious practice. In its first phase, it transformed the Slavic communities, but not the others. The Balts were untouched; Scandinavia still bowed to the Old Norse Gods. The Khazar khanate, predominantly Muslim, was ruled by an elite that eccentrically adopted Judaism.[36]

Kievan Rus' had long been in contact with Byzantium, and it was the Greek Orthodoxy of the Byzantine Empire that gradually infiltrated the East Slavs. A century earlier, the Byzantine missionaries, Saints Cyril and Methodius, had developed both an alphabet and a composite language, known respectively as Cyrillic and as Old Church Slavonic, to facilitate the conversion of the Slavs. Their efforts had borne early fruit among the Bulgars, a Slavicized Turkic people living on the Black Sea coast close to Constantinople.[37]

Nonetheless, religious conversion was nowhere a simple matter, and the Rurikid ruling houses of Rus' were not easily detached from their Varangian roots. The Kievan Prince Ingvar, whom the Slavs called Ihor or Igor, had a Christian wife, the sainted Olga (Helga). He built a fleet of ships that terrorized all parts of the Black Sea; after twice besieging Constantinople, he entered into formal diplomatic relations with the Empire, but consistently rejected his wife's pleas to accept her religion. His death in 945 was described by a Byzantine chronicler. He had attempted unwisely to exact tribute twice in the same month from one of his subject tribes. The tribesmen captured him, bent two birch trees double, and tied his legs to the tips of the trees; then they let them spring back to their full height.[38]

It is impossible to say how exactly the Rurikids viewed their Varangian ancestry, or whether they cultivated their Norse gods in order to distance themselves from their Slav subjects. Over time, their 'Norseness' would have been diluted. Svyatoslav, son of Ingvar and Olga, seems to have been the first of the line whose Slav name does not also appear in a Norse form in any source.

Ingvar's grandson, Valdemar/Volodimir (r. 980–1015), was born illegitimate, and therefore had marginal chances of scooping the dynastic jackpot. Yet he surmounted all obstacles. Raised at the feet of his Christian grandmother, the Regent Olga, he was sent from Kiev to rule over Novgorod, and in the war of succession that followed his father's death in 972, he seems to have called on his Scandinavian kinsmen, notably Haakon Sigurdsson of Norway. First, he invaded Polatsk, killed its ruler, Rogvolod, and carried off Rogvolod's daughter, Rogneda. Then, victorious over his brothers, he re-entered Kiev, settled down as ruler of a reunited Rus', and took Rogneda as his bride. His name in the Old Church Slavonic of the chronicles was Vladimir – meaning 'World-Ruler'.

The most portentous event of Vladimir's reign occurred in 988. Having sent out envoys to observe all the religions of the day, the 'World-Ruler' rejected Latin Catholicism, Islam and Judaism, and decided to introduce Christianity into his land in its Byzantine form. The envoys who had attended the Mass in St Sophia's cathedral in Constantinople had reported: 'We knew not whether we were in heaven or on earth.' Christian missions were then sent to the different parts of Rus'. An Orthodox *eparch*, or metropolitan bishop, was installed in Polatsk in 992.

In the next generation, the Rurikid dynasty splintered again. Prince Izyaslav (d. 1001), son of Vladimir and Rogneda, returned to his mother's home of Polatsk to re-establish the ruling line of so-called *Rogvolodichi*. Kiev and Novgorod passed to his brother, Yaroslav the Wise, between whom and the rest of Vladimir's brood a complicated fratricidal feud broke out. As a result, Polatsk was able to break away to become an independent political entity. Novgorod did the same slightly later. In due course, Rus' was divided into seven or eight separate principalities.

Between the eleventh and thirteenth centuries, the Principality of Polatsk under the descendants of Rurik governed the 'Land of the Headwaters' in north-west Rus' without serious interference. It was subdivided into five dependent 'lands' – Polatsk (Polotsk), Smalensk (Smolensk), Turaŭ (Turov), on the Pripyat', Chernigaŭ (Chernigov), which bordered Kiev, and Navahrudak (Novogrudok), which bordered Aukštota. At some point, it lost control of Smalensk, whose ruler emerged as an independent prince. Like all the nascent principalities of medieval Europe, it spent much time warring. There were campaigns to the east against Pskov and Novgorod, conflicts to the south with Kiev, and constant skirmishes with the Balts to the north-west. In this context, the chroniclers begin to record the presence of a people described as 'Lituvins'. The first mention occurs in the German Quedlinburg Chronicle in an entry for 1009. Modern Lithuanians regard this date as their entry into history.[39]

In those same centuries, further headway was made in the grounding of the Orthodox Church. St Efrosinia of Polatsk (*c.* 1120–73) was an abbess, bibliophile and church-builder; her bejewelled cross, plundered

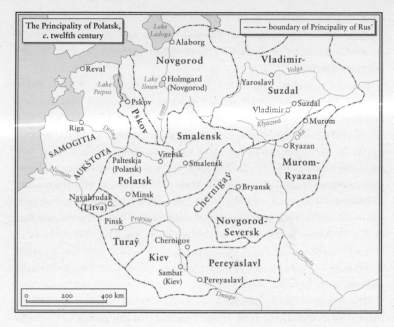

during the Second World War, was long regarded as the supreme treasure of local art.[40] She died on pilgrimage to Jerusalem, and her church of St Saviour still stands. Her contemporary, St Kiryl of Turaẙ (c. 1130–82) was a monk, a bishop, a famous preacher and the author of prayers that are still in use.[41] Smalensk was home to an icon of great antiquity traditionally attributed to St Luke.[42]

One may assume that people in Polatsk would have heard of the founding of *Moskva* (Moscow), which occurred in 1147 some 300 miles away. Yet they would have had little reason to regard it as a major event in their lives. Moscow was just one of several cities newly founded by Yuri Dolgorukiy, prince of Vladimir-Suzdal, whose writ did not run in the Land of the Headwaters. The political loyalty of the citizens of Polatsk was quite separate from that to which the infant Moscow belonged. Their ecclesiastical obedience was to the metropolitan of Kiev, who in turn owed allegiance to the patriarch of Constantinople. At that stage of their history, the different parts of Rus' were set on centrifugal courses.

In the thirteenth century two external dangers appeared whose impact was to be lasting. The first was the Teutonic Knights, a German crusading order that had assumed the mission of converting the Baltic pagans. The second, the Mongol Horde of Genghis Khan, galloped out of Central Asia into the heart of Europe. The principalities of Rus' were caught between the two.

German crusaders landed on the Baltic coast at the very start of the century. Their fort at Riga, founded in 1204, served as the base for their northern province of Livonia, the *Terra Marianna* ('Land of the Virgin Mary'). Their southern province of Prussia, founded in 1230, became the base for operations driving eastwards towards Samogitia and Aukštota (see pp. 339ff.). Before long, the Knights controlled access to the sea via the estuaries of the Nieman and the Dvina, and the leaders of Polatsk, Novgorod and Vladimir felt sufficiently threatened to take common action. Prince Alexander Nevsky (1220–63) of Novgorod had already made his name battling the Swedes on the River Neva; in 1242 he and his allies won a still more spectacular victory over the Teutonic Knights on the ice of Lake Peipus. He is regarded nowadays as Russia's most popular hero.[43]

The Mongol Horde attacked when Alexander Nevsky was heavily embroiled in the north. Tens, if not hundreds, of thousands of nomadic horsemen rode out of the steppe into the ill-defended borders of eastern Rus'. Moscow was totally destroyed in 1238, less than a century after its foundation. Kiev suffered the same fate in 1240. The Horde stormed on through Poland, razing Kraków, and cutting down the assembled knights of Silesia. Tribute was exacted by the Mongol khan from all parts of Rus' that his riders could reach, and Alexander Nevsky was obliged to submit to the Horde for confirmation of his titles.

The twin threats from north and south produced a predictable reaction from the lands caught in the middle. The Baltic tribes of Samogitia and Aukštota, under pressure from the Teutonic Knights, found common cause with the Orthodox Christian princes of Polatsk. At this distance, it is impossible to tell whether the Baltic party simply attacked their weakened Ruthenian neighbours and annexed their land, or whether something closer to a voluntary merger was engineered. The well-established Principality of Polatsk need not have been razed and destroyed in the manner of Moscow and Kiev. It is more likely that the constituent districts of the principality submitted successively to Baltic overlords, until a point was reached at which the new overlords gained a controlling interest.

However it came about, the key figure henceforth is best identified as the 'High King' Mindaugas (1203–63), otherwise Mindoug or Mendog, who was crowned in 1253 with the German-derived title of *konung*. He could not have attained this position without the benefit of a preceding period of state-building. Recent scholars have emphasized that the Baltic tribes had been organizing military formations, tax collection and manorial enterprises for at least a century.[44] One of them proposes 1183 as the date when the new Baltic state was launched. Another suggests that Mindaugas, though originally a pagan warrior, had fought as a mercenary in the land of Navahrudak, had converted to Orthodox Christianity, and had then used Navahrudak as a power-base for further expansion. His religious elasticity was notorious. At another time, he was baptized into the Catholic faith, and later abandoned it. Yet he was certainly strong enough to attack Novgorod in the early 1240s, and, following his repulse, to pick off Polatsk, Vitebsk and Minsk in turn. His coronation must have been the culmination of a series of political and military triumphs. As a sign of his enhanced dignity, his entourage gave him the same status of 'grand duke' or 'grand prince' that Alexander Nevsky had recently negotiated for himself from the Mongols, and they called his new state the Grand Duchy of Litva. In the practice of the Ruthenian scribes, the name was usually shortened to VKL: 'V' for *Vielkie* or 'Grand', 'K' for *Knyaztva* or 'Duchy' and 'L' for *Litvy*. In the practice of Latin scribes, VKL was transcribed as MDL, and Litva was translated as 'Lithuania': *Magnus Ducatus Lithuaniae*.

The name Belarus – or some earlier form of it – also came into currency in this same era. Its literal meaning of 'White Ruthenia' is not in doubt, but its derivation has been the subject of endless speculation. Most plausibly, 'white' had the connotation of a free territory, and 'black' that of territory that was occupied, or tribute-paying. It certainly fits the circumstances. White Ruthenia was the only part of Rus' to stay free of the Mongol yoke. The name of *Czarnorus'* or 'Black Ruthenia', which became attached to the Land of Navahrudak, might conceivably be explained in the same way, since it was probably the first part of the Principality of Polatsk to be occupied by the Balts.

The territory of the grand duchy in this earliest emanation was roughly equivalent to a combination of present-day Lithuania and present-day Belarus, and the creation of the new state dealt a heavy blow to the idea of a united Rus'. White Ruthenia parted company from eastern Rus' for many centuries, developing along different lines and acquiring a separate identity. Its imminent reunion for a long spell with Kievan/Ukrainian Ruthenia would give the Belarusians and Ukrainians much in common, and would project the expanded concept of 'Litva'

far beyond its modest Baltic origins. At the same time, in the late thirteenth century, that new state was entering a cultural and political
sphere which was quite foreign to Mongol-controlled Moscow.

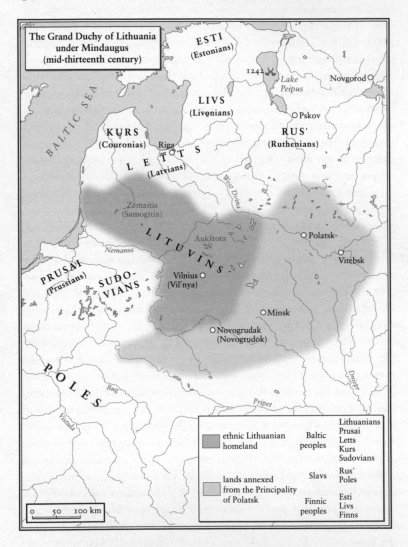

The Grand Duchy of Lithuania under Mindaugus (mid-thirteenth century)

	Baltic peoples	Lithuanians Prusai Letts Kurs Sudovians
ethnic Lithuanian homeland		
lands annexed from the Principality of Polatsk	Slavs	Rus' Poles
	Finnic peoples	Esti Livs Finns

Once the grand duchy had been established, its particular characteristics would probably have caused less surprise to its subjects than to
outsiders. A caste of pagan warriors held sway over a predominantly
Christian population that had adopted its Orthodox ties nearly three

centuries earlier. Vestal virgins tended the sacred flame in oak groves, while Christian preachers strove alongside them to inculcate a totally different religion and culture. Christianization had been in progress in Europe for more than 1,000 years; as it proceeded, all public manifestations of paganism were generally suppressed. But circumstances in the MDL did not conform to a simple pattern. The arrival of Orthodox Christianity had indeed led to the suppression of the Norse and Slavic variants of paganism. Nevertheless, resistance was protracted; the Balts of the region were not yet affected; and memories of former beliefs must surely have lingered on. Such memories would have functioned in a setting where the paganism of the late Varangian elite probably differed little from the dying Slavic paganism of the populace at large. Pagan practices often went underground or morphed into pseudo-Christian rituals, and the supposedly Christianized people of early White Ruthenia may have passed through several generations during which the continuing pagan religion of their Baltic neighbours would not have looked particularly strange or offensive. Hence, when a Baltic warrior caste stepped into the Varangians' shoes, there was no violent reaction.

The Ruthenians' acceptance of Baltic overlordship would have been strengthened by the growing opportunities for territorial expansion and military adventure. At the time of the coronation of Mindaugas, the Mongol Horde ruled supreme at all points to the south. In the following decades, however, Mongol power declined; the 'Golden Horde' settled far away on the lower Volga; and Ruthenian princes were tempted to stray, their temerity varying in proportion to their distance from the Mongols' revenge. The Muscovites, for instance, did not make their decisive bid for freedom until the 1380s. But the princes of southern Ruthenia, in Ukraine, grew restless a century earlier, when the fading of Mongol control created a vacuum into which the warriors of the grand duchy charged with alacrity. Under Grand Duke Gediminas (r. 1316–41), they reached Kiev for the first time, ruling it for several decades in conjunction with the Tartars. In addition, a broad band of territory was annexed stretching from Podolia and Volhynian Lutsk on the Polish border to Chernigov and Bryansk on the confines of Muscovy. Brest on the River Bug was captured, together with the district of Polesie beyond the Bug.

Gediminas is generally taken to have been the founder of the grand duchy's capital, although it may well have been built on the site of the unidentified Voruta, the principal residence of Mindaugas. According to legend, he had been hunting on the borders of Baltic and Ruthenian settlement and had a dream in which he saw an iron wolf howling on the top of a hill; a shaman told him to erect a castle on a nearby bluff overlooking three rivers. The wooden castle was soon surrounded by houses and streets running down to the River Vilnya. Its earliest mention in the historical record dates from 1323, soon before the grand duke invited foreign traders and craftsmen to live there. Municipal rights on the model of Magdeburg were granted six decades later. For the grand duchy's original Baltic elite, the city's name was *Vilnius*: for the Ruthenians, *Vil'nya*, like the river: for the Poles, who would soon arrive in force, *Wilno*.[45]

Under Grand Duke Algierdas (r. 1345–77), the tempo quickened. Algierdas, one of Gediminas's seven sons, was a pagan warrior chief par excellence, who appears to have maintained internal peace by dividing his dominions with his brother, Kestutis. He battled the Teutonic crusaders and the Tartar hordes with equal enthusiasm, and twice besieged Moscow. Although held posthumously to have been a champion of Orthodoxy, his marriage to an Orthodox princess, Maria of Vitebsk, had no special significance. In 1349 the lands of 'Red Ruthenia' – so-called because they centred on the 'Red Town' of Chervien – were divided with Poland. And in 1362, at the Battle of the Blue Water near the Black Sea coast, the supremacy of the Mongol-Tartar Horde was broken for good. The consequences were immense. The grand dukes of Litva took over Kiev permanently, absorbing the southern expanses of Ukraine and putting themselves in a position to influence the metropolitan of Kiev, the highest authority of the Orthodox Church in East Slavdom. In the course of a century of raiding, of castle-building and of rewarding their followers with handsome lands, they came to govern a state that was larger than either France or the Holy Roman Empire, and was going to grow still further.

The city of Kiyiv/Kiev was the most ancient and most venerable in the whole of Slavdom. Legend attributes its foundation to the year AD 485, when the valiant Kie and his brothers set up their homes on three adjacent hills beside the Dniepr. In that remote era the various Slavic peoples were as yet undifferentiated. Thanks to modern politics, however, the city of Kiev is more usually associated in people's minds with 'ancient Russia' than with medieval Lithuania; indeed, it is frequently billed as 'Russia's birthplace'. So a word of clarification may be in order. When the grand duchy overran it in 1362, the city was a shadow of its former self; its population had greatly declined, and the metropolitan himself was living elsewhere. The cathedral church of St Sophia founded by Yaroslav the Wise, together with its 'indestructible wall', which depicted the Virgin Oranta in golden mosaics, was still intact. But recovery from the Mongols' ravages had been slow, and the city's political importance was minimal. Nonetheless, the so-called 'Lithuanian occupation', which was to last for more than 200 years, was no fleeting episode; and it was undertaken by a successor state to Kievan Rus' whose rule was perfectly acceptable to most contemporaries. One cannot judge medieval events by the teleological standards of a Russia that had yet to be created.

Muscovy also stood to reap its rewards from the Mongols' retreat. Following the example of Algierdas, the ruler of Moscow, Dmitri 'Donskoy', was expanding his frontiers towards the Don, and preparing to form a coalition of eastern princes that would throw off the 'Mongol yoke' for ever. In this way, Moscow and the grand duchy became rivals to inherit the legacy of a divided Rus'.

Despite the waning of the Mongolian threat, however, the grand duchy knew little respite, for the Teutonic Knights were still on the march. Having subdued Prussia and Livonia, the Knights were entering a long period of hostility and intermittent conflict with Poland; their greedy crusading eyes also descended on the defiant paganism of the Lithuanians. The strategic grounds for a rapprochement between the grand duchy and Poland grew ever more apparent.

Unlike most monarchs of the age, the grand dukes of Litva, not being Christians, naturally exhibited no special preference between Catholicism and Orthodoxy, and they married their daughters to Catholic or to Orthodox princes as convenience dictated. Yet a view has persisted that Grand Duke Gediminas in particular had been grooming his court and country for conversion to Roman Catholicism; it is supported by the phraseology of a letter which Gediminas wrote to the pope in 1322 and which contains an expression of his readiness '*fidem catholicam recipere*'. A recent study, however, concludes that the grand duke's intentions were strictly limited. The letter was sent in a tricky international phase when he was fighting fiercely against the Catholic Teutonic Order and, at the same time, seeking assistance from Catholic Poland. Gediminas was assuring the pope that he was not anti-Catholic, and that, as a gesture of goodwill, he would admit Dominican and Franciscan missions; but he was not considering wholesale conversion.[46] Indeed, he may well have hoped that the Vatican might abolish the Teutonic Order in the way that it had abolished the Knights Templar. Gediminas did not hesitate to execute Catholic priests judged to have insulted the pagan religion, and his own funeral in 1342 displayed all the features of traditional ritual.

The grand duke's body was placed on an open pyre. His favourite servant and his favourite horse were cast into the flames to accompany their master, and a group of German slaves, bound and gagged, were heaped on top for good measure. Algierdas, too, departed this life like his father, with no hint of Christian sensitivities.

Religious life in Litva, therefore, was far from straightforward. On the surface, there appeared to be a high degree of tolerance. Muslim Tartar communities were welcomed. So, too, were Jewish Karaites from Crimea, and special provisions were made for Catholic knights to marry the daughters of the grand duke's pagan entourage. Under the surface, however, there were ugly tensions. In 1347, when Vilnius was still a pagan capital, three Christian Ruthenian brothers – Anthony, John and Eustaphy – were put to death for some minor insubordination. These three 'Vilna Martyrs' were duly revered by the Orthodox faithful, and their relics preserved in the Trinity church.[47]

When Grand Duke Jogaila (r. 1377–1434) mounted the throne still a bachelor, he knew that any marriage he might make would be overshadowed by strategic considerations. He had no special love for the Poles, worshippers of 'the German God' and a target for his raiding parties. His first inclination was to explore the possibility of marrying a princess from Moscow. Yet in 1382 a prime opportunity occurred. Louis of Anjou, king of Poland and Hungary, died suddenly without male issue; Louis's younger daughter Jadwiga (or Hedwig) was designated by the magnates of Poland as the prospective successor and *rex*:

> In 1385, as soon as Jadwiga arrived in Cracow, the Lithuanian matchmakers made their first approaches. A conjugal and a political union were proposed. It was a decisive moment in the life of two nations . . . The Polish barons, too, had their reasons. After thirteen years of Angevin rule, they were not now disposed to submit to the first man, who by marrying Jadwiga, could impose himself on them. [Further] having rejected Louis's elder daughter, Maria, on the grounds that she was [betrothed] to Sigismund of Brandenburg, they could hardly accept Jadwiga's present fiancé, Wilhelm von Habsburg, Prince of Austria . . . The Lithuanian connection was much more interesting. Jadwiga could be told to do her duty. Maidenly and ecclesiastical reticence could be overcome.
>
> On 14 August 1385, therefore, at Kreva (Krewo) in White Ruthenia, an agreement was signed, in which the Polish barons persuaded Jogaila to concede a number of very advantageous undertakings. In return for the hand of Jadwiga, the Lithuanian prince was ready to accept Christian

baptism, to convert his pagan subjects to Roman Catholicism, to release all Polish prisoners and slaves, to co-ordinate operations against the Teutonic Knights, and to associate the Grand Duchy of Lithuania with the Kingdom of Poland in a permanent union. On this basis, in February 1386 a great assembly of Polish barons and nobility at Lublin elected Jogaila, whom they knew as 'Jagiełło', as their king.[48]

The grand duchy was embarking on a Polish–Lithuanian orientation that would accompany it for as long as it lasted. 'For four long generations spanning 186 years, Jogaila and his heirs [would drive] the Kingdom of Poland and the Grand Duchy of Litva in harness, like a coach-and-pair. They presided over an era when the Lithuanian and Ruthenian elite [would be] polonized, and the Poles [would accede] to the problems of the east.'[49] For much of that time it appeared that the Jagiellons were building one of Europe's strongest monarchies.

The consequences of the Union of Kreva were felt more immediately in the grand duchy than in the Kingdom of Poland. The pagan religion of the Lithuanian elite was prohibited. The sacred groves were felled. The pagan priests and vestal virgins were banished, and mass Christian baptisms were enacted in the River Vilnya on the orders of the now Catholic monarch. Henceforth, Roman Catholicism became the official religion of court circles in Vilnius, and increasingly of the more ambitious nobles. Adopted by a substantial minority of the grand duchy's population, it existed in uneasy cohabitation with the Byzantine Orthodoxy of the majority. At the same time, traditional political culture was undermined. In theory, the grand duke lost none of his autocratic powers; in practice, he was obliged to grant wide privileges to influential subjects, who quickly learned the habits of their more rebellious Polish counterparts.

The minting of coinage, however, has traditionally been one of the marks of sovereignty, and the grand duchy was no exception. Until recently, it was thought that the first coins could be dated to the early fourteenth century, but analysis of a major hoard discovered in the grounds of the lower castle at Vilnius has confirmed that the first minting took place under Jogaila in 1387. The triangular silver alloy *kapros*, which at first sight appear to be more primitive and older, actually date from the fifteenth century. Henceforth, the coinage regularly bore the emblem of the grand duchy – the mounted rider known as the *vytis* or *pahonia* – which has continued in use to the present day.[50]

Jogaila's cousin Vytautas (1350–1430) caused constant trouble in the grand duchy for decades. Already disaffected before the Union with Poland, he was imprisoned in the castle of Kreva, during negotiations there with the Poles, won the sympathy of many *boyars*, that is, of senior members of the grand ducal entourage,* escaped and took refuge with the Teutonic Knights; he may even have toyed with the idea of an alliance with Muscovy. But he was lured back to obedience by Jogaila, signed the Union of Kreva, accepted baptism and actively supported the Christianization campaign. Shortly afterwards, however, he fell out with Jogaila yet again, this time over the grant of the Duchy of Trakai to someone else. He fled once more to Prussia, and remained the focus of dissent throughout the 1390s. Only defeat by the Tartars tamed his opposition, and thanks to the Vil'nya-Radom Act of 1401 (see below) he was able to emerge as Jogaila's partner and near-equal, running the grand duchy while Jogaila ran the kingdom. In 1408, he recovered Smalensk at the third attempt before loyally leading the grand duchy's army into battle alongside the Poles. Nonetheless, he jealously guarded Lithuania's separate status for a further thirty years, gaining the epithet of 'Vytautas the Great' and becoming an international figure. He received the obeisance of Tartar khans and Russian princes, exacted rich tribute from Novgorod, and conducted diplomatic relations with both the pope and the German emperor. At the time of his death in 1430, news spread that he had been planning to have himself crowned as 'king of Lithuania'.[51]

The death of Vytautas led first to civil war and then to reconciliation under the main branch of the Jagiellonian dynasty. The civil war lasted throughout the 1430s as Jogaila's brother battled with a brother of Vytautas, while the Teutonic Knights did their best to meddle. At one point, it was announced that the grand duchy had been annexed by Poland. Yet Jogaila's passing defused tensions. One of his young sons, Władysław III (r. 1434–44), took the throne of Poland under the guidance of the great Cardinal Oleśnicki, who dominated the royal court, while Jogaila's younger son, Kazimierz Jagiellończyk (1427–92), was brought up to rule the grand duchy. In the end, weary of bloodshed, the *boyars* of Litva acclaimed the thirteen-year-old Jagiellończyk grand duke in 1440 without seeking Polish approval. Their choice proved judicious. The young prince grew into one of the great father-figures of

---

* *Boyar* meaning 'warrior' is a term that can be found in Kievan Rus', in the grand duchy and later in Muscovy. It refers to a military elite who over time also formed the circle of the prince's senior political advisers.

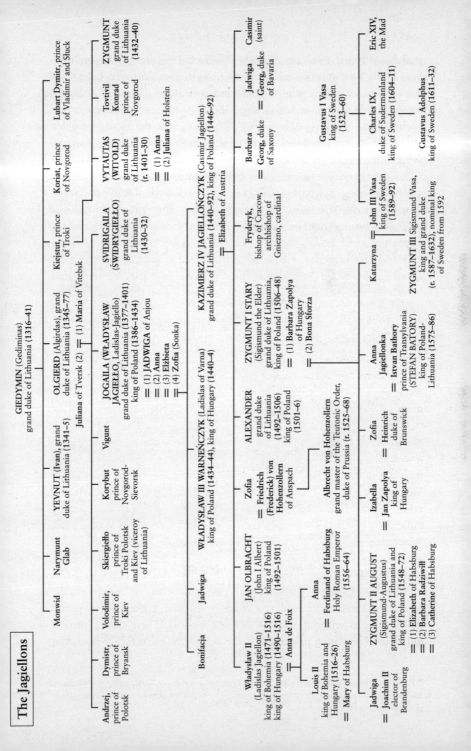

The Jagiellons

GIEDYMIN (Gediminas) grand duke of Lithuania (1316–41)

Children:
- Monwid
- Narymunt Glab
- **YEVNUT (Ivan)**, grand duke of Lithuania (1341–5)
- **OLGIERD (Algirdas)**, grand duke of Lithuania (1345–77) = (1) Maria of Vitebsk; Juliana of Tversk (2)
- Kiejstut, prince of Troki
- Koriat, prince of Novgorod
- Lubart Dymitr, prince of Vladimir and Shuck

Next generation:
- Andrzej, prince of Polotsk
- Dymitr, prince of Bryansk
- Volodimir, prince of Kiev
- Skiergiełło prince of Troki Polotsk and Kiev (viceroy of Lithuania)
- Korybut prince of Novgorod-Sievorsk
- Vigunt
- **JOGAILA (WŁADYSŁAW JAGIEŁŁO, Ladislas-Jagiello)** grand duke of Lithuania (1377–1401) king of Poland (1386–1434)
  = (1) JADWIGA of Anjou
  = (2) Anna
  = (3) Elżbieta
  = (4) Zofia (Sonka)
- **SVIDRIGAILA (ŚWIDRYGIEŁŁO)** grand duke of Lithuania (1430–32)
- **VYTAUTAS (WITOLD)** grand duke of Lithuania (r. 1401–30)
  = (1) Anna
  = (2) Juliana of Holstein
- Tovtivil Konrad prince of Novgorod
- **ZYGMUNT** grand duke of Lithuania (1432–40)

Next generation:
- Bonifacja
- Jadwiga
- **WŁADYSŁAW III WARNEŃCZYK (Ladislas of Varna)** king of Poland (1434–44), king of Hungary (1440–4)
- **KAZIMIERZ IV JAGIELLOŃCZYK (Casimir Jagiellon)** grand duke of Lithuania (1440–92), king of Poland (1446–92) = Elizabeth of Austria
- Barbara = Georg, duke of Saxony
- Jadwiga = Georg, duke of Bavaria
- Casimir (saint)

Children of Kazimierz IV:
- **Władysław II (Ladislas Jagiellon)** king of Bohemia (1471–1516) king of Hungary (1490–1516) = Anna de Foix
- **JAN OLBRACHT (John I Albert)** king of Poland (1492–1501)
- Zofia = Friedrich (Frederick) von Hohenzollern of Anspach
- **ALEXANDER** grand duke of Lithuania (1492–1506) king of Poland (1501–6)
- **ZYGMUNT I STARY (Sigismund the Elder)** grand duke of Lithuania, king of Poland (1506–48)
  = (1) Barbara Zapolya of Hungary
  = (2) Bona Sforza
- Fryderyk, bishop of Cracow, archbishop of Gniezno, cardinal

Children of Władysław II:
- **Louis II** king of Bohemia and Hungary (1516–26) = Mary of Habsburg
- Anna = Ferdinand of Habsburg Holy Roman Emperor (1556–64)

Child of Zofia:
- Albrecht von Hohenzollern grand master of the Teutonic Order, duke of Prussia (r. 1525–68)

Children of Zygmunt I Stary:
- Jadwiga = Joachim II elector of Brandenburg
- **ZYGMUNT II AUGUST (Sigismund-Augustus)** grand duke of Lithuania and king of Poland (1548–72)
  = (1) Elizabeth of Habsburg
  = (2) Barbara Radziwiłł
  = (3) Catherine of Habsburg
- Izabela = Jan Zapolya king of Hungary
- Zofia = Heinrich duke of Brunswick
- Anna Jagiellonka = Istvan Bathory prince of Transylvania (**STEFAN BATORY**) king of Poland-Lithuania (1575–86)
- Katarzyna = John III Vasa king of Sweden (1589–92)

Child of Katarzyna and John III Vasa:
- **ZYGMUNT III** Sigismund Vasa, king and grand duke (r. 1587–1632), nominal king of Sweden from 1592

Swedish Vasa line:
- **Gustavus I Vasa** king of Sweden (1523–60)
  - Eric XIV, the Mad
  - **John III Vasa** king of Sweden (1589–92)
  - Charles IX, duke of Sudermanland king of Sweden (1604–11)
    - Gustavus Adolphus king of Sweden (1611–32)

medieval Europe. He added the throne of Poland to his position in the grand duchy after his crusader-brother was killed by the Turks at Varna in 1444, and, by marrying a Habsburg, was able to place his numerous sons and daughters in positions of influence far and wide. Apart from rescuing the Polish-Lithuanian Union, he oversaw the rise of Jagiellons to the thrones of Bohemia and Hungary. Indeed, for a time in the late fifteenth century, the prospects of the Jagiellonian dynasty looked considerably stronger than those of their Habsburg relatives.

Notwithstanding stresses and strains, therefore, the dual state proved more resilient than many had feared. It adjusted to successive crises, its constitutional structures evolving accordingly:

> The [Act] of Kreva was abrogated by Jadwiga's death [in 1400], but the political arguments which inspired it remained operative throughout the Jagiellonian era. On every occasion that difficulties arose, the Polish-Lithuanian Union was renewed on terms of ever increasing intimacy . . .
>
> The first stage [had been] effected in 1401. As Jogaila and Jadwiga were childless, it was necessary to design the machinery of a future succession. Meeting in their separate camps at Radom and Vilna the Polish and Lithuanian barons agreed that nothing should be decided in future without mutual consultation. In the so called 'Vilna-Radom Act', Jogaila's cousin Vitautas (Witold) was to rule Lithuania for life . . . If Jogaila were to die without natural heirs, the future of his two realms was to be determined by common assent.
>
> The second stage was effected in an agreement signed at Horodło in Volhynia on 2 October 1413. Here, in effect, the Polish lords and Lithuanian boyars formed themselves into a joint estate. Among the many provisions it was agreed that matters of concern touching both countries should be settled in joint assemblies of the nobility, and that the Polish lords should participate in the electoral confirmation of the Lithuanian Grand Duke . . .
>
> Most remarkable, however, was the spirit in which the agreements were reached . . . The Polish nobility were obtaining a permanent stake in the internal affairs of their partners: the Lithuanians were receiving a guarantee of the separate identity of their state. Cynics would say that in such circumstances it is easy to be noble-minded. Even so . . . the words of the Preamble to the Act of Horodło are worth noting: '*Whoever is unsupported by the mystery of Love*', it began, '*shall not achieve the Grace of salvation . . . For by Love, laws are made, kingdoms governed, cities ordered, and the state of the commonweal is brought to its proper goal. Whoever shall cast Love aside, shall lose everything.*' In later times, when a weakened Polish-

Lithuanian state became ... the prey of stronger enemies, these words served ... as a reminder of the Union's high founding principles.

Thus the Polish and Lithuanian nobility looked forward to the future with confidence. To all intents and purposes, they became one, political nation. Henceforth, to be 'Polish' was to be a citizen of the Polish-Lithuanian state.[52]

One persistent nuisance to the security of the united polity continued to be posed by the Teutonic Knights. Despite the fact that the crusaders' original *raison d'être* had vanished with the conversion of Lithuania, they doggedly defended their power and sought to extend the Order's lands. Most descriptions of the wars between the Teutonic Order and Poland-Lithuania view them as a simple clash between Prussian and Polish interests. Conventional interpretations of the great battle at Grunwald in 1410, at which the Order was decisively defeated (see pp. 346–7), provide a good example. Yet the grand duchy's priorities necessarily diverged from the kingdom's. The 'Great War' with the Knights (1409–22) certainly brought Poland and Lithuania closer, but in matters of foreign policy and military preparedness, the grand duchy had to reckon with other issues relating to Livonia, Muscovy and Crimea which affected the Poles only tangentially.

After 1418 Livonia evolved into an unusual confederation of mini-states, less than half of which was occupied by the Livonian province of the Teutonic Order. It was joined in the greater part by the four self-governing bishoprics of Riga, Courland, Ösel and Dorpat. A Livonian Diet regularly convened at Walk (a town which today is divided between Valka in Latvia and Valga in Estonia), and was dominated by a Germanized nobility. The fragmented character of the confederation reduced its capacity for offence. Nonetheless, it was the nearest foreign state to Vilnius, and it had to be watched at all times.[53]

Muscovy aroused fears that were by no means confined to its growing military strength. Having extracted the lands of the eastern Rus' from the Mongol yoke, it grew in power and prestige, and by gaining control of the Republic of Novgorod by stages, it became the equal of the grand duchy in terms of inhabited territory and population. Its culminating assault arrived in 1478, when large numbers of Novgorod's citizens were massacred. Yet the source of Moscow's unparalleled pretensions lay far over the horizon in ideas born in Byzantium. In 1453, when the Ottoman Turks finally captured Constantinople, they put the Byzantine Empire out of its terminal agony; but they also planted the seed of a megalomaniac idea in Muscovite minds. Byzantium, the

'Second Rome' was dead. Long live Moscow, therefore, the 'Third Rome'! Ivan III (r. 1440–1505), known as 'the Great', was the first Muscovite prince to take the idea seriously, to adopt the Byzantine two-headed eagle as his emblem, and thereby to spread the notion that he was the only true successor of the Roman Caesars, the 'tsars'. The prospects from the religious perspective were particularly threatening. The patriarch of Constantinople, to whom all Orthodox Slavs had hitherto owed allegiance, had now fallen into infidel hands. According to Moscow's logic, his authority passed automatically to the metropolitan of Moscow, who would eventually be raised to the self-appointed rank of patriarch. All Orthodox Slavs, not least in Ukraine and White Ruthenia, quaked.[54]

The Khanate of Crimea was another menacing newcomer. The remnants of the original Mongol Horde had dispersed; but an important fragment of it, which had taken over the Crimean peninsula and converted to Islam, revived former fears. These Crimean Tartars enjoyed a near-impregnable base, and they grew rich from Black Sea trade and piracy and from inland raids; they also benefited from the protection of the Ottoman sultan.[55] In 1399, on the River Vorskla near Ukrainian Poltava, they routed a grand ducal army under Vytautas, effectively terminating his political plans, and in the fifteenth century their raiding parties began to penetrate deep both into Muscovy and the grand duchy. These activities on the 'Wild Steppes' of the grand duchy's southern expanses gave rise to the formation of self-defence communities of 'Cossacks' on the lower Dniepr (*Kozak* is a Turkish word meaning 'adventurer' or 'freebooter'). Here was Europe's ultimate borderland. Its Slavonic name, *Ukraina*, meant 'On the Edge': a counterpart to the American 'Frontier'. Cossacks and Tartars were Europe's 'cowboys and Indians'. Centuries would pass before they were tamed.[56]

Kiev in particular remained exposed to Tartar attacks. One such assault in 1416 preceded a siege that was successfully resisted; another in 1483 led to the city's sacking. The return of the metropolitans to residence there proves that ancient traditions were still alive. So, too, does the magnificent Kievan Psalter (1397), containing more than 300 spectacular miniatures.[57] The growth of municipal pride is evidenced by the introduction of Magdeburg Law (the most widespread set of municipal rights used for the incorporation of cities in Eastern Europe), by the construction of a wooden *Ratusha*, or 'town hall', that lasted until modern times, and by the adoption in 1471 of the city's emblem, the Archangel Michael. Merchants continued to be drawn to fairs where the river trade met the steppe trails. But Kiev trailed behind Vil'nya.

The grand duchy was to reach its farthest limits when the Crimean khans ceded sections of the Black Sea coast in the mid-fifteenth century in return for military assistance. The territory, largely uninhabited, was known as *Dykra*, the 'Wasteland'. It contained a couple of fortified ports, Kara Kerman (later Ochakiv) and Hacibey (later Odessa), and apart from some nomadic tribes, nothing much else. The grand duchy could neither defend it nor develop it, and eventually abandoned it to the Ottomans.[58]

The Grand Duchy of Lithuania with the other Jagiellonian lands, *c.* 1500

Over the decades, the Jagiellons and their entourage, who left Vilnius in 1386 and took up residence in the Royal Castle at Kraków, became thoroughly Polonized. Jogaila and his two sons were bilingual, as was Jogaila's grandson, Alexander Jagiellończyk, who ruled in the grand duchy before ruling Poland as well. But by the sixteenth century, the royal and grand-ducal courts were almost exclusively Polish-speaking. Back home in Vilnius-Vil'nya, the dominant administrative language was Slavonic *ruski*, not Baltic Lithuanian.

Similar adjustments occurred among the grand duchy's nobility. Prior to the Union of Horodło, power had rested firmly in the hands of a ruler whose subjects owed him absolute fealty. Under Vytautas, however, a policy of enfeoffment was instigated, that is, of investing nobles with fiefs and creating a class of feudal vassals. The ruler increasingly exercised power indirectly through loyal courtiers and servants who were rewarded with huge grants of land in each of the main localities. In due course, as the distant grand dukes grew less and less inclined to interfere, a small number of powerful families put down roots and turned themselves into hereditary lords. Some of them were destined to become the largest landowners in the whole of Europe. With few exceptions, these fortunes were created by individuals of either Lithuanian or Ruthenian descent, such as Gostautas (Gasztold) or Ostrozki (Ostrogski), but their descendants functioned effortlessly in the highest circles of all the Jagiellonian realms. By the sixteenth century, a score of magnates controlled 30 per cent of the grand duchy's land, leaving the remaining 70 per cent in the hands of some 19,000 minor *boyars*, of the Church, or of the grand duke's domain. A military register (see Table 2) drawn from 1528 clearly displays the magnatial preponderance. These names would reverberate throughout the grand duchy's history.

Table 2. Military Register (1528)[59]

Family	Knights due for service	Number of villages
Kesgaillos (Kezgajllo)	768	12,288
Radvilaos (Radziwiłł)	760	12,160
Gostautas (Gasztold)	466	7,456
Olelko (Olelko, prince)	433	6,928
Ostrozki (Ostrogski, prince)	426	6,816
—— (Ostrzykowicz)	338	5,408
Hleb (Hlebowicz)	279	4,464
—— (Zabrzeziński)	258	4,128
The bishop of Vilnius	236	3,776
—— (Kiszka)	224	3,548
Chodko (Chodkiewicz)	201	3,216
—— (Sanguszko, prince)	170	2,720
—— (Illnicz)	160	2,560
Sapiegos (Sapieha)	153	2,448
—— (Holszański, prince)	122	1,952
—— (Pac)	97	1,552

The Early Radziwiłłs

Krystyn Ościk (1364–42)
|
Radzivil Ościkowicz (1384–1477)
|
Mikołaj Radziwiłłowicz (d. 1509)

| Mikołaj Radziwiłł (1470–1521) | Jan Radziwiłł (1474–1532) | Adalbert Radziwiłł (1476–1519) | Anna Radziwiłłówna (1476–1522) | Jerzy Radziwiłł (1480–1541) |

Mikołaj 'the Black' Radziwiłł (1515–65)

Mikołaj 'the Red' Radziwiłł (1512–84)

Barbara Radziwiłł (1520–51)

None of the magnates of Litva faced a more star-studded future than the Radziwiłłs, yet their origins were obscure, and their rise to prominence occurred late and quickly. The legend that they were descended from the last pagan archpriest of Vilnius is a fabrication. The first of the clan was Krystyn Ościk, the castellan of Vil'nya from 1417 until 1442, whose son's first name became the family's surname. Long life, lavish dowries, numerous offspring, high office and territorial appetite did the rest. The clan was firmly ensconced by the time the Jagiellonian era came to an end. From then on, their record of office in the grand duchy was unrelenting: 7 hetmans or 'Supreme Commanders', 8 chancellors, 5 marshals, 13 palatines of Vil'nya, 6 palatines of Troki, 2 bishops, 1 cardinal and a total of 40 senators. Their motto read: '*Bóg Nam Radzi*' – 'God Advises Us'.[60]

The assembling of the largest estate lands in the grand duchy took about a century. Krystyn Ościk had no great fortune, but his great-grandsons accumulated *c.* 14,000 homesteads with a serf population of *c.* 90,000. There were three branches: the Radziwiłłs of Rajgród and Goniądz on the Polish frontier, who died out in 1542, the Radziwiłłs of Nieśwież and Ołyka in the south, and the Radziwiłłs of Birze close to Livonia. They obtained properties by serving the grand dukes, who rewarded them well, and by marrying wealthy wives. But they also purchased land, broke new ground in the wilderness, and took in estates as security against loans. Their key property of Nieśwież arrived in their portfolio with Jan I's third wife in 1523. Mir was received in grant. Ołyka, on the other hand, which lay beyond the Pripyat' in Volhynia, was discarded, and eventually became the seat of the Czartoryskis. Yet, by the 1550s, when Mikołaj 'the Black' and Mikołaj 'the Red' were the favourite ministers of the king and grand duke Sigismund-August, and Mikołaj the Red's sister, Barbara, was queen, they had outrun all competitors. The permanence of their fortunes was to be sealed in 1586. In return for supplying the Crown with an annual quota of troops, the Radziwiłł estates were raised to the status of an *Ordynacja* (entail), which could never be legally dispersed.

Their palace at Nieśwież lies in the rolling country near the source of the Nieman, halfway between Minsk and Pinsk. It was one of the three Radziwiłł estates entailed in 1586, and was developed by Jan I's son, Mikołaj Krzysztof 'Sierotka' (1549–1616), 'the Orphan'. Completed in 1599, it was graced by Bernadoni's Baroque Corpus Christi church to mark the family's return to Catholicism at various times during the Counter-Reformation. Its five wings boasted 106 main rooms, an entrance gate, a clock tower, a parade ground and park. It was later extended by Prince Michał Kazimierz 'Rybeńko' (1702–62), the ninth *ordinatus*, whose wife Franciszka Wiśniowiecka was a playwright, who demanded and received her own theatre. Though robbed and sacked in various wars, the fabric was never destroyed, and it has survived, like the castle of Mir, to be designated a UNESCO World Heritage Site.[61]

Each of the key castles of the magnatial estates grew into a small-scale capital, overshadowing the modest incorporated towns. The growth of the magnates was also accompanied by an influx of Jews, who were attracted both by the commercial possibilities and by the demand for literate administrators. In this, the grand duchy followed in the footsteps of Poland, which since the mid-fourteenth century had been Europe's main safe haven for persecuted Jewry. The stereotypical image of rural towns throughout the grand duchy presents a picture of a Polish or Polonized landowner, a small middle class of strong Jewish complexion, and a surrounding peasant mass of illiterate serfs, Lithuanians or Ruthenians.

Given the increased influence of the magnates, the governments of Jagiellonian Litva took the form of a partnership between the grand duke or his deputies and the Lords' Council. (As yet, there was nothing equivalent to the Polish *Sejm* or parliament that first assembled in the late fifteenth century.) The grand dukes never formally surrendered their absolute powers, but since they were frequently absent in Poland, the Council was able to assume far-reaching responsibilities. At the regional level, the Polish model was followed. The grand duke's representative, the *wojewoda* or 'palatine', exercised supreme political and military authority in each of the palatinates except in the far south beyond Kiev, where Tartars and Cossacks roamed at will. 'Ukraina' only felt the rod of government intermittently from the rewards and punishments meted out by royal/grand-ducal expeditions.

The great offices of state were reserved for a narrow circle of magnates. The same surnames recur. The *hetman wielki* or 'great hetman' commanded the military forces of the grand duchy, and was expected to lead them in person; he supervised a network of castellans charged with defending the grand-ducal castles and organizing regional defence. The *kanclerz* or 'chancellor' headed the civilian administration, based in Vil'nya, and was assisted by the palatines and district *starostas*, whose function had originally been military but was gradually transformed into that of regional and local executives.

Attempts to modernize the administration of the grand duchy were hampered by the absence of a uniform legal code, but this deficiency was remedied in 1522 by a commission convened on the grand duke's orders. The 'First Lithuanian Statute' was implemented seven years later. It consisted of 282 articles in 13 chapters, many of them drawn from the ancient code of Kievan Rus', the *Russkaya Pravda*. It was handwritten in the *ruski* language of White Ruthenia, and has survived in several copies. The first article states that 'all citizens of the grand duchy of Lithuania shall be judged by the same court regardless of their rank and title'. Chapter 3 summarizes the privileges of the nobility, chapter 4, family law, and chapters 11, 12 and 13, criminal law. Many extravagant claims have been made about the Lithuanian Statutes, suggesting, for instance, that they were the only comprehensive legal codex between Justinian and Napoleon. If this is an exaggeration, the achievement was certainly real.[62]

In matters of religion, the grand duchy of the early sixteenth century was characterized by great diversity. Since Ukraine as well as White Ruthenia formed part of the state, Orthodox Christians formed a heavy majority of the population. They adhered to the traditional Slavonic liturgy of Kievan Rus', not to the Muscovite 'Russian Orthodoxy' that was enforced beyond the eastern border. They had little direct contact with their distant patriarch and the clergy was left largely to its own devices, the Ostrogski princes acting as their secular 'guardian'. Their holiest shrines in the north were at Trokiele near Lida and at Zhirovice near Hrodna, where a wonder-working statuette of the Virgin was revered; and in the south at the monastery of Lavra Pecherskaya in Kiev, founded by St Theodosius in the eleventh century. Several proposals to create a separate patriarchate for the grand duchy were never realized.

Roman Catholicism, introduced into Baltic Lithuania by Jogaila in the 1380s as the second Christian denomination in the grand duchy, was strengthened by the Polonization of the nobility; the bishop of Vil′nya became a powerful figure. St Casimir Jagiellon, son and brother of kings and grand dukes, died at Hrodna in 1484. Canonized in 1522, he was declared patron saint of Lithuania.[63] Nevertheless, the Calvinist Reformation made surprising headway in the grand duchy, especially among the magnates. Mikołaj 'the Red' Radziwiłł, grand hetman and chancellor, was a convert, and protector of a Protestant community at Birze. The Holy Bible, translated into Polish for the first time ever, was published at Brest in 1562. (The first accessible Lithuanian equivalent of the Brest Bible did not appear until 1735 when published in Prussian Königsberg; a translation into Lithuanian undertaken in Oxford during Cromwell's Protectorate had little popular impact.)[64]

Judaism was also present throughout the grand duchy, and Jewish numbers increased steadily due to migration from Poland. Quaint wooden synagogues were a feature of many small towns. A community of *karaim* or 'Karaites', originally from Crimea, had been settled in Troki since the time of Vytautas.[65] The Karaites do not accept the validity of the Talmud, and are regarded by the proponents of rabbinical Judaism as heretics. They, like the Protestant Christians, put strong emphasis on the written word, and were drawn into the printing trade, thereby contributing to the general growth of education and literacy.[66]

Vil′nya-Vilnius in the early sixteenth century was a city of many traders, many languages and many religions. The grand duchy's capital since the fourteenth century, it was unrivalled in size and influence after the loss of Smalensk, and had been walled against possible Tartar attack. In 1522, the year that the walls were finished, it welcomed the grand duchy's first print shop. Its owner was the humanist and bibliophile Francysk Skaryna (*c.* 1485–1540), who gained the reputation of being the founding father of Belarusian letters.[67] The royal and grand-ducal palace stood on the site of a pagan temple destroyed only 150 years before. The Ruthenians congregated on the eastern side around the

Gate of Dawn and their Orthodox church; the Jews dominated the western quarter, and its 'German Street'. The Poles and the Catholics were in a distinct minority until the court moved there in 1543.

Kiyiv/Kiev struggled to compete. In a charter of 29 March 1514, the king and grand duke, Sigismund the Elder, reconfirmed the municipality's right to be governed by the Magdeburg Law, which had evidently lapsed:

> The mayor [*voit*] and townspeople of Kiev have petitioned us and informed us that our brother, His Grace . . . Alexander of glorious memory . . . had granted them in his benevolence the German or Magdeburg law . . . so that in the future the townspeople would be governed in accordance with all the articles of that law. Taking into consideration their services, therefore, and the losses they suffer from our enemies in the borderland [the Tatars], and desiring that this town of ours should increase in population and prosperity, we have done as they petitioned . . . And they shall observe this law in every respect, just as our town of Vil'no observes it; and by this our charter we confirm eternally and inviolably for all time to come . . . all those rights and exemptions which we have granted.[68]

The most acute concern of the grand duchy, however, lay with the rise of Muscovy under Ivan 'the Great'. The ideology of the 'Third Rome' no doubt seemed far-fetched to many non-Muscovites, since it was saying, in effect, that the grand duchy had no legitimacy. It underpinned the dubious proposition that Moscow possessed a divine, imperial mission to unite all of ancient Rus' under its rule, thereby justifying the policy of the 'Gathering of the Lands'. According to this ideology, the majority of the grand duchy's inhabitants, being Orthodox Slavs and descendants of Kievan Rus', should now defect. The message received little or no support among White Ruthenians and Ukrainians, who valued their political separation and their religious liberty, but from Moscow's viewpoint it provided a constant and convenient *casus belli*. Alexander Jagiellończyk, son of Casimir the Great, was married to Ivan's daughter, Helena, but when he approached his father-in-law to discuss improved relations, he was told that there could be no discussions until the whole of the 'tsar's birthright' had been returned. Helena wrote to her father: 'Everyone here thought that I would bring all good things, love, friendship, eternal peace and co-operation: instead, there came war, conflict, the ruin of towns, the shedding of Christian blood, the widowing of wives, the orphaning of children, slavery, despair, weeping and groans.'[69]

Ivan III began the campaign to recover the lands of Rus' in 1485. It would proceed, with intervals, for three centuries, but it opened with five Muscovite wars against the grand duchy in fifty years. Vyazma was the first grand-ducal fortress to be lost, in 1494; but the most critical battle of the near incessant fighting was contested near the city of Orsha on 8 September 1514. The Muscovites had just captured Smalensk by siege with a huge array of men and machines, carrying off the city's holy icon and immediately laying the foundations of the largest of all their kremlins. They were moving deeper into the grand duchy when confronted by a much smaller force under Hetman Konstanty Ostrogski. They attacked at dawn, enjoying a 3 : 1 advantage and confident of success. Assault and counter-assault followed, until the massed Muscovite spearhead was drawn into a trap. The Lithuanian lines parted suddenly to reveal banks of concealed artillery. Cannon mowed down the advancing infantry. Polish cavalry swept in from the wings, and, as reported with considerable exaggeration, 30,000 Muscovite dead were left on the field; all 300 of their guns were captured. Returning to Vil'nya in triumph, Ostrogski celebrated the victory by building two Orthodox churches: of the Trinity and of St Nicholas.[70] Yet repeated attempts to recover the lost lands met only modest success. When a longer interval in hostilities was called in 1537, the Muscovites were still holding on to broad expanses of the borders including Polatsk, Smalensk, Chernigov and Seversk; Homel alone was retained.

Military problems demanded constant attention. Until the middle of the fifteenth century, the old feudal levy performed well. Poland alone put 18,000 knights into the field and the grand duchy was not far behind. Fortresses and cities were protected by dirt-and-stone walls to meet the challenge of siege artillery. In later decades, however, difficulties arose. The old type of army was no longer suited to the open warfare of the south against the Crimean Tartars. Knights could hardly arrive on the scene of distant action before the season's campaign was ending. Casual finances, which had to be spent before the land tax was collected, no longer sufficed. The *levée-en-masse* had to be supplemented. In the 1490s a limited move in this direction was taken when an *obrona potoczna* or 'current defence force' of some 2,000 men was created to defend Red Ruthenia from Tartar raids. In 1526 it received an established financial grant. The trouble was that the system needed extending. Without a permanent standing army, each campaign required an extraordinary financial grant, and the numbers of men who could be fielded were constantly declining, forcing commanders to rely on the resourcefulness and (variable) quality of their troops.

In this regard, Crown Hetman Jan Tarnowski (1488–1561), was an outstanding figure. Though not a subject of the grand duchy, he played an important role in its affairs. Like his contemporary in the west, the Chevalier de Bayard, 'the knight without fear of reproach', he was a small man with an immense reputation. It was Tarnowski who modified the Hussite concept of the *tabor* or 'military train' for use in the east, and turned it into the vehicle of repeated victory against overwhelming odds. The stores of his entire army were carried in huge six-horse wagons, which could stay on the move over vast distances or which could be chained together and formed up into a square to make an instant fortress anywhere in the wilderness. A Polish-Lithuanian *tabor* besieged by twenty or thirty thousand Tartars must have closely resembled the overland wagon trains of American pioneers attacked by the Sioux or the Cherokee. Tarnowski also developed the headquarters services of a modern army: horse-artillery, field hospitals, the corps of *Szancknechte* (sappers), the *Probantmajster*'s logistical department, the 'Hetman's Articles' or code of discipline, courts martial and the corps of army chaplains. His experiences were summarized in a book of theory, *Consilium Rationis Bellicae* ('An Outline of Military Method'), published in 1558. His watchword was 'Know your adversary'; and he preached the doctrine of military flexibility.[71]

Sigismund-August (1520–72) was to be the last of the Jagiellonian king-grand dukes, and his personal tragedy was somehow symptomatic of a hereditary system that was nearing its end. Subjected as a boy in Kraków to a hasty and irregular coronation, where the customary procedures were not observed, he was made painfully aware of the dynasty's anxieties; the Jagiellons were losing their thrones in Hungary and Bohemia. Yet as the son of Sigismund the Elder and of Queen Bona Sforza, he grew up in the midst of Poland's 'Golden Age', surrounded by Italian-inspired art, architecture and literature; he matured to be a true Renaissance man, noted for his patronage of the humanities, his religious toleration, his interest in administrative reforms and his passion for maritime affairs. He was given control of the grand duchy when still a teenager, and Vil'nya was the scene of his happiest moments.

The young Jagiellon met Barbara Radziwiłł in Vil'nya when he was a twenty-four-year-old widower and she the twenty-four-year-old widow of the grand duchy's richest man, Stanisław Gasztołd. Their romance was sweetened by the opposition of many courtiers and by their secret marriage in the palace chapel in 1547. But Barbara was sick and childless.

She was not crowned as queen and grand duchess, and soon died from malignant cancer. Her husband was heartbroken. The dynasty was entering a cul-de-sac.

The rest of Sigismund-August's reign proceeded in the shadow of the broken dream. The king-grand duke's miserable third marriage, to a Habsburg archduchess, highlighted the contrast between the stricken Jagiellons and the meteoric rise of their Habsburg relatives. (This was the age of Emperor Charles V, so different from the prospects of fifty years earlier.) What is more, the pressures for political integration, which grew in the 1550s, were not generally welcomed. The brooding monarch had not been keen on it in his early years, and confessed that he was likely to die before the future of his two states had been properly resolved.

A favourable turn in foreign affairs, however, occurred in 1561. Gotard Kettler (1517–87), grand master of the Knights of the Sword in Livonia,* was troubled by the vulnerability of the federation to which he belonged, fearing the depredations of Danes, Swedes and Muscovites. He was also swept along by the full flood the Protestant Reformation, which was sapping the foundations of the state. Appealing to Sigismund-August for help, he decided on the same course of action which had been followed a generation earlier by the grand master of the Teutonic Knights in Prussia (see below, p. 351): he disbanded his Order; converted to Lutheranism; and turned Livonia into a secular state. After a brief multi-sided war, the grand duchy annexed southern Livonia, and Kettler became duke of Courland, which he held from Lithuania in fief. Sigismund-August, already the overlord of Prussia in his capacity as king of Poland, now became, in his capacity as grand duke, overlord of Courland-Livonia as well.

In 1566 the Second Lithuanian Statute was published, a revised and expanded version of the First. It now consisted of 14 chapters and 367 articles, written in the same *ruski* language that was declared the sole medium of court hearings. (One senses a vested interest of entrenched Ruthenian lawyers, who held a virtual monopoly.) Innovations included confirmation of the equality of Catholic and Orthodox Christians before the law, the extension of Lithuanian justice to the south-western province of Volhynia, and the introduction of new noble privileges in line with Poland, where the king's powers were already formally limited. The

---

* The Livonian Knights of the Sword were a crusading order founded in Riga in 1202 and merged with the Teutonic Knights in 1236, thereby forming the Livonian province of the Teutonic State.

23. Barbara Radziwiłł (1520–51), the tragic wife of Sigismund-August: queen of Poland and grand duchess of Lithuania for six months.

24. Title page of the Third Lithuanian Statute, 1588.

25. 'The Polish Plum Cake', 1773: cartoon satirizing the First Partition of Poland-Lithuania.

26. Stanisław-August Poniatowski (r. 1764–95): born at Volchin in White Ruthenia, died in St Petersburg, 'repatriated' 1938.

27. *Stetl Juden*, orthodox Jews, from one of Galicia's many Jewish towns.

28. Hutsul man and horse from eastern Galicia.

29. Polish *Górale*, or 'Highlanders', from the Tatra mountains.

Lwów. Plac św. Ducha.
Lemberg. Heiligen-Geist-Platz.

30. Lwów–L'viv–Lemberg, capital city of Habsburg Galicia.

31. Joseph II (r. 1780–90), emperor and first king of Galicia and Lodomeria.

32. Franz-Josef (r. 1848–1916), emperor and last king of Galicia and Lodomeria.

33. The Vistula Lagoon (the *Kalingradskiy Zaliv*, formerly the *Frisches Haff*): the Baltic coast in the watery homeland of the *Prusai*.

34. Malbork, Poland: formerly the Marienburg, headquarters of the Teutonic Knights and the world's largest brick castle.

35. The Battle of Grunwald (in the German tradition, Tannenberg), 15 July 1410, as depicted by Jan Matejko (1878): the Death of Grand Master Ulrich von Jungingen.

36. The Tannenberg Memorial, 1927–45, marking the German victory of September 1914 and the 'Teutons' Revenge' for Grunwald.

37. (*top*) *The Prussian Homage*, Krakow, 1525, as depicted by Matejko. Albrecht von Hohenzollern kneels before Sigismund I, king of Poland

38. (*middle left*) Albrecht von Hohenzollern (1490–1568), last grand master of the Teutonic Order and first duke of Prussia.

39. (*middle right*) Frederick I (r. 1688–1713), first king in Prussia, Königsberg, 1701.

40. (*left*) Frederick William I (1620–88), the 'Great Elector' of Brandenburg and last duke of Prussia.

Polish statute of *Nihil Novi* (1505), for example, had established the parliamentary principle of *Nic o nas bez nas*, roughly 'Nothing about us without us'; it was very similar to the idea of 'no taxation without representation', which some readers may imagine to have been invented elsewhere. The traditional governance of the grand duchy had tended towards the autocratic end of the spectrum. The legislation of 1566 formed part of a move in the opposite direction of limited monarchy.

Throughout Sigismund-August's reign, no stable peace was achieved with Muscovy. The fifth Muscovite War had ended in 1537 with a truce, not a treaty. The grand duchy had been strengthened by a second victory at Orsha in 1564 during the Livonian crisis, and by gaining direct access to the sea at Mittau and Riga; but Moscow had also gained its first ever foothold on the Baltic at Narva. Further hostilities were awaited.[72]

By the mid-1560s, the most pressing concern by far was the imminent extinction of the Jagiellonian dynasty. Sigismund-August was convinced that his death would bring chaos if the grand duchy were not integrated with Poland. The *Sejm*, which assembled in Lublin three days before Christmas in 1568, had been convoked for the express purpose of forging a constitutional union between kingdom and grand duchy. Sigismund-August was in a hurry. This was the fourth such meeting in five years, and was attended by both Lithuanian and Polish representatives; the arguments were well rehearsed. The common danger from Muscovy, the exposure of the south-eastern provinces to the Tartars, the convergence of political cultures and the inadequacy of existing military and financial practices all pointed to the necessity of fundamental change. But there was added urgency. The king's third marriage had failed definitively. Divorce was impossible. A legitimate heir could not be born. The Jagiellons were sure to die out.

The king-grand duke, tired and sick, roused himself for the last great effort of his life. He alone could break the barriers to reform. In the last decade, he had tried many devices to unify mechanisms in the two parts of his realm. In 1559 he had instituted a *Sejm* for the grand duchy, and in 1564 provincial *sejmiki* or regional assemblies of nobles on the Polish model. At the same time he surrendered all of his prerogatives which limited the nobility's property rights, and extended full legal privileges to Orthodox gentry. He knew, of course, that habits do not change overnight. He knew that the Lithuanian representatives were fearful of Poland's greater numbers, and had been selected by the magnates under threat of punishment. He watched at Lublin how the three leading Lithuanians – Mikołaj 'the Red' Radziwiłł, Jan Chodkiewicz and Ostafi

Wołowicz – simply ordered the rest of their delegation to keep silent. After one month of formalities, and a further month of crossed purposes, the king summoned Radziwiłł and Chodkiewicz to appear in person and explain themselves. When they fled in the night he reacted angrily. Over the following days three provinces of the grand duchy – Podlasie, Volhynia and Kiev – were incorporated into the kingdom by royal decree. Two Podlasian officers, on refusing to swear allegiance to the Polish Crown, were promptly stripped of their posts. The implication was clear: if the Lithuanian lords refused to behave like Polish noblemen and debate the issue openly, the king would turn on them with all the fury of former Lithuanian autocrats.

In April the leading lords of the Ukraine* – Ostrogski, Czartoryski, Sanguszko and Wiśniowiecki – took their places in the Senate (the upper chamber of the *Sejm*). On 17 June 1569 Chodkiewicz himself reappeared, and, in the name of his peers, tearfully implored the king 'not to hand them over to the Polish Crown by hereditary will, to the slavery and shame of their children'. Sigismund-August replied, also in tears: 'God dwells where Love is, for such is his Divine Will. I am not leading Your Lordships to any forced submission. We must all submit to God, and not to earthly rulers.' It was the moment of decision. Chodkiewicz accepted the terms of the proposed Union. The Senate rose to its feet and roared its thanks. Poland and Lithuania were to be joined together, 'freemen with free, equals with equal'.[73] There was to be one *Rzeczpospolita*, one 'Republic or Commonwealth'; one indivisible body-politic; one king, elected not born; one currency, and one *Sejm*, whose deputies were to form the state's most powerful institution. The Lithuanians were to keep their own law, their own administration, their own army, and the titles of their princely families.

The king-grand duke laboured incessantly on the details for hours on end, day after day. 'These are great matters,' he said, 'which are to last for centuries; they require long deliberation and good counsel.' Finally, on 1 July 1569, the Act of Union was sealed. Standing hat in hand, and surrounded by the clergy, Sigismund-August received the oaths of loyalty from each of the signatories. Then, he led the entire assembly to the church of St Stanisław, knelt before the altar and sang the *Te Deum* in a strong voice.[74]

---

* *Ukraina*, very roughly the territory between Kiev and the Black Sea coast, was Europe's equivalent of the later American frontier. It was dominated by wide open steppes, and, except for the river valleys of the Don, the Dniepr and the Dniester, it was not permanently settled until early modern times under Polish rule.

The Polish-Lithuanian
Commonwealth from 1572

0   100   200 km

commonwealth

fiefs and
dependencies

DENMARK

BALTIC SEA

LIVONIA

Pskov

Novgorod

MUSCOVY

Riga

COURLAND

Moscow

Gdańsk

DUCAL

PRUSSIA

Wilno
(Vilnius)

Polotsk

Dźwina

Niemen

GRAND

Minsk

Nowogródek

DUCHY

Poznań

Warsaw

Vistula

Bug

Oder

Volhynia

Kijów

Kraków

Lwów

Galicia

ORON

(Crown of Poland)

Ukraine

Dniepr

HABSBURG

DOMAINS

Vienna

ROYAL
HUNGARY

Dniester

OTTOMAN   EMPIRE

In Muscovy, Ivan IV, angered by news of the Union of Lublin, hastened to one of the crimes which earned him the name of 'Terrible'. Novgorod, like the new Poland-Lithuania, despised Moscow's autocratic tradition. Forged letters were produced to show that the archbishop and governor of Novgorod were guilty of treasonable contacts with Sigismund-August. The tsar administered punishment in person. The inhabitants of Novgorod were systematically seized and killed in batches of 500 or 1,000 every day. In five weeks, Russia's most civilized city was depopulated and reduced to a smouldering heap. Ivan returned to Moscow to prepare the cauldrons of boiling oil and the meat hooks which were to chastise some hundreds of Muscovites suspected of sympathizing with Novgorod. What future for the 'Republic of goodwill' with such a neighbour?

Sigismund-August's last years were tinged with remorse. His constant appeals for love and harmony were bred by the fear that love and harmony were in short supply. In 1569 the *Sejm* insisted on debating his marital affairs and rose on 12 September without attending to his requests. The provisions for drafting electoral procedure, for creating a central treasury and for preparing judicial reforms were postponed. 'You see that I am a servant of Death,' he had told them, 'no less than Your Lordships. If you do not pay heed, then my work and Yours will be turned to nought.'[75] They paid little attention.

Sigismund-August relapsed into despair and insomnia. He locked himself into his castle at Knyszyn near the Lithuanian border and refused to receive his senators. He died on 7 July 1572, surrounded by a motley company of quacks, astrologers and witches, in a room hung in black in memory of Barbara Radziwiłł. His last will repeated his beautiful lifelong wishes which were so unlikely to come true:

> By this our last testament, We give and bequeath to our two realms, to the Polish Crown and to the Grand Duchy of Lithuania, that love, harmony, and unity ... which our forebears cemented for eternity by strong agreements, mutually confirmed ... And to whomsoever of the two nations shall hold firmly to the Union ... We bequeath Our blessing, that the Lord God in his favour shall grant them honour and power [and] fame both at home and abroad ... But whosoever shall profess ingratitude and follow the paths of separation, may they quake before God's wrath, who in the words of the prophet, hates and curses them who sow dissension between brother and brother ...[76]

The last of the Jagiellons was buried on Wawel Hill in Kraków. The private person of the king-grand duke was dead; his public person rode in effigy to the burial. The royal standard was broken asunder and, with the royal jewels, cast into the grave. This same act symbolized the transfiguration of the Kingdom of Poland and of the grand duchy. The late king had ruled as the hereditary monarch of two separate principalities. He was leaving them united in one elective republic.[77]

Within the dual *Rzeczpospolita*, the grand duchy found itself both diminished and strengthened. By losing the southern steppelands in Ukraine (see p. 262), it was reduced to less than half its former size, and with the Ukrainian lands added to the kingdom, its relative size vis-à-vis Poland fell to perhaps 1 : 1.5. It had returned to the traditional Lithuanian-White Ruthenian base of the distant days of Mindaugas. Observers of the *Rzeczpospolita* would wonder whether, if Ukraine had been set up as a third pillar of the state instead of passing under Polish rule, the resultant triple structure might not have been more balanced. As it was, the grand duchy played a junior role in the Polish-Lithuanian partnership. Yet it possessed a guarantee of internal inviolability, and its representatives could participate in full in both the common *Sejm* and the royal elections. The so-called Noble Democracy gave the great Lithuanian lords inordinate influence.

The administrative units and regional jurisdictions of the *Rzeczpospolita* were finally defined in 1581. The grand duchy possessed its own supreme judicial tribunal, which circulated between sessions in three centres: nine palatinates, plus the Duchy of Samogitia, and Livonia. The palatinates were Vilna, Troki, Brest, Minsk, Vitebsk, Mtislav, Polatsk, Seversk and Smalensk, the latter being no more than a residual entity. Each of them was divided into *poviats* or 'districts', and each held its own *sejmik* or 'regional assembly of nobles', sending delegates to the central Diet in Warsaw with precise instructions. The Duchy of Samogitia functioned as a palatinate except that it was divided into twenty-eight 'tracts' instead of districts. Livonia would be handed to Sweden in 1621; Seversk in 1634 and the remnant of Smalensk in 1667 to Muscovy. The rest remained intact to 1773, or in some cases to 1795.

One of the characteristics of the commonwealth's nobility was their distaste for titles: in theory, they were all equal, whether aristocrat or lowly squire. Hence, unlike the rest of Europe, there were no native counts, earls or dukes. Nonetheless, one of the ways in which the king had overcome the doubts of the Lithuanian magnates in 1569 was by allowing most of them to keep their princely titles. (The offer was not available to the kingdom's greatest lords, like the Zamoyski or the Potocki.) Two categories existed. The old Ruthenian title of *Knyaz* was reserved for descendants of the Rurikid, Gediminid and Rogvolodichi ruling houses. The Latin titles of *princeps* and *dux* had usually been awarded either by the pope or by the Holy Roman Emperor. Both, after 1569, passed into Polish as *ksiąze*, 'prince'. The Ruthenian princely families included the clans of Giedroyć, Puzyna, Sanguszko, Sapieha and Czartoryski. The imperial and papal princes were headed by the Radziwiłłs, who had been granted the honour twice. Henceforth, almost all of these names were the *magnati magnatorum* – the 'greatest of the great'.

Within the *Rzeczpospolita*'s dual framework, the leaders of the grand duchy were eager to maximize their freedom of action. To this end, state laws were reviewed, and in 1588 a third version of the grand duchy's law code was published. This Third Lithuanian Statute had been in preparation since the Union of Lublin. The committee which prepared the drafts was drawn from a cross-section of nationalities and religions, and seems to have intended a collation of Polish and Lithuanian laws. But the moving spirit of the exercise was Prince Lev Sapieha (1557–1633), Lithuanian chancellor from 1581; and the end product was clearly designed to preserve the grand duchy's special interests. Its fourteen chapters were approved by Sigismund Vasa in the first year of his reign, confirmed by the joint *Sejm* and printed in Vil'nya in 1588. Its third chapter, which states that no lands would be ceded to anyone,

The Grand Duchy of Lithuania,
1572–1795

— · — · — frontiers of the Polish-Lithuanian Commonwealth
— — — — frontiers of the grand duchy

defiantly introduces the corporate concept of the grand duchy's nature.
The relevant passage brims with defiance:

> RAŹDZEŁ TRECI: 'Ab šlachieckich volnaściach i pašyreńni Vialikaha
> Kniastva Litoŭskaha.' My, Haspadar, abiacajem, taksama, i śćviardžajem
> toje za Siabie j naščiadkaŭ Našych ... My, nia budziem nikomu nijakim
> čynam bajaraŭ, šlachtu dy ichnaja majontki, abšary i ziemli addavać ...

CHAPTER THREE: 'On the Freedoms of the nobility and the development of the Grand Duchy of Lithuania.' We, the *Haspadar*, the Ruler, by custom and by confirmation, for Ourselves and Our heirs, and by the Oath that We took with all the assemblies of all the lands of the Grand Duchy . . . Art. 5. We declare for all time, and undertake to preserve, that We like our forebears . . . will never hand over to anyone, by any act, the property, territories and lands of the *boyars* and nobles.[78]

Religion posed the greatest challenge. The *Rzeczpospolita* took shape in the year of the St Bartholomew's Eve massacre, when 20,000 Protestants were murdered in Paris. Much of Europe was ablaze with wars of religion. In Warsaw, the nobles of the newborn commonwealth, exceptionally, formed a solemn league to avoid violence through religious differences. And so it proved. Although the Counter-Reformation was to recover much lost ground from the Protestants, in the commonwealth it could only do so by peaceful means. In Lithuania, a chain of Jesuit colleges established at Vil'nya, Polatsk, Dorpat, Orsha and Vitebsk was particularly successful in revitalizing Catholicism, and conflict between Catholics and Orthodox was rare. The threat was mainly external. Muscovy persisted in its efforts to draw the Ruthenians away from Byzantine Orthodoxy and to persuade them to recognize the authority of the patriarch of Moscow. After decades of such harassment, the majority of Slav Orthodox bishops summoned a Church Council at Brest in 1596 and formed a new Greek Catholic Church, which was to preserve the Slavonic liturgy while adopting papal supremacy.[79] Henceforth, the Orthodox community in the grand duchy was to be divided, as in Ukraine, between 'Uniates' and 'Disuniates'. The Uniates were in communion with Rome; the disuniates continued to recognize the patriarch of Constantinople. Even so, simple Orthodox believers were sometimes reluctant to accept the Greek Catholics. St Jozephat Kuntsevich (1580–1623), Uniate archbishop of Polatsk, was murdered in Vitebsk by an angry mob and cast into the Dvina. The Ukrainian Cossacks, who often rampaged into the *Rzeczpospolita*, were also fierce defenders of the old Orthodoxy. The Orthodox martyr St Athanasius of Brest (d. 1648) appears to have been murdered by Catholics in retaliation for the Cossacks' misdeeds.

To most Europeans in that Age of Monarchy, a royal election sounded like a contradiction in terms. But in the Polish-Lithuanian Commonwealth, as in the Holy Roman Empire, it was a fundamental constitutional procedure for centuries. All nobles were entitled to participate, providing an electorate of 5 to 6 per cent of the population. They were required to attend armed and mounted, and between 30,000 and 40,000 would gather on the Wola Field near Warsaw, staying there until a unanimous decision was obtained. Some of the magnates, like the Radziwiłłs, would bring along a regiment or two, and a battery of artillery, to help win over the opposition. They were choosing a man who would automatically become grand duke as well as king of Poland.

The first election, in 1573, passed off quietly, but it produced a dud from France. Henry de Valois fled to Paris three months after his coronation, having succeeded to the French throne. The second election in 1576 was a procedural shambles, provoking civil war. But it eventually produced a brilliant warrior and statesman from Transylvania – Stefan Batory – who brought the rebellious elements to heel, and devoted much energy to the grand duchy's foreign policy. The third election, in 1587, initiated a series of kings from the Polish-Swedish Vasa dynasty:

Henryk Walezy (Henri de Valois) (r. 1573–4)
Stefan (Stephen) Batory (Istvan Bathory) (r. 1576–86)
Zygmunt III Waza (Sigismund III Vasa) (r. 1587–1632)
Władysław IV Waza (Ladislas IV Vasa) (r. 1632–48)
Jan Kazimierz Waza (John Casimir Vasa) (r. 1648–68)

By custom, the Catholic primate of Poland presided over the state during the interregnum between the death of a king-grand duke and a successor's coronation.

Batory's war against Moscow in 1579–82 aimed to recoup the grand duchy's losses and to put an end to the constant wrangling over Livonia. The Muscovites had taken advantage of Batory's other preoccupations, principally in suppressing the revolt of Danzig, and had overrun almost all of Livonia; a response was called for. Most of the fighting took place along the eastern border, where the Russian city of Pskov was besieged by a huge force, which built a wooden city outside the walls to survive the winter. The Russian chronicler saw it as a trial of strength between two opposing religious faiths:

The siege of Pskov began in the year 7089,* in the month of August and the 18th day, on the feast of the holy martyrs Frol and Laurel. The Lithuanian people started to cross the river and to appear before the city with

* Until 1699 the Russian calendar calculated the years since the date of the Creation of the World, and placed New Year's Day on 1 September. After 1699 the Julian not the Gregorian Calendar was adopted.

their regiments . . . The king himself came before Pskov. In that same month of August on the 26th day, on the feast of the holy martyrs Adrian and Natalya, this man, the Lithuanian king, drew close . . . like a wild boar from the wilderness.[80]

The purpose of the operation was to cut off Moscow's line of communication with Livonia. The tsar wrote to the pope, complaining that Batory was 'a Turkish employee'. The pope responded by sending a Jesuit legate, Possevini, to see if there was any chance of compromise. But the siege continued, even though cavalrymen were frozen dead in their saddles. The Poles and Lithuanians, having put their strategic garrotte into place, were not going to relent until the tsar conceded. His position secure, the 'much-proud Lithuanian King Stephan' left the 'evil-hearted and greatly-proud chancellor-Pole', Jan Zamoyski, in command. Negotiations began in the presence of Possevini. At the Peace of Yam Zapolski (January 1582), Moscow abandoned the whole of Livonia, and returned Polatsk to Batory. The besiegers hung on at Pskov until the tsar's commissioners handed over the keys to all the Livonian castles:

And so, by the great and ineffable grace of the Holy Trinity, of our helpers . . . from the whole family of Christ . . . by the intercessions of the great miracle-workers . . . by defenders of the God-preserved city of Pskov, by the leaders in Christ . . . of the whole Russian land . . . by the prayers of the true-believing and God-loving Grand Duchess Olga . . . and of all the saints; by the Lord the tsar, the true-believing grand duke, Ivan Vasil'evich, beloved of Christ, who holds all Russia in his patrimony; indeed, by all God's wonders, the city of God with all its people was saved from the Lithuanian king . . .

Then, on the fourth day of February, the Polish hetman and lord chancellor moved off with all his array to the Lithuanian land. In the city of Pskov, the gates were opened. And I, having completed this story in all its fullness, have brought it to its end.[81]

Thus did the Muscovites record a severe defeat. They would not regain another viable opening onto the Baltic, a 'window on the West', for 120 years.

The Vasa period started on a note of continuity because the successful candidate of 1587, the Swedish Prince Sigismund Vasa (Zygmunt Waza), was the son of a Jagiellonian mother. But the Swedish connection proved deeply conflictual. As leader of the defeated pro-Catholic party in the Swedish civil war, Sigismund lost control of his native

country and fell into long-running hostility with his victorious Protestant relatives, not least over control of Livonia. Once again, the grand
duchy was exposed. What is more, the outbreak in 1606 of a noble
revolt in Poland, the Zebrzydowski Confederation, demonstrated that it
was perfectly legal to take up arms against the king if strict rules were
observed. A baleful precedent was set for the Lithuanian magnates. In
1621, the Swedish Vasas took over Livonia by force of arms, leaving the
Rzeczpospolita only the province of Letgalia at Dunabourg, on the
grand duchy's northern border.

The reign of Władysław IV brought a period of political calm, economic prosperity and social peace. The *Rzeczpospolita* even managed
to avoid involvement in the protracted violence of the Thirty Years War
in neighbouring Germany. In reality, however, deep-seated problems
were accumulating.

One of the prominent social and cultural features of Poland-Lithuania
in the early seventeenth century was a phenomenon that has been dubbed
the 'noble–Jewish alliance'. In the grand duchy, as in the Ukrainian palatinates now separated from it, the wealth and influence of the landed
magnates increased. And a literate class of Jewish managers, lawyers and
administrators was imported from Poland to run the estates and to col-
onize the small towns. The Jews had often faced discrimination in the
urban centres, especially from the guilds. But in the east of the state,
which was less urbanized, they met fewer barriers. In Vilnius, they established a very strong community where Yiddish culture was cherished and
eminent scholars of the Torah welcomed.[82]

The grand duchy also provided refuge for radical religious thinkers.
A group of Polish anti-Trinitarians settled at Troki, where they analysed
biblical texts alongside members of the Jewish Karaites.[83] The *Hizzuq
Emunah* ('Fortress of Faith') of Isaac ben Abraham of Troki (1525–86),
though not translated into Latin until 1681, was regarded by the *philosophes* of the Enlightenment as one of the founts of their thought.[84] 'Even
the most determined freethinkers', wrote Voltaire, 'have proposed virtually nothing that cannot be found in *Le Rampart de la Foi du Rabbin
Isaac*.'[85] The Karaites of Troki would have appreciated the compliment
but not the reference to one of their leading intellectuals as a rabbi.

In those same decades, royal patronage was a chosen instrument of
the Counter-Reformation no less than education. The Polish Vasas were
Catholic devotees by definition – having lost their throne in Sweden for
the Faith – and the preferences of the court affected the ecclesiastical
alignment of the nobles. Father Piotr Skarga SJ (1536–1612), sometime

rector of the Jesuit Academy at Vil'nya, confessor to the king-grand duke and the Catholic Church's most eloquent ideologue, foresaw a day of reckoning for the sinful republic.[86] Another Jesuit, St Andrew Bobola (1591–1657), who worked as a rural missionary first in Polatsk and later in Pińsk, was to be martyred in the Cossack wars.[87]

Disaster struck in 1648. A Cossack rebellion in Ukraine headed by Bogdan Chmielnicki sent Cossack armies flooding westwards into Poland, and provoked a chain of further invasions. In 1654 the Muscovites joined in after reaching an understanding with the Cossacks. This development provoked Swedish armies to march both into northern Poland and into the grand duchy, where Vil'nya was occupied. The treasonable surrender of the Lithuanian grand hetman, Janusz Radziwiłł, who was contemplating a permanent union with Sweden, created shock waves of despair. In 1655 one Russian army entered Ukraine, and another invaded the grand duchy, recapturing Vil'nya from the Swedes and perpetrating a horrific pogrom. In 1655–6 the king-grand duke, Jan Kazimierz, fled to his wife's possessions in Habsburg-ruled Silesia. These terrible years became known as the *Potop*, the 'Flood'.

During the Cossack wars, the government of the *Rzeczpospolita* was plagued by a form of constitutional abuse that would become notorious. In a system where the nobles were both law-makers and law-enforcers, it made good sense for the *Sejm* to work on the principle of unanimity; deputies had habitually held up proceedings until particular points of a bill were clarified or dropped; this *liberum veto* or 'right of veto' had served its purpose for years. Yet in 1652 a Lithuanian deputy called Siciński, acting on the orders of his Radziwiłł patron, exercised the veto in the final minutes of an overextended parliamentary session, immediately before the state budget was to be approved. In a finely calculated act of legislative vandalism, he then left the chamber without justifying his protest, and rode out into the night. The veto was judged valid, and the entire legislation of the session remained unratified. Much to the amusement of some of the grand duchy's magnates, one imagines, an aristocratic troublemaker had demonstrated how the state could be held to ransom.

In 1656 and 1657 the *Rzeczpospolita* staged a remarkable revival. The king-grand duke returned. New troops were raised, and Catholic sentiment was aroused by appeals to fight the heretical, Protestant invaders. The Virgin Mary was proclaimed Queen of Poland. The Swedes were expelled from both the kingdom and the grand duchy, and the Muscovites pushed back. Polish-Lithuanian troops even attacked enemy positions on the Danish islands, which the Swedes had reached by marching across the ice. At Hadziacz in 1658 Cossack elders signed an agreement which appeared to end their alliance with Moscow and to initiate a tripartite *Rzeczpospolita*. At the Treaty of Oliwa in 1660 a general settlement of the First Northern War* was concluded, though Livonia and Ducal Prussia had to be abandoned. But then, exactly when Polish-Lithuanian forces were taking the offensive against the Muscovites, another crippling noble rebel confederation shattered the common resolve. Kiev and the eastern Ukraine were lost for ever; and in 1668, after six years of fraternal fighting, Jan Kazimierz, the last Vasa monarch, abdicated. During his reign, 25 per cent of the *Rzeczpospolita*'s population died of fire and sword, hunger and plague.

The reign of Jan Sobieski (1673–96) is most often viewed, especially by outsiders unfamiliar with internal affairs, as the last grand flourish of Polish-Lithuanian power and glory. Certainly, as a fearless warrior and war leader, who had made his name as crown hetman during the Swedish wars, he put on a grand show. By breaking the Ottoman Siege of Vienna in 1683, he secured his place as one of Europe's greatest heroes. Yet Sobieski's foreign wars, financed by foreign subsidies, masked deep internal weaknesses. One of his most intractable problems persisted in the grand duchy, where the vendettas of the magnates ran completely out of control. While the king-grand duke battled the Turks on the Danube, the Sapieha faction battled the Pac faction in the grand duchy, and all semblance of co-ordinated government broke down. In itself, the breakdown was not terminally destructive – the *Rzeczpospolita* had recovered from similar episodes before – but the timing was fatal. The grand duchy was paralysed at a juncture when Swedish–Muscovite rivalry was coming to a head in the adjoining lands; any major war between Sweden's Baltic Empire and Muscovy was bound to see the grand duchy trampled between the two.

In 1696, on Sobieski's death, the official language of the grand duchy's administration was changed from *ruski* to Polish. The change marked the point where the ruling nobility had become so Polonized that the grand duchy's principal native language was no longer readily intelligible to the upper classes and to the bureaucracy. The Chancellery scribes had to make another adjustment. What for centuries had been

---

* Given the Polish–Swedish conflict of 1621–35 during the continental campaigns of Gustavus Adolphus, Polish usage prefers to call the conflict of 1654–60 the 'Second Northern War'. Robert Frost (*The Northern Wars: War, State and Society in North-eastern Europe, 1558–1621* (Harlow, 2000)) concurs.

either VKL or MDL now became WXL: 'W' for *Wielkie*, 'X' for *Księstwo* and 'L' for *Litewskie*; and Vil'nya, for official purposes, became Wilno. It was highly ironic; the Polishness of the grand duchy's elite was intensifying at the very time when Russian influences among them stood on the brink of marked expansion.

The era of the Saxon kings that followed Sobieski is traditionally seen as the nadir of the *Rzeczpospolita*'s fortunes, although some historians have sought to rehabilitate it.[88] August II the Strong (r. 1697–1733), elector of Saxony, and his son, August III (r. 1733–63), accepted the Polish-Lithuanian throne in order to outflank their German neighbours and rivals in Brandenburg-Prussia. They only achieved their goal by pocketing Russian gold, by bribing electors with fake coins, by promising to convert to Catholicism, and afterwards by signing up to a permanent alliance with the tsar. In the ensuing decades, they used their new acquisition as a milch cow and dragged it into endless wars, quarrels and occupations, from which, whatever their wishes, they were impotent to escape. Formally, they held the triple title of 'elector, king and grand duke'.

The Great Northern War (1700–21) essentially pitted Russia against Sweden, although other powers were also involved. Peter the Great, the aspirant emperor of Russia, and Charles XII, king of Sweden, were the principal combatants. The former, a physical giant, was 'a typical fanatic, who never questioned the correctness of his ideas'; the latter, sexually ambiguous, was eulogized by Voltaire as 'a king without weaknesses'.[89] August the Strong, however, was deeply enmeshed in the political intrigues from the start, and much of the fighting was conducted in Poland and Lithuania. His entry into the war as Peter's ally sucked Charles XII's army into the *Rzeczpospolita*, and the Swedes' long march to destruction at Poltava in 1709 brought a trail of devastation throughout the grand duchy. The Polish-Lithuanian nobility were divided into pro-Russian and pro-Swedish factions: a Swedish placeman, Stanisław Leszczyński (later duke of Lorraine) contrived to sit on the throne between 1704 and 1709; and the subsequent arrival of the Russian army virtually turned the *Rzeczpospolita* into a Russian protectorate. In 1717, when Russian mediators did nothing to calm interfactional animosities, the noble deputies were driven into passing laws in silence, at a cowed *Sejm* that assembled under the menace of Russian guns, effectively depriving the state of the means of its own defence. Military spending was drastically curtailed. State taxation could only support a standing army limited to 18,000 men, at a time when the Prussians could field 200,000 and the Russians 500,000. The grand duchy's military establishment was now smaller than the Radziwiłłs' private army.

Under August III, the central organs of the *Rzeczpospolita* ceased to function. The elector-king-grand duke resided in Dresden, and ruled through viceroys. Attempts to convene the *Sejm*, and hence to raise taxes, were repeatedly blocked by use of the *liberum veto*. For thirty years, the *sejmiki*, the regional noble assemblies, provided the sole source of co-ordinated administration. The magnates grew stronger than ever. They cultivated an outlook called 'Sarmatism', proclaiming – ostrich-like – that 'Polish freedom' was incomparably wonderful. Both the Prussians in northern Poland and the Russians in the grand duchy billeted their troops on the countryside for free, by charging the cost of their upkeep to the local population. Europe of the Enlightenment looked on, and complacently equated 'Poland' with 'anarchy'.

Nothing better illustrates the political decadence of the Saxon era than the workings of the so-called 'Familia'. A group of magnates headed by the Czartoryskis and Poniatowskis took advantage of the political vacuum, seeking to replace the authority of the absent monarch with their own. They came together in the 1730s, when a royal election was in prospect, and were active until the 1760s, when one of their number was the successful candidate in the next. Proposing a single centralized state, the abolition of the *liberum veto*, and a modernized financial system, they aroused the opposition of the Potocki faction in the kingdom and of the Radziwiłłs in the grand duchy. Among the Familia's most active members among the older generation was General Stanisław Poniatowski (1676–1762), sometime adjutant to Charles XII and treasurer of the grand duchy, and in the younger generation, Prince Adam Kazimierz Czartoryski (1734–1823), probably the most enlightened reformer of the age. Their flamboyant aristocratic lifestyles contrasted blatantly with that of the countless serfs who maintained it. One sees parallels with progressive elements among the French nobility of the *ancien régime*, and with the more enlightened slave-owners, who, a continent away, were preparing the American Revolution.

It would be unwise, however, to generalize too drastically about the peasantry. It is true that the society of the grand duchy was marked for centuries by serfdom, and the misery of the serfs could be dire. In 1743–4, in the *starostvo* (county) of Krychev in eastern White Ruthenia, a local war was fought between the Radziwiłł regiments and an 'army' of rebellious serfs. Petitions to the lords, known as *supliki*, begging for easement, were sometimes granted, sometimes ignored. Yet islands of hope could flourish amid the sea of poverty. Although about 30 per cent of the population was controlled by the magnatial estates, about 70 per cent was not. A class of free peasants held their own in the eastern palatinates, paying rent and prospering from the production of flax and timber. In the southern palatinates, flight to 'Cossackdom' or to estates in Ukraine, where colonists received favourable terms, was always an option for disaffected peasants.

Moreover, the later eighteenth century saw a considerable increase in the overall size of the economy, in agricultural improvements, and even in manufacturing. Efforts to rationalize river transport were crowned in 1785 by the opening of canal systems linking both the Nieman and the Dniepr and, via the Royal Canal, the Pripyat' and the Bug. The grand duchy was well placed to export corn, timber and potash. The improvers aimed to direct trade both to the Vistula and to the Black Sea, in addition to the traditional exit via Riga. The great estates were equipped with flour mills, lumber machines and breweries. The first textile factory in the grand duchy began working in 1752 at Nieśwież, and the Radziwiłłs thereafter constructed twenty-three further industrial works, producing everything from glass to paper, bricks to gunpowder.[90]

Stanisław-August Poniatowski (r. 1764–95), the last king-grand duke of Poland-Lithuania, was the Familia's candidate for the throne and a former lover of the Russian empress, Catherine the Great. As a young diplomat employed in St Peterburg by both the British and the Saxon embassies, he had made a huge impression on the German-born future empress, who selected him for protracted romantic services. A decade later, he easily won her support in the royal election. As monarch, however, he saw his task as one of urgent reform, reanimating the vital organs of the moribund state, modernizing society, promoting culture and relaxing the stranglehold of the pro-Russian magnates elevated by his Saxon predecessors. The empress wished to maintain the status quo from which Russia greatly benefited. The two of them were on a collision course. Every time the beleaguered monarch showed signs of pulling his country from the quagmire, his patroness pushed it back in.[91]

The three decades of Stanisław-August's reign witnessed a dramatic spectacle rarely seen in European history. One of the largest states in Europe fought for its life, while the wisecrackers of the Enlightenment, led by Voltaire, mocked its impotence. Stanisław-August and his circle desperately sought to restore the *Rzeczpospolita* to health and viability, while the so-called 'Enlightened Despots'* sought not only to obstruct him, but to exploit their victim's vulnerability and to dismantle the repairs. A maritime metaphor might be appropriate. The captain and crew strive valiantly to keep their stricken vessel afloat, while pirates moored alongside help themselves to the ship's timbers chunk by chunk. The captain is then declared (by the pirates) to have been a poor seaman, and his ship a wreck that was not worth saving. The drama usually appears in the history books as the 'Partitions of Poland', but this, of course, is a misnomer. The state being dismantled was not 'Poland', but the dual 'Commonwealth of Poland and Lithuania'. Moreover, the catastrophe was less catastrophic in the long run for Poland than for the grand duchy. Though the kingdom was dismembered like the grand duchy, large parts of Poland were destined to be salvaged. The wreck of the grand duchy would sink for ever.

The First Partition, in 1773, was enacted as punishment for a decade of successful progress. It was conceived by Frederick II of Prussia, approved by Catherine the Great and then foisted on a supposedly reluctant empress of Austria, Maria Theresa. As the Prussian king explained: 'She wept as she took, and the more she wept the more she took.' Since the *Rzeczpospolita* was essentially defenceless, the international bandits were able to carve out large slices of territory for themselves, and then to persuade the victim to cede their plunder by formal treaty. The Prussians took a slice out of northern Poland. The Austrians were given a bigger slice in the south. The Russians annexed roughly one-quarter of the grand duchy, including the palatinates of Polatsk, Vitebsk and Mtislav. A chorus of Russian spokesmen and apologists explained that the noble empress was merely repossessing her own property.[92]

The following decades nonetheless saw the heyday of the Polish Enlightenment. The leading spirits of the movement, inspired by the king-grand duke himself and resigned to the futility of political activities, made great strides in education, agriculture, administration, history and the arts. Modern schools were opened, the latest farming methods introduced, a national history project launched, civil servants were trained, and writers and painters sponsored. The magnates played their part, some of them voluntarily emancipating their serfs. The banishment of the Jesuit Order in 1773 threatened to devastate schooling,

---

* Notably Frederick the Great of Prussia and Catherine the Great of Russia, whose rational approach to state-building was lavishly praised by apologists living at a safe distance from their habitual depredations and warmongering.

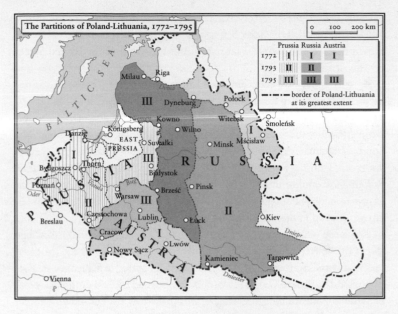

The Partitions of Poland-Lithuania, 1772–1795

but the National Education Commission that was tasked with addressing the crisis set up a far-flung school system, which functioned far into the nineteenth century. It would train several generations in the language, culture and heritage of the *Rzeczpospolita*. 'If there are still people in two hundred years time who think of themselves as Poles,' declared Stanisław-August, 'my work will not have been in vain.' The Commission's first director was Jakub Massalski (1727–94), bishop of Vil'nya. The *Korpus Kadetów*, founded to train an administrative elite, was pioneered by Prince Michał Kazimierz 'Rybeńko' Radziwiłł; while his son, Prince Karol Stanisław, 'Panie Kochanku' (1734–90), though a dyed-in-the-wool reactionary, raised his palace at Nieśwież into a major centre of theatre, music and opera.[93]

The Second Partition was preceded by an intense period of political reform embodied in the Great *Sejm* of 1788–92. It was a race against time between the reformers, who sought to regain the *Rzeczpospolita*'s independence, and the pro-Russian opposition, hampered by Russia's preoccupation with an Ottoman war. If the Turks continued to pin the Russians down, the Polish-Lithuanian reformers might find the space to attain their goals. If not, a Russian expedition would march. At first, the reforms prospered: taxes were voted. A professional standing army was financed and put into training, and the core offices of a modern administration were established. Finally, on 3 May 1791, on the initiative of the king-grand duke, a fine written constitution was passed, the first in Europe and second in the world only to that of the United States of America.[94]

By this time, however, and tragically for the reformers, the international climate had fundamentally shifted. The outbreak of the French Revolution in 1789 had convinced Europe's absolute rulers that moderate constitutionalists and flaming Jacobins were indistinguishable. The Polish-Lithuanian experiment was doomed. A Russo-Turkish truce cleared the ground, and in St Petersburg the empress collected a group of handpicked Russophiles, all subjects of the *Rzeczpospolita*, who raised the flag of rebellion on the south-eastern frontier at Targowica. Then the Russian army marched in their support.

The Russo-Polish war of 1791–2 was not a foregone conclusion. The forces of the *Rzeczpospolita*, though outnumbered, slowed the progress of the advancing Russian columns. At two battles in Ukraine, at Zieleńce and Dubienka, General Kościuszko proved to be a commander of unusual talent. But then the king-grand duke lost his nerve and capitulated, the constitution was declared invalid, and the traitorous victors were invited by their Russian paymasters to plunder and to persecute. Those treacherous 'Targovicians' included General Szymon Kossakowski, the grand duchy's grand hetman, and his brother Josef Kossakowski, bishop of Livonia.

General Tadeusz Kościuszko (Tadevish Kastiushka, 1746–1817) was a professional soldier, the son of Polonized gentry from the Brest region of White Ruthenia. Educated in Warsaw and Paris, he had spent 1776–83 in the service of the infant United States, where he is remembered as a friend of Thomas Jefferson and a founder of the West Point military academy. His views on freedom and democracy were strengthened by his American experience. He was about to become the chief hero of the *Rzeczpospolita*'s demise.[95]

The details of the Second Partition were worked out in protracted negotiations. By a Russo-Prussian treaty of 23 January 1793, the Prussians were to take Danzig and the Russians were to absorb most of the grand duchy's palatinates except for Vil'nya, Brest and Samogitia. This time the Austrians were left out. By a second treaty, signed at Hrodna on 25 September by representatives of Prussia and of the *Sejm* of Poland-Lithuania, the king-grand duke was obliged to accept the emasculation of his regal powers. The treaties were implemented later in the year.[96]

For two years, what was left of the *Rzeczpospolita* – a clutch of territories in central Poland and the rump of the grand duchy, including Warsaw, Lublin, Poznań, Kraków and Vil'nya – fought desperately to survive. Kościuszko raised his standard in March 1794, swearing the oath to king and country in the Great Square of Kraków. In one battle, at Racławice, the Russians were routed. In Vil'nya, a soldier of Jacobin leanings, Jakub Jasiński, expelled the Russian garrison. But at the Battle of Maciejowice, Kościuszko fell wounded from his horse; according to legend, his last words before capture were '*Finis Poloniae*'. In Warsaw, a true Jacobin-style rising broke out, and a number of clerics and nobles were strung up by the mob. Finally, as the Russian General Suvorov entered the capital, the whole population of the suburb of Praga were massacred. Suvorov's laconic message to the empress read: 'Hurrah. Praga. Suvorov.' Her reply read, 'Bravo Fieldmarshal, Catherine.' After that, the Third Partition, an act of liquidation, could be imposed without any pretence of negotiation.[97]

During those two final years, the territory of the grand duchy was systematically overrun and pillaged. The Russians retook Vil'nya, and formally abolished the ancient state of which it was the capital. All nobles who had taken up arms lost their lands, and all the traditional civil and military offices were closed. Lithuania and Poland had been joined, for better and for worse, for 409 years. They were now extinguished together, and the link was severed.

The exact moment at which a body-politic dies is sometimes hard to determine. In legal terms, it could be defined by an act of abdication unaccompanied by an act of succession, or by the withdrawal of international recognition. In the kingdom-grand duchy, it arrived for practical purposes on the day when the last of the offices of state stopped functioning: 25 November 1795, symbolically St Catherine's Day. By then, Warsaw had been handed over to the Prussians, who expelled all remaining foreign diplomats. The Austrians were organizing Galicia. The Russians were digesting the grand duchy whole.

One last scene was enacted. After the formal abdication of Stanisław-August on the morning of 25 November, he was escorted from Warsaw under guard, and condemned without trial to lifetime captivity in Russia. He was, as it were, acting out the fate of his ex-subjects. After crossing the border and stopping in Hrodna in 'Black Ruthenia', the military column attending his carriage wound its way through the wintry landscape from one end of the grand duchy to the other. His captors would have been told that they were crossing 'western Russia'. Such was the formula

that would henceforth be taught to the world at large. But Stanisław-
August knew otherwise. He and his memories were bound for St
Petersburg on a journey of no return.

III

The legacy left by the demise of a state is markedly more complex than
that which follows the death of an individual. There is, to begin with, a
large physical residue of land, cities, government buildings and other
assorted assets that have to be reallocated by the new owners. There is a
considerable collection of legal and financial issues – claims, titles, debts
and outstanding cases – that must somehow be resolved. As likely as not,
there is also a huge cultural deposit, the accumulated literature, music, art,
legends, history, languages, laws and customs that live on even when their
authors do not. Most importantly, there is a community of people, thousands or millions strong, the former citizens, subjects and servants of the
defunct state, who will now be pressed to change their identities, their
attitudes and their allegiances. Finally, there are, or there ought to be, the
state archives: the collections of official files and government records,
which attest to the functioning of the late body-politic, and which enable
historians to trace its progress and to preserve its memory. In the case of
the grand duchy, all these elements can be identified, and more besides.

After 1793 the lands and peoples which had for centuries formed
part of the grand duchy passed in their entirety to the Russian Empire.
They were supplied not only with a new administration, a new ruling
class, a new official language and a new Russian-based educational system, but also with a new history. They were declared, quite falsely, to
have been reunited with the ancient Russian homeland, from which,
supposedly, they had once been torn away. The Empress Catherine celebrated her acquisitions in true Spartan manner by striking a notorious
medal which read: 'That which was torn away, I have recovered.'[98]
Wilno/Vil'nya, no longer a state capital, became the provincial city of
Vilna. Hence, when Napoleon arrived on the Nieman only a dozen
years later, the world was told he was about to invade 'Russia'.

Everyone interested in international affairs knows that shorthand
forms are widely used in place of cumbersome state titles. People say
'America' instead of 'the United States of America', ignoring the protests
of the Canadians. They still say 'England' instead of 'the United Kingdom

of Great Britain and Northern Ireland', though 'the UK' is increasingly common. And throughout the twentieth century, they have invariably said 'Russia' when referring to 'the Empire of all the Russias', 'the Union of Soviet Socialist Republics', or, since 1992, 'the Russian Federation'. This practice is bearable so long as its users understand what the short forms are replacing. There is a very real danger, however, that by hearing nothing but the short forms endlessly repeated, the unwary public may be misled. For it is all too easy – and completely erroneous – to believe that the UK is equivalent to 'the land of the English' or to assume that 'Russia' is inhabited exclusively by Russians.

The issue is particularly relevant to the fallout from the suppression of the Grand Duchy of Lithuania. The peoples of the former grand duchy disappeared from view in the late eighteenth century and, with a brief exception during the Russian Revolution, only resurfaced in the late twentieth. Suddenly in 1989–91, the world woke up to the news that the western regions of the Soviet Union had not really been Russian at all. New nation-states, such as Latvia, Lithuania, Belarus and Ukraine appeared as if from nowhere, and precious few commentators were able to explain where they came from.

After the Russian Empire's annexation of the grand duchy, all the historic administrative structures were replaced by centralized *gubernias* or 'governorships', which took their orders from the tsarist government in St Petersburg. The six *gubernias* of Vilna, Kovno (including Courland), Grodno, Minsk, Mogilev and Vitebsk were grouped together in a north-western *Kray* or 'Land' ruled by a governor-general. The entire nomenclature was changed. Russian names took the place of Polish names, and map-makers round the world came to terms with 'Western Russia' or 'the North-western Gubernias'. The old names of 'Lithuania' and 'Belarus' were banished. 'White Ruthenia' was presented as 'White Russia', and an international treaty was signed to suppress the name of Poland for ever.[99]

In this first Russian period, the administrative rearrangements included the creation of the so-called Pale of Jewish Settlement in 1791. The Jewish Pale was a clearly defined region – essentially the lands of Russian-occupied Poland-Lithuania – within which all Jews were now required to reside. Henceforth, no Jew could legally reside elsewhere in the Russian Empire without special permission; and no Jew could reside in one of the closed cities, like Kiev, within the Pale. The boundaries of the Pale were to vary, but the legal restrictions remained in place until 1917. As

Western *gubernias* of the Russian Empire
in the nineteenth century

FINLAND   OLONETS

St Petersburg

ESTLAND   ST PETERSBURG   NOVGOROD

BALTIC SEA   LIVLAND   YIAROSLAV

Riga   PSKOV   TVER   VLADIMIR

KOVNO   VITEBSK   MOSCOW   Moscow

Kovno   Vilna   Vitebsk   SMALENSK   VLADIMIR

VILNA   Minsk   Mogilev   KALUGA   RYAZAN

PRUSSIA   Grodno   MOGLILEV   TULA

Warsaw   GRODNO   MINSK

POLAND   OREL

Chernigov   KURSK

VOLYNIA   CHERNIGOV

AUSTRIA-HUNGARY   Zhitomir   Kiev   VORONEZH

Kamenets Podolsky   KIEV   POLTAVA   KHARKOV

PODOLIA   Poltava

BESSARABIA   EKATERINOSLAV

ROMANIA   KHERSON   Ekaterinoslav

Kishinev   Odessa

TAURIDA

- - - - Russian western frontier
▨ Pale of Jewish settlement
KIEV *gubernia* name
Minsk city name   Simferopol

BLACK SEA   0   50   100 km

a result, the former grand duchy, together with Austrian Galicia, and the
Kingdom of Poland as resurrected by the Congress of Vienna, became
the parts of Europe where the percentage of Jews within the general
population was highest.

The existing laws were too extensive and too firmly established to be
replaced wholesale or overnight. Russian decrees were introduced gradually, and sections of the old Lithuanian Statutes remained in force for
decades. Yet one area where radical change was introduced quickly pertained to the status of the nobility. In Poland-Lithuania, the nobles had
formed an independent legal estate. They had elected the monarch, governed the localities, convened regional assemblies and enjoyed the rights
to own land and to bear arms. Such 'Golden Freedoms' were unthink-

able in the tsarist autocracy, so early in the 1790s the privileges of the
grand duchy's nobility were arbitrarily rescinded. The only families
permitted to apply for noble status were those who could produce documents to prove it. Since no such documentation had been produced
systematically in Poland-Lithuania, over 80 per cent of the existing
nobility were cast into a legal limbo, uncertain about their title to their
estates and land and their qualifications for public office.

In 1806 the armies of Napoleon's French Empire advanced eastwards, to establish the French-controlled Duchy of Warsaw. Hopes rose
high that Napoleon would liberate the population of the whole region
from both social and political oppression. In the event he did neither,
although he did raise huge numbers of Polish troops for the French service. The peace negotiations held in 1807, between Napoleon and Tsar
Alexander I on a raft moored in the Nieman, proved only temporary.

Much of the fighting of the 1812 campaign, which Napoleon called
his 'Second Polish War', was contested on lands which until recently had
formed part of the grand duchy. The *Grande Armée* crossed the Nieman
at Kovno, and reached Vilna on Sunday, 28 June. 'Our entry into the
city was triumphal,' wrote one of Napoleon's Polish officers.

> The streets ... were full of people; all the windows were garnished with
> ladies who displayed the wildest enthusiasm ... The Polish patriots of
> Vilna held a solemn [service] in the cathedral, followed by a ceremonial act
> of reunification of Lithuania and Poland ... 'Everyone, in the manor and
> the village, felt that they were going into battle in the Polish cause,' wrote
> [a landowner] ... In Grodno, the French forces were met by a procession
> with [icons], candles, incense and choirs. In Minsk ... a *Te Deum* was held
> to thank God for the liberation. Resplendent in his full dress uniform,
> General Grouchy personally handed around the plate at Mass, but at the
> other end of town his cuirassiers were breaking into shops and ware-
> houses ... As soon as they saw how the French behaved, [the country folk]
> took themselves and their livestock off to the forests ... 'The Frenchman
> came to remove our fetters,' the peasants quipped, 'but he took our boots
> too.'[100]

With some delay, the French moved off towards Moscow. The Battle
of Borodino was fought on the first section of historic Russian territory
that they entered. Moscow burned. Napoleon's retreat, which began in
December, proceeded over the same ground. The icy crossing of the
River Berezina, an exploit that became legendary, brought the *Grande
Armée* back into the former grand duchy. The Cossacks harassed the

frozen French columns as they shuffled through the snow towards a mirage of safety. Long before the spring came, it was clear that all hope for the restoration of the commonwealth was lost.

At the Congress of Vienna in 1815, the victories of the tsar's armies were reflected in political arrangements that would last until the First World War. A Russian-run Kingdom of Poland, of which the tsar was king, was established, but the former grand duchy in its entirety returned to being part of the Russian Empire. For the next three or four generations, Poles, Lithuanians, Ruthenians and Jews were subject to an unrelenting campaign to turn them into model subjects of the tsar.

Before the Partitions, every elected Polish-Lithuanian monarch had borne the dual titles of 'king of Poland' and 'grand duke of Lithuania'. After 1795, when the titles became vacant, they were snapped up by the tsars. Yet they were still kept strictly separate. As from 1815, all the Romanovs adopted the three-part style of 'emperor and autocrat of all the Russias', 'tsar (or sometimes king) of Poland' and 'grand duke of Finland, etc. etc.' Lithuania did not appear in the short title, being subsumed according to tsarist ideology in the category of 'all the Russias'.[101]

In time, as the nineteenth century progressed, a proportion of the wealthier and more influential landowners of the former grand duchy were able to have their nobility confirmed by the Office of Heralds in St Petersburg. Not surprisingly the Radziwiłłs were among those who adjusted well. But the tsarist authorities made political loyalty an iron condition of any such confirmation and refusals were common. So, too, were confiscations. A large number of estates, and all the most important offices, were taken over by incoming Russian officials, adventurers and carpetbaggers. At the head of them were figures like General Alexander Rimsky-Korsakov (1753–1840), who lived in the extravagant Tuskulanai manor near Vilnius, or Count Mikhail Muravyov (1796–1866), later known as Muravyov-Vilensky, who held a series of high government positions, and who was instrumental in suppressing local resistance. 'What Russian guns can't accomplish', Muravyov once said, 'will be accomplished by Russian schools.'

In Muravyov's time, serfdom was the burning social issue. It had been avoided during the Napoleonic Wars, and shelved during the ultra-conservative post-war era, but it arose again under Alexander II, the so-called 'Tsar Liberator' (r. 1855–81). Together with those in other parts of the Tsarist Empire, the serfs of the former grand duchy, an absolute majority of the population, were released from their feudal bonds in 1861, but not from the grinding poverty of backward rural life. Yet emancipation brought hope. It meant that the former serfs could move away to seek work, that they could learn new crafts and skills, and open businesses; and that they could educate their children. Reality moved slowly; aspirations rose fast.

Education, therefore, became a battleground of competing interests. Tsarist officialdom saw an opportunity for far-reaching Russification, which involved not only the teaching of the Great Russian (Muscovite) language but also reverence for the tsar and the promotion of Russian Orthodoxy. For the population at large, the problem was how to give their children a schooling without handing them over unconditionally to the ambitions of the Russian state. Both the Poles and the Jews possessed their own school systems, and, from the 1840s, the Catholic bishops of Wilno (Vilnius) successfully sponsored primary classes for Lithuanian-speaking children. The harshest battles centred on the fate of White Ruthenians, whose language was treated as a Russian dialect and whose conversion to Russian Orthodoxy was taken for granted.

The overall effectiveness of Russification is hard to measure. The currency of Russian certainly increased, and a proportion of the people became functionally bilingual. One of the few groups to be more thoroughly Russified belonged to a sector of the Jewish community who adopted Russian in place of their native Yiddish. These people were known as *Litvaks*, literally 'Jews of the grand duchy'; their linguistic choice marked their desire of escaping from traditional Jewish society. They naturally made up most of the first wave of Jews who decided to emigrate.

Religion remained a bone of contention. Some groups and individuals were willing to bear the civil penalties which their religious allegiance entailed. Yet there was no move to close down either Roman Catholic churches or Jewish synagogues. Tsarist animosity focused on the Ruthenian Greek Catholic Uniates, who were treated as traitors to the nation. In 1839 and again in 1876 decrees were issued to ban Greek Catholicism outright and to force its adherents into Russian Orthodoxy. In order to practise their religion, many Uniates fled to Austrian-ruled Galicia.

Nonetheless, despite the tensions, the human mass of the former grand duchy stayed largely *in situ*. For the first two or three generations, prevalent attitudes were characterized by mainly passive resistance to Russian rule, although it sporadically turned active. For two or three generations after that, the former grand duchy was deeply affected by the rise of a variety of new political and national movements. Until 1864, the sense of disillusionment was heightened by the bitter consequences of three successive failed risings – in 1812, 1830–31 and 1863–4. On each occasion, patriots from the former kingdom fought and died along-side volunteers from the former grand duchy, hoping that the late *Rzeczpospolita* could somehow be revived. On the contrary, the risings were crushed; repressions multiplied; tsarist rule was strengthened.

The former grand duchy supplied many of the insurrectionary lead-ers. Romuald Traugutt (1826–64), head of a clandestine national government declared in Warsaw during the January Rising of 1863–4, was the son of a gentry family from the Brest palatinate. Jakub Gieysz-tor (1827–97), a Polish nobleman who had freed his Lithuanian serfs, believed that the rising was premature, but joined all the same. Antanas Mackievičius (1828–63), later seen as a Lithuanian nationalist, none-theless fought for the restoration of the multinational grand duchy. Zygmunt Sierakowski (1826–64) led bands of rural guerrillas in Samog-itia. Kastuś Kalinoŭski (1838–64), now counted among the pioneers of Belarusian identity, addressed social distress as well as national issues. All fought in vain. Traugutt and his associates were executed in front of Warsaw's Russian citadel. Sierakowski and Kalinoŭski were executed in Vilnius. Their dreams of the grand duchy's revival died with them.

In this era of insurrections, the poet Adam Mickiewicz (1798–1855), born and raised in Novogrudok – the town in 'Black Ruthenia' where the very name of *Litva* was said to have been born – penned the most eloquent and lasting lament for the late grand duchy. His epic poem *Pan Tadeusz* (1834) has the subtitle 'The Last Raid in Lithuania', and describes the life of a rural community at the time of Napoleon's inva-sion in 1812. In matchless language, it evokes both the colourful traditions of the past, and the dreams for liberation. Mickiewicz wrote in Polish, and the opening lines of *Pan Tadeusz* have become the most famous lines in the language:

> O Litwo! Ojczyzno moja, Ty jesteś jako zdrowie.
> Ile Cię cenić trzeba, ten tylko się dowie,
> Kto Cię stracił. Dziś piękność Twą w całej ozdobie
> Widzę i opisuję, bo tęsknię po Tobie.

('O Litva! My homeland, you are like health. / How to gauge your worth, only he can know / who has lost you. Today I see your full beauty / and describe it, because I long for you.') Irony of ironies, Poland's national bard did not come from Poland. It is as if William Shakespeare had lived in Dublin. But such is his stature that Lithuanians, too, take 'Adomas

Mickievičius' to be their own; and Belarusians consider 'Mitskieyvitch' to be theirs:

Tėvyne Lietuva, mielesnė už sveikatą!	*Літва! Ты, як здароўе ў нас, мая Айчына! . . .*
Kaip reik tave branginti, vien tik tas pamato,	*Што варта ты, ацэніць той належным чынам,*
Kas jau tavęs neteko. Nūn tave vaizduoju	*Хто цябе ўтраціў. Вось красу тваю жывую*
Aš, ilgesy grožiu sajaudintas tavuoju.	*Зноў бачу і апісваю, бо скрозь сумую.*

All the millions of people who still read this poetry, translate it, learn it by heart, or teach and study it in school as part of the official curriculum, are perpetuating the grand duchy's heritage.

Opposition to tsarist rule after 1864 was channelled in new directions. The anarchists, for example, believed in direct action. The *Narodna Vol'ya* ('National Will') organization, attracted recruits from all over the Russian Empire. But the man who threw the bomb that killed Tsar Alexander II in 1881 was a déclassé nobleman from the district of Bobruisk, Ignacy Hryniewiecki (1856–81). The socialists long remained undistinguished from the anarchists, and until the end of the century were largely undifferentiated between the democratic and undemocratic tendencies. Józef Piłsudski (1867–1935), who hailed from a minor landowning family from the Vilna district, became a leading light in the illegal Polish Socialist Party (PPS), having spent five years in exile in Siberia. He was to emerge in 1918 as the first head of state of a reborn Poland. Yet he always stayed true to the multinational traditions of the grand duchy, contesting nationalism in all its forms and longing for close co-operation between Poles, Jews, Lithuanians and Belarusians. The *Bund*, or Jewish Labour League, came into being in Minsk in 1897. (Ironically enough, Piłsudski's ethnic, social and geographical origins were almost identical to those both of Ignacy Hryniewiecki and of Feliks Dzierżyński (1877–1926).

In late nineteenth-century Europe, nationality issues rose to the top of the agenda almost everywhere. Any number of national movements took to the field in opposition to the central authorities, aiming in the first instance to capture cultural affairs – to promote a national language, to publicize national literature and to formulate a national history. Then they moved on to demand political autonomy, and, as the final stage, the creation of a national state.

In this context, the lands of the former grand duchy offered abun-
dant, politically fertile ground. The brutal tsarist regime invited resistance,
and social structures were crumbling due to the proscription of the
nobility and the liberation of the serfs. The result was fierce competition, not only between tsarist officialdom and its opponents, but equally
between nationalist and socialist groupings and between rival national
movements. A spectrum of separate national dreams arose that could
not be satisfied without conflict.

The Russians had developed a state-backed nationalism of their own
that was projected from Moscow and St Petersburg into the imperial
provinces. It viewed the Poles, dominant in the former ruling class of the
Rzeczpospolita, as the prime enemy. The Lithuanians (though Roman
Catholic) and the Jews were seen as prospective allies against the Poles,
while the Ruthenians were classed as Russians. In the past 'Polishness'
had been associated both with the landowning nobility and with Roman
Catholicism, but these associations gradually broke down. Increasingly
it was linked to all Polish-speakers, irrespective of social, economic or
religious status. A large group of déclassé Polish nobles strove to keep
up appearances. A Polish bourgeoisie held the fort in Wilno, as they
called it, and a sizeable Polish sector of the peasantry was concentrated
in the surrounding district. All tended to show solidarity with their
compatriots in the former kingdom.

The Ruthenians, almost entirely enserfed until 1861, possessed little
awareness of nationality. If asked about their national affiliation, they
were famous for replying that they were *tutejsi* or 'locals'. Nonetheless,
they were deeply offended by the forcible introduction of Russian Orthodoxy, and grew more receptive to the activists who were collecting and
publishing Belarusian folklore and codifying the Belarusian language for
educational purposes. Contrary to some predictions, they never sought
to join their fellow Ruthenians in Ukraine. Instead, some of them sought
to imitate Polish culture. Jan Czeczot (1796–1847), who was Polish, is
often regarded as the pioneer of Belarusian identity. Vincent Dunin-
Marcinkiewicz (1807–84) initiated the Belarusian literary tradition by
translating *Pan Tadeusz*.

The Lithuanian national movement started from similarly humble
beginnings. Church-based Lithuanian primary schools had long functioned, but a sixty-year struggle with the Russian authorities had to be
fought before permission was given for Lithuanian to be written in the
Latin alphabet. By the early twentieth century, however, the first generation of Lithuanian-educated Lithuanians was coming to the fore. They

were passionate about language and literature, about separating their own ethnic history from that of their neighbours and about gaining recognition.

In 1800 the Jewish community of the former grand duchy had been defined exclusively by religion. By 1900, after exposure to an unprecedented demographic explosion, to pogroms and to a series of modernizing movements, it had emerged as a recognized nationality. The *Haskalah* or 'Jewish Enlightenment', which urged Jews to assimilate into public life while preserving their religious practices in private, operated throughout the century. Yet the spread of the Hasidic movement, demanding new forms of strict religious observance, worked in the opposite direction. One of its prominent sects, the *Lubavicher*, gained many devotees in the southern districts.[102]

Zionism, in contrast, grew out of Jewish secular culture and the Hebrew Revival, that is, the campaign to adapt the Hebrew language to everyday purposes. The Second Zionist Congress, held at Minsk in 1902, revealed the existence of a fully fledged Jewish nationalist movement. Its main goals were to sharpen Jewish identity against other nationalities, to encourage emigration to Palestine and, like nationalists the world over, to complain of discrimination and persecution (quite justifiably, in this case, after the passing of the discriminatory May Laws of 1882). It inevitably collided with the *Bund*, which sought to reconcile Jews with their neighbours and to build a better world for all.

By 1914, therefore, the political scene was fragmented in the extreme. Visions of the future were irreconcilably diverse:

> [T]he old capital of the Grand Duchy of Lithuania was a desired political capital to Lithuanians, Belarusians, and Poles ... a spiritual capital to the Jews ... and an ancient Russian city to the officials who exercised power. Most of the city's schools taught in Russian, most of its churches were Roman Catholic, more than a third of its inhabitants were Jews ... The city was ... 'Vilnius' in Lithuanian, 'Wilno' in Polish, 'Vil′nia' in Belarusian, 'Vil′na' in Russian and 'Vilne' in Yiddish ...
>
> Vilnius was for Lithuanian activists the capital of the Grand Duchy, built by Grand Duke Gediminas at the dawn of Lithuania's glory. Increasingly, they saw the medieval Grand Duchy as the antecedent of an independent Lithuanian state ...
>
> Belarusian national activists, too, harkened back to the Grand Duchy, regarded themselves as its heirs, and claimed Vil′nia as their capital. Unlike [the Lithuanians] ... they favored a revived Polish-Lithuanian

Commonwealth ... The Belarusian idea began to compete seriously with
the imperial idea [of] 'West Russia.' In Vil'nia city, Belarusian speakers far
outnumbered Lithuanian speakers. In the Vil'nia province ... [they] were
more than half the population. The first important Belarusian periodical,
Nasha Niva (Our Soil), appeared in 1906.

Under Russian imperial rule, a special sort of Polish culture consolidated
its hold on ... the Wilno region (*Wileńszczyzna*). Despite a series of [discrim-
inatory] laws ... Poles still owned most of the land, [and] were probably
the city's plurality ... Assimilation to Polish language was regarded not so
much as joining a distinct national [group] as joining respectable society ...
Aware of their families' roots ... and often bilingual or trilingual themselves,
[such Poles] regarded the Grand Duchy as the most beautiful part of the
Polish inheritance ... In the early twentieth century, their political views
were given a federalist structure by patriotic socialists such as Józef
Piłsudski ...

The Jews, who represented 40 percent of the city's population and
perhaps three quarters of its traders ... had inhabited the 'Jerusalem of
Lithuania' in large numbers for four hundred years. The 'Lithuania' in
question was the old Grand Duchy, which had included cities such as Minsk
(by this time about 51 percent Jewish), Homel (55 percent), Pinsk (74
percent), and Vitebsk (51 percent). The Vitebsk of this era is best known
from the paintings of its native son, Marc Chagall (1887–1985).[103]

Thanks to international convulsions beyond their control, all the
national movements that had taken root in the former grand duchy
were about to be overwhelmed by outside interests. During the First
World War (1914–18), the area saw fierce fighting between German and
Russian armies on the Eastern Front; and after the outbreak of the Russian Revolution and Civil War it was subjected to a series of political
experiments. In March 1918 at Brest (which the Poles call Brześć
Litewski and the Germans Brest-Litowsk), Leon Trotsky signed away a
large swathe of the dead Tsarist Empire, including most of the former
grand duchy, where the experiments mushroomed. The stunted Republic
of Lithuania, founded with German support in 1917 in Kaunas (Kovno),
could not realize its claims on Vilnius; and the resultant Polish-Lithuanian
feud ever the city obstructed all attempts at post-war co-operation.[104]
The Byelorussian National Republic, created by local activists in Minsk,
lasted for little more than a fortnight.[105] The Communist-run Lithuanian-
Byelorussian Republic which succeeded it, the 'Lit-Byel', created in
conjunction with the Bolsheviks, endured barely a year.[106] In 1919–20

the Polish army of Józef Piłsudski established a brief interval of dominance in the region. After its victory in the Polish–Soviet War of 1919–20,
Poland held onto 'Middle Lithuania' and partitioned Byelorussia with
the Soviets.[107] The official name of Vilna reverted back to Wilno.

In the inter-war period, the Lithuanian Republic lost its democracy
to the regime of Antanas Smetona (1874–1944), while partitioned
Byelorussia lost all prospect of self-government. Western Byelorussia,
under Polish rule, remained a backward region, but its difficulties bore
no comparison to the horrors taking place beyond the Soviet frontier.
Under Lenin's auspices, the Byelorussian SSR – in eastern Belarus – was
granted use of the Byelorussian language and a nominally autonomous
administration in Minsk. In reality, it was run from Moscow through
the iron dictatorship of the Soviet Communist Party. The Uniate Church,
which had resurfaced during the German occupation of the war years,
was eradicated even more viciously than in tsarist times. Under Stalin,
the young Byelorussian intelligentsia, educated in the 1920s, was almost
annihilated; the leaders of the Byelorussian national movement were
shot. Any independent peasants were destroyed during the collectivization campaign. The Jewish community was deeply split between the
secular, pro-Soviet element organized by the all-powerful *Yevsektsiya* or
Jewish section of the Communist Party and the traditional, religious
and non-Communist majority. Many decades later, the Kuropaty Forest
near Minsk would reveal the secret mass graves of hundreds of thousands of unidentified victims of Stalin's 'Great Terror'.[108]

In the Second World War the former grand duchy lay in the eye of the
storm from beginning to end, being subjected to an ordeal unparalleled
in the whole of European history. Both Western Byelorussia and Lithuania were awarded by the Nazi–Soviet Pact to the Soviet sphere of influence.
A joint Nazi–Soviet victory parade was staged in Brest in September
1939, and Lithuania was overrun by Stalin's Red Army in June 1940. The
first Soviet occupation was marked by mass executions, deportations and
repressions. German occupation followed when 'Operation Barbarossa'
crashed over the frontier in June 1941; it spurned all the many opportunities that arose to present the Nazi regime as a liberator. A quick glance
at the wartime map reveals that (with the exception of Leningrad/St
Petersburg) the weight of devastation and Nazi oppression were not
inflicted on Russia but on the non-Russian republics. (The German military *Reichskommissariat Ostland* coincided in large measure with the
post-1569 grand duchy.) The year 1941 also signalled the onset of the

Nazis' two largest crimes: the genocidal Holocaust against Jews and the liquidation of Soviet prisoners by starvation. The scene of these crimes largely coincided with the horrors of unbelievably ferocious anti-partisan warfare. In 1944 the victorious and vengeful Red Army smashed its way west regardless of the human cost. The retreating Germans created 'scorched-earth' zones and last-ditch 'fortresses' to be defended to the death. In one single campaign, Operation Bagration, which drove the front to the River Vistula, Marshal Rokossowski reoccupied the whole of Byelorussia and destroyed more than fifty German divisions. In the process, Minsk and several other cities were completely razed, with enormous loss of civilian life. Then the world's record-breaking murder machine, Stalin's NKVD, appeared to filter, arrest, shoot, torture, deport and terrorize the survivors.

A land so afflicted could never be the same again. The Lithuanians had been severely depleted by Soviet actions in 1940–41 and 1944–5. The Poles were decimated, partly by the early Soviet deportations, partly by the German occupation, and partly by the post-war 'repatriation campaign'. The Jews, murdered by the Nazi SS during the Holocaust, had been virtually exterminated. The Byelorussians suffered from all sides. By 1945 human losses in Byelorussia were estimated at 25 per cent of the population. No other part of Europe – not Poland, not the Baltic States, not Ukraine and not Russia – had sustained such mind-numbing levels of slaughter.[109]

For forty-six years after the war, Lithuania and Byelorussia sweated out a further spell within the Soviet Union, where the question of their reintegration was not even considered. Not only were they behind the Iron Curtain in the post-war period; they were corralled behind the extra grille that separated them from other countries of the Soviet bloc. The watchword was reconstruction. But they were poorly treated compared to more favoured republics. Politically and economically, they were held in the stranglehold of Communist Party control and of centralized command planning. Socially, they had been artificially homogenized, and they could exploit a tiny margin of autonomy only culturally and lin-guistically. In the Lithuanian SSR, the Lithuanian language was retained as the principal medium of education and administration, and a Lithua-nian Communist elite took pains to keep the influx of Russians at bay. By the late twentieth century over 80 per cent of the citizenry remained Lithuanian by speech and nationality. As the Soviet Union began to crumble, Lithuania became a viable candidate for separation. Early in 1991 it was the first of the Soviet republics to demand independence.[110]

The Byelorussian SSR was less coherent in its ethnic composition and far more confused in its objectives. It had never recovered fully from its wartime devastation. The inflow of ethnic Russians was not stemmed, especially into top positions, and Russophile sentiment came in with them. The great mass of people were indigent, collectivized state serfs, whose knowledge of their own history and culture was minimal. Religion was sorely curtailed. The native Uniates were not reinstated and the Roman Catholic churches stayed shut, as they had since 1917. The Byelorussian language, written exclusively in Cyrillic, was rarely a vehicle for subversive thoughts. And the border with Poland remained closely guarded.

Nonetheless, when the moment of Soviet collapse arrived, the Byelorussian Communist Party did not falter. It acted as host to a secret meeting held in the tsar's former hunting lodge at Viskuli in the Belovezh Forest on 9 December 1991, when the representatives of Russia, Byelorussia and Ukraine declared the USSR to be extinct. The world's largest state expired painlessly. It met a much easier death than that suffered by the grand duchy almost two centuries earlier.

Archives are, in a sense, the dust and ashes of a dead polity. They contain the records of monarchs who reigned, of institutions that functioned and of lives that were lived. Like boxes of family papers in the attic, they are an indispensable aid to accurate memory and to trustworthy history.

The condition of archives, therefore, gives a good indication of the strength of memory and the reliability of the history books. If archives are well ordered, one may conclude that the legacy of past times is respected. If not, it is likely that memory and history have been neglected. One of the first decisions of ill-willed regimes is to order the destruction or sequestration of their predecessors' archives. In the case of the grand duchy, large parts of the archives have totally disappeared.

The *Metryka Litevska* or 'Lithuanian Register' is the commonest collective name for the original indexes/archival inventories of the grand duchy's central chancery. Since it no longer exists in one place, it is difficult to estimate its size. But, at a minimum, it was made up of a thousand huge, leather-bound ledgers, and it contained six main divisions: Books of Inscriptions (i.e. summaries of laws and decrees), Books of 'Public Affairs' (records of the Chancellor's Office), *Sigillata* (copies of documents issued under the grand-ducal seal), Court Books, Land Survey Books, and Legation Books relating to foreign affairs. The time-span stretches from the very early thirteenth century to the very late eighteenth century. The principal languages employed are *ruski* (Old Belarusian), Latin and Polish.

Locating and reconstructing the *Metryka Litevska* has demanded a
fascinating saga of academic sleuthing that could only be undertaken
with modern technology. It was long delayed, partly because the most
interested parties had no access, and partly because Russian and Soviet
archivists were following their own agenda. Nowadays, one can state
with some confidence that the dispersal of the grand duchy's records
took place in nine or ten stages:

- In 1572, following Union with Poland, the main body of
  documents (though not the registers) was taken by the last
  chancellor of the pre-Union grand duchy, Mikołaj 'the Red'
  Radziwiłł, and was housed in the Radziwiłłs' palace at
  Nieśwież. According to the Radziwiłłs, the priceless papers had
  been consigned to them for safe-keeping; according to others
  they were stolen.

- From 1572 to 1740 the archives of the post-Union period,
  together with the older registers, were kept in the Chancery in
  Vilnius. Most papers relating to foreign policy were filed in the
  Metryka Koronna. The *Metryka Litevska* received numerous
  files relating to Muscovy and the Tartars.

- During the Swedish invasion of 1655–6, large quantities of
  documents and inventories were plundered and taken to
  Stockholm. Part of the loot was returned by the Treaty of
  Oliwa (1660), but an important group of registers remained
  in Sweden.

- In 1740 the grand-ducal Chancery and its records were moved
  to Warsaw; sometime later a joint Polish-Lithuanian archival
  administration was established. After 1777, since the majority
  of clerks could no longer read Cyrillic, Polish summaries were
  added to the contents of each ledger. A start was made on a
  huge project aiming to produce a full copy of the entire archive
  and to transcribe all the *ruski* texts into the Latin alphabet.

- In 1795 the contents of Warsaw's archives and libraries,
  together with the surviving registers, were seized by the Russian
  army, and transported to St Petersburg, where they were duly
  joined by the archives from Nieśwież.

- In the course of the nineteenth century Russian imperial
  archivists broke up the Polish-Lithuanian records to suit their
  own administrative purposes. Anything relating to Ukraine, for
  example, was sent to Kiev.

- In 1887 an incomplete and inaccurate catalogue of the *Metryka Litevska* was compiled and published in St Petersburg.
- In 1921 the Treaty of Riga between Poland and the Soviet republics made provision for the restoration of all archives carried off from Warsaw in 1795. The provision was largely observed in the breach.
- In 1939, the Polish Archive Service removed as many records as possible from central Warsaw, but large parts of the pre-war collections were destroyed during the war by fires, bombing and German looting.

One obvious conclusion is that Vilnius and Minsk are probably not necessarily the best places to locate the basic sources for study of the grand duchy.

The task of piecing together the archival jigsaw was first undertaken by Polish scholars in the 1920s and 1930s, but the work was far from complete when overtaken by redoubled wartime disasters. Post-war conditions, which gave absolute priority to the sensitivities of the Soviet Union, were not conducive to impartial research.

So with much delay the star role eventually fell to a heroic American scholar from Harvard University, whose findings began to appear in the 1980s. Her original concern was to summarize the holdings of the Soviet state archives in general, since their guardians treated catalogues as state secrets. But she came to realize that many records originating from the grand duchy, though broken up and widely scattered, had survived under misleading headings and identification numbers. She also realized that the registers in Stockholm, to which she had unrestricted access, were invaluable. They helped her to trace papers which were housed in various parts of Poland or the Soviet Union and whose existence would otherwise have been impossible to pinpoint. The net result was an unrivalled degree of understanding of the grand duchy's archival legacy.[111]

Since then, primary research has been greatly facilitated, and scholars of many nationalities toil to make up the backlog of two centuries. Enormous gaps and problems remain, yet it is a great consolation to know that all was not lost. Even for the amateur historian with no special expertise, it is extraordinarily exciting to open one of the inventories, and to gaze on the raw material of the grand duchy's history with one's own eyes.

One important relic, however, was never in the archives. The body of the last king-grand duke, buried appropriately in the church of St Catherine in St Petersburg in February 1798, rested untroubled in its tomb for 140 years. Then, in 1938, by agreement of the Soviet and Polish authorities who were tasked with fulfilling the restitution clauses of the Treaty of Riga, the sarcophagus was broken open and the coffin dispatched to Poland. However, since pre-war Poland's official view of Stanisław-August was not positive, the government opposed the plan of reburial in the royal crypt at Wawel Castle in Kraków, and the coffin was transported instead to the chapel at Volchin (Wołczyn) near Brest, to Stanisław-August's birthplace in the former grand duchy. During the war and in the post-war Soviet period, Volchin was totally devastated and the derelict chapel used as the fertilizer store of a Soviet collective farm. So the pulverized human remains 'brought home' to St John's cathedral in Warsaw in 1995 were not in reality homeward bound; nor, with any certainty, were they the remains of Stanisław-August.[112]

In the fields of art, architecture and social history, another single-handed labour of love was undertaken by an archivist and librarian who passed the second half of his life in Silesia. In the 1930s the late Roman Aftanazy had been a keen cyclist and photographer, touring the eastern borders of Poland's Second Republic with a camera and notebook, and starting a collection of annotated pictures of castles and country houses. After the war, when many of the historic buildings had been destroyed, he realized that his collection, though incomplete, was unique. And he spent the next forty years compiling a detailed photographic and descriptive record of every single landed estate in Lithuania, Byelorussia and Ukraine. He contacted all the surviving former owners or their neighbours, persuading them to submit every available photograph, plan, inventory or family history. His daring operation in Communist times was completely illegal, but its results were sensational. In 1986 he published the first volumes (out of a total of twenty-two) of a work which lists and describes in detail more than 1,500 residences. Part I, consisting of four volumes, deals with the former grand duchy, and is organized by the palatinates that existed in the seventeenth and eighteenth centuries. There are 148 substantial entries, from Abele to Żyrmuny, for the Palatinate of Vilnia alone. This is no mere catalogue. It is a comprehensive compendium, giving full accounts of almost every landed family and their estates, together with their homes, their galleries, their gardens, their furniture, their genealogies, their legends and their fortunes. It is an intellectual rescue operation of a lost world on a grand scale.[113]

The volume on the residences of the Palatinate of Brest contains a description of the birthplace of the last king-grand duke:

The Volchin estate lay to the north-west of Brest, close to the junction of the Bug and Pulva rivers. In the mid-16th century it had belonged to the Soltan family, and in 1586 Jarosław Soltan, Starosta of Ostryn built an Orthodox church there. In 1639, the first wooden Catholic church was erected by the next owner, Alexander Gosiewski, Vojevoda of Smolensk ... Between 1708 and 1720 [during the Great Northern War] the property passed by sale or inheritance to the Sapiehas, the Flemings, the Czartoryskis, and the Poniatowskis ...

Stanisław Poniatowski proved to be an excellent manager. While enlarging the palace initiated by the Sapiehas, he re-modelled a score of farms, built seven water mills, reduced the obligations of his serfs, bred a herd of pedigree cattle, and constructed a fleet of ships for carrying grain [by river] to Danzig. In 1733, he opened the octagonal chapel in which his son, the future king, was christened.

Nonetheless, the estate was sold in 1744 to Poniatowski's son-in-law, Michał Czartoryski, the Lithuanian chancellor, who completed the palace in mid-century, adding stone-built wings to the central section built of spruce logs. As well as the 92 main rooms, there was a library, a theatre, an orangerie, a frescoed altana, and a home park of 60 morgs. The furniture and tapestries were French, and the paintings mainly Italian. Portraits of Charles XII, of August II and III, and of Stanisław Poniatowski himself held pride of place ... Since Volchin was relatively close to the capital, Warsaw, it was the scene of numerous balls, garden parties, theatrical performances and boat races.

[Thanks to the First Partition, however,] the Czartoryskis moved their main residence in 1775 to Puławy [near Lublin], and Volchin was neglected. [After the Third Partition of 1795, it found itself in the Russian Empire, and was abandoned.] It was eventually sold in 1838 to settle the family's debts, and in the mid-nineteenth century the [ruined] palace was demolished.

After that, only the chapel survived, having been converted by the tsarist authorities for the purposes of Orthodox worship. The chapel register, which contained the record of King Stanisław-August's baptism, was preserved in a nearby Catholic parish. Restoration of the chapel, which accompanied its reconversion to a Catholic sanctuary, was completed in time for the arrival of the king's coffin from Leningrad in 1938.[114]

Even diligently reconstructed records and material remains, however, do not tell the whole story. Some people, by religious analogy, might believe that the grand duchy had a soul or spirit as well as a mortal body. For the grand duchy continues to generate all manner of intangibles – myths, legends, stories and literary echoes – that many observers notice, and some try to analyse.

One of the best known poetical statements about life in the twentieth century proposes that the modern world was built on 'a heap of broken images'. And one of the very first of many enigmatic fragments scattered through T. S. Eliot's *The Waste Land* refers to Lithuania. 'Bin gar keine Russin, stamm' aus Litauen, echt deutsch,' says an unidentified female voice. ('I'm no sort of Russian woman: I come from Lithuania, pure German.') The words are so deliberately obscure and enigmatic they come close to nonsense, and they inevitably invite speculation. They might refer, as the poet's widow has proposed, to a real woman encountered in Paris. Alternatively, they could well be a sly and deliberately distorted reference to a character in H. G. Wells's *New Machiavelli* (1911), who was not a Lithuanian but a Lett from Courland. 'The line is not a direct quote,' says the latest of literary detectives, 'but a transposition made ... to hear all the voices as one voice, all the women as one woman.'[115] The historian refrains from joining in. The important point is that echoes of something called 'Lithuania', but very different from modern Lithuania, continued to circulate long after its death, and that, as the poet was aware, Russia was something else. The grand duchy is one of the countless 'broken images' which contribute to our imperfect understanding of European civilization.

6

Byzantion

The Star-lit Golden Bough
(330–1453)

Istanbul is the fourth largest city in Europe, and the largest in Turkey. It straddles the waters of the magnificent Bosporus, its ancient suburbs lying on the European shore and the newer eastern suburbs on the Asian side. Founded as *Byzantion* in the seventh century BC by Greek colonists from Megara, it changed its name to Constantinople in AD 330, when it became the capital of the Roman Empire, and to Istanbul in 1453, when it became the capital of the Ottoman Empire. Since it commands the only passage for shipping between the Mediterranean and Black Seas, its strategic and commercial importance is unsurpassed. Its historical monuments include, from the Greek period, the Serpentine Column, which has stood in the centre of the hippodrome for nearly 2000 years; from the Roman period, the cathedral of St Sophia, the Aqueduct of Valens and the matchless Theodosian Walls; and from the Ottoman period, the sultan's Topkapi Palace and the Suleymaniye Mosque. The Golden Horn, the natural harbour which first attracted Greeks, Romans and Turks alike, is the heart of the city. It provides Europe's closest view of Asia. The posters say '*Hoş karşılamak türkiye*' ('Welcome to Turkey').[1]

Anyone wishing to look deeper into the life of Istanbul will probably be told to turn to the novels of Orhan Pamuk, and in particular to his *Istanbul: Memories and the City*. In the citation for his Nobel Prize for Literature in 2006, the Swedish Academy wrote: 'In the quest for the melancholic soul of his native city, [Pamuk] has discovered new symbols for the clash and interlacing of cultures':

A lovely spring breeze was wafting through the balcony's grand doors, carrying the scent of linden trees. The lights of the city shone on the Golden Horn below. Even the slums and shanty-towns of Kasimpasa looked beautiful.

I thought how happy I was, even feeling as if this was a prelude to yet greater happiness. The gravity of what had transpired with Fusun confused me, but I told myself that everyone has his secrets, fears, and moments of worry. No one could guess how many of these elegant guests felt similarly uneasy or carried secret, spiritual wounds.[2]

Pamuk certainly writes of Istanbul's pains and of his own inner life with emotional precision. Of himself, he says: 'I am the living dead'; and of his hometown: 'Istanbul is no longer a city of consequence ... It is an insular little place sinking in its own ruins.'[3] In this introspective mode, his writing has depth, and his interest in varied social milieux and competing intellectual traditions gives it breadth, too.

Yet in some respects, Pamuk's vision is surprisingly blinkered. Readers will search in vain for many of the symbols and references which might be conjured up by such a rich history. His much-vaunted exploration of 'a vast cultural history' turns out to be entirely Turkocentric. 'The East' of his experience means the flotsam of the late Ottoman Empire. 'The West' stands for Atatürk's secular, Europeanized, national republic and its foreign sources of inspiration. The past, it seems, goes no further back than the world of his parents and grandparents. Pamuk's gloomy artistry is the work of a modern *Istanbullu* with marked historical myopia: a writer blind to all but the most recent remains of what went before.

Throughout 2010, together with the Ruhr region in Germany and Pécs in Hungary, Istanbul served as one of the three chosen European Capitals of Culture. Having created the 'Istanbul 2010 ECOC Agency', it participated with energy and elan under the slogan of '*Avrupa Kültür Başkenti*'. Hundreds of events took place spanning the visual arts, music, film, literature, theatre, traditional arts, urban culture, education, cultural heritage, museums, tourism and sports. The year-long festival opened on 10 January with a rally in the Golden Horn Congress Centre attended by the president of Turkey, Abdullah Gül, and the Turkish prime minister, Recep Tayyip Erdoğan. 'I salute everyone: from Emperor Constantine to Sultan Mehmet the Conqueror,' Mr Erdoğan said, 'from Sultan Suleyman all the way to Mustafa Kemal Atatürk, who have since its foundation ornamented Istanbul like an embroidery.'[4] Proceedings ended twelve months later at a closing ceremony addressed by State Minister Egemen Bağiş. 'The world has re-discovered Istanbul with this project,' the minister said boldly; 'Istanbul is [not just] a European city; it is the city which shaped European Culture.'[5]

II

Byzantium – whose English name was taken from the Latin, not the Greek – is a piece of historical reality; despite its changing appellations, it has had a continuous and evolving existence since the day of its foundation. The 'Byzantine Empire', in contrast, is no more than an intellectual construct, an abstraction, some might say, that never really existed. Promoted by the *philosophes* of the Enlightenment – the Byzantines themselves continued to call their territories the 'Roman Empire' – it is a label of convenience invented long after the state in question had disappeared, a substitute for another artificial name – the 'Greek Empire' – which some historians (including Gibbon) preferred. Its inventors disliked theocratic states in principle, and could not stomach the idea of a Roman Empire that was not ruled by Rome.

The translation of the Roman Empire from a state whose centre of gravity lay in Italy to one based further east took place very gradually. Its division into Western and Eastern sub-states, each with its own emperor, was introduced by Diocletian in AD 285; the choice of Byzantium as the new capital was made by Constantine I in 330; the Western Empire collapsed in 476; and the definitive loss of Italy occurred in stages between the initial invasion of the Lombards in 567 and their much delayed entry into Rome in 772. This was the latest point, 440 years after the founding of Constantinople, when the Empire can be said to have shed its former western provinces for good, and when, looking at its history in retrospect, westerners felt it had ceased to be 'theirs'. Yet another thousand years would pass before the Enlightenment concocted a new designation for this political entity with which the 'West' no longer identified.

The Roman Empire was never in fact primarily western, nor purely Roman. The Romans had conquered Greece and the Greek-speaking Hellenic world (including Byzantion) in their republican days, long before they intervened in more distant places like Gaul, Germany or Britain; and the intermingling of Greek and Roman traditions played a fundamental role in all subsequent developments. Shortly after the death of the first *Augustus*, Octavius Caesar (r. 726–767 AUC: 27 BC–AD 14), the wealthiest and most populous imperial province was in Hellenized Egypt. Christianity, the future imperial religion, came out of the East in the same era, and four out of the five Church patriarchs would reside there. When the forty-ninth emperor, Diocletian, divided the Empire into two halves, he himself chose to be *Augustus* of the East; and when the fifty-sixth decided to move the capital from the Tiber to the Bosporus, he did so in response to a well-established political, commercial and cultural shift.

From then on, the Roman Empire grew ever more oriental, both in geography and civilization. As from 380, under the sixty-sixth emperor, Theodosius I (r. 379–95) Christianity gained a religious monopoly, soon causing 'Caesaro-papism' to become the norm. The *basileus* (emperor) ruled both as *autocrator* and as *pontifex maximus*; Church and State were inseparable. In the fifth century, the provinces of Britannia, Gallia, Germania and (northern) Africa were overrun by 'barbarian' hordes; in the sixth, despite a brief resurgence under the eighty-eighth emperor, Justinian (r. 527–65), Hispania and Italia began to peel away. The Empire was being reduced to what in modern terms might be called the Balkans and the Levant. In the seventh century, as the Lombards bit off most of Italy, the first attacks were launched by the rising power of Islam, with whose adherents the imperials would fight to the death for more than 800 years. In the eleventh century the Great Schism cut the Empire off from the Latin Church of the West, creating the lasting division between Orthodoxy and Catholicism. All the while, despite their use of the Greek language, the Empire's rulers and subjects continued to think of themselves as Romans and to call their homeland either *Romania* or *Pragmata Romaion*, the 'Land of the Romans'. This was the offence for which Westerners in general, and the *philosophes* in particular, could not forgive them.

To all who have been seduced by the concept of 'Western Civilization', therefore, the Byzantine Empire appears as the antithesis – the butt, the scapegoat, the pariah, the undesirable 'other'.[6] Although it formed part of a story that lasted longer than any other kingdom or empire in Europe's past, and contains in its record a full panoply of all the virtues, vices and banalities that the centuries can muster, it has been subjected in modern times to a campaign of denigration of unparalleled virulence and duration. The fashion, if not initiated by Voltaire, was certainly inflated and disseminated by him. '*Byzance*', wrote the Sage of Ferney in 1751, was 'a story of obscure brigands', and 'a disgrace to the human mind'.[7]

Montesquieu wrote an early work on the decadence of the late Roman Empire, for which he invented the adjective 'byzantine' in its modern sense. His chief contribution to political thought lay in his definition of 'the separation of powers'; and since Byzantium knew no such separation, he was necessarily hostile. 'Henceforth', he wrote after dropping the Roman name, 'the Greek Empire is nothing more than a tissue of revolts, seditions and perfidies ... Revolutions created more revolutions, so that the effect became the cause.'[8] The flail was then taken up by Georg Hegel, founder of the modern philosophy of history. 'Byzantium', Hegel opined, 'exhibits a millennial series of uninterrupted crimes, weakness, baseness, and want of principle: a repulsive and hence an uninteresting picture.'[9] Such was the Enlightenment's prevailing wisdom. Did the Empire of Augustus know no crimes?

Yet predictably no one matched the great Edward Gibbon in the eloquence of his disdain. Thanks to Gibbon, the whole of Byzantine history came to be conceived as the inexorable progress of Decline, varied only by the welcome moment of its Fall. Gibbon's notorious chapter 48, which traces the reigns of the Byzantine emperors from Heraclius (no. 93, r. 610–41) to Alexius V (no. 151, r. 1204), overflows with the relish of his wilful prejudice. The Greek empire, Gibbon wrote in his chapter

48, saw the triumph of barbarism and superstition; '[its fate] has been compared to that of the Rhine, which loses itself in the sands before its waters can mingle with the ocean'.[10] Or again:

> [T]he subjects of the Byzantine Empire, who assume and dishonour the names both of Greeks and Romans, present a dead uniformity of abject vices, which are neither softened by the weakness of humanity nor animated by the vigour of memorable crimes ... on the throne, in the camp, in the schools, we search, perhaps with fruitless diligence, the names and characters that may deserve to be rescued from oblivion.

The negativity is relentless:

> Of a space of eight hundred years, the four first centuries are overspread with a cloud interrupted by some faint and broken rays of historic light ... The four last centuries are exempt from the reproach of penury: and with the Comnenian family the historic muse of Constantinople again revives, but her apparel is gaudy, her motions are without elegance or grace. A succession of priests, or courtiers, treads in each other's footsteps in the same path of servitude and superstition: their views are narrow, their judgment is feeble or corrupt: and we close the volume of copious barrenness, still ignorant of the causes of events, the characters of the actors, and the manners of the times.

The Gibbonian lash spares none of the sixty rulers mentioned in that long chapter. On the subject of the Empress Irene, for example, the last of the Isaurian dynasty (no. 110, r. 797–802), who had blinded her son (and about whom Voltaire wrote a play), his outrage assumes cosmic proportions:

> The most bigoted orthodoxy has justly execrated the unnatural mother, who may not easily be paralleled in the history of crimes. To her bloody deed superstition has attributed a subsequent darkness of seventeen days, during which many vessels in mid-day were driven from their course, as if the sun, a globe of fire so vast and so remote, could sympathise with the atoms of a revolving planet. On earth, the crime of Irene was left five years unpunished; her reign was crowned with external splendour; and if she could silence the voice of conscience, she neither heard nor regarded the reproaches of mankind. The Roman world bowed to the government of a female; and as she moved through the streets of Constantinople the reins of four milk-white steeds were held by as many patricians, who marched on foot before [her] golden chariot ... But these patricians were for the most part eunuchs; and their black ingratitude justified, on this occasion, the popular hatred and contempt.

In other cases, mockery was the chosen weapon:

> The name of Leo the Sixth has been dignified with the title of *philosopher*;
> and the union of the prince and the sage ... would indeed constitute the
> perfection of human nature. But the claims of Leo are far short of this ideal
> excellence. Did he reduce his passions and appetites under the dominion of
> reason? His life was spent in the pomp of the palace, in the society of his
> wives and concubines; and even the clemency which he showed, and the
> peace which he strove to preserve, must be imputed to the softness and
> indolence of his character. Did he subdue his prejudices, and those of his
> subjects? His mind was tinged with the most puerile superstition; the influ-
> ence of the clergy and the errors of the people were consecrated by his laws;
> and the oracles of Leo, which reveal in prophetic style, the fates of the empire,
> are founded on the arts of astrology and divination. If we still inquire the
> reason of his sage appellation, it can only be replied, that [he] was less ignor-
> ant than the greater part of his contemporaries in church and state.

Gibbon had run into a crisis in the writing of *The Decline and Fall*.
After forty-seven chapters he had only reached the end of the sixth century, and he had nearly nine more centuries to cover. He desperately
needed to change the pace, and chapter 48 was his vehicle for doing so.
Rhetorically, it was magnificent; but as even his admirers admit, 'historically, it was the weakest section'.[11]

The onslaught of the Enlightenment all but obliterated the earlier
school of Byzantine scholarship which had been started in Italy by academic refugees from Constantinople in the mid-fifteenth century; and the
rehabilitation of the Byzantine Empire as a worthy subject of study has
occupied the best part of the last 200 years. The first steps towards greater
discrimination were taken in Germany, by Winckelmann and others. In
Britain, the art historian John Ruskin (1819–1900) made a powerful case
for the originality of Byzantine art, especially in *The Stones of Venice*
(1851–3); and the work of his older contemporary George Finlay (1799–
1875) re-created a historical continuum which links the revered world of
ancient Greece both with Byzantium and with the newly independent
Greek kingdom of his own day.[12] As Finlay demonstrated, the Empire died
twice: once at the hands of Western crusaders, who seized Constantinople
between 1204 (the perverted Fourth Crusade) and 1261, and the second
time at the hands of the Ottoman Turks in 1453. In its terminal phase, the
Empire shrivelled in almost botanical style, having repeatedly flowered
and borne its fruit. Eventually, reduced to the confines of the single city, it
was ready, like the last living twig on an ancient stump, to perish.

In the twentieth century, three scholarly names stand out. J. B. Bury (1861–1927), an Irishman, is often credited with the revival of Byzantine studies in Britain. Editor both of Gibbon and of the *Cambridge Ancient History*, he held chairs at Trinity College, Dublin, and at Cambridge. A brilliant Hellenist, he wrote extensively on Classical Greek, Roman and Byzantine subjects.[13] Professor Sir Steven Runciman (1903–2000), an eccentric gentleman scholar, claimed to have been Bury's 'first and only student' at Cambridge. He was conversant with an astonishing array of languages, including, reputedly, Greek, Latin, Turkish, Farsi, Arabic, Georgian, Armenian, Russian and Bulgarian, and in the title of an influential early work he bravely linked 'Byzantine' with 'Civilisation'.[14] In his *History of the Crusades* (3 vols., 1951–4), he constantly battled the self-centred prejudices of the 'West', preferring to believe that the Easterners were guardians of Europe's culture and refinement, and Westerners the barbarians.[15] 'There never was a greater crime against humanity', he wrote, 'than the Fourth Crusade.'[16] Professor Sir Dimitri Obolensky (1918–2001), a Russian-born Oxonian, displayed similar inclinations. His work was notable for revealing that the Byzantine Commonwealth had been a multinational community of faith, and that its legacy was still alive among the Eastern Slavs.[17]

Once Byzantine Studies were established in the academic world,[18] the next task was to raise awareness among the public at large. In this regard, Judith Herrin, a professor from King's College, London, relates the sort of incident that turns other historians green with envy:

One afternoon . . . two workmen knocked on my door in [London University]. They were doing repairs . . . and had often passed my door with its

notice: 'Professor of Byzantine History'. Together, they decided to stop by
and ask me 'What *is* Byzantine history?' They thought that it had something
to do with Turkey. And so I found myself trying to explain briefly what
Byzantine history is to two serious builders in hard hats and heavy boots . . .
They thanked me warmly, said how curious it was, this Byzantium, and
asked why didn't I write about it for them?[19]

Those two builders were in the same position as 99 per cent of the
population, including 98 per cent of educated Westerners.

Another distinguished Byzantinist, meanwhile, had been applying her-
self to some of the basic questions. 'For most historians,' Professor Averil
Cameron begins, 'Byzantium is an absence.'[20] Her answer to 'What was
Byzantium?' sounds very straightforward: 'Byzantium is the modern name
given to the state and society ruled almost continuously from Constantinople (modern Istanbul) from the dedication of the city by the Emperor
Constantine in AD 330 until its sack by the Ottomans under the young
Mehmed ('The Conqueror') in 1453.'[21] 'But Byzantium is hard to grasp,'
she continues, 'and "the Byzantines" even more so.'[22] Her perception that
Byzantine history began in AD 330 is not shared by everyone. Many scholars put the transition from Roman to Byzantine significantly later, either
with Justinian or with Heraclius or even with Leo III (r. 717–41). It is common practice nowadays to use the framework of five Byzantine dynasties:
the Heraclian (610–717), the Isaurian (717–867), the Macedonian (867–
1081), the Comnenian (1081–1258) and the Palaeologan (1258–1453).

In answer to 'Who were the Byzantines?' Professor Cameron is intent
on dispelling misconceptions:

> The Byzantines were not a 'people' in any ethnic sense. If we consider only
> Anatolia, the population had been thoroughly mixed for many centuries.
> Nor did an education in classicising Greek, which was normal for Christians
> and pagans alike when Constantinople was founded, and which continued
> to be the badge of culture in Byzantium, carry any ethnic implications. In
> this sense, advancement in Byzantium was open to anyone who was able
> to obtain the education in the first place.[23]

Under 'Attitudes to Byzantium', Cameron quotes a well-known academic
reference work with dismay. 'The term "Byzantine", its editors pro-
nounce, 'is a) something extremely complicated, b) inflexible, or c) carried
on by underhand means.'[24] Non-expert reactions are little better:

> In the western public consciousness mention of Byzantium attracts two
> main responses: either it is still thought of as irrelevant or backward, the

precursor of the Ottoman Empire and somehow implicated in the political and religious problems of the contemporary Balkans, or else it seems in some mysterious way powerfully attractive, associated as it is with icons and spirituality or with the revival of religion in post-Communist Europe. Each of these responses reveals the persistence of deep-seated stereotypes, and neither does justice to Byzantium or the Byzantines as they actually existed.[25]

Progress, in other words, is slow.

In 2008–9, the Royal Academy in London staged an epoch-making exhibition in collaboration with the Benaki Museum in Athens, and entitled simply *Byzantium*. It contained 350 objects, many of stunning beauty. The magnificent catalogue was assembled by 100 contributors.[26] Reviewers, as if rediscovering a forgotten truth, wrote of 'the intensity of sacred art'. The president of the Academy enthused about the 'huge crowds', which surged past half a million.[27] The biggest wonder was that nothing like it had been staged before.

The book Professor Herrin promised to the builders appeared shortly before the exhibition, after five years' preparation. In her introduction to what she calls 'a different history of Byzantium', Herrin talks appetizingly of 'an image of opaque duplicity', and of 'a mystery' associated with this 'lost world'. In her conclusions, she appeals for Byzantium to be 'saved from its negative stereotype'. The chapter headings include items such as 'The Largest City in Christendom', 'The Ravenna Mosaics', 'The Bulwark against Islam', 'Icons', 'Greek Fire', 'Eunuchs' and 'Basil II, the Bulgar-slayer'. In addition to scenes from Constantinople, the illustrations show Mount Athos and Mount Sinai, Cappadocia, the Fourth Armenia, Moscow, Sicily, Greece, Venice and Muslim Córdoba. This may not be what the average reader expects. Least expected of all was the headline of one of the book's enthusiastic reviews: 'Brilliant, Beautiful and Byzantine'. These were not adjectives that would have naturally been associated with the subject fifty years earlier.[28]

Fortunately, awareness of Byzantium is not quite so limited in other parts of Europe. Educated Russians, for example, conscious of the Orthodox tradition, are very aware of their debt. 'We have taken over the best parts of our national culture from Tsargrad,' a Professor Granovsky once exclaimed,[29] using the old Russian name for Constantinople. Even in Catholic countries, where people are generally less sympathetic, the response is unlikely to be a blank stare. In April 1962 a young historian from Oxford was travelling across Poland with a group of British students, almost all of them totally devoid of any knowledge of the country's history. As their train approached Warsaw, the tall outline of a huge, ugly building appeared on the horizon. Unbeknown to the student-traveller it was the much-hated Palace of Culture which Joseph Stalin had donated to the Polish capital a dozen years earlier. Braving the language barrier, a gentleman in the compartment pointed through the window to explain what the building was. He tried in Polish; he tried in German; he tried in Russian; all to no avail. But then he found the one word that conveyed his meaning. '*Byzancjum*,' he cried with a broad Eureka grin. '*To jest Byzancjum*' ('This is Byzantium').[30]

Every scrap of knowledge leads inexorably to the day when the real, the historic Byzantium ceased to exist. 'The one thing we think we know is that the Byzantines were doomed.'[31] When Constantinople was founded, the Roman Empire had stretched from the Atlantic to the bounds of Persia, from Hadrian's Wall to the Sahara. Together with China and the Gupta Empire in India, it was one of the largest political states in the world, and it is all too easy to imagine that its subsequent career followed a steady, monotonous, uninterrupted downwards slide. Yet Doomsday *did* occur in the spring of 1453. The Ottoman Turks had been camping on the Asian shore of the Bosporus for over a century. The Roman Empire, once covering the whole of the 'known world', had shrunk to the bounds of the Theodosian Walls:

> The impaling of Christian prisoners in view of the Walls was calculated to cause panic. On 12 April a naval attack on the boom failed. The great cannon, firing once every seven minutes from sunrise to sunset, day after day, reduced large sections of the outer wall to rubble. But the gaps were filled at night . . . On 20 April an imperial transport flotilla fought its way into the harbour . . .
>
> But then, in a masterstroke, the Sultan ordered his fleet of galleys to be dragged overland behind Pera and into the Golden Horn. The City lost its harbour. From then on, the defenders had only three options: victory, death, or conversion to Islam . . .
>
> The decisive assault was launched about half-past one in the morning of Tuesday, 29 May, the fifty-third day of the siege. First came the bashi-bazouk irregulars, then the Anatolians, then the Janissaries:
>
> > 'The Janissaries advanced at the double, not rushing in wildly . . . but keeping their ranks in perfect order, unbroken by the missiles of the

enemy. The martial music that urged them on was so loud that the sound could be heard between the roar of the guns from right across the Bosphorus. Mehmet himself led them as far as the fosse, and stood there shouting encouragement ... Wave after wave of these fresh, magnificent and stoutly armoured men rushed up to the stockade, to tear at the barrels of earth that surmounted it, to hack at the beams that supported it, to place their ladders against it ... each wave making way without panic for its successor ...'

Just before sunrise, Giustiniani took a culverin shot on his breastplate and retired, covered in blood. A giant janissary called Hasan was slain after mounting the stockade; but he showed it was possible. A small sally-port, the Kerkoporte, was left open by retreating Greeks, and the Turks swarmed in. The [166th] Emperor dismounted from his white Arabian mare, plunged into the fray, and disappeared.

Constantinople was sacked. Gross slaughter and rapine ensued. St Sophia was turned into a mosque:

'The *muezzin* ascended the most lofty turret, and proclaimed the *ezan* or public invitation ... The imam preached; and Mohammed the Second performed the *namaz* of thanksgiving on the great altar, where the Christian mysteries had so lately been celebrated before the last of the Caesars. From St Sophia, he proceeded to the august but desolate mansion of a hundred successors of the great Constantine ... A melancholy reflection on the vicissitudes of human greatness forced itself on his mind, and he repeated an elegant distich of Persian poetry. "The spider has woven his web in the Imperial Palace, and the owl hath sung her watch song on the towers of Afrasiab." '[32]

One thousand, one hundred and twenty-three years had passed since the refounding of the city by the Emperor Constantine: 2,211 years since the Megarans had laid the first stone.

III

Describing or summarizing Europe's greatest 'vanished kingdom' is almost too much to contemplate. Like European history in general, the story is too long, too rich and too complex; and if Orhan Pamuk is typical of his compatriots, it is virtually forgotten among the Byzantines' most immediate successors. Despite their hard-won achievements, professional historians struggle with the enormity of their task. Summary evocations are perhaps best left to poets, especially to one who was once the pupil of J. B. Bury:

> The unpurged images of day recede;
> The Emperor's drunken soldiery are abed;
> Night resonance recedes, night-walkers' song
> After great cathedral gong;
> A starlit or a moonlit dome disdains
> All that man is,
> All mere complexities,
> The fury and the mire of human veins.
>
> Before me floats an image, man or shade,
> Shade more than man, more image than a shade;
> For Hades' bobbin bound in mummy-cloth
> May unwind the winding path;
> A mouth that has no moisture and no breath
> Breathless mouths may summon;
> I hail the superhuman;
> I call it death-in-life and life-in-death.
>
> Miracle, bird or golden handiwork,
> More miracle than bird or handiwork,
> Planted on the star-lit golden bough,
> Can like the cocks of Hades crow,
> Or, by the moon embittered, scorn aloud
> In glory of changeless metal
> Common bird or petal
> And all complexities of mire or blood.
>
> At midnight on the Emperor's pavement flit
> Flames that no faggot feeds, nor steel has lit,
> Nor storm disturbs, flames begotten of flame,
> Where blood-begotten spirits come
> And all complexities of fury leave,
> Dying into a dance,
> An agony of trance,
> An agony of flame that cannot singe a sleeve.

Astraddle on the dolphin's mire and blood,
Spirit after spirit! The smithies break the flood,
The golden smithies of the Emperor!
Marbles of the dancing floor
Break bitter furies of complexity,
Those images that yet
Fresh images beget,
That dolphin-torn, that gong-tormented sea.[33]

7

Borussia

Watery Land of the Prusai
(1230–1945)

I

Kaliningrad is the most westerly city of the Russian Federation. Capital of the surrounding autonomous *oblast* or 'administrative district', it was named in Soviet times after one of Stalin's many disreputable henchmen, Mikhail Kalinin (1875–1946), sometime president of the USSR. It lies on the Pregolya river, 30 miles from the Baltic coast and the ex-Soviet naval base of Baltiysk. The city centre, which straddles a number of islands, was extensively damaged during the Second World War, and the ruins of its historic buildings were long left uncleared by the controlling Soviet military. Now, restored to civilian rule, Kaliningrad possesses the full infrastructure of a modern, developing city: an international airport, a direct rail link to Moscow, a business park, an industrial zone and a university. Its ex-Soviet population of 430,000 consists almost entirely of Russian-speakers drawn from all the former Soviet republics.[1]

Thanks to wartime devastation, grandiose plans were drawn up in 1945 to design 'a Russian and socialist city' worthy of 'our Soviet Man, victor and creator . . . of a new, progressive culture'. The chief architect, Dmitri Navalikhan, assumed that building would start from a tabula rasa, that is, on a site from which all traces of the past had been erased; the style was to be a 'New Brutalism'. In practice, nothing so ambitious proved possible. Navalikhan's plans still lie in the Moscow archives, the object of art historians' curiosity.[2] When rebuilding did start, attempts were made to demonstrate that Kaliningrad was an ancient Russian city returning to its roots. The first statue to be erected, in 1946, was to the eighteenth-century soldier Generalissimo Alexander Suvorov, whose father had briefly served as governor of the city during the Seven Years War. Only then was the main street, the *Leninskiy Prospekt*, laid out from the railway station to the city centre, and lined with statues of Lenin, Stalin, Kalinin, Kutuzov and Pushkin.

Kaliningrad's present, anomalous situation is the result of the simultaneous collapse of both the Soviet bloc and the Soviet Union itself.
Having been assigned after the Second World War to the Russian
SFSR,* the Kaliningrad *oblast* served as the linchpin of Soviet strategic
defences in the Baltic region. But in 1990–91, when adjoining parts of
Poland and Lithuania left the Soviet bloc, it suddenly found itself cut off
from the rest of Russia, and the demise of the USSR rendered the
concept of a Soviet military zone redundant. Surrounded by foreign
countries, the stranded Russian enclave, with a total population close to
1 million, became a sad anachronism.

The full history of Kaliningrad's unenviable fate in the 1990s has
still to be written, but there can be no doubt that it was characterized
by a large measure of neglect and an almost total lack of financial
investment. Submarines of the ex-Soviet fleet rusted at their moorings;
ex-Soviet soldiers and their dependants lost all means of providing for
themselves; environmental pollution mushroomed. The ensuing vacuum was filled by social, economic and political pathologies of all sorts.
Crime syndicates flourished. A scheme was afoot to declare independence from Moscow. In 1998, to retake control, Moscow declared a state
of emergency.[3]

At the very end of the century, concerted efforts were made to rescue
the failed city by the rehabilitation both of its physical infrastructure
and its social fabric. Modern buildings were constructed, eyesores were
cleared, roads mended and trees planted. Drug gangs were rounded up,

* Russian Soviet Federative Socialist Republic, the predecessor of the present-day Russian
Federation and prior to 1992 the largest of fifteen constituent Republics of the Soviet Union.

protection rings closed down, and foreign smuggling stifled. The aim was to turn Kaliningrad into the hub of a Special Economic Zone, a 'Baltic Hong Kong' attracting new enterprises, casinos and tourist hotels. The European Union, eager to contain the danger on its borders, offered far-reaching advice and co-operation.[4]

In the course of Vladimir Putin's two presidential terms, from 2000 to 2008, Russia, though patently only pseudo-democratic, made considerable progress towards greater stability and prosperity, and Kaliningrad's downward slide was halted. New industry arrived, notably in the form of a television assembly plant that now supplies one in three television sets throughout Russia, and a BMW car factory, whose products go mainly to Germany. Hotels, a casino and tourist agencies have been established, and an Agreement of Special Association signed with the European Union. City-twinning partnerships have been created, not only with fellow Baltic ports like Kiel, Gdynia or Klaipeda, but also with Norfolk (Virginia) and Mexico City. High-powered delegations visited, including European Commissioner Chris Patten and German Chancellor Gerhard Schröder. Conferences were held, an EU-Russia Parliamentary Co-operation Committee was formed, and in December 2006 a casino law aimed to confine gambling to a special zone within the Special Zone. Most importantly, travel and transport arrangements were eased so that people and goods could move freely to the rest of Russia. It did no harm that the president's wife, Russia's first lady, Lyudmila Putina, had been born and raised in Kaliningrad. And though formally only prime minister after 2008, Putin clearly remains master of the Kremlin.

VIP visitors are customarily taken to inspect drilling rigs, new business enterprises and the Kaliningrad *duma* or 'parliament'. A Working Group of the EU-Russia Parliamentary Co-operation Committee in October 2006, for example, was shown round the LUKOIL D6 offshore rig, the Georgenburg Studfarm, the Taranova Brewery, and the Lesobalt wood-processing factory.[5] Overall, the European visitors were impressed both by recent economic recovery and by the colossal gulf still to be bridged. Economic growth in 2001–5 was reported at 25 per cent, 6 per cent per annum, but 25 per cent of zero is still zero. All thoughtful visitors are dumbfounded by the crime figures, and by living standards that one scholar has put at sixty-five times lower than the EU average.[6]

All but the most partial observers would agree that the potential of the 'Baltic Hong Kong' has yet to be realized. Over-enthusiastic proponents of

'Transition' assumed that free markets and Western-style democracies would develop of their own accord. In fact, the Soviet legacy is proving stubborn. One reason lies in the very low starting point: once a city has gained the reputation of 'cesspit of cesspits', the tarnished image does not improve overnight.[7] Negative statistics, which may or may not be out of date, continue to circulate. Kaliningrad has (or had) a murder rate 20–30 per cent higher than the Russian average. Kaliningrad is (or was) the scene of Europe's highest rates of HIV infection, tuberculosis and diphtheria. Kaliningrad is still reputed to support Europe's most persistent network of white slave trafficking. And though the Kaliningrad *oblast* regenerates, the adjacent districts in Poland and Lithuania, now inside the European Union, regenerate much faster.[8]

Two factors inhibit Kaliningrad's would-be renaissance. One derives from the nature of the Putin regime itself. If crime, corruption and a hidden local hierarchy lie at the heart of the problem, the centralized authoritarian system is unlikely to cure it; the Special Economic Zone may well prove to be more of a money-spinning outpost of Kremlin Corp than a motor of local well-being. One of the most successful, government-backed enterprises, the Baltic Tobacco Factory (BTF), turns out to be specially designed for smuggling cigarettes into Germany. It mass-produces the ex-Chinese Jin Ling brand in packets that are suspiciously similar to those of Camel cigarettes, except that a goat has replaced the camel.[9]

Further inhibitions stem from the pathological proportions of the Russian military presence. Since the Soviet army's withdrawal from East Germany, the Kaliningrad *oblast* harbours the largest concentration of military equipment, personnel and installations in the whole of Europe, and the cash-strapped ex-Soviet military is widely suspected of playing godfather to the notorious crime syndicates. What is more, militarization may actually increase. In the summer of 2007, when Russia's foreign minister first hinted at relocating nuclear missiles to Kaliningrad in response to US proposals for a Central European 'Missile Shield', none but the generals rejoiced. Headlines about 'a return to the strategic frontline' do not encourage investors and developers.*

President Putin's governor in Kaliningrad, Georgiy Boos, was appointed in September 2005 to preside over celebrations of the city's 750th anni-

---

* It is not true that Kaliningrad houses the mission control centre of the Russian Space Agency (ROSKOSMOS). Numerous misleading comments on this subject derive from the fact that prior to 1996 the small town of Korolev near Moscow, which does house the centre, also used the name of Kaliningrad.[10]

versary. A pretext was found in the slender thread of continuity since 1255, and the festivities were attended by presidents Putin and Chirac of France, and Germany's Chancellor Schröder. Governor Boos stressed the necessity for dialogue on all fronts, especially with Germany and the EU, and acted as the genial host to numerous delegations.[11]

Visitors to the enclave, therefore, have many interesting things to look out for. They usually arrive either at Khrabrovo Airport, which serves international destinations such as Copenhagen, Warsaw and Prague, or at the Bagrationovsk border crossing with Poland. Europeans accustomed to border-free journeys can relive their past experiences of visa controls, police questions and customs examinations. Rumours of an unavoidable thirty-six-hour wait are exaggerated.

Landmarks of the Soviet era are much in evidence. The *Dom Sovietov*, or 'House of Soviets', a high-rise pile from the 1960s, occupies the site of the former Royal Castle. The *Rossiya* cinema is an architectural exhibit of some distinction. The *Ploshad Pobiedy* or 'Victory Square' is named after Stalin's triumph in the 'Great Patriotic War', and a triumphal arch reminds visitors to the Baltic Stadium of the same event. The City Hall or 'White House' vies in its oversized proportions with the gleaming new Russian Orthodox cathedral of Christ the Saviour. Deliberately or accidentally, the statue of Lenin – a brutal proponent of atheism, but still apparently revered – stands right in front of the cathedral.[12]

Shopping is not Kaliningrad's forte. A Benetton shop has opened in place of an abandoned Italian restaurant. Another store, clearly a champion of endurance, sports a sign 'Founded in 1932'. But generally speaking, there is nothing to make the experience of consumption here anything but the most mundane.

Among the restored historical monuments, pride of place must go to the medieval cathedral. Built over fifty years in the fourteenth century, it was destroyed in 1944 in as many minutes by RAF bombs. One can view three of the city's fortified gates, now adapted for motor traffic, the former opera house, now a museum, the city zoo, and, allegedly, the wartime headquarters of the Nazi Gestapo.[13] Visitors with a sense of the past, however, may have difficulty in locating the remnants of pre-Soviet times:

> Occasionally, signs of another, older order poked through the wreckage of the new. In one place, a concrete pavement came to an abrupt end revealing a well-laid cobblestone road lying just beneath its surface; somewhere else,

an old building leaned sideways in an empty lot, surrounded by nothing. It was possible, almost, to see how the streets of the old town – once narrow and twisted and lined with the tall houses of the merchants – had disappeared beneath Soviet avenues of cracked concrete; how variety . . . had vanished behind spectacular monotony . . .

Yet the city seemed unconscious of its history. After an hour of searching, map in hand, I found the only monument to the Soviet destruction of [the city]: a tiny underground museum hidden away in a war bunker. Most of its displays contained battle dioramas, and a series of diagrams plotted the Red Army's advance . . . The final room contained before-and-after photographs. Brick homes and churches before: identical concrete blocks after. Mediaeval churches before: empty lots after.

Outside, I tried to walk through the old heart of the city, but the street plan made no sense. The centre of the town seemed jagged, unfinished: it was as if someone had thrown down the mismatched boulevards and drab buildings on top of the older landmarks by accident, and then gave up the whole project for lost when he saw the hideous result.[14]

Only two of the city's famous inhabitants have left a discernible spoor. One, Leonhard Euler (1707–83) was a celebrated mathematician who went off to St Petersburg. Before leaving he set his fellow citizens the impossible task of finding a route round the city's islands in such a way that returned them to their starting point after crossing each of its then seven bridges not more than once.[15] The puzzle cannot be tackled in its original form, since only five bridges have survived. Even so, 'Euler's Path' is a pleasant tourist trail which takes one round the Old City's islands.

Unlike his colleague and critic, J. G. Hamann (1730–88), Immanuel Kant (1724–1804) never set foot outside his home town. His lectures are reputed to have been attended by Russian officers during the Seven Years War. His tomb is still marked in the restored cathedral, and a moving souvenir lurks in an easily missed corner of the former castle precinct, where a small inscribed bilingual plaque bears a quotation from Kant's *Critique of Practical Reason*. 'There are two things', it reads, 'which the more I think of them, the more they inspire awe: the starry heavens above me, and the moral law within.' A small posy of flowers is usually left on the lintel of this plaque.[16]

Many visitors drop into the former Kaliningrad State Pedagogical Institute, which since 2005 has been upgraded to full university status as the Russian State University 'Immanuel Kant', or 'ISKUR'. The institution claims to be successor to the sixteenth-century Albertina College, and is unusually keen to establish international connections. As of March 2008, it was claiming forty-four partner universities, including four in Lithuania, ten in Poland, fourteen in Germany, and Europe's oldest university at Bologna.[17]

Yet the intellectual horizons of Kaliningrad's educated citizens can be very limited, especially in regard to history. A brilliant American historian of the region, then a young journalist, was looking in the early 1990s for assistance from the editor of a newspaper previously called *Komsomolskaya Pravda*; she found out how little her Russian colleague could tell her:

> She had been born in Siberia, and spent her childhood at an army base in the Kurile Islands. Her parents had escaped the cold and poverty of Asiatic Russia by joining the army [and] moving west ...
>
> The editor had lived in Kaliningrad for most of her life, but in school she had not learned that Kaliningrad had ever been a German city. History began with the Russian Revolution, and the next important event was the Great Patriotic War. After the war, her teachers told her, Stalin liberated Kaliningrad from Nazi occupation, but no-one ever said anything about the city prior to this event. Now she knew more. She had seen photographs of the cathedral, and she was very proud of Kant: she thought that Kaliningrad should be renamed Kantgrad. Already, she said, her generation considered itself 'different' from Russian Russians. They were Baltic Russians, a new nationality ...
>
> Yet her knowledge of the city's past was shallow. She spoke of Kant with the same veneration that Russians reserve for their canon of cultural heroes – Pushkin, Tolstoy, Dostoyevsky – yet she had not read any of Kant's books: 'I don't think they are published in Russian' ... Her interest in Germany was an interest in German tourism, German commerce, not an interest in the German past. Her plans for 'her city' were plans that would bring in German money.[18]

A worthwhile diversion is to explore the Kutuzovsky suburb, the only pre-war district to have survived intact and where ancient pre-war trams were still running in the 1990s. It is free of the otherwise ubiquitous *khrushchyoba*, the Khrushchev-era housing blocks, and is filled instead with once elegant villas, each now divided into seven or eight apartments. Nowadays, the Kutuzovsky is also punctuated with the vulgar, fenced-off residences of the super-rich. Outside Kaliningrad, visitors can enjoy a curious mixture of verdant countryside (where brooding lakes and forests alternate with agricultural settlements) and small towns caught in a time warp. With few exceptions, these tattered places have preserved their grandiloquent Soviet names: Sovyetsk Gvardejsk ('Red Guard-town'), Slavsk ('Gloryville'), Krasno-Znamensk ('Red Banner'), Pravdinsk (after *pravda*, 'the truth') and Pionerskii (after the Communist Youth Organization). No one tells you that Sovyetsk was formerly Tilsit, where Tsar Alexander I met Napoleon on a raft on the Nieman in 1807. Tourists can visit the naval base at Baltiysk if armed with a *propusk* or 'pass'. The giant sand-dunes of the Curonian Spit are a UNESCO World Cultural Heritage Site. The more adventurous can plunge into the forests to discover the romantic ruins of Teutonic castles at Balga, Polessk (Labiau) and Saalau (Kamenskoe).[19] The *Kaliningradtsy* console themselves with the none-too-gallant saying, as one moves away from Poland, that 'the cows get prettier – unlike the women'.

On the coast, beyond Baltiysk, lie a couple of half-empty seaside resorts: Svetlogorsk and Zelenogradsky. The strangely dilapidated town of Yantarny is said to be the source of 80 per cent of the world's amber, and hence of the smuggling trade. Hardy souls who venture out of Kaliningrad to savour these places, however, must be prepared for a lesson in Communist-era planning:

> I made my way up the filthy staircase and down the dark hall. Opening the door, I beheld a remarkable sight. It was not just that the hotel room was badly designed. It was as if someone had purposefully set out to create a room where . . . nothing worked at all.
>
> Every item in the bathroom was poorly constructed, as if stray bits of old junk had been reassembled there . . . The sink had no drainpipe, so water leaked straight onto the floor. The toilet flushed not with a handle, but with a bit of twisted wire. The shower head was so low that any normal adult would have to kneel to wet his head. An inoperable ventilator, unconnected to any source of electricity, hung from the wall.
>
> In the bedroom, the walls were covered in unmatching tiles. Half of the room was muddy blue, and the other half hospital green. No-one had made the tiles reach the ceiling, so several inches of unadorned cement lined the top of the walls. The beds lacked sheets and pillows. A small but vigorous cockroach was crawling across the floor.
>
> Someone had ordered the construction of this hotel. Someone else had built it. Someone had placed the mismatching tiles on the walls, someone had installed the ill-fitting sink . . . someone had failed to make the beds.

Many decisions had been made, but no-one had been responsible for the hotel room . . . It was just a place, created to fill the plan of a distant bureaucrat who would never see it and would never care.[20]

The region's best asset is its climate. Apart from faraway Murmansk, this is Russia's only section of northern coastline that is ice-free throughout the year. Twenty years ago, the USSR had six Baltic naval bases. Today's Russia has only two: Kronstadt near St Petersburg and Baltiysk.

So far, Kaliningrad and its beleaguered enclave have failed to change their name. The city of Kalinin, in central Russia, has reverted to the ancient name of Tver, and the broad Kalininskaya Boulevard in central Moscow is the 'Tverskaya' again. The citizens of Leningrad voted overwhelmingly in 1991 to recover the city's original identity of St Petersburg. So there is no shortage of precedents, but no consensus has emerged in the enclave about a new name. The front-runners in the 1990s were 'Kantograd' and 'Korolovsk'. At present, the Russian slang-name of 'Kyonig' is said to have the edge. But cultural sensibilities are still heavily Sovietized, and rallies are still held to mark the Bolshevik Revolution.

As the second post-Soviet decade reached its end, the city held its breath to see if the stand-off over nuclear missiles could be defused. In 2008 hopes were sinking. The government of Poland had agreed in principle to admit the American 'Shield'; and Russia's new president, Dmitri Medvedyev, threatened to install short-range Iskander missiles in the enclave. Then in 2009 tensions relaxed. The incoming Obama administration in the United States curtailed the chances of the 'Shield' being built,[21] and the Iskanders were sent back. The signing of a new Russo-American START Treaty on 26 January 2011 promised a period of calm.

Nonetheless, the Kalingrad enclave remains a place of tangible unease. Some still blame external threats. 'Russia is like a wolf,' one Kaliningrader has said enigmatically, 'a wolf that has been trapped by hunters.'[22] So far no one has caught sight of the hunters; others underline internal shortcomings. On 2 February 2010 tens if not hundreds of thousands of protesters gathered in central Kaliningrad to demand the removal not only of Governor Boos but also of Vladimir Putin. The placards targeted Putin's *YedRo* or 'United Russia' Party; '*Partiya YedRo*', the jingle read, '*pomoinoye vyedro*' ('United Russia [is] a bucket of filth').[23] The Kremlin ordered a high-level inquiry, but fresh demonstrations broke out exactly six months later. This time Governor Boos was immediately fired, and replaced by the local YedRo Secretary, Nikolay Tsukanov.

Suddenly the air was thick again with ambitious plans. Visions of the Baltic Hong Kong resurfaced as the federal government proposed yet another 'new economic status' for the enclave. Governor Tsukanov proposed his home town of Gusev as a centre of expansion parallel to Kaliningrad. The Regional Development Agency announced multi-billion-rouble grants to accelerate stalled projects for a new seaport and a nuclear power station.[24] Even the outlook for gay tourism was explored. Then, as if to go back to basics, a Russo-German scheme was unveiled at Zeleniogorsk to prepare an Open Air Museum of the Ancient Prussians.[25]

II

One thousand, two thousand years ago, the land that lies on the southern shore of Europe's second inland sea was virtually *terra incognita*. If it was known beyond its own shores at all, it was as the 'Amber Coast', the source of the shimmering translucent gold-brown stones which were highly prized for jewellery in the ancient world. The native tribes who lived in the dark forests of the Baltic coastland had few contacts with outsiders. They lived from fishing, hunting and raiding their neighbours. They called themselves *Prusai*, or *Pruzzi* – a name that has been traced to an Indo-European root connected with water. Since they would have identified themselves above all with their natural surroundings, there is some basis for thinking of them as the 'Water Tribes' or the 'Lakeland Folk', or possibly, through the striking configuration of their coastline, as the 'People of the Lagoons'.[26]

The *Prusai* thrived untouched by civilization until the thirteenth century AD. They were pagan, illiterate, pre-agricultural and, in the eyes of their neighbours, primitive predators. All the great events of early European history passed them by. Hoards of Roman coins, deriving no doubt from the amber trade, indicate that they must have been aware of the wider world,[27] yet the Roman Empire rose and declined without altering their way of life. The invading Asiatic nomads rode across the open plains to the south, and the westward passage of Germanic, and later of Slavic tribes, did not penetrate their homeland. The empire of Charlemagne and his successors never reached them; nor did the religion of the Nazarenes, which gradually overtook the north European mainland in the tenth century and Scandinavia in the twelfth.

Apart from occasional and ambiguous references by early geographers, the first event to bring the *Prusai* into the historical record occurred in 997. In that year the Czech Prince Vojtech of Prague, a missionary bishop, took ship in the Vistula delta intending to convert them. Instead, he was murdered by his prospective flock. A search party ransomed his body, and brought it back as a holy relic to the newly founded Polish cathedral of Gniezno. Vojtech was better known by his baptismal name of Adalbert, and as St Adalbert of Prussia he was destined to become the heavenly patron of the land which had rejected him.[28]

The *Prusai* formed the westernmost grouping within a larger collection of Baltic peoples, including the Lithuanians and Latvians and who spoke related languages and followed similarly traditional ways of life. The names of their constituent tribes were recorded in Latin forms by the Catholic monks who first accumulated knowledge of the region. Already in the ninth century, the so-called Bavarian Geographer* had recorded the Latin name of *Borussia* – that is, the land of the *Prusai* – from which all modern variants of the country's name are derived: *Prussia* (Latin and English), *Preussen* (German), *Prusse* (French) and *Prusy* (Polish). Five hundred years later, when the conquest of Borussia

---

* An anonymous author, the Geographus Bavarus, probably a monk of Reichenau; his work entitled *Descriptio civitatum et regionum ad septentrionalem plagam Danubii* was not discovered until 1772, in Munich in the Bavarian State Library.

by Christian knights was in progress, the priest Peter Dusberger compiled a much fuller list of tribes. Among the Balto-Prussian ethnic group, he noted the Varmians, the Pomesanians, the Natangians, the Sambians, the Skalovians, the Nadruvians, the Bartians, the Sudovians and the Galindians. Each of them possessed their own territory within the expanse lying between the Vistula and Nemanus (Nieman) rivers. The first six on the list were settled on the coast, the others in the interior. There may have been others.

The geography of *Borussia* added greatly to its isolation. The coastal strip was bordered by a string of maritime lagoons, which had formed behind long sandy spits and which obstructed easy access to the rivers. The interior consisted largely of the vast lines of morainic stones which marked the stages of retreat of the last northern ice cap. The result was a tangle of fantastically shaped lakes interspersed by winding chains of pine-covered heights. There were no straightforward routes or trails, no safe refuges for intruders. Most of the ground was unsuitable for growing crops. The temptation to mount cattle-raids into the open country beyond the lakes, and to seize the produce of foreign barns, was great.

By the thirteenth century, however, the *Prusai* were effectively surrounded on all sides. The area to the west beyond the Vistula had been settled by Western Slavs, notably by the Kashubs, who formed part of the Duchy of Pomerania. To the south lay the Polish Duchy of Mazovia, centred on Warsaw, which during 'the era of fragmentation', was enjoying a state of semi-independence. To the east, beyond the Nieman, other Baltic groupings were embarking on adventures of their own that would lead to the states of Livonia and of the Grand Duchy of Lithuania.

The principal motor of change in East Central Europe in that era was the arrival of the Mongol Horde. Streaming out of the Asian steppes, the Mongols destroyed Moscow in 1238, before wreaking death and pillage through what is now southern Poland and Hungary. The resultant insecurity encouraged two developments. One was the establishment of crusading orders to strengthen Christendom's eastern borders. The other was the mobilization of German colonists to repopulate the devastated districts.

In its previous phase, Germanic colonization did not affect *Borussia*. After 1180, when the Slavonic duke of Pomerania, Boguslav III, had sworn fealty to the Holy Roman Empire, settlers from the latter crossed the River Oder and edged along the Pomeranian coast. After 1204, when one of the military orders, the Knights of the Sword (see p. 270n.), established a base at Riga in Livonia and when the Danes built their fort at Tallinn in Estonia, the Northern Crusades* were underway.[29] But the *Prusai*, sandwiched between the advancing colonists on one side and the warring crusaders on the other, remained unscathed.

Such was the situation in the 1220s, when Conrad, duke of Mazovia, lost patience with the perpetual raiding of the *Prusai*. Earlier attempts to subdue them with the help a minor Polish crusading order, the Knights of Dobrzyn, had failed, so in exchange for a grant in fief of the district of Chełmno (Kulmerland) the duke called in an outfit of far greater capacity, inviting the Knights of the Teutonic Order to use their fief as a base for containing the *Prusai*. From what was said later, it seems Conrad envisaged nothing more than a local and limited operation. He would certainly not have anticipated that his guests would soon grow far more powerful than himself.[30]

The 'Order of the Brothers of the Teutonic House of the Virgin Mary in Jerusalem' had been founded in the previous century as one of several military organizations spawned by the crusader states of *Outremer* in the Holy Land devoted to converting 'infidels'. It thrived through control of the port of Acre, but after the Saracen reconquest of Jerusalem in 1187 its knights increasingly gained a living as mercenaries in Greece, in Spain and then in Hungary. Yet its essential ethos and ambitions remained intact. The Teutonic Knights were looking for projects that would sustain a way of life devoted to fighting infidels but free from Europe's feudal hierarchies.[31]

The key figure in their schemes was Hermann von Salza (*c.* 1179–1239), who ruled the Order for thirty years as grand master, and who possessed connections both at the imperial court and at the Lateran Palace. This was the time when the emperor, Frederick II of Hohenstaufen (r. 1215–50), held sway in Sicily, and when his wars with the Papal States led to his excommunication (see p. 192). Von Salza, whose career began as a knight in the Hohenstaufen entourage, acted as mediator in their disputes, and his familiarity with successive popes gave him a position which he exploited to great advantage. In essence, he contrived to place the Knights under direct papal patronage, and thereby to secure immunity from unconditional loyalty to the various secular rulers in whose lands they operated. The strategy failed in Hungary, whence the Order was expelled in 1225. In Mazovia, it worked to perfection.

---

* So-called by historians to distinguish them from the Crusades in the Holy Land, in Languedoc or in Iberia.

Apart from anything else, Grand Master von Salza was an expert in legal trickery. Each stage of his scheming was supported by fine-sounding documents which gave the Order important rights without corresponding obligations. In 1226, the emperor's Golden Bull of Rimini stated that the duke of Mazovia should equip the Order to fight the pagans, and that the conquered territory should be *Reichsfrei*, that is, beyond imperial jurisdiction. In 1230 the Treaty of Kruszwica, supposedly signed both by the Order and by the duke but leaving no later documentary trace, stated that Kulmerland was to be held by the Order in fief from Mazovia. In 1234, the self-contradictory Golden Bull of Rieti of Pope Gregory IX confirmed these arrangements, while also subjecting the Order exclusively to papal authority. Thus, having secured their foothold, the Knights felt that they possessed legal immunity. Any protests by the duke of Mazovia could be ignored. The emperor and the pope were far away, and the throne of Poland was vacant.

Within a short time, the Teutonic Order created a socio-military machine that could sustain unbroken campaigns of conquest and that turned the frontline in *Borussia* into the scene of non-stop operations. Both the Order of Dobrzyn and the Order of the Sword were absorbed into it, providing a pool of knights to support a regular army. Recruits appeared from all over Christendom, attracted by the adventure of combat and the lust for land. Peasant colonists, mainly Germans and Flemings, were imported on favourable terms to work the land and to ease the manpower problem. Towns were built, marshes drained, trails cut through the wilderness and trade routes opened up. The amber monopoly was appropriated, taxes collected, troops raised, trained and paid, and the war against the infidels incessantly pursued. The killing, burning and deportation of the native *Prusai* was pursued in the name of the Faith, and the 'Black Knights', who wore a white cloak emblazoned with the black cross, assumed the divine mantle. They and their dependants spoke German, and it was among them that the name of *Preussen* gained currency.

The political organization of the *Ordensstaat*, as it came to be known – the State of the Teutonic Order – was built up in the course of the conquest. To begin with, its headquarters remained in Acre, but then moved to Venice; it did not come to *Borussia* until 1309. The grand masters were chosen by the Brother-Knights through an electoral committee. Once confirmed by the pope, they served both as commander-in-chief and as chief executive, appointing the subordinate *Landmeisters*, the provincial governors, and *Komturs*, the district commanders. Altogether, during the 327 years of the Order's existence in its medieval form, thirty-five grand masters held office for an average of nine years each. The first of von Salza's successors was Conrad of Thuringia (1239–40), and the last Albrecht von Hohenzollern (1510–25). The longest serving grand master was Winrich von Kniprode, from 1351 to 1382.

The conquest of *Borussia* proceeded over six decades, and was formally completed in 1283. Unfortunately, since the *Prusai* left no records, the story has only been told from the Order's perspective. The chief source is the four-volume *Chronicon Terrae Prussiae*, composed by Peter Dusberger half a century later, probably in Königsberg. Peter saw the Order's work as a sacred mission, and his Brother-Knights who died in battle assured of a place in Heaven. The pagans, he acknowledged, were also to be admired for their unwavering devotion to their misguided beliefs. Many Christians, he laments, could learn from their example.[32]

There can be no doubt that these Northern Crusades were contested with great ferocity on both sides. It was said that captured knights were roasted alive inside their armour. The *Prusai*, if they resisted conversion, could expect no better. All forms of violence and cruelty were justified. Captives were routinely tortured, settlements systematically razed, and survivors of both sexes were forced into slavery, from which baptism was the only exit. Their huts and homes were cleared to make way for incoming colonists. Large numbers were deported to reservations; others fled to neighbouring Lithuania. Thus did 'Western Civilization' advance.

The *Livonian Rhymed Chronicle*,* written in the late thirteenth century, described the initial offensive:

> Being on a peninsula, the land is almost surrounded by the wild seas ...
> No army had ever invaded there, and on the [seaward] side no one can fight
> against it because a wild stream, wide and deep, flows along it ... A narrow
> strip extends towards [Lithuania] and there the Christians came with their
> stately army. The Christians rejoiced. They found the great forest of the
> Samites there ... [made] of trees so large that they served as a bulwark ...
> The Christians ... vowed not to rest till it had been cut in two ... Then,
> when they had ... slashed through the forest, the army advanced directly
> into the land. The Samites learned that they were visited by guests who
> wished to do them harm.[33]

* The *Livlandische Reimchronik*, composed in Low German by anonymous authors and intended to be read aloud to the Knights during their mealtimes, covers the years 1180–1290.

On that occasion, the crusaders had fallen into a trap. Deep in the wilderness, they were ambushed and annihilated.

As the crusaders progressed, they planted many fortified towns and castles in the wilderness. Elbing, Thorn, Allenstein and Marienwerder were all Teutonic foundations. Königsberg ('King's Mountain') was founded in 1255 on a site sacred to the *Prusai* called *Tvangste*. It was named in honour of King Ottakar II of Bohemia, who had participated in the fighting personally. But nothing rivalled the size and grandeur of the Marienburg, the 'Fortress of the Virgin', erected from 1274 on the banks of the River Nogat. Four times larger than the royal castle of the English kings at Windsor, it was almost certainly the biggest medieval castle in Europe, and could be approached from the sea. Its vast walls, soaring towers and bristling battlements exude a sense of triumph and permanence. When completed in the early fourteenth century, it became the seat of the Order. By then, the land of the *Prusai* had been subdued, and the new country of *Preussen* established.[34]

The advance of the Teutonic Order naturally went hand in hand with the power of the Roman Catholic Church which had blessed its activities. The first, missionary, bishop of *Borussia*, Christian of Oliva (d. 1245), was a Cistercian monk with Polish connections who had worked with the Order of Dobrzyn. But the Teutonic Knights preferred the Dominicans, and in the 1330s, when Bishop Christian was being held for ransom by the *Prusai*, they made fresh arrangements. A papal legate arrived to mediate, and in 1243 he divided the country into four dioceses: Chełmno, Pomesania, Varmia and Sambia. He placed the new church province under the archbishop of Riga.

Kulmerland had formed the northern border of the Polish Duchy of Mazovia, and contained the towns of Kulm (Chełmno), Thorn (Toruń), Graudenz (Grudziądz) and Płock. The castle at Dobrzyn had belonged to the eponymous knightly order. Once the lakeland area to the north was cleared of its native inhabitants, it was settled by Polish colonists from Mazovia known as Mazurs, thereby receiving its name of Mazury (Mazuria/Masuren). According to later folklore, Pomesania enshrined the name of Pomeso, son of a legendary king, Vudevuto. It occupied the maritime district to the east of the Vistula. Its principal town Elbing (Elbląg) replaced the former port of the *Prusai* at Truso. Varmia or Emeland was the homeland of a Baltic tribe descended from a legendary chieftain, Varmo. It became the seat of a powerful line of bishops, prince-bishops and, eventually, archbishops. The first of the bishops never assumed office, but the second and third, Anselm von Meisser and

Heinrich Fleming, ruled the see until the turn of the fourteenth century. Their cathedral was built at Frauenburg (Frombork), which in 1310 became the first Prussian city to be incorporated, as was common in the Baltic according to the Law of Lübeck. In due course, Frauenburg would become the home of its cathedral's canon-astronomer, Nicholas Copernicus.[35] Sambia or Samland remained beyond the control of the Teutonic Order until the 1250s. It consisted largely of the maritime peninsula which separates the two principal coastal lagoons – subsequently known as the *Frisches Haff* and the *Kurisches Haff*. The city of Königsberg was surrounded by countryside in which the native Old Prussian language persisted long after being suppressed elsewhere.

The most easterly parts of *Borussia* were not conquered until the early 1280s. The key moment came with the fall of the island fortress within the 'Salmon Lake' of Ełk. German settlers renamed the fortress 'Lyck', and the Poles 'Łęg'. But the salmon motif was not forgotten. Nearly 700 years later, when another population transfer took place, the Old Prussian name of Ełk was restored and a salmon reappeared in the town's coat of arms.[36]

Despite the neglect with which the heritage of the *Prusai* was once treated, enough remnants of their language, Prusiskan, have survived for it to be reconstructed by modern scholars. It is classified as 'Old Prussian' to distinguish it from various Germanic dialects, such as Low Prussian, which developed in the province subsequently. It is one of the oldest known forms of Indo-European, and is closest to modern Latvian.[37]

Old Prussian was written down in the Latin alphabet from the thirteenth century onwards. The so-called Basel Epigram, which was probably inscribed in the margin of another manuscript by an educated Prussian sent to study in Prague, reads: '*Kayle rekyse, thoneaw labonache theywelyse. Eg koyte, poyte, nykoyte, penega doyte.*' This has been rendered as: 'Hello, sir! You are no longer a kind uncle, if you want to drink yourself but don't give a penny to others.' The so-called Elbing Vocabulary, dating from *c.* 1400, records 802 words in their German and Old Prussian versions, and a fifteenth-century fragment records the first line of the paternoster: '*Towe Nüsze kas esse andangensün swyntins.*' By far the fullest texts are to be found in three catechisms printed in Königsberg in 1545–61 in the hope of converting the last surviving *Prusai* to Protestantism.[38]

The Germanization of the conquered province, therefore, was a very long process. Though the Knights and the majority of colonists were

German-speaking, the official language of the Church and of administration was Latin. What is more, once the Old Prussian population was
baptized, the campaign to eradicate their culture waned. Many Old
Prussian place names and river names (Tawe, Tawelle, Tawelninken)
and even personal names survived, as did small rural pockets of native
speakers. As things worked out, the *Ordensstaat* disappeared before the
Old Prussian language did.

No sooner had the *Ordensstaat* been established than it ran into open
conflict with its neighbouring Polish duchies. The Knights had never
shown much respect for their neighbours, and for most of the thirteenth
century, when the fragmented Kingdom of Poland was unable to stand
up for itself, they probably imagined that they could exploit their military
advantage unopposed. In the long run, however, they were awakening a
powerful rival who would eventually bring them low.[39] The Poles always
felt cheated by the way that their Teutonic 'guests' had 'abused their
hospitality'; but so long as the Order confined itself to battling the
pagans they were not unduly concerned. Yet the Order's threat to the
lower Vistula valley commanding Poland's access to the sea could not
be ignored. The Polish–Teutonic contest over this crucial territory would
last for nearly 200 years.

Ever since the Goths had moved away from the lower Vistula in the
early part of the first millennium AD, the area had been systematically
settled by Slavic tribes. Together with the port of Gdańsk, the area had
formed part of the Polish realm for centuries, and was the funnel
through which Poland's contacts with the sea had to pass. It was now
coming under double pressure – from the creeping growth of Brandenburg along the coast to the west, and from the Teutonic State to the east.

Brandenburg, it should be stressed, had no earlier connection with
Prussia. Based on an infertile and unpromising piece of territory beyond
the River Oder, in the Empire's *Nordmark* or 'North March', it was originally inhabited by Slavs, who knew it as Brennibor. It was not yet an
electorate of the Empire, and was still to fall into the grasp of the
Hohenzollern family. It was ruled by the House of Ascania, heirs of
Albert the Bear (*c.* 1100–70), first margrave of Brandenburg and the
founder of Berlin. A century after Margrave Albert's death, the Brandenburgers had crossed the Oder and were entrenched on its eastern bank
in their so-called *Neumark* or 'New March'. Two hundred miles and
more of Poland and of Polish-controlled Pomerania separated them
from the nearest holdings of the Teutonic Order.[40]

The Poles were either too divided, or too slow, to avert the danger. Their capital lay far over the horizon in Kraków, and their rulers had grown careless of northern interests. In the decade starting in 1300 the Polish throne fell temporarily to the Bohemian Premyslid dynasty, which also ruled Hungary, and which cared nothing for Baltic affairs. The key moment arrived in 1308–9, when a party of magnates in eastern Pomerania, seeing the distractions of their nominal Polish overlords, transferred their allegiance to the Brandenburgers. Then, in a repetition of Conrad duke of Mazovia's fatal blunder eighty years before, a pro-Polish party in Pomerania called on the Teutonic Knights to help them retain Gdańsk. The Knights rode in, and kept Gdańsk for themselves. According to one report, to ease the introduction of submissive German colonists, they massacred the entire population of the city. Within a short time they had annexed the entire lower Vistula, and the Polish court was left appealing in vain to a papal tribunal. The Knights had turned from fighting pagans to fighting fellow Catholics.

In the fourteenth century the territorial possessions of the *Ordensstaat* reached their maximum extent. Courland and Livonia had been merged. The last native rebellions had been suppressed, the rural economy thrived, and several cities – Danzig (Gdańsk), Marienburg, Elbing and Königsberg – joined the international trading network of the Hanseatic League. Fine churches were built, like the Marienkirche in Danzig or the cathedral at Frauenburg; monasteries were planted in the countryside; church schools trained an educated class. Crusading continued beyond Prussia, settling down into a routine of seasonal campaigns in Lithuania, where many a foreign knight won his spurs. The Knights had created a disciplined, purposeful and prosperous medieval state, and the fame of *Preussen* spread far and wide. Chaucer's Knight from the *Canterbury Tales* had been there:

> A knight ther was and that a worthy man
> That fro the tyme that he first bigan
> To ryden out, he loved chivalrye
> Trouthe and honour, fredom and curtesie.
> . . .
> At Alisaundre he was, when it was wonne;
> Ful oft tyme he hadde the bord bigonne
> Aboven all naciouns in Pruce:
> In Lettow hadde he reysed and in Ruce.[41]

So, too, in his youth, had the English king, Henry IV.[42]

The Order's wars with Poland are too extensive, and perhaps too tedious, to recount in detail. There were endless skirmishes and numerous lengthy conflicts. As time wore on, however, the Poles gradually strengthened their position. In 1320 the Kingdom of Poland was reunited. In 1333–70, under Casimir the Great, it rationalized its holdings by incorporating Red Ruthenia and voluntarily ceding Silesia to the Holy Roman Empire. In 1385, at the Union of Kreva, it established a personal union with the Grand Duchy of Lithuania, thereby creating the largest state on the European map (see pp. 254–5 above). The threat posed by the Teutonic Order lay at the root of the Poland-Lithuania Union. Henceforth, the Jagiellonian dynasty consciously set out to dig the Order's grave.

The Battle of Grunwald, which was fought on open ground near the town of Allenstein (Olsztyn) on 15 July 1410, saw the Teutonic Knights humbled. In later times, it would be presented as a decisive clash of arms between 'Teuton' and 'Slav'. In reality, its significance was regional, not racial, but it certainly marked the watershed of the Order's military power. The victor, Władysław Jagiełło, king of Poland and grand duke of Lithuania, captured the Teutonic camp, where he found a score of wagons loaded with iron shackles prepared for the intended prisoners, now turned victors. Resplendent in silver armour on the crest of a hillock, he received the standard of the bishop of Prussian Pomerania, and sent it to Kraków as a trophy. With it he dispatched a letter to his queen:

> Most serene, excellent Princess, dearest Spouse! On Tuesday, the Feast of the Apostles, the grand master with all his power drew close, and demanded that battle be joined ... After we had watched each other for a time, the grand master sent two swords over to us with this message: 'Know you, King and Witold, that this very hour we shall do battle with you. For this, we send you these swords for your assistance.' ... At which, with the troops standing in full order, we advanced to the fray without delay. Among the numberless dead, we ourselves had few losses ... We cut down the Master, and the Marshal, SCHWARTSBURG, and many of the *Komturs*, forcing many others to flee ... The pursuit continued for two miles. Many were drowned in the lakes and rivers, and many killed, so that very few escaped.

Before Grunwald, the Knights could think of themselves as all but invincible. After Grunwald, they were thrown onto the defensive.

The battle may equally be seen as a confrontation between two opposing strains of Christianity. The Teutonic Knights belonged to the brutal, supremacist crusading tradition of Western Europe, built on the assumption that infidels and 'other-believers' were for extirpating. The Jagiellons, in contrast, whose realms contained a great plurality of religious belief, deplored both the crusading tradition and the theory of papal supremacy behind which the Knights concealed their rapacity. On the eve of Grunwald, the Polish contingents intoned their 'Hymn to the Virgin', the *Bogurodzica*, thereby underlining their conviction that the Knights' own cult of the Virgin Mary was false. They were joined in the fray by ranks of Orthodox Ruthenians and by Muslim Tartar cavalry. This was the era which witnessed the beginnings of the conciliar movement, which sought to subordinate the papacy to the decisions of Church Councils. One of the members of the Polish-Lithuanian delegation to the Council of Constance, Paulus Vladimiri (Paweł Włodkowic, c. 1385–1435), rector of the Jagiellonian University in Kraków, led the intellectual assault on the Teutonic Order's pretensions. His *Tractatus de potestate papae et imperatoris respectu infidelium*, a 'Treatise on the power of the pope and the emperor with regard to non-believers', did not immediately win universal support. But it sowed the first seeds of serious doubt concerning the validity of the Order's mission.[43]

The first cracks in the *Ordensstaat*'s fabric appeared in the mid-fifteenth century. To bolster their flagging military machine, the Knights mercilessly raised taxes to the point at which their commercial cities sought to escape. The Prussian League, first formed with like-minded municipalities in 1440 by the city fathers of Danzig, appealed to the Polish king for protection. An act of incorporation issued by King Casimir Jagiellończyk in 1456 provided the immediate cause of the third, thirteen-year Polish-Teutonic War. The outcome, following another Polish victory, was exactly what the Order had sought to prevent. The Treaty of Thorn (1466) divided the *Ordensstaat* into two. The western part, henceforth known as Royal Prussia, and which included Danzig, was returned to the Kingdom of Poland after a gap of 157 years. The eastern part, centred on Königsberg, remained in Teutonic hands as a Polish fief. The Order lost more than half of its human and economic resources. Königsberg became its fourth capital.

The division of the *Ordensstaat* in 1466 created distinctions that lasted until the Second World War. Despite a complicated political history, and repeated changes of nomenclature, the western section (Royal Prussia/Polish Prussia/*Westpreussen*, and, in large part, and using Nazi terminology, the 'Polish Corridor') was never again fully merged with the eastern section (East Prussia/Ducal Prussia/Prussian Prussia/*Ostpreussen*). In the eyes of those who admire the *Ordensstaat* and regret its misfortunes, the Treaty of Thorn has been described as the start of the 'partitions of Prussia'.[44]

The history of Royal Prussia, which fell into the Polish orbit, is little known to those who approach the Prussian story from an exclusively German perspective. (The subject was actively suppressed by bans and book-burnings when the Hohenzollerns eventually took over.) Yet for 300 years this 'Other Prussia' flourished, not only as a separate institutional entity, but as the source of a separate political ideology and culture, based on concepts of freedom and liberty. Though the population was ethically mixed, Polish and German – with a strong German predominance in the cities – the corporate identity and fierce local patriotism of

Royal Prussia digressed markedly from the values with which the name of 'Prussia' is usually associated.[45]

Royal Prussia's territory consisted of the valley of the lower Vistula from the river's 'elbow' near Thorn to the Baltic coast, plus the protruding province of Varmia. Its three major centres were Danzig (Gdańsk), Elbing (Elbląg) and Thorn (Toruń), together with a constellation of lesser towns. These prosperous urban communities provided the motor both for commercial dynamism and for startlingly original cultural developments.

The government of Royal Prussia was based on the municipal liberties granted to the towns, and on the provincial Diet, which provided a forum for a politically active nobility. Following the statute of *Nihil Novi* (see p. 271, above), courts and provincial assemblies developed in the wider Kingdom of Poland too. When the constitutional Commonwealth of Poland-Lithuania was created in 1569, Royal Prussia was formally incorporated. From then until the First Partition of Poland of 1773, it was divided into the palatinates of Pomerania (Danzig), Kulm and Marienburg, and the autonomous diocese of Varmia. Deputies were sent to the central Diet in Warsaw and to royal elections, while *sejmiki* or district noble assemblies functioned in each palatinate.

The high degree of self-government enjoyed by Royal Prussia's burghers and nobles fostered a high degree of originality in the realms of history-writing and myth-making. Simon Grunau's *Preussische Chronik*, produced in fifteenth-century Elbing, was fundamentally hostile to the record of the Teutonic Knights. The scholar Erasmus Stella (d. 1521) explored the origins of Prussia, presenting the ancient *Prusai* as a 'people born to freedom', and publicizing the legend of 'Mother Borussia' and her many sons. In due course, both the Gothic Myth and the Sarmatian Myth* were adapted to reinforce the idea that 'the Prussians will not suffer a lord amongst them'. The Sarmatian strand in this ideology invented a common oriental origin for Prussians, Poles and Lithuanians, so that the authors' contemporary attachment to the right of resistance could be shown to have ancient roots. It was an effective barrier to absolutist ideas coming from the West, and a fertile seed-bed for the 'Royal Prussian Enlightenment' centred in the eighteenth century around the figure of Gottfried Lengnich (1689–1774).[46]

All in all, Royal Prussia generated a strong sense of 'pre-modern identity' that stands apart from ethnic nationalism, but was firmly grounded in the experience of a long-lasting political community. This identity, which saw Poland as protector and its easterly neighbour, the growing Hohenzollern state, as a menace, inspired heart-warming loyalty in successive wars, and exercised a significant influence on oppositional circles in adjacent Königsberg. It would persist until the eventual arrival of the army and officialdom of Frederick II of Prussia in 1773, after which it was suppressed by force.

In the fifty or sixty years following the Treaty of Thorn, the Teutonic Knights gradually lost their *raison d'être*. They had no more pagans to convert, and the twin stars of their ideological firmament, the Empire and the papacy, were both in disgraceful disarray. Their former subjects in Royal Prussia had won impressive liberties, and were now surging ahead in prosperity. After losing their edge in the latest armed conflicts with Poland, many of the Knights in Teutonic Prussia could have seen little hope in a future of endlessly lost battles. Their state was ripe for a revolution that none saw coming.

The Knights had a further problem. The Treaty of Thorn required their grand masters to pay homage to the Polish king. The act of homage was normal feudal practice, and since the Order's lands lay outside the Empire, it was not an issue on which the Empire could intervene. Even so, it grated. Later German commentaries would invariably call it 'humiliating'. Each subsequent homage strengthened the feeling among the Knights that arrangements had to change, and after 1493 the Knights

---

* The Gothic Myth among Germans and the Sarmatian Myth among Poles propagated the idea that the modern descendants of ancient Goths and Sarmatians inherited their forebears' inborn love of freedom.

tried to withdraw their Polish allegiance. Moreover, two grand masters enjoyed strong political connections in Germany. Friedrich von Sachsen (r. 1497–1510) was a prince of Saxony. His successor, Albrecht von Hohenzollern (r. 1510–25), was a scion of the dynasty that had taken over the imperial Electorate of Brandenburg.

It was in 1517 that Martin Luther (probably) nailed his ninety-five theses to the door of the castle church in Wittenberg. Even he could not have guessed that the Teutonic Knights, long famed for their militant Catholicism, would prove to be one of his most receptive audiences. Within a couple of years, however, Grand Master von Hohenzollern had been won over to the need for radical measures to reform the Church. After consultations with Martin Luther in person, he determined to transform the Catholic *Ordensstaat* into a confessional state devoted to what would soon be called Protestantism. This meant that the grand master would have to resign from his office and assume a secular title, that the Order would have to be disbanded or dismissed, and that individual Knights would have to choose between joining the new state or leaving. Most crucially, approval would have to be obtained from Poland-Lithuania. If it was not, the chances were that the Order's part of Prussia would simply be annexed, or that the Knights would be sent by their feudal superior on military service against his enemies elsewhere (Poland-Lithuania was sorely troubled at the time by marauding Tartar hordes: see p. 260).

Such was the genesis of the solution that was duly put into effect in 1525. The grand master resigned. The Order, together with any Knights who so chose, retired to its northern province of Courland-Livonia (see p. 270), and the rest swore allegiance to the new Lutheran faith. Then, by prior agreement, Albrecht von Hohenzollern travelled to Kraków to proclaim his fealty to the king of Poland, and to receive Prussia in fief. According to the Treaty of Kraków, the ex-grand master became a duke, and his possessions a duchy.

The act of Prussian homage, which was staged in public on 10 April 1525 in Kraków's great market square, did not belong to the historic scenes which the Hohenzollerns would later care to publicize, but it formed an essential element in the make-up of sixteenth-century Europe. As depicted by the Romantic painter Jan Matejko, it would become a favourite prop to Polish national pride. In the painting, Sigismund-August, King Sigismund I, sits grandly on his throne. Albrecht von Hohenzollern, bareheaded and dressed in full armour, kneels before him, holding the Prussian standard of the black eagle. A Prussian knight touches the hem of the standard in a gesture which was later said to have rendered the homage invalid.[47] The series of ducal acts of homage to Poland was to continue with every change of duke or king: 1569, 1578, 1611, 1621, 1633, 1641 ... Europe would forget, but time was when the king of Poland was boss and the Hohenzollern was an underling.

The second stage of Duke Albrecht's investment took place in Königsberg, where he arrived on 9 May 1525, seeking the formal approbation of the Prussian Estates:

> The whole city welcomed [the duke] with the ringing of bells and the firing of cannon. The Confirmation Diet, assembled on 25 May, was attended by three Polish commissioners – the *wojewoda* of Marienburg, the Chamberlain of Pomerania, and the *starosta* of Bratian ... The viceroy, Jerzy Polentz, feared opposition ... Albrecht personally justified the need for the Treaty with Poland, blaming all previous misfortunes on the bad conduct of the Order.
>
> On the 28th, Georg Kunheim stated the willingness of the Estates to accept the authority of the duke and of the royal commissioners ... Only the City Council of Königsberg demurred, but it was won over by the efforts of Friedrich Heydeck. That same day, the Estates paid homage to the duke in front of the Castle steps; and on the 29th and 30th, they passed resolutions to give Albrecht a significant financial grant of 82,000 guilders ...
>
> On the 31st, during the last session, a nobleman calling himself 'the Old Pilgrim' cut out the [black] cross from the cloak of one of the Knights, Caspar Blumanau. With this gesture, the Teutonic Order ceased to exist in Prussia.[48]

Much scholarly comment about the events of 1525 is coloured by knowledge of subsequent developments. It assumes that Poland was bound to weaken, and that the Hohenzollerns were destined for greatness. No one at the time possessed such knowledge. The king of Poland was by far the stronger player. He had weighed the plan to create the duchy against an alternative of sending the Order to Ukraine to crusade against the Tartars. He would have been advised that the Order had lost much of its military potential, and chose the option of transforming the remnant of the *Ordensstaat* in the hope of creating a powerful and lasting Polish-Prussian unit. Success or failure depended on the evolution of Catholic–Protestant relations, on the uncertain fortunes of the Hohenzollerns and, above all, on the shifting balance of power. If the Kingdom of Poland were to remain dominant, the Duchy of Prussia would remain dependent. If Poland faltered, the duchy might try to cut loose.

Historical judgements on the Teutonic State differ widely. Heinrich von Treitschke, court historian at Berlin in the late nineteenth century, idolized it:

What thrills us ... in the history of the *Ordensland* ... is the profound doctrine of the supreme value of the state and of civic subordination to the purposes of the state, which the Teutonic Knights proclaimed [so] clearly ... The full harshness of the Germans favoured the position of the Order amidst the heedless frivolity of the Slavs. Thus Prussia earns the name of the new Germany.[49]

Polish historians, whose views receive less publicity, find less to enthuse them.[50] Treitschke's ethnic comparisons, though typical for his age, presaged much worse to come. An exiled German historian who took refuge in Britain during the Second World War sought to balance the extremes by talking economics. 'All in all,' he wrote, 'the image of the Teutonic Order as the agent of extermination is a cliché no longer tenable ... The most lasting legacy of [their] state ... was its economic system based on large-scale agricultural production.'[51] To impartial ears, this opinion may sound like a faint-hearted attempt to avoid troublesome issues.

For the century following 1525, the Duchy of Prussia, the successor to the Teutonic *Ordensstaat*, remained a dependent fief of the Kingdom of Poland; it maintained its status in 1569 when, by the Union of Lublin, the kingdom joined the Grand Duchy of Lithuania to form the *Rzeczpospolita* or Commonwealth of Poland-Lithuania (see p. 272). It was undoubtedly one of the jewels in the Polish Crown during Poland's 'Golden Age' and, as such, is well known to students of Polish history. Yet in the annals of the Hohenzollerns it is often skipped over by those eager to reach the age of the 'Great Elector' and of Frederick the Great. In the later age of nationalism, Germans were disinclined to remember how Germany's premier dynasty played a subservient role to the Jagiellons and their successors.[52]

It is entirely anachronistic, however, to regard Albrecht of Hohenzollern, duke of Prussia, as a defiant Germanic champion. To be exact, he was the son of Jagiellons on his maternal side, and hence half-Polish; and he kept in close contact with his Polish relatives: King Sigismund I was his uncle and Sigismund II August his cousin. Furthermore, since Albrecht's conversion to Lutheranism had resulted in his excommunication by the papacy and banishment from the Empire, he naturally relied

all the more on Poland as the duchy's chief guarantor. When Prussian
Lutheranism was rent by an internal schism involving the duke's protégé, Andreas Osiander, for example, it was Sigismund-August who
acted as mediator. The Polish king, who had to cope with Protestants
among his own nobles, was no champion of the Counter-Reformation.
He was to say that he wanted 'no windows into men's souls'; his toler-
ant attitude to religious differences certainly helped the first Lutheran
state to take root.

Sixteenth-century Königsberg, known in Polish as Królewiec, blossomed into the capital city of this small state. It was the site both of an
independent Protestant university – the Albertina (from 1544) – and of
the ducal mint, which issued some fine coins bearing the inscription
'JUSTUS EX FIDE VIVIT', 'The Just Man Lives By Faith'. It was also the
seat of the Prussian Estates, an assembly which acted as a brake on the
duke's arbitrary tendencies, and enjoyed the right of appeal to the Polish
overlord. Like the burghers of neighbouring Danzig, many of the Prussian nobles greatly appreciated the liberties which the Polish connection
afforded them.

Duke Albrecht's reign in Prussia lasted more than forty years. It was
severely disturbed in the 1520s by the Peasants War, which the duke
suppressed with ferocity and which confirmed the continued existence
of serfdom. From 1530, the duchy was drawn into the Wars of the
Schmalkaldic League, fought against the German emperor to confirm
the right of the Protestant states to self-determination, and ended by
acceptance of the principle *cuius regio, eius religio* – the religion of a
state's ruler was the religion which was to prevail there. In the 1550s the
duchy was disturbed by a storm in court politics provoked by the
intrigues of a Croatian adventurer, Paul Skalić, and the duke participated somewhat fitfully in the campaign against Emperor Charles V. Yet
his ambitions turned increasingly to his own dynastic matters. Since he
was one of eight brothers, the duke had a superabundance of relatives.
Thanks to his newfound Protestantism, the previously celibate grand
master had been able to marry; and his marriage to Dorothea of Denmark produced another large brood of children. According to a
proclamation of 1561, in addition to his Prussian dukedom, he claimed
to be margrave of Brandenburg and of Stettin in Pomerania, duke of the
Kashubians and Wends, burgrave of Nuremberg, and count of Rügen.[53]

Nonetheless, during the duke's lifetime, religion raised a near-
insurmountable barrier to any thoughts of uniting the two main
Hohenzollern lines. The duke's cousins, the Hohenzollern margrave-

electors* of Brandenburg, were staunch Roman Catholics. Joachim I Nestor (r. 1491–1535) forced his sons, on pain of disinheritance, to swear eternal loyalty to the Catholic faith. Nevertheless, Joachim II Hector (r. 1535–71), though married to Jadwiga Jagiellonka, daughter of the Polish king, gradually embraced the growing Protestant faction in Berlin, and formally proclaimed Lutheranism as Brandenburg's religion in 1555.[54]

Throughout the sixteenth century, in fact, Prussia's connections with Poland stayed stronger than those with the Holy Roman Empire in Germany. Royal or West Prussia, joined to the Kingdom of Poland, was largely inhabited by Poles. Ducal or East Prussia, though mainly Lutheran and German-speaking, was a Polish fief and dependent on Poland's goodwill.

The gradual rapprochement between the Hohenzollerns of Königsberg and the Hohenzollerns of Berlin did not start until after Duke Albrecht's death. The principal cause lay in the protracted bouts of mental illness which afflicted the duke's son and heir, Albrecht Friedrich (r. 1568–1618) throughout another very long reign. According to custom, a fief could be revoked in cases of heirlessness or incapacity, and the family was forced to take precautions. First, the Berlin Hohenzollerns persuaded the Polish king to sell them the legal rights to the duchy's reversion. This meant that, if Albrecht Friedrich were to be incapacitated permanently, the Brandenburgers were entitled to act as if they were his legal heirs. Secondly, they appointed a Berliner as regent (effectively viceroy) in Prussia. Thirdly, in 1594, they married the duke's daughter, Anna, to the margrave-elector's son, Johann Sigismund (1572–1619). By that time, the Jagiellons had died out; the elective monarchy of Poland-Lithuania had been dragged by a Vasa king into the civil wars of Sweden, and its close supervision of Prussian affairs was slipping.

From the viewpoint of Hohenzollern dynastic planners, everything fell into place in 1618, though not without complications. Duke Albrecht Friedrich finally died on the eve of the Thirty Years War, and was succeeded without contest by his son-in-law, Johann Sigismund, thereby creating a personal union between Prussia and Brandenburg. But barely a year later Johann Sigismund died unexpectedly, and his twenty-four-year-old son, Georg Wilhelm (r. 1619–40), was not able to assume his

---

* Together with the kings of Bohemia, the counts palatine of the Rhine and the dukes of Saxony, the margraves of Brandenburg served as one of the Holy Roman Empire's four secular and hereditary electors, participating in imperial elections and enjoying the prestigious title of *Kurfürst* or 'Prince-Elector'.

legacy so smoothly. This time the court lawyers in Warsaw took a close interest, and insisted that procedures be followed. Margrave-Elector Georg Wilhelm was kept waiting two years before claiming his right of succession to the duchy.

The merger of the Hohenzollerns' twin states can be viewed from different perspectives. From Berlin, no doubt – especially in later times – it was seen as a magnanimous gesture by the senior branch to graciously open the family firm to their country cousins. From Königsberg, in contrast, it looked more like a voluntary decision taken between equal partners. In the first phase of the Thirty Years War, both Brandenburg and the Empire to which it belonged were deeply traumatized. Prussia, in contrast, was enjoying an enviable position on the Baltic as the natural 'halfway house' between the Commonwealth of Poland-Lithuania, on which it was constitutionally dependent, and the nearby Swedish Empire, which shared its Protestant and commercial interests. The decisive trials of strength still lay in the future. It was to stand aloof from the wars in Germany, and would be neutral in the Polish-Swedish conflict, when Gustavus Adolphus blazed his trail of glory and destruction across the Continent. At that time, Poland-Lithuania, unlike the Empire, was avoiding religious embroilments. Anyone peering into the future would have had grounds to suppose that Prussia's destiny in the Polish-Swedish Vasa orbit was no less stable than Brandenburg's precarious position in a divided and warring Germany.

The admission of the Brandenburgers into Prussia was not just a simple decision between monarchs. The king of Poland was not an absolute ruler, and in order to implement the agreement with Berlin over the fusion of the two Hohenzollern possessions, he was obliged to obtain the assent both of the commonwealth's Diet and of the Prussian Estates. The procedures were cumbersome, and the negotiations tortuous. What might have looked to the court at Berlin as a foregone conclusion proved in Warsaw and Königsberg to be a protracted political cliffhanger.

The key session of the Estates of Ducal Prussia lasted from 11 March to 16 July 1621 in the thirty-fourth year of the reign of Sigismund III Vasa. It opened with a protest from the court in Berlin, which regarded the confirmation procedures in general, and the presence of the king of Poland's commissioners in particular, as unwanted interference in the duchy's internal affairs. Georg Wilhelm had imagined that he could be invested first and discuss conditions later, but the opposite applied. The king's commissioners, led by the royal secretary, Stefan Zadowski, faced

Hohenzollerns and Jagiellons

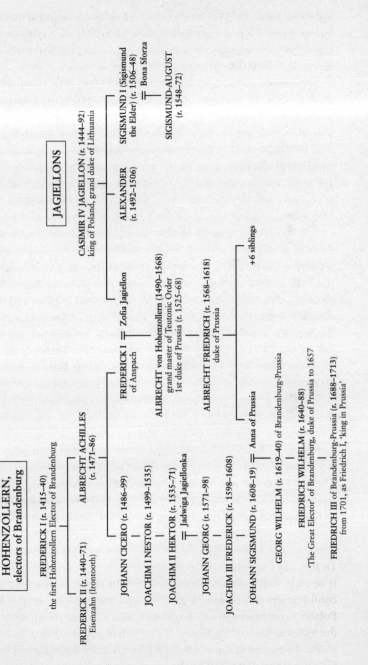

HOHENZOLLERN, electors of Brandenburg

FREDERICK I (r. 1415–40)
the first Hohenzollern Elector of Brandenburg

FREDERICK II (r. 1440–71)
Eisenzahn (Irontooth)

ALBRECHT ACHILLES (r. 1471–86)

JOHANN CICERO (r. 1486–99)

JOACHIM I NESTOR (r. 1499–1535)

JOACHIM II HEKTOR (r. 1535–71)
‗ Jadwiga Jagiellonka

JOHANN GEORG (r. 1571–98)

JOACHIM III FREDERICK (r. 1598–1608)

JOHANN SIGISMUND (r. 1608–19) ‗ Anna of Prussia

GEORG WILHELM (r. 1619–40) of Brandenburg-Prussia

FRIEDRICH WILHELM (r. 1640–88)
'The Great Elector' of Brandenburg, duke of Prussia to 1657

FRIEDRICH III of Brandenburg-Prussia (r. 1688–1713)
from 1701, as Friedrich I, 'king in Prussia'

FREDERICK I of Anspach

ALBRECHT von Hohenzollern (1490–1568)
grand master of Teutonic Order
1st duke of Prussia (r. 1525–68)

ALBRECHT FRIEDRICH (r. 1568–1618)
duke of Prussia

+6 siblings

JAGIELLONS

CASIMIR IV JAGIELLON (r. 1444–92)
king of Poland, grand duke of Lithuania

ALEXANDER (r. 1492–1506)

SIGISMUND I (Sigismund the Elder) (r. 1506–48) ‗ Bona Sforza

SIGISMUND-AUGUST (r. 1548–72)

Zofia Jagiellon ‗

the Estates with four demands before he agreed to continue: an increase in the subsidy for the Turkish War, the building of a second Catholic Church in Königsberg, the appointment of a royal naval inspector at Pillau and the fortification of the port of Pillau against Swedish attack. A walk-out by the pro-Brandenburg faction had little effect, since they proved to be in a minority. So the session resumed with an agreement to discuss the list of *gravamina* or local 'complaints' alongside the king's demands. Another wrangle concerned appointments to vacant offices. The would-be duke was informed in writing that he had no right to make appointments until he had performed the act of homage. In response, Berlin refused to recognize the speaker of the Diet, a royal candidate, and objected to the custom whereby the duchy's officials swore dual oaths of allegiance both to the king and to the duke.[55]

The Brandenburg party eventually gained the upper hand, possibly by bribery; the royal commissioners suddenly announced the imminent handover of the duchy's administration at the end of May. After that, the king concentrated on winning Georg Wilhelm's co-operation in his dynastic feud with the Swedish Vasas.[56] He never managed to insist on the reinstatement of the speaker, who had been physically ejected from Königsberg by guardsmen from Brandenburg. The game closed with the would-be duke's candidature approved. Georg Wilhelm was received in Warsaw, where he was obliged to swear on oath that his sister's marriage to Gustavus Adolphus of Sweden had been arranged without his knowledge. The act of homage was performed on 23 October. The dual state of Brandenburg-Prussia was finally under way.

From 1621 to 1657 the Duchy of Prussia was ruled from Berlin but as a distinctly separate element of the doubly dependent, dual state of Brandenburg-Prussia. Its continuing feudal link to Poland required some residual obligations, but in practice it meant little more than an understanding not to oppose the overlord's interests in foreign policy. The reign of Margrave-Duke-Elector Georg Wilhelm was overshadowed by the Thirty Years War, from which he sought to stay aloof. In this he was successful with respect to Prussia, but unsuccessful with respect to Brandenburg. In 1631 he was drawn into the campaigns of Gustavus Adolphus. His tiny army was unable to compete and large parts of his ancestral lands were ravaged. He retired exhausted to Königsberg six years later, and was succeeded by his only son, Friedrich Wilhelm (r. 1640–88), known to Berlin-biased history as 'The Great Elector', *Der Grosser Kurfurst*.[57]

The constitutional position of the Great Elector is worth elucidating. Later German history would always present him as a prince of the German Empire with subsidiary interests in the distant outpost of Prussia. The key to his policies, however, lay in the fact that he was bound by two loyalties, not one. As elector of Brandenburg, he was a dependant of the Habsburg-run Empire. But as duke of Prussia he was a dependant, and a formal vassal, of the Kingdom of Poland. Especially in the early years of his reign, it was far from clear which of the two allegiances would be the more important. He later became a past master of playing off one against the other, but prior to the Treaty of Westphalia in 1648, when the Thirty Years War finally ended, Poland attracted much of his loyalty. The court of Ladislas IV Vasa in Warsaw, where religious tolerance prevailed, could be reached in a day from Königsberg, at least on a winter sleigh ride, and the young Hohenzollern loved to go there. He spoke bad Polish fluently, and as a 'prince of Poland' was eager to participate in all the gatherings, rites and ceremonies. His own act of homage was performed on 6 October 1641 in the courtyard of Warsaw's royal castle. This outlook would not be modified until the following decades, when Poland would be overtaken by calamities every bit as horrendous as those visited earlier on Germany.

The lessons which the young margrave-duke-elector learned from his father's unhappy experiences were threefold. First, since he had forsaken Lutheranism for the Calvinism of his mother and his uncle Frederick, elector palatine, the 'winter king' of Bohemia, he cannot have failed to realize that Poland's religious pluralism brought many benefits. Secondly, seeing Poland's vulnerability despite its size, he decided that a large standing army was a sine qua non for self-protection. Thirdly, he calculated that the fiscal and commercial policies of smaller states would have to be unusually efficient if they were to support a viable military establishment. In short, he was encouraged to adopt the inimitable mixture of toleration, militarism and mercantilism for which the Hohenzollern state would become famous. In this, the margrave-duke-elector's chief adviser was to be J. F. von Blumenthal (1609–57), sometime chief military commissar of the Empire, diplomat, administrator and financier.

The establishment of Brandenburg-Prussia encouraged the consolidation of a social class whose fortunes would for ever be tied to the image of the Hohenzollern state. Landowning and military service had gone hand in hand throughout European history; but conditions to the east of the Elbe in the seventeenth century fostered a very special breed of noble families, whose rise has been extravagantly described as 'the

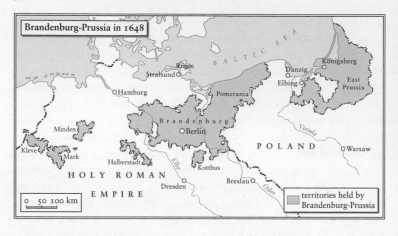

most important factor in German History'.[58] The *Junkers** benefited
both from the availability of large expanses of uncultivated land, which
enabled them to build up unusually extensive estates, typically of
5,000–7,000 acres, and from a dynamic state machine eager to employ
them. As a result, they would acquire a near-monopoly on higher posts
in the Hohenzollerns' army and bureaucracy; and they cultivated a corporate ideology and ethos which has been defined as 'the opposite of
everything bourgeois'.[59] Combining land improvement with soldiering,
the typical Junker was a patriarchal *Hausvater*, a stickler for discipline,
a political loyalist, a social conservative, an agrarian capitalist, a cultural philistine, a devotee of his honour, duty and masculinity, and the
self-appointed master of his home locality. He had more in common
with his brothers and neighbours, the Polish *szlachta*, than with counterparts in France or England. Several of the largest Junker families, like
the Donhoffs of Friedrichstein, had close relatives, like the Denhoffs of
Parnava, who lived and served in Poland and Lithuania.[60] But one
should take care not to run ahead too fast. 'In early modern times,'
writes a specialist, 'the Junkers were interested above all in farming;
their military inclinations date from the eighteenth century.'[61]

In 1648 the Commonwealth of Poland-Lithuania was struck by an
explosion of chaos similar to that which had hit Germany in 1618. It

---

*Junker, literally *Jung Herr* or 'Young Lord' and originally a colloquial phrase, came to
denote a whole social class. Its members often had roots in Germany's medieval aristocracy,
the *Uradel*, but in early modern times, as the 'Ostelbien nobility', they were concentrated in
Brandenburg-Prussia, whence they later migrated into all the Hohenzollern provinces. Their
surnames were usually preceded by *von* or *zu*.

was brought low in the first instance by a long-running and destructive rebellion of the Ukrainian Cossacks. But then the Muscovite armies invaded, followed in close order by those of Charles X of Sweden, who launched simultaneous attacks from both north and west. These were the years of the Swedish 'Flood', the *Potop*. Pillage, rapine, plague and hunger ensued. A quarter of the population died. The royal government virtually collapsed. The king, Jan Kasimierz Vasa, fled his kingdom (see p. 281).[62] In the midst of the anarchy, the duke of Prussia attempted to stay neutral. But in 1656, when another Swedish army landed in Danzig, Brandenburg-Prussia could either join the invader or risk being invaded. Moreover, the Swedish campaign was dressed up as a Protestant crusade, to which the Protestant Prussians were expected to adhere. Also, since Charles X Vasa was posing as the rightful king of Poland, he could reward the Hohenzollern duke by releasing him from his feudal dues. Friedrich Wilhelm made his choice, and in late July the Prussians entered Warsaw in triumph with the Swedes. Charles X then declared that the Duchy of Prussia was sovereign and independent.

The next year, however, saw the beginnings of a strong Polish revival. At the Treaty of Wehlau (September 1657) the margrave-duke-elector agreed to abandon the Swedes, but only if the Polish negotiators matched the Swedes by conceding Prussia's sovereign status. Poland could not refuse. And the concession was incorporated into the Treaty of Oliwa (1660) that ended the *Potop*.

In later times, the Treaty of Wehlau and its consequences have caused considerable controversy. German historians have usually seen it as an inevitable step in Prussia's rise to power. Polish historians have often seen it as a shameless act of blackmail, carried out by a grasping Prussian who had treacherously deserted his duty. All agree that it was an important milestone, and few could deny that the feudal contract was broken. As a vassal of Poland, the margrave-duke-elector definitely had an obligation of loyalty; equally, as the feudal liege, the Polish king had an obligation to protect his vassal. Both sides had broken their bond. It is also beyond dispute that the Treaty of Wehlau was never constitutionally ratified by the *Sejm* of the Commonwealth, and that many clauses remained a dead letter. One, for example, granted Poland-Lithuania the right of reversion to the Duchy of Prussia, much as the Hohenzollerns had obtained in the previous century. Another, which granted Brandenburg-Prussia the income of Lauenburg and Bütow, was made conditional on Berlin supplying 1,500 infantrymen and 500 cavalrymen for the commonwealth's campaigns against Muscovy. By a similar arrangement, the elector was to enjoy the city of Elbing's income until the common-wealth refunded the costs of his operations against the Swedes. Neither side observed these near-impossible commitments, thereby storing up a mass of unresolved disputes for the future.

From 1657 to 1701 the Duchy of Prussia was thus an independent state attached by personal union to the dependent, imperial state of Branden-burg. It was already a monarchy in substance, if not in name, and though its ruler did not change his titles, he had definitely improved his status. The margrave-duke-elector of Brandenburg-Prussia, like the Stu-art kings of England-Scotland-Ireland in the same period, was moving from the third class to the second class of European rulers.

This was the age of Louis XIV, when the absolutist model of govern-ment in France was widely praised, and the Hohenzollern elector was one of many who was attracted to it. In Brandenburg, Blumenthal pro-posed that nobles committed to military service be relieved of taxation in return for surrendering their rights to assemble in the Estates. Even-tually, in 1678, he would succeed in founding and financing a substantial standing army. His master was moving along an authoritarian, if not a strictly absolutist, road.

Huge resentment built up in the duchy. The governor, whose first act had been to hang two of Königsberg's burghers accused of collaboration with the Swedes, was seen to violate the guarantee of self-government which the Prussian Estates had received; they protested in fury. The imperial envoy to Poland, Franz von Lisola, expressed his surprise:

> [A] strong aversion to the Elector [prevails] in the whole Duchy of Prussia, not just among the Catholics but also among the Lutherans and the common folk ... They all plan rebellion as soon as possible, mainly because of reli-gion, [but also] because the Elector aims ... to subject Prussia to the arbitrary power of his ministers from Brandenburg and to abolish all privileges. The Elector joined the Swedish party without the consent of the estates, thereby provoking the revenge and the hatred of the Poles against them.[63]

The elector's own chancellor, Otto von Schwerin, shared the opinion. 'Your Electoral Highness would not believe to what extent the Polish crown is dear to their hearts,' he reported in 1661, 'and how they all seek their good in this connection.' A decade later he wrote, 'As long as one generation lives who remembers Polish rule, there will be a source of resistance in Prussia.'[64]

The reasons for constitutional conflict between Brandenburg and Prussia ran deep. The two states drew on different traditions concerning the relationship between ruler and ruled:

> While pro-Hohenzollern theorists proclaimed the duty of the ruled to believe and trust in the good intentions of the ruler *legibus solutus*, some among the Ducal Prussian estates, including the burghers of Königsberg, defended the principle of fundamental laws restricting the power of central government. [It was] the outsider from Berlin who diminished their liberties, while the Polish crown, with whom they had formed 'one body', was their natural home. The belief that they were dealing with a foreign ruler provoked a refusal to finance the Elector's other domains and provinces in the Empire, which had no connection with Prussia but through the dynasty: 'Shall the last drop of blood be wrung from the Prussian nobility, although they have nothing to do with the Holy Roman Empire?'
>
> What separated the Elector and his advisors from the Prussian opposition was a fundamental difference in the understanding of human nature, the function of government, and . . . the common good.[65]

Hohenzollern military policy was soon tested. Sweden, though it had its wings clipped in 1660, still possessed a fine army and a first-rate navy, and the Swedes were unhappy with their rivals' diplomatic intrigues. In 1675 they launched a lightning attack on Berlin from Stettin. The local defences were overrun, and the margrave-duke-elector was obliged to march his Prussian army 155 miles in ten days to rescue Brandenburg. At Fehrbellin, the Prussians gained a famous victory, and showed that a new power had entered the European stage. The date of 28 June remained a national holiday in Berlin until 1918, and the 'Fehrbelliner March' supplied one of the finest tunes in the European military repertoire.[66] The victor was raised in popular parlance to the ranks of 'the Great'.

Three years later, the Swedes tried another manoeuvre. This time, the margrave-duke-elector had to deploy his troops by sleigh, in the depths of winter, capturing Stralsund and the island of Rügen. He showed that his new standing army – already 40,000 professional men strong – was as mobile as it was muscular. Even so, one is not entitled to imagine that Brandenburg-Prussia had already overtaken Poland-Lithuania in every respect. The Great Elector's last years coincided with the career of Poland's greatest warrior king, Jan Sobieski.

Poland-Lithuania was apparently recovering well from the catastrophes of preceding reigns, and Sobieski's pet project was the reconquest

of Prussia. He swore 'to reduce the Hohenzollerns to the Polish obedience': that is, to reverse the Treaty of Wehlau, which in Polish eyes had
been signed under duress. But in 1672 the Ottoman Turks invaded the
province of Podolia, and Sobieski's attention was diverted to the south.
By the mid-1670s, the Ottomans were overrunning Hungary, and by the
early 1680s were heading for Austria. In the end, Sobieski found glory
in 1683 at the Siege of Vienna (see p. 282), only to be endlessly bogged
down thereafter in his Danubian campaigns. He never brought Prussia
to heel: the Great Elector died in 1688, unpunished, head of a state that
was fast developing into one of the wonders of the Continent.

The next margrave-duke-elector, Friedrich or Frederick III (r. 1688–
1713), did not at first seem particularly adventurous. His inheritance
was put in jeopardy in 1697 when his neighbour and chief rival in Germany, the elector of Saxony, was unexpectedly crowned king of Poland
in succession to Sobieski. Brandenburg-Prussia was now all but surrounded by a Saxon-Polish-Lithuanian combination that enjoyed a
marked preponderance of territory and resources. The Saxon elector-
king, August II the Strong, whose amorous adventures have gained him
a place in the *Guinness Book of Records*, was intent on competing in
the military as well as the erotic lists. The dangers rose dramatically in
1700, when Charles XII of Sweden set out to rekindle the northern
wars and August set out to oppose him. As in 1656, Brandenburg-
Prussia threw in its lot with the Swedes.

Such was the setting for one of the most astonishing events of self-
promotion in modern history. No one could have guessed what the
outcome might be of the two vastly complicated European wars then
beginning, nor how Hohenzollern Brandenburg-Prussia would emerge
from them. The War of the Spanish Succession had thirteen years to run.
The Great Northern War was to last for twenty-one years. In the politics
of the north, no one could have foretold whether Charles of Sweden,
Peter of Russia or even August of Saxony-Poland-Lithuania would prevail. Yet the margrave-duke-elector, as the proud owner of a fine army,
knew he was going to be courted by all sides, and would be able to exact
a price for his support. He wanted to bring recognition to his father's
achievements, to draw level with his Saxon rival (who had already been
crowned in Kraków), and to ensure that his representatives would be
sitting at the top table when fighting gave way to diplomacy. To this end,
he determined to raise his international status to that of a crowned king.

There was more to royal titles than met the eye. They were symbols
of legitimacy, and were fiercely guarded. Negotiations between the

Hohenzollern and the Holy Roman Emperor, the ageing Leopold I, were pursued by Charles Ancillon, son of the leader of the Huguenot community in Berlin. The emperor was a stickler for protocol. He was, or had been, the holder of the only royal titles permitted in the Empire: 'king of the Germans', 'king of the Romans' and 'king of Bohemia'. On the other hand, Ancillon noticed that the formation of a new grand alliance against Louis XIV was causing anxiety; the emperor's advisers were inclined to make concessions. So he argued that his master, as duke of Prussia, already enjoyed the rights of an independent sovereign and, most importantly, that the status of Brandenburg would not be affected. If the elector of Saxony could be crowned outside the Empire, why couldn't the Hohenzollern? The deal was struck. In exchange for an alliance against France and a contingent of 8,000 grenadiers, the margrave-duke-elector was to be granted a coronation.

One crucial detail remained, namely the wording of the royal title. The margrave-duke-elector could not become 'king of Brandenburg', because Brandenburg was part of the Empire. Nor could he become 'king of Prussia', because the western half of Prussia belonged to Poland, over which his Swedish allies also claimed suzerainty. (In 1704, when Charles XII invaded Poland, one of the first things he did was to declare himself Polish king.) So what could the prospective realm be called? The title had somehow to be based on Frederick's duchy. The solution was found with 'the Kingdom *in* Prussia'.*

Frederick's coronation took place in Königsberg, the city where he had been born in the year of the Treaty of Wehlau. It required a colossal logistical operation: 1,800 carts and carriages pulled by 30,000 horses dragged 200 courtiers and their paraphernalia from Berlin over 400 miles of unpaved roads. For a substantial part of the journey the travellers were crossing Polish territory. The expedition took exactly four weeks – with Christmas celebrated on the way:

> By January 18, 1701 everything was ready – trumpeters, drummers, bells. The King-to-be created a scenario for his own coronation. The people of Koenigsberg saluted Friedrich and his wife Sophie Charlotte as their King and Queen. Friedrich put the crown onto his own head and after that let the [specially created] bishops bless him ... [so that] the kingship [be] considered as God-given. Thus Friedrich III became Friedrich I King in Prussia ...

* *Das Königreich in Preussen* as distinct from *Das Königreich Preussen* from 1772.

After the self-coronation, he called for his wife in order to crown her a Queen. She came in a gorgeous golden dress all shining with diamonds, with a wonderful pearl bouquet fastened onto the dress, and wearing the purple mantle with crowns and eagles similar to her husband's. She [knelt] before the King, and he put the crown onto her head. Sophie Charlotte, being a ... highly intellectual woman, perceived the event as a farce ...

Not seeing ... the Queen's sufferings, the King continued his perform-ance. The servants brought the best piece of roasted ox and two rummers of wine for the royal couple. The feast began. Gold and silver coins to the sum of 6000 thalers were scattered among the crowd. The first day of cele-bration finished with fireworks and illuminations. The whole celebration continued till spring and finished in Berlin. Afterward it occurred that the event had cost the King ... six million thalers![67]

Frederick's annual income was 4 million thalers. Prussia's pretentious-ness became something of a joke. Stories, true and false, were retailed around Europe:

Frederick imitated the rigid etiquette of the Spanish court in his little king-dom, surrounded his palace with Swiss guards, and indulged his taste for pomp and magnificence ... [His ministers] drew funds from the unfortunate people in various and novel ways. Taxes on wigs, dresses, and hogs' bristles were imposed; and it is scarcely necessary to say that the extortionate [chief] minister took good care to fill his own pockets ... He even had recourse to alchemy to procure gold; and one alchemist [called] ... the Conte de Ruggiero, was put to death (... for deceiving the King) ... being hanged on a gilded gallows, in a toga made of gilt paper.[68]

The coronation did not increase the territory of Brandenburg-Prussia by one square inch, but its rulers could now regard themselves as kings and be so regarded by others. They had broken the unseen barrier which, in an age of faith, divided the company of the Lord's Anointed from mere chief executives. In the new century, their kingdom and its fortunes would advance from strength to strength.

As from 1701, therefore, the meaning of 'Prussia' shifted once again. It ceased to be a geographical term, and, in a brilliant act of political branding, was turned into a dynastic one. At the start of Frederick III's reign, it had referred exclusively to the eastern segment of Brandenburg-Prussia. After the coronation (when he adopted the style of Frederick I), it was applied to all parts of the king's realms, and the change required a deliberate mental adjustment. Every person who let the word 'elector' pass their lips paid a one-thaler fine into the charity box. Henceforth, every single place on which the Hohenzollerns laid their hands was officially designated as 'Prussian' – any number of distant localities from Poznan to Neuchâtel to Mönchengladbach were destined to be called 'Prussian'. Strange to say, Berlin became Prussian. Still more strangely, Brandenburg became Prussian. Duke Albrecht would never have believed it.

One of the very first and most famous products of the new kingdom was discovered by mistake. In 1704 a couple of Berlin paint-makers were trying to mix a red pigment. The potash which they used was contaminated, so, instead of red, they precipitated a beautifully stable, synthetic and light-fast blue. Its chemical name is ferric hexacyanoferrate. They called it Prussian Blue, 'PB' for short. Had their discovery occurred only four or five years earlier, it probably would have been called Brandenburg Blue.[69]

All stories, like all good essays, have a beginning, a middle and an end. The Prussian story is no exception – the only difficulty is to specify its start point, mid-point and end point. If the exercise is confined to recorded history, the total span, from the Golden Bull of Rimini in 1226 to Law No. 46 of 1947, measures 721 years. This would put the mathematical mid-point at 1586, in the era when Prussia's association with Brandenburg was just breaking into bud. If on the other hand one counts the span less mechanically in round centuries, the central period is occupied by the sixteenth and seventeenth centuries, the early period by the thirteenth century to the fifteenth and the terminal period by the eighteenth century to the twentieth.[70] By this reckoning, the coronation of 1701 marks the start point of Prussia's final flourish.

It is not hard to see therefore that the 'Rise of Prussia', traditionally dated from 1640, as generally conceived is a manifest misnomer. It would be better described as the 'Rise of Hohenzollern Prussia', or perhaps of the 'Fifth Prussia'. Indeed, the conventional 'Rise of Prussia' owes its very existence to a group of nineteenth-century historians, known as the 'Borussian School', who were working for the Hohenzollern court. Scholars such as J. G. Droysen (1808–40), Heinrich von Sybel (1817–95) and, above all, Heinrich von Treitschke (1834–96), were partisans of the Hohenzollerns' historic mission, of Prussian Protestantism as opposed to Austrian Catholicism, of the 'Prussian Spirit' and of the *Kleindeutsch* solution of the German Question in their own day. They lionized the Teutonic Knights, but shunned those parts of the story that tied Prussia neither to Germany nor to the Hohenzollerns.[71] They cemented the notion that Prussia and Germany were one and the same thing. Among foreign scholars, their views have won a near-monopoly. 'When we speak of Germany we think of Prussia,' wrote two distinguished British authors from the same era, 'and when we speak of Prussia we are thinking of Germany.'[72]

The Berlin-centred and rarely questioned 'Borussian approach' has benefited greatly from the disappearance of all Prussia's rivals which had once figured prominently, but which from a later standpoint can appear insignificant. Several powerful countries disappeared not only from the forefront of international politics but also from the front pages of historiography. Sweden's power was demolished by Peter the Great. Saxony lost much ground after its separation from Polish-Lithuania in 1763. Poland-Lithuania collapsed catastrophically during the Partitions of 1773–93, when it was physically swallowed by its neighbours (see pp. 285–90). The Holy Roman Empire was destroyed in 1806 during the Napoleonic Wars. Its demise left Prussia vying with Austria for supremacy in the German world, and with the Russian Empire for dominance in the East.

Yet in 1701, when Frederick I proclaimed the 'Kingdom in Prussia', the map of Europe looked very different from that of a later age. The Grand Duchy of Moscow had already taken to calling itself *Rossiya* or 'Russia', and its recent seizure of Ukraine from Poland had given it territorial weight in Europe to match its vast, empty holdings beyond the Urals. But the Russian Empire did not formally exist. In 1703, in an act of bravado parallel to that of Frederick I's, Grand Duke Peter Romanov laid the foundations of his imperial city-to-be on Swedish land at the mouth of the River Neva, and called it *Sankt Petersburg*. Russia, like Prussia, was gambling on the outcome of the Great Northern War. Henceforth, the competition between these two gamblers introduced a new factor into European history, matching in their rivalry for control of the East the older, Franco-Imperial competition for supremacy in the West.

At the time, neither Frederick nor Peter could be classed as premiership players. The Hohenzollerns were preoccupied with Brandenburg's neighbour, Saxony. The Romanovs were preoccupied with Sweden, whose provinces on the southern Baltic shore promised a future 'window on the West'. As yet, the Hohenzollerns could not dare to challenge their German masters, the Habsburg emperors, and the Romanovs, though masters of the limitless wastes of Siberia, had so far failed to

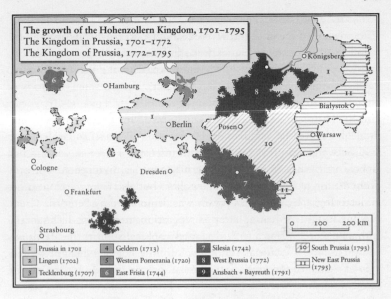

The growth of the Hohenzollern Kingdom, 1701–1795
The Kingdom in Prussia, 1701–1772
The Kingdom of Prussia, 1772–1795

1	Prussia in 1701	4	Geldern (1713)	7	Silesia (1742)	10	South Prussia (1793)
2	Lingen (1702)	5	Western Pomerania (1720)	8	West Prussia (1772)	11	New East Prussia (1795)
3	Tecklenburg (1707)	6	East Frisia (1744)	9	Ansbach + Bayreuth (1791)		

establish a permanent outlet either to the Baltic or to the Black Sea. To the west, they faced Poland-Lithuania, whose internal maladies were masked by Sobieski's military reputation; in the south, they were hemmed in by the lands of the Ottoman sultan.

Given these constraints, the modern Prussian story centres on the ways and means whereby a peripheral, partly dependent and initially third-class outfit contrived in the space of five or six generations to become Europe's leading power. The transformation is surrounded by the aura of a near-miracle. The main stages can be summarized under five headings: (1) the international recognition of Prussia's royal status by the Treaty of Nystadt in 1721; (2) the phenomenal military feats of Frederick II the Great (r. 1740–86), whose acquisition of 'Royal Prussia' inspired him to change his title to 'King *of* Prussia'; (3) the astonishing revival of the kingdom and the Prussian army after their defeat and near-extinction during the Napoleonic Wars; (4) Prussia's colossal territorial gains at the Congress of Vienna (1815), which laid the foundations of its subsequent industrial pre-eminence; and (5) the three textbook wars of Chancellor Otto von Bismarck, who in less than a decade turned Prussia into Europe's supreme military power. The zenith of Prussia's success arrived after victory in the Franco-Prussian War of 1871, when, in the great Hall of Mirrors at Versailles, the Prussian king was declared emperor of Germany.[73]

The most precarious moment in the whole saga occurred in January 1762 towards the end of the Seven Years War. Königsberg, captured by Russian forces four years earlier, was administered by military governors and for practical purposes had been annexed to the Russian Empire. After the storming of the fortress of Kolberg in Pomerania, Berlin was put under siege, and was on the point of capitulating. Frederick II, whose army had lost half its troops, was said to be on the point of suicide. But suddenly the Russian empress died; her nephew Peter III succeeded, and as a declared Prussophile, called off the offensive; Frederick was offered an honourable exit from the war. He called his lucky escape the 'Miracle of the House of Brandenburg'. Prussia survived, recovered and went on to outperform the aspirations of even her most fervent admirers.

Infuriatingly for Berlin, many Europeans reacted to Prussia's success with a mixture of fear and ill-disguised jealousy. Some turned to satire and caricature: a Victorian schoolbook from England, which presented a 'brief sketch of the growth of Prussian power', speaks for the whole genre:

> By her insatiable ambition, guided by consummate skill and complete disregard of what is lawful and right, she [Prussia] has succeeded within the last century of robbing Austria, Poland, Saxony, Denmark, Hanover and France of provinces belonging to their respective empires. And thus, for a season, [she has] succeeded in making herself the head boy of Dame Europa's School.[74]

How, one wonders, can the head boy be a 'she'? The gender confusion may be symptomatic. 'Prussian militarism', which all the other powers were trying to emulate, would soon be denounced as a fundamental cause of Europe's miseries.

Herein lie the roots of another historiographic phenomenon. Having been made the centrepiece of a dubious moral parable about Good and Evil in modern times, German history in the nineteenth and twentieth centuries has reached unequalled prominence in the academic syllabus, commanding by far the largest number of theses, textbooks, courses and researchers. Especially in Anglo-American opinion, whose English-language media rule the globalized roost, former complaints about 'Prussian militarism' have merged with the horror of Nazism, the culmination of all past evil. Adolf Hitler (who was not a Prussian), the author of the Holocaust and warlord of the Axis, has been presented not only as an ogre to obliterate all other ogres, but also as the inevitable product of long-term German trends. Hitler, as one gadfly historian put it, was no more of an accident than 'when a river flows into the sea'.[75]

The Later Hohenzollerns, 1701–1918

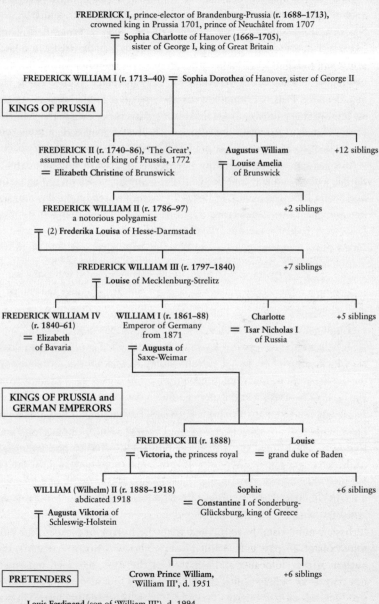

KINGS IN PRUSSIA

FREDERICK I, prince-elector of Brandenburg-Prussia (r. 1688–1713), crowned king in Prussia 1701, prince of Neuchâtel from 1707
= **Sophia Charlotte** of Hanover (1668–1705), sister of George I, king of Great Britain

FREDERICK WILLIAM I (r. 1713–40) = **Sophia Dorothea** of Hanover, sister of George II

KINGS OF PRUSSIA

FREDERICK II (r. 1740–86), 'The Great', assumed the title of king of Prussia, 1772
= **Elizabeth Christine** of Brunswick

Augustus William = **Louise Amelia** of Brunswick   +12 siblings

FREDERICK WILLIAM II (r. 1786–97) a notorious polygamist   +2 siblings
= (2) **Frederika Louisa** of Hesse-Darmstadt

FREDERICK WILLIAM III (r. 1797–1840)   +7 siblings
= **Louise** of Mecklenburg-Strelitz

FREDERICK WILLIAM IV (r. 1840–61) = **Elizabeth** of Bavaria

WILLIAM I (r. 1861–88) Emperor of Germany from 1871 = **Augusta** of Saxe-Weimar

Charlotte = Tsar Nicholas I of Russia   +5 siblings

KINGS OF PRUSSIA and GERMAN EMPERORS

FREDERICK III (r. 1888) = **Victoria**, the princess royal

Louise = grand duke of Baden

WILLIAM (Wilhelm) **II** (r. 1888–1918) abdicated 1918
= **Augusta Viktoria** of Schleswig-Holstein

Sophie = **Constantine I** of Sonderburg-Glücksburg, king of Greece   +6 siblings

PRETENDERS

Crown Prince William, 'William III', d. 1951   +6 siblings

Louis Ferdinand (son of 'William III'), d. 1994
George Frederick (son of Louis Ferdinand), b. 1976

Other tyrants, other victims, other tragedies, have been pushed aside or emotionally defused. Among them is the tragedy of Prussia itself.

This 'Allied Scheme' has the further effect of endowing Russia with a relatively benign image. Since the Empire of the tsars, and later the Soviet Union, fought stoutly as allies of the West in two world wars, 'Russia' is not judged by the same standards by which Prussia and Germany are judged. People talk of Prussian militarism but not of Russian militarism; of the 'German jackboot' but not of the Russian or the Soviet jackboot (even though goose-stepping was introduced into Russia by Prussian military advisers). Russian imperialism and expansionism, though far more extensive than anything in the German record, are somehow taken to be normal. German ideas of *Lebensraum*, 'living space', which long predated Hitler, are uniquely aggressive and obnoxious. Russia's development, especially in its Soviet form, which under Lenin and Stalin followed a course filled with human misery and mass murder, has sometimes been described as a noble experiment that lost its way. Until very recently, German development has been widely described in terms of its *Sonderweg*, a sinister 'Special Path' that was leading in the wrong direction from the start. Communist crimes are rarely measured by the same criteria as Nazi crimes, and, despite a plethora of historical truth-telling in recent decades, Russia is still perceived, on balance, as having been a force for good.[76] Young scholars who challenge the German-centred consensus can still sometimes expect a roasting.[77]

A better balance between East and West is called for. Thanks to Prussia's location on Germany's eastern flank, Russia always loomed large on the Prussian mental map. Once Poland-Lithuania was removed from the reckoning, Prussia and Russia gained a common frontier, and fear of Russia nourished many Prussian attitudes. By the same token, thanks to repeated bloody campaigns, it was the Prussian element within Germany that Russians learned to hate. These tendencies need to be recognized, and correctives applied. Western strands in German history must not be forgotten. But Russo-Prussian relations must feature with due prominence in the long, last act of the tale which leads eventually to Prussia's annihilation.

Such is the context within which one of the most formidable of recent history books needs to be examined. Few writers can ever have received such an extravagant shower of plaudits as the author of *Iron Kingdom: The Rise and Downfall of Prussia*. To almost universal acclaim, Christopher Clark, a Cambridge don of Australian provenance, has written a text whose intellectual content is as cogent as its style is lucid. The reviews bristle with flattering adjectives: 'riveting', 'illuminating', 'profoundly satisfying', 'enthralling', 'authoritative', 'shrewd' and 'judicious'. Clark rejects the jaded accusations against the Hohenzollern state, offering in their place a portrait of a polity that was progressive, cosmopolitan and enlightened. His tour de force is all the more welcome because it undermines the framework of prejudice into which German history has so often been forced.

Nonetheless, at least one half sentence in Clark's text must be called into question. It is not insignificant, since it makes up the first clause of the first sentence on the first of 688 pages. The words read: 'In the beginning, there was only Brandenburg', and they are conditioned by a further phrase, 'the heartland of the future state of Prussia'.[78] One has to wonder. It is hard to see why the eastern part of the equation is ignored. A better opening might have read: 'Once upon a time, there was a place called Brandenburg, and another called Prussia.' It might have prepared the reader better for the long exposition which follows, and which shows how Brandenburg and Prussia came together. In fact, *Iron Kingdom* does not start at the beginning either of Prussia or of Brandenburg or indeed of the kingdom. It picks up the thread in the year 1600, more than halfway through Prussian history, and more than a century before the kingdom's launch. And one cannot help noticing the book's final sentence. 'In the end', it states, 'there was only Brandenburg.' It is an elegant flourish to bring the argument full circle, but it also reveals the author's secret. He has adopted the standpoint of a latterday liberal Berliner; he has not been relating the history of 'all the Prussias'. Despite the very original interpretation, the focus, like that of the Borussian School, is firmly placed on the Hohenzollerns' creation: its origins, its prime and its sorry end. Once this is understood, all further quibbles can be forgotten. The remaining 99.99 per cent of *Iron Kingdom* can be read with great benefit. It deals in depth with the 250-year period that the present sketch is regrettably obliged to skimp.

In the nineteenth century Hohenzollern Prussia bore little resemblance to the kingdom of Frederick I, still less to the Prussia of Duke Albrecht. Its possessions stretched from Aachen to Tilsit, from the Danish frontier to Switzerland. It had many heartlands: the twin industrial heartlands of the Ruhr and of Silesia, the state heartland in Brandenburg and the historical heartland in a province that had now become 'East Prussia'. It was Europe's leading industrial power, and its huge military-industrial complex explains the basis of its leading role in the German Empire.

The Kingdom of Prussia, 1807–1918

Königsberg
Danzig   East
Pomerania   Prussia
Hamburg
Hanover   Brandenburg
Berlin   Posen
Westphalia   Warsaw
Cologne
Hesse   Dresden
Saxony   Breslau   RUSSIAN
Rhine Province   Silesia   EMPIRE
Frankfurt   Prague
Alsace-Lorraine   Württemberg
Strasbourg   Bavaria
Baden
Munich

Prussian lands in 1807
territory gained or regained in 1815
territory gained 1865–6
— · — border of the German Empire, 1871–1918

0   50   100 km

Russia, meanwhile, having acquired the largest slice of Poland-Lithuania and most of the Ottoman Empire's Black Sea lands, had become Prussia's immediate neighbour. It was by far the largest state in the world, possessing a larger population than all the German states together, untold natural riches and gargantuan ambitions. Once France had been humbled in 1871, it was self-evident that the Empire of the tsars was the only continental power that might one day challenge Prussian-controlled Germany.

As these circumstances became apparent, Prussia adopted a policy of studied non-confrontation. For decades on end, Berlin avoided all hints of wishing to extend Prussia's eastern frontier. During the Crimean War it stayed aloof from Britain and France's quarrel with Russia; each of Bismarck's short wars – in 1864, 1866 and 1870–71 – were conducted exclusively in Western or Central Europe. In his testament, the first modern German emperor, Wilhelm I, proffered the crucial advice to his son, 'never to provoke those Russian barbarians'. His restraint postponed, but did not dispel, the conflict which many considered inevitable.

Prussia's westward expansion could not but dilute the multinational character of Prussian society. In 1800, when Prussia had held Warsaw,* the Slav element in its population reached a peak of about 40 per cent.

* From 1795 to 1806, following the Third Partition of Poland.

Thereafter it gradually declined, and receptiveness to German nationalism rose accordingly. 'Old Prussia' had been staunchly monarchist, stressing duty to the state, not the nation. Loyalty was its only yardstick for judging Germans, Poles and Danes alike. The Hohenzollerns looked askance at German unification until the very last moment. When the German Empire was declared in 1871, Poles still formed 10 per cent of the population, and had a huge cohort in Berlin. Their Germanized offspring sprinkled the provinces and the football teams with Polish surnames.[79] Similarly, as Berlin grew mightily, the significance of the original, the historic, the 'real Prussia' shrank accordingly. Königsberg remained a substantial provincial town and the coronation city. No expense was spared to equip it with impressive modern fortifications. But compared to Berlin it was a backwater:

KOENIGSBERG (Polish *Królewiec*), a town of Germany, capital of the province of East Prussia and a fortress of the first rank ... Pop. (1905), 219,862 ... It consists of three parts: the Altstadt (old town), to the west, Löbenicht to the east, and the island Kneiphof, together with numerous suburbs ...

Among the more interesting buildings are the *Schloss*, a long rectangle begun in 1255 ... and the cathedral, begun in 1333, adjoining which is the tomb of Kant. The *Schloss* was originally the residence of the Grand Masters of the Teutonic Order and later of the dukes of Prussia. Behind is the parade-ground, with the statues of Albert I and [many others] ... To the east is the *Schlossteich*, a long narrow ornamental lake ... The north-west side of the parade-ground is occupied by the new university buildings, completed in 1865, the finest architectural features of the town. The university (Collegium Albertinum) was founded in 1544 by Albert duke of Prussia, as a 'purely Lutheran' place of learning. It is chiefly distinguished for its mathematical and philosophical studies, and possesses a famous observatory ...

Koenigsberg is a naval and military fortress of the first order. The fortifications were only completed in 1905 ... The works consist of an inner wall ... and of twelve detached forts ... on [either] bank of the Pregel. Between them lie two great forts, that of Friedrichsburg on an island, and the Kaserne Kronprinz on the east of the town ... The protected position of its harbour has made Koenigsberg one of [Germany's] most important commercial cities. A new channel has recently been [opened to] Pillau, 29 miles distant on the outer side of the Frische Haff ...

The Altstadt grew up around the castle built ... on the advice of Ottaker II. King of Bohemia ... Its first site was near the fishing village of

Steindamm, but after destruction by the Prussians in 1263 it was rebuilt in
its present position ... In 1340 [the city] entered the Hanseatic League ...

Koenigsberg suffered severely during the war of liberation ... The opening of a railway system [later] gave a new impetus to its commerce, making
it the principal outlet for Russian grain, seeds, flax and hemp. It has now
regular steam communication with Memel, Stettin, Kiel, Amsterdam and
Hull.[80]

Despite the initial hint, few people reading this entry would have guessed
which part of the city's history had been quietly omitted.

A day on which at least some of Königsberg's past glories returned
was 18 October 1861. King Wilhelm I (r. 1861–88) arrived with his new
chancellor, Otto von Bismarck, to initiate what became Prussia's most
glorious decade. The painter Adolf Menzel attended the coronation to
make sketches, and four years later, after completing 152 portraits of the
participants, he produced a vast documentary canvas, overwhelming
in its detailed realism. Unfortunately, Menzel's conceit of showing the
king and future emperor swinging his ceremonial sword in a gesture
worthy of Grand Master von Salza was not thought appropriate. The
picture was duly consigned to a bedroom in the Sanssouci Palace at
Potsdam.[81]

The standard text on nineteenth-century Prussian military attitudes
was composed by General Friedrich von Bernhardi (1849–1930), a
Baltic German, a cavalryman, a military writer and a pupil of Treitschke.
Born in St Petersburg, he may conceivably have absorbed something
from the country of his birth, though his main claim to fame was to
have been the first German soldier to ride through the Arc de Triomphe
in Paris at the head of the victory parade in 1871. His *Germany and the
Next War* (1912) was copiously quoted by Allied apologists eager to
justify their anti-German animosity. From Treitschke's *Politics* (1897) it
borrowed 'The end-all and be-all of a State is power, and he who is not
man enough to look this truth in the face should not meddle with politics'. And 'God will always see to it that war always recurs as a drastic
medicine for the human race'. Bernhardi's own epigrammatic contributions include: 'War is a biological necessity'; 'The maintenance of peace
can never be the main goal of policy'; 'War is the greatest factor in the
furtherance of culture and power'; 'The State is a law unto itself. Weak
nations do not have the same right to live as powerful and vigorous
nations'; and 'Any action in favour of collective humanity outside the
limits of the State and nationality is impossible'.[82]

Bernhardi's detractors did not always notice that his rant was framed as an attack on the treatise on 'Perpetual Peace' by Immanuel Kant, who was rather more Prussian than he was; Bernhardi's admirers, who could be found everywhere Europe, did not enquire too closely why warmongering was right in one country but wrong in others. Patriotism and partisanship framed most people's views on the cause of the First World War; they have started to fade only lately. 'It was the British government', writes a prominent British historian, 'which ultimately decided to turn the continental war into a world war.'[83]

Nonetheless, it would be unwise to distance Prussian-led Germany very far from the heart of debates on the road to war. German unification had been achieved in 1871 through Prussia's crushing military victory over France, and the next four decades were overshadowed by the near-universal conviction that military preparedness was the key to the successful pursuit of international relations. No one was more convinced than Kaiser Wilhelm II, the last German emperor and the last king of Prussia (r. 1888–1918), and no country was better equipped than the homeland of Alfred Krupp, the world's largest industrial firm, for making elaborate preparations. When Wilhelm set his 'New Course' and dismissed Bismarck in his reign's second year, France was already engaged with Russia in building a military counterweight and the British Empire was soon fearing for its naval supremacy. Rightly or wrongly, he was widely regarded as the embodiment of Prussian values:

> He believed in force and 'the survival of the fittest' in domestic as well as foreign politics. [He] did not lack intelligence but he did lack stability, disguising his deep insecurities by swagger and tough talk ... He was not so much concerned with gaining specific objectives, as had been the case with Bismarck, as with asserting his will. This trait in the ruler of the most important Continental power was one of the main causes of the prevailing uneasiness in Europe at the turn-of-the-century.[84]

According to an unattributed but shrewd assessment, the Kaiser, 'if not the father of the Great War, was its godfather'.

By 1914, Europe's two strongest military powers, Russia and Prussian-led Germany, were poised on the verge of a trial of strength, before which neither would flinch. Indeed, both Berlin and St Petersburg were convinced that the coming clash had better be fought sooner than later.

Russia was aligned with France and Britain. Germany stood alongside Austria and Italy at the head of the so-called Central Powers. The 'Great War' exploded very nearly 100 years after Waterloo had ended the last Continent-wide conflagration. All sides blamed their opponents for the conflict. Western analysts, who denounced 'the Kaiser's War', pointed to Germany's 'Schlieffen Plan', the tactics of which determined that Germany should strike first before being struck a double blow. Though his original plan was modified, the dead General Schlieffen was roundly denigrated as a treacherous Prussian warmonger. Germany's fears of encirclement were given little credence.

Russia's equally ambiguous actions attracted less criticism in the West. Yet in the chain reaction that led from the assassination at Sarajevo to the outbreak of war, Russia's unconditional support for Serbia matched Germany's 'blank cheque' to Austria, and it was Russia's provocative mobilization that finally pushed Germany over the edge.[85] The speed of the Russian army's double-pronged attack on the Eastern Front showed how the tsarist military command, like its German counterpart, had been planning a pre-emptive blow. Kaiser Wilhelm II and his entourage were undoubtedly paranoiac, but their readiness to resort to war did not exceed that of the Russians.

Western commentators have not generally wanted to hear how their Russian allies hoped to harm Germany, but war aims published by the Russian foreign office in September 1914 reveal their intentions. They foresaw (a) the total liquidation of East Prussia; (b) the re-creation of a Russian-run Kingdom of Poland; and (c) the establishment of a new Russo-German frontier on the Rivers Oder and Western Neisse (exactly as eventually happened in 1945).[86] From Germany's viewpoint, they were deeply threatening. They do not absolve the German leadership, but they certainly show that Prussia's militarism was not unique. Of course, Russia's plans were quickly forgotten. The attack on East Prussia was efficiently repulsed; the Russian 'steamroller' repeatedly stalled and after 1915 German forces carried all before them on the Eastern Front. Even so, the Prussians who dominated Germany's military circles had received a nasty shock, a shock which goes a long way to explaining their punitive terms imposed on Soviet Russia at the Treaty of Brest-Litovsk (1918). The chief German negotiator at Brest-Litovsk, General Max Hoffmann (1869–1927), had been Field Marshal Hindenburg's chief-of-staff in East Prussia four years earlier. It was Hoffmann who suggested changing the name of the victory of 1914 to the 'Battle of Tannenberg',* thereby claiming revenge for the defeat of the Teutonic Knights at nearby Grunwald 500 years before.[87]

Any narrative which stresses the Russian dimension in the First World War automatically invites protests about neglect of the French dimension. Surely, one hears, the Russo-German contest in the East must be discussed in conjunction with the centuries-old Franco-German saga in the West. This is true. Yet a contradistinction between the French and Russian factors is not entirely valid. Unlike in 1871, the French had forged a close military partnership with Russia, ensuring that in 1914 Germany faced a concerted challenge on two fronts. As seen from Berlin, the hostile double-headed Franco-Russian hydra was a monster which no one else had to face. What is more, the hydra's Russian head was judged more dangerous than the French one. Schlieffen and his colleagues reckoned that France had to be dealt with first, because Russia, with far more territory and far more troops, could not be neutralized so readily.

Berlin, moreover, was still looking at the military landscape through Prussian spectacles. The Kaiser and his Junker-dominated staff had good reason to worry about the proximity of the Russian frontline. At its nearest point, Russian troops were deployed within 60 miles of Königsberg, and in the border province of Grenzmark Posen, less than 200 miles from Berlin. The French frontier was much more distant. If the campaigns were to go badly, the French might retake Alsace and Lorraine, or invade the Rhineland. The Russians would capture the Empire's capital.

For all these reasons, the outcome of the First World War was deeply bewildering. By late 1918, the German army had gained a complete victory on the Eastern Front, had eliminated its most dangerous enemy and had dictated the terms of peace. Its stalwart performance on the Western Front, against an array of powerful allies, had not faltered for more than four years; and it was brought to an end without experiencing anything that might have been described as a rout. Yet the German Empire collapsed. Revolution erupted in Berlin; the Kaiser was forced to abdicate; the Hohenzollerns were banished; the invincible 'Iron Kingdom', around which Germany's imperial personality had been forged, was demolished; and the victorious Allies, representatives of the 'Western civilization' with which most Germans identified, chose to act

* Hindenburg's attack on 29 August 1914 centred on the 2th Russian Army, which was surrounded near the village of Frogenau. Tannenberg, nearly 20 miles away, did not feature until a report was written that evening.

vindictively and to punish Germany for all the war's disasters and
bloodshed. The resultant bewilderment opened the door to a variety of
political hucksters and fanatics whose very existence was previously
unknown.

Strategic thinking with strong nationalist and racial overtones was
very much in fashion in those days, not only in Germany. Already before
the war, strident publicists and learned professors from various countries
had raised the so-called 'Jewish Question' or the 'Thousand-Year Struggle
between Teuton and Slav'; the success of Bolshevik revolutionaries, who
made no secret of their international aspirations, greatly heightened existing tensions. As the Armistice silenced the guns on the Western Front, the
prospects of a lasting peace in the East were receding fast. The Bolsheviks
were promising to export their Revolution to the heart of 'capitalist
Europe'. If and when they decided to put their promises into practice,
the eastern provinces of Germany would find themselves in the first line
of attack. Western Europeans were breathing a sigh of relief, but the
nations of Eastern Europe were bracing themselves for further conflict.
As subsequent history proved, the stay of execution lasted for just thirty
years. In late August 1914 the Cossacks of Russia's General Ren-
nenkampf had ridden up to the outer walls of Königsberg. Given the
historical inclinations of Russian 'imperial tourism', there was every
possibility that in one guise or another they would be back.

The abolition of the Kingdom of Prussia in November 1918 is often
mistaken for the end of the Prussian story. In reality, it marked the end
of Hohenzollern rule, but not of the Prussian state. Yet another variant
on Prussian statehood, a *Freistaat Preussen* or 'Free State of Prussia'
lived on, first as a self-governing component of the post-war 'Weimar
Republic' and then, from 1933, of the Third Reich – though by then the
self-government was only nominal.

Nonetheless, the outcome of the First World War left little more than
an uneasy truce in many parts of Europe. The settlement of Versailles,
bypassing the Bolsheviks, failed to address the problems of the East. The
reborn Polish Republic, invaded by the Red Army in 1920, was forced
to defend its independence unaided, interrupting Lenin's revolutionary
march on Berlin in the process.[88] Both the Weimar Republic and Soviet
Russia were treated as pariahs by the Western Powers. Millions of Europeans were left either fearful or resentful, and the possibility of a
renewed conflagration was always present. Even though the Central
Powers had won a comprehensive victory on the Eastern Front, the

people of Prussia suffered the heaviest territorial losses and bore a dis-
proportionate share of the opprobrium. It was no accident that the
myth of the 'stab in the back'* was launched by Hindenburg and General Ludendorff.

After the abolition of the Prusso-German monarchy, the *Freistaat
Preussen*, though substantially reduced by cessions to Poland, remained
the largest territory in Germany. Its government was dominated by Social
Democrats. A single SPD politician, Otto Braun, served as Prussian prime
minister from 1920 to 1932.[89]

Prussia's brief era of democracy was overthrown by the arbitrary
actions of Germany's central government. In 1932 the German chancellor,
von Papen, suspended Braun's administration in the so-called *Preussen-
schlag* or 'Prussian coup', citing 'electoral turbulence'. His dubious
decision facilitated the introduction of one-party rule by the Nazis, who
appointed Hermann Göring as the Prussian premier only one year later.
Göring gloated over 'the marriage of old Prussia with young Germany'.

Traditional Prussian society, still led by the landed Junker class, did
not provide a natural hunting-ground for the Nazis. Prussia's cities,
including Berlin, leaned decidedly to the Left. Very few Nazi leaders were
born in East Prussia. Even so, some Nazi ideas did resonate strongly.
Protests against the '*Diktat* of Versailles', for example, made more sense
in Danzig or in Königsberg than in Hamburg or Munich. Claims about
the German master race could also appeal to people who had long cultivated the ethos of hardy pioneers, and the concept of *Lebensraum* was
associated exclusively with the East. The idea that Germany's natural
'living space' was there for the taking did not seem particularly outland-
ish after the German army's recent victory in those parts. In East Prussia,
above all, still shaken by the Russian invasion of 1914, proposals for the
eastward extension of German settlement could be seen as a necessary
defensive measure.

Voting trends in Weimar Prussia followed no simple pattern. While
the provincial *Landtag* had a socialist majority, the city of Königsberg
itself was run by a right-wing nationalist, Carl Goerdeler (1884–1945),
Bürgermeister from 1920 to 1930. In the two elections of 1932, the
Nazis made significant advances, but failed to win an outright victory.
In the last democratic contest in Königsberg, the Nazis received 62,888

---

* The *Dolchstosslegende*, traced to a conversation between General Ludendorff and Sir
Neil Malcolm in 1919, gained wide currency by claiming that the German military had
been betrayed by politicians.

votes from 173,154 cast (36.3 per cent); the left-wing vote of 75,564 was divided almost equally between socialists and Communists.[90]

Inter-war Prussia did not share a frontier with the Soviet Union, but many of Prussia's discontents were shared by the Bolsheviks. Both sides hated the Versailles settlement, and despised the new, Western-backed national states. The Bolsheviks were free of Nazi-style racism, but they shared an appetite for mass killing by category and assumed that ideological conflict would lead to military conflict. They knew that their attempt in 1920 to export Communist Revolution with bayonets had failed miserably.[91] So when Stalin launched his Five Year Plans, he famously predicted that, if the breakneck programme did not succeed within a decade, 'we will be annihilated'. He was counting on war.[92]

The Second World War in Europe, therefore, must be conceived above all as a fight to the death between two totalitarian monsters. The Greater Reich and the Soviet Union were the largest combatant powers by far. Both aimed to recoup losses incurred since 1914. And their titanic, savage struggle on the Eastern Front accounted for perhaps three-quarters of the fighting and casualties.[93] The future of East Prussia hung in the balance throughout. Each stage of the war, therefore, has to be defined by the changing relations between Germany and the Soviet Union. During the currency of the Nazi–Soviet Pact in 1939–41 East Prussia was protected by its location in the German sphere of influence. After the start of 'Operation Barbarossa' on 22 June 1941, when Hitler assaulted his erstwhile partner, it was left far behind the area of operations. Within a couple of years, when the tide changed, its prospects quickly grew precarious.

The outcome of the war was decided by the unexpected survival of the Red Army, and by the series of colossal, almost unimaginably expensive victories that began with Stalingrad and Kursk. From mid-1943 onwards, Stalin's triumphant forces smashed their way westwards, until they won the shattering Battle for Berlin in April 1945 without even calling on Western assistance. The final layout of Europe on VE Day saw perhaps one-quarter of the Continent neutral, one-quarter under Western control, and one-half under Soviet control. Though the Third Reich was totally destroyed, the principal victor was not 'Freedom, Justice and Democracy'. It was a second totalitarian regime, which had killed millions, which ran the world's largest network of concentration camps, and which had triumphed by exacting unparalleled human sacrifices. This second evil monster would keep the free world busy for the next forty-five years. The Prussia of the Teutonic Knights, of Duke Albrecht and of Immanuel Kant, lay entirely at its mercy.

The sentence hanging over Prussia could not be executed by one blow. The first phase began in the late summer of 1944. When Soviet troops approached, the decisive move appeared imminent. A Red Army sortie into the frontier village of Nemmersdorf left a trail of atrocities behind it. But Stalin had given priority to the conquest of the Balkans, and his northern armies halted on the Nieman and the middle Vistula.

Adolf Hitler's main military command post was located at the Wolfsschanze or 'Wolf's Lair' near Rastenburg in East Prussia from June 1941 to November 1944. The unsuccessful bomb plot against him took place there on 20 July 1944, yet the headquarters was not relocated for a further four months. In that time, the central Soviet spearhead forces stayed encamped before Warsaw; three Soviet 'fronts' in Lithuania surrounded East Prussia's northern border, while the Red Army's attack columns were surging through Bulgaria, Romania and Hungary. The Western Allies were still crawling up Italy, and pushing stolidly on through France. Their one contribution to the reduction of East Prussia occurred when the RAF twice raided Königsberg.

In the records of RAF Bomber Command, the Königsberg operation is justified by the target being 'an important supply port for the Eastern Front' and is described as 'one of the most successful of the war'. For 'successful' read 'devastating'. Two consecutive raids were necessary before the desired effect was achieved. On the night of 26/7 August, 74 Avro Lancasters of 5 Group flew in: 4 were lost, and little damage was inflicted. So on the night of 29/30 August, 189 Lancasters were sent, dropping 480 tons of incendiaries, and losing 15 of their number. Their controllers noted 'significant fighter activity'. The fires burned for three days. The inner suburbs of Altstadt, Löbenicht and Kneiphof, which had no port facilities, were obliterated.[94] In the local record, 25,000 people were killed.

The firestorm of August 1944 figures prominently in explanations of the disappearance of the famous Prussian treasure, the *Bernsteinzimmer* or 'Amber Room' presented to Peter the Great during the Great Northern War. Fifty-five amber panels decorated with gold leaf and crystal mirrors and weighing six tons adorned the Imperial Palace at Tsarskoye Selo near St Petersburg from 1716 to 1941. During the Siege of Leningrad, they were 'reclaimed' by German troops, reassembled in Königsberg, and put on public display in the Royal Castle. Since 1944, their whereabouts have been unknown.[95]

By January 1945 the Soviet conquest of East Prussia had been awaited for many months, and the Red Army rapidly overran the whole

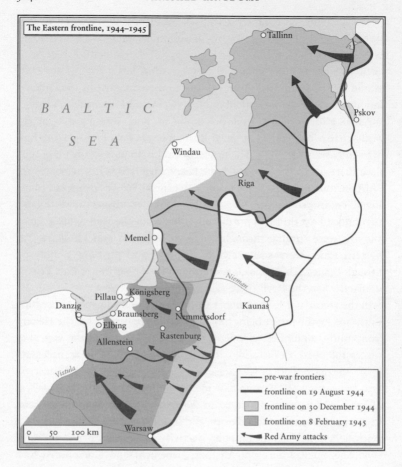

The Eastern frontline, 1944–1945

BALTIC SEA

Tallinn

Pskov

Windau

Riga

Memel

Nieman

Pillau Königsberg

Danzig

Braunsberg

Nemmersdorf

Kaunas

Elbing

Rastenburg

Allenstein

Vistula

Warsaw

0   50   100 km

— pre-war frontiers
— frontline on 19 August 1944
frontline on 30 December 1944
frontline on 8 February 1945
Red Army attacks

province except for Königsberg. The purpose of the operation, which
began on 13 January, was to engage the large German Army Group
Centre and to prevent it from assisting other German defence lines.
Marshal Zhukov's principal offensive, which set off from the vicinity of
Warsaw, was pointed directly at Berlin; and Marshal Rokossovsky was
tasked with ensuring that no German units from East Prussia could
interfere. This objective was achieved, though progress was slow, and
heroic efforts by German defenders managed to reopen the supply road
from Königsberg to Pillau.

The most obvious, immediate consequence, however, was to sow panic
among East Prussia's civilian population, and to trigger the terrible *Flucht
aus dem Osten* or 'Flight from the East'.[96] The winter was unusually

harsh. Deep snow covered the ground. All the rivers and canals were frozen hard, and the *Frisches Haff*, the 'Freshwater Lagoon', had turned into
a vast slab of solid ice. The Gauleiter of the province, Erich Koch, resisted
the orderly evacuation of the population until it was too late, condemning disobedient civilians to be shot. So when he finally relented on
20 January, he started a stampede. Germans living north of Königsberg
had no chance of escape. Those living further south had ten days before
the roads to Elbing and Danzig were cut. Tens of thousands of people set
off in carts, on bicycles, horse or foot, hoping to reach safety.

To begin with, the Königsbergers were only half-trapped. Once the
railway to Allenstein was cut, the best way out was to cross the ice to
Pillau. Hundreds and thousands attempted the crossing every day for several weeks. Many dropped from cold and exhaustion. Many were strafed
by Soviet fighters, or fell into holes in the ice. But many struggled on to
Pillau to wait for help.

Fortunately for them, the *Kriegsmarine* had prepared plans for a
large-scale humanitarian rescue. Admiral Dönitz gave orders on 21
January for 'Operation Hannibal' to begin. A thousand merchant ships
and naval vessels operated a non-stop service between Pillau, Danzig
and Stettin, running the gauntlet of Soviet bombers and submarines.
They suffered horrendous losses, including the sinking of the *Wilhelm
Gustloff*, the greatest maritime disaster in world history, when 10,000
may have died.[97] But they also saved very many lives.

The final battle for Königsberg – what the Russians now call the
Shturm Kenigsberga, the 'Storming of Königsberg' – was mounted in the
first week of April under General Chernyakovsky. The attackers faced
four concentric defensive lines, twenty modernized forts, and five full
divisions of the 3rd Panzer Army. Calls for surrender were ignored.
Chernyakovsky moved to the assault, deploying four armies, massed
artillery at a density of 250 guns per half-mile, and a fleet of warplanes.
Shelling pulverized the outermost defences. Day 1 of the ground assault
brought the attackers to the second line in the south. Day 2 was marked
by fierce resistance and by Hitler's repeated refusal of permission to
capitulate. On Day 3, in better weather, the Soviet air force wreaked
havoc in the city centre. Day 4 dawned with the defences hopelessly
fragmented, and finished with the forbidden capitulation.[98] An estimated
80 per cent of Prussia's one-time capital lay in ruins. The surviving
defenders were marched off, and the remaining civilians subjected to a
reign of murder, rape and pillage. 'The robbers' lair of German imperialism', *Pravda* announced in Moscow, 'has been liquidated.'

A German, who had been working during the siege as a doctor, took a walk to see for himself:

> Slowly, systematically, Soviet soldiers were blowing holes in the streets, wrecking churches, burning houses, raping women. The scale of the destruction is difficult to imagine. The idea was not simply to defeat Königsberg, but to destroy its history ...
>
> Up the Königstrasse, over the Rossgartenmarkt and beyond, wound an enormous coil of incoming troops, in which we now became engulfed. I pinched my thigh hard to convince myself that all of this was no dream ... 'Königsberg in 1945,' I told myself repeatedly ...
>
> Just about here was where our dentist used to live. He worked up there – in the air. Perhaps in those days ... he may have looked down at the peaceful street below ... Now, between flaming ruins, a wildly yelling throng, without beginning or end, was pushing its way along the same street.[99]

The confusion is indicative of the conditions that reigned amid the post-war ruins of Königsberg. There are many mysteries. What happened, for example, to the German civilians who were still alive at the war's end? Of East Prussia's population of 2.2 million, an estimated 300,000 were killed during the fighting; 193,000 were still trapped in the city before the final assault, but only 50,000 were sent to Germany in 1949, having been used for forced labour. The figures do not add up. The deficit appears to total 100,000 at the very least.*

A Königsberger, having fled the city, joined a group of refugees in an empty village:

> In the farmyard further down the road stood a cart, to which four naked women were nailed through their hands in a cruciform position ... In the dwellings we found a total of seventy-two women, including children, and

---

* The Soviet assault of April 1945 is the second event which features in the Amber Room mystery. A recent study claims that the treasure was destroyed on 9–11 April by high explosives and fire, but this assumes that no attempt had been made to crate the treasure up or remove it to safety in the previous five months, and that six tons of amber could evaporate in heat without leaving even microscopic chemical traces. So the hunt continues. One theory holds that the Amber Room sank with the *Wilhelm Gustloff*; a second that it was buried with Nazi gold in a Saxon mine; a third that it lies beneath a Lithuanian lagoon; and a fourth that it forms part of the undeclared loot in Moscow's Trophy Archive. The word on the street in Kaliningrad is that it was drowned in the concrete foundations of the *Dom Sovietov*.[100]

one old man, all dead, all murdered in a bestial manner, except only for a few who had bullet holes in their necks. Some babies had their heads bashed in ... All the women, as well as the girls ... had been raped.[101]

Five decades later, a visiting historian who saw the place with her own eyes, made a considered judgement:

[Königsberg was] one of the few places where Stalin succeeded completely in what he set out to do. He exterminated the East Prussians as thoroughly as the Teutonic Knights once exterminated the Prus, taking a few years instead of a century. He filled the city with outsiders. He destroyed the churches and the houses and the trees. He put concrete blocks in their place. He obliterated the past. 'If I were dropped in this town by parachute and asked where I was,' wrote [Marion von Dönhoff] who spent her childhood near Königsberg and returned long after the war, 'I would answer: perhaps Irkutsk.'[102]

The formal termination of Prussia's existence was delayed for a while more. Here, historians must distinguish between the province of East Prussia and the state of Prussia. The province was liquidated by the Potsdam Conference; the state was not. Despite Allied assertions to the contrary, the Potsdam Conference, which lasted from 17 July to 2 August 1945, possessed no legal standing. It was a makeshift arrangement between the victorious Allied leaders, who met to discuss the management of a defeated Germany and, pending an intended peace conference, to make interim judgements on urgent matters. A Council of Foreign Ministers prepared the peace conference's agenda, but the conference never met, so the decisions taken at Potsdam, unlike those embodied in the Treaty of Versailles, did not receive the endorsement of an international treaty. In relation to Königsberg and East Prussia, they were extremely vague and tentative:

The Conference examined a proposal by the Soviet Government to the effect that pending the final determination of ... the peace settlement, the section of the [USSR's] western frontier adjacent to the Baltic Sea should pass from a point on the eastern shore of the Bay of Danzig to the east, north of Braunsberg-Goldap, to the meeting point of the frontiers of Lithuania, the Polish Republic and East Prussia. The Conference has agreed in principle ... concerning the ultimate transfer to the Soviet Union of the City of Königsberg and the area adjacent to it as described above subject to expert examination ...

The President of the United States and the British Prime Minister have declared that they will support the proposal of the Conference at the forthcoming peace settlement.[103]

Nothing was spelled out in the Potsdam Agreement about the division of East Prussia. Though the new Soviet frontier was to pass 'north of Braunsberg-Goldap', the Allied negotiators did not indicate that the area to the south of the line was to be handed to Poland. This not-so-trivial matter was left to a private understanding between the Soviet Union and its Polish Communist clients, and to a separate, Polish-Soviet Treaty signed on 16 August 1945.[104] Only then did the map emerge that held good for the rest of the century.

For the time being, the Allied Control Authority, which was running occupied Germany, put the Prussian question aside. The Council of the Four Powers – the United States, the Soviet Union, Britain and France – which administered the four zones of occupation plus Berlin, were overburdened by pressing issues of emergency welfare, reconstruction, economic re-priming, and de-Nazification. They only remembered Prussia when they began to prepare a new, comprehensive network of German administrative units.

Prussia presented an unforeseen problem. The *Freistaat Preussen* had been overthrown illegally in 1932–3, and could now be regarded as a victim of Nazi aggression. Its long-serving prime minister Otto Braun had returned from Swiss exile. Like his protégé Willi Brandt, he was an acknowledged anti-Nazi, and was back in Berlin lobbying strongly for the restoration of the state from whose helm he had been abruptly removed a dozen years earlier. The fact was, of course, that Prussia's former provinces had already been broken up, and the would-be state had no territory left to administer. In any case, the Soviets were implacably opposed. Their thinking was reflected in the Allied Control Authority's Law No. 46 of 25 February 1947. Not only was the State of Prussia peremptorily abolished; it was characterized as 'a bearer of militarism and reaction'.[105]

Law No. 46 merely put the final nail in Prussia's empty coffin. The body of Prussia, the living substance, the community of human beings that had stayed intact until January 1945, had already been dispersed. By 1947 there was virtually nothing left. Prussia suffered the fate of Carthage: '*ubi solitudinem faciunt, pacem appellant*', 'they create a desert, and they call it peace'.

III

Since the fall of the Iron Curtain, the memory site* par excellence of all things Prussian has been established in Berlin. After a break of forty-five years, reunited Berlin returned to its position at the head of a united Germany, and is booming, not least as a cultural centre. Despite the passage of time, however, Berliners cannot help being reminded that they are reclaiming a historically polluted space, which served not too long ago as capital both of the Third Reich and of the German Democratic Republic. So anything which diverts attention from the 'bad old days' is welcome, and deliberately cultivated memories of Prussia constitute an effective antidote to the otherwise unsavoury odours of the *Hitlerzeit*, the *Mauer* and the *Volksrepublik*. Sighs of relief are everywhere audible, thanking the stars that many aspects of the city's Prussian connection can be celebrated with pride and enthusiasm. Even so, observers puzzle over the exact causes:

> It is more than a 'yearning for Prussia', more than a passing nostalgic whim
> which prevents the ghost of Prussia from being laid to rest . . . ; it is more
> than a mere escapist tendency or wish to flee into the past. This new sensi-
> tivity towards Prussia more likely expresses growing dissatisfaction with
> the shallowness of the present, a desire to see it more deeply rooted in the
> soil of history. Far from indicating a 'flight from Federal Republican reality',
> it suggests an attempt to safeguard the reality in its entirety, no matter how
> dubious its constituent elements might be.[106]

In the early twenty-first century, therefore, nostalgia about parts of the past mingles with optimism about the future. Berliners and tourists alike ogle the cranes and skyscrapers of the Potsdamer Platz that is rising from the ruins left during the Cold War. They admire the restored Reichstag, which still retains its dedication 'DEM DEUTSCHEN VOLKE', 'To the German Nation', but whose heavy stone dome has been replaced by a light and airy glass one by the British architect Norman Foster. They gaze at the restored Brandenburg Gate, past which the Berlin Wall ran until recently, or at the re-gilded *Siegessäule*, the 'Victory Column', which commemorates the Franco-Prussian War. The mindless triumphalism of

---

* Thanks to the work of the French scholar Pierre Nora, in *Les Lieux de mémoire* (1984–92), 'memory site' now forms part of the established vocabulary of studies on collective memory. It refers to places, objects and buildings that are deliberately selected and promoted over others to preserve the memory of people or events.

former times has gone, but there is no reluctance to recall Prussia's days of non-military glory. The royal palaces at Potsdam and Charlottenburg are popular destinations; a decision was taken in 2010 to ignore financial prudence and to rebuild the Hohenzollerns' *Stadtschloss* or 'City-centre Palace', that was demolished by the GDR. With every day that passes, *Preussentum*, the 'Prussian Spirit', is taking on friendlier connotations.

Nowhere can this wind of historical change be felt more keenly than on Museum Island, in the middle of the River Spree. The *Altes Museum* was founded there in 1830, and joined by the *Neues Museum* in 1859, the *Alte Nationalgalerie* in 1876, the *Bode Museum* in 1904, and finally the *Pergamon Museum* in 1930. Enthusiasts call it 'Prussia's Most Beautiful Jewel':

> Museum island is a product of what was surely the happiest and most prestigious [of decades], around 1820–30 ... The philosopher, Hegel, regarded that Prussian heyday as evidence that the 'world spirit' thrives at a certain time, in a certain place, and with particular fervour ...
>
> When you first step onto this island you cannot believe your eyes – right in the middle of the city you are surrounded on two sides by water and by five examples of monumental architecture. Sitting on a summer's evening on the grass in front of the Altes Museum, on which the words 'ALL ART IS AND WAS CONTEMPORARY' [stand out] in neon lettering, you see the old reconciled with the new. You hear the bells of Berlin cathedral behind you, watch the glowing red sunset ... and for a few moments are transported back to the Prussian Arcadia. The fact that the lawns and the flower-beds ... are still known by the wonderful name of *Lustgarten* (literally, Garden of Pleasure) says a lot about the often underestimated sensual delights of supposedly ossified Prussianism.[107]

Some dictionary definitions of 'Prussianism' still hold to outdated views. *Merriam-Webster*, for example, defines it as: 'the despotic militarism and harsh discipline of the Prussian ruling class'.[108] It will clearly have to be modified.

Other exhibitions in Berlin display a similarly strong Prussian accent. The German Historical Museum (DHM) does not possess a separate Prussian section; but the Hohenzollern state takes second place there only to the Holy Roman Empire. The Prussia Exhibition of 1981 in West Berlin – *Preussen Versuch einer Bilanz*, 'Prussia: an Attempted Balance Sheet' – attracted enormous attention, not least because East Germany at the time was assuming shades of Prussian Blue.[109] In 2001 Berlin and Brandenburg joined forces to celebrate the 300th anniversary of the

Prussian Kingdom's foundation; and more than a hundred exhibitions were staged.[110] A show on *Prussia's Women*, for example, examined the neglected half of the Prussian story. Others explored 'Prussia's Sense of Art', 'Prussia: a European Story' and 'Prussian Science and Technology'.[111] A more recent exhibition of *Power and Friendship* put on by the German foreign office about the relations between Prussia and Russia in the years 1800–1917 demonstrates what can achieved by discreet, diplomatic selectivity.[112]

For selectivity, whether of location or date or theme, is the key to understanding all appeals to history, and one should not pretend that it is risk-free. From the historian's standpoint, Berlin's current Prusso-mania is harmless, but only as long as it does not assume monopolistic proportions. Two dangers come to mind. One is that Prussia's multi-national history be seen exclusively from the German perspective. The other is that Brandenburg's image becomes so fused with Prussia's that the two are thought inseparable. This would be an injustice. After all, Prussia's origins lie far beyond Berlin, just as Berlin's own origins lay outside the Hohenzollern and Prussian parameters. When the Hohen-zollerns moved to Brandenburg in the early fifteenth century, Prussia was already a well-established state. When the Prussian label was first attached to Brandenburg in 1701, the Hohenzollerns had been sover-eign rulers for only forty-four years. Before that, Brandenburg's non-Prussian and initially non-German storyline tells of the early mar-graves, of the electorate, of the *Nordmark*, of Albert the Bear, and of the Slavic land of Brennibor.

In short, those who are inspired to reflect on the past in the beguiling environment of Berlin's *Lustgarten* should not allow their thoughts to be constrained by their immediate surroundings. They should certainly read and learn about the Hohenzollerns' 'Iron Kingdom'; but they should also read something about other Prussian worlds that have van-ished even more comprehensively. On this subject, the popular poet Agnes Miegel (1879–1964), a Königsberger, skilfully invokes the anguish of her compatriots:

O kalt weht der Wind über leeres Land,	Oh cold blows the wind o'er the empty land,
O leichter weht Asche als Staub und Sand!	Ashes waft lighter than dust and sand.
Und die Nessel wächst hoch an geborstner Wand,	And nettles grow high on the broken wall,

VANISHED KINGDOMS

*Aber höher die Distel am Acker
rand!*

*Es war ein Land – wir liebten dies
Land –*

*Aber Grauen sank drüber wie
Dünensand.*

*Verweht wie im Bruch des Elches
Spur*

*Ist die Fährte von Mensch und
Kreatur –*

*Sie erstarrten in Schnee, sie verglühten
im Brand,*

*Sie verdarben elend in Feindes-
land,*

Sie liegen tief auf der Ostsee Grund,

*Flut wäscht ihr Gebein in Bucht und
Sund,*

*Sie schlafen in Jütlands sandigem
Schoss –*

*Und wir Letzten treiben heimat-
los,*

*Tang nach dem Sturm, Herbstlaub im
Wind –*

Vater, Du weisst, wie einsam wir sind!

Higher yet is the thistle on the acre's
edge.

There once was a land which we
dearly loved;

Horrors engulfed it like sand-
dunes.

As the spoor of the elk is dissolved in
the bog,

So, too, is the passage of man and
beast.

They froze in the snow, or burned in
the fire,

Or perished in misery on hostile
ground.

Deep they lie on the East Sea's bed,

The tides wash their bones round
bays and straits,

They sleep in Jutland's sandy
lap –

And we, the last of them, wander
homeless,

Like storm-tossed seaweed, or
wind-blown leaves.

Father, You alone know Your
children's desolation.[113]

Berliners in particular might keep constantly in mind that the Iron Kingdom was only one of several Prussias. In the not too distant future, they will be able to visit the exhibition and documentation centre of the proposed Centre for Flight and Expulsion, approved by the Bundestag in March 2008 amidst great controversy. The Centre is the brainchild of the League of German Expellees (BdV) and its doughty chairperson, Erika Steinbach, who is determined to add a story of German wartime suffering to the more familiar narrative of German guilt. Among the two million members of her League, there is a strong contingent of East Prussians and Königsbergers, whose perspective does not chime with that of the typical Berliner or casual visitor. For they and their descend-ants, like assorted Poles from the former Royal Prussia or Russians from Kaliningrad, are likely to show little inclination for nostalgic Prus-sian fashions. They will know that in the long centuries before Friedrich

392

Wilhelm's coronation in Königsberg, the land where Kaliningrad now stands was ruled by grand masters of the Teutonic Order, by dukes of Prussia, by duke-electors and by kings of Poland. They may even have heard of *Tvangste* and of the shadowy, anonymous, 'People of the Lagoons'.

All the nations that ever lived have left their footsteps in the sand. The traces fade with every tide, the echoes grow faint, the images are fractured, the human material is atomized and recycled. But if we know where to look, there is always a remnant, a remainder, an irreducible residue.

In this case, the residue is quite large. The last of the Prussias is not long dead. There are living people who remember it. There are men and women who were born Prussian and who, in part at least, have retained their Prussian identity. They have been scattered to the ends of the earth, but some still belong to the associations of exiles and expellees, who talk of the old times, and who write books about the *Unvergessene Heimat*, the 'Unforgettable Homeland'.[114] There are even those who dream of Prussia's resurrection. Yet these are all relicts from just the latest Prussian generation. They are descendants not only of German forebears but also of several earlier incarnations of Prussia. Somewhere among them roam the genes of the *Prusai*.

8

Sabaudia

The House that Humbert Built

(1033–1946)

Rome, 2 June. Italy's Day of the Republic, the *Festa della Repubblica*, is celebrated on the same date every year. The president comes down from the Quirinale Palace, lays a crown of laurels on the tomb of the Unknown Soldier and gives the signal for a grand military parade. RAI news, the Italian news agency, issues the usual bulletin: 'The celebrations of the anniversary of the Republic were initiated today by the President ... Escorted by the cuirassiers of the guard of the Corps of Carabinieri, he laid the Crown on the Altar of the Fatherland, and sent the parade on its way from the Imperial Forum ...'[1] Italian commentators liken their republican *Festa* to Bastille Day in France or to Independence Day in the United States. A similar event will be staged on 4 November, *la Giornata dell'Unità*, to mark Italy's annual Armed Forces Day.

In 2010 Giorgio Napolitano (b. 1925), Italy's eleventh president, had reached the fifth year of his seven-year term. Trained as a lawyer, he used to be an activist of the Italian Communist Party (PCI), until it was dissolved in 1992; he then served as a member of the European Parliament. His nicknames include *Il Principe Rosso*, 'The Red Prince', and *Il Re Umberto*, 'King Umberto'. His personal contribution to the national day was to invite the public into the house and gardens of the Quirinale.[2] He has been characterized as Italy's 'enduring president',[3] a pillar of stability in an unstable country.

The tomb of Italy's Unknown Soldier, the *Milite Ignoto*, stands beside the Altar of the Fatherland at the centrepoint of the monumental complex on the Piazza Venezia – the *Vittoriano*. It dates from 1911, and is surrounded by an array of patriotic symbols – including the columns of Winged Victory, the four-horse chariot, the *Quadrighe*, and the Fountain of the Two Seas.[4] On the steps of the altar, the president of state is awaited by the presidents of the Senate, of the chamber of deputies, of

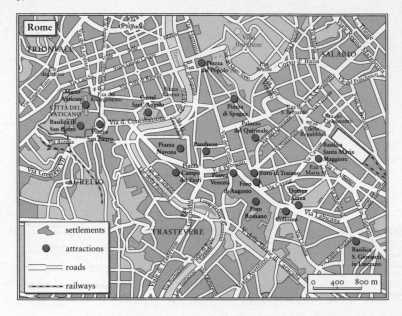

the constitutional court and of the council of ministers. After laying the crown of laurels, he reviews the guard of honour, presents a short address, then leaves the square with the minister of defence and the chief of the defence staff.

The military parade presents a stunning show made up from all branches of the Italian armed forces and police. The crowds applaud, listening to the bands of the *Esercito* (army), the *Marina Militare* (navy), the *Aeronautica* (air force), the *Arma dei Carabinieri*, the *Polizia di Stato* (state police), and other formations. The traditional *Corsa degli Bersaglieri* raises a special cheer: the 'Sharpshooters Regiment' (including its musicians) does not march past the stands, but runs. The soldiers step out most willingly to the strains of the *'Canzone del Piave'*, the 'Song of the Piave', a popular melody from the First World War (and between 1943–6 the national anthem). Warplanes scream overhead, releasing jetstreams of green, white and red. (In 2008 heavy rain was falling, and no planes flew.)

The symbols of the Italian Republic are displayed everywhere. The national flag, the green-white-red tricolour, dates from the Cispadane Republic of 1797. The Republic's emblem consists of a five-pointed red star surmounting the toothed wheel of labour, encircled by garlands of oak and olive. It rests on the gold letters of 'REPUBBLICA ITALIANA' on

a red field. The national anthem, '*Il Canto degli Italiani*', is popularly
known after its author as 'Mameli's Hymn'. Composed in Genoa in 1847,
it was always sung by republicans in defiance of their monarchist rivals:

> *Fratelli d'Italia!*
> *L'Italia s'è desta;*
> *Dell'elmo di Scipio*
> *S'è cinta la testa.*
> *Dov'è la Vittoria?*
> *Le porga la chioma,*
> *Ché schiava di Roma;*
> *Iddio la creò.*
> *Stringiamci a coorte*
> *Siam pronti alla morte*
> *L'Italia chiamò.*

('Brothers of Italy! / Our land has awoken. / Her head is ringed / by
Scipio's Helmet. / Where's our Victory? / The roll-call summons you, /
once the slave of Rome. / God has created Her. / Let's line up in our
cohorts, / we're ready for death. / Italy has called.')[5]

The foul weather of 2008 matched a tense political situation. The leaders of the *Lega Nord*, the 'Northern League', Italy's most bumptious
party, were boycotting the parades; they do not believe in the permanence
of the present political order. When pressed by a reporter, the president
issued a stark warning: '*Basta ribellioni contro lo stato*', 'Enough rebellions against the state!' Before the parade finished, an incident occurred
on the Fori Imperiali. The president's open-topped limousine had already
passed. When Prime Minister Silvio Berlusconi's car appeared, a girl ran
forward calling '*Presidente, presidente, una foto . . .*' (In Italian usage, as
president of the council of ministers, the premier enjoys the same form of
address as the president of the Republic.) The cavalcade halted. The
crowd started chanting: 'Silvio! Silvio!' Berlusconi obliged. Leaping out of
his car, he strolled the full length of the Fori surrounded by his admirers.
A voice in the crush shouted '*Silvio santo subito*'* in mock blasphemy; '*Ci
proverò*,' he promised, 'I'll show you; I'll solve all the problems.' The press
reported widely on the 'Berlusconi show' and the *bagno di follia*, 'the
forty minutes of delirium'. The Day of the Republic, ran the headline, 'has
been turned into the *Festa di Silvio*'.[6]

*

* *Santo subito*, meaning 'an instant saint', was the cry raised on the death of Pope John Paul
II in 2005, when many of his admirers were demanding beatification without delay.

The annual *Festa della Repubblica* is staged to remember one of the
closest-run political events in Italy's history. On 2 June 1946 Italians were
asked to vote in an 'institutional referendum' to decide whether their
country should remain a kingdom or become a republic. The result was
announced next day. The monarchy received 10,719,284 valid votes – 46
per cent; the republic 12,717,923 – a victorious 54 per cent. The country
was geographically divided. The north supported the republic; the poor,
less populous Mezzogiorno favoured the monarchy. Ravenna voted 91.2
per cent for the republic; Messina 85.4 per cent for the king.[7]

The last king of Italy, Umberto II (1904–83) was forty-two years old
when, from his point of view, the referendum was lost. Having mounted
the throne a month earlier as a result of his father's abdication, he had
reigned for only thirty-three days, and thereby earned the unkind sobriquet of *Il re di maggio*, 'The king of May'. In the three preceding years
he had served with some acumen as 'royal lieutenant', putting his com-
promised father into the background and easing the country's transition
from Mussolini's Fascism. In this respect, his role was not dissimilar to
that of his Spanish relative, Juan Carlos, during the aftermath of Franco.[8]

Post-war Italy, however, was less forgiving than post-Franco Spain.
Italy's royals had worked with Mussolini over two decades, and the
wounds of dictatorship, defeat, foreign occupation and civil war were
still festering. The anti-clerical and anti-monarchist Left, urged on by
the Communists, was rampant. Umberto's father had been slow to
adapt. By clinging to his throne for as long as he did, he had lessened the
chances of the monarchy's survival.

The consequences of the referendum were swift and stark. The constituent assembly resolved that the monarchy was abolished, that the
monarchy's symbols were illegal, that the royal family's property was to
be confiscated and that the king and his close male relatives were to be
banished. The king's home, the Quirinale Palace, was to be handed to
an acting head of state, Alcide de Gasperi. The royal standard, with its
eagle and four crowns, was to be hauled down, and the shield of the
House of Savoy was to be torn from the central section of the national
tricolour. The anthem of the '*Marcia Reale*', the 'Royal March', already
suspended, was to be permanently silenced. All the signs and symbols
associated with the Italian state since its birth in 1861 were to disappear.
The kingdom was ordered to dissolve; the date was set for 18 June.

The king hesitated for over a week, ceasing only when riots in Naples
were suppressed by bloody violence and civil war loomed. He formally
put an end to his brief reign on 12 June 1946, setting aside the royal

insignia, consigning the royal jewels to the Banca d'Italia and signing away his birthright. The next day he drove to Ciampino Airport, whence he flew into exile for life. His first port of call was his elderly father, who had left after the abdication a month earlier and had taken up residence in Egyptian Alexandria under the name of the count of Pollenzo. At the invitation of King Farouk, his Belgian-born queen, Marie-José, and their four children would shortly arrive to join him. As his plane soared out over the Tyrrhenian Sea, the last Umberto and his kingdom vanished over the horizon. He took with him the legacy of the first Umberto, nearly a thousand years old.

II

Humbertus or Hupertus I (*c.* 980–1047), otherwise Humbert of the White-hand, was the first count of Sabaudia. Since he lived at a time when all written sources were in Latin, the vernacular versions of his name and his county can only be guessed. But later records refer to him either as '*Humbert aux Mains Blanches*' (in French) or as '*Umberto Biancamano*' (in Italian), and to his county either as *Savoie* or *Savoia*. His possessions in the upper reaches of the Two Burgundies (see pp. 115 ff) stretched from the shores of Lake Leman to the Alpine fastnesses round Mont Blanc. He and his court would have spoken an old form of Franco-Provençal, a predecessor of the language now known as *Savoyard*. He was a direct progenitor of the king of Italy who was dethroned by the referendum of June 1946.

Like all self-respecting medieval rulers, Humbertus boasted a very long genealogical tree. Copied uncritically on numerous modern websites, it starts in AD 390 with a Roman senator called Ferreolus. Verifiable accuracy is never a characteristic of such productions. Any such claims made on behalf of Humbertus by his descendants were certainly not taken up by a historically minded Victorian travel-writer who visited the region at a time when it was achieving international fame and who confined himself to its medieval connections:

> Next day I reached St Jean de Maurienne. We seem to know nothing of [its] early history except that it was governed by bishops before ... Humbert of the White Hands ... obtained his investiture from the Emperor Conrad the Salic, towards the commencement of the eleventh century. The Christian world had just recovered from the abject fears of the year 1000 ... and its princes had [returned to] fighting and murdering one another ...

The Bishops of Savoy ... [had] declared themselves independent ...
Humbert, who ... had raised himself by his personal merit to be a Marquis,
or Lieutenant of the Emperor ... fought the Bishop, defeated him, razed
his city to the ground; and thus caused himself to be named Sovereign Count
of that wild district.[9]

The intrepid author of these words, Bayle St John, walked the length
and breadth of that 'wild district' in 1856, when it was fast becoming
one of Europe's most unstable trouble spots. He was a well-read Francophile, fascinated by political developments in the region, and it would
have been out of character if he had not been familiar with a learned
history of Savoy recently published in Annecy. Its author, like St John,
gave no credence to any rumours of Humbert's exotic ancestry, but provided more details of the county's rise to prominence:

> In 1033, the Emperor Conrad the Salic was absent in Hungary, and Eudes,
> Count of Champagne, benefited from his absence to take possession of
> Cisjuran Burgundy ... The Emperor then returned ... and marched against
> the rebels. One of his lieutenants, meanwhile, a descendant of Boso ... laid
> siege to [the episcopal town of] St Jean de Maurienne, leaving the Emperor
> to deal with Geneva. The siege was long: the sorties numerous and bloody:
> the Bishop sought every means to free himself ... In the end, taken by storm
> and razed, the town of St Jean was left completely deserted ... The lieuten-
> ant of whom we have spoken, was called Humbert, commander of the
> March of Maurienne. Conrad created a sovereign county for him – *comes
> in agro Savojense*.[10]

Henceforth, the counts of Sabaudia were both subjects of the Holy
Roman Empire and for practical purposes lords of all they surveyed.
They flourished by the usual medieval strategies of exploiting their vassals, fighting their neighbours, expanding their territories and marrying
well. Since their immediate neighbours to the west, the counts of Vienne,
were increasingly drawn into the growing French sphere, they themselves concentrated their efforts on control of the Alpine passes, and on
links with the eastern (Italian) side of the Alps in the *Piemonte*, the 'Foot
of the Mountains'. As a result, the heartland of Sabaudia soon consisted
of a clutch of 'provinces' which surrounded the meeting point of the
modern frontiers of France, Switzerland and Italy: namely, Savoy proper
(its *chef-lieu* Chambéry), the Genevois (Annecy), the Chablais (Thonon),
Faucigny (Bonneville), the Tarentaise (Moûtiers), the Maurienne (St
Jean) and the Val d'Aosta (Courmayeur). The administrative centre was

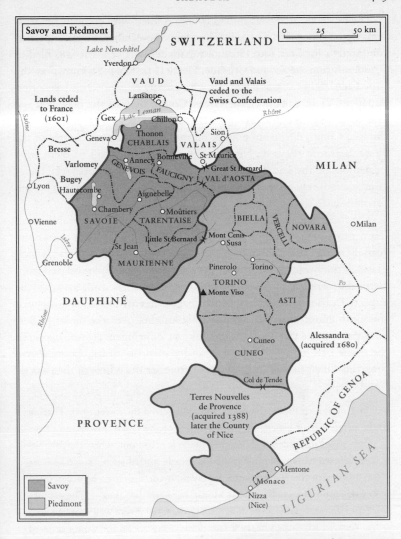

Savoy and Piedmont

SWITZERLAND

Lake Neuchâtel

0   25   50 km

Yverdon

VAUD

Lausanne

Vaud and Valais
ceded to the
Swiss Confederation

Lands ceded
to France
(1601)

Saône

Gex

Lac Léman

Chillon

Geneva

Thonon

CHABLAIS

Sion

Rhône

St Maurice

VALAIS

MILAN

Bresse

Annecy

Bonneville

Great St Bernard

Varlomey

GENEVOIS

FAUCIGNY

VAL d'AOSTA

Lyon

Bugey

Hautecombe

Aiguebelle

Chambéry

Moûtiers

BIELLA

VERCELLI

NOVARA

Milan

SAVOIE

TARENTAISE

Little St Bernard

Mont Cenis

Susa

St Jean

Vienne

Isère

MAURIENNE

Pinerolo

Torino

Grenoble

Rhône

DAUPHINÉ

TORINO

Monte Viso

ASTI

Po

Cuneo

Alessandra
(acquired 1680)

CUNEO

Col de Tende

REPUBLIC OF GENOA

PROVENCE

Terres Nouvelles
de Provence
(acquired 1388)
later the County
of Nice

Mentone

Monaco

LIGURIAN SEA

Nizza
(Nice)

Savoy

Piedmont

moved from St Jean to Camberiaco (Chambéry) in 1232, but the counts'
favourite residences were at Avigliana (Viana, Veillane) near Susa, and
later at Aiguebelle (Acqua, Aigue) in the Maurienne. Their prize assets,
however, were the mountain trails leading across the high ridge of the
western Alps, namely the Great St Bernard, the Little St Bernard, the
Mont Cenis and, further south, the Col de Maddalena (Largentières).
The counts adopted the sobriquet of *gardien des cols*, 'guardian of the
Alpine passes'.

The list of the early Sabaudian counts is filled with colourful characters. Otto/Oddon I (r. 1051–60), by marrying Adalina da Susa, carried the family's fortunes into Piedmont. Amadeus III (r. 1103–48) died in Rhodes during the Second Crusade. Pierre II (r. 1263–8), known as 'the little Charlemagne', was a warrior who greatly expanded his territories. Amadeus VI (r. 1343–83), the Green Count, died of the plague at the end of a long military career.[11] His son, Amadeus VII (r. 1383–91), the Red Count, died from poison, but not before gaining control of the *Paese Nizzardo* (Pays de Nice) to the south. Almost all of them were buried beside the Lac du Bourget in the crypt of the Abbey of Hautecombe, whose chantries would not be silenced until the arrival of French revolutionary troops in 1796.

The rise of the medieval counts is known in some considerable detail thanks to a French chronicle compiled in the early fifteenth century by Jean d'Orville, also known by his surname of 'Cabaret'. The text, which exists in thirty copies but which has only been recently translated from Latin into French, is full of adventures, curiosities and, as might be expected, obsequious flattery. Much space is devoted to the conquests of the ninth count, Pierre II, who led his knights over the Great St Bernard pass in 1263 to confront the duke of Zähringen. Having captured the castle of Chillon on Lake Leman by surprise attack, Count Pierre took the duke prisoner, and set out to conquer the whole of the Pays de Vaud:

> The Count rode first to Moudon, where he seized the lower town. Fearing the projectiles of his *engins*, the defenders of the Great Tower and of the upper town surrendered . . . He then made for Romont, where the inhabitants refused to capitulate. But the Savoyards hurled such a huge number of stones that the walls crumbled. Having made his entry, he ordered the construction of a small castle at Morat, between the lakes . . . The capture of Yverdon was much more difficult. The defenders were well supplied with artillery, which caused heavy losses in his army . . . So the Count ordered his prisoners to be brought from Chillon, and demanded of the Duke that all the barons and knights of the Vaud be permitted to pay him homage. If the Duke refused, he would be put to death . . . The Duke saw that no other solution was possible . . . The Vaudois paid homage to the Count . . . And the Duke returned freely to his duchy in Germany.[12]

At the time, the Pays de Vaud formed part of the imperial Kingdom of Burgundy; Switzerland had not been invented. The Kingdom of France, which watched the expansion of Savoy with suspicion, was still confined

Counts of Savoy

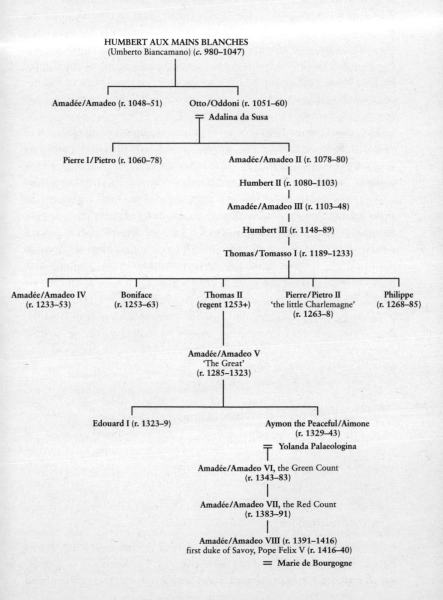

HUMBERT AUX MAINS BLANCHES
(Umberto Biancamano) (*c.* 980–1047)

Amadée/Amadeo (r. 1048–51)   Otto/Oddoni (r. 1051–60)
= Adalina da Susa

Pierre I/Pietro (r. 1060–78)   Amadée/Amadeo II (r. 1078–80)

Humbert II (r. 1080–1103)

Amadée/Amadeo III (r. 1103–48)

Humbert III (r. 1148–89)

Thomas/Tomasso I (r. 1189–1233)

Amadée/Amadeo IV   Boniface   Thomas II   Pierre/Pietro II   Philippe
(r. 1233–53)   (r. 1253–63)   (regent 1253+)   'the little Charlemagne'   (r. 1268–85)
(r. 1263–8)

Amadée/Amadeo V
'The Great'
(r. 1285–1323)

Edouard I (r. 1323–9)   Aymon the Peaceful/Aimone
(r. 1329–43)
= Yolanda Palaeologina

Amadée/Amadeo VI, the Green Count
(r. 1343–83)

Amadée/Amadeo VII, the Red Count
(r. 1383–91)

Amadée/Amadeo VIII (r. 1391–1416)
first duke of Savoy, Pope Felix V (r. 1416–40)
= Marie de Bourgogne

to the west of the Rhône. Thanks to a common rivalry with France, however, Sabaudia developed a special relationship with England and in 1236, Count Pierre II travelled to London with his niece Eleanor of Provence, for her marriage to King Henry III. Known in England as the earl of Richmond, the count became one of the king's favourites and leader of an influential court faction. In 1246 Henry III granted the Savoyards a manor on the banks of the Thames, halfway between the City of London and Westminster. This Savoy Manor gave rise to a thriving district, graced in due course by the Savoy Palace, the Savoy Chapel and the Savoy Hotel.[13]

Count Amadeus VIII (r. 1391–1440) is celebrated on many scores. On coming of age, he formulated the statutes of his dynasty's premier order of chivalry, the Order of the Collar, modelled (like the Burgundian Order of the Golden Fleece) on England's Order of the Garter. Dedicated to the Virgin Mary, the Order was repeatedly to change its name, but never to drop its enigmatic motto of 'FERT'.* In 1416, the count moved up a rank in the medieval hierarchy by obtaining the title of 'duke' from the emperor, together with formal recognition of his independence. Shortly afterwards, he took possession of Torino (Turin), henceforth the richest item in his portfolio. He and his heirs would doggedly exploit their position as lords of the joint state of Piedmont-Savoy, ruling over lands stretching from the environs of Lyon to the source of the Rhône near Andermatt, and from the Lake of Neuchâtel to the Tyrrhenian Sea.

Nonetheless, it could be said that the greatest achievement of Amadeus VIII, now Duke Amadeus, was to be elected pope, or at least anti-pope. After the deaths of his wife and eldest son, he had retired to the Château de Ripaille on the shores of Lake Leman, where he was living as the master of an order of knights-hermit. Fame of his saintliness spread, and in 1439 he found that an irregular conclave of cardinals, appointed by the Church Council of Basle, had raised him to the throne of St Peter. Taking the papal name of Felix V, he failed to exert his authority and resigned a decade later, accepting a cardinal's hat in consolation.[14] His position as duke, meantime, had been assumed by his second son, Louis (r. 1440–65), who raised the family's status still higher by gaining possession of the wonder-working Shroud of Turin.[15]

* The Order, now known as the Order of the Most Holy Annunciation, still exists. Its motto is variously taken to stand either for the Latin word *fert*, 'he bore', as in 'Christ bore our sins', or for a hidden message such as FORTITUDE EIUS RHODUM TULIT, which would refer to the conquest of Rhodes by Amadeus III, or FOEDERE ET RELIGIONE TENEMUR, 'We are held together by the constitution and by religion'.

From the time of the duke-pope, the succession to the ducal title
passed smoothly by hereditary right through fourteen generations. (The
only serious difficulty arose in 1496 when the direct line became extinct;
it was solved by the accession of Philippe de Bresse, lord of Bugey, the
late duke's great-uncle.) None of the dukes was more resplendent or
more successful than Emanuele-Filiberto (r. 1553–80), who made Turin
his permanent capital in 1563 and who greatly strengthened Italian
influence throughout his dominions. Nonetheless, the devastation caused
by the Franco-Imperial Habsburg wars of the sixteenth century was colossal – at the start of his reign the whole of the duchy had been occupied
by the French. The Venetian ambassador to Turin reported desperate
conditions:

> Uncultivated, no citizens in the cities, neither man nor beast in the fields,
> all the land forest-clad and wild: one sees no houses for most of them are
> burnt, and of nearly all the castles, only the walls are visible; and of the
> inhabitants once so numerous, some have died of the plague or of hunger,
> some by the sword, and some have fled elsewhere, preferring to beg their
> bread abroad.[16]

The delicacy of the duke's predicament can be judged by the fact that
he served as an imperial general while married to the sister of the French
king. His fortunes were restored by his victory at the head of Spanish
forces at Saint-Quentin in August 1557; the full restitution of his lands
following the Peace of Cateau-Cambrésis (1559) permitted him to dis-
pense with income granted by the duchy's Estates and to rule as an
absolute monarch. By skilful diplomacy, he persuaded the French to
vacate the fortress of Pinerolo, the Spaniards to leave Asti, and, at the
cost of abandoning the Vaud, the Bernese to restore Gex, the Chablais
and the Genevois. A form of Italian now became the main language of
administration and education, and the ruling house identified ever more
strongly with its Italian name of *Casa Savoia*.

In the early seventeenth century a Francophile and Francophone reaction grew in strength in the duchy's Savoyard districts. The *Académie
Florimontane*, founded at Annecy in 1606, served as an inspiration for
the Académie Française founded in Paris twenty-nine years later by
Cardinal Richelieu, and served as a counterbalance to official, Italianate
influence. Conflicts between Catholics and Protestants also arose.
St Francis de Sales (1567–1622), born in the Château de Thorens near
Annecy, made his saintly name by calming religious passions. Originally
a pupil of the Jesuits, he studied in both Paris and Padua before returning

to Annecy and devoting himself to 'the devout life'. His sermons were spellbinding, his books beautifully written and his peaceable methods of evangelism inspired numerous Catholic Orders, including the Sisters of the Visitation of Holy Mary, the Missionaries of St Francis and the Salesians of Don Bosco. In due course he became bishop of Geneva, although based in Annecy because the city of Geneva remained in Calvinist hands. He was named patron of the deaf on account of his invention of a sign language.[17]

Despite de Sales' example, religion continued to be the source of major conflict. A non-Catholic Christian community, the *Valdenses* or Vaudois, that long antedated the Protestant Reformation, had taken deep root in the Alpine valleys. In the sixteenth century the Valdenses joined forces with the Calvinists, and probably represented a majority of Christian believers in the duchy's Alpine districts. The Counter-Reformation authorities were determined to eradicate them. In 1535 they had been extirpated in French-ruled Provence, and long awaited a similar fate in Switzerland. It was eventually inflicted upon them by Duke Carlo Emanuele II in 1655. The duke's army took up positions, and drove its victims to the heads of the valleys, then, at 4 a.m. on 24 April, proceeded to a general massacre. It was a bloodbath such as Europe had not seen since the massacre of St Bartholomew's Eve eighty years before. Protestant Europe was outraged. Oliver Cromwell, Lord Protector of the British Isles, threatened to intervene; Cromwell's Latin secretary, John Milton, composed a sonnet, 'On the late Massacher in *Piemont*':

> Avenge O Lord thy slaughter'd Saints, whose bones
> 　　Lie scatter'd on the Alpine mountains cold,
> 　　Ev'n them who kept thy truth so pure of old
> 　　When all our Fathers worship't Stocks and Stones,
> Forget not: in thy book record their groanes
> 　　Who were thy Sheep in their antient Fold
> 　　Slayn by the bloody *Piemontese* that roll'd
> 　　Mother with infant down the Rocks. Their moans
> The Vales redoubl'd to the Hills, and they
> 　　To Heav'n. Their martyr'd blood and ashes sow
> 　　O're all th'*Italian* fields where still doth sway
> The triple Tyrant: that from there may grow
> 　　A hunder'd-fold, who having learnt their way
> 　　Early may fly the *Babylonian* wo.

Astonishingly, no general amnesty was granted to the Vaudois until 1848.

Nothing seemed to bring any serious interruption to the onward march of the *Casa Savoia*. From 1630 the dukes had assumed the additional title of 'princes of Carignano', a lowly Piedmontese village, and henceforth as self-styled 'prince-dukes' were buried in a purpose-built mausoleum within the cathedral complex in Turin. The widowed queen-regent, Marie-Christine de France (d. 1663), '*Madama Reale*', was a dominant figure in the mid-seventeenth century. It was for her that the ducal palace in Turin was misleadingly named the 'Palazzo Reale'. The domed San Sidone chapel (1694) was constructed to provide a suitable setting for the Shroud. The dynasty's sense of self-importance was plain to see.

Madama Reale's son, Carlo Emanuele II (r. 1638–75), extirpator of the Vaudois, also set his heart on strengthening access to the Mediterranean seaboard. Thwarted in a war with Genoa, he chose instead to develop the port of Nizza/Nice, to which he built a transalpine road over the Col de Tende.[18] The three different parts of the duchy – Savoy, 'New Provence' (Nice) and Piedmont – were heading towards economic as well as political integration. Their borders had stabilized, and when Switzerland gained international recognition at the Treaty of Westphalia in 1648, the House of Savoy resigned all thoughts of recovering any parts of the new state that it had once possessed. Prince Eugene of Savoy (1663–1736), the greatest military commander of the early eighteenth century, was one of Carlo Emanuele's grandsons.[19]

It was Prince-Duke Vittorio Amadeo II/Victor Amadeus II (r. 1675–1730) who finally secured a royal throne, by manoeuvring astutely during the War of the Spanish Succession. At the Treaty of Utrecht (1713), he was among the beneficiaries, being rewarded with the ex-Spanish Kingdom of Sicily – hardly the most convenient of acquisitions, but newly anointed monarchs cannot afford to look a *cavallo di presente* in the mouth. The obvious policy was to accept the gift graciously, to bask in the title of 'king of Sicily' and to bide one's time.

An excellent opportunity arrived only five years later. The *Casa Savoia* was not alone in its dissatisfaction with its gains from Utrecht, and during the territorial redistribution that took place during preparations for the Treaty of The Hague (1720), it proved possible to do business with the Austrians, specifically to swap Sicily for Sardinia. The arrangement was still not ideal, but it made the dynasty's territorial agglomeration slightly more cohesive, while preserving the monarch's all-important royal status. For the next eighty years, as 'kings of Sardinia', the heirs of Vittorio Amadeo II could enjoy the uninterrupted fruits of

The Kingdom of Sardinia, c. 1750

their second kingdom in the curious configuration of Piedmont-Savoy-Nice and Sardinia.[20]

More stable conditions in the eighteenth century raised the House of Savoy to its apogee. Apart from the strange attempt of Vittorio Amadeo II to reclaim his throne after abdicating and retiring to Chambéry with his mistress, there were no dynastic crises; there were no destructive wars, and there was plenty of room for improvement and steady enrichment. Carlo Emanuele III (r. 1730–73) proved himself an able administrator and diplomat, confining his involvement in the Wars of the Polish and Austrian Successions to limited and lucrative campaigns. His son,

Vittorio Amadeo III (r. 1773–96) was religiously devout, politically conservative and temperamentally generous, being a great benefactor and a popular 'Father of his People'. Their kingdom could not be counted among Europe's greatest powers, but it was sturdily independent and frequently courted as an ally. A British strategist, surveying the state of the Continent in 1761, rated it highly:

> The Dominions of His Sardinian Majesty, considered as Duke of Savoy and Prince of Piedmont, have always been regarded as the Key of Italy ... and in latter times this Prince has been justly looked upon as the natural Master of the Ballance in Italy ... Because of its being His interest to affect Peace rather than War, Reason and Experience dictate that he will never want Allies ... for the Preservation of His Territories.[21]

The resources at the king's disposal impressed the foreign observer:

> The island of Sardinia, next to Sicily, is the largest in the Mediterranean ... The people are rough and unpolished, but live in a kind of barbarous Plenty, which, affording them much Meat and little Labour, they look on their Island as a Paradise from which they are drawn with Reluctancy ... The Dutchy of Savoy is a large but far from fruitful Country; however, the Inhabitants are a hardy and laborious People, and by their Industry subsist tolerably well. The Principality of Piedmont is very large and the best part of it very fertile and well-cultivated, much less exposed than Savoy ... very strong by Nature and well fortified by Art. *Turin*, which is the royal residence, is a very large and beautiful city standing by the River Po and admirably well fortified. The County of Nice is less fruitful but of great importance as it is the only [continental] Part ... which lies upon the Sea ... The districts acquired from the Dutchy of Milan have augmented both the Power and the Revenue of his Sardinian Majesty, so he is justly esteemed one of the most considerable Potentates ...
>
> The Commerce of these Countries was scarce worthy of Notice, but by degrees Things have been very much changed. The Staple Commodity of Piedmont is a kind of Silk indispensably necessary in many Manufactures ... The Navigation of the Po enables the inhabitants of Turin to carry on considerable Trade to Venice ... Besides all these, His Sardinian Majesty has gradually and silently possessed himself of all the Passages whereby the Inland Trade is carried on between France and Italy, and having it in his Power to lay what Duties he thinks proper, derives thence an additional Revenue, keeping the neighbouring States in a kind of Dependence ...

Even as Things stand now, it is apparent that the Territories of this Monarch are very populous, and the People of *Savoy* and of the Vallies are naturally martial, so that under these last two reigns a very considerable Army of regular Troops has been kept up, and the King can never be at a loss to bring forty or fifty Thousand Men into the Field when Occasion require it . . . Besides this, the Fortresses of Piedmont are in so good order that his Sardinian Majesty can always make a Stand until supported by the Autrians . . . Upon these Principles, therefore, we may safely lay it down that . . . he is one of the great powers of Italy."[22]

The rosy tone of this account may be explained in part by its author's wish to encourage an alliance between Great Britain and the House of Savoy. But it was by no means eccentric in seeing that 'Sardinia', like its northern counterpart 'Prussia', was currently moving up the international league table. Progress continued for another generation until Vittorio Amadeo III put everything at risk by declaring war on revolutionary France.

Ever since France's Italian wars of the late fifteenth century, French troops on their way down the Italian peninsula had repeatedly marched through Savoy and Piedmont, sometimes staying for decades at a time. But Napoleon's 'Army of Italy', which crossed the Alps in 1796, brought a new dimension to the practice. The troops of the revolutionary French Republic were intent on sweeping away all the *anciens régimes* which they encountered, and they spared the Roman Catholic Church no mercy. The abbey of Hautecombe, for example, was sacked, and turned into a tile factory. Savoy was annexed to the French Republic as the Département du Mont-Blanc, without a fight; Piedmont was turned into a French military district; a Département des Alpes-Maritimes was formed round Nice; and the 'king of Sardinia' with his son and heir were driven out of their mainland dominions and forced to live in exile in the Sardinian rump of their kingdom. All these drastic arrangements proved temporary.

The general restoration of Europe's monarchies that followed Napoleon's defeat at Waterloo was confirmed by the Congress of Vienna (1815), and the exiled king of Sardinia was not forgotten. He recovered his lost lands, returned to Turin, and promptly attempted the restoration of the *status quo ante*. Yet post-Napoleonic Europe was very different from pre-revolutionary Europe. Many of the ideas spawned and exported by the French Revolution continued to circulate, posing a near-ubiquitous challenge to the natural conservatism of the restored monarchs. The ideas of 'the nation', endowed with a life of its own, and of the inborn right of its inhabitants to liberty, equality and social fraternity, were particularly strong, beginning to undermine the post-Napoleonic order as soon as it was established. Three parts of Europe where 'the nation' felt most excluded from politics were specially susceptible; and popular demands grew for the creation of nation-states on the French model. Poland, which had been carved up by three neighbouring empires (see pp. 285–90), was to strive in vain throughout the nineteenth century to win back its independence; but Germany and Italy were to succeed where Poland failed. Germany was divided by the intense rivalry of Protestant Prussia and Catholic Austria; advocates of the German national movement, the *Vormärz* ('pre-March'), could at first see no easy way to do so. Italy's divisions were still more marked. The north was dominated by the Austrian Empire, which held onto both Venice and Milan; the centre was run by a gaggle of reactionary monarchs, including the Roman pontiff in his Papal States; and the south remained in the grip of the Bourbon Kingdom of the Two Sicilies. In face of the restored hereditary rulers, the advocates of the Italian national movement, the Risorgimento or 'Resurgence', did not possess a common strategy.

For Italian nationalism encompassed several competing interests. One wing placed the emphasis on cultural objectives, notably on education, the promotion of a single, standardized Italian language, and the promotion of national consciousness. The central figure in this was the Milanese writer, Alessandro Manzoni (1785–1873), author of the first novel written in standard Italian, *I promessi sposi* (*The Betrothed*, 1827). Another wing was dedicated to political radicalism. Here the central role was played by the secret and revolutionary Society of the Charcoal burners, the *Carbonari*, whose activities were formally banned; one of its members, a Sicilian soldier called Guglielmo Pepe (1783–1855), launched the first of many abortive risings in Calabria in 1820. There was even a tradition of support for the Risorgimento by ruling monarchs; Napoleon's stepson and viceroy in Italy, Eugène de Beauharnais, had set the example, which was followed by the emperor's brother-in-law, Joachim Murat, when King of Naples (see p. 523, below). It seemed to create the perceived need for a political patron of established authority, who could curb the hotheads while giving heart to the moderates and negotiating with the powers.

The things that all Italian nationalists shared were dismay at the failure of early constitutional projects, opposition to the political role of the papacy, and resentment against the 'foreign presence' of Austria in Lombardy, Venice and the Trentino. They operated in all parts of Italy, though less successfully in some states than in others, and from early on saw Piedmont as fertile ground. In March 1823 a nationalist insurrection was organized in the town of Alessandria by a professional officer of the Sardinian army, Count Santorre de Santarosa (1783–1825), who was hoping to unite Italy under the House of Savoy by waging war on the Austrians. He persuaded the regent of Piedmont to issue a short-lived Constitution before the absent king returned and ordered the insurrectionaries to be crushed. Despite its failure, Santarosa's enterprise showed that Piedmont was already moving in a different political direction from Savoy.

The seeds of nationalism had been sown in Savoy during the years of occupation by armies of the revolutionary Republic and Empire. After 1815, voices were again raised for the removal of the 'foreign kings' and the reinstatement of a French administration, and steps were taken to forge a separate Franco-Savoyard identity. This was done in part by cultivating the idea that the modern, French-speaking inhabitants of Savoy were the direct descendants of a Celtic tribe, the Allobroges, who had lived in the region in Roman times. A key figure in this movement was Joseph Dessaix (1817–70), a writer, sometime political prisoner and admirer of the Risorgimento. He was the author both of a popular historical encyclopedia[23] and of the definitive Savoyard song, 'Le Chant des Allobroges':

> Je te salue, ô terre hospitalière,
> Où le malheur trouva protection
> D'un peuple libre arborant la bannière.
> Je vins fêter la Constitution.
>
> Allobroges vaillants! Dans vos vertes campagnes
> Accordez-moi toujours asile et sûreté;
> Car j'aime à respirer l'air pur de vos montagnes.
> Je suis la Liberté! La Liberté!

('I greet you, hospitable land, / where misfortune found protection / from a free people displaying their banner. / I came to celebrate the constitution. // Valiant Allobroges! In your green countryside / grant me always refuge and security; / for I love to breathe the pure air of your mountains. / I am Liberty! Liberty!')[24] This song was not sung in Piedmont.

Yet nationalism, whether French or Italian, did not enjoy a monopoly on the political spectrum. Conservatism was also strong, and a long struggle between monarchists and republicans was only just beginning. Many people simply clung to the status quo, fearing a return to the turbulence of Napoleonic times. In both Piedmont and Savoy, a middle way appealed, combining the maintenance of the monarchy with a programme of gradual constitutional reform. In the peculiar arrangements of what officialdom now called *I Stati Sardi*, 'the Sardinian States', many Savoyards and Piemontesi felt that they could find common cause. Growing currency was given to the concept of 'the Subalpine Kingdom' – *il Regno Subalpino, le Royaume Subalpin*.

The 'king of Sardinia' who returned from exile in 1815 was the fifth of his line to bear the royal title, and the fifth of eight 'Sardinian' monarchs in all. Vittorio Emanuele I (r. 1802–21) was the second son of the late Vittorio Amadeo III and had briefly been preceded during their exile by his elder brother, Carlo Emanuele IV (r. 1796–1802). During his stay in Cagliari, he formed the Corps of Carabinieri, which remains a colourful feature of Italian life to this day. After the Congress of Vienna handed him the lands of the former Genoese Republic, he founded the Sardinian navy, which was henceforth based in the port of Genoa.

Carlo il Felice/Charles le Heureux/Félix (r. 1821–31) was the younger brother of his two predecessors. He was particularly proud of the Bourbon heritage of his mother, Maria Antonia, an infanta of Spain, and a zealous defender the royal prerogative. After the suppression of Santarosa's rising, he was known to his subjects not as *Il Felice*, but as *Il Feroce*, 'The Ferocious'.

His successor, Carlo Alberto (r. 1831–49), was less ferocious but not easily swayed by radical demands. He introduced a bureaucratic, paternalistic administration dubbed *Il Buon Governo* or 'Good Rule', and in 1834 ordered the suppression of the next attempted insurrection, in Turin, for which the young Giuseppe Mazzini (see below) was handed a death sentence. Carlo Alberto also took special pains to reassert the dynasty's standing by restoring its monuments. He renovated the family mausoleum at Hautecombe and relaunched it as the prime symbol of the family's continuity. The revolutionary wreckage at the abbey was removed, a grandiose Gothic church was erected on the ruins, and the ducal tombs were lovingly reconsecrated. A steamship service was introduced to take visitors back and forth to Aix-les-Bains, and in 1849 Carlo Alberto himself was buried there among his ancestors. The record of his self-proclaimed *Buon Governo* was not entirely negative. A memorial column erected in his honour still stands beside the Pont d'Arve at Bonneville.[25]

Before his death, Carlo Alberto had succumbed to the Continent-wide clamour of 1848 to issue liberal constitutions, in his case *lo Statuto Albertino*. The remarkable thing was not that the *Statuto* was intro-duced, but that it was never rescinded. While reserving all executive decisions to the king, including declarations of war and peace, it guar-anteed freedom of speech and assembly and made provision for a two-chamber parliament, made up of an appointed Senate and a cham-ber of elected deputies.[26] The king equally ensured the survival of the Valdenses. After centuries of persecution he granted them toleration, decorating the one-legged British missionary, John Beckwith, who had taken up their cause. Henceforth their main centre would be located near Ivrea in Piedmont, at La Torre on the eastern slopes of the Gran Paradiso.[27]

Piedmont-Savoy did not witness any of the more extreme manifesta-tions of the 'Springtime of Nations'. Public meetings in Chambéry and Turin did not disintegrate into the sort of riots and revolutions that were witnessed in Paris, Milan or Rome. Nonetheless, the old king's proclamation of the *Statuto* had far-reaching consequences, and his refusal to heed the resurgent conservatives or to limit the constitution kept the ferment of 1848 bubbling throughout the following decade. It opened the way in Savoy for pro-French republicans to agitate in favour of reunion with France; and, on the other side of the Monte Viso, for activists of the Risorgimento to press for the adoption of Piedmont as the springboard of Italian unification. Neither the Francophiles in Savoy nor the Italophiles in Piedmont enjoyed a monopoly. Yet the resultant stresses grew ever more visible. Savoy and Piedmont were being pulled in opposite directions. This was what Bayle St John had set out to observe.

Unfortunately, Vittorio Emanuele II (r. 1849–61 and 1861–78) was temperamentally indisposed to plotting a firm course between the com-peting whirlpools. In his youth he had dallied in *Carbonaro* circles, and was familiar with the aims of the radicals, though he sympathized more with those of the moderates. On the other hand, as a crowned king, he was loath to join the hue and cry against other divinely appointed mon-archs. It was not his choice that the reactionary stand of other Italian rulers, including the pope, should have pushed him into the role of the Risorgimento's chief patron, yet neither could he bring himself to shun the conceited motto of '*VERDI*' – 'Vittorio Emanuele Re d'Italia'. As part of a dubious claim to have shown bravery in battle, he also adopted the sobriquet of *Il Re Galantuomo*, 'the Hero King'. In reality, he was one of the world's ditherers. The British foreign minister, the earl of Clarendon, was less than generous: 'There is universal agreement that Vittorio Emanuele is an imbecile. He tells lies to everyone. At this rate, he will end up losing his crown and ruining Italy.'[28] In foreign affairs the king relied on the advice of his foreign minister, the devious Count Cavour (see below).[29] 'I have discovered the perfect means of deceiving diplomats,' Cavour once said; 'I tell them the truth and they never believe me.'[30]

The political condition of Savoy at this juncture was extremely fragile.[31] The Sardinian Restoration had been accompanied by an influx of Italian-speaking bureaucrats and by a resurgence of 'the noble-clerical reaction', and pro-French sentiment had been growing ever since: large numbers of Savoyards had emigrated to Lyon and Paris, and the republicans among them instinctively sought rapprochement with a French republic. On the other hand, as carefully reported by Bayle St John, the pro-French party received a series of hard blows in the 1850s. The opening of the 'subalpine parliament' in Turin, attended by deputies from every part of the state, won over many sceptics. The invasion of Chambéry in 1848 by a republican rabble from Lyon calling themselves the 'Voraces' infuriated the citizenry,[32] and the violence in Paris surrounding Napoleon III's *coup d'état* in 1851, widely reported in Chambéry, tarnished France's image. From then on, there was no French republic for Savoyard republicans to join.

Chambéry in the 1850s was a small provincial town still harbouring memories of its past glory. It was increasingly overshadowed both by the nearby spa of Aix-les-Bains, with its boisterous casino, and, across the frontier, by the French city of Grenoble, which was more than twice its size. Bayle St John liked it:

> Chambéry is the capital of the province of Savoy; and, it has . . . a far more complete and metropolitan character than might have been expected. There is no trace of the village about it . . . evidently a place accustomed to be the seat of government [and] somewhat annoyed to be so no longer . . . Everything seems to be arranged for making the city a comfortable winter-quarter . . . During the summer everyone who can afford it disperses . . . up the lower slopes of the mountains which are dotted with villas . . .
>
> However, the streets and . . . the Place Saint Léger, where the band played each evening, were sufficiently well-thronged . . . The aristocracy of the

place being away, the middle classes tried to lord it ... I wished to change
some English sovereigns. The money-changer had gone to Paris. This is
confirmation of a truth ... that the English ... all go to Switzerland, or
only make a dash into northern Savoy to visit Mont Blanc ...

The fountain of De Boigne, with its four half-elephants stuck together is
one of the ugliest things I have ever seen ... M. de Boigne ... earned a
colossal fortune in India ... He built the long street through the centre of
town, adorned like the Rue de Rivoli [in Paris], with porticos ...

Then there is the old castle – so many times rebuilt that only a scrap is
really old ... Underneath the terrace of the castle ... not far from the place
where Mme. de Warens once [held] ... her extraordinary interviews with
Jean Jacques [Rousseau], extends a botanical garden.[33]

Travellers usually reached Chambéry from France by crossing the
frontier station on the River Guiers at le Pont de Beauvoisin, some 15
miles west of the city. St John reported a succession of peculiarly pedantic and intrusive customs examinations conducted by teams of French
and 'Sardinian' inspectors. In local parlance, 'beyond the Guiers' meant
'in France', and 'this side of the Guiers' meant 'in Savoy'. On leaving the
city, travellers could go either north to Geneva and the Swiss frontier,
south towards the border with Dauphiné, or east on the road to Italy.
Fifteen miles from Chambéry, the eastbound road divides. The left fork
takes one to Albertville, Moûtiers, Bourg St Maurice and via the Little
St Bernard pass to the Val d'Aosta. The right fork, which Bayle St John
preferred, leads to St Jean de Maurienne, the Mont Cenis and, through
the Val di Susa, to Turin.

The capital of Piedmont lies 138 very precipitous miles from the capital of Savoy. On reaching it, having crossed the Mont Cenis on foot,
Bayle St John did not conceal his distaste:

Turin has been suddenly swelled out to suit the convenience of a new
royalty ... [It] disappoints the stranger, not because it is uglier or meaner
than he expects, but because of its audacious air of pretension ... Every
street, every square manifestly asserts its right to be admired, and fails at
first because the mind puts itself into a hostile attitude. Instead of noticing
the real beauties, we notice at once the tedious provoking uniformity ...

Numbers of the houses and palaces are built of brick in a dirty London
hue ... The Carignan Palace, where the Chamber of Deputies sits, is a huge
ugly pile ... The palace of the king upon the Piazza Castello is nothing to
look at, but its apartments are superbly laid out and decorated ... The

Palazzo Madama is an old brick house . . . To make it uglier than it would otherwise be, they have built an observatory on the top . . .

The court is as elaborate as the court of an empire, with all the same accumulation of useless offices and degrading titles, which are ludicrous . . . in so small a kingdom. If every soldier is a general, every man has two confessors.[34]

As a Victorian liberal and an Anglican Protestant, the itinerant Englishman was perhaps predisposed against 'the Sardinian monarchy' and its hallmark Catholicism. Yet an inventory of the royal palaces in Turin and its surroundings listed twenty-two major buildings; the charge of overblown pretentiousness was well targeted, and the fact that he had to walk over the central section of the route between Chambéry and Turin, in a year when the railway between Chambéry and Paris was on the verge of completion, revealed the relative attractions of the two sides of the Alps. Even eighty years earlier, observers including both Voltaire and Gibbon had reacted exactly as St John did. They felt that the extravagant Sardinian monarchy was living it up at the expense of its impoverished Alpine subjects. 'In every gilded moulding', wrote Gibbon during a visit to the royal palace in Turin in 1764, 'I see a Savoyard village dying of hunger, cold and poverty.'[35]

The catalogue of the royal titles, almost one hundred long, was no less extensive than that of the royal palaces:

Victor Emmanuel II, by the Grace of God, King of Sardinia, Cyprus, Jerusalem, Armenia, Duke of Savoy, count of Maurienne, Marquis (of the Holy Roman Empire) in Italy; prince of Piedmont, Carignano, Oneglia, Poirino, Trino; Prince and Perpetual vicar of the Holy Roman Empire . . . prince bailiff of the Duchy of Aosta, Prince of Chieri, Dronero, Crescentino . . . Duke of Genoa, Montferrat, Aosta . . . Chablais, Genevois, Piacenza, Marquis of Saluzzo (Saluces), Ivrea, Susa . . . Ginevra, Nizza, Tenda, Romont, Asti . . . Novara, Tortona, Bobbio, Soissons . . . Baron of Vaud e del Faucigni, Lord of Vercelli, Pinerolo, Lomellina . . . Overlord of Monaco, Roccabruna and 11/12th of Menton, Noble patrician of Venice, patrician of Ferrara.[36]

Soon yet another title would be added.

It was well known that the Emperor Napoleon III looked with favour on the Italian Risorgimento, but many observers in the late 1850s wondered whether sympathy would ever be translated into action. It *was*, but only after some extraordinary skulduggery. In January 1858, a group of Italian revolutionaries unsuccessfully bombed the emperor's carriage on its way to the Paris Opéra; disillusioned by his prevarications, they were convinced that he was blocking all hopes for change in Italy. The chief conspirator, Felice Orsini, soon captured by the police, was a disciple of Mazzini. Before he was guillotined, he apparently penned two death-cell letters, which were duly published in the press. 'Unless Italy is free,' they said, 'the peace of Europe will be no more than a delusion.' Much, much later it was discovered that the letters' author was not Orsini but an imperial aide.[37] Napoleon III spent many hours in the following weeks poring over Italian maps; he had decided to prevaricate no further.

At this stage, three men were driving the 'Italian Question' forward. All three were subjects of the House of Savoy; and all contested Metternich's cynical saying that 'Italy is merely a geographical expression'. Giuseppe Mazzini (1805–71), founder of the 'Young Italy' movement and the theorist of Italian republicanism, had never reconciled himself to the Congress of Vienna which had handed his native Genoa to the Piedmontese. In 1858 he was still under sentence of death in Turin for fomenting failed insurrections; and, as one of the leaders of the ill-fated Roman Republic of 1848–9, was still operating from exile in London.[38] Giuseppe Garibaldi (1807–82), a Nizzardo sea-captain and once Mazzini's partner, already had a rich revolutionary career behind him, both in Italy and in South America. In 1858, having recently established his home on the island of Caprera off Sardinia, and with his hopes for support from the House of Savoy reviving, he was preparing to be elected to the subalpine parliament as the member for Nice.[39] Camillo Benso, Count Cavour (1810–61), an aristocratic liberal with Piemontese, French and Savoyard connections, had been prime minister of the Sardinian kingdom for six years. He had already steered the House of Savoy through the Crimean crisis. He was less interested in patronizing the Risorgimento than in furthering his royal master's fortunes, and he regarded the activities of Mazzini and Garibaldi as an infernal nuisance.[40]

In the early summer of the same year, an obscure emissary from Paris arrived in Turin unannounced. He told Count Cavour that Napoleon III wished to see him privately, preferably during the emperor's annual visit to the spa at Plombières-les-Bains in the Vosges. Cavour hardly needed to be briefed. He knew about the turn in French policy through the wife of the crown prince of Savoy, Napoleon III's daughter; and he was receiving information from his own cousin, Virginia Oldini, countess of

Castiglione, whom he had deliberately inserted into the imperial court in Paris to add her to the emperor's lengthy list of mistresses.* Cavour thereon ordered a false passport, and travelled to the Vosges incognito and by a roundabout route. His secret meeting with Napoleon at Plombières on 21 July 1858 was conducted in a semi-conspiratorial setting, although his presence was leaked to the French press. What exactly happened can only be reconstructed from a report composed by Cavour; none of the emperor's ministers were involved and many details remain vague. But it is clear Cavour learned that the French were itching to attack Austria, and were willing to do so in partnership with Sardinia. He did not learn the emperor's final aims, however, and he was taken aback by the harsh terms proposed. In essence, the emperor offered to send his army to liberate northern Italy from Austria, but only if the counties of Savoy and Nice were ceded to France in return. Cavour swallowed his pride and, in principle, accepted. He was risking the loss of perhaps a third of his sovereign's possessions in the uncertain hope of winning something more extensive.[42]

Over the next two years Italian politics evolved rapidly, and all the while the agreement of Plombières was kept conveniently secret. In June 1859 the French army marched 'to free Italy' from its oppressors – the Austrian imperialists, the pope and other 'reactionary' rulers. At Magenta and Solferino it won decisive but particularly bloody victories against the Austrians. (The terrible suffering of the soldiery at Solferino prompted the creation of the Red Cross.) The Sardinian army, assisted by Garibaldi's volunteers, the *Cacciatori d'Italia*, had played a supporting role. The Austrians, despairing, agreed to withdraw from Lombardy. As they left Milan, the 'Sardinians' marched in. The House of Savoy was preparing to form its third kingdom, just as Cavour had planned.

Yet several things did *not* go to plan. Shortly after Solferino, Napoleon III made a separate peace with Austria at Villafranca di Verona, failing to consult Cavour and sorely displeasing his Italian clients. He was said to be traumatized by the appalling battlefield bloodshed, and appeared to be abandoning the scheme for an expanded Sardinian kingdom in favour of a French-protected Italian confederation. Cavour resigned in disgust, and for six months the path towards a mutually agreed solution became severely fogbound.

* Oldini, '*la comtesse divine*', often reckoned one of the great beauties of the age, fascinated Parisian high society, lived luxuriously in a grand *Hôtel* on the place Vendôme and became one of the stars of early photography.[41]

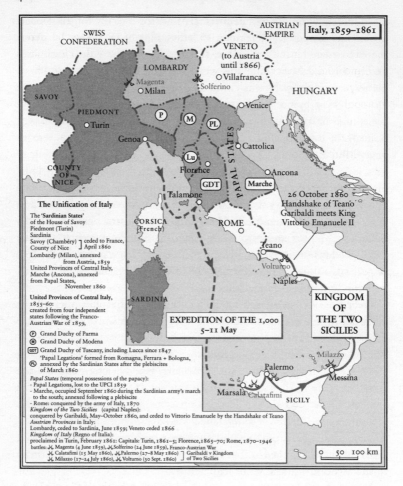

Italy, 1859–1861

The Unification of Italy

The 'Sardinian States'
of the House of Savoy
Piedmont (Turin)
Sardinia
Savoy (Chambéry) ⎤ ceded to France,
County of Nice   ⎦ April 1860
Lombardy (Milan), annexed
        from Austria, 1859
United Provinces of Central Italy,
Marche (Ancona), annexed
from Papal States,
        November 1860

United Provinces of Central Italy,
1855–60:
created from four independent
states following the Franco-
Austrian War of 1859.

ℙ Grand Duchy of Parma
𝕄 Grand Duchy of Modena
ᴳᴰᵀ Grand Duchy of Tuscany, including Lucca since 1847
   'Papal Legations' formed from Romagna, Ferrara + Bologna,
ℙᴸ annexed by the Sardinian States after the plebiscites
   of March 1860

Papal States (temporal possessions of the papacy):
- Papal Legations, lost to the UPCI 1859
- Marche, occupied September 1860 during the Sardinian army's march
  to the south; annexed following a plebiscite
- Rome: conquered by the army of Italy, 1870
Kingdom of the Two Sicilies (capital Naples):
conquered by Garibaldi, May–October 1860, and ceded to Vittorio Emanuele by the Handshake of Teano
Austrian Provinces in Italy:
Lombardy, ceded to Sardinia, June 1859; Veneto ceded 1866
Kingdom of Italy (Regno di Italia):
proclaimed in Turin, February 1861. Capitals: Turin, 1861–5; Florence, 1865–70; Rome, 1870–1946
battles: ⚔ Magenta (4 June 1859), ⚔ Solferino (24 June 1859), Franco-Austrian War
⚔ Calatafimi (15 May 1860), ⚔ Palermo (27–8 May 1860) ⎤ Garibaldi v Kingdom
⚔ Milazzo (17–24 July 1860), ⚔ Volturno (30 Sept. 1860) ⎦ of Two Sicilies

EXPEDITION OF THE 1,000
5–11 May

26 October 1860
Handshake of Teano:
Garibaldi meets King
Vittorio Emanuele II

KINGDOM
OF
THE TWO
SICILIES

0   50   100 km

In the second half of 1859 developments in north-central Italy came to
the fore. Having lost the protection of their Austrian allies, the dukes of
Parma and Modena and the grand duke of Tuscany were all overthrown
by local revolutions. In Florence, Grand Duke Leopold II, who had
rescinded Tuscany's constitution in the way that Vittorio Emanuele had
not done, was forced to abdicate. Papal administrators were driven out of
the Romagna, the northernmost section of the Papal States. All the liberated territories then joined forces in a pro-Sardinian grouping called the
United Provinces of Central Italy. They elected one Sardinian governor,
only to find that Vittorio Emanuele insisted on appointing a different one.
Confusion reigned. Napoleon III in particular had lost his way.

At this juncture, Cavour realized that an opportunity for diplomatic action had reopened. Returning to office in January 1860, he determined to mend fences with the French and to resuscitate the Plombières agreement. Essentially, if Paris were prepared to approve a series of plebiscites in the United Provinces of Central Italy with a view to their incorporation by Sardinia, Turin would agree to hold parallel plebiscites in Nice and Savoy with a view to their cession to France. These terms were drawn up and signed in Turin at the Franco-Sardinian Treaty of 24 March 1860.[43]

The difference between a referendum and a plebiscite is a fine one. Both pertain to collective decisions made by the direct vote of all qualified adults. The referendum, which derives from Swiss practice, involves an issue that is provisionally determined in advance, but that is then 'referred' for a final decision by the whole electorate. This would have suited the circumstances envisaged by the Treaty of Turin, but 'plebiscite' was the term that the treaty used.

Plebiscites were common in nineteenth-century Europe, especially in France. The *scitum plebis* or 'people's choice' had its roots in ancient Rome and was revived during the French Revolution, when popular support was sought for successive constitutions. Louis-Napoleon's *coup d'état* was approved by plebiscite in 1851, as was the restoration of the French Empire in 1852. The plebiscites in Nice and Savoy were to form part of a series starting in Parma, Modena, Tuscany and Romagna. Plebiscites are often criticized for being open to manipulation. The wording, the timing, the local circumstances and the degree of impartial supervision can all affect the outcome. In 1860 in Nice and Savoy, none of the basic safeguards were in place. The plebiscites were staged for the purpose of obtaining a preconceived result; Napoleon III aimed to keep procedures under close French control; the press was subjected to censorship; and the 'Sardinian' government obligingly resigned all responsibility.

The inhabitants of Savoy were told nothing of what was being prepared until some astonishing posters, dated 10 March 1860, were put up in all the main localities. In Chambéry, Governor Orso Serra announced the referendum and appealed for calm: 'HABITANTS DE LA PROVINCE DE CHAMBÉRY. *Envoyé ici par le Gouvernement du Roi . . .*,' he began. 'Sent here by the king's government in order to strengthen the ancient ties which unite the populations of the monarchy, I could not foresee the events which . . . are rendering the accomplishment of my

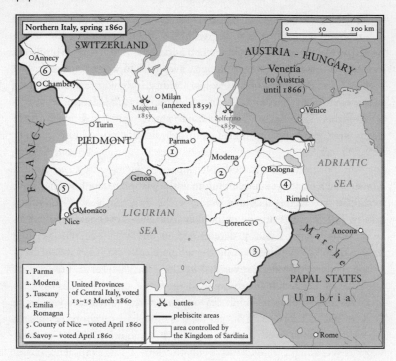

Northern Italy, spring 1860

1. Parma
2. Modena
3. Tuscany
4. Emilia Romagna
   United Provinces of Central Italy, voted 13–15 March 1860
5. County of Nice – voted April 1860
6. Savoy – voted April 1860

⚔ battles
▬ plebiscite areas
☐ area controlled by the Kingdom of Sardinia

mission very difficult.' He then blamed 'the events' on a *sourde agitation* – literally on 'deaf' or 'thoughtless trouble-making' – and gave the distinct impression that the government had been forced to organize the referendum against its better judgement. His summary of the king's attitude was, at best, curious:

> You will be called on to choose between this ancient monarchy of Savoy, to which you are united by the affection of centuries and by limitless devotion, and the Nation, which has so many claims to your sympathy ... However keen would be the regret experienced in the king's heart if the provinces which were the glorious cradle of the monarchy were to decide to separate ... he would not refuse to recognise the validity of the peaceful and orderly manifestation [of your will].[44]

The terms of the Turin Treaty were then published and 'Sardinian' troops were ordered to withdraw from the plebiscite areas. On 1 April 1860 Vittorio Emanuele formally released his Savoyard and Niçois subjects from their oath of allegiance. The voters could hardly have failed to guess that the monarchy intended to abandon them.

They also knew that the French emperor believed the outcome to be a foregone conclusion. He had ignored a petition sent to him from northern Savoy asking for wider consultations, and on 21 March his words to a delegation of well-known Savoyard Francophiles were made public. 'I am able without failing in any international duty to testify to you my sympathy,' he told them. 'It is neither by conquest nor by insurrection that Savoy and Nice will be united to France, but by her legitimate sovereign supported by popular consent.'[45]

In the brief period when debate was permitted, the plebiscite organizers did not reinstate suspended newspapers, such as the *Courrier des Alpes*, which had been demanding that all options be openly discussed. In theory, the options in Savoy were fivefold. The first was for the status quo to be maintained. The second would see Savoy become an independent state. The third would see Savoy joined to Switzerland. The fourth would allow districts with pro-Swiss, pro-'Sardinian' or pro-French sentiments to decide for themselves. The fifth was that the whole of Savoy would be taken by France. In the event, only one question was put: '*La Savoie, veut-elle être réunie à la France?*' ('Does Savoy want to be reunited with France?') The word 'reunite' was in itself obviously provocative.[46] The voters were only able to choose between '*Oui*' and '*Non*'.

In the spring of 1860 the Italian peninsula found itself in almost total turmoil. As yet, no Kingdom of Italy existed. The future of the United Provinces of Central Italy hung in the balance; and, though nationalist ferment was spreading to Sicily, Garibaldi and his 'Thousand' were still waiting to sail into the fray there. The autocratic King 'Bomba' – Ferdinand II – was still entrenched in Naples, as was the pope in Rome. Despite much criticism, Austria was holding on both to Venice and to the surrounding *Terraferma*. To hold a plebiscite amid such uncertainty was tantamount to offering a choice, not between France and Italy, but between France and chaos.

The plebiscite planners were especially worried about pro-Swiss sentiment. Switzerland, unlike France or Italy, was both stable and democratic. The Swiss cantons adjacent to Savoy, having the same Burgundian origins, were French-speaking, and the northern Savoyard districts of Chablais and Faucigny were known to possess a clear, pro-Swiss majority. So the planners added an extra 'box' headed '*oui et Zone*' to the voting paper. This gave voters who accepted annexation to France the extra possibility of supporting a 'Free Trade Zone' in the northern districts. There was no extra box marked '*Non et Zone*', and no opportunity to opt for incorporation into Switzerland. Women (as usual) were excluded.

April 1860 provided the occasion for popular poetry. One of the less gruesome verses was written by a M. Turbil, the inspector of elementary schools in Savoy, who expressed appreciation of the 'Sardinian' past along with fervent expectation of the French future:

> Nous l'aimions cependant l'antique dynastie
> Dont nos superbes monts couvrirent le berceau,
> Et le Roi-Chevalier qu'acclame L'Italie,
> Et notre vieille croix, et notre vieux drapeau!
> Aujourd'hui le Piémont, trouvant pour sa couronne
> Un plus riche fleuron, déserte nos firmas ...
> O mon charmant pays! Volontiers on pardonne
> Quand la France nous tends les bras!

('We loved the ancient dynasty / whose cradle is surrounded by our sublime peaks, / and the knightly king, whom Italy now acclaims, / and our old Cross and our old flag. / But today, finding a richer emblem for its Crown, / Piedmont is deserting our frosty land ... / Oh, my charming country! One freely forgives / when we are offered France's embrace.')[47]

The plebiscite in Savoy did not take place until voting in Central Italy and in Nice had been completed. Parma, Modena, Tuscany and Romagna, which all voted on 22 March, showed strong majorities for incorporation into Piedmont, thereby creating a setting where the traditional Franco-Italian balance in the *Stati Sardi* had already been overturned. The County of Nice voted on 15/16 April in an event marked by a low turnout and a high rate of abstentions. Nonetheless, the French were able to claim that 25,743 Niçois had voted '*Oui*' and only 100 '*Non*'. Presented as a 99.23 per cent victory for France, the result gave the impression of an unstoppable trend. Garibaldi, for one, was furious at the cession of his native town. He voiced his outrage loudly in the sub-alpine parliament, before returning home to Caprera.

Voting in Savoy was organized collectively, inhibiting dissent. It started on Sunday, 22 April. Parishioners were led to the voting booths by stewards. Cards marked '*Oui*' were distributed for men to stick on their hats. An engraving from Chambéry shows voters lined up by profession in front of the Grenette (today the Musée des Beaux-Arts). Doctors and lawyers wore their academic robes. The band of the

National Guard was playing cheerful music. French flags waved on all sides. The first group of voters, the customs officers, were brought in at 7 a.m. At nine o'clock it was the turn of the archbishop and his chapter; at 9.30, the farmers from the suburbs. Secret balloting was not practised. Scrutiny of the votes proceeded on the 23rd and the 24th, and the final count for the whole of Savoy was proclaimed on 29 April: Registered voters: 135,449. Votes cast: 130,839. Favourable: 130,523. Against: 235. '*Oui et Zone*': 47,000. Abstentions: *c.* 600. Spoiled papers: 71. Majority: 99.76 per cent.[48]

In Chambéry itself, the majority of pro-French votes was declared to be only 99.39 per cent. 'There were no winners and losers today', an imperial proclamation commented. 'In the midst of such imposing unanimity, the old hatreds have disappeared.'[49] Within a week, Garibaldi sailed with his 'Thousand' from Genoa, heading for the conquest of Sicily, and Savoy faded from the forefront of Europe's attention.

Ratification of the plebiscite was scheduled for 29 May in the subalpine parliament in Turin, and for early June in the French Senate. The session in Turin proved tumultuous. Only three of the eighteen Savoyard deputies bothered to attend, and Cavour was shouted down. But he had little to fear. The results were safely ratified. French troops held a grand parade in Chambéry in front of the Fontaine des Éléphants.

Two matters remained: the transfer of powers, and the division of the armed forces. The former was staged in the castle at Chambéry on 14 June 1860. The French emperor's representative, Senator Laity, arrived to take possession of the territory from the Sardinian commissioner, M. Bianchi. The two men drove to the castle in one carriage. The documents of transfer were signed in the antechamber of the Grand Salon. M. Bianchi then left by the back door, as Senator Laity proceeded to announce that annexation was complete. The archbishop made a short speech: 'For eight centuries,' he said, 'the clergy of Savoy always maintained a sense of loyalty and of perfect submission to the royal family to whom Providence had assigned our destiny ... Subject now to a new sovereign, we shall grant him the same respect, obedience and loyalty.' The senator responded gracefully. At 12.15 p.m. the French flag was raised, and cannon roared out a salute.[50] At the time of the plebiscite, 6,350 Savoyards were serving in the Sardinian army; 6,033 had voted '*Oui*' and 282 '*Non*'. The officers were now given a free choice either of staying in the Sardinian service, or of resigning their commissions. Most of them stayed. But the 'Brigade de Savoie' was disbanded:

When Victor Emmanuel presided [in Turin] over the last parade of the
Brigade of Savoy, before sending the soldiers home over the Alps, which
had now become a state frontier, it is said that the troops and the sovereign
were both deeply moved ... The ancient alliance between the Savoyard
soldiers and the House of Savoy was coming to an end amid the ritual and
fanfares of a military review; and eight centuries of history were reaching
their term. One of the oldest and most stable monarchies in Europe was
dying ... There was much ... to impress every man of honour, even the
most passionate democrat.[51]

When it was all over, the Emperor Napoleon and the Empress Eugénie
paid their first official visit to Savoy between 27 August and 5 September. The celebrations were extravagant. The streets were hung with
bunting and with loyal placards. Parades, receptions, balls, banquets,
concerts and theatre visits followed in dizzy succession, and the emperor
graciously ate a meal of *chamois aux épinards*. The empress graciously
waved to every shout of the crowd. A memorable gas-lit tableau was
erected on the station platform at Chambéry showing an imperial eagle,
with a wing-span of 30 feet, clutching in its talons a board bearing the
figure 141,893 – supposedly the total tally of votes cast for France.[52]

No one knew what the results of the plebiscite might have been if all
options had been offered. Britain and Switzerland protested in vain. France
and 'Sardinia' insisted that they had fulfilled their obligations, and that the
result had been lawfully ratified; a Free Trade Zone was in place along
France's new border with Switzerland. The king and Count Cavour had
more pressing matters to worry about. The *fait* was *accompli*. Yet the
divorce between Savoy and Piedmont can only be seen as a historic rupture.
It ended a union that had been in place since 1416, and it rode roughshod
over a number of democratic choices. It also separated the ruling house
from its ancestral land, cutting them adrift like a boat without moorings,
a flimsy vessel tossed like a bottle onto the stormy seas of Italian politics.

The Kingdom of Italy did not materialize until the year following the
transfer of Nice and Savoy. Garibaldi's expedition to Sicily, and subsequently to Naples, proved a decisive catalyst, and for several weeks in
the late summer of 1860, the prospect loomed that the 'Sardinian' monarchists would be sidelined. However, neither Cavour nor Napoleon III
was prepared to contemplate failure. On 11 September, the Sardinian
army marched south to take control of all the Papal States and to keep

Garibaldi's republicans out of Rome. The race was on. 'If we do not reach the Volturno before Garibaldi reaches La Cattolica,' Cavour said, 'the monarchy is lost, and Italy will remain in the prison-house of the revolution.'[53]

Garibaldi lost the race. Marching up from the south, he never reached Rome and had to settle for a triumphal entry into Naples in the company of Vittorio Emanuele II. Then, having been refused the Neapolitan viceroyalty for life, he retired in pique. The king of Sardinia was left in command of virtually the whole country. The last major obstacle had fallen. The House of Savoy was indeed entering its third kingdom.

Arrangements were finalized in the winter of 1860/61. An all-Italian parliament was summoned to Turin and voted decisively for the creation of a national Kingdom of Italy, of which Vittorio Emanuele was to be the first monarch. The proclamation was made in February 1861 and the coronation staged on 17 March. Count Cavour officially became Italian prime minister, but he was also mortally exhausted, and died of a stroke within months. His last words, as reported, were 'Italy is made. All is safe.'[54] Napoleon III was aghast at the news. 'The driver has fallen from the box,' he remarked, 'we must see if the horses will bolt.'[55]

After four years, the kingdom's capital was moved from Turin to Florence. In 1866, following the Austro-Prussian War, Venice was incorporated into Italy. Finally in 1870, Rome fell; and the Papal States were abolished. The pope lost all temporal power. Vittorio Emanuele took up residence in the former papal palace on the Quirinale. When he died in 1878, victorious and revered, the foundation stone of the *Vittoriano* was laid in his honour.

During the next sixty-eight years three monarchs reigned in Italy: Vittorio Emanuele II's son Umberto I (r. 1878–1900), Vittorio Emanuele III (r. 1900–46) and Umberto II (r. 1946). None of their reigns was terminated by natural causes. Umberto I, who had fought at Solferino, had been christened with the name of the dynasty's founder, and changed his regnal number from IV to I. By contemporary standards, he was not the most oppressive of monarchs, and was dubbed *Il Buono*. Nonetheless he did little to calm a wave of violent bread riots that broke out in the late 1890s, and he made himself unpopular by rewarding the general, Bava-Beccaria, who had violently suppressed rioters in Milan. Like his maternal Habsburg relatives, he became the target for nihilist assassins. In July 1900, at Monza, he was shot dead.

The House of Savoy entered the twentieth century, therefore, visibly chastened. In conservative eyes, the assassination of 1900 simply added to the continuing humiliation of a Catholic nation evident in the fate of a 'captive papacy'. Monarchs relying solely on Divine Right were evidently unsafe. In any event, the elaborate bronze and marble complex of seventeen sculptures of princes of the House of Savoy from Umberto Biancamano on, executed in 1903 by Canale and displayed in the Valentino Garden in Turin, was to be the last of its kind. The First World War was a time of intense ordeals for Italy as for many countries, and it proved fatal for several ancient monarchies. If the Habsburgs, the Hohenzollerns and the Romanovs could be toppled, the *Casa Savoia* had to watch its step.

Fortunately, the new king, Vittorio Emanuele III, had sworn loyalty to the constitution without demur, and was widely judged to be a man of 'energy and a lofty sense of duty'.[56] Italian Fascism was not his creation, and his policy of trying to tame it rather than confront it cannot be attributed to cowardice. It all happened by a process of creep and fudge. Nonetheless, as the true nature of Europe's first Fascist regime was revealed in the 1920s, the monarchy undoubtedly complied with some of its excesses. And in one important symbolic respect, by accepting a panoply of phoney titles, it lent its name to the regime's aggressions. Vittorio Emanuele III did not object when offered the crown of the 'emperor of Abyssinia' or the 'king of Albania'. One of his relatives basked in the title of 'Zvitomir II, king of Croatia'.

Nevertheless, throughout the war years, the monarchy acted as a force for stability and continuity. Many of Italy's elite regiments, like the *Cavalleggeri Savoia* or the *Granatieri di Savoia* – named after the House not the Duchy of Savoy – prided themselves on traditions going back to the seventeenth or eighteenth century. '*Avanti Savoia*' remained the standard battle cry of Italian troops, and high-quality equipment such as the Savoia Marchetti SM 79 bomber benefited from the royal brand. In August 1942, while fighting the Red Army on the River Don at Izbushensky, 600 dragoons of the Prince of Aosta Celere Division achieved a signal victory against overwhelming odds. As they trotted, cantered and then galloped into 'the last major cavalry charge of European history', they whirled their sabres and roared out their cries of '*Carica!*' ('Charge!') and '*Savoia!*'

Whether or not the dynasty could be forgiven was the issue posed by the referendum of 1946. For the first time in Italy's history, women were permitted to participate in the voting. The opinion of a leading British historian betrays no regrets about the people's choice: 'Like the [English] in 1688 and the French in 1789, the Italians had thus carried out their own constitutional revolution ... The oldest surviving dynasty in Europe had run its course. After eighty-five years, during which it presided over national unification and enjoyed many triumphs as well as failures, the end came in tragedy and anticlimax'.[57] But once again the wording of the referendum may be pertinent. At the time it was first discussed, Vittorio Emanuele III had already ceded his official duties to his son; and it would have been perfectly possible for the referendum to have posed the question whether or not the king should officially abdicate. In that case, the nation could have passed its verdict on one man's record, while leaving the monarchy intact. Yet the referendum's authors, heavily influenced by ex-Partisans and Communists, were determined that the vote should be aimed directly at the institution of monarchy. As a result, the king's conduct and the suitability of his son were overshadowed by weightier considerations. The question posed was 'republic' or 'king'. The House of Savoy was presented as being out of its depth in an age of populist politics and democratic manipulation. Just as it had discarded the Duchy of Savoy through a plebiscite, it now lost the Kingdom of Italy through a referendum. The long story, which began nearly ten centuries before with one Umberto, ended with another. And the vision of Mazzini and Garibaldi finally triumphed over that of Cavour.

III

In the view of monarchical purists no throne ever falls vacant. There is always an heir apparent, always a successor, always a claimant (even if some see the claim as that of a false pretender). 'The king is dead', they say. 'Long live the king!'

Ex-King Umberto II, therefore, was not really an ex-king in the eyes of his most fervent subjects and followers. He was simply an unfortunate monarch in temporary exile – exactly as his great-great-grandfather Carlo Alberto had been, or his maternal grandfather, King Nikola of Montenegro (see Chapter 12). After leaving Italy, and arranging his father's funeral in 1947, he and his family settled in Switzerland. The royal couple's marriage, however, had never been happy; and exile permitted them to separate. The ex-queen, Marie-José, who was a Saxe-Coburg-Gotha by birth, stayed in Geneva with her children, and later moved to Mexico. Umberto took up residence in the Villa Italia at Cascais in Portugal, whence, as 'Europe's Grandfather', he could sally forth to royal weddings or jubilees at the invitation of the dwindling company of reigning monarchs. According to gossip, he was bisexual – a personal trait which might explain the Vatican's strange silence during the referendum of 1946. He died in 1983 and was laid to rest at Hautecombe, where Marie-José would join him twenty years later.[58] His last act, irksome to many of his relatives, was to bequeath the Shroud of Turin in his will to the Roman Catholic Church.

Umberto's death led automatically to the elevation of his only son and heir to Italy's virtual throne. Vittorio Emanuele IV, prince of Naples (b. 1937), had shot and killed a man in Corsica and had spent a dozen years proving his innocence in the French courts. (He had fired a rifle in anger at night-time intruders on his yacht, and hit a sleeping tourist on an adjacent boat.) He was also pressing the Italian government to lift the ban on his return to Italy, entering a plea to the European Court of Human Rights. His wish was finally granted in 2002 on condition that he formally renounce all claims. This done, he proceeded to sue the Republic both for compensation, and for restitution, among other things, of the Quirinale Palace. In 2006 he was briefly imprisoned on charges of benefiting from the profits of prostitution at his casino at Campione on Lake Como.[59]

In the eyes of true monarchist circles, however, more serious offences had been committed. After quarrelling with his father and marrying a commoner without royal permission, Vittorio Emanuele had long feared that he might be dispossessed, and so claimed that Umberto II had forfeited the crown by agreeing to the referendum of 1946. Though the father was still alive at the time, the son proclaimed himself 'king'. At this, his angry relatives mounted a counter-claim. By negotiating with the government of the Italian Republic, they argued, Vittorio Emanuele had implicitly acknowledged the Republic's legitimacy, and had *ipso facto* committed treason against himself. A substitute claimant was found in his cousin Amadeo, 'duke of Aosta' (b. 1943), who during Mussolini's occupation of Yugoslavia had been the infant 'king of Croatia'.[60]

The two well-funded camps were well capable of pursuing long campaigns of litigious attrition. One of them drew income from the Campione casino, from arms dealing and from a hedge fund registered in Geneva. The other supported itself from the wine trade and from the appellation of *Vini Savoia-Aosta*. In May 2004 both claimants were invited to a royal wedding in Madrid. There, in full view of the cameras, the elder titular king landed two punches on the nose of the younger one.[61] Their battles continued inconclusively in the courts. In January 2010 a court in Arezzo ordered the duke of Aosta to drop the name of

Savoia, and to confine himself, like his wines, to the Savoia-Aosta label; another court in Piacenza dismissed the charges of criminal corruption levelled at Vittorio Emanuele. But no ruling was made on the contested headship of the House. Increasingly, it seemed that the issue would eventually be settled by the age-old competition between longevity and fertility; the most likely winner in the long term was yet another Umberto (b. 2009), the duke of Aosta's grandson. To keep the rumour mill turning, Vittorio Emanuele has been caught on video boasting how he duped the French courts over the murder of which he had once been acquitted. Neither murder nor manslaughter is a bar to the succession, but the prince's outburst that preceded the killing cannot have endeared him to his subjects. '*Voi, italiani di merda*', he was reported to have shouted, 'You Italian sh–ts, I'll kill the lot of you'.[62]

The land from which the *Casa Savoia* took its name has now belonged to France for more than a century and a half. The *départements* of Savoie (*chef-lieu* Chambéry) and of Haute-Savoie (*chef-lieu* Annecy) form part of the Rhône-Alpes region. They are endowed with huge areas of exceptional natural beauty, including (western) Europe's highest mountain, Mont-Blanc (15,771 feet), France's first National Park in the Vanoise, and scores of world-famous ski-resorts – Chamonix, Megève, Val d'Isère, Les Arcs, Meribel, Tignes and Flaine, among others. They also encompass an officially denominated wine-growing region, which stretches from Crépy overlooking Lake Geneva to the flank of the Massif des Bauges south of Chambéry. The AOC *Vin de Savoie*, much neglected in Paris, includes fine white, red and rosé wines, the most renowned among its twenty-two registered *crus* being the aromatic, golden Chignin-Bergeron, the dry Apremont made on the slopes of Mont Granier from white Jacquère grapes, the deep-red Mondeuse d'Arbin, and the Roussette de Savoie cru Marestel, which comes from the village of Jongieux, perched on a plateau high above the abbey of Hautecombe.[63] These are among the modern successors to the *Vitis Allobrogica*, recorded in ancient times by both Pliny and Plutarch.

Popular guides to the history of Savoy, however, rarely enter into the historical nuances:

- Early 11th century, 'Humbert aux Blanches Mains', Count of Maurienne ... receives the title of Count of Savoy. His dynasty became 'Guardians of the Passes'.
- 1419, Savoy is united with Piedmont.

- 1860, April. Savoyard Plebiscite. A crushing majority of 'Yes' votes hands Savoy to France.

  The Savoyards, weary of government by Piedmont . . . turned to France. In 1858, at the interview of Plombières, Napoleon III and Cavour decided that, in exchange for French help in the struggle against the Austrian occupation, Italy would cede Savoy and Nice to France if the population concerned consented. This led to the Plebiscite of April 1860. By a vote of 130,533 for 'Yes' against 235 for 'No', the Savoyards expressed their desire to become French.[64]

This assumes, among other things, that an Italian state existed at the time of the plebiscite.

An official website explains the plebiscite in terms of discontent with some poorly identified kings:

  The kings of Savoy began to spend increasing amounts of time in their Italian territories and the Savoyards, who had always spoken French, found it difficult [after 1815] to accept the return of the Piedmontese administration . . . In 1858, during the Plombières talks between Napoleon III and Cavour, minister of the King of Piemonte and Sardinia, France promised to provide military aid against Austria on the condition that Nice and Savoy would be returned to France. King Vittorio-Emmanuele II, whose ambition was the unification of Italy, accepted the deal.[65]

  The modern visitor to Chambéry is treated to all the sights that pleased Bayle St John more than 150 years ago, and more besides. The castle, adorned with a classical façade, is nowadays the Préfecture, but the cathedral, the rue de Boigne, the place St Léger and the Fontaine des Éléphants are much as they were. The Musée Savoisien, lodged in a former Franciscan convent, contains an extensive collection of religious art, much of it brought from Hautecombe. St John, who devoted a whole chapter to Mme de Warens and Rousseau, would be delighted to learn that Les Charmettes has been preserved and restored: 'The memory of the philosopher inhabits the rooms . . . which are decorated in the late 18th century style . . . The house opens onto a terraced garden in a wooded valley . . . closed on the horizon by the Dent du Nivolet. It's here that the visitor will best recover the charm of this "sojourn of happiness and innocence".'[66]

  In Bayle St John's time, alpinism was in its infancy, and skiing had not been invented. The very first ski-station in Savoie, at Megève, was opened in 1921. Nowadays, such places support the region's biggest business. Most visitors rush past everything else to reach the slopes, or in the summer to power their speedboats across the green-blue waters of the Lac du Bourget and the Lac d'Annecy. But several fine historical sites survive. The ferries still sail to the abbey of Hautecombe, now in the care of an ecumenical order.[67] The Château de Thorens, 12 miles up the mountain from Annecy, exudes the atmosphere of pre-plebiscite Savoy. And in Cavour's former study it displays the table on which the treaty of annexation was signed.[68]

The pilgrim route to St Jean-de-Maurienne, where it all began, leads for 40 miles up the valley of the Arc beneath the towering peaks of the Vanoise. On approaching St Jean, one passes the ruined ramparts of the Château de Charbonnières, the earliest known seat of the counts of Maurienne. Immediately before the town, a round tower, La Tour du Châtel, marks the place where Count Humbertus I expired in 1047. In the town square, the eleventh-century cathedral is signalled in the guide-book for its coloured medieval frescoes, its pre-Romanesque crypt, its cloister and garden, and for the side chapel of St Thècle, which houses a most holy relic: the three fingers of St John the Baptist, brought from Alexandria in early Christian times, which give the town its name. The cathedral is a strange building. Its ancient interior and leaning tower are masked by an incongruous, three-arched neo-classical façade erected in the reign of Carlo Emanuele III. But in the shade of the front portico, the destination of all historical pilgrims awaits. The tomb of Humbert aux Mains Blanches shows a warrior reclining on his sarcophagus under a pointed Gothic arch. It is covered by an iron grille bearing the signs and symbols of his house: the Cross of Savoy, the double Savoyan love-knot, and the FERT motto. It was built in 1826 by King Carlo il Felice, at the time when he was restoring Hautecombe and when he hoped that Savoy and Piedmont would stay together for ever.[69]

None of which prepares the visitor for the news that chronic criticism of the Annexation of 1860 has rumbled on ever since. A dissident minority has always existed in Savoie, and if anything is now gaining strength. Only ten years after the Annexation, the French Second Empire of Napoleon III collapsed and was replaced by the Third Republic. The occasion was used by Savoyard republicans to voice their opinion that the plebiscite had been rigged. At Bonneville in Faucigny, a local committee resolved that the vote 'did not represent the will of the people'. Paris reacted by sending 10,000 extra troops to Savoy.[70]

After the First World War, the French government's actions were challenged in the International Court of Justice, and the Free Trade Zone was
summarily abolished. As part of the proceedings, the full text of the
secret Franco-Sardinian agreement was made public. It transpired that
France had given guarantees about the demilitarization of Savoy which
were subsequently ignored.[71]

During the Second World War Savoie was invaded first by Italian and
then by German forces. In 1944 the French Resistance suffered a bloody
defeat at the Plateau de Glières, the Savoyard counterpart to the fortress
of Vercors in Dauphiné. Pro-French sentiment revived. In 1960 festivities marking the centenary of the plebiscite were held without opposition.
After 1965, however, a movement for regional autonomy (MRS) began,
part of a broader surge of sentiment in France against over-centraliza-
tion. It did not succeed either in turning Savoie into an official region or
in joining Savoie to Dauphiné.

With some delay, therefore, the *Ligue Savoisienne* was founded in
1994 with an openly separatist agenda. Its performance in local elections – 6 per cent of the vote in Haute-Savoie, and 5 per cent in Savoie – was
modest, but its adherents have since entered into competition with a
restructured regionalist movement. With the aid of the Internet, they are
conducting a lively 'identity campaign' to raise awareness of the distinct-
ness of the Savoyard language and to clarify the contested issues of
modern history. They argue, for instance, that the Franco-Sardinian
Treaty of Turin of 24 March 1860 has lapsed through non-observance;
that the subsequent plebiscite was a travesty; and that the democratic will
of the Savoyard nation has never been tested. In 1998, having made a
declaration of independence that everyone else ignored, they published a
Constitutional Project for the Federation of Savoy.[72]

Preparations in Savoie for the 150th anniversary of the Annexation in
2010 were understandably somewhat muted. The state archive in
Chambéry staged an exhibition of posters from 1860; and the official
website was adorned by a collection of impartial historical dossiers on
la période sarde, 'the Sardinian Period'.[73] Neither Chambéry nor Annecy
thought fit to mount a Franco-Italian festival to match that organized in
2008 by the town of Plombières-les-Bains.[74] The Savoyard separatists
had roundly condemned that festival, denouncing 'the celebration of a
conspiracy which united a dictator and his accomplice in fomenting
conquests and massacres'.[75]

The one thing missing was any trace of curiosity, let alone regret,

concerning the fate of the *Casa Savoia*. The mixed feelings described by
Bayle St John in the days of the 'subalpine kingdom' have completely
evaporated. According to today's Savoyards, the *Casa Savoia* turned
their backs on their homeland, and their homeland has forgotten the
Savoia. Whatever their origins, the ex-kings of Italy are seen as irrelevant foreigners; they belong to a well-known category of Savoyard
migrants – local lads who left home to make their fortune, but who lost
touch with their roots. As the sorrowful Savoyard proverb puts it: '*Toujours ma chèvre monte, et mon fils descend*',* 'My goat always goes up
the mountain, and my son is always going down.'

Preparations for celebrations of the 150th anniversary of Italian Unification in 2011 were concentrated very naturally in Turin, although
many events were held elsewhere.† Turin's festival, entitled '*Esperianza
Italia 150*', was poised to present hundreds of concerts, operas, exhibitions, plays and parades. The royal palaces had been renovated, and the
ex-royal hunting lodge, the *Reggia di Venaria Reale*, was fitted out as
the venue for an extravagant artistic display.

Yet an embarrassing background of political turmoil could not be
wholly concealed. The prime minister, Silvio Berlusconi, a vulgar bil-
lionaire, a media baron, is the longest serving leader of a major European
country, and a serial offender against good taste and responsible conduct. Having survived decades of accusations of corruption, he was
finally stripped of his legal immunity, and faced four trials for tax fraud,
bribery and sordid sex offences. Italian women were staging demonstrations against him in all the major cities. When his government proposed
to introduce 17 March as an extra national holiday to mark the proclamation of the Kingdom of Italy, his coalition partners walked out. His
public standing, which only three years previously had produced the
'*Festa da Silvio*', was sinking to the level of the *Casa Savoia*. To say that
the international reputation of a wonderful country was being tarnished
by its political elite was an understatement.

Historians increasingly believed that Italy's malaise had deeper causes.
Dysfunctional politics are perhaps the outward symptom of more fundamental flaws. The Unification of Italy, once held up as a glorious
achievement, was proving at best a partial success. The manner of its

* Alternatively, '*Toujours, ma chèvre monte et ma femme descend.*'
† A fine evening of '*Melodie e poesie*' was staged in the Italian embassy in London, featuring
Neapolitan songs and readings from Dante and Petrarch, and among the guests, Fabio
Capello, the football coach, and Antonio Carluccio, the master chef. By a happy coinci-
dence, Capello was born on 18 June 1946, the birthday of the Italian Republic.

execution, as an instrument of the ambitions of the *Casa Savoia*, never engendered a sense of solidarity between Italy's diverse regions, and even when the *Savoia* left, centrifugal forces remained strong:

> Geography and the vicissitudes of history made certain countries ... more important than the sum of their parts might have indicated. In Italy the opposite was true. The parts are so stupendous that [some of them] would rival every other country in the world in the quality of its art or the civilization of its past. But the parts have never added up to a coherent whole. United Italy never became the nation its founders had hoped for because its making had been flawed both in conception and in execution ... 'a sin against history and geography'. It was thus predestined to be a disappointment ... [The Italians] have created much of the world's greatest art, architecture and music ... Yet the millennia of their past and the vulnerability of their placement have made it impossible for them to create a successful nation-state.[76]

The president of the Republic, who had often railed bitterly against his countrymen's quarrels, must have been holding his head in despair. Giorgio Napolitano could only have reflected on the absence of fundamental consensus throughout his long career. He would certainly have remembered the day of the referendum in June 1946, when he and his Communist comrades in Naples had tried to celebrate the republic's victory. They hung out their Red Flag alongside a national tricolour from which the coat of arms of the *Savoia* had been ripped out. Their headquarters was promptly stormed by a baying mob of monarchists, who had won an overwhelming majority in the city.[77] Disunity threatened then, and has continued to do so ever since.

9

Galicia

Kingdom of the Naked and Starving
(1773–1918)

I

The road to Halich is very wide, extremely bumpy and almost empty. It runs across rolling open countryside for 60 miles south from L'viv, the chief city of western Ukraine. Every now and again one passes through a roadside village with its goose-pond, its old wooden houses and flower gardens, and its rebuilt, onion-domed church. Though the fact is nowhere advertised, one is travelling over part of the 'continental divide', the watershed between the Baltic and the Black Sea. To the west and north-west, all waters flow into the basin of the Vistula. To the east and south, they flow either into the Dniepr or the Dniester. Our road, via Rohatyn, is heading for the Dniester.[1]

Our driver, Pan Volodymyr, belongs to the middle-aged generation that learned to drive during the Soviet era. Indeed, one could talk of a Red Army driving style – utterly fearless and completely regardless of human life. Pan Volodymyr seems to care nothing either about his own skin or about passenger welfare. His main technique is to charge at full speed down the middle of the road, wheels straddling the centre line. In this way, he avoids the steep camber and the deepest of the potholes that multiply on the tarmac's outer edges, but the main purpose, one suspects, is to be lord of the road. He careers along, oblivious to the bucking motion, the constant jumps and jolts, and the non-stop judder of an over-stressed chassis. He constantly takes left-turning corners blind, then fights with the shaking steering wheel as the vehicle yaws back over the hump into the dangerous pothole zone. He spurns his seat belt, except for a short stretch where the police are known to lurk; and he clearly has no use for the handbrake, which lies buried under a pile of bottles and magazines. Worst of all, when he sees another car approaching, he refuses either to slow down or to move over. Instead, he clings to a position within inches of the centre line, daring the oncomer to give

way, and only veering outwards at the very last second. He is equally
contemptuous of combine harvesters, of massive swaying timber-trucks,
and of drivers from the same school of driving as himself. When asked
if he could possibly keep his speed below 75 mph, he presses on regardless in sullen silence.

In Rohatyn, we circle the square looking for a place to stop. An over-
size statue of the beautiful Roxolana stands in the centre. This daughter
of a local Orthodox priest was seized as *yasir* or 'human booty' during
a Tartar raid in the early sixteenth century, sold in the slave market of
Istanbul and raised to be the consort of the Ottoman sultan, Suleiman
the Magnificent: a local girl lost but not forgotten. The date of birth that
appears on her statue is questionable, but her story is authentic.
Renamed Hurrem, 'the Smiling One', she bore the sultan six children;
her son Selim succeeded to the Ottoman throne; and the resplendent

Baths of Roxolana (1556) are still one of Istanbul's prominent tourist attractions.

The traffic on the road to Halich says much about contemporary Ukraine. Pan Volodymyr, who is reputed to be a bishop's chauffeur, an aristo of his profession, drives a gleaming Renault Espace, which keeps company with similarly up-to-date Toyotas and Skodas and an occasional BMW, but most of the vehicles are twenty or thirty years older. In L'viv, we had ridden in a colossal Volga taxi, which thundered over the cobbles at perhaps 10 mph and was easily overtaken by a student jogger.

Here, in the countryside, one sees why the road has to be 10 yards wide. Soviet designs, especially of trucks, combined gargantuanism with pre-war technology. Many such monsters are still crawling around like decrepit dinosaurs, indeed one of them is edging painfully up a steep slope and being imperceptibly overtaken by a dilapidated ex-German charabanc belching heavy black smoke. As Pan Volodymyr roars up behind, blasting his horn and aiming for the narrow gap between them, another huge truck comes into view at the top of the hill, broken down and stranded on the verge, which our cavalcade has somehow to pass. The roadway is wide enough for three vehicles, but not for four. I close my eyes in prayer.

Ordinary Ukrainians do not have such problems. They usually walk, or ride between the villages on creaking bicycles; they drive a horse and cart, a *fura*, or they stand for hours at forlorn crossroads in the shade of derelict bus shelters, waiting for the lift that may or may not come. They push sacks of potatoes on handcarts, or pull wooden beams on improvised trailers, or, with no shop in sight for miles, they trudge homewards with bulging shopping bags. They try to flag us down, or to sell us a jar of forest berries, but Pan Volodymyr careers on. Episcopal drivers stop for no man.

Like the roads, the Ukrainian countryside is only partly de-Sovietized. The collective farms which once turned the peasants into state serfs have been disbanded, but they have not been replaced by a viable system of private farming. 'The young people are leaving for the cities in droves,' one of our companions says sadly, 'or are working abroad.' One sees the results. An old woman, bent double, holds a single cow on a rope in the pasture. The ex-Soviet dairy stands abandoned nearby. A ragged lad watches a herd of grazing goats. A grandfather dangles his grandchild on the porch of their cabin. The plots and strips and orchards adjacent to the village are tilled and tended, full of fruit and vegetables, but the great open fields, untouched for years, have gone to seed, turned into oceans of bracken and meadow-wort. 'No one knows who owns what,' we are told; 'they are waiting for legislation.' One thinks: for legislation, like the bus which may or may not come.

The town of Burshtyn is announced miles away by a soaring yellow cloud that rises into the summer sky. It is a prime relic of Soviet times, a whole community dependent on one colossal coal-burning power station in the heart of a rural region. The coal comes from the Donbass (the Donetsk Basin), almost 1,000 miles away. Three red-and-white chimneys, extraordinarily tall and covered in soot, belch out their pungent filth perhaps 900 feet above the ground. Acres of rusting gantries line the streets. The wrecks of abandoned boilers, trucks and railway equipment litter the townscape; a thick layer of ubiquitous grey powder stifles the weeds that grow between the sleepers and the rails that no longer lead anywhere. The installation is too vital to discard and too costly to replace, so it continues to produce and to pollute.

Halich comes into view over the brow of a hill not far beyond Burshtyn. A medieval miracle takes the place of a modern monstrosity. Our companion points to a Romanesque hilltop tower on the right. 'That's the twelfth-century church of St Pantaleimon,' she announces, 'recently restored.' A roadside sign says 'ГАЛИЧ'. The Cyrillic letter Г, which in Russian is pronounced 'G' as in 'Gal', is pronounced 'H' in Ukrainian, as in 'Hal'. The sunlit valley of the Dniester, already a sizeable stream, glistens ahead. A couple of bridges, one old and one new, cross the river in the direction of a huddle of roofs surrounded by tall trees. Beyond rises a steep, wooded scarp surmounted by red-brick fortifications.

We drive into town, crossing the new concrete bridge over the Dniester, and passing a *fura* with a tethered foal trotting behind. The square is spacious, dusty, windblown and almost deserted. A large cobbled expanse rings an ill-defined central area where a tall statue stands amid a clump of much taller trees. The pines and planes have somehow been grafted and pollarded to produce a high panoply of leaf cover supported by bare trunks. A tiny goose-pond shimmers alongside. This is not just a country town, but a town with a patch of countryside right in the middle of it.

A small gaggle of men are sitting or squatting in the shade, waiting for something to happen. A couple of them struggle to their feet to watch us arrive. A Renault Espace with plates from L'viv provides them with the event of the morning. We rumble over the cobbles round three sides of the square until we reach a shady parking space near the local

reception committee. Two dilapidated vehicles nearby look more abandoned than parked. Nothing moves. We climb out to take our bearings.

Halich does not look the least bit historic. It appears to have been hit
by a cyclone, most probably the Second World War, and then by a Five
Year Plan that ran for only two or three. At one time, the square must
have been lined with shops and houses on all four sides. Only one line
of older buildings remains, on the northern side. It backs onto the Dniester, and contains the 'Pharmacy', a bookshop and a store selling
glassware. The other three sides are largely open to the elements. Even
on this summer's day, the wind blows a cloud of dust through the trees.
The western side is half-filled by a Soviet-era pavilion from the 1960s or
1970s covered with wooden scaffolding. It is being prepared either for
reconstruction or for demolition, but no workers are in sight. The eastern side is defaced by an incongruously modern furniture store, not yet
completed, and by a gaping open space through which the corrugated-
iron or green-painted roofs of the cabins of the locals can be glimpsed.
The southern side, under the lea of the wooded scarp, displays a small
wooden-built, onion-domed church, an overgrown paddock confined
by a fence, and a crumbling Soviet cinema.

Curiosity encourages a stroll through the trees to the statue. It turns
out to be as grandiose as its surroundings are shabby. A monumental
bronze horseman, sword in hand, rears above a white marble plinth.
The inscription reads 'король данило халицкии', 'Korol' Danylo Halitsky'. Pan Volodymyr announces that Korol' means 'König' – 'King'. It's
both a surprise and a puzzle. So, too, is the date: '1998', less than ten
years before our visit. One of our party wonders how a poverty-stricken
community can afford an inordinately lavish historical symbol. Someone else adds that another monument must have stood here until quite
recently: most probably a statue of Lenin. At all events, we are seeing
signs of what we came for. This is where the name of Galicia began.

Lunchtime. The Restaurant 'Mirage' is open. One notes a delicious sense
of irony. Food in Soviet times was often a mirage; now one can buy it.
The fare is modest but appetizing: red beetroot soup, a thick slice of roast
pork and a tomato salad. All the wooden houses on the street have their
own little gardens and apple trees. The supply of fruit and vegetables is
plentiful.

After lunch, we wander back across the square to the wooden church
spotted earlier. Outside is a tablet dated 1929 that we try to decipher. It
is a memorial to a group of twenty-one locals, 'WHO SUFFERED FOR

THE RUSSIAN NAME IN THE TALERHOF CAMP UNDER THE AUSTRO-
HUNGARIAN YOKE'. This is tricky. The inscription obviously relates to
the First World War, when Halich would have been occupied by the
Russian army before being recaptured by the 'Royal and Imperials', and
its Russophile flavour explains why it survived the Soviet era. Talerhof
sounds Austrian. But why had the victims suffered 'for the Russian
name'? Perhaps they were people whom the Austrians had regarded as
collaborators. Someone had wanted to remember them, and some official had allowed them to do so; 1929 could have been the year of their
return, or more likely of its tenth anniversary.

Inside the church, an elderly woman is sweeping the floor; a still
older man rises from his seat and offers to show us round. Pan Roman
speaks Ukrainian, Polish, Russian and German. He was born in 1925,
he says, after his Ukrainian father married his Polish mother. He stands
beside a nineteenth-century iconostasis adorned with folk-style icons,
and tells us his story, which, like the ill-lit church, is filled with confusing details. When he talks of the German army, it is not clear whether
he is referring to the First or the Second World War. Between the wars,
he had 'finished seven classes', meaning that his schooling ended when he
was thirteen or fourteen. He does not say so, but the school, like his
mother, must have been Polish. He leaves us in no doubt about the
defining moment of his life. In 1946 he and his mother were deported to
Siberia, where they were 'thrown out of the train' and 'buried in snow'.
He does not explain how a young man of conscript age could have survived the war, or when they returned from Siberia.

We decide to walk up the hill to explore the castle. When we reach it,
we find that the impressive red-brick construction is modern. As Pan
Roman had told us, the original was levelled by Red Army artillery in
the summer of 1944 after the Wehrmacht had set up a defensive position there. There are no medieval ruins to be seen, and there is nothing
to say whose castle it once was. The view across the valley to the distant
church of St Pantaleimon is ravishing.

Returning to the square and the bookshop, we purchase a small
guidebook to try to solve some of the basic questions.[2] We are apparently in the so-called New Town, founded in the fourteenth century,
while the ancient 'Princely City' lies several miles away on the top of a
plateau. A picture from before the First World War shows that the
square had indeed been enclosed and lined with houses, and that its
extended oblong had stretched from the foot of the castle scarp to the

line of riverside houses that still survive. The iron footbridge across the river was already *in situ*, built by the Austrians to take passengers from the square to the railway station. In those days, trains would have gone up and down the Dniester line from Stryj to Stanislavov, Chernovtsy, and eventually to Moldavian Kishinev.

The town's links with the south are emphasized by the fact that for centuries it was one of the chief refuges of the Jewish Karaite sect, which originated in Crimea (see p. 266). The Karaites, who spoke Tartar as their everyday speech, survived in Halich until sometime after the arrival of the Nazis in 1941. Their *kenasa* or 'temple' was blown up by the Soviets in 1985. Their memory survives in the name of 'Karaitsky Street'.

The guidebook presents us with an elaborate chronology, starting in AD 290 with the earliest mention of Halich in a work by Jordanes and ending in 2001 when Halich joined the Association of West Ukrainian Towns. In between, sixty or seventy entries recount a wide selection of events:

981	Volodymyr the Great annexes Halich to Kievan Rus'.
1156–7	The Halich bishopric is founded.
1189	Hungarian King Bela II occupies Halich.
1199	Halychyna and Volhynia united in a single principality.
1241	The (Mongol) host of Batu Khan captures Halich.
1253	Danylo Halitsky crowned in Drohobych.
1349	Polish King Kazimierz III captures Halich.
1367	Halich is granted the Magdeburg Law.
1772	Halich passes to Austrian rule.
1886	Construction of the L'viv to Chernovtsy railway line.
1915	Occupation by the Russian army.
1918	Halich becomes part of the West Ukrainian People's Republic.
1919–39	Halich is under Polish rule.
1939–91	Halich is under the Soviets.
24 August 1991	Halich joins independent Ukraine.

Nothing of significance, apparently, happened for 400 years before 1772 or in the three years of German occupation 1941–4.[3]

The tone of the guidebook outdoes the photos in Technicolor:

> It was on the banks of the age-old Dniester ... that the princely town of
> Halich – a powerhouse of Ukrainian statehood – was destined to appear.
> It was here that the Ukrainian spirit was nurtured, tempered in vilest
> battles ... moulded by the will-power of lion-hearted and wise princes,
> covered with the glory of victorious Halich regiments, rinsed with tears,
> and braced with thousands of Halichians slaughtered in massacres ... under
> the foreign yoke. [They are] brought back to life in chronicles, gospels and
> songs ... in cathedrals, churches and whatnot.[4]

The author is at pains to stress that under presidential decrees of 11
October 1994, ancient Halich was granted the status of a 'National Preserve', also that the same decrees saw 'the beginning of the process of
the restoration of historical justice'. Ancient Halich and its Ruthenian
inhabitants are strongly connected to the task of reconstructing contemporary Ukraine's identity.

To reach the *Knyazhi Horod* or 'Princely City', one has to drive five
or six miles out of Halich and up a long hill to the village of Krylos. Pan
Volodymyr sets off enthusiastically. He draws up on a steep slope in
front of the rural museum, searches desperately for the handbrake, and
announces that from here on we have to walk. In the museum, skipping
through displays of prehistoric pots and modern folk culture, we learn
that the exact location of the Princely City was not found until the
second half of the twentieth century and that a huge archaeological project is still in progress. A gang of student volunteers armed with spades,
sieves and cameras walks past, proving the point. These modern Ukrainians think of the medieval Ruthenians as their ethnic ancestors.

The *Knyazhi Horod* occupies *c.* 120 acres of land which exploits the
natural defensive features of a wedge-shaped mountain. It is contained in
a double ring of ramparts, one lining the outer circle that runs inland
from the high bluffs overlooking the Dniester, the other surrounding the
inner fortress on Krylos Hill. The oldest point is the tenth-century burial
mound of a prince, possibly the founder of Halich, who was interred with
his weapons and the remains of his burned ship. The largest complex of
foundations belongs to the twelfth-century cathedral of the Assumption.
The most significant item is probably the Prince's Well, the only safe
source of water for the garrison and inhabitants, who must have numbered several thousand. The site was large enough to include grazing
pasture for livestock, orchards and market gardens. Its military decline

coincided with the fall of the Ruthenian principality of Halich in the mid-fourteenth century, when a Polish royal stronghold was built nearby. Its use continued, however, as a local religious centre, first by the Orthodox Church, and from the end of the sixteenth century by Greek Catholics. The Palace of the Greek Catholic metropolitans stood here. The church of the Assumption began to rise alongside the ruins of the preceding cathedral in 1584, the work of a local *boyar* Shumliansky family, but was razed to the ground by a Tartar raid in 1676 and never properly restored. In Soviet times, the buildings were used as a museum. Like their tsarist predecessors, who ruled here briefly in 1914–15, the Soviets did not tolerate the Greek Catholic Church, and were fiercely hostile to any remnants of independent Ruthenian or Ukrainian history. Only now is the ancient legacy of Halich being put back together, piece by piece.

The name of Danylo Romanovych Halitsky (r. 1245–64), prince and conceivably 'king' of Halich, is well known to all Ukrainians as the founder of L'viv. He is said to have received his crown from an emissary of Pope Innocent IV, the most politically powerful pontiff of the Middle Ages and the sworn enemy of German emperors. Three years after his coronation, Halitsky laid the foundations of the new capital, which he named after his infant son Liv – Leo, 'the Lion'. His own emblem was a raven, which figures prominently on his coat of arms and on all subsequent heraldic compositions derived from it. Our return journey, therefore, with 'Volodymyr the Great' raring for the chase, led from the Raven's Perch to the Lion's Den.

To travellers in the first decade of the twenty-first century, Halich is just a small, Ukrainian town of no special interest except to archaeologists and enthusiasts of medieval history. Yet throughout the nineteenth century it was a hallowed spot of unusual distinction, indeed it was the place which gave a sense of historical purpose and identity to one of Central Europe's most famous kingdoms.

II

The Kingdom of Galicia and Lodomeria was created in 1773 from the acquisitions of the Austrian Empire during the First Partition of Poland, and was destroyed in October 1918 at the end of the First World War. Throughout its existence of 145 years, it was designated as a *Kronland*, one of the Empire's 'Crownlands', and the kingdom's crown was vested from start to finish in the imperial monarchs of the House of Habsburg. In all, there were seven of them:

Maria Theresa (r. 1740–80)
Joseph II (r. 1780–90)
Leopold II (r. 1790–92)
Francis II (r. 1792–1835)
Ferdinand I (r. 1835–48)
Franz-Joseph (r. 1848–1916)
Charles (r. 1916–18)

The kingdom's name was invented by Maria Theresa's advisers in Vienna in accordance with a complicated historical conceit. Many centuries earlier – before their annexation by medieval Poland – the districts of Halicz (Galicia) and Volodymyr (Lodomeria) had briefly belonged to the kings of Hungary, who had thereon assumed the title of 'dukes of Galicia and Lodomeria'. Four hundred years later, since the empress was also queen of Hungary, her advisers decided to revive the ancient ducal title, upgrade it to royal status, and apply it to a much wider area.

The kingdom's territory was increased and diminished on various occasions, but was never inconsiderable. The core area established in 1773 covered *c*. 30,000 square miles, similar in size to Scotland or Bavaria, and consisted of two distinct parts. Western Galicia coincided in large measure with the historic Polish province of Małopolska (Lesser Poland), whose roots went back to the eleventh century, occupying a broad tract of land between the upper valley of the Vistula and the Carpathian ridge. Eastern Galicia, beyond the River San, largely coincided with the former palatinate of Ruthenia, a province which had been annexed by Poland in the fourteenth century. Its chief city – L'viv – which the Austrians renamed Lemberg, became the kingdom's seat of government.

The kingdom's population, which was to grow dramatically during the nineteenth century, numbered some 3 million in 1773. It was mainly composed of three ethnic groups, each associated with a different religion. The Polish-speaking Poles were predominantly Roman Catholic. The Ruthenians, who spoke *ruski*, a form of old Ukrainian, were predominantly Greek Catholic Uniates (see p. 277). The Jews, if not assimilated into Polish society, mainly spoke Yiddish, and were divided between the adherents of Orthodox Judaism and of Chassidism (see below, p. 463). The population was overwhelmingly rural. With the exception of Lemberg itself, the towns were small; the villages were numerous. In western Galicia, Poles and Jews lived cheek by jowl. In eastern Galicia, Polish nobles lived in their country houses, while Ruthenian peasants tilled the soil, and Jews formed a strong majority in their *shtetln* or 'little towns'.

The kingdom's history can be divided into three periods. During its first twenty years Galicia was deeply influenced by the enlightened reforms of Joseph II. In the next twenty, which were dominated by the Napoleonic Wars, it experienced successive bouts of political instability and territorial transformation. Only after 1815 did it settle down to the more stable but less optimistic existence which persisted until the end. One mid-century change, however, was important. In 1846 Poland's ancient capital, Kraków, which the 1815 Congress of Vienna had turned into a city-republic, lost its sovereign status and was merged with Galicia. From then on Kraków and Lemberg were rival centres.

The kingdom's character escapes easy categorization. It was determined by its artificial creation, by its geopolitical location and by its legendary poverty. Far from Vienna but close to the Empire's most vulnerable frontiers, life in Galicia was full of pains and problems. Its citizens were never in full control of their destiny, developing a strong sense of fatalism combined with a famous brand of humour. At some point, some Galician wag made play on the kingdom's name. Since *goły* means 'naked' and *głód* means 'hunger', it didn't take much to adapt the kingdom's name to 'Golicia and Glodomeria' – 'Kingdom of the Naked and Starving'.[5]

The reforms of Joseph II, an enlightened despot par excellence, were radical but mainly short-lived. A serious attempt was made, for example, to improve the lot of the illiterate, rural serfs. Taxes were imposed on landowners and numerous monasteries were dissolved to provide the income for a state-backed scheme of primary education. Yet the emperor's centralizing policies underestimated both provincial particularities and the force of conservative opposition. At the end of his ten-year reign, in the shadow of the French Revolution, he was forced to rescind much of his reform programme.[6] The dissolution of monasteries did, however, have lasting effects. The social influence of the Roman Catholic Church was diminished, and former monastic lands were frequently used to attract German colonists and to settle them as free farmers. In several districts, compact German communities came to form a substantial minority.[7]

Galicia's fate during the French revolutionary wars was closely bound up with that of its Austrian masters. The Habsburgs, relatives of Marie-Antoinette, were viewed in Paris as the lords of reaction, and for twenty years after 1793 France and Austria were almost continually at war. Although the revolutionary armies never set foot in Galicia, they inspired the creation of the neighbouring Duchy of Warsaw, with which conflict was unavoidable. Throughout those two decades large numbers of Galician men were conscripted into the Austrian army, and the province was obliged to pay its tribute in blood and taxes.

Such was the setting for the romantic and tragic story of the three Polish Legions, which cut a dashing figure on many a battlefield. About 30,000 Galician soldiers, who had been taken to Italy by the Austrians, volunteered in 1797 to change sides and to fight for Napoleon. Their commander, General Jan Henryk Dąbrowski (1755–1818), found favour with his men by pressing Napoleon to overthrow the Partitions of Poland (see pp. 285–90). In the event, the Legions were employed everywhere except on the road to Poland, and deep disillusionment set in. Their last, desperate mission was to Haiti, where many of them changed sides for a second time to fight against French colonialism. Nonetheless, the 'Song of the Legions', set to the tune of a lively mazurka, long outlived the original singers:

> Jeszcze Polska nie zginęła, póki my żyjemy,
> Co nam obca przemoc wzięła, szablą odbierzemy!
> Marsz, marsz, Dąbrowski, z ziemi włoskiej do Polski,
> Pod Twoim przewodem, złączym się z narodem.

('Poland has not perished yet so long as we still live. / That which foreign force has seized we'll with sabres drawn retrieve! / March, march, Dąbrowski, to Poland from the Italian land. / So let us join our nation, under Thy command'.)[8] Nearly a century would pass before these words could be freely sung in Galicia.

Having missed out on the Second Partition of Poland in 1793, the Austrian authorities participated in the Third two years later, accepting a large tract of land north of the Vistula containing both Kraków and Lublin. They renamed it 'New Galicia'. Their acquisition provided one of the causes of the brief war of 1809 with the Napoleonic Duchy of Warsaw, but the expanded territorial arrangements did not survive the Napoleonic Wars; at the Congress of Vienna, New Galicia disappeared from the map.[9] Kraków was elevated to be a small independent republic; Lublin was given to Russia.

Prince Metternich, the Austrian chancellor from 1815 to 1846, famously remarked that 'Asia begins at the Landstrasse', a street in Vienna's eastern suburbs. The Viennese were apt to regard anywhere and everywhere to the east of their magnificent city as backward and exotic, and they played a prominent role in launching the stereotype of 'Eastern Europe' as a reservoir of underdevelopment and inferiority. Travellers to Galicia habitually wrote of dirty inns, bad roads and savage peasants. After 1846, however, the *Kaiser-Ferdinands-Nordbahn* linked Vienna with Lemberg. The railway provided a convenient means whereby Austrians could discover Galicia, and Galicians the rest of the Empire. The author of one well-known travelogue called it *Aus Halbasien*: 'Halfway to Asia'. 'Anyone taking that line will die of boredom,' he wrote, 'if not of hunger.'[10]

As the crow flies, Lemberg is some 340 miles north-east of Vienna, but the rail journey was considerably longer. The first stage crossed the provinces of Moravia and Austrian Silesia; the Galician frontier was reached either at Oświęcim (Auschwitz) or at Bielsko (Bielitz). Beyond Bielsko lay the lands of the medieval Duchy of Oświęcim and Zator. A short ride to the south lay the Habsburg castle of Żywiec (Saybusch), seat of an imperial archduke and from 1856 home to an imperial brewery. To the left, one skirted the fertile valley of the Vistula; to the right the rolling Beskid Hills. At Kęty stood the chapel of the Saint-Professor Johannes Cantius (1390–1473), patron of academic study. At Wadowice, the Austrians were to build a large barracks, and the garrison town would become the birthplace of a pope. At Kalwaria Lańckorona one passed a hilltop Franciscan monastery, scene of a popular annual pilgrimage. In the early days the train did not cross the river into Kraków but stayed on the south bank at Franz-Jozef Stadt (Podgórze). From 1815 to 1846, the Vistula formed the frontier between the Austrian Empire and the Republic of Kraków.

Further east, as Galicia widened out, the railway left the Vistula and made for the San. Wieliczka and Bochnia possessed ancient salt mines, once the source of great wealth. Tarnów and Rzeszów were bishoprics. Travellers pausing for refreshment might have noticed that peasants coming from the villages in the wooded hill country to the south of the line were no longer speaking Polish. They were Ruthenian Lemkos – one of several distinct ethnic communities. Przemyśl (Peremyshl) on the River San commanded Galicia's central crossroads, the dividing line between west and east. It was the site of the kingdom's largest fortress, of two cathedrals, Roman Catholic and Greek Catholic, and of several synagogues.

Despite its historic origins in a Ruthenian principality, Lemberg had become an island of Polishness. As time passed, it also attracted a

The Kingdom of Galicia
and Lodomeria, *c.* 1900

substantial Jewish community and an influential body of Austrian bureaucrats, many of them Germans from Bohemia. It was Galicia's principal
centre of urban life and of refined culture, and it developed a unique personality (see below). In due course, the railway was extended beyond
Lemberg, in the first instance to join Galicia with the neighbouring province of Bukovina. Later on, it linked the Austrian Empire with the Russian
port of Odessa. Galicia's eastern frontier was passed at Śniatyń. In that
district, locals still called the northern bank of the Dniester the 'Polish
side', and the southern bank the 'Turkish side'.

   The landscape of Galicia was (and still is) extremely picturesque. The
rivers flowing down from the snowbound Carpathian ridge are filled
with broad, deep and powerful streams feeding numerous lakes and
waterfalls, and range after range of hills are piled up against the ridge,
creating row after row of valleys, great and small. The woods and forests were varied and extensive. The hilltops were often crowned with
dense pinewoods, while high stands of beech stretched out below the
rocky summits of the main ridge. The valley floors and broad plains were
filled with farmland. Agriculture was traditional, not to say primitive.
The peasants lived in wooden cabins, spun yarn for their own clothes,
and tilled the fields by hand in timeless routine. They donned their
colourful costumes on Sundays or for religious festivals, or to ride to

the markets that were run by Jews. It was a land which tourists would increasingly seek to visit, and which peasants would increasingly want to leave.

Galicia's mountain districts presented remarkable variety, both in their inhabitants and their scenery; they were to prove attractive for hikers, ethnographers, painters, poets and photographers, especially from Germany and Austria. *Podhale*, the 'Land of the *Górale*' or 'Polish Highlanders', snuggled among the subalpine peaks of the Tatra Mountains to the south of Kraków.[11] It was famed for its wood-carving, its white felt clothing and its inimitably raucous music. Further east, the *Lemkivshchyna* or 'Land of the Lemkos' occupied both sides of the Carpathian ridge among the tree-clad Lower Beskid hills. The Greek Catholic Lemkos spoke a Ruthenian dialect quite different from the speech of the *Górale*, and were famed for their choral singing.[12] Beyond the San round Sambor lay the *Boykivshchyna*, the 'Land of the Boykos', another Ruthene group which included a substantial minority of Orthodox. Boyko villages were marked out by their unusual triple-domed, beehive churches.[13] The *Hutsulshchyna* or 'Land of the Hutsuls' backed onto the mountainous frontier with Hungary to the south-east of Lemberg.[14] The Hutsuls specialized in metalwork and horse-breeding, lived in widely scattered hamlets, and were said to be riddled with syphilis. All these districts boasted wild scenery, severe winters, remote pastoral homesteads, archaic dialects, vivid costumes and treasured folklore.

Galician society was formally feudal until the mid-nineteenth century, and remained traditional and pre-modern until the end of its existence. Most of the landed estates, where serfdom remained in force until 1848, belonged to a score of powerful Polish magnates. The free peasantry was largely confined to pastoral communities in the southern highlands. The middle classes were undeveloped, the commercial and professional sectors often being in Jewish hands. Religious practices were strong. Churches and synagogues usually provided the most substantial buildings.

A small number of the grandest Galician landowners could boast some of the largest fortunes in Europe. Each of them governed scores of scattered districts from their *klucz* or 'home estate' – the Branickis at Sucha, the Czartoryskis at Sieniawa, the Potockis at Łancut and Rymanów, the Sapiehas at Krasiczyn, the Dzieduszyckis at Jezupol and the Lubomirskis at Czerwonogród. These families attended court in Vienna and assumed Austrian titles. Their extravagant lifestyle, filled with balls, banquets, foreign tours and international gatherings, was vulnerable to the vagaries of fortune. Though they prospered as a class, individual families rose and fell like football clubs in a premiership league table.[15]

The peasantry, in contrast, were as indigent as their masters were affluent. Men, women and children toiled in the fields from dawn to dusk. They had a few basic implements, an ox-team or possibly a horse, but before the twentieth century little or no machinery. Until 1848 the men were obliged to work for several days a week on the lord's demesne, leaving their wives and offspring to cultivate the family plot. They attempted to survive outside the money economy, suspicious of the Jews who ran it, fearful of debt, and only going to market to sell a pig or to buy a fork or a foal. Like the aristocrats, they watched their family fortunes rise and fall in response to the vicissitudes of health, weather, fertility and the birth of sons, but the tenor of their communal life was remarkably constant. Peasant speech, peasant customs and peasant dancing were all peculiar to their particular social estate. Even after the abolition of serfdom, partly thanks to illiteracy and the scarcity of alternative employment, the peasantry stayed firmly tied to the land. Polish and Ruthenian peasants in Galicia had much more in common with each other than with the rest of society.

Debates over serfdom multiplied after the Congress of Vienna, but the issue did not come to a head in Galicia until 1846, when disastrous floods coincided with a political upheaval in the Republic of Kraków. Some Austrian officials, it seems, actively encouraged serfs to rebel against their masters in order to nip the Cracovian conspiracy in the bud. A peasant called Jakub Szela from the village of Smarzowy near Tarnów assembled a gang of men intent on violence against the local nobility. When the authorities failed to intervene, bands of rebel serfs toured the countryside, beating, burning and butchering noblemen and their families. Bounties were paid for severed noble heads. At least 1,500 murders were perpetrated, and none was punished. When the military finally moved in, Szela was exiled to Bukovina, and the emperor was eventually forced to sign the decree of abolition. This *Rabacja* or 'Peasant Rising' of 1846 (otherwise known as the 'Galician Slaughter') sent ripples of horror round Europe.[16] Everyone who had thought that the social order was God-given and immutable was obliged to think again.

The abolition of serfdom brought only partial relief for the peasants. The strong conservative lobby in Vienna was able to insist that the state compensation payable to the landowners for the loss of their serfs be financed from long-term mortgage payments imposed on the ex-serfs.

The supposed beneficiaries of abolition were indeed freed from bondage and were theoretically free to leave their villages, yet they were not given anywhere to go, and, if they stayed on to work the land which they still regarded as 'theirs', they moved at a stroke from serfdom to deeply indebted tenancies, typically condemned to pay off their mortgage over thirty or forty years. To make things worse, all sorts of traditional practices, such as the right to graze cattle on common land or to collect firewood in the forest, were thrown into dispute, where the advantage belonged to the landowner and his lawyers. Serfdom had provided security of tenure in exchange for bondage. Now, both bondage and security had ended.[17]

Nonetheless, over the decades, new horizons opened up for the former serfs, who were forced to take responsibility for their own destiny. They could buy and sell their produce more effectively, and exploit crafts for monetary gain. They looked forward to educating their children, and began to campaign for village schools. With some delay, they took to various new forms of collective activity, organizing both economic co-operatives and political parties.

All the textbooks state that in the second half of the nineteenth century Galicia's economy remained seriously retarded. Certainly it did not possess the dynamism either of its neighbour, Prussian-ruled Silesia, or of Austrian-ruled Bohemia. Yet it did not stand still either. After 1848 a wider railway network was built; export businesses increased, especially of timber, paper, sugar and tobacco; and several mechanized industries were launched.

Oil, however, supplied the only resource to promise industrial development of more than provincial importance. Discovered in the 1850s in the district of Borysław-Drohobycz, it grew explosively into a wild oil-rush area of near-unregulated drilling and exploration. Foreign investment, mainly French and German, poured in. Borysław and nearby Tustanowice saw hundreds of oil shafts spring up in the muddy fields alongside the district's only paved road, and 100 trains a day left the state refinery at Drohobycz. In 1908 the Galician oilfield claimed to be the third largest in the world after those of Texas and Persia.[18]

Even so, the deep-seated problems of Galicia's rural economy deteriorated. After devastating floods in the early 1880s, rural poverty reached catastrophic proportions. Famine stalked both the villages and the Jewish *shtetln* that lived from the peasants' trade. A study published in 1887, which historians now consider exaggerated, purported to show that Galicia had become Europe's poorest province.[19] Paradoxically, the population had more than doubled in less than a century, while agricultural productivity lagged far behind. Galicia appeared to be falling victim to the Malthusian nightmare which most of Europe had avoided. Overpopulation underlay all other socio-economic ills. Food production had fallen well below rates in neighbouring countries in every crop except potatoes. The birth rate soared to 44/1,000 per annum. The death rate was dropping. The total population was heading for 9 million. Galicia could no longer feed its sons and daughters.

Mass migration was the result. Migrant workers no longer returned home after a seasonal spell in Germany or in Western Europe, but went further and further afield. The coal mines of Ostrava or of Upper Silesia were a frequent destination, but once the railways were built, it was a relatively simple matter to take a train to Bremen or Hamburg and to sail for America. The station at Oświęcim provided the main point of departure. Special barracks were built to house the crowds of paupers who thronged the platforms, and fourth-class wagons were laid on to transport them to the north German ports. The exodus gathered momentum in the last decades before 1914. The annual outflow was counted in hundreds of thousands, and the total ran into millions.[20] Most of them would never see Galicia again. The Poles usually headed for the new industrial towns of the American Midwest like Chicago, Detroit or Cleveland, Ohio. The Ruthenians preferred the prairie provinces of Canada. The Jews made for Vienna, and then for New York.

Though many emigrants would not have known how to read and write, some did; and the letters sent back home constitute an eloquent source of information on their experiences.[21] The pains of emigration also form the subject of Galicia's best-loved popular song:

> Góralu, czy ci nie żal
> Odchodzić od stron ojczystych,
> świerkowych lasów i hal
> I tych potoków srebrzystych?
> Góralu, czy ci nie żal?
> Góralu, wracaj do hal!

('Oh, Gooral, are you not weeping / to walk from your own native land, / from the pine trees, mountains and pastures, / from the silver torrent's bright strand / Oh, Gooral, are you not weeping? / Oh, Gooral, come back to home!')[22] In the nature of things, Galicia's cities were untypical. The urban population never exceeded 20 per cent of the country. Yet its importance should not be underestimated: the cities were the focal point of administrative, commercial and cultural activities that kept the kingdom functioning. Lemberg, though a Polish city in the eyes of its Polish majority, strongly exuded the flavours of the multinational Habsburg Empire. Its Jewish community, increasingly assimilated, represented perhaps a third of its population, while the other minorities – Ruthenian, German, Czech and Armenian – created a variegated ethnic patchwork.

A large number of imposing public buildings in the grandiose Viennese style sprang up round the older, historic centre. The university, refounded in 1817, the renowned *Politechnika* (1877) and the building of the Galician *Sejm* or Diet were all examples of modern neo-Gothic design. The three cathedrals – Roman Catholic, Greek Catholic and Armenian – set the tone of religious plurality, and the erection of a full range of theatres, opera house, art galleries and museums attested to the city's cultural vitality. The late nineteenth century saw the arrival of railway stations, municipal waterworks, tramways, parks, prisons and sports clubs. Lemberg was famed for its lively café life. Numerous monuments and institutions dedicated to King John (Jan) Sobieski, the 'Saviour of Vienna' (see p. 282), the district's most illustrious son, were entirely appropriate.

For the first 100 years, the Austrian authorities in Lemberg pursued a policy of steady linguistic Germanization. But from 1870, the introduction of municipal autonomy led to re-Polonization. Streets, like Sapieha Boulevard, the main thoroughfare, were given Polish names. A statue to Poland's national bard, Adam Mickiewicz (who never visited), was placed in the Mariacki Square. And the amazing Panorama Racławicka, a theatrical battle-scene presented 'in the round', was opened on the centenary of Kościuszko's famous victory over the Russians at Racławice in 1794 (see p. 289). The city's motto, '*Semper Fidelis*', which had distinct Roman Catholic overtones, was now taken to refer unambiguously to the memory of Poland's tragic past.[23]

By the late nineteenth century Lemberg had found its way into the leading European tourist guides:

LEMBERG – Population, c 160,000 Hotels. Hot.George, R from 3K, B.90h; Imperial, Grand, Metropole, de L'Europe, de France. Restaurants. At the hotels, also Stadtmuller, Krakowska Str; Rail Restaurant at the chief station. Cafes. Theatre Café, Ferdinands Platz; Vienna Café, Heilige-Geist Platz. Electric Tramway from the chief station to the Wały Hetmanskie, and thence to the Kilinski Park and to the Cemetery of Łyczaków. Horse cars also traverse the town. British Vice-Consul: Prof. R. Zaliecki . . .[24]

Unlike Lemberg, nineteenth-century Kraków was struggling to recover from a long period of decay. When Galicia was first formed, grass had been growing through the cobbles of its magnificent medieval square, the *Rynek*. More recently, the successive collapse of New Galicia, of the Duchy of Warsaw and of the Republic of Kraków all dashed the city's hopes of regaining its former status. Kraków was smaller than Lemberg, and returned to Galicia in 1846 as a distinctly poor and battered relation. To disarm the city, the medieval walls were razed and replaced by a municipal garden, the *Planty*, encircling the central area.

Nonetheless, in the last quarter of the century Kraków's ancient splendour started to revive. The Jagiellonian University, re-Polonized and rehoused, became a powerhouse of modern Polish culture. Art, science and learning flourished as never before. And Kraków's Polishness, radiating from the most Polish part of Galicia, heralded further changes to come:

> Gdy chcesz wiedzieć, co to chowa
> Nasza przeszłość w swojém łonie,
> Jako stara sława płonie:
> To jedź bracie do Krakowa.

('If you want to see what here is bred / our heritage in its very womb / like an ancient flame that catches fire: / ride, brothers! Go to Krakow!')[25]

Galicia's linguistic kaleidoscope exuded both charm and complications. The main secular tongues of German, Polish, Ruthenian and Yiddish were accompanied by the sacred languages of Latin, Old Church Slavonic, Old Armenian and Hebrew.

In Galicia's early days, German was less developed as a governmental and literary medium than Polish. (It was only starting to develop in those roles in Prussia.) As a result, the Habsburg bureaucrats of Lemberg cultivated a highly stilted and artificial style of their own. Galician Polish, too, was relatively archaic. The nobles held forth in forms filled with third-person titles, rhetorical flourishes and elaborate courtesies. The peasants used the second-person form, and were given to rural idioms, popular proverbs and down-to-earth vocabulary. Ruthenian, that is, Galician *ruski*, which would be classified nowadays as Old West Ukrainian, was the language of illiterate serfs and their descendants, and of the Greek Catholic clergy who served them; it shared many of the characteristics of White Ruthenian *ruski* in the former Grand Duchy of Lithuania (see p. 243). Its vocabulary had been subjected to a tidal wave of Polonisms, and its orthography long wavered between the Latin and the Cyrillic alphabets. In the mountain districts, it fragmented into numerous local dialects.

Historically, the native language of Galicia's Jews was Yiddish; they prayed and studied in Hebrew. As the nineteenth century wore on, however, the trend towards assimilation in secular matters led to the widespread adoption either of German or, especially in Kraków, of Polish. Jews in the country towns also needed to understand the language of the surrounding peasantry. Trilingualism or quadrilingualism was not uncommon.

The depth of the cultural gulf which separated town from country, and class from class, can be gleaned from the exceptional memoirs of Jan Słomka, that is, 'Jack Straw' (1848–1929), who was born in a village near Dębica in western Galicia in the last year of serfdom. As an illiterate farmboy, he writes, he had no conception of being Polish. The peasants of his district called themselves 'Mazury', having migrated from further north in Mazovia many generations earlier. The label of 'Pole' was reserved for nobles. Only when he learned to read and write in his twenties did he realize that he belonged to the same Polish nation as Prince Sapieha or Adam Mickiewicz.[26]

Galicia's linguistic diversity was nicely demonstrated in the singing of the imperial anthem, which was adopted in 1795 with words by Lorenz Leopold Haschka and melody by Joseph Haydn:

> Gott erhalte Franz den Kaiser,
> Unsern guten Kaiser Franz,
> Hoch als Herrscher, hoch als Weiser,
> Steht er in des Ruhmes Glanz . . .[27]

(The music was to be adopted later by the German Empire, and sung to 'Deutschland, Deutschland über alles'.) After 1848, however, the practice spread whereby the anthem could be sung by each of the emperor's subjects in their own language. In Galicia, the Polish version competed mainly with Ruthenian:

> Boże wspieraj, Boże ochroń   Bozhe, budy pokrovytel'
> Nam Cesarza i nasz kraj,   Cisariuh, Ieho kraiam!
> Tarczą wiary rządy osłoń   Kripkyj viroiu pravytel'
> Państwu Jego siłę daj.   Mudro nai provodyt' nam!

('God assist and God protect / our Emperor and our land! / Guard his rule with the shield of faith / and hold his state in Thy hand!') The text was also available in Yiddish and Hebrew, and if necessary in Friulian.[28]

By the turn of the century, each of the Empire's nationalities was singing their own national anthem alongside, or even in place of the imperial one. The Poles of Galicia did not favour Dąbrowski's '*Mazurek*' or the '*Warszawianka*' that were popular across the Russian frontier. Instead, they preferred the lugubrious choral hymn composed by Kornel Ujejski in shock from the Galician *Rabacja*:

> *Z dymem pożarów, z kurzem krwi bratniej*
> *Do Ciebie, Panie, bije ten głos . . .*
>
> Through fiery smoke, through brothers' blood and ashes,
> To Thee, O Lord, our fearful prayers ring out
> In terrible lamentation, like the Last Shout.
> Our hair grows grey from these entreaties.
> Our songs are filled with sorrow's invocation.
> Our brows are pierced by crowns of rooted thorn.
> Our outstretched hands are raised in supplication,
> Like monuments to Thy wrath, eternally forlorn.[29]

The Ruthenians, for their part, adopted a song that was first printed in Lemberg in 1863. Appropriately composed by a lyricist from Kiev and a musical cleric from Peremyshl, it embodied the spiritual link between the Ukrainian national movement in the Russian Empire and the Ruthenians of Galicia, and was destined to become the national anthem of Ukraine. Its first line parodied the first line of Dąbrowski's '*Mazurek*': 'Poland has not perished yet'. The pro-Ukrainian Ruthenians sang '*Shche ne vmerla Ukraina*', 'So far Ukraine has not perished'.

The Zionist anthem '*Hatikvah*', though rarely heard in conservative Galicia, was predictably composed by a Galician Jew.[30]

Galicia's religious culture was traditional, compartmentalized and very demanding. It was designed for people who craved guidance and solace in hard, uncertain lives and who rarely questioned either the strict observances or the unbending authority of their religious leaders. Piety both in public and in private marked a way of life accepted by Christians and Jews alike.

The main branches of the Catholic faith, Roman and Greek, operated throughout the kingdom. The Roman Catholic Church was closely associated both with the Habsburg establishment and with the Polish community. In western Galicia it provided the religion of all classes: in the east, of the gentry.

The Greek Catholic (Uniate) Church, in contrast, served a Ruthenian community that was only slowly emerging from serfdom and from cultural isolation. It had retained the liturgy of its Byzantine roots, while adhering to the principle of papal supremacy. Being viewed with intense hostility by the Russian Orthodox Church across the eastern frontier, it blended well with Austria's anti-Russian political stance. Its most outstanding hierarch was Andrei Sheptytskyi (Andrzej Szeptycki, 1865–1944), metropolitan of Lemberg-Halich, who was cousin to a Roman Catholic general and nephew to the dramatist Alexander Fredro. Scion of a leading landed family and a graduate of the Jagiellonian University, he chose a Ruthenian and Uniate identity of his own free will, and became the true shepherd of his flock, both politically and spiritually. In the Second World War he was one of the few churchmen to dare to denounce Nazi crimes from the pulpit.[31]

The Russian Orthodox Church, despite (or perhaps because of) its dogged attempts to recruit Slav Christians, was not well viewed in Galicia. The so-called 'Russophiles' in the central Carpathian area were the only substantial group to embrace it.[32] The old-established Armenian Church served a community of merchants and exiles who had fled Ottoman rule, and whose adherents were thoroughly Polonized in everyday life. But their cathedral in Lemberg preserved the rites and language of Christianity's oldest denomination.[33]

The Protestants of Galicia were fish in the wrong sort of water. They were either German Lutherans, who had settled in a number of rural colonies, or Polish Evangelicals, who had spilled over the border from Austrian Silesia (where the Catholics were Czech and the Protestants Polish). They were strong in Lemberg, in Stanisławów and in Biała.

As defined by religious practice, the Jews formed over 10 per cent of Galicia's population and were often an absolute majority in particular localities. Yet traditional Orthodox Judaism was strongly challenged by the rise of the Hassidic sects, who had started to proliferate in the late eighteenth century. The Hassids, or Chassids, meaning the 'Pious', rejected the rabbis and their teaching of the Talmud. They observed their own strict rules of dress and diet, and lived in separate communes, each headed by its *zaddik* or 'guru'. Their emphasis lay on the mystical aspects of religion, on the practice of Cabbala and on their rapturous singing and dancing. They were especially resistant to assimilation and modernity, and increasingly set the tone for the *Galizianer*, the stereotypical 'Galician Jew'. The Karaites, who also shunned Judaic Orthodoxy, were another minority within the minority.[34]

Monasteries had long been a feature of the Galician landscape, and they suited the kingdom's conservative ethos. Many of the dissolutions enacted by Joseph II, therefore, were reversed; many ancient foundations, Roman Catholic and Uniate, continued to flourish. Here and there – in the Benedictine ruins of Tyniec near Kraków, or of the former Basilian cloister at Trembowla – there were reminders of hostile secular forces. But they were exceptions. The approaches to Kraków continued to be dominated by the towers of the Camaldulensian monastery at Bielany, and by the imposing battlements of the Salvator convent.

All denominations made public displays of their piety. Galician life was punctuated by a great variety of saints' days, processions and pilgrimages. The Cracovian Feast of St Stanisław was celebrated in May with great pomp, while the Corpus Christi parade in June attracted still greater crowds. The annual pilgrimage in August to the Franciscan cloister at Kalwaria Zebrzydowska in west Galicia was attended by tens of thousands of peasants who dressed up in their finest clothes to camp out in the vicinity for days. (It was a central event in the peasants' marriage market.)

The Jews, too, had their pilgrimages. At Passover in the spring or at Yom Kippur in the autumn visitors would congregate round prominent synagogues or at the homes of 'miracle-working' zaddiks. Belz and Husiatyn were two of many favourite destinations.

Among the Catholics, the cult of the Virgin Mary was widely practised. Many Polish pilgrims headed across the frontier to Częstochowa, to the shrine of the Black Madonna, who had long been revered as 'Queen of Poland'. Attempts by the Austrian authorities to declare her 'Queen of Galicia and Lodomeria' did not meet with much success.

Galicia's secular culture has to be divided into two parts: the folk culture of the peasant majority, which was rooted in immemorial customs; and the more intellectual activities of educated circles, which were the product of growing European interchanges in science and the arts.

Despite the age of its roots, Galician folk-culture cannot be regarded as static. After the abolition of serfdom, the speech, the costumes, the music, the legends, the songs and dances and the everyday practices of various regions all became badges of pride for the newly liberated rural class, and were standardized and formalized in new ways. They also attracted the attention of early ethnographers. František Řehoř (1857–99) was a Czech who was taken in his boyhood to a farm near Lemberg, and who spent a lifetime recording Ruthenian folklore.[35] Semyon Ansky (1863–1920) was a Jewish socialist who made a now classic study of

Galician Jewry during the First World War.[36] Stanisław Vincenz (1888–1971) was a Pole born in Hutsul country who was to spend most of his life in exile. His famous analysis of Hutsul culture, *Na Wysokiej Połoninie*, 'On the High Pasture', was not published until the world of his youth had been destroyed.[37]

Education, of course, was the key to social advancement. But, despite many improvements, it remained the preserve of relatively few beneficiaries. Generally speaking, Jews who learned to read and write as a religious duty were better served than Christians, and enjoyed a distinct headstart on the route into the professions, commerce and the arts. In the early nineteenth century the provision of primary schools, largely by the Churches, was woefully inadequate. After the reign of Joseph II the Austrian state was interested in little other than the training of its German-speaking bureaucracy. From the 1860s onwards, however, important changes were made. First, though elementary education was never compulsory, the number of schools multiplied greatly. Secondly, both the secondary schools and the universities were largely taken over by Polish educators. By 1914 Galicia possessed sixty-one Polish *gymnasia* or grammar schools, but only six Ruthenian ones. The Jagiellonian University in Kraków, the University of Lemberg and the Lemberg *Politechnika* were all Polish institutions.

For obvious reasons, historians rose to special prominence. Everyone wanted to know how the old Polish-Lithuanian Commonwealth had been destroyed, and why Galicia had been created. The Stańczyk Group of historians in Kraków – so named after a mordant royal jester – held that the Polish nation had no one to blame for its misfortunes but itself. Count-Professor Stanisław Tarnowski (1837–1917) was a central figure in the group.[38] Alexander Brückner (1856–1939), professor of Slavic History and Philology at Berlin, was also, despite his name, a Galician Pole.[39] Professor Szymon Azkenazy (1866–1935), a specialist in diplomatic history, contested the Stańczyks' 'pessimism'.[40] It was entirely fitting that one of the last governors of Galicia, Professor Michał Bobrzyński (1849–1935), was a popular Cracovian medievalist.

Yet no one was more influential in the long run than Mikhail Hrushevsky (1866–1934), the founding father of Ukrainian history. Though employed in St Petersburg, Hrushevsky could only publish freely in Lemberg, and his *Traditional Scheme of Russian History* (1904) demolished the widespread Russocentric myth that Moscow and its successors had been the sole legitimate heirs of Kievan Rus'.[41] Meir Bałaban (1877–1942), a graduate of Lemberg, wrote a series of groundbreaking works on the Jews of Kraków, Lemberg and Lublin, thereby earning the reputation as the pioneer of modern Polish-Jewish history.[42]

Literature, too, blossomed in Galicia, partly because many foreign writers chose to live there. Thanks to the rise of national languages, Polish, Ruthenian and Jewish letters flourished in parallel. Among Galicia's native sons, the poet Wincenty Pol (1807–72), offspring of an Austrian family in New Galicia, took brilliantly to the local Polish idiom.[43] Count Alexander Fredro (1793–1876), whose estate lay at Surochów near Jarosław, is best characterized as the father of Galician comedy.[44] Kazimierz Tetmayer (1865–1940) was the principal promoter of the 'Tatra Legend' and of associated regional culture, and the patron of Zakopane as a literary centre.[45] Elements of the legend included a romantic cult of the high mountains, tales of freedom-loving heroes (especially of Janosik, the 'Robin Hood' of the Tatras), and a movement for stylized regional architecture and design.

An eclectic group of artists and writers calling themselves *Młoda Polska*, 'Young Poland', made their name around the turn of the century. By far the most significant figure among them was the Cracovian Stanisław Wyspiański (1869–1907) – poet, dramatist, painter, architect, designer and professor of Fine Arts. His play *Wesele* (1901), 'The Wedding Feast', bristling both with historical references and contemporary issues, is a dramatic masterpiece.[46] *Wesele* was inspired by a real event – the marriage in the village of Bronowice near Kraków of a young university lecturer and a peasant girl. The Cracovian snobs no doubt viewed the event as a social *mésalliance*. But Wyspiański saw it as an allegory of reconciliation leading to national unity. In the play's final scene, a little girl is brought forward and asked to put her hand on her heart: 'Something is throbbing,' she says.

— 'And do you know what it is?'
— 'It's my heart.'
— 'Yes, and that's what Poland is!'[47]

Wyspiański would be counted among the highest pantheon of Polish writers.

Among the many exiles who moved to Galicia, Jan Kasprowicz (1860–1926) won perhaps the greatest reputation. The child of illiterate parents, he had fled Prussia, but so educated himself that he translated Dante, Shakespeare and Dostoyevsky into Polish. He worked for thirty years in Lemberg, before retiring to his *Harenda* at Poronin near Zakopane.[48]

The Ruthenian literary movement, which started virtually from scratch in the 1830s, had a multitude of obstacles to overcome. The *Rusalka Dnistrovaia*, the very first joint publication of three writers calling themselves the 'Ruthenian Triad', was composed in Lemberg in 1837, but for fear of the state censorship was published in Budapest;[49] it was not until 1848 that activists were successful in asserting the right of Ruthenian/Ukrainian to be officially regarded as a distinct language. Henceforth, the 'Ukrainian Awakening' would proceed in parallel in Austrian Galicia and in Russian-ruled Ukraine. Its most important member, Ivan Franko (1856–1916), enjoyed little esteem during his lifetime. He was the orphaned son of a blacksmith from a village near Drohobych, an active non-Marxist socialist, a powerful prose writer, and an academic. After his death, he came to be seen alongside the poet Taras Shevchenko as one of the fathers of modern Ukrainian literature; the university from which he was expelled would later be given his name. In Galician times he made a major contribution to the cultural advance of his national community by translating the classics of European literature, including works by Dante, Shakespeare, Byron, Hugo and Goethe.[50]

Vasyl Stefanyk (1871–1936) was an accomplished writer of Ruthenian short stories. Born in Pokutia, East Galicia, he studied medicine in Kraków and became acquainted with members of the *Młoda Polska* group. His chosen theme was the travails of emigration. One of the stories, '*Kaminnyi Khrest*', 'The Stone Cross' (1900), was turned into an early film; a monument to its real-life hero, who died in Canada in 1911, was raised in Hilliard, Alberta.[51]

Galicians often used German as a literary medium, either because they had gone off to study in Austria or because they sought to address a wider European public. Leopold von Sacher-Masoch (1836–95) fitted both criteria. He was the son of the police director of Lemberg, and was not a native German-speaker. But on returning from studies in Graz he made his name in the 1860s as a writer of short stories inspired by Polish, Jewish and Ruthenian folklore. His trademark work, however, *Venus in Pelz* ('Venus in Furs', 1869), explored his sexual proclivities, and gave rise to the psychiatric term 'masochism'.[52]

Jewish writers plied their craft in German, Polish, Yiddish or Hebrew according to circumstance. The leading literary critic Wilhelm Feldman (1866–1919), for example, born in Zbaraż, educated in Berlin and resident in Kraków, mainly chose Polish.[53] Mordechai Gebirtig (1877–1942), poet and song-writer, is celebrated as Kraków's 'Last Yiddish Bard'. His song, '*S' Brent*', 'Our little town is burning', has become a Jewish standard. His 'Farewell to Kraków' can be taken as a lament for the lost world of Galician Jewry:

> *Blayb gezunt mir, Kroke!*
> *Blayb zhe mir gezunt.*
> *S'vart di fur geshpant shayn fur mayn hoyz*
> *S'traybt der wild soyne,*
> *Vi m'traybt a hunt,*
> *Mit akhzoriyes mikh fun dir aroys.*

('Farewell for me, my Kraków! / Farewell, my country. / The harnessed cart is waiting outside. / The wild enemy / is driving me out like a dog / to destinies unknown.')[54]

Sooner or later, all attempts to describe Galicia's qualities and characteristics reach the subject of humour. Galicians tended to be both sardonic – since they had little faith in their ability to change anything – and, as a way of softening the blow, addicted to jokes. A famous story, told by Galicians about the Galician Front in 1914, says it all. A German officer reports: 'The situation is serious, but not hopeless.' An Austrian officer retorts: 'No, it's hopeless, but not serious.'

Many of the jokes centred on the long-lived Emperor Franz-Joseph. In the winter of 1851, when he visited the Jagiellonian University, the professors were told that they must stand when the emperor was standing, and sit when the emperor was seated. Outside the venerated *Collegium Maius*, the emperor slipped on the icy cobblestones and fell flat on his face. All the professors immediately flung themselves headlong onto the ice. On another occasion, the emperor lost his way when hunting in the mountains, taking refuge after nightfall in a remote tavern. The emperor knocks on the bolted door. 'Who's there?' the innkeeper calls. 'We are,' comes the reply. 'And who, for God's sake, are *We*?' 'We, by God's Grace,' the visitor recites, 'are His Royal and Imperial Majesty, the Apostolic King of Jerusalem, Emperor of Austria, King of Hungary, Bohemia, Moravia, Dalmatia, Croatia, Slovenia, Galicia and Lodomeria ...' 'In that case,' the innkeeper relents, 'come in, but by God's grace, will We please wipe Our boots.'

True to his ascetic lifestyle, whereby he wore the same old army jacket for decades, Franz-Joseph was said to allow himself only one mistress. Anna Nakowska, wife of a Galician railway official, claimed to have made numerous discreet visits to the Hofburg in the 1870s. She

reportedly benefited from discounted railway fares, and her husband
from regular promotions. But she was not alone, being superseded in
the emperor's affections by his long-term companion, the actress Katharina Schratt. In 1880, during the emperor's second visit to Galicia, the
station at Bochnia was decorated with a banner bearing the imperial
motto, '*Viribus Unitis*'. The workmen responsible did not notice that
the banner was hanging directly over the station conveniences. The
combined message read: 'Strength in Union: Ladies and Gentlemen'.

In 1915 an Austrian officer of Polish descent was overheard deriding
his emperor as a '*stary pierdola*'. In the ensuing court martial, three professors of the Jagiellonian University solemnly testified that the offending
expression could indeed be construed as 'Old Fart'. On the other hand,
they asserted, it was also an archaic form of endearment meaning 'Fine
elderly gentleman'. About the same time, a Russian revolutionary was
stopped on the frontier. A police officer asks him: 'For what purpose do
you intend to visit Galicia?' 'My purpose is to support the international
struggle of the Working Class against Capitalism!' 'In that case,' says the
officer, 'since no one here does much work, and we don't have any
money, please come in.'

Jokes and gossip are excellent subjects for dividing historians. The
purists say, correctly, that they cannot be verified. The realists maintain,
with equal correctness, that they provide vital insights into the tenor of
everyday life.[55]

For the first century of its existence, Galicia's government was entirely
centralized. The emperor and his ministers in Vienna ruled through
governors resident in Lemberg. Politics, such as it was, consisted of
delivering petitions to the governor, or, for influential aristocrats, of
seeking the emperor's ear at court. From 1772 to 1848, every single
name on the list of governors or 'governors-general' – eighteen in total,
from Graf Anton von Pergen to Freiherr Wilhelm von Hammerstein –
was an Austrian German.

In 1848, during the 'Springtime of Nations', Galicia played a minor
part in the Europe-wide disturbances, and Galician delegates attended
the Slav Congress in Prague. The Congress assisted in the recognition of
Ukrainian identity despite Russian protests, while discovering that the
Poles and pan-Slavism do not mix. Little could be achieved beyond the
talking. Imperial forces were on hand to bombard first Lemberg and
then Kraków into obedience.[56] Nonetheless, the consequences were
far-reaching. A lively Galician delegation had lobbied the emperor in

Vienna for the abolition of serfdom, and at home a rash of political organizations formed to channel the growing demands for representation. A strong body of the emperor's Galician advisers were convinced that constitutional reform was unavoidable. Among them was Count Agenor Gołuchowski, a native Galician who went on to serve several terms as governor from the 1850s to the 1870s.

Two new organizations with lasting influence were both Ruthenian in orientation. The Supreme Ruthenian Council (*Holovna Ruska Rada*, HRR) set out not just to gain influence with the Austrian government, but also to prevent the Poles from gaining a monopoly on language and educational issues. It rapidly mobilized a network of local councils, which were to be the foundation of the future Ruthenian/Ukrainian movement. The Ruthenian Congress (*Ruskyi Sobor*), in contrast, was set up by conservative landowners in order to counter the HRR's more radical aspirations. Between them, these two organizations would ensure that the Galician Poles would not henceforth have everything their own way.

After the 'Springtime of Nations', Polish leaders headed by Gołuchowski pressed for provincial autonomy in the name of political restraint. They were effectively telling Vienna that if put in charge, they would keep the lid on radicalism. At the same time, a group calling themselves the 'Podolians' followed the example of Prince Lev Sapieha and emphasized charitable works and social relief. Perhaps as a result, compared to the situation in Russian-ruled Poland, Polish national sentiment in Galicia was relatively subdued. In 1863–4, when the January Rising was raging over the border (see pp. 295–6), active support for the insurrectionaries was limited.

Galicia was finally granted autonomy in 1871 following the transformation of the Empire into the dual Austro-Hungarian monarchy four years earlier. Galicia was to enjoy less self-government than Hungary but more than other imperial provinces. There was to be a *Sejm* with three chambers; a separate Ministry of Galician Affairs in Vienna; and the governors were given the title of *namiestnik* or 'viceroy'. Polish was to be the principal language of administration and education. Conservative landowners were left in a dominant position, and the more assertive Poles began to think of the kingdom as the 'Piedmont' of a reunited Poland, that it might mirror Piedmont's role in Italy's Risorgimento. Ruthenians and Jews felt increasingly excluded. Between 1871 and 1915, every viceroy, every minister of Galician affairs and every marshal of the Galician Diet, was Polish. The Galician Diet, also dominated by Poles, was notorious for long-winded speech-making and for lack of effective action. The Polish expression of '*austriackie gadanie*', literally 'Austrian babbling', possesses similar connotations to English phrases such as 'hot air' or 'prattle'.

Nonetheless, social and political conditions in Galicia were conducive to nationalist ideas gaining most ground among the Ruthenians. One group, the 'Old Ruthenians', gathered in the parish halls of Uniate churches. A second, the Kachkovskyi Society, named after its founder, was suspected of Russophile tendencies. A third, the *Narodovtsy* or 'Populists', gradually won the support of a clear majority. Backed by the educational Prosvita Society, they made a telling symbolic step when they established their headquarters in the Lubomirsky Palace, formerly the governor's residence. They too thought of Galicia as being like Piedmont – but of a future Ukrainian state.[57]

By 1907, democratic institutions had been introduced throughout the Empire. Male suffrage, which had already functioned for several years, was replaced by universal suffrage for elections to the imperial *Reichsrat* in Vienna, where Galician deputies took their places alongside Germans, Czechs, Slovenes, Bukovinians and many others. Nationalists of many hues mingled alongside conservatives, socialists and the first Zionists. In 1908 Galicia sent the largest of all delegations, some on horseback, others on foot, and all in brilliant costumes, to the emperor's diamond jubilee celebrations.

Yet in that same year, the viceroy of Galicia was murdered in Lemberg by a Ukrainian extremist. The assassination made it to the front page of the *New York Times*:

STUDENT MURDERS GOVERNOR OF GALICIA
Count Andreas Potocki Victim of Bitter Enmity between
Ruthenians and Poles
SHOT WHILE GIVING AN AUDIENCE
Poles crying for vengeance – Great Excitement at Lemberg[58]

Five years later, on the eve of the First World War, another political bombshell exploded. Austrian counter-intelligence agents checking suspicious parcels of money in Vienna's main post office, uncovered a traitorous liaison between the former chief of their military intelligence service and the Russian government. Colonel Alfred Redl (1864–1913), born in Lemberg, part Jewish and part Ukrainian, had been a brilliant officer. But he was also homosexual, and vulnerable to blackmail. Over a decade, he is thought to have supplied the Russians with the Austro-Hungarian masterplan for war against Serbia and details of all the main fortifications in Galicia. When he shot himself in disgrace, the emperor was said to be most upset by the bad example of an officer dying in mortal sin.[59]

By the turn of the century, therefore, several social and political chasms were opening up in Galicia. The aristocrats had been joined in the wealthiest sector of society by a small but very affluent bourgeois class, frequently Jewish, while the Polish Socialist Party (PPS) was mobilizing support among a small but militant working class, especially in the oil-field. A sturdy Polish Peasant Movement (PSL), markedly anti-clerical and undeferential, was courting a large constituency. Poor Jews and still poorer peasants were emigrating in droves. Above all, rival nationalist movements were eyeing each other with deepening suspicion. Galicia had little to offer to those demanding 'Poland for the Poles', 'Ukraine for Ukrainians' or 'Zion for the Jews'.

Nowhere could these divisions be seen more clearly than in Krynica, a small spa town nestling in the hills 60 miles south-east of Kraków. Mineral springs had been discovered there and a fine Renaissance-style pump-house had been built in the 1890s beneath the pine-clad slopes. Railway lines connected Krynica-Muszyna both with Kraków and with Budapest. Rich clients, many Jewish and many from Russia and Hungary, came to take the waters, to relax in the mudbaths, to stroll along the elegant Parade and to enjoy the luxurious hotels, villas and restaurants. Elegant Polish ladies showed off the latest Parisian fashions. At the same time, a half-hidden slum of Jewish paupers huddled behind the town hall, and ragged peasants from the surrounding Ruthenian villages drifted into town to seek work as servants or chambermaids, or sometimes to beg. One of them, a deaf-mute Lemko washerwoman, gave birth in 1895 to one of Galicia's most remarkable sons. Epifanyi Drovnyak, like his mother, suffered from a speech impediment, and spent much of his life begging on the Parade. Yet as 'Nikifor' he eventually won recognition as a unique, 'naive' (or stylistically 'primitive') painter.[60] Just as his contemporary L. S. Lowry painted Lancashire cotton mills and matchstick people, Nikifor loved to draw Galician train stations and their passengers.

A couple of hours on the slow local train to the north of Krynica brought one to Bobowa – an archetypal Jewish *shtetl* in the middle of verdant Polish countryside. In 1889 the village had burned down. The original inhabitants moved out, and the followers of a Chassid *zaddik*, Salomon ben Natan Halberstam, moved in. A new *yeshivah* or Talmudic academy was founded. The old wooden synagogue was rebuilt in stone, and on feast days thousands of Chassidic pilgrims would arrive from far and wide. The owners of the town were the counts Długoszowski, refugees from Russian-ruled Poland. In the years before 1914, the son of the family, Bolesław Wieniawa-Długoszowski, was studying in Paris. But he returned home in time to fight with Piłsudski's Polish Legions during the First World War. His relations with the Jews exemplify the way in which, at their best, different Galician religions and ethnic communities could live beside each other before 1914. Photographs have survived of him in officer's uniform entertaining Salomon Halberstam's son – the silver-haired, bemedalled general with the smiling, bearded, fur-hatted Chassid.[61]

When war broke out in August 1914, everyone knew that Galicia's fate was precarious. It was strategically exposed, and fighting between the Austrian and Russian armies immediately took place on Galician soil. Fear of the 'Russian steamroller' was great: if the tsar's armies were victorious, Galicia would be annexed to Russia. If the Central Powers held firm, almost everyone assumed that Galicia would remain a Habsburg Crownland indefinitely.

Most Galician men who enrolled for military service served in the Imperial and Royal Army. The casualty rate among them was high. A much smaller number, perhaps 30,000, found their way either into Józef Piłsudski's newly formed Polish Legions or into their Ukrainian equivalent, the United Sich Riflemen. Both of these formations grew out of scouting, sporting or paramilitary groups that had come into being in the previous decade. Piłsudski's men, who belonged to the anti-nationalist branch of Polish patriotic opinion, upholding the country's multi-religious and multi-cultural traditions, contained a strong contingent of Jews. And, like Dąbrowski's men a century earlier, they were fired up by the call to fight for the restoration of Polish independence. They actually started the fighting on the Galician Front on 6 August, when they crossed the Russian frontier near Kraków in an act of deliberate bravura. But they soon retreated, and took their place on the frontline alongside all the other formations of the Central Powers. After three years of hard fighting, they were pulled out of the line in preparation for transfer to the Western Front. Having refused to take an oath of allegiance to the German Kaiser, however, they were disbanded. Piłsudski

Galicia in Austria-Hungary, c. 1914

was imprisoned, his officers interned, and the rank and file redistributed among other units. As a result, they played no further part either in the war or in Galicia's future.[62]

The Austrian authorities were equally keen to mobilize Ruthenian manpower. A Ukrainian army corps assembled round the Sich Riflemen by drawing on recruits from eastern Galicia. Their ultimate political aims were not clarified, but their eagerness to fight Russia was shared by their Polish counterparts and satisfied Vienna. Since they stayed in the field, they were able to influence events at the war's end.[63]

At first, Galicia's prospects had looked grim. The Russian steamroller rolled, driven by huge numerical superiority. Lemberg was occupied, and the fortress at Przemyśl was subjected to a five-month siege. The Austrians pulled back. By early December 1914 Cossack patrols were raiding the outskirts of Kraków. (One of them was captured at Bierżanów, now within the city limits.) But then the line held. In a Christmas counter-offensive, the Austrians recovered almost half the lost ground, retaking most of west Galicia.[64]

In 1915 the initiative passed to the Central Powers. Having knocked out one of the two Russian army groups in East Prussia, and having established a trench-line deep inside France, the German command felt free to reinforce its hard-pressed Austrian allies. A massive combined operation pushed off in July from the district of Gorlice (adjacent to Krynica) and all resistance was swamped for a couple of hundred miles. The Germans swung north to capture Warsaw. The Austrians reached Lublin, recovering both Przemyśl and Lemberg. The German and Austrian emperors met to agree on the re-creation of a subservient Polish kingdom in Warsaw and Lublin. Galicia breathed again.

The next year was one of renewed alarms, heightened by the death of Franz-Joseph. General Brusilov launched a fresh Russian offensive. Lemberg changed hands once again, and Przemyśl was subjected to a second siege. This time, however, the Russians drove south over the Carpathians into Hungary. They eventually ran out of steam, and their positions in the winter of 1916–17 were not dissimilar to those of two winters previously. War-torn Galicia was holding on. It provided the setting for one of the most celebrated fictional treatments of life on the Eastern Front in *The Adventures of the Good Soldier Švejk*.[65] Švejk's Czech creator, Jaroslav Hašek, served in Galicia.

It was not long before the crash of the cannon was joined by the rumblings of revolution. In the course of 1917 the Russian army fell apart. Mutinous soldiers shot their officers and refused to fight, appealing to the rank and file of their German and Austrian enemies to follow suit. In March the 'February Revolution' overthrew the tsar. In November the Bolsheviks' 'October Revolution' overthrew Russia's provisional government. In consequence, though the fighting raged on in Western Europe, peace was clearly coming to the East. The armies of the Central Powers surged forward, occupying the Baltic provinces, Lithuania, Byelorussia and Ukraine. Both Lithuania and Ukraine declared their independence from Russia, and Lenin, the desperate Bolshevik leader, was forced to sue for peace. The Treaty of Brest-Litovsk in March 1918 was signed at the dictate of Berlin and Vienna. Soviet Russia was forced to resign from huge swathes of territory, and Galicia was reconfirmed as a Habsburg possession.[66]

The main civilian concerns were now for epidemic diseases and for refugees. Typhoid broke out, followed by the worldwide epidemic of Spanish influenza. Well over a million Galician civilians had been displaced, their sufferings inspiring appeals for international aid.

The impact of the Bolshevik Revolution on Galicia is difficult to gauge. It may have encouraged the new Emperor Charles to seek a separate peace. Some soldiers, infected by the revolutionary bacillus, threatened to mutiny; most simply demanded to go home. Many of them, while marching off, turned against their imperial rulers less in the name of international revolution than in that of national liberation. Czech and Slovak regiments demanded a Czech-Slovak state; Croats and Slovenes aspired to a new Yugoslavia; Poles talked about a Polish Republic; and Ukrainians about a free Ukraine.

The ferment came to a head in October 1918. The Central Powers were now falling back in disarray on the Western Front, and the emperors in Berlin and Vienna were facing calls for abdication. In Galicia, the troops of the Royal and Imperial Army, together with Austrian officialdom, were melting away. Officers threw away the keys of their fortresses. Appeals to Vienna went unanswered, and in any case Vienna seemed to be issuing no orders. Kraków was left in the hands of the local garrison. Lemberg was handed over to a division of Ukrainian Riflemen. In west Galicia, a Polish Liquidation Committee declared itself guardian of all ex-imperial assets. In east Galicia, a 'West Ukrainian Socialist Republic' was surfacing in parallel to an Austro-German Republic in Vienna. On 11 November the Emperor Charles declared that he was withdrawing from government, and absolved all officials from their oath of office. Unlike the German Kaiser, he did not abdicate but withdrew to his country house at Eckertsau to await developments. After four months, he left for Switzerland, and the Empire just petered out. Ironically, since the emperor had also been king of Galicia and Lodomeria, the helpless kingdom petered out with it. After months of huge confusion, it was joined to the reborn Polish Republic, whose head of state, freshly released from his German prison, was Józef Piłsudski.

Galicia's afterlife lasted at the most for one generation. The kingdom itself was never restored, but the multinational community which it had fostered lived on under a succession of political regimes and was not definitively broken up until the Second World War. In 1918–21, the partition of Galicia led to violent conflicts. The Poles of Lemberg rebelled against the West Ukrainian Republic within a week, drove the Ukrainian troops out by their own efforts, and then, calling on military assistance from central Poland, freed the whole of Galicia from Ukrainian control.[67] They then embarked on a political campaign to ensure that all of the former Galicia be awarded to the Polish Republic. At the same time, the territory became embroiled in a wider war between Poland and the Soviet Republics. In spring a 1920 it provided the base for Piłsudski's march on Kiev in the company of his allied Ukrainian armies. That summer, it was the scene of a Bolshevik invasion, headed by the fearsome *Konarmiya* of 'Red Cossacks'. In the autumn, following Poland's decisive victory over the Red Army at Warsaw, it returned in its entirety to Polish rule.[68]

In the 1920s and 1930s, reunited and forming a composite part of inter-war Poland, the former Galicia enjoyed a brief period of respite. West Galicia, centred on Kraków, returned to its historical name of Małopolska. East Galicia/West Ukraine, centred on Lemberg (now Lwów), was given the unhistorical name of 'Eastern Little Poland'. As in late Austrian times, the Poles held the reins of power. Administration and education were strongly Polonized, and for the first time illiteracy was largely abolished. In several easterly districts, substantial numbers of Polish settlers, usually war veterans from 1920, were given grants of land to strengthen the border areas. Loyalty was maintained by a relatively benign regime, by a strong military presence, and by fear of the neighbouring Soviet republics, where political, social and economic conditions were infinitely more oppressive. Refugees reaching the former Galicia from Lenin's 'Red Terror', from Stalin's forced collectivization or from the Ukrainian Famine of 1932–3 left little doubt in people's minds about the horrors of the 'Soviet paradise'.

The problems encountered by Galicia's non-Polish minorities, which were to be a favourite topic of Communist propaganda in the decades that followed, have often been exaggerated. The Jews did encounter a certain measure of discrimination, especially during the Polish–Soviet War. But stories of widespread pogroms, though oft repeated, were dismissed by successive international inquiries. The notorious 'Lemberger Pogrom' of November 1918 turned out to be a military massacre in which three-quarters of the victims were Christian.[69] The Ruthenians/Ukrainians, too, encountered painful episodes. Rural poverty continued to afflict the villages of so-called 'Polska B', that is, the poorer, eastern part of inter-war Poland. Though the constitution guaranteed the equality of all citizens, Ukrainian language and culture were never put on an equal footing with Polish. In 1931 a rural strike was countered by brutal pacifications from the Polish military; in 1934 the murder by Ukrainian terrorists of the Galician-born minister of the interior, Bronisław Pieracki, provoked harsh repressions. Even so, none of these ordeals bore any resemblance either to the atrocities in progress across the Soviet border or to the catastrophes that were about to strike.

Ex-Galicians who became prominent after 1918 were legion. They included Wincenty Witos, peasant politician and premier;[70] Stefan Banach, mathematician;[71] Karel Sobelsohn, 'Radek', Bolshevik;[72] Leopold Weiss (Muhammad Asad), Muslim convert;[73] Michał Bobrzyński, historian;[74] Martin Buber, philosopher;[75] Joseph Retinger, a 'Father of Europe';[76] Omelian Pritsak, Harvard orientalist;[77] Joseph Roth, Austrian writer;[78] Bruno Schulz, Polish writer and artist;[79] S. Y. Agnon, Israeli novelist;[80] Władysław Sikorski, general and politician;[81] Archduke Albrecht von Habsburg, Polish officer;[82] Rudolf Weigl, microbiologist;[83] Ludwig von Mises, economist;[84] Stepan Bandera, Ukrainian nationalist;[85] and Simon Wiesenthal, Nazi-hunter.[86]

Space permits only one of these diverse figures to be described. The highly eccentric career of Leopold Weiss (1900–92) was prompted by circumstances that were fairly common among educated Galicians. Weiss was born in Lemberg to a family of liberal Jewish professionals, who took religious tolerance for granted. His father, the son and grandson of rabbis, had broken with tradition to become a lawyer; and, though the young Leopold's parents gave him a standard Talmudic education, they took great care not to press religious views on him. The result, he said, was a feeling that they lacked any real conviction. Hence, when he arrived in Palestine in the 1920s he parted company with his Zionist colleagues from Galicia, made friends with Arabs, converted to Islam, and took the name of Muhammad Asad. He was the author of *The Message of the Qur'an* (1964), one of the best-known introductions to Islamic teaching for foreigners. After living for a time in Saudi Arabia and befriending King Saud, he married a Saudi wife, and moved to British India, eventually serving as Pakistan's first ambassador to the United Nations. In 1939 he was arrested by the British as an enemy alien. His parents, who had stayed in Lemberg, perished in the Holocaust.[87]

In 1939–45 the former Galicia belonged to the slice of Europe which suffered greater human losses than anywhere in previous European history. The Polish Republic was destroyed in four weeks in September 1939 by the collusion of Hitler's Wehrmacht with Stalin's Red Army. By the Nazi–Soviet Pact of 28 September, the land and people of the defunct Republic were divided between German and Soviet zones of occupation. The southernmost stretch of the dividing line ran along the River San (along the old border between west and east Galicia). Then the killings and deportations began. In the German zone, Kraków, renamed Krakau, was made the capital of the SS-ruled General Government; Oświęcim, renamed Auschwitz, saw the installation of the Nazis' largest concentration camp. In the Soviet zone, Lemberg (now Lvov) became the headquarters of a brutal Communist regime enforcing Stalinist norms. Up to a million people – Poles, Ukrainians and Jews – were condemned either to the Soviet concentration camps of the Gulag, or to exile in the depths of Siberia or of Central Asia.[88]

In the middle years of the war, 1941–4, following Hitler's reneging on the Nazi–Soviet Pact and 'Operation Barbarossa', the area of German occupation was extended far to the east. East Galicia, now *Distrikt Galizien*, was added to the General Government, and Nazi policies for reconstructing the racial composition of their *Lebensraum* swung into action. Virtually all Galician Jews were murdered, either shot in cold blood or transported to the gas chambers of Auschwitz or Sobibor.[89] Slightly later, part of the Ukrainian underground launched a programme of ethnic cleansing in which hundreds of thousands of Poles were murdered.[90] The Waffen-SS raised only one division of Ukrainian volunteers in the former Galicia, the XIV Waffen-SS *Galizien*, exclusively for military duties against the Soviet Union;[91] two or three Waffen-SS divisions were typically raised in each of many other occupied countries, such as Belgium, the Netherlands and Hungary. On the other side, scores of Ukrainian divisions fought in the Red Army. The clandestine Ukrainian Insurrectionary Army (UPA) duly launched a desperate campaign to defend its homeland simultaneously against both Hitler and Stalin. They, their dependants and their sympathizers were annihilated.[92]

In 1944–5 the Red Army returned with a vengeance. The Stalinist authorities were determined to uphold the frontier-line agreed with the Nazis in 1939, and hence to perpetuate the division of the former Galicia. What is more, they ruled that the remaining Polish population was to be concentrated to the west of the line, and Ukrainians to the east. Vast tides of fugitive humanity flowed back and forth. Recalcitrants were driven out of their homes. The Poles of east Galicia/eastern Małopolska/*Distrikt Galizien*, now labelled 'repatriants', were packed onto trains and dispatched from Soviet territory. Almost the entire surviving Polish population of Lemberg was sent to Wrocław/Breslau, the capital of Silesia, where it replaced the expelled German citizenry.[93] This was social engineering on an unprecedented scale.

The districts adjoining the new Polish–Soviet frontier were hit particularly hard. One example must suffice. Ustrzyki Dolne lay on the bank of the River San. Its multinational Galician make-up had stayed intact till 1939. A Jewish majority predominated in the town, though there were also some Poles and a few Ruthenians. One of its prominent Jewish citizens, Moses Fränkel, had been a long-serving mayor. In the

surrounding mountainous countryside, a Ruthenian Lemko peasantry
lived alongside an old German rural colony. None of these groups survived the war. The Poles of Ustrzyki were deported en masse by the
Soviets in 1939, almost all of them dying from maltreatment or the Siberian cold.[94] The Germans, by Nazi-Soviet agreement, were forcibly sent to
the so-called 'Warthegau' to replace expelled natives.* In 1942 the Jews
of Ustrzyki were rounded up by the Wehrmacht, marched to a temporary
transit station, and then sent to the extermination camp at Sobibór. This
only left the Ruthenian Lemkos, who were rounded up and dispersed by
the Communist authorities in 1946–7 in an act of ethnic cleansing called
'Operation Vistula', launched on the pretext of rooting out the remnants
of the wartime Ukrainian underground.[95] By that time, Ustrzyki was a
ghost town, emptied of all its pre-war inhabitants. The mountain villages
were deserted, the houses had been torched and razed, the orchards had
turned wild; the fields, untended, were overgrown. All that remained were
a few ruined churches and synagogues, and the vandalized tombstones of
the cemeteries.[96] The former east Galicia, forcibly Ukrainianized, now
formed part of the Ukrainian SSR. The former west Galicia, artificially
Polonized, belonged to the Polish People's Republic. The new Soviet–
Polish frontier reduced contacts to a minimum. The Ustrzyki district was
finally restored to Poland by the Soviet Union in 1951.

The Kingdom of Galicia and Lodomeria had died in 1918. Thirty years
later, the community of ex-Galicians had effectively been broken up and
dispersed. Their multinational homeland had been completely ground to
pieces. In the end, ex-Galician society fell victim to the two great totalitarian monsters of the twentieth century. But clearly it also harboured
elements within its own make-up that could be driven to ugly, murderous violence. Some of its Ruthenians/Ukrainians had voluntarily joined
the Nazi service, and some in the wartime countryside had engaged in
Nazi-style crimes against Poles. Some of its Poles and Jews had joined
Stalin's cause, and became complicit in Soviet crimes, especially in
1939–41. Seventy years after the event, revelations are emerging only
now about shameful crimes perpetrated by Polish peasants against fugitive Jews.[97] Observers will be tempted to ask whether the Galicians, if
left to their own devices, might not have descended to the sort of intercommunal atrocities that broke out, for example, in Yugoslavia. The
question is unhistorical, and the answer can never be known – though

* The Warthegau, i.e. the District of the River Warthe, was the Nazi name for Great Poland.

it can be easily asked by people whose country has never been occupied or subjected to the sort of apocalypse which struck the former Galicia.

III

Museums are an established feature of contemporary cultural, social and intellectual life. They are the conscious product of attempts to keep in touch with the past, and sometimes to reconstruct it systematically. Traditionally, they have displayed a strong material emphasis – on the collection, preservation, analysis and display of historical objects – and a tendency, perhaps inevitable, to reflect the priorities of their paymasters. Few museums set out to be completely impartial or inclusive, and none succeed in being so.[98]

Modern museums have grown from a very long tradition that goes back to ancient Greece. The *Mouseion* or 'Seat of the Muses' at Alexandria, which housed the famous Library, was the prototype of many later institutions. During the Renaissance a *cabinet de curiosités* or *Raritätenkammer* became essential for self-respecting rulers and aristocrats. The collections of Cosimo I de' Medici in Florence and Rudolf II in Prague were unsurpassed. Claims to be Europe's oldest public museum are disputed between the Grimani Collection in Venice (1523), the Ole Worm Collection in Copenhagen (1654) and the Ashmolean Museum in Oxford (1677). Europe's leading state museums include the Vatican's Capitoline Museum (1734), the British Museum in London (1759), the Prado in Madrid (1784), the Louvre in Paris (1793) and the Rijksmuseum in Amsterdam (1800). The theory and practice behind museums used to be called museography, but nowadays museology, or museum studies, is more common.[99] Not everyone, though, is impressed. 'A museum', said Pablo Picasso, 'is just a collection of lies.'[100]

The Kingdom of Galicia and Lodomeria flourished in an era when state and national museums were becoming a fixture of every major European capital. The complex of Royal Museums in Berlin (see pp. 390–91) was particularly imposing. Not to be outdone, Emperor Franz-Joseph opened two grand museums on adjacent sites in Vienna in 1891 to form his own *Museumviertel* or 'Museum Quarter'. One, the *Kunsthistorisches Museum*, was devoted to art history; the other, the *Naturhistorisches*, to natural science. The older Germanic National Museum at Nuremberg, which was launched in 1853 by patrons linked to the movement for German unification, had a consciously national and non-dynastic purpose.

So too did the magnificent Szépművészeti Museum of Fine Arts in Budapest (1906). These were the benchmarks to which all Central European museum creators aspired.

Galicia possessed its own more modest array of museums. In Lemberg, the oldest, the Ossolineum, was founded in 1817 by (and named after) a local landowner and literary patron. Its origins and contents were later described in a popular guidebook:

> At Ossoliński Street 2, in an extensive park, stands the Ossolineum (The National Ossoliński Institute). It consists of two parts: the Library founded by Count Jozef Maksymilian Ossoliński ... and the Museum initiated in 1823 by a grant from Prince Henryk Lubomirski. The collections are located in a former Carmelite Convent, which was once ... a military cookhouse. [Before] 1869 ... they were subjected to all sorts of governmental interference. The Library consists of 142,000 books, 5,000 manuscripts, 5,300 autographs and 1,700 documents. The Lubomirski Museum ... [that merged] in 1870 with the rest of the collections ... has since grown enormously.[101]

In addition to books and documents, the collection contained historical paintings, costumes, coins, flags, armour and assorted militaria. The Dzieduszycki Museum, founded in 1855, was devoted primarily to ornithology and ethnography. Its prize exhibit was a prehistoric hairy rhinoceros unearthed near Stanisławów.[102] A small Ruthenian exhibition was a distinctly poor relation.

The twin stars of Kraków's museums were the Czartoryski and the *Narodowe* or 'National'. Set up within a year of each other in 1878–9, the former originated in a private aristocratic collection. The latter was launched by a municipal committee determined to display the grandiose canvases of the Polish National School.

Princess Izabella Czartoryska (1746–1835) née Fleming was as rich as she was patriotic as she was debauched. At a juncture when one of her sons was the leading minister of the tsar, she set out to collect everything and anything that would help preserve the memory of the late Polish-Lithuanian Commonwealth, and much else besides. Her estate at Puławy near Lublin had just been incorporated into 'New Galicia', and she created two collections there, one in the Temple of the Sibyl (1801) and the other in the Galician House (1803). Within a few years, however, Puławy found itself again under Russian control. Exhibitions of Polish patriotism were not tolerated, and the remnants of the plundered contents were transferred, after many peripatations, to Kraków, where in the late nineteenth century visitors could admire them in peace. By then, the husband rather than the wife was being given the credit:

> *The Museum of the Princes Czartoryski* represents first-class scientific and artistic value ... Its origins go back to the end of the XVIII Century, when General Adam Czartoryski ... began to collect souvenirs of the past in Puławy ... After the catastrophe of [the November Rising] in 1831, [important sections] were lost. But others survived in Paris [and elsewhere] ... Only *c.* 1880 were they reassembled by Prince Władysław Czartoryski in Kraków, in the former Piarist Monastery ... The pearls of the collection are a Marble Venus from Naples, the Etruscan Ware, Egyptian antiquities, 12th Century enameled Limoges crosses, 7000 pieces of armour, 4000 coins and medals, 500 paintings and miniatures, 20,000 prints and drawings ... and the grand standard of the Russian Tsar captured [in 1610] by [Hetman] Żółkiewski.[103]

These Galician museums stayed intact until the Second World War. But in 1939–45, state-backed looting was only one of many disasters to befall them. The Czartoryski Museum eventually recovered its Leonardo, *Lady with an Ermine*, but not its Raphael, *Portrait of a Young Man*. The Ossolineum lost its Dürers, presumably to Nazi looters, before the institution was broken up by Soviet decree. One half was to remain in L'viv to form part of a purely Ukrainian complex. The other half, including the original manuscript of Mickiewicz's *Pan Tadeusz*, was to be shipped to Wrocław in Silesia, where, following post-war frontier changes, the Polish collection was to be resurrected.

In the Soviet-run world, however, no museum managers would have dared to celebrate the Galician heritage as such. Their focus lay instead on Communist class themes or on exclusively national stories. Soviet Ukraine cultivated a uniquely hostile vision of the former Galicia. All ills were attributed to Polish class oppression; the oppressors were Poles, and all the oppressed were Ukrainians. Galicia's multinational panorama was equally unwelcome to officials of the post-war Polish People's Republic. Poland's historic link with the eastern part of the kingdom, and with L'viv, was a taboo subject, where numerous blank spots were kept deliberately blank. At the same time, Communist cultural policy recognized the importance of museums as instruments of educational and social control, which ensured they were completely subordinated to ideology and to current political goals.

By the time the Soviet bloc disintegrated in 1989–91, Galicia had been seventy years in the grave. Both the museologists and the public at large had grown accustomed to a highly selective view of the past. Henceforth the Marxist approach was condemned, but nationalist assumptions persisted. Financial resources and new ideas were in short supply. Change came slowly.

Given that Ukrainian L'viv had spent 145 years as the capital of the Kingdom of Galicia and Lodomeria, one might expect that the city's museums would devote substantial space to the 'Austrian Period'. Visitors soon discover that the expectation is misplaced. Contemporary L'viv betrays little interest either in Galicia as a whole or in the former realities of 'Lemberg'. Two decades after the fall of Communism, no prominent exhibition in seven main museums addresses Habsburg times. In the L'viv Historical Museum on the central *Rynok* there is an exhibition on the ancient world, another on the medieval world and a third on 'Literary L'viv in the early 20th Century'. A special department concentrates on everyday life in bygone 'Halichyna'; and there are galleries displaying paintings, jewellery, porcelain, military orders and armour. A permanent exhibition celebrates 'The Struggle of the Ukrainian People for National Independence', but treats Austrian Galicia as just one of successive foreign occupations – in which 'the people' are assumed to be exclusively Ukrainian. One meets no awareness that 'Halichyna' and 'Galicia' are not quite the same thing.[104]

In Kraków, sometime chief city of western Galicia, one can encounter the same lack of interest. The focus here is Polish as opposed to Ukrainian, but the prevailing myopia is remarkably similar. The Muzeum Narodowe in Kraków, housed in the medieval Cloth Hall and splendidly renovated, cultivates the national strand of memory and little else – just like its counterpart in L'viv. In the main displays and in the principal buildings, the emphasis is on the nineteenth-century school of Polish art; the star exhibits are the colossal canvases, often on historical subjects, by painters such as Matejko, Chełmoński or Malczewski. As one enters, one still sees the inscription which announces that this is a shrine to the culture of the Polish nation. A certain indulgence towards late Austrian times when the Polish element had gained the upper hand can be sensed. Even so, the strength of the chosen perspective is striking. It was reinforced during the decades of the People's Republic when officialdom was bent on promoting a sense of national identity among a distressed, displaced and often disaffected population.[105]

A visit to the Czartoryski Museum prompts different thoughts. Paintings and antiquities apart, the exhibits include a remarkable *cabinet de curiosités*. The original intention, one suspects, was to simply impress the multitude, though today's viewers may find themselves wondering whether the identifications of the objects are true or false:

- The harp of Marie Leszczyńska, queen of France (1703–68).
- The violin of her father, Stanisław Leszczyński, king of Poland.
- The silver hat badge of King Stefan Batory (r. 1576–86).
- The knife and fork of Queen Barbara Radziwiłł (d. 1551).
- Jan Sobieski's camp bed from the Siege of Vienna (1683).
- Voltaire's quill.
- Rousseau's briefcase.
- The Marshal's tipstaff from the Diet of 3 May 1791.
- Kościuszko's standard (1794).

The most dramatic exhibit of all, proudly displayed behind plate glass, is a half-gnawed, rock-solid, bright green chunk of mouldy bread. It was allegedly cast aside by the none-too-hungry Napoleon on the morning when he re-crossed the Berezina in December 1812, then picked up and preserved by his hungry but loyal soldiers. Like all holy relics, genuine or fake, it has immense powers of imaginatory stimulation. Above it, there hangs the inscription that once hung over the entrance to the Temple of the Sibyl in Puławy. It reads 'PRZESZŁOŚĆ PRZYSZŁOŚCI', 'The Past in the Service of the Future'.[106]

Whose past and whose future? one wonders. Two hundred years ago, the 'Past' for the Czartoryskis was that of the late Polish-Lithuanian Commonwealth, and the 'Future' was the happy time when the Commonwealth was going to be restored. The collection was established before the Congress of Vienna dashed all hopes of a restoration, so its conceptual basis has stood still for two centuries. It is no place to learn about Galicia. The museum's planned reorganization, which may return part of the holdings to Puławy, clearly offers opportunities for reflection.[107]

Most museologists would recognize here the clutch of problems that centre on the near-universal idea of the 'excluded past'. They struggle to find ways of reintroducing topics that for one reason or another have been neglected or actively suppressed.[108] In the United States, for example, the Native American heritage and the history of slavery long suffered from official denial, and it is only recently that the omissions have been rectified.[109] In Australia, it was the appalling history of the near-extermination of the Aborigines. In Russia, despite the efforts of the Memorial Association, the crimes of the Soviet regime largely escape attention; there is certainly no museum recording the history of its victims. In most countries, including Britain, the histories of women, of children, of the poor, have not been expounded with enthusiasm. In Poland and Ukraine, the successor states to Galicia, a great deal remains to be done if Galicia's memory is not to fall into oblivion.

A step in the right direction was taken in 1995 when a new *Muzeum Galicja* opened in the Kazimierz district of Kraków. It has won many plaudits for its innovatory methods of recovering 'The Traces of Memory'. Its basic collection has been assembled round photographs by the late Chris Schwarz, who travelled far and wide to record 'what could still be recorded of a lost civilisation'. Yet, as its English name indicates, the Galicia Jewish Museum was conceived as a tribute to Jewish life in the former Galicia, not to Galician life as a whole. There are five sections:

- Jewish Life in Ruins.
- Jewish Culture as it once was.
- Sites of Massacre and Destruction.
- How the Past is being remembered.
- People Making Memory.

In 2008, three additional exhibitions were on view: 'Fighting with Dignity: Jewish Resistance in Kraków, 1939–45', 'March '68 in the Kraków Press', and 'Polish Heroes: those who rescued Jews'. *Muzeum Galicja* is an admirable antidote both to the effects of the Holocaust and to the lamentable tendency to bypass the age-old Jewish presence, yet it too presents something short of the full story.[110] The fact remains that the sum total of current memory-making leaves much to be desired. The rich, multi-layered legacy of Galicia stays in the shadows. The kingdom 'as it really was' remains at best half-forgotten or half-remembered.

One ray of hope in this regard may well be found beyond the territory of the former Galicia, in Silesia. Contacts between the Ossolineum Institute, relocated to Wrocław in 1946, and its sister institution in L'viv, were all but eliminated. After 1991, however, it reorganized itself as a private foundation, and secured legal ownership of its most important possessions,[111] and now has an explicit mission to bridge the gap between Poland and Ukraine. Rehoused in the former German Gymnasium of St Matthias, and magnificently refurbished, it operates in an environment where international reconciliation is an everyday issue, and where knowledge of Polish-German issues may assist in the handling of Polish-Ukrainian issues. Since German Breslau, like Austrian Galicia, possessed a strong Jewish presence, it may help to reintegrate Jewish memory, too. The Stefanyk Library in L'viv, less accustomed to the new opportunities and more strapped for cash, adapted more slowly,[112] but practical co-operation and a measure of trust are being re-established. New vistas are opening up in the new era of digitization and of exhibition-sharing. In the twenty-first century this L'viv–Wrocław axis offers one of the best prospects for resuscitating Galician heritage.

Another positive development of a completely different type is located in the town of Nowy Sącz, not far from Krynica, where an open-air ethnographic museum admirably illustrates the difficulties of adapting to a new political environment and of recovering comprehensive memories. The exhibits consist mainly of rural buildings, transported from their original sites and carefully reassembled. The most interesting aspect, though, is that in Galician times the surrounding district straddled the divide between predominantly Polish and predominantly Ukrainian settlement; the adjoining township of Stary Sącz was home to a vibrant Jewish community.

When the museum was first conceived in the 1960s, the cultural authorities of the Polish People's Republic were eager to promote a strange mixture of Marxist historical materialism and old-fashioned 'Blood and Soil' nationalism. It was judged essential to pretend that the territory of the Republic coincided exactly with Poland's immemorial 'historic lands'. Talk of 'ethnic minorities' was suppressed; all museums were subject to rigorous state censorship; and any deviation risked punishment. It was not possible, for example, to let it be known that the area south-east of Nowy Sącz had been inhabited until recently by people of Ruthenian/Ukrainian descent. And any hint of the ethnic cleansing undertaken by the Communist regime during 'Operation Vistula' would have been construed as a criminal offence.

In the museum's early days, therefore, nothing was said directly about Poles, Ukrainians or Jews. Instead, the exhibition space was divided into four sectors, each devoted to one of four 'ethnographic groups' – *Pogórzanie* (Hill People), *Górale* (Highlanders) *Lemkos* and *Lachy*. Each of the groups, it was explained, enjoyed their own dress, customs, dialects and socio-economic organization. The use of the term *Lachy* is particularly curious. It is the standard Ukrainian word for Poles, and it was presumably chosen to avoid explaining that the neighbouring Lemkos were a branch of the Ukrainians. In all probability it referred to the Polish peasants of the mid-Galician plain, who practised arable farming as opposed to the pastoral economy of the hill and mountain groups.

To be fair, the museum's initial *raison d'être* was to provide a record of traditional rural life, which was fast disappearing under the pressures of industrialization. Care was taken, in good Marxist style, to distinguish between the primitive cabins of landless labourers and the more substantial dwellings of richer owners. Even so, there were glaring omissions. There was no church, no manor house, and not a single reminder of the Jewish presence.[113]

Since 1989 the contents of the museum have evolved in several directions. First, the updated guidebook now speaks of three 'ethnic minorities' – Germans, Jews and Roma – alongside the four 'ethnographic groups', and exhibits have been added relating to each of them. Secondly, a number of rural churches and chapels have been introduced. There are fine examples of wooden sacral architecture, Roman Catholic, Uniate, Orthodox and Lutheran, but as yet no sign of a synagogue. Thirdly, with assistance from European Union funds, a separate area has been set aside to reconstruct a typical *miasteczko galicyjskie* or 'Galician townlet'. As of 2009, when building works were still incomplete, the Yiddish word of *shtetl* was not being used, but it would be very surprising if the overall Jewish accent were not considerably strengthened. For the time being, visitors are greeted with a photographic exhibition of Jewish sites and cemeteries in Galicia, and also with a klezmer concert and an introduction to Jewish cooking.[114]

A stroll round the museum takes two or three hours, or more if the richly furnished interiors are properly inspected. Over sixty buildings offer great variety, from a poor peasant's cabin from Lipnica Wielka (*c.* 1850), to an early nineteenth-century linseed oil-mill from Słopnice; from a thatched cottage of a country labourer from Podegrod (1846), to a wooden Greek Catholic church of St Demetrius from Czarne (1786); from a Roma complex of two dwellings and a forge from Czarna, to an early eighteenth-century manor house from Rdzawa near Bochnia. For all its dilemmas, this collection of Galician rural architecture and folklore is more typical of the former Galicia, and is more inclusive, than are the art galleries and highbrow museums.[115] Yet it can never be complete. The 'real', the authentic, the 'total Galicia' remains tantalizingly out of reach.

The present challenge facing local historians and museologists would have been well understood by Galicians. In the wake of the latest political shift in 1989, the bearers of the Polish, Ukrainian and Jewish heritages are confronted, like their ancestors, by the need to find paths towards compromise and cohabitation. They have somehow to shelve their selfish interests, and to seek out themes of common concern. It is to be hoped that something can be achieved before the centenary of Galicia's demise in 2018. A touch of Galician humour would help. So, too, would the old Habsburg motto: '*Viribus Unitis*'.

Etruria

French Snake in the Tuscan Grass

(1801–1814)

I

Florence – Firenze – the chief city of Tuscany and cradle of the Renaissance – is the Mecca of all art-seekers. They come in their millions from all over the world, gazing at the buildings, the paintings and the sculpture, walking the streets that were walked by Dante, Fra Angelico and Michelangelo, breathing the air inhaled by Giotto, by Leonardo and by Galileo. I myself was one of them, taken at a tender age to see the great masterpieces, and shortly afterwards to the gates of Paradise Lost at nearby Vall'Ombrosa, where John Milton imagined Satan's legions as 'Angel Forms'

> who lay intrans't,
> Thick as Autumnal Leaves that strow the Brooks
> In *Vallombrosa*, where th'*Etrurian* shades
> High overarch't imbowr;[1]

Milton was consciously writing in the epic tradition of Homer, Virgil and Dante. James Joyce, another literary pilgrim to Italy, described *Paradise Lost* as 'a Puritan transcript of the Divine Comedy'.[2]

Like all medieval cities, Florence has an ancient heart that covers just a couple of square miles. The only good way to see it is on foot. A stroll from the Ponte Vecchio, the 'Old Bridge', across the River Arno to the central Piazza della Signoria takes only a few minutes, and one can walk round the line of the medieval walls in a morning or an afternoon. On arriving in Florence, therefore, one is faced by a mass of adverts and agencies which offer the services of private guides and of guided tours. A typical enterprise offers six alternative tours: 'Introduction to Florence', 'The Golden Age', 'The Medici Dynasty', 'Life in Medieval Florence', 'Unusual Florence' and 'Florence for Children'. The last of these options,

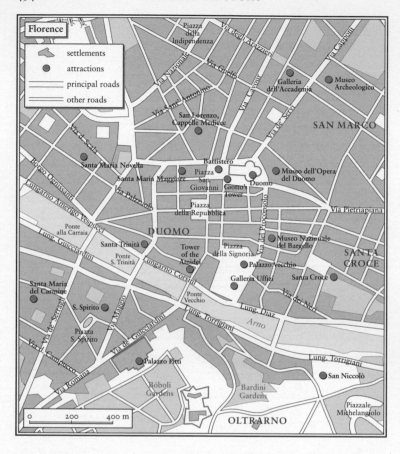

it is promised, can be enjoyed no less by accompanying adults. The attractions include 'climbing the Duomo tower', 'visiting a castle', 'how children lived', 'trying on period clothing' and 'watching artists at work.'[3]

Most guidebooks recommend a one- or two-day tour in the company of an interpreter, followed by a lifetime of individual exploration. After all, one is entering a city that claims to possess one-fifth of all the world's 'Old Masters':

Day 1
The Accademia Gallery, starring Michelangelo's *David*.
The Monastery of San Marco: Fra Angelico murals.
The Medici Chapels.

The Cathedral Baptistery and Ghiberti's Bronze Doors.
Giotto's Tower.
Dinner near the Piazza della Signoria.

Day 2
The Bargello Museum.
The Duomo Museum, including Donatello.
The Church of Santa Maria Novella, Masaccio.
The Uffizi Galleries: reserve a month in advance.
Dinner in the Oltrarno district.[4]

Why do they say Oltrarno in Florence, but Trastevere in Rome?*

The literary cognoscenti choose the Dante Trail. Dante Alighieri (1265–1321) not only pioneered vernacular literature in Europe, he preceded all the other geniuses that Florence produced, and set the Renaissance in motion. The trail always begins at the Sasso di Dante, 'Dante's Stone', from which the poet is said to have watched the laying of the cathedral's foundations in 1296. Next, inside the cathedral, one gazes at Domenico di Michelino's astonishing depiction of *Dante and his Poem* (1465), which portrays the garlanded and red-robed poet holding up a copy of his *Divine Comedy*. On the right of the picture rise the walls and turrets of Florence, with the Duomo behind; on the left, the pit of Hell, the mountain of Purgatory and the heaven of Paradise.

From the cathedral, the guide leads his party along the trail to the houses of the Portinari family. Dante's Beatrice, the idealized woman who leads the poet from *Purgatorio* to *Paradiso*, was a Portinari who died young. The group passes thence in a couple of minutes to Dante's own home, La Casa di Dante. Nearby stands the Palazzo del Bargello, a glowering structure that was once the seat of the *podestà* or 'governor'. It was here, in 1301, that Dante's banishment from Florence was proclaimed; a sentence that flowed from some obscure factional feud, it was a cruel prelude to a lifetime's exile and to the endless moods of simmering anger and gnawing nostalgia that drove his pen through a hundred cantos. Outside the church of Santa Croce, one sees Pezzi's over-life-size statue of Dante (1865) and inside, Ricci's cenotaph to the Altissimo Poetà (1829). Santa Croce contains the tombs of Michelangelo

---

* Florence's district of Oltrarno, literally 'on the other side of the Arno', is the counterpart of Trastevere, 'on the other side of the Tiber', in Rome.

and of Galileo, but not, of course, of Dante. Florence's greatest son was not allowed home even to die.

Passing along the Via dei Neri, the 'Street of the Blacks', one is reminded of the rival factions whose feuds ruined Florentine politics. The Guelphs drove out the Ghibellines, before the victorious Guelphs themselves split into Blacks and Whites. Dante had belonged to the Whites, who lost out. At the former Palazzo dei Priori, one can still see the rooms where Dante participated in municipal meetings before his banishment.

In Dante's time, the great open space of the Signoria was filled by the palaces of the powerful Uberti clan. Earlier in the thirteenth century the Uberti had championed the pro-imperial Ghibelline party. After the triumph of their anti-imperial Guelph enemies, their palaces were razed, leaving a void that can be seen and felt to this day.

Beside the Ponte Vecchio, the Tower of the Amidei is associated with the murder in 1215 of a young nobleman, Buondelmonte dei Buondelmonti, who had spurned a daughter of one of the oldest Florentine families, the Amidei. The murder is alluded to in Dante's *Paradiso*, and was said to have sparked the original feud between Guelphs and Ghibellines. The nearby church of Santa Trinità used to house Cimabue's *Madonna* (c.1280), which would have been known to Dante but which now hangs in the Uffizi. In Santa Maria Maggiore lies the tomb of Brunetto Latini, the Florentine philosopher to whom Dante was intellectually indebted. Despite placing him in the *Inferno* in the Ring of the Sodomites, Dante says to him: *'m'insegnavate come l'uom s'etterna'*, 'you taught me how man makes himself eternal'.[5] The tour ends at the church of Santa Maria Novella, where one admires the frescoes of the Strozzi chapel painted by Filippino Lippi, and the great crucifix painted by Giotto, Cimabue's pupil and Dante's contemporary.[6]

The poet, torn between admiration of his native city and disgust at its vices, railed bitterly in the *Inferno* against the ingratitude of his compatriots, who appeared to forget him:

> *Godi, Fiorenza, poi che se' sì grande,*
> *che per mare e per terra batti l'ali,*
> *e per lo 'nferno tuo nome si spande!*

> Rejoice, O Florence, you are so great
> That your wings beat over land and sea,
> And your name resounds through Hell![7]

Or again:

> Florence mine, you might well be content . . .
> You are rich, you're at peace, and you're wise . . .
> [Yet], if you recall your past, and think clearly,
> You will see yourself like a woman fallen sick
> Who cannot find repose on the softest down,
> Twisting, turning and seeking to ease her pain.[8]

Dante called her Fiorenza – half-way between the Latin Florentia and the modern Firenze – but he need not have worried about his reputation in his native city. As we can see in a second set of frescoes in Santa Maria Novella, painted by Nardo di Cenio in the 1350s, Dante became a celebrity within a generation of his death.

Niccolò Machiavelli (1469–1527) is another towering genius whose presence in Florence can sometimes be overshadowed by his contemporaries. His tomb in Santa Croce bears the inscription 'TANTO NOMINI NULLUM PAR ELOGIUM': 'No praise is sufficient for so great a man.' Machiavelli was a man after Dante's own heart: mordant, searingly honest, frequently funny, sardonic, and breathtaking in every other line he wrote. They would have got on famously. Machiavelli was an accomplished historian. His *History of Florence* (1520–25) is sometimes regarded as the pioneering work of modern European history; yet he is best known for his scintillating political commentary, *Il Principe*, *The Prince*. His no-nonsense advice to ruling princes made him famous. 'A prince must learn *not* to be always good,' he wrote, 'but to be good or not as needs require.' In the future, several of the world's greatest statesmen were to keep a copy of Machiavelli in their pocket or at their bedside.[9]

Such is the force of the Renaissance, however, that many visitors to Florence fail to realize that the city's history cannot fairly be confined to one brilliant age. The city's website lists thirteen main periods:

Foundation of the Roman colony, Florentia (59 BC).
Byzantine and Lombard periods.
The Carolingians.
Florence of the Communes.
13th Century: Guelphs and Ghibellines.
From the 14th Century to the Renaissance.
The Renaissance.

Great names of the 16th Century.
Decline of the Medici to 1737.
The Lorraine Period.
Risorgimento.
Florence as the capital of the Kingdom of Italy.
Florence of the Novecento (20th Century).[10]

Two or three more periods may safely be added, especially if Florence's
surroundings are included. One of them, prior to Florentia's founding,
was that of the Etruscans, when present-day Tuscany lay at the centre of
Italy's most prominent prehistoric civilization. Another, in our own day,
sees Florence at the heart of a huge influx of migrants and foreigners,
who come to savour the 'simple life' that has been drowned elsewhere
by modern living.[11] The world of Dante and Machiavelli forms a suitable backdrop to a countryside where medieval villages and ancient
farmhouses snuggle among the olive groves, and where the rich bask in
the sun, sip Chianti, lament the modern rat race, and idealize vigor-
ously:

> For dinner tonight, we've stopped at the *rosticceria* and picked up some
> divine *gnocchi* made from semolina flour. I've made a salad. Ed brings out
> the Ambrae from Montepulciano and holds it up to the light. *Ambrae* . . .
> must be Latin, possibly for amber. I take a sip – maybe it *is* ambiance, the
> way dew on lilacs and oak leaves might taste. *Wine is light, held together
> by water.* I wish I'd said that, but Galileo did.
>
>   From the yard above the road, I see the cypresses graph a rise and fall
> against a sky blown clean of clouds by this afternoon's wind. Stars are
> shooting over the valley, stars that fell even before the Etruscans watched
> from this hillside . . . Five, six, stars streak across the sky. I hold out my
> hand to catch one.[12]

This is not a backward-looking city, however. Its president (that is,
mayor), elected in February 2009, is a young, dynamic, centre-left politician, who is tipped to leap to the forefront of Italy's national politics.
Matteo Renzi (b. 1975) is demanding a clean-out of Berlusconi's Augean
Stables. His views are condensed in a book entitled *Fuori!* ('Out!').
'I get nauseous thinking about Italy's political class,' he says; 'it has
done nothing in thirty years, and spends its time arguing on chat
shows.'[13]

*

Florence guards its secrets well. Those who know the city best are aware
of things that never cross the path of the average tourist. The British
colony in Florence, for example, goes back to medieval times. It did not
originate with the stream of temporary visitors, like John Milton in
1638, who came here on the Grand Tour but then returned home,
though it obviously did much to enliven the stay of such artistic tourists.
It has been graced, among others, by such notables as George Nassau,
3rd Earl Cowper and Reichsfürst of the Holy Roman Empire (1739–89);
Lord Henry Somerset (1849–1932), songwriter, sometime comptroller
of Queen Victoria's household and former husband of Lady Isabella
Somers-Cocks; Una, Lady Troubridge (1887–1963), sculptress and
sometime wife of an admiral; the inter-war group of English ladies
known as *I Scorpioni* ('The Scorpions'), who featured in Franco Zef-
firelli's film *Tea with Mussolini* (1999); and most recently Sir Harold
Acton (1904–94), author of the inimitable *Memoirs of an Aesthete*
(1948). A parallel list of literary names would include Radclyffe Hall
(1880–1943), author of *The Well of Loneliness* (1928); Violet Paget
(Vernon Lee, 1856–1935), novelist and inventor of the concept of
'empathy'; Violet Keppel-Trefusis (1894–1972), daughter of King
Edward VII's mistress;[14] and the extraordinary double-bodied poet
Michael Field (Katherine Bradley, 1846–1914 and Edith Cooper, 1862–
1913), affectionately known as 'the Mikes'. All of these exiles (and
many more) can be described as art-lovers, bohemians and connoisseurs, and many were aristocrats, real or imagined. Yet they did not
advertise the most important cause of their exile. All, or nearly all, were
fugitives from the British law, and many were devoted to personal rela-
tionships that in Dante's time – as in the case of Brunetto Latini – would
have alerted the so-called 'Office of the Night'. Habitual pretence was
part of the game. Harold Acton threatened to sue on hearing that he
might be 'outed' by a biographer and, while claiming to be merely
observing 'certain men in Florence', coined the immortal phrase, 'the
queerer, the dearer'.[15]

Another secret pertains to a further period of Florentine history,
which followed the 'Lorraine Period' and preceded the Risorgimento,
but which the city's website fails to mention. For reasons not entirely
clear, few guidebooks even mention its leading figure, the ghost that
stalks the Florentine feast. He was a great man with Florentine roots,
who transformed Europe and was said always to carry a copy of *Il
Principe* on his person.

I I

Napoleon Bonaparte, as he became, was not a Frenchman. Born in
Ajaccio in 1769, he was a Corsican, and his native language was *corsi-*
cano, an Italian dialect similar to Genoese. Admittedly, he was a French
subject from birth, having entered this world just a year after France
bought Corsica from the city of Genoa; but he did not start to learn
French until he was ten, nor Frenchify his name until the age of twenty-
six. Less well known is the fact that the Buonaparti were a family of
Florentine descent. The main branch had been lords of Fucecchio
between Florence and Pisa in Dante's time, and a lesser branch left Tuscany for Corsica in the sixteenth century. Except for a flying visit in
1784, when he needed to obtain a certificate of noble origin in order to
start officers' training in the French army, Napoleon did not see Italy
until his late twenties. When he finally arrived for a longer stay, on what
might now be thought of as a business trip, one of the first things he did
was to visit Florence and look up his long-lost relatives.

Like many Corsicans, Nabuleone Buonaparte possessed a potent sense
of family solidarity. His parents and their seven other children were to play
a central part in his life. His father, Carlo-Maria Buonaparte (1746–85)
died young, aged thirty-nine; his mother, Maria-Letizia Ramolino (1750–
1836), lived fifty years a widow. Except for Giuseppe (Joseph, 1768–1844),
all of Nabuleone's siblings were born after him. His three younger brothers
were Luciano (Lucien, 1775–1840), Luigi (Louis, 1779–1846) and Girolamo (Jérôme, 1784–1860); his three sisters were Maria-Anna
(1777–1820), Maria-Paolina (1780–1825) and Carolina-Maria (1782–
1839). They collectively milked the connection with their celebrated
brother for all they were worth.[16]

It was the Italian campaign of 1796 – Year V according to the revolutionary calendar – that brought the young General Bonaparte to the
notice of the whole Continent, and vaulted him into the upper reaches
of French politics and international affairs. He set out in the spring of
that year to carry the war to the Austrian Empire, which had been a
thorn in the flesh of the French Republic for the previous three years;
and he ended the campaigning season having conquered great swathes
of Austrian territory in Italy. He had been sent out from France as a
servant of the collective leadership of the revolutionary Directory, and
returned as the arbiter of its decisions. Surrounded by a crowd of imper-

ial provinces, Italian duchies, Papal States and city-republics, he became the destroyer of crowns, a maker of kingdoms.[17]

The sheer speed and brilliance of that first Italian campaign created the emotional shock which drove forward the subsequent torrent of political changes. The twenty-six-year-old took command of the Army of Italy immediately after marrying Joséphine de Beauharnais on 9 March, scattering the Austrians at Millesimo on 13 April and the Piedmontese at Mondovi on the 22nd. Within three weeks he had crushed the main Austrian force at Lodi, and on 15 May entered Milan. The Kingdom of Sardinia made peace, France annexed Nice and Savoy, and the puppet Lombardic Republic was launched. Fighting resumed in the late summer, ending with yet another victory for Bonaparte over the Austrians at the Battle of Arcola (15–17 November). By that time, the Cispadane Republic was already in business at Bologna.*

General Bonaparte visited Florence during the summer interval between the two rounds of campaigning. On 29 June he arrived at the little town of San Miniato in the Val d'Arno,† and met the Abbé Filippo Buonaparte, who was described as his *zio* or 'uncle'. They talked of changing family fortunes, and visited the family tombs in the church of San Francesco. San Miniato is often publicized as Italy's 'capital of truffles', of which Napoleon was inordinately fond. 'Triumphant on the battlefield,' writes one connoisseur, 'Napoleon also ate truffles for strength in his tussles between the covers with the fiery Josephine.'[18] The Tartuffians do not record whether it was before or after his visit to San Miniato that he gained an appetite for the reputed aphrodisiac. Yet the encounter with his ancestors would undoubtedly have strengthened Bonaparte's feeling that he and his siblings might be destined for greater things in Italy.[19]

Bonaparte had driven to San Miniato from the coast at Livorno, which French troops had entered a couple of days earlier on the pretext of the French flag being insulted there. Livorno was the chief port of the Grand Duchy of Tuscany, with which France was not officially at war, but everyone knew that Tuscan troops had been sent to bolster the Austrians and that Tuscany's neutrality was observed in the breach:

---

* Like the names of the French Republic's *départements*, all the names of republics created in Italy were based on geographical features. 'Lombardic' refers to the Plain of Lombardy; 'Cispadane' means 'On this side of the River Po'; 'Cisalpine' means 'On this side of the Alps'.
† Not to be confused with San Miniato del Monte, which directly overlooks the city.

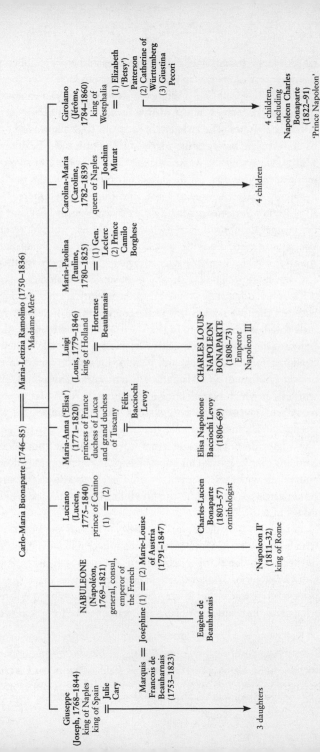

I Buonaparti: the Bonapartes

Carlo-Maria Buonaparte (1746–85) ══ Maria-Letizia Ramolino (1750–1836) 'Madame Mère'

Giuseppe (Joseph, 1768–1844) king of Naples king of Spain ══ Julie Cary

3 daughters

NABULEONE (Napoléon, 1769–1821) general, consul, emperor of the French

Marquis ══ Joséphine (1) ══ (2) Marie-Louise François de Beauharnais (1753–1823)

Eugène de Beauharnais

Marie-Louise of Austria (1791–1847)

'Napoléon II' (1811–32) king of Rome

Luciano (Lucien, 1775–1840) prince of Canino (1) ══ (2)

Charles-Lucien Bonaparte (1803–57) ornithologist

Maria-Anna ('Elisa') (1771–1820) princess of France duchess of Lucca and grand duchess of Tuscany ══ Félix Bacciochi Levoy

Elisa Napoleone Bacciochi Levoy (1806–69)

Luigi (Louis, 1779–1846) king of Holland ══ Hortense Beauharnais

CHARLES LOUIS-NAPOLEON BONAPARTE (1808–73) Emperor Napoleon III

Maria-Paolina (Pauline, 1780–1825) ══ (1) Gen. Leclerc (2) Prince Camilo Borghese

Carolina-Maria (Caroline, 1782–1839) queen of Naples ══ Joachim Murat

4 children

Girolamo (Jérôme, 1784–1860) king of Westphalia ══ (1) Elizabeth ('Betsy') Patterson (2) Catherine of Württemberg (3) Giustina Pecori

4 children, including Napoleon Charles Bonaparte (1822–91) 'Prince Napoleon'

On the 27th of June the French entered [Livorno], and a few hours previous to their arrival, every English ship in the mole, twenty-three in number, sailed for Corsica, conveying a considerable quantity of merchandize, two hundred and forty oxen, and most of the families belonging to the English factory; for our minister at Florence, Hon. W. F. Wyndham, and our consul at Livorno [John Udney, Esq.] who had both been indefatigable in procuring good intelligence, knew of the scheme long before its execution.[20]

Livorno would not cease to be a source of trouble.

On 1 July, the general paid a visit to Grand Duke Ferdinando III of Tuscany at the Pitti Palace in Florence. The grand-ducal residence, one of Florence's most historic buildings, lacked nothing for such important occasions, its external surroundings in the Boboli Gardens being no less splendid than the grand interior:

> The Palazzo Pitti was begun after the design of Filippo di Ser Brunellesco, the most celebrated architect of the fifteenth century, and finished by Ammannati. In the courtyard is the basso-rilievo of a mule, who constantly drew the sledge which contained the materials employed in the building; and over [it] is a statue of Hercules, and near it a group like that called Ajax Telamon, of a soldier going to inter his dead comrade. The ceilings of this palace painted in *tempera* by Pietro de Cortona and his scholars, represent the patriotic action of the Medici family, under emblems taken from heathen mythology ...
>
> The Royal Apartments are splendidly adorned with gilding, beautiful tables of Florentine mosaic-work, superb silver statues, and some of the most celebrated pictues in the world, namely by Salvator Rosa, Rubens, Fra Bartolomeo, Titian, Carlo Dolci, Raphael!!!, Andrea del Sarto, Vandyck!!!, Buonarotti!!!, and Rembrandt!!! ...
>
> The *Giardino di Boboli* is very large, and contains several pieces of sculpture, the most remarkable of which are the fountain of the great walk decorated with a colossal Neptune standing on a granite bason, by Giovanni di Bologna ... [It] is open to the public.[21]

The Pitti would soon see many new faces, and many of its art treasures would disappear to Paris.

The grand duke was a prominent member of the House of Habsburg-Lorraine, the ruling house of Austria, against whom Bonaparte had been fighting. His late father, the Holy Roman Emperor Leopold II, had been grand duke of Tuscany before him; the present emperor, Francis II, was his elder brother. His grandmother, the Empress Maria Theresa, had been the dynasty's matriarch for forty years, and it was her husband, Francis of Lorraine, who had gained possession of Tuscany after the death of the last of the Medici. In the young Corsican's eyes, these people were quintessential aristos, international parasites of the sort that the French Revolution was intent on driving out.

Grand Duke Ferdinando was obviously unable to refuse the general's proposed visit and received him politely. Yet the meeting was necessarily fraught: the grand duke was nephew to the late French queen, Marie-Antoinette, whose head had rolled under the guillotine only three years earlier. A near-contemporary account confirms the dinner guest's insolent mood:

> Bonaparte . . . resolved, that the brother of the emperor should pay for his presumed inclinations. For the present, the Florentine museum and the grand duke's treasury were spared; but [Livorno], the seaport of Tuscany and the great feeder of its wealth, was seized without ceremony. The grand duke, in place of resenting these injuries, was obliged to receive Bonaparte with all the appearance of cordiality, and the spoiler repaid his courtesy by telling him, rubbing his hands with glee, during the princely entertainment provided for him, 'I have just received letters from Milan; the citadel has fallen; – your brother no longer has a foot of land in Lombardy.' 'It is a sad case,' said Napoleon himself, long afterward, 'when the dwarf comes into the embrace of the giant, he is like enough to be suffocated; but it is in the giant's nature to squeeze hard.'[22]

In effect, the upstart general was putting his host on notice: Florence could go the same way as Milan. More to the point – there was no need to spell it out – Ferdinando's head could end up in the same sort of bloody basket as that of his aunt.[23]

A different account of the event suggests that the grand duke played his part very skilfully:

> Bonaparte came to Florence accompanied by Berthier [his chief of staff] and part of his *état-major*, but no privates except those who commonly attended his person, and these mounted guard at the Pitti Palace, while the Tuscan troops attended the French general who was invited to dine with the Grand Duke. The entrance of the French was orderly, but . . . not one Tuscan subject welcomed them with 'Viva la Repubblica!'
>
> The Grand Duke, however, received Bonaparte with affability, untinctured by fear; making him magnificent presents, and doing the honours of a splendid table with apparent ease and cheerfulness; and though during

dinner a French courier arrived to announce that the citadel of Milan had surrendered, the Grand Duke was so master of himself as to betray no concern: but conversed with his guest respecting the Bonaparte family, which is of Tuscan origin, and at the general's instance conferred upon his uncle the order of S. Stefano.

In the evening the Duke accompanied Bonaparte to the theatre, where the audience received their prince with uncommon plaudits. – 'You seem to reign in the hearts of your subjects, sir', said the general; 'but have you always such full houses as this?' 'Usually a great deal fuller,' replied the Duke.[24]

Soon after leaving Florence, Bonaparte was told that the Royal Navy had seized the island of Elba. Activity at sea was one of the few things that the British could do to impede French progress. Elba, though adminstered from Naples as part of the *Stato dei Presidii*, otherwise known as the 'Tuscan ports', lay within historic Tuscany; and its loss would have prompted the grand strategist to contemplate further conquests as a means of protecting his fragile gains. For the British, Tuscany held no great strategic interest. Its main claim to fame at the time lay in the Etruscan-style pottery that was all the rage among Britain's wealthy classes. Josiah Wedgwood, who had died the year before, had called his ceramics factory in Staffordshire's Black Country 'Etruria'.

Bonaparte returned to Paris in November, leaving the French army in Italy to the command of General Charles Leclerc (1772–1802). But he was soon forced to retrace his steps, and had to spend a second year campaigning in Italy before a firmer peace with Austria could be signed at Campo Formio in October 1797. In the process, the French army wrested the Romagna from the Papal States, marched into Tyrol, and sent off an expedition to capture the Ionian Islands. A new crop of French-sponsored republics sprouted in its wake – the Ligurian at Genoa, the Lemanic at Geneva, then the Helvetian in Switzerland and the Roman in the realms of the pope. The Cisalpine Republic engorged itself by swallowing the Cispadane.

A powerful backlash followed this avalanche of change, and in 1798–9 French forces in Italy struggled to contain it. Bonaparte, who sailed romantically to Egypt in May 1798, could not intervene in person. The exiled pope, Pius VI, implacable after being stripped of his temporal powers, inspired resistance. Britain marshalled a second anti-French coalition. The Russians sent a powerful army into Italy under Field Marshal Suvorov, and a fleet under Admiral Gorchakov to join the

Royal Navy in the Mediterranean. The king of Naples, seizing the opportunity provided by Bonaparte's absence in Egypt, recaptured Rome, only to flee as soon as the French counter-attacked, sailing in haste from Naples aboard Nelson's flagship. Pending Bonaparte's return to Europe, all arrangements necessarily seemed temporary.

Italian affairs were vastly complicated by the far-reaching tentacles of the House of Bourbon. The late Louis XVI of France had been a Bourbon; the king of Spain was a Bourbon; the king of Naples was a Bourbon; and so, too, was the duke of Parma, whose possessions almost touched Tuscany in the north. The duke tried to secure his position by paying the French a million *livres* and sending twenty-five of his best paintings to the Louvre, hoping to turn himself into a key pawn on the political chessboard. It was of the Bourbons that France's foreign minister, Talleyrand, was much later to say: 'They have learned nothing, and forgotten nothing.'[25]

French diplomacy at this point was juggling with half a dozen issues, most of which had a Tuscan aspect. Negotiations with Spain, which

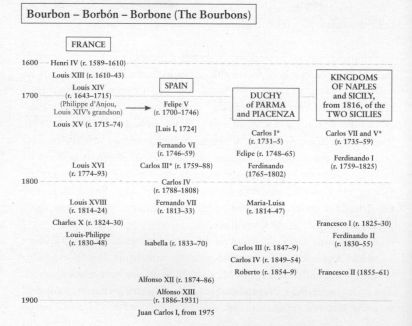

Bourbon – Borbón – Borbone (The Bourbons)

FRANCE	SPAIN	DUCHY of PARMA and PIACENZA	KINGDOMS OF NAPLES and SICILY, from 1816, of the TWO SICILIES
1600 Henri IV (r. 1589–1610)			
Louis XIII (r. 1610–43)			
Louis XIV **1700** (r. 1643–1715) (Philippe d'Anjou, Louis XIV's grandson) →	Felipe V (r. 1700–1746)		
Louis XV (r. 1715–74)	[Luis I, 1724]	Carlos I* (r. 1731–5)	Carlos VII and V* (r. 1735–59)
	Fernando VI (r. 1746–59)	Felipe (r. 1748–65)	
Louis XVI (r. 1774–93)	Carlos III* (r. 1759–88)	Ferdinando (1765–1802)	Ferdinando I (r. 1759–1825)
1800	Carlos IV (r. 1788–1808)		
Louis XVIII (r. 1814–24)	Fernando VII (r. 1813–33)	Maria-Luisa (r. 1814–47)	
Charles X (r. 1824–30)			Francesco I (r. 1825–30)
Louis-Philippe (r. 1830–48)	Isabella (r. 1833–70)	Carlos III (r. 1847–9)	Ferdinando II (r. 1830–55)
		Carlos IV (r. 1849–54)	
		Roberto (r. 1854–9)	Francesco II (1855–61)
	Alfonso XII (r. 1874–86)		
1900	Alfonso XIII (r. 1886–1931)		
	Juan Carlos I, from 1975		

* **NB.** Carlos III of Spain, Carlo I of Parma, Carlo VIII of Naples and Carlo V of Sicily were the same man.

eventually led to the secret treaty of San Ildefonso (October 1800), aimed to facilitate the purchase by France of Spain's American province of Louisiana; Tuscany was being dangled in front of the Spanish Bourbons as an inducement to accept the deal. Negotiations with Naples were conducted in Florence, where the Neapolitan Bourbons were being offered the restoration of their kingdom on condition that their ports remained closed to Britain's Royal Navy. Negotiations with Portugal sought likewise to exclude the British. Negotiations with Britain itself at Amiens were leading at snail's pace towards a formal treaty that would not be signed until March 1802; the British were characteristically most concerned about the freedom of maritime trade. Negotiations with the papacy assumed that revolutionary, anti-religious fanaticism was running its course; the proposed Concordat would restore Catholicism to France but not the Papal States to the papacy.

Tuscany, which depended on overseas trade and was the immediate neighbour of the Papal States, could not be indifferent either to commercial negotiations or to the Franco-papal conflict. The French army's occupation of Rome in February 1798 caused passions to rise, and the grand duke's decision to welcome the fugitive pope raised tensions. The grand duke was acutely aware of French suspicions, so when he gave shelter in 1798–9 not only to the pope but also to a varied company of 'reactionary' exiles, including the king of Sardinia, he cannot have been totally surprised by the consequences. Pius VI, frail and eighty-one years old, was accommodated throughout the winter in the *Forestiera* or 'Forest Lodge' of the Carthusian Certosa di Galluzzo near Florence, a favourite destination for day trippers from the city:

> The monastery is built on a circular hill; the building is extremely irregular . . . [But] there are few subjects in Tuscany which a painter would rather study. The great square within the monastery is surrounded by a colonnade supporting the roof.
>
> Each hermit has two or three small rooms to himself and a little plot of ground. Some were employed in reading; some cultivated their gardens, while others would mope in gloomy melancholy . . . they seldom spoke, silence being a virtue of the Order of St Bruno . . . One of their favourite amusements after meals was to feed some two hundred cats, which came mewing and squalling beneath the windows from the woods below.[26]

But the Directory in Paris feared a rescue, so on 28 March 1799 the pope was plucked from his Florentine asylum and transported across

the Alps under duress. He died in captivity at Valence after reigning
twenty-four years. His death was a black omen for his erstwhile Tuscan
hosts.[27]

Worse was to follow. In the summer of 1799 Florence was the scene
of violent commotions. A republican faction took control of the municipality and invited a small French force into the city. An *Albero della
Libertà*, a 'Tree of Liberty', was raised in the Piazza della Signoria, the
revolutionary calendar was imposed, together with heavy taxes, and the
militants forced the grand duke and many clerics to depart. A violent
counter-revolution then broke out in nearby Arezzo. Fomented by the
new pope, Pius VII (r. 1800–1823), who had been elected in an emergency conclave in Venice, bloodthirsty peasant bands roamed the
countryside to cries of '*Viva Maria!*' before storming into Florence and
slaughtering any Frenchman too slow to escape. The grand duke's supporters restored order with the help of Austrian troops. They won but a
short stay of execution.

The turbulence in Tuscany coincided with still more gruesome horrors in the south. French difficulties in southern Italy had multiplied in
proportion to the extreme violence sanctioned by the royalist Neapolitan opposition. The king of Naples, Ferdinand IV, was a son of the
former Spanish king, Charles III; his wife, the Archduchess Maria Carolina, was the daughter of the Empress Maria Theresa and sister of
Marie-Antoinette, the executed wife of Louis XVI. After the declaration
of the Neapolitan Parthenopean Republic in 1799, they had retired
with their court to Palermo in Sicily, whence a ferocious campaign of
resistance was organized. The peasant *lazzaroni* – counterparts of the
Spanish *guerrillas* – fought the French with great courage and cruelty,
while a 'Christian Army of the Holy Faith', the *Sanfedisti*, advanced
from Calabria under the none-too-Christian Cardinal Ruffo. Fire, plunder and massacre spread far and wide; the cardinal's irregulars were
supported both by a squadron of the Russian navy and by Admiral
Horatio Nelson, who was rewarded with the title of duke of Brontë.
The return of the royal couple to Naples in December 1800 was attended
by mass executions and punitive trials.

In 1800, having effectively appointed himself first consul in France,
Bonaparte returned to Italy with a vengeance. Crossing the Great
St Bernard for a second time, he descended onto the plain of Lombardy
and blew his enemies away like chaff. At Marengo in June, he defeated
the Austrians so thoroughly that the rest of the peninsula lay at his feet.
The Second Coalition was dead; the French resurgence was unstoppable.

Negotiations began at Lunéville for a comprehensive European settlement that was finally signed the following February. France gained the left bank of the Rhine. Six French-run republics, four of them in Italy, received international recognition; Tuscany was to be disposed of as the first consul thought fit. In October 1800 General Joachim Murat (1767–1815), Napoleon's aide-de-camp and brother-in-law, led a large French force into Tuscany which occupied the whole region, broke into Florence, sacked churches and perpetrated atrocities. Murat, a cavalryman dubbed the 'First Horseman of Europe', placed himself at the head of a provisional Tuscan government. He was accompanied by his eighteen-year-old wife of several months, the former Carolina Buonaparte, the first consul's youngest sister. She was one of three Buonaparte sisters who would enliven the Florentine scene.

Such was the state of affairs that prevailed while the diplomatic settlement over Tuscany was being concluded. The full terms were revealed in the final Franco-Spanish Treaty of Aranjuez (21 March 1801) and in the Franco-Neapolitan Treaty of Florence signed by Murat on 28 March 1801. Grand Duke Ferdinando's Tuscan possessions were to be confiscated and pass to his neighbours, the Bourbons of Parma, who were to be given royal status and the title of 'kings of Etruria'.[28] Ferdinando was to be compensated from lands seized by the secularization of the archbishopric of Salzburg. The Bourbons of Naples, who had ruled over the *Stato dei Presidii* since the 1730s, were required to cede their possession and to withdraw its garrisons. The *Stato dei Presidii* would then be amalgamated with the territory of the dissolved Grand Duchy of Tuscany to create the Kingdom of Etruria, so reuniting historic Tuscany with much of the adjacent coastline.

Despite their elevation to nominal royalty, the Bourbons of Parma cannot have been particularly delighted by this turn of events; their home base in Parma was to be annexed directly to France as the Département de Taro (it was contiguous on its western border with Piedmont, which had already been incorporated). What is more, the duke of Parma was to be passed over in Etruria in favour of his son, Lodovico di Borbone, otherwise known as Louis de Bourbon, who was married to a Spanish cousin and was presumably judged more malleable. The new king's father, who had paid so heavily to sweeten the French, declined in health and shortly died, no doubt rueing his investment.

The Kingdom of Etruria was the first of Napoleon's monarchical experiments. All the earlier states and statelets thrown up by the French

Revolution, from Batavia to Helvetia, had been republics modelled on
the French Republic itself. But by 1801, as first consul for life, Napoleon
was free to indulge his own autocratic tendencies. His new attitude was
bound up with the growing reaction against republicanism both in
France and in Italy, which encouraged him to seek common cause with
moderate (and especially with dependent) monarchists. He would continue on this path until in four years he was crowned emperor of the
French, and in five, king of Italy.

By public proclamation, Etruria was declared to be a sovereign kingdom, and as such it would receive foreign ambassadors; in reality, it was
a client state which paid tribute to France – partly to maintain the French
garrison and partly to swell Napoleon's general war chest. Because of the
Bourbon connection, it is sometimes described as belonging to the Spanish dominions, but this is nominally correct at best. It owed everything
to its French sponsors. It had been invented by the French, and could be
dismantled by the French. As soon as its existence became inconvenient,
it would be wiped out at the stroke of a Parisian pen.

Etruria's king, Lodovico I (or Louis Ier d'Étrurie, 1773–1803), was
barely twenty-eight years old when handed his kingdom without warning. By royalist standards, his pedigree was impeccable. His father's
family, the Bourbons of Parma, were close relatives of Spain's ruling
house, who called him *El Niño*, 'The Child'. His mother's family, the
Habsburg-Lorrainers, linked him both to Austria and to the previous
rulers of Tuscany. His nineteen-year-old wife, Maria-Luisa di Borbone,
was an infanta of Spain. A famous group portrait, *The Family of
Charles IV*, was painted by Goya in 1800–1801. It shows Lodovico and
Maria-Luisa holding their baby son and standing in a place of honour
immediately behind the Spanish monarch. Whether or not the half-
Spanish client of an increasingly autocratic French dictator could gain
control over his manufactured Italian realm was open to question.

There was no time for a coronation. On hearing of their good fortune, the king and queen rushed from Spain to Paris in May 1801 to
undergo a civilian induction, and no doubt to be given advice and
instructions. Napoleon organized two military parades in their honour
in front of the Tuileries. The royal couple sat in Napoleon's box at the
Opéra during a performance of Gluck's *Iphigénie en Aulide*. Commemorative medals were struck, and complimentary verses composed:

> *La Toscane autrefois nous donna Médicis,*
> *Aujourd'hui la vertu va régner dans Florence.*

('Tuscany in former times gave us the Medicis, / today in Florence Virtue is going to reign.') The appearance of a young Bourbon couple so soon after the end of the revolutionary wars could not fail to intrigue Parisians, not least because they were only thinly disguised as the 'count and countess of Livorno'. They became the talk of the town, and the subject of gossip in the first consul's entourage, which knew very well that this was 'Don Louis I of Etruria' and 'Maria-Luisa, infanta of Spain'. They made a mixed impression, as the emperor's chief valet recalled:

> The King of Etruria was not fond of work, and . . . did not please the First Consul, who could not endure idleness. I heard him one day severely score his royal protégé (in his absence of course). 'Here is a prince,' he said, 'who . . . passes his time cackling to old women, to whom . . . he complains in a whisper of owing his elevation to the chief of this cursed French Republic . . .' 'It is asserted,' remarked [an officer of the household to Bonaparte], 'that you wished to disgust the French people with Kings by showing them such a specimen, as the Spartans disgusted their children with drunkenness by exhibiting to them a drunken slave.' 'Not so, my dear sir,' replied the First Consul, 'I have no desire to disgust them with royalty, but the sojourn of the King of Etruria will annoy a number of good people, who work incessantly to create a feeling favourable to the Bourbons.'[29]

Maria-Luisa had some success in creating that favourable feeling:

> The Queen of Etruria was, in the opinion of the First Consul, more sagacious and prudent than her husband . . . [She] dressed herself in the morning for the whole day, and walked in the garden, her head adorned with flowers or a diadem, and wearing a dress, the train of which swept up the sand of the walk: often also carrying in her arms one of her children . . . ; by night the toilet of her Majesty was somewhat disarranged. She was far from pretty, and her manners were not suited to her rank. But, which fully atoned for all of this, she was good-tempered, much loved by those in her service, and scrupulous in fulfilling the duties of wife and mother. In consequence, the First Consul, who made a great point of domestic virtue, professed for her the highest esteem.[30]

A concert and extravagant farewell party were organized for the visitors at the Château de Neuilly by Talleyrand. The chateau and park were illuminated with coloured lights, and one end of the hall was filled by a tableau of the Piazza della Signoria replete with fountains and 'Tuscans singing couplets in honour of their sovereigns'. There was a grand ball hosted by the first consul's sister Paolina, and the evening closed with a

display of rockets, fireworks and 'Bengal Fire'. Then the happy couple
set off and travelled by stages to Florence. When they entered their
capital on 2 August, they were greeted by representatives of the municipality; a new royal flag was flying, and a royal medal had been struck in
celebration.[31] The streets were thronged with curious people, and General Murat was waiting with his staff and a detachment of cavalry to
escort them into their residence in the Pitti Palace.

The Kingdom of Etruria's territory of *c.* 7,700 square miles formed a
rough rectangle, bounded in the west by the sea, and in the north, east
and south by high mountains. Northern Tuscany was separated from the
basin of the Po by the Apennines, which at Monte Cimone rose above
6,000 feet. Travellers coming from the north, from Bologna, faced a wild
tract of country:

> Two miles before and after Scarico l'Asino, where the Italian customs house
> stands, the mountains become so black and barren that you discover noth-
> ing but naked crags and crumbled rocks . . . Farther on, Nature assumes a
> more cheerful face, the heights and bottoms being clad with spreading
> forests of chestnuts . . . Groves of fig-trees succeed them, and these are
> relieved by extensive plantations of olives, which in Etruria seem to have
> displaced every other fruit.[32]

Florence, the kingdom's capital, was circled by a ring of ancient Tuscan
towns – Prato, Arezzo, Cortona, Siena and San Gimignano – and was
linked by the lower valley of the Arno to Pisa and the sea. Southern
Tuscany round Pitigliano adjoined the frontier of the Papal States
(which had been resuscitated in 1800) and the coastal strip extended
southwards for some 90 miles as far as the peninsula of Monte Argentario. Etruria's main outlet to the sea, Livorno, had been developed by
the Medici as a free port, and had attracted an unusually cosmopolitan
population. There were colonies of Greeks and Turks, a large Jewish community and, as the Protestant cemetery attests, a prosperous group of
English merchants, who called it 'Leghorn'. It had been relieved from the
French occupation of 1796, but in 1798–9 it had been forced to supply
ships and men for the Egyptian campaign. Suspicions of its pro-British
sympathies persisted. The kingdom's other ports, formerly part of the
Stato dei Presidii, included Piombino, Talamone and Orbetello.[33]

   Etruria was not poor. The Tuscan countryside was productive as
always, and the cities maintained strong ties with international commerce; hence the continuing British interest. Foreign visitors were

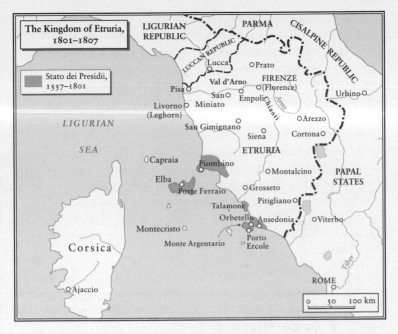

The Kingdom of Etruria,
1801–1807

Stato dei Presidii,
1557–1801

LIGURIAN REPUBLIC

PARMA

CISALPINE REPUBLIC

LUCCAN REPUBLIC

Lucca

Val d'Arno

Pisa

San
Miniato

Livorno
(Leghorn)

Empoli

Prato

FIRENZE
(Florence)

Urbino

San Gimignano

Arezzo

Siena

Cortona

ETRURIA

Chianti

Arno

LIGURIAN

SEA

Capraia

Piombino

Elba

Porte Ferraio

Montecristo

Corsica

Ajaccio

Montalcino

Grosseto

Talamone

Orbetello

Monte Argentario

Ansedonia

Porto
Ercole

PAPAL
STATES

Pitigliano

Viterbo

Tiber

ROME

0   50   100 km

pleasantly surprised by the relatively low cost of living: 'This city is not
calculated to drain the traveller's pocket ... Bread and wine are still
cheaper than in Rome; and a pot of excellent coffee with cream and
cakes cost only five *grazie*. This coin, worth about a penny, appears to
have taken its name from the Austrian *kreutzer* ... It is singular that the
Austrian ducats are all over Italy ...'[34] Indeed, multiple currencies operated. The Florentine system, which was similar to the £, *s., d.* of England,
was different from the Pisan. One Tuscan pound or *lira* was equivalent
to 20 *soldi*, and 1 *soldo* to 12 *denari*. Intermediate coins called *paoli* and
quatrini also circulated. Austrian gold ducats and Maria Theresa silver
thalers were highly valued.

   An Englishwoman living in Tuscany at the time has left some vivid
descriptions of the condition of the people and the country. In addition
to the grand duchy's artistic heritage, she writes enthusiastically about
the vitality of urban life, the vigour of the peasantry and the enlightened
nature of the prevailing laws. In Florence, for example, she was excited
by the ceremonies surrounding the Feast of St John, the city's patron,
which took place every June. There were chariot-races, exhibitions
of *pallone*, a game said to be the ancestor of baseball, and elaborate
processions:

On the morning of the festa of S. Giovanni homage is paid by all the Tuscan cities to their prince; and this ceremony passes in the Piazza del Granduca; the throne of the sovereign being erected under the Loggia, which is hung with a fine tapestry, as is the royal box. The balconies and scaffoldings for the people are likewise handsomely decorated. No sooner has the prince ascended the throne (which is surrounded by the household and the great officers of state) than the procession commences with men on horseback dressed in ancient habits . . . ; then come gentlemen [from] the neighbourhood of Pisa, then come immense wooden towers representing the several cities of Tuscany . . . ; but when the citizens of Siena arrive, they are summoned to stop and their leader makes an oration expressing sorrow for the revolt some hundred years ago and promising they will always be loyal in future . . . After the Sanesi come the citizens of Florence followed by the little Tuscan army, which pays the military compliments to its sovereign and closes the procession.[35]

The English resident found the Florentines very hospitable, 'fond of learning, the arts and sciences', and 'generally speaking, good-humoured, warm-hearted and friendly'. The greatest impression, however, was made by the peasants of the countryside:

The Tuscan peasantry, considered collectively, are pure in their morals and pastoral in their lives; and the peculiar comeliness of both sexes is very striking, especially in the environs of Florence . . . The men are tall, robust, finely proportioned, and endowed with that self-possession, which at once excites respect . . . The women are of a middle stature, and were it not for bad stays, would be well made. They have large, languishing black eyes accompanied by that expressive brow which constitutes the most captivating part of an Italian countenance. Their manners are uncommonly graceful, and instead of curtseying, they gently bow their bodies and kiss the hand of a superior . . . The upper class of farmers usually possess a horse, a waggon or two, and a pair of large, dove-coloured oxen, whose beauty is as remarkable as their masters . . . Shoes and stockings are deemed superfluous even by the women, who carry them in baskets on their heads until they reach town . . . The phraseology of Florentine peasants is wonderfully elegant, indeed their Italian is said to be the purest now spoken; but the most remarkable quality in these people is their industry: for during the hottest weather they toil all day without sleep . . . yet they live almost entirely upon bread, fruit, pulse, and the common wine of the country. Though their diet is light and their bodily exertions are almost perpetual, they commonly attain old age.[36]

In the two preceding decades, Tuscany had benefited greatly from the progressive social policies of the Habsburg grand dukes, who were paragons of the 'enlightened despotism' then in fashion. The contrast with England could not have been greater:

> According to the law of the late Emperor Leopold, no one can be imprisoned for debt, though creditors have power to seize the property of their debtors; and no offence is punishable with death, though murderers are condemned to perpetual labour as galley-slaves; and to these and many other wise regulations are attributable the almost total exemption from robbery and murder which this country enjoys and the increase to its population . . . I have never heard of house-breaking, nor of more than one highway-robbery (and that committed by an Irishman) during my long residence . . .[37]

Modern historians confirm this positive picture. 'Tuscany, insignificant in terms of *Realpolitik*,' writes one British expert on the era, 'was renowned throughout the civilised world . . . not only through its unique cultural heritage, but because of its enactment of some of the most enlightened principles of the Enlightenment.'[38] The incoming Etrurian management would be hard pressed to match its predecessor.

The formation of a royal government, however, was severely constrained by the king's French supervisors; all of Lodovico I's appointments had to be made in consultation with the resident French ambassador and his legation. General Henri-Jacques Clarke (1765–1818), seconded to Florence from other duties in Italy, did not shrink from giving vociferous opinions. The king and the ambassador decided to retain the council of state and its subordinate ministries that had operated under the previous grand-ducal regime, but the French were adamant that no persons of the 'Austrian persuasion' could continue to hold senior office. The choice of chief minister fell on Count Odoardo Salvatico. The king and council established their own direct link with France by appointing Count Averardo Serristori as their ambassador to the first consul; in practice, to Talleyrand. A papal nuncio, Mgr Caleppi, was present, though his traditional influence was much reduced. On 29 August 1801 the king addressed his subjects in his first *motu proprio* or 'decree', which enjoined them to put the past into 'perpetual oblivion' and to heal their divisions.[39] Over him hovered the shadow of 6,000 French troops, one-third of them men from the Polish Legions.

The outlines of local politics were clear to see. Small groups of Jacobin sympathizers and Freemasons existed in the cities, and tended to look to the French for radical measures. Conservative, anti-revolutionary circles were more numerous, especially in the countryside, often enjoying the support of the clergy. The middle ground was held by the so-called 'Patriotic Party', attached to Tuscany's enlightened heritage and aiming to steer between the extremes; the University of Pisa was said to be its powerhouse. The prospects for moderation, however, were favourable. The violent events of 'il '99' had discredited doctrinaire positions, and the kingdom started life in the year of the Concordat, whereby the first consul was reconciled to the Roman Church. Italy appeared to be stabilizing. The French were making peace with Austria and with Britain, extricating themselves from their disastrous Egyptian expedition and evacuating Naples.

Within Napoleonic Italy, Etruria was surrounded by a patchwork of petty principalities, all dependent on France but each with a different regime. To the north, administered from Milan, lay the enlarged Cisalpine Republic. To the east and south, ruled from Rome, lay the restored but still occupied Papal States. To the north-west, lay the Ligurian Republic of Genoa and the Republic of Lucca.* Further north, Piedmont had been declared a French military district. In each of these places, as in Etruria, French-inspired republicans were vying with papal-backed 'reactionaries'.[40] Etruria found itself in a category in which local rulers possessed some leeway in internal affairs while deferring to France in external affairs.

The arrival of the royal couple in their residence, as described in the queen's memoir, was less than auspicious. Their predecessor, the Grand Duke Ferdinando, had stripped the Pitti Palace of everything he could carry off, and the queen complained that she had to organize a whipround of local sympathizers to provide some basic furniture and cooking utensils. As an infanta of Spain, accustomed to dining off gold and silver plate, she was reduced for the first time in her life to eating off porcelain. Worse, she suffered the first of two miscarriages.

Nonetheless, as she recalled, modest progress was made:

> My husband's first object was to try to get rid of the French troops which occupied Tuscany and which pressed very heavily on the people; but under a variety of pretences, his demands . . . were constantly refused . . . All that we could obtain was that Murat's troops should quit the capital as soon as a noble guard would be formed; but they neither quitted Leghorn nor Pisa nor the other parts of the state.[41]

---

* They inspired the opening sentence of Tolstoy's *War and Peace* (1869): '"*Eh bien, mon prince*, so Genoa and Lucca are now no more than private estates of the Bonaparte family."'

In 1802, however, Napoleon's restless spirit destroyed hopes for an extended period of calm. The Cisalpine Republic, now renamed the 'Italian Republic', became the focus of his attention. Its constitution required the election of a president, so a *consultation* was convened at Lyon to consider the candidates and a suitable hint from Talleyrand persuaded the delegates to elect Napoleon himself. Later that year, French troops reoccupied Switzerland. The terms of the treaties of Lunéville and Amiens were flouted everywhere. Napoleon defiantly declared, 'It is recognized by Europe that Holland and Italy, as well as Switzerland, are at France's disposal.'

Etruria saw little of its royal couple. Both of them were frequently indisposed, and the queen took to attending functions alone. Then in September they sailed for Spain to attend a family wedding. The queen gave birth to a premature baby girl aboard ship near Barcelona; the king was so ill from epilepsy that they missed the wedding. They did not return till the end of the year.

By 1803, Napoleon was again preparing for war. To this end, he crudely extracted subsidies from his satraps, disregarded their nominal neutrality and threatened the non-compliant with punishment. He was especially rapacious in his support for the state-sponsored looting of art. Visitors to the Uffizi found that the gallery's most famous exhibit was missing:

> The Venus of the Medici is here no more; she was torn from the pedestal by the French and sent to the depot of spoils in Paris. Her place is now vacant; she stood in the beautiful octagonal hall among the choicest forms of antiquity . . . You miss her with a peculiarly painful sensation. Florence during two centuries was her assigned abode; every traveller sought her here . . . and now she is gone.[42]

Successive events sent ripples of foreboding through the little Etrurian court. One was Napoleon's cynical resale of Louisiana to the United States for 60 million francs, less than three years after the deal of which the creation of Etruria had formed part. The first consul's greed seemed boundless. Shortly afterwards, in May 1803, Etruria was cast into mourning by the sudden and unexpected death of its young king, who died from an epileptic fit when barely thirty years old. His body was carried back to Spain and buried in the Pantheon of the Infantes in the Escorial.

Nothing was more shocking for the royalists, however, than the kidnapping and execution of the duc d'Enghien, the last of the French Bourbons and a symbol of the royalist cause throughout Europe. The dashing duke was an émigré who had taken up arms against the French Republic. In March 1804 a military snatch squad crossed the Rhine, raided the duke's residence in Germany, and carried their captive back to France for trial. Napoleon refused all pleas for mercy, and ordered that the duke be executed in the palace ditch at Vincennes. His judicial murder attracted the comment by France's chief of police, later attributed to Talleyrand: *C'était pire qu'un crime; c'était une faute* ('It was worse than a crime; it was a mistake'). After that, no Bourbon or royalist could feel safe, and Napoleon's reputation plummeted.

Lodovico I was automatically succeeded in Etruria by his infant son, Carlo-Luigi (Charles-Louis), aged four. Executive powers were placed in the hands of the late king's widow and the child's mother, herself only twenty years old, who took the title of queen-regent. A 10-lira silver coin, minted at this time, announced the new reign. The inscription reads: 'CAROLUS LUDOVICUS DEI GRATIA REX ETRURIAE ET MARIA ALOYSIA REGINA RECTRIX'.[43]

For four years, as Etruria's boy monarch grew up, the kingdom was administered by the queen-regent with the guidance of her ministers. Following Salvatico's dismissal, two men came to the fore. One was Count Fossombroni, a prudent and experienced servant of the previous regime, who still had a long career in front of him, and the other Jean-Gabriel Eynard (1775–1863), an enterprising Franco-Swiss businessman. Eynard came to Florence in 1803 from Genoa, where he had made a fortune supplying the French army with blue denim cloth, 'Bleu de Gênes', and is said to be the inventor of 'blue jeans'. He used his money to buy the sole subscription to an Etrurian government bond, which gave him a built-in interest in the kingdom's welfare. Working in partnership with the queen-regent, he reorganized the tax system, created taxable manufactures, such as tobacco and porcelain companies, and closely monitored military procurement, travelling to Paris in person to ensure that the promised subsidies were paid. Some measure of his success may be seen in the queen-regent's announcement of an extraordinary levy of 20,000 troops. In total, the Kingdom of Etruria raised no fewer than twenty-six regiments, including the Reggimento Real Toscano, the Compagnia Dragoni d'Etruria, the Pompatori Militari di Firenze and the Corpore Reale dei Cacciatori della Città di Firenze.

The queen-regent spent lavishly on educational projects too, founding a Higher School for Science, and a Museum of Natural History; she once threw a party in the Loggia dei Lonzi where 200 poor children were entertained before being told to take the cutlery and crockery home. (Perhaps it was the despised porcelain.) Slowly, she regained her optimism:

> When I assumed the reins of government, my sole idea was to promote the happiness of my subjects ... An epidemic fever had recently broken out at Leghorn, and a great number had fallen victims to it. The French troops continued to occupy the country, without the least necessity ... and occasioned exorbitant expenses. I saw myself reduced to increasing the taxes. At last, however, I succeeded in obtaining a Spanish general to be sent with some troops of that nation in place of the French ... I then enjoyed perfect tranquillity.[44]

She also derived much satisfaction from her children:

> The King, my son, was everything I could wish; good, docile, and already gave indications of a noble character. He made great progress in his studies; his health was strong, and every day saw an increase in the tender affection which his subjects bore to him. My only ambition was to be able some day to show him the deplorable state in which I had found the kingdom, and that in which I expected to deliver it into his hands.[45]

Princess Marie-Louise-Charlotte, three years younger than her brother, had recovered well from the adverse circumstances of her birth.

In December 1803 the queen-regent entertained a surprise visitor to the Pitti in the person of Paolina, Napoleon's second sister. The two women had met two years earlier at Neuilly. Both had since been widowed; both understood the fragility of their respective positions. In the space of a few months, Paolina had buried her first husband, General Leclerc, who had died campaigning in San Domingo, and had entered a second marriage with a Roman aristocrat, Camillo Borghese, prince of Salmona, to whose estates she was now travelling. She sincerely liked the queen-regent, asked for a portrait and a lock of her hair for keepsakes, and begged to keep in touch. On receiving the keepsakes, she thanked 'ma chère Louise' warmly in her none-too-grammatical French: 'Adieu, ma Louise, adieu! Je vous aime et ce n'est pas pour dire ... Si vous désires me sentir heureuse, aimes moi toujours: je suis pour la vie vostre Paulette [sic].'[46] The letter was signed, 'Borghese, née Bonaparte'. Since the queen-regent's French was not much better, the two wrote henceforth in Italian.

Princess Paolina's visit must have been all the more intriguing for the Florentines, because she and her siblings were attracting ever more sensational headlines. The first consul's genius for self-promotion was now extending to the promotion of his four brothers and three sisters, all of whom were showered with offices, titles, marriage partners and publicity. He employed the neo-classical sculptor Antonio Canova, for example, to glorify the Buonaparte brood in marble nudes. In 1804 he commissioned a topless, reclining figure of *Paulina Borghese as Venus Victrix*, and a vulgar imitation of Michelangelo's *David* entitled *Napoleon as Mars the Peacemaker*. The former caused a minor sensation; the latter was so embarrassing that its originator refused to put it on public display.* Nepotism came naturally in such a climate. A fresh French ambassador arrived in Florence, the Marquis François de Beauharnais (1753–1823), the brother of Joséphine's first husband.

In December 1804 the 'first consul for life' invited the pope to Paris to officiate in Notre-Dame at his coronation as the 'emperor of the French'. As part of the proceedings, he awarded all of his siblings the title of *altesse impériale* or 'imperial highness', while naming his brothers Giuseppe (Joseph) and Luigi (Louis) as his official heirs. At the climatic moment in the service, he took the imperial crown out of the pope's hands and, spurning divine assistance, placed it on his own head. Six months later, having waved his wand to turn the Italian Republic into the Kingdom of Italy, he organized a second coronation for himself in Milan. He then set up his favourite sister 'Elisa', Signora Bacciochi, first as princess of Piombino and then as duchess of Lucca.

Elisa was the family nickname for Maria-Anna Buonaparte, the fourth surviving child of Napoleon's parents, who had been close to Napoleon since their time together in pre-revolutionary Paris. She was well educated, having attended the Maison Royale de Saint-Louis at St Cyr, and socially ambitious, having run a literary salon with her other brother, Luciano. Above all, she was quite capable of standing up for herself. She was the dominant partner in a long-lasting if unequal marriage to a bumbling Corsican officer, Pasquale Bacciochi Levoy, who had also changed his first name – in his case from Pasquale to Felice/Félix – and who after their wedding in 1797 commanded the citadel at Ajaccio. Many thought that it was Elisa's idea to turn Italy into a political playground for the Buonaparti, and to put her in charge of the first experiment. In the next year, the district of Massa and Carrara, which contained Europe's most valuable marble quarries, was specially detached

* Bought for a song by the Duke of Wellington in 1815, it is now housed in Apsley House, London.

from her brother's Kingdom of Italy for their benefit. Félix was promoted to the rank of général de division.

Elisa threw herself into her task with zest. She created an Academy of Fine Arts in Lucca, founded the Banque Elisienne, reformed the clergy and promulgated new legal codes. She was assiduous in financing her extravagances through the confiscation of Church property. Her methods could not fail to be compared to those of the queen-regent in Etruria; the Palazzo Lucchese and the Palazzo Pitti were in open competition. Yet the two women behaved to each other with propriety. Letters and gifts were exchanged. Maria-Luisa sent a pair of pure bred horses to Lucca; Elisa responded by sending a consignment of fine Parisian dress materials in return.

In Florence, it was easy to feel that the Bonaparte tribe were getting uncomfortably close. It was no secret that they were looking for suitable lands and titles for themselves in Italy, rather than elsewhere. When Napoleon was overheard saying 'Luciano would restore the glory of the Medici', strong rumours spread that the emperor's second brother, who was performing well in Paris as the minister of the interior, had been earmarked to take over Etruria. In the event, Luciano (Lucien), who was a convinced republican, had to be content with the title of prince of Canino; Luigi was made king of Holland, Girolamo king of Westphalia, Paolina duchess of Guastalla, and Eugène de Beauharnais, Napoleon's stepson, viceroy of Italy. The emperor was losing the patience to work with foreign royals.

In the years 1805–7 Napoleon was preoccupied with the affairs of northern Europe. His great victories of Austerlitz, Jena, Auerstadt and Friedland destroyed the Holy Roman Empire, reduced Prussia to ruins, drew the French into Poland and threatened Russia. Problems in Spain and Portugal also demanded his attention. In Italy, left to its own devices, crushing taxation and merciless recruiting were provoking popular resistance. Pope Pius VII was unreconciled to the French regime. Rome spawned a rebellion. Southern Italy was in uproar and the French hold on Naples tenuous. When cities like Genoa caused trouble, the instinctive reaction was to incorporate them into France. Napoleon grew especially impatient with the Bourbon Kingdom of Naples, and, as he saw it, with the king's ingratitude. Both Giuseppe Bonaparte and Joachim Murat were still waiting for thrones. When he discovered that the Neapolitans had been conspiring yet again with the British, he abruptly announced: 'The Bourbon dynasty has ceased to reign.' Giuseppe arrived in Naples in February 1806 to replace them.

In that same year, Napoleon systematized his attempts to stifle Britain's trade with the Continent. His Berlin Decrees (November 1806) forbade the import of British goods, thereby initiating the 'Continental System'; his Milan Decree (December 1807) ordered the confiscation of any vessel that had called at a British port. The System held firm in France and Germany, but was widely circumvented in the Mediterranean and came at a high political cost. None of the French-occupied countries liked being told what they could or could not buy. The Kingdom of Etruria, which as the Grand Duchy of Tuscany had been suspected by the French of 'Austrophilism', now gained the reputation of being 'Anglophile'. Livorno was seen as the port where the Continental System leaked most.

Napoleon's growing problems in Spain were compounded by yet another showdown with the ruling Bourbons. Charles IV and Maria-Luisa, parents of the Etrurian queen-regent, had reigned since 1788. The king was rated 'despotic, sluggish and stupid', a former wrestler who spent his time hunting; the queen, 'coarse, passionate and narrow-minded', acted as their political manager. Together, they were the most reactionary couple still seated on a European throne. Through the 1790s, they had been unswerving opponents of the French Revolution, and during the negotiations at San Ildefonso they had fought hard to uphold Bourbon interests. In the following years, however, they sought an accommodation with France. Their one-time chief minister, Godoy, duke of Alcudia, who contrived to be both the king's favourite and the queen's lover, was restored to power by the first consul, and set out to satisfy French demands.[47] Spain undertook to pay France a monthly tribute of 6 million francs and to prevent Portugal from breaking the continental blockade. Neither obligation was fulfilled. Godoy was deeply unpopular, and the heir apparent, Ferdinand, led an abortive plot against him.

In 1806–7 the crisis in Iberia slipped out of control, until in November 1807 General Junot was ordered to march through Spain with a French army and to punish the Portuguese. He only succeeded in provoking a general Spanish collapse amid what became the Peninsular War. In March 1808 the Spanish king abdicated and took refuge in France at Bayonne. Napoleon toyed for a while with his son, Ferdinand (in royalist eyes Ferdinand VII), before luring him to join his father in France. There he was arrested, and, like the rest of the Spanish royals, pensioned off. Ex-King Charles and ex-Queen Maria-Luisa were packed off to Rome, while ex-King Ferdinand was imprisoned for six years at

Talleyrand's castle of Valençay. Napoleon coolly sent his brother Giuseppe to Madrid to take the prisoners' throne, and Murat replaced Giuseppe on the throne in Naples.

These degrading events can only have been followed in the Pitti Palace with dismay. The queen-regent of Etruria was the daughter of the abdicated Charles IV, the sister of the imprisoned Ferdinand VII, and grand-niece of the deposed king of Naples. By the autumn of 1807, increasingly isolated, she was the last of the Bourbons in power. The marquis de Beauharnais was posted to Spain and replaced by a less congenial ambassador to Etruria, Count Hector d'Aubusson de la Feuillade, the Empress Joséphine's chamberlain; the queen-regent suspected the new-comer of intriguing with the Princess-Duchess Elisa. Long before the final scene, she must have trembled at the way the drama was unfolding.

In Paris, too, doubts must have been raised about the Kingdom of Etruria's future. Though more docile than the Kingdom of Naples, it had failed to become a bastion of French influence and had turned instead into the last Bourbon outpost. Florence was again serving as a haven for anti-French refugees, and Etruria's ports were acting as ready loopholes for British goods. Although one British historian states confi-dently that the queen-regent of Etruria 'was abruptly removed for failing to enforce the Continental blockade',[48] the explanation is insufficient; very little time had elapsed to assess whether the 'Continental System' was working or not. It seems more likely that Napoleon had made up his mind during his dealings with the Bourbons in Bayonne, and was simply waiting for a convenient moment to act.

The causes of Etruria's demise, therefore, must be sought in a wider context; the breaching of the ban on British trade was important, but so too were the perception of Etruria's deepening disaffection and Napo-leon's escalating dispute with the papacy. Pius VII and his chief minister, Consalvi, had tried repeatedly to find a modus vivendi with France. But in 1806 he had declined to grant a divorce to the emperor's youngest brother, Girolamo, who had rashly married an American woman called Betsy Patterson; and in 1807, reacting to Napoleon's insistence on the removal of Consalvi, he refused to give public support to the Continen-tal System. The Papal States and their neighbour, Etruria, together looked set to become a theatre for anti-French activities in Italy, and the emperor baulked. As part of the settlement with the Spanish Bourbons, a legal but little publicized decree signed by the emperor late in 1807 at Fontainebleau announced the abolition of the Kingdom of Etruria. The following February a column of troops was despatched to reoccupy

Rome. The pope protested. The emperor joined the four remaining Papal States to his Kingdom of Italy. The pope thereon excommunicated the emperor, and the emperor gave orders for the arrest and deportation of the pope.[49]

The queen-regent of Etruria would later claim that she had been taken by total surprise:

> On the 23rd November 1807, while I was at one of my country residences [at Castello], the French Minister, D'Aubusson la Feuillade, came to inform me that Spain had ceded my kingdom to France; . . . and that the French troops ordered to take charge of my dominions had arrived. I immediately despatched a courier to the King [of Spain], my father, to ask for an explanation . . . The answer which I received . . . was that I must hasten my departure, as the country no longer belonged to me, and that I must find consolation in the bosom of my family . . . At the moment of our departure the French published a proclamation in which they released our subjects from their oath of fidelity . . . In this manner, at the worst season of the year, I took leave of a country where my heart has remained ever since.[50]

In contemplating the dissolution of Etruria, French bureaucrats would certainly have weighed the advantages and disadvantages of two solutions. On the one hand they would have pondered the replacement of the Bourbon-Parmas by an alternative client ruler. On the other, they would have discussed the benefits of annexing the kingdom to the French Empire. In the event, they decided to do both. The kingdom's territory was divided into three, and added to the Empire as the *départements* of the Arno, Mediterranée and Ombrone. Shortly afterwards, the Princess-Duchess Elisa was given the additional resuscitated title of grand duchess of Tuscany. Maria-Luisa di Borbone, ex-queen-regent of Etruria, vacated the Pitti Palace with her children on 10 December 1807. As she left, the kingdom expired, after an existence of less than seven years.

For the next eighteen months the territorial and administrative reorganization of the former kingdom was accompanied by widespread civil disobedience and in the countryside by the rise of banditry. Pending the arrival of their new grand duchess, who had fallen seriously ill, the three new imperial *départements* were subordinated to a military general-government, which also oversaw the island of Elba. Civil prefects were appointed: Jean-Antoine, baron Fauchet for the Arno at Florence, Ange Gandolfo for the Ombrone at Siena, and Guillaume Capelle for La

Mediterranée at Livorno; each of the *départements* was divided into sub-prefectures on the French model (Elba was transferred from Lucca to La Mediterranée in 1811 as the Arrondissement of Portoferraio). All these territories were put under the supreme command of a *Giunta* or 'Joint Command' headed by the governor-general, Jacques-François de Menou (1750–1810).

Menou was one of most colourful characters of revolutionary France; he has also been characterized as 'probably the hardest man in Napoleonic Europe'.[51] As the baron de Boussay, he had been a noble deputy to the Estates-General of 1789. Later, he made his name as the Republic's enforcer in the horrific war of the Vendée, and rose to be general in chief of the Army of the Interior. Surviving a treason trial, he accompanied Napoleon to Egypt, where he converted to Islam and, after the assassination of General Kléber, accepted the overall command of the expeditionary force. In line with his newfound faith, he changed his first name to Abdullah, and named his infant son Suleyman after Kléber's assassin. Forced to capitulate by the defeat at Aboukir, Menou returned to France, served on the *Tribunat* and then moved to Turin as administrator-general of militarized Piedmont. There, for his private devotions, he built himself a golden-domed mosque beside the Chapel Royal.

'When Menou went to Florence, he left his wife behind, took up with the lead dancer at the Milan opera, staged stunning equestrian shows for the public, and threw lavish parties in the beautiful Pitti Palace.'[52] Yet the emperor had sent Menou to Tuscany to restore discipline and to combat the anticipated reaction to the introduction of universal male conscription – one of the necessary consequences of being incorporated into the Empire. In 1808 he oversaw the formation of several new Tuscan regiments, among them the 29th Division of *Veliti*, the famous 'Vélites de Florence', a quick-marching infantry unit that distinguished itself all over Europe. The Tuscans, however, had repeatedly shown their displeasure at heavy French taxation, requisitioning and military recruitment, and conscription meant a further tightening of the screw. Men placed on the military register were likely to abscond, to take to the woods and to live from brigandage; if forced into uniform, they were likely to desert and to take their arms with them. As a veteran of some of the toughest fighting of the last twenty years, Menou believed their insubordination could only be countered by terrorizing the population that gave the bandits and deserters sustenance. His chosen technique was to organize 'flying columns' that took recalcitrant villages by surprise, destroyed farmsteads, seized hostages and meted out

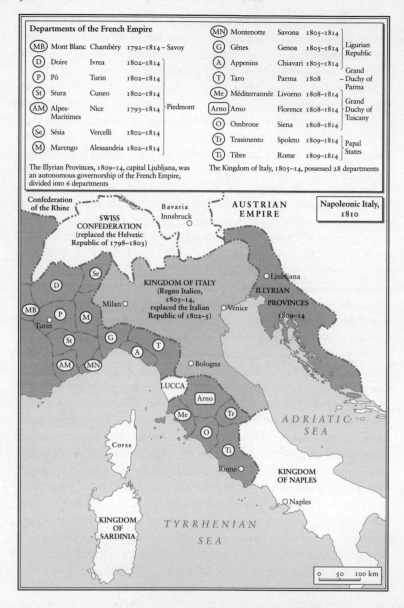

Departments of the French Empire

(MB)	Mont Blanc	Chambéry 1792–1814 – Savoy	
(D)	Doire	Ivrea 1802–1814	
(P)	Pô	Turin 1802–1814	
(St)	Stura	Cuneo 1802–1814	
(AM)	Alpes-Maritimes	Nice 1793–1814	Piedmont
(Se)	Sésia	Vercelli 1802–1814	
(M)	Marengo	Alessandria 1802–1814	

(MN)	Montenotte	Savona 1805–1814	
(G)	Gênes	Genoa 1805–1814	Ligurian Republic
(A)	Appenins	Chiavari 1805–1814	
(T)	Taro	Parma 1808	Grand Duchy of Parma
(Me)	Méditerrannée	Livorno 1808–1814	
(Arno)	Arno	Florence 1808–1814	Grand Duchy of Tuscany
(O)	Ombrone	Siena 1808–1814	
(Tr)	Trasimeno	Spoleto 1809–1814	Papal States
(Ti)	Tibre	Rome 1809–1814	

The Illyrian Provinces, 1809–14, capital Ljubljana, was an autonomous governorship of the French Empire, divided into 6 departments

The Kingdom of Italy, 1805–14, possessed 28 departments

summary executions. The hallmark tool of his trade was the mobile guillotine.[53] His name is listed on the Arc de Triomphe.

Menou's right-hand man in Tuscany was General Étienne Radet (1762–1825), a comrade-in-arms since the pacification of the Vendée.

Radet was by now inspector-general of the Gendarmerie, his task to expand the service into the Empire's new *départements*; he supervised the creation of the 29ᵉ Légion de Gendarmerie de Florence, who were both trained soldiers and an arm of the judicial police. The 29ᵉ Légion sought to be ubiquitous, being formed into units of six, which occupied posts for surveillance and control in every suburb, every valley and every district. They lived in the heart of bandit country, directly confronting the brigands, smugglers and deserters. They were largely made up of French veterans, since the proposal to mix Frenchmen with locals proved impractical. Two successive conscriptions in 1808 and 1809 kept them very busy.

In the summer of 1809, Radet received the most important order of his life: on the emperor's direct authority, he was told to take 1,000 men to Rome and to kidnap the pope. On the night of 5 July they scaled the walls of the Quirinal Palace, where Radet raced round the darkened corridors until he burst into the pontiff's private rooms. '*Saint-Père*,' he began, 'Holy Father, I come in the name of my sovereign, the emperor of the French, to tell you that you must renounce the temporal domains of the Church.' '*Je ne le puis*,' Pius VI is said to have replied, '*je ne le dois pas, je ne le veux pas*' ('I can't do it, I oughtn't to do it and I don't want to do it'). So the raiding party bundled their prisoner into a carriage; Radet locked the door, and climbed on top beside the coachman. Before dawn, they were racing along the northern road out of Rome.

Despite the political tensions and the social unrest, Princess-Duchess-Grand Duchess Elisa Bacciochi thrived. Separated from her husband, she applied herself to the administration and adornment of her extended realms, showing signs of her brother's flare and energy. Her pet project was the complete refurbishment of the Pitti Palace and Boboli Gardens, which she raised to the condition which has distinguished them ever since, and where she prepared a lavish apartment for Napoleon's use on the return visit which he promised to make. She also placed herself at the heart of Florentine artistic life. A painting commissioned from Pietro Benvenuti, now at Versailles, may be regarded as her manifesto: entitled *Elisa Bonaparte entourée d'artistes à Florence*, it shows Elisa wearing a tiara and a dazzling white Empire dress looking down from an elevated throne onto an adoring company of equally resplendent courtiers, soldiers, painters, sculptors and craftsmen. In the foreground, wearing a cocked hat, Antonio Canova is presenting the grand duchess with his latest marble bust, *Elisa en Polymnie*.[54]

Late in July 1809, soon after the grand duchess was installed, the Florentines hardly noticed an incident that was hidden from public view. After a prolonged and nightmare journey from Rome, during which the captive pontiff suffered acute gastric attacks and General Radet was injured when their carriage overturned, Pius VII was brought in the night to the Certosa di Galluzzo, the self-same monastic house at which his late predecessor had resided ten years before. One of his attendants later published an account of their experiences:

> Our approach to this holy spot was known before hand by that worthy sister of Buonaparte, the soi-disante Grand-Duchess of Tuscany, who had the insidious and malignant courtesy to send a message to the Holy Father ... to ask whether there was anything he wanted ... To so unexpected and artful a message, the Pope only answered with his customary heroism: 'I do not know this lady of whom you speak, and I have no need of her services for anything.'[55]

In the morning, since the grand duchess had no intention of taking him in, the captive's involuntary journey restarted. He was taken over the Alps to Briançon and thence, after a change of orders, to indefinite house arrest at Savona on the Riviera.

Meanwhile, the fortunes of the ex-queen-regent were equally sliding from bad to worse. After her expulsion from Florence, she had travelled to Milan for a meeting with Napoleon. He promised her compensation in the dual form of the Principality of Northern Lusitania in Portugal (which he did not control) and marriage to his brother Luciano (who was already married). Unsurprisingly, she rejected both propositions. From Milan, she travelled to her family home at Aranjuez in Spain, which she reached in the wake of her father's abdication. She eventually caught up with her parents and brother on their way into exile: 'I knew nothing of what had been going on, and almost the first words which my father addressed to me on my arrival were: "You must know, my daughter, that our family has for ever ceased to reign." I thought I should have died at the intelligence ... I took leave of my parents and retired to my chamber more dead than alive.'[56]

Yet her ordeal deepened. She plotted to escape with her children to England, but was trapped by the French police, summarily tried, deported to Rome and incarcerated:

> I remained two years and a half in this monastery, and a whole year without seeing a soul, without speaking to a creature, and without being allowed

to write or to receive news, even of my son ... Exactly a month after my entry into the convent, M. Janet, intendant of the treasury, paid me a visit and took from me the jewels I had brought with me ... Once a month only, General Miollis brought my parents and son to see me, but I was not allowed to kiss the dear child more than once.[57]

*

As the ex-queen-regent languished in detention, the French masters of her son's former kingdom were losing the will to stamp their mark on a reluctant population. General Menou left in 1809; General Radet did not return; and the drive to build imperial institutions and to enforce the imperial law gradually lost momentum. 'Quiet reigned in Tuscany,' writes one historian of the years 1809–13, 'but it was the quiet of exhaustion and fear.'[58] Despair set in when many of the recruits and conscripts failed to come home. Food prices soared, bread riots erupted and hunger stalked the countryside. The news from Russia in 1812 was bad, and from the Battle of the Nations at Leipzig in 1813 catastrophic. The Empire was crumbling; its servants lost heart, and the bandits grew bold. Faced by a powerful brigand called Bonaccio, the increasingly impotent prefect of the Arno proposed that he and his band of deserters be offered an amnesty if only they would volunteer to be transported to Spain. In Florence, the prefect only had one depleted Croat regiment at his disposal. Yet his superiors in Paris overruled him. 'All wrongdoers must be captured,' they wrote indignantly, 'or driven beyond the borders of the empire.'[59] By that time, no one in Florence knew where the borders were.

The final act of Tuscany's *anni francesi*, the sad 'French Years', was delivered in the spring of 1814 by a man who had once been present at their launch. Marshal Murat, as he now was, the 'king of Naples', had abandoned Napoleon after Leipzig and changed sides; the Austrians put him in charge of a mixed army of imperial regulars and captured Italians. At their head, he traversed half of Italy, heading for Rome and Naples, and liberating towns and cities from his French compatriots. As his men entered Florence on 23 February, Princess-Grand Duchess Elisa fled, the administration dissolved, the residue of the garrison surrendered and negotiations started almost immediately for the restoration of Grand Duke Ferdinando.

Ex-Queen-Regent Maria-Luisa was already free, liberated on 14 January 1814 when Neapolitan troops drove the French from Rome.

Reunited with her royal parents, she took up residence in the Quirinale Palace, where she was among the dignitaries who welcomed Pope Pius VII in May following his release. During the weeks of waiting, she was writing her memoir in the hope that it would help her to reach England. It ends with a defiant declaration:

> Such is the calamitous history briefly told, which I could spin out into volumes ... I have been the unhappy victim of the blackest treachery, the football of a tyrant who made sport of our lives and properties ... I trust that England, the asylum of unfortunate princes, will not refuse to take under her protection an unhappy widow and mother, with two children ... all three without any support; although we have undisputable rights as sovereigns to the states of Parma, Piacenza and Guastalla as well as Etruria ...[60]

*

At that very time, Napoleon was himself being forced to abdicate. For many months since Leipzig, he had conducted a fighting retreat from Germany. But every victory was pyrrhic; every week his armies dwindled, and every day his supporters grew wearier. Despite dazzling manoeuvres in north-eastern France, he proved incapable of defending Paris. Finally, he bowed to the demand of his generals, and on 11 April 1814 signed an act of unconditional abdication. Though he never revisited Florence as he had promised, he did return to the former Kingdom of Etruria, and in the most unforeseen of circumstances. In return for his agreeing to abdicate, the tsar of Russia insisted that he be given the island of Elba as his private, sovereign domain, and he landed there on 4 May, disembarking from the appropriately named British warship the *Undaunted*. He was allowed to keep 500 officers in his retinue, and 1,100 soldiers for his guard; his house at Portoferraio was dubbed the imperial palace. Prior to his arrival, the populace were said to have burned him in effigy, protesting at the heavy taxes and military conscription still in force; but when they saw him in person, they took him to their hearts, hoping that he could better their lot. They led him in procession to the harbour church, sang a *Te Deum* and presented their petitions.

During the 297 days that Napoleon spent on Elba, he conducted himself with exemplary energy and initiative, setting a shining example for all sovereigns of small states and accomplishing considerably more in those ten months than the Bourbon-Parmas had done in Etruria in six years. He was following in the footsteps of the island's Renaissance ruler, Cosimo I de' Medici, who had founded the town of Cosmopolis (now Portoferraio) in 1548. He designed a flag, issued a constitution, built roads, repaired the harbour, organized plantations and irrigation schemes, reviewed his troops, opened a hospital, reorganized the iron mines and the granite quarry, introduced running water and drainage, and grandly restored three of the island's villas. He was helped, of course, by a generous Allied pension. Despite the close attentions of his mother, 'Madame Mère', he even managed to smuggle in his favourite mistress, Maria Walewska, for a two-day tryst. (His wife, daughter of the Austrian emperor, and his son were in Vienna.) Much of the time, though, was passed in playing the game of spies and counter-spies, in duping his British guards wherever possible, and in seeking information about the growing crisis in France. His entourage of generals, Bertrand, Drouot and Cambronne, was probably more anxious than he.[61]

On arrival on Elba, Napoleon had declared '*Ce sera l'île des repos*' ('This will be the Isle of Relaxations'). He had been on the move, more or less non-stop, for twenty years. He had fought sixty major battles, criss-crossed the Continent from Madrid to Moscow, and had seen millions of men die. The break was welcome, but his health faltered. He put on weight and suffered from urine retention. He lavished attention on his residences, building an Egyptian room at the Palazzo Mulini and an ornamental garden at the Villa San Martino. In high summer he was particularly fond of the hermitage of La Madonna del Monte, whence he strolled around the hills and looked out over the sea to his native Corsica. His favourite viewpoint lay atop a rocky perch still known as the *Sedia de Napoleone*, 'Napoleon's Seat'.

According to the leading nineteenth-century historian of the consulate and Empire, the exiled ex-emperor displayed fine qualities of character:

His life was quiet and fulfilled, for it is in the nature of superior minds to know how to submit to the severities of fate, especially when deserved ... His mother, tough and imperious, but very conscientious ... enjoyed a place of honour ... And Princess Pauline Borghese pushed friendship for her brother to the point of passion ... She was the centre of a small company of people on the island, who ... treated [Napoleon] as their sovereign. He showed himself to be gentle, well-mannered, serene and attentive. When his monarchical duties were done, he spent his time with Bertrand and Drouot, walking, or riding round the island, or sailing a canoe ... He cherished the idea of writing a history of his reign, discussing the more controversial aspects of his career with great frankness. He often returned to the subject of the

failed Peace of Prague*– the only mistake to which he readily admitted ...
He read the newspapers with a remarkable intellectual penetration, that
helped him to find the truth among the thousand assertions of the journalists ... According to him, the march of the French Revolution had only been
halted for a moment ... Further conflicts between [the supporters of] the
ancien régime and of the Revolution were to be expected; and they would
provide the opening for him to reappear on the scene.[62]

Plans for *L'Envol de L'Aigle*, 'The Eagle's Flight', were veiled in
secrecy. The Bonapartists in France had certainly not lost hope; and the
return of thousands of French prisoners from Germany, Russia and
Spain was feeding a large pool of trained but unemployed veterans. The
freshly restored Bourbon king of France, Louis XVIII, was showing no
talent, and had broken an undertaking to pay the ex-emperor a subsidy
of 2 million francs. The Allied Powers had dropped their guard. Napoleon's chief jailer, Sir Neil Campbell, instead of watching his charge, was
in the habit of sailing over to Livorno for entertainment.

A plot, therefore, could be hatched. Whether Napoleon was the insti-
gator or the willing accomplice is immaterial. His troops trained for
a journey. A sloop appeared off the coast during the night of 25/26
February 1815. In the morning, the escape route was open:

Napoleon allowed the soldiers to continue their duties until midday, when
they were given some soup. They were then assembled in the harbour with
their arms and baggage ... Although no one said that they were about to
sail for France, they never doubted it, and broke into transports of indes-
cribable joy! They were immensely excited by the prospect of ... seeing
France again, and of entering once more on the path of power and glory.
And they filled the bay of Porto Ferraio with shouts of *Vive l'Empereur!*[63]

At the last moment, the 'king of Elba' stepped into a rowing boat to be
ferried to the sloop and to seek his destiny once more. Landing near
Antibes on the French Riviera, he set out on the road for Grenoble and
Paris. Somewhere before Grasse, he passed the carriage of the prince of
Monaco. 'Where are you going?' he enquired. '*Chez moi*,' the prince
replied. '*Moi aussi*,' said Napoleon.[64]

---

* More usually, the Congress of Prague, June–August 1813, when Napoleon had the opportunity of making peace with Russia and Prussia during an extended truce. After he rejected
the terms offered, Austria joined the coalition against him, and he was forced into the
unsuccessful campaign that led to his defeat at the Battle of the Nations at Leipzig.

The Battle of Waterloo followed in June. The British army under the duke of Wellington was drawn up to the south of Brussels. The Prussians under Field Marshal Blücher were approaching from the east. Napoleon was confident of victory. His fellow exiles from Elba were with him. But finally the fortunes of war turned against them, and Napoleon quitted the field defeated. General Cambronne, gravely wounded, was lying in a pool of his own blood when called on to surrender by a British officer. According to the official version, he replied, '*La Garde meurt, mais ne se rend pas*' ('The Guard dies, but doesn't surrender'). Rumour spread, however, that '*le Mot de Cambronne*' was not *meurt*, but a different five-letter m-word. A hundred years later, French encyclopedias were still refusing to quote him exactly.[65] 'A mistake may be admitted after one day,' it has been said; 'if delayed, the truth will emerge after one century.'[66] Bertrand would survive to accompany his master on the second exile.[67] Drouot lived on, and was made famous by his great oration when Napoleon's remains were interred in Les Invalides in 1840.[68]

The subsequent fate of the main players in the drama of 'Etruria' can be shortly told. The Emperor Napoleon, of course, was shipped off to St Helena, whence he did not escape. By decree of the Congress of Vienna, his empress, Marie-Louise of Austria (1791–1847) – of whom he had said unkindly '*Je marie un ventre*' ('I am marrying a belly') – was given the former Bourbon Duchy of Parma for life. Her son, the consumptive *Aiglon* or 'Eaglet' (1811–32), was raised and educated in Vienna, where he used the title of duke of Reichstadt; in the view of the Bonapartist purists, he was the Emperor Napoleon II. After his death the Napoleonic succession passed to the *Aiglon*'s uncles, first to Giuseppe and in 1844 to Luigi. Countess Maria Walewska, whom Napoleon last saw briefly on Elba, returned to Poland, divorced her husband and was remarried to one of Napoleon's marshals, Count Philippe Antoine D'Ornano (1784–1863), another Corsican. Maintained by an estate near Naples, she died in 1817 leaving three sons from three different fathers, and some highly controversial memoirs. The handsome son born from her liaison with Napoleon, Alexander Florian Colonna-Walewski (1810–68), fled from service in the Russian army, emigrated to France, served in the Foreign Legion and rose under Napoleon III to be senator, duke and minister of foreign affairs. He married the daughter of Princess Poniatowski in Florence in 1846, resolutely insisting to the last that he was the son of his mother's first husband.[69]

The Grand Duchy of Tuscany, including Florence and Elba, was restored in 1815 to Ferdinando III of Habsburg-Lorraine, who returned to the Pitti Palace after an absence of fifteen years and found it in much better condition than when he had left it. He and his descendants reigned in Florence until 1859–60, when the French came back and the second Kingdom of Italy was formed (see Chapter 8). The former grand duchess of Tuscany, Elisa Buonaparte-Bacciochi, pregnant and still only thirty-eight, was arrested in March 1814 and spent some months in detention in Austria; she took up residence near Trieste, where she died prematurely from a contagious disease, predeceasing her imperial brother. Her husband, Félix Bacciochi, survived her by twenty-one years, but was buried alongside her in the Basilica of St Petronius in Bologna. Her daughter, Elisa Napoleone Bacciochi Levoy (1806–69), sometime princess of Piombino, became the duchess of Camerata by marriage, and her eldest brother, Giuseppe, sailed away to make a new life in the United States.[70] Her ex-royal brother-in-law, Joachim Murat, who changed sides for a second time in 1815, ended up being executed by the post-war Neapolitan authorities. Fearless to the last, he put himself in command of the firing squad that killed him. '*Soldats, faites votre devoir,*' he ordered; 'Soldiers, do your duty. Aim straight at the heart, and spare the face. Fire!'[71]

The *dramatis persona* of the story who recovered against the greatest odds was the ex-queen and ex-queen-regent of Etruria, Maria-Luisa. Resisting multiple misfortunes, she secured a future both for her children and for herself. The Congress of Vienna rewarded her with the Duchy of Lucca, where she replaced the deposed Bacciochi, and where a memorial now stands in the palace that was grandly restored under her guidance. She developed the port of Viareggio, and founded seventeen monasteries. Sadly, she lost the affection of her son, Charles-Louis/Carlo-Luigi (1799–1884), once the boy-king of Etruria and known after 1815 as the 'prince of Lucca', who claimed to have been ruined by her 'physically, morally and financially'. Despite strenuous efforts, she failed to find a new spouse for herself, but arranged her son's marriage to a princess of Savoy, and that of her daughter, Marie-Louise-Charlotte (1802–57), to a prince of Saxony. She died of cancer in Rome in 1824, and her body was taken to the Escorial for burial beside her late husband. She is not short of biographers.[72] Twenty-three years later, her thankless son succeeded to the Duchy of Parma after Napoleon's ex-empress, and lived to a ripe old age.

Of the people who had worked with her in Florence, Count

Fossombroni resumed his earlier career as chief adviser to Grand Duke Ferdinando. Jean-Gabriel Eynard stayed on after 1807 to work for Grand Duchess Elisa. He then settled in Geneva, and became a pioneer of daguerreotype photography and one of Europe's leading philhellenes; he was a co-founder of the Bank of Greece. General Clarke rose to be Napoleon's minister for war; the Marquis de Beauharnais headed several Napoleonic embassies. General Menou died in service on leaving Florence. General Radet was made a baron of the Empire for his exploits in Italy, only to be court-martialled during the Restoration and to serve a four-year sentence of imprisonment.

After Napoleon's death, the surviving Buonaparti felt much more comfortable in Italy than anywhere else. 'Madame Mère' went from Elba to Rome with her daughter, Paolina Borghese, whom she outlived, and died at an advanced age in 1836, never having learned a word of French.[73] Her personality was described by an English art collector, who met her in 1817, when he called to examine her brother's pictures:

The mother of Napoleon . . . resides with her brother, Cardinal Fesch, in the Palazzo Falcone. She was even said to have become a devotee . . . She affects none of the reserve of Lucien in certain matters, but speaks with tears in her eyes about the ex-emperor, displays the feeling of a mother in her language, and laments that he has not written since being on St Helena, fondly cherishing the hope that the English government would finally set him at liberty . . . Madame has evidently been a very fine woman; she still looks well with the aid of her toilette, and her manners are ever dignified. She appears a queen, and refutes those notions, so easily accredited in Britain, [about] the vulgar manners of the Bonaparte family.[74]

The same art collector also records seeing 'Papa Chiaromonti', Pius VII, General Radet's former prisoner:

We have often met his Holiness taking his favourite walk near the Coliseum. His morning dress is a scarlet mantle, a scarlet hat with a very broad brim edged with gold, and scarlet stockings and shoes. When he is met by the Romans, they invariably fall on their knees, and he gives them his blessing. The British stand and take off their hats, and their bows are graciously returned . . . His Holiness's carriage, which is a plain, crazy-looking machine drawn by six horses with riders in purple livery, always follows him.[75]

Paolina, in contrast to her mother, became extravagant in her later years, insisting, it was said, on being carried to her bath by African slaves.[76] Luciano, prince of Canino, the ex-Jacobin, also chose Rome, devoted himself to Etruscan archaeology and died in Viterbo in 1840.[77] His son, Charles-Lucien Bonaparte (1803–57) became a zoologist and ornithologist of international fame, and compiled the first major survey of Italy's natural fauna.[78]

Camillo Borghese, the Roman prince, chose Florence over Rome. Long separated from Paolina, he spent seventeen peaceful years living by the Arno with his mistress and dabbling in Bonapartist plots. For a brief period, when Paolina was mortally sick, Pope Leo XII persuaded him to take in his dying wife. He never left Florence, and both he and Paolina were laid to rest in the Borghese Chapel at the Roman church of Santa Maria Maggiore. Carolina Buonaparte-Murat, the ex-queen of Naples, was the subject of scandalous rumours during the Congress of Vienna about her alleged dalliance with Prince Metternich. It is more certain that Talleyrand said of her, 'she has Cromwell's head on the shoulders of a pretty woman.' ('Cromwell's head' presumably meant ruthless brains.) She moved to Florence in 1830 with her second husband, Francis Macdonald, residing in the Palazzo di Annalena on the Via Romana. A cenotaph in her memory stands by the Murat family tomb in the Père Lachaise cemetery in Paris.[79] Giuseppe, the eldest brother and sometime king of Naples and of Spain, sailed back from the United States to settle in Florence too, and died there in 1844.[80] Girolamo Bonaparte, the youngest brother and erstwhile king of Westphalia, lived in Florence with his third wife until 1853 before moving to Paris as a 'prince imperial' under the Second Empire.[81] Luigi, the ex-king of Holland, who was expelled from his much-loved kingdom by Napoleon and dispossessed by the Restoration, formally renounced French citizenship and spent the second half of his life abroad. But he, too, found his way to Tuscany and died in Livorno.[82] Ironically, it was Luigi's son, Charles Louis-Napoleon (1803–73), who finally inherited the Bonapartist mantle, climbed the political ladder and emerged as the Emperor Napoleon III.[83] Except for his aunt Carolina, who had once sought brief asylum in Ajaccio when Murat was on the run,[84] no single member of the Buonaparte clan ever returned to Corsica.

Nabuleone, Giuseppe and Girolamo were buried in the Parisian Invalides. They were joined in 1940 by the *Aiglon*, whose remains were sent to Paris from Austria with the compliments of Adolf Hitler. In some people's eyes, as veterans of the French service, they rightly belong there. Yet they and their kin were all, in essence, outsiders – as the French might say unkindly, *des intrus*, or as their mother would have said, *intrusi*.

III

So who cares to remember the Kingdom of Etruria? Not the Italians, for whom it occurred during a period of national humiliation. It barely gets a mention in the Museo Napoleonico in Rome.[85] Not the French either, for whom it was a far-away, dead-end episode; nor the Spaniards, for whom the Napoleonic era is both painful and embarrassing. And certainly not the Florentines, who have so many more uplifting things to remember. The answer, therefore, is 'not many'. Historians who study Italy in the early nineteenth century do so to 'the almost total exclusion of the direct and indirect impact of the French Revolution'.[86] One interested party (one imagines) is the Bourbon family, which has survived intermittently on the throne of Spain and whose followers maintain a thriving genealogical industry.[87] Apart from them, there is only the occasional Bonapartist pilgrim, and the faithful readers of nonconformist historians. Elba is for ever associated with Napoleon. Florence is not.

Yet a 'Napoleonic Tour' of Florence and Tuscany might prove a worthy addition to those already operating. Day 1 could start at the Piazza della Signoria, to see if anyone among the admirers of Michelangelo's *David* has heard of the *Albero della Libertà* or of *Napoleon as Mars the Peacemaker*. An extended stop at the Pitti Palace, where Napoleon met the grand duke of Tuscany, could concentrate on the contrasting management styles of the queen-regent of Etruria and of Grand Duchess Elisa Bacciochi. A short trip out to the beautiful Certosa di Galluzzo, where two popes were held prisoner, would serve as a reminder of the ingrained coercion of Napoleonic regimes. In the evening, there is time to drive down the Val d'Arno to the ruined castle at Fuccechio and the church at San Miniato, whose hillside perches face each other across the valley. San Miniato del Tedesco, to give its full name, once an imperial residence on the pilgrim route to Rome, where Napoleon met the Abbé Filippo Buonaparte, is a good place to stay overnight. The Torrione Tower was the scene of the suicide of Pier della Vigna, secretary to Emperor Frederick II, as recounted in Dante's *Inferno*;[88] the Palazzo Buonaparte still stands in the town square and a copy of Napoleon's death mask is on display nearby.[89] The best time to visit is mid-November, when one can combine historical explorations with the *Mostra Mercato Nazionale del Tartufo Bianco* ('National Commercial Fair of the White Truffle').[90] Truffle-based recipes can be sampled at the *Ristorante Accademia degli Affidati* on the Piazza Napoleone.[91]

Day 2 starts with a gentle downhill trip to Lucca, where the palace is stocked not only with more memories of Elisa and Maria-Luisa but with many art treasures. In the afternoon, one sails across the strait on the ferry from Piombino to Portoferraio on Elba, admires the Villa San Martino and finishes with the steep climb above Marciana to a well-deserved rest at La Madonna del Monte. Sunset over the sea, as viewed from the *Sedia de Napoleone*, provides the finest of settings for thoughts on the fickleness of fortune both for individuals and for kingdoms.

On this issue, both Dante and Machiavelli have much to say. Machiavelli regards Fortune as the creator of opportunities, which some men exploit to their advantage and others neglect at their cost. The important thing is for a ruler to be flexible, adaptable and enterprising. 'It is better to be bold than timid and cautious,' he wrote, 'because Fortune is a woman, and the man who wants to control her must treat her roughly.'[92]

Dante, like most of his educated contemporaries, was heir to the classical tradition where the Goddess Fortuna dispenses good luck and bad luck by turns. As a reader of Boethius, he was familiar with the image of Fortuna's Wheel, whose four axes were marked with the words *regno* ('I reign'), *regnavi* ('I have reigned'), *sum sine regno* ('I am without a kingdom') and *regnabo* ('I shall reign'). In the *Inferno*, he put his views into the mouth of his guide Virgil, whose exposition nevertheless assumes unexpected Christian overtones. Dante held that what unbelievers might call Chance is really the work of Divine Providence, whose dispensations govern the Wheel of Fortune no less than the motions of the universe. Lady Fortuna is praiseworthy, therefore, and men are foolish to 'crucify her' simply because the causes of her actions are not fully understood:

> *per ch'una gente impera e l'altra langue*
> *seguendo lo giudicio di costei*
> *che è occulto, com'in erba l'angue.*

('For one nation rules and another languishes / according to her hidden judgement, / hidden like a snake in the grass.')[93]

11

Rosenau

The Loved and Unwanted Legacy

(*1826–1918*)

Coburg, sometimes spelled Koburg, is a tidy country town close to the dead centre of the German Federal Republic. It sits astride one of the streams that flow down from the Thüringian forest into the circle of Upper Franconia in northern Bavaria. It makes its living from wood-working and furniture-making, and is home to some 42,000 inhabitants. Its historical monuments include the medieval hilltop fortress, the *Veste Coburg*, and the ostentatious former ducal palace, the *Schloss Ehrenburg*.[1] Bayreuth, the city of Wagner, lies some 40 miles distant.

The town of Gotha, some two hours' drive to the north, lies at the foot of the opposite slopes in the Free State of Thüringia, whose dense forests have given it the label of the 'green heart of Germany'. It is a local administrative centre and, with 46,000 inhabitants, is slightly larger than Coburg; its name, meaning 'Waters of the Goths', appears as *Gotaha* in a document of Charlemagne's era. Its principal modern attraction is the Friedenstein, a former ducal palace and 'pearl of the early Baroque'.[2] Eisenach, overlooked by the Wartburg castle where Martin Luther took refuge, lies only 16 miles to the west, and Erfurt, the *Land* capital, a similar short distance to the east.

In the course of their long history, the towns of Coburg and Gotha and their dependent districts were sometimes ruled separately and sometimes together. Their part of Germany was famous for its teeming mass of small states, all of which had once claimed to be equal members of the Holy Roman Empire; Coburg and Gotha, on the borders of Saxony and Bavaria, usually fell within the Saxon political orbit. In the early nine-teenth century, however, the two statelets were joined together in a territorial reorganization agreed among descendants of the kings of Sax-ony; and for the nine decades up to 1918, a sovereign duchy functioned there under a single line of ruling dukes.[3] In that era, the principal ducal

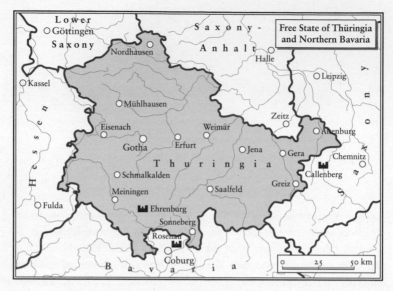

seat lay neither in Coburg nor in Gotha, but at *Schloss Rosenau*, near
Rodenthal. The united duchy was broken up after the First World War,
when the citizens of Coburg voted to join Bavaria. After the Second World
War, from 1949 to 1990, Coburg found itself in West Germany, while
Gotha belonged to the Communist-ruled German Democratic Republic.

Nowadays, Rosenau Castle is owned by the Bavarian government.
Originally founded in the fourteenth century as the hunting lodge of a
rich merchant, the castle was bought by a duke of Saxe-Gotha in 1721
and remained in the possession of his descendants for two hundred
years. It was twice allowed to fall into rack and ruin, once during the
Napoleonic Wars and again after the Second World War. Having ceased
to be a private property in 1918, it was taken over during the Third
Reich by the National Socialists' Women's Service and then by the Luft-
waffe. After the war, when General Eisenhower's headquarters was
located for a time at Gotha, it was used by the US army. By the 1970s,
it became a derelict 'national monument'.

The more recent restoration of Rosenau by Bavaria's *Schlösser- und
Gärtenverwaltung*, the 'Castle and Garden Administration', was started
in 1990, and completed by the turn of the century. The aim was to bring
the house and park back to the prime condition which they had enjoyed
in the 1840s. 'The palace, basically a medieval structure, had been
rebuilt from 1808 to 1817 in the neo-Gothic style,' explains the English
website of the 'Bavarian Palace Department':

1. The Abbey of Hautecombe, Lac du Bourget, Savoy: site of the mausoleum of the *Casa Savoia*.

2. *Mont Blanc*, painted by J. M. W. Turner in 1837, when Western Europe's highest peak ormed part of the Sardinian 'Sub-alpine Kingdom'.

VOTING AT CHAMBERY FOR THE ANNEXATION OF SAVOY TO FRANCE.

43. (*above*) April 1860: voters line up in Chambéry for the Plebiscite on the future of Savoy.

44. (*left*) Vittorio Emanuele II (r. 1849–78), king of Sardinia and, from 1861, of Italy.

45. (*left*) 1910: the fiftieth anniversary of Savoy's 'reunion' with France.

Le Petit Journal

SUPPLÉMENT ILLUSTRÉ

DIMANCHE 18 SEPTEMBRE 1910

CINQUANTENAIRE DE LA RÉUNION DE LA SAVOIE A LA FRANCE

46. (*below*) Referendum of 1946: Italian monarchists support 'Umberto II, the Monarchy and the Soldier King'.

47. Maria-Luisa di Borbone (1782–1824) as Queen Regent of Etruria, c. 1804, with her son, King Carlo Lodovico II, and her daughter, Maria Luisa Carlota.

48. A 10-lira silver florin of the Kingdom of Etruria (1803), showing the infant king with his mother and, on the reverse, the kingdom's coat-of-arms.

49. *Elisa Bonaparte entourée d'artistes à Florence* (1809) by Pietro Benvenuti. Antonio Canova presents a marble bust to Napoleon's eldest sister who was the duchess of Lucca, grand duchess of Tuscany and princess of Piombino.

50. San Miniato in Val d'Arno: sometime home of the Buonaparti and of superb white truffles.

NAPOLÉON À L'ILE D'ELBE

51. Napoleon's First Exile, Elba, 1814: behind him Generals Bertrand, Drouot and Cambronne, who may or may not have said '*La Garde meurt*'.

52. Royal *Wedding*, 1840, at the Chapel Royal, St James's Palace: Victoria, who had proposed to Albert, nonetheless promised 'to serve and obey' him.

53. Queen Victoria and family, Coburg, 21 April 1894: Kaiser Wilhelm II, the Queen, Dowager Empress 'Vickie' of Germany (*front row seated L to R*); also, the Queen's surviving sons, in uniform – Edward (*middle, L*), Alfred, (*back R*) and Arthur (*second row, R*); the future Tsar, Nicholas II with fiancée Alix of Hesse (*second row*); 3 Russian grand dukes, 3 Battenbergs, 10 Saxe-Coburg and Gothas, and 13 princesses; Prince 'Alfie' of Saxe-Coburg and Gotha, d. 1899 (*standing extreme L*).

S. K. H. Herzog Carl Eduard
von S.-Coburg-Gotha.

54. (*left*) Prince Charles Edward (1884–1953): Victoria and Albert's youngest grandson, the last duke of Albany and the last duke of Saxe-Coburg and Gotha.

55. (*below*) Princess Elizabeth and Prince Philip: but for the name-changing, their wedding in 1947 would have seen a Saxe-Coburg and Gotha marrying a Schleswig-Holstein-Sonderburg-Glücksburg.

56. (*below*) The funeral of King George V, January 1936. The late king's cousin, Charles Edward, brings up the rear of the procession wearing a steel German helmet.

57. (*above*) Adolf
Hitler enters
Prague, 15 March
1939.

58. (*left*) Khust:
capital for one day
of the Republic of
Carpatho-Ukraine

Particular highlights are the Marble Hall with its three aisles, and the residential apartments with their colourful wall decoration and original Biedermeier furniture from Vienna. Among the structures that have survived in the landscaped park with its 'Swan Lake' and 'Prince's Pond' are the orangery, the tea-house (today the park restaurant), the Jousting Column (sundial), and parts of the hermitage.[4]

Once the restoration was in progress, Rosenau attracted interest from connoisseurs of art and architecture the world over. British magazines sent experts out to report: 'Today, after years of neglect, Rosenau has become once more the perfect Biedermeier dream of a little Gothic castle. Its small but pretty interiors full of stained glass, brightly colored painted and papered walls, and elaborately decorated ceilings are all now exquisitely restored to their former glory after a decade of patient work.'[5] Guided tours are provided every hour on the hour.[6] Visitors are impressed by the fact that Rosenau has been rescued from ruin twice over. Art and architecture, however, do not explain everything. Fascination with 'the perfect Biedermeier dream' far exceeds the intrinsic merit of Rosenau's romantic views or its fine Marble Hall. Much of the excitement derives from its connections with a world-famous man and wife who loved each other deeply and who both loved Rosenau. In 2011, the 150th anniversary of the husband's death provided the pretext for a series of exhibitions, concerts and readings, not only at Rosenau but also at the Callenberg and Ehrenburg palaces. The festivities were modestly billed 'Coburg Commemorates One of its Famous Inhabitants'.[7]

II

Franz Albrecht Karl August Immanuel (1819–61) was not a king. But he was definitely royal, both by birth and later by marriage. He was the second son of Ernst III, duke of Saxe-Coburg-Saalfeld, and of Louise, princess of the neighbouring Duchy of Saxe-Gotha-Altenburg, and as such a scion of the senior, Ernestine branch of the Wettins, the royal House of Saxony.* As he grew up, his relatives long pondered the possibility of exploiting their links with leading foreign monarchies.

---

* *Saxe* is the French name for Saxony, as opposed to *Sachsen* in German. Since the German aristocracy had the habit of speaking French, however, they often wrote their titles in the French form, and it was the French form that passed into English usage. '*Saxe Coburg*' stands for 'Coburg Saxony' and '*Saxe Gotha*' for 'Gotha Saxony'.

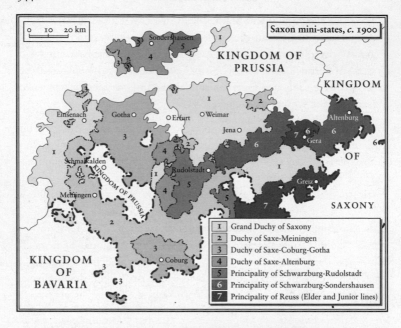

The prince was born and raised at Rosenau. The day following his birth, his paternal grandmother, the dowager duchess of Coburg-Saalfeld, wrote to her married daughter in England:

> *Rosenau, August 27, 1819*
>
> [Louischen] was yesterday morning safely and quickly delivered of a little boy. Siebold, the *accoucheuse*, had only been called at three, and at six the little one gave his first cry in this world, and looked about like a little squirrel with a pair of large black eyes. At a quarter to 7 I heard the tramp of a horse. It was a groom, who brought the joyful news. I was off directly, as you may imagine, and found the little mother slightly exhausted, but *gaie et dispos*. She sends you and Edward [the duke of Kent] a thousand kind messages . . .[8]

'The little boy is to be christened tomorrow', his grandmother continued. 'The Emperor of Austria, the old Duke of Saxe-Teschen, the Duke of Gotha, Mensdorff, and I are to be sponsors.' Baptism into the Lutheran Protestant faith was performed by an archbishop in Rosenau's Marble Hall. Since the Austrian emperor was Catholic, he was appointed 'sponsor' rather than godfather; it was in his honour that the infant's first given name was Franz. But for everyday purposes, his parents intended to call him Albrecht after the duke of Saxe-Teschen.

After the duke of Gotha's death, when Albrecht was six, the two families of Coburg and Gotha decided to merge their duchies in a personal union. The result from 1826 was a united Duchy of Saxe-Coburg and Gotha – in German, *Das Herzogtum Sachsen-Coburg und Gotha* – whose two parts were separated by a substantial band of territory belonging to the Kingdom of Saxony. Albrecht's father changed his title, becoming Duke Ernst I; and his elder brother, also Ernst, became the heir apparent. The new duchy's attractive bicolour standard, the *Landesflagge*, displayed two horizontal halves: the upper half in apple green, the lower half in white.[9]

Rosenau during Albrecht's boyhood was basking in the glory of its first renovation. A local almanac noted the stark contrast with its condition only a few years earlier: 'The busy court ladies enjoy views of beautiful nature, where not so long ago pigeons and swallows, owls and bats nested ... When the present re-shaping of the castle began it was just the dirty and uncomfortable dwelling of boorish tenants; the fine Marble Hall was a dust-tip and wood-store.'[10] The Duchess Louise was particularly pleased with her own quarters: 'I live on the second floor ... I have a little living room, where if there are not too many visitors we generally drink our tea. The wallpaper is gold with dark blue vine leaves ... My sitting-room ... is grey, dark blue and gold.'[11]

A more extensive description can be found in the volume compiled long afterwards by Albrecht's widow:

> Distant about four miles from Coburg, it is charmingly placed on a knoll that rises abruptly ... from a range of wooded hills which divide the lovely valley of the Itz from the broad and undulating plain ... The knoll on which the house stands ... falls precipitously on the east side to the Itz, and by a very steep descent on the other three sides to the plain ...
>
> The top forms a small plateau, on the southern edge of which stands the house, a solid oblong building ... with high gable-ends. The entrance is in a round tower on the west side of the house, to which the approach ascends through a thick grove of young spruce firs ... A broad winding staircase in the tower leads upwards to the principal rooms on the first floor, and downwards to the Marble Hall, or dining-room ...
>
> A small terrace-garden at the north end ... commands a lovely view of the Itz, beyond which ... the country is broken up into a succession of wooded hills and picturesque valleys, with ... smiling, tidy villages standing in the middle of rich meadows and orchards, the hills gradually rising up to the highest points of the Thüringerwald ...

The Marble Hall ... opens on a small gravelled space, bounded by a neatly trimmed hedge of roses, and communicating ... by a long and irregular flight of stone steps, with the walk along the banks of the [river] below. Standing on this space in the early morning ... or in the afternoon ... it is difficult to imagine anything more bright or enjoyable.

Prominent amongst the trees which grow and thrive at the Rosenau is the Abele poplar, of which there are many very good specimens here ... This accounts at once for this tree having always been a favourite one with the Prince, for surely no man was ever endowed with a stronger feeling of love for all the recollections and associations of his youth, and of his native place.[12]

Albrecht would tell his wife that his childhood at Rosenau had been 'paradise'. He and his older brother had been handed over at an early age to the care of a tutor called Christopher Florschütz, who attended the boys night and day, being responsible for all aspects of their upbringing:

The children soon discovered that Florschütz's stern exterior hid a heart of gold. Although only twenty-five, he had already been ... tutor to the two youngest sons of duke [Ernst]'s eldest sister, Alexander and Arthur Mensdorff. Many of duke [Ernst]'s old-fashioned friends deplored the choice of a man of known liberal principles ... (later on, some of them even blamed Florschütz for letting them attend lectures in philosophy at Bonn, on the ground that such studies might lead to anarchy!) Mathematics and Latin formed the basis of Florschütz's teaching ... together with wide reading of modern literature in German, French and English. Florschütz spoke English well, so that [his younger pupil] was familiar with it from the age of four ...

Florschütz ... was a born teacher who [imparted] a love of learning for its own sake, and there is no doubt that [Albrecht]'s passionate interest in science was a direct result of having physics and chemistry presented to him in an interesting way as a boy ... Above all, Florschütz taught them to go to the root of everything, to accept nothing at second hand, to use their eyes and to look about them for beauty in nature, art, literature and humanity.[13]

By speaking English with Florschütz, Albrecht would have learned for the first time to think of himself sometimes as Albert, and of his brother as Ernest; it was an important transition. He would have known from an early age that his paternal aunt, Victoria of Saxe-Coburg-Saalfeld, his father's widowed sister, was now duchess of Kent and living in

London with her three children. Having cousins in London, he would have seen the point of giving English an equal place in his studies with the more usual French. His diligence, aged fourteen, may be gauged from a timetable that he prepared for himself in 1833 (see p. 548).

The paradise, however, had its dark side. Albert's immediate family could not give him the warmth and encouragement on which children thrive. His father, the duke, was a shameless syphilitic rake, said to organize orgies in one of his other residences at Callenberg. He had brought a mistress from France, Mme Panam, whose insufferable son used the self-styled name of 'prince de Coburg', and whose memoirs, published in 1823, brought shame on all concerned.[14] Albert's mother, the Duchess Louise, disgusted by her husband's debauchery, chose a formal separation, even though this most cruelly forced her to abandon her children. When she was leaving, a large crowd of well-wishers gathered at Rosenau to see her off. Her sons, confined in the nursery with whooping cough, could not join them. In due course, she divorced and remarried, but died young, of cancer. She was replaced at Rosenau by the duke's cousin and second wife, Antoinette-Marie of Württemberg, who failed to establish a warm relationship with her stepsons. Worse still, though they rarely quarrelled openly, Albert did not really find a soulmate in the elder brother, who shared his fate for more than twenty years:

These brothers, born in 1818 and 1819, were so dissimilar in character and appearance that there were mischievous rumours that the younger one was illegitimate ... Almost from the day of his birth Albert's beauty was remarked upon. 'Lovely as a little angel,' his mother recorded in his infancy. His eyes, like his mother's, were deep blue and his curly hair was at first fair.

Albert's brother Ernest 'was as unattractive as Prince Albert was attractive. His complexion,' ran [one] harsh description, 'was sallow with liver spots, his eyes were bloodshot, and his lower teeth, like those of a bulldog, protruded far above his upper ones.' He was 'a mighty hunter of wine, women and song'. Even from their infancy, it was plainly evident that the elder son took after his father ... while Albert strongly resembled his mother ...

[Another relative] found it puzzling that [Prince Albert] turned out to have so fine a character 'with such a father and such a brother, both equally unprincipled'. When Albert was still only four, his mother suddenly disappeared from his life for ever ... it was typical of the boy, and later of the man, that he never uttered a bitter comment on this occurrence, and always thought of his mother with great tenderness.[15]

Table 3. Albert's timetable[16]

Hours	Monday	Tuesday	Wednesday	Thursday	Friday	Saturday
6–7	Translation from the French	Exercises in music	Reading	Exercises in memory	Exercises in music	Correspondence
7–8	Repetition and preparation in history	Preparation in religion	Riding	Repetition and preparation in history	Exercises in memory	Riding
8–9	Modern history	Religious instruction	Exercises in German composition	Religious instruction	Ancient history	Exercises in German composition
10–11	Ovid	Ovid	Music	Modern history	Exercises in Latin composition	Music
11–12	English	Logic	English	English	Natural history	English
12–1	Mathematics	Geography	French	Cicero	Logic	French
1–2			Drawing			Drawing
6–7	French	English exercises	French	English exercises	French	Geography
7–8	Exercises in Latin composition	Written translation of Sallust	Mathematics	Mathematics	Latin exercises Sallust	Correspondence

The 'mischievous rumours' were generated by speculation that his mother may have indulged in a secret liaison before his birth, possibly with an army lieutenant or with a Jewish chamberlain at Coburg.[17] Closer examination of the circumstances leads to the unproven hypothesis that the child's biological father could have been Prince Leopold, the future king of the Belgians and the most likely source of allegations designed to cover his own tracks.[18]

Albert of Saxe-Coburg-Gotha and Victoria of Kent were introduced to each other in May 1836 by their hopeful relatives. He was still sixteen; she had just passed her seventeenth birthday. 'Uncle Leopold', who by now was King Leopold, was brother both to Albert's father and to Victoria's mother; and it was he who arranged for his two Saxon nephews to travel to London to meet their cousin, already the heiress to the British throne. The scheme worked to perfection. Victoria wrote to her uncle thanking him for 'the prospect of great happiness . . . in the person of dear Albert'. There was no question at this stage of an engagement. The old king, William IV, disapproved. But the emotional bond, at least on the girl's side, was sealed.

Victoria's family, the Hanoverians, were no less German than Albert's, having consistently imported brides from Germany for all their heirs apparent, and they were even more painfully dysfunctional. Victoria, who had been conceived in Saxony and born in England,* was surrounded by German women in her infancy and only began English lessons from the age of five. She never knew her father, the duke of Kent, who died young; indeed, cruel gossip hinted that she, too, was not her father's biological child.[19] Three of her four surviving paternal uncles, including the king, were estranged from their wives; bastard cousins proliferated;[20] sexual and hereditary diseases, especially porphyria, were rampant; premature deaths were commonplace.[21] Victoria had only become heir apparent in 1830 because all three of her father's older brothers died without legitimate issue. Her mother, the duchess of Kent, never gained a proper grasp of English; she had two older, German-speaking children from a previous marriage, and lived in London with a lover thinly disguised as her household comptroller;† she was jealous and overprotective of her latest offspring, preventing Victoria making friends and subjecting her to a

---

* By a curious coincidence, the same midwife, Frau Siebold, had attended Victoria's birth at Kensington Palace three months before officiating at Albert's birth at Rosenau. The Kents' wedding had taken place at the bride's home in the Ehrenburg Palace at Coburg in May 1818. Shortly after, the duchess of Kent announced her pregnancy and promptly left for England to ensure that her child would be British-born, taking Frau Siebold with her.
† Sir John Conroy.

The Hanovers and the Wettins

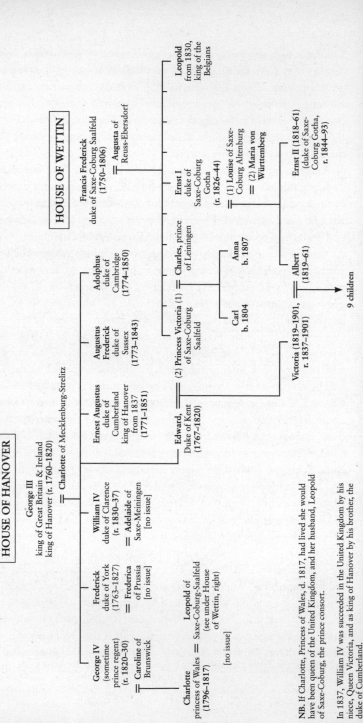

HOUSE OF HANOVER

George III
king of Great Britain & Ireland
king of Hanover (r. 1760–1820)
= Charlotte of Mecklenburg-Strelitz

Georg IV (sometime prince regent) (r. 1820–30)
= Caroline of Brunswick

Frederick duke of York (1763–1827)
= Frederica of Prussia [no issue]

William IV duke of Clarence (r. 1830–37)
= Adelaide of Saxe-Meiningen [no issue]

Ernest Augustus duke of Cumberland king of Hanover from 1837 (1771–1851)

Augustus Frederick duke of Sussex (1773–1843)

Adolphus duke of Cambridge (1774–1850)

Edward, Duke of Kent (1767–1820)

Charlotte princess of Wales (1796–1817) = **Leopold** of Saxe-Coburg-Saalfeld (see under House of Wettin, right) [no issue]

HOUSE OF WETTIN

Francis Frederick duke of Saxe-Coburg Saalfeld (1750–1806)
= Augusta of Reuss-Ebersdorf

Ernst I duke of Saxe-Coburg Gotha (r. 1826–44)
(1) Louise of Saxe-Coburg Altenburg = (2) Maria von Württemberg

Leopold from 1830, king of the Belgians

Charles, prince of Leiningen = (2) **Princess Victoria** (1) of Saxe-Coburg Saalfeld

Carl b. 1804   Anna b. 1807

Albert (1819–61)

Ernst II (1818–61) (duke of Saxe-Coburg Gotha, r. 1844–93)

Victoria (1819–1901, r. 1837–1901) = **Albert** (1819–61) → 9 children

NB. If Charlotte, Princess of Wales, d. 1817, had lived she would have been queen of the United Kingdom, and her husband, Leopold of Saxe-Coburg, the prince consort.

In 1837, William IV was succeeded in the United Kingdom by his niece, Queen Victoria, and as king of Hanover by his brother, the duke of Cumberland.

repressive daily regime. Fearful of the illicit liaisons with which the royal
court was riddled, she even forced her adolescent daughter to sleep with
her in the same room. The lonely teenager, locked up in Kensington Palace for longer than she could remember, sought solace with her spaniel,
Dash, and with her beloved governess, Louise Lehzen, a Coburger.

Victoria, in short, had much in common with her handsome Saxon
cousin; and she determined to resist all alternative suitors. William IV
died a year after his visit and she was crowned queen in 1838. Albert
was invited back the following year. He meanwhile had been patiently
studying at the University of Bonn, staying with Uncle Leopold in Brussels and undertaking a 'Grand Tour' of Italy. He arrived in Windsor on
15 October 1839, and the queen proposed marriage on the morning of
the fourth day of his return. Her journal overflowed with superlatives:

> Oh! to *feel* I was, and am loved by such an *Angel* as Albert was *too great
> a delight to describe!* He is *perfection*; perfection in every way – in beauty –
> in everything! I told him I was quite unworthy of him and kissed his dear
> hand – he said he would be very happy '*das Leben mit dir zu zubringen*'
> and was so kind . . . it was the happiest, brightest moment of my life, which
> made up for all I had suffered and endured. Oh! *how* I adore and love him,
> I cannot say!![22]

Albert's account of the betrothal is contained in a letter which he
wrote shortly afterwards to his grandmother, the dowager duchess of
Gotha; it was to be translated into English for the authorized description of his early years compiled under Victoria's supervision:

> *Liebe Grossmama . . .*
> The Queen sent for me alone to her room . . . and declared to me in a genuine
> outburst of love and affection (*in einem wahren Ergusse von Herzlichkeit und
> Liebe*) that I had gained her whole heart (*ich habe ihr ganzes Herz gewonnen*)
> and would make her intensely happy (*überglücklich*) if I would make her the
> sacrifice of sharing my life with her (*wenn ich das Opfer bringen wolle, mit ihr
> mein Leben zu theilen*) . . . ; the only thing that troubled her was that she did
> not think herself worthy of me (*das sie meiner nicht werth ware*) . . .[23]

Both the queen and the prince were native German-speakers; it would
have been strange, when pledging their troth, if they had turned to some
other language. Certainly, German was the idiom that they would use
for personal and domestic purposes for the rest of their life together.

Prince Albert's journey to England in anticipation of their wedding occupied two freezing weeks early in 1840. He started on 28 January from his grandmother's house in Gotha:

> The streets were densely crowded, every window was crammed with heads, every house-top covered with people waving handkerchiefs, and vying with each other in demonstrations of affection ... The carriages stopped in passing the Dowager Duchess's, and Prince Albert got out with his father and brother to bid her a last adieu ...
>
> Having passed in a long procession through the town ... the Princes took a final leave at the Last Shilling, and got into one of the Queen's travelling-carriages. The Duke, attended by Colonel Grey, went another German mile to the frontier, where an arch of green fir-trees had been erected, and a number of young girls dressed in white, with roses and garlands, and a band of musicians and singers ... were assembled to bid a final 'Godspeed', as he left his native land behind him.
>
> The travelling-carriages, with the fourgons, were eight in number ... The Duke and Princes were attended, in addition to the three English gentlemen (Lord Torrington, Colonel Grey, and Mr. Seymour), by Counts Alvensleben, Kolowrath, Gruben, and Pöllnitz ...
>
> A little before nine [a.m.], the party left Cassel to go seventeen German miles to Arnsberg, where they only arrived as the clock was striking ten in the evening. The following night was passed at Deutz ...
>
> The Rhine ... had to be crossed the next morning in boats, a tedious and a cold operation, made more disagreeable by the heavy rain ... The party left Cologne about half past nine, dined at Aix-la-Chapelle about three, and arrived at Liège, where they slept, about ten. At Aix-la-Chapelle the Prince heard the news of the rejection of the proposed grant of £50,000 ... It led him to fear that the people of England were not pleased with the marriage ...
>
> Before leaving Liège, the Duke received all the authorities, civil and military, who were severally introduced ... At ten, the whole party was conveyed, in one large omnibus, to the railroad terminus at Ans, where a special train had been provided, by which they were taken in four hours to Brussels ...
>
> On Wednesday the 5th February, at half past seven, the journey to England was resumed, by rail as far as Ostend, and thence posting along the coast by Dunkirk and Gravelines to Calais ... At half past eleven the two Princes arrived at Calais, where, notwithstanding the lateness of the hour, they found all the officers of the garrison waiting at the hotel to receive them ... Lord Clarence Paget, who had been sent in the *Firebrand* to escort the Prince over, also met the party at the hotel ...

[Early on] Thursday the 6th February, the weather was beautiful, with a light air from the N.W. Unfortunately the tide was too low to admit of sailing before half past eleven; and in the meantime the day changed. A strong breeze freshened up from the S.E., and increased almost to a gale. The *Firebrand* not being able to get out so soon, the whole party had embarked in the *Ariel*, one of the Dover packets . . . But the passage was long (five hours and a half); and the deck of the little steamer was a scene of almost universal misery and seasickness. The Duke had gone below, and on either side of the cabin staircase lay the two Princes, in an almost helpless state. The sea got heavier as the vessel approached the land, and it was by no common effort . . . that Prince Albert, who had continued to suffer up to the last moment, got up as it entered between the piers to bow to the people by which they were crowded.

The inhospitable mood of the English Channel could easily have been taken as a bad omen. But as soon as they docked the Prince's spirits rose rapidly:

Nothing could exceed the enthusiasm which greeted the Prince when he set his foot on shore as the affianced husband of our Queen . . . The night was spent at Dover, at the York Hotel, and after a very poor attempt by most of the party at dinner, everyone was glad to get to bed.

It had been arranged that the Prince should not arrive at Buckingham Palace till Saturday. A short journey was therefore made the next day to Canterbury . . . The Royal party arrived accompanied by an escort of the 11th Hussars, and having received an address from the city authorities, the Prince, with his brother, attended the service of the Cathedral at three. In the evening the city was illuminated, and a vast crowd assembled before the hotel, cheering for the Prince, who answered their call by appearing, to their great delight, on the balcony.

From Canterbury the Prince sent on his valet with his favourite greyhound, Eôs, and the Queen speaks in her journal of the pleasure which the sight of 'dear Eôs' gave her . . .

On Saturday morning, the 8th, after receiving an address from the Dean and Chapter, the Prince left at ten for London, meeting with the same enthusiastic reception along the whole line of route to Buckingham Palace. Here the party arrived at half past four o'clock, and were received at the hall-door by the Queen and the Duchess of Kent, attended by the whole household. At five o'clock the Lord Chancellor administrated the oaths of naturalisation to the Prince, and the day ended by a great dinner, attended by the officers of State, Lord Melbourne, etc., the Queen recording in her journal, in warm terms, the great joy she felt at seeing the Prince again . . .

But amidst ... all the rejoicings and festivities ... the grandmother left behind at Gotha ... was not forgotten ... And the Prince himself, on the morning of his wedding-day, sent her these few touching lines:

'Dear Grandmama, In less than three hours I shall stand before the altar with my dear bride! In these solemn moments I must once more ask for your blessing, which I am well assured I shall receive, and which will be my safeguard and my future joy! I must end. God help me!

Ever your faithful Grandson.
London, Feb. 10, 1840.'[24]

The royal wedding took place in the Chapel Royal of St James's Palace. It gave the bridegroom the title of His Royal Highness, the House of Lords having refused to make him a peer of the realm, and the Commons awarding him only a reduced grant from the Civil List. The prime minister, Lord Melbourne, parried the queen's request for the elevation of her husband to 'king-consort'; seventeen years would pass before the lesser title of 'prince consort' would be granted. Albert feigned indifference. 'It would almost be a step downwards,' he wrote. 'As a Duke of Saxony I feel myself much higher than a Duke of York or Kent.' His consolation was that by marrying Victoria he had given his own name of Saxe-Coburg and Gotha to the British royal family. He had also the gratification of hearing his bride promise 'to obey him and serve him'. Five months earlier, the queen's advisers had insisted that he would *not* be allowed to propose marriage during their engagement but that the proposal must be made by her. Yet now, when it came to the wedding, they did not interfere with the traditional service. Albert was required 'to love, comfort, honour and keep' his wedded wife, but Victoria was further required to proffer both obedience and service to her wedded husband.[25] This was no mean concession. And he had entered the Chapel Royal surrounded by the knighthood, chivalry, pomp and insignia of his homeland:

THE BRIDEGROOM

HIS ROYAL HIGHNESS, FIELD-MARSHAL PRINCE ALBERT, K.G.

Wearing the Collar of the Order of the Garter
Supported by their Serene Highnesses, the reigning Duke of
Saxe-Coburg and Gotha
And the Hereditary Prince of Saxe-Coburg and Gotha,
Each attended by the Officers of their Suite, namely
Count Kolowrath, Baron Alvensleben and Baron de Lowenfels.[26]

His father, the duke, wore the dark-green uniform with red piping of his duchy's army, thigh-length military boots and the Grand Cross of the highest ducal order. His brother, Prince Ernst, wore a light-blue cavalry uniform, adorned by the Star of Coburg-Gotha and the Collar of the Garter, and carried an officer's helmet. They had entered their carriages amid the sound of trumpets and 'all the honours paid to the Queen herself'; and they left the Palace escorted by a squadron of Life Guards.

Some historians do not accept the conventional picture of an ecstatic, well-matched couple, each content in their complementary roles. They suggest that Albert in particular was unhappy in his subordinate position, presuming that the emotional rigours of his childhood had made him a dissembler. He was never so deeply in love as the besotted Victoria, they say; he plotted his life's course as he played chess, move by move, and callously exploited his wife's numerous pregnancies in order to strengthen his hold over her. He was a voracious, obsessive hunter, killing animals en masse for pleasure, and a harsh father to his sons. In the political sphere he did far more than hold the blotter while his wife signed the state papers: he maintained a clandestine correspondence with his kinsmen in Germany, especially in Prussia, using Rothschilds Bank as a conduit for letters. He refused to stay out of controversies, and appeared in the public gallery of the House of Lords, for example, to air his views on the Corn Laws.[27]

Nonetheless, Albert's ascent to the highest level of royal and aristocratic society cannot have failed to arouse some sense of satisfaction, not least because his native duchy was home to the most prestigious of publications on these matters. The *Almanach de Gotha* was Europe's most authoritative genealogical guide for nearly 200 years. First issued in 1763, it listed names in three sections: I. Sovereign Houses, II. German Nobility, and III. Selected Nobility of other European countries; each annual edition recorded all relevant births, deaths, marriages and titles. Throughout the nineteenth century, in order to preserve their status, all aristocrats were obliged to marry persons of equivalent rank. The *Almanach*, therefore, had the last word on who was permitted to marry whom. It is absolutely certain that there would have been a copy on the shelves at Coburg and Rosenau.

Due to their deference to their local dukes, the *Almanach*'s editors customarily listed the House of Saxony in pole position among the sovereigns. The Emperor Napoleon had once taken offence at this practice, but in the 1820s, when Albert's name first appeared, the Ernestine

(Lutheran) branch of Saxony again led the field; and Albert's mother appeared in the same subsection as Victoria's mother. In accordance with the traditional linguistic practices of the German aristocracy, the information was presented in French:

GÉNÉALOGIE DES SOUVERAINS DE L'EUROPE
ET DES MEMBRES VIVANTS DES LEURS FAMILLES

SAXE
BRANCHE ERNESTINE (Luth.)

SAXE-GOTHA
Duc Frédérick IV, né le 23 Nov 1774, succ. à son frère le Duc Auguste, 17
    Mai 1822 ...
SAXE-MEININGEN ...
SAXE-HILDBOURGHAUSEN ...
SAXE-SAALFELD-COBURG
  1) Duc Ernest, n. 2 Janv. 1784, succ. à son père le Duc François, le 9 Dec
     1806, mar 31 Juill 1817 à la D. Louise, F. d'Auguste, Duc de Saxe-Gotha,
     n. 21 Déc 1800
Fils
  2) D. Ernest Auguste Charles Jean Léopold Alexandre Edouard, Pr.Héréd.
     n.21 Juin 1818
D. Albert François Auguste Charles Emmanuel, n. 26 Août 1819
Frères et Sœurs ...
  5) D. Marie Louise Victoire, n. 17 Août 1786. v. Grande-Bretagne
     [Londres] ...[28]

Great Britain is listed twenty-one pages further on:

GRANDE BRETAGNE (Engl. Anglic.)
Roi Georges IV, Frédéric Auguste, né 12 Août 1762 ... succ. à son père le
    Roi Georges III 29 Janv. 1820 ...
Frères et Sœurs
  4) Venue du Frère le Pr. Eduard, Duc de Kent (quatrième Fils du Roi Georges
     III), Pr. Marie Louise Victoire, né 17 Août 1786, F. de François Duc de
     Saxe-Cobourg ...
Enfant
Pr. Alexandrine Victoire, n. 24 Mai 1819.[29]

Four years after Albert married Victoria, the old duke of Saxe-Coburg-Gotha, Albert's father, died, and the ducal title passed to Albert's elder brother, Ernest II (r. 1844–93). Since his brother had fathered no children (and did not seem about to do so), Albert assumed the position of heir apparent, and Albert's sons moved up in the duchy's line of succession. Nothing changed in this regard for the rest of the consort's life.

Victoria's diaries for 1845 gush with enthusiasm during the young couple's first visit to Germany. They travelled to Coburg, and then to Rosenau: 'I cannot say how much affected I felt in entering this dear old place and with difficulty I resisted crying; the beautifully ornamented town, all with wreaths and flowers, the numbers of good and affectionate people, the many recollections all connected with this place, all was so affecting.' Victoria's delight was unbounded as she toured her husband's birthplace; he showed her the nursery, the table on which he would stand to be dressed as a small boy, and the cuts in the wallpaper left from his fencing fights with his brother.

Albert, in contrast, was troubled. On the journey from Cologne on the Prussian royal train, they had been treated to the sight of 4,000 Prussian soldiers lining the banks of the Rhine as they passed, firing thunderous volleys. During a brief reception in the Augustusburg Palace at Brühl, the king of Prussia had delivered an overblown speech on the theme of 'Waterloo-Victory-Victoria'. And not everything at Coburg was to Albert's liking:

> Since he had particularly asked that there should be no fuss, Albert was annoyed that Ernest received them . . . with a guard of honour and his little army on parade. Because it was bound to be an emotional experience to take Victoria to the Rosenau, he arranged for them to be alone when he showed her his old bedroom under the roof . . . In the Veste [Coburg's fortress] he took her to see the Cranachs, the new Ernst-Albrecht Museum, the chapel with Luther's pulpit and the marvellous view from the terrace. Everything was as it had always been, except that he now had a wife by his side.
>
> Yet he himself had changed . . . He was amazed that he had never noticed that the peasants lived in hovels, that their wives worked in the fields even in the last stages of pregnancy, and that there were no schools to speak of. It was a shock to find the great contrast between Coburg and Gotha . . . There was much more evidence of culture in his maternal grandfather's palace than in all his father's houses put together . . . Albert had not realised how many of his interests were inherited from [his maternal great-

grandfather] . . . and how much his four years in England had done to develop them.[30]

The ten years that followed brought the royal pair their longest period of calm and fulfilment. Victoria was a self-assured monarch, surrounded by a fast-growing family. Albert was devoted to his work as chairman of the committee preparing the Great Exhibition, and he adored his daughters, particularly the eldest, 'Vickie', who grew up to be his favourite companion. In the census return completed on 30 March 1851 the royal family are recorded as living in Buckingham Palace with only a few servants. 'Her Majesty Alexandrina Victoria' is listed first; her 'Relationship to Head of Household' was 'Wife', her 'Condition' 'Mar[ried]', her age thirty-one, and her 'Rank, Profession or Occupation' 'The Queen'. 'HRH Francis Albert Augustus Charles Emmanuel', also thirty-one and married, was described as 'Head' of the household, and 'Duke of Saxony, Prince of Coburg and Gotha'. He apparently had no British 'Rank, Profession or Occupation'. One suspects that it was Albert who answered the census official's questions.[31]

Queen and consort would see Rosenau together only one more time, although Victoria would go there alone on five further occasions. During their visit in the summer of 1860, she waxed particularly eloquent. 'If I weren't the person whom I am,' she said, 'my home would be here,' adding cautiously, 'though it would be my second home.' Albert broke down in tears. 'I shall never see my birthplace again,' he exclaimed prophetically. Within the year he was dead, struck down at the age of forty-two, officially by typhoid.

Contrary to the legend of a perfect marriage, there is reason to suppose that Albert's shockingly early death could indeed have been hastened by the unseen stresses of mounting matrimonial discord. After the birth in 1857 of their ninth child, Princess Beatrice, the queen's doctors ruled that her life would be endangered by further pregnancy, and the couple were forced to make separate sleeping arrangements. She grew irritable, and occasionally hysterical; he became depressed, withdrawn and exhausted by overwork. In that same year he was deeply pained by the fact that his title of prince consort had to be granted through the queen's personal intervention because no one else in authority had cared to take the initiative. The queen did not support him in his ill-concealed feud with Lord Palmerston. Albert felt unloved, and ashamed by the realization that his eldest son, the future Edward VII, was turning, like his own father and brother, into a brazen lecher. He was already weak and drained, therefore, when he set out in the cold, damp November weather of 1861 to visit the prince of Wales in Cambridge and to administer a paternal reprimand. He took Edward for a long walk and caught cold. Returning to Windsor with a high fever, he suffered complications and never recovered.[32]

If this version of events is accepted, Queen Victoria's descent into lifetime mourning was caused as much by guilt as by grief; her determination to perpetuate Albert's memory in a worldwide array of monuments and memorials was certainly inconsistent with his wishes. She also felt compelled persistently to revisit the scene of their lost bliss in Germany. In the summer of 1863 the black-robed widow stayed with Albert's aunt at Coburg, where she received the emperor of Austria, Franz-Joseph. Her ministers in London fretted at her absence. 'Your Majesty,' advised Benjamin Disraeli, 'you cannot rule the Empire from Coburg.'

By the mid-nineteenth century, the name of Saxe-Coburg had assumed continental proportions. Most of Albert and Victoria's nine children were married into Europe's most prestigious ruling families. They and their progeny were to occupy the thrones not only of the British Empire but also of Germany, Russia, Norway, Spain, Romania and Bulgaria. Uncle Leopold's line of Saxe-Coburgs held its own in Belgium for five generations, and extended its tentacles as far as Mexico; the Saxe-Coburg-Koharys were prominent in Hungary, and gave rise to the Coburg-Braganzas who ruled Portugal until 1910. The Palais Coburg in Vienna, built between 1840 and 1845 for General Ferdinand Sachsen-Coburg-Kohary, was one of the architectural treasures of the Habsburg capital; and Saxe-Coburg soup, made from Albert's favourite Brussels sprouts, was a worthy counterpart to the Brown Windsor soup on which the British Empire was said to have been built.

Albert's homeland did not enjoy the formal status of a kingdom, but it was a hereditary monarchy, and was accepted as a constituent member of the German Empire from 1871 to 1918. Like its neighbours, Saxe-Altenberg, Saxe-Meiningen and Saxe-Weimar-Eisenach (where Goethe had served as chancellor), it was tiny, but clearly attractive:

SAXE-COBURG-GOTHA (Ger. *Sachsen-Koburg-Gotha*), a sovereign duchy of Germany, in Thuringia ... consisting of the two formerly separate duchies of Coburg and Gotha, and of eight small scattered enclaves ... The total area is 764 sq. m., of which about 224 are in Coburg and 540 in Gotha. The duchy of Coburg is bounded by Bavaria, and by Saxe-Meiningen, which

separates it from Gotha ... The duchy of Coburg is an undulating and
fertile district, reaching its highest point in the Senichshöhe (1716 ft.) near
Mirsdorf. Its streams, the chief of which are the Itz, Biberach, Steinach and
Rodach, all find their way into the Main. The duchy of Gotha, more than
twice the size of Coburg, stretches from the borders of Prussia ... to the
Thuringian Forest, the highest summits of which (Der grosse Beerberg, 3225
ft. and Schneekopf, 3179 ft.) rise within its borders. The more level district
on the north is spoken of as the 'open country' (*das Land*) in contrast to
the wooded hills of the 'forest' (*der Wald*).[33]

Duke Ernst II was active in Germany's court politics and in the German national movement, for whose benefit he was known for hosting
prestigious shooting rallies. But his management of his own duchy was
far from ideal, and there can be no doubt that its affairs exercised the
hearts and minds of both Albert and Victoria throughout their marriage. Little, however, was done, and it was a great misfortune that
Albert had been dead for more than thirty years before matters came to
a head. By that time, the sons of Albert and Victoria had hearts and
minds of their own, and the duchy had become a fully constitutional
state. Coburg had possessed a constitution since 1821; Gotha followed
suit during the 'Springtime of Nations' that swept Central Europe in
1848–9. Throughout those early years the two territories had been
joined to their ruler in personal union; but from 1852 they were legally
united under him, like the several parts of Britain's United Kingdom:

Constitution and Administration. – Saxe-Coburg-Gotha is a limited hereditary monarchy, its constitution resting on a law of 1852, modified in 1874.
For its own immediate affairs each duchy has a separate diet, but in more
important and general matters a common diet ... meeting at Coburg and
Gotha alternately, exercises authority. The members are elected for four
years. The Coburg diet consists of eleven members and the Gotha diet of
nineteen. The franchise is extended to all male taxpayers of twenty-five
years of age and upwards ... The united duchy is represented in the imperial Bundesrat by one member and in the Reichstag by two members ... By
treaty with Prussia the troops of the duchy are incorporated with the Prussian army. The budget is voted ... for four years, a distinction being made
between domain revenue and state revenue. The receipts ... on behalf of
Coburg were estimated for 1909–1910 at about £100,000 and those for
Gotha at about £200,000, while the common state expenditure amounted
to about the same sum. The civil list of the reigning duke is fixed at £15,000
a year, in addition to half the proceeds of the Gotha domains, and half the

net revenue of the Coburg domains ... The duke of Saxe-Coburg-Gotha [also] enjoys a very large private fortune, amassed chiefly by Ernest I., who sold the principality of Lichtenberg, which the Congress of Vienna had bestowed upon him in recognition of his services to Prussia.[34]

Over the decades the name of Gotha came to be associated with three very different spheres of life: engineering, left-wing politics and aeronautics. All three derived from one source. The *Gothär Waggonfabrik* started producing rolling stock in the 1840s; it rapidly attracted a large industrial workforce that became one of the breeding grounds of German socialism. The German Social Democratic Party (SPD) was founded in the town in 1854, and its 'Gotha Programme' of 1875 became a central subject of debate within the movement. Karl Marx's *Critique of the Gotha Programme* introduced the world to concepts such as the 'dictatorship of the proletariat' and 'proletarian internationalism', propagating the famous principle of 'From all according to ability, to all according to need'.[35] Its tardy publication in 1891, eight years after its author's death, prepared the theoretical ground for the transition from Marxism to Marxism-Leninism. By that time, the *Waggonfabrik* was one of the Empire's leading producers of electric trams. After the turn of the century, it would diversify still further when it moved into airplane construction. The Gotha Ursinus G-1 biplane was to become the mainstay of the imperial strategic bomber fleet.[36]

Duke Ernest II of Saxe-Coburg-Gotha died in 1893. He had been Victoria's brother-in-law for more than fifty years and was great-uncle to Kaiser Wilhelm:

> It appears the end was paralysis of the larynx caused by the state of the brain ... which in its turn was the result of the terrible fast life he had led in Berlin from the time he was seventeen; put into the 1st Prussian Corps, the fastest of all the regiments, with a thoroughly bad man to look after him. He simply had no chance whatever, and humanly speaking his life has just been drained away. How strange Royalties are, their children seem to lack the ordinary care bestowed on our own humblest middle class.[37]

The duke's death was greatly mourned in Berlin; he had been the first person to congratulate the Kaiser on his accession. He was buried in the Moritzkirche in Coburg.

The succession passed automatically to the late duke's Germano-British nephews. The snag was that none of them really wanted it. Victoria and Albert's eldest son, Edward, renounced his claim, having better things to do as prince of Wales. Their second son, Alfred, duke of Edinburgh (b. 1844), who had pursued a successful career in the Royal Navy and sailed the world, accepted it reluctantly. He was probably motivated by the interests of his only son, Prince Alfred ('Alfie'), the wayward offspring of an unhappy marriage to a Russian princess. Having sworn allegiance to the duchy's constitution, Duke Alfred (r. 1893–1900) settled in at Rosenau, busying himself with his music-making and his ceramics collection, bringing order to the duchy's finances, and slowly overcoming the locals' resistance to a 'foreigner'. He was rewarded the following year by his mother's last visit and by one of the most inclusive gatherings of European royalty ever staged. In addition to the Queen-Empress Victoria, he acted as host to Kaiser Wilhelm II, to the future Tsar Nicholas II and to the future British kings Edward VII and George V. His reign was also enlivened by the presence in Coburg of Johann Strauss II, the 'Waltz King', who had left Vienna following his third marriage to a Protestant. Strauss's opera *The Gypsy Baron* (1885) and his famous '*Kaiser-Waltzer*' ('Emperor Waltz', 1889) were both composed in Saxe-Coburg-Gotha.

Deaths in the ruling family then struck a double blow. In 1899 the heir apparent, Prince 'Alfie', who was both syphilitic and haemophiliac, shot himself during his parents' silver wedding celebrations, despairing both at his medical condition and at the implications of his secret marriage to a commoner.[38] Barely a year later, Duke Alfred died at Rosenau of throat cancer, exactly as his uncle had done. News of his death made world headlines:

DUKE OF SAXE-COBURG DEAD
Expired Suddenly at Rosenau Castle on Monday
QUEEN VICTORIA'S SECOND SON
was afflicted with cancer, but did not know of his malady[39]

A few weeks earlier, the next step in the saga of succession had been settled in the most unsatisfactory manner imaginable: by hunting for the least unwilling candidate. Victoria and Albert's third son, Arthur, duke of Connaught, already a general in the British army, was not going to endanger his chance of receiving a field marshal's baton, and Connaught's own son, Prince Arthur (b. 1883), a schoolboy at Eton College, was apparently terrified of the inheritance. Victoria and Albert's fourth son, Leopold, duke of Albany (1853–84), another haemophiliac, was already dead, struck down by a botched injection following a fall at Cannes. So the royal courtiers' search moved with awful inevitability to another Eton schoolboy: Leopold's helpless and posthumous son, Queen Victoria's youngest grandson, Prince Charles Edward (b. 1884). Rumours surfaced that the elder prince, Arthur, had given his younger cousin, Charles Edward, a good public-school thrashing in order to deflect the hand of fate. The ultimate decision would have been taken by Queen Victoria herself.

The Diet of the duchy made a rare show of dissatisfaction. As reported in the *New York Times*, which could take liberties unthinkable in London, the atmosphere had turned sour:

> The Diet of the Duchy as well as the people at large is protesting most energetically against this intention of the British Royal Family, and declare that they will not allow these British princes to shake the dice for the ducal crown of Saxe-Coburg-Gotha. The Diet has proclaimed its right to say the directing word about the succession to the throne.[40]

The protesters were presumably told to mind their own business.

Thus began the sad public career of Prince Charles Edward (Carl-Eduard), the last duke of Albany and the last duke of Saxe-Coburg-Gotha. In theory, like his uncles and cousins, he could have tried to renounce the claim. In practice, he was trapped. Despite having a German mother, the former Princess Helena of Waldeck-Pyrmont, he was exceptional in the family for speaking no German; it had been assumed that he would have to earn his living in England. He knew of no one to whom he might have passed the burden of his succession, and had no means of gauging how poisoned the chalice would prove to be. His mother told him, or so his descendants would say, that to acquiesce in his fate was the most dutiful way of honouring his dead father's memory.[41]

At first, the prospects did not seem too bad. Carl-Eduard was allowed to finish his English education, and to begin with he reigned in name only under joint regents. He would have known that his predecessor, Duke Alfred, an accomplished musician, had won his subjects' confidence and that in seven years' occupancy of the throne had managed to flit happily between Rosenau and his London residence at Clarence House.

> Joint regent for the boy-Duke, with his mother, was . . . Prince Hohenlohe. But it was the Kaiser himself who superintended his education, and 'Charlie' and his sister Alice spent many holidays with the imperial family . . . There

The British Saxe-Coburgs and Gothas

ERNST I
1st duke of Saxe-Coburg and Gotha (r. 1826–44)

ERNST II
duke of Saxe-Coburg and Gotha, (r. 1844–93)

Albert of Saxe-Coburg and Gotha (1819–61) Prince Consort = **VICTORIA** of Hanover (1819–1901) queen of Great Britain and Ireland empress of India (r. 1837–1901)

- Victoria ('Vickie'), the princess Royal (1840–1901) princess of Prussia, empress of Germany

- Albert Edward prince of Wales (1841–1910) (**EDWARD VII**, r. 1901–10) = Alexandra of Sonderburg-Glücksburg

- Alice (1843–78) grand duchess of Hesse

- **ALFRED** (1844–1900) duke of Edinburgh duke of Saxe-Coburg and Gotha (r. 1893–1900)
  - 'Alfie', d. 1899

- Helena (1846–1923) princess of Schleswig-Holstein

- Louise (1848–1939) duchess of Argyll

- Arthur (1850–1942) duke of Connaught
  - Prince Arthur (1883–1938)
  - Princess Alice (1883–1981) countess of Athlone duchess of Cambridge = Alexander of Teck

- Leopold (1853–84) duke of Albany = Helene of Waldeck-Pyrmont
  - Charles Edward ('Carl-Edward') (1884–1954) duke of Albany duke of Saxe-Coburg and Gotha (r. 1900–18) = Victoria Adelaide of Sonderburg-Glücksburg
    → 5 children

- Beatrice (1857–1944) princess of Battenberg

GEORGE V (r. 1910–36) = Mary of Teck

- **EDWARD VIII** (r. 1936)

- **GEORGE VI** (r. 1936–52) = Elizabeth Bowes-Lyon
  - **ELIZABETH II** (r. 1952+) = Prince Philip of Sonderburg-Glücksburg (Mountbatten) duke of Edinburgh (b. 1921)
  - Princess Margaret (1930–2002)

was, occasionally, some embarrassment about the young people's divided loyalties, but they solved it in their own way: during the Boer War the Crown Prince [of Prussia] bet Alice a diamond brooch against a diamond pin that the Boers would win – he duly paid up when the British were victorious. A few years later ... the new Coburgs' link with the imperial family was tightened, when Duke Charlie married [the Empress's niece] and the couple divided their time between Coburg and Berlin ... Princess Alice, on the other hand, had reforged the link with Britain by marrying Prince Alexander of Teck ... whose sister Mary had married Prince George, the future George V. Alexander largely had been educated in Britain and was an officer in the British army.[42]

Duke Carl-Eduard's accession to Saxe-Coburg-Gotha at the age of twenty-one took place in July 1905. His entry into his duchy was attended by much ceremony, and much unguarded comment. He was received at the railway station at Gotha with full military honours, before proceeding to the Friedenstein Palace, where his mother was waiting. He swore the constitutional oath in the throne room of the palace, watched by representatives of the Kaiser and King Edward VII, by ministers of the duchy's government, and by an array of officials and their ladies. Some of the press reports, while sympathizing with the new duke, did not mince words about the manner of his succession:

UNWILLING PRINCE IS NOW A GERMAN DUKE
Charles Edward of Saxe-Coburg Attains his Majority
HIS HEAD WAS NOT PUNCHED
Cousin to whom the Dukedom was also offered
Threatened to Whip Him if he refused it[43]

One small source of satisfaction arose from Carl-Eduard's right to a magnificent, newly designed personal standard, the *Herzogstandarte*, neatly combining his British and Saxon connections. The design showed the royal banner-of-arms of Saxony – a field of ten black and gold horizontal stripes – surmounted by a diagonal *Rautenkranz* or 'crancelin', and a heraldic canton. The crancelin, running from upper left to bottom right, took the form of a crenellated garland in deep green. The heraldic canton placed in the top-left corner was made up from the quartered arms of a royal British prince 'defaced' by a white 'label' bearing red hearts and red crosses.

Very soon the first international storm clouds appeared on the horizon. The 'Dreadnought race' was driving a wedge between Britain

and Germany, and the young duke's chief patron and cousin, Kaiser
Wilhelm, was proving particularly bullish. The Kaiser had already
nominated the duke's bride, Princess Victoria Adelaide of Schleswig-
Holstein-Sonderburg-Glücksburg – a relative both of Britain's Queen
Alexandra and of Prince Andrew of Greece (father of the yet-unborn
Prince Philip) – and he now ordered his protégé to attend an officer
school of the Prussian army. This assignment must have been especially
uncomfortable. Carl-Eduard had been taking German lessons, but, as a
lifelong sufferer from rheumatoid arthritis, he had no military ability or
inclination. Fortunately, his marriage was a happy one. He married his
bride at Glücksburg in Holstein – in the 'Lucky Castle'. His wife and
five children provided a source of solace in a life that was to grow
increasingly bleak.

   The First World War saw the duke raised to the rank of general, yet
abruptly removed from his nominal command. Though he volunteered
to fight on the Eastern Front, he saw no active service. No doubt to
mask this embarrassment, a medal was struck in 1916 to celebrate his
non-existent military record. The Diet of his duchy revived the issue of
the succession, voting that 'all foreigners' and 'persons who have waged
war on the German Empire' should be excluded; at the same time, in
Britain, he was struck off the list of Knights of the Garter. In July 1917,
nearly three years into the war, his British relatives abandoned the German family name of Saxe-Coburg-Gotha by an Order in Council, and
were magically transformed into 'Windsors'. His sister Alice and her
husband, the duke of Teck, were reinvented as the countess and earl of
Athlone, but he was not offered the same option. Still worse, since he
was judged to have 'adhered to His Majesty's enemies', Britain's Titles
Deprivation Act (1917) empowered the Privy Council to investigate his
alleged treason and to decide on the punishment.

   The Titles Deprivation Act was peculiarly vindictive with regard to
those members of the British royal family for whom, like Duke Carl-
Eduard, much more was at stake than a mere name change. It was one
thing to legislate for British royals at home, quite another to lay down
the law for 'all descendants of Queen Victoria':

> We, of our Royal Will and Authority [proclaimed George V], do hereby declare
> and announce that as from the date of this Our Royal Proclamation Our
> House and Family shall be styled and known as the House and Family of
> Windsor ... And We do hereby further declare that We for Ourselves and ...
> for all other descendants of Our ... Grandmother Queen Victoria who are

subjects of these Realms, relinquish and enjoin the discontinuance of the use
of the degrees, styles, dignities, titles and honours of Dukes and Duchesses of
Saxony and Princes and Princesses of Saxe-Coburg and Gotha, and all other
German degrees, styles, dignities, titles, honours and appellations.[44]

The Privy Council's verdict was delivered in January 1919. Together
with three other 'enemy peers', Carl-Eduard was to lose the dukedom of
Albany, the earldom of Clarence, the barony of Arklow and the style of
Royal Highness. His standards were removed from St George's Chapel,
Windsor. In short, he was turned into a pariah.*

Meanwhile, as the German Empire folded, all the hereditary rulers in
Germany were forced to abdicate. Carl-Eduard renounced his dukedom on
14 November 1918, five days after the announcement of the Kaiser's own
abdication. Then, as the Weimar Republic stuttered into life, the German
populace took revenge on its aristocracy. The Workers' and Soldiers' Council of Gotha invaded the ex-duke's castle at Rosenau, abolished his duchy
and confiscated his lands. He was now a private citizen, a condemned man
in his homeland, an outcast in his adopted country and a lodger in his own
home. He had done nothing except to behave well and do what he was
told. The humiliation was acute.

It is not true, however, that the ex-duke was penniless. With some
delay, he received a compensation settlement from the state, and possessed other sources of income that enabled him to sustain a comfortable
family life. His mother, the dowager-duchess of Albany, came to visit
him and his family for vacations, delighting in her grandchildren. They
were all spending a family holiday together at Hinterreis in the Austrian
Tyrol when she died there suddenly in September 1922.

Inter-war Germany was a hotbed of radical politics and a cauldron of
economic distress. Industrial production faltered, unemployment soared
and the currency collapsed. The nation lost its established leaders, the
middle classes lost their savings and large sections of the public lost all
hope. The vacuum was filled by wild radicals from both the Right and the
Left. Fascist and Communist Party gangs battled each other in the streets.

On 14 October 1922 a little-known group of right-wing thugs from
Munich decided to target the town of Coburg, which they knew to be,
like Gotha, a nest of their left-wing opponents. Their leader, a former

---

* The three other 'discontinued peers' were the crown prince of Hanover (the duke of Cumberland), the duke of Brunswick and Viscount Taafe.

corporal called Adolf Hitler, announced that he was going to stage a 'German Day' in Coburg, and hired a train for the purpose. He arrived with a brass band and 800 flag-waving supporters (practically the whole National Socialist Party at the time), who promptly brawled with policemen attempting to maintain order. When a crowd of locals tried to bar the way, a general fracas ensued. Stones were thrown, insults hurled and bones broken. The Nazis then pressed on to the town centre, where Hitler held a rally, announcing that Coburg had been cleansed of 'Red tyranny'. Back at the train station, the railwaymen refused to release the Nazis' train. Hitler responded by threatening to kidnap every 'Red' in sight and to take them hostage to Munich. His bluster and brutality won the day. Seven years later, Coburg was the first city in Germany to give the Nazis an absolute majority of votes in a municipal election. In 1932 Hitler issued one of the most prized Nazi Party decorations, the 'Coburg Badge', showing a wreathed swastika. The inscription reads: 'MIT HITLER IN COBURG, 1922–32'.[45]

It is not possible to say whether ex-Duke Carl-Eduard watched Hitler at work on the 'German Day' in Coburg; if not, he would certainly have heard first-hand reports. He was an example of those who cared little for the Nazis' radical ideology, but who shared their outrage at Germany's shabby post-war treatment; he would have approved of their hostility to the Communists, who had destroyed his duchy. At first he was associated with one of the more conservative groupings, the Harzburg Front, which sought to unify the German right-wing opposition, and which made a tactical alliance with the Nazis in the early 1930s. In 1932, however, when right-wing politics were in some disarray, he was persuaded to join the SA, the Nazi Brownshirts, and rose quickly to the high rank of *Obergruppenführer*. He may have been influenced by his wife's brother-in-law, ex-Prince August Wilhelm of Prussia, who had joined the Nazi Party before him.

After Hitler's election to power in 1933, the ex-duke was singled out as an instrument for cultivating the British establishment and was made president of the Anglo-German Friendship Society. In this capacity he kept in close touch with the British ambassadors in Berlin, Sir Eric Phipps and Sir Nevile Henderson, and attended the funeral in London of his cousin George V in January 1936. Limping along far behind the late king's coffin as the official German emissary, he was completely ignored by his British relatives. A solitary figure, he shuffled along painfully, shoulders stooped and feet splayed, struggling to keep pace with the procession. Incongruously, he wore a green, German-style trenchcoat bereft of insignia and a stormtrooper's iron helmet. His influence, such as it was, came to an end less than a year later with the abdication of his cousin's son, Edward VIII, of whom the Nazis had entertained high hopes.

Whatever the ex-duke's exact opinions, there is no doubt that he and his distinguished lineage were exploited by the Nazis, even though they may have seen him more as a victim of 'the Reds' than as an enthusiast for 'the Browns'. In 1932, for example, when Carl-Eduard's daughter Sibylla was married in Coburg to Prince Gustav Adolf of Sweden, Hitler sent a personal telegram of congratulations. In the evening, during a torchlight procession by the local branch of the Nazi Party, the revellers marched round the statue of Prince Albert that stood in the town square.[46] Carl-Eduard also contrived to hold on to some of his aristocratic privileges, continuing to award medals and decorations to his 'House Order' of Saxe-Coburg Gotha. As a wartime aviation ace, Hermann Göring was awarded the Order's Commander's Cross.

During the Second World War the ailing Herr von Saxe-Coburg lived with his family in seclusion. Though he kept his honorary presidency of the German Red Cross, on whose behalf he visited the United States and Japan in 1940, henceforth he played little active part in public life. One of his sons was killed on the Eastern Front; two others served in the armed forces. Allegedly, he received another telegram in April 1945 from the Führer, urging him to avoid the invading Americans. By then, most of his remaining property had been seized by the Soviet army, which also smashed the presses of the *Almanach de Gotha* and carried off their priceless archives. The husband of his much-loved sister, Princess Alice, was now the governor-general of Canada,[47] yet none of the ex-duke's connections would save him. He was arrested in 1946 by the American Military Administration of Bavaria and hauled before a de-Nazification court. The prosecution argued that he could not possibly have been unaware of Nazi atrocities. He denied the accusation and pleaded not guilty, but was given a crushing fine, and further detained. By early 1947, sick and undernourished, he was succumbing to the rigours of a prison camp. 'Crippled by arthritis, the old man stumbled painfully round a rubbish dump, scrabbling in the rotting refuse until he found an old tin can. Starving, he pulled up grass to add to the thin soup which his American captors allowed him.'[48] That same year, his sister Princess Alice and her husband the earl of Athlone travelled to Germany and successfully effected his release.

Ironically, the Americans then assigned the ex-duke and ex-duchess a servant's lodging in the stables of *Schloss Callenberg*, the scene of his great-grandfather's orgies. According to his granddaughter, 'he thought it was wonderful'.[49] He had contracted cancer, and had lost the sight of an eye. But he lived long enough to buy a ticket to a public cinema at Gotha in June 1953, and to watch the coronation of Elizabeth II in Technicolor. 'That must have been the worst moment'[50] – the young British queen was his nephew's daughter, and he was the second most senior living member of her father's family. He died in 1954 aged sixty-nine. His eldest son and heir, Johann Leopold, had renounced all rights of inheritance. Carl-Eduard's only consolation was that he died in a bed that had been brought from his birthplace at Claremont House, Esher, in Surrey. It was, he said, 'his little bit of England'.

III

When the Duchy of Saxe-Coburg-Gotha was founded in 1826, European monarchy was at its peak. All the leading powers – France, Britain, Prussia, Austria and Russia – were monarchies; and every time that a new state was formed, like Greece in 1828 or Belgium in 1831, new monarchs were selected and installed. Republicanism appeared discredited. The revolutionary Corsican general who terrified Europe for twenty years had abandoned his original principles by crowning himself emperor of the French and king of Italy in the middle of his career. After France's defeat, the victorious monarchs thanked God for His blessings, and forgot why the Revolution had happened.

By 1919, when the Duchy of Saxe-Coburg-Gotha was abolished, monarchy was in serious decline. The Romanovs had been toppled and savagely murdered; the Hohenzollerns and the Habsburgs had been forced out; France had reached its Third Republic. Both Austria and Germany were in the process of adopting republican regimes. Among the states formed by the post-war settlement, republics outnumbered monarchies by four to one. The minority of monarchs who had not lost their thrones, in countries like Britain or Italy, feared for their future.

European monarchy was deeply bound up with the mystical registers of Christian religion. The example of the United States was not yet strong enough for Europeans to accept that republican ideals were compatible with a religious society. Kings and emperors were not just crowned; they were anointed with holy oil and installed amid oaths, prayers, anthems, divine invocations and clouds of incense. In 1914 they had all received the Almighty's blessing for prosecuting war against each other and for sending millions of their subjects to the slaughter. Monarchists did not notice the discrepancy, doing their utmost to convince the world that monarchy was God-given and virtuous, that republicanism was godless and morally deficient.

Yet the systemic vindictiveness with which the last duke of Saxe-Coburg-Gotha was treated by his own kind, suggests that there is little to choose in terms of morality between royalty and republicans. When dynastic interest or national pride are at stake, the Sermon on the Mount counts for little, and common human decency is set aside. Generally speaking, British attitudes have followed suit. Whenever Carl-Eduard's name crops up in the British press, all the old epithets about the 'traitor peer' resurface, and new ones are added: 'a scandalous life', one of 'Hitler's most fervent supporters', 'a top Nazi official' and 'a convicted Nazi'.

After Carl-Eduard's death, his offspring were divided over what to do. Some of them retreated into private life; his daughter Sibylla became mother to the king of Sweden. His widow, the ex-Duchess Victoria Adelaide, lived on until 1970. But his fifth child, Friedrich Josias (1918–98) decided to revive his late father's claims, and it is Friedrich Josias's son, Andreas von Saxe-Coburg-Gotha (b. 1943), who now heads the line descended from the duke of Albany. The outcome of a short-lived wartime marriage, the self-styled 'Prince Andreas' is the grandson of Albert and Victoria's grandson.[51] The heir apparent, 'Prince Hubertus', was married to Kelly Rodestvedt in Coburg on 23 May 2009.[52]

Using a variety of strategies, other members of the Saxe-Coburg-Gotha clan fared better than the luckless Carl-Eduard. One branch, for example, had been raised in 1878 to the throne of Bulgaria. Their last representative, the Bulgarian Tsar Simeon (b. 1937), started his reign in 1943 aged six, only to be driven out after a couple of years by the Soviet-backed Communists, who shot his uncle, the regent, and abolished the monarchy. He lived in Spain, graduated from a US army cadet school and prospered in business. Then, when the Communist regime in Bulgaria collapsed, he reinvented himself, formed a democratic political party and in 2001–5 served as Bulgaria's prime minister under the unlikely name of 'Sakskoburggotski'.[53]

Further branches of the family strove to survive by disguising their identity. The Saxe-Coburg-Gothas of Belgium, for example, simply stopped using their family name in the correct belief that it would soon be forgotten.[54] Their British relations, in contrast, embarked on an elaborate strategy of concealment, marshalling a mixture of legal ploys, image-management and historical propaganda. They repeatedly changed their family name by proclamation or by Acts of Parliament, successfully masking the fact that the Windsor-Mountbatten wedding of 1947 would otherwise have seen a Saxe-Coburg-Gotha marrying a Schleswig-Holstein-Sonderburg-Glücksburg. The bride's father, as seen above, had changed his surname before she was born, and changed his first name from Albert or 'Bertie' to George on ascending the throne; the bridegroom had assumed an Anglicized form of his mother's name. A future queen, of course, could not stay as 'Mrs Mountbatten' for long, so after her marriage her surname was changed back to 'Windsor' (despite her husband's displeasure) and in 1960, for the benefit of the children, it was modified again to 'Mountbatten-Windsor'.[55] Through all of this, the royals honed their upper-class English accents, threw themselves into patriotic and charitable activities, spoke no German in public, deflected awkward questions, avoided their German relatives and, in a sustained campaign of genealogical legerdemain, massaged their family tree beyond recognition. Most of their subjects do not know that Lady Diana Spencer (1961–97) was the very first person of primarily English descent who ever came near the British throne in the whole of its 300-year history. They had to wait until the twenty-first century before Camilla Parker-Bowles, by a civil marriage, and Kate Middleton, in a grand church wedding, were allowed to follow her example.

Pretence, therefore, is an essential part of the royal performance; some might call it adaptability. Albert and Victoria would have understood perfectly, both having embarrassing relatives to dispel. They would also have known (since the operation started in their own times[56]) that royal genealogists can achieve wonderful results through imaginative misrepresentation; vulgar forgery is unnecessary. By the skilful use of Englished forms, by an emphasis on titles as opposed to surnames, and above all by the selective filtration of unwanted bloodlines, dedicated family-tree-surgeons have transformed the dominant flavour of their product. No doubt with the best patriotic motives in mind, they have persuaded the unsuspecting public that British royalty's closest ancestral ties are with English and Scottish monarchs all the way back to William the Conqueror and beyond.[57] In the process, they have sidelined the royal family's far closer ties with the Hanovers, the Tecks, the Brandenburg-Ansbachs, the Brunswick-Wolfenbüttels, the Württembergers and the Schleswig-Holstein-Sonderburg-Glücksburgs. If only the truth were known, the degree of consanguinity between the 'Mountbatten-Windsors' and the Normans, Plantagenets, Tudors and Stuarts is almost astronomically remote.

Anyone wishing to reconstruct the basic kinship group of the British queen and her consort only needs to list the parents and grandparents of their respective forebears. In addition to the Bowes-Lyons, the Cavendish-Bentincks, the Smiths (of Blendon Hall), the Burnabies and the Romanovs, they will soon discover their most intimate connections to be with the Anhalt-Zerbsts, the Altenbergs, the Barby-Mühlingens, the Battenbergs, the Braunschweig-Lüneberge, the Castell-Castells, the Castell-Reinlingens, the Dohna-Schlobittens, the Erbach-Ehrbachs, the Erbach-Schönbergs, the Ebersdorfs, the Hesses, the Hesse-Darmstadts, the Hesse-Kassels, the Hesse-Philippstals, the Hohenzollerns, the Holstein-Gottorps, the Jülich-Kleve-Bergs, the Kiz-Rheides, the Lehndorffs, the Leiningen-Dagsburgs, the Lippes, the Mecklenburg-Strelitzes, the Nassau-Usingens, the Nassau-Weilbergs, the Neubergs, the Oettingen-Oettingens, the Pfalz-Zimmerns, the Reuss von Ebersdorfs, the Saxe-Altenbergs, the Saxe-Coburg-Saalfelds, the Saxe-Eisenachs, the Saxe-Gothas, the Saxe-Hildeburghausens, the Saxe-Lauenbergs, the Saxe-Weimars, the Saxe-Weissenfels, the Sayn-Wittgensteins, the von Schliebens, the Schönburg-Glauchaus, the Schwarzburg-Rudolfstadts, the Schwarzburg-Sonderhausens, the Solms-Laubachs, the Solms-Sonnenwalde und Pouches, the Stolberg-Gederns, the Waldecks, the Waldeck-Eisenbergs, the Wettins and three times over with the Saxe-Coburg-Gothas.

None of which, one hastens to add, implies that Germans make undesirable relatives; international match-making cannot be reduced to any such crude formula. What it does show, thanks in no small part to Albert and Victoria, is that British public opinion adopted markedly pro-German sympathies for much of the nineteenth century, but, thanks to two world wars, decidedly Germanophobe antipathies for most of the twentieth. To navigate a path of survival through the minefield of these shifting prejudices, Britain's royal family decided to pretend that it was something it wasn't, and isn't. The late Princess Diana was thus perhaps more right than she knew when she regretted 'having married into a German family'.[58] Prince Albert, of course, never had such regrets.

12

Tsernagora

Kingdom of the Black Mountain

(1910–1918)

I

Montenegro is the 192nd member of the United Nations, received into membership on 28 June 2006. It is one of only three states to have been so inducted in the twenty-first century, the others being the Federal Republic of Yugoslavia in 2000 and Switzerland in 2002. To make matters suitably confusing, Montenegro had formed part of the Federal Republic of Yugoslavia between 1992 and 2002, until the Federation changed its name to 'Serbia and Montenegro'.[1] It can at least take comfort from being one important step ahead of its neighbour, the self-styled Republic of Kosovo, which declared its independence on 17 February 2008, but which has not gained full international recognition.

The establishment of state sovereignty is a complex business. For practical purposes, a political entity may gain its independence by its own efforts, but to enjoy sovereign status in international law it needs to be recognized as such by others. Similarly, a recognized state may cease to function *de facto*, but its disappearance does not become an established fact *de jure* until accepted internationally. In the twenty-first century, the international body that usually confirms a candidate state's full sovereignty by admitting it to membership, or crosses it off the list, is the United Nations. UN procedures require that membership is granted or withdrawn by a decision of the General Assembly acting on the advice of the Security Council. Montenegro, however, has made it. Today, together with five other post-Yugoslav republics, it looks forward to a brighter future than at any time in the last generation.

Montenegro has a population of 620,000 living in a territory of 5,332 square miles. As in neighbouring Bosnia and Albania, the population has traditionally been divided along religious lines, although proportions differ. According to the last census (2003), three-quarters are Orthodox Christians. The remainder are either Roman Catholics,

living mainly on the coast, or Muslims. All speak a dialect of the same language, which is variously designated as Serbian, Serb-Croat or Montenegrin, and is written in Montenegro in modified forms either of the Cyrillic or the Latin alphabet.

After the dismemberment of Yugoslavia in the 1990s, and the consequent humbling of Serbia, Montenegro is no longer overshadowed by its overweening Serbian neighbour. Democratization of a sort is afoot, and a market economy is taking root. A fully fledged diplomatic service has been established. There are Montenegrin embassies to the UN in New York, to the EU in Brussels, to the Organization for Security and Co-operation in Europe (OSCE) in Vienna, to all the other post-Yugoslav republics, to the Holy See and to a dozen major capitals on all continents, including the United Kingdom and the United States.[2]

Tourism is professionally promoted. Montenegro can be reached by road, rail, sea and air. Frontier crossings are open with Croatia, Bosnia and Herzegovina, Albania, Serbia and, most recently, with Kosovo (which Montenegro recognized in October 2008). The bus-line *Autosaobracaj* links Croatian Dubrovnik with Herceg-Novi. A railway link runs from Podgorica to Bar, a regular ferry sails to Bar from Bari in Italy, and two international airports function at Podgorica and Tivat. Flights to the majority of European capitals are assured by two national carriers: Montenegro Airlines and Adria Airways. The well-established Croatian airport at Dubrovnik lies only 20 miles from the border. It is no longer true that Montenegro is remote or inaccessible.

The tourist brochures and websites gush with superlatives about the 'Pearl of the Adriatic':

> The sea, the lakes, the canyons, the mountains enable everyone to decide on the best way to enjoy quality vacation. In one day, a traveller can have a coffee on one of the numerous beaches of the Budva Riviera, eat lunch with the song of the birds on the Skardar Lake, and dine beside the fireplace on the slopes of the Durmitor mountain . . .
>
> Turbulent history . . . has left behind an invaluable treasure in numerous historic monuments throughout this proud country. The blue sea with endless beaches, restless waters of the clear rivers and beautiful mountain massifs, mixed with the spirits of the old times, have given Montenegro everything one needs for an unforgettable vacation.
>
> Montenegro is an ecological state . . . A large number of sunny days in the summer months and a large quantity of snow in the winter, determine the two most developed forms of tourism . . . In recent times, following global trends, Montenegro is developing extreme sports that the tourists can enjoy as well.[3]

Rafting down the Tara Riva in the Durmitor National Park is strongly recommended.[4]

Montenegro's two inland capitals, Podgorica and Cetinje, compete for visitors, but the main destinations for holidaymakers lie on the coast, where they are regaled with stunning natural beauty and historical charm. Ulcinj has 'the longest sandy beach on the Adriatic'. Kotor is a UNESCO World Heritage Site. Petrovac hosts Roman and Venetian remains. The island-hotel of Sveti Stefan, joined to the mainland by a causeway, boasts a long list of famous guests from Sophia Loren and Princess Margaret to Elizabeth Taylor, Richard Burton, Yuri Gagarin, Alberto Moravia, Sidney Poitier, the president of Outer Margolia and Willy Brandt (which says something of its vintage); it has recently re-opened after renovation, its monastic-style rooms blended with modern luxury and costing from £770 per night upwards.[5] The port of Bar contains both the Turkish fortress of Haj Nehaj and the Castle of King Nikola.

Podgorica is the country's largest town, with 135,000 inhabitants, and is the present-day capital. It stands near the site of a prehistoric Illyrian settlement, and developed during the Middle Ages as a commercial centre. Razed to the ground during the Second World War, its most dynamic period of growth occurred during post-war industrialization, when it was renamed Titograd.[6] Cetinje is barely one-tenth the size of Podgorica but it is the country's historical and religious centre. Founded in the fifteenth century at the foot of the imposing Mount Lovćen, it provided a secure refuge against Ottoman power spreading from the interior and Venetian power dominating the coast. Its long record of resistance earned it the nickname of the 'Serbian Sparta'. Its principal monuments include the Cetinje Monastery, the Lokanda Hotel and the Biljarda House (1838), formerly the Royal Palace, which contains the ultimate symbol of nineteenth-century Europeanization, a billiard room. The plentiful iron railings in Cetinje were cast from captured Ottoman cannon.[7]

Not everything in Montenegro, however, is quite as transparent as the crystal waters of the Adriatic. The economy conceals some very murky sectors; the citizens continue to be torn by a fundamental identity problem, and the political system is decidedly Putinesque.

One of the strongest arguments for Montenegro's withdrawal from Yugoslavia was to protect the economy from rampant hyperinflation, which in 1994 reached a world record level of 3.13 million per cent per month. In 1999, therefore, the dinar was dropped in favour of the Deutschmark, and in 2002 the Deutschmark was replaced by the euro. Montenegro, in the view of informed commentators, was already preparing to separate.[8] Even so, the economy has struggled to recover. It is buoyed up by endemic smuggling, by widespread money-laundering and by dubious foreign investors, especially Russians, who have found a safe haven for their activities. On the international Corruption Chart Index, Montenegro occupies 85th position out of 179 countries listed.[9]

The core of the identity problem lies in the issue of whether or not Montenegrins are really Serbs. In the census of 2003, only 270,000 or 43 per cent declared themselves to be ethnic Montenegrins; 200,000 or 32 per cent preferred self-designation as Serbs. Several surveys were undertaken, and the percentages fluctuated wildly according to the questions asked – in the view of an émigré website, Montenegrins constitute 62 per cent of the population, and Serbs only 9 per cent.[10] The distinction rests less on religious practice and more on attitudes towards the Serbian state and to the highly politicized Serbian Orthodox Church, which insists that all its adherents are Serbs whether they like it or not. In 1993, when the first referendum on independence was held in a setting dominated by the Serbia of Slobodan Milošević, and by his campaign to maintain Yugoslav unity by force, the vote unsurprisingly produced a pro-Serbian majority. But it also provoked the appearance of a breakaway Montenegrin Orthodox Church, which rejects the automatic association of its members with Serb identity, and which was restored after an interval of seventy-five years. This showed that strong resentments persisted against Serbian domination, and not only in the political sphere. In 2006, when a second referendum was held after Milošević had been deposed, a pro-independence majority was returned by the modest margin of 55.5 per cent for and 44.5 per cent against.[11]

Throughout this period, Montenegro's political scene was dominated by one party and by one man. The party, the Democratic Socialist Party of Montenegro (DSPM), was a reconstructed continuation of the Montenegrin branch of Tito's old League of Yugoslav Communists. The man was Milo Djukanović (b. 1962), the party leader and a prime example of an ex-Communist who knew how to adapt to the post-Communist era. Djukanović is a former basketball player, with the tall stature of a natural leader, the face of a film star and the eloquence of a practised populist. He first came to prominence as a close associate of Milošević, who helped him to apply Serbia's 'anti-bureaucratic revolution' and to remove the party's Old Guard. He then elbowed his colleagues aside, and in 1991 entered office at the age of twenty-nine in the first of his six terms as prime minister. Except for a four-year break in 1998–2002, when he served as president, his premiership continued until December 2010. He parted company with Milošević in the mid-1990s over the Dayton Accords, which he considered too conciliatory, and was slowly converted to the movement for independence round the turn of the century. He stepped down as premier at the end of the decade, being replaced by his deputy, Igor Lukšić, but retained the key post of Chairman of the DSPM. He is said to be concentrating on Montenegro's bid to join the European Union; still only forty-nine, he has by no means bowed out of politics.

The power of the Montenegrin political elite is said to rest on a seamless alliance between the ruling Party and members of the former Yugoslav security services; their wealth is certainly connected to a number of family-controlled banks and businesses, such as Capital Invest, Primary Invest and Select Investment. The international reputation of Djukanović stood high, especially with American representatives, during the Bosnian and Kosovo crises, but passed temporarily under a cloud when Italian police laid charges laid against him over alleged links with the Mafia and the Camorra; the charges have since been dropped. Djukanović has been described as 'the kind of Marxist who keeps a picture of Margaret Thatcher on his desk' and as 'the Smartest Man in the Balkans'.[12]

Like all EU candidates, Montenegro faced a long process of verifications and negotiations. Formal application was made in 2008, and candidate status granted in December 2010. When negotiations opened in the following New Year, an assessment of Montenegro's chances of meeting the criteria for the thirty-five chapters of the Union's *acquis communautaire* was issued by the EU team in Brussels. Reading very much like an old-fashioned school report, their statement listed the current position regarding each chapter under one of five categories: 1. 'No major difficulties expected', 2. 'Further effort needed', 3. 'Considerable effort needed', 4. 'Nothing to adopt', and 5. 'Totally incompatible with the acquis'. It placed eight subjects starting with 'Taxation' into the first category; thirteen starting with 'Labour Mobility' into the second; eighteen starting with 'Free Movement of Goods' into the third; two including 'Institutions' into the fourth; and only one, 'Environment', into the fifth. Why exactly policy to the environment should be judged 'totally incompatible' in Montenegro, which has declared itself 'an ecological state', would now have to be investigated. It may have something to do with the plan for multiple dams on the Moraca river.[13] An overall Action Plan was proposed and accepted on 23 February 2011. All applicants must pass through this mill, and a final result cannot be expected for some years.[14] For the time being, the world watches and waits, pondering the well-known television advertisement broadcast alongside 'Incredible India' and 'Malaysia Truly Asia' – 'Montenegro – Experience the Wild Beauty'.[15]

II

The Lycée Louis-le-Grand is one of France's most prestigious boys' schools. Once a Jesuit college, it changed its name when it received the royal patronage of Louis XIV, but still stands on the rue St Jacques in the heart of Paris, in the *Quartier Latin*, surrounded by the hallowed halls of the Sorbonne and the Collège de France. Its graduates, named '*magnoludoviciens*', are envied for their success in gaining competitive entry to the elite '*grandes écoles*'. They include some of the best-known names of French culture and politics, from Molière and Voltaire to presidents Pompidou, Giscard d'Estaing and Chirac. They also include a number of sons of distinguished foreign families who have been sent to Paris to be subjected to an educational experience of international renown.[16]

One of the latter, Nikola Mirkov Petrović-Njegoš (1841–1921) studied at Louis-le-Grand in the second part of the 1850s. He was a Balkan prince from a country which most of his classmates could hardly have marked on the map, heir to a near-legendary line of hereditary and celibate prince-bishops or *vladikas*, who traditionally passed their sovereign titles to their nephews. He had been raised in the Serbian Orthodox Church, schooled both in the martial arts and in poetry, and was not well suited to his academic hothouse. He undoubtedly regarded himself as a Serb, and belonged to a dynasty that openly spoke of the restoration of the 'tsardom of Stefan Dušan', destroyed by the Ottoman Turks nearly 500 years earlier. Like all his compatriots, he had been brought up to believe that the Ottoman victory over the Serbs at the Battle of Kosovo in 1389 was the greatest catastrophe in world history. Now he was living in an age when the Ottoman Empire was the 'Sick Man of Europe'. Serbia, Greece and Romania had already broken free of its grip. Hopes were rising that others would soon follow.

In 1860, when his country's call came, Prince Nikola was just nineteen years old. His uncle, Danilo I, had been assassinated. There was no time to finish his baccalaureate. The ex-schoolboy hurried to Marseille, took ship and sailed home to become the crowned head of a state whose future was as uncertain as its past was obscure.[17]

Crna Gora, as its inhabitants call it, the 'land of the Black Mountain', lay inland from the Adriatic coast, squeezed between Bosnia and Albania. It took its name from the dark, pine-clad massif of Mount Lovćen (5,653 feet), which rises to the west of Cetinje; when the country first made the headlines during Prince Nikola's long reign, Victorian newspapers often transliterated the Cyrillic form of the name as 'Tsernagora'. Today, it best known to the outside world by the old Venetian name of Montenegro. Its total area is smaller than that of Wales or of Connecticut. The fertile landscape of the northern district contrasts sharply with the sterile, calcinated mountains of the centre and south, known as the *Brda* or 'Highlands'. At the prince's accession, landlocked Montenegro was separated from the Adriatic by a long coastal strip known to locals as *Primore* and to others as *Albania veneziana*.[18]

In the distant past, the Principality-Bishopric of Montenegro had been ruled by non-hereditary clerics; Prince Nicola's family established the right of hereditary succession in 1696, and Nicola was the seventh of the Petrović-Njegoš line. His uncle and immediate predecessor, however, had secularized the state, separating it from the Orthodox Church in 1852 and changing the ruler's title from 'prince-bishop' to 'prince'. This meant that Nicola's duties were entirely non-ecclesiastical, and that the headship of the Church was no longer joined to the headship of the principality.

Montenegrin society was organized round a traditional system of

The tribes of Montenegro, *c.* 1900

USKOKI

HERCEGOVINA

Banjani

Ozrinići

Moračani

Rovčani

Vasojevići

SEVEN HILLS

Cuce

Pješivci

Bjelopavlii

Piperi

Bratonožići

Drekalovići

Kuči

Lim

Čeklići

Njeguši

Kosijeri

Zagarač

Podgorica

Kotor

Cetinje

Cetinjani

Dobrsko Selo

Ceklin

ALBANIA

Maini

Podgor

Ljubotin

Grazani

Budra

Brajevići

Dupilo

Brcele

Sotonice

Lake Shkoder

Paštrovići

Boljevice

ADRIATIC SEA

Gluhi Do

Limljani

Highland clans
Rijecka clans
Katunska clans
Crmnica clans
Coastal clans

0   20   40 km

tribes or clans, which had led the struggle against Ottoman domination from the sixteenth century onwards. The clans were contemptuous of all outside government, and resistant to taxation. They also cultivated the inimitable Montenegrin code of chivalry, summarized by the slogan '*Čojstvo i Junaštvo*' – 'Humanity and Bravery' – that characterized the ideals of a warrior people. Vendettas and feuding were an integral part of their way of life.[19]

The distinction between tribes and clans is simple in theory, but less easy to make in practice. In essence, the clans were patrilineal kinship groups similar to those in Scotland, each claiming descent from a historical or legendary ancestor. Petrović, for example, meaning 'Son of Peter', was Prince Nikola's clan name; some of the larger clans were divided into sub-clans, which used separate names. Men and women from the same clan were forbidden to marry. The tribes, in contrast, were larger groupings made up of all the clans inhabiting a particular territorial district. Each of them held regular gatherings or *zbori* in traditionally designated villages, where matters of common interest were discussed and tribal chiefs were elected. The Njeguši tribe, for example, to which the Petrovići clan belonged, took its name from the village where it held its tribal meetings. In districts inhabited by a single clan, the tribe and the clan became indistinguishable. In Prince Nikola's lifetime, some thirty tribes were active in Old Montenegro or in the adjacent Highlands and Coastland.[20]

Once the tribes had liberated the most remote mountain districts from the Ottomans in the sixteenth century, a proto-national movement began to form round the authority of the Orthodox metropolitan of Cetinje. This movement, partly religious and partly political, gave rise to the independent principality of the *vladikas*.[21] Such at least is the romantic version of history that became popular in Prince Nikola's day. Later historians have grown increasingly cautious about declarations of the country's 'age-old freedom'. They now paint a picture in which the principality did indeed enjoy a large measure of self-government but only in close association with the Ottomans. As elsewhere in the Balkans, the Sublime Porte was willing to arrange special rules for taxation and military service, but not to resign its claim to overlordship.[22]

Montenegro's status in 1860, therefore, can best be described as disputed. In the eyes of the outside world, it was still an integral part of the Ottoman Empire. But since it had enjoyed self-rule under its prince-bishops for nearly two centuries, increasing numbers of its people tended to think of it as an independent, sovereign state. In the age of the

Risorgimento, which was blossoming just across the Adriatic, they were not alone in harbouring nationalist ideas. On the other hand, thanks to the Orthodox connection, the Russian Empire began to act as if Montenegro were some sort of informal protectorate. Prince Nikola's main aim during his reign was to gain full international recognition for the independence from both these behemoths which he and many of his subjects took to be their birthright.

Nikola's fervent sense of a national mission was fostered by the romantic literature of the day, and in particular by the writings of the last of the ecclesiastical *vladikas*, Petar II Petrović-Njegoš (r. 1830–51), a man whom he would have known before departing for Paris. Prince-Bishop Petar's *Gorski Vijenac*, 'The Mountain Wreath', is counted a jewel of Serbian poetry and by some as a major engine in what has been called the 'slavic myth-making factory'; it was certainly a work of great popularity that helped cement nineteenth-century Serbian identity. Published in 1847, it runs on through 2,819 epic verses, celebrating the people's struggle for freedom and describing the cultural interplay of the Montenegrin tribes with Ottoman Muslims and decadent Venetians. It centres on a period in the early eighteenth century, when significant numbers of Montenegrins had converted to Islam and the survival of Christian Slavs was perceived to be in danger. Petar was rousing his countrymen to fight for their traditions or to see them perish:

> . . . After the storm the sky grows clearer;
> The soul grows serene after sorrow's pain;
> The song waxes joyous after tears have been shed.
> Oh that mine eyes could be opened to watch
> As our homeland regains all that which was lost,
> As Tsar Lazar's crown shines bright in my face
> And Milos returns to his Serbian kin.
> Then would my soul be truly content,
> Like a peaceful morn at the height of Spring
> When the winds of the sea and the darkest clouds
> Sleep calm o'er the heaving waves . . .
> Let the struggle continue without respite,
> Let it bring what men thought never could be.
> Let Hell and the Devil devour us all.
> Flowers will grow and bedeck our graves,
> For the sake of those who are still to come . . .[23]

In recent times, Petar's poetry has been judged incendiary, accused of inciting conflict between Christian and Muslim;[24] in its day, it gave heart to a weak Christian community that felt oppressed by a powerful Ottoman and Muslim establishment.

At all events, the Montenegrins faced a formidable task. In the late nineteenth century they were surrounded on all sides by stronger neighbours. In 1862, when the prince's father, Prince Mirko, took an army into neighbouring Herzegovina to help some fellow Christian rebels, the incursion ended in defeat and a punitive peace. Bosnia and Herzegovina were ruled by Austria after 1878, but both the Sandžak of Novi Pazar* and Albania (to which the coastal *Primore* belonged) remained integral parts of the Ottoman Empire. The strategic environment was taut.[25]

For fifteen years, therefore, awaiting more favourable international circumstances, Prince Nikola applied his mind to domestic reforms in the spirit of Petar II, who had been devoted not only to poetry but also to constitutionalism and to popular education; regarded as the father of his people, he had been buried on the very summit of Mount Lovćen. Prince Nikola drove his reforms forward. He surrendered some of his prerogatives to the Senate, initiated a programme of general primary education and, with notable assistance from Russia (which he was quite willing to accept), restructured and re-equipped the army.

Much effort was put into public relations, and a number of foreign tours were staged. In 1867 Nikola returned to Paris to meet Napoleon III, and the following year he toured St Petersburg, Berlin and Vienna. As a champion of Orthodoxy he was well favoured by the Romanovs, who sent military missions and supplies to Cetinje and who strengthened their own dynasty with an influx of Montenegrin brides.

By 1876, Nikola felt strong enough to declare war on the Ottomans, and in conjunction with Serbia to wage what amounted to a war of independence. Like his father, he personally led his troops into battle. Initial fortunes were meagre, but when the Russian army opened up a front on the Black Sea, the Ottomans were forced to withdraw their troops to defend Bulgaria, and the Montenegrins were free to conquer their seaboard. They were praised by the British prime minister, William Gladstone, who called them 'a bunch of heroes . . . whose braveries surpass those of the ancient Hellenes at Thermopylae and Marathon'.[26] They were rewarded at the Congress of Berlin, convened in 1878 to

---

* A district of Bosnia. The Ottoman *sandjak* was a second-level administrative unit, less than a province.

terminate the Russo-Turkish War, with a declaration by the Great Powers of Montenegro's sovereign status. Its frontiers were extended, and Prince Nikola announced that the Battle of Kosovo had been revenged. The date of the Berlin Declaration – 13 July – was adopted as Montenegro's National Day.

Gladstone's concern for Montenegro derived from his long-standing crusade in defence of the Ottoman Empire's Slav and Christian subjects, and was a natural sequel to his denunciation of the 'Bulgarian Horrors'. In 1877 he wrote a learned but highly romantic article about Montenegrin history, stressing its centuries-old record of resistance and the 'honourable sentiment of gratitude' owed by Western nations. 'Among the Serbian lands', he wrote of the fifteenth century, 'was the flourishing Principality of Zeta':

> It took its name from the stream which flows southward ... toward the Lake of Scutari. It comprised the territory now known as Montenegro, or Tsernagora, together with the seaward frontier ... and the rich and fair plains encircling the irregular outline of the inhospitable mountain. Land after land had given way; but Zeta ever stood firm. At last, in 1478, Scutari was taken on the South, and in 1483 ... Herzegovina on the north submitted to the Ottomans. Ivan Tchernoievitch, the Montenegrin hero of the day, applied to the Venetians for the aid he had often given, and was refused. Thereupon he, and his people with him, quitted the sunny tracts in which they had basked for some seven hundred years, and sought, on the rocks and amidst the precipices, surety for the two gifts most precious to mankind – their faith and their freedom. To them, as to the Pomaks of Bulgaria and the Bosnian Begs, it was open to purchase by conformity a debasing peace. Before them, as before others, lay the *trinoda necessitas*: the alternatives of death, slavery or the Koran. They were not to die, for they had work to do. To the Koran or slavery, they preferred a life of cold, want, hardship and perpetual peril. Such is their Magna Charta; and without reproach to others, it is, as far as I know, the noblest in the world.
>
> Then and there, [they] voted unanimously their fundamental law, that, in time of war against the Turk, no son of Tsernagora would quit the field without the order of his chief: that a runaway would be forever disgraced and banished; that he should be dressed in woman's clothes ... and that the women striking him with their distaffs should hunt the coward away from the sanctuary of freedom. And now for four centuries wanting only seven years they have maintained the covenant of that awful day, through an unbroken series of trials and exploits, to which it is hard to find a parallel in the annals of Europe, perhaps even of mankind.[27]

Gladstone was especially impressed by the fact that, when fleeing to the interior mountains in 1484, only seven years after Caxton had produced England's first book, the Montenegrins had carried a printing-press with them. More critically, he noted two uncivilized practices: the public display of severed Turkish heads, and the mutilation of prisoners. The former was dismissed, since the British government had done the same to Jacobite rebels not long previously, but the latter found no excuse.[28]

Not to be outdone, Alfred, Lord Tennyson, Gladstone's exact contemporary, penned a sonnet:

> They rose to where their sovran eagle sails,
> They kept their faith, their freedom, on the height,
> Chaste, frugal, savage, arm'd by day and night
> Against the Turk; whose inroad nowhere scales
> Their headlong passes . . .
> O smallest among peoples! rough rock-throne
> Of Freedom! warriors beating back the swarm
> Of Turkish Islam for five hundred years,
> Great Tsernogora! never since thine own
> Black ridges drew the cloud and brake the storm
> Has breathed a race of mightier mountaineers.[29]

*

Owing to the publicity generated by his tours, the prince of Montenegro could only grow in political stature. In 1891 he visited the Ottoman sultan, who implicitly, though not formally, relinquished all rights over his former province. In 1896, he attended the coronation of Tsar Nicholas II in St Petersburg, and on his way home won the ultimate accolade of taking afternoon tea with Queen Victoria at Windsor Castle. In line with other progressive monarchs, he was preparing a constitution, launched a national currency, the *perper*, and promoted the idea of a national Church.

In June 1903 Montenegro's royal court was deeply shaken by a crisis in neighbouring Serbia. The king of Serbia, Aleksandar I Obrenović, had caused great offence among his subjects by arbitrary acts such as suspending the constitution for half an hour in order to dismiss some unwanted senators, and in the teeth of fierce criticism had recently married a commoner, Queen Draga. A dispute then arose over the naming of an heir apparent. King Aleksandar wanted to elevate Queen Draga's brother, against whom the twenty-four-year-old Prince Mirko of

Montenegro, Prince Nikola's second son, who was married to an Obren-ović, was put forward as a counter-candidate. Senior members of the Serbian military were so incensed that they plotted a royal assassination, and in Belgrade on 11 July Aleksandar and Draga were shot, mutilated and disembowelled. The assassins then rejected Prince Mirko, choosing the exiled Serbian Prince Petar Karadjordjević in his stead. King Petar I, as he became (r. 1903–21), had lived in Cetinje during his exile and had married Nikola's eldest daughter, Zorka; he was a mild and liberal man, who had translated John Stuart Mill into Serbian. Even so, fear and sus-picion entered into relations between the courts of Cetinje and Belgrade.

In February 1904 the Russo-Japanese conflict broke out in the Far East, and Prince Nikola felt obliged to declare war on Japan in support of the tsar; several hundred Montenegrins travelled to Manchuria to join the ranks. Among them was the prince's godson, Dr Anto Gvozde-nović (1853–1935), who rose to be a general in the Russian, and later the French, armies. After the fighting ceased, no steps were taken to end the state of war between Montenegro and Japan.

Also in 1904, the traditional system of tribes and clans was reorgan-ized. Four *nahija* – 'provinces' or 'captaincies' – were created, the tribes were redistributed within them, and every province received its state-appointed elder. Prince Nikola was smoothing the ground for the introduction of more modern state structures.

In 1905, Montenegro became a constitutional monarchy following the adoption of an elaborate constitution of 222 articles, modelled in large part on its Serbian equivalent. A British Foreign Office Handbook would use Serbian terminology to describe the arrangements:

> The Prince continued to represent the State in all its foreign relations; primogeniture in the male line was declared to be the law of succession; the Senate was preserved; the country was divided into departments (*oblasti*), districts (*capitanie*) and communes (*opshtine*); a free press and free compul-sory elementary education, a Council of State of six, and a Court of Accounts of six members formed part of the Charter. A National Assembly of sixty-two deputies (the *Narodna Skupshtina*), partly elected by universal suffrage and partly composed of ex officio nominees of the Prince, was to meet annually on 31 October ... Deputies must be 30 years of age and pay 15 kronen in taxes annually.[30]

The first general election was held in November of the same year. There were no established political parties; deputies mainly represented local

Petrović and Karadjordjević

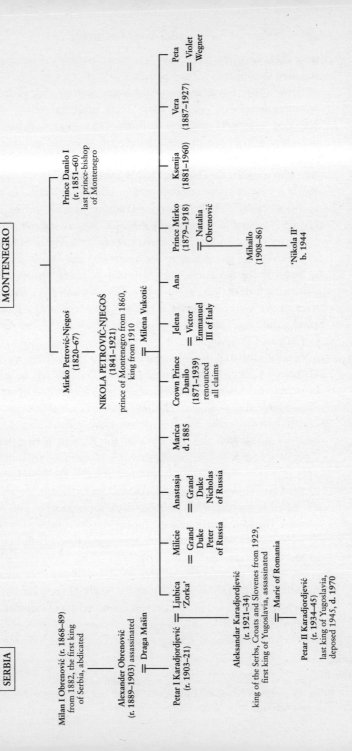

or tribal interests; and the National Assembly's recommendation required the approval of the prince.

After 1907, however, two embryonic parties did arise. One, the *Naradna Stranka* or 'People's Party' (NS), was organized by and Italian-educated engineer, Andrija Radović (1872–1947), who aimed to introduce a more modern and democratic system. The other, the 'True People's Party' (PNS) or 'Rightists', was organized by Prince Nikola himself, who resented the challenge to his prerogatives. Radović survived for barely a year as prime minister, and briefly found himself in prison. Yet in 1913 his People's Party won a landslide victory and he retuned to favour. Prospects for constititional evolution were improving.

In 1910 Montenegro celebrated its prince's golden jubilee. The court of St Petersburg raised him to the honorary rank of field marshal[31] and, as befitted the occasion, the National Assembly petitioned him to assume the title of 'king', which he graciously accepted. The representatives of the Great Powers applauded and Montenegro took its place among the kingdoms of Europe on Proclamation Day, 28 August 1910 (15 August Old Style).*

In a parallel step, a decree gave effect to the decision to declare the Orthodox Church in Montenegro autocephalous, that is, independent of patriarchal jurisdiction. Previously the Church had operated under the nominal jurisdiction of the patriarch of Constantinople, as did its counterpart in Serbia. But the decree now asserted that Montenegro had never accepted the abolition of the Serbian patriarchate by the Ottomans in 1766, and hence that the Montenegrin Church was the only true successor of the tradition of St Sava, the founder of Serbian Orthodoxy. This was no trivial matter. The Orthodox clergy traditionally acted as guardians not only of religious practice but also of national identity. The Montenegrins now appeared to be claiming that their form of adherence to Serbian traditions was more correct than that practised in Serbia. This was asking for trouble.[32]

An official photograph of the royal family on Proclamation Day records the Petrović-Njegoš clan at the height of their success. The gentlemen are decked out in a variety of exotic military uniforms; the ladies in regulation ankle-length, white silk dresses and cartwheel hats. King Nikola sits in national costume in the centre alongside the matronly

* Like other Orthodox countries, Montenegro adhered to the old Julian Calendar, which was thirteen days behind the Gregorian Calendar used by Western countries. Dates were usually expressed in both New Style and Old Style.

Montenegro and neighbours, 1911

Voivodina

AUSTRIA-
HUNGARY

Belgrade

Bosnia

SERBIA

○ Sarajevo

Dalmatia

Hercegovina

Sandžak of
Novi Pazar

Novi Pazar ○

Montenegro

Dubrovnik ○

Podgorica ○

Cetinje ○

OTTOMAN
EMPIRE

A D R I A T I C

○ Scutari

S E A

Albania

○ — 40 — 80 km

Tirana ○

Queen Milena, a landowner's daughter who had married him when she
was only thirteen. They are surrounded by their seven surviving daughters, their three sons, one grandson and a collection of spouses. Their
eldest son-in-law, Petar I of Serbia, is missing, but three others, including King Vittorio Emanuele III of Italy, are present. Crown Prince
Danilo (1871–1939), their fifth child, stands in the middle of the back
row; their twenty-one-year-old grandson, Crown Prince Aleksandar of
Serbia, reclines in the foreground.[33]

In the summer of 1911 an American reporter, who was seeking a
scoop on the current Albanian crisis but had heard of King Nikola's
love for poetry and plays, obtained an interview at the 'Biljarda House'
by announcing that he was a New York literary critic. Fighting had

flared on the nearby frontier, but 'Nikita' was not going to miss an
opportunity to discuss literature. 'There is no vanity so deep', the reporter
remarked, 'as that of authorship':

> The King soon joined me – a fine, old, sturdy gentleman turned seventy, with
> rugged features, a coarse mouth, and a good forehead. A heavy moustache lent
> picturesqueness to a massive face, lit up by shrewd and rather kindly eyes . . .
> Nikita seemed oblivious of his Ministers . . . He plunged into literature, [speak-
> ing] in faultless French – the French of a professor . . . He touched on Lamartine,
> and eulogised Chateaubriand. From poetry we passed on to drama.
>
> 'Yes,' said the King, 'I have written plays myself. The best known,
> produced in the Royal Theatre here, is a drama called the "Empress of the
> Balkans". The heroine was suggested by my wife.'
>
> I knew nothing of the 'Empress', but it seemed courteous to inquire if
> the King would not like to have the work performed in France or England
> or America. The question seemed to change Nikita instantly from the ruler
> of a brave and restless land into an author . . . He gave me a copy of his
> play in Montenegrin (which resembles Serb or Russian). He also favoured
> me with his autographed photograph.
>
> Being now in high good spirits, he obliged me quite spontaneously with
> his opinion on the impending crisis. To my distress, I found that he had
> resolved to avoid war, for the time, and to drop the Albanian cause.[34]

The Balkan Wars – wars of liberation from the Ottoman Empire, complicated by conflicts between the liberated for the spoils – erupted the
very next year notwithstanding, and Montenegro found itself in a cauldron of swirling conflicts in which stronger parties always held the
initiative. King Nikola plunged into the fray alongside Serbia. He still
had his lyrical foreign admirers:

> He speaks as straight as his rifle's shot,
> As straight as a thrusting blade,
> Waiting the deed that shall trouble the truce
> His savage guns have made . . .
>
> Stern old King of the stark black hills,
> Where the fierce lean eagles breed,
> Your speech rings true as your good sword rings –
> And you are a king indeed![35]

The First Balkan War of 1912, in which several states participated
against the Ottomans and Montenegro fired the first shot, ended the

age-old dominance of the Ottoman Empire. The Second Balkan War of 1913, in which 10,000 Montenegrin troops were sent to the Bulgarian Front, ended with Montenegro winning a common border with Serbia. But it also led to disputes with the Great Powers. King Nikola had captured the Albanian port of Shkoder (Scutari) in defiance of Western advice, only pulling out after vociferous Austrian protests.[36] Vienna viewed Montenegro as a Russian surrogate.

As if on cue, as soon as peace was declared, King Nikola's play, *Balkanska Carica*, was published in London in an English translation. A signed portrait of the author faced the title page:

THE EMPRESS OF THE BALKANS: A DRAMA IN THREE ACTS
BY NICHOLAS I PETROVITCH-NIEGOSH,
KING OF MONTENEGRO
Adapted from the Servian . . .
London
(Eveleigh Nash)
1913

The text was preceded by a detailed 'Description of the Characters', one or two quite recognizable:

PRINCE EEVAN, the Ruler of Montenegro, age 70 – a majestic old man, a warrior and a stern ruler, but kind-hearted.

PRINCE GEORGE, the Heir-Apparent, age 26 – young and strong, very polite and kind, and of a quiet disposition.

PRINCE STANKO, the second son, age 24 – strong and very ambitious: vigorous, fearless and brave, but of changeable moods, easy to persuade.

VOIVODA DEHAN, age 65 – old, but bears his age well, being full of life: a great hero and warrior, yet not vain.

VOIVIDA PERUN, Prince Eevan's guest, age 60.

DANITZA, Perun's daughter, aged 20 – a firm character and very patriotic: in love with Stanko: full of pluck, very resolute, and of pleasant manners.

IBRAHIM AGA, Envoy of the Sultan, aged 50 – slight and medium height, dark yellowish complexion, and cunning looking, full of compliments and a very deceitful character.[37]

The time of the action is given as 'the end of the Fifteenth Century'. The American, who had brought the original text to London, thought that the royal drama lacked 'imaginative charm'. 'It did not make me very anxious to adapt the play for Broadway,' he wrote. 'It had been written in fair verse, under the influence of Schiller, [but] had no "punch" . . . It might have proved the germ of a good musical comedy.'[38] Unfortunately, musical comedy was the image which Europeans as well as Americans continued to have of Montenegro:

> There was a whiff of the Middle Ages about King Nicholas: his insistence on leading his troops into battle, his dispensing of justice under an ancient tree, and the magnificent medals he awarded himself and his friends . . . His capital, Cetinje, was merely a large village, the Bank of Montenegro a small cottage, and the Grand Hotel a boarding-house . . . [The king's] new palace was more like a German pension, with the royal children doing their home-work in folk costume . . . and the King sitting on the front steps waiting for visitors. Franz Lehár used Montenegro as the model for *The Merry Widow*.[39]

Lehár's operetta, first performed in Vienna in December 1905, was a popular sensation in the years before the Great War; between 1907 and 1910 it received nearly 800 performances in London alone. In the libretto, the scene of action is barely disguised as the Principality of 'Pontevedro', and its capital as Letigne. The Pontevedran ambassador is Baron Zeta, his first secretary – Count Danilo, and his assistant – Njegus. 'Vilya's Song' is presented as an 'old Pontevedran melody':

> *Vilja, O Vilja! Du Waldmägdelein,*
> *Fass' mich und lass' mich*
> *Dein Trautliebster sein.*

('Vilya, O Vilya, you forest maiden, / take me and let me / be your own truest love.')[40] If Europeans thought about Montenegro at all before the war, most of them would have done so in terms of Lehár's happy romp.

Montenegro's story is well illustrated on its early postage stamps. The first issue of the Montenegrin post office, from 1874, was inscribed exclusively in Cyrillic and shows the head of Prince Nikola. A commemorative issue in 1893 marked the 400th anniversary of Montenegro's oldest surviving printed book, and another in 1896 the 200th anniversary of the hereditary state of the *vladikas*. In 1910 a coronation issue appeared, and was followed by a set of definitive designs which showed the king sporting traditional regal headdress and which proved to be the country's last.[41]

In August 1914, the assassination of Archduke Franz-Ferdinand in Sarajevo took place within thirty miles of the Montenegrin frontier, and fighting was started by the Austrian attack on Serbia. The Montenegrins rushed to bolster Serbian resistance, declaring war against Austria, only to find themselves caught up in a long and bitter conflict. They also hoped, as the Serbs did, to obtain hefty slices of the Adriatic coast and of northern Albania; indeed they were formally promised important acquisitions, including Dubrovnik, during negotiations preceding the Treaty of London (1915) which brought Italy into the war on the Allied side. But the outcome of the fighting was less favourable. In 1916–17 the Serbian army was forced to retreat, conducting a long march over the mountains into Albania, and eventually taking refuge on the island of Corfu. As the Austrians surged forward, Montenegro was cast into intense distress.[42] At the Battle of Mojkovac in January 1916, the Montenegrin army made great sacrifices to enable their Serbian allies to escape, but their own country fell into enemy hands, and King Nikola was persuaded to go into exile in France. He left his kingdom to a plight that was as ambiguous as it was perilous. After complicated negotiations, he reached an agreement with Vienna whereby the royal administration and the authority of the clans would be left in place under the overall control of an Austrian commander. These negotiations in their turn provoked not only the unintended capitulation of the Montenegrin army but also a bitter split within the Montenegrin government-in-exile. Andrija Radović, who had served a further spell as prime minister, parted company with the king permanently. The exiled monarch was rapidly losing control of his destiny.

In the remaining years of the war, as Austrian power faded, political ferment accelerated. One part of Montenegrin opinion was drawn to the 'Yugoslav Idea', the scheme whereby all the southern Slavs – Serbs, Montenegrins, Croats, Slovenes and Macedonians – would join together to form a common state. Another part gave more attention to the 'Pan-Serbian Idea', which proposed that the existing Kingdom of Serbia should be expanded to draw in all ethnic Serbs, including those living in Bosnia, Montenegro, Kosovo and Macedonia. Crucially, though the concept of a united Yugoslavia and that of a 'Greater Serbia' each had their enthusiasts, they were not necessarily incompatible. Such, indeed, was the view of Andrija Radović. Henceforth, Montenegro's best-connected politician contacted Serbia's exiled government and made common cause with them.

The wider diplomatic framework was also changing shape. In 1914 Montenegro's interests had been protected by Russia, and by Russia's ally, France. After the Treaty of London, however, Italy entered the equation and King Nikola shared Italian aspirations for territorial reconstruction in the Adriatic region, as did Radović. Then in 1917 the Bolshevik Revolution knocked Russia off the chessboard; the French duly drew closer to Serbia; and Italian plans for the Adriatic lost Western support. The Americans, in particular, were opposed to the Treaty of London, which they saw as a wicked example of the old secret diplomacy. King Nikola was losing his international friends.

According to one witness, 'the Austrian occupation was not a brutal one'; at least in its first phase. 'Not a child was killed, not a woman violated.'[42] Yet matters soon deteriorated. The Montenegrin army's capitulation spread dismay, and the exiled government gave contradictory explanations. For example, it issued a declaration stating that the agreement with the Austrians had only been made to gain time; that the King was urging resistance, and that nobody had the right to negotiate an armistice, let alone make peace.[43] As a result, many of the king's loyal subjects were unclear as to whether they should co-operate with the occupying forces or not. The Austrians ordered the internment of all adult males as a precaution. This sparked acts of defiance, which in turn provoked reprisals. Austrian soldiers were shot, and the offenders were hanged. Worst of all, the clans broke ranks. Montenegrins started to skirmish with Montenegrins. As the international conflict drew to a close, civil war was looming.

Thanks to the Austrian occupation and King Nikola's exile, Montenegro played little part in the rapidly moving but ill co-ordinated plans to create a united state of Yugoslavia. The principal protagonist in this venture was a Dalmatian Croat, Ante Trumbić (1864–1938), sometime mayor of Split, further up the Adriatic coast from Kotor. Trumbić's Yugoslav Committee had been launched in London, working closely with the scholar R. W. Seton-Watson and his journal *New Europe*; but in 1917–18 it was engaged in its key task of finding suitable Serb partners in order to outflank the alternative project of a Greater Serbia. On 17 July 1917, in conjunction with the slippery Serb politician Nikola Pašić (1845–1926), sometime mayor of Belgrade, Trumbić signed the Corfu Declaration, which envisaged a future Kingdom of the Serbs, Croats and Slovenes. The Declaration named the House of Karadjordjević as the future ruling dynasty, and it made no mention of Montenegro.[44] This was ominous. And Pašić proved himself to be thoroughly unreliable. Seton-Watson said of him: 'The old man changes his mind every few hours, and cannot be trusted for five minutes with his word of honour or anything else.'[45] Pašić was soon indicating that the Corfu Declaration had been a passing dalliance, and as late as July 1918 appeared to be paying attention exclusively to pan-Serbian aspirations. 'Serbia', he told Trumbić opaquely, 'internationally represents our nation of three names.'

Following the Corfu Declaration, Radović surfaced in Switzerland, where he established the Central Montenegrin Committee of National Reunification. The extent of his support cannot be gauged, but one should note that the nation which he aimed to reunite was not Montenegro; it was the nation of all Serbs wherever they lived. For practical purposes, he was campaigning against Montenegro's restoration.

Inside Montenegro, therefore, confusion reigned. Contact with the exiled king had virtually been lost. There was no Montenegrin radio service, the telephones were controlled by the Austrians, and the illiterate majority of the population could not make sense of the few foreign newspapers that crept past the censors. The Yugoslav project was left in the hands of distant outsiders. There can be little doubt that the Montenegrins, like most Europeans, were expecting change. They knew that King Nikola's chief patron, the Russian tsar, had been overthrown, and that parts of his Empire, like Ukraine, had broken away. But for the most part they were waiting patiently for the king to return and for the international situation to stabilize.

The last fortnight of the war caused the greatest confusion of all. On 28 October 1918, the Austro-Hungarian Empire collapsed, the Emperor Charles withdrew from government, and the Austrian occupation forces pulled out from Montenegro. In all the great cities of the dying Empire – in Vienna and Budapest, in Zagreb, Ljubljana, Prague, Lemberg and Sarajevo – national committees sprang up to demand the formation of new states. Then, on 4 November, revolution broke out in Berlin. The Kaiser abdicated, German forces on the Western Front retreated, and the Central Powers, which had appeared invincible only six months earlier, cracked. The Western Allies, 'who were not expecting victory when it came',[46] emerged triumphant. They dictated the terms of the Armistice of 11 November, and announced that a general Peace Conference would convene in Paris on 31 January. Montenegrins were not the only ones to wonder what the fast-moving events would bring.

At the very end of the Great War, in the interval between the Armistice and the start of the Peace Conference, Montenegro was hit by the cruellest of blows. The war had apparently been won. The country was freeing itself from the Central Powers. As a member of the victorious Allies, it was looking forward to receiving its due rewards. Yet a completely different scenario arose. A hastily convened meeting of a 'Grand National Assembly' calling itself the *Skupština* voted in favour of union with the nascent Yugoslav kingdom. Executive decisions passed immediately to Belgrade. King Nikola lost his throne. His kingdom, a Serbian Sparta only eight years old, was put out on the mountainside like a Spartan child, and left to die in its infancy. It was the only Allied state to disappear from the map.

The sequence of events whereby Montenegro lost its statehood deserves closer examination. After all, the standard procedure for an occupied Allied country would have seen the state and its territory restored as soon as victory was assured. Belgium, for example, which had been occupied by Germany between 1914 and 1918, was fully restored to the king of the Belgians and his government at the end of hostilities. Albert I made his triumphal re-entry into Brussels on 22 November 1918, two days before the 'Grand National Assembly' of Montenegro convened. Allied declarations had consistently bracketed Montenegro with Belgium and Serbia as countries whose restoration was guaranteed. What in 1918 made Montenegro different?

The collapse of Austria-Hungary in October 1918 left a vacuum in the territories which the Royal and Imperial Army had occupied. In Montenegro, no provision was made for an orderly transfer of power. The Montenegrin army had no time to reconstitute itself. After the capitulation of January 1916, some of its units had handed in their arms to the Austrians and disbanded; others had left the country and were serving under Serbian command. All the Balkan allies were subordinated in theory to the French General Franchet d'Espérey in distant Salonika; the western part of the Balkan theatre had been entrusted to his deputy, General Venel. Yet little direct control could be exercised and few military resources could be spared for the Montenegrin backwater. The coastal region was assigned to the French or to British and Italian units brought in by sea. The mountainous interior was assigned to the Serbian army, the only substantial ground force in the region, while eastern border districts were infiltrated by Serbian 'irregulars'. In short, in the weeks both before and after the Armistice, no coherent Montenegrin formation was on hand to defend Montenegro's interests.[47]

The standing of the Montenegrin monarchy was definitely diminished. King Nikola's wartime actions had provoked a wave of criticism. Some denounced him for treating with the enemy, others for deserting his country or betraying the Serbs, and a few for 'behaving like a despot' or for living well off Allied subsidies. He had quarrelled with some of the politicians, and calls for his abdication had emanated from his own entourage.[48] Yet there had been no concerted campaign in the country to remove him, still less to abolish the institution of monarchy; a deal with the king's Serbian relatives was still on the cards. A measure of qualified sympathy for the king can be found in an unexpected source. Milovan Djilas (1911–95), later one of Tito's comrades and prisoners, and himself a Montenegrin, remembered the episode from his childhood. 'There had actually been no betrayal,' he wrote. 'What could [the king] have done? . . . [He] did not betray the Serbs. If he betrayed anything – and he did – it was the Montenegrin Army and the Montenegrin state.'[49]

As for relations between the House of Petrović-Njegoš and the House of Karadjordjević, little was known in public. The kings of Montenegro and Serbia were both old men; both were looking to the younger generation; both had been forced into exile, Nikola in Antibes, Petar in Corfu; and both hoped for co-ordinated policy. Crown Prince Aleksandar of Serbia, Nikola's grandson, was a key figure; he was already the acting Serbian regent, and was obviously ambitious. In London in 1915, he had been the first person ever to talk about 'our Yugoslav people'[50] – though such sentiments did not necessarily indicate ill will to his grandfather. A highly impractical scheme floated by Radović foresaw the Montenegrin and Serbian dynasties reigning over Yugoslavia jointly, with a Petrović and a Karadjordjević taking turns to mount the throne. Nobody took the idea seriously.

Montenegro's isolation was increased by tensions in neighbouring Albania, which was the subject of acute international disagreements. The Serbian army had laid waste to large parts of northern Albania in late 1918, devastating over 150 villages in the Drin valley. The depredations were encouraged by the French, who wanted post-war Serbia to be strong and were hatching a plot to partition Albania. In order to undermine a fragile government in Tirana, an insurrection was then fomented among the Catholic Mirdita clan, which was to declare its mountainous retreat to be an independent republic. Far away in Paris, a French-dominated committee announced that Albania was to be partitioned (according to the provisions of the Treaty of London), while the United States recognized Albanian independence and received an Albanian ambassador to Washington. This complicated dispute distracted attention from developments elsewhere.

Inside Montenegro, two opposing political camps were forming but with no established forum in which to compete. The pan-Serbian camp inspired by Radović was pressing both for unification with Serbia and for the creation of a Yugoslav state under Belgrade's leadership. It assumed that Montenegro's pre-war constitution had lapsed, and sought to achieve its end by imposing its own unilateral procedures: a classic case of self-styled democrats impatient of democratic methods. The rival royalist camp aimed to restore the Kingdom of Montenegro first and to address the Yugoslav issue later. Its sympathizers, though badly organized, probably represented majority opinion; they certainly reflected the stated intentions of the Allied Powers.

It is worth quoting Clause 11 of President Wilson's Fourteen Points of April 1917, which had gained the adherence of both Britain and France, and which was widely seen to embody the guidelines of Allied policy. 'Romania, Serbia and Montenegro should be evacuated,' it read, 'occupied territory restored, Serbia accorded free and secure access to the sea, and the relations of the several Balkan states to one another determined by friendly counsel.' Further: 'International guarantees should be entered upon for the political and economic independence and territorial integrity of the several Balkan states.'[51] From this, it is clear that the Allied leaders intended to restore the statehood of all their Balkan allies and to secure it by treaty.

In the circumstances of November 1918, however, there was no question of 'friendly counsel' or a level political playing field. The Serbian army, which had marched into the void left by the Austrians, gave its backing to the pan-Serbian group in Montenegro, which immediately set up a so-called National Council, together with a Provisional Executive Committee to organize elections to a 'Grand National Assembly'. The plan was masterminded by Radović. The country's political class as a whole were given no chance to compete on equal terms. The king and government were still abroad; they commanded no independent troops and few officials; and the effective influence of their supporters outside Cetinje was minimal.[52] From his French exile, King Nikola issued a decree on 12 November, the day after the Armistice, for convening the Montenegrin parliament or *Skupština*; but his loyal subjects had no way of implementing it.

So far, no fundamental disagreement had arisen over the joint Yugoslav project. Serbs, Croats, Slovenes, Bosnians and Montenegrins had all felt the weight of Austrian rule or occupation, and all saw the benefits of future co-operation. A Yugoslav state suited the purposes of the

Western Allies, who saw it as a desirable replacement for Austrian influence, and the smaller nations were enthusiastic. King Nikola himself had expressed his willingness to join. He was thinking, no doubt, of a federal Yugoslav state modelled on the German Empire, in which several reigning monarchs had retained their separate crowns. Here was an issue on which 'friendly counsel' was certainly needed.

Montenegrins, therefore, had many worries. It was not clear how Montenegro's territory was to be fully restored, or how the Yugoslav project might be realized. Disagreements were always in the air; pessimists might have despaired. Yet it was a great relief to hear that the Armistice had been declared, and a comfort that Montenegro was accepted as one of the victorious allies. In such circumstances, small nations are naturally inclined to put their faith in the benevolence of the Great Powers; Montenegro, it appeared, was not in so sorry a pass as Hungary or Bulgaria, which had backed the wrong side.

The Serbs, in contrast, would have spotted several major obstacles from the start. Time, for them, was of the essence. If they were to realize their dream of a state in which Serbia would play the same dominant role as Prussia played in Germany, they had to act quickly. In particular, they had to forestall their principal partners and rivals, the Croats, who were still extricating themselves from the old Austro-Hungarian institutional structures. The outcome of the Peace Conference and its deliberations was uncertain. The Serbian delegation would be in a far stronger position if preliminary arrangements to Serbia's liking were put in place in advance.[53]

The Serbs were equally concerned about the future of their monarchy. One might have expected the monarchists of Serbia and Montenegro to act in harmony, if only to keep the republicans at bay. After all, King Petar I of Serbia was King Nikola's son-in-law, had lived in Cetinje and shared a very similar background. He, too, had been educated in France; he was a graduate of the military academy at Saint-Cyr, and had served (as 'Pierre Kara') as a French officer during the Franco-Prussian War. The two monarchs were of the same age and of the same outlook and had a very great deal in common. But there lay the problem. There were generals and courtiers in Belgrade who regarded the House of Petrović-Njegoš as a dangerous challenger. They had brought King Petar to the throne in 1903 through a murderous military *coup d'état*, and were fearful of something similar happening again. Moreover, their king was sick, and had ceded his prerogatives to his Montenegrin-born son. In the race for the throne of Yugoslavia – there were no kings in Slovenia or Croatia – the Montenegrin dynasty was the Serbians' only serious competitor.

In addition, Serbia was a landlocked country. There were four possible directions in which her promised 'access to the sea' could be projected: over Croatian territory to the north-west, over Albanian territory to the south-west, over Greek territory to the south, or directly over Montenegro. Greece and Croatia were strong enough to resist. Albania was in turmoil. Montenegro offered the easiest target.

At the turn of October 1918 the stalled Yugoslav project had suddenly come to life. Another National Committee appeared in Croatian Zagreb on 29 October, announcing the creation without warning of a 'State of Slovenes, Croats and Serbs'. Its president, Dr Anton Korošec, was a Slovene who had been active in the imperial *Reichsrat* in Vienna, and its vice-presidents were a Croat and a Serb from Croatia. Its putative territory was made up exclusively of lands from the dying Habsburg Empire – the Serbs in its title referring to inhabitants of Bosnia and Hercegovina, not of Serbia or Montenegro. Nonetheless its appearance opened up opportunities which the exiled government of Serbia could not ignore. Nikola Pašić immediately saw the chance of building a 'Greater Serbia' within a still larger Yugoslavia, and he sought a swift encounter with the politicians from Zagreb. Korošec was equally eager to do business with Pašić, because conflict was looming with Italy over the Adriatic littoral from Trieste to Dubrovnik. (In a last act of Austro-Hungarian desperation, Korošec had been handed control of the entire Royal and Imperial Fleet.)

The resultant Conference of Geneva was attended by Pašić, Korošec and Trumbić, representatives respectively of the government of Serbia, the National Council from Zagreb and the Yugoslav Committee, but with no authorized representative from Montenegro. On 6 November, after four hectic days, it reached an agreement whereby the newly announced State of Slovenes, Croats and Serbs would be merged with the Kingdom of Serbia. An expanded National Council was recognized as the provisional government of the merged states, while parallel ministries would function in Zagreb and Belgrade. The name of the new entity, subtly modified, was to be the 'Kingdom of the Serbs, Croats and Slovenes'.

Serbia, therefore, had the strongest of motives for eliminating Montenegro without delay, and the chance of exploiting a golden opening presented itself before the war had formally ended. The chosen course of action, adopted with lightning speed, was to bring all Serbs into the Yugoslav fold on Belgrade's terms. It was applied to ex-Austrian Bosnia and Hercegovina and to the ex-Hungarian Vojvodina as well as to Montenegro. In all cases, the organizers achieved their goals with the tacit assistance of the Serbian army. In Montenegro's case, they selected Podgorica, not the royal capital of Cetinje, as the meeting-place for the 'Grand National Assembly', and quickly distributed white and green voting cards: white for the pro-Serbian Yugoslav option; green for advocates of the restoration of the Kingdom of Montenegro. The timetable was draconian, and the sleight of hand brazen. The few foreign observers who learned of the elections were blissfully unaware that the 'Grand National Assembly' was something quite different from the constitutional *Skupština*, whose convocation the king had decreed.

Two short weeks, starting on 10 November, were allotted for the election campaign, which was marked and marred by a tide of anti-Petrović smears and insinuations. Brochures and press articles fanned hostile rumours. The absent King Nikola's dealings with the Habsburgs were described as selfish and unpatriotic: he was said to have amassed a huge personal fortune in (unspecified) British banks. Rallies were limited to seven days only (and in Cetinje to three days). The Serbian army was ordered to arrest all 'agitators', and to prevent the return of Montenegrin exiles. A council of compliant bishops announced the reunion of the Montenegrin and Serbian Orthodox Churches.

In this stage-managed scenario, the result of the 'plebiscite' was entirely predictable: 168 delegates were chosen with a crushing majority for the pro-Serbian Whites, the *bjelaši*, and the resulting 'Grand National Assembly' met on 24 November. During the Assembly's second session two days later a 'Decision Document' stated first that 'the Serbian people of Montenegro share one blood, language, religion and tradition with the people of Serbia', and secondly, that the unification of Montenegro with Serbia offers 'the only possible salvation for our people'. No debate was permitted.

Four resolutions were then passed:

1. to dethrone King Nikola I Petrović-Njegoš and his dynasty
2. to unify Montenegro and Serbia into one state under the [Serbian] Karadjordjević dynasty, and thus unified . . . to join the common mother country . . . of Serbs, Croats and Slovenes
3. to select an Executive Committee of five persons to manage all activities until unification is complete: [and]

4. to inform the former King, his Government, the Allied Powers,
and all non-aligned states about this decision.[54]

Out of 168 delegates, 160 assented. 'With Serbian troops in occupation,' writes one disinterested historian, 'a national assembly, apparently
made up only of those with the correct views, voted hastily to depose
their king and to unite with Serbia.'[55]

Contemporary descriptions of the Podgorica Assembly do not reflect
well on its participants:

> They smoked, talked, shouted as in a café; the resolutions were declared to
> have been carried by unanimity. Anyone who attempted to object was
> howled down. Objections were raised that some members present, even
> those from Cetinje itself, were not the persons elected. But no hearing could
> be obtained. Some Albanians had been sent forcibly to represent the county
> of Pec, but they protested in vain that they had no wish to take part in the
> proceedings. All this was under the shadow of the bayonet.[56]

Protests made no difference, and once the vote had been recorded, the
Assembly's participants were surplus to requirements. On 1 December
a Serb-appointed Montenegrin Council invited the Serbian regent, Prince
Aleksandar, to assume power, and Montenegro was annexed to Serbia
by royal decree; Aleksandar had already assumed the additional post
of regent of the Yugoslav kingdom. On 4 December, in Belgrade, the
invalid Petar I was proclaimed king of the Serbs, Croats and Slovenes,
making his last public appearance. His new style made no mention of
Montenegro. The Serbian Yugoslav authorities severed relations with
King Nikola, assuring the Allied Powers that the demise of his kingdom
had come about through his subjects' democratic choice.

The backlash was not slow in coming. The royalist Greens or *zelenasi*
appealed to General Venel to annul the Podgorica resolutions and to
support free elections. Fighting broke out in Cetinje on Christmas Eve,
24 December. The royalists, already classed as 'rebels', suffered dead
and wounded. During a brief visit to Cetinje, General Venel called for a
ceasefire, ordering the rebels (but not the Serbian army) to lay down
their arms. In essence, Montenegro had been pacified before the Peace
Conference in Paris had even started work.[57]

King Nikola and his ministers still had the use of their embassy in
Paris, in addition to the royal residence in Antibes and their offices in
Neuilly-sur-Seine and Bordeaux, where a Montenegrin military camp
was located. They approached all and sundry with pleas that Monte-

negro's independence be respected; the king was personally assured by
Woodrow Wilson, David Lloyd George and President Poincaré that they
all understood his position. He publicly appealed to his subjects to
renounce violence. But no practical assistance was forthcoming. The
king's letters to the Allied leaders usually went unanswered, or, if
answered, were degraded by high-flown but evasive replies. On 24
November 1918, the day of the king's deposition, Poincaré wrote:
'Your Majesty may rest assured that the Government of the [French]
Republic . . . will lend itself to no attempt which would aim to force the
will of the people of Montenegro and to deny their legitimate aspirations.'[58] President Wilson only replied after two months' delay: 'A good
opportunity will soon be offered to the Montenegrin people', he opined,
'to express themselves freely upon the political form of their future
Government.'[59]

The Greens launched a more determined rising on the day of the
Orthodox Christmas, 7 January 1919. Their temerity quickly ignited a
civil war, which divided the traditional tribes. The Serbian army carried
out fierce reprisals, provoking counter-reprisals. Both sides perpetrated
atrocities; the house of Andrija Radović in Martinici was torched by
marauders, his mother kidnapped and his father shot. But the Greens
were no match for Serbian fire-power. 'Their houses were burned down.
They were pillaged and beaten. The women had cats sewn into their
skirts, and the cats were beaten with rods. The soldiers mounted astride
the backs of old men and forced them to carry them across streams.
They attacked girls. Property and honour and the past: all this was
trampled on.'[60] Montenegrin soldiers were required to swear a new oath
of allegiance to King Petar I. Those who refused were arrested. Serbian
jails filled up with Montenegrin inmates.

The Peace Conference proved a disaster for Montenegro. In the
absence of Russia owing to the Bolshevik Revolution, King Nikola's
kingdom found itself friendless. The seat reserved for the country's dele-
gate remained empty. The explanation offered by the Supreme Council
on 13 January 1919 stated that 'the seat could not be allocated until
the political situation in the country had clarified'.[61] The Yugoslav delegation, in contrast, headed by Trumbić and Pašić, took their seats
without difficulty. They were accompanied by Andrija Radović, the
head of their Montenegrin Section, and were able to feed their views
to the conference almost unopposed. Their publicity materials, including a book by Radović, were widely translated and widely distributed,
greatly outnumbering the pro-Montenegrin offerings.[62] King Nikola's

representative, General Gvozdenović, was only invited to address the
Supreme Council on one occasion, on 6 March, but to no effect. In May
the Conference extended formal recognition to the Kingdom of the
Serbs, Croats and Slovenes, of which Montenegro, willy-nilly, now
formed part.[63] Thereafter the Serbian government had nothing to do but
to protect its gains; King Nikola would be hammering on a door that
was already shut.

Despite continuing international concern, the whole of 1919 passed
without any meaningful discussion about Montenegro. The British
government sent out a prominent diplomat, the earl de Salis, to make
enquiries on the spot. An Irish landowner and a count of the Holy
Roman Empire, Sir John De Salis-Soglio (1864–1939) had held several
posts in the Balkans, including that of British envoy at Cetinje in 1911–
16; he deposited his report in the Foreign Office in September, but the
foreign minister, Lord Curzon, told Parliament that its publication was
impossible.[64] Questions were tabled both in the House of Commons
and in the House of Lords, to no avail. Rumours spread that De Salis
had disappeared, that he had been rescued by a British warship, or that
his life was in danger. A parliamentary review prepared by Major Temperley* duly informed the House of Commons that nothing improper
had occurred.[65] Yet the feeling grew that the British government knew
far more that it was prepared to concede.

Once the main sessions of the Peace Conference were over, Britain's
Foreign Office published all the handbooks which it had earlier prepared for the use of its officials and diplomats. No. 20 in the series was
devoted to Montenegro. Its eighty-two pages contained copious information on history, geography and social and economic conditions, but
only a few lines on developments since 1913:

> Especially since the two Serb states have been coterminous, contact with
> Serbia has led the Montenegrins to make comparisons not to the advantage
> of their own country; and a movement for the abdication of King Nikola
> so as to unite the two countries under the Karageorgevich dynasty was
> publicly started by the ex-Premier M. A. Radovich in 1917. The conference
> of Jugo-Slav delegates held at Geneva in 1918 discussed the relation of
> Montenegro to the new Jugo-Slav state; and a specially summoned Skup-

---

* H. W. V. Temperley (1879–1939) was a historian, Fellow of Peterhouse and later Professor
of Modern History at Cambridge. In 1919, having fought at Gallipoli and published his
History of Serbia, he was working for the War Office in military intelligence.[66]

shtina deposed the king and declared for incorporation ... This decision, however, has been challenged on constitutional grounds.[67]

This summary could easily have been written in Belgrade. The failure to distinguish between the 'Grand National Assembly' and the constitutional *Skupština*, which never convened, was fundamentally misleading.

In 1920–21 Britain, France and the United States proceeded one by one to withdraw their representatives from the Montenegrin government-in-exile. They had decided that the king's ministers had lost their ability to influence developments, and, since fresh elections were being held throughout Serbia, accepted the view that the people of Montenegro were participating in a democratic system. They were deeply at odds by now with the Italian government, which was voicing its displeasure over the Adriatic settlement, and which saw itself alongside Montenegro as a fellow victim of Allied callousness. It was left to the American press, and to a lesser extent to the Italians, to tell the world some basic and long overdue details. Early in April 1920 the *New York Times* published a sensational article entitled 'Serbs Arrest De Salis':

Paris, April 2. The Count de Salis, formerly British Minister to Montenegro and a special envoy to the Vatican ... has been arrested and imprisoned by the Serbians while executing a mission of investigation into Montenegro for his Government. This information is contained in a declaration made to King Nicholas, who is now in Paris, by the Montenegran Foreign Minister ... The declaration alleges that the [count's] Report was to the effect that the Serbian Army 'which overran Montenegro after the armistice terrorized the population', [and that] the reign of terror continues.

In conclusion, the complaint is made that 'Europe knows what is happening to Montenegro, but remains indifferent' and that President Wilson, 'the great champion of small nations, persistently turns a deaf ear'.[68]

Prime Minister Bonomi of Italy told his parliament at this time: 'The Montenegrin question has *not* been discussed by the powers, and the state of affairs created by Serbia has never received international sanction.'[69] The queen of Montenegro asked for a meeting with Lloyd George when he visited Cannes. The request was refused. The powers were giving their former ally the cold shoulder. The contents of the De Salis report were not disclosed, though historians now know how damning it was. Among other things, Montenegro was 'under occupation by a strong Serbian force', Montenegrin officials had been replaced by Serbians, elections to the Podgorica Assembly had been illegal, the prisons were full and the present regime was hated.[70]

Meanwhile, the Serbian army began an annual series of expeditions into the mountains to round up the 'rebels'. Barbarous acts multiplied. Villages were torched. Bounties of 100,000 dinars were placed on the heads of fugitives. Locals were beaten or bribed to turn informer, and prisoners faced torture and execution. The Belgrade press showed no restraint in publishing the grisly photographs. A Canadian staff officer, resident in the Balkans, gave testimony: 'I know the case of a certain Bulatovich called "the Colonel" found in the hands of the Serbs. This unfortunate man was three times hung . . . At the last moment, the rope was cut so that he would not die immediately . . . Afterwards, they broke his arms and legs. Finally, still living, they removed his skin, like that of a beast.'[71] Reports from Montenegro recorded 6,000 houses burned, and many more pillaged. Damage caused by the Serbian army exceeded that of the Austrian occupation, and was estimated at 723 million francs. More than 5,000 Montenegrin civilians were languishing in Serbian internment camps. Another Canadian, who had been running a war hospital at Dulcigno (Ulcinj), wrote to the British government in July 1920 saying that his charity could no longer do its work. 'The Serbs have done every dirty trick they could think of,' he wrote. 'There are not many Montenegrins, and in another year there will be none left.'[72] To cap it all, the Serbian government passed a law for 'The Protection of the State', permitting its security forces to use whatever means they pleased.

Owing to continued protests, the British government called for still more inquiries. In mid-1920 further reports were commissioned from Major Temperley, and from Ronald Bryce, a professional diplomat, who were sent out to observe the elections. Neither discovered serious irregularities. Bryce concluded (a) that fresh elections had taken place satisfactorily, and (b) that the people of Montenegro were in favour of a 'Jugo-Slav State'.[73] Temperley concurred. What they failed to report was that the Serbian government had vetted all the electoral candidates, and that membership of the 'Jugo-Slav State' was not at issue. It was one thing to favour the formation of Yugoslavia; it was something quite different to be tricked and shackled into joining Yugoslavia with no opportunity to negotiate the terms. For its part, the government of Montenegro in exile appealed to the Supreme Allied Council for the creation of a commission of inquiry.

By this time, despairing of their alliance with Britain and France, King Nikola and his ministers placed their last hope in the good faith of the United States; General Gvozdenović was dispatched as the royal ambassador to Washington. In January 1921, therefore, when the US administration followed the British and French lead in withdrawing recognition from Montenegro's representatives, the reaction was understandably bitter. J. S. Plamenatz, premier and foreign minister of the royal Montenegrin government, signed a strong, not to say intemperate diplomatic protest. He reminded the Americans of 'the annexation of Allied Montenegro by force and bloodshed' and of President Wilson's assurances about the Montenegrin people's 'right to self-determination':

> Taking into consideration all the foregoing facts, the royal Government of Montenegro cannot believe that the government of the United States – the most civilized country in the world – would contemplate an act [leading to] the breaking off of diplomatic relations with Montenegro. Such an action would not only aid the criminal intentions of Belgrade, but would ignore all the principles of international morality and justice; the United States would be guilty of not respecting its given word and not respecting the sovereignty of Montenegro.[74]

King Nikola of Montenegro died on 1 March 1921 at Antibes aged eighty, and was buried at San Remo. A terminal act of submission appeared to have been played out on the 21 October following, when Queen Milena, the king's widow, dissolved the Montenegrin government-in-exile and released the ministers from their oath of allegiance, so detaching herself from the only focus round which the royalist cause might have coalesced. Her decision was reported in the *New York Times* under the headline of 'Exit Montenegro':

> News has reached Rome that the Montenegrin Government has ceased to exist ... Queen Milena has recognised the inopportuneness of giving the name of Government to a body of ministers who no longer have any power ... The handful of soldiers remaining ... have agreed to disband ... The act of Queen Milena ... marks the passing of one of the most interesting little states of Europe, and removes from the Supreme Council and the League of Nations one of their most afflicting burdens ... It is unlikely that agitation for an independent Montenegro will be continued.[75]

By that time, the former kingdom was losing its very name. After incorporation into a newly centralized Serbia, Serbian officials increasingly referred to it as the *Banovina Zetska*, the 'Region of the Zeta', a formula officially adopted in 1929; the Montenegrin constitution, together with the authority of the tribes and clans, had been swept away.

The House of Petrović-Njegoš was brought low by Nikola's death. The heir apparent, Prince Danilo, had renounced his rights in favour of his cousin, King Aleksandar. His brother, Prince Mirko, had predeceased their father; the next in line, Prince Mirko's son Mihailo, was a boy of thirteen. There was no hope of a quick recovery. In due course Mihailo, who had been at school at Eastbourne in England, accepted the role of pretender, and General Gvozdenović was appointed regent.

A 'League of Montenegrin Emigrants' thereupon published a brochure entitled *Le Plus Grand Crime de la Guerre Mondiale*, 'The Greatest Crime of the World War'. Its subtitle read: *La Tentative d'escamoter un état allié*, 'The Attempt to Cause an Allied State to Vanish'. The book consisted of page after page of quotations from Allied statesmen:

'Great Britain will continue to pursue the war energetically until Belgium, Serbia and Montenegro are restored.' Herbert Asquith, 10 January 1916.

'The restoration of Belgium, Serbia and Montenegro.' David Lloyd George, in response to a question from the German delegation to the Peace Conference concerning the conditions of peace, 16 April 1919.

'The question of Montenegro will not be discussed at Pallanza [during Yugoslav-Italian negotiations] but at a later date by all the Powers.' Bonar Law, British Conservative Party leader, 11 May 1920.

'Montenegro's only fault is to have participated in the war and to have believed the promises of her allies.' C. Treves, Italian socialist.

'Germany's crime against Belgium is not so great as that committed by Serbia . . . against Montenegro. The first of those crimes has been repaired; the second still enjoys the support of the Powers.' Hugo Mowinckel, Norwegian minister, August 1920.[76]

The final curtain, however, had not yet fully descended. Between April and May 1922 the delegates of thirty-four countries convened at the Genoa Conference to discuss the post-war reconstruction of Eastern Europe. The conference was heading for fruitless deadlock, but one of the items on its agenda related to the work of the Inter-Allied Reparations Commission, and discussion revealed that Montenegro's share of reparations had never been paid. Absurd though the argument sounded, the Commission had retained the $2 million collected and due to Montenegro because 'it apparently doesn't know to whom to pay it'.[77] The occasion provided a pretext for further protests on Montenegro's behalf. Gabriele d'Annunzio, the firebrand Italian nationalist and 'the first duce',

made an impassioned speech; and a Dr Chotch, still described as Montenegro's foreign minister, presented a formal appeal to each of the delegations:

> With its note of 1 November 1920 to the Supreme Allied Council and
> the League of Nations, the Government of Montenegro ... asked for the
> appointment of an international commission of investigation ... [into] the
> crimes and offences committed ... against the Montenegrin people. Unfor-
> tunately, this cry of despair ... did not find the response which we hoped
> its justice would inspire.
>
> The Montenegrin people and Government firmly believe that the exalted
> assembly of the representatives of the nations gathered at Genoa will not
> ignore the martyrdom of the Montenegrin people and the unheard-of
> barbarity of which they are the victims.
>
> Consequently, in the name of the Montenegrin Government, I have the
> honor to pray the International Conference to deign to inaugurate a commis-
> sion of investigation charged with verification of the [said] crimes and
> offences ...[78]

'Montenegro's Plea' was accompanied by piles of documents detailing
Serbian atrocities. It received no known reply, and no investigation ever
materialized. The *New York Times*, which had pursued the story with
determination, spoke the last word, publishing a long article on 16 April
1922 and recounting the events of the last four years; the headline read
'Annihilation of a Nation'.[79]

Montenegro's friends in the outside world were now few and far
between. One of them, an Englishman who had once been tutor to King
Nikola's sons, wrote a searing denunciation in 1924, which excoriates
the Allied Powers no less than Serbia. It opens with a scene from the
heart of London:

> On the walls of the top of the grand staircase in the Foreign Office in White-
> hall a number of decorative panels have been painted in honour of our
> Allies in the Great War. The centre panel, entitled 'BRITANNIA PACIFICA-
> TRIX', depicts all the Allies and includes Montenegro as a separate state.
> Britannia is represented welcoming her loyal comrades in arms; some –
> France, Italy, America and Japan – are glorious figures; others, who suffered
> more bitterly – Belgium, Roumania, Serbia, Montenegro – are mournful
> with bleeding wounds. The official description of the panel contains the
> following words: 'Serbia is clasping Montenegro in her arms.'[80]

*

For the next eighty-seven years, the former subjects of the Kingdom of Montenegro lived their lives as citizens of Yugoslavia. In the inter-war period, they were integrated into Serbia within the Kingdom of Serbs, Croats and Slovenes. During the Second World War they endured harsh occupations, first by the Italian Fascists and then by the German Nazis. In post-war, Communist-run Yugoslavia, their land was reconstituted by Tito as one of the country's six federal republics.

King Nikola's legacy was not insignificant. For one thing, he left a dozen sons and daughters who, through numerous strategic marriages, played a significant role in Balkan and Orthodox politics, and he was remembered as the 'father-in-law of Europe'. (His daughter Yelena, as Queen Elena of Italy during Mussolini's regime, had some influence in an Axis attempt to restore a Montenegrin state.) For another, he left a considerable poetic and literary oeuvre that now forms part of the standard Serbo-Croat repertoire. Most ironically, perhaps, he had done much through his earlier writings and pronouncements to strengthen the cause of pan-Serbian nationalism, fanning the flames of romantic exclusivity without knowing what the flames might consume. His own career was ruined by the cause which he had once encouraged.

Once Tito's Communist regime had passed, King Nikola's memory could again be honoured. In 1989 his body and that of Queen Milena (who had died at Cap d'Antibes only two years after her husband) were brought home from San Remo and reinterred in the Cupiro Chapel at Cetinje. The former royal palace reopened as a royal museum. Shortly after, the Montenegrin Orthodox Church, which Nikola had sponsored, was re-established. In 1997, the elderly Archbishop Mikhailo of Cetinje, who had worked in exile as Queen Elena of Italy's archivist, assumed the position of the metropolitan of Montenegro, thereby challenging the hierarchy of the Serbian Orthodox Church. His rival was Archbishop Amfilohije, metropolitan of Montenegro and the Littoral, who made headlines by denouncing Prime Minister Djukanović as the 'Pagan King'.[81] Archbishop Mikhailo gained the allegiance of perhaps 30 per cent of the faithful.[82]

During the terrible Yugoslav wars of the 1990s, Montenegro stood by Serbian-led Yugoslavia for longer than any other republic. No less than a third of the officers of the Yugoslav army were Montenegrins, as were large numbers of officials and Party leaders in Yugoslavia's central administration. Montenegrin forces participated in the attacks on Croatian Dubrovnik and on the Muslim-inhabited areas of Bosnia.[83] Both Slobodan Milošević and Željko Ražnatović, the paramilitary leader known as

Yugoslavia after 1945

'Arkan', were Serbs of Montenegrin descent.[84] So, too, is Radovan Karadzič, the former leader of the Bosnian Serbs.[85]

Yet from 1997 onwards the Montenegrin Communist Party, which had stayed in charge throughout the wars, split into pro- and anti-Milošević factions, and the stronger anti faction gradually distanced itself from Belgrade. In its brief, last emanation, the Yugoslav Federation took a dual form, within which Serbia and Montenegro were assigned an equal voice in foreign and defence policy, adopting the sort of arrangement which King Nikola and his ministers might once have accepted.

Montenegro's disaffection with Serbia grew markedly in 1999 during 'Operation Noble Anvil', NATO's bombing campaign launched to protect neighbouring Kosovo, then a province of Serbia (with a largely Albanian population) which, as we saw at the outset, declared its independence in 2008. Kosovan refugees poured over the frontier; NATO planners targeted Montenegrin ports and communications; and collateral casualties were caused when bombs fell on peaceful villages. Montenegro was paying heavily for a Serbian connection of rapidly decreasing benefit.

Once Slobodan Milošević had been overthrown in Serbia in October 2000, the Montenegrin leadership talked openly of its aspirations for an agreed divorce. Preparations took time, but on 22 May 2006, after nearly ninety years' delay, the crucial referendum was held. The motion for independence narrowly gained the required majority of votes, despite EU monitors having raised the threshold from 50 to 55 per cent; the winning margin of 0.5 per cent was more respectable than it seemed.[86] Montenegro joined the United Nations and the Council of Europe. The sovereign state which had vanished in 1918 was restored.[87]

In the period preceding the referendum, the government of Prime Minister Djukanović systematically promoted all the symbols of Montenegro's separate identity. In addition to supporting the Montenegrin Orthodox Church, it renamed the country's official language. The school curriculum replaced Serbian language classes with 'native language classes', and the University's Department of Serbian Language and Literature became the 'Department of Serbian, Montenegrin, Bosnian and Croat Studies'.[88] In 2004 a new state anthem was introduced in reaction to Serbia's reintroduction of the old royal anthem of the House of Karadjordjević. Since then Montenegrins sing '*Oj svijetla majska zoro*', 'Oh, bright dawn of May', which recalls the conquest of Kosovo.[89]

Finally, on 12 December 2005 the prime minister unveiled a long-awaited statue in a spacious park of Podgorica. 'Montenegro', Djukanović said, 'was, is and should be a friend of all nations, especially of the South Slavs. But never again [will she become] someone's friend to her own detriment.'[90] An opposition spokesman dismissed the event as 'a dictator's act of personal promotion'. Yet it was welcomed by Prince Nikola II Petrović (b. 1941), an architect resident in Paris and son of the late Prince Mihailo.[91] The statue showed King Nikola mounted, but wearing the same national dress as he had worn on Proclamation Day in 1910.

III

The theory and practice of state sovereignty is a complex subject. Few would deny that the destruction of a recognized state through foreign interference is illegal. One may draw a parallel with the death of individuals. If a man or a woman dies from age or sickness, the event may be regretted, but it cannot be morally denounced. Yet if the loss of life is due to the action or inaction of others, it is automatically classed as a crime – manslaughter or murder or involuntary homicide.

With respect to sovereign states, the wider context is crucial. Few politicians or international lawyers would oppose the idea that a supranational order exists, and that the conduct of sovereign states is subject to collective rules and sanctions. Such, after all, are the foundations of international law. The failure in Montenegro's case, therefore, was not confined to the fact of the state's demise through foreign fraud and violence: it was equally a failure of what would now be called the 'international community'. Montenegro had been a member of the war-time entente, and her legal personality was still intact as the war ended. Whether or not it was formally terminated by the decisions of the Paris Peace Conference is open to debate. For reasons that are hard to pin-point, Montenegro's fate completely escaped the international agenda.

King Nikola's kingdom sank before the legal framework of state sovereignty was strengthened by the Estrada Doctrine of 1930 and the Montevideo Convention of 1933, which expounded the principles of sovereign equality and of non-intervention. It certainly met Montevideo's four criteria of sovereignty: namely, a permanent population, a defined territory, a recognized government, and the capacity to conduct foreign relations.[92] But in 1918–21, when the Allied Powers and then the League of Nations had to deal with numerous cases of disputed sovereignty, none of these principles had been formally established. The Åland Isles, for example, objected to automatic incorporation into Finland, which had recently declared its independence. The Ålanders were 90 per cent Swedish-speaking, and claimed the right to remain in Sweden. The Swedish government sponsored their claim, and the League of Nations convened its very first commission of inquiry. In 1921, to the surprise of many, the commission's recommendation was to leave the islands under Finnish jurisdiction, but with a firm guarantee of their autonomy. This judgment has held good ever since.[93]

In Albania, another dispute was not settled so peaceably. The Serbian army launched a further advance in an attempt to pre-empt the out-come, but its offensive helped the Allied Powers to resolve their differences in precisely the opposite way to the Serbs' intentions. In November 1921, by a decree of the Allied Conference of Ambassadors, Albanian independence was recognized and, with minor changes, the frontiers of 1913 were reconfirmed.[94]

The question arises, therefore, why Montenegro could not have benefited from similar arbitration. Both the Peace Conference and the League of Nations were aware of the problem, yet failed to act. The League's excuse may well have been a technical one: once incorporated into Serbia, the Montenegrins became a minority, and the League had a rule that claims by minorities had to be sponsored by the claimants' 'mother country'. Sweden sponsored the Ålanders, but Serbia was obviously not going to sponsor a Montenegrin complaint against Serbia.

One can only think that the Supreme Council at the Peace Conference was gripped by the fatal 'friendly ally syndrome'. Montenegro was shunned for the same reason that the Irish Republic or Corsica was shunned. Allied leaders were quick to champion the victims of the defeated enemy, but they had neither the will nor the courage to investigate injustices caused by their own major partners. At one point, for example, President Wilson agreed to meet a Corsican delegation, not realizing that Corsica formed part of metropolitan France. When reprimanded by Clemenceau, he cancelled the appointment, telling his secretary: 'I cannot interfere with the internal affairs of a friendly ally.' Lloyd George pounced. 'I hope your Excellency will apply the same rule to Ireland,' he said, 'which I need not remind you is still a part of Great Britain ... After all, are we not your ally?' 'Associate,' the President responded sourly, 'not ally.'[95]

Assessments of Montenegro's unification with Serbia have varied greatly over the decades. Inter-war Serbian scholars regarded it as an entirely natural event. Yugoslav scholars of the Tito era, strongly influenced by Communist ideology, showed no sympathy for a dead monarchy. Now that an independent Montenegro has re-emerged, however, a new historical consensus appears to be emerging with it. A textbook published in Podgorica in 2006 and a scholarly monograph both present interpretations that coincide in large measure with the once lonely voice of the author of *Martyred Nation*.[96]

One is tempted to enquire whether any other European states have been treated as shabbily as Montenegro was, especially by an ally or by self-styled benefactors. Austria's *Anschluss* with Germany in 1938, as engineered by Adolf Hitler, is an obvious candidate,[97] and Stalin's takeover of the three Baltic states in 1940 is another.[98] Yet the fate of Poland in 1944–5 must surely top the list. Poland was a comparatively large country, a combatant Allied state, and a formal ally of the Western Powers. Nonetheless, the formula which could be dubbed the 'Montenegrin Gambit' worked like a dream for Poland's post-war oppressors. In stage one, the Soviet Union's Red Army overruns Poland in the closing campaign of the war against Germany; one Allied country is said to be liberating another. In stage two, in the shadow of Red Army bayonets, a bogus committee is formed to undermine the reputation of the exiled government in London, and to demand a common political front with the USSR. Their programme is presented as the product of honest differences within Polish democratic opinion. In stage three, a pre-printed manifesto is suddenly produced, and in the name of the people a self-appointed gang of Soviet stooges usurp the prerogatives of the legal but absent government. In stage four, the Communist security forces classify all political opponents as 'bandits', and calmly pulverize the independence movement. The Western leaders thereon submit to the 'friendly ally syndrome' in the manner of the Foreign Office panels, as 'Russia clasped Poland in her arms'.[99]

Surprising parallels can be observed during the Yugoslav wars of the 1990s. The militaristic, centralizing Serbia that swallowed Montenegro in 1918 seems to have been reborn in the militaristic, centralizing Serbia of Slobodan Milošević. Once again, shameless intrigues in neighbours' affairs, the deployment of military force, and murderous reprisals against 'rebels' became the order of the day. Once again, most Western leaders stood aloof in impotent embarrassment. Yugoslavia fell apart amid a worse wave of thuggery and chicanery than that attending her birth.[100] Fortunately, after years of bloodshed and hand-wringing, the Western Powers eventually overcame their inhibitions. Peace-keeping forces were sent to Bosnia and to Kosovo and the warring parties were brought to the negotiating table at Dayton, Ohio. The Serb-led Yugoslav army was restrained, Yugoslavia was selectively bombed by NATO, and Milošević eventually faced charges of war crimes before an international tribunal.[101]

One wonders what King Nikola might have made of it all, had he or his successors had ever returned to pot the ivories in the Biljarda House or to bask on the sun-baked battlements of Bar. Nikola had belonged to a generation for whom 'Serb' and 'Montenegrin' were almost interchangeable terms, and for whom the enemy was almost invariably an outsider – usually a Turk or an Austrian. Familiar with tribal feuds, he could hardly have imagined the scale of the fratricidal slaughter that was perpetrated by Yugoslavs against Yugoslavs in 1918–21, in 1941–5 and again in 1991–5. Moreover, Nikola was overthrown not by republicans but by fellow monarchists, and his memory was reinstated by an ex-Communist. So he might have concluded that neither monarchy nor republicanism, which gained an incontestable lead in Yugoslavia during the Second World War, were necessarily virtuous. The only true guide to human behaviour, perhaps, is the ancient Montenegrin code of 'Humanity and Bravery'. In this spirit, Montenegrins of all persuasions can still enjoy the rousing song, which King Nikola himself composed:

> Онамо, 'намо, 'hamo . . . За брДа она
> Милошев, кажу, пребива гроб!
> Онамо покој добију души
> Кад Србин више не буде роб.

> Onamo, 'namo . . . za brda ona
> Milošev, kažu, prebiva grob!
> Onamo pokoj dobiću duši
> Kad Srbin više ne bude rob.

> There, over there . . . beyond the hills,
> Miloš, they say, is laid in his grave!
> There my soul will obtain rest
> When the Serb will no more be a slave.[102]

As Lord Curzon apparently failed to recognize, it is the Montenegrin counterpart to 'Rule, Britannia'.

13

Rusyn

The Republic of One Day

(15 March 1939)

I

'Ruthenia' sounds vaguely similar to 'Ruritania': or rather, it sounds suspiciously like a whimsical cross between Ruritania and Slovenia. It is, of course, a real place, as opposed to the fictional kingdom invented by the Victorian novelist Anthony Hope for *The Prisoner of Zenda*.[1] Ruritania never vanished, because it never existed. Ruthenia, in contrast, like Slovenia, belonged in Hope's day to the Austro-Hungarian Empire, and in official Hungarian terminology was called *Kárpátalya*. After the First World War, it was joined to Czechoslovakia as *Podkarpatsko* or 'Sub-Carpathian Ruthenia'; and after the Second, to the Soviet Union. It now forms the Zakarpattia region of the Ukrainian Republic. Nowadays, the preferred name for the region in English is 'Carpatho-Ukraine'. Its largest town and the most westerly in Ukraine, Uzhgorod, lies very close to the frontier of Slovakia and hence of the European Union. One can get there from Western Europe by driving due east from the Czech Republic or by taking a cheap flight to Uzhgorod from Prague, Warsaw or Kiev.

The dominant ethnic group in Carpatho-Ukraine call themselves *Rusyns* or 'Ruthenians'; under Hungarian rule before 1918, they were often referred to as *Ukro-Rusyns* or 'Ruthenians of Hungary'. They are a small branch of a much larger East Slavic grouping that includes the Belarusians and Ukrainians, both of whom at one time called themselves by the same name (see Chapters 5 and 9), but from whom the Carpatho-Rusyns would think themselves distinct. Prior to 1945, their homeland on the sunny southern slopes of the central Carpathian Mountains was never incorporated into the same state as Belarus or Ukraine, and the different historical environment inevitably fostered different customs and characteristics. The landscape below the subalpine peaks is dominated by tree-clad hills, deep valleys and broad rivers, by flower-filled

summer meadows, and by a climate that encourages fruit-growing and
wine-production. Apart from Uzhgorod and Mukachevo, the towns are
few and insignificant. The typical village is no more than a cluster of
farm buildings watched over by a carved wooden church. Overpopulation and rural poverty, however, forced many to flee abroad. Robert
Maxwell (1923–91), the British press magnate, was born Ján Ludvík
Hoch at Solotvyno near Tyachiv on the Romanian frontier; popularly
known as 'the bouncing Czech', he was a Czechoslovak citizen at birth
but not ethnically Czech. Adolph Zukor (1873–1976), the founder of
Paramount Pictures, was born in a Rusyn village just across the frontier
with Slovakia, as were the parents of American artist Andrij Warhola
(Andy Warhol, 1928–87).

   Not everyone will see the point of visiting Zakarpattia. It does not
top the bill of Ukraine's tourist destinations, just as Ukraine does not
top Europe's. Yet the point is not trivial. It is not just about gazing on
Uzhgorod's ancient castle, or strolling carefree across the footbridge
over the River Uzh, or sampling the local Pancake Festival, Zarkapat-
tia's answer to Mardi Gras. For some, it may involve seeking the traces
of the venerable Jewish *yeshivah*, which once flourished at Khust. But

for most, it is mainly concerned with proving that this little part of the world exists.

II

In the early twentieth century the Rusyns of Carpatho-Ukraine possessed a strong sense of national consciousness, reinforced by an active émigré community in the United States. Their identity was closely bound up with the Greek Catholic Church, which had been established in the Kingdom of Hungary since the Union of Uzhgorod of 1646. But the Church's influence was fractured by the presence of Russophile and Orthodox elements, and later, in the 1920s, by that of Communists. Their political aspirations were constantly thwarted by the indifference of the Great Powers and by the presence among them of Hungarian, Slovak, Romanian, German and Jewish minorities.[2]

Carpatho-Ukraine's two decades in the inter-war Republic of Czechoslovakia were not happy. The government in Prague constantly postponed action on its undertaking to give a wide measure of autonomy to *Podkarpatsko*, as demanded by the Treaty of St Germain (1919), which had formally abolished the Austro-Hungarian Empire. The population of 814,000 (1938), of whom about 15 per cent were Jews, suffered the lowest living standards in the country. Politics were stifled by the wrangles of pro-Hungarian, pro-German and pro-Soviet groupings. During the Munich Conference of September 1938, when substantial slices of Bohemia were repackaged as the 'Sudetenland' and ceded to Nazi Germany, the impotence of the central government caused dismay; and matters deteriorated further in November when German arbitrators at the so-called Vienna Awards forced both Slovak and Ruthenian delegates to cede territory to Hungary. *Podkarpatsko* lost a broad swathe of land that included both Uzhgorod and Mukachevo.

Nonetheless, on 22 November 1938 Prague granted the much-delayed autonomy to Slovakia and Ruthenia in a desperate attempt to hold the state together. An executive Regional Council was established at Khust (Huszt), headed by the Revd Avgustyn Voloshyn (1874–1945), a Greek Catholic clergyman and former professor of mathematics, who had chaired the committee that had recommended Ruthenia's entry into Czechoslovakia twenty years before. A regional assembly was planned. A nationalistic paramilitary formation, the Sich Guard, received official recognition.

These arrangements, however, only created deeper tensions. The Slovaks, in particular, felt dangerously exposed to further Hungarian encroachments, and prepared to seek independent status under German protection. The Rusyns formed the helpless last link at the end of the chain. Slovak independence would cut them off from Prague completely. They had little enthusiasm to attach themselves to Poland; Polish–Ukrainian relations were not the best. And, though some sympathy existed for the theoretical concept of a Greater Ukraine, they had no wish in practice to join Stalin's blood-soaked Soviet Union. To stand any chance of survival, Carpatho-Ruthenia's only sensible course of action would be to declare independence itself.

The match was struck at 5.00 a.m. on 15 March 1939, when the German army marched into the rump of Czechoslovakia, occupied Prague and proclaimed Bohemia and Moravia to be a 'Protectorate' of the Reich. Hitler cited prevailing civil unrest (created by the Nazis) as a threat to German security. Father Tiso, the Slovak leader, was already declaring Slovakia's secession, forewarned thanks to a recent meeting with the Führer. The Rusyn leaders, whom no one had consulted and who were totally isolated, decided they had no alternative but to follow the Slovaks' lead.

The Republic of Carpatho-Ukraine, therefore, was proclaimed that same day. Its government was to be led by the Revd Voloshyn as president, and by Julian Revay as prime minister. Its constitution stated that a democratically elected Diet was to enjoy supreme control; that the state language was to be Ukrainian; that the flag was to consist of two blue and yellow horizontal bands; and that the new measures were to be implemented immediately. The words of the national anthem, '*Shche ne vmerla Ukraina*', 'Ukraine has not perished yet', borrowed from Poland's, were aptly defiant. Since Uzhgorod was already occupied by Hungary, Khust was to be the state capital.

Ethnic violence instantly spilled over into Carpatho-Ukraine from Slovakia. The Sich Guard became embroiled both with stranded Czechoslovak army garrisons and with Slovak and Hungarian irregulars on the frontiers. Three-sided skirmishes were in progress when unexpected news arrived in the afternoon. The Hungarian army, having condemned the civil unrest, had crossed the border from the south.

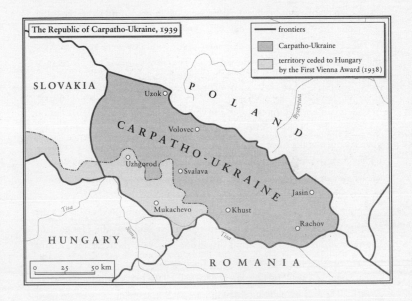

Thanks to the close proximity of Hungary and Romania, Khust had been attracting an unusual crowd of foreigners. A substantial German delegation had arrived, and had persuaded German peasants from some of the nearby villages to come into town and wave their swastika flags. There was an elderly American missionary, Mrs McCormick and her husband, and a Polish photographer. There were at least two Britons. One of the Britons, Commander Wedgwood-Benn MP, spoke none of the local languages and left, but not before he was overheard (as reported by the other Englishman) telling someone in Latin, '*Adolfus Hitler bonus vir!*'*

Michael Winch, a travel-writer, claimed to be there conducting research. He was expecting the Sich Guards to come to blows with the police and army. He was able to present an eyewitness account of events from his hotel window, which is worth quoting at length:

In twenty-four hours we lived in three different states. We woke up in the Czechoslovak Republic. By the evening Carpatho-Ukraine was a free land. Next day the Hungarians came in . . .

At quarter-past six [in the] morning, Tuesday, [15 March] I was woken up by banging in the courtyard. At first, I had thought they were beating carpets . . . Jumping up, I looked out of the window . . . and dived straight under my bed. In the archway to the back street a boy was standing with a smoking revolver in his hand. Rifles were banging off, and from the other side came the rat-tat-tat of a machine-gun.

Then I realized that the Czech gendarmes and military were at last making the long-planned attack on the Sitch . . . Two tanks arrived and it seemed likely that gendarmes would soon come bursting up the stairs . . .

Suddenly there was an appalling noise of splintering glass, and a shower of bullets came whizzing through the windows . . . We were all lying flat on our stomachs on the cold cement floor, but the porter crept along and gingerly opened the door. All eyes were transfixed as the opening gradually widened. Across the threshold two legs were lying immobile. I thought their owner was dead. Then . . . a man came crawling out of the room, followed by two others. They were Slovak lorry drivers . . .

About half an hour later a messenger arrived from [Father-President] Voloshyn and ordered the Sitch to surrender. He said that the Hungarians had taken advantage of internal dissension to renew their claims . . . and all were to combine together to keep them out . . .

The square . . . was still absolutely deserted. All the heavy iron shutters were down . . . The only living things in sight were a horse, standing in an unattended cab . . . and a soldier looking very comic as he crouched behind the petrol pump and covered a nearby window with his rifle . . . In the hotel everyone's nerves were getting strained. The little waiter took refuge in drink. 'The Czechs are pig-dogs, the Poles are pig-dogs,' I heard him shouting . . . The restaurant was a shambles; no furniture, the mirrors shattered, the curtains torn down, the walls pitted by bullets, dirt and paper everywhere . . .

* Most unlikely; Commander William Wedgwood-Benn, Viscount Stansgate (1877–1960), was a long-serving Liberal and then Labour MP, who served in the RAF in both world wars.

Life at once returned to normal. In a few minutes I saw a peasant from Apeza, with a bundle of carpets over his shoulder, hawking along the street, and a Jew setting off with a chicken under his arm to be killed by the ritual slaughterer. The outside of the hotel [was] all pitted and blackened . . . The Sitch barracks had had every single window blown out . . .

Czech rule was shortlived. At one o'clock it was announced over the wireless that Slovakia had proclaimed its independence. This inevitably meant the end of the Czechoslovak State, and the future of Carpatho-Ukraine was in the balance . . . In the afternoon, a Council of Ministers decided that it would follow Slovakia's example. So the slaughter of forty people in the morning had been to no purpose . . .

At about six-thirty, in falling snow, we all collected outside the Government building to hear the Proclamation of Independence. There were [some] seven hundred persons present . . . Father Voloshyn, the Prime Minister, Gren-Zedonsky, a patriotic writer, and other representative persons spoke from the balcony. A new Ministry was announced . . . No one demonstrated, no one sang, no one even raised a patriotic shout for the new Republic. Even after the speeches there was little enthusiasm. Gendarmes . . . guarded the doors, and Czech soldiers . . . preparing for evacuation, continually ploughed their way through the crowd . . . The people seemed drugged by bewilderment.

No mention had been made in the speeches of German protection. Voloshyn was still full of hope, but so far a telegram which had been sent to Hitler at midnight on Monday-Tuesday, asking that Carpatho-Ukraine should be accepted as a full German Protectorate, had not been answered . . . We went to bed in a free Ukraine.[3]

The next day, 16 March, dawned with the Republic still intact:

On our last morning in Chust, we were woken by the Sitch marching down the street and singing patriotic songs. They had been released from gaol, had been re-armed and were to take over the defence and policing of the country. The Czechs . . . were in full retreat. Boxes were being carried downstairs, furniture, bicycles and people were being piled on to lorries. A small boy was waiting for transport with a huge white pig held by a rope round its hind leg.

The Ukrainians were at last a free people. Every house was flying a yellow and blue flag. Blue and yellow were in every buttonhole, on every horse, on every café table. The Jews, in terror, were even painting bands of blue and yellow round their shop windows. The first meeting of the Diet, so long postponed, was to take place that very afternoon. Apart from the

Government, we seemed to be the only people in town who knew that the Hungarians were advancing. But where were the German aeroplanes? . . .

With the country's future decided both the McCormicks and ourselves felt that there was no reason for stopping longer.

So the Anglo-Americans decided on evacuation:

But what route should we leave by? . . . We piled fifteen pieces of luggage into my ten-pound car, while the McCormicks, C and five more pieces of luggage were squeezed into a taxi, whose driver we had bribed heavily . . .

When we left [Khust] at mid-day all the gendarmes had disappeared. The streets were being policed by the Sitch and by German colonists [wearing] swastikas . . . We felt as if we were leaving helpless children to be slaughtered.

At Sevlus, some fifteen miles west of Chust, we found a very different scene. Not a single flag; and all the shops were shut. I suggested that it might be as well to inquire from the local commander [about] conditions on the frontier. We went into . . . the headquarters of the frontier guard. We . . . eventually found [the commandant] across the road. The remnants of the Czech Army were to evacuate the town in ten minutes, he said, and the Hungarians were only three kilometres away.

'I suppose we can go through all right?' asked Mrs McCormick.

'You can of course do whatever you like,' he said, 'but listen!'

From down the road came the steady rat-tat-tat of a machine-gun.

'We shall have to go back,' I said.

'Oh no, it will be quite all right,' said Mrs McCormick, 'we're Americans, no one will shoot at us.' . . .

We hurried back, ran our cars into the [Polish] Consulate's garden and were given coffee and liqueurs . . . while the battle went on outside. There was a good deal of noise, but . . . no one seemed to get killed. From the verandah we heard the command 'Forward, boys!' and saw the first Hungarians, the 'irregulars', with rifles slung over their shoulders on pieces of string, come clambering over the fence . . .

Then came the Hungarian Army. Most of them were old warriors, some with falling moustaches, and they drove in aged cars most of which had been [requisitioned] . . . The local population, the majority of which is Hungarian, gave them a hastily improvised welcome. As many Hungarian flags [had been] hidden away . . . as there had been Ukrainian flags in Chust . . .

As soon as the troops had passed, a lawyer in the house opposite darted out and put a Hungarian name-plate on his door. It was the fifth time he had changed it in the last twenty years, he said.

After the [Hungarian] Colonel had come and drunk sherry with the [polish] Consul we proceeded on our way. We were in Ukrainian registered cars – but no one stopped, or even questioned us.[4]

Hungarian forces pushed steadily forward, dispersing all opposition and arresting both Czechoslovak and Carpatho-Ukrainian officials. During the afternoon, Budapest radio announced that *Kárpátalya* had been reunited with the motherland after twenty-one years' separation. Hitler had secretly authorized the action. By the evening, it was all over. The Hungarians captured Khust. Most of the Rusyn leaders escaped into Romania. The Sich fought on in the mountains. Hundreds were killed outright, while more than 1,000 reached Bratislava, only later to find their way into German camps.[5] On 17 March Hungarian soldiers occupied the Polish frontier and completed their short campaign. They were met by Polish units, who helped them deal with captured Sich Guards. Prisoners suspected of coming from the Polish side were taken into Poland. The others were taken by their captors to the banks of the Tisa river, and (reportedly) massacred. The Hungarians then crossed into Slovakia to secure the frontier zone there.

These events, though they involved military action, a substantial death toll, the invasion of a member state of the League of Nations, and the suppression of a democratic government, might well qualify as a prelude to the Second World War. Alas, they very rarely find mention.

Carpatho-Ruthenia survived much of the war under Hungarian rule in relative quiet. But in 1944 the long-delayed arrival of the Nazis paved the way for the Holocaust's last major operation and the extermination of the entire Jewish population. The arrival of the Red Army in turn spelled disaster for the Hungarians, many of whom were deported to the Gulag. A Czechoslovak delegation which hoped that the Soviets would relinquish control made a brief appearance, but swiftly departed. The Revd. Voloshyn, who had passed the war teaching quietly in Prague, was taken to Moscow and shot.[6]

Fifty years of Soviet silence followed. In 1991 Zakarpattia resurfaced as a district of independent Ukraine, in 2002 the Revd Voloshyn was officially declared a Hero of Ukraine. In October 2008 an Orthodox priest from Uzhgorod, Abbot Dmitri Sidor, assembled a group of Russophiles, all conveniently armed with Russian passports (exactly as their counterparts in South Ossetia), and publicly announced the restoration of the Republic of Carpatho-Ruthenia.[7] Once again, the world paid no attention whatsoever.

III

In the eyes of most Westerners, nothing could be more 'Ruritanian' than the story of Carpatho-Ukraine's one-day republic. All the necessary ingredients are present: a diminutive East European country; a squabbling mix of obscure ethnic groups; a mass of near-unpronounceable names in unfamiliar languages; a brew of 'fanatical nationalisms'; and a tragi-comic outcome for which the Ruritanians alone need be blamed.

These attitudes about Eastern Europe have surfaced many times in the thinking of Western intellectuals. They are part of a widespread, but often unspoken assumption about Western superiority. They are implicit in several of the influential theories of economic history, such as those of Immanuel Wallerstein[8] or Robert Brenner, and explicit in works of political science by Hans Kohn,[9] Ernest Gellner[10] and John Plamenatz.[11] In one of his choicer passages, Plamenatz contrasts the healthy 'civic nationalism' of Western countries with the supposedly unhealthy nationalism of their Eastern counterparts. Western nationalism, Plamenatz maintains, was 'culturally well equipped'. 'They had languages adapted ... to progressive civilisation. They had universities and schools ... importing the skills prized by that civilisation. They had ... philosophers, scientists, artists and poets ... of world reputation. They had medical, legal and other professions ... with high standards.'[12] In other words, their inherently liberal attitudes were supposedly born from superior education and culture.

From this one might deduce that Eastern Europe had no modern languages, no schools or universities (like Prague or Kraków), no scientists (like Copernicus) or poets (like Pushkin), and, despite the lawyer of Sevlus who dashed out to change his name-plate, no professionals. 'What I call eastern nationalism has flourished among the Slavs as well as in Asia and Africa ... and Latin America,' Plamenatz explains. 'I could not call it non-European, and have thought it best to call it eastern because it first appeared to the east of Western Europe.'[13] In other words, the inherently illiberal attitudes of Eastern Europe were supposedly derived from inferior culture. It may not be completely irrelevant that Plamenatz, though an Oxford don, was born in Cetinje in Montenegro, the son of King Nikola's prime minister-in-exile (see Chapter 12). A similar air of deprecation pervades the ethnic slurs and jokes purveyed by the science-fiction writer Isaac Asimov, who would habitually translate them into a Ruritanian context, not mentioning any real countries by name. A well-known conflict-resolution game, 'Equatorial Cyberspace', uses a highly nationalist country called Ruritania as the base model for its conflicts.

The critical dimension in these false scenarios can be found in an ingrained leniency towards the conduct of the Great Powers and of Western countries in general. Any group of Ruritanians can be made to look ridiculous if one omits to make the necessary comparisons. In the case of the break-up of Czechoslovakia, for instance, it is not irrelevant to ask how the crisis started. Is the wild nationalism of the East Europeans to be condemned, and the measured civic nationalism of Adolf Hitler (who stirred up the conflict to begin with, and incited others to follow his example) to be praised? In the wider context of Ukrainian politics, are the minor iniquities of minor parties to be highlighted while the colossal mass murders in Soviet Ukraine are passed over in silence?

Questions of the same sort can be asked about international diplomacy. It is easy enough to point out blameworthy faults among assorted Czechs, Poles, Hungarians, Slovaks and Ruthenians. Yet all these most interested parties were excluded from the Munich Conference, as were the Soviets. The prime responsibility, therefore, lay with those who arrogated the decisions to themselves – notably with Adolf Hitler, the host, and with Neville Chamberlain, the British prime minister and principal guest. Here is the context within which some telling comparisons can be made. Can one seriously suggest that the brands of nationalism favoured by Hitler or Mussolini should be characterized as civic or liberal? Will anyone dare to say that Julian Revay and the Revd Voloshyn were selfish, parochial and short-sighted politicians, unlike the generous, broad-minded and far-seeing statesman from Downing Street? All judgements about the luckless Republic of Carpatho-Ukraine should start from the fact that the Rusyn leadership was desperately trying to cope with the fall-out of policies which were none of their making.

Fortunately, the 'Ruritanian syndrome' is now a well-recognized phenomenon in intellectual discourse and is the subject of numerous studi~ and analyses. Terms such as the 'imperialism of the imaginati~ 'narrative colonization' are coined by scholars exploring Eu~ tal maps and 'orientalist discourses of otherness'. 'Bal~ stereotype with little more validity than Erewhon, ~ Land'; and it is harmless so long as it is kept ~ operetta. Nonetheless, 'it is [still] possible for . . . European multicultural ideals', writes one indign~

about Albanians, Croats, Serbs, Bulgarians and Romanians with the sort of generalised, open condescension which would appall if applied to Somalis or the people of Zaire'.[14] *Nota bene*: the Carpatho-Rusyns don't even make it onto the list of the slighted.

14

Éire

The Unconscionable Tempo of the Crown's Retreat

since 1916

I

By all accounts, Prince Albert's visit to Dublin was a huge success. As befitted a state occasion, he was greeted by a 21-gun salute. He planted an Irish oak, sported a green tie embroidered with shamrocks and drew a large crowd as he strolled along Kildare Street on his way to tea at the Shelbourne Hotel. After visiting a local school, he took leave of the children with the Gaelic words: *go raibh mile maith agat*, meaning 'Thank you a thousand times'. 'Prince Albert', gushed the *Irish Times* (founded 1859), 'brought a touch of class and ceremony to Dublin.' Some readers might have blinked and reread the headline. For this was April 2011; it was the Irish Republic; and the visitor was the son of the film star Grace Kelly, Prince Albert II of Monaco.[1] Observers of Ireland beware: it is full of unexpected echoes of the past.

Until very recently, Ireland was widely esteemed as a fortress of democratic republicanism, and a model of self-made prosperity; it is the republican David, who slung his shot at the British imperial Goliath, and escaped. Ireland is now a sovereign member both of the United Nations and of the European Union. The republican image is strong. Its head of state, the *uachtarán* or 'president' of the Republic, is elected directly for a term of seven years, renewable once; the present incumbent is Mary McAleese, a former professor of law born in the Ardoyne district of Belfast.[2] The bi-cameral parliament, the *Oireachtas*, consists of a Senate of 60 members, and the lower house or *Dáil*, whose 166 members are elected under a system of proportional representation and single transferable votes. The *taoiseach* or 'prime minister' is appointed by the president after nomination by the parliament. The Republic's capital is Baile Atha Cliath (Dublin), its official languages Irish Gaelic and English. Its coat of arms displays a golden harp on a deep blue field, its flag is a green-white-and-orange tricolour. And its national anthem is the '*Amhrán na bhFiann*' or 'Soldier's Song', invariably sung in Gaelic:

> *Sinne Fianna Fáil*
> *Ata fá gheall ag Eirinn,*
> *Buidhean dar sluagh tar ruinn do rainig*
> *Chughainn . . .*[3]

The official use of Gaelic, which is no longer the language of everyday speech, is an essential part of the state ethos; the Irish don't understand much of it, but the English can't get a word.

Visitors to Dublin see evidence of Ireland's democratic and republican traditions on every hand. The castle, founded by King John and once the seat of English colonial power, is nowadays used for presidential receptions and inaugurations. Leinster House, once the palace of the Fitzgerald dukes of Leinster, is the home of the Dáil. The Bank of Ireland building, which faces Trinity College, once housed the parliament of the pre-1800 kingdom. The city's main street is named after Daniel O'Connell (1775–1847), 'the Liberator', who fought for Catholic Emancipation. It shelters the old General Post Office, where the Irish Republic was first proclaimed in 1916, and, at its northern end, a Garden of Remembrance dedicated to 'all who gave their lives in the cause of Irish Freedom'. The Mansion House, the home of the lord mayor, where the Republic was proclaimed for the second time in 1919, is situated close to St Stephen's Green across the river on Dawson Street. The Green saw fierce fighting during the Easter Rising, and entered people's hearts because both sides stopped firing to let the ducks in the pond be fed.[4] It now shelters a monument to Ireland's most revered female revolutionary, Countess Constance Markiewicz (1868–1927), who fought there as a soldier. The bronze bust sits atop a stone pedestal inscribed: 'CONSTANCE MARKIEVICZ, MAJOR IRISH CITIZEN ARMY, 1916'.

The Republic's territory, some 27,450 square miles, is divided into twenty-six counties (since 1999, the Republic does not lay formal claim to the six counties of British-ruled Northern Ireland). Its area is smaller than both England and Scotland, but almost four times larger than Wales. The island forms a rough rectangle, the western coast constituting Europe's most westerly rampart against the Atlantic Ocean.

The Republic's population, which stands at 4.442 million (2008) is considerably lower than the highest historical levels. In 1800 Ireland was home to some 8 million inhabitants, not far behind England's then total of *c*. 10 million, a ratio of 1:1.25. Largely as the result of famine,

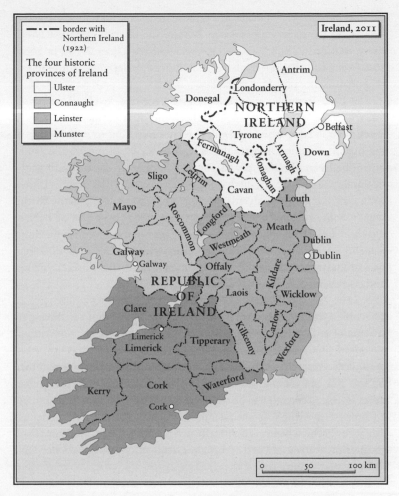

emigration and the absence of Irish modernization and industrialization, the ratio had fallen by 1900 to 1 : 12.

Ireland's political system survived great turbuluence before it gained
stability. Two main political parties trace their roots to the 1920s.
Fianna Fáil or 'Soldiers of Destiny', once the party of Éamon de Valera,
the 'Father of the Republic', has often dominated, forming the government for sixty of the state's eighty years and most recently from 1997 to
February 2011.[5] The rival *Fine Gael* or 'Clan of the Gaels', otherwise
the United Ireland Party, which also boasts republican roots, has usually
headed the opposition. Its father-figure is De Valera's rival, Michael

Collins.[6] Three other parties are represented. The Labour Party has a similar profile to its namesake in Britain; the environmentalist Green Party, founded in 1981, entered government with Fianna Fáil in 2007; and *Sinn Féin*, the oldest of Irish republican groupings, is looking to rebuild after decades of marginality.

The Irish Republic experienced unprecedented levels of economic growth in the late twentieth and early twenty-first centuries. Thanks to investment in education and modern technology, and to membership of the European Union, remarkable advances took place from the 1960s onwards; Ireland's GDP per capita rose decade by decade until at the beginning of the twenty-first century it overtook that of the United Kingdom. For a time, Irish citizens enjoyed the top ranking in the Worldwide Quality of Life Index.[7] Not until the global recession of 2008–9 did the 'Celtic Tiger' (so named in 1994) stumble, and with it the political elite's reputation. Out of Prince Albert's hearing, the talk in Dublin was of ineffectual leadership, and of 'a culture of clientilism, cronyism and corruption'.

The official Irish version of Irish history is built round a three-part scheme of periodization. Two or three millennia of the 'Era of Ancient Celtic Freedom', stretching from prehistory to the twelfth century AD, are followed by the 'Era of Foreign Domination' (1171–1916) and then by the 'Era of National Liberation', which is still in progress. (Liberation is judged incomplete because the Republic's territory does not yet encompass the whole of the island of Ireland.) Present-day academics might reject the scheme as politically driven and 'archaic' in comparison to their own advanced researches; but academic histories do not have the last word in any country.

Ireland's Era of Ancient Celtic Freedom is by any standards one of the marvels of European history. The Gaelic-speaking nation, secure in its seagirt fortress, was ruled by bards and tribal chieftains, among whom a long succession of *ard rí* or 'high kings' exercised supreme authority. The Irish king lists, compiled by medieval monks, contain some 200 names, the earliest of which, like Slaine (1934–1933 BC) or Bres (1897–1890 BC), are clearly mythical; the precise-looking dates are the product of pure guesswork. The latest names such as Muirchertach Mac-Lochlain (d. AD 1166) or Ruaidre Ua Chobar (d. 1186) were unable to exert anything more than nominal authority.[8] The high point is often taken to have been reached by Brian Bóraimhe, Brian Boru (r. 1002–14), who is described in the medieval *Book of Armagh* as *Imperator Scottorum* or 'emperor of the Irish'.[9] He battled the Vikings, briefly established hegemony over all the island, and died at the Battle of Clontarf, the 'Bull's Meadow', near Dublin. Mael Sechneill mac Domnaill, king of Meath (r. 980–1002, 1014–22), known as Malachi Mor, was deposed by Brian Boru, but regained the high kingship after Clontarf.[10]

The Era of Foreign Domination, which lasted more than 700 years, is conventionally divided into three sub-periods. The first, under the heading of the 'Lordship of Ireland (1171–1541)', saw the kings of England ruling as overlords but not annexing the country. The second, under the heading of the 'Kingdom of Ireland (1541–1801)', was launched by Henry VIII's Crown of Ireland Act and terminated by the the Napoleonic Wars; it saw the English monarchs (and from 1707 British monarchs) reigning in parallel over realms joined by personal union. The third sub-period, under the heading of 'British Ireland (from 1801)' saw 'John Bull's Other Island' integrated into the expanded United Kingdom of Great Britain and Ireland. Presuming that British rule in Ireland can be recognized as legitimate – which purists do not accept – republican teaching holds that it ended in the years 1916–18; in the eyes of unreconciled unionists, it has never ended.

Official accounts sometimes circumnavigate a number of episodes which the majority of Irish people would prefer not to have happened. One of these, the Plantation of Ulster, saw a Protestant colony, mainly of Scottish Presbyterians, established in northern Ireland in the early seventeenth century (exactly the same era in which the Pilgrim Fathers established similar colonies in North America).[11] Other regrettable episodes deriving from religious conflicts include the reconquest of Ireland by Oliver Cromwell in 1649–52[12] and the victory of Protestant forces under William of Orange at the Battle of the Boyne in 1689.[13] Nonetheless, the Irish show few signs of forgetting the suffering of their forebears; memories remain alive of Cromwellian atrocities such as the Siege of Drogheda or of the discriminatory, anti-Catholic Penal Laws enforced after 1691.[14]

The last decades of the Kingdom of Ireland, however, are usually viewed with favour. In the era of the American War of Independence, an Irish Patriot Party came to the fore, demanding the repeal of the Penal Laws, seeking to share English traditions of liberty, and aiming to establish a degree of constitutional autonomy. Their leader was Henry Grattan (1746–1820), a member of the Anglo-Irish Protestant elite, who worked for the emancipation of the Catholic majority. 'Patriots of Ireland,' declared George Washington in 1788, 'your cause is identical with mine.' In 1782 Grattan persuaded the British government to grant self-government to the Irish parliament in Dublin – henceforth 'Grattan's Parliament' – and to sever many mechanisms of British control save for the Crown and the Crown's representative, the viceroy. His policy, which imitators called 'Home Rule', was summed up by the slogan: 'The [Irish] Channel Forbids Union, the Ocean Forbids Separation'. It came to grief thanks to fears in London generated by the French Revolution and by the rebellion of the United Irishmen in 1798. But it was long remembered as an experiment ahead of its time.

The nineteenth century, therefore, is often regarded by the Irish as a time when foreign oppression returned with a vengeance. The first phase of life in the United Kingdom was dominated by O'Connell's campaign for freedom of religion and the rights of the Roman Catholic Church; the second phase by a great national awakening of the sort which occurred in many European countries. The roots of the movement lay in the realization in the decades after the Great Famine of 1846–9 that the lifeblood of traditional Irish culture had been haemorrhaging for generations and that only a concerted effort could prevent the country being turned into a 'West Britain' as advocated by British officialdom. The result was an explosion of interest in national history, Gaelic language, Celtic myths, Irish literature and folk music. Its heroes were not rebels or soldiers, but poets like Brian Merriman (1749–1805), scholars like James Hardiman (1782–1855) or Samuel Ferguson (1810–55), and writers like William Carleton (1794–1869). Their work came to fruition in the Gaelic Revival at the century's end.

No activity was more typical of this movement than the collection, distribution and writing of popular songs. And no member of it was more influential than the great poet song-writer Thomas Moore (1779–1852), friend of Byron and Shelley, and author of 'The Minstrel Boy', 'The Meeting of the Waters', 'The Last Rose of Summer' and many others. Fired by Moore's example, a veritable torrent of lyrics and melodies poured forth. Almost all of the songs which were to feature in Ireland's twentieth-century history had been composed before the First World War. They included 'A Nation Once Again' (1854), 'The Wearing of the Green' (1864), 'God Save Ireland' (1867), 'The Soldier's Song' (1907), 'Danny Boy' (1913) and Thomas Moore's 'Let Erin Remember':

> Let Erin remember the days of old
> 'Ere her faithless sons betrayed her,
> When Malachi wore the collar of gold

Which he won from the proud invader:
When her kings, with standard of green unfurl'd,
Led the Red-branch knights into danger,
'Ere the emerald gem of the western world
Was set in the crown of the stranger.[15]

Tone-deaf historians may dismiss these songs and their lyrics as 'doggerel'; if so, they may be ignoring a valid point of entry to the mood and spirit of some important historical moments. Irish intellectuals have also tended to be dismissive; they could be envious of Tom Moore's enduring popularity. As all would have agreed, however, 'the stranger' was the king of England.

Monarchy has featured in the Irish story, therefore, in a variety of periods and in a number of guises. The native high kings of ancient Ireland were a historical reality of which the modern Irish are inordinately proud. The medieval lords of Ireland were for practical purposes English kings by another name; the Kingdom of Ireland, which Henry VIII bequeathed to his heirs and successors in perpetuity, was an evolving polity, parts of whose heritage persist to the present. The British monarchs of the nineteenth century reigned over a sorrowing Ireland plagued by the death and departure of millions. Queen Victoria visited Dublin four times between 1864 and 1900, Edward VII and George V just once each, in 1904 and 1911 respectively. On these occasions, the desire of the inhabitants to please their guests without compromising their principles could prove hilarious. When Edward VII visited the Catholic seminary at Maynooth, he found the buildings bedecked not with red, white and blue but with the royal horse-racing colours; when he drove into the south-western village of Tully in his fleet of open-topped Panhards and Cadillacs, he was greeted by a group of pony riders holding up a banner: 'FRIEND OF OUR POPE'.[16]

As the nineteenth century drew on, the main thrust of Irish politics was directed to the struggle for Home Rule, that is for autonomous self-government under the British Crown. Its minimum goal was to restore institutions similar to those of the pre-Union kingdom. The period is for ever associated with the name of Charles Stewart Parnell (1846–91), who commanded the political scene for only a short period but with immense panache. The son of an Anglo-Irish-American Protestant family, he turned the Irish Parliamentary Party into a major political force, and concentrated all his efforts on gaining influence with the British establishment. He took advantage of the uproar in the Irish countryside during the Land War, when tenants battled landowners (like the notorious Captain Boycott), and he won over many voters who might otherwise have espoused radicalism. While campaigning for the restoration of the pre-Union Irish parliament, he kept his ultimate objectives deliberately obscure. 'No man has the right', he once declared, 'to say to his country: "Thus Far, and No Further".' He made a huge impression on Britain's Liberal prime minister, William Gladstone, not least when Parnell's party held the balance of power at Westminster after the election of 1885. Gladstone duly performed a volte-face and adopted the principle of Home Rule. But Parnell's sudden and early death, aged forty-five, robbed Ireland of its 'uncrowned king'; the Home Rule Bill lost its most powerful motor; and a series of Conservative governments after Gladstone played the Irish Question out of court.[17]

Parnell's democratic strategy overshadowed all other Irish political trends. A revolutionary, republican movement certainly existed; the Irish Republican Brotherhood (IRB), known as the Fenians, had been founded in 1858 by people with strong Irish-American connections. They had organized an abortive rising in 1867 and a number of sporadic acts of violence continued to be perpetrated. But by the century's end, their tiny, clandestine membership was judged marginal to the mainstream.[18]

During Parnell's lifetime, Irish society was revitalized by the Roman Catholic Church, which achieved a position of unprecedented authority. No longer the patron of a dispossessed and starving nation served by a downtrodden clergy, it came into its own as a major force in education, social care and nation-building. Its four archdioceses and its thousand parishes became the focus of activities and enterprises. They were supported by a wide variety of religious orders and lay organizations such as the Ancient Order of Hibernians (originally founded in the sixteenth century) or the Knights of Columbanus (1915). The Irish Church was deeply conservative in temper; it preserved and promoted many traditional customs such as the worship of relics, the veneration of saints and adoration of the Virgin Mary; its idea of progress was to adopt Vatican-sponsored cults like that of the Immaculate Conception or the Sacred Heart of Jesus. When in 1879 the Mother of God was judged to have appeared in person at Knock in County Galway, the Church's special mission to the Irish people was confirmed.[19]

Predictably, Ireland's ancient Christian tradition was enriched by her equally strong musical inclinations; the encounter has borne much fruit, not least in hymnology. Yet the best known of Irish hymns was slow to take its final form. The Gaelic words of '*Rop tú mo Baile*' are attributed to a sixth-century monk, Dállan Forgaill; the folk melody '*Slane*' is named after a battle of the same era. The two were not put together until Mary Byrne translated the Gaelic into English in 1905, Eleanor Hull versified it in 1912, and the verse joined the tune in a hymnary of 1927. The English version has become a worldwide favourite among hymn-singers, and has been translated back into modern Gaelic many times:

Be Thou my vision, O lord of my heart,	*Bí Thusa 'mo shúile a Rí mhór na ndúil*
Naught be all else to me, save that Thou art;	*Líon thusa mo bheatha mo chéadfaí 's mo stuaim*
Thou my best thought by day or by night,	*Bí thusa i m'aigne gach oíche 's gach lá*
Waking or sleeping, Thy presence my light.	*Im chodladh no im dhúiseacht, líon mé le do ghrá.*
Be Thou my wisdom, Thou my true word,	*Bí Thusa 'mo threorú i mbriathar 's imbeart*
I ever with Thee and Thou with me, Lord	*Fan thusa go deo liom is coinnigh mé ceart*
Thou my great Father, I Thy true son,	*Glac cúram mar Athair, is éist le mo ghuí*
Thou in me dwelling, and I with Thee, one.	*Is tabhair domsa áit cónaí istigh i do chroí.*

In all, four Home Rule bills were introduced into the Westminster Parliament – in 1886, 1892, 1912 and 1920. The third one was critical because the Irish Party held the balance at Westminster. Facing ferocious opposition from the Ulster Unionists, it started its passage through Parliament in April 1912 under the sponsorship of Herbert Asquith's Liberal government, cleared the House of Lords after three rejections, received royal assent, and entered into British law as the Government of Ireland Act on 18 September 1914. The widespread impression was that a suitable compromise had been found, that Parnell's dream had been realized. The suspension of the Act due to the outbreak of the Great War did not cause the expected uproar; and wartime preoccupations defused the looming confrontation between the armed Ulster Volunteers in Belfast and their counterparts in Dublin, the Irish Volunteers. Hundreds of thousands of Irishmen served in the British forces in 1914–18, some 50,000 of them sacrificing their lives.

Given what was to happen within a matter of months, therefore, it is pertinent to ask about Irish attitudes to the Crown. Curiously, information on this subject is not readily forthcoming. The essay on 'Ireland in the Twentieth Century' on the Irish government's official website[20] makes no single mention of monarchy whatsoever. More surprisingly, the distinguished Irish historian most closely associated with this period has little to say either. Roy Foster's chapter entitled 'The New Nationalism', covering the years between Parnell's death and the First World War in his now standard account, contains no single sentence about republicanism; and it makes only two passing references to the IRB in the context of its rivalry with the Gaelic League.[21] The important issues according to him were cultural nationalism, the Gaelic language, the Land Question, the socialist movement, opposition to the Boer War, Anglophobia and anti-Protestant sentiment, but not, apparently, the monarchy. This must surely be an omission. For kings and queens, royal titles and the 'Crown' figured in political debates at the time, and have never ceased to do so.

Politics, however, cannot explain everything. The years of the struggle over Home Rule were equally the years when both Britain and America were swept by a popular craze for Irish songs. The star turn was the tenor John McCormack (1884–1945), an opera singer who took to the concert platform. His signature song was 'The Wearing of the Green', whose words referred to the United Irishmen of 1798:

> Oh Paddy dear, and did ye hear the news that's going round
> The shamrock is by law forbid to grow on Irish land.
> No more Saint Patrick's Day we'll keep: his colour can't be seen
> For there's a cruel law agin' the Wearing of the Green.[22]

And no number rivalled the success of a song that exuded pure contentment:

> When Irish eyes are smiling sure 'tis like a morn in spring;
> With a lilt of Irish laughter you can hear the angels sing.
> When Irish hearts are happy all the world is bright and gay,
> And when Irish eyes are smiling sure they'd steal your heart away.[23]

Nor were the smiles confined to the native Irish. Parts of Ireland in that era were the preserve of the British elite, the playground of the highest servants of the Crown; some of them would look back on those halcyon pre-war days as the happiest in their lives. One of the most evocative of memoirs was written by a future British prime minister:

My father had gone to Ireland as secretary to his father [who had been] appointed Lord-Lieutenant by Mr Disraeli ... We lived in a house called 'The Little Lodge', about a stone's throw from the Viceregal [residence]. Here I spent nearly three years of childhood ... I remember my grandfather, the Viceroy, unveiling the Lord Gough statue in 1878. A great black crowd, scarlet soldiers on horseback ... the old Duke, the formidable grandpapa, talking loudly to the crowd. I recall even a phrase he used: 'and with a withering volley he shattered the enemy line.' I quite understood ... that a 'volley' meant what the black-coated soldiers used to do with loud bangs so often in the Phoenix Park where I was taken for my morning walks ...

In one of these years we paid a visit to Emo Park, the seat of Lord Port-arlington, who was explained to me as a sort of uncle ... The central point in my memory is a tall white stone tower ... [which] had been blown up by Oliver Cromwell. I understood definitely that he had blown up all sorts of things and was therefore a very great man.

My nurse, Mrs Everest, was nervous about the Fenians. I gathered these were wicked people ... On one occasion when I was out riding on my donkey, we thought we saw a long dark procession of Fenians approaching. I am sure now it [was] the Rifle Brigade ... But we were all very much alarmed, particularly the donkey, who expressed his anxiety by kicking. I was thrown off and had concussion of the brain. This was my first introduction to Irish politics!

It was at 'The Little Lodge' I was first menaced with Education. The approach of a sinister figure described as 'the Governess' was announced ... Mrs Everest produced a book called *Reading without Tears*. It certainly did not justify its title in my case ... [When] the Governess was due to arrive, I did what so many oppressed peoples have done in similar circumstances: I took to the woods. I hid in the extensive shrubberies ... which surrounded 'The Little Lodge' ...

My mother took no part in these impositions ... My picture of her in Ireland is in a riding habit, fitting like a skin and often beautifully spotted with mud. She and my father hunted continually on their large horses ... [She] always seemed to me a fairy princess: a radiant being possessed of limitless riches and power ... She shone for me like the Evening Star.[24]

Anyone who spends a few carefree hours in Phoenix Park today will still find many of the attractions that so delighted the young Winston Churchill over a hundred years ago. The ancient herd of fallow deer still grazes on the park's verdant grassland; the wide open spaces where Lord and Lady Randolph spurred their chargers still welcome riders. The Furry Glen, the People's Garden and the Dublin Zoo are in place, as are the ruins of the Magazine Fort (1611) and the Testimonial Monument (1864) to the celebrated Dubliner, the duke of Wellington, who was (probably) born at 24 Upper Merrion Street.

Other landmarks have either changed or disappeared. The Viceregal Lodge is now the *Áras an Uachtárain*, the official residence of the Irish president. The Little Lodge is called Ratra House, in memory of the Republic's first president, Douglas Hyde, who died there; and its shrubberies still bloom. They even tell visitors about the ghost of a little boy who wanders the park in search of his grandfather.[25] The Deerfield Residence, once the home of Ireland's chief secretary, now houses the US ambassador, and medieval Ashdown Castle, newly renovated, the visitors' centre. There one can buy refreshments, souvenirs and guidebooks. One learns, for example, that the park's name has nothing to do with phoenixes, but is a corruption of the Gaelic name, *fionn uisce*, meaning 'clear water'. One can also read about the Phoenix Park murders of 6 May 1882, when two leading British officials were knifed to death by a Fenian group calling themselves the 'Irish National Invincibles'. One of the victims, Lord Frederick Cavendish, was the chief secretary; the other, Thomas Henry Burke (1829–82), was the permanent secretary, the top civil servant of the day. Burke was a Catholic from Galway, but seen by his assailants as a 'castle rat'. Three years earlier, he met his young neighbour, Winston Churchill, and gave him the present of a toy drum. The death and the drum are both recalled in *My Early Life*. The statues to Lord Carlisle and to Field Marshal Gough – the latter unveiled by 'the formidable grandpapa' – stood in the park until the 1920s, but have since vanished.

The purging of British statues in Dublin went to considerable lengths, but was never completed. In addition to Carlisle and Gough, the nationalists expunged Admiral Nelson from O'Connell Street, King William III from College Green, and Queen Victoria herself from Merrion Square. But interesting exceptions were made. One statue, which once held pride of place in front of Leinster House, was moved to the side of the Dáil, to Leinster Lawn, and is still there in the company of assorted republicans and nationalists. Queen Victoria repeatedly begged for it to be erected, as it was in 1908, seven years after her death, to the memory of Albert – not of Monaco, but of Saxe-Coburg-Gotha. Since that time, Ireland has been a central player in a historical process that may be described without too much hyperbole or sense of anticipation as the break-up of the United Kingdom. The process, whose seeds were barely perceptible in the early twentieth century, was to surface fifteen years after Queen Victoria's death and continued to develop for the rest of the century amid the alternating pulsations of centrifugal and centripetal forces. In the early twenty-first century it reached a significant new stage after the introduction of devolution, but was still some distance, even in Ireland, from its ultimate vanishing point.

II

If Ireland's contemporary history begins anywhere, it is with the Easter Rising of 24 April 1916. In a move calculated to exploit Britain's wartime preoccupations, a few hundred Irish patriot-rebels stormed the General Post Office in Dublin, raised republican flags and pronounced the advent of the Irish Republic:

POBLACHT NA hÉIREANN
THE PROVISIONAL GOVERNMENT
OF THE IRISH REPUBLIC
TO THE PEOPLE OF IRELAND
Irishmen and Irishwomen. In the name of God and of the
dead generations, from which she receives her old tradition
of nationhood, Ireland, through us, summons her children
to the flag and strikes for her freedom.[26]

Fighting with British forces lasted for seven days. The surviving insurgents were rounded up, and their leaders tried for treason; ninety were condemned to death. Fifteen of them, including the seven signatories of the Republic's Proclamation – Clarke, MacDiarmid, MacDonagh, Ceannt, Pearse, Connolly and Plunkett – were executed. The British response was harsh, perhaps because plans for German involvement had been uncovered; the insurgents would not have risked a military operation without hopes of heavyweight foreign assistance. As it was, the executions were creating martyrs. Éamon de Valera, commander of the Irish Volunteers' Third Brigade, was lucky to be reprieved (see below).[27] A republican song from the days immediately after the Rising exudes undiluted bitterness:

Take away the blood-stained bandage from off an Irish brow;
We fought and bled for Ireland and will not shirk it now.
We held on in her struggle, in answer to her call
And because we sought to free her / we are placed against a wall.[28]

In those same years, the strong Irish presence in the British army was underlined by the most famous of all the Great War's marching songs.

A battalion of the Connaught Rangers was heard singing it as they marched out of Calais for the Front. Recorded by John McCormack, it quickly became a runaway hit:

> It's a long way to Tipperary
> It's a long way to go.
> It's a long way to Tipperary
> To the sweetest girl I know.
> Good-bye, Piccadilly,
> Farewell Leicester Square,
> It's a long, long way to Tipperary
> But my heart's right there.[29]

The unhurried beat is perfect for swinging along in unison. The melody is compelling. And the bittersweet words are anything but warlike. Tipperary is now known to untold millions round the world who would not otherwise know where it is.

As Britain concentrated all her resources and attention on the war effort, attitudes in Ireland fermented. The insurgents' political organization, Sinn Féin, meaning 'Ours Alone', and its secret military wing, the IRB, attracted far more sympathizers after the Rising than before it. It claimed that the British were reneging on Home Rule, not merely postponing it, that the British government was beholden to the Unionist lobby, and that Irish patriots would have to fight for their rights. In October 1917, Sinn Féin's convention openly advocated 'international recognition of Ireland as an independent Irish Republic'.[30] De Valera, amnestied, became the party's chairman.

The Unionists, for their part, were dedicated to the integrity of the United Kingdom and regarded Sinn Féin and their like as a bunch of mutineers. Men like Sir Edward Carson – a Protestant barrister from Dublin, who had brought down Oscar Wilde – or Churchill's friend F. E. Smith, later earl of Birkenhead, saw British law as the sole fount of legitimacy. They waved their Union Jacks, and revered the Ulster Volunteers who had been slaughtered on the Western Front. With few exceptions, they were also supporters of the Protestant Ascendancy. Both the Anglo-Irish landowning class and the Presbyterians of Ulster were embattled Protestant minorities in a largely Catholic land.

The songs to which the Unionists marched drew on a rich and ancient repertoire. 'King Billy', that is, William III of Orange (d. 1694), invariably figures as the chief hero, and the pope as the chief villain:

Sons, whose sires with William bled
Offspring of the mighty dead
When the Popish tyrants fled
And this fair land left free.

Yield not now to Popish guile
Trust them least when most they smile
Sun the crafty fowler's toil.
And keep your liberty![31]

The sectarian fervour gripping 'loyalists' and 'Unionists' had barely changed since the seventeenth century.

In 1917–18 the British government organized a multi-party convention which debated the implementation of Home Rule inconclusively. Then, early in 1918, it sought to bring Ireland into line with Great Britain by introducing military conscription. Objectively, the policy appeared even-handed, and in fact was never applied. But in the fragile Irish context it provided the pebble that set off a landslide,[32] refanning passions that might otherwise have died down. Almost everyone united against it – the Church, the unions, the Parnellite Irish Parliamentary Party and the local councils. Prime Minister David Lloyd George thereupon made the fatal mistake of threatening to withhold Home Rule 'until the condition of Ireland makes it possible'.[33]

A new chapter opened as the Great War closed. At the general election of December 1918, Lloyd George was whipping up support for 'squeezing Germany till the pips squeak'. But in Ireland, demands for total independence had risen to the top of the agenda, and pushed out other concerns. Of 105 Irish MPs elected, 73 belonged to Sinn Féin. They promptly turned their backs on Westminster, and on 21 January 1919 those of them who were not in British prisons assembled in the Round Room of Dublin's Mansion House as a separate Dáil or parliament. The Papal Count George Plunkett (1851–1948), father of three condemned sons, and Eoin (John) MacNeill (1867–1945), military commander and medieval historian, kept order. The Assembly voted to sever links with Great Britain, and the Republic of Ireland was proclaimed for a second time, in Gaelic, as if the United Kingdom did not exist. Éamon de Valera was appointed the chief executive, and the Republic's armed force, the Irish Republican Army (IRA), was formed from a variety of amalgamated units, including the IRB. Instructions were drawn up for ambassadors to be sent to the Peace Conference in Paris, and an 'Address to the Free Nations of the World' was framed. The session was finished within an hour and a half.

The British press watched in disbelief. British journalists, like many participants, were not well attuned to the proceedings:

> Twenty-eight Sinn Féin members of parliament were here . . . But there must have been at least two thousand others in an improvised Strangers' Gallery. Many other thousands waited outside, but a strong body of the Sinn Féin Volunteers kept an effective and sometimes a rather stupid guard.
>
> It would have offended against the national spirit, of course, to carry on the debates of the National Assembly in the language of the Sassenach, and the result was a self-denying ordinance which kept some members quite silent and even reduced others to mere French.
>
> It was a very quiet and rather stilted National Assembly. Probably nine-tenths of those there did not know what it was saying, and when the instructed raised a cheer, the Speaker broke into English to tell them that the rules of parliament did not allow it. The Mansion House, which gives it hospitality to all comers, had provided a few seats for the benches, and, roped off from [the rest the room] these made the House.[34]

In 1919–20 a massive campaign of civil disobedience brought the British administration in Ireland to its knees. Taxes went unpaid, government offices were boycotted, dockers refused to handle British army supplies, orders from London went unheeded. But formal recognition proved more elusive. The British government was not willing to recognize a state within the state; and it persuaded foreign countries to follow suit. Representatives of the Irish Republic who travelled to the Peace Conference in Paris were not admitted. Lenin, who accepted a loan from Ireland for Soviet Russia, was the sole foreign leader to acknowledge the Irish Republic's existence.

The first hostile act against British forces occurred on 21 January 1919, when a couple of lone marksmen killed some officers of the Royal Irish Constabulary (RIC) in Tipperary. The British government reacted with restraint, merely designating a Special Military Zone in the southwest. Similarly, the Dáil made no haste to declare war. The majority of IRA leaders favoured guerrilla-style tactics like those of the South African Boers, whom they greatly admired, and a minority led by Arthur Griffith favoured passive resistance. Even so, violence spread. IRA raids provoked RIC reprisals. Hundreds of policemen were shot, and scores of country houses belonging to Anglo-Irish landowners were torched. By the summer, an undeclared armed conflict variously called the 'Anglo-Irish War' or the 'War of Irish Independence' was well and truly ignited.

In 1920, the British government lost patience. Reluctant to deploy the regular British army, which was in the throes of demobilization, it raised two notorious auxiliary formations to bring the rebels to heel. One of them, the RIC Reserve Force, universally known from the colour of their uniforms as the 'Black and Tans', were recruited from hardened war veterans, paid 10 shillings per day, and exempted from normal military discipline. The other, the Auxiliary Division of the RIC, known as the 'Auxies', were drawn exclusively from ex-British army officers. Together, they burned, plundered and murdered their way round Ireland. Regular courts were suspended, and subsidies halted to non-loyalist districts. In the autumn Westminster introduced new legislation. The Restoration of Order in Ireland Act (1920) provided for martial law, internment and death sentences without trial. In December the Government of Ireland Act (1920), passed under Unionist pressure, attempted to limit the contagion by dividing the island into two parts – Southern Ireland, made up of twenty-six counties, and Northern Ireland, containing the remaining six. Each was to have its own assembly. Contrary to intentions, the partition proved permanent.

The initial years of military struggle against the British brought the IRA to the peak of its popularity. Lacking comparable firepower, its leaders avoided open battle with professional British troops, and were duly denounced as terrorists. But by keeping up their attacks and staying in the field, they created an impasse in which the British began to review their policies. The misdeeds of the 'Black and Tans' strengthened the Irish cause with every day that passed:

> They burned their way through Munster,
> Then laid Leinster on the rack.
> Thro' Connacht and thro' Ulster
> Marched the men in brown and black.
> They shot down wives and children
> In their own heroic way, but
> The Black and Tans like lightning ran
> From the Rifles of the IRA![35]

Over the winter of 1920–21, bloodshed intensified. The worst episodes occurred in Belfast, where 'loyalist' mobs attacked Catholic enclaves indiscriminately. The creation of paramilitary 'B-specials' to support the Ulster Constabulary was opposed by the Catholic hierarchy, but few Protestant leaders publicly reprimanded loyalist violence.

Three men co-operated in the construction of a truce. General Smuts, the South African champion of the Boers, suggested to King George V that he make a 'speech for conciliation in Ireland'. The idea was taken up by Lloyd George, who persuaded a reluctant Cabinet to comply. The king's speech, delivered in Belfast on 22 June 1921, called on all Irishmen 'to pause, to stretch out the hand of forbearance and conciliation, to forgive and forget, and to join in making for the land they love a new era of peace, contentment and goodwill'.[36] The words were judged to match the public mood. A truce came into effect on 11 July 1921. The forces of the Crown and their militant opponents appeared to have fought each other to a standstill.

At this point, Éamon de Valera (1882–1975) reached the first pinnacle in a long career characterized by successive peaks and troughs. Born in the United States, the son of an Irish mother and a reputedly Cuban father, he had grown up in Ireland with his maternal relatives, had learned Gaelic and qualified as a teacher. Known as 'the Long Fellow' because of his height, he was a principled republican among comrades holding a variety of constitutional views. He had been saved from execution after the Easter Rising by his American citizenship, and was pushed into prominence by being a rare survivor of the original leadership. In 1917–19 he rose from the position of Sinn Féin's chairman, to that of president of the *Dáil Éireann*, and of *príomh aire* or 'prime minister'.[37]

For the whole of 1920, however, the *príomh aire* had absented himself, disappearing from Dublin to raise funds in the United States. In consequence, he lost ground to his deputies, notably to Michael Collins, 'the Big Fellow', sometime head of the IRB and another survivor of the Rising,[38] and to Arthur Griffith, one of the original founders of Sinn Féin.[39] Griffith, a surprising voice of moderation, had long advocated a 'two kingdom solution', such as had pertained prior to 1801, publicizing the idea of a dual, Anglo-Irish monarchy similar to that of Austria-Hungary.[40] Among these leaders, there was no common blueprint regarding the nature of the future state.[41]

Three days after the truce, Éamon de Valera went to Downing Street to sound out Lloyd George, and a priceless scene ensued. De Valera was used to thinking of Ireland's oppressors as 'the English'. He had not counted on his British adversary being both a Celt and a native Welsh-

speaker. He read out his declaration in stilted Gaelic, then handed Lloyd
George an English translation. The 'Welsh Wizard' played along with
him. 'So what's the Gaelic name for your state?' he enquired. '*Saorstát*'
('Free State') came the reply. 'I see,' said Lloyd George. 'I didn't hear the
Gaelic word for "Republic" in your speech.' He then launched into a
lengthy discussion in Welsh with his personal secretary, T. J. Jones. De
Valera, flustered, couldn't follow. Eventually, reverting to English, Lloyd
George delivered the knock-out blow. 'We Celts don't have a word for
a Republic,' he announced, 'because we've never had one.'[42] If this
account reflects even part of the truth, De Valera already knew that one
of his key demands – the recognition of the Irish Republic – was unlikely
to be met. Nonetheless, on returning to Dublin, he persuaded the Dáil
to proclaim him president of the Republic. He was throwing down the
gauntlet not only to the British but also to many Irish colleagues.

Work began soon after on an Anglo-Irish Treaty. Its main aims were
to design a new political order for Southern Ireland, and to define the
border with Ulster, which was to have the right to secede. The Irish delegation at the negotiations was led by Arthur Griffith, assisted by Michael
Collins and others, who installed themselves at 44 Hans Crescent in
Kensington. Its secretary was the English novelist and Hibernophile,
Erskine Childers. The negotiators wrestled in London, while killings in
Ireland persisted; they only reached a conclusion after the British threatened to restart a full-scale war. Ratification had to be undertaken in
triplicate – by the Dáil, by the British-backed House of Commons of
Southern Ireland and by the British Parliament in Westminster. All was
completed in January 1922. The king had reason to be satisfied. After a
civil war (as he would have seen it) a wayward realm had returned to the
fold, and had made its peace with the home country.

The details, however, were crucial. As determined by the treaty, the
Irish Free State was to take the form of a constitutional monarchy, not
a republic. It was to resemble the existing dominions, such as Canada or
Australia, thereby achieving more than the pre-war Home Rule Act,
which had only promised self-government within the United Kingdom;
but the king was to remain head of state – albeit of a different state – and
was to be represented in Dublin by a governor-general. The legislative
Dáil, elected by universal suffrage, was to name its candidate for prime
minister for the governor-general's approval. The national anthem, as
previously, was to be 'God Save the King'. These arrangements were the
fruit of a reluctant compromise between the British hard line, which

upheld the rights of the Crown, and the initial Irish demands, which had
hoped to preserve their Republic. They were set to take effect on 6
December.[43]

Reactions to the treaty were threefold. First, the Unionists in Northern
Ireland hastened to exercise their opt-out. At the province's first general
election in May 1921, they had won a 66 percent majority. A second
vote was staged with certain outcome. Sir James Craig MP, sometime
organizer of the Ulster Volunteers, took the night ferry from Belfast carrying a loyal petition to the king. The whole operation was completed
within a month, and six of the nine historic counties of Ulster adopted
the position from which they have never since wavered. Secondly, the
Irish Free State applied for membership of the League of Nations.
Thirdly, the politicians in Dublin who appeared to have achieved a large
part of their objectives fell into deadly dispute.

The Anglo-Irish Treaty passed in the Dáil by only sixty-four votes
to fifty-seven; the treaty's opponents, who lost out, flatly refused to
accept the result. De Valera resigned, and started making provocative
speeches about 'Irishmen wading through Irish blood'. Michael Collins,
who had prosecuted the war against the British but who had also signed
the treaty, was denounced as a renegade. In order to prove his patriotic credentials, he launched an abortive attack on Ulster, in the first
of the so-called 'Border Wars', before entering into armed conflict with
his 'irreconcilable' Irish adversaries. Nineteen twenty-two, therefore,
was a year of civil war. The 'Free Staters' and their army were pitted
against the rump of the IRA, and were subjected to the same guerrilla-
style attacks that the British had endured earlier. Before the treaty
entered into force, Collins was killed in an ambush. He claimed to have
won 'the freedom to win freedom', and he was eventually proved right.
Arthur Griffith, too, died that year, from a heart attack. But the pro-
treaty forces prevailed, and the Free State took flight as envisioned.
George V was the king; Tim Healy (1855–1931), a lawyer and former
Westminster MP, was the first governor-general, and W. T. Cosgrave
(1880–1965), once sentenced to death, the first *taoiseach*. As one of the
Free State leaders put it: 'We were probably the most conservative-
minded revolutionaries ever.'[44]

The central cause of the civil war had lain in the decision to sacrifice
the Republic. The tragedy was all the greater since 'feeling in the country at large was far more decisively in favour of the Treaty than in the

committed republican atmosphere of the Dáil'.[45] In this regard, Roy
Foster has written reprovingly of 'the obsession with "the Crown".[46]
The fact is that two opposing groups were obsessed with the Crown: the
Irish ultra-republicans and the British establishment. Constitutionally,
the Anglo-Irish settlement introduced a system that was halfway
between the abandoned Home Rule project and full sovereignty. What
it most nearly resembled was the separate but dependent 'Kingdom of
Ireland', abolished in 1801 to make way for the Union.

In the final phase of the civil war, which continued into the late spring
of 1923, exasperated Free State ministers adopted ruthless measures to
fight violence with violence. Once masters of their own legislation, they
introduced an Emergency Powers Act which sanctioned summary executions. Before the fighting petered out, the forces of the Free State had
killed more IRA men than the British ever did. Erskine Childers was
among the victims.[47] De Valera, having denounced the treaty and praised
the 'Legion of the Rearguard', was arrested and interned.[48]

Not surprisingly, most of the songs generated by the Irish Civil War
emanated from the defeated republicans. The Free Staters, though they
won, had little to crow about. 'The Drumboe Martyrs' laments one
batch of executed victims, while the satirical 'Irish Free State', 'which
ran up the red-white-and-blue', accurately reflects republican bitterness.
Yet nothing offended republicans more than the Free State's adoption of
the green-white-and-gold tricolour of the late Republic:

> Take it down from the mast, Irish traitors,
> It's the flag we republicans claim.
> It can never belong to Free Staters,
> For you've brought on it nothing but shame.
>
> Why not leave it to those who are willing
> To uphold it in war and in peace,
> To the men who intend to do killing
> Until England's tyrannies cease?
>
> You have murdered our brave Liam and Rory,
> You have murdered young Richard and Joe.
> Your hands with their blood is still gory,
> Fulfilling the work of the foe.[49]

Taken together, the Anglo-Irish War, the Anglo-Irish treaty and the
Irish Civil War changed the face of southern Ireland. After 1919, large

numbers of Anglo-Irish landowners, the backbone of British rule, left their estates and never returned. After 1922, the treaty made provision for the orderly exodus or retirement of British officials, whom the Free State compensated. The survivors of fratricidal slaughter were left in a state of deep trauma that took decades to heal.

In March 1924, Sir Charles Villiers Stanford died in Cambridge, where he had been Professor of Music for almost forty years. He was a musician of the highest standing both as conductor and composer; his contribution to church choral music in particular passed into the standard repertoire.[50] But the professor had equally produced a lengthy series of collections of Irish folk songs and of Irish-inspired compositions. For he was an Irishman, born in Dublin, who never cut his roots. His works included a comic opera, *Shamus O'Brien,* six orchestral *Irish Rhapsodies*, *Irish Fantasies* and *Six Irish Sketches* for violin, *Intermezzo on the Londonderry* Air for organ, a *Limmerich ohne Woerte* under the pseudonym of Karel Drofnatski, and three song cycles for voice and piano: *A Sheaf of Songs from Leinster*, *Six Songs from the Glens of Antrim* and *An Irish Idyll*:

> In summer time I foot the turf
> And lay the sods to dry;
> South wind and lark's song
> And the sun far up in the sky.
>
> I pile them on the turf stack
> Against the time of snow;
> Black frost, a gale from the north.
> Who minds what winds may blow?
>
> Now winter's here, make up the fire,
> And let you bolt the door.
> A wind across the mountains,
> And a draught across the floor.
> . . .
>
> I see myself a barefoot child,
> I see myself a lad,
> When the gold upon the gorse bush
> Was all the gold I had.

> I do be having some fine old dreams
> Of days were long ago,
> When the wind keens, the night falls
> And the embers glow.[51]

Stanford was witness in his generation to the deep interpenetration of English and Irish life.

The Irish Free State could not have experienced a worse start, and acute problems pressed on many fronts. The coffers, for example, were virtually empty, and confusion reigned over the nature of the Free State's monarchy. Some sources list George V and his two sons, Edward VIII and George VI, as 'kings of Ireland'.[52] In the light of subsequent Commonwealth practice, this looks logical. But contemporary documents contain no such title. In reality, the exact relationship between the Free State and its monarch had been left curiously (and perhaps deliberately) ambivalent. Article 4 of the treaty laid down an oath of allegiance to be taken by all members of the Dáil, binding them 'to be faithful to HM King George V . . . in virtue of the common citizenship of Ireland with Great Britain . . . and her membership of the British Commonwealth of Nations'.[53]

The so-called National Anthem also caused trouble. 'God Save the King' is a royal anthem, not a national one, and nowhere does it mention the country whose monarch God is asked to save. More seriously, the words were still the same as in Britain. In consequence, they stuck in many an Irish throat. Though the Free State bands would dutifully play the melody on official occasions, it was often met either with stony silence or with counter-chants. Gaelic-speakers usually sang 'The Soldier's Song'. Others preferred a favourite from the American Civil War, sung to the rousing tune of 'Tramp, Tramp, Tramp – the Boys are Marching':

> 'God Save Ireland,' said the heroes,
> 'God Save Ireland,' said they all.
> Whether on the scaffold high
> Or the battlefield we die,
> Oh, what matter when for Erin dear we fall.[54]

From its inception the Free State was closely intertwined with the Roman Catholic Church, which, thanks to the exodus of Anglo-Irish Protestants, garnered the loyalties of 93 per cent of the population. The Church, having supported Parnell and the Home Rule Bill, had formally condemned the IRA's violence, and after the civil war it was the only institution with the resources to assist an impoverished government in the fields of education, healthcare and social reform. The majority of schools were run by Catholic orders, which insisted on Catholic instruction in the classroom. In 1924 divorce was banned and the sale of contraceptives made illegal; abortion was unavailable. After 1930, most Irish hospitals were funded by a sweepstake whose tickets were routinely distributed by priests and nuns, and the Eucharistic Congress of 1932 was treated as a state event. Suggestions have been made that the loss of royal ritual made people more susceptible to the charms of religious ritual.[55] The authoritarian ethos of the Irish Church could not be easily contested. For practical purposes, the ecclesiastical Index of banned books functioned as a system of state censorship. Ulster Protestants had always held that 'Home Rule means Rome Rule', and the Free State's early years did little to discredit the equation.

Nonetheless, during the rest of the 1920s, the two parts of Ireland settled down to an uneasy truce in which open conflict was avoided. In the North, which was more industrialized, competition for work in a sluggish post-war economy led to increasing and blatant discrimination against Catholics in key enterprises such as the Belfast shipyards. A government plan to introduce non-sectarian education was blocked by opposition from Protestants and Catholics alike. In the South, where over half the population still worked the land, the government put its mind to maximizing agricultural commerce, especially with Britain, and to relieving social poverty. Gaelic education represented another priority, which addressed the demands of cultural nationalism. 'The prosecution of the Irish language became the necessary benchmark of an independent ethos.'[56] At the same time, care was taken to strengthen democratic stability round the Dáil, the Free State army and the unarmed police, the *Garda Síochána*. When Éamon de Valera re-emerged from detention to found Fianna Fáil in 1926, promising to promote republicanism through the Free State's institutions, he caused the Sinn Féin movement to splinter yet again. From then on, republicans still bent on armed struggle were reduced to a very small rump.

No privileged status was offered to the Roman Catholic Church, despite its long-standing ties to Irish nationalism. Some Catholic politicians harboured anti-clerical tendencies, just as many Catholic priests had shunned the IRA. In any case, the British guardians of the treaty, conditioned by the Protestant Ascendancy, were unwilling to envisage a theocratic state on Britain's doorstep. So Free State leaders had to be cautious. *Taoiseach* Cosgrave expressed his country's undying allegiance to the papacy, but the more extreme advocates of Catholic control were disappointed. Deep-seated tensions between Church and State in Ireland did not surface for over half a century.[57]

With some delay, the British government responded to the division of Ireland by passing the Royal and Parliamentary Titles Act (1927). Ever since his pre-war coronation, George V had used the formula of 'king of the United Kingdom of Great Britain and Ireland, of the Dominions, and of other realms beyond the seas'. Now the initial part of his title was changed to 'king of Great Britain, Ireland, the Dominions, and . . .'.[58] The replacement of the first 'and' by a comma pointed unambiguously to Ireland being accepted as a separate realm. In consequence, the king was advised to accept the nomination of the next governor-general from the Irish government, not from the British. At the Imperial Conference of 1926, when the structures of the British Commonwealth were first mooted, the Irish Free State was listed among its constituent dominions, alongside Australia, Canada, New Zealand and South Africa. Cosgrave participated without apparent demur.

The 1930s witnessed a republican revival. Membership of the Commonwealth did not give the Free State any marked benefits; and, as the Great Depression deepened, socio-economic ills in Ireland mounted. After five years' preparation, De Valera's Fianna Fáil, drawing on pro-republican sympathies that had gone underground since the civil war, won the election of 1932, and formed a radical government. For its party anthem, it had adopted the melody and bilingual lyrics that had been sung before the General Post Office in 1916. The original words of 'Amhrán na bhFiann' were in English:

> Sons of the Gael! Men of the Pale!
> The long-watched day is breaking;
> The serried ranks of Innisfail
> Shall set the tyrant quaking.
> Our campfires now are burning low;
> See in the east a silvery glow,
> Out yonder waits the Saxon foe,
> So chant a soldier's song.[59]

De Valera assumed office shortly after the Statute of Westminster of 1931 had retracted Britain's right to legislate for the dominions. As a result, he was able to use legalistic 'salami tactics' to slice up the Free State's constitution bit by bit. First to go was its reference to the Anglo-

Irish Treaty. Then, in successive amendments, he abolished or limited the Senate, the governor-generalship and appeals to the Privy Council. Short of declaring war, the British were helpless. The second governor-general, James McNeill (1928–32), grew so irritated that he resigned early; and the third, Donald Buckley (1932–6), was simply told by De Valera to keep a low profile, effectively neutered by a hint about suspending the Irish government's payment of the lease on his luxurious residence. When he welcomed the French ambassador he performed the only official function in the whole of his tenure.[60]

The prime opportunity for more extensive change came about through a crisis in the British monarchy. The old king, George V, died in January 1936, breaking the thread of continuity with pre-Rising times. He was succeeded by the playboy Edward VIII, whose association with an American divorcee scandalized Catholic Ireland, no less than Britain. Preparations for a secular coronation broke the sacred spell that monarchists had long cultivated. De Valera seized the opportunity to abolish the oath of allegiance in Ireland, and, through the External Relations Act (1936), to deny Britain control over foreign affairs. He also wrote directly to the new king, giving notice that his government intended to replace the Free State's constitution. Paralysed by the abdication crisis, the British government barely noticed what was happening.

In December 1936 a curious monarchical moment occurred. Edward VIII abdicated on the 10th, the decision being immediately confirmed by the Westminster Parliament. But the Dáil in Dublin was unable to follow suit until the 12th. This meant that for one whole day – 11 December 1936 – the duke of Windsor retained his status as king in Ireland (if not as 'king *of* Ireland') without being the United Kingdom's sovereign.

Such was the prelude to De Valera's boldest step. In 1937 he introduced a bill to the Dáil proposing that the constitution of 1922 be repealed. The Free State was to disappear, and a draft *Bunreacht na hÉireann* or 'Constitution of Ireland' was put forward to replace it. The Gaelic version of the Preamble and fifty articles was to be regarded as definitive; the state's official name was to be changed to *Éire*. The governor-general was to be replaced by the *uachtarán* or 'president', and the will of the people was to be supreme. The draft was accepted by popular plebiscite on 1 July 1937.[61]

The British government in London did not yet accept the change explicitly. But it was recognized implicitly by the monarchy when George VI was crowned in May 1937 as 'king of Great Britain and Northern Ireland'. However, since Éire had not withdrawn from the

Commonwealth, and since the king's claim to reign over 'the dominions' was not altered, Britain and Ireland both acknowledged some residual and purely theoretical role for the Crown.

The *Bunreacht* generated many hostile misunderstandings. The Preamble, for example, was worded, 'In the name of the most Holy Trinity ... to Whom all actions of men and states must be referred.' This gave rise to wild accusations that the text as a whole discriminated against non-Roman Catholics. In reality, religious freedom together with the rights of all Christian faiths and of the Jewish community were guaranteed; and a reference to 'the special position of the Holy Catholic, Apostolic and Roman Church', though deliberately deferential in tone, made no provision for practical action. The first president of Éire, Douglas Hyde (1860–1949), founder of the Gaelic League, who was famous for lecturing forty years before 'On the Necessity of De-anglicising the Irish People', was a Protestant.[62] De Valera resisted persistent demands to give Roman Catholicism the status of a state-backed religion, and on issues such as divorce or the role of women simply followed the social teaching of his day.

Article 2 of the *Bunreacht* reasserted the concept of a national territory covering the whole island of Ireland, as in the Act of 1542. This provoked howls of protest in Belfast, which claimed that Northern Ireland's existence was denied. Yet Article 3 specifically stated that Éire would not govern anywhere beyond the twenty-six counties. Widest of the mark was the accusation that the *Bunreacht* of 1937 had created an Irish 'Republic'. Acutely conscious of the painful sensitivities of the 1920s, De Valera needed no instruction on this point. Neither 'the Republic' in English, nor any Gaelic equivalent, found a mention. He had long since learned the virtue of constructive obfuscation.

In this same period, De Valera was extremely active in the League of Nations. His speech in 1936 on 'The Failure of the League' underlined the selfishness of the Great Powers and their disregard for small nations. It helped him to the League's presidency, and strengthened his hand in dealings with Britain.[63] In 1938 Éire succeeded in terminating an Anglo-Irish trade war, and in regaining the three 'Treaty Ports' of Spike Island, Berehaven and Lough Swilly which the Royal Navy had occupied since 1922. It was edging its way towards full sovereignty.

During the Second World War, Ireland immediately declared an 'Emergency' accompanied by strict neutrality. The Emergency was explained by the need to restrain the IRA, which had traditional pro-German sympathies and which perpetrated several anti-government bombings. (Evidence would emerge long afterwards of De Valera's complicity with British Intelligence on this issue.) The policy of neutrality was genuine, seeking to avoid commitment either to Britain or to Germany. De Valera's temerity caused immense anger in London, where the British government had assumed that all the dominions would automatically take Britain's side. British attitudes were still largely configured in imperial mode, and, since Irish harbours were sorely needed for the campaign against German U-boats, a real danger arose that British forces would reoccupy them. Churchill first tried to tempt De Valera by dangling the prospect before him of a reunited Ireland. When this failed, he swallowed his fury. He knew how much trouble the 'Irish Question' had caused only twenty years earlier. In any case, Britain's resources were hopelessly overstretched. But Éire did not tempt fate by cosying up to the Third Reich. Indeed, as the Nazi star waned, intelligence was shared with the British. Nonetheless, De Valera's defiant, not to say gratuitous gesture in April 1945, when he visited the German embassy in Dublin to present his condolences on Adolf Hitler's death, exceeded the normal demands of protocol. Despite his American roots, he made no parallel gesture on the death of President Roosevelt.[64]

After the war, Ireland could have expected British retribution. Yet Clement Attlee's Labour government was less bullish than Churchill's Conservatives might have been, and amid a torrent of post-war crises Ireland did not figure high on Britain's priorities. The decision in 1947 to abandon India, and the collapse of the Empire, deflated Britain's imperial pretentions for good.

By 1948, therefore, having after some delay repealed Emergency powers, John Costello's interparty coalition, which had taken over from De Valera , felt confident enough to initiate the final break with Britain, and the British government felt sufficiently contrite to bow to the inevitable. On 18 April the Republic of Ireland Act was introduced to the Dáil. In five brief clauses, it renamed the state, cancelled the External Relations Act (1936), gave executive authority to the president, formally withdrew from the Commonwealth, and established the date of its completion exactly one year later.[65] De Valera, the republican, though out of office, had finally triumphed after thirty-three years of struggle. Asked what his greatest mistake had been, he confessed: 'to have opposed the Treaty'. Foster calls him an 'old political shaman'.[66] He would serve two presidential terms under the new dispensation.

In the meantime, the rules of the British Commonwealth were amended so that republics were not automatically excluded. Ireland did not seek to benefit. Then Attlee's government moved the Ireland Act (1949), which both recognized the Republic and confirmed Northern Ireland's separate status. The British were at pains not to disturb the huge number of Irish people who were living and working in Britain.

Nonetheless, the clumsy wording of the Ireland Act sowed the seeds of future conflict. One clause stated, bizarrely, that 'Ireland shall not be regarded as a foreign country for the purpose of any law'. Another stated that the status quo in Northern Ireland could not be changed without the express consent of the Stormont parliament,[67] effectively handing the Unionists a built-in veto on all reforms. This created the impression that the British government was retracting with the left hand what had just been granted by the right, and, in the eyes of many, provided the rallying point round which the near-defunct IRA could rise again. Henceforth, the clandestine IRA reverted to the fundamentalist brand of republicanism that condemned it to be treated as a pariah both in the South and the North.

The clause also lay at the root of a long-running wrangle between Britain and Éire's head of state. According to the *Bunreacht* of 1937, the head of state's official title in English was 'president of Éire'. But British officialdom refused to use it, and invitations were politely turned down for decades. When the Commonwealth Conference determined in 1953 to regulate its affairs at the start of a new reign, therefore, Ireland was no longer a member. Queen Elizabeth II became 'queen of Canada' and 'queen of Australia' but not 'queen of Ireland'. Though Irish people had played a prominent part in creating the human substance of Empire and Commonwealth, their representatives did not participate in the post-imperial club. Instead, they poured their enthusiasm into the Marian Year of 1954, an ultra-Catholic occasion that jarred with prevailing attitudes in Britain.

In 1962 an embarrassing legal anomaly was discovered. As part of a legislative spring-cleaning exercise, it was found at Westminster that the original Crown of Ireland Act (1542) was still on the statute books. It had been left untouched in 1801 when the Kingdom of Ireland had supposedly been abolished; and again in 1921–2, when the Irish Free State seceded from the United Kingdom. Henry VIII's Act laid down, among other things, that all the Tudor monarch's heirs and successors were to be 'kings of Ireland' in perpetuity. For the legal purists, the implications were astonishing. Elizabeth II did indeed belong to the heirs and successors of Henry VIII. So by right of inheritance if not by coronation, she was still queen of Ireland. The Act was promptly repealed.[68]

Also in 1962, the latest of the IRA's long-running 'border campaigns' came to an end. Notwithstanding appearances, pockets of the diehard IRA had lived on, and for six years they had pursued a series of typical hit-and-run actions on the border of Northern Ireland. One incident, the inglorious raid on the Brookeburgh barracks of the RUC in County Fermanagh on New Year's Day 1957, left two young men dead and produced one of the most poignant of modern Irish ballads. Written by Dominic Behan, brother of the playwright Brendan, 'The Patriot Game' pours scorn on the Irish Republic and on British forces alike:

> Come all ye young rebels, and list while I sing,
> For the love of one's country is a terrible thing.
> It banishes fear with the speed of a flame,
> And it makes us part of the patriot game.
>
> This Ireland of ours has too long been half free.
> Six counties lie under John Bull's tyranny.
> But still De Valera is greatly to blame
> For shirking his part in the patriot game.
>
> And now as I lie here, my body in holes
> I think of those traitors who bargained in souls
> And I wish that my rifle had given the same
> To those Quislings who sold out the patriot game.[69]

It was recorded by Liam Clancy and in the United States by Bob Dylan, who said of Clancy: 'the best ballad singer I've ever heard'.

Nonetheless, despite such setbacks, relations between the Irish and British governments had been slowly but steadily improving. Both had sought to join the European Economic Community, and both had been fended off by General de Gaulle. It was a welcome milestone, therefore, when the Republic of Ireland joined in 1972 with the United Kingdom and Denmark as entrants to the EEC. It was a day when Irish eyes were indeed smiling.

Unfortunately, the same half-century in Northern Ireland was marked by rigid ossification. The Unionist-Loyalist majority in the six counties, having gained control in 1920, strained every sinew to maintain its dominance; in time their intransigence led to a violent backlash from the excluded minority. Ironically, at the very time when Britain and Ireland were entering into neighbourly partnership, the Unionist and Nationalist communities of Northern Ireland were entering into a thirty-year intercommunal bloodbath.[70]

The regime which prevailed in Northern Ireland from 1922 to 1972 was based on an anachronistic mixture of sectarian prejudice, pseudo-democratic manipulation and social oppression. Arguably, in a segregated society, it was also responsible for the defensive, introverted and sometimes extremist attitudes that grew up on the opposite side of the sectarian divide. The province's parliament, which met at Stormont Castle, had a built-in Protestant-Unionist majority that was maintained by gerrymandering in marginal constituencies. The province's long-serving prime ministers, notably Viscount Craigavon (formerly Sir James Craig), 1922–40, and Lord Brookeburgh, 1943–63, were paragons of immobility. The province's twelve Westminster MPs, a bulwark of the Conservative and Unionist Party, allied with the British Tories in all the most reactionary causes of the day, and the Province's police force, the Royal Ulster Constabulary, recruited almost exclusively from Protestants, routinely turned a blind eye to all misdemeanours except those committed by Catholics. The province's oldest and most influential organization, the Orange Order, was devoted to the defence of the Protestant Ascendancy, and its own parades in the annual marching season in July used the anniversary of the Battle of the Boyne as the pretext for celebrating anti-Catholic triumphalism. Thousands of marching columns, bedecked in bowler hats, pinstripe suits and umbrellas flaunted their Orange sashes and Union Jacks, deliberately passing through Catholic districts in order to cow the natives. The whole tenor of official life was conducted in the aggressive-defensive mode initiated before the First World War. 'Ulster will fight and Ulster will be right' was a common cry. Marching, drilling, flag-waving, loyalty to 'the Crown', and shouts of 'We will never surrender' set the dominant tone. The minority community – Catholic, Irish Nationalist, Republican, and roughly 40 per cent of the population – were simply expected to knuckle under. While attitudes both in Britain and in southern Ireland evolved, attitudes in Ulster froze.

One element of the Ulster mind-set stressed the ancient link with Scotland. Scottish Presbyterians, though numerically dominant, had long played second fiddle to the Unionist establishment, which tended to have English landowning and (Anglican) Church of Ireland connections. (The Democratic Unionist Party (DUP) of the Revd Ian Paisley would

eventually get the upper hand over the official Unionists.) Especially
when supporting Glasgow Rangers football club, the Ulstermen sang of
'The Hands across the Water' – the common Scottish bond:

> And it's hands across the water
> Reaching out for you and me,
> For King, for Ulster, for Scotland
> Helping keep our people free!
> Let the cry be 'No Surrender'
> Let no one doubt our Loyalty
> Reaching out to the Red Hand of Ulster,
> Is the hand across the sea.[71]

The immediate origins of Northern Ireland's 'Troubles' can be traced
to the late 1960s. A republican celebration in Belfast of the fiftieth anniversary of the Easter Rising – to match the concurrent festival in
Dublin[72] – provoked a public declaration from the newly formed paramilitary Ulster Volunteer Force (UVF) that all IRA supporters would be
killed. The first murders began. Two years later, the Northern Ireland
Civil Rights Association (NICRA), modelled on its counterpart in the
United States, started mass demonstrations calling for an end to discrimination against Catholics in housing, employment, healthcare and
political representation. The demonstrators were brutally assaulted
both by Protestant mobs and by the RUC. Their first rally, on 27 April
1968, was to protest against a ban on republican Easter parades.

In August 1969 the 'Battle of the Bogside' in Derry (or Londonderry
as it was more generally known in the north) saw a more menacing outbreak of rioting. It also saw the emergence of the Provisional IRA, the
'Provos', an armed paramilitary splinter group, which promised to take
on the UVF using its own methods.[73] The Northern Ireland prime minister of the time, Sir Terence O'Neill, milder and less confrontational
than his predecessors, had once caused a scandal by visiting a Catholic
school, and showed sympathy for the besieged minority. He called in
the British army to protect them. The decision proved fatal. Instead of
holding the ring, the army took sides, identifying loyalists as allies and
'Provos' as the enemy. In January 1972, on 'Bloody Sunday', soldiers
of the Parachute Regiment gunned down thirteen unarmed Catholic
demonstrators.[74] Further rioting ensued. The British government blamed
the government of Northern Ireland. The parliament at Stormont was
suspended. The province looked forward to three decades of military
law and of 'Direct Rule' from London.

Britain's good intentions of ruling impartially soon lapsed. The Sunningdale Agreement of December 1973, which proposed power-sharing between the two communities,[75] was aborted by a paralysing wave of loyalist strikes. No effective action was taken against them. Thereafter, the British authorities merely sought to contain the violence. The army, military intelligence and MI5 worked closely with the RUC. The Ulster Defence Regiment (UDR), a new security force, was largely Protestant in its make-up, and was infiltrated by the UVF. The Provos and other clandestine republican formations were classed as criminals and terrorists, whereas, despite their similarly brutal conduct, the UVF and Ulster Defence Association (UDA) were not. The policy of internment without trial in the purpose-built Maze Prison at Long Kesh was directed overwhelmingly at Catholic suspects, provoking hunger strikes and a further downward turn in the spiral of violence. Nothing was done to rein in loyalist marches, and well-meaning reconciliation groups, including churchmen from both sides and the 'Peace People' who received the Nobel Prize for their efforts, were sidelined.[76]

Intercommunal atrocities proliferated, with a constant stream of murders, reprisals, bombings, shootings, house-burnings, beatings, kneecappings, disappearances, collective punishments, as well as the harshest of words. Belfast was divided into fearful armed camps, each sheltering behind barbed wire, high walls and bricked-off streets. There were parts of town where Catholics or Protestants could not tread for fear of their lives; and in the countryside, there were districts such as South Armagh where British soldiers walked at their peril. The British media made great play at specific outrages such as the assassinations of Airey Neave MP in 1979[77] and of Lord Mountbatten, the last viceroy of India, in the same year;[78] far less attention was paid to the unceasing bloodletting of lesser human beings in Belfast. Frustrations on the nationalist side of the barricades reached boiling point. A hunger strike began in the Maze Prison when an IRA activist, Bobby Sands, elected to Westminster during his sentence, starved himself to death.[79] Recruitment for the Provos soared.

The Northern Ireland 'Troubles' produced a new wave of republican minstrelsy. Ballads and protest songs proliferated, and recordings went round the world. 'My Little Armalite' celebrated the favourite weapon of the Provos, and 'Fighting Men of Crossmaglen' the struggle in South Armagh. 'The Men behind the Wire' highlighted the endless ordeal of the internees:

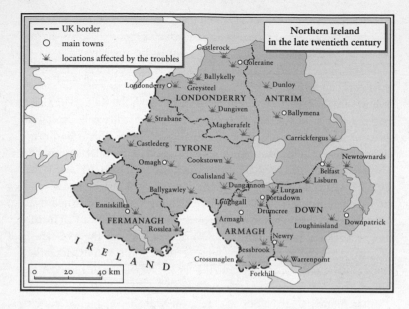

Armoured cars and tanks and guns
Came to take away our sons
But every man will stand behind
The Men behind the Wire.
Not for them a judge or jury
Or indeed a crime at all.
Being Irish makes them guilty,
So we're guilty one and all.
Round the world the truth will echo
Cromwell's men are here again.
England's name again is sullied
In the eyes of honest men.[80]

Fresh calls came from the Republic to end the 'Occupation'. The language could be less than polite:

Go home, British soldiers, go on home!
Have you got no f—ing homes of your own?
For eight hundred years, we've fought you without fears
And we'll fight you for eight hundred more.

If you stay, British solders, if you stay
You'll never ever beat the IRA.

So f— your Union Jack, we want our country back.
We want to see old Ireland free once more.[81]

Yet gentler tones were heard among the truculence. One of the most
popular recordings of the era derived from the revival of an ancient
Irish air by the 'Blind Harper', with modern words added:

> Just give me your hand
> Is '*tabhair dom do lamh*'.
> Just give me your hand
> And I will walk with you.
> For the world it is ours,
> All the sea and the land.
> To destroy or command,
> If you give me your hand.[82]

In the 1970s and 1980s, the singing and the weeping continued, with no
sign of resolution.

In those same decades the grip of the Roman Catholic Church on life in
the Republic finally began to slip. The hierarchy opposed a state scheme
for free public secondary schools, presumably because it would compete with the Church's own; censorship and the constitutional ban on
divorce were only removed in 1966. Changes introduced by the Second
Vatican Council, notably to the celebration of Holy Mass in Latin, helped
undermine a priesthood accustomed to the idea of an eternal status quo.
But reform was driven above all by demands for women's rights. The
Health (Family Planning) Act of 1979, which permitted the sale of contraceptives on prescription, was a landmark, though it also demonstrated
the Church's powers of obstruction. A Church-backed 'Pro-Life' campaign battled its 'Pro-Choice' adversaries on abortion, routinely issuing
injunctions against actual and would-be offenders. These petty skirmishes concealed a volcano ready to erupt. In 1984–5 the first of an
endless flow of sex scandals broke surface. The seminarians of Maynooth
College publicly accused their reverend head of predatory homosexual
habits; in County Offaly an unmarried fifteen-year-old schoolgirl died
horribly giving birth alone on a beach; and in County Clare, a local priest
was found battered to death in suspicious circumstances. Step by step, the
press gained courage, official denials lost credibility and the truth seeped
out. Throughout the twentieth century, and contrary to their own teaching, all levels of the Catholic clergy had been involved in all manner of

sexual abuses, from secret concubinage and fathering of children, to rape, molestation, beatings and exploitation of minors. The *Garda Síochána* had been complicit in the hierarchy's cover-up. The standing of the Church slumped; the Church's link to the state weakened, and the country's image was sullied.

In retrospect, one could see that the visit of Pope John Paul II in 1979, when more than a third of the Republic's population flocked to greet him in Phoenix Park, had marked the high point of traditional Irish attitudes and practices. Ninety per cent of the population were still attending Mass at least once a week. In the subsequent decades numerous incremental changes took place which some observers believe have added up to a social revolution, notably in the fields of public and private morality, the position of women, the relations of Church and State, of declining deference to authority and of increased understanding of the North. 'The first two decades of the 20th century brought Ireland independence,' wrote an Oxford historian, 'but the final two brought a social revolution whose consequences were probably even more far reaching.'[83]

In the 1990s, headlines from Ireland placed these moral upheavals in the Republic alongside a political impasse in the North and signs of a historic economic reversal. The Republic's presidential election of 1990 was won by Mary Robinson, an activist of the Pro-Choice movement; after one term she departed to become UN Commissioner for Human Rights and to be replaced by another woman of similar profile, Mary McAleese. In 1992, the appalling 'X-Case', in which the attorney-general of the Republic had taken steps to prosecute a teenage victim of rape, provoked a national referendum on the right to information on abortion; the Church's defeat on this relatively minor issue punctured its dictatorial pretensions for good.

In the North, a beleaguered IRA had redirected its bombing campaign onto the British mainland. The Brighton Bombing of 1984 nearly killed the British prime minister, Margaret Thatcher.[84] Frightful atrocities occurred at Canary Wharf in London and in Manchester. But a parallel policy of the 'bullet and the ballot-box' was then adopted. While the Provos persisted – as they saw it – in matching violence with violence, their political wing, Sinn Féin, sought to reap the benefits of open politics. The architect of the policy was Gerry Adams (Gearóid MacAdhaimh, b. 1948), the grandson and great-grandson of Fenians, an activist of NICRA, an ex-internee, a survivor of assassins, allegedly an ex-IRA commander, and the president of Sinn Féin since 1983.[85] To avoid prosecution, Adams claimed disingenuously that his party was totally independent of the Provo terrorists. Yet his strategy bore fruit. Mainstream nationalists found their way into public discussions, floating the possibility of a settlement. In the crucial Downing Street Declaration of 15 December 1993, Prime Minister John Major joined the Republic's *taoiseach* in affirming that the Northern Ireland Question should be solved exclusively by Irish people from North and South. The British government was distancing itself from the fighting. The first of a string of ceasefires followed. They happened to the accompaniment of an unprecedented boom in the Republic's economy; never before in living memory had Dublin been far more prosperous than Belfast.

In the later 1990s sporadic violence recurred. But as the death toll passed the 3,500 mark, killing fatigue set in on all sides. Senator George Mitchell, the US president's emissary, breathed life into preliminary talks. The war of words did not abate. The loudest mouth in Northern Ireland characterized the pope as 'the Anti-Christ', called Gerry Adams 'the devil's dinner partner', President McAleese 'dishonest' and the queen 'a parrot'.[86] But prospects of peace were improving.[87]

The Belfast Agreement of April 1998 – otherwise known as the Good Friday Agreement – was clearly a very important if ambiguous achievement. To some, it was only 'a Sunningdale for slow learners', for others a masterly model for all long-running 'peace processes'. It was signed by Prime Minister Tony Blair for the United Kingdom, by *Taoiseach* Bertie Ahern for the Republic, and by all the Northern Ireland parties except the Democratic Unionists. Put to referendums in both the North and the Republic, it won approval by 71 per cent and by 84 per cent respectively. Of its eighteen provisions, a key clause bound all signatories to the pursuit of their objectives 'by peaceful and democratic means'. Groups and individuals were henceforth free to work for a reunited Ireland or for the preservation of the United Kingdom, but not with guns or bombs. There were three additional strands: one devoted to internal arrangements in Northern Ireland, a second to contacts between Northern Ireland and the Republic and a third to the British Isles and Ireland as a whole. In the view of Britain's Northern Ireland Office, 'the political and peace processes . . . have brought huge benefits and change'.[88]

The most immediate response, however, was horrific. On 15 August 1998, four months before the Agreement came into force, a car bomb exploded without warning in Omagh, killing 29 people and maiming 300. A dissident group calling itself the 'Real IRA' was publicizing its dissent.[89] In that same year, the Nobel Peace Prize was awarded jointly to the leaders of Northern Ireland's two moderate parties. David Trimble of the Ulster Unionist Party and John Hume of the Social Democratic Labour Party (SDLP) had shunned the violent elements within their respective Unionist and Nationalist communities, and were judged to be makers of peace.[90]

On Armistice Day 1998 President McAleese joined Queen Elizabeth II in a symbolic act of reconciliation at the Messines Ridge near Ypres in Belgium. Messines was the site of a battle in June 1917 where 20,000 Irish soldiers – Protestants from the 6th Ulster Division and Catholics from the 16th Irish Division – had shed their blood side by side in the British service. Now, after eighty years' silence, the two women stood facing the sunset, and paid their respects to the fallen. After the ceremony, they inaugurated the Island of Ireland Peace Tower.

Nonetheless, years passed before some of the Agreement's main provisions bore fruit. The creation of a governmental Executive from all parties elected to the Northern Ireland Assembly was made possible by Sinn Féin's willingness to suspend its ideological objections and to work *pro tempore* within an institution that was ultimately responsible to the British Crown. The first attempt, under David Trimble as first minister, broke down over slow progress in disarming the paramilitaries. The setback was remedied by the St Andrews Agreement of 2006, and the Executive finally got down to business the next May. Votes were moving from the moderate centre towards the two extremes, but not to the detriment of co-operation. The redoubtable Ian Paisley of the DUP,[91] now more restrained in his public pronouncements, and Martin McGuinness of Sinn Féin,[92] once sworn enemies, became first minister and deputy first minister respectively.

Other elements had moved faster. By the Good Friday Agreement, the Republic dropped its constitutional claim to the six counties. The North-South Ministerial Council, and the potentially important British-Irish 'Council of the Isles', started work.[93] British army bases were closed. Reform of the police system was initiated, and commissions on human rights, equal opportunities and parades went into business.

As with every previous step, the Good Friday Agreement brought about a new round of singing. One of the themes hailed hopes of reconciliation:

> In the battered streets of Belfast,
> Can't you hear the people cry?
> For justice long denied them
> And their crying fills the sky.
> But the winds of change are singing

> Bringing hope from dark despair.
> There's a day of justice dawning.
> You can feel it in the air.
>
> There's a time laid out for laughing,
> And a time laid out to weep
> There's a time laid out for sowing
> And a time laid out to reap
> There's a time to love your brother
> And a time for hate to cease,
> If you sow the seeds of justice
> Then you'll reap the fruits of peace.[94]

Simultaneously, with no ulterior motives in mind, the BBC World Service held a competition to find the world's most popular song. The winner could hardly have been predicted. Beating India's national hymn '*Vande Mataram*', it was a very old song from Ireland:

> When boyhood's fire was in my blood
> I read of ancient freemen,
> For Greece and Rome who bravely stood
> Three hundred men and three men.
> And then I prayed I yet might see
> Our fetters rent in twain,
> And Ireland long a province, be
> A Nation Once Again.
> (refrain) A Nation Once Again,
>   A Nation Once Again,
>   And Ireland long a province, be
>   A Nation Once Again.[95]

One suspects that the e-mail voting skills of Irish expatriates in 2002 were still superior to those of the average Indian.

In the decade when Northern Ireland was tending its wounds, the Republic was stoking the fires of a different sort of catastrophe. The economic boom went to Irish heads. People told 'We are richer than the Germans', felt that they could spend money like water. Property developers launched grandiose projects; consumers piled up mountains of debt, splashing out on luxurious homes, foreign holidays and expensive cars; and irresponsible bankers handed out excessive credit without a thought for tomorrow. Politicians acted as if the party would never stop. 'The

boom is getting boomier,' chortled Bertie Ahern, in 2006. 'We behaved
like a pauper who had won the lottery,' said someone else. The behaviour
seemed all the more reprehensible since it coincided with the
inquiries and reports that comprehensively exposed the shortcomings of
the Catholic Church. Eventually a leading Irish commentator, foreseeing
disaster, described his country as 'A Ship of Fools'.[96]

Damien Dempsey was the songster who set the national mood to
music:

> Greedy, greedy, greedy, greedy, greedy
> So greedy, greedy, greedy, greedy, greedy
>
> Now they say the Celtic Tiger in my home town
> Brings jewels and crowns, picks you up off the ground
> But the Celtic Tiger does two things
> It brings you good luck or it eats you for its supper.
> It's the tale of the two cities on the shamrock shore.
> Please Sir can I have some more,
> Cos if you are poor you'll be eaten for sure.
> And that's how I know the poor have more taste than the rich
> And that's how I know the poor have more taste than the rich.
>
> Hear the Tiger roar – I want more
> Hear the Tiger roar, I want more, more, more.[97]

The Republic's distress coincided with the North's convalescence. No
one could pretend, of course, that the 'Irish Question' had reached its
terminus. Pockets of tension remained in Ulster. Various minorities still
felt embattled. The Orangemen were still marching, and protesters still
attempting to block their way. Dissident IRA-men were still planning
their 'spectaculars', and exploding bombs. Mind-sets changed slowly.
Yet a return to large-scale bloodshed was unlikely,[98] and a distinct shift
in attitudes to Ireland's painful history could be observed. 'Where previously
our history has been characterized by a plundering of the past
to separate and differentiate us,' said the Irish president in a London
lecture, 'our future now holds the optimistic possibility that . . . we will
re-visit the past more comfortably and find . . . elements of kinship long
neglected, of connections deliberately over-looked.'[99] 'Today we salute
Ulster's honoured and unageing dead,' declared Northern Ireland's
incoming first minister, '. . . Protestant and Roman Catholic . . . Unionist
and Nationalist, male and female, children and adults, all innocent victims
of the terrible conflict.'[100] 'The reality is, that it's now 2009,' wrote

the president of Sinn Féin in his *Leargas* blogspot, 'not 1969 or 1920 or for that matter 1690. And we're all living in an Ireland governed democratically by all-Ireland institutions, and by powersharing mechanisms in the six counties.'[101] In January 2010 a marathon negotiating session involving both British and Irish prime ministers broke the latest deadlock in Northern Ireland, enabling the Executive to resume business.

The British government itself was experiencing a change of heart. The Saville Inquiry into the events of 'Bloody Sunday' reported in June 2010, firmly rejecting the whitewash of the earlier Widgery Report and condemning killings by the British army as 'unjustified and unjustifiable'. It destroyed the notion that the 'Provos' could be blamed for everything. The new prime minister, David Cameron, made an unreserved apology in the House of Commons, and the chairman of the official Unionists (the Ulster Unionist Party, UUP), once the bedrock of British control in Ulster, resigned: in 2010 the UUP vote had slumped from 46 per cent in 1974 to 15 per cent.[102] The first minister of the province, Peter Robinson of the DUP, was embroiled in a damaging scandal.[103] Times were changing. The city of Derry/Londonderry, where the initial killings had taken place in 1972, was chosen as the UK's 'City of Culture'.

The Republic, meanwhile, was sinking deeper into the mire. Though the financial bubble had burst in 2008 in line with the global recession, the most serious consequences did not surface immediately. The Fianna Fáil government took over the debts of two failing banks, the Anglo-Irish and the Ulster, and pretended that the problem was solved. In the spring of 2010, when Greece was forced to accept a Eurozone bail-out, ministers in Dublin were still mocking suggestions that Ireland might have to follow suit. But self-criticism crept into public debate. 'We're very narcissistic,' one woman lamented; 'we believed our boom was better than anyone else's.' And moral reflections returned. 'People lost interest in the other world,' commented the abbot of Glenstal, 'while they were so successful in this one.'[104] The government denied all until reality caught up with them in November. Inspectors from the EU Commission and the IMF flew in to examine Ireland's books. Their investigations led to an 85-billion-euro rescue package that would tie the Republic into austerity, tax rises and social pain for decades to come.[105] The Celtic Tiger, if not dead, was floored. The Republic found itself in intensive care; a land of smiles became a land of woe, and its image as a brave pioneer evaporated.

Political meltdown followed swiftly on economic meltdown. The *taoiseach*, Brian Cowen, announced his imminent departure, his government's reputation in shreds. In a mere five years, Ireland's position in the Quality of Life Index had dived from 5th in the world to 41st, sixteen places behind the United Kingdom. Inward immigration had stopped, and outward emigration had restarted at the rate of 1,000 per week. Unemployment was soaring. Popular anger reached fever pitch. A general election brought forward to 25 February 2011 voted massively for change. Fianna Fáil was battered by the voters, its representation in the Dáil falling from 70 to 16. Its coalition partner, the Green Party, was annihilated. Fine Gael triumphed, increasing its seats from 51 to 68; its leader, Enda Kenny, hastened to form a cabinet. The Labour Party almost doubled its representation, from 20 to 35, and Sinn Féin's tiny support was more than tripled, from 4 seats to 13. Gerry Adams, who had resigned from his unoccupied seat at Westminster, topped the contest in County Louth, in the nearest part of the country to Belfast; he had declared his ambition of becoming the Republic's president within five years. Sinn Féin's decline had been arrested, but the 'fortress of democratic republicanism', which it had once founded, looked distinctly sick.[106] Éamon de Valera 'was spinning in his grave'.[107]

James Joyce's novel *Ulysses* (1922) was completed in the year that the Irish Free State was proclaimed. One of the characters says, 'History is a nightmare from which I am trying to awake.' Despite the passage of nearly a century, the sentiment still strikes chords. The British nightmare is perpetuated by the Irish Question still hanging like a millstone round London's neck; the Republic's nightmare is fed by shame that so many accomplishments have repeatedly been squandered, and the nightmare of principled republicans by their inability to win majority backing. In Northern Ireland, the most recent nightmare has ended, but people have woken up to an apparent stalemate.

Hence, as the centenary of the Easter Rising rose over the horizon, the main participants in the chain of conflicts – the British, the Irish, the Unionists and the republicans – had all been duly chastened; everyone's pride had been humbled in turn. The long retreat of British rule in Ireland had slowed to an imperceptible crawl. The British queen, who still reigned over six Irish counties, accepted an invitation to visit Dublin for the first formal royal visit there since her grandfather's in 1911.[108] Unionists were holding on to their corner of the island, but only by sharing power. Nationalists and republicans, in whose eyes the country was only three-quarters free, were marking time, believing it to be on their side. Monarchy in Ireland had still not vanished. It had reached a moment reminiscent of a king of Ireland's famous last words; lying on his deathbed in 1685, Charles II, who was equally king of England and king of Scotland, apologized for being 'an unconscionable time a-dying'.[109]

III

That the United Kingdom will collapse is a foregone conclusion. Sooner or later, all states *do* collapse, and ramshackle, asymmetric dynastic amalgamations are more vulnerable than cohesive nation-states. Only the 'how' and the 'when' are mysteries of the future.

An exhaustive study of the many pillars on which British power and prestige were built – ranging from the monarchy, the Royal Navy and the Empire to the Protestant Ascendancy, the Industrial Revolution, Parliament and Sterling – indicated that all without exception were in decline; some were already defunct, others seriously diminished or debilitated; it suggests that the last act may come sooner rather than later.[110] Nothing implies that the end will necessarily be violent; some political organisms dissolve quietly. All it means is that present structures will one day disappear, and be replaced by something else.

The contending forces of centralization and decentralization have ebbed and flowed in modern British history like the tides of the sea. The Home Rule Bill for Ireland (1912) was matched by a Scottish Home Rule Bill (1914); both suffered the same fate, because the Great War demanded the tightening of ties to the imperial government in London. Lloyd George, one of Britain's wartime prime ministers, had started his career calling for Welsh Home Rule and working for an organization, *Cymru Fydd* or 'Young Wales', that also faded. But the Armistice was followed in the inter-war period by the opposite tendency. Ireland's secession from the United Kingdom was accompanied by the founding in 1920 of the Scottish National League, the forerunner of the Scottish National Party (SNP), and in 1925 of *Plaid Cymru* in Wales; as we have seen, Home Rule for Northern Ireland began to operate in 1921.

The Second World War reinvigorated the centre, only to be followed once again by a centrifugal surge. Ireland's exit from the Commonwealth in 1949 formed part of the general retreat from Empire; the outbreak of the Troubles in Northern Ireland in 1969 coincided with a phase when the SNP and Plaid Cymru had been winning their first seats in Westminster, where they joined the Ulster Unionists in a spectrum of regional parties. As half a century earlier, when Constance Markiewicz had been elected the first British woman MP, Sinn Féin refused to take the oath to the Crown or to occupy the seats it had won. Yet the tide was already on the turn when the British government ceded referendums on devolution in Scotland and Wales in 1979, and defeat of the devolutionists preceded twenty years of respite.[111]

The demands from the 'UK's regions' inexorably built up again in the 1990s, and immediately after their general election victory in 1997 the 'Scotto-Brits' of New Labour introduced a devolved parliament and government in Edinburgh for Scotland, a devolved Assembly and Executive in Cardiff for Wales, and proposals for similar devolved arrangements in Northern Ireland.[112] They had come together under the late John Smith, MP for North Lanarkshire and leader of the Labour Party 1992–4, in circumstances making them acutely conscious of the electoral threat to the Scottish Labour Party from the SNP; they understood far better that any English politicians that the interplay of Westminster politics with that of the new 'regional centres' was becoming a key feature of the overall system. Under Tony Blair in 1997–2007 and Gordon Brown in 2007–10, they stayed loyal to their devolutionary principles, but took no steps either to apply them to the regions within England or to create a devolved English legislature. Their hesitations have left the political architecture of the United Kingdom in the early twenty-first century inherently unbalanced. Scotland, Wales and Northern Ireland cannot develop any sense of equality with their overmighty English partner; and the English have little incentive to address the inbuilt instability. The kingdom is not well prepared for the next turn of the tide; resentments grow, and solidarity is sapped.

The introduction of self-government undoubtedly deflates centrifugal pressures, and wins time for re-consolidation. But the history of other empires that decided to decentralize – like Austria-Hungary after 1867 – proves equally that life in autonomous provinces provides a school for separatists, who see their autonomy as a step towards national independence. (Before 1916, as we saw, Arthur Griffith had been pressing for an Austro-Hungarian solution in Ireland.) The British case is interesting because the united state has always contained within itself three consciously non-English nations, whose tectonic plates have long been drifting away from London's central control. There may be a devolutionary lull, but it will not last for ever. The events of 1998 are still too close to see if devolution – which has a secondary meaning of 'degeneration'[113] – is going to hold up for another generation or not. Time is always the hardest dimension to judge.

Ireland played the key role in the first stage of the United Kingdom's disintegration in 1919–22, and it will no doubt play its part in the stages still to come. It split off in less than ideal circumstances when British imperial confidence was still strong; it took dominion status within the Commonwealth as a stepping stone towards the final shore; and it weathered many adverse forecasts. Yet it held its own, and in due course reached its intended destination. The little boy from the Little Lodge lived to see it pass most of the stops on the way: from Republic to Free State, from Free State back to Republic, and from Commonwealth member to aspirant candidate of the European Economic Community. 'We have always found the Irish a bit odd,' Churchill once remarked, no doubt with a grin. 'They refuse to be English.' Ireland's present financial plight is bad – worse, it is said, than the United Kingdom's – but is unlikely to be terminal given the prop supplied by the Eurozone. Assuming that it recovers, the Republic will again be minded to assist any who contemplate following its lead. For the time being, a significant new factor lies in the rise of the Nationalists in the North and their growing impact on the Republic. In the British general election of 2010, the combined vote of the Unionist parties (DUP plus UUP) fell below that of the combined anti-Unionists (Sinn Féin plus SDLP). Gerry Adams was preparing to present himself not only as the democratic majority leader in the North but also as the only true champion of republicanism in the island as a whole.

However, just as the construction of the British state and nation took place by stages over many years, its deconstruction can only be expected to proceed in like manner – in an extended process involving successive lurches, lulls and landslips. It will also depend on the continued health and strength of the European Union. Would-be separatists in Britain are encouraged by the existence of a European home, where they can take refuge. Yet in the wake of the Lisbon Treaty, the Community is less open to newcomers than previously, and it is far from certain that the EU can continue to drift in its present unwieldy and ineffectual form.[114] The immediate future may be determined by a race between the United Kingdom and the EU over which beats the other to a major crisis.

The fate of the monarchy will inevitably form another element in the drama. The United Kingdom has been a monarchical state from the start, and the weakening or termination of the monarchy must necessarily have far-reaching consequences. Most analysts, however, do not look beyond the hoary arguments between constitutional monarchy and republicanism.

More recently, the monarchists appeared to have the upper hand, maintaining that the modern monarchy, far from being democracy's enemy, adds stability and legitimacy to the democratic institutions, with which it co-operates.[115] One prominent pundit wrote a book *On Royalty* only to find that he was losing faith in his initial republican sympathies.[116] Criticism is widespread about individual royals, as it is about primogeniture and the exclusion of Catholics, but not about the basic issue of the monarchy's existence. British republicanism remains weak. A campaign group called 'Republic' was founded in 1983, and is frequently asked politely for comments.[117] Its activities have been facilitated by a ruling of the law lords which determined in 2003 that the moribund Treason (Felony) Act could not be invoked against peaceful advocacy of a republic. The realms of possibility do not exclude the chance that the heirs and successors of Elizabeth II might just fall by the wayside without warning; no one who remembers the abdication crisis of 1936 would bet on the monarchy failing to serve up a surprise. But the joyous wedding of Prince William and Kate Middleton in April 2011 seemed to be pointing in the opposite direction, as were the opinion polls.[118] All indications suggested that nothing radical would happen during Elizabeth II's lifetime, and her longevity looked assured.

Yet polls are poor long-term predictors, and in any case the future of the monarchy and the potential break-up of the British state are two very different things. If by some stroke of fortune, the republicans were to prevail, they would rebuild the machinery of government and change the states's name, perhaps to the 'United British Republic'; but the elementary facts of the state's territory, population and make-up would remain intact. Not so if the United Kingdom were to disintegrate, and spawn a series of new sovereign entities from its constituent parts. In the latter case, the monarch of the day would pushed into a choice between retiring gracefully or soldiering on in reduced circumstances. It is perfectly possible to imagine a small group of stoical, diehard royals clinging to the throne, stiffening their upper lips, and watching with noble resignation as their kingdom crumbled around them. That the captain goes down with his ship is an honourable British tradition.

Nonetheless, the monarchy's fate is of secondary significance, if not largely irrelevant to the more profound issue of the state's survival; the United Kingdom will still be facing dissolution whether a king or queen continues to reign or not. Permutations in the most likely sequence of future political landslips are numerous, offering a variety of alternative scenarios. Scotland, almost certainly, will make the first move, although it is not yet ready to do so. The SNP has held the reins of government in Edinburgh from 2009 and openly favours separation; its electoral triumph in May 2011 increased its standing but its further success is dependent on numerous unknowns.[119] Even if it manages to organize a referendum on Scottish independence, it is very unlikely to succeed at the first attempt. It was given a huge boost by the hostile stance of Mrs Thatcher's right-wing regime in the 1980s, and a similar effect could be forecast if Westminster were to revert to a Thatcherite position. As matters stand, they were complicated in 2010 by the formation of a British coalition government of Conservatives and Liberal Democrats, who were less abrasive than a straight Tory administration might have been. The Liberal Democrats, in particular, had still to prove whether they could salvage a support-base in Scotland.[120] If they fail, the British government will be dependent for the first time ever on almost exclusively English representation.

Even so, the long-term trends are clear enough. English resentment against the 'peripheries' is sure to balloon in times of austerity, boosting support for specifically English-orientated organizations like the Campaign for an English Parliament[121] or, on the right-wing fringe, the English Defence League;[122] this resentment as much as Scottish nationalism will be decisive in driving the Scots from the Union. What exactly will trigger the breach can only be imagined, but the ongoing problems of the euro conjure up some menacing perspectives. If the bail-out of Ireland in 2010, which cost 85 billion euros, were to be followed by a more costly emergency in a much larger country like Spain or Italy, one can well postulate that the British government would refuse to contribute; and in the ensuing fracas, it would reasonable to expect that a body of English Eurosceptics would seize the opportunity to demand Britain's withdrawal from the EU. Such a demand could be the match that fires the keg. The Europhile Scots, the Europhile Welsh and the Europhile Irish would be enraged. If the SNP were to stage its referendum at a juncture when voting for Scottish independence was posed in terms of leaving the United Kingdom but staying in the EU, the SNP's chances of winning would be greatly enhanced. If they won, the Act of Union would be revoked; Scotland would take its place alongside Ireland as a sovereign member of the EU, and the United Kingdom as we know it would disappear. Other Scottish escape routes can be plotted.

When Scotland departs, a crestfallen England – frustrated, diminished and shorn of its great-power pretensions – will be left in the company of two far smaller dependencies. Resultant discomforts will grow sharply. Autonomous Wales will compete with autonomous Northern Ireland to make the next move. Timescales are hard to estimate, but in ten or twenty years' time, political evolution may have progressed further in Ulster than is Wales. Throughout the twentieth century Ulster Unionists could afford to be intransigent, because they possessed a local, democratic majority; in the twenty-first century they will be squeezed by the growing demographic advantage of the Catholic and nationalist community. How will they react? The Protestant heirs of Edward Carson and Ian Paisley are never going to be dragged willingly into the bosom of the Irish Republic, but they will have to compromise; and since they have long viewed Scotland as their ancestral home, they may well seek a rescue through some form of partnership 'across the water', jumping before they are pushed. Difficult adjustments would be necessary on all sides; the Irish counties may have to be repartitioned, and sectarian sensitivities calmed. European mediators may play a part. But a generation that has grown up in peace will strain every sinew to avoid a return to the Troubles. And once the Anglo-Scottish union has been broken, the environment for Belfast, Dublin and Edinburgh to seek a common destiny will be much improved.

That would leave Wales standing alone with England. Nothing could be more conducive to a sharpening of Welsh political instincts, to demands in Cardiff for further devolution and to a comprehensive rapprochement between 'Welsh Wales' and South Wales. The English would be losing heart; the Red Dragon's departure would only be a matter of time. The Welsh, who once were the original Britons, would end up being the last of the Britons.

If by any chance the monarchy were to keep functioning, it would be obliged to readapt its titles to each successive shift. When Scotland leaves the United Kingdom, 'Great Britain' will be dropped from the royal title, which will change perhaps to the neologism of 'kings (or queens) of England, Wales and Northern Ireland'. When Northern Ireland leaves, the title could revert to that of 'kings (or queens) of England and Wales', as under Henry VIII in 1536. If a monarch were still in post when Wales leaves, he or she will be back to being 'king (or queen) of England'. This is a title which many misguided English subjects believe to have been current all along. It would not apply, of course, if an English Republic had been declared in the meantime, or if at some point the House of Windsor had morphed into the House of Balmoral and had mounted the Scottish throne.

As ever, when a political community dissolves, the residue will include a collection of songs, and of emotions which the songs embody. The key emotion will be nostalgia, that is, a wistful sentiment inspired by loss, the pain of being separated from one's home. Nothing is more powerfully nostalgic than the words and haunting melody of Ireland's most deservedly famous song:

> Oh, Danny boy, the pipes, the pipes are calling
> From glen to glen, and down the mountain side.
> The summer's gone, and all the roses falling.
> 'Tis you, 'tis you must go, and I must bide.
>
> But come ye back, when summer's in the meadow,
> Or when the valley's hushed and white with snow.
> 'Tis I'll be there, in sunshine or in shadow.
> Oh, Danny boy, oh Danny boy, I love you so![123]

Saturated with 'Celtic melancholy', these words were written, surprisingly and appropriately, by an Englishman.[124] The melody, the incomparable 'Londonderry Air', is classed as Irish Traditional.

ÉIRE

59. The 'Black and Tans': Royal Irish Constabulary Reserve Force, 1920, during the Anglo-Irish War.

0. The Anglo-Irish Treaty signed y Michael Collins, December 921.

61. Irish women singing hymns and political songs under guard in Dublin, 1921.

2. Eamon de Valera takes the lute at an IRA parade, 1922, uring the Irish Civil War.

63. King George V and Queen Mary, monarchs of Great Britain and Ireland, ride through Kingstown (now Dun Laoghaire), July 1911.

64. The Imperial Conference, London, 1926. George V and his prime ministers; W. T. Cosgrave of the Irish Free State (*back row, right*).

65. Queen Elizabeth II, Queen of Great Britain and Northern Ireland, speaking three words of Gaelic in Dublin Castle, watched closely by the Irish Republic's *taoiseach*, Enda Kenny, and President Mary McAleese: May 2011, one century after her grandfather's visit.

66. (*left*) British stamps of 1912 bearing the head of King George V, overprinted in Gaelic. (a) 'Provisional Government of Ireland 1922' during the currency of the Republic, and (b) 'Irish Free State 1922' after the Anglo-Irish Treaty came into force.

(a)   (b)

67. (*right*) Irish Free State, First Series, 1922, 1d Red. Although George V remained king, the design omits both the king's head and the new state's name, showing instead a map of all Ireland and the unofficial name of Éire.

68. (*left*) Latin was admissible, but not English. (a) The International Eucharistic Congress, 1932, and (b) The Holy Year of 1933–4: 'In the Cross is Salvation'.

(a)   (b)

(a)   (b)

69. (*above*) Postage stamps in the service of republican history – (a) 2p, mauve, 1937. 'The constitution of Ireland', which officially introduced the name of Éire – Hibernia turns the pages of history; (b) 2½p black, 1941. twenty-fifth anniversary of the Easter Rising: a volunteer before Dublin's General Post Office.

70. (*right*) The centenary of the late President's birth, 1982: 26p commemorative issue, 'Eamon de Valera, 1882–1975'.

73. King Nikola in exile: Antibes, France, *c.* 1921. Montenegro, after annexation by Serbia, was the only Allied country to lose its independence after the First World War.

MONTENEGRIN POSTAL HISTORY

74. (*above left*) 3 nović red, from the country's first issue in 1874; (*below left*) 1 nović blue and brown from the 200th anniversary series, 1896.

75. Stamps celebrating the fiftieth year of Nikola's reign and the Proclamation of the Kingdom, 1910. (*left*) 1 para black, Nikola *magnoludovicien*; (*centre*) 2 para purple, King Nikola and Queen Milena; (*right*) 5 para green, the King on horseback.

76. *Kalevipoeg*, 'The Son of Kalevi' Estonia's foundation myth.

77. The *Pronkssödur* or 'Bronze Soldier': a Soviet war memorial, whose removal to a war cemetery in Tallinn caused the cyber war of 2007.

78. The pre-war Linda Monument: used in Soviet times as an unofficial memorial site for Estonians killed or deported by Stalin.

79. Red Army cavalry enters Tallinn. The forces of the Soviet Union occupied Estonia twice, in 1940–41 and for a second time between 1945 and 1991.

80. A Latvian battalion of the Waffen SS marches through Tallinn. The forces of the Third Reich occupied Estonia from July 1941 to September 1944.

81. The Baltic Chain, 23 August 1989, marking the fiftieth anniversary of the Nazi–Soviet Pact: two million protesters link hands over the 350 miles from Estonia to Latvia and Lithuania.

82. Moscow, August 1991: Mikhail Gorbachev, secretary general of the Soviet Communist Party and president of the USSR, is publicly berated by Boris Yeltsin, president of the RSFSR (Soviet Russia). Fifteen Soviet republics, including Russia, were starting out on their road to sovereign independence, and the Soviet Union was about to vanish.

15

CCCP

*The Ultimate Vanishing Act
(1924–1991)*

I

Estonia reaches the world headlines only sporadically. It did so in 1994, when a sea-going ferry sank in the night in the Gulf of Finland with the loss of nearly a thousand lives, and it did so again in April 2007. On the latter occasion, the Estonian government had ordered the removal of a war memorial from the centre of the capital to a suburban cemetery. The result was violent rioting, followed by a strange episode that some commentators called 'the world's third cyber war', organized, or so it appeared, by or from the country's largest neighbour.* A very tiny flea had somehow enraged a very big bear.

Estonia joined the European Union in 2004. One of ten new member states, it was one of three entrants which, until recently, had formed part of the Soviet Union. Its accession substantially extended the EU's frontier with Russia that had first come into being to the north of St Petersburg, Russia's second city, as a result of Finland's accession in 1995.

Estonia, 17,370 square miles in area, is twentieth in size of the EU's present member states, larger than Denmark but smaller than Slovakia. In terms of population, with 1.3 million inhabitants, it ranks twenty-fourth, between Cyprus and Slovenia.[1] Its culture and history are nearest to those of its northern neighbour, Finland, from which it is separated by an arm of the Baltic Sea. Its name for itself, as seen on its postage stamps, is *Eesti*, which derives from a Scandinavian label given to the peoples of the eastern Baltic, and which even appears in Tacitus.

The Estonian language belongs to the Finno-Ugrian group; apart from Finnish, it has no major close linguistic relatives in Europe (its other

* The first cyber war was fought in 1998 between NATO and Serbia, the second in 2006 by Israel and Hisbollah.

geographical neighbours – Swedish, Latvian and Russian – are Indo-
European). It owes its origin to a prehistoric migration from western
Siberia, where other Ugric peoples still survive. Its sound system is characterized by an unusual triple gradation of phoneme length – short,
long and overlong. Its morphology, like that of Turkish or Hungarian, is
'agglutinative', meaning that simple verbal units are often 'glued
together' to form lengthy compounds; its orthography has been adapted
since the seventeenth century to the Latin alphabet. It has three main
dialects – one connected with Tallinn; another with Tartu; and a third
called *Kirderannikumurre* based on the north-east coastland. The final
amalgam is almost totally incomprehensible to the outside world. The
opening sentence of the Universal Declaration of Human Rights in
Estonian reads '*Kõik inimesed sünnivad vabadena ja võrdsetena oma*

väärikuselt ja õigustelt' ('All people are born free and equal in their dignity and rights').[2]

Tallinn, the capital, is a Baltic port city of some 400,000 people. Its name is usually explained by the phrase '*Taani-linna*', meaning 'Danish castle', which reflects the fact that it was long dominated by foreign seafarers, while the Estonians lived primarily in the interior. (For much of its long history, it was best known by its German, Swedish, Russian and Danish name of Reval.) There are three distinct quarters. The *Toompea* or *Domberg*, 'Cathedral Hill', was formed round the original medieval fortress built in 1219; the Lower City crowds round the port area; and the outer suburbs developed in the nineteenth and twentieth centuries when rural Estonians moved in to work in the city's expanding industries. The ethnic breakdown of the citizens (2007) indicates 54.9 per cent Estonians, and 42 per cent Slavs, mainly Russian. These figures are very different from those of the period immediately before 1940, when few Russians but many Germans were present.[3]

Travel to Estonia is easy, either by air to Tallinn, by ferry from Helsinki, or by rail from Riga or St Petersburg. The country has become something of a Mecca for the adventurous traveller who wants to explore unfamiliar places that until recently were completely out of bounds. The tourist brochures recommend a combination of sightseeing in Tallinn and Tartu and of communing with nature in the many forests, lakes and islands. The Toompea castle, the Toomkirik church and the medieval ramparts top the sightseeing list in Tallinn. The summer Estonian Song Festival is a big draw to Tartu, which is also a university town. The Lahemaa National Park lies only 30 miles east of Tallinn along the coast. Bear, moose, boar and wolves roam the woods. Fishing for northern pike or eel, or bird-watching along the expansive shore of Lake Peipus, offer unusual experiences. Beach-walking at Pirita or Pärnu can be exhilarating.[4]

The walk up Cathedral Hill in Tallinn reveals many layers of history. Once the northernmost member of the Hanseatic League, the city passed through phases of rule by Denmark, the Teutonic Order, Sweden and, from 1721, the Russian Empire. The sixty-six towers of the heavily fortified walls indicate how successive governors valued their prize. The slender spire of St Olav's, once the tallest in Europe, belongs to the late medieval period before the arrival of Lutheranism. Yet it is striking that the prime location at the top of the hill continues to be dominated by the Russian Orthodox church of St Alexander Nevsky, which overshadows the Lutheran cathedral and which was completed in the last years of tsarist rule. A plan in 1924 to demolish this exuberant symbol of foreign power was not carried out by Estonia's first independent government; in the 1990s, following Estonia's second independence, it has been meticulously restored.

As an ex-Soviet state, Estonia naturally takes pride in its multi-party parliamentary democracy introduced after the constitutional referendum of 1992, and in its free-market economy. The present prime minister, Andrus Ansip (b. 1956), head of the Reform Party and a former mayor of Tartu, has run a coalition government since 2005. The president, Toomas Hendrik Ilves (b. 1953), born in Sweden and educated in the United States, a former foreign minister, was elected in 2006. The Bertelsmann Transformation Index places Estonia first out of fifteen 'post-Soviet states' in its final, weighted average for all-round political, economic and social performance.[5]

Controversies arise, as in any democracy. In March 2010 several newspapers printed blank pages in protest against a government bill requiring journalists to disclose their sources of information in certain well-defined areas. *Pravda* in Moscow regarded the bill as outrageous and Estonian democracy 'a profanation'. 'The level of democracy there is similar to that of ancient Athens,' *Pravda*'s correspondent commented; 'it's democracy for the privileged.'[6] This view may be compared with that of the Press Freedom Global Rankings (2009). Estonia with a status of 'Free' comes 6th out of 175, higher than both the United Kingdom and the United States; Russia with a status of 'Not Free' comes 153rd.[7]

Surprisingly perhaps, the aspect of life in Estonia which many choose to praise is not democracy, sightseeing or communing with nature, but the electronic revolution. Tallinn, the home of Kazaa and Skype, is publicized as the 'super-connected capital' and the 'champion of the digital age':

Estonia has broken free from its Eastern bloc shackles to emerge anew as European champion of the digital age ... In Tallinn free internet access is taken for granted and the acceptance of digital ID cards has opened up a world of mobile phone-enabled e-commerce. Not only do Estonians buy lottery tickets, annual travel passes, and beer at a concert via SMS, they also carry out the majority of their banking transactions electronically ...

Practising what they preach, the country's leaders have also embraced wireless technology; documents are reviewed from internet terminals and laptops provided in parliament. Laws are filed electronically ... The public can access draft laws and minutes from parliamentary debates online ...

Estonia became the first nation to allow electronic voting for parliamentary elections in 2007 . . .

It's little wonder, then, that the world's most talented young IT professionals have flocked to Estonia's capital to establish e-businesses. It's quite a transformation . . . 'Back in 1991, Estonia wanted to be the best in something, and it seized the opportunity with IT.'[8]

In January 2009 Tallinn was named as one of the world's top seven 'Intelligent Communities'.[9]

Nevertheless, visitors to Estonia will soon encounter the strong attachment to folk culture, and to the feeling that land and people are one. A nation which lived for centuries on the edge of civilization and which had no name for itself other than *maarahvas*, meaning 'locals', has been deeply impressed by the age-old struggle for survival and identity. Before the nineteenth century, there was little written literature, and, exactly as in Finland, the movement of national awakening was launched by writers who collected oral legends and transposed them into modern imitations of what they imagined to be ancient poetry. In Finland, the task was undertaken by Elias Lönnrot (1802–84), author of the world-famous *Kalevala*, and in Estonia by his exact contemporary, Friedrich Reinhold Kreutzwald (1803–82), author of the *Kalevipoeg* or *Kalevide* (1853), the 'Son of Kalev'. Both men were country physicians, and neither, despite their German names, was German. Kreutzwald's parents had been serfs. He himself had been a village schoolteacher before qualifying in medicine. He only took up the challenge of reconstructing the tales of Kalev and Linda after his colleague, Dr Faehlmann, the original pioneer, died young.

Kreuzwald's *Kalevipoeg* is universally regarded in Estonia as the national epic. It recounts the adventures of the giant Soini in 19,000 verses arranged in twenty cantos, which to outsiders (except perhaps Finns) are written in pure gobbledegook:

> *Sõua, laulik, lausa suuga,*
> *Sõua laululaevakesta,*
> *Pajataja paadikesta –*
> *Sõua neid senna kaldale,*
> *Kuhu kotkad kuldasõnu,*
> *Kaarnad hõbekuulutusi,*
> *Luiked vaskseid luaastusi*
> *Vanast ajast varistanud,*
> *Muiste päivist pillutanud . . .*[10]

According to tradition, Kalev and his spouse Linda were regarded as the protoplasts of the modern nation; and their story is told to every Estonian child:

> Kalev foretold the glory and greatness of [their] last son to Linda, indicating [Soini], still unborn, as his heir, and shortly after fell dangerously sick.
>
> Then Linda took her brooch, and spun it round on a thread, while she sent forth the Alder-Beetle . . . to beseech the aid of the Moon. But the Moon only gazed on him sorrowfully . . .
>
> Again Linda spun the brooch and sent forth the beetle . . . as far as the Gold Mountain, till he encountered the Evening Star, but he also refused him to answer.
>
> Next time, the beetle took a different route, over wide heaths and thick fir-woods till he met . . . the rising sun. [And], on a fourth journey, [he] encountered the Wind-Magician, the old Soothsayer from Suomi, the great Necromancer himself. But they replied with one voice that . . . what the moonlight had blanched . . . could never bloom again. And before the beetle returned from his fruitless journey, the mighty Kalev had expired.
>
> Linda sat weeping by his bedside without food or drink for seven days and seven nights, and then began to prepare [him] for burial. First she bathed him with her tears, then with salt water from the sea, rain water from the clouds, and lastly water from the spring. Then she smoothed his hair with her fingers, and brushed it with a silver brush, and combed it with a golden comb . . . She drew on him a silken shirt, a satin shroud, and a robe confined with a silver girdle. She dug his grave herself, thirty ells beneath the sod, and grass and flowers soon sprang from it.

> From the grave the grasses sprouted,
> And the herbage from the hillock;
> From the dead man dewy grasses,
> From his cheeks grew ruddy flowers,
> From his eyes there sprang the harebells,
> Golden flowerets from the eyelids . . .

> Linda mourned Kalev for three months and more . . . / She heaped a cairn of stones over his tomb, / which formed the hill where / the Cathedral of [Tallinn] now stands . . . The Upper Lake, on Tallinn's inland side, was said to be formed from Linda's tears.[11]

If the folk legends of the Baltic region occupy the most distant part of Estonia's timeline, the most recent period is taken up with the Soviet years of 1940–91. Many foreign observers will find much to admire in current efforts to cope with the Soviet legacy. The Russian Federation, a fellow post-Soviet state, is 358 times Estonia's size, and to keep an even keel in the turbulent wake of the giant neighbour demands great skill and nerve.

The strategy of the Estonian government is based on membership of two international organizations, the European Union and NATO, which provide a measure of political, economic and military security that Estonia on its own could not dream of. Many people in the West are not always aware that Russia still upholds the concept of the 'near-abroad', that is, an extraterritorial sphere of influence in which Moscow feels entitled to interfere.

The Museum of Occupations, opened in 2003, is the product of an information policy that is calmly undermining the shibboleths of the Soviet era. The name says it all. Estonia in the Second World War suffered invasions both by the Nazis and by the Soviets, and large numbers of citizens were killed by each set of invaders. It is a vital service to historical truth, therefore, that the word 'occupation', with all the terrible things it implies, be employed in its plural form. To the Soviet mind-set, as to the present-day Kremlin, this simple rectification of the historical record is anathema. In Soviet usage, as in that of many Britons and Americans, the negative word 'occupation' is applied exclusively to the misdeeds of the Nazis, while all actions of the anti-fascist alliance are referred to as 'liberation'.[12]

Rectifying the history books is equally necessary. In 1998 the Estonian president convened an International Commission for the Investigation of Crimes against Humanity, which has produced a huge volume of 1,337 pages chronicling the basic facts of the wartime experience.[13] The book's cover shows a Nazi swastika and a Soviet Red Star both dripping blood. Difficult issues, such as the reasons why different groups of Estonians fought either on the German or on the Soviet side, are confronted. In the realm of film, an Estonian-Canadian has produced an award-winning documentary entitled *Gulag 113* (2005), the name of a Soviet concentration camp near Kotlas in the Arctic, based on personal testimonies.[14]

The 'War of Symbols' has its roots in the baleful legacy of Soviet fictions which modern Estonia constantly seeks to counter. After the Red Army's triumph in 1944–5, like all other 'liberated countries', Estonia was covered by a rash of grandiose monuments hailing Soviet achievements. One of the largest is the *Monument Sovietskiy* at Paldiski, where a Soviet submarine base once functioned. Another, the *Maarjamäe* Memorial by the seaside at Pirata, is a concrete and iron complex surrounding a tall obelisk. An extra spire was added in 1960 to mark Russian soldiers killed in 1918. A third, known as the *Pronkssödur*, or *Bronze Soldier*, stood in the centre of Tallinn until 2007.

It needs to be borne in mind that while the Soviet authorities expended considerable money and energy restoring monuments with Soviet or Russian connections, including the Palace of Catherine the Great at Kadriorg, they forcibly suppressed all memory sites associated with Estonia's own independent history. As a result, the Soviet memorials, which were viewed by Russians as symbols of pride, were viewed by Estonians as symbols of oppression. What is more, having no places to pay respect to their own dead, Estonians were forced to improvise. The pre-war Linda Monument, for example, which depicts the legendary heroine mourning Kalev, took on new connotations during the Cold War. Standing on a street in the Lower City, it became the unofficial site for remembrance of the post-war Stalinist terror. People leaving flowers there risked arrest. Nowadays, a modern plaque reads: 'TO REMEMBER THE PEOPLE WHO WERE TAKEN AWAY'.[15]

In the continuing climate of recrimination, the decision of the Estonian government to relocate the *Bronze Soldier* is variously judged either highly offensive or perfectly reasonable. By Soviet standards, the memorial was a modest one. A six-foot-tall statue, modelled on the figure of a pre-war Olympic wrestler, stood in a thoughtful pose, with bowed head, in front of a simple wall of dolomite stone. The problem lay in its prime location and in the inscription: 'TO THE LIBERATORS OF TALLINN', which the great majority of citizens felt inappropriate. So in April 2007 it was relocated to the war cemetery, to join the Soviet war graves. It was not destroyed or blown up, as some reports insisted, or defaced or banished out of sight.[16] Yet the resultant outburst was immediate and violent. Thousands of ethnic Russians marched on downtown Tallinn, waving Russian flags and shouting anti-Estonian slogans. Rioting raged for two days. Shops were looted and windows smashed; 300 disturbers of the peace were detained.[17]

Not content with the strength of this reaction, Vladimir Putin, president of the Russian Federation, used the occasion of the annual Red Square parade on 9 May to fuel the fire: 'Those who are trying today to desecrate memorials to war heroes are insulting their own people and sowing enmity and new distrust,' he told thousands of veterans and soldiers.[18] Kremlin sources accused Estonia of 'blasphemy' and of 'indulging neo-fascists'. Members of a Kremlin-backed youth movement barricaded the Estonian embassy in Moscow.

Such was the context of the mysterious 'cyber war'. The basic facts are not in dispute. The websites of Estonian government ministries, political parties, newspapers, banks and businesses were disabled by tens of thousands of simultaneous electronic 'hits'. Their servers were swamped, and a domino-style sequence of Distributed Denial of Service (DDS) was triggered: in other words, paralysis. The attacks came in three waves: one starting on 27 April, just after the relocation of the *Bronze Soldier*; a second on 9 May, after Putin's speech; the third a week later. They were on a scale that could only be achieved by mobilizing a worldwide network of up to a million co-ordinated computers which had either been hijacked or rented through the so-called 'botnet' system. Fortunately, as a member of the EU and NATO, Estonia could draw on international assistance, and, with the help of the Asymmetric Threats Contingency Alliance (ATCA), was successful in ending the emergency.[19]

The outstanding question is who was responsible. In talking to the Russian authorities, EU and NATO officials were careful to avoid direct accusations, and Kremlin officials were quick to deny them, suggesting instead that sophisticated Estonian computer specialists had masterminded a cyber offensive against their own government. Many things are possible, but some possibilities are more probable than others, and there are certain similarities between these and other mysterious events such as the murder in London of Russian dissident Alexander Litvinenko in November 2006 by radioactive polonium 210. Very few countries, companies or individuals possess the resources to launch sting operations at $200 million a shot. The cyber offensive against Estonia does not fit into the same category as other known episodes, such as Moonlight Maze (1999), when unidentified hackers penetrated the Pentagon, or Titan Rain (2003), which apparently came out of China, both of which are classed as simple info-gathering, 'phishing' exercises. According to one expert, the sole purpose of repeatedly using a vast stream of ten Mbit/s for ten hours, as occurred in Estonia, is to cripple the victim's infrastructure.[20]

International law was not very helpful. As things stood in 2007, an attack on a member state's communications centre by bombs or missiles would automatically have invoked Article V of the NATO Treaty as an act of war, but an anonymous 'botnet' attack fell into a grey area. It may just be a coincidence that during the attack on Estonia attack the National Center for Supercomputing Applications (NCSA), 'the first line of defence against cyber-terrorism', happened to be holding a conference in Seattle.[21] It may be irrelevant that some attackers could be traced to Internet addresses in Moscow. And it may be true, as one Finnish expert commented, that 'the Kremlin could inflict much more serious cyber-damage if it chose to'. Yet someone, somewhere, was going to extraordinary lengths to send a message.

The Estonian government's determination to press ahead and join the Eurozone as planned on 1 January 2011 can only be seen in the light of the cyber-experience. Sceptical commentators said that it had bought 'the last ticket to the *Titanic*'. The previous year, 2010, had witnessed a major sovereign debt crisis in which the future of the euro was repeatedly called into question. Two countries in the zone, Greece and Ireland, had been forced to accept painful bail-outs, and several others were thought to be teetering on the same brink. It was not a moment of confidence in the euro, yet Estonia did not falter. It had recovered from the global recession, returning to GDP growth at +2.4 per cent after 12 months of headlong fall in 2009 of -13.9 per cent. On New Year's Day, therefore, it became the seventeenth member of the Eurozone; the *kroon* ceased to circulate, being exchanged for euros at the rate of 1E = 15.6466 *krooni*. 'Estonia is too small', said the finance minister, 'to allow itself the luxury of full independence.'[22] The flea, it seemed, was seeking safety in numbers against the unwelcome attentions of the bear.

II

Many myths and misunderstandings persist about Soviet history. As often as not, textbooks state quite inaccurately that the Soviet Union was founded in 1917 by the Bolshevik Revolution. They imply that Lenin's party had been the principal revolutionary force in the Russian Empire and overthrew the tsar, and that the Soviet Union was just a further stage in the seamless continuum of Russia and the Russians. The so-called 'Russian Civil War' is usually presented as a domestic affair, fought out between Russian 'Whites' and Russian 'Reds'. In more recent times, the Russian Federation of Boris Yeltsin and Vladimir Putin is frequently presented not as one of the fifteen post-Soviet states, but rather as the product of a mere change of government, as just the latest variant on the unchanging Russian theme. Some may be surprised to learn, therefore, that the Soviet Union was created on 1 January 1924 and dissolved on 31 December 1991.[23]

In formal terms, the Tsarist Empire of 'all the Russias', which reached its end in February 1917, had been created by Peter the Great in 1721. But Peter's empire prolonged and expanded the political and territorial complex that had been assembled earlier by the grand dukes or 'tsars' of Muscovy. 'The gathering of the lands', a long process whereby Moscow aimed to take control of all the East Slavs, had been proclaimed in the fifteenth century. Expansion across the Urals into Siberia and Central Asia, the largest demographic vacuum on the globe, was launched at the end of the sixteenth century; the conquest of lands in the west and north-west possessed by Sweden and Poland began in the mid-seventeenth. The pace of expansion was relentless. Between 1683 and 1914 it averaged 53 square miles per day, and may be characterized as a case of *bulimia politica*. Despite some regurgitations, the result by the early twentieth century was an imperial domain of unparalleled dimensions in which ethnic Russians represented barely half of the population.[24]

If the Russians constituted the largest of the seventy or so nationalities in the Tsarist Empire, the Estonians were one of the smallest. Like the Finns, they had spent most of modern history within the political sphere of Sweden. Much of their homeland lay within the historic Swedish province of Ingria, or in Livonia; the Russian connection did not impinge until the Russo-Polish and Russo-Swedish wars of relatively recent times. Russia's imperial capital, St Petersburg, was founded in 1703 in a Swedish-Estonian-Finnish district without the slightest reference either to international law or to the local inhabitants. Russia's possession of Estonia was confirmed by the Treaty of Nystadt (1721) at the close of the Great Northern War.

After the emancipation of their serfs under Alexander I – earlier than in Russia as a whole – Estonians rapidly acquired a strong sense of their national identity. As Protestants, they were devoted to education in their own language, and resisted the imposition of Russian. Yet demands for an independent Estonian state only found expression at the turn of the twentieth century, and with very meagre chances of realization. In order to succeed, a very diminutive David would somehow have to challenge a super-colossal Goliath.

To compound these problems, Estonian society had its own internal divisions. The Estonian-speaking majority were mainly rural peasants. The administration was controlled by Russians, while commercial and landowning interests were largely in the hands of Baltic Germans and of

a small Jewish community. The main port, Reval (Tallinn), was especially
lacking in Estonian flavour. The whole country was garrisoned by a
large Russian army.

The condition of the Estonians in the early twentieth century was
conveyed to the world by the *Encyclopaedia Britannica* in bilious tones:

> The Esths, Ehsts, or Esthonians, who call themselves Tallopoeg and
> Maamees, are known to the Russians as Chukhni or Chukhontsi, to the
> Letts as Iggauni, and to the Finns as Virolaiset. They belong to the Finnish
> family, and consequently to the Ural-Altaic division of the human race.
> Altogether they number close upon one million, and are thus distributed:
> 365,959 in Esthonia (in 1897), 518,594 in Livonia, 64,116 in the govern-
> ment of St. Petersburg, 25,458 in that of Pskov, and 12,855 [elsewhere]. As
> a race they exhibit manifest evidences of their Ural-Altaic or Mongolic
> descent in their short stature, absence of beard, oblique eyes, broad face,
> low forehead and small mouth. In addition, they are an under-sized, ill-
> thriven people, with long arms and thin, short legs. They cling tenaciously
> to their native language, which is closely allied to the Finnish . . . Since 1873
> the cultivation of their mother tongue has been sedulously promoted by an
> Esthonian Literary Society (*Eesti Korjameeste Selts*), which publishes *Toime-
> tused*, or 'Instructions' on all sorts of subjects. They have a decided love of
> poetry, and exhibit great facility in improvising verses and poems on all
> occasions, and they sing, everywhere, from morning to night . . .

One can easily imagine a Victorian empire-builder describing the Welsh or
the Irish in similarly dismissive style. Astonishingly, the author goes on to
express the opinion that Estonia's lot had improved through Russification:

> Since 1878, however, a vast change for the better has been effected in their
> economic position . . . The determining feature of their recent history has
> been the attempt made by the Russian government (since 1881) and the
> Orthodox Greek Church (since 1883) to russify and convert the inhabitants
> of the province . . . by enforcing the use of Russian in the schools and by
> harsh and repressive measures aimed at their native language.[25]

In all probability, these words reflect the views of a Russian contributor,
Prince Piotr Kropotkin.

The encyclopedia's account of Estonia's capital puts a heavy accent
on its Russian and German connections:

> REVAL, or REVEL (Russ. *Revel*, formerly *Kolyvañ*; Esthonian, *Tallina*
> and *Tannilin*), a fortified seaport town of Russia . . . situated on . . . the gulf

of Finland, 230 m. W. of St. Petersburg by rail. Pop by nail. (1900) 66,292, of whom half were Esthonians and 30% Germans. The city consists of two parts – the Domberg or Dom, which occupies a hill, and the lower town on the beach. The Dom contains the castle (first built in the 13th century . . .), where the provincial administration has its seat, and an [Orthodox] cathedral (1894–1900) with five gilded domes . . . The church of St. Nicholas, built in 1317, contains many antiquities . . . and old German paintings. The Dom church contains . . . the graves of the circumnavigator Baron A. J. von Krusenstern (1770–1846), of the Swedish soldiers Pontus de la Gardie (d. 1585) and Carl Horn (d. 1601), and of the Bohemian Protestant leader Count Matthias von Thurn (1580–1640) . . .

The oldest church is the Esthonian, built in 1219. The public institutions include a good provincial museum of antiquities; an imperial palace, Katharinenthal, built by Peter the Great in 1719; and very valuable archives, preserved in the town hall (14th century). The pleasant situation of the town attracts thousands of people for seabathing. It is the seat of a branch board of the Russian admiralty and of the administration of the Baltic lighthouses. Its port . . . freezes nearly every winter.[26]

*

The break-up of the Tsarist Empire began during the First World War, two years before the Russian revolutions of 1917. In the summer of 1915, German forces broke through Russian lines on the Eastern Front, and occupied large swathes of imperial territory, from Poland and Lithuania in the north to Ukraine in the south. Russian counter-offensives failed, arousing much anger. In February 1917 the tsar was overthrown and imprisoned by his own courtiers, and his autocratic regime replaced by constitutionalists who formed a provisional government. But in November 1917* the provisional government, headed by the socialist Alexander Kerensky, was overthrown by Lenin's Bolsheviks, a smaller but more ruthless socialist faction, in what was effectively a *coup d'état*. Constitutional socialists were replaced by totalitarian socialists (and to add extra irony, Kerensky's father had once been Lenin's headmaster). In their origins, the Bolsheviks had been part of the clandestine Russian Social Democratic Party, but after seizing power they broke with all

---

* Owing to tsarist Russia's use of the Julian Calendar, the 'October Revolution' actually took place on 7 November 1917 (New Style). To bring Russia into line with the rest of Europe, a Bolshevik decree abolished the Julian Calendar one month later; 17 December 1917 (Old Style) was inmediately followed the next day by 1 January 1918 (New Style).

their former comrades, like the Mensheviks, and treated them with the same absolute disdain that characterized their dealings with all opponents.* In March 1918, at Brest-Litovsk, they were forced to make peace with Germany, and to abandon most of the territory which the Germans had occupied since the outbreak of war. (see p. 378 above).

As self-proclaimed internationalists, Lenin and his circle were not especially interested in frontiers and territory. They believed that all such matters would be sorted out amicably once the international revolution had destroyed all existing regimes and had joined up with fraternal proletarians in foreign countries. Two events, however, intervened. The first was the outbreak of the Russian Civil War, in which the infant power of the Bolshevik 'Reds' was contested by a variety of adversaries, usually called 'Whites' but made up of conservatives, non-Bolshevik leftists and non-Russian nationalists. The second was the revolt of the many non-Russian nationalities, all of whom chose to break free and to form their own national republics. In 1918–19, therefore, the Bolsheviks' area of control, which is best called Soviet Russia, covered only a fraction of the former Tsarist Empire.† The tasks of the Red Army were threefold: to secure the Russian heartland; to reconquer the breakaway national republics; and to march into Central Europe to provoke the prophesied international revolution.[27]

The Bolsheviks' bid to engineer revolution throughout Europe by force was launched in 1920, but failed miserably. Lenin on this occasion was the enthusiast, and Leon Trotsky, as commissar for war, despite his reputation, the sceptic.[28] The Red Army marched westwards in May, naming its destination as Berlin or even Paris. They didn't get past Warsaw. They were badly beaten in August by the army of the Polish Republic – one of the breakaway national states, which had no desire to return to Russian rule, Red or White.[29] From then on, the Bolshevik leaders had to think more seriously about organizing and centralizing power in the lands that they actually controlled.

The overall performance of the Red Army in those years was very erratic. Finland, the Baltic States and Poland were not brought under Soviet

---

* The Bolsheviks described themselves by the formula of Russian Social Democratic Workers Party (Bolsheviks), usually reduced to RSDRP(b). Like most of the contorted acronyms of the revolutionary period, this name was repeatedly altered.
† The official name was the Russian Soviet Federative Socialist Republic (RSFSR). Many Westerners, who grew accustomed to the name of Soviet Russia in this initial period, continued to apply it inappropriately after 1924 to the wider Soviet Union, of which the RSFSR was only one part.

control. But Byelorussia, Ukraine and the vast expanses of Siberia, south-ern Russia and the Far East were reconquered. So, too, was the Caucasus. Many parts of Central Asia were still being contested in the mid-1920s.

In 1922, however, Lenin suffered a series of strokes and Joseph Stalin emerged as general secretary of the ruling Bolshevik Party. He rejected Lenin's internationalist priorities, and launched the policy of 'Socialism in One Country'. His purpose was to postpone foreign adventures while building up political, economic and military power. Such was the context for the formation of a Soviet Union. The Bolshevik Party had no inten-tion of relinquishing its dictatorial hold on power, but its doctrine of the 'Party-State' permitted the organization of a number of nominally autonomous but dependent republics; answering to the central Party dic-tatorship, these republics were also to be joined in federal union. The plans were passed by the Supreme Soviet in December 1923 and put into effect on the first day of the following year.[30] The name of the new fed-eral state was to be the Union of Soviet Socialist Republics, USSR in short: in transliterated Russian, '*Soyuz Sovetskikh Sotsialisticheskikh Republik*', or *SSSR*. The acronym written in Cyrillic was 'CCCP'.

Moscow thereupon became the dual capital both of the Soviet Union and of Soviet Russia. The All-Union government and the subsidiary government of the RSFSR were separate bodies, staffed by different officials. Even so, political power continued to be concentrated, as always, not in Soviet state structures but in the parallel organs of the dictatorial Bolshevik Party, which oversaw the work of all other institu-tions. In 1925, the Bolsheviks changed their name once more to 'All-union Communist Party' (*Vsesoyuznaya Komunistichestkaya Partiya*, or VKP). The VKP's general secretary, Joseph Stalin, the supreme dictator, saw no need to appoint himself to subordinate positions such as president or prime minister of the USSR. The inner sanctum of power was located in Stalin's office in the VKP's headquarters in the Kremlin.

The events that unfolded in Estonia during those same years combined to bring about a result that few would have thought possible, namely, the declaration of Estonia's independence. During the First World War the German army had in 1915–16 swept into the Baltic provinces of the Rus-sian Empire in, fatally weakening tsarist power in ways that the local population could never have achieved on its own. The Germans encour-aged the national aspirations of non-Russian peoples, and in some places such as Lithuania and Ukraine, they actively supported moves to create sovereign republics. They occupied Reval and Dorpat (Tartu), but stopped short of Petrograd (as St Petersburg had recently been renamed).

In March 1917 the Russian provisional government proclaimed its intention of continuing the war against Germany and of reuniting the Russian Empire. To counter this policy, the Bolsheviks called for peace, and for the recognition of the national rights of all subject peoples. Estonia, on the doorstep of revolutionary Petrograd, was inevitably excited by the passions of the day. The Baltic Germans were at best unsure. During the civil war which followed, Estonia was the scene of several multi-sided conflicts. It provided the base for one of the 'White' armies attacking Bolshevik Petrograd. At the same time, it witnessed a complicated civil war of its own, in which Bolshevik sympathizers, Estonian national patriots and the German *Baltikum* army struggled to gain supremacy.

Seen from the Estonian perspective, the key events in that turbulent period were the granting of autonomy to Estonia in March 1917, following a mammoth demonstration in Petrograd, and the peace treaty with Soviet Russia in February 1920. Kerensky, the head of the provisional government, was a liberal and favoured self-government of the non-Russian provinces, which he wanted to keep loyal for the continuing war effort. So on 30 March 1917 a decree was passed consolidating all Estonian-inhabited districts into one province, and authorizing the formation of an administrative executive and a parliament, the *Maapäev*.[31]

In the summer of 1917, however, the provisional government in Petrograd started to lose control. The Bolsheviks were undermining stability in the country and the Germans were advancing up the Baltic coast. At this juncture, an Estonian radical, Jaan Tõnisson, proposed the creation of a Northern Union of all the Baltic countries, including Finland. The goal, as yet out of reach, was independent statehood. 'We can't stand by while our fate is left to the mercy of others,' he declared. 'It's now, or never.'[32]

When the Bolshevik coup occurred in November 1917, therefore, an Estonian independence movement was already in existence; and on the following 24 February, the country's future National Day, a declaration of independence was promulgated in Tallinn.[33] It had little prospect of general acceptance: it was opposed by local Communists, who among other things had set up a Soviet mini-republic on the island of Naissaar off Tallinn; all was soon overturned by the extension northwards of the area of German occupation, the *Ober Ost*. The Germans were not welcomed with any enthusiasm, but their presence at least blocked a possible Bolshevik takeover; the Estonian Committee of National Salvation, which had issued the declaration, was forced underground and its emissary to Finland captured by the Germans and shot. Recognition by the Western Allies did not materialize until May. At this stage, however, the Bolsheviks' stance towards breakaway republics was still ambiguous; in some places, notably in Ukraine and the Caucasus, they were crushing the separatists by force, but in the Baltic region they refrained from outright denunciations of national movements. On Armistice Day, 11 November 1918, when the Germans laid down their arms, the National Committee resurfaced in Tallinn and reconfirmed their earlier pronouncements.[34]

In Estonian eyes, the War of Independence began at that point. Lenin did not recognize Estonia's freedom; Red Guards overran many districts, and briefly seized Tallinn. The 'Red Terror' was unleashed in support both of social revolution and of Russian control. Many atrocities were perpetrated, and for a time it appeared that the 'Reds' would prevail. Yet Estonian defences held. A small Estonian army, under General Johan Laidoner, used armoured trains to disrupt Bolshevik communications. Britain's Royal Navy landed supplies, and Finnish volunteers crossed the Gulf of Finland. No clear verdict had been achieved when a new enemy appeared in the form of German volunteers, the *Baltikum Landwehr,* marching out of Latvia. Three-sided hostilities persisted until the end of 1919.[35]

By that time, Trotsky's main Red Army was winning the Russian Civil War, and a major attack on Estonia was daily awaited. Yet Lenin's inner circle had other ideas. They had always argued that a proletarian revolution in Russia must necessarily link up with a wider revolution in the major capitalist countries, so now, having secured Russia and set their minds on a strategic offensive through Poland to Germany, they abandoned secondary operations such as the conquest of Estonia. The attack on Narva with 160,000 men had brought no results. It was opportune to sue for peace, and a truce was arranged before Soviet Russian and Estonian negotiators assembled at Tartu.

The Tartu Treaty between Estonia and Soviet Russia was signed on 2 February 1920:

> Russia recognised Estonia's independence, 'giving up of free will and for ever all the sovereign rights that Russia had over the Estonian people and country.' Soviet Russia paid Estonia 15 million gold roubles from the tsarist gold reserves. Under the peace treaty Estonia agreed to disarm the White Russian army on its territory, for which [the] Whites later bitterly reproached [her]. Larger countries were also not enthusiastic . . . According to the western

countries Estonia should have fought Russia until the fall of communism and the restoration of the White government, after which it should have peacefully reunited with Russia. It is understandable that Estonia was not interested in such a future . . .[36]

The dissonance between the interests of small nations and the ideas of Westerners, who pursued stability at anyone's cost but their own, was manifest.

Estonia's independence, therefore, was achieved almost exclusively by Estonian efforts. It had little to do with the Western Powers or their Versailles settlement. What is more, it came about well before the creation of the Soviet Union and the stabilization of Soviet affairs by Joseph Stalin. 'Today Estonia commands its future for the first time,' declared the chief Estonian representative at Tartu, Jaan Poska. But he added: 'The threat has not yet passed.'[37]

Under Stalin's direction, the USSR was transformed in less than two decades from a backward, largely peasant country into a modern power of considerable industrial and military potential. Stalin was driven partly by Communist ideology and partly by memories of the humiliating defeat of the Great War. When he launched his accelerated programme of Five Year Plans and collectivized agriculture in 1929, he said: 'If we don't transform this country in ten years, our enemies will destroy us.'

This socio-economic transformation, however, was achieved through the most appalling cruelty, violence, terror and mass murder. The USSR built the world's first major concentration camp system: the Gulag.[38] Millions died during forced collectivization and during the artificial famine produced in Ukraine.[39] The Communist Party itself was subjected to violent purges and disgraceful show trials, and in the 'Great Terror' of 1937–9 vast numbers of ordinary men and women were simply shot at random to create the ultimate totalitarian climate where no one felt safe. The Soviet economy, which many foreign observers imagined to be a fascinating experiment, was made to work by suppressing all normal human incentives and spontaneous initiatives: 'Stalin built this Brobdingnagian economy on the bones of kulaks and prisoners . . . It was not designed to generate the stream of information necessary for self-regulation, but to respond to orders from the regime. It was an economy planned for total control. But control in the absence of terror cannot be total.'[40] Westerners, distracted by the rise of fascism,

The Baltic States between the wars

FINLAND

Lake Ladoga

SWEDEN

Helsinki

Leningrad

○ Stockholm

Tallinn ○

BALTIC

ESTONIA

Lake Peipus

SEA

Tartu ○

○ Pskov

USSR

○ Riga

LATVIA

Daugavpils ○

Klaipėda ○

LITHUANIA

Kaunas ○

○ Vilnius

Gdynia ○
Danzig ○

○ Königsberg

○ Minsk

EAST PRUSSIA
(to GERMANY)

POLAND

Memelland, occupied by Lithuania 1923,
annexed by Germany in March 1939

Wilno district, annexed by Poland 1922

0   50   100 km

were notoriously slow to recognize the true nature of the USSR. Anyone living in the countries bordering the USSR was likely to be better informed.[41]

Throughout the inter-war period, the Estonian Republic made rapid progress towards the creation of a modern state and society. The Bolshevik model did not appeal. A democratic republican constitution was passed on 15 June 1920. All the national institutions – civil service, education, justice, welfare and armed forces – had to be organized from scratch, and the Estonian language itself had to be adapted. All this, not surprisingly, caused considerable difficulties, not least since the Estonians were used to being governed either in Russian or in German.

After joining the League of Nations in 1920 as a founder member, Estonia gained universal recognition. It played a full part in international trade, in various pan-European cultural projects, and in numerous international bodies from the Red Cross to the International Postal Union. In foreign policy, the Estonian government was naturally drawn to the company of Western democracies, which had championed the cause of national self-determination. As in the parallel case of Finland, considerable tact and restraint had to be exercised so as not to arouse the ire of the giant neighbour.

Yet there were limits to what could be achieved. Communist agitation persisted, despite the Tartu Treaty, and in 1924 Estonia survived a brazen attempt to overthrow it:

> With Comintern's support, the leaders of the putsch received training and equipment in the Soviet Union from where they were then secretly taken to Estonia. The Soviet embassy in Estonia participated actively in the preparations. Military forces were massed on the Estonian borders, and the Red Navy's Baltic Fleet set out to sea. Soviet journalists started a fierce campaign of anti-Estonia propaganda. On December 1, 1924 several hundred insurgents attacked the more important strategic points and military units in Tallinn. Their goal was to take power in the capital for a couple of hours and then send a request for help to the 'friendly' Red Army . . .
>
> However, events did not evolve as planned. At Tondi military school, at the War Ministry, and in many other places the attack was resisted. Attempts to get workers to join the uprising also failed. Fighting groups, some of them spontaneously formed, began to take back sites held by communist attack groups. In this way the unit formed by General Põdder won back the Central Telegraph before a victory call could be sent to the Red Navy waiting for the raid. Within six hours the coup attempt had been put down . . . Some of those captured were executed. Over 20 people died on the Republic's side, civilians among them.[42]

Moscow's intentions had been fully revealed; tensions did not subside until the Soviet Union joined the League of Nations in 1935, after which Moscow adopted the less abrasive concept of an international 'Popular Front' and made a show of co-operating with foreign partners against fascism. It seemed that the ground was being prepared for a programme of collective security, which Estonia could join.

Nonetheless, the attempt to introduce Estonia to Western-style democracy also ran into trouble. A multi-party parliamentary system functioned in the 1920s, but the largest single political group, the Estonian Peasant Party, was inevitably the advocate of sectional interests. The propertied and landed classes, mainly German, who had the upper hand under tsarist rule, felt threatened; and a small pro-Bolshevik minority was raring to denounce the 'bourgeois' state. The financial crisis of 1929–30 caused the collapse of Estonia's main bank, and was followed by severe unemployment. In the political sphere, the populist VAPSI movement (which began as an association of army veterans) gained support, demanding authoritarian government. In 1933 the currency, the *kroon*, had to be devalued; and in the ensuing rumpus, Jaan Tõnisson, now head of state, declared a state of emergency. His desperation opened the door to more unrest, a national referendum, a new constitution and the emergence of an authoritarian regime dominated by the Peasant Party of Konstantin Päts:

> As the new constitution came into force, the first step was the election of a president. Four candidates [competed]: August Rei, Päts, [General] Laidoner, and Vapsi leader A. Larka. In reality only the latter two stood a chance . . . Päts, fulfilling the duties of the head of state, decided not to wait for the election results. He made an agreement with Laidoner and on March 12, 1934 they carried out a coup . . . giving Laidoner extraordinary authority to guarantee the security of the state. Vapsi organisations were closed and their leaders arrested. Elections were postponed . . .
>
> The coup was at first welcomed by a lot of Estonians, but it soon became clear that Päts . . . planned to govern Estonia on the basis of the authoritarian constitution of the Vapses . . . On October 2, 1934 Päts dissolved the parliament, which had been demanding a restoration of democracy, and did not recall it. The silent era, as it became known, started, during which the government curtailed many civil rights . . . On March 5, 1935 the activity of political parties was suspended, the only one that remained being the Fatherland Union (*Isamaaliit*) . . . Silencing the opposition enabled the government to carry out centralised reforms . . .[43]

The Estonian dictatorship of 1935–40 had certainly digressed from the democratic path, but it was not in the same horrific league as that of the totalitarians. One of the last peacetime acts of President Päts was to give amnesty to all political prisoners.

There can be no doubt that the Soviet Union was the largest combatant state in the Second World War in Europe, and that it ended the war as the principal victorious power.[44] In the first phase of the war, during the currency of the Nazi–Soviet Pact, the USSR was the Third Reich's partner, and behaved accordingly. The Red Army participated in the annihilation of Poland,[45] invaded Finland in the Winter War of 1939–40[46] and forcibly annexed the Baltic States, Moldova and Bukovina. In the spring and summer of 1940, the Germans rapidly overran Belgium and northern France in an astonishing blitzkrieg, but throughout the war operations on the Western Front were of little interest and no benefit to Estonia.

In the second phase, which started in June 1941 with 'Operation Barbarossa', the Soviet Union sustained a massive attack by its erstwhile German partner. Few experts gave the Red Army much chance of survival. But it fought on against the odds, manoeuvring in the vast spaces of the Eastern Front, evacuating industry and sacrificing colossal numbers of men. The German invaders were repulsed at Moscow,[47] stopped in their tracks at besieged Leningrad[48] and soundly beaten at Stalingrad.[49]

In the third and conclusive phase, which began with the destruction of Germany's largest Panzer tank force at Kursk in July 1943, the Red Army relentlessly drove the Wehrmacht back.[50] US aid via Lend-Lease came on stream, and the pre-war Soviet frontier was reached a year later. The Soviets moved so much faster than the Western Allies that the whole of Eastern Europe was overrun before Berlin was stormed without Western help.[51] By May 1945, Stalin's victory was complete. At Yalta and Potsdam, he was able to drive a very hard bargain with the Americans, who were still fighting the Japanese. Despite unprecedented losses, which may have reached 27 million, the USSR had emerged as one of the world's two superpowers.[52]

During the Second World War, Estonia found itself in a zone of Europe that was occupied in turn both by the Stalinist Soviets and by the Nazi Germans. The resultant miseries were multiplied by the fact that it lay close to the German–Soviet frontline for three whole years.

In 1939, the secret protocols of the Nazi–Soviet Pact consigned Estonia to the Soviet sphere of influence, where Stalin could act with impunity. Estonians watched helplessly as the Red Army assaulted their Finnish neighbour, and then in June 1940 as it invaded the three Baltic states. In Soviet parlance, this operation was labelled 'liberation', though it involved mass repressions, deportations and massacres. By agreement with the Nazis, Estonia's German community was expelled en masse to German-occupied Poland. That first Soviet occupation of Estonia in

1940–41 was to last for only one year, but it was organized in a manner that smacked of careful planning. It was preceded by a harsh diplomatic campaign, and was facilitated by the expulsion of the Estonian Germans. It was achieved by blackmail and threats, and, technically, by a Council of State that voted obediently for incorporation into the USSR.

The shameless arrogance of Soviet conduct, however, can only be believed if described in detail. Stalin's manipulation of force and fraud was superlative. The opening gambit was to surround Estonia's frontiers with Red Army divisions and to demand, in the name of security, that Soviet military bases be built on Estonian territory. Next, after the Red Army had moved in, it transpired that the Soviet troops had been accompanied by thousands of slave labourers brought in by the NKVD to build the bases. The operation was overseen in person by the notorious Andrei Zhdanov, a member both of Stalin's Politburo and of the Supreme Soviet. In the third stage, Zhdanov delivered the master stroke. The men from the Soviet labour battalions were marched under guard into central Tallinn to lead a 'public demonstration' against the Estonian government and to call for an end to 'bourgeois power'. Appropriate revolutionary placards were distributed for the benefit of the foreign press. Order was maintained by a self-appointed 'People's Self-defence' organization; the Estonian police were warned to stay away. The Estonian tricolour was hauled down from the mast on Toompea hill and replaced by the 'Hammer and Sickle'. The parliament buildings and the president's palace at Kadriorg were taken over, together with the offices of press and radio. Two days later, on 21 June, Zhdanov instructed President Päts whom to appoint as prime minister and whom to dismiss. A month of purges followed. All Estonian institutions, including the civil service and the political parties, were stripped of unsuitable personnel. In the general election of 14–15 July, the 'Union of Working People' claimed a 92.9 per cent victory. The way was open for the declaration of the Estonian Soviet Socialist Republic beneath the portraits of Lenin and Stalin and the gunbarrels of Soviet tanks.[53]

Estonian reactions were recorded by a British diplomat from Moscow. 'The feelings of the Estonian people at present', he noted, 'are a mixture of apathetic resignation to their fate, forlorn hope for an ultimate delivery by Great Britain or Germany, fear of the OGPU [secret police], contempt for their conquerors, and bitter regret that they did not, like the Finns, make a bid for freedom.'[54]

Once incorporation was effected, all existing state institutions were dissolved. The police force was reorganized, and the Estonian army disbanded. All professional associations were banned. The press was censored, and independent journalists dismissed. Sovietization proceeded apace in the economy, in education and in the judicial system. These changes were accompanied by violent repressions. Arrests and interrogations were commonplace. Some cases were tried in court; most were not. Executions were perpetrated in NKVD prisons and in the forests. Mass deportations began, especially of professional people who might rally opposition. The conscription of Estonian men into the Red Army was followed by the evacuation of factories and factory workers to the 'rear areas' deep in Russia.

In the course of several weeks, a fully fledged Soviet system of government was installed and running. The Estonian Soviet Socialist Republic officially came into being on 6 August 1940, but all power was vested in the centralized Communist Party of the Soviet Union and its local appointees. An Estonian Supreme Soviet took the place of the *Maapäev*, and a hand-picked Council of People's Commissars under Johannes Lauristin headed the executive. All local government bodies were Sovietized. There was, however, some resistance: although the Red Army's Winter War against Finland had finished before the Soviet occupation of Estonia began, Finnish sympathies were strongly pro-Estonian, and, with clandestine Finnish help, bands of 'Forest Brothers' conducted a partisan summer war against the occupiers.[55]

In June 1941, following Hitler's dramatic renegation of the Nazi–Soviet Pact, the German Wehrmacht arrived, and turned Estonia into the base area for the long-running Siege of Leningrad. People suspected of collaboration with the recent Soviet regime were rounded up. Those Estonians who welcomed the German occupation, however, mainly did so from relief at seeing the back of Stalin's henchmen. As in other countries occupied by the Third Reich, the Waffen SS established an Estonian Legion for recruits willing to sign on for service on the Eastern Front.

The dilemmas faced by Estonia and other East European countries during the German occupation are rarely understood by Westerners, who have been led to believe that only one 'Evil Force' had to be confronted. In reality, the Germans wielded ruthless power and resistance was near-impossible. There were also sound patriotic reasons for joining the 'war against Bolshevism', particularly after a measure of self-government was introduced, extremely welcome after the preceding 'Great Terror'. In the second half of 1941, therefore, a joyful interlude arrived when the symbols of Soviet oppression were torn down. A series of investigations uncovered the sites of Soviet massacres and executions.

Estonia, like Finland, was needed by Germany for the war against the USSR. Hope rose among Estonians that a bearable modus vivendi would be found.

Nonetheless, the true nature of the Nazi regime quickly became evident. The Gestapo and Security Police (SD) proved themselves the equals of the NKVD. A concentration camp was opened in Tartu, and a new wave of arrests and executions took place. The extermination of Estonia's small community of about 1,000 Jews was perpetrated in January 1942, followed by the creation of extermination centres for imported Czech and German Jews. Soviet prisoners of war were killed in still larger numbers.[56]

During the three years when the German–Soviet front lay close to Estonia's north-eastern border, Estonian soldiers served both in German-sponsored and in Soviet-sponsored formations. Before the German invasion, the Red Army had trained Estonian officers, formed Estonian regiments set up an Estonian branch of the Political-Military Department. Two Soviet divisions, the 180th and 182nd, were largely Estonian in composition, as were the 8th and 22nd Territorial Rifle Corps. They were pulled back as the Wehrmacht advanced. A few senior Estonian officers, such as Major-General Jaan Kruus, passed into Soviet service, though every single one of them who was not killed at the front, including Kruus, was eventually murdered by the NKVD. General Laidoner, the pre-war commander-in-chief, was held in the Gulag until his death in 1953.[57]

On the German side, Estonian recruits were taken into the *Omakaitse* ('Home Guard'), into Estonian security groups within the Wehrmacht, into so-called Defence Battalions, into Border Defence Regiments and into the Estonian SS-Legion. None of these formations was necessarily sinister in character, and, in theory at least, all were assigned to purely military duties. In February 1944 general conscription was imposed on all males of military age.

Like all other SS-Legions in other German-occupied countries, the Estonian Legionnaires were composed mainly of volunteers. After training, they were transferred either to the Waffen-SS 20th Grenadier Division or to one of the SS-Ostland reserve battalions, where their senior officers were German. They saw combat service in various sectors of the Eastern Front, suffering heavy casualties. Their toughest engagement, in February 1943, was in the Narva sector. The survivors were withdrawn for retraining in Germany, and then saw action in Silesia, where their commander, SS-*Standartenführer* Franz Augsberger, was killed in battle.[58]

In the summer of 1944 the pendulum of war swung again. The Siege
of Leningrad was lifted, the Red Army returned and the German Army
Group North pulled out successfully into Latvia in 'Operation Aster'.
The Estonian population was left to cope with the aftermath. The
NKVD set to work again with a vengeance, and another wave of Estonians was consigned to the Gulag or to mass graves. The second Soviet
'liberation' rendered the topic of Estonian independence impossible to
mention. This time, the Soviets let it be known that they intended to stay
for ever.

Nonetheless, in the brief interval between the German retreat and the
Soviets' return, a small group of Estonian politicians attempted to
organize an independent government in Tallinn. Jüri Uluots (1890–
1945), who had been both the last pre-war prime minister and chairman
of a German-sponsored National Committee, issued a declaration of
Estonian neutrality. On 18 September 1944, acting in his capacity as the
sole legal representative of the pre-war republic still at liberty, he
appointed a government headed by a lawyer, Otto Tief. The blue-black-
and-white flag flew on the Pikk Hermann tower for two days. A party
of German marines, sent from evacuation duties in the port to crush the
'mutiny', was repulsed. But on the 22nd, Soviet tanks drove in, and the
flag was hauled down. The government fled to Pogari, whence they
hoped to escape to Finland. Scattered resistance briefly slowed the Red
Army down. Tief and most of his ministers were arrested and sent to the
Gulag. Uluots and a small company reached Stockholm, where an
Estonian government-in-exile was formed. Their principled action was
doomed to failure, but, like the contemporaneous Warsaw Rising, had
enormous symbolic resonance.[59]

The reimposition of Soviet rule in 1944–5 sparked a repeat performance of all the horrors and ordeals of 1940–41. A Communist government,
handpicked in Moscow, arrived on the coat-tails of the Red Army. Its
most prominent figure, Johannes Vares Barbarus (d. 1946), a doctor and
poet, had briefly served in similar circumstances in 1940. The Estonian
Communist Party was reinstated, intent on wreaking revenge on its
compatriots. Estonian territory east of Narva and much of the Petseri
eastern district were arbitrarily annexed by the Russian Soviet Federative Socialist Republic (RSFSR), the largest of the Soviet republics.

On 2–3 July 1945 a military court of the Supreme Soviet held a show
trial to condemn the ministers of the last Estonian government. Uluots
was condemned *in absentia* (and died – unusually – of natural causes).
His minister of defence, Jaan Maide, was shot. Others were imprisoned.

The Great Terror raged once again. In 1944–53, c. 30,000 Estonians were consigned to prison camps. Tens of thousands more were arrested, interrogated, tortured, raped, 'disappeared' or executed. The largest single deportation, involving 76,000 individuals from all three Baltic States, was carried out in March 1949. Their destination was eastern Siberia. The re-deportation of children who had been taken to Siberia in 1941 and who had somehow found their way home was peculiarly sadistic. Soviet citizens repatriated from Germany and returning prisoners of war could expect no mercy. Low-level armed resistance continued for years.[60]

One small footnote raises a wry smile. One of Otto Tief's ministers, Arnold Susi, who fell into the clutches of the NKVD in 1944, made friends in the Gulag with Alexander Solzhenitsyn. Both men were eventually released; it was at Susi's country home in Estonia that Solzhenitsyn would later hole up in secret to write *The Gulag Archipelago*, the book which would do so much to undermine belief in the Soviet system.[61] The pre-war Estonian president, Konstantin Päts, like General Laidoner, was not so lucky. He spent sixteen years in a Soviet camp before dying there in 1956. The exiled Estonian government, sheltered in Stockholm, carried the baton of legality from 1940 to 1992.

In the eyes of the Western Powers, the Soviet annexation of Estonia in 1940 had been judged illegal; no retraction was ever issued to change the official opinion. The 4221st Estonian Guard Company, formed by the US army from selected prisoners of war in 1946, saw duty at the Nuremberg War Tribunal, wearing American uniforms.[62] Yet nothing practical was done to challenge Estonia's captivity.

For forty years after the war, the Soviet Union strove to compete with the United States in all fields, and to prove the vaunted superiority of its system. In 1952 it introduced a model, but totally bogus and irrelevant constitution, and changed the ruling party's name to the 'Communist Party of the Soviet Union', KPSS or, in English, CPSU. Despite such window dressing, it remained not just a 'one-party state' but a complicated amalgamation of union and autonomous republics, shackled at every level by the parallel structures of the Party dictatorship. Throughout the Cold War it held its own. Not only was it the largest country in the world territorially; it possessed the world's most numerous nuclear arsenal, and a vast array of naval, air, ground and rocket forces. For a time after the launch of the Sputnik spaceship in 1957 it seemed to be gaining an edge in science and technology too. It looked completely invincible.

After Stalin's death in 1953, the crimes of the early Soviet era were selectively denounced, and a limited 'thaw' under the leadership of Nikita Khrushchev removed the worst excesses. Yet the essence of latter-day Soviet Communism was immobility. There was no serious modification of Marxism-Leninism, no retreat from a command economy, no lowering of the censorship and no real margin of freedom. In the 1970s, under Leonid Brezhnev, a permanent state of international impasse was reached under the name of 'détente'.[63] Neither the United States nor the USSR was winning the arms race. The Soviets' former pupil, Communist China, was brought to the fore in the international arena in 1972 by an American diplomatic manoeuvre following the Sino-Soviet split.[64] In the 1980s the Soviet leadership grew more rigid in response to the challenge from US President Ronald Reagan, who spoke openly of the 'evil empire'. Poland's Solidarity movement was crushed, as previous acts of defiance in Hungary and Czechoslovakia had been. The Soviet bloc appeared to be gripped in the same vice that had gripped the Soviet Union for three generations.[65]

Throughout the post-war era the Estonian Soviet Socialist Republic (ESSR) was the smallest of the Soviet Union's fifteen republics. Its territory was essentially the same as that of pre-war Estonia, but its population was somewhat different. The Jews (exterminated) and Germans (expelled or killed) had gone, and their absence was more than made up by a massive influx of Russian settlers. Estonia was governed by the standard dual Party-State system imposed on all the Soviet republics. State institutions were largely run by locals, especially by Estonian nationals born elsewhere in the USSR. The Estonian branch of the Soviet Communist Party was also largely in Estonian hands but it was directly subordinated to Moscow, which charged it with keeping all state organs in line. In reality, therefore, the country was locked into a Russian-run collective dictatorship. Elections were held for councils and assemblies. But since all candidates were appointed by Party-run electoral commissioners, voters were given no meaningful choice.

The history of the Estonian Communist Party, especially in the last phase of Stalinism from 1945 to 1953, makes for sorry reading. One chairman, Barbarus, committed suicide little more than a year after his appointment. A successor, Nikolai Karotamm, was purged in 1950, charged with 'bourgeois nationalism'. A third, Johannes Käbin, emerged as the Party's strongman for twenty years. Yet personalities held only secondary importance. All factions in the Party competed to win Moscow's approval, and all were ultimately dependent on the presence of the Red Army and the KGB, the Soviet Security Service.

Stalinist repression was followed by the post-Stalinist 'thaw' and then by the long era of Brezhnevian stagnation. During the 'thaw', Käbin's close links with Khrushchev bore fruit in the shape of reduced food requisitions and improved economic conditions. Under Brezhnev, however, Russification gathered pace once again. Käbin was succeeded by a Russified Estonian, Karl Vaino, who had been born in Tomsk and could not speak his mother-tongue fluently. The official policy of bilingualism did not apply to Russians, laying the seeds of a later conflict. Bureaucratic centralization had the effect that 'the recipes of all cakes baked in Estonia were drawn up in Moscow'.[66]

Information in the West about Soviet-era Estonia in this period was peculiarly inadequate. An encyclopedia of Russia published in London in 1961, for example, was not so much factually inaccurate as incapable of distinguishing the wood from the trees:

Estonia (Estonian Eesti or Eestimaa), Union Republic of the U.S.S.R, bordering on the Gulf of Finland, Latvia, the Baltic Sea and Lake Chudskoye in the east; it is mainly lowland plain, partially forested, with many lakes and marshes and a soft, almost maritime climate; Area 17,800 sq. m.; population (1959) 1,197,000 (56 per cent urban), mostly Estonians (73 per cent), also Russians (22 per cent), before the war also Germans. There are oil-shale extraction and processing, electrical engineering, textile, wood-processing and food (bacon and butter) industries; dairy farming and pig raising are carried on, and grain, potatoes, vegetables and flax cultivated. Principal towns: Tallinn (capital), Tartu, Pärnu, Narva, Kohtla-Järve . . . During the period of Estonian independence (1919–40) the country's industry declined, being cut off from the Russian market, but agriculture flourished with the export of butter and bacon to Britain and Germany. At first independent Estonia was a democratic republic, but in 1934 a dictatorship was established under President Päts . . . though a kind of representative assembly with limited powers was introduced. A Communist uprising in Tallinn was suppressed in 1924.[67]

This entry could easily have been written by the propaganda department of the Soviet embassy. It concentrates on economic issues, avoids controversial historical matters, says nothing of the Second World War, and gives the impression that the pre-war Estonian Republic (but not Stalin's Soviet Union) deserved the label of a dictatorship. It omits the important fact that both Britain and the United States regarded Estonia's incorporation into the USSR as illegal.

Indeed, each of the assertions in the extract above needs a gloss. The influx of Russians, for example, was not just a happenstance, but part of a systematic policy aimed at strengthening Moscow's influence and weakening Estonian identity. The city of Narva illustrates the point. Completely destroyed during the war, it was placed out of bounds to Estonians after 1945. The large-scale presence of the Soviet military had the same effect. Several Estonian garrison towns, like Paldiski, were closed to civilians for decades.

In the socio-economic sphere, it is true that Soviet planning promoted industrialization and urbanization, yet one can hardly refer to the subject without discussing the harsh, exploitative methods and their baleful consequences. The unrestrained exploitation of Estonia's oil-shale beds for the benefit of Leningrad, for example, has ruined the town of Kohtla-Järve, which is now overshadowed by towering slag heaps. The nearby town of Ailamae was blessed with a Soviet nuclear processing plant, and has been left with a hopelessly polluted man-made lake that was used as a dump for dangerous waste. In Tallinn, the suburb of Lasnamäe, once touted as a workers' paradise, is stranded as a museum for the maltreatment of the proletariat.

Culturally, the Soviet authorities sponsored purposeful activities, some of which were undoubtedly beneficial. State education ensured almost universal literacy, and Estonian remained the main language of instruction in most schools. In literature, despite official promotion of the great Russian classics, some local writers were able to flourish. The sentimental and uncontroversial Oskar Luts (1887–1953), author of *Kevade* (*The Spring*, 1913) had started to publish in tsarist times and remained popular. The historical novelist Jaan Kroos (1920–2007) established himself as a 'State Artist of the ESSR' after his return from the Gulag; his favourite theme, which pitted Estonian peasants against Baltic German barons, suited Soviet political interests but could also be read as a surreptitious metaphor for the contemporary scene. The arts were encouraged, especially film, music, dance and opera, and imposing state-sponsored venues were provided. The bass-baritone Georg Ots (1920–75), one of the Soviet Union's most thunderous opera-singers, contrived to include Estonian songs and productions in his repertoire.[68]

But the overall balance-sheet is not easily assessed. Russification intensified in the 1970s as the Estonian proportion of the population shrank; religious observance was decimated; the Estonian Lutheran Church and the Russian Orthodox Church were sorely harassed, and ubiquitous state censorship enforced whatever it regarded as the Soviet norm. The cultural environment, therefore, could be stifling, and leading figures, like the conductor Neeme Järvi (b. 1937), fled abroad; taking his wife and family to Sweden in 1980, he settled for many years in Gothenburg. He was soon followed by his contemporary, Arvo Pärt, the modern minimalist composer, who chose Vienna. Emigration, which was illegal, was often the only option for creative people, who wanted to further their careers unhindered.[69]

Estonia would be a good place, in fact, to study the consequences of the Soviet Union's deeply ambiguous cultural policies in detail. Soviet cultural planners aimed to achieve the impossible: to encourage national and linguistic diversity and at the same time to mould people in the image of their ideal *Homo sovieticus*, 'national in form, but socialist in content'. What they meant was that Estonians, Ukrainians, Georgians, Uzbeks and all the others would be allowed to speak their national languages but not to express any independent ideas; and they failed to publicize the ultimate goal, which was a generalized Communist-inspired culture plus Russification. This was the approach to all branches of cultural activity: a superficial variety was tolerated, but only as part of a far-reaching conformity.[70] The author of the strategy, Joseph Stalin, who was not a native Russian, made no bones about the ultimate purpose, which was 'the fusion [of cultures] into one General Culture,

socialist in both form and content and expressed in one general language'.[71] Russian, the language of the imperial capital, was the only
possible candidate for promotion as the universal lingua franca. In
practice, it was taught rigorously in all Estonian schools of the ESSR as
a compulsory second language, though of course no serious effort was
made to teach Estonian to Russians, even those living in Estonia.

Looking back on Soviet cultural policy, which had such a critical
impact on Estonian national identity, some Estonians may conclude
that it was an improvement on the openly Russificatory, pre-Revolution
schemes. Most, however, will have their doubts, and will probably realize how lucky Estonia was to have been exposed to Soviet social
engineering for only two or three generations. There was no support for
genuine bilingualism, and all the non-linguistic aspects of culture were
subordinated to foreign priorities. One need look no further than the
Kreutzwald State Library of the ESSR (now the National Library) in
Tallinn. Housed in a gigantic concrete bunker-building never completed
in Soviet times, its first priority after 1945 was to expand its Russian
collection; and throughout its existence, large numbers of Estonian, pre-
Soviet or foreign books were held under lock and key in a special section
of prohibita closed to ordinary readers.[72]

Given the vigilance of the KGB, no opposition movement could
expect to operate in Soviet Estonia for long. But games of cat and mouse
were played incessantly, and relays of groups and individuals constantly
gave new life to dissident impulses. The armed opposition of 'Forest
Brothers' stayed at large until the mid-1950s, supported by agents of
Western intelligence; and a small number of 'lone rangers' until the
1970s. Various forms of civilian protest surfaced from time to time. In
1946 a group of schoolgirls blew up a Soviet war memorial in Tallinn.
After 1975, the Helsinki Agreement, which encouraged so-called 'legal
opposition', and the so-called Baltic Appeal of 1979, which demanded
publication of the Nazi–Soviet Pact's protocols, made world headlines;[73]
in 1980 youth riots were reported. Reprisals were severe, but noncon-
formism never dried up.

Throughout those long decades, it was illegal to wave the Estonian
colours of blue, white and black; it was illegal to sing the pre-war
national anthem; and it was treasonable to talk in public about independence. Above all, it was unwise to dream.

When the young, dynamic and affable Mikhail Gorbachev stepped onto
the world scene in March 1985 as the new general secretary of the

Soviet Communist Party, no one thought that the Soviet Union's funeral was approaching. Gorbachev came to save the USSR, not to bury it. Western politicians, and the Western public, were enchanted by him. His determination to end the Cold War naturally played well, while the slogans of *glasnost* (often taken, wrongly, to mean 'openness') and *perestroika* ('reconstruction') were universally applauded. Few outsiders could understand why Gorbachev was so heartily distrusted among many of his own people.[74]

In retrospect, one can see that Gorbachev was poorly suited to act as the Soviet Union's saviour, partly because he was poorly informed, notably about the history and make-up of the mammoth state which he dismantled by mistake. He failed to realize that the USSR had been assembled from a collection of captured nationalities held together by coercion. As soon as the coercion was removed, almost all the non-Russian republics prepared to leave, exactly as they had in 1918. In only a few cases did the Russian-dominated elites of Central Asian republics like Kazakhstan or Uzbekistan hesitate. When Gorbachev let it be known that East Germany could not count on the Soviet army to intervene, as it had in Hungary in 1956 and in Czechoslovakia in 1968, all the Communist leaders of the satellite states (except Ceauşescu in Romania) saw the game was up, the Soviet bloc disintegrated and the Berlin Wall collapsed. Similarly in August 1991, when Gorbachev attempted to relax the terms of the Union Treaty (which defined the role of the USSR's constituent republics), his own colleagues launched an abortive coup against him. His political credit was exhausted. Boris Yeltsin, the leader of the RSFSR (the Russian Soviet Federative Socialist Republic), led a movement to recognize the independence of the fifteen Soviet republics, and in effect to terminate the Soviet story.

When Gorbachev first appeared, no one in Estonia, or in the other Soviet republics, had been thinking about national independence. The new general secretary had not been shaped by the Stalinist era, but all the talk concerned the reform of the Soviet system, not its replacement. In any case Gorbachev was slow to show his hand. When he did, his main concerns centred on foreign policy, not on the internal structures of the Soviet State. In 1987, the eightieth-anniversary celebrations of the October Revolution were staged with all the usual Soviet bombast, and everyone assumed that similar anniversaries would continue into the foreseeable future. Even when *glasnost* and *perestroika* got under way, they were presented as the twin pillars of a controlled experiment, aiming for a degree of welcome relaxation, not for radical change.

Yet Estonians by then could receive Finnish television, so they knew that their Finnish cousins across the water enjoyed a far higher standard of living, and much greater freedoms. But they were not inclined to raise their hopes. Twice in the twentieth century they had escaped from the Soviet grasp, only to be twice recaptured. In the early 1980s they had watched the Solidarity episode in Poland intensely, and had seen the movement crushed.

Nineteen eighty-seven was the year when Soviet-watchers noticed that Moscow's grip on the Soviet republics was slipping. When a local war broke out between Armenia and Azerbaijan over the remote enclave of Nagorno-Karabakh, Gorbachev took no active steps to stifle it. Communist leaders in each of the republics, including Estonia, realized that their room for manoeuvre was widening. *Glasnost*, too, was getting out of hand. Contrary to Western belief, the Russian word means 'publicity',[75] and was initially used by Gorbachev to encourage Party activists to stand up for his policies against hostile criticism. Yet once unleashed the slogan soon spread into areas of previously taboo subjects. In Estonia, it gave rise to uninhibited historical discussions and to an unparalleled tide of national reawakening.

The first buds of the coming 'Baltic spring' had appeared in October 1986 with the foundation of the harmless-sounding Estonian Heritage Society. This was soon followed by public protests, apparently unconnected, against phosphorite mining. But history and ecology were joining hands. What they had in common was a determination to resist Moscow's dictatorial habits.

Mass demonstrations began in 1987. They were entirely peaceful, but unauthorized. One, on 23 August, was held in the Hirvepark in Tallinn to mark the anniversary of the Nazi–Soviet Pact – hitherto an unmentionable event. Another, in October, gathered in Võru to remember the War of Independence. This was the first occasion for forty-seven years when the Estonian flag flew freely in public. A third meeting, in February 1988, was called to mark the Tartu Treaty of 1920 and faced police with dogs and riot shields. From then on the ferment gathered pace in the guise of the 'Singing Revolution'. Ever-greater crowds would assemble spontaneously to sing forbidden patriotic songs and to wave flags. Emotions rose inexorably. Finally, on 11 September 1988 at the Tallinn Song Festival, the leader of the Heritage Society demanded the restoration of Estonia's independence.

Defiance of Soviet authority was now out in the open. Gorbachev's reaction was to replace the ruling Party's first secretary in Estonia, while promoting constitutional reform and the creation of a National (Soviet) Delegates Congress. His position weakened, however, when people across the USSR sensed that he was unwilling to sanction the use of force. As a result, the Supreme Council of the ESSR decided of its own accord on 16 November 1988 to issue a declaration of Estonian sovereignty. Soviet laws were only to be regarded as valid when ratified in Tallinn. Moscow protested, but no one was disciplined. The outside world was still largely oblivious to the implications.[76]

In 1989 Estonian politics followed two paths. One group, headed by Estonian Communists, participated in Gorbachev's Moscow-centred reform movement. The other, based in Tallinn, pressed for autonomy and, increasingly, for independence. The climate was changing rapidly. In June the world outcry against the Tiananmen Square massacre in China lessened the chances of Soviet hardliners regaining control, and the triumph of the Solidarity movement in the partial elections in Poland showed that the monolith was cracking. On 23 August 1989, 2 million people linked hands in the 'Baltic Chain', which stretched all the way across the Baltic States from Tallinn to Vilnius in Lithuania. It showed that Estonians were not isolated.[77] The fall of the Berlin Wall in November, regarded in the West as a world-historical event, did not make the same impact on Soviet citizens, who had still to break the bars of their cage.

In 1990 and 1991 the Estonian national movement adopted the strategy of pursuing its own programme while ignoring whatever Moscow did. In February 1990 elections to a Congress of Estonia turned into a de facto referendum on national statehood. The Congress then announced 'a period of transition awaiting developments'. Pro-Moscow elements staged impotent counter-demonstrations. Violent events occurred in Lithuania and Latvia, where in January 1991 Soviet special forces attempted and failed to suppress the 'separatists'. Gorbachev's one and only resort to force produced, from his viewpoint, far too little and was much too late. Even so, an Estonian referendum on 3 March produced a 77 per cent majority in favour of independence. The three Baltic republics then seceded, regardless of the consequences. On 17 September 1991 the flags of Estonia, Latvia and Lithuania were flown at the UN building in New York. They had been recognized by Iceland, by the UN and by Yeltsin's Russia even while the USSR was theoretically still intact.[78] Estonia soared into free flight as the Soviet Union slumped onto its deathbed. On 31 December 1991 'Lenin's only child' finally succumbed.

III

The Soviet Union was a major player on the world stage for most of the twentieth century. From the day of its creation to the day of its dissolution it was bigger than any other territorial entity on the globe, and its sheer size gave it enormous geopolitical significance. But it made still greater impact for both ideological and military reasons. In the 1920s and 1930s, as the 'world's first socialist state', it delivered the single most serious challenge to a reigning international order dominated by the Western Powers. Thanks to its stunning victory in the Second World War, it passed four decades as one of only two world superpowers, vying with the United States for influence, and (prior to the Sino-Soviet split) commanding a bloc of states containing almost one-third of mankind.

According to their own propaganda, Soviet leaders had discovered the secrets of the 'scientific system of the future'; they were looking forward to a continuing existence where defeats and disasters would be unknown. Their utopian ideology produced a scenario which described the road to the end of the world. They would resist all attempts to divert their mission until a perfect, classless and 'Communist' society was achieved. Foreign states would gradually be won over. When a critical mass of progressive nations had joined the Soviet camp, the remaining fortresses of reaction would surrender, and all conflict would cease. States would then become redundant. Frontiers, governments and armies would wither away, and mankind would prosper for ever in a condition of bliss, as promised by the socialist prophets. 'Day by day, hour by hour,' every schoolchild was taught, 'the Soviet people are building the radiant edifice of Communism with joy and pride.'[79] As many observers have remarked, Soviet Communism was less of a political creed, and more like a pseudo-religion;[80] it rested on belief, not on experience or knowledge.

Many factors contributed to the Soviet Union's downfall. They include defeat in Afghanistan, an unsustainable arms race, financial bankruptcy, laggardly technology, sclerotic political structures, a discredited ideology, a generation gap between rulers and ruled, and much else besides; discussion of them fills any number of weighty tomes,[81] but none in itself gives a sufficient explanation. The essence lies deeper, and is not complicated. The Soviet system was built on extreme force and extreme fraud. Practically everything that Lenin and the Leninists did was accompanied by killing; practically everything they said was based on half-baked theories, a total lack of integrity and huge, barefaced lies – what the Russians would call *naglaya lozh'*. The Soviet economy had been assembled over decades by eliminating all market mechanisms, by suppressing the flow of economic information and by terrorizing the population into subservience. When a general secretary finally came along who was no longer prepared to perpetuate the fantasies and the coercion, all the circuits fused, and total paralysis rapidly ensued. Gorbachev, the well-intentioned reformer, was as shocked by this as anyone. His predicament was likened in Russia to an apocryphal story about an old man who flushed his toilet at the exact moment of the Tashkent earthquake. 'If I'd known what was going to happen,' the old man exclaimed as he climbed from the rubble, 'I would never have pulled the chain.'[82]

This gulf between the idealized scenario and the reality may well explain why Soviet leaders behaved like frightened rabbits, mesmerized by the headlights of history, as the juggernaut of unexpected events was about to run them over. Gorbachev and his comrades, trained from childhood in the Soviet fictions, simply could not respond appropriately; they tried to grapple with accumulating problems, but found them insoluble. No one could have guessed at the magnitude of their incompetence or self-deception. No one could have predicted that the Soviet Union, which possessed the most elaborate security apparatus ever assembled, would prove incapable of self-defence, or would have expired without a spirited rearguard action. The August coup of 1991, mounted by Gorbachev's closest colleagues, proved a total fiasco; it discredited Gorbachev as well as those who had arrested him, and it triggered the very collapse that its authors had wanted to avoid. One can only conclude that the dinosaur was already brain-dead before it died from the political equivalent of a paralytic stroke.

The departure of the Soviet Union left a political void in large expanses of Eurasia, and an accompanying vacuum in the international arena. Fifteen dependent Soviet republics were transformed into fifteen independent states, the largest of them the giant Russian Federation,[83] the smallest tiny Estonia. The other thirteen ranged from Estonia's Baltic neighbours Latvia and Lithuania to Uzbekistan, Kirghizstan and Turkmenistan in Central Asia. Some of them joined the so-called Commonwealth of Independent States (CIS), a supposedly voluntary association of Russian-led ex-Soviet republics. Others, including Estonia, declined, and within a short time were heading eagerly towards membership both of NATO and of the European Union.

The vacuum in international politics took at least a decade to fill. Some American analysts, preoccupied for the whole of their adult lives by rivalry with the Soviet Union, assumed that US-led capitalist democracy would henceforth have no more major competitors, that they had reached the 'End of History'.[84] Others concluded that the twenty-first century would be the 'American Century'. All of this was questionable. It was just as possible to argue, as one prescient historian did in 1988, that American power had passed its peak,[85] that the US lead had been squandered by a neo-conservative administration, or that the new century heralded the rise of new powers like China, India and Brazil.[86] The geopolitics of the world were changing from 'bipolar' to polygonal.

At all events, the reconfigured map of the globe threw up a number of unforeseen patterns. The European Union, for example, which had been formalized by the Maastricht Treaty on the same day in December 1991 on which the leaders of Russia, Byelorussia and Ukraine put the Soviet Union out of its misery, expanded exponentially into the post-Soviet void. By 2007 it had a membership of twenty-seven states with more than 500 million inhabitants; ten of the twenty-seven, including Estonia, had only recently escaped from Communist tyranny. In terms both of GDP and of population, it far outstripped anything that the former Soviet Union could boast.

At the same time, since the ex-Soviet republics in Central Asia were found to be rich in oil, they were drawn into a new version of the Great Game.[87] The United States now vied with Russia over the control of new oil reserves, the politics of the Middle East gained a new northern flank and the future of countries like Iran, Iraq, Afghanistan and Pakistan became the object of intensified international concern.

Estonia's restoration in the midst of the turbulence was especially remarkable, and by no means preordained. Estonian leaders had set a skilful course around the obstacles blocking their progress, but the odds for success were not favourable. They possessed guile and popular support, but no serious instruments of power. One forgets just how hostile and touchy official Soviet opinion was; it had been looking forward to the demise of the separate personalities of the USSR's constituent republics and to their assimilation into 'universal Soviet Man'. According to another apocryphal story, a visiting Oxford academic had ventured to say in the 1980s that he rather liked Estonia. 'In that case,' his host had retorted, 'you must obviously be anti-Soviet.' And yet the daunting chasm of transition was safely crossed. As one prime minister reported with satisfaction, Estonia had performed a miracle that was psychological no less than political and economic.[88]

A pertinent remark in this context was voiced by Vladimir Putin, the second president of the Russian Federation. In 2005, looking back, he said that 'the collapse of the Soviet Union had been the greatest geopolitical catastrophe of the century'.[89] He was referring in particular to the fate of ethnic Russians stranded outside Russia's borders. But he had been a career officer of the KGB, which, despite its ruthless reputation, had signally failed in its prime duty of protecting the Soviet state. His regret was tinged by pangs of corporate guilt.[90]

Putin's sense of humiliation was shared by millions of Russians for whom the loss of superpower status had been accompanied by the loss

of a large part of their colonial empire. His determination to recover
lost prestige, by fighting the Chechen war or by appearing to 'stand up
to the Americans', was more important to them than his half-measures
in establishing a 'managed democracy'. These attitudes, macho and defiant, underpinned his undoubted popularity.[91] One must presume that
Putin shared with his compatriots a strong sense of bafflement about
how the great calamity had actually happened. There had been no time
to reflect. The Soviet Union had been there one day, and had gone the
next. Contrary to the wishes of its supporters, and the efforts of its
guardians, it had performed world history's ultimate vanishing act.

How States Die

The strange death of the Soviet Union – which played no small part in the trains of thought behind the present studies – suggests that a typology of 'vanished kingdoms' is worth attempting. Bodies politic clearly expire for a variety of reasons, and it is perhaps important to ask whether their disappearances follow discernible patterns. Historians are not comfortable with the idea of random causation, and some sort of analysis, however tentative, is desirable.

Political pathologies can be observed in endless guises. But the theme here is neither 'revolution' nor 'regime-change' nor 'system-failure'. Revolution and regime-change refer to events where the social order or the government is overthrown, but where the territory and population of the state remain intact. 'System-failure' is concerned with political organisms which lose the capacity to function effectively, but do not necessarily collapse completely; they may be compared to a motor car that has broken down but has not yet been scrapped. This brief enquiry is limited to the more drastic phenomenon of states that cease to exist.

Political philosophers, whose known ruminations began in ancient Greece, have been thinking about statehood for millennia, though state demise has seldom been at the forefront of their preoccupations. By describing the state as a 'creation of nature', and man as a 'political animal', Aristotle can be read as implying, among other things, that states, like other natural life forms, might be subject to cycles of birth and death.[1] Thomas Hobbes, though mainly interested in the foundation and perpetuation of states, was more explicit about their demise. In *Leviathan*, he expounded on the 'internall diseases' that tend to 'the dissolution of the Commonwealth'. The ultimate factor is war: 'When in a warre (forraign, or intestine,) the enemies get a final Victory; so as ... there is no farther protection of Subjects in their loyalty; then is the Commonwealth DISSOLVED.' At the last, 'Nothing can be immortall, which mortals make.'[2] Rousseau in his *Social Contract* reached the same conclusion. 'If Sparta and Rome perished,' he asked rhetorically, 'what state can hope to last for ever?' 'The body politic, no less then the body of a man, begins to die as soon as it is born, and bears within itself the causes of its own destruction ... the best constitution will come to an end.'[3]

Christian theologians and biblical scholars, whose traditions are almost as long as those of the philosophers, have constantly been exercised by the rise and fall of states, though less by related questions of causation; they have usually been satisfied by explanations based on divine providence or the Wrath of God. The Fall of Babylon of 539 BC, which was a major historical event in the Old Testament, is presented in the Book of Revelation as a metaphor for the end of the existing world order and the advent of Christ-ruled 'New Jerusalem'. Every good Christian had heard the story of Belshazzar's Feast, where the prophet Daniel deciphered the writing on the wall: 'MENE, MENE, TEKEL UPHARSIN ... God hath numbered thy kingdom, and finished it; ... thou art weighed in the balances and found wanting';[4] and few would be unaware of the words of the angel from heaven who 'cried mightily with a strong voice, saying, Babylon the great is fallen, is fallen, and is become the habitation of devils, and the hold of every foul spirit.'[5] St Augustine of Hippo (354–430), the senior Father of the Church, expounded these matters in his *City of God*; all human history, he writes, consists of a confrontation between the *civitas hominis*, the World of Man, and the *civitas Dei*, the divine World of the Spirit. The passing of the former is a necessary prelude to the triumph of the latter.[6] St Thomas Aquinas OP (*c.* 1225–74), Christian theologian par excellence, dominated Catholic thought into modern times. In his *Summa Theologica*, he consigned political questions like the birth and dissolution of states to the realm of universal or natural law, disentangling them from divine law and opening them up to the general, non-theological, discussions, in which all could participate.[7] The Protestant reformers developed their own schools of politico-theological scholarship. In England, Thomas Cromwell, in his preamble to the Henrician Act of Supremacy, was at pains to deny the link between royal authority and traditional Catholic teaching, inventing a new scheme of English history to match.[8] In Germany, Martin Luther's doctrine of the Two Kingdoms was a new take on St Augustine's old theme of the City of God.[9]

In the nineteenth century, anarchists like Proudhon or Bakunin, believing all government to be pernicious, were the first to postulate that 'the destruction of the state' was actually admissible.[10] The Marxists talked in similar vein, though with different goals in mind. Marx himself denied that he aimed at 'the complete destruction of the state'; the 'withering of the state' which Engels described was only to occur at a late stage when the sources of class conflict had been eliminated.[11] But Lenin in his *State and Revolution* (1917) called openly for the 'destruction of the bourgeois state', as a prelude to the 'Dictatorship of the Proletariat'.[12]

In the twentieth century international lawyers have explored the subject in their own right and with their own methods. The defining term which they chose for it in English was the 'extinction of states'.[13] One of the most recent contributors to the debate argues that in a world where *terra nullius* ('no one's land') no longer exists, the extinction of pre-existing states is a precondition for the creation of new ones.[14]

Political scientists entered the field relatively recently. All too often their hallmark has been prolix argumentation leading to blindingly obvious conclusions. So it is reassuring to see that the English term on which they appear to have settled, 'State Death', is uncharacteristically concise.[15] Their approach, which depends heavily on factorial modelling and on comparison of case studies, is closely allied to analyses of territorial disputes and of conflicts preceding the outbreak of wars. Yet their arguments would carry greater weight if they did not rely so much on data originating in the simplistic Correlates of War Project (COW). To every historian's despair, COW takes 1816 as the arbitrary start point of history, uses patently invalid definitions of state sovereignty and apparently (in studies written in the twenty-first century) does not yet include the USSR among its obituaries.[16] It is a hopeful sign that a call has been made to revise the COW data.[17]

In the last decade, a further sub-field of study has appeared under the heading of 'Failed States'. The term is clearly a misnomer, since the bodies concerned, though infirm, have still not reached the international graveyard. They should probably be called 'Failing States', and are said to be 'in danger of disintegration'. As from 2005, an annual Index of sixty such invalids has been published, supported by quantitative measurements of their distress and dividing them into 'critical', 'in danger' and 'borderline'.[18] Somalia, Chad and Sudan topped the Index for 2010. Europe was represented by Georgia (no. 37), Azerbaijan (no. 55), Moldova (no. 58) and Bosnia and Hercegovina (no. 60).

Vocabulary is important, and terminological proliferation is indicative of a sorry pass where modern scholars betray little ability of harmonize their practices with neighbouring disciplines. If the 'dissolution of the state' was good enough for Hobbes and Locke (and for the

French philosophers as well), one wonders why it should be dismissed by lesser mortals. As it is, on top of 'dissolution', one is now forced to worry about 'destruction', 'withering', 'extinction', 'expiration', 'death', 'failure', 'disintegration' and no doubt many more. One is reminded of the parrot which was 'demised', 'passed on', 'expired', 'stiff', 'deceased', 'bereft of life' 'off the twig', 'gone to join the bleedin' choir invisible' – 'in fact, an ex-parrot'.[19] Likewise, the focus here is on the past tense and on the ex-state. In this connection, the term 'extinct states' has again been gaining currency; a popular website lists no fewer than 207 extinct states in Europe's past, a definite underestimate.[20]

At one time, it was only thought necessary to consider two categories of dissolution, one caused by external force and the other by internal malfunction: in Hobbesian language, 'forraign warre' was contrasted with 'internall diseases'. John Locke took a similar line in his *Two Treatises on Civil Government*. Having discussed how 'the inroad of foreign force' was 'the usual and almost the only way whereby [a commonwealth] is dissolved', he goes on to say: 'Besides this overturning from without, governments are dissolved from within,' and then explains the circumstances in which this takes place.[21]

The international lawyers also preferred a dual scheme, distinguishing the voluntary from the involuntary. 'Voluntary extinction' was exemplified in the British Isles, where 'the Kingdoms of England, Scotland and Ireland were extinguished as states' in order to create the United Kingdom.[22] 'Involuntary extinction' is illustrated by 'Poland, destroyed in 1795'.[23]

Nowadays, most scholars would agree that external, internal, voluntary and involuntary factors are all observable, and that dual schemes no longer suffice. Among the case studies in this book, at least five mechanisms appear to be at work: implosion, conquest, merger, liquidation and 'infant mortality'.

The Soviet Union is often said to have 'imploded'.[24] The metaphor may well be taken from the realm of astronomy where stars and other heavenly bodies, often large and apparently solid, are known to collapse in on themselves and atomize. It suggests that outside pressures may be present, but the essential event pertains to a catastrophic malfunction at the centre; a vacuum is created, the constituent parts disengage, and the whole is destroyed. Some such catastrophe occurred in Moscow in the autumn of 1991. The Soviet political system had been constructed round the centralized dictatorship of the Communist Party and the command economy. Hence, as soon as Gorbachev lost the ability or the will to command, all the Party-State structures ground to a halt. Fifteen orphaned republics were pushed into taking the terminal step beyond mere 'system-failure'. Implosion, therefore, must be counted as a form of death by natural causes.

Scholarly attempts to explain the demise of the USSR follow as many lines of argument as there are specialists to pursue them. Sovietologists frequently point to economic failings. Some also stress the ideological black hole created by Gorbachev's decision to end the Cold War, which deprived the 'first socialist state' of its *raison d'être*, and others the revolt of the nationalities, which led to the fateful scheme to reform the Union Treaty and to the abortive coup of August 1991. Each of these has merit. But deeper questions centre on the puzzle of why the elaborate machinery of the Party-State proved incapable of responding. Here, one enters the unfathomable realm of the unintended consequences of *glasnost* and *perestroika*.[25]

The Federation of Yugoslavia, which fell apart in stages between 1991 and 2006, displayed many similar features to those in the USSR. Power leeched away from Belgrade, as it did from Moscow, as each of the federation's republics ignored instructions from the centre. In Yugoslavia, however, the central institutions of the state rallied; and a long rearguard action was mounted from the Serbian-controlled centre to rein in the separatist inclinations of its neighbours. In time, however, Serbia's brutal campaign to rescue the federation by military means reinforced the centrifugal forces already in motion. The more Milošević raged, the more surely the constituent republics were alienated, including, in the end, Serbia's most faithful partner, Montenegro. Here one wonders whether 'explosion' might not be a more appropriate description.[26]

The Austro-Hungarian Empire, which collapsed in 1918, would seem to be another example of implosion. In that case, external pressures were more in evidence thanks to the military operations of the First World War. Yet the Empire survived the fighting intact, only to fall victim to the catastrophic failure of imperial authority at the war's end. After peace had been signed on the Eastern Front in March 1918, the imperial heartland was no longer under threat from a major 'inroad of force'. The conflict on the Italian Front, though intense, was essentially a regional affair. But in the following months the Habsburgs and their officials lost the ability to command. By October, the emperor's writ no longer ran; and the Empire's various provinces were making their own arrangements. Galicia, for example, did not rebel. It was deserted by an impotent Vienna besieged by Austro-German republicans. Then, lacking all guidance, it disintegrated amid the general chaos.[27]

As Locke observed, the 'inroad of foreign force' supplies the most usual cause of state death. The Kingdom of Tolosa, the States of Burgundy, the Byzantine Empire, the Commonwealth of Poland-Lithuania, and Prussia (as an element of the Third Reich) were all destroyed by conquest. Yet conquerors do not always proceed to destroy their defeated adversaries; both the Byzantine and the Polish examples suggest that the health and strength of a conquered country plays a part, alongside the conqueror's intentions, in the loser's fate. By 1453, for example, the once-mighty Byzantine Empire had shrunk to the dimensions of a tiny city-state, before being picked off by the final siege. Before 1795, the Polish-Lithuanian Commonwealth had endured a century of encroachments, debilitating malfunctions and internal haemorrhages before it faced the wars of the Partitions. The question posed, therefore, is whether the weakness of the state or the malevolence of its enemies was primarily responsible for its decease. Here, the moment of truth only arrives when the conquered state lies prostrate at the conqueror's mercy, and the decision is taken to reprieve or to destroy. The sages of the Enlightenment mocked the commonwealth's impotence. The patient was undoubtedly sick, but that sickness, in itself, was not decisive. The key lies in the knowledge that the commonwealth's neighbours were planning to kill their victim and to seize his assets. The Partitions of Poland-Lithuania can rightly be likened to a sustained campaign of bullying and assault which ended with the murder of a battered invalid. 'Poland-Lithuania was the victim of political vivisection – by mutilation, amputation, and in the end by total dismemberment: and the only excuse given was that the patient had not been feeling well.'[28] In coroner's language, the outcome would be described as 'death by unnatural causes'.

Conquest, in other words, is not necessarily the prelude to annihilation, although it often may be. Cato might cry 'Delenda est Carthago', 'Carthage must be destroyed', but the advice does not have to be heeded. In the case of Prussia – which, though merged into Germany, still existed in 1945 – the Allied Powers waited almost two years before delivering the coup de grâce. In other instances, countries can be conquered, occupied, absorbed and at some later date revived. Rousseau was well aware of this possibility when asked to analyse Poland-Lithuania's predicament in 1769. 'You are likely to be swallowed whole,' he predicted correctly, 'hence you must take care to ensure that you are not digested.'[29] The experience of the Baltic States in the twentieth century fits the same pattern. Estonia, Latvia and Lithuania were invaded by the Soviet Union in June 1940, occupied and annexed. But they were not fully digested. Fifty years later, like the biblical Jonah, they re-emerged from the belly of the whale, gasping but intact.

Geopolitical factors obviously play a role. Some states, like eighteenth-century Sweden or nineteenth-century Spain, can decline and degrade to the point where they become sitting ducks for would-be aggressors. They survive because no one takes the trouble to finish them off. States occupying more sensitive locations have no such luck. The leading scholar in 'State Death' theory places special emphasis on this mechanism.[30]

Many political organisms start life through the amalgamation of pre-existing units; the degree of integration achieved by such amalgams differs widely. Dynastic states are particularly susceptible to the collect-or's syndrome. The Kingdom-County of Aragon was one such example; the fifth Kingdom of Burgundy another; and the United Kingdom of Great Britain and Ireland a third. By the same token, if the process is reversed, the likelihood of a collection breaking up into its original units can be high. Such operations are probably best described in the corporate language of merger and de-merger.

The 'Kingdom of Sardinia', 1718–1861, must be rated a dynastic amalgam par excellence. Its four main constituent elements – Savoy, Piedmont, Nice and Sardinia – had been assembled by the *Casa Savoia* much as multinational corporations now assemble a portfolio of brands and companies. After the Napoleonic Wars, the parts had little in common except the common subjection to the ruling house. In the 1860s, therefore, as the Risorgimento reached its height, the dynasty took a conscious decision to offload the Savoyard and Nizzardo parts of its portfolio to clear the ground for a new corporation, to be called the 'Kingdom of Italy'. The Sardinian brand was sacrificed together with Savoy because they were incompatible with the dynasty's new business plan.

Political dynasties, however, employ a variety of strategies, among which the marriage of heirs and heiresses is arguably the most important. Furthermore, since patriarchal cultures can normally insist that a wife's assets be automatically subsumed into those of her husband, the realms of a sovereign heiress would usually lose their separate identity on marriage, as they did in the cases of Jadwiga of Poland in 1385 or of Mary of Burgundy in 1477. In practice, a great deal depended on the conditions agreed during pre-nuptial negotiations or succession contracts, and all sorts of variant settlements have resulted. British readers will be most familiar with the differences between the settlement for a personal union of 'England and Wales' and Scotland in 1603 after the death of Elizabeth I, and those for the constitutional union of England and Scotland in 1707 and of Great Britain and Ireland in 1801.

The case of the Crown of Aragon is particularly interesting in this regard. The dual state first came into being in 1137 due to a marriage contract sealed on behalf of the heiress of Aragon and the heir to the County of Barcelona. Formally, Aragon and Catalonia were still distinct entities more than three centuries later in 1469 when the prospective King-Count Ferdinand of Aragon married the Infanta Isabella, heiress to Castille. So, too, was their Kingdom of Valencia. These three heartland units, while being incorporated into the Spanish realms, remained juridically and administratively distinct for nearly 250 years after that second landmark marriage; the Crown of Aragon did not finally fade away until the aftermath of the Treaty of Utrecht in 1713. By that time, Spain was struggling with the tangled succession of the Bourbon and Habsburg dynasties – neither of which had been heard of in the distant days of Queen Petronilla and Count Ramón Berenguer.

Liquidation is a concept well understood in company law; and there is no good reason why it should not be applied by analogy to the particular circumstances in which a state entity or 'political company' is deliberately suppressed. The clearest example that comes to mind is when the leaders of the two parts of Czechoslovakia reached agreement on their 'velvet divorce' by consent in 1993. Since then, both the Czech Republic and the Republic of Slovakia have taken their places as sovereign states and good neighbours within the European Union.[31]

Of course, the trickiest question is to determine which liquidations are genuinely consensual and which are not. Many of them are not. In November 1918 the handpicked 'Grand National Assembly' which enabled Serbia to seize and liquidate the Kingdom of Montenegro by outwardly democratic means may be regarded a classic example of gangster-led political theatre. The Allied Powers, alas, were not very nimble or astute at spotting the rogues; they certainly let the Montenegrin question slip past the Paris Peace Conference, perhaps because they had no means of constraining wayward allies like Serbia. At least one British statesman, a future Nobel Peace Prize winner and serving in the founding commission of the League of Nations, seems to have seen what was happening; Lord Robert Cecil (1864–1958) summed up the Serbian delegates of the Peace Conference as 'a band of dishonest and murderous intriguers', and he was not taken in, as many were in that era, by the posturing of the Bolsheviks.[32] On the other hand, six months before the Japanese invasion of Manchuria in 1931, Cecil had the misfortune to tell the council of the League: 'There has scarcely ever been a period in the history of the world when war was less likely than at present.' Even perspicacious statesmen have their moments of credulity.

In 1940, the Soviet takeover of the Baltic States was also accompanied by a combination of military invasions, phoney 'referendums' and international perplexity. Handpicked delegates were assembled. Portraits of Stalin were paraded. The public was terrorized. Critics were harassed or physically removed. The result was known in advance, and the world was told that the victimized countries had joyfully petitioned Moscow for admission to the USSR. In the process, the 'bourgeois republics' were liquidated. 'Suicide by coercion' might also fit.

Irish republicans would maintain that their Republic had been liquidated in like manner by the Anglo-Irish Treaty of 1921. In their view, the treaty was invalid because the Irish delegates had been browbeaten into submission by the British threat of full-scale war, and they were not mistaken in their belief that browbeating had been applied. The Free Staters and their friends, in contrast, argued that the content of the treaty was not so drastic, and that the charge of 'liquidating the Republic' hid a more complicated reality. The facts are on their side. Though the name and form of the 'Republic' were indeed surrendered under pressure, the substance of a separate, self-governing Irish state was upheld. Despite everything, the treaty did not re-incorporate Ireland into the United Kingdom, and it provided the foundations on which the Irish Republic was subsequently constructed.

There remains a category which, for want of something more precise, may be described as the political counterpart of infant mortality. In order to survive, newborn states need to possess a set of viable internal organs, including a functioning executive, a defence force, a revenue system and a diplomatic service. If they possess none of these things, they lack the means to sustain an autonomous existence, and they perish before they can breathe and flourish. The 'Republic of One Day' in Carpatho-Ukraine illustrates the point nicely. Since its executive body did nothing other than to declare its independence, it may be said to have been stillborn.

Other young states succumb after a brief struggle. No state is as vulnerable as in the very early days of its existence, and the vultures begin to hover as soon as the infant takes its first breath. Many such infants falter because they are incapable of independent sustenance if the parent's life support is withdrawn. All the Napoleonic creations, such as the Kingdom of Etruria, belong to this category. Others collapse because the political, military or economic environment is too hostile. Several can be found in the brief outline of Soviet history sketched in Chapter 15. One such state would be Kerensky's would-be constitutional and republican Russia, which had overthrown the tsar's government in February 1917 but whose provisional government was snuffed out by the Bolsheviks after only eight months. Another might be the Byelorussian National Republic of 1918 or the Ukrainian National Republic in the same era. A third would be the homeland of the Soviet Union's founder, the Republic of Georgia, which held out for three years in its first incarnation from 1918 to 1921, and which is again gasping for air nearly ninety years later in the hostile environment of Russia's 'near abroad'.[33]

Successful statehood, in fact, is a rare blessing. It requires health and vigour, good fortune, benevolent neighbours and a sense of purpose to aid growth and to reach maturity. All the best-known polities in history have passed through this test of infancy, and many have lived to a grand old age. Those which failed the test have perished without making their mark. In the chronicles of bodies politic, as in the human condition in general, this has been the way of the world since time immemorial.

From the time of the ancient Greeks, and no doubt longer, the death of a monarch entailed a grand funeral, an oration, a burial or a burning pyre, an epitaph on the tomb and an obituary. Alaric's committal to the Busento was but a specific variant to normal practice. The Anglo-Saxons and Vikings often buried their chieftain in his ship, to mark the end of his rule and the start of a new voyage either to Valhalla or to Heaven:

> Scyld was still a strong man when his time came
> And he passed over into Our Lord's keeping.
> His warrior band did what he bade them
> When he laid down the law among the Danes.
> They shouldered him out to the sea's flood,
> the chief they revered who had ruled them.
> A ring-necked prow rode in the harbour,

clad with ice, its cables tightening.
They stretched their beloved lord in the boat,
laid out amidships by the mast,
the great ring-giver ... The treasure was massed
on top of him: it would travel far
on out into the sway of the ocean ...
And they set a gold standard up
high above his head and let him drift
to wind and tide, bewailing him
and mourning their loss. No man can tell,
no wise man in the hall or weathered veteran
knows for certain who salvaged that load.[34]

Generally speaking, the death of a ship of state was not so fêted, though the occasional fine obituary has been penned. William Wordsworth mourned the passing of a state far older than the Kingdom of Etruria, but another of those which were snuffed out by a Napoleonic whim:

Once did she hold the gorgeous East in fee;
And was the safeguard of the West: the worth
Of Venice did not fall beneath her birth,
Venice, the eldest Child of Liberty.
She was a maiden City, bright and free;
No guile seduced, no force could violate;
And, when she took unto herself a Mate,
She must espouse the everlasting Sea.
And what if she had seen those glories fade,
Those titles vanish, and that strength decay;
Yet shall some tribute of regret be paid
When her long life hath reached its final day:
Men are we, and must grieve when even the Shade
Of that which once was great is passed away.[35]

Notes

INTRODUCTION

1. John Hunt, *The Ascent of Everest* (London, 1953); R. Mantovani, *Everest: The History of the Himalayan Giant* (Shrewsbury, 1997); J. R. Smith, *Everest: The Man and the Mountain* (Caithness, 1999). 2. T. Gwynn Jones, *Geiriadur: Cymraeg–Saesneg a Saesneg–Cymraeg* (Cardiff, 1953). 3. William Johnson Cory (1823–92), after Callimachus (third century BC). 4. Edward Gibbon, *The Decline and Fall of the Roman Empire*, Everyman edn., 6 vols. (London, 1910); *The Autobiography of Edward Gibbon* (London, 1910). 5. Norman Davies, *The Isles: A History* (London, 1999). 6. 'The Day Thou gavest Lord is ended' (1870), words by John Ellerton, melody of 'St Clement' by Clement Scholefield. 7. 'Nazi Gold: Publishing the Third Reich', BBC Radio 4, 17 March 2011. 8. A. J. P. Taylor, *The Struggle for Mastery in Europe* (Oxford, 1954); *English History, 1914–45* (Oxford, 1965); *The Habsburg Monarchy, 1809–1918* (London, 1948); *Bismarck: The Man and the Statesman* (London, 1955); *The Course of German History* (London, 1945); *The Origins of the Second World War* (London, 1961); etc. 9. H. Trevor-Roper, *Historical Essays* (London, 1957), foreword, quoted by Adam Sisman, *Hugh Trevor-Roper: The Biography* (London, 2010), p. 293. 10. Ibid., pp. 168, 294. 11. See R. B. Cunninghame Graham, *A Vanished Arcadia: Some Account of the Jesuits in Paraguay, 1607–1767* (London, 1901); B. L. Putnam Weale, *The Vanished Empire* (London, 1920), on China; Mabel Cabot, *Vanished Kingdoms: A Woman Explorer in Tibet, China, and Mongolia, 1921–25* (New York, 2003); or Oriental Institute Museum, Chicago, *Vanished Kingdoms of the Nile: The Rediscovery of Nubia. An Exhibition* (Chicago, 1995). 12. Murry Hope, *Atlantis: Myth or Reality?* (London, 1991); R. Vidal-Naquet, *The Atlantis Story: A Short History of Plato's Myth* (Exeter, 2007). 13. www.jewishvirtuallibrary.org/jsource/archaeology/bethsaida.htm. See also P. R. Davies, *In Search of Ancient Israel* (Sheffield, 1992). 14. 2 Samuel 13: 37. 15. Thomas Gray, 'Elegy Written in a Country Church-yard' (1751). 16. John Keats, 'La Belle Dame Sans Merci' (1819). 17. Percy Bysshe Shelley, 'Ozymandias' (1818). Rameses II, pharaoh of the XIXth dynasty, was known to the Greeks as Ozymandias. His statue, 'the Younger Memnon', which inspired Shelley, is in the British Museum. 18. Horace, *Odes*, book I, ode 14, lines 1–4. 19. From Henry Wadsworth Longfellow, 'The

Building of the Ship' (1849).   20. W. S. Churchill, *The Second World War*, vol. 3:
The Grand Alliance (London, 1950), p. 24.

CHAPTER I. TOLOSA

Bibliographical Note. Until recently, the Visigoths have not been treated favour-
ably by historians. The decline of the Roman Empire in the West was conventionally viewed from the imperial perspective and through Latin sources. And the
transitional fifth century did not get much coverage. The *New Cambridge Medieval History*, vol. 1 (Cambridge, 2005), for example, does not address the period
before AD 500. Two relevant collections of academic studies are available in English: P. Heather (ed.), *The Visigoths from the Migration Period to the Seventh
Century: An Ethnographic Perspective* (Woodbridge, 1999), and A. Ferreiro (ed.),
The Visigoths: Studies in Culture and Society (Leiden, 1999). A synthesis of the
subject has recently been published in German: Gerd Kampers, *Geschichte der
Westgoten* (Paderborn, 2008). A chapter on 'The First Gothic Successor State' is
well hidden in Peter Heather's *The Goths* (Oxford, 1996), pp. 181–215.

I

1. See www.lescommunes.com/communie-vouille-86294.html (2009). See also
15e Centenaire de la Bataille de Vouillé, 507–2007, foreword by Ségolène Royal
(Poitiers, 2007), p. 29.   2. www.507vouillelabataille.com (2008).

II

3. After J. B. Bury, *The History of the Later Roman Empire, 395–800* (London,
1889), vol. 1, ch. 6.   4. See H. Wolfram, *History of the Goths* (Berkeley, 1998);
P. Heather, 'The Fourth Century Goths', in P. Heather and J. Matthews, *The
Goths in the 4th Century* (London, 1991), pp. 51–94.   5. Themistius, *Orations*,
quoted by Heather, and Matthews, *The Goths in the 4th Century*,
p. 47.   6. Edward Gibbon, *The History of the Decline and Fall of the Roman
Empire*, Everyman edn., 6 vols. (London, 1911), ch. 31.   7. Marcel Brion, *Alaric
the Goth* (London, 1932).   8. Paulus Orosius (d. 418), *Historia Adversos Paga-
nos*, quoted Gibbon, *Decline and Fall*, ch. 31.   9. See R. Mathisen and H. Sivan,
'Forging a New Identity: The Kingdom of Toulouse and the Frontiers of Visigothic Aquitaine, 418–507', in Ferreiro, *The Visigoths*, pp. 1–62.   10. Septimania,
'the province of the Seven Cities' on the Mediterranean coast, was made up of the
modern districts of Béziers, Elne, Agde, Narbonne, Lodève, Maguelonne and
Nîmes.   11. See Mathisen and Sivan, 'Forging a New Identity'.   12. St Jerome
(342–420), translator of the Latin Vulgate Bible. His Chronicle built on the earlier
work of St Eusebius and became the basic source on the history of the early
Christian Church. See also L. Valentin, *St Prosper d'Aquitaine* (Paris,

1900). 13. E. A. Thompson, *The Huns* (Oxford, 1999); Christopher Kelly, *Attila the Hun: Barbarian Terror and the Fall of the Roman Empire* (London, 2008). 14. Sidonius Apollinaris, *Letters*, trans. O. M. Dalton (Oxford, 1915). 15. K. Zeumer (ed.), *Leges Visigothorum Antiquiores* (Hanover, 1894). 16. Pablo C. Diaz, 'Toulouse: The Shadow of the Roman Empire', in Heather, *The Visigoths*, pp. 330 ff. 17. See Ian Wood, in Kathleen Mitchell and Ian Wood (eds.), *The World of Gregory of Tours* (Leiden, 2002). 18. T. Hodgkin, *Theodoric the Goth: The Barbarian Champion of Civilization* (London, 1923). 19. See J. Gaudemet, 'Bréviaire d'Alaric', in Jean Leclant (ed.), *Dictionnaire de ll'antiquité* (Paris, 2005). 20. See Edward James, *The Franks* (Oxford, 1998). 21. Gregory of Tours, *Historia Francorum*, 2.35; Latin text at www. thelatinlibrary.com/gregorytours/gregorytours2.shtml; a translation is available at www.fordham.edu/halsall/basis/gregory-hist.html. 22. Ibid., 2.37. 23. Ian Wood, in Rosamund McKitterick and Roland Quinault (eds.), *Gibbon and Empire* (Cambridge, 1997). 24. Gibbon, *Decline and Fall*, ch. 38. 25. See John Moorehead, *Justinian* (London, 1994). 26. See B. Young, 'The Missing Archaeology of the Visigoths', in *The Battle of Vouillé: Symposium Commemorating the 1500th Anniversary*, University of Indiana at Urbana Champaign, 12 April 2007; http://theheroicage.blogspot.com/2007_04_01_archive.html.

III

27. 'La Bataille de Voulon', http://voulon.fr/histoire_42.htm (2010). 28. www. jacobins.mairie-toulouse.fr/patrhist/edifices/menu/listeed_.htm (2010); www. visite.org/aquitaine/fr/patrimoine.php (2010). 29. A. Ferreiro, *The Visigoths in Gaul and Spain, AD 418–711: A Bibliography* (Leiden, 1998). 30. 'Cloîtres et monastères disparus de Toulouse', http://pedagogie.ac-toulouse.fr/culture/religieux/clodaurade.htm (2010). 31. www.corbieresweb.com/montagne-d-alaric (2010). 32. Henry Lincoln, *The Holy Place: Decoding the Mystery of Rennes-le-Château* (Moreton-in-Marsh, 2005); www.rennes-le-chateau-archive. com/ (2010). 33. Henri Boudet, *La Vraie Langue celtique et le cromlech de Rennes-les-Bains* (Carcassonne, 1886; Nîmes, 1999). 34. http://redpill.daily grail.com/wiki/rennes_le_chateau (2010); http://dreamscape.com/morgana/metis. htm (2010); www.magie-arcadie.be/rennes-le-chateau.htm (2010). 35. Gérard de Sède, *L'Or de Rennes, ou La vie insolite de Bérenger Saunière* (Paris, 1967); Michael Baigent, Richard Leigh and Henry Lincoln, *The Holy Blood and the Holy Grail* (London, 1982, 2005); R. Andrews and P. Schellenberger, *The Tomb of God* (London, 1996); Lynn Picknett and Clive Prince, *The Templar Revelation: Secret Guardians of the True Identity of Christ* (London, 1997, 2007); Christian Doumergue, *Rennes-le-Château, le grand héritage* (Nîmes, 1997); Dan Brown, *The Da Vinci Code: A Novel* (London, 2003). 36. See Joseph O'Callaghan, *A History of Mediaeval Spain* (Ithaca, NY, 1975), ch. 1, 'The Visigothic Kingdom'; Harold Livermore, *Twilight of the Goths: The Rise and Fall of the Kingdom of Toledo, 575–711* (Bristol, 2006). 37. D. A. Pharies, *A Brief History of the*

Spanish Language (Chicago, 2007). **38.** http://rickmk.com/rmk/pray/got-our.html (2010). **39.** V. Kouznetsov, *Les Alains: cavaliers des steppes, seigneurs du Caucase* (Paris, 1997). **40.** August von Platen (1796–1835), 'Das Grab in Busento' (1820).

CHAPTER 2. ALT CLUD

Bibliographical Note. There is no dedicated monograph in English on this subject, and only a handful of scattered academic articles such as Alan Macquarrie, 'The Kings of Strathclyde', in A. Grant and K. Stringer (eds.), *Mediaeval Scotland: Crown, Lordship and Community* (Edinburgh, 1993), pp. 1–20, or, for the later period, Davitt Broun, 'The Welsh Identity of the Kingdom of Strathclyde, 900–1100', *Innes Review*, 55 (2004), pp. 111–80. Growing piles of information, of variable reliablility, are available on a rising tide of internet sites, including www.templum.freeserve.co.uk/history/strathclyde/localkings.htm and http://en.wikipedia.org/wiki/list_of_kings_of_strathclyde. The background is beautifully presented by Alistair Moffat, *Before Scotland: The Story of Scotland before History* (London, 2005), especially ch. 7, 'The Last of the British'.

I

1. A panoramic view of the Rock can be seen at www.flickr.com/photos/ccgd/5512793/. Also *Dumbarton Rock*, photo by John Crae; www.clydesite.co.uk/articles/upperriver.asp. **2.** R. Jeffrey and I. Watson, *Doon the Watter: A Century of Holidays on the Clyde*, 2 vols. (Edinburgh, 1999). **3.** Iain McCrorie, *The Royal Road to the Isles* (Glasgow, 2001); F. M. Walker, *Song of the Clyde: A History of Clyde Shipbuilding* (Edinburgh, 2001); see also www.shipsofcalmac.co.uk/history_timeline.asp. **4.** www.traditionalmusic.co.uk/folk-song-lyrics/roamin_in_the_gloamin_.htm; see also Gordon Irving, *Great Scot: The Life Story of Sir Harry Lauder* (London, 1968). **5.** Quoted in www.turningwood.fsnet.co.uk/dumbarton.html (2004); www.undiscovered-scotland.co.uk/dumbarton/dumbartoncastle (2008); see also Iain MacIvor, *Dumbarton Castle* (Edinburgh, 2003). **6.** See Brian Lavery, 'The British Government and the American Polaris Base on the Clyde', *Journal of Martime Research* (Sep. 2001). **7.** www.whiskymag.com/whisky/brand/ballantine_s (2004); www.ballantines.com. **8.** Incorporated 1765, see www.dunbartonnh.org.

II

9. T. Mommsen, 'Petrarch's Conception of the Dark Ages', *Speculum*, 17/2 (1942), pp. 226–42. **10.** K. H. Schmidt, 'Insular Celtic: P and Q Celtic', in M. J. Ball and J. Fife (eds.), *The Celtic Languages* (London, 1993); Paul Russell, *An Introduction to the Celtic Languages* (London, 1995). **11.** W. F. Skene, *The Four Ancient*

Books of Wales, 2 vols. (Edinburgh, 1868).   12. http://en.wikipedia.org/wiki/ Cumbric_language (2008). Most recently, and after the completion of the present essay, a Cumbric Revival Community has been launched on the Internet at www. cumbricrevival.com.   13. See Peter Brown, *The Rise of Western Christendom* (Oxford, 2003).   14. Elizabeth Sutherland, *In Search of the Picts: A Celtic Dark Age Nation* (London, 1994).   15. Possibly confused with another Alauna, south of Hadrian's Wall, usually located at modern Maryport (Cumbria). See also I. A. Richmond, 'Ancient Geographical Sources for Britain North of the Cheviot', in his *Roman and Native in North Britain* (Edinburgh, 1958); G. W. S. Barrow, 'The Tribes of North Britain Revisited', *Proceedings of the Society of Antiquaries of Scotland*, 119 (1989), pp. 161–3.   16. In July 2008, the Antonine Wall was adopted by UNESCO as a World Heritage Site. See www.antonineway. com.   17. See Michael Jones, *The End of Roman Britain* (Ithaca, NY, 1996).   18. Peniarth MS 45, National Library of Wales: translated online at http://www.maryjones.us/ctexts/bonedd.html (2010).   19. 'Yr Hen Ogledd', in John Koch (ed.), *Celtic Culture: A Historical Encyclo-pedia* (Oxford, 2006).   20. C. T. Greenhead, quoted in Moffat, *Before Scotland*, p. 305.   21. Old Kilpatrick, West Dunbartonshire, which is situated on the Clyde at the western end of the Antonine Wall. See www.rcag.org.uk/parishes_st.patricks_oldkil-patrick.htm.   22. Macquarrie, 'The Kings of Strathclyde', p. 4, and A. Boyle, 'The Birthplace of St. Patrick', *Scottish Historical Review*, 60 (1981). Boyle's identifi-cation of Fintry near Old Kilpatrick with the *Ventre* of Miurchu's *Vita sancti Patricii* (seventh century) and with W. J. Watson's *Venn tref* or 'White House' is rejected, somewhat unconvincingly, on the grounds that Kilpatrick is supposedly a Gaelic name of much later vintage; W. J. Watson, *The History of Celtic Place-names of Scotland* (Edinburgh, 1993). See J. B. Bury, *The Life of St Patrick and his Place in History* (London, 1905).   23. St Patrick, 'Letter to Coroticus', in R. P. C. Hanson, *The Life and Writings of the Historical Saint Patrick* (New York, 1983), pp. 58–73.   24. Daphne Brooke, *The Search for St Ninian* (Whithorn, 1993).   25. Leslie Alcock, 'A Multi-Disciplinary Chronology for Alt Clut, Castle Rock, Dumbarton', *Proceedings of the Society of Antiquaries of Scotland* (1975–6), p. 105.   26. See Kathleen Hughes, 'The Welsh Latin Chronicles: *Annales Cam-briae* and Related Texts', in Hughes, *Celtic Britain in the Early Middle Ages: Studies in Scottish and Welsh Sources* (Woodbridge, 1980), pp. 67–85.   27. Nennius, *Historia Brittonum* ('A History of the Britons'), ed. D. Dum-ville (Cambridge, 1985).   28. Moffat, *Before Scotland,* p. 320.   29. Adamnan, *Life of St Columba*, ed. W. Reeves (Lampeter, 1988); Adamnan of Iona, *Life of St Columba*, trans. R. Sharpe (London, 1995).   30. http://www.clanarthur.com (2008); http://www.scottishweb.net/...clans-clanmacarthur/ (2010).   31. At Strathblane. In *Arthur and the Lost Kingdoms* (London, 1999), Alistair Moffat argues for King Arthur's base to have been located at Roxburgh Castle in the Borders.   32. John Bruce, *History of the Parish of West or Old Kilpatrick and of the Church and Certain Lands in the Parish of East or New Kilpatrick* (Glasgow, 1893); Joseph Irving, *History of Dumbartonshire* (Dumbarton, 1860).   33. James Knight, *Glasgow and Strathclyde* (London, 1930). The references to Bruce, Irving,

Knight and others are at www.templum.freeserve.co.uk/history/strathclyde/arthur.htm. **34.** The Life is by Jocelyn of Furness. See John Glass, *The Mission of St Mungo* (Twickenham, 2007). **35.** 'The University of Glasgow Story' at www.universitystory.gla.ac.uk/coat-of-arms/. **36.** See www.catholicireland.net/church-a-bible/church/january-saints/1226-14-st-kentigern-or-mungo. Many versions of the legend exist. **37.** Adamnan, *Life of St Columba*, ch. 8. See also 'Rhydderch Hael', www.celtnet.org.uk/gods_rh/rhydderch.htm. **38.** See M. Lapidge and D. Dumville, *Gildas: New Approaches* (Woodbridge, 1984). **39.** A. Marette-Crosby, *The Foundations of Christian England: Augustine of Canterbury and his Impact* (York, 1997). **40.** J. T. Koch (ed.), *The Gododdin of Aneirin: Text and Context from Dark-Age North Britain* (Cardiff, 1997), p. 52. **41.** Ibid., pp. 10–11. **42.** Ibid., pp. 12–13. **43.** From 'The Stanzas of the Graves', in *The Black Book of Carmarthen*, http://www.celtic-twilight.com/camelot/poetry/yrhengerdd/englynion_y_beddau.htm. (2008). **44.** Moffat, *Before Scotland*, p. 326. **45.** Bede, *Ecclesiastical History*, book 4, ch. 26. **46.** James Fraser, *The Pictish Conquest: The Battle of Dunnichen 685 and the Birth of Scotland* (Stroud, 2006). **47.** Moffat, *Before Scotland*, pp. 328–9. **48.** See W. D. Simpson, *The Early Christian Monuments at Aberlemno, Angus* (Edinburgh, 1969). **49.** P. C. Bartrum (trans.), *Early Welsh Genealogical Tracts* (Cardiff, 1966): also online at http://kmatthews.org.uk/history/harleian_genealogies/5.html. **50.** 'Pittin the mither tongue online', www.scots-online.org (2010). **51.** Macquarrie, 'The Kings of Strathclyde', p. 1. **52.** See John Bannerman, *Studies in the History of Dalriada* (Edinburgh, 1974). **53.** N. A. M. Rodger, *The Safeguard of the Sea: A Naval History of Britain, 660–1649* (London, 1997), p. 5. **54.** From Bede, book 1, chs. 1, 12, quoted in Alcock, 'A Multi-Disciplinary Chronology for Alt Clut', pp. 104–5. **55.** *Brut y Tywysogion* ('Chronicle of the Princes'), ed. Revd John Williams ab Ithel (London, 1860), pp. 6–7. **56.** Otherwise Teudibar map Beli, see www.earlybritishkingdoms.com/lists/strathclyde.html. **57.** N. Aitchison, *Scotland's Stone of Destiny: Myth, History and Nationhood* (Stroud, 2000). **58.** Macquarrie, 'The Kings of Strathclyde', pp. 12, 18. **59.** *Brut y Tywysogion*, pp. 14–15; *Nennius: British History and the Welsh Annals*, ed. J. Morris (London, 1980), pp. 48, 89; *The Annales Cambriae: Texts A–C in Parallel*, ed. D. Dumville (Cambridge, 2002); *The Annals of Ulster*, quoted by Alcock, 'A Multi-Disciplinary Chronology for Alt Clut', p. 106. **60.** Text reconstructed by author. **61.** A. A. M. Duncan, *Scotland: The Making of the Kingdom* (Edinburgh, 1995), p. 90. **62.** Macquarrie, 'The Kings of Strathclyde', p. 12. **63.** Ibid., pp. 12–13. **64.** See John Davies, *A History of Wales* (London, 1993), pp. 62 ff. **65.** Norman Davies, *The Isles: A History* (London, 1999), pp. 216–17. **66.** *Brut y Tywysogion*, pp. 20–21. **67.** See Broun, 'The Welsh Identity of the Kingdom of Strathclyde'. **68.** See e.g. Nicholas Aitchison, *Macbeth: Man and Myth* (Stroud, 1999). **69.** *The Chronicle of John of Worcester*, ed. R. Darlington and P. McGurk (Oxford, 1998). **70.** A. A. M. Duncan, *Kingship of the Scots, 842–1292* (Edinburgh, 2002), pp. 37–41. **71.** Cynthia Nevile, *Native Lordship in Mediaeval Scotland: The Earldoms of Strathearn and Lennox, 1140–1365* (Portland and Dublin, 2005). **72.** Michael, bishop of Glasgow. According to English sources, two earlier bishops of Glasgow were appointed by the archbishops of York. Bishop Magsuen (*fl.* 1055–60) may well have owed his see to the conquest of Earl Siward.   73. A. Dooley and H. Roe, *Tales of the Elders of Ireland* (Oxford, 1998), p. 13.   74. F. Mort, *Renfrewshire* (Cambridge, 1912).   75. A. A. M. Duncan, 'William, Son of Alan Wallace: The Documents', in J. Cowan (ed.), *The Wallace Book* (Edinburgh, 2007), pp. 42–63.   76. Fiona Watson, 'Sir William Wallace: What We Do – and Don't Know', in Cowan, *The Wallace Book*, p. 27.   77. J. C. Borland, *William Wallace: His Birthplace and Family Connections* (Kilmarnock, 1999).   78. James A. Mackay, *William Wallace: Brave Heart* (Edinburgh, 1996).   79. George Fraser Black, *The Surnames of Scotland: Their Origin, Meaning and History* (New York, 1946).   80. See also M. Stead and A. Young, *In the Steps of William Wallace* (London, 2002).   81. Alistair Moffat, *The Highland Clans* (London, 2010), p. 151.

III

82. See G. W. S. Barrow, *Kingship and Unity: Scotland 1000–1306* (London, 1981)   83. John Prebble, *Culloden* (London, 1973); J. Sadler, *Culloden: The Last Charge of the Highland Clans* (Stroud, 2006).   84. John Prebble, *The Highland Clearances* (London, 1963).   85. Wilson McLeod, *Revitalising Gaelic in Scotland* (Edinburgh, 2006).   86. R. Renwick and J. Lindsay, *The History of Glasgow*, 3 vols. (Glasgow, 1934).   87. James Macpherson, *The Poems of Ossian and Related Works* (Edinburgh, 1896).

CHAPTER 3. BURGUNDIA

Bibliographical Note. The overwhelming mass of general works on Burgundy are written from the French perspective, and the great majority of them concentrate heavily on the history of the late medieval duchy. See, for example, Henri Drouot, *Histoire de Bourgogne* (Paris, 1927), or Jean Richard, *Histoire de Bourgogne* (Paris, 1957). There is no standard study of the imperial Kingdom of Burgundy in English, and no broad survey of Burgundian history as a whole.

I

1. See www.brk.dk; also http://en.wikipedia.org/wiki/bornholm (2007).   2. See www.cimber.com (2010), www.airliners.net/aviation-forums/general_aviation/4474449 (2010).   3. http://en.wikipedia.org/wiki.bornholmsk_dialect (2011); J. D. Prince, 'The Danish Dialect of Bornholm', *Proceedings of the American Philosophical Society,* 63/2 (1924), pp. 190–207.   4. 'Bornholmsk Folkemusik', http://www.myspace.com/habbadam (2010).   5. J. H. Hopkins, 'Bornholm Disease', *British Medical Journal,* 1/4664 (May 1950).   6. Martin Anderson Nexo, *Pelle Eroberen* (1910), translated as *Pelle the Conqueror* (London, 1916) and

turned into a film directed by Bille August in 1987. 7. http://www.iau.org.
tw. 8. 'Trolling Master Bornholm Allinge', http://www.eventful.com/events/
trolling-master . . ./ (2001). 9. Danish Naturists Federation, http://www.
strandguide.dk (2010). 10. 'Bright Green Island', http://www.brk.dk/bornholm/
site=aspx?p=45 (2010). 11. Erling Haagense, *The Templars' Secret Island*
(Moreton-in-Marsh, 2000). 12. R.Guichard, *Essai sur l'histoire du peuple Bur-
gonde de Bornholm* (Paris, 1965); I. Wood, 'Ethnicity and the Ethnogenesis of the
Burgundians', in H. Wolfram and W. Pohl (eds.), *Typen der Ethnogenese unter
besonderer Berücksichtigung der Bayern* (Vienna, 1990). 13. See Knud Jes-
persen, *A History of Denmark* (Basingstoke, 2004). 14. 'Danish Island Calls for
Help', 28 December 2010, www.swedishwire.com/nordic/7860 (2010).

II

15. James Bryce, *The Holy Roman Empire* (London, 1901), p. 434. 16. Ibid.
17. Odet Perrin, *Les Burgondes* (Neuchâtel, 1968). 18. Guichard, *Essai*.
19. G. W. S. Friedrichsen, *The Gothic Version of the Epistles* (London, 1939);
Charles A. Anderson Scott, *Ulfilas: Apostle of the Goths* (Cambridge, 1885).
20. From *Widsith*, ed. K. Malone (London, 1936). 21. Perrin, *Les Burgondes*,
pp. 270–73. 22. Translation by author. 23. Edward Peters, 'Introduction', to
Katherine Drew, *The Burgundian Code: Book of Constitutions or Law of Gundobad* (Philadelphia, 1963), pp. 1–2. 24. C. E. Stevens, *Sidonius Apollinaris and
his Age* (Oxford, 1933). 25. J. Favrod, *Les Burgondes: un royaume oublié au
cœur de l'Europe* (Lausanne, 2002), pp. 32 ff. 26. Ibid., p. 235. 27. Perrin, *Les
Burgondes*, p. 537. 28. See P. Grierson and M. Blackburn, *Medieval European
Coinage* (Cambridge, 1986), vol. 1, pp. 75 ff. 29. 'St Clothilda', *Catholic Encyclopedia* (New York, 1907). 30. 'The Burgundian Civil War', *Burgundians in the
Mist*, http://www.theburgundian.blogspot.com/2010/06/burgundian-civil-war.
html (2010). 31. Drew, *The Burgundian Code*, contains the text of the code in
translation. 32. Ibid., p. 31. 33. Ibid., p. 84. 34. Ibid., p. 86. 35. Ibid., p.
17. 36. F. Paxton, 'Power and the Power to Heal: The Cult of St Sigismund
of Burgundy', *Early Modern Europe*, 2 (1993), pp. 95–110. 37. D. Shanzer and
I. Wood, *Avitus of Vienne: Letters and Selected Prose* (Liverpool, 2002). 38. P.
Bouffard, *Saint-Maurice d'Agaune* (Geneva, 1974). 39. J. von Pflugk-Harttung,
A History of All Nations from the Earliest of Times (Philadelphia, 1905),
p. 399. 40. See Guy Raynaud de Lage, *Introduction à l'ancien français* (Paris,
1975); P. Porteau, 'Langue d'oc et langue d'oïl', in his *Deux études dans l'histoire
de la langue* (Paris, 1962). 41. Gregory of Tours, *Historia Francorum*, 4.25. See
Medieval Online Sourcebook, www.fordham.edu/halsall/basis/gregory-hist.
html. 42. Ibid., 3.19. 43. J. Favrod (trans.), *La Chronique de Marius
d'Avenches* (Lausanne, 1991). 44. W. E. Klingshirn, *Caesarius of Arles: The
Making of a Christian Community in Late Antique Gaul* (Cambridge, 1994).
45. F. MacManus, *St Columban* (New York, 1963); Katherine Lack, *The Eagle
and the Dove: The Spirituality of the Celtic Saint Columbanus* (London,

2000). **46.** J. M. Wallace-Hadrill, 'The Bloodfeud of the Franks', in his *The Long-Haired Kings and Other Studies in Frankish History* (London, 1962). **47.** J. M. Wallace-Hadrill, 'Fredegar and the History of France', ibid., p. 87. **48.** Ibid., p. 92. **49.** Ibid., p. 147. **50.** L. Theis, *Dagobert: un roi pour un peuple* (Paris, 1952). **51.** Antonio Santosuosso, *Barbarians, Marauders and Infidels: The Ways of Medieval Warfare* (Boulder, Colo., 2004). **52.** Alessandro Barbero, *Charlemagne: Father of a Continent* (Berkeley, 2004), pp. 28-33. **53.** Jean Richard, *Les Ducs de Bourgogne et la formation du duché* (Paris, 1954). **54.** Lucy Smith, *The Early History of the Abbey of Cluny* (London, 1930); Edwin Mullins, *In Search of Cluny: God's Lost Empire* (Oxford, 2004). **55.** Gillian Evans, *Bernard of Clairvaux* (Oxford, 2000). **56.** 'A Thousand Years of Monastic Winegrowing', www.bourgogne-wines.com. **57.** 'Le Duc de Bordeaux', http://wn.com/un_deux_rab (2010). **58.** R. Poupardin, *Boson et le royaume de Provence* (Châlons-sur-Saône, 1899). **59.** Mireille Labrousse, *St Honorat: fondateur de Lérins et Évêque d'Arles* (Bégrolles, 1995). **60.** Favrod, *La Chronique de Marius d'Avenches*, p. 122. **61.** R. Lane Poole, *Burgundian Notes: The Union of the Two Kingdoms of Burgundy* (Oxford, 1913). **62.** Geoffrey Barraclough, *The Origins of Modern Germany* (London, 1947), pp. 50-51. **63.** *Alpes du Nord*, Michelin, Guide Vert (Paris, 2007), pp. 338-9. **64.** R. W. Dixon, *The Close of the Tenth Century of the Christian Era*, Arnold Prize Essay (Oxford, 1858), p. 2. **65.** E. Taylor (ed.), *Lays of the Minnesingers or German Troubadours of the Twelfth and Thirteenth Centuries* (London, 1825), pp. 15-16. **66.** D. Stich, *Parlons francoprovençal: une langue méconnue* (Paris, 1998); www.arpitania.com. **67.** R. Lane Poole, *Burgundian Notes: The Supposed Origin of Burgundia Minor* (Oxford, 1915). **68.** See Adam Wandruszka, *The House of Habsburg: Six Hundred Years of a European Dynasty* (London, 1994). **69.** 'Zaehringen', *Encyclopaedia Britannica*, 11th edn. (1911). **70.** Peter Munz, *Frederick Barbarossa: A Study in Medieval Politics* (London, 1969). **71.** K. Leyser, 'The Crisis of Medieval Germany', in his *Communications and Power in Medieval Europe*, vol. 2 (London, 1994). **72.** Barraclough, *Origins of Modern Germany*, p. 146. **73.** David Abulafia, *Frederick II: A Medieval Emperor* (London, 1988). **74.** See J. Boichard, *Histoire de la Franche-Comté* (Toulouse, 1978). **75.** See Rudolf Massini, *Des Bistums Basel zur Zeit des Investiturstreites* (Basle, 1946). **76.** Reginald Abbot, *The Rise of the Swiss Confederation* (Oxford, 1861). **77.** M. Aurel *et al.*, *La Provence au Moyen-Âge* (Aix-en-Provence, 2005). **78.** A. Latreille, *L'Histoire de Lyon et du Lyonnais* (Toulouse, 1975). **79.** J. Charay, *Petite histoire politique et administrative du Vivarais* (Lyon, 1959). **80.** F. Benoit, *La Provence et le Comtat Venaissin* (Paris, 1949); B. Guillemain, *La Cour pontificale d'Avignon* (Paris, 1962). **81.** Françoise Gasparri, *La Principauté d'Orange au Moyen Âge* (Paris, 1985). **82.** Council of Lyon, 1245. See www.piar.hu/councils/ecum13.htm#bullofex-communication; full text at www.intratext.com/ixt/eng0066/. **83.** W. L. Wakefield, *Heresy, Crusade and Inquisition in Southern France, 1100-1250* (London, 1974); A. Monaster, *History of the Vaudois Church* (London, 1848). **84.** See Joseph Strayer, *The Reign of Philip the Fair* (Princeton, 1980). **85.** B. Bligny, *L'Histoire du Dauphiné*

(Toulouse, 1973). 86. See www.identitecomtoise.net/histoire, a website on the language and history of Franche-Comté. 87. From 'Philip I of Burgundy', http://en.wikipedia.org/wiki/philip_1%2c_duke_of_burgundy (August 2007). 88. Richard Vaughan, *Philip the Bold: The Formation of the Burgundian State* (London, 1979). 89. Richard Vaughan, *Valois Burgundy* (London, 1975). 90. J. Billioud, *Les États de Bourgogne aux XIVe et XVe siècles* (Dijon, 1922). 91. J. Calmette, *The Golden Age of Burgundy* (London, 2001). 92. G. Attinger, *L'Histoire du Pays de Neuchâtel* (Neuchâtel, 1979). 93. W. Blockmans and W. Prevenier, *The Promised Lands: The Low Countries under Burgundian Rule, 1369–1530* (Philadelphia, 1999), pp. 164–5. 94. Jean Froissart, *The Chronicles of England, France and Spain etc.* (London, 1906), p. 464. 95. J.-M. Cauchies (ed.), *A la cour de Bourgogne: le Duc, son entourage, son train* (Turnhout, 1998). 96. Myriam Cheyns-Condé, 'L'Épopée troyenne dans la "Librairie" ducale bourguignonne', in Cauchies, *A la cour de Bourgogne*. See also N. F. Blake, *William Caxton and English Literary Culture* (London, 1992). 97. H. Liebaers, *Flemish Art from the Beginning till Now* (Antwerp, 1985); Dirk De Vos, *The Flemish Primitives* (Amsterdam, 2002). 98. K. Morand, *Claus Sluter: Artist at the Court of Burgundy* (London, 1991). 99. J. Lestoc-quoy, *Deux siècles de l'histoire de la tapisserie* (Arras, 1978). 100. 'Un tres doulx regard: the blossoming of the Burgundian spirit in song, 1390–1440', www.asteriamusica.com/programs.html (2007). 101. D. Fallows, *Dufay* (New York, 1998); W. H. Kemp, *Burgundian Court Song* (Oxford, 1990); H. M. Brown, *Josquin and the Fifteenth-Century Chanson* (Oxford, 1985). 102. L. E. Halkin, *Erasmus: A Critical Biography* (Oxford, 1993). 103. J. Huizinga, *The Waning of the Middle Ages* (London, 1924), p. 1. 104. See 'Johan Huizinga', at www.kirjasto.sci.fi/huizin.htm (2008). 105. From Froissart, *Chronicles*. 106. http://www.chateau-de-santenay.com (2010). 107. 'Le Palais des Ducs de Bourgogne', http://dijon.free.fr/visite/palais1.htm (2010). 108. Richard Vaughan, *John the Fearless: The Growth of Burgundian Power* (London, 1966). 109. Richard Vaughan, *Philip the Good: The Apogee of Burgundy* (Woodbridge, 2002). 110. Edward Tabri, 'The Funeral of Duke Philip the Good', *Essays in History*, 33 (1990–91). 111. Richard Vaughan, *Charles the Bold: The Last Duke of Burgundy* (Woodbridge, 2002); Henri Dubois, *Charles le Téméraire* (Paris, 2004). 112. Philippe de Commynes, *The Universal Spider: The Life of Louis XI of France*, trans. and ed. Paul Kendall (London, 1973), p. 212. 113. Ibid., p. 213. 114. Ibid., pp. 198 ff. See also Musée Historique de Berne, *Le Butin des guerres de Bourgogne et œuvres d'art de la cour de Bourgogne*, catalogue raison-née (Berne, 1969). 115. Luc Hommel, *Marie de Bourgogne ou le grand héritage* (Brussels, 1945); G. Dumont, *Marie de Bourgogne* (Paris, 1982). 116. Martyn Rady, *The Emperor Charles V* (London, 1988). 117. See http://en.wikipedia.org/wiki/reichskreis. 118. See Pieter Geyl, *The Revolt of the Netherlands* (London, 1988). 119. Jean Schneider, *L'Histoire de la Lorraine* (Paris, 1961). 120. Francisco Elías de Tejada y Spínola, *El Franco-condado hispánico* (Seville, 1975); François Pernot, *La Franche-Comté espagnole* (Besançon, 2003). 121. See http://fr.wikipedia.org/wiki/anciennes_provinces_de_france

(2008).   122.   http://regionsdefrance.wikispaces.com/   (2008).   123.   www.
rhonealpes.fr/ (2008).   124. Apparently a transposition of the French motto
'*Autre n'auray*', also used by the dukes; see R. Prosser, *The Order of the Golden
Fleece* (Iowa City, 1981), p. 5.

III

125. 'Burgundy',www.answers.com (2009).   126. 'Burgundy (region)', http://
en.wikipedia.org/wiki/burgundy_(region) (2008). Some of the problems are sorted
out at http://fr.wikipedia.org/wiki/bourgogne_(homonymie).   127. www.burgun
dynet/history-burgundy.html.   128. *Shorter Oxford English Dictionary* (Oxford,
2000), vol. 1, p. 253.   129. *Oxford English Dictionary*, compact edn. (Oxford,
1971), vol. 1, p. 1187.   130. Dictionaries listed above include: www.meriam-
webster.com. Émile Littré (Paris, 1956); Paul Robert (Paris, 1966); Paul lmbs
(Paris, 1975); *New Encylopaedia Britannica*, macropedia, vol. 3, p. 497; and
Nouveau petit Larousse (Paris, 1969).   131. *Brockhaus: die Encyclopädie* (Leipzig, 1996), vol. 4, pp. 196–8.   132. *Encyklopedia Powszechna PWN* (Warsaw,
1973), vol. 1, pp. 379–80.   133. Saul Cohen (ed.), *The Columbia Gazetteer of
the World* (New York, 1998), vol. 1, pp. 470–71.   134. Andrew Dalby, *The
World and Wikipedia: How We Are Editing Reality* (Draycott, 2009).   135. To
be fair, the chapter closes with 'the history of the various Burgundian regions was
far from simple'; *New Cambridge Medieval History* (Cambridge, 1999), vol. 3, pp.
328, 345.   136. Robert J. Casey, *The Lost Kingdom of Burgundy* (London, 1924),
pp. 3, 6, 8.

CHAPTER 4. ARAGON

Bibliographical Note. Library catalogues contain more entries on the writer
Louis Aragon than on the Crown of Aragon. Apart from Thomas Bisson's *The
Medieval Crown of Aragon: A Short History* (Oxford, 1986), there is no satisfac-
tory work in English on the overall subject. Henry Chaytor's *History of Aragon
and Catalonia* (London, 1933), which is now available online, starts with 'the
grand-sons of Noah' and is far too densely detailed for comfort. Numerous documentary sources have been collected and translated, such as the *Llibre dels Fets*
of James the Conqueror (see note 51 below) or *The Chronicle of Muntaner* (see
note 37). And it is not difficult to find excellent monographs or academic articles
on particular aspects and episodes. But the inclusive approach is signally lacking,
especially in work inspired by national Catalan or regional Aragonese perspectives. Readers seeking introductory matter need to explore books on the Iberian
peninsula as a whole, such as Jocelyn Hillgarth's *The Spanish Kingdoms, 1250–
1516* (Oxford, 1976) or Stanley Payne's 'The Rise of Aragón-Catalonia', in his *A
History of Spain and Portugal*, 2 vols. (Madison, 1973), vol. 1, ch. 5.

I

1. www.perpignan.cci.fr/2-13674-accueil.php (2007). 2. 'Office de Tourisme de la Ville de Perpignan', www.mairie-perpignan.fr (2007). 3. http://france-for-visitors.com/pyrenees/roussillon/perpignan.html (2007). 4. http://www.usap. com (2010). 5. Marcel Durliat, *L'Histoire du Roussillon* (Paris, 1962), pp. 6, 40. 6. http://www.estivales.com (2010). 7. http://www.villagesdefrance.free.fr (2010). 8. Horace Chauvet, *Folklore du Roussillon* (Perpignan, 1943). 9. Festival of Amélie-les-Bains: http://www.kadmusarts/festivals/932.htm (2010). 10. Alicia Marcet i Juncosa, *Abrégé d'histoire des terres catalanes du nord*, traduction du catalan (Canet, 1994). 11. http://en.wikipedia.org/wiki/el_gran_carlemany (2010). See also A. Degage and A. Duro i Arajol, *L'Andorre* (Paris, 1998).

II

12. *The Song of Roland*, trans. Glyn Burgess (London, 1990), lines 1-9. 13. Barton Sholod, 'The Formation of a Spanish March', in his *Charlemagne in Spain: The Cultural Legacy of Roncesvalles* (Geneva, 1966), pp. 44 ff. 14. Ralph Giesey, *If Not, Not: The Oath of the Aragonese and the Legendary Laws of Sobrarbe* (Princeton, 1968). 15. A. Ferreiro, 'The Siege of Barbastro, 1064-5: A Reassessment', *Journal of Medieval History*, 9/2 (1983), pp. 129-44. 16. Ibn Bassam, quoted by Christopher Dawson, 'The Origins of the Romantic Tradition', in his *Mediaeval Religion and Other Essays* (London, 1934), p. 146. 17. Gerald Bond (ed. and trans.), *The Poetry of William VII, Count of Poitiers, and IX Duke of Aquitaine* (New York, 1982). 18. Richard Fletcher, *The Quest for El Cid* (Oxford, 1991); David Nicolle, *El Cid and the Reconquista* (London, 1988); Ramón Pidal, *The Cid and his Spain* (London, 1924). 19. *The Poem of the Cid: A New Critical Edition*, ed. Ian Michael, trans. Rita Hamilton and Janet Perry (Manchester, 1975), ll. 1 ff. 20. Ibid., ll. 955-61 ff. See T. Montgomery, 'The Cid and the Count of Barcelona', *Hispanic Review*, 30/1 (1962), pp. 1-11. 21. R. W. Southern, *The Making of the Middle Ages* (London, 1953), p. 129. 22. George Beech, *The Brief Eminence and Doomed Fall of Islamic Saragossa* (Zaragoza, 2008). See http://en.wikipedia.org/wiki/taifa_of_zaragoza (2008). 23. J. Boutière and A. H. Schutz (eds.), *Biographies des troubadours* (Paris, 1964). 24. From the Provençal poem *Sainte Foy*, quoted by Chaytor, *History of Aragon and Catalonia*, ch. 4. See also H. J. Chaytor, *The Provençal Chanson de Geste* (London, 1946). 25. Dawson, *Mediaeval Religion and Other Essays*, pp. 125, 128. 26. John Shideler, *A Medieval Catalan Noble Family: The Montcadas, 1000-1230* (Berkeley, 1983). 27. Attributed to Ferdinand the Catholic. On Aragonese constitutional matters, see J. M. Mas i Solench, *Les Corts a la Corona Catalono-Aragonesa* (Barcelona, 1995); Xavier Gil, 'Parliamentary Life in the Crown of Aragon', *Journal of Early Modern History*, 6/4 (2002), pp. 362-95. 28. Georges de Manteyer, *La Provence, du premier au douzième siècle* (Paris, 1908). 29. E. Le Roy Ladurie, *L'Histoire du Languedoc* (Paris, 1962). 30. Bernard Reilly, *The*

Kingdom of León-Castilla under King Alfonso VII (Philadelphia, 1998).   31. Southern, *The Making of the Middle Ages*, pp. 122–7; 'The Family of the Counts of Barcelona', Genealogical Table, ibid., p. 125. Count Wilfred is buried at his foundation, Santa Maria di Ripoll.   32. Peter Sahlins, *Boundaries: The Making of France and Spain in the Pyrenees* (Berkeley, 1989).   33. Norman Davies, *Europe: A History* (Oxford, 1996), pp. 427–8.   34. Jocelyn Hillgarth, 'The Problem of a Catalan Mediterranean Empire', *English Historical Review*, 90 (1975), pp. 3 ff.   35. J. H. Elliott, *The Revolt of the Catalans: A Study in the Decline of Spain, 1598–1640* (Cambridge, 1963), p. 3. See also his 'A Europe of Composite Monarchies', *Past and Present*, 137/1 (1992), pp. 48 ff.   36. http://en.wikipedia. org/wiki/lista_de_reis_d'aragon (Catalan). In the present study, the Aragonese style will be followed, but the Catalan form is equally correct.   37. Pass of Manzana, from *The Chronicle of Muntaner*, trans. from the Catalan by Lady Goodenough (London, 1921).   38. Philippe III le Hardi, during the 'Aragonese Crusade'. See Ivan Gobry, *Philippe III, fils de Saint Louis* (Paris, 2004).   39. *The Chronicle of Muntaner*, vol. 1, pp. 16–17.   40. K. L. Reyerson, 'Flight from Prosecution: The Search for Religious Asylum in Mediaeval Montpellier', *French Historical Studies*, 17/3 (1992), pp. 602–26.   41. See Y. Baer, *A History of the Jews in Christian Spain*, 2 vols. (Philadelphia, 1961).   42. Francesca Español, 'El salterio y libro de horas de Alfonso el Magnánimo y el cardenal Joan de Casanova 28962 (British Library, Add. 28962)', *Locus Amoenus*, 6 (2002–3).   43. Coronation of Alfonso El Benigno, 1328, from, *The Chronicle of Muntaner*, vol. 2, pp. 722–8.   44. Dawson, *Mediaeval Religion and Other Essays*, p. 135.   45. John Boswell, *The Royal Treasure: Muslim Communities under the Crown of Aragon* (New Haven, 1977).   46. *Gesta Comitum Barcinonensiam*, ed. L. Barrau Dihigo and J. Massó i Torrents. (Barcelona, 1925).   47. Ana Isabel Lapeña Paúl, *Selección de documentos del monasterio de San Juan de la Peña, 1195–1410* (Zaragoza, 1995), p. 388.   48. Felipe Fernández-Armesto, *Barcelona: A Thousand Years of the City's Past* (London, 1991).   49. Susan Rose, 'Christians, Muslims and Crusaders: Naval Warfare in the Mediterranean at the Time of the Crusades', in her *Medieval Naval Warfare* (London, 2002), ch. III.   50. *The Chronicle of Muntaner*, vol. 1, pp. 50–52; J. A. Robson, 'The Catalan Fleet and Moorish Sea-power (1337–1344)', *English Historical Review*, 74 (1959), pp. 386–408.   51. *The Book of Deeds of James I of Aragon: A Translation of the Medieval Catalan Llibre dels Fets*, Crusade Texts in Translation, 10, trans. Damian Smith and Helena Buffery (Aldershot, 2003), pp. 78–81.   52. Ibid., p. 84.   53. Ibid., p. 86.   54. http://en.wikipedia.org/wiki/valencian (2007); see also http://en.wikipedia.org/ wiki/kingdom_of_valencia (2008).   55. R. I. Burns, 'Muslims in the Thirteenth-Century Realms of Aragon', in J. Powell (ed.), *Muslims under Latin Rule, 1100–1300* (Princeton, 1990).   56. *Spain*, Dorling Kindersley series (London, 2000), pp. 240–43.   57. J. L. Sotoca García, *Los amantes de Teruel: la tradición y la historia* (Zaragoza, 1979).   58. Marta VanLandingham, 'The Domestic Influence of the Queen', in her *Transforming the State: King, Court and Political Culture in the Realms of Aragon (1213–1387)* (Leiden, 2002), pp. 187–94.   59. See Chaytor, *History of Aragon and Catalonia*, ch. 8.   60. Denis Mack Smith, *Mediaeval*

Sicily (London, 1968); Clifford Backman, *The Decline and Fall of Medieval Sicily: Politics, Religion and Economy in the Reign of Frederick III, 1296–1337* (Cambridge, 1995). **61.** Steven Runciman, *The Sicilian Vespers* (Cambridge, 1958). **62.** Lawrence Mott, *Sea Power in the Medieval Mediterranean: The Catalan-Aragonese Fleet in the War of the Sicilian Vespers* (Gainesville, Fla., 2003). **63.** 'Roger of Loria', *Columbia Electronic Encyclopedia*, www.education.yahoo (2011). **64.** Michele Amari, *History of the War of the Sicilian Vespers* (London, 1850), vol. 2, pp. 231–3. **65.** Dante Alighieri, *Purgatorio*, canto III, ll. 114–17 (translation by author). **66.** Ibid., canto VII, ll. 70–129. **67.** http://en.wikipedia.org/wiki/category:kings_ of_ sicily (2008). **68.** See Neil Wilson, *Malta* (London, 2000). **69.** *The Chronicle of Muntaner*, vol. 2, pp. 507–9. **70.** K. M. Setton, *The Catalan Domination of Athens, 1311–88* (London, 1975). **71.** Ibid. **72.** David Abulafia, 'The Aragonese Kingdom of Albania: An Angevin Project of 1311–16', in B. Arbel (ed.), *Intercultural Contacts in the Medieval Mediterranean* (London, 1996), pp. 1–13. **73.** See Paul Kennedy, *The Rise and Fall of the Great Powers* (London, 1988). **74.** Burns, 'Muslims', pp. 67 ff. **75.** David Abulafia, *A Medieval Emporium: The Catalan Kingdom of Majorca* (Cambridge, 1994). **76.** Ibid. **77.** A. L. Isaacs, *The Jews of Majorca* (London, 1936). **78.** E. A. Peers, *Ramon Lull: A Biography* (London, 1929). **79.** *The Chronicle of Muntaner*, vol. 2, p. 661. **80.** Pere III of Catalonia (Pedro IV of Aragon), *Chronicle*, trans. Mary Hillgarth (Toronto, 1980). **81.** http://en.wikipedia.org/wiki/james_iii_of_majorca (2008). **82.** T. N. Bisson, *Tormented Voices: Power, Crisis and Humanity in Rural Catalonia, 1140–1200* (Cambridge, Mass., 1998). **83.** In his will, Pedro IV had appointed his daughter and only child, Constanza, as his successor. His temerity in this matter was seen by many nobles as a direct threat to their own, more normal practice of male primogeniture. **84.** www.1902encyclopedia.com/s/spa/spain-24htm (2010). **85.** Pere III (Pedro IV), *Chronicle*, pp. 431–9. **86.** J. N. Hillgarth, 'The Royal Accounts of the Crown of Aragon', in her *Spain and the Mediterranean in the Later Middle Ages* (Aldershot, 2003), study III, p. 15. **87.** Josep Brugada i Gutiérrez-Ravé, *Nicolau Eimeric (1320–1399) i la polèmica inquisitorial* (Barcelona, 1998). **88.** Mack Smith, *Mediaeval Sicily*, ch. VII, 'The New Feudalism'. **89.** Bianca Pitzorno, *Vita di Eleonora d'Arborea: principessa medioevale di Sardegna* (Brescia, 1984). **90.** Eleonora d'Arborea, *Carta de Logu* (Sassari, 2002, facsimile of the 1805 edn.). **91.** VanLandingham, *Transforming the State*, 'Introduction'. **92.** Ferran Soldevila, *Història de Catalunya* (Barcelona, 1962). **93.** Norman Davies, 'Xativa', in *Europe: A History*, p. 350. **94.** VanLandingham, *Transforming the State*, p. 195. **95.** Pedro de Luna, Benedict XIII, antipope, 1394–1423. Ironically, Benedict had supported Ferdinand's candidacy for the Aragonese throne; J. N. D. Kelly, *The Oxford Dictionary of Popes* (Oxford, 1986), pp. 232–4. **96.** 'Titles of European Hereditary Monarchs', Doc. 149, Dec. 1413, www.geo-cities.com/eurprin/aragon.html (2009). **97.** Alan Ryder, *Alfonso the Magnanimous: King of Aragon, Naples and Sicily* (Oxford, 1990). **98.** Paul Arrighi, *Histoire de la Corse* (Paris, 1966); M.-A. Ceccaldi, *Histoire de la Corse, 1464–1560* (Ajaccio, 2006). **99.** 'Titles of European Hereditary

Monarchs', Aragon, Doc. 1, March 1458, www.geocities.com/eurprin/aragon. html (2009). 100. Quoted by George Hersey, *Alfonso II and the Artistic Renewal of Naples* (New Haven, 1969). 101. Harry Hodgkinson, *Scanderbeg* (London, 2004); O. G. S. Crawford (ed.), *Ethiopian Itineraries, c. 1400–1524* (Cambridge, 1958), pp. 12ff. 102. David Abulafia, 'The Crown of Aragon in the Fifteenth Century', unpaginated draft article to appear in the catalogue of the 'Crown of Aragon' Exhibition, Philadelphia Museum of Art (planned for 2010 but postponed). With permission. 103. 'Callistus III', in Kelly, *The Oxford Dictionary of Popes*, pp. 179–80. 104. Marion Johnson, *The Borgias* (London, 2001). 105. Felipe Fernández-Armesto, *Ferdinand and Isabella* (London, 1975); J.-H. Mariejol, *The Spain of Ferdinand and Isabella* (New Brunswick, NJ, 1961). 106. Marie-Louyse Des Garets, *Le Roi René* (Paris, 1980). 107. John Elliott, *Imperial Spain* (London, 1963), pp. 24, 30–31. 108. P. Vilar, 'Le Déclin catalan du bas Moyen Âge', *Estudios de Historia Moderna*, 6 (1956–9), pp. 1–68. 109. Abulafia, 'The Crown of Aragon'. 110. Jozef Pérez, 'The Inquisition in the Kingdom of Aragon', in his *The Spanish Inquisition: A History* (New Haven, 2005), pp. 30–33; Henry Kamen, *The Spanish Inquisition* (London, 1965). 111. Abulafia, 'The Crown of Aragon'. 112. Felipe Fernández-Armesto *1492: The year our World Began* (London, 2010). 113. Mariejol, *The Spain of Ferdinand and Isabella*, *passim*. 114. Published as Marineo Lucio, *Crónica d'Aragón* (Barcelona, 1974). 115. Henry Kamen, *Spain's Road to Empire: The Making of a World Power, 1492–1763* (London, 2003). 116. Geoffrey Parker, *Philip II* (London, 1979). 117. See Ernle Bradford, *The Great Siege of Malta: 1565* (London, 1969). 118. V. Titone, *La società siciliana sotto gli spagnoli* (Palermo, 1978). 119. 'Battle of le Puig', *Malta Times*, 5 January 2007, 'Expert Concludes Mattia Preti Painting Depicts Famous 13th Century Battle.' 120. M. Mignet, *Antonio Perez and Philip II* (London, 1846). 121. Elliott, *The Revolt of the Catalans*. 122. See Henry Kamen, *Spain in the Later Seventeenth Century* (London, 1983). 123. Henry Kamen, *The War of the Spanish Succession in Spain, 1700–15* (London, 1969); David Francis, *The First Peninsular War, 1702–13* (London, 1975). 124. Henry Kamen, *Philip V of Spain: The King who Reigned Twice* (New Haven, 2001).

III

125. www.spain-flag.eu/region-spain-flags/aragon.htm (2008). 126. Armand de Fluvià i Escorsa, *Els quatre pals: l'escut dels comtes de Barcelona* (Barcelona, 1994). 127. See J. Llobera, *The Role of Historical Memory in (Ethno) Nation-Building* (London, 1996). 128. http://en.wikipedia.org/wiki/els_segadors (2011). 129. http://en.wikipedia.org/wiki/himno_de_aragon (2011). 130. http:// en.wikipedia.org/wiki/himno_de_la_comunidad_valenciana (2011). 131. 'The Anthem of Majorca', http://www.consellmallorca.net/?&id_parent=272&id_ section=1855&id_son=749& (2011). 132. 'Hymne á la Catalogne', http:www.

oasisdesartistes.com/modules/newbbex/viewtopic.php?   (2011).   133.   Bisson, *Medieval Crown*, pp. 189–90.

CHAPTER 5. LITVA

Bibliographical Note. The historiography of the Grand Duchy of Lithuania is extremely fragmented, and preliminary introductions in English are hard to find. A start could be made with Jerzy Lukowski, *Liberty's Folly: The Polish-Lithuanian Commonwealth in the Eighteenth Century, 1697–1795* (London, 1991), Daniel Stone, *The Polish-Lithuanian State, 1386–1795* (Seattle, 2001) or even with Norman Davies, *God's Playground: A History of Poland*, 2 vols.(Oxford, 1981), vol. 1, which provides the background to the long period of union with Poland between 1385 and 1795. More serious researchers will need to have half a dozen languages at their fingertips, and must be prepared to wrestle with conflicting Lithuanian, Belarusian, Polish and Russian perspectives. See Stephen Rowell, *A History of Lithuania* (Vilnius, 2002), Nicholas Vakar, *Belorussia: The Making of a Nation* (Cambridge, Mass., 1956) and John Fennell, *The Crisis of Medieval Russia, 1200–1304* (London, 1983). A multinational survey of the Grand Duchy's history is eagerly awaited from the pen of Professor Robert Frost of Aberdeen University.

I

1. CIA, World Factbook, www.cia.gov/library/publications/the-world-factbook/geos/bo/html (2008); www.alternativeairlines.com/belavia.   2. The website for 'International Tourist Rankings' names fifty countries. The Corruption Perception Index is produced by Transparency International. The 'Quality of Life Index' and the 'Democracy Index' are both produced by the Economist Intelligence Unit, London, www.eiu.com.   3. BBC News online, Stephen Mulvey, 'Profile: Europe's Last Dictator?',10 September 2001; see also http://president.gov.by/en.   4. Piers Paul Read, *Ablaze: The Story of Chernobyl* (London, 1993); Alex Kirby, 'Analysis: The Chernobyl Legacy', BBC News online, 5 June 2000; John Vidal, 'Hell on Earth', *Guardian*, 26 April 2006; USA Nuclear Regulatory Commission, 'Fact Sheet on the Accident at the Chernobyl Nuclear Power Plant', www.nrc.gov/reading-rm/doc-collections/fact-sheets/fschernobyl.html (2008).   5. http://www.massviolence.org/kurapaty-1937-1941-nkvd-mass-killings (2010).   6. Ivan Lubachko, *Belorussia under Soviet Rule* (Lexington, Ky., 1973); Keith Sword (ed.), *The Soviet Takeover of the Polish Eastern Provinces, 1939–41.* (Basingstoke, 1991); David Marples, *Belarus: From Soviet Rule to Nuclear Catastrophe* (Basingstoke, 1996).   7. European Humanities University, Vilnius, http://en.ehu.lt/about (2008).   8. 'Alexander Lukashenko: Dictator with a Difference', *Daily Telegraph*, 25 Sept. 2008; BBC News online, 'Observers Deplore Belarus Vote', 24 April 2004.   9. For an eccentrically apologetic assessment, see Stewart Parker,

The Last Soviet Republic: Alexander Lukashenko's Belarus (Minsk, 2007).
10. Helena Golani, 'Two Decades of the Russian Federation's Foreign Policy in the CIS: The Cases of Belarus and Ukraine', Hebrew University, 2011: http://www.ef.huki.ac.il/publications/yakovlev%20golani.pdf (2011). **11.** 'Eastern Partnership', European Union External Action: http://eeas.europa.eu/eastern/index-en.htm (2011). **12.** http://charter97.org/en/news/2011/5/22/38809/?1 (2011). **13.** 'Wikileaks, Belarus and Israel Shamir', http://www.indexoncensorship.org/,,,wikileaks-belarus-and-israel-shamir (2011). **14.** David Stern, 'Europe's Last Dictator Goes to the Polls', BBC News online, 17 December 2010. **15.** 'As Belarus Votes, World Settles for Lukashenko as the Devil it Knows', Radio Free Europe, 31 Jan. 2011. **16.** Evgeny Morozov, *The Net Delusion: How Not to Liberate the World* (London, 2011); see also Timothy Garton Ash, *Guardian*, 19 Jan. 2011. **17.** The Soviet era memorial was designed to divert attention from the none-too-distant site of the NKVD's massacre at Katyn: www.belarus-misc.org/history/chatyn.htm (2008). **18.** Captured from the Poles in September 1939, the old fortress of Brest (Brest-Litovsk) was the scene of a heroic stand by the Red Army at the start of Operation Barbarossa. See 'Brest Hero Fortress', www.absoluteastronomy.com/topics/brest_fortress (2007). **19.** The Virtual Belarus Guide, www.belarusguide.com/travel1 (2007). **20.** http://www.belarus.by/en/travel/adventure-sports (2011). **21.** www.belintourist.by/travel (2007). **22.** Sergei Mel'nik, *МИР – MIR* (Minsk, 2007), p. 18; see also http://whc.unesco.org/en/lis (2009). **23.** Mel'nik, *MIR*, pp. 2–5. **24.** Ibid., p. 5. **25.** Ibid., *passim*. **26.** http://www.radzima.org/eng/locality/dzyarzhynava.html (2011). **27.** www.soviet.bunker.com (2011). **28.** Dan Hancox, 'Back in the USSR', *Guardian*, 2 May 2011. **29.** www.belarusguide.com/as/history/vklintro.html (2007).

II

30. Marija Gimbutas, *The Balts* (London, 1963); Alfred Senn, *The Lithuanian Language: A Characterization* (Chicago, Ill., 1942). **31.** Bryan Sykes, *Blood of the Isles: Exploring the Roots of our Tribal History* (London, 2006); idem, *One World – Many Genes* (Cedar City, Ut., 2003). **32.** On Slavic prehistory, see Marija Gimbutas, *The Slavs* (London, 1971). I am indebted to Michał Giedroyć of Oxford for guidance in crossing this minefield, and for his unpublished notes on 'Belarus: The Missing Link' (2007). **33.** Reginald De Bray, 'Byelorussian', in his *Guide to the Slavonic Languages* (London, 1961), pp. 129–92; also 'The Belarusian Language', http://languages.miensk.com/lang_eu_as_af/indoeuropean/belarusian.htm (2007). **34.** The outlines of the controversy over 'Litva' can be followed on the Internet in the conflicting information supplied by Lithuanian and Belarusian sites. Compare 'Lithuanian History, A Brief Chronology', www.balticsworldwide.com/tourist/lithuania/history.htm, and 'History of Belarus in Dates', http://xz5.org, or 'The Origins of the Grand Duchy of Litva (Lithuania)', www.belarusguide.com/as/history/jermal1.html. The rudiments of the problem, but not a solution, can be observed in W. Ostrowski, *The Ancient Names and Early Cartography of Byelorussia* (London, 1971). **35.** D. Ostrowski (ed.), *The Povest' vremennykh let: An Interlinear Collation and Paradosis* (Cambridge, Mass., 2003). **36.** Arthur Koestler, *The Thirteenth Tribe: The Khazar Empire and its Heritage* (London, 1976). **37.** See Richard Fletcher, *The Barbarian Conversion: From Paganism to Christianity* (Berkeley, 1999). **38.** As per *The History of Leo the Deacon*, ed. A.-M. Talbot and D. F. Sullivan (Washington, 2005). **39.** *Die Annales Quedlinburgenses*, ed. Martina Giese (Hanover, 2004), entry for AD 1009. The Lithuanian millennium was celebrated in July 2009; www.kulturkompasset.com/2009/06/lithuanian_millenium_celebration_in-vilnius. **40.**'StEuphrosyneofPolotsk',www.belarus/by/.../famous_belarusians (2007). **41.** http://en.wikipedia.org/wiki/cyril_of_turaw (2007); A. Mel′nikaŭ, *Kiryl, episkap Turaŭski* (Minsk, 1997). The cathedral of St Kiril of Turau of the Belarusian Autocephalous Orthodox Church is located at 401, Atlantic Avenue, Brooklyn, NY 11217. **42.** 'Smolensk Icon Mother of God', http://www.icon.lt/list/smolensk.htm (2011). **43.** M. Isoaho, *The Image of Aleksandr Nevskiy in Medieval Russia: Warrior and Saint* (Leiden, 2006). **44.** Michał Giedroyć, *The Rulers of Thirteenth-Century Lithuania* (Oxford, 1994). **45.** S. Žukas, *Vilnius: The City and History* (Vilnius, 2001); J. Harasowska, *Wilno* (Glasgow, 1944). **46.** See Stephen Christopher Rowell, *Lithuania Ascending: A Pagan Empire within East-Central Europe, 1295–1345* (Cambridge, 1994). **47.** Saints' Day, 14 April, www.missionstclare.com/english/people/apr14.htm (2009). **48.** Davies, *God's Playground*, vol. 1, pp. 116–17. **49.** Ibid. **50.** 'Pocket Book of Lithuanian Coins, 1386–1938', www.freshwap.net/forums/e-book-tutorials/247084-a.html (2009); http://en.wikipedia.org/wiki/pahonia (2009). **51.** G. Mickūnaitė, *Making a Great Ruler: Grand Duke Vytautas of Lithuania* (Budapest, 2006). **52.** Davies, *God's Playground*, vol. 1, pp. 119–21. **53.** Livonian confederation, http://en.wikipedia.org/wiki/livonian_confederation (2007). **54.** M. Stremoukoff, 'Moscow the Third Rome: Sources of the Doctrine', *Speculum* (Jan. 1953), pp. 84–101, repr. in M. Cherniavsky (ed.), *The Structure of Russian History: Interpretative Essays* (New York, 1970). **55.** Alan Fisher, *The Crimean Tartars* (Stanford, Calif., 1978). **56.** 'Zaporizhian Cossacks', in Volodymyr Kubijovyč (ed.), *Encyclopedia of Ukraine* (Toronto, 1970). **57.** http://www.svgatayarus.ru/pda/data/...267_kiev_psalter/index.php?lang (2011). **58.** http://en.wikipedia/wiki/dykra (2009). **59.** From J. Ochmański, *Historia Litwy* (Wrocław, 1979), p. 106. **60.** S. Mackiewicz, *Dom Radziwiłłów* (Warsaw, 1990); see also 'Radziwill Family', http://en.wikipedia.org/wiki/radziwi%c5%82%c5%82_family (2008). **61.** Mirosława Malczewska, *Latyfundium Radzwiłłów w XV do połowy XVI wieku* (Warsaw, 1985); *World News*, http://wn.com/niasvizh_castle (2010). **62.** Karl von Loewe (ed.), *The Lithuanian Statute of 1529* (Leiden, 1976). **63.** Feast Day, 4 March; see 'St. Casimir', in *Catholic Encyclopedia* (New York, 1907). **64.** *Biblia święta: to jest Księgi Starego i Nowego Zakonu* (Brest, 1563; facsimile, Paderborn, 2001); S. B. Chyliński, *An Account of the Translation of the Bible into the Lithuanian Tongue* (Oxford, 1659). **65.** See 'Lithuania', *Encyclopedia Judaica* (Jerusalem, 1971), vol. 11; 'Belorussia', ibid., vol.

4. 66. Meira Polliack, *Karaite Judaism: A Guide* (Leiden, 2004). 67. 'Francis Skaryna', http://www.belarusguide.com/culture/people/skaryna.html (2010). 68. George Vernadsky *et al.* (eds.), *A Source Book for Russian History from Early Times to 1917*, 3 vols. (New Haven, 1972), vol. 1, pp. 109–10. 69. Ochmański, *Historia Litwy*, p. 117. 70. See 'Battle of Orsha', www.kismeta. com/digrasse/orsha.htm (2008). In September 2005 four citizens of Belarus were heavily fined for celebrating the 491st anniversary. 71. W. Dworzaczek, *Hetman Jan Tarnowski* (Warsaw, 1985). 72. See Robert I. Frost, *The Northern Wars: War, State and Society in Northeastern Europe, 1558–1721* (Harlow, 2000). 73. See M. Koialovich, *Dnevnik liublinskogo seima 1569 goda* (St Petersburg, 1869). 74. H. E. Dembkowski, *The Union of Lublin: Polish Federalism in the Golden Age* (Boulder, Colo., 1982). 75. Anna Sucheni-Grabowska, *Zygmunt August: król polski i wielki książę litewski* (Warsaw, 1996). 76. Quoted in Davies, *God's Playground*, vol. 1, p. 155. 77. Sucheni-Grabowska, *Zygmunt August*. 78. www.geocities.com/paris/chateau/7855/kasic/statut/artykul_3.htm. 79. On the origins of the Greek Catholic Church, and the Council of Brest, see Oskar Halecki, *From Florence to Brest, 1439–1596* (New York, 1968). 80. Siege of Pskov, V. I. Malyshev (ed.), *Pov'est' o prikhozhenii Stefana Batoriya na grad Pskov* (Moscow and Leningrad, 1952), pp. 55 ff. 81. Ibid., p. 98. 82. 'Vilna', in *Encyclopedia Judaica*, vol. 16, pp. 138 ff. 83. The anti-Trinitarian movement in Poland-Lithuania was founded by Fausto Sozzini (1539–1604), whose followers were variously known as Arians, Socinians, Racovians and Polish Brethren. See P. Hewett, *Racovia: An Early Liberal Religious Community* (Providence, RI, 2004). 84. Isaac of Troki, *Hizuk Emunah, or Faith Strengthened* (New York, 1970). 85. Voltaire, *Mélanges*, vol. 3 (Paris, 1961), p. 334. 86. Janusz Tazbir, *Piotr Skarga: szermierz kontrreformacji* (Warsaw, 1978). 87. 'St Andrew Bobola', in *Catholic Encyclopedia*. 88. See J. Gierowski and A. Kamiński, 'The Eclipse of Poland', in *New Cambridge Modern History*, vol. 6 (Cambridge, 1970), pp. 681–715, trans. Norman Davies. 89. Margus Laidre, 'On Personalities', in his *The Great Northern War and Estonia* (Tallinn, 2010), pp. 218–36. 90. Marceli Kosman, *Historia Białorusi* (Wrocław, 1979), pp. 172–83. 91. On Stanisław-August, see Adam Zamoyski, *The Last King of Poland* (London, 1992). 92. Jerzy Lukowski, *The Partitions of Poland* (London, 1999). 93. Andrzej Ciechanowski, *Nieśwież: międzynarodowy ośrodek kultury na Białorusi* (Warsaw, 1994), pp. 21–8. See also Richard Butterwick (ed.), *Peripheries of the Enlightenment* (Oxford, 2008). Naturally, Lithuanian commentators talk of the 'Lithuanian Enlightenment'. See 'Age of Enlightenment in Lithuania', http:// lietuva1000.lt/lietuvos-istorija/.../svietimo-epocha-lietuvoje/fulltext (2009). 94. M. Hillar, 'The Polish Constitution of May 3, 1791: Myth and Reality', *Polish Review*, 37/2 (1992), pp. 185–207. 95. M. Haiman, *Kościuszko: Leader and Exile* (New York, 1977). 96. R. H. Lord, *The Second Partition of Poland: A Study in Diplomatic History* (Cambridge, Mass., 1915). 97. R. H. Lord, 'The Third Partition of Poland', *Slavonic Review*, 9 (1925).

III

98. Catherine's Medal, 1793; R. Bideleux and I. Jeffries, *A History of Eastern Europe: Crisis and Change* (London, 1998), p. 164. According to Sparta's founding myth, the Sons of Heracles recovered their ancestral lands which the Mycenaeans had taken from them, and then turned the Mycenaeans into helots. **99.** Davies, *God's Playground*, vol. 1, p. 542. **100.** Adam Zamoyski, *1812: Napoleon's Fatal March on Moscow* (London, 2004), pp. 161–3. **101.** N. Riazanovsky, *A History of Russia* (New York, 1963). **102.** G. Dynner, *Men of Silk: The Hasidic Conquest of Polish Jewish Society* (New York, 2006). **103.** Timothy Snyder, *The Reconstruction of Nations: Poland, Ukraine, Lithuania, Belarus, 1569–1999* (New Haven, 2003), pp. 53–6. **104.** Edvardas Tuskenis (ed.), *Lithuania in European Politics: The Years of the First Republic, 1918–40* (New York, 1999). **105.** *Byelorussia's Independence Day, March 25, 1918: Documents, Facts, Proclamations, Statements and Comments* (New York, 1958). **106.** See Norman Davies, 'The Genesis of the Polish-Soviet War, 1919–20', *European History Quarterly*, 5/1 (1975), pp. 47–67. **107.** See Norman Davies, *White Eagle, Red Star: The Polish-Soviet War, 1919–1920* (London, 1972). **108.** http://www.massviolence.org/kurapaty-1937-1941-nkvd-mass-killings (2010). **109.** Timothy Snyder, *Bloodlands* (New Haven, 2010). **110.** D. J. Smith, *The Baltic States: Estonia, Latvia, Lithuania* (London, 2002). **111.** Patricia Kennedy Grimsted, *The Lithuanian Metryka in Moscow and Warsaw: Reconstructing the Archives of the Grand Duchy of Lithuania* (Cambridge, Mass., 1984). **112.** Zamoyski, *The Last King of Poland.* **113.** Roman Aftanazy, *Dzieje rezydencji na dawnych kresach Rzeczypospolitej*, 2nd edn., 11 vols. (Wrocław, 1991–7). **114.** Ibid., vol. 3. **115.** H. A. Mason, 'The Lithuanian Whore in *The Waste Land*', *Cambridge Quarterly*, 18 (1989), pp. 63–72.

CHAPTER 6. BYZANTION

Bibliographical Note. It is invidious to make suggestions for reading in a field that is headed by Edward Gibbon. In addition to sampling Gibbon, whose prejudices need to be recognized, my own recommendations would be, for sheer *joie de vivre*, Steven Runciman, *Byzantine Civilisation* (London, 1933), plus two recent books: Judith Herrin, *Byzantium: The Surprising Life of a Medieval Empire* (London, 2007), and Averil Cameron, *The Byzantines* (Oxford, 2006). Exciting introductions are also provided by Cyril Mango, *Byzantium: The Empire of the New Rome* (London, 1988), and John Julius Norwich, *A Short History of Byzantium* (London, 1998)

I

1. www.istanbulcityguide.com (2008); *Time Out Istanbul* (London, 2004). **2.** Orhan Pamuk, *The Museum of Innocence* (London, 2009), p. 33. **3.** Pamuk, *Istanbul: Memories and the City*, quoted by Christopher Bellaigue, 'A Walker in the City', *New York Times*, 5 June 2005. 4. Erdoğan, 17 January 2010, Anadolu Agency, http://www.highbeam.com/doc/IGI-216976898.html (2010). 5. Egemen Bağiş, 23 February 2010, http://abgs.gov.tr/index.php?p=4567641=2 (2010).

II

6. Norman Davies, 'Western Civilisation versus European History', in his *Europe East and West* (London, 2006), pp. 46–60. 7. Voltaire, from *Micromégas, Avec une histoire des croisades* (1752). 8. Charles-Louis de Secondat, baron de Montesquieu, *Considérations sur les causes de la grandeur des Romains et de leur décadence* (1734), ch. 21. 9. Georg Hegel, *The Philosophy of History* (New York, 2007), p. 338. 10. Edward Gibbon, *The History of the Decline and Fall of the Roman Empire*, Everyman edn., 6 vols. (London, 1911), ch. 48. 11. Runciman, *Byzantine Civilisation*. 12. George Finlay, *Greece under the Romans* (Edinburgh, 1844), *History of the Byzantine and Greek Empires* (Edinburgh, 1853), *The Hellenic Kingdom and the Greek Nation* (London, 1836). 13. J. B. Bury, *A History of Greece to the Death of Alexander the Great* (London, 1900), *The Hellenistic Age* (Cambridge, 1923), *A History of the Roman Empire from its Foundation to Marcus Aurelius* (London, 1893), *A History of the Later Roman Empire, 395– 800* (London, 1889), *A History of the Eastern Roman Empire, 802–867* (London, 1912). 14. Runciman, *Byzantine Civilisation*. 15. Anthony Bryer, 'Sir Steven Runciman: The Owl, the Spider and the Historian', *History Today* (May 2001); for collected obituaries, see http://homepage.mac.com/paulstephenson/madison/byzantium/notes/runcimanobit.html. 16. See Michael Angold, 'The Road to 1204', *Journal of Medieval History*, 25/3 (1999), pp. 257–78. 17. Dimitri Obolensky, *The Byzantine Commonwealth: Eastern Europe, 500–1453* (London, 1971); *The Byzantine Inheritance of Eastern Europe* (London, 1982); *Byzantium and the Slavs* (Crestwood, 1994); *Russia's Byzantine Inheritance* (Oxford, 1950). 18. See the journal *Byzantine and Greek Studies* (1975–). 19. Herrin, *Byzantium*, p. xiii. 20. Cameron, *The Byzantines*, p. viii; Averil Cameron, *The Uses and Abuses of Byzantium: An Essay* (London, 1992). 21. Cameron, *The Byzantines*, p. 1. 22. Ibid. 23. Ibid., p. 8. 24. J. Pearsall (ed.), *Oxford English Reference Dictionary* (Oxford, 1996); see Cameron, *The Byzantines*, p. 3. 25. Ibid. 26. R. Cormack and M. Vassilaki, *Byzantium 330–1450*, Royal Academy of Arts (London, 2008). 27. http://static.royalacademy.org.uk/files/ra-annual-report-2009-653.pdf (2011). 28. G. W. Bowersock, 'Brilliant, Beautiful and Byzantine', *New York Review of Books* (25 Sept. 2008). 29. Unlocated. See Priscilla Roosevelt, *Apostle of Russian Liberalism* (Newtonville, Mass., 1986). 30. Norman Davies, personal recollection from April 1962. 31. Cameron, *The Byzantines*, p. 4. 32. Norman Davies, *Europe: A History* (Oxford, 1996), pp. 448–50, with extracts from Gibbon, *Decline and Fall*, ch. 68.

III

33. William Butler Yeats, 'Byzantium' (1930).

CHAPTER 7. BORUSSIA

Bibliographical Note. Any survey of Prussian history is contingent on what is understood by the term 'Prussia'. The principal focus among Germans and Germanists has always been on the possessions of the Hohenzollern dynasty and on their kingdom founded in 1701. The most up-to-date and rightly praised work on this hugely documented subject is Christopher Clark, *Iron Kingdom: The Rise and Downfall of Prussia, 1600–1947* (London, 2006). Readers seeking information in English about pre-Hohenzollern Prussia, or non-German Prussia, face a more difficult task. The best introduction in English would be Karin Friedrich, *The Other Prussia: Royal Prussia, Poland and Liberty, 1569–1772* (Cambridge, 2000).

I

1. http://russia.rin.ru/guides_e/2780.html (2008).   2. Bert Hoppe, 'Traces of a Virtual History in a Real City', National Centre for Contemporary Art, http://www.art-guide.ncca-kaliningrad.ru (2010).   3. A. Torello, 'Kaliningrad, Adrift in Europe', *SAIS Review*, 25/1 (2005), pp. 139–41.   4. Special Economic Zone, www.kaliningrad-rda.org/en/kgd/sez.php (2008).   5. Camiel Eurlings (ed.), *Report: Kaliningrad Region*, Working Group of the EU-Russia Parliamentary Co-operation Committee, 9–11 October 2005. European Parliament, PE.358.347.   6. Grant Heard, 'The Baltic Kaliningrad', http://depts.washington.edu/baltic/papers/kaliningrad.html (2008). Massive protests were staged in Kaliningrad in February 2010 against continuing economic hardships.   7. Angus Roxburgh, 'Why the Russian Cesspit is No Hong Kong', *Sunday Herald* (18 Feb. 2001), http://findarticles.com/p/articles/mi_qn4156/is_20010218/ai_n13957352 (2008).   8. Beyond Transition, online newsletter, 'Kaliningrad: Uncertain Future of Russia's Baltic Enclave', www.worldbank.org/html/prddr/trans/...pgs41-42.htm (2008).   9. M. Sobczyk, 'Illicit Cigarettes Flood into EU from the East', Emerging Europe, *Wall Street Journal* (22 Feb. 2011).   10. Roskosmos, www.federalspace.ru/main/php?lang=en (2008).   11. http://en.wikipedia./wiki/georgi_boos (2008).   12. http://en.wikipedia.org/wiki/kaliningrad (2008).   13. www.lonelyplanet.com/russia/western...russia/kaliningrad/472292 (2008).   14. Anne Applebaum, *Between East and West: Across the Borderlands of Europe* (New York, 1994), pp. 22–3.   15. Euler's Seven Bridges, http://mathforum.org/isaac/problems/bridges1.htm (2008); http://people.engr.ncsu.edu/mfms/sevenbridges/ (2008).   16. Allen Buchler, 'Kaliningrad Revisited' (2004), www.electric-review.com/archives/000010.html (2008).   17. Immanuel Kant State University of Russia, http://intdep.albertina.ru/index4.html (2008).   18. Applebaum, *Between East and*

West, p. 27. 19. Kaliningrad region, http://myazcomputerguy.com/everbrite/page6d.html (2008). 20. In Svetlogorsk: Applebaum, *Between East and West*, pp. 30–31. 21. 'US, Poland, Reach Deal on Anti-Missile Defense Shield', *Huffington Post* (14 Aug. 2008), www.huffingtonpost.com/2008/08/14/html (2008); Luke Harding, 'Living on the Frontline of the New Cold War', *Guardian* (8 Nov. 2008). 22. Buchler, 'Kaliningrad Revisited'. 23. Luke Harding, 'Kremlin Shocked as Kaliningrad Stages Huge Anti-government Demonstration, *Guardian* (2 Feb. 2010). 24. http://www.bruecke-osteuropa.de/kaliningrad/rda-kaliningrad.ppt (2011). 25. See www.lagomar.de/index.php?id=58 (2011).

II

26. Henryk Łowmiański, *The Ancient Prussians* (Toruń, 1936). 27. See J. Mortimer Wheeler, *Rome Beyond the Imperial Frontiers* (London, 1955). 28. D. Attwater, *Penguin Dictionary of Saints* (London, 1976), p. 30; Gerard Labuda (ed.), *Święty Wojciech w polskiej tradycji historiograficznej* (Warsaw, 1998). 29. Eric Christiansen, *The Northern Crusades: The Baltic and the Catholic Frontier, 1100–1525* (London, 1997). 30. Henryk Samsonowicz, *Konrad Mazowiecki* (Warsaw, 2008); Karol Górski, *Zakon Krzyżacki a powstanie państwa pruskiego* (Wrocław, 1977). 31. William Urban, *The Teutonic Knights: A Military History* (London, 2003); Udo Arnold (ed.), *Contributions to the History of the Teutonic Order* (Marburg, 1986). 32. Peter of Duisberg, *Chronicon Terrae Prussiae* (Jena, 1679). 33. *Livonian Rhymed Chronicle*, trans. Jerry Smith (Bloomington, Ind., 1977), quoted by Christiansen, *The Northern Crusades*; see also William Urban, *The Prussian Crusade* (Langham, Md., 1977). 34. A. Chodzyński, *Malbork Castle* (Warsaw, 1982); Karol Górski, *Dzieje Malborka* (Gdynia, 1960). 35. Fred Hoyle, *Copernicus: His Life and Work* (London, 1973); Maria Bogucka, *Copernicus: The Country and Times* (Wrocław, 1973). 36. http://en.wikipedia.org/wiki/e%c5%82k (2008). 37. http://donelaitis.vdu.lt/prussian/index.htm (2008). 38. http://en.wikipedia.org/wiki/old_prussian (2008). 39. Marian Biskup, *Zakon Krzyżacki a Polska w średniowieczu* (Toruń, 1987). 40. E. Schmidt, *Die Mark Brandenburg unter den Askaniern, 1134–1320* (Cologne, 1973). 41. Geoffrey Chaucer, *The Canterbury Tales*, 'The Prologue', ll. 43–6, 51–4. 42. R. Kyngeston, *Expeditions to Prussia and the Holy Land made by Henry, Earl of Derby (afterwards King Henry IV)* (London, 1894). 43. Stanisłaus F. Bełch, *The Contribution of Poland to the Development of the Doctrine of International Law: Paulus Vladimiri, decretorum doktor, 1409–1432* (London, 1964). 44. www.absoluteastronomy.com/topics/partition(politics) (2008). 45. Friedrich, *The Other Prussia*. 46. Ibid., ch. 9, 'Myths Old and New: The Royal Prussian Enlightenment.' 47. Jan Matejko, *Hold Pruski*, 'The Prussian Tribute' (1882): http://entertainment.webshots.com/photo/14196440230 74695728kkcxmn (2008). 48. Janusz Małłek, *Dwie części Prus: studia z dziejów Prus Książęcych i Prus Królewskich w XVI i XVII wieku* (Olsztyn, 1987), pp. 37–8. 49. Treitschke, quoted Friedrich, *The Other Prussia*, introduc-

tion. 50. M. Biskup (ed.), *The Teutonic State of Prussia in Polish Historiography* (Marburg, 1982). 51. F. L. Carsten, *The Origins of Prussia* (Oxford, 1954). 52. See Benedikt Stuchtey, 'Imperialism and Frontier in British and German Historical Writing around 1900', in B. Stuchtey and P. Wende (eds.), *British and German Historiography, 1750–1950* (New York, 2000). 53. W. Hubatsch, *Albrecht of Brandenburg-Ansbach: Teutonic Grand Master and Duke of Prussia* (Heidelberg, 1967). 54. See H. W. Koch, *A History of Prussia* (New York, 1978). 55. Barbara Janiszewska-Mincer and Franciszek Mincer, 'The Diet of 1621', in their *Rzeczpospolita Polska a Prusy Książęce w latach 1598–1621: Sprawa Sukcesji Brandenburskiej* (Warsaw, 1988), pp. 245ff. 56. As from the Swedish civil war of the 1590s, the Polish Vasas claimed to be the legitimate kings of Sweden and the Swedish Vasas claimed to be the legitimate kings of Poland-Lithuania. 57. Derek McKay, *The Great Elector* (Harlow, 2001). 58. A. J. P. Taylor, *The Course of German History* (London, 1945), p. 28. 59. Max Weber, 'National Character and the Junkers', in his *Essays on Sociology* (London, 1998); see also C. Torp, *Max Weber and the Prussian Junker* (Tübingen, 1998). 60. Piers Paul Read, *The Junkers* (London, 1968); F. L. Carsten, *A History of the Prussian Junkers* (Aldershot, 1989). 61. Ibid., p. vii. 62. Norman Davies, 'Vasa – the Swedish Connection', in his *God's Playground: A History of Poland* (Oxford, 1981), vol. 1, pp. 433–669. 63. Quoted in Friedrich, *The Other Prussia*, p. 152. 64. Quoted ibid., p. 154. 65. Ibid., pp. 154–5. 66. R. Herion, 'Fehrbelliner Reitermarsch', www.amisforte.nl/fehrbelliner.htm (2008). 67. http://www.germanculture.com/ua/library/weekly/aao11801a.htm. 68. M. A. D. [*sic*], *The History of Prussia* (London, 1869), pp. 10–11. 69. http://en.wikipedia.org/wiki/prussian_blue (2008). 70. Rudolf von Thadden, 'Prussia: When Was It?', in his *Prussia: The History of a Lost State* (Cambridge, 1987). 71. G. P. Gooch, 'The Prussian School', in his *History and Historians in the Nineteenth Century* (London, 1913); R. Southward, *Droysen and the Prussian School of History* (Lexington, Ky., 1995). 72. J. A. R. Marriott and Sir Charles Grant Robertson, *The Evolution of Prussia: The Making of an Empire* (Oxford, 1915), p. 11. 73. A. J. P. Taylor, *Bismarck: The Man and the Statesman* (London, 1955); David Hargreaves, *Bismarck and German Unification* (Basingstoke, 1991). 74. An Old Westminster King's Scholar, *The Growth of Prussia from AD 1271 to AD 1871* (London, 1871), p. 30. 75. Taylor, *Course of German History*, p. 7; http://gotterdammerung.org/books/reviews/c/course-of-german-history.html (2010). 76. G. Hosking and R. Service (eds.), *Re-interpreting Russia* (Basingstoke, 1998); Robert Service, *Stalin: A Biography* (London, 2004); Richard Pipes, *Three 'Whys' of the Russian Revolution* (London, 1998); Robert Conquest, *The Dragons of Expectation: Reality and Delusion in the Course of History* (London, 2005). 77. See Richard Evans on Timothy Snyder, *London Review of Books* (4 Nov. 2010). 78. Clark, *Iron Kingdom*, p. 1. 79. Norman Davies, 'Preussen – the Prussian Partition, 1772–1918', in his *God's Playground*, vol. 2, pp. 112–38; see also E. Martuszewski, *Polscy i nie polscy Prusacy* (Olsztyn, 1974). 80. 'Koenigsberg', in *Encyclopaedia Britannica*, 11th edn. (1911). 81. Adolf Menzel, *Coronation of Wilhelm I in Koenigsberg in the Year 1861* (1865): http://germanhistorydocs.ghi-dc.org/print_document.cfm?document_id=304 (2008). 82. Friedrich von

Bernhardi, *Germany and the Next War*, trans. Allen H. Powles (London, 1912). 83. Niall Ferguson, *The Pity of War* (London, 1998), p. 461. 84. W. L. Langer *et al.*, *Western Civilization* (Chicago, 1968), p. 528. 85. Sergei Dobrorolski, 'On the Mobilisation of the Russian Army, 1914', in his *Voienniy Sbornik* (1922), trans. www.vlib.us/wwi/resources/archives/texts/t040831b.html (2008). 86. K. Rosen-Zawadzki, 'Karta buduszczej Jewropy' ('Map of the future Europe'), *Studia z dziejów ZSRR i Europy Środkowej* (Wrocław, 1972), vol. 8, pp. 141–5, with map. 87. Holger Herwig, 'Tannenberg: Reality and Myth' and 'The Use and Abuse of History and the Great War', in Jay Winter *et al.* (eds.), *The Great War and the Twentieth Century* (New Haven, 2000). 88. Norman Davies, *White Eagle, Red Star: The Polish-Soviet War, 1919–20* (London, 1972). 89. Dietrich Orlow, *Weimar Prussia, 1918–25: The Unlikely Rock of Democracy* (Pittsburgh, 1995); idem, *Weimar Prussia, 1925–33: The Illusion of Strength* (Pittsburgh, 1991). 90. Michael Behrent, 'Weimar Koenigsberg', from 'Research for the Max & Gilbert film *Koenigsberg is Dead* (2004)': www.do4d.de/k/ii_nation.html (2008). 91. Ibid. 92. Service, *Stalin*, p. 273. 93. Norman Davies, *Europe at War, 1939–1945: No Simple Victory* (London, 2006). 94. RAF Bomber Command, campaign diary, August 1944, www.raf.mod.uk/bombercommand/aug44.html (2008). 95. http://en.wikipedia.org/wiki/amber_room (2008). see also Catherine Scott- Clark, *The Amber Room: The Untold Story of the Greatest Hoax of the Twentieth Century* (London, 2004). 96. A.-M. De Zayas, *A Terrible Revenge: The Ethnic Cleansing of East European Germans, 1944–50* (Basingstoke, 2006); Christopher Duffy, *Red Storm on the Reich: The Soviet March on Germany* (London, 1991). 97. C. Dobson *et al.*, *The Cruellest Night: Germany's Dunkirk and the Sinking of the* Wilhelm Gustloff (London, 1979). In 2002 a monument was raised in Kaliningrad to Alexander Marinesko, the captain of the Soviet submarine which sank the *Gustloff*. See photo: www.flikr.com/photos/sludgeulper/3273776945/ (2008). 98. http://en.wikipedia.org/wiki/battle_of_k%c3%b6nigsberg; see also Isabel Glenny, *The Fall of Hitler's Fortress City: The Battle for Koenigsberg, 1945* (London, 2007); Antony Beevor, *Berlin: The Downfall, 1945* (London, 2002). 99. Graf Hans von Lehndorff, quoted by Applebaum, *Between East and West*, pp. 18–19. 100. David Shukman, 'On the Trail of the Amber Room', BBC News, 1 August 1998: http://news.bbc.co.uk./1/hi/world/europe/143364.stm (2008). 101. Karl Potrek, quoted by Applebaum, *Between East and West*, p. 19. 102. Applebaum, *Between East and West*, pp. 25–6. Marion Dönhoff, *Before the Storm: Memories of my Youth in Old Prussia* (New York, 1990). 103. 'Agreements of the Berlin (Potsdam) Conference, 17 July–2 August 1945', www.pbs.org/wgbh/amex/truman/psources/ps_potsdam.html (2008). 104. Polish–Soviet Treaty of Friendship and Co-operation, 21 April 1945; see Davies, *God's Playground*, vol. 2, pp. 558–9. 105. 'Abolition of the State of Prussia', US State Department, *Germany, 1945–47: The Story in Documents* (Washington, 1950), p. 151.

III

106. Thadden, *Prussia: The History of a Lost State*, p. 125. 107. Florian Illies, 'Prussia's Most Beautiful Jewel', *dot De Magazin-Deutschland* (13 Nov. 2009). 108. Merriam-Webster online, www.yourdictionary.com (2009). 109. Ausstellungskatalog, *Preussen versuch einer Bilanz* (1981): www.hdg.de/lemo/objekte/pikt/...katalogpreussen/index.htm (2008). 110. 'Prussia 2001', www.germanculture.com.u/library/weekly/aa01118o1a.htm (2008). 111. www.preussen-2001.de/en/programm/landesausstellung.html (2008). 112. *Power and Friendship: Berlin–St Petersburg, 1800–1917: Rediscovering an Era of European History*, www.spsg.de/macht_und_feundschaft_pressetext/eng.pdf (2008). 113. Agnes Miegel, from 'Es war ein Land', http://www.alt-rehse.de/heimat-preussen.htm (2011), trans. Norman Davies. 114. Bernd Längin, *Unvergessene Heimat Ostpreussen: Städte, Landschaften, und Menschen auf alten Fotos* (Dusseldorf, 1995).

CHAPTER 8. SABAUDIA

Bibliographical Note. Since it cannot be fitted tidily into French, Swiss or Italian history, Savoy is frequently overlooked. No standard survey has been published in English, either of the land of Savoy or of the House of Savoy. Indeed, British library catalogues give more space to religious matters in seventeenth-century Savoy than to all other Savoyard topics. Of course, specific studies have been addressed to particular people, periods or episodes. But an introduction to the historical identity of Savoy remains extremely elusive. French historians, such as Henri Ménabréa, *Histoire de Savoie* (Paris, 1933, 1960), find great difficulty in transcending the concept of Savoy merely as a province of France. Interest in the *Casa Savoia* is largely, if not exclusively, Italian. Jacques Lovie, *Savoie* (Grenoble, 1973) is much quoted; and a recent study by Robert Colonna d'Istria, *Histoire de la Savoie* (Paris, 2002) brings an open-minded approach to the subject. A polemical study by Jean Pignon, *Savoie française: histoire d'un pays annexe* (St Gingolphe, 1996), illustrates the convictions of the separatist minority.

I

1. RAI bulletin, 3 June 2008: www.televideo.rai.it/televideo/pub/popupultimanotizia.jsp?id=393939. 2. 'Napolitano alla Festa del 2 giugno', www.repubblica.it/2008/06/sezioni/politica/due-giugno-2008 (2008). 3. P. Kammerer, 'Italy's Enduring President', *Le Monde diplomatique* (English edn.) (1 Aug. 2008). 4. www.quirinale.it/simboli/emblema/emblema-aa.htm (2008). 5. 'L'inno nazionale', www.radiomarconi.com/marconi/mameli1.html (2010). 6. 'E la festa della Repubblica diventa la festa di Silvio', www.repubblica.it/2008/06/sezioni/politica/due-giugno-2008/ (2008). 7. http://ena.lu/referendum-

constitution-italy-1946-020703683.html (2010). **8.** http://en.wikipedia.org/wiki/umberto_ii_of_italy (2008).

II

9. Bayle St John, *The Subalpine Kingdom: or, Experiences and Studies in Savoy, Piedmont and Genoa*, 2 vols. (London, 1856), vol. 1, pp. 141–3. **10.** Claude Genoux, *Histoire de Savoie* (Annecy, 1852), p. 68. **11.** E. Cox, *The Green Count of Savoy* (Princeton, 1967). **12.** Jean d'Orville 'Cabaret', *La Chronique de Savoie* (Les Marches, 1995), 'Comment le comte Pierre devint seigneur du Pays de Vaud', pp. 108–9. **13.** Robert Somerville, *The Savoy: Manor, Hospital, Chapel* (London, 1960); Compton Mackenzie, *The Savoy of London* (London, 1953). **14.** J. N. D. Kelly, *The Oxford Dictionary of Popes* (Oxford, 1986), pp. 243–4. **15.** A. S. Barnes, *The Holy Shroud of Turin* (London, 1934); H. E. Gove, *Relic, Icon or Hoax? Carbon Dating the Turin Shroud* (Bristol, 1996); R. Hoare, *The Turin Shroud is Genuine: The Irrefutable Evidence* (London, 1994). **16.** Quoted by E. Ricotti (1861) in *Encyclopaedia Britannica*, 11th edn. (1911). **17.** Margaret Trouncer, *The Gentleman Saint: Francis de Sales and his Times* (London, 1973). **18.** J.-P. Fouchy, *Et Nice devient le port de Savoie* (Cannes, 2008). **19.** Nicholas Henderson, *Prince Eugen of Savoy* (London, 1964). **20.** C. Storrs, *War, Diplomacy and the Rise of Savoy, 1690–1720* (Cambridge, 1999). **21.** John Campbell, *The Present State of Europe*, 6th edn. (London, 1761), p. 380. **22.** Ibid., pp. 398–402. **23.** J. Dessaix, *La Savoie historique et pittoresque*, 2 vols. (Annecy, 1854). **24.** http://en.wikipedia.org/wiki/chant_des_allobroges (2008). One of several stanzas that are often omitted refers to Poland's struggle for freedom: '*Relève-toi ma Pologne héroïque / Car pour t'aider je m'avance à grands pas, / Secoue enfin ton sommeil léthargique / Et je le veux, et je le veux, tu ne périras pas!*' ('Arise, my heroic Poland, / for I'm striding to your aid. / Shake off your lethargic sleep / I wish it, wish it: you will not die!'). Quoted by Liliana Batko-Sonik, 'Stan wojenny w Małopolsce: relacje i dokumenty' (Kraków, n.d.), p. 19. **25.** César Vidal, *Charles Albert et le risorgimento italien* (Paris, 1932). **26.** C. Jemolo *et al*., *Lo Statuto Albertino* (Florence, 1946). **27.** 'John Beckwith', *Encyclopaedia Britannica*, 11th edn. **28.** Quoted at www.search.com/reference/victor_emmanuel_ii_of_italy (2008). **29.** Denis Mack Smith, *Victor Emanuel, Cavour and the Risorgimento* (London, 1971); idem, *Cavour* (London, 1985); Maurice Paléologue, *Cavour* (London, 1927, 1970). **30.** www.quotesdaddy.com (2010). **31.** Sylvain Milbach, *L'Éveil politique de la Savoie: conflits ordinaires et rivalités nouvelles, 1848–1853* (Rennes, 2008). **32.** Justin Godart, *A Lyon, en 1848: les Voraces* (Paris, 1948). **33.** St John, *The Subalpine Kingdom*, vol. 1, pp. 19–20, 72–4. **34.** Ibid., pp. 156–64. **35.** Edward Gibbon, *Gibbon's Journey from Geneva to Rome ...*, ed. G. A. Bonnard (London, 1961), p. 18, quoted by H. Trevor-Roper, *History and Enlightenment* (London, 2010), p. 10. **36.** http://en.wikipedia.org/wiki/house_of_savoy

(2008). 37. Orsini Letters, in Paléologue, *Cavour*, ch. IV, pp. 105–46. 38. C. Bayly (ed.), *Mazzini and the Globalisation of Democratic Nationalism* (Oxford, 2008). 39. Donn Byrne, *Garibaldi: The Man and the Myth* (Oxford, 1998). 40. Denis Mack Smith, *Cavour and Garibaldi: A Study in Political Conflict* (Cambridge, 1985). 41. Claude Dufresne, *La Comtesse de Castiglione* (Paris, 2002); Giuseppe Borghetti, *L'Ambasciatrice di Cavour* (Rome, 1933); P. Apraxine and X. Demange, *La Comtesse Divine: Photographs of the Countess of Castiglione* (New Haven, 2001). 42. Paléologue, *Cavour*, ch. V, pp. 149–71. 43. Franco-Sardinian Treaty, 1860: http://fr.wikipedia.org/wiki/traite_de_turin_1860 (2008). 44. 'Annonce d'un referendum et appel au calme', 10 March 1860: www.savoie.fr/archives73/expo-affiches-1860/index.html (2010). 45. Napoleon III, 21 March 1860: http://newspapers.nla.gov.au/ndp/del/article/1206057. 46. Lovie, *Savoie*, pp. 38–41. 47. Ibid., p. 37. 48. Ménabréa, *Histoire de Savoie*, pp. 231–2. 49. Lovie, *Savoie*, p. 41. 50. Ibid., pp. 43–5. 51. Ménabréa, *Histoire de Savoie*, p. 347. 52. Lovie, *Savoie*, p. 48. 53. *Encyclopaedia Britannica*, 11th edn. 54. www.quotesdaddy.com. 55. www.biographicon.com/view/5r0il (2010). 56. Cecil Headlam, in *Harmsworth Universal Encyclopedia* (London, 1925). 57. Denis Mack Smith, *Italy and its Monarchs* (New Haven, 1969), p. 342.

III

58. Robert Katz, *The Fall of the House of Savoy: A Study in the Relevance of the Commonplace or the Vulgarity of History* (London, 1971). 59. See: www.regalis.com/reg/savgen, also http://en.wikipedia.org/wiki/…htm, Category: 'Pretenders to the Italian Throne'. 60. www.crocerealedisavoia.it/index.htm (2010). 61. 'Right Royal Punch-up', *Guardian* (29 May 2004); see also http://en.wikipedia.org/wiki/vittorio_emanuele,_prince_of_naples (2010). 62. 'Prince admits killings on video', *Sunday Times*, 27 Feb. 2011; Birgit Hamer, *Delitto senza Castigo: la vera storia di Vittorio Emanuele* (Civitavecchio, 2011). 63. http://www.vin-de-savoie.fr. 64. *Alpes du Nord*, Michelin Guide Vert (Paris, 2007), p. 30. 65. www.tourisme.savoiehautesavoie.com (2008). 66. *Alpes du Nord*, p. 88. 67. Communauté du Chemin Neuf, *L'Abbaye de Hautecombe* (Lyon, n.d.). 68. www.chateauthorens.fr (2008). 69. Maison de la Maurienne, *Guide Patrimoine* (St Jean, n.d.), pp. 7–8; also www.maurienne-tourisme.com (2010). 70. Ménabréa, *Histoire de Savoie*, p. 674. 71. Colonna d'Istria, *Histoire de la Savoie*, pp. 243–4. 72. Projet de Constitution de la Federation Savoisienne, http://notre.savoie.free.fr/infos/info52.htm (2008). 73. www.sabaudia.org/v2/dossiers/dos-histoire.php (2010). 74. '150ème Anniversaire de l'Entrevue de Plombières', www.categorynet.com/communiques-de-presse/histoire (2008). 75. Open letter to the president of the Rhône-Alpes region, Arpita News, 27 June 2008, http://blog.regionleman.com/2008/06/07 (2008). 76. David Gilmour, *The Pursuit of Italy: A History of a Land, its Regions and their Peoples* (London, 2011), p. 399. 77. Kammerer, 'Italy's Enduring President'.

CHAPTER 9. GALICIA

Bibliographical Note. Library systems which fail to distinguish between 'Galicia' as a province of Spain and 'Galicia' as a province of the Austrian Empire can cause needless confusion. So, too, do entries which insist on placing historic entities into modern categories, such as 'Galicia (Ukraine)' or 'Galicia (Poland and Ukraine)'. The sole overview of the subject in English, Paul Magocsi's *Galicia: A Historical Survey and Bibliographical Guide* (Toronto, 1983) is written very deliberately from a Ukrainian standpoint, while Polish, Jewish and Austrian imperial perspectives are equally important. Readers are best advised to start with the relevant chapters in one of the general introductions to the Habsburg monarchy – such as that by Henry Wickham Steed (1913), by A. J. P. Taylor (1948, 1990), or by Robert Kann (1977) – and then to move on to studies of the different ethnic communities. In addition to Magocsi, it is possible to explore Galicia's Polish connections in the chapter 'Galicia' in Norman Davies, *God's Playground: A History of Poland* (Oxford, 1981), vol. 2, and Galicia's Jewish heritage in Jonathan Webber, *Rediscovering Traces of Memory* (Bloomington, Ind., 2009).

I

1. Journey undertaken in May 2006. 2. Yury Lukomsky and Mariya Kostik, *Putyvnik-Halych* (L'viv, 2003). 3. 'Korotka istorichna kronika Halicha', ibid. 4. Ibid., p. 1.

II

5. Stanislaw Grodziski, *W Królestwie Galicji i Lodomerii* (Kraków, 1976); see also Henryk Wereszycki, *Niewygasła przeszłość* (Kraków, 1987); H.-C. Maner, *Galizien: eine Grenzregion im Kalkül der Donaumonarchie im 18. und 19. Jahrhundert* (Munich, 2007). 6. T. C. W. Blanning, *Joseph II and Enlightened Despotism* (London, 1994); S. K. Padover, *The Revolutionary Emperor: Joseph II of Austria* (London, 1967). 7. *Galizien*, Deutsche Geschichte im Osten Europas (Berlin, 1999). 8. W. J. Podgórski, *Pieśń Ojczyzny pełna: Mazurek Dąbrowskiego w dziejowych rolach* (Warsaw, 1994). 9. http://en.wikipedia.org/wiki/west_galicia (2008). 10. Karl Emil Franzos, *Aus Halbasien: Culturbilder aus Galizien* (1876), quoted by Marcin Pollack, *Nach Galizien*, trans. as *Po Galicji* (Wołowiec, 2007), p. 12. 11. M. Orłowicz, *Ilustrowany Przewodnik po Galicji, Bukowinie, Spiszu, Orawie, i Śląsku Cieszyńskim* (Lwów, 1919, repr. Krosno, 2004). 12. J. Czajkowski (ed.), *Łemkowie w historii i kulturze Karpat* (Rzeszów, 1992). 13. http://www.wrota.podkarpackie.pl/en/culture/minority/ethnic/boykos (2011). 14. F. A. Ossendowski, *Huculszczyzna: Gorgany i Czarnohora* (Wrocław, 1990). 15. Daniel Beauvois, *Trójkąt ukraiński: szlachta, carat i lud . . ., 1793–1914* (Lublin, 2005), brilliant but bilious, contains many references to Galicia;

see also his 'Szlachta w Galicji Wschodniej', *Studia Historyczne*, 34/2 (1991).   16.
M. Sliwa (ed.), *Rok 1846 w Galicyji* (Kraków, 1997); see also Davies, *God's Play-ground*, vol. 2, pp. 147–8.   17. Stefan Kieniewicz, *The Emancipation of the Pol-ish Peasantry* (Chicago, 1969).   18. S. Unger, *The Galician Petroleum Industry* (London, 1907); Norman Davies, 'Brytyjski kapitalizm a nafta galicyjska', *Studia Historyczne*, 13 (1970), pp. 283–9; Alison Frank, *Oil Empire: Visions of Prosper-ity in Austrian Galicia* (Cambridge, Mass., 2005).   19. S. Szczepański, *Nędza galicyjska w cyfrach* (Lwów, 1888), quoted by Davies, *God's Playground*, vol. 2, p. 146.   20. Dorota Praszałowicz *et al.*, *Mechanizmy zamorskich migracji łańcuchowych w XIX wieku* (Kraków, 2004).   21. W. Thomas and F. Znaniecki, *The Polish Peasant in Europe and America* (Boston, 1998).   22. www.vbvm.org/polish/song.html (2008).   23. John Czaplicka (ed.), *Lviv: A City in the Crosscur-rents of History* (Cambridge, Mass., 2002); S. Wasilewski, *Lwów* (Wrocław, 1990); P. Fässler *et al.*, *Lemberg, Lwów, Lviv – eine Stadt im Schnittpunkt europäischer Kulturen* (Cologne, 1995).   24. From K. Baedeker, *Austria-Hungary* (London, 1905).   25. From Wincenty Pol, 'Pieśń o ziemi naszéj' (1843), 'A Song of Our Land'.   26. Jan Slomka, *From Serfdom to Self-Government: The Memoirs of a Polish Village Mayor (1842–1927)* (London, 1941).   27. 'Austria-Hungary, Die Kaiserhymne', http://david.national-anthems.net/ath.htm (2008).   28. http://en.wikipedia.org/wiki/translations_of_gott_erhalte_franz_den_kaiser (2008).   29. Kornel Ujejski, from *Skargi Jeremiego* (Paris, 1947), trans. Norman Davies.   30. Naphtali Herz Imber (1855–1909). See J. Kabakoff, *Master of Hope: Selected Writings of N. H. Imber* (New York, 1985).   31. A. Krawczuk, *Christian and Social Ethics in Ukraine: The Legacy of Andrei Sheptytskij* (Edmonton, 1997).   32. A. V. Wendland, *Die Russophilen im Galizien* (Vienna, 2001).   33. K. Stopka, *Ormianie w Polsce dawnej i dzisiejszej* (Kraków, 2000).   34. Mikhail Kizilov, *The Karaites of Galicia: An Ethno-religious Minority, 1772–1945* (Oxford, 2009).   35. P. Palys, 'The Road to Galicia: František Rehor and Every-day Life in Galicia in the Second Half of the 19th Century', *Studia Historyczne*, 50/1 (2007).   36. S. Ansky, *The Enemy at his Pleasure: A Journey through the Jewish Pale of Settlement during World War One* (New York, 2002).   37. Stanisław Vincenz, *On the High Uplands: Sagas, Songs, Tales and Legends of the Carpathians* (London, 1955).   38. Marcin Król, *Stańczycy: antologia myśli społecznej i politycznej konserwatystów krakowskich* (Warsaw, 1982).   39. W. Berbelicki, *Aleksander Brückner* (Warsaw, 1989); M. Katz (ed.), *Aleksander Brückner: ein polnischer Slavist in Berlin* (Wiesbaden, 1991).   40. J. Dutkiewicz, *Szymon Askenazy i jego szkoła* (Warsaw, 1958).   41. Mikhailo Hrushevsky, *The Traditional Scheme of Russian History* (Winnipeg, 1958).   42. Isaac Biderman, *Mayer Balaban, Historian of Polish Jewry* (New York, 1976).   43. J. Rosnowska, *Dzieje Poety: o Wincentym Polu* (Warsaw, 1963).   44. B. Lasocka, *Aleksander Fredro: drogi życia* (Warsaw, 2001).   45. K. Przerwa-Tetmajer, *Poezje wybrane*, ed. J. Krzyżanowski (Wrocław, 1968); K. Przerwa-Tetmajer, *Tales of the Tatras* (New York, 1943).   46. Kazimierz Wyka, *Młoda Polska* (Kraków, 1987); S. Pigoń, *Śpiewak wielkości narodu* (Wrocław, 1957), on Wyspiański.   47. From S. Wyspiański, *Wesele (1901): The Wedding*, trans. Gerald Karpolka (Ann Arbor,

2001). **48.** J. J. Lipski, *Twórczość Jana Kasprowicza* (Warsaw, 1975). **49.** *Rusalka dniestrovaia: ruthenische Volks-Lieder* (Budim, 1837) **50.** J. Kozik, *The Ukrainian National Movement in Galicia, 1815–49* (Edmonton, 1986); 'Ivan Franko', in *Encyclopedia of Ukraine* (Toronto, 1970). **51.** Elżbieta Wiśniewska, *Wasyl Stefanyk w obliczu Młodej Polski* (Wrocław, 1986). **52.** James Cleugh, *The First Masochist: A Biography of Leopold Sacher-Masoch* (London, 1967). **53.** Wilhelm Feldman, *Dzieje polskiej myśli politycznej* (Warsaw, 1991). **54.** From Mordechai Gebirtig, *Mayne Mider* (New York, 1948); G. Schneider (ed.), *Mordechai Gebirtig: His Poetic and Musical Legacy* (London, 2000). **55.** See Leszek Mazan, *Zdarzenia z życia naszego monarchy* (Kraków, 2003). **56.** On 1848, L. B. Namier, *The Revolution of the Intellectuals* (Oxford, 1992). Namier, formerly Bernstein-Niemirowski, was himself a Galician; see Julia Namier, *Lewis Namier* (Oxford, 1971). **57.** Paul Magocsi, *The Roots of Ukrainian Nationalism: Galicia as Ukraine's Piedmont* (Toronto, 2002). **58.** *New York Times* (13 April 1908). **59.** Robert Asprey, *The Panther's Feast* (London, 1959); see also Janusz Piekałkiewicz, *World History of Espionage* (Washington, 1998). **60.** M. Kilowska-Lysiak, 'Nikifor', in Visual Arts Profiles, www.culture.pl/en/culture/artykuly/os_nikifor_krynicki (2008). **61.** 'Bober (Hasidic Dynasty)', http://en.wikipedia.org/wiki/bobov.html (2008). **62.** W. Milewska *et al.*, *Legiony Polskie, 1914–18* (Kraków, 1998); Waclaw Jędrzejewicz, *Joseph Piłsudski: A Life for Poland* (New York, 1982). **63.** They are not to be confused with the Ukrainian Legion raised by the Waffen-SS in the Second World War. They were to form the basic military force of the West Ukrainian Republic in 1918–19. See Stepan Ripetsky, *Ukrainske sichove striletstvo* (New York, 1956). **64.** Mark Von Hagen, *War in a European Borderland: Occupations and Occupation Plans in Galicia and Ukraine* (Seattle, 2007); see also Norman Stone, *The Eastern Front, 1914–17* (London, 1988). **65.** Jaroslav Hašek, *The Good Soldier Svejk and his Fortunes during the Great War*, trans. Cecil Parrott (London, 1998); Cecil Parrott, *The Bad Bohemian: The Life of Jaroslav Hašek, Creator of the Good Soldier Svejk* (London, 1978). **66.** J. W. Wheeler Bennett, *The Treaty of Brest-Litovsk and Germany's Eastern Policy* (London, 1940). **67.** Mikhailo Hutsuliak, *Pershyi Listopad 1918 roku na zakhidnikh zemlyakh Ukrainy* (Kiev, 1993); Artur Leinwand, *Obrona Lwowa: 1–22 listopada 1918r* (Warsaw, 1991); Oleksa Kuz'ma, *Lystopadovi dni 1918r* (L'viv, 2003); Maciej Kozłowski, *Między Sanem a Zbruczem: walki o Lwów i Galicję Wschodnią, 1918–19* (Kraków, 1991). **68.** Norman Davies, *White Eagle, Red Star: The Polish-Soviet War, 1919–1920* (London, 1972); Michał Klimecki, *Galicja Wschodnia 1920* (Warsaw, 2000); idem, *Galicyjska Socjalistyczna Republika Rad* (Toruń, 2006); Michael Palij, *The Ukrainian-Polish Defensive Alliance, 1919–20* (Edmonton, 1995). **69.** See Norman Davies, 'Great Britain and the Polish Jews, 1918–20', *Journal of Contemporary History*, 8 (1973), pp. 119–42. **70.** A. Zakrzewski, *Wincenty Witos: chłopski polityk i mąż stanu* (Warsaw, 1977). **71.** P. Kaluza, *A Life of Stefan Banach* (Boston, 1976). **72.** W. Łerner, *The Last Internationalist* (Stanford, Calif., 1979). **73.** Muhammad Asad, *Islam at the Crossroads* (New York, 1934), *The Road to Mecca* (New York, 1954; London, 1996), *The Principles of State and Government in Islam* (Berkeley, 1961), etc. **74.** W. Łazuga, *Michał Bobrzyński: myśl* *historyczna a działalność polityczna* (Wrocław, 1982). 75. M. Friedman, *Encounter on the Narrow Ridge: A Life of Martin Buber* (New York, 2003). 76. Jan Pomian, *Joseph Retinger: Memoirs of an Eminence Grise* (London, 1972); G. Witkowski, *Ojcowie Europy* (Warsaw, 2001). 77. F. E. Sysyn, *Adelphotes: A Tribute to Omeljan Pritsak* (Cambridge, Mass., 1990). 78. W. von Sternburg, *Joseph Roth* (Cologne, 2009). 79. J. Jarzębski, *Szulz* (Wrocław, 1999). 80. B. Hochman, *The Fiction of S. Y. Agnon* (Ithaca, NY, 1970). 81. Keith Sword (ed.), *Sikorski, Soldier and Statesman* (London, 1990). 82. Timothy Snyder, *Red Prince: The Fall of a Dynasty* (London, 2008). 83. W. W. Szybalski, *The Genius of Rudolf Stefan Weigl, a Lvovian Microbe Hunter* (Madison, 1957). 84. Javier Aranzadi, *Liberalism against Liberalism: The Works of Ludwig von Mises* (London, 2006). 85. K. Anders, *Murder to Order* (London, 1965). 86. T. Segey, *Simon Wiesenthal* (London, 2010). 87. Asad, *The Road to Mecca*. 88. Keith Sword, *The Soviet Takeover of the Polish Eastern Provinces, 1939–41* (Basingstoke, 1991). 89. 'Galicia Memorial Sites', www.chgs.umn.edu/museum/memorials/galiciapoland (2011). 90. T. Piotrowski, *Polish-Ukrainian Relations during World War Two: Ethnic Cleansing in Volhynia and Galicia* (Toronto, 1995). 91. M. O. Logusz, *Galicia Division: The 14th Waffen SS Grenadier Division Galizien* (Philadelphia, 1997). 92. V. Humeniuk and L. Luciuk, *Their Just War: Images of the Ukrainian Insurgent Army* (Toronto, 2007). 93. Norman Davies and Roger Moorhouse, *Microcosm: Portrait of a Central European City* (London, 1999). 94. Information on Ustrzyki Dolne provided by the late Professor Eugeniusz Waniek of Kraków, 2009. 95. http://www.dpcamps.org/operationvistula.html (2011). 96. http://borsuczyna.pl/en/bieszczady (2011). 97. J. Grabowski, *Judenjagd: polowanie na Żydów, 1942–45. Studium dziejów pewnego powiatu* (Warsaw, 2011).

III

98. Neil MacGregor, *A History of the World in 100 Objects* (London, 2010), 'Introduction'. 99. Eilean Hooper-Greenhill, *Museums and the Shaping of Knowledge* (London, 1992). 100. http://www.brainyquote.com/quotes/authors/p/picasso_2html (2001). 101. M. Orłowicz, *Ilustrowany Przewodnik po Galicji*, pp. 68–70. 102. Ibid., p. 62. 103. Ibid., pp. 297–9. 104. http://www.lvivbest.com/en/museums (2011). 105. Muzeum Narodowe, Kraków, www.muzeum.krakow.pl (2011). 106. Fundacja Książąt Czartoryskich, www.muzeum-czartoryskich.krakow.pl (2011). 107. Ibid. 108. P. Stone and R. Mackenzie, *The Excluded Past: Archaeology in Education* (London, 1990). 109. National Museum of the American Indian, Washington, DC, http://www.nmai.si.edu/subpage.cfm?subpage=visitor (2011). 110. Muzeum Galicja, Kraków, www.galicjajewishmuseum.org (2011). 111. http://en.wikipedia.org/wiki/ossolineum (2011). 112. 'V. Stefanyk National Lviv Academic Library', http://www.nas.gov.ua/en/structure/dhpl/lsl/pages/default.aspx (2011). 113. Magdalena Kroch, *A Guide to the Sącz Ethnographic Park* (Nowy Sącz, 2003). 114. Joanna Holda,

Sącz Ethnographic Park: Supplement to the Guide, 2003 (Nowy Sącz, 2006)   115. www.muzeum.sacz.pl/47.17.wiecej_o_sadeckim_parku_etnograficznym.htm.

CHAPTER 10. ETRURIA

Bibliographical Note. There is no monograph in English devoted to the Kingdom of Etruria. Interested readers will need to burrow both into works dealing with Italy as a whole, such as C. Duggan, *The Force of Destiny: A History of Italy since 1796* (London, 2008) or into accounts of Napoleon's Italian campaigns. There is one standard item in Italian, Giovanni Drei, *Il Regno d'Etruria* (Modena, 1935), and two recent studies: Romano Coppini, *Il gran-ducato di Toscana dagli 'anni francesi' all'Unità* (Torino, 1993), and Edgardo Donati, *La Toscana nell'impero napoleonico* (Florence, 2008).

I

1. John Milton, *Paradise Lost* (1664), book I, ll. 301–304.   2. James Joyce, quoted by R. J. Schork, in *American Notes and Queries*, 4 (1991), p. 1.   3. Florentia Agency, www.florentina.org/florentia_walking-tours/pdf (2008).   4. www.ricksteves.com/plan/destinations/italy/florence3.htm (2008).   5. Dante Alighieri, *Inferno*, canto XV, l. 85.   6. 'The Florence of Dante', www.aboutflorence.com/itineries-florence/dante.html.   7. Dante, *Inferno*, canto XXVI, ll. 1–3.   8. Dante, *Purgatorio*, canto VI, ll. 127, 137, 148–51.   9. J. R. Hale, *Machiavelli and Renaissance Italy* (London, 1961); Quentin Skinner, *Machiavelli: A Very Short Introduction* (Oxford, 2000); Niccolò Machiavelli, *The Prince*, ed. Q. Skinner (Cambridge, 1988).   10. www.aboutflorence.com/history (2008).   11. Frances Mayes, *Bella Tuscany: The Sweet Life in Italy* (London, 1999); Beth Elon, *Tasting Tuscany* (London, 2006); see also Kinta Beevor's exquisite *A Tuscan Childhood* (London, 1993).   12. Mayes, *Bella Tuscany*, pp. 56, 364.   13. Tom Kington, 'Italy's Rising Star Vows to Banish Berlusconi Sleaze', *Observer* (20 Feb. 2011).   14. Philippe Jullian, *Violet Trefusis: A Biography* (London, 1976).   15. David Leavitt, *Florence: A Delicate Case* (London, 2002), p. 87. See also: Oreste del Buono *et al.*, *Gli Anglo-Fiorentini: una storia d'amore* (Florence, 1987).

II

16. A. H. Hilliard, *Napoleon's Brothers* (Stroud, 2007); Margery Weiner, *The Parvenu Princesses: Elisa, Pauline and Caroline Bonaparte* (London, 1964).   17. David Chandler, *The Campaigns of Napoleon* (London, 1966).   18. E. Luard and J. Heseltine, *Truffles* (London, 2006), p. 37.   19. Andrea Corsini, *Il Bonaparte a Firenze* (Florence, 1961).   20. Marianna Starke, *Letters from Italy* (London, 1815), vol. 1, pp. 71–2.   21. Ibid., pp. 203–12.   22. J. G. Lockhart,

The History of Napoleon Bonaparte (London, 1830), vol. 1, p. 41.   23. 'Bonaparte chez le Duc de Toscane, 1796', lithographe, Paris, c. 1830. Kunstantiquariat Poligraphicum, www.poligraphicum.de/napoleon.html (2008).   24. Starke, *Letters from Italy*, vol. 1, pp. 74–5.   25. John Bergamini, *The Spanish Bourbons: History of a Tenacious Dynasty* (London, 1974).   26. H. W. Williams, *Travels in Italy, Greece and the Ionian Islands* (Edinburgh, 1820), vol. 1, pp. 176–7.   27. R. Duppa, *A Brief Account of the Subversion of the Papal Government, 1798* (London, 1807).   28. F. C. Schneid, *Napoleon's Conquest of Europe: The War of the Third Coalition* (Westport, Conn., 2005), p. 220.   29. Constant [Louis Wairy], *The Private Life of Napoleon Bonaparte* (London, 1895), vol. 2, ch. VII.   30. Ibid.   31. www.cgb.fr/monnaies/vso/v31/gb/monnaiesgbcbf6.htm (2007).   32. Teodor Uklanski, *Travels in Upper Italy, Tuscany, and the Ecclesiastical States ... in 1808–9* (London, 1816), pp. 38–9.   33. 'Royaume d'Étrurie', http://fr.wikipedia.org/wiki/royaume_d'etrurie (2007).   34. Uklanski, *Travels*, p. 94.   35. Starke, *Letters from Italy*, vol. 1, pp. 243–5.   36. Ibid., pp. 249–53.   37. Ibid., pp. 258–9.   38. Stuart Woolf, 'Introduction' to Ivan Tognarini, *La Toscana nell'età rivoluzionaria e napoleonica* (Naples, 1985), p. 15.   39. Giovanni Drei, *Regno d'Etruria (1801–1807)* (Modena, 1935), p. 46.   40. Stuart Woolf, 'Rationalisation and Social Conservatism, 1800–14', in his *A History of Italy, 1700–1860: The Social Constraints of Political Change* (London, 1979), pp. 188ff.   41. *The Memoirs of the Queen of Etruria, written by herself (an addition to the memoirs of the Baron de Kolli)* (London, 1823), pp. 309–10.   42. Uklanski, *Travels*, p. 67.   43. 'Royaume d'Étrurie'.   44. *Memoirs*, pp. 313–14.   45. Ibid., p. 314.   46. Ibid., p. 137.   47. Douglas Hilt, *Godoy and the Spanish Monarchs* (London, 1987).   48. Woolf, 'Rationalisation', p. 206.   49. Margaret O'Dwyer, *The Papacy in the Age of Napoleon and of the Restoration: Pius VII, 1800–23* (Langham, Md., 1985).   50. *Memoirs*, pp. 315–16.   51. Michael Broers, *Napoleon's Other War: Bandits, Rebels and their Pursuers in the Age of Revolutions* (Witney, 2010), p. 90.   52. Ibid., p. 91.   53. Ibid.   54. Philippe Bordes, 'Les Peintres Fabre et Benvenuti à la cour d'Elisa Bonaparte', in P. Rosenberg (ed.), *Florence et la France: rapports sous la Révolution et l'Empire* (Paris, 1979), pp. 187–207.   55. *Narrative of the Seizure and Removal of Pope Pius VII on 6 July 1809 ...*, trans. from the Italian (London, 1814), pp. 106–7.   56. *Memoirs*, p. 318.   57. Ibid., pp. 335–6.   58. Roman Coppini, *Il gran-ducato di Toscana*, p. 187.   59. Broers, *Napoleon's Other War*, p. 92.   60. *Memoirs*, pp. 339–40.   61. Robert Christophe, *Napoleon on Elba* (London, 1964); Guy Godlewski, *Napoléon à l'île d'Elbe* (Paris, 2003).   62. Adolphe Thiers, *Histoire du Consulat et de l'Empire* (Paris, 1861), vol. 19, pp. 51–3.   63. Ibid.   64. Norman Mackenzie, *The Escape from Elba: The Fall and Flight of Napoleon, 1814–15* (Oxford, 1982); Alan Schom, *One Hundred Days* (London, 1993).   65. 'Mot de Cambronne', in *Dictionnaire encyclopédique Quillet* (Paris, 1935).   66. Compare Dom Pierre, 'La Vérité sur le Mot de Cambronne', based on the testimony of a French eyewitness, http://napoleon1er.perso.neuf.fr/mot_de_cambronne.html (2009), with John White, 'Cambronne's words' based on British testimony and discussed at www.napoleon-series.org/research/miscellaneous/c_cambronne.html

(2010). In all probability Cambronne uttered both of the 'm-words' but prior to his capture. 67. J. T. Tussaud, *The Chosen Four* (London, 1938). 68. G. Ambert, *Le Général Drouot* (Tours, 1896). 69. Antoine D'Ornano, *Maria Walewska, l'épouse polonaise de Napoléon* (Paris, 1937); C. Sutherland, *Napoleon's Great Love* (London, 1979); Marian Brandys, *Kłopoty z panią Walewską* (Warsaw, 1969); Françoise de Bernardy, *Alexandre Walewski: le fils polonais de Napoléon* (Paris, 1976); C. Hibbert, *Napoleon's Women* (New York, 2002). 70. Owen Connolly, *The Gentle Bonaparte: A Biography of Joseph, Napoleon's Eldest Brother* (New York, 1968). 71. Marcel Dupont, *Murat: cavalier, maréchal, prince et roi* (Paris, 1980). 72. W. R. Villa-Urrutia, *La Reina de Etruria, doña Maria Luisa de Borbón* (Madrid, 1923); Sixte, Prince of Bourbon-Parma, *La Reine d'Étrurie* (Paris, 1928). See also http://en.wikipedia.org/wiki/maria_louisa_of_spain.duchess_of_lucca (2008). 73. Alain Decaux, *Napoleon's Mother* (London, 1962). 74. Williams, *Travels*, vol. 2, pp. 4-5. 75. Ibid., vol. 1, p. 453. 76. Len Ortzen, *Imperial Venus* (London, 1974). 77. A Pietromarchi, *Lucien Bonaparte: prince romain* (Paris, 1985). 78. P. T. Stroud, *The Emperor of Nature: Charles-Lucien Bonaparte and his World* (Philadelphia, 2000). 79. Joan Bear, *Carolina Murat: A Biography* (London, 1972). 80. Owen Connolly, *The Gentle Bonaparte: A Biography of Napoleon's Elder Brother* (New York, 1968). 81. F. M. Kircheisen, *Jovial King: Napoleon's Youngest Brother* (London, 1932). 82. http://www.biography.com/articles/louis-bonaparte-9218602. 83. F. S. Bresler, *Napoleon III: A Life* (London, 1999). 84. Hubert Cole, *The Betrayers: Joachim and Caroline Murat* (London, 1972).

III

85. C. Pietrangeli, *Il Museo Napoleonico* (Rome, 1950). 86. Woolf, 'Rationalisation'. 87. Charles Petrie, *The Spanish Royal House* (London, 1958); J. H. Shennan, *The Bourbons: History of a Dynasty* (London, 2007). See also www.casareal.es/casareal and www.borbonparma.org. 88. Dante, *Inferno*, canto XIII, ll. 58-60. 89. D. Facaros and M. Pauls, *Tuscany, Umbria & the Marches*, Cadogan guides (London, 1990), pp. 212-13; http://www.san-miniato.com (2010). 90. http://jobili.com/festival/white_truffle_festival_in_san_miniato_12438 (2011). 91. http://www.ristorantedegliaffidati.it (2011). 92. Machiavelli, *The Prince*, ch. 25. 93. Dante, *Inferno*, canto VII, ll. 82-4.

CHAPTER 11. ROSENAU

Bibliographical Note. There is no single monograph in English which covers the whole of this chapter's subject. The ancestry and life of Albert, the prince consort, have generated a huge literature. Leading biographies include Theodore Martin, *The Life of HRH the Prince Consort*, 5 vols. (London, 1875-80); Daphne Bennett, *King without a Crown* (London, 1977); David Duff, *Albert and Victoria* (London, 1977); Robert Rhodes James, *Albert, Prince Consort* (London, 1983);

and Stanley Weintraub, *Albert: Uncrowned King* (London, 1998). The history of the British royal family after Albert's death has also attracted much attention. Relevant works include Sidney Lee, *Queen Victoria: A Biography* (London, 1902); John Van der Kiste and Bee Jordaan, *Dearest Affie: Alfred, Duke of Edinburgh* (Stroud, 1984); Lance Salway, *Queen Victoria's Grandchildren* (London, 1991), and E. J. Feuchtwanger, *Albert and Victoria: The Rise and Fall of the House of Saxe-Coburg-Gotha* (London, 2006). Interest in the royal family's German duchy, however, falls off sharply during the First World War. There is no account of the duchy's final years, and no biography of the last duke. Studies of the politics and administration history of the duchy are only available in German.

I

1. www.coburg-tourist.com (2008). 2. http://english.gotha.de (2008). 3. See entry 'Rosenau' in *Encyclopaedia Britannica*, 11th edn. (1911). 4. www. schloesser.bayern.de/englisch/palace/objects/co-rosen.htm (2008). 5. Stephen Calloway, in *Antiques* (8 Jan. 1994). 6. www.sgvcoburg.de. 7. 'Bayern Tourismus', http://www.bavaria.by/en/in-2011-coburg-commemorates-one-of-its-famous-inhabitants.html (2011).

II

8. Charles Young, *The Early Years of the Prince Consort*, compiled for and annotated by Queen Victoria (London, 1867), pp. 22–3. 9. Duchy of Saxe-Coburg-Gotha (Germany), civil and state flag: www.crwflags.com/fotw/flags/de-sg%5ed.html#1897. 10. *Coburgischen Taschenbuch, 1821*, quoted by Calloway in *Antiques*. 11. Calloway, ibid. 12. *The Early Years*, pp. 85–8. The description is annotated by Queen Victoria: 'The peaceful beauty of the scene is, perhaps, still more striking by moonlight.' 13. Bennett, *King without a Crown*, p. 18. 14. Pauline Adelaide Panam, *Memoirs of a Young Greek Lady, Madame Pauline Adelaide Alexandre Panam . . . versus the reigning Duke of Saxe-Coburg* (London, 1823). 15. See Elizabeth Scheeben, *Ernst II: Herzog von Saxe-Coburg und Gotha* (Frankfurt, 1987). 16. Bennett, *King without a Crown*, p. 18. 17. Baron von Mayern; story discounted by Feuchtwanger, *Albert and Victoria*, p. 30. 18. Richard Sotnick, *The Coburg Conspiracy: Royal Plots and Manoeuvres* (London, 2010) 19. On Victoria's disputed ancestry, see D. M. and W. Potts, *Queen Victoria's Gene* (Stroud, 1995). 20. Notably the FitzClarences; see Roger Fulford, *Royal Dukes: The Father and Uncles of Queen Victoria* (London, 2000). 21. John C. G. Röhl, Martin Warren and David Hunt, *Purple Secret: Genes, Madness and the Royal Houses of Europe* (London, 1998). 22. Quoted by Feuchtwanger, *Albert and Victoria*, p. 39. 23. Young, *The Early Years of the Prince Consort*, pp. 239–41, 422–3 24. Ibid., pp. 197–205. 25. Ibid.,

p. 453. 26. Ibid., p. 447. 27. See UKTV History, *Prince Albert of Saxe-Coburg-Gotha* (2010), a documentary film by Griffin Nary, parts 1–3, including interviews with Stanley Weintraub, Theo Arnson and Monica Charlot. 28. *Almanach de Gotha*, 60th edn. (Gotha, 1823), pp. 1–3. 29. Ibid., pp. 20–21. 30. Bennett, *King without a Crown*, p. 133. 31. 'Queen Victoria's Census Return' (1851), www.nationalarchives.gov.uk/museum/item.asp?item-id=35 (2011). 32. *Prince Albert of Saxe-Coburg-Gotha*, film, parts 4–6. 33. 'Saxe-Coburg-Gotha' in *Encyclopaedia Britannica*. 34. Ibid. 35. Karl Marx, *Critique of the Gotha Programme* (1875). 36. http://encyclopedia.farlex.com/gotha+bomber (2008). During the Second World War a prototype 'Gotha jet fighter' was developed, first as the Ho-IX, then as the Go229: see www.aviastar.org/air/german/horten_ho-9.php (2008). 37. Dulcie M. Ashdown, *Victoria and the Coburgs* (London, 1981), p. 174. 38. Van der Kiste and Jordaan, *Dearest Affie*. 39. *New York Times* (1 Aug. 1900). 40. Ibid. (8 June 1899). 41. Charlotte Zeepvat, *Prince Leopold: The Untold Story of Queen Victoria's Youngest Son* (Stroud, 1998). 42. Ashdown, *Victoria and the Coburgs*, p. 178. 43. *New York Times* (20 July 1905). 44. Quoted by Ashdown, *Victoria and the Coburgs*, p. 186. 45. Robin Lumsden, *Medals and Awards of the Third Reich* (Shrewsbury, 2001). 46. Ashdown, *Victoria and the Coburgs*, pp. 191–2. 47. Theo Aronson, *Princess Alice: Countess of Athlone* (London, 1998). 48. Michael Thornton, 'The Nazi Relative that the Royals Disowned', *Mail on Sunday*/Mail Online (1 Dec. 2007). 49. Victoria Huntington-Whitely, in the Channel 4 documentary *Hitler's Favourite Royal*, 2 June 2008. 50. Ibid.

III

51. http://www.facebook.com/pages/prince-andreas-of-saxe-coburg/136732246347101?sk=wrki (2011). 52. Royal News of 2009, I, www.angelfire.com/realm/gotha/news/2009_1.htm (2010). 53. www.fact-archive.com/encyclopedia/simeo_ii_of_bulgaria (2008); see also John D. Bell, *Bulgaria in Transition* (Westview, conn., 1998). 54. 'The Belgian Royal Family', http://www.monarchie.be/en (2011). 55. Mountbatten-Windsors, see Ben Pimlott, *The Queen: A Biography of Elizabeth II* (London, 1996). 56. E. Tauerschmidt, *Prince Albert's Ancestry* (London, 1840). 57. Dulcie M. Ashdown, *The Royal Line of Succession: The British Monarchy from Egbert AD802 to Queen Elizabeth II* (Andover, 1992). 58. To her divorce lawyer, Anthony Julius; see Sally Bedell Smith, *Diana: The Life of a Troubled Princess* (London, 2007).

CHAPTER 12. TSERNAGORA

Bibliographical Note. Surprisingly enough, the history of Montenegro has been well served by English-language historians, although the short-lived Montenegrin Kingdom is inevitably treated as a passing episode. The most up-to-date works are: Elizabeth Roberts, *Realm of the Black Mountain: A History of Montenegro* (London,

2007), and Kenneth Morrison, *Montenegro: A Modern History* (London, 2009). It is well worth dipping into some of the older books to sample the period flavour. See, for example, R. Wyon and G. Prance, *Land of the Black Mountain* (London, 1903), or Mary Edith Durham, *Through the Lands of the Serb* (London, 1904). H. W. V. Temperley's chapter 'Montenegro and her Share in Serbian National Development', in his *History of Serbia* (London, 1917), gives a distinctly pro-Serb slant, while the Handbook No. 19, *Montenegro*, issued by the Historical Section of the British Foreign Office in 1919, is informative both about the country's past and about the attitudes of the Great Powers. A monograph by Srdja Pavlovic, *Balkan Anschluss: The Annexation of Montenegro and the Creation of the South Slav State* (West Lafayette, Ind., 2008) was not available when the present study was being prepared.

I

1. http://un.org/members/list.shtml (2008).   2. http://montenegro.embassy homepage.com (2008). 3. www.visit-montenegro.com/tourism-mcc.htm (2008).   4. http://www.summitpost.org/durmitor/152176 (2011).   5. Claire Wrathall, 'A Star Reborn', *Financial Times* (4–5 June 2011); http://www.amanre sorts.com.   6. http://en.wikipedia.org/wiki/podgorica (2008).   7. http://en. wikipedia.org.wiki/cetinje (2008).   8. BBC News, 14 November 2002; Steve Hanke, 'Inflation Nation', *Wall Street Journal* (24 May 2006).   9. http://media. transparency.org/news_room/in_focus/2008/cpi2008 (2008); Russia weighed in at 147th, and Belarus at 151st. Denmark is top, Somalia bottom.   10. 'Controversy over Montenegrin ethnic identity', http://en.wikipedia.org/wiki/montenegrins.   11. 'Montenegro's Referendum', www.crisisgroup.org/home/index.cfm?=4144 (2006).   12. Radio Free Europe, 17 October 2008.   13. www.earthconserva tion.net/dam-effect-on-environment.html (2011).   14. http://www.eupolitics.ein news.com/news/eu-enlargement-montenegro (2011).   15. As seen on CNN and on the BBC World Service.

II

16. *La Dictionnaire encyclopédique Quillet* (Paris, 1935).   17. www.montene gro.org/kirigniki.html (2008). This source is a website of the Montenegrin Association of America.   18. Wyon and Prance, *Land of the Black Mountain*.   19. Christopher Boehm, *Blood Revenge: The Enactment and Management of Conflict in Montenegro and Other Tribal Societies* (Philadelphia, 1987).   20. See Germaine Tillon, *My Cousin, my Husband: Clans and Clanship in Mediterranean Societies* (London, 2007).   21. E. D. Goy, *The Sabre and the Song* (Belgrade, 1995).   22. See Branislav Djurdjev, *Turska vlast u Crnoj Goriu XVI i XVII veku* (Sarajevo, 1953).   23. Adapted by Norman Davies from *The Mountain Wreath*, by Petar Petrović-Njegoš, trans. Vasa D. Mihailovich (Belgrade, 1997).   24. S. Pavlović, 'The Mountain Wreath: Poetry or a Blueprint for the

Final Solution?', *spacesofidentity.net*, 1/3 (Oct. 2001).   **25.** George Brodrick *et al.*, 'Montenegro and its Borderlands: A Discussion', *Geographical Journal*, 4/5 (1894), pp. 405–7.   **26.** As quoted in 'Montenegro: A Commentary', *Ambassadors' Review* (Fall 2008).   **27.** W. E. Gladstone, *Montenegro or Tsernagora: A Sketch* (London, 1913), pp. 4–5; repr. from *Nineteenth Century* (May 1877).   **28.** Ibid., p. 18.   **29.** Alfred, Lord Tennyson, 'Montenegro' (1877), from *Ballads and Other Poems* (1880).   **30.** *Montenegro*, FCO Handbook No. 19, p. 36.   **31.** 'Montenegro', in *Encyclopaedia Britannica*, 11th edn. (1911).   **32.** C. Mylonos, *Serbian Orthodox Fundamentals* (Budapest, 2003).   **33.** 'The Family of King Nikola Petrovic-Njegos', www.njegos.org/petrovics/family.htm (2010).   **34.** Charles Henry Meltzer, 'Nicholas of Montenegro, King and Dramatist', *New York Times* (11 Nov. 1917).   **35.** Don Marquis, 'Nicholas of Montenegro' (1912).   **36.** See Richard Hall, *The Balkan Wars, 1912–13: Prelude to the First World War* (London, 2000); also Brian Pearce (ed.), *The Balkan Wars: The War Correspondence of Leon Trotsky* (London, 1980).   **37.** Nicholas I Petrovitch-Niegosh, *The Empress of the Balkans*, trans. W. M. Petrovitch and D. J. Volnay (London, 1913).   **38.** Meltzer, 'Nicholas of Montenegro'. His article, which was prompted by the announcement of King Nicola's exile, contained reminiscences of events some six years earlier.   **39.** Margaret MacMillan, *Peacemakers* (London, 2001), p. 129.   **40.** 'Vilya's Song' for *Die lustige Witwe* ('The Merry Widow'), music by Franz Lehár, libretto by Victor Leon and Leo Stein; see J. Kenrick, 'The History of a Hit' (2004), www.musicals101.com/widowhist/htm.   **41.** Montenegro postal history: Kingdom of Montenegro from 1874, Austrian occupation, 1917–18, Italian occupation, 1941–3, German occupation, 1943–4, *Scott Standard Postage Stamp Catalogue* (New York, 1984), vol. 3, pp. 890–92.   **42.** See Jan Gordon, *Two Vagabonds in Serbia and Montenegro, 1915* (London, 1939).   **43.** Milovan Djilas, *Montenegro* (London, 1964), p. 107.   **44.** Corfu Declaration (1917), www.firstworldwar.org/source/greaterserbia_corfudeclaration.htm (2010).   **45.** Hugh Seton-Watson (ed.), *R. W. Seton-Watson and the Yugoslavs: Correspondence 1906–41*, 2 vols. (London, 1976), vol. 1, p. 359.   **46.** MacMillan, *Peacemakers*, p. 27.   **47.** Roberts, *Realm of the Black Mountain*, pp. 218 ff.   **48.** Andrija Radović to R. W. Seton-Watson, *R. W. Seton-Watson and the Yugoslavs*, vol. 1, p. 304.   **49.** Djilas, *Montenegro*, pp. 108–9.   **50.** Hugh Seton-Watson, *The Making of a New Europe: R. W. Seton-Watson and the Last Years of Austria-Hungary* (London, 1981), p. 157.   **51.** Wilson's Fourteen Points, quoted by Roberts, *Realm of the Black Mountain*, p. 330.   **52.** Šerbo Rastoder, 'Twentieth Century Montenegro', in his *The History of Montenegro from Ancient Times* (Podgorica, 2006), pp. 159 ff.   **53.** Ivo Banac, *The National Question in Yugoslavia: Origin, History, Politics* (Ithaca, NY, 1984), especially part II, 'Great Serbia and Great Yugoslavia', pp. 141–214.   **54.** Rastoder, 'Twentieth Century Montenegro', p. 160.   **55.** MacMillan, *Peacemakers*, p. 126.   **56.** Quoted by Roberts, *Realm of the Black Mountain*, p. 320.   **57.** Rastoder, 'Twentieth Century Montenegro', p. 162.   **58.** Quoted in Alex Devine, *The Martyred Nation: A Plea for Montenegro* (London, 1924), p. 13.   **59.** Ibid.   **60.** Milovan Djilas, *Land Without Justice* (New York, 1958), quoted by Roberts, *Realm of the Black*

Mountain, p. 326.   61. J. Ciubranovitch (ed.), *Le Plus Grand Crime de L'histoire* (Rome, 1928), p. 10.   62. A. Radović, *Le Monténégro: son passé et son avenir* (Paris, 1918); Janko Spasojevic, *Le Roi Nicholas et l'Union du Montenegro avec la Serbie* (Geneva, 1918); Alex Devine, *Montenegro in History, Politics and War* (London, 1918); Yovan Plamenatz, *Le Monténégro devant La Conférence de la paix* (Paris, 1919).   63. On Montenegro at the Peace Conference, see Dejan Djokić, *Nikola Pašić and Ante Trumbić: the Kingdom of Croats, Serbs and Slovenes* (London, 2010) (the Peace Conferences of 1919–23 and their aftermath), and Whitney Warren, *Montenegro: The Crime of the Peace Conference* (New York, 1922); also Ivo Lederer, *Yugoslavia at the Peace Conference* (New Haven, 1963).   64. Report by earl de Salis on Montenegro, 21 August 1919, PRO (London) FO 608/46: referenced by Roberts, *Realm of the Black Mountain*. Text published in R. L. Jarman (ed.), *Yugoslavia Political Diaries, 1918–65* (Cambridge, 1997), vol. 1.   65. Temperley Report, 12 October 1919, in Jarman, *Yugoslavia Political Diaries*, vol. 1.   66. See J. D. Fair, *Harold Temperley: A Scholar and Romantic in the Public Realm* (London, 1992).   67. *Montenegro*, FCO Handbook No. 19, p. 38.   68. *New York Times* (4 April 1920).   69. Devine, *Martyred Nation*, p. 34.   70. Report by earl de Salis, in Jarman, *Yugoslavia Political Diaries*, vol. 1.   71. Col. Burham, quoted by Devine, *Martyred Nation*, pp. 19–20.   72. Enclosure in George Grahame (Paris) to Earl Curzon, 19 August 1920. National Archives, LG/F/57/2//4.   73. Bryce Report, 12 December 1920, in Jarman, *Yugoslavia Political Diaries*, vol. 1.   74. Published in the *New York Times* in 1922.   75. *New York Times* (22 Oct. 1921).   76. Ciubranovitch, *Le Plus Grand Crime*.   77. Ibid.   78. 'Montenegro's Plea as Made at Genoa', *New York Times* (4 June 1922).   79. Walter Littlefield, 'Annihilation of a Nation: Montenegrins' Effort to Prevent Annexation of their Country to Serbia', *New York Times* (16 April 1922).   80. Devine, *Martyred Nation*, p. 1.   81. 'Serbian Bishop Condemns Supporters of the Montenegrin Church', BBC – IMR, 7 January 2006.   82. www.moc-cpc.org/index_e.htm (2010).   83. See T. Judah, *The Serbs: History, Myth and the Destruction of Yugoslavia* (New Haven, 1997).   84. Lenard Cohen, *Serpent in the Bosom: The Rise and Fall of Slobodan Milošević* (Boulder, Colo., 2001).   85. Nick Hawton, *The Quest for Radovan Karadžić* (London, 2009).   86. 'Serbia accepts Montenegro Result', BBC News, 23 May 2006, news.bbc.co.uk/1/hi/world/Europe/5009242.stm (2011).   87. Florian Bieber (ed.), *Montenegro in Transition: Problems of Identity and Statehood* (Baden-Baden, 2003).   88. http://www.montenegro.org/language.html (2011).   89. http://www.youtube.com/watch?v=gptpjmdtofk (2011).   90. 'PM Unveils Monument to Last Montenegrin King, Vows to Renew Independence', BBC – IMR, 20 December 2005.

III

91. http://njegos.org/past/petrovics/family.htm (2008); see also Olga Opfell, *Royalty Who Wait* (Jefferson, NC, 2001).   92. See www.cfr.org/publication/15897/

montevideo_convention.html (2008). 93. James Barros, *The Åland Islands Question* (New Haven, 1968). 94. Miranda Vickers, The Albanians: A Modern History (London, 1999). 95. E. J. Dillon, *The Inside Story of the Peace Conference* (London, 1919), p. 98. 96. Roberts, *Realm of the Black Mountain*; Rastoder, 'Twentieth Century Montenegro'; Devine, *Martyred Nation*. 97. Pavlovic, *Balkan Anschluss*, not consulted. 98. See Andres Küng, *A Dream of Freedom* (Cardiff, 1981). 99. See Stanislaw Mikolajczyk, *The Rape of Poland* (London, 1948). 100. Laura Silber, Alan Little and A. Ciric, *The Death of Yugoslavia* (London, 1995); Misha Glenny, *The Fall of Yugoslavia: The Third Balkan War* (London, 1996); Mark Almond, *Europe's Backyard War* (London, 1994). 101. Human Rights Watch, *Weighing the Evidence: Lessons from the Slobodan Milosevic Trial* (New York, 2006). 102. http://en.wikipedia.org/wiki/onamo_'namo! (2008).

CHAPTER 13. RUSYN

Bibliographical Note. Thanks to the work of American and Canadian Ukrainians, the history of Carpatho-Ruthenia is reasonably accessible in English. The principal scholar in the field is Paul Robert Magocsi, whose titles include *The Rusyn-Ukrainians of Czechoslovakia* (Vienna, 1983), *Carpatho-Rusyn Studies: A Bibliography* (New York, 1988), and *Our People: Carpatho-Rusyns and their Descendants in North America* (Toronto, 1994). The region also attracted a number of Western travellers with a taste for the exotic, notably Henry Baerlein, *In Czechoslovakia's Hinterland* (London, 1938).

I

1. Anthony Hope, *The Prisoner of Zenda* (London, 1894).

II

2. Paul Magocsi, 'National Assimilation: The Case of the Rusyn-Ukrainians of Czechoslovakia', *East Central Europe*, 11/2 (1975), pp. 101–31. 3. Michael Winch, *Republic for a Day: An Eye-witness Account of the Carpatho-Ukraine Incident* (London, 1939), pp. 275 ff. 4. Ibid. 5. Ibid. 6. www.ucrdc.org/hi-augustyn-voloshyn.html. 7. Yuri Snegirev, 'A New Republic is Close to Appearing in Transcarpathia', *Izvestiya* (14 Nov. 2008), trans. at www.robertamsterdam.com/2008/11/when_in_ruthenia.htm.

III

8. Immanuel Wallerstein, *Modern World Systems: Capitalist Agriculture and the Origins of the European World Economy* (New York, 1974). 9. Hans Kohn,

The Idea of Nationalism: A Study of its Origin and Background (New York, 1944). 10. Ernest Gellner, *Nations and Nationalism* (Oxford, 1983). 11. John Plamenatz, *Man and Society: A Critical Examination of Some Important Social and Political Theories* (London, 1963). 12. Ibid., quoted by Norman Davies, *Europe East and West* (London, 2006), pp. 29–32. 13. Ibid. 14. Vesna Goldsworthy, *Inventing Ruritania: The Imperialism of the Imagination* (London, 1998), p. xi. See also Norman Davies, 'Fair Comparisons and False Contrasts', in his *Europe East and West*, pp. 22–45.

CHAPTER 14. ÉIRE

Bibliographical Note. Despite an enormous literature, Ireland's twentieth-century history is not particularly accessible. Many authors are manifestly partisan, and others assume exacting levels of knowledge that their readers may not possess. General surveys of the subject have been published by Mary Collins (London, 1970), Edward Norman (London, 1971), J. J. Lee (Cambridge, 1989), Tony Gray (London, 1996), Alvin Jackson (Oxford, 1999), Richard Killeen (Dublin, 2003) and Tim Pat Coogan (London, 2004). Roy Foster, who brings strong cultural insights into his political analysis, is the acknowledged authority. Senia Pašeta, *Modern Ireland: A Very Short Introduction* (Oxford, 2003) provides a good entry point. *The Oxford Companion to Irish History*, ed. S. J. Connolly (Oxford 1998), offers a mine of reliable information. Recordings of all the songs in this chapter can be found on the website of www.youtube.com.

I

1. *Irish Times* (4 April 2011). 2. Ray MacManais, *The Road from Ardoyne: The Making of a President* (Dingle, 2004). 3. http://en.wikipedia.org/wiki/amhran_ na_bhfiann (2008). 4. www.visitdublin.com/seeanddo/historicsites/dublin.aspx (2008). 5. www.fiannafail.ie (2010). 6. www.finegael.org (2010). 7. 'Worldwide Quality of Life Index, 2005', www.economist.com/media/pdf/quality_of_ life.pdf (2008). Interestingly, a rival index produced by the Irish-based organization International Living.com placed France in first place, and Ireland in 57th; www.il-ireland.com/qofl2008/ (2009). 8. http://en.wikipedia.org/wiki/ list_of_high_kings_of_ireland (2009). 9. M. Mahoney, *Brian Boru: Ireland's Greatest King* (Stroud, 2002). 10. See Cecelia Holland, *The Kings in Winter* (New York, 1968) and Morgan Llywelyn, *Lion of Ireland* (New York, 1980), historical novels; also www.doyle.com.au/battleclontarf.htm. 11. Philip Robinson, *The Ulster Plantation: British Settlement in an Irish Landscape, 1600–1607* (Belfast, 2005); Cyril Falls, *The Birth of Ulster* (London, 1996). 12. R. Dunlop (ed.), *Ireland under the Commonwealth* (Manchester, 1913). 13. P. B. Ellis, *The Boyne Water* (London, 1976). 14. M. Wall, *The Penal Laws, 1691–1760* (Dundalk, 1961). 15. 'Let Erin Remember', Thomas Moore, *Poetical Works* (Edinburgh, n.d), pp. 440–41. 16. As recounted by Mary Kenny, *The Crown and the*

Shamrock: Love and Hate between Ireland and the British Monarchy (Dublin, 2009). **17.** Roy Foster, *Charles Stuart Parnell: The Man and his Family* (Hassocks, 1979); Paul Bew, *Parnell* (Dublin, 1991). **18.** R. V. Comerford, *The Fenians in Context, 1858–82* (Dublin, 1998). **19.** D. O'Corrain and T. O'Riordan, *Ireland, 1815–70: Emancipation, Famine, and Religion* (Dublin, 2011). **20.** Diarmaid Ferriter, 'Ireland in the Twentieth Century', www.gov.ie/en/essays/twentieth.html (2009). **21.** Roy Foster, 'The "New" Nationalism', in his *Modern Ireland, 1600–1972* (London, 1988), pp. 450, 454. **22.** www.ireland-information.com/irishmusic/thewearingofthegreen.shtml (2010). **23.** 'When Irish Eyes Are Smiling', from *The Isle O' Dreams* (1912) by Chauncey Olcott, www.contemplator.com/ireland/irisheye.html (2009). **24.** W. S. Churchill, *My Early Life* (London, 1930). **25.** Michael O'Riain, 'Queen Victoria and her Reign at Leinster House', *Dublin Historical Record*, 1 (1999), pp. 75–86.

II

26. Full text in Foster, *Modern Ireland*, pp. 596–7. **27.** Brian Barton and Richard Foy, *The Easter Rising* (Stroud, 1999). **28.** www.triskelle.eu/lyrics/bloodstainedbandage.php?index (2009). **29.** www.firstworldwar.com/audio/itsalongwaytotipperary.htm (2009). **30.** Foster, *Modern Ireland*, p. 489. **31.** www.loyalist.lyrics.co.uk/index-s.html (2009). **32.** Foster, *Modern Ireland*, p. 489. **33.** Ibid., p. 490. **34.** 'Sinn Fein's Declaration of Independence', *Manchester Guardian* (22 Jan. 1922). **35.** 'The Rifles of the IRA', http://ingeb.org/songs/inninet.htm (2009). **36.** C. L. Mowat, *Britain between the Wars* (London, 1968), pp. 84–5. **37.** See Ronan Fanning, 'De Valera', in *Dictionary of Irish Biography* (Cambridge, 2009). **38.** Tim Pat Coogan, *Michael Collins: A Biography* (London, 1990). **39.** R. Davis, *Arthur Griffith* (Dundalk, 1976). **40.** See Arthur Griffith, *The Resurrection of Hungary: A Parallel for Ireland* (Dublin, 1904). **41.** Calton Younger, *A State of Disunion* (London, 1972). **42.** See Thomas Jones, *Diary with Letters* (London, 1954). **43.** See Frank Pakenham (Lord Longford), *Peace by Ordeal* (London, 1962). **44.** Kevin O'Higgins, quoted in J. Cannon (ed.), *The Oxford Companion to British History* (Oxford, 1997), p. 515. **45.** Foster, *Modern Ireland*, p. 509. **46.** Ibid., p. 506. **47.** Tom Cox, *The Damned Englishman: A Study of Erskine Childers* (Hicksville, NY, 1975). **48.** See Tim Pat Coogan, *De Valera: Long Fellow, Long Shadow* (London, 1993). **49.** 'Take it down from the Mast', www.free-lyrics/thedubliners/274859.html. **50.** Jeremy Dibble, *Charles Villiers Stanford: Man and Musician* (Oxford, 2002); C. V. Stanford, *Pages from an Unwritten Diary* (London, 1914). **51.** 'A Fire of Turf', op. 139, nr. 1 (1913), words by Winifred Letts, from *An Irish Idyll*. **52.** e.g. George VI, 'the last King of Ireland', www.answers.com/topic/king-george-vi (2009). **53.** Text of the Anglo-Irish Treaty 1921: National Archives of Ireland, *Documents on Irish Foreign Policy*, vol. 1: *1919–21* (Dublin, 1998), also online. **54.** 'God Save Ireland', www.celtic-lyrics.com>forum>lyrics. **55.** By Mary Kenny, in *The Crown and the Shamrock*. See also N. Browne, *Church and State in Modern Ire-*

land (Belfast, 1991). 56. Foster, *Modern Ireland*, p. 518. 57. Enda Macdonagh, 'Church–State Relations in Independent Ireland', in James Mackey (ed.), *Religion and Politics in Ireland* (Dublin, 2003). 58. http://en.wikipedia.org/wiki/monarchy_of_ireland (2009). 59. www.iol.ie/~dluby/anthem.html (2009). 60. Brendan Sexton, *Ireland and the Crown, 1922–36: The Governor-Generalship of the Irish Free State* (Dublin, 1989). 61. '*Bunreacht na hÉireann*', www.constitution.ie/constitution-of-ireland/default.asp (2009). 62. J. E. and G. W. Donleavy, *Douglas Hyde: A Maker of Modern Ireland* (Oxford, 1991). 63. Coogan, *De Valera*. 64. Ian Wood, *Ireland during the Second World War* (London, 2002); E. O'Halpin (ed.), *MI5 and Ireland, 1939–45* (Dublin, 2003); Brian Girvin, *The Emergency: Neutral Ireland* (London, 2006); Clair Wills, *That Neutral Island: A Cultural History of Ireland during the Second World War* (London, 2007). 65. http://en.wikipedia.org/wiki/republic_of_ireland_act_1948 (2009), with text. 66. Foster, *Modern Ireland*. 67. 'Ireland Act, 1949, c41, 12 and 13 Geo 6', full text at http://en.wikisource.org/wiki/ireland_act_1949 (2009). 68. 'Crown of Ireland Act, 1542, c. 1 33 Hen. 8', full text at www.opsi.gov.uk/revisedstatutes/acts/aip/1542/caip_15420001_en_1 (2009). This Act, including the clause on 'High Treason', still applies in Northern Ireland. 69. www.thebards.net/music/lyrics/patriot_game.shtml (2010). 70. Paul Bew *et al.*, *Northern Ireland, 1921–2001: Political Forces and Social Classes* (London, 1995). 71. www.loyalistlyrics.co.uk/index-h.html (2009). 72. Mary E. Daly and Margeret O'Callaghan (eds.), *1916 in 1996: Commemorating the Easter Rising* (Dublin, 2007). 73. Patrick Bishop and Eamonn Mallie, *The Provisional IRA* (London, 1987). 74. Eamonn McCann, *Bloody Sunday in Derry* (Dingle, 1998); idem, *The Bloody Sunday Enquiry* (London, 2006). 75. Conflict Archive on the Internet (CAIN) Webservice, 'The Sunningdale Agreement': http://cain.ulst.ac.uk/events/sunningdale/agreement.htm (2009). 76. Mairead Corrigan and Betty Williams, Nobel Prize Winners, 1976: www.peacepeople.com/pphistory.htm (2009). 77. Paul Routledge, *The Elusive Life and Violent Death of Airey Neave* (London, 2003). 78. Philip Ziegler, *Mountbatten: The Official Biography* (London, 2001). 79. J. M. Feehan, *Bobby Sands and the Tragedy of Modern Ireland* (Sag Harbor, NY, 1985). 80. 'The Men behind the Wire', composed by Paddy McGuigan of the Barleycorn group, who was himself interned as a reward for writing the song. See http://unitedireland.tripod.com/id110.htm (2009). 81. 'Go home, British soldiers' (1972), composed by Tommy Skelly of the South Dublin Union. See R. Daly and D. Warfield, *Celtic and Ireland in Song and Story* (Glasgow, 1990), pp. 38, 150–55. 82. From *The Wolfe Tones Song Book*, vol. 2 (1990). 83. Pašeta, *Modern Ireland: A Very Short Introduction*, p. 146. 84. http://www.youtube.com/watch?v=j61grao2x9g (2011). 85. Ed Moloney, *The Secret History of the IRA* (London, 2002). 86. Ian Paisley, MP, www.allgreatquotes.com/ian_paisley_quotes.shtml (2010). 87. Kevin Bean, *The New Politics of Sinn Fein* (Liverpool, 2007). 88. www.nio-gov.uk/the agreement/political background_8_august_2004 (2009). 89. BBC News, 16 August 1998, http://news.bbc.co.uk/1/h/events/northern_ireland/latest_events/152156.stm (2009). 90. Dean Godson, *Himself Alone: David Trimble and the Ordeal of Unionism* (London, 2005); Frank Millar, *David Trimble: The Price of Peace* (Dublin, 2008); George Drower, *John Hume: Man of Peace* (London, 1996); Paul Routledge, *John Hume: A Biography* (London, 1998). 91. Steve Bruce, *God Save Ulster: The Religion and Politics of Paisleyism* (Oxford, 1986); idem, *Paisley: Religion and Politics in Northern Ireland* (Oxford, 2007). 92. L. Clarke and M. Johnston, *Martin McGuinness: From Guns to Government* (Edinburgh, 2003); see also Gerry Adams, *Hope and History: Making Peace in Ireland* (Dingle, 2003). 93. Officially the British-Irish Council first convened in 1999; see http://en.wikipedia.org/wiki/british%e2%80%93irish_council. 94. 'A Day of Justice Dawning' or 'The Winds are Singing Freedom', by Terry Makem, http://merryploughboys.com/cd-lyrics/3_01twasf.html (2009). 95. 'A Nation Once Again', composed by Thomas Osborne Davis (1814–45), http://en.wikipedia.org/wiki/a_nation_once_again (2009); see also http://www.bbc.co.uk/worldservice/us/features/topten (2009), with audio recording by the Wolfe Tones. 96. Fintan O'Toole, *Ship of Fools: How Stupidity and Corruption Killed the Celtic Tiger* (London, 2009). 97. Damien Dempsey, 'Celtic Tiger', http://www.justsomelyrics.com/1511874 (2011). 98. Michael Cox *et al.*, *A Farewell to Arms: Beyond the Good Friday Agreement*, 2nd edn. (Manchester, 2006). 99. Mary MacAleese, 'Changing History', Longford Lecture, 23 November 2007, quoted Margaret Macmillan, *The Uses and Abuses of History* (London, 2009), p. 72. 100. Ian Paisley, 8 May 2007, www.allgreatquotes.com. 101. Gerry Adams, 4 December 2009, http://www.leargas.blogspot.com/2009/12/lesson-of-history.html (2010). 102. 'No MPs and no Empey', *Guardian* (10 Aug. 2010). 103. http://noplaceinthesun.com/page15.htm (2011). 104. Quoted in 'After the Race', *The Economist* (19 Feb. 2011). 105. Peter Topping, 'Ireland's 2010 Deficit Largest in the EU', *Inside Ireland* (27 June 2011). 106. http://fairocracy.com/general_election_results_2011/irish_general_election_full_results.html (28 Feb. 2011). 107. Diarmaid Ferriter, 'The People's Act of Revenge', *Guardian* (24 Feb. 2011). 108. http://www.fco.gov.uk/en/about-us/whatwe.../state-visit-ireland-2011 (2011). 109. http://www.englishmonarchs.co.uk/stuart-3.htm (2011).

III

110. Norman Davies, *The Isles: A History* (London, 1996), pp. 697–1017. 111. Tam Dalyell, *Devolution: The End of Britain?* (London, 1977). 112. Vernon Bogdanor, *Devolution in the United Kingdom* (Oxford, 1999). 113. *Shorter Oxford English Dictionary*. 114. Timothy Garton Ash, 'Wake up Europe', *Guardian* (June 2010); David Marquand, *The End of Europe* (London, 2011). 115. See Vernon Bogdanor, *The Monarchy and the Constitution* (Oxford, 1995). 116. Jeremy Paxman, *On Royalty* (London, 2006). 117. See www.republic.org.uk. 118. An ICM poll for the BBC in 2009 found 76 per cent in favour of the monarchy continuing after the reign of Elizabeth II, with 18 per cent against and 6 per cent undecided; news.bbc.co.uk/1/hi/7967142.st (2011).

See also http://www.officialroyalwedding2010.org (2011). **119.** http://www.
bbc.co.uk/news-scotland-13305522 (2011). **120.** Martin Kettle, 'Scotland will
tell. . .', *Guardian* (9 April 2011). **121.** See http://www.cep.org.uk (2011). **122.**
See http://www.englishdefenceleague.org (2011). **123.** 'Danny Boy', words
(1910) by F. E. Weatherly, published 1913. Davies, *The Isles*, app. 62, pp. 1010–
11. **124.** Frederick Weatherly (1848–1929), composer of 'The Holy City', 'Roses
of Picardy', 'Yesteryear', 'Beauty's Eyes', etc. See 'Danny Boy – the Mystery
Solved', http://www.standingstones.com/dannyboy.html (2009).

CHAPTER 15. CCCP

Bibliographical Note. No subject has been more blighted than Soviet history by
political passions and by special pleading. The best overview is that of Geoffrey
Hosking, *History of the Soviet Union* (London, 1985); Bertrand Russell's *Theory
and Practice of Bolshevism* (London, 1919), written by a former sympathizer
whose eyes were opened, remains a valuable antidote to the thousands of Westerners who took Soviet propaganda at face value. The authors to avoid include Sidney
Webb, E. H. Carr and Jerry Hough. Even among sceptical commentators, however,
a strong tendency remains to equate the Soviet Union with Russia, and readers
need to make a conscious effort to supplement their general reading with an outline knowledge of the fifteen Soviet republics. The most convenient introduction to
the history of Estonia is by Mati Laur, *A History of Estonia* (Tallinn, 2004).

I

1. Statistics from *Whitaker's Almanack 2007* (London, 2006); see also, *Country
Report: Estonia*, Economist Intelligence Unit (London, 1998). **2.** http://en.wiki-
pedia.org/wiki/estonian_language (2008); ibid., /estonian_vocabulary; Mare Kit-
snik and Leelo Kingisepp, *Teach Yourself Estonian* (London, 2008). **3.** 'Tallinn:
An Introduction', www.balticsww.com/tourist/estonia/sights.htm (2008). **4.**
Neil Taylor, *Estonia: The Bradt Travel Guide* (Chalfont, 2005); Robin Gauldie,
Estonia (Peterborough, 2006); http:/visitestonia.com/index.php (2008). **5.** Bertelsmann Transformation Index, www.nationmaster.com/country/en-estonia/
dem-democracy (2010). **6.** Sergei Balsamov, 'Profane Estonian Democracy and
Blank Newspaper Pages', *Pravda*, www.english.pravda.ru/world/ussr/19-03-
2010/112645-democracy-0 (2010). **7.** Reporters Without Borders, www.rsf.org/
only_peace_protects_freedoms-in.htm (2010). **8.** *Easyjet*, in-flight magazine
(April 2008), p. 98. **9.** www.intelligentcommunity.org/client-uploads./icf-il-2009
(2009). **10.** Fr. R. Kreutzwald, *Kalevipoeg*, canto I, ll. 1–8, after the critical edition of 1961, www.kalevipoeg.info/texteestoniencadres.html (2008). **11.** 'Death
of Kaleb', www.sacred-texts.com/neu/hoe/hoe1-07/htm (2008). **12.** Museum of
Occupations of Estonia, www.okupatsioon.ee/english (2008). A similarly
imaginative museum can be visited in Riga: www.occupationmuseum.lv. **13.**

Estonian International Commission for the Investigation of Crimes against Humanity, *Estonia, 1940–1945* (Tallinn, 2006). **14.** Eduard Kolga; http://nationalalliance.org/gulag/5gulag.htm (2007). **15.** K. Brueggemann and A. Kasekamp, 'The Politics of History and the "War of Monuments"', *Estonia: Nationalities Papers*, 36/3 (3 July 2008), pp. 425–48. **16.** Monument controversy, http://en.wikipedia.org/wiki/bronze_soldier_of_tallinn (2008). **17.** Gary Peach, 'Estonia Removes Disputed Soviet War Memorial', *International Herald Tribune* (27 April 2007). **18.** Adrian Blomfield, 'Putin Criticises Estonia over War Memorial', *Daily Telegraph* (12 May 2007). **19.** Ian Traynor, 'Russia Accused of Unleashing Cyberwar to Disable Estonia', *Guardian* (17 May 2007); 'A Cyber-riot', *The Economist* (10 May 2007). **20.** www.security-gurus.de/papers/cyberwarfare.pdf (2010). **21.** www.ncsa.illinois.edu (2010). **22.** 'Estonia Joins Euro as Currency Expands into former Soviet Bloc', http://www.bloomberg.com/news/2010-12-31.html (2011).

II

23. Richard Pipes, *The Formation of the Soviet Union* (Cambridge, Mass., 1964). **24.** Geoffrey Hosking, *Russia: People and Empire, 1552–1917* (London, 1997). **25.** 'Estonia', in *Encyclopaedia Britannica*, 11th edn. (1911). **26.** 'Reval', ibid. **27.** Evan Mawdsley, *The Russian Civil War* (Edinburgh, 2000). **28.** Robert Service, 'The Polish Corridor', in *Stalin: A Biography* (London, 2004), pp. 175–85. **29.** See Norman Davies, *White Eagle, Red Star: The Polish-Soviet War, 1919–1920* (London, 1972); and Adam Zamoyski, *Warsaw 1920* (London, 2008). **30.** N. Bukharin, *Building up Socialism* (London, 1925); Service, *Stalin*. **31.** Georg von Rauch, *The Baltic States: The Years of Independence* (London, 1974), pp. 24–39. **32.** Ibid., p. 31. **33.** Estonia's Declaration of Independence, 1918, www.president.ee (2010). **34.** 'The German Occupation, 1917–18', in Rauch, *Baltic States*, pp. 39–49. **35.** 'War of Independence', ibid., pp. 49–70. See also www.allempires.com/article/index.php?q=estonian_liberation_war (2008). **36.** Mart Laar, *Estonia's Way* (Tallinn, 2006), p. 126. **37.** See M. W. Graham, *The Diplomatic Recognition of the Border States* (Berkeley, 1939). **38.** Anne Applebaum, *Gulag: A History of the Soviet Camps* (London, 2003). **39.** Stefan Oleskiw, *Agony of a Nation* (London, 1983); Robert Conquest, *The Harvest of Sorrow: Soviet Collectivisation and the Terror-Famine* (London, 2002); L. Luciuk (ed.), *Holodomor: Reflections on the Great Famine in Soviet Ukraine, 1932–33* (Kingston, Ont., 2008). **40.** Scott Shane, *Dismantling Utopia: How Information Ended the Soviet Union* (Chicago, 1994), p. 90. **41.** Robert Conquest, *The Great Terror: A Reassessment* (Oxford, 2008); idem, *Stalin: Breaker of Nations* (London, 1998); idem, *The Dragons of Expectation: Reality and Delusion in the Course of History* (London, 2005). **42.** Laar, *Estonia's Way*, p. 130. **43.** Ibid., pp. 135–6. **44.** See Norman Davies, *Europe at War, 1939–1945: No Simple Victory* (London, 2006). **45.** Steve Zaloga, *Poland 1939: The Birth of Blitzkrieg* (Oxford, 2002). **46.** William Trotter,

The Winter War: The Russo-Finnish War of 1939–40 (London, 2002). 47. Rodric Braithwaite, *Moscow 1941: A City and its People at War* (London, 2006). 48. Harrison Salisbury, *The Siege of Leningrad* (London, 1969). 49. Antony Beevor, *Stalingrad* (London, 1999). 50. Janusz Piekalkiewicz, *Operation Citadel: Kursk and Orel. The Greatest Tank Battle of the Second World War* (Novato, Calif., 1987). 51. Antony Beevor, *Berlin: The Downfall, 1945* (London, 2002). 52. See Richard Overy, *Russia's War* (London, 1999). 53. Jan Lewandowski, *Estonia* (Warsaw, 2001), pp. 137–45. 54. J. W. Russell, quoted by David Kirby, 'Incorporation', in G. Smith (ed.), *The Baltic States* (London, 1996), p. 80. 55. 'Soviet Occupation, 1940–41', in *Estonia, 1940–1945*, pp. 1–410; Meelis Maripuu, 'The Deportations of 1940–41', ibid.; see also Imbi Paju, *Memories Denied* (Helsinki, 2006). 56. 'German Occupation, 1941–44', in *Estonia, 1940–1945*, pp. 521–766; Riho Vastrik, 'The Tartu Concentration Camp', Meelis Maripuu, 'The Execution of Estonian Jews', 'The Annihilation of Czech and German Jews', 'Soviet Prisoners of War in Estonia', ibid. 57. Indrik Paavle, 'Fate of the Estonian Elite', in *Estonia, 1940–1945*, pp. 391–410. 58. T. Hiio and P. Kaasik, 'Estonian Units in the Waffen SS', in *Estonia, 1940–1945*, pp. 927–68; P. Kaasik, 'The 8th Estonian Rifle Corps in North-Western Russia', ibid., pp. 909–26. 59. Lauri Malksoo, 'The Government of Otto Tief', in *Estonia, 1940–1945*, pp. 1107–12. 60. 'Phase III, The Soviet Occupation of Estonia from 1944', www.historycommission.ee/temp/pdf/conclusions_en_1944.pdf (2008); see also M. Laar, *War in the Woods: Estonia's Struggle for Survival, 1944–56* (Ann Arbor, 1992). 61. Alexander Solzhenitsyn, *Invisible Allies* (New York, 1997), pp. 46–64. 62. *Estonia, 1940–1945*, p. 1031. 63. Robert Litwak, *Détente: American Foreign Policy, 1969–76* (Cambridge, 1986). 64. Margaret MacMillan, *Nixon and Mao: The Week that Changed the World* (New York, 2006). 65. Leonard Shapiro, *The Government and Politics of the Soviet Union* (London, 1970); Martin Malia, *The Soviet Tragedy: A History of Socialism in Russia, 1917–91* (New York, 1994); Alec Nove, *Stalinism and After* (Boston, 1989). 66. T. Parming and E. Jaervesoo, *Case Study of a Soviet Republic: The Estonian SSR* (Boulder, Colo., 1978). 67. S. Utechin, *Concise Encyclopaedia of Russia* (London, 1961), pp. 172–3. 68. Maxim Waldstein, 'Russifying Estonia? Iurii Lotman and the Politics of Language and Culture in Soviet Estonia', *Kritika*, 8/3 (2007), pp. 561–96. 69. Paul Hillier, *Arvo Pärt* (Oxford, 1997); Eesti Musika, *Estonian Music Guide* (Tallinn, 2004). 70. Marina Frolova-Walker, 'Nationalist in Form, Socialist in Content: Musical Nation-building in the Soviet Republics', *Journal of the American Musical Society*, 51/2 (1998), pp. 331–71. 71. Quoted in Stalin, *Marxism and the National and Colonial Question* (n.p., 1934). 72. http://www.nlib.ee/html/inglise/rr/hist.html (2011). 73. The Appeal was signed by prominent names in all three Baltic States. See 'Estonia Today: The Molotov–Ribbentrop Pact and its Consequences', http://web-static.vm.ee/static/failid/493/mrp.pdf. 74. Stephen White, *Gorbachev and After* (Cambridge, 1993). 75. 'Glasnost', in *Oxford Russian–English Dictionary* (Oxford, 1972). 76. Estonian national awakening: Clare Thomson, *The Singing Revolution* (London, 1992); Henri Voigt, *'Estonia – the Singing Revolution': Between Utopia and Disillusion-*

ment (Oxford, 2005), pp. 20–35. 77. Meldra Usenko, *Akcija Baltijas Cels, 1989 - The Baltic Way* (Riga, n.d.), illustrated. 78. 'Estonia – Independence Reclaimed', http://countrystudies.us/estonia/5.htm (2008).

III

79. Yuri Meltsev reviewing Shane, *Dismantling Utopia,* in *Independent Review,* 1 (1996). 80. See Emilio Gentile, *Politics as Religion* (Oxford, 2006). 81. Archie Brown, *The Gorbachev Factor* (Oxford, 1997); idem, *Seven Years that Changed the World: Perestroika in Perspective* (Oxford, 2007). 82. Leonid Batkin, as quoted by Shane, *Dismantling Utopia*, p. 5. 83. Edward Lucas, *The New Cold War: How the Kremlin Threatens Both Russia and the West* (London, 2007). 84. Francis Fukuyama, 'The End of History?' *National Interest,* 16 (1989). 85. Paul Kennedy, in *The Rise and Fall of the Great Powers* (London, 1988). 86. Michael Cox, *US Foreign Policy after the Cold War: Superpower without a Mission* (London, 1995); Bill Emmott, *Rivals: The Power Struggle between China, India and Japan* (London, 2008); Martin Jacques, *When China Rules the World: The Rise of the Middle Kingdom and the End of the Western World* (London, 2009); Lauren Phillips, *International Politics in 2030: The Transformative Power of Large Developing Countries* (Bonn, 2008). 87. Lutz Kleveman, *The New Great Game: Blood and Oil in Central Asia* (London, 2004). 88. Mart Laar, 'The Estonian Economic Miracle', Backgrounder 2060, *The Heritage Foundation* (7 August 2007); www.heritage.org/isses/worldwidefreedom/bg2060.cfm. 89. Andrew Osborn, 'Putin: Collapse of the Century', *Independent* (26 April 2005). 90. Lilia Shevtsova, *Putin's Russia* (Washington, 2005). 91. Anna Politovskaya, *Putin's Russia: Life in a Failing Democracy* (London, 2004); Anders Aslund, *Putin's Decline and America's Response* (Washington, 2005); Bertil Nygren, *The Rebuilding of Greater Russia* (London, 2008).

HOW STATES DIE

1. Aristotle, *Politics*, book I, parts 1–2. 2. Thomas Hobbes, *Leviathan* (1651), part II, ch. xxix 'Of those things that weaken or tend to the Dissolution of a Commonwealth'. 3. J.-J. Rousseau, *Social Contract* (1762), book III, ch. 11, 'The Death of the Body Politic', trans. Maurice Cranston (London, 1968). 4. Daniel 5: 25–7. 5. Revelation 18: 2. 6. Augustine, *City of God*, trans. J. Healey (London, 1931). 7. T. Gilby, *The Political Thought of Thomas Aquinas* (Chicago, 1958); E. L. Fortin, 'Thomas Aquinas as a Political Thinker', *Perspectives of Political Science*, 26/2 (1997), p. 92. 8. Edwin Jones, *The English Nation: The Great Myth* (Stroud, 2003). 9. W. Cargill Thompson, *The Political Thought of Martin Luther* (Totowa, NJ, 1984). 10. See James Joll, *The Anarchists* (London, 1965). 11. Karl Marx, in his *Critique of the Gotha Programme* (1875); Friedrich Engels, in the *Anti-Dühring* (1878), as expounded by Lenin, 'On the Withering of the State and Violent Revolution', in his *State and Revolution* (1917), ch.

2. **12.** Lenin, 'On the Eve of Revolution', in his *State and Revolution*, ch. 2: www.marxists.org/archive/lenin/works/1917/staterev/cho2.htm   (2009).   **13.** John Westlake, 'On the Extinction of States', in his *International Law*, Part 1 (Cambridge, 1904), pp. 63–8.   **14.** James Crawford, *The Creation of States in International Law*, 2nd edn. (Oxford, 2006).   **15.** Tanisha Fazal, *State Death: The Politics and Geography of Conquest, Occupation and Annexation* (Princeton, 2007).   **16.** 'COW, Project History', www.correlatesofwar.org/cowhistory. htm (2009).   **17.** Fazal, *State Death*, pp. 243–58.   **18.** 'Index of Failed States, 2009', from the journal *Foreign Policy* www.foreignpolicy.com/articles/2009/06/22/ 2009_failed_states_index_interactive_map_and_rankings   (2010).   **19.**   *Monty Python's Flying Circus*, 'Dead Parrot Sketch', www.mtholyoke.edu/~ebarnes/ python/dead-parrot.htm   (2009).   **20.**   www.en.wikipedia.org/wiki/list_of_ extinct_states (2011).   **21.** John Locke, 'Of the Dissolution of Government', *Two Treatises on Civil Government* (1690; London, 1960), ch. XIX, pp. 252–3.   **22.** Westlake, 'On the Extinction of States', p. 64.   **23.** Ibid., p. 66.   **24.** See Saul Bernard Cohen, 'Implosion of the Soviet State', in his *Geopolitics of the World System* (Langham, Md., 2003), pp. 198 ff.; Robert Miller, 'The Implosion of a Superpower' (1992), http://history.eserver.org/gloss/ussr-in-1991.txt (2010).   **25.** 'The Collapse of Communism: A Re-examination', British Academy Symposium, 15–16 October 2009.   **26.** Laura Silber and Allan Little, *The Death of Yugoslavia* (London, 1995).   **27.** Mark Cornwall (ed.), *The Last Years of Austria-Hungary* (Exeter, 2002); Oszkar Jaszi, *The Dissolution of the Habsburg Monarchy* (Chicago, 1966).   **28.** Norman Davies, *God's Playground: A History of Poland* (Oxford, 1981), vol. 1, p. 551.   **29.** J.-J. Rousseau, *Considérations sur le Gouvernement de la Pologne et sa réforme projetée* (London, 1782).   **30.** Fazal, *State Death*.   **31.** Jiři Prehe, 'The Split of Czechoslovakia: A Defeat or a Victory?', www.prehe.cz/prednasky/2004 (2009).   **32.** Lord Robert Cecil, quoted by Harry Hanak, 'The Government, the Foreign Office and Austro-Hungary, 1914–18', *Slavonic and East European Review*, 47/108 (1969).   **33.** David Marshall Lang, *A Modern History of Georgia* (London, 1962); A. K. Niedermaier (ed.), *Countdown to War in Georgia* (Minneapolis, 2008).   **34.** *Beowulf*, prologue, ll. 26–52, trans. Seamus Heaney as 'The Ship of Death', from *The Haw Lantern* (London, 1987).   **35.** William Wordsworth, 'On the Extinction of the Venetian Republic' (1802).

Acknowledgements

Research on this book began in April 2006, when I set off with my wife Maria for the Firth of Clyde on the first of successive expeditions to explore the site of a vanished kingdom. For the next five years we shared the ardours and pleasures of an enterprise in which I was the pen-pusher cum designer and she the undisputed *chef des idées* and manager of life-support systems. Once again, Roger Moorhouse provided sterling assistance as picture-researcher, map-drawer and adviser in matters German. Katarzyna Pisarska has served throughout as my virtual PA, skimming over all obstacles whether in Harvard, Uzbekistan or Nepal. I acknowledge my debt to several institutions, including the Fundacja Nauki Polski and Carta Blanca S.A. in Warsaw, the Jagiellonian University in Kraków, Clare Hall and Peterhouse, Cambridge, and St Antony's College, Oxford; and I wish to express my special gratitude to numerous individual contributors. Almost every chapter has been read and improved by consultants of the highest calibre, whose comments calmed doubts and fears while leaving ultimate responsibility with the author. The long list of names is headed by that of my late friend and colleague Rees Davies, who was in at the start and who was followed by Jorg Hensgen, Peter Heather, James Campbell, Conrad Leyser, David Abulafia, Robert Frost, Robert Evans, Philip Mansel, Noel Malcolm, Roy Foster, Geoffrey Hosking, Margus Laidre and Chris Clark, who proved particularly generous. Additional advice was kindly supplied by Alexandra Loewe, Alba and Andrea Skidmore, and Thomas Charles-Edwards. The digitalized text was beautifully produced from a large manuscript by Gosia Figwer, Malgorzata Ciszewska and the late Miranda Long, ably supplemented by Heather and Sebastian Godwin and Hazel Dunn. Professional editorial work was undertaken by David Milner, Charlotte Ridings and Elizabeth Stratford. The project was launched by Will Sulkin, who gave valuable early support, but came to fruition through the combined efforts of my irreplaceable agent, David Godwin, and of my literary adviser, fellow Boltonian and publishing director of Allen Lane, the indefatigable Stuart Proffitt.

Index

Page references in *italic* indicate maps or figures, which can also be found listed in full at the front of the book.

Aachen 122
Aberlemno Stone 60–61
Abernethy, Treaty of 75
Académie Florimontane 407
Acallan na Senórach ('Old Men's Colloquy') 78–9
Acton, Sir Harold 499
Adalbert of Prussia, St (Vojtech of Prague) 337
Adamnan 53, 57
Adams, Gerry 672–3, 677, 678, 681
Adelheid (St Adelaide) 117, 118
Aderydd (Arhuret) 59
Aedan macGabrain 53, 56
Aeron (Ayrshire) 49, 62
Aetius, Flavius 21, 93, 94
Aftanazy, Roman 306
Agaunum (St Maurice-en-Valais), abbey of 99
Agde, General Church Council of 19
Agnon, S. Y. 478
Ahern, Bertie 673, 676
Aidan, St 60
Ailamae 718
Aix-en-Provence 118, 217
Aix-les-Bains 415, 417
Alaborg 243
Åland Isles 617
Alans 17, 18, 31
Alaric I 16–17, 31
Alaric II 18, 24–5, 26, 30, 31
Alaric, Montagne d' 27
Alauna 46, 47
Alba 66, 70–71, 72, 74, 75–6
Alban, St 46
Albania 197, 587, 597, 601, 617
Albert I of Belgium 600
Albert II of Monaco 637
Albert, prince 543–9, 551–9, 573, 637

timetable he prepared for himself, aged fourteen 547, 548
Albert the Bear 344
Albigensian Crusade 125, 179
Albon, counts of 118, 127
Albrecht Friedrich von Hohenzollern 355
Albrecht von Habsburg 478
Albrecht von Hohenzollern 341, 351, 352, 353–4
Alcañiz, fortress 184
Alcluith 39, 64
Alclut 69
Aleksandar, crown prince of Serbia 593, 601, 606, 612
Aleksandar I Obrenović 589–90
Alemanni 24
Alessandria 414
Alexander I, tsar 293, 334, 699
Alexander II, 'Tsar Liberator' 294, 297
Alexander VI, Roderic Llançol de Borja 215, 218
Alexander of Teck, 1st earl of Athlone 566, 569
Alexandria, Egypt 401, 435
museum 481
Alexandria, Vale of Leven 37
Alfons de Borja, Pope Callistus III 215
Alfonso I El Batallado 169, 170
Alfonso II of Aragon and I of Barcelona 171
Alfonso II of Naples 214
Alfonso V the Magnanimous, of Aragon 210, 211–12, 213–14
Alfonso VII of Castile 175
Alfonso of Aragon, Infante Alfonso 201–2
Alfonso of Aragon, son of Fernando I 209
Alfred, duke of Edinburgh and of Saxe-Coburg and Gotha 562, 563
Alfred, hereditary prince of Saxe-Coburg and Gotha 562

Alfred of Wessex, king 68
Alfred the Great 89
Alghero 202
Algierdas 252, 254
Alicante 189
Alice, countess of Athlone 566, 569
Aljaferia Castle 169, 184
Allenstein 342
Allobroges 414
Alt Clud, Kingdom of the Rock 42–83
    5th century 49–52
    6th century 52–57
    7th century 57–62
    8th to 9th centuries 62–72
    10th century 72–5
    11th century 75–7
    12th century 77–80
Amadeo, 'duke of Aosta' 432–3
Amadeus VI, the Green Count 404
Amadeus VII, the Red Count 404
Amadeus VIII (Felix V) 406
Amalfings 18
Amalric 26
Amanieu de Sescars, *il dieu d'amor* 172
Ambaciensis (Amboise) 24
Amber Room (*Bernsteinzimmer*) 383,
    386n
Amfilohije, Archbishop 614
Amiens, Treaty of 507, 517
Anatolia 196, 319
Ancient Order of Hibernians 644
Ancillon, Charles 365
Andemantunnum (Langres) 95
Andorra 159–60
Andreas von Saxe-Coburg-Gotha 571
Andrew, St 66
Angevins, relations with Aragon 174,
    192–3, 195, 197, 211
Angles 53, 56, 57–60, 62, 64
Anglo-Irish Bank 677
Anglo-Irish Treaty 655–7, 661–2, 737
Anglo-Saxon Chronicle 66, 73–4
Anglo-Saxons 42, 44, 738
    see also Angles
Anna of Prussia 355
Annales Cambriae 52
Annecy 118, 407–8, 436
Anselm von Meisser 342–3
Ansip, Andrus 692
Ansky, Semyon 464–5
Antoinette-Marie of Württemberg 547
Antonine Wall 46, 48, 64
Aquitania/Aquitaine 17, 18–20, 24, 27, 30
Arago, François 154
Aragon, empire 161–227, *166*, *178*, *192*,
    735

and the Angevins 174, 192–3, 195, 197,
    211
Aragonese language 171
and the Balearic Islands 185, 187–9,
    197–200, 202–3, 226
and Castile 163, 165, 166, 169, 170–71,
    175, 189, 204–5, 207–10, 211,
    215–17, 217, 218–19, 220, 223
and the Catalans 166, 171, 174–5, 177,
    189, 196, 199, 200, 202, 206–7, 210,
    217–18, 222–7, 736
and the Church 169, 181–3, 184
coronation ceremonies 182–3
and Corsica 197, 201, 210
Crown of Aragon 176, 177, 180, 183–4,
    190, 195, 206–7, 209–10, 217–18,
    221–7, 736
General Privilege 191
and Gozo 196
and Greece 191, 196, 199
House of Ramiro 164–5, *165*
and Jaime I 185–6, 187–9, 197
and the Jews 183–4
and Mallorca 187–8, 197–200, 202–3,
    226
and Malta 191, 195–6
and Menorca 188–9, 199
and Montpellier 179–81, 184, 202–3
and Naples 184, 193, 197, 210–14,
    211–13, 216–18
navy 205
origins of the kingdom 161–4,
    165, *166*
and Pedro IV 174, 202–7
Privilege of Union 203
and the Pyrenees 156–60
and the *Reconquista* 164, 166–9, 173,
    181, 183, 184
and Rosselló 177–9, 200, 222
and Sardinia 197, 201–2, 206, 220
and Sicily 191–5, 197, 206, 212, 220
and Teruel 190–91
House of Trastámara 207, *208*,
    210, 216
Union of Liberties 191, 203
union with Barcelona 170–71, 174–6;
    see also Barcelona
and Valencia 176, 189–90
Aragon, river 161
Aranjuez, Treaty of 509
Arborea 201, 206
Arcola, Battle of 501
Arelate (Arles) 20, 109
Argyll 37n, 53, 65, 66
Arianism 16, 20, 30, 93, 98–9
Ariège 157

Aristotle 729
Aristra, Inigo 155
Arius of Alexandria 16n
Arles 104, 116, 119, 122
  Arelate 20, 109
  Kingdom of (Kingdom of the Two
    Burgundies) 115–19, *116*
Armagnacs 131
Armenia 722
Armenian Church 463
Arnau de Grub, St 182
Arnaut Catalan 172
Arpitan 120
Arpitania *121*
Art, son of Conn 47
Arthgal, king 69–70
Arthur, duke of Connaught 562
Arthur, king 54
Arthur, prince, of Connaught and
    Strathearn 562, 563
Arthurian legend 54–55, 56
Arvernis (Clermont) 20
Asad, Muhammad (Leopold Weiss) 478
Ascania, House of 344
Ascendancy, Protestant 650, 660, 667,
    679
Asimov, Isaac 632–3
Aster, Operation 714
Asti 407
Asymmetric Threats Contingency Alliance
    (ATCA) 697
Ataulf, the 'Noble Wolf' 17–18
ATCA (Asymmetric Threats Contingency
    Alliance) 697
Athanasius of Brest, St 277
Athelstan 72, 73, 74
Athens 196
Atholl 65
Atlakvida 94
Attila (Atli) 94, 103
Auberge d'Aragon 220
Auerstadt 521
Augsberger, Franz 713
August II the Strong 283, 364
August III 283, 284
August Wilhelm of Prussia 568
Augustine of Hippo, St 730
Augustodunum (Autun) 95
Augustus Caesar 314
Aukštota 248
Aurausion (Orange) 125
Auschwitz 478, 479
Austerlitz 521
Austria/Austrians
  and France 451–2, 500–501, 505,
    508–9, 516

and Galicia 289, 292, 295, 449–
    50, 451–3, 455–6, 470, 473–5, 474;
  see also Galicia
  Habsburgs see Habsburgs
  and Italy 425, 500–501
  and Montenegro 597–9
  and Napoleon I 500–501
  and Poland 286
  and Serbia 597–9
  Vienna see Vienna/Viennese
Austria-Hungary 470, 472
  Carpatho-Ukraine see Carpatho-Ukraine
  collapse of Empire 599, 600, 733–4;
    Treaty of St Germain 625
Austrian Netherlands 141
Avenio (Avignon) 95
Avignon 104, 125, 128, 153, 205
  Aouenion 95
Avitus, Eparchius 22
Avitus of Vienne 99
Azerbaijan 233, 722, 731
Azkenazy, Szymon 465

Babylon, Fall of 730
Bacciochi Levoy, Elisa Napoleone 534
Bacciochi Levoy, Maria-Anna ('Elisa')
    Bonaparte 500, 520–21, 523, 524,
    527, 529
Bacciochi Levoy, Pasquale/Félix 520–21
Bağiş 313
Bagration, Operation 302
Bakiyev, Kurmanbek Saliyevich 235
Bakunin, Mikhail 730
Bałaban, Meir 465–6
Balearic islands 185, 187–9, 197–200,
    202–3, 226
Balkans 214, 314, 383
  Balkan Wars 594–5
  Montenegro see Montenegro/Tsernagora
Balmoral 83
Baltic Appeal (1979) 720
Baltic/Balts 240–42, 244, 245, 618, 702
  'Baltic Chain' 723
  and the birth of the Grand Duchy of
    Litva 248–9
  deportations under Soviet Great Terror 715
  Estonia see Estonia
  inter-war Baltic States 707
  Latvia see Latvia/Latvians
  Lithuania see Litva/Lithuania
  and the Mongol Horde 248, 251, 252,
    260, 338
  Prussia see Prussia/Borussia and the
    Prussians
  Soviet 1940 takeover of the Baltic States
    301–2, 618, 710–12, 737

Baltic/Balts – *cont.*
  and the Teutonic Knights 248, 252, 253, 259
  World War II 710
Baltic Tobacco Factory (BTF) 330
Baltiysk 334, 335
Bamburgh Castle 53, 56
Banach, Stefan 477–8
Bandera, Stepan 478
Baou, lords of (Les Baux) 119, 125
Bar, Montenegro 580
Barbarossa, Operation 301–2, 382, 479, 710
Barbarus, Johannes Vares 714, 717
Barbastro 166–7
Barcelona 160, 162, 170, 171, 173, 175, 183, 185–6, 200, 203, 222, 223, 224
  Church Council of 181
  Disputation of 184
  House of 163n
  union with Aragon 170–71, 174–6
  university 184
  Usatges de Barcelona 174
Barretinas, Revolt of the 222
Bartians 338
Basle, Council of 215
Batory, Stefan 278–9
Batowski, Henryk 7
The Battle of Brunanburh 73
Battle of the Nations, Leipzig 529
Baussenque Wars 119
Baux, counts/lords of 119, 125
Bavarian Geographer (Geographus Bavarius) 337
Beatrice, princess 558
Beatrice I, countess of Burgundy 122
Béatrice de Provence 174
Beauharnais, Eugéne de 413, 521, 523, 535
Beauharnais, Joséphine de 501
Beaune 137
Beckwith, John 416
Bede 39, 42, 52, 53, 60, 64
Behan, Dominic 666
Beinnie Britt 47
Belarus/Byelorussia 231–9, 232, 249, 291, 301, 302, 303, 703; *see also* White Ruthenia
  Byelorussian National Republic (BNR) 233, 301, 738
  Lukashenkism 233–5
  and the Wikileaks scandal 235
Belfast 653–4
Belfast Agreement 673–5
Belgium 600, 710
Belgrade 590, 600, 602, 604, 605–6
Beli (Bili I) 61

Bellver Castle 199
Benaki Museum, Athens 320
Benedict XIII 209
Benso, Camillo, Count Cavour 417, 420–21, 423, 428, 429
Benveniste de Porta 183
Benvenuti, Pietro 527
Bera, count 171
Berber states 199
Berehaven 663
Berenguela of Barcelona 170–71, 175
Berenguer de Anglesola 182
Berenguer Ramón I El Corbat 163
Berenguer, House of 171, 175
Berlin 367, 370, 375, 379, 382
  1918 revolution 599
  Congress of 587–8
  fall of the Berlin Wall 721, 723
  Museum Island 390
  Potsdam Conference 387–8
  Prussian memory site 389–93
Berlusconi, Silvio 399, 437
Bernard, St 107–8
Bernard de Got 126
Berne 122
Bernhardi, Friedrich von 376–7
Bernicia (Berneich/Bryneich) 49, 53, 56, 60
Bernsteinzimmer (Amber Room) 383, 386n
Berthold V, count 121–2
Bertrand, Henri Gatien 531, 533
Besalú 174, 175
Besanz/Besançon 141
  Diet of Besanz 123
  Vesontio 95, 118
Bevar Bornholmsk 87–8
Bianchi, M. 427
Bismarck, Otto Edward von 369, 376, 377
Black Death 128, 202, 204–5
Black, George Fraser 80
Blair, Tony 673, 680
Bloody Sunday 668
  Saville Inquiry 677
Blücher, Gebhard Leberecht von 533
Blue Water, Battle of 252
Blumenthal, J. F. von 359, 362
Bobola, Andrew, St 281
Bobowa 472
Bobrzyński, Michał 465, 478
Boccanegra of Genoa 205
Bogside, Battle of the 668
Boguslav III 338
Bohemia 258, 269, 454, 457, 625, 626
  Premyslid dynasty 345
Bologna 501
Bolsheviks 233, 335, 380, 382, 701–5

Bolshevik Revolution 335, 380, 475–7, 598, 607
Red Army *see* Red Army
Red Cossacks 477
Bonaparte, Carlo Maria 500
Bonaparte, Carolina-Maria, later Carolina Buonaparte-Murat 500, 509, 536
Bonaparte, Charles Louis Napoléon *see* Napoleon III
Bonaparte, Charles-Lucien 536
Bonaparte, Filippo, Abbé 501
Bonaparte, Girolamo (Jérôme) 500, 521, 523, 536
Bonaparte, Giuseppe (Joseph) 500, 520, 521, 523, 533, 536
Bonaparte, Letizia, 'Madame Mère' 531, 535
Bonaparte, Luciano (Lucien) 500, 520, 521, 528, 535–6
Bonaparte, Luigi (Louis) 500, 520, 521, 533, 536
Bonaparte, Maria-Anna ('Elisa') 500, 520–21, 523, 524, 527, 529
Bonaparte, Maria-Paolina, later Paolina Borghese 500, 511, 519–20, 521, 531, 535, 536
Bonaparte, Nabuleone/Napoleon *see* Napoleon I
Bonaparte family 502
Bonedd Gwyr y Gogledd ('The Descent of the Men of the North') 49, 57
Bonhill, Vale of Leven 37
Boniface VIII 201
Bonifacio, fortress 210
Bonneville 402, 415, 435
Bonomi, Ivanoe 609
Book of Aneurin 58
Boos, Georgiy 330–31, 335
Borbetomagus (Worms) 93
  massacre at 93, 94
Bordeaux 102
Borghese, Camillo 519, 536
Borghese, Paolina, née Bonaparte *see* Bonaparte, Maria-Paolina
Borja 215
Bornholm 87–90, 89
  see also Burgundia/Burgundians
Bornholm disease 88
Bornholmsk 87–8
Borodino, Battle of 293
Borussia *see* Prussia/Borussia and the Prussians
Borussian School 367–8
Borysław 457
Bosnia 587, 605, 614–15, 619, 731
Boso, count 110

Boso II, count of Arles, margrave of Tuscany 112
Bosonids 110, *111*, 118–19
Boudet, Abbé 27–8
Bourbon, House of 506, *506*, 537
  Bourbons of Parma 506, 509, 510; Lodovico I 509, 510–12, 515, 516, 517; Maria-Luisa di Borbone 510–12, 516, 517, 518–19, 521, 522, 523, 528–30, 534
  Louis Antoine de Bourbon, duc d'Enghien 517–18
Bourbon Kingdom of Naples 521
Bourgogne province 139, 141, 142
Boycott, Captain Charles Cunningham 644
Boykivshchyna 455
Boyne, Battle of the 641
  anniversary 667
Bradley, Katherine 499
Brandenburg/Brandenburgers 344, 345, 355–6, 358, 363, 390–91
  state of Brandenburg-Prussia 358–60, 360, 361–2, 363–6
Brandt, Willi 388
Branickis 455
Braun, Otto 381, 388
Brenner, Robert 632
Bres (Irish king) 640
Brest 251, 266, 275, 301
  Brest-Litowsk Treaty 300, 378, 702
  Church Council of 277
Breviarum Alarici 24
Brezhnev, Leonid 716
Brian Bóraimhe/Boru 640–41
Bridei map Bili 60, 61
Brighton Bombing 672
Britain
  army *see* British Army
  Battle of Waterloo 533
  and France 507, 516, 522; anti-French coalition 505
  and Germany: Anglo-German Friendship Society 568; 'Dreadnought race' 565–6; royal families 572–3
  and the House of Saxe-Coburg and Gotha 554–70
  and Ireland 641–2, 643–4, 649–85; *see also details under* Ireland
  and Montenegro 608–9
  New Labour 680
  Northern, ninth to tenth centuries 71
  RAF 383
  royal family 566–7, 571–3; fate of the monarchy 681–2
  Royal Navy 40, 41, 505, 506, 507, 663, 679, 705

Britain – *cont.*
  Titles Deprivation Act 566–7
  see also Britannia; Britons, Ancient;
    United Kingdom
Britannia 17, 44–9
  Northern (*c*. AD 410) 47
  the Old North *see* Old North
British Army 533, 649–50, 652, 653, 668,
  674, 677
British Commonwealth 661, 663, 664,
  665, 679
British Stone (*Clach nam Breatan*) 63
Britons, Ancient 42–3, 44–5, 56–57, 62
  of 'The Rock' *see* Alt Clud, Kingdom of
    the Rock
Bronze Soldier (*Pronkssödur*) 696
Brookeburgh, Basil Stanlake Brooke, 1st
  Viscount 667
Brookeburgh barracks 666
Brown, Dan: *The Da Vinci Code* 28
Brown, Gordon 680
Brückner, Alexander 465
Brude (Bridei) 61
Bruges 137
Brunanburh, Battle of 73–4
Brunechildis 103
Brusilov, Alexei Alekseevich 475
Brut y Tywysogion ('Chronicle of the
  Princes') 64, 68, 70, 74
Bryce, James 90–91, 120, 142
Bryce, Ronald 610
Bryneich (Bernicia) 49, 53, 56, 60
Brythonic language 43–4, 45, 72, 77
Buber, Martin 478
bubonic plague 128
  see also Black Death
Buckley, Donald 662
Budapest, Szépmüvészeti Museum of Fine
  Arts 482
Bukovina 454, 456, 710
Bulgars 245
Bund (Jewish Labour League) 297, 299
Bunreacht na hÉireann 662, 663,
  665
Buonaparte family *see* Bonaparte family;
  Napoleon I; Napoleon III, *and under*
  the surnames Bonaparte
Buondelmonte dei Buondelmonti 496
Burdigala (Bordeaux) 24, 25
Burgdorf 121
Burgundia/Burgundians 89–149, 129
  arts 135–6
  Bryce and 90–91, 120, 142
  Burgundian Circle 139–41, *140*
  Burgundian Code 97–8
  Burgundian School of music 135

County-Palatine of Burgundy (Franche-
  Comté) 124–5, 127–8, *130*, 131,
  138–41
  definitions of Burgundy: online 143–5;
    reference works 144, 145–9
  disintegration of imperial Burgundy
    123–5, 124, 127
  duchy-county 131
  Duchy of *Burgundia Minor* 121
  Duchy of Burgundy (French) 105, *105*,
    106–8, *107*, 113, *130*
  within the Frankish realms (mid-sixth
    century) *101*
  Franko-Burgundian wars 99
  kingdoms: first (Kingdom of Gundahar)
    91–5, 92; second (founded by
    Gundioc) 24, 95, 94–100; third
    (*Regnum Burgundiae*) 100–104;
    fourth (Lower Burgundy/Kingdom of
    Provence) 109, *109*–12, 113, 147; fifth
    (Upper Burgundy) 112–15, *113*, 735;
    sixth (Kingdom of Arles/of the Two
    Burgundies) 115–19, *116*; seventh
    (imperial Burgundy) 119–23, 123–5,
    124, 127
  Landgravate of Burgundy 121
  language 96, 100
  and Lotharingia *105*, 105
  States of Burgundy (Duchy of Burgundy)
    131–9, *133*, 734
  the three Burgundies (*c*. AD 1000) 112,
    113
  see also Lower Burgundy; Upper
    Burgundy
Burgundy wine 108
Burke, Thomas Henry 648
Burns, Robbie 38, 83
Burshtyn 444
Bury, J. B. 318
Bute, Isle of 38
Byelorussia *see* Belarus/Byelorussia
Byelorussian National Republic (BNR)
  233, 300–301, 738
Byrne, Mary 645
Byzantine Empire/Byzantines 23–4,
  25, 196, 245, 259–60, 312, 313–
  24, 734
  contraction of the empire *318*
  and Kievan Rus' 245
Byzantine Orthodoxy 30, 255, 277
Byzantion/Byzantium 259–60, 311–13,
  314
  see also Constantinople; Istanbul

Cabillo (Chalon-sur-Saône) 102
Cadzow (Hamilton) Castle 78

Caer Ligualid (*Luguvalium*/Carlisle) 49, 56
Caesarius of Arles, St 102
Cagliari 201, 202
Caílte 78
Calabria 166, 211, 413, 508
Caledonian-MacBrayne 37
Caledonii 46, 47
Caleppi, Mgr 515
Callistus III, Alfons de Borja 215
Calvinism 266, 359, 408
Cambronne, Pierre 531, 533
Cameron, Averil 319
Cameron, David 677
Camorra 582
Campagna 212
Campaign for an English Parliament 683
Campbell Clan 80
Campbell, Sir Neil 532
Campin, Robert 135
Canaries 199
Candida Casa 52
    see also Whithorn
Canova, Antonio 520, 527
Cantius, Johannes 453
Capelle, Guillaume 524
Caracall, emperor 48
Carbonari 413
Cardona, fortress 184
Caretana 97
Carham, Battle of 76
Carlat 175
Carleton, William 642
Carlo Alberto 415–16, 431
Carlo Emanuele II, duke 408
Carlo Emanuele III 410
Carlo Emanuele IV 415
Carlo Félice/Charles le Heureux/Charles
    Félix 415, 435
Carolingians 100, 104–6, 111
Carpatho-Ukraine/Carpathian Ruthenia
    623–34
    constitution 626–7
    declaration of independence 626
    under Hungarian rule 631
    in inter-war Republic of Czechoslovakia
        623, 625, 626
    landscape 623–4
    map of Carpathian Ruthenia 624
    and the Holocaust 631
    Republic of Carpatho-Ukraine 626–31,
        627, 737
    and the Soviet Union 631
Carson, Sir Edward 650
Carta de Logu 206
Casimir III the Great 346
Casimir Jagiellon, St 266

Castile, relations with Aragon 163, 165,
    166, 169, 170–71, 175, 189, 204–5,
    207–10, 212, 215–17, 217, 218–19,
    220, 223
Catalaunian Fields, Battle of 21, 94
Catalina, Catherine of Aragon 219
Catalonia/Catalans 154, 158, 159, 160
    and Aragon 166, 171, 174–5, 177, 189,
        196, 199, 200, 202, 206–7, 210,
        217–18, 222–7, 736
    Catalan Company 196, 218
    Catalan language 158, 162, 171, 223
    Catalan Revolt 222
    flag 224
    French in 179, 199, 222
    legal code, *Usatges de Barcelona* 174
    Llibre dels Fets ('Book of Deeds') 185,
        187–8
Catania university 184
Cateau-Cambrésis, Peace of 407
Cathars 28, 179, 181
Catherine of Aragon 219
Catherine the Great 285, 286, 290
Catherine of Lancaster 207
Cato the Elder 734
Catraeth, Battle of 57–59
Caucasus 703, 705
Cavendish, Lord Frederick Charles 648
Cavour, Camillo Benso, count 417,
    420–21, 423, 428, 429
Caw 52
Caxton, William 135
Cecil, Robert, 1st Viscount 737
Celts 42, 43, 60
    battles against Angles 57–59
    Brythonic (P-Celtic) 43–4
    Gaelic/Goidelic 43–4
    Kingdom of the Rock see Alt Clud,
        Kingdom of the Rock
    Old North see Old North
Cennrigmonoid monastery (St Andrews)
    66
Central Asia 248, 479, 699, 703, 721, 725,
    727
Centre for Flight and Expulsion, Berlin 392
Cerdagne/Cerdanya 158, 174, 175, 222
Ceretic Guletic (Coroticus) 51–2
Certosa di Galluzzo 507, 528, 537
Cesare Borgia 215
Cetinje 579, 580, 585, 587, 590, 605, 606,
    614
Chablais 402, 407, 425
Chaca 164
Chad 731
Chalon 106
Chamberlain, Neville 633

Chambéry 402, 416, 417–18, 423, 426–7,
    428, 434, 436
Charbonnieres, Château de 435
Charlemagne (Charles the Great) 100, 104,
    161–2
    Marches of Charlemagne's Empire 162,
    163
Charles I of Austria 450, 475, 476, 599
Charles II of England, Scotland and
    Ireland 679
Charles II, the Bewitched of Spain 220
Charles II, duke (later Charles V) 139
Charles IV of Spain 522–3
Charles V, Holy Roman Emperor 139,
    219–20, 354
Charles X of Sweden 361
Charles XII of Sweden 283, 364, 365
Charles d'Anjou 174, 195
Charles the Bald 106, 110
Charles Edward, duke of Saxe-Coburg and
    Gotha 563–7, 568–70, 571
Charles Félix/Charles le Heureux/Carlo il
    Felice 415, 435
Charles the Great see Charlemagne
Charles-Louis/Carlo-Luigi, boy-king of
    Etruria 518, 534
Charles Martel 100, 104
Charles de Navarre 128
Charles le Téméraire (Karel de Stoute) 132,
    137–8
Chassidism 299, 463, 473
Chastellain 137
Chaucer, Geoffrey: Canterbury Tales 345
Chechen war 728
Chełmno/Kulmerland 339, 340, 342
Chernigov 268
Chernobyl disaster 233
Chernyakovsky, Ivan 385
Chester, Battle of 44
Childebert II 102
Childers, Erskine 655, 657
Chilperic I 96
China 618, 716, 723, 726
Chirac, Jacques 331, 583
Chmielnicki, Bohdan 281
Chodkiewicz, Jan 271–2
Chotch, Dr 612–13
Christian of Oliva 342
Christianity
    Aragon and the Church 169, 181–3, 184
    Arianism 16, 20, 30, 93, 98–9
    Armenian Church 463
    and the Burgundians 97–9, 107–8, 110
    Byzantine Orthodoxy 30, 255, 277
    Caesaro-papism 314
    Calvinism 266, 359, 408

Church's war against the Cathars 181
and Clovis and Clothilda 97
Crusades see Crusades
dialogue with Jews and Muslims 182
in Estonia 719
in Galicia 462–3, 464
and Germanic codifying 97–8
Great Schism 315
Greek Catholic (Uniate) Church 237,
    277, 295, 301, 463, 625
Greek Orthodoxy 245
Inquisition 218, 221
in Ireland 641, 644–5, 659–61; and the
    Northern Ireland 'Troubles' 667–9;
    Protestants 641, 650, 654, 660, 667–9,
    674, 684; Roman Catholic Church
    644–5, 659–61, 671–2; tensions
    between Church and State 661, 668–9,
    672
in late Roman Britain 46
in Litva 250–51, 253–5, 265–6, 277;
    under Russian annexation 295
Lutheranism 270, 353–4, 355, 359, 463
monastic foundations in Duchy of
    Burgundy 107–8
Montenegrin Orthodox Church 581,
    592, 605, 614, 616
and the Moors 161–2; see also
    Reconquista against the Muslims
papacy see papacy
and the Picts 63–4, 65
pilgrimage see pilgrimage
Roman Catholicism see Roman Catholic
    Church
Roman Church in Iberia 181
and Rus' 245, 246–7
Russian Orthodoxy 265, 295, 298, 463
in Sabaudia 407–8
Scottish Presbyterians 641, 667
Second Council of Lyon and the filioque
    126
Serbian Orthodox Church 581, 592,
    605, 614
and the Slavs 245
Teutonic Knights see Teutonic Knights
Valdensians/Vaudois 126, 408
'Chronicle of the Princes' (Brut y
    Tywysogion) 64, 68, 70, 74
Churchill, Winston 10, 646–7, 664, 681
Cid, El (Rodrigo Díaz de Vivar) 167–9
Cimabue 496
Cinbellin 57
Cinuit 52
Cione, Nardo di 497
Cisalpine Republic 505, 517
Cispadane Republic 398–9, 501, 505

Cîteaux, abbey of 107
Civitas Turonum (Tours) 20
Clach nam Breatan (British Stone) 63
Clancy, Liam 666
Clark, Christopher: *Iron Kingdom* 372–3
Clarke, Henri-Jacques 515, 535
Clemenceau, Georges 618
Clement V, pope 126
Clinoch 57
Clontarf, Battle of 641
Clota, River 48
Clotaire II 102
Clotaire III 102
Clothilda 97, 99
Clovis, king of the Franks 24–5, 30, 31, 97, 99
Clovis II 102
Cluny, house of 107
Clyde, Firth of 36, 36–7, 38, 64, 78, 83
    Dumbarton Rock 35–42
Clyde Valley (*strath Cluatha*), Battle of 48
Clydeside 40, 41, 55, 72, 83
Cnut Sweynsson the Great 75, 76
Coalburners, Society of 413
Coburg 541–2, 557, 559, 560, 567–8
    Duchy of Saxe-Coburg and Gotha 545, 557, 559–70; *see also* Saxe-Coburg and Gotha
Coburg-Braganzas 559
Codex Euricianus 23
Coel Hen (King Cole) 49, 52
Colanica 46
Cold War 8, 89, 389, 696, 715, 721, 733
Collar, Order of (now Order of the Most Holy Annuciation) 406
Collins, Michael 639–40, 654, 655, 656
Colliure (Collioure) 178
Colonia Julia Vienna (Vienne) 95, 97
Colquhouns of Luss 77
Columba, St 53, 57, 60
Columbanus, St 102
Columbus, Christopher 218
Comet 37
Commonwealth of Independent States (CIS) 234, 725
Communism
    Communist China 716, 723; *see also* China
    Estonian Communist Party 714, 717
    League of Yugoslav Communists 581
    Montenegrin Communist Party 615
    Soviet Communism 716, 724; Soviet Communist Party 301, 302, 706, 712, 715, 717, 721, 732–3; *see also* Soviet Union (CCCP)

Communist Party of the Soviet Union (KPSS/CPSU) 715
Commynes, Philippe de 138
Compromise of Caspe 207
Comtat Venaissin 118, 123, 125
Connaught Rangers 650
Conrad I of Burgundy (Conradus Pacificus) 114, 117
Conrad II, emperor 119
Conrad IV 127
Conrad, duke of Mazovia 339
Conrad, son of Frederick II 192
Conradye of Thuringia 341
Conrad von Zähringen 120–21
Consalvi, Ercole 523
Consilium Rationis Bellicae (An Outline of Military Method) 269
Constantine I the Great 314, 319, 322
Constantine I, king of the Picts 66, 70
Constantine II, king of Scots 66, 72
Constantinople 214, 259–60, 311, 317, 319; *see also* Byzantion/Byzantium; Istanbul
    Patriarch of 260
Constanza di Hohenstaufen 191, 195
Continental System 522, 523
Cooper, Edith 499
Copenhagen, Ole Worm Collection 481
Copernicus, Nicholas 343
Corbeil, Treaty of 185
Coria 46
Coroticus (Ceretic Guletic) 51–2
Corps of Carabinieri 415
Corpus de Sang 222
Correlates of War Project (COW) 731
Corsica 197, 201, 210
Cosgrave, W. T. 656, 660–61
Cosimo I de' Medici collection, Florence 481
Cossacks 260, 265, 277, 281–2, 293–4, 361, 380
Côte d'Or 108, 137
Counter-Reformation 408
Courland 259, 270, 291
    Courland-Livonia 345, 351
Courrier des Alpes 425
courtly love 172
COW (Correlates of War Project) 731
Cowen, Brian 677–8
Cowper, George Nassau, 3rd Earl 499
Coyanza, Council of 163
Craig, Sir James/Viscount Craigavon 656, 667
Crimean khanate 260, 261, 268

Croatia/Croats 476, 602, 604
  see also Serbs, Croats and Slovenes,
    Kingdom of
Cromwell, Oliver 82, 408, 641
Cromwell, Thomas 730
Crown of Ireland Act (1542) 641, 665–6
Crusades
  Second Crusade 108
  Fourth Crusade 317, 318
  Albigensian Crusade 125, 179
  Crusade of Barbastro 167
  Iberian 218
  Northern 339, 341–2
  Teutonic Crusaders see Teutonic Knights
  see also Reconquista against the
    Muslims
Culloden, Battle of 82
Cumbria 45, 70, 78
Cumbric 45, 79
Cunedda ap Edern 49
Curzon, George, Earl Curzon of Kedleston
    608, 620
Cuthbert, St 60
Cymru Fydd (Young Wales) 679
Cynon, son of Clydno Eidyn 58, 59
Cyril, St 245
Cyrillic 245
Czartoryski, Adam Kazimierz 284, 483
Czartoryski, Izabella (née Fleming) 482
Czartoryski Museum 482–3, 484–5
Czartoryskis 264, 272, 284, 455
Czechoslovakia 7, 623, 625, 626, 626, 627,
    633, 736
  Czech Republic 736
Czeczot, Jan 298

da Susa, Adalina 404
Dąbrowski, Jan Henryk 452
Dagobert 102, 103–4
Dalriada, Kingdom of 53, 61–2, 63, 65
Damnonia/Damnonii 46, 47, 54
Danelaw 68
Danes 65, 72, 90, 338–9
  see also Burgundia/Burgundians
Danilo, crown prince of Montenegro 593,
    612
Danilo I of Montenegro 583
d'Annunzio, Gabriele 612
Dante Alighieri 172, 194–5, 495–7, 538
Danzig/Gdańsk 344, 345, 348, 349, 361
  revolt of 278
Darentasia, abbey of 117
'Dark Ages' 42, 70, 81
Datini, Francesco 200
Dauphiné 112, 118, 123, 127
David, St 55

David, prince of the Cumbrians, later
    David I 77–8
David MacBrayne Ltd 37
Dawson, Christopher 183
Dayton Accords 581
de Gasperi, Alcide 400
de Gaulle, Charles 666
De Salis report 608, 609
De Salis-Soglio, Sir John 608
de Valera, Éamon 639, 649, 650, 651,
    654–5, 656, 657, 660, 661–2, 663,
    664
Deakin, William 8
death of states, theories of 729–39
Deira/Deur 53, 59
Democratic Socialist Party of Montenegro
    (DSPM) 581
Democratic Unionist Party (DUP) 668,
    677, 681
Dempsey, Damien 676
Denhoffs of Parnava 360
Derry/Londonderry 677
  Battle of the Bogside 668
'The Descent of the Men of the
    North' (Bonedd Gwyr y Gogledd) 49,
    57
Dessaix, Joseph 414
Diana, princess of Wales 572, 573
Díaz de Vivar, Rodrigo (El Cid) 167–9
Dieupentale (Tarn-et-Garonne) 27
Dijon 106–7, 134
  see also Divio
Din Guauroy 53
Dinant 138
Diocletian 314
Disraeli, Benjamin 559
Divio 95, 101–2
  see also Dijon
Djilas, Milovan 601
Djukanović, Milo 581, 582, 614, 616
Dmitri 'Donskoy' 253
Dobrzyn 342
  Knights of 339, 340
Dolgorukiy, Yuri 247
Domingo, Plácido 225
Domitian, emperor 19
'Don Carlos' von Habsburg 222, 223
Donation, Bull of 215
Dönitz, Karl 385
Donnchad (Duncan) I 76
Dorothea of Denmark 354
Dorpat see Tartu/Dorpat
Douce de Provence 174–5
Draga, queen 589–90
Dragovichi 243
'Dreadnought race' 566

Drogheda, Siege of 641
Drohobycz 457
Drouot, Antoine 531, 533
Drovnyak, Epifanyi (Nikifor) 472
Droysen, J. G. 367
DSPM (Democratic Socialist Party of
    Montenegro) 581
Dubienka 288
Dublin 68, 637, 638, 642, 643, 648–9,
    649, 678
  Phoenix Park 647–8, 672
  purging of British statues 648
Dubrovnik 597, 614
Dufay, Guillaume 135
Dumbarton 37–42
  Castle 39
  global use of the name 41
  and the Kingdom of the Rock see Alt
    Clud, Kingdom of the Rock
  Rock 35–7, 39, 48, 54, 79
  shipyard 37
Dumbarton, Confederate vessel 41
Dumbarton Castle, HMS 41
Dumnagual Hen 57
Dumnonii 47, 54
Dun Eidyn (Edinburgh) 49, 58, 59
  see also Edinburgh
Dun Rheged (Dunragit) 56
Dunblane 68
Duncan (Donnchad) I 76
Dundonald, Castle 39
Dunin-Marcinkiewicz, Vincent 298
Dunkeld 65
Dunmail Raise 72–3
DUP (Democratic Unionist Party) 668,
    677, 681
Durazzo 197
Dusberger, Peter 338, 341
Dylan, Bob 666
Dynfwal III 74
Dynfwal map Teudebur 64
Dyrka ('The Wasteland') 261
Dzieduszycki Museum 482
Dzieduszyckis 455
Dzierżyński, Feliks 237, 297
Dzyarzhynovo (formerly Oziembłów)
    Manor 237

Eadberht, king of Northumbria 64–5
Eamont Bridge 72
East Anglia 68
East Prussia 348, 355, 373, 378, 381, 382,
    383–8
Ebling 342
Ebrovaccus 96
Eburodunum (Embrun) 95

Ecgfrith, son of Oswy 60, 61
Edgar, king 74
Edinburgh 75
  see also Dun Eidyn
Edmund the Elder 74
Edward, duke of Kent 549
Edward VII/Edward Prince of Wales 558,
    559, 562, 569, 643, 659, 662
Edwin of Northumbria 60
EEC (European Economic Union) 666
Efrosinia of Polatsk, St 246–7
Egypt 199
Éire see Ireland/Éire
El Cid (Rodrigo Díaz de Vivar)
    167–9
Elba 214, 505, 524, 530–32
Elbing (Elbąg) 342, 345, 349
Elderslie 79, 80
Eleanor of Aragon 207
Eleanor of Provence 406
Elena of Italy 614
Eleonora d'Arborea 206
Eliot, T. S.: The Waste Land 308
Elizabeth II 570, 665–6, 674, 678
Ełk 343
Emanuele-Filiberto, duke of Savoy 407
Embrun (Eburodunum) 95
Emeland see Varmia/Varmians
Eneci see Annecy
Engels, Friedrich 731
Enghien, Louis Antoine de Bourbon, duc d'
    517–18
England/the English 6, 42
  Hundred Years War 128
  occupation of Paris 131
  and Sabaudia 406
English Defence League 683
Enrique of Castile, El Impotente 216
Eochaid map Rhun 71
Eogan II (Owain the Blind) 76
Epaon, Council of 99
Epila, Battle of 203
Erasmus of Rotterdam 135
Erbin 52
Erdoğan, Recep Tayyip 313
Ernst II, duke of Saxe-Coburg and Gotha
    545, 546, 547, 555, 557, 560–61
Ernst III , duke of Saxe-Coburg-Saalfeld,
    later Duke Ernst I 543, 545, 547, 555,
    557
Erwig (Euric/Evaric) 18, 23
Espérey, Franchet d' 600
Estonia 689–728, 690, 709
  1917 declaration of independence 704–5
  1988 declaration of sovereignty 723
  1991 UN recognition 723

Estonia – *cont.*
  arts 719
  Committee of National Salvation 704–5
  'cyber war' 697–8
  and democracy 707, 708–9
  Estonian Soviet Socialist Republic
    711–12, 714–23
  exiled government in Stockholm 714,
    715
  expulsion of German Estonians 711
  German occupation 712–14
  inter-war period 707–9
  Jewish extermination 713
  language 689–90, 719, 720
  Moscow's 1924 attempted coup 708
  national identity 699
  national movement 723
  and the Nazis 695, 710, 712–14
  Nystadt Treaty 699
  Tallinn *see* Tallinn
  Tartu Treaty 705–6
  VAPSI movement 709
  War of Independence 705
  'War of Symbols' 695–7
  World War II 695, 710–15
Estonian Communist Party 714, 717
Estonian Guard Company, 4221st 715
Estonian Heritage Society 722
Estonian Lutheran Church 719
Estonian Peasant Party 709
Estrada Doctrine 617
Etruria, Kingdom of 509–38, *513*
  creation of 509–10
  dissolution of 523–4
  Florence *see* Florence/Florentines
  and France 509–10, 515, 516, 524–7,
    529–33
  local politics 515–16
  regiments 518
  see also Tuscany
EU *see* European Union
Eucharistic Congress (1932) 660
Eugène de Beauharnais 413, 521, 523,
  535
Eugene of Savoy 409
Eugénie, Empress 428
Euler, Leonhard 332
Euric (Evaric/Erwig) 18, 23
European Economic Union (EEC)
  666
European Union (EU) 234–5, 681, 697,
  727
  Commission 677
  and Estonia 689, 695, 697, 725
  and Montenegro 581, 582
Everest, mount 1

Evissa (Ibiza) 189
Experius, St, bishop of Toloso 20
External Relations Act (Ireland, 1936) 662,
  664
Eyck, Jan van 135
Eymerich, Nicolau 205
Eynard, Jean-Gabriel 518, 535

Farouk, king 401
Fascism 430
Fauchet, Jean-Antoine, baron 524
Faucigny 402, 425, 435
Federal Republic of Yugoslavia 577, 614,
  615
Fehrbellin 363
Feldman, Wilhelm 467
Felipe II (Philip II, the Prudent) 220,
  221
Felipe III (Philip III, the Pious) 220
Felipe IV (Philip IV, the Great) 220
Felipe V (Philippe de Bourbon) 223
Felix V (Amadeus VIII) 406
Fenians (IRB) 644, 646, 647, 650, 651,
  654
Ferdinand I, Holy Roman Emperor 219
Ferdinand I of Austria 450
Ferdinand I, of Leon and Castile, the Great
  163–4
Ferdinand II, king of Aragon 210, 215,
  216, 218, 219
Ferdinand IV, king of Naples 506, 508
Ferdinand VII of Spain 522–3
Ferdinando III of Tuscany 503, 504, 507,
  508, 516, 534
Ferguson, Samuel 642
Fernando d'Antequera, Fernando I of
  Aragon 207–9
Fernando I of Naples, Don Ferrante 214,
  218
Fernando II of Naples 214
Fernando El Católico 214, 216, 218
Fiachna of Ulster, king 56
Fianna Fáil 639, 660, 661, 677, 678
Field, Michael (Bradley and Cooper,
  'the Mikes') 499
Filips de Goede (Philippe le Bon) 132
Filips de Stoute *see* Philip the Bold
Fine Gael 639, 678
Finland 693, 702, 704, 710, 712
Finlay, George 317
Finnic tribes 242, 244
fitzAlan-Stewart family 79, 80
Flaochad 103
Flemish School of painting 135
Florence/Florentines 429, 493–9, *494*, 512,
  513–14, 521, 523, 527, 529

29e Légion de Gendarmerie de Florence 527
British colony of 499
Cosimo I de' Medici collection 481
Franco-Neapolitan Treaty of 509
and Napoleon Bonaparte 500–510, 519–20
periods 497–8, 499
Pitti Palace 503, 504, 512, 516, 524, 525, 527, 534, 537
'Vélites de Florence' 525
Florschütz, Christopher 546
Fontainebleau decree 523
Forez 118
Forgaill, Dallan 645
Formentera 189
Fortriu 61, 63, 66
Fossombroni, Vittorio, count 518, 535
Foster, Norman 389
Foster, Roy 646, 657
Fourcalquier 119
France
1797 campaigns and new republics 505
and Albania 601
and Austria 451–2, 500–501, 505, 508–9, 516
and Britain 505, 507, 516, 522
Burgundian–Armagnac civil war 131
and Catalonia 179, 199, 222
and Etruria 509–10, 515, 516, 524–7, 529–33
Franco-imperial Habsburg wars 407
Franco-Sardinian Treaty 423–5, 436
French Revolution 288, 412, 423, 642
Hundred Years War 128, 131
and Italy 508, 521; Italian campaign of 1796 500–501
Kingdom of 104, 128, 139, 141, 404–6
modern 141–2
and Napoleon I 500–510; 'Second Polish War' 293–4
Nice see Nice
and Poland 521
and Sabaudia 404–6, 407, 412, 414, 417, 435, 436; annexation 412, 425–7, 435, 436, 501; Napoleon III 419–22, 423, 425; Nice 409, 410, 412, 421, 423–5, 426; plebiscite 423–8, 435; Treaty of Turin 423–5, 436
and Spain 506–7, 522–3; Franco-Spanish War 222–3; Treaty of Aranjuez 509
and Switzerland 517
Third Republic 435

and Tuscany 509, 525
War of the Sicilian Vespers 193
war with Aragon 210
West Francia's rebranding as 115
World War I 379
Franche-Comté 128, 141, 142, 147
County-Palatine of Burgundy 124–5, 127–8, 130, 131, 138–41
Francis de Sales, St 407–8
Francis I, duke of Lorraine 504
Francis II, Holy Roman Emperor 450, 503
Franciszka Wiśniowiecka 264
François VI de Beauharnais 520
Fränkel, Moses 479–80
Frankish language 100
Franko, Ivan 467
Franks 24–6, 30, 97, 99, 104
Catalans see Catalonia/Catalans
Franko-Burgundian society of Regnum Burgundiae 100–104
Franko-Burgundian wars 99
Franz-Ferdinand of Austria 597
Franz-Joseph I of Austria 450, 468–9, 475, 481, 559
Frauenburg (Frombork) 343
Fredegar/Fredegarius/Pseudo-Fredegarius 102–3
Frederick I, Barbarossa 120, 122, 124
Frederick I of Prussia (Frederick III Elector of Brandenburg) 364–7
Frederick II of Hohenstaufen 123, 126, 192, 339
Frederick II The Great, king of Prussia 286, 350, 369, 370
Frederick III Elector of Brandenburg (Frederick I of Prussia) 364–7
Frederico II of Sicily 195
Frederico IV of Naples 214
Fredro, Alexander 463, 466
Free Trade Zone, French–Swiss border 425, 428, 436
Freemasons 515
Fribourg 121
Friedland 521
Friedrich Josias, prince of Saxe-Coburg and Gotha 571
Friedrich von Sachsen 351
Friedrich Wilhelm, The Great Elector 358–9, 361, 362, 363, 364
Fuero d'Aragon, 'Codex of Huesca' 174

Gaelic language 41, 43–4, 76–7, 78, 80, 637, 638, 660
Gaelic Revival 642–3

Gaels 37n, 42, 43, 46, 53, 62, 71, 81–3
  of Argyll 53–54
  Picto-Gaelic fusion 37n, 63, 65–6
  see also Scots
Gaeltacht 38, 75, 82
Galbraith Clan 77
Galicia 289, 292, 295, 734
  and the Bolsheviks 475–7
  east Galicia/West Ukraine 441–9, 442,
    450–51, 477, 478, 480, 481–2;
    Distrikt Galizien 479
  Galician Diet 470–71
  Jews 450, 454, 459, 461, 463, 464, 465,
    467–8, 470, 472, 473, 477
  Kingdom of Galicia and Lodomeria
    449–81; c. 1900 454; c. 1914 in
    Austria-Hungary 474; afterlife (after
    1918) 476–80; creation of 449;
    economy 457–8; education 465; end
    of 476; folk culture 464–5;
    government 469–71; humour 468–9;
    literature 466–8; and museums 481–9;
    national anthems 462; population
    450, 458; religious culture 462–4;
    serfdom 455, 456–7, 469–70; society
    455–7; suffrage 471; World War I
    473–6
  landscape 454–5
  languages 460–61, 470
  migration 458
  New Galicia 452
  'Peasant Rising'/'Galician Slaughter'
    456
  railway from Vienna to Lemberg and
    beyond 453, 454
  and Vienna 452–3, 455–6, 734
  west Galicia 450, 474, 476, 477, 480
Gallia Aquitania 17, 18–20, 24
Gallinians 338
Galloway (Galwyddel) 49, 62
Gallura 201
Galwyddel (Galloway) 49, 62
Gandolfo, Ange 524
Garci Ximenez 185
Garibaldi, Giuseppe 420, 425, 428, 429
Gastaustas (Gasztold) 262
Gasztołd, Stanisław 269
Gaul
  and the Burgundians see Burgundia/
    Burgundians
  and the Kingdom of Tolosa 18–31
  Roman 17
Gdańsk see Danzig/Gdańsk
Gebirtig, Mordechai 467–8
Gediminas 251–2, 253
Gellner, Ernest 632

Geneva (Genava) 95, 97, 104, 408, 505
  Conference 604
Génévois 402, 407
Genghis Khan 248
Genoa/Genoese 199, 202, 205, 206, 210,
    212, 420, 505, 518, 521
  Conference 612–13
Geoffrey of Monmouth 54
Georg Wilhelm, Elector of Brandenburg
    355–6, 358
George, St 169, 221
George IV 82
George V 562, 566–7, 568, 643, 654, 656,
    659, 661, 662
George VI 659, 662–3
George Ballantine & Son Ltd 40
Georgia/Georgians 719, 731, 738
Gereint 52
German Historical Museum (DHM) 390
German Social Democratic Party (SPD)
    561
Germany
  Brandenburg see Brandenburg/
    Brandenburgers
  and Britain: Anglo-German Friendship
    Society 568; 'Dreadnought race' 566;
    royal families 572–3; see also
    Saxe-Coburg and Gotha
  and Carpatho-Ukraine 626, 627
  Coburg see Coburg
  and Czechoslovakia 626
  East Germany 390, 721
  fall of the Berlin Wall 721, 723
  and Galicia 474–5; Distrikt Galizien
    479
  Gotha see Gotha
  and the idea of nation 413
  inter-war 567–9
  and Ireland 664
  Kingdom of 123
  and the Mongol Horde 338
  Nazis: and Estonia 695, 710, 712–14;
    Holocaust 302, 479, 480; and
    Lithuania 381–8; and Prussia 381–8;
    and Sudetenland 625; World War II
    301–2, 382–6, 478–9, 710, 712–14;
    see also Nazism
  and Prussia 340, 343–4, 345, 351–3,
    364, 367–8, 373, 375–80, 381–8
  Rosenau see Rosenau Castle
  and Russia 377–80, 701–2,
    703–4
  and Ruthenia 625
  Saxony see Saxony
  and Slovakia 625
  and the Soviet Union 301–2, 382–8,

478–9, 710, 712–14, 721; Operation
  Barbarossa 301–2, 382, 479, 710
Teutonic Knights *see* Teutonic Knights
Thuringia 542
World War I 377–80, 474–5, 701, 703
World War II 301–2, 382–6, 478–9, 710,
  712–14; *see also* Nazism
Gévaudan 175
Gévaudan, Gilbert de 175
Gex 407
Ghent 136, 139
Ghibellines 192, 496
Gibbon, Edward 2, 21, 23, 26, 94, 315–17,
  419
Gibica 91
Gibraltar, Straits of 205
Gierowski, Józef 7
Gieysztor, Jakub 296
Gilchrist Breatnach 77
Gildas the chronicler 57
Giovanni, duke of Gandia 215
Giric MacRath 71
Girona 153, 173, 181
Giscard d'Estaing, Valéry Marie 583
Gladstone, William 587–9, 644
Glas-gau 55
Glasgow 79, 83
Glasgow Celtic 83
glasnost 721, 722
Glycerius, emperor 97
Gobharaidh (Gowrie) 65
Godesigel 97
Gododdin, Land of 49, 53, 59
Godomar/Gundimor 96, 99
Godoy, duke of Alcudia 522
Goerdeler, Carl 381
Golden Bull (1356) 128
Golden Fleece, Order of 134–5
Gołuchowski, Agenor 470
Gonzalo de Cordoba 218
Good Friday Agreement 673–5
Gorbachev, Mikhail 720–21, 722–3, 725,
  733
Gorchakov, Admiral 505–6
Göring, Hermann 381
Gotha 541, 542, 560, 561
  Duchy of Saxe-Coburg and Gotha 545,
    557, 559–70; *see also* Saxe-Coburg
    and Gotha
  Workers' and Soldiers' Council of
    567
Gotha Ursinus G-1 biplane 561
Gothär Waggonfabrik 561
Gothic language 29
Gothic myth 350
Govan 69, 70, 78

Government of Ireland Act (1914) 645
Government of Ireland Act (1920) 653
Goya, Francisco José de 510
Gozo 191, 195, 220
Grandson in the Vaud 138
Grattan, Henry 641, 642
Gray, Thomas 6
Greece, and Aragon 191, 196, 199
Greek Catholic Church 277
Greek Catholic (Uniate) Church 237, 277,
  295, 301, 463, 625
Greek Orthodoxy 245
Green Party (Ireland) 640, 678
Gregory IX, pope 340
Gregory of Tours 23, 24, 26, 100–102
Grenoble 417
Griffith, Arthur 652, 654, 655, 656, 680
Grimani Collection, Venice 481
Grodno 291, 293
Gruadenz 342
Grunau, Simon 349
Grunwald, Battle of 346–7
Guallauc 56
Guelphs 192, 496
Guifré El Pilós (Wilfred the Hairy) 175,
  184, 224
Guigues d'Albon 118
Guillaume de Poitiers 172
Guillaume VIII 167
Guillem Ramón, Great Seneschal 173
Gül, Abdullah 313
Gulag 706, 714
Gulag 113 695
Gundahar 91, 93–4
  Gundahar's kingdom 91–5, 92
Gundimor/Godomar 96, 99
Gundioc/Gunderic 94–5, 96
Gundobad 96, 97
Guntram 100–102
Guotadin 49
Gusev 335–6
Gustav Adolf of Sweden, prince 569
Gustavus Adolphus of Sweden 356, 358,
  569
Gvozdenović, Anto 590, 608, 611, 612
Gwynedd 49, 55, 70
gypsies 237

Haakon Sigurdsson 246
Habichtsburg/Habsburg (Hawk's Castle)
  121
Habsburgs 139, 220, 258, 270, 478, 570,
  733
  Franco-imperial Habsburg wars 407
  and Galicia 450, 451–2, 460,
    468–9

Habsburgs – *cont.*
  House of Habsburg-Lorraine 503, 510, 534; Ferdinando III of Habsburg-Lorraine 503, 504, 507, 508, 516, 534 and Nikola I 605
  and Tuscany 503, 504, 507, 508, 510, 515, 516, 534
Hacibey (later Odessa) 261
Hadrian's Wall 48
Hadziacz 282
Hague, Treaty of the 409
Halich 444–9
Halitsky, Danylo Romanovych 449
Hall, Radclyffe 499
Halley's comet 215
Hamann, J. G. 332
Hammershus Castle 89
Hannibal, Operation 385
Hanoverians 549, 550
  see also Victoria, queen
Hanseatic League 345
Hanulfus 93
Harald Sigurdsson, 'Hardrada' 75
Hardiman, James 642
Harleian Genealogies 50, 64
Harzburg Front 568
Haschka, Lorenz Leopold 461
Hašek, Jaroslav 475
Hasidic movement 299, 463, 473
Hautecombe, abbey of 404, 412, 432, 435
Haydn, Joseph 461
Hayward, Max 8
head-binding 93
Health (Family Planning) Act (Ireland, 1979) 671
Healy, Tim 656
Hegel, Georg Wilhelm Friedrich 315
Heinrich Fleming 343
Heinrich (Henry) II, king of the Germans 119
Helena, daughter of Ivan III 267
Helena of Waldeck-Pyrmont 563, 567
Helsinki Agreement 720
Helvetii 95
Henderson, Sir Neville 568
Hengerdd 45
Henry (Heinrich) II, king of the Germans 119
Henry III El Doliente 207
Henry III of England 406
Henry IV 345
Henry VIII 643
  Crown of Ireland Act 641, 665–6
Henry de Valois 278
Heraclitus 2

Heraclius 319
Hermann von Salza 339–40
Herrin, Judith 318–19, 320
Herzegovina/Hercegovina 587, 588, 604, 605, 731
Hibernia 17
  Ancient Order of Hibernians 644
  Scotti (Hibernian pirates) 37
Hilarius of Poitiers, St 20
Hindenburg, Paul von 379n, 381
Hingley, Ronald 8
Historia Brittonum 49, 53, 54
Hitler, Adolf 370, 382, 383, 385, 479, 568, 569, 618, 626, 631, 633, 664, 712
Hobbes, Thomas 729, 731
Hoch, Jan Ludvik (Robert Maxwell) 624
Hoffmann, Max 378–9
Hohenzollern, Albrecht Friedrich von 355
Hohenzollern, Albrecht von 341, 351
Hohenzollerns 348, 351–2, 354–6, 357, 358–9, 361–2, 363–7, 368, 371, 379, 391, 570
Holmgard *see* Novgorod
Holocaust 302, 479, 480, 631, 713
Holovna Ruska Rada (HRR, Supreme Ruthenian Council) 470
Holy Loch 39–40
Holy Roman Empire 115, 128, 174, 346
  destruction of 368, 521
  of the German Nation 119
  imperial Circles 139–41, *140*
  and Prussia 338
  Sabaudia *see* Savoy/Sabaudia
Homedes, Juan de 220–21
Homel 268, 300
Honoraus, St 110
Honorius, emperor 18
Hope, Anthony 623
Hospitallers 220
Hroerekh (Rurik) 243, 244
Hrushevsky, Mikhail 465
Hryniewiecki, Ignacy 297
Hubertus, Hereditary prince of Saxe-Coburg and Gotha 571
Huesca 164–5, 174, 181, 184, 207
Hugh of Arles 110, 114, 118
Hugonids 117
Hugues Capet 115
Huguet de Mataplana 172
Huizinga, Johan 135–6
Hull, Eleanor 645
Humberside 68
Humbertus I 401–2, 435
Hume, John 674
Hundred Years War 128, 131
Hungary 339, 364, 450, 627

Hungarian Army 627, 630–31
and the Red Army 631
Ruthenians of 623, 631; *see also* Rusyns
see also Austria-Hungary
Huns 17, 21, 31, 93, 94
Hurrem/Roxalana 442–3
Hutsulchyzna 455
Hyde, Douglas 648

Iberia 17, 115, 163, 522–3
Aragon *see* Aragon
Charlemagne and Muslim Iberia 162
Iberian Jews 190
Iberian Peninsular in 1137 172
and the *Reconquista* 115, 164, 166–9,
173, 181, 183, 184
Roman Church in 181
and the Visigoths 20, 23, 26, 28, 29
see also Portugal; Spain
Ibn Adret, Rabbi 181
Ibn Bassam al-Shantarini 167
Ida the Flamebearer 53
Ilergertes 165
Ilves, Toomas Hendrik 692
indulgences 215
Ingvar/Ihor/Igor (Kievan prince) 245
Innocent I 20
Innocent IV 449
Inquisition 218, 221
International Commission for the
Investigation of Crimes against
Humanity 695
Intervallum 46, 49, 53
Investiture Contest 122–3
Iona 53, 66
IRA (Irish Republican Army) 651, 652–3,
656–7, 660, 663–4, 665, 666, 668,
672, 676
Provisional IRA 668, 669, 672, 677
Real IRA 673
IRB (Irish Republican Brotherhood,
Fenians) 644, 646, 647, 650, 651, 654
Ireland/Éire 43, 637–85, 639
1937 change of name to Éire 662
20th century 640, 649–74
21st century 674–8
abortion 671–2
Anglo-Irish trade war 663
Anglo-Irish Treaty 655–7, 661–2, 737
Anglo-Irish War/War of Irish
Independence 653
Belfast/Good Friday Agreement 673–5
Border Wars 656, 666
and the British Commonwealth 661,
663, 664, 665, 679
British Ireland 641

Church–State tensions 661, 668–9
civil disobedience 652
civil war 656–7
Constitution of (*Bunreacht na hÉireann*)
662, 663, 665
'Council of the Isles' 674
Crown of Ireland Act (1542) 641, 665–6
cultural nationalism 660
Dáil 637, 638, 651, 652, 655, 656, 659,
660, 662, 664, 678
division into Southern and Northern
Ireland 653
Easter Rising 638, 649
economy 640, 673, 675–6, 677; IMF/EU
bailout 677
Emergency Powers Act 657
emigration 678
Era of Celtic Freedom 640–41
Era of Foreign Domination 640, 641
Era of National Liberation 640
External Relations Act (1936) 662,
664
Fianna Fáil 639, 660, 661, 677, 678
Fine Gael 639, 678
Gaelic education 660
Gaelic Revival 642–3
Government of Ireland Act (1914) 645
Government of Ireland Act (1920) 653
Green Party 640, 678
Health (Family Planning) Act (1979)
671
Home Rule 642, 643–4, 645, 650,
651, 679; Act/bills 644, 645, 655, 659,
679
IRA *see* IRA (Irish Republican Army)
IRB *see* Irish Republican Brotherhood
Ireland Act (1949) 665
Irish Free State 655–8, 659–62
Irish presence in British army 649–50
Kingdom of Ireland 641–2, 643, 657
Labour Party 640, 678
Lordship of Ireland 641
loyalists 651, 653–4, 666–7, 668–9
military conscription 651
national anthems 638, 655, 659
North-South Ministerial Council 674
Northern Ireland *see* Northern Ireland
Northern Ireland relations: in the 1990s
672–4; Bloody Sunday 668–9, 677;
the 'Troubles' 667–9, 677, 679–80
oath of allegiance 659, 662
Peace People 669
Penal Laws 641
political system 637, 639–40
population 638–9
property boom 675–6

Ireland/Éire – *cont.*
  Protestants in 641, 650, 654, 660, 674,
    684; and the Northern Ireland
    'Troubles' 667–9; Protestant
    Ascendancy 650, 660, 667, 679
  Republic of 637–40, 649–57, 664–84;
    Republic of Ireland Act 664
  Restoration of Order in Ireland Act
    (1920) 653
  Roman Catholic Church in 644–5,
    659–61, 671–2
  Royal and Parliamentary Titles Act
    (1927) 661
  St Andrews Agreement 674
  songs 646, 650–51, 658–9; from the
    Irish Civil War 657; 'The Patriot
    Game' ballad 666; of reconciliation
    674–5; republican ballads and protest
    songs 669–71
  Sunningdale Agreement 669
  Ulster *see* Ulster
  unemployment 678
  Unionists 641, 645, 650–51, 665, 666–8,
    673, 677, 678, 679–80, 681, 684
  women's rights 671
  World War II, Emergency and neutrality
    663–4
Irene, Empress 316
Irish Church 644–5, 660
'Irish National Invincibles' 648
Irish Parliamentary Party 643–4
Irish Patriot Party 641–2
Irish Republican Army *see* IRA
Irish Republican Brotherhood (IRB,
    Fenians) 644, 646, 647, 650, 651, 654
Irish Volunteers 645
Isabella I of Castile 210, 215, 216, 218
Isabella of Taranto 214
Islam and the Muslim people
  Christian dialogue with 182
  in Montpellier 179
  Moors *see* Moors
  Muslim Tartars in Litva 254
  Muslims of Mallorca 200
  Muslims of Menorca 199
  and the *Reconquista* 115, 164, 166–9,
    173, 181, 183, 184
  in Valencia 189–90
Island of Ireland Peace Tower 674
Isle of Man 66
Istanbul 311–13, 443
  see also Byzantion/Byzantium;
    Constantinople
Italy
  1810 517
  1859–61 422

  1946 constitutional referendum 430–31
  and Austria 425, 500–501
  Cispadane Republic 398–9
  Fascism 430
  Festa della Repubblica 397–400
  and France 500–501, 508, 521
  House of Savoy *see* Savoy/Sabaudia
  institutional referendum (1946) 400
  Italian campaign of 1796 500–501
  Italian peninsular, 1860 425
  Italian Republic 517
  Kingdom of 119, 400–401, 428, 429,
    431, 437, 735
  and the Lombards 314–15
  nationalism 413–14; Risorgimento *see*
    Risorgimento
  Northern, Spring 1860 424
  Piedmont *see* Piedmont
  plebiscite 423–8, 435
  Rome *see* Rome
  tarnishing by Berlusconi 437
  Unification *see* Risorgimento
  United Provinces of Central Italy 422
  World War I 430
Ivan III the Great 260, 267–8
Ivan IV the Terrible 273
Ivar Beinlaus 69
Izyaslav, prince 246

Jaca 164
Jacobins 288
  sympathizers 515
Jadwiga (Hedwig) of Poland 254, 735
Jagiełło, Władysław 347
Jagiellończyk, Alexander 261, 267
Jagiellończyk, Kazimierz 256–8, 348
Jagiellonian dynasty 256–8, 257, 261,
    264–6, 269–74, 346–7, 357
  Jagiellonian lands (*c.* 1500) 261
Jagiellonian University 460, 465, 468, 469
Jagiellonka, Jadwiga 355
Jaime I El Conquistador 180, 185–6,
    187–9, 197
Jaime II El Justo 193–4, 195
Jaime II of Mallorca 197, 198–9
Jaime III of Mallorca 199, 203
Jaime IV 203, 211
Jamestown, Vale of Leven 37
Jan I 264
Jan Kasimierz Vasa (John II Casimir) 278,
    361
Jan zonder Vrees (Jean sans Peur) 132, 137
Japan 590
Järvi, Neeme 719
Jasiński, Jakub 289
Jean II de Valois 128

Jean le Bon 130
Jean sans Peur (Jan zonder Vrees) 132, 137
Jeanne III de France 127–8
Jefferson, Thomas 288
Jena 521
Jesuit Order 286
Jews
    in Aragon 183–4, 205
    in Belarus 237
    in Carpatho-Ukraine 625, 631
    Christian dialogue with 182
    under Ferdinand and Isabella 218
    of Galicia 450, 454, 459, 461, 463, 464,
        465, 470, 472, 473, 477; literature
        467–8
    Hasidic movement 299
    Holocaust 302, 479, 480,
        631, 713
    Iberian 190
    Karaites 254, 264, 280, 447, 463
    in Litva 254, 264, 266, 267, 291–2;
        Bund (Jewish Labour League) 297,
        299; Jewish Enlightenment 299;
        Litvaks 295; the noble – Jewish
        alliance 280
    in Mallorca 200
    in Montpellier 179, 181
    Pale of Jewish Settlement 291–2
    pogroms 182, 477
    of Ustrzyki Dolne 479–80
    Zionism see Zionism
    see also Judaism
Joachim I Nestor 355
Joachim II Hector 355
Joan de Casanova OP 182
Joan of Arc 215
Joanna I of Naples 203, 211
Joanna II of Naples 211
Jofre de Foixà 172–3
Jogaila 254–5, 256, 261, 266
Johann Leopold 570
John II Casimir Vasa (Jan Kasumierz Vasa)
    278, 361
John VIII, pope 110
John, king of England 122
John the Fearless (Jean sans Peur) 132, 137
John Paul II, pope 672
Jones, T. J. 655
Joseph II, Holy Roman Emperor 450, 451
Josquin des Prez (Joskin van de Velde) 135
Jovinus 91–2
Jovis Villa (Jupille) 100
Joyce, James 493
    Ulysses 678
Juan II of Aragon 209–10, 216, 217
Juan II of Castile 209

Juana la Loca of Castile 219
Judaism 185, 245, 266, 450, 463
    Hasidic movement 299, 463, 473
    see also Jews
Julia Vienna (Vienne) 95, 97
Junkers 360, 381
Junot, Marshall Jean-Andoche 522
Justinian I 314, 319

Käbin, Johannes 717
Kachkovski Society 471
Kalevipoeg (Kreuzwald) 693–4
Kalinin, city (Tver) 335
Kalinin, Mikhail 327
Kaliningrad 327–33, 335–6
    oblast 327, 328, 330
Kalinoŭski, Kastuś 296
Kalwaria Zebrzydowska 464
Kant, Immanuel 332, 377
Kara Kerman (later Ochakiv) 261
Karadjordjević, House of 591, 597, 601
    Petar I 590, 601, 603
Karadzić, Radovan 615
Karaites 254, 264, 280, 447, 463
Karel de Stoute (Charles le Téméraire) 132,
    137–8
Karotamm, Nikolai 717
Kárpátalya see Carpatho-Ukraine
Kashubs 338
Kasprowicz, Jan 466
Kastiushka, Tadevish (Taduesz Kościuszko)
    288, 289
Kaunus/Kovno 291, 293, 300
Kazakhstan 233, 721
Kazimierz IV Jagiellończyk 256–8, 348
Kazimierz, Jan 281, 282
Kazimierz 'Rybeńko', Michał 264
Kenny, Enda 678
Kerensky, Alexander 701, 704
Kestutis 252
Kettler, Gotard 270
Khazars 242–3, 245
Khrushchev, Nikita 716
Khust (Huszt) 624, 625, 627, 631
Kie 252
Kiev/Kiyiv 244, 246, 248, 251, 252–3,
    260–61, 267, 272, 282, 476
    Lavra Pecherskaya monastery 266
Kievan Psalter 260
Kievan Rus' 244, 245
    liturgy 265
Kincaids 77
Kirghizstan 725
Kiryl of Turaŷ, St 247
Kiyiv see Kiev/Kiyiv
Knight, James 54–55

Knights of Columbanus 644
Knights of Dobrzyn 339
Knights of St John 220
Knights of the Teutonic Order *see* Teutonic Knights
Knights Templar 28, 89, 183, 253
Kniprode, Winrich von 341
Knyazhi Horod ('Princely City') 448–9
Koburg *see* Coburg
Koch, Erich 385
Kohn, Hans 632
Kohtla-Järve 718
Kolberg, fortress 370
Königsberg 342, 343, 345, 348, 350, 352, 354, 356, 365, 370, 375–6, 381–2, 383, 385–7
Storming of 385–7
Korošec, Anton 604
Kościuszko, Taduesz 288, 289
Kosovo 577, 579, 615, 616, 619
Battle of 583
Kotor 579
Kovno 291, 293, 300
Kraków 248, 261, 269, 274, 289, 478
and Galicia 451, 452, 456, 460, 476
Jagiellonian University 460, 465, 468, 469
museums 482–3, 484–5, 486
Treaty of 351
Wawel Castle 306
Kreutzwald, Friedrich Reinhold 693–4
Kreva, Union of 254–5, 256, 258, 346
Kroos, Jaan 719
Kropotkin, Piotr 700
Kruszwica, Treaty of 340
Kruus, Jaan 713
Krychev 284–5
Krylos 448
Krynica 472
Kryvichi 243
Kulm 342, 349
Kulmerland 339, 340, 342
Kuntsevich, Jozephat, St 277
Kuropaty Forest 233, 301
Kursk 382, 710

la Feuillade, Count Hector d'Aubusson de 523
Labour Party (Ireland) 640, 678
Ladislas IV Vasa (Władysław IV Waza) 278, 280
court of 359
Laidoner, Johan 705, 715
Laity, Senator 427
Lake District 68, 72–3
Lallans 38, 62

Lanark 80
Languedoc 104, 125
Languedoc-Roussillon 153, 226
Languoreth, queen 56
Latini, Brunetto 499
Latinus Stone 52
Latvia/Latvians 240, 242, 291, 337, 690, 705, 714, 723, 725, 735
Lauder, Harry 38
Lauria, Ruggiero di 193
Lauristin, Johannes 712
Lavra Pecherskaya monastery 266
'Lay of Atli' 94
lazzaroni 508
League of German Expellees (BdV) 392
'League of Montenegrin Emigrants' 612
League of Nations 611, 613, 617–18, 656, 663, 708, 737
League of Yugoslav Communists 581
Leclerc, Charles 505, 519
Lee, Vernon (Violet Paget) 499
Leghorn *see* Livorno
Lehár, Franz: *The Merry Widow* 596
Lehzen, Louise 551
Leipzig, Battle of the Nations 529
Lemberg, Ukraine *see* L'viv/Lemberg
Lemkivshchyna 455
Lengnich, Gottfried 350
Lenin, Vladimir Ilyich 475, 652, 702, 703, 705, 724–5, 731
Leningrad *see* St Petersburg/Leningrad/Petrograd
Lennox Clan 77
Leo III 319
Leo VI 317
Leo XII 536
Leon 162, 163
Leonora of Portugal 202
Leopold, duke of Albany 562–3
Leopold I, Holy Roman Emperor 365
Leopold I of Belgium 549
Leopold II, Holy Roman Emperor 450, 503
Leopold II, grand duke of Tuscany 422
Lerinum (Lérins), abbey of 110
Leszczyński, Stanisław 283
Letgalia 280
Leven, Vale of 37–8, 40, 41–2
Lex Gundobadana 97
Lex Romana Burgundionum 97
Liberal Democrats 683
Ligue Savoisienne 436
Linda Monument, Tallinn 696
Lindisfarne (Medcaut) 56–57, 66
Lindon 46–7
Lippi, Filippino 496

Lisbon Treaty 681
Lisola, Franz von 362
Litva/Lithuania 238–308, 241, 250, 261,
    276, 723
  from 1914 299–302
  Aftanazy's volumes on 306–7
  annexation into the Russian Empire 290,
    291–302
  birth of the Grand Duchy of Litva
    (VKL/MDL) 248–9
  and Christianity 250–51, 253–5, 265–6,
    277
  civil war 256
  coinage 255
  era of the Saxon kings 283–90
  and the 'Familia' 284
  industry and trade in the eighteenth
    century 285
  Jagiellonian dynasty 256–8, 261, 264–6,
    269–74, 346; Jagiellonian lands (c.
    1500) 261
  Jews in see Jews: in Litva
  and Kievan Rus' 244, 245
  and the Kingdom of Poland 253, 254–5,
    256, 258–9, 268, 360–61, 734; Act of
    Union 272; Partitions of Poland
    286–9, 287, 732, 734; Polish
    Lithuanian Commonwealth c. 1635
    273; Rzeczpospolita 272–84, 286–90;
    Union of Kreva 254–5, 256, 258, 346
  'Land of the Headwaters' 241, 241, 242,
    243, 245, 246, 247
  language 238, 240, 261, 282, 298–9,
    302
  Lithuanian-Byelorussian National
    Republic 301
  Metryka Litevska (Lithuanian Register)
    303–5
  military register 262
  modern Lithuania contrasted with
    Belarus 238–9
  name 'Litva' 243
  and Prussia 349
  river networks 240–41, 241
  royal elections 277–8
  and Rus' see Rus'
  Sejm 271, 272, 273, 274, 275, 281, 283,
    284, 287, 288
  serfs 284–5, 286, 294–5, 296, 298
  under Soviet occupation 301–3
  Statutes 265, 270–71, 275–7
  and the Teutonic Knights 252, 253, 259,
    345
  World War I 300–301
  World War II 301–2
Litvinenko, Alexander 697

Livonia 259, 270, 275, 278, 280, 282
  Courland-Livonia 345, 351
Livonian Knights of the Sword 270, 338,
    340
Livonian Rhymed Chronicle (Livlandische
    Reimchronik) 341
Livorno 501–3, 512, 522, 525
Llançol de Borja, Roderic, Pope Alexander
    VI 215, 218
Llanwlwy (St Asaph) 55
Lleddiniawn (Lothian) 49
Lleida (Lerida) 153, 177, 181
Llibre dels Fets ('Book of Deeds'), Catalan
    185, 187–8
Llívia 158–9
Lloyd George (of Dwyfor), David, 1st Earl
    607, 609, 651, 654–5, 679
Llull, Ramón 200–201
Llywarch Hen 59
Loarre, fortress 184
Locke, John 731, 732, 734
Lodi 501
Lodomeria 450
  and Galicia see Galicia: Kingdom of
    Galicia and Lodomeria
Lodovico I di Borbone (Louis de Bourbon)
    509, 510–12, 515, 516, 517
Logudoro 201
Lombards 314–15
  Lombard War 104
  Lombardic Republic 501
London 68
  Treaty of 597, 598, 601
Londonderry see Derry/Londonderry
Longfellow, Henry Wadsworth 10
Lönnrot, Elias 693
Lorraine, Duchy of 141
Lothar I 106, 108
Lothar II 108
Lotharingia 105, 105, 106, 110
Lough Swilly 663
Louis, duke of Savoy 406
Louis, St, king of France 125
Louis XI 210
Louis XIV 365, 582
Louis XVI 506
Louis XVIII 532
Louis de Bourbon see Lodovico I di
    Borbone
Louis of Anjou, king of Poland and
    Hungary 254
Louis the Blind 110, 112
Louis-le-Grand, Lycée 582–3
Louise, princess of Saxe-Gotha-Altenburg
    543, 545, 547, 556
Louisiana 507, 517

Lower Burgundy 108, *109*, 109–12, *113*, 118–19, 147
Lublin 255, 271–2, 289, 452
 Union of 272–3, 353
Lubomirski Palace 471
Lubomirskis 455
Lucrezia Borgia 215
Lugdunum (Lyon) 95, 96, 97, 125–6
Luguvalians 59
Lukashenko, Alexander Grigoryevich 233–5
Lukšić, Igor 581
Luna, Juan de 222
Lunéville, Treaty of 508–9, 517
Luther, Martin 351, 730
Lutheranism 270, 353–4, 355, 359, 463
Luts, Oskar 719
L'viv/Lemberg 441, 442, 449, 450, 451, 453–4, 459, 475, 476, 478–9
 museums 484; Ossolineum 482, 483
 pogrom 477
 Stefanyk Library 487
Lyon 106, 108, 118, 126–7
 Lugdunum 95, 96, 97, 125–6
Lyon, Second Council of 126

Maarjamäe Memorial 696
Maastricht Treaty 727
Mac-Lochlain, Muirchertach 640
McAleese, Mary 637, 672, 673, 674
macAlpin, Kenneth (Cinaed mac Alpin) 66
macAlpin, House of 75–6
MacArthur Clan 54, 77
 MacArthurs of Strachur 80
MacBethad mac Findlaich 76
McCormack, John 646, 650
Macdonald, Francis 536
McFarlane, K. B. 7
McGuinness, Martin 674
Machiavelli, Niccolò 497, 538
Maciejowice, Battle of 289
Mackievičius, Antanas 296
MacNeill, Eion (John) 651
McNeill, James 662
Macpherson, James 83
Macsen Wledig 48
Madauc/Madawg 58
Madina (Ciutat de Mallorca/Palma) 188
Mafia 582
Maforian, emperor 23
Magdeburg Law 260, 267
Magenta 421
Magyars 115, 117
Mahon 199
Maide, Jaan 714
Maimonides, Moses 181

Main, River 92
Major, John 673
Malachi Mor 641
Malcolm I 76
Malcolm III Canmore 76, 77
Mallorca 187–8, 197–200, *198*, 202–3, 226
Małopolska 450, 477
 see also Galicia: east Galicia/West Ukraine
Malta 220
 and Aragon 191, 195–6
Manau (Clackmannan) 49
Manfred, son of Frederick II 192, 195
Mantaille, Synod of 110, 112
Manzoni, Alessandro 413
Marca Hispanica 162
Marches of Charlemagne's Empire 162, *163*
Marchidun (Roxburgh) 48, 54
Marcilla, Diego 190–91
Marcinkiewicz, Jan 237
Marengo 508
Margaret, St 77
Margaret, countess-palantine of Burgundy 128
Marguerite de Dampierre (Marghareta van Male) 130–31, 132
Mari of Montpellier, Abba 181
Maria, princess of Castile, Queen Mary of Aragon 209
Maria of Aragon, Maria of Castile 209
Maria of Vitebsk 252
Maria Antonia, infanta of Spain 415
Maria Carolina of Austria, archduchess 508
Maria Theresa, Empress of Austria 286, 450, 503–4
Maria-Luisa di Borbone 510–12, 516, 517, 518–19, 521, 522, 524, 528–30, 534
Maria-Luisa of Parma 522
Marie-Antoinette 504, 508
Marie-Christine de France 409
Marie de Montpellier, Dame 180
Marie-José, queen of Italy 401, 431
Marie-Louise-Charlotte, princess of Etruria 519, 534
Marie-Louise of Austria, duchess of Parma 533
Marienburg 342, 345, 349
Marienwerder 342
Marius d'Avenches (later St Marius Aventicensis) 102
Markiewicz, Constance 638, 680

Marseille 116, 211–12
    Massilia 20
Martin I El Humano 207
Marx, Karl 730–31
    Critique of the Gotha Programme 561
Marxism 730
Mary Magdalene 28
Mary of Burgundy 139, 735
Mary, Virgin 281
    cult of 347, 464, 644
Massalski, Jakub 287
Massilia (Marseille) 20
    see also Marseille
Mataro 222
Matejko, Jan 351
Maurice, emperor 103
Maximilian von Habsburg 139
Maximus, Magnus (Macsen Wledig) 48
Maxwell, Robert 624
Maynooth seminary 643, 671
Maze Prison 669
Mazovia 338, 339–40, 342
Mazurs 342
Mazzini, Giuseppe 415, 420
Mdina 195–6, 221
Medcaut (Lindisfarne) 56–57, 66
Mediterranean naval and mercantile
    network 213
Medvedyev, Dmitri 235, 335
Mehmed II the Conqueror 319
Melbourne, William Lamb, 2nd Viscount
    554
Memling, Hans 135
Mendog/Mindaugas/Mindoug 248–9
Menorca 188–9, 199
Menou, Jacques-François de 525–6, 529,
    535
Menzel, Adolf 376
Mercia 44, 72
Merewig/Merovée 99
Merovingians 99–100, 102–4
Merriman, Brian 642
The Merry Widow, Lehár 596
Messines 674
Methodius, St 245
Metryka Litevska (Lithuanian Register)
    303–5
Metternich, Prince Klemens Wenzel von
    452, 536
Mezzogiorno 218
MI5 669
Mickiewicz, Adam 296–7, 459
Middleton, Kate 572, 682
Miegel, Agnes 391–2
Mihailo, prince of Montenegro 612
Mikhailo of Cetinje 614

Milan 501
    Decree (1807) 522
    Edict of 46
Milena of Montenegro 593, 609,
    611, 614
Mill of Haldane estate 40
Millau 175
Millesimo 501
Milošević, Slobodan 581, 614, 615, 619,
    733
Milton, John 408, 493, 499
Mindaugas/Mindoug/Mendog 248–9
Minsk/Miensk 231, 232, 249, 275, 291,
    297, 299, 300–301, 302
    University of 234
Mir 237, 264
    Castle 236–7
Miramar monastery 200
Mirdita clan 601
Mirko Petrović-Njegoš (Nikola I's father)
    587
Mirko, prince of Montenegro (Nikola I's
    son) 589–90, 612
Mises, Ludwig von 478
Mitchell, George 673
Mloda Polska (Young Poland) 466
Modena 422, 423
Mogilev 291
Moguntiacum (Mainz) 92
Mojkovac, Battle of 597
Moktadir 167
Moldova 710, 731
Molière 583
Mondovi 501
Mongol Horde 248, 251, 252, 260, 338
Montcada clan 173
Monte Aragon castle 165
Montearagon 207
Montenegrin Communist Party 615
Montenegrin Orthodox Church 581, 592,
    605, 614, 616
Montenegro/Tsernagora 577–620, 578
    19th century 583–90
    20th century 589–616, 733,
    736–7
    and Austria 597–9
    and the Balkan Wars 594–5
    Central Montenegro Committee of
        National Reunification 599
    code of 'Humanity and Bravery' 620
    Democratic Socialist Party of
        Montenegro (DSPM) 581
    and the Grand National Assembly 600,
        602, 605–6, 609, 736
    joined to the UN and Council of Europe
        616

Montenegro/Tsernagora – *cont.*
  loss of statehood at end of the Great
    War 600–613, 617, 618
  the modern state 577–82, 616
  and neighbours, 1911 593
  People's Party (NS) 592
  postage stamps 596
  and Russia 587–8, 597–8
  Serbian identity question 580–81, 586–7
  taken into Yugoslavia 614–16
  tribes and clans 584–5, 584
  True People's Party (PNS) 592
  war with Japan 590
Montesquieu, Charles-Louis de Secondat,
  baron de La Brède et de 315
Montevideo Convention 617
Montfort, Simon IV de 185
Montmajour, abbey of 117
Montpellier 177, 179–81, 202
  university 184, 200
Montserrat, abbey of 184
Moonlight Maze 697
Moore, Thomas 642–3
Moors 155, 161–2, 169, 173, 177, 183,
  189–90, 221
  under Ferdinand and Isabella 218
  and the *Reconquista* 115, 166–9, 173,
    181, 183, 184
Morat, lake of (Murten) 138
Morgant of South Gododdin 56
Morozov, Evgeny 235
Moscow (Moskva) 247, 252, 253, 259–60,
  267, 271, 293, 703, 710, 732–3
  Batory's war against 278–9
  and 'the gathering of the lands'
    699
  Grand Duchy of *see* Muscovy/
    Muscovites
  Mongol destruction (1238) 248, 338
  see also Soviet Union (CCCP)
Mountbatten, Louis, 1st Earl 669
Mountbatten-Windsors 572
Mtislav 275, 286
Mukachevo 624, 625
Mungo, St (Kentigern) 54–56
  cult of 78
Munich Conference (1938) 625, 633
Murat, Carolina Buonaparte- 509, 536
Murat, Joachim 413, 509, 512, 521, 523,
  529
Muravyov, Mikhail 294
Murcia 189
Murten (Morat) 121
Muscovy/Muscovites 251, 253, 259–60,
  268, 271, 273, 277, 278, 281, 282,
  361, 368

Museum Island, Berlin 390
Museum of Occupations, Tallinn 695
Myrddin (Merlin) 59

Nadruvians 338
Nahmanides (Moses ben Nahman
  Gerondi) 183–4
Nakowska, Anna 468–9
Namatius of Saintes 19
Nancy 138
Naples 193, 212–13, 429, 516
  and Aragon 184, 193, 197, 210–14,
    211–13, 216–18
  Bourbon Kingdom of 521
  Castel d'Ovo 212
  Castel Nuovo 212
  castle of St Elmo 212
  Kingdom of (Neapolitan Sicily) 193,
    194, 211
  monastery of San Domenico Maggiore
    212
  riots (1946) 400
  university 184, 212
Napoleon I 290, 293, 334, 412, 452, 485,
  500–506, 508–10, 517–18, 520,
  521–3, 525, 528, 530–33, 536, 555
  abdication 530
  Battle of Waterloo 533
  and the duc d'Enghien 517–18
  and Etruria 509–10
  excommunication 524
  in exile on Elba 530–32
  sent to St Helena 533
Napoleon II, duke of Reichstadt, *Aiglon*
  533, 536
Napoleon III 419–22, 423, 425, 428, 429,
  536, 587
Napolitano, Giorgio 397, 438
Narbo Martius (Narbonne) 20
Narbonne 25
Narodna Vol'ya ('National Will') 297
Narodovtsy 471
Narva 705, 718
Nassau, George, 3rd Earl Cowper 499
Natangians 338
National Center for Supercomputing
  Applications (NCSA) 698
nationalism 632, 633
  culturual 660
  Estonian 723
  German 413; *see also* Nazism
  Italian 413–14; Risorgimento *see*
    Risorgimento
  Polish 487
  Russian 298
  in Sabaudia 414–15

NATO 89, 615, 619, 695, 697
Navahrudak 244, 249
Navalikhan, Dmitri 327
Navarre 157, 163, 164, 165, 169, 170,
    185, 210
Nazism 381–8, 568–9
    and Carpatho-Ukraine 631
    and Estonia 695, 710, 712–14
    and former Galicia 478, 479
    Holocaust 302, 479, 480, 631, 713
NCSA (National Center for
    Supercomputing Applications) 698
Neave, Airey 669
Nechtan, king of Fortriu (d. c 621) 61
Nechtan, king of the Picts
    (r. 706 – 24) 63
Nechtansmere, Battle of 57, 60–61, 62
Nelson, Horatio 508
Nemmersdorf 383
Neopatria 196
Nepos, Julius 23
Nestorianism 20
Nestorius 20n
Neuchâtel 132
Neustria 100, 103
Nevsky, Alexander 248
New Labour 680
Nibelungen 93–4
Nice 409, 410, 412, 421, 423–5, 426, 501
Nicholas II, tsar 562
NICRA (Northern Ireland Civil Rights
    Association) 668
Nieśwież 263, 264, 285, 287
    Corpus Christi church 264
Niflungar 93–4
Nijmegen, Treaty of 141
Nikifor (Epifanyi Drovnyak) 472
Nikola I of Montenegro 431, 583, 584,
    586, 587–8, 590, 592, 593–4, 596,
    598, 600–601, 603, 614, 619–20
    Balkanska Carica 595–6
    death 611
    in exile 597, 600, 602, 605, 606–8,
        610–11
    legacy of 614
Nikola II Petrović 616
Ninian, St 52, 60
Njeguši 585
NKVD 302, 712, 713, 714
Noble Anvil, Operation 615
Norse culture 68, 72, 81
North-South Ministerial Council
    674
Northern Ireland 653, 660, 670, 678
    Belfast/Good Friday Agreement 673–5
    British government's distancing itself
    from the Northern Ireland Question
    673
    Democratic Unionist Party 667–8, 677,
        681
    Ireland Act (1949) 665
    Omagh bombing 673–4
    OUP see Ulster Unionist Party
    and the Republic in the 1990s 672–4
    St Andrews Agreement 674
    Saville Inquiry 677
    SDLP 674, 681
    'Troubles' 667–9, 679–80; Bloody
        Sunday 668–9, 677
    Ulster see Ulster
    UUP see Ulster Unionist Party
    Widgery Report 677
Northern Ireland Civil Rights Association
    (NICRA) 668
Northern War, First 282
Northern War, Great 283
Northumbria 53, 60, 63, 72, 75
Nostra Domina Daurata 20, 27, 29
Novantae 46, 47
Novgorod (Holmgard) 243, 244, 246, 246,
    249, 256, 259
    Ivan IV's massacre in 273
Novi Pazar 587
Novogrodok/Novogrudok/Nowogrodek
    244, 296
Nowy Sącz ethnographic museum 487–8
Nuits St George 137
Nuremberg, Germanic National Museum
    481
Nwython 61
Nystadt, Treaty of 369, 699

Obolensky, Sir Dimitri 318
O'Connell, Daniel 638
Odo II of Champagne 119
Odoacer 24
Oengus I 63–4, 65
Oengus II 65
Official Unionist Party see Ulster Unionist
    Party
oil 234, 235, 457, 718, 727
Olaf the White 69
Old Church Slavonic 245
Old French 100
'Old Men's Colloquy' (Acallan na
    Senórach) 78–9
Old North 41, 42–3, 45–6, 50, 54, 57, 72,
    81
    Kingdom of the Rock see Alt Clud,
        Kingdom of the Rock
    language 45–6
Old Ruthenians 471

Oldini, Virginia 420–21
Ole Worm Collection, Copenhagen 481
Oleg 244
Olegarius, St (Oleguer Bonestry) 181
Oleśnicki, cardinal 256
Olga, St (Helga) 245
Oliwa, Treaty of 282, 361
Ołyka 263, 264
Omagh bombing 673–4
O'Neill, Sir Terence 668
Onuist, king of the Picts 64–5
Operation Aster 714
Operation Bagration 302
Operation Barbarossa 301–2, 382, 479, 710
Operation Hannibal 385
Operation Noble Anvil 615
Orange 118
   Aurausion 125
Orange Order 667, 676
Order of the Collar (now Order of the Most Holy Annunciation) 406
Ornano, Philippe Antoine d' 533
Orosius, Paulus 17–18
Orsha 268, 271
Orsini, Felice 420
Orville, Jean Cabaret d' 404
Osca see Huesca
Ościk, Krystyn 263
Osiander, Andreas 354
Ostrogoths 23, 24, 30
Ostrogski, Konstanty 268, 272
Ostrozki (Ostrogski) 262
Oswy of Northumbria 60
Ots, Georg 719
Ottaker II of Bohemia 342
Otte-Guillaume/Otto-Wilhelm of Burgundy 118
Otto/Oddon I, count of Sabuadia 404
Ottomans 259–60, 261, 282, 287–8, 317, 321, 364
   Balkan Wars 594–5
   and Montenegro 580, 583, 585, 586–7, 587–8, 594–5
   and Russians 288, 587–8
Owain the Blind (Eogan II) 76
Owen of Cumbria (Ywain map Dynfwal of Strathclyde) 72
Owen/Owain (Ywain of 'The Rock') 61
Oxford, Ashmolean Museum 481

Padarn Pesrut 48
paganism 30, 81, 242, 245, 250–51, 253–4, 255
Paget, Violet (Vernon Lee) 499
Paisley, Ian 667–8, 673, 674

Paldiski 718
Palermo 192, 508
   university 184
Palladia Tolosa (modern Toulouse) 18–20
Pallas Athena, goddess 19
Palma 173, 199
Palmerston, Henry John Temple, 3rd Viscount 558
Palteskja see Polatsk
Pamplona 162
Pamuk, Orhan 311–13, 322
Panam, Madam Pauline 547
Panorama Racławicka, Lemberg 459
papacy 30, 110, 122
   Investiture Contest 122–3
   loss of temporal power 429
   papal schism 128
   and the Teutonic Knights 340
Papal States 192, 339, 413, 422, 428, 501, 505, 512, 516, 523–4
   abolishment of 429
Papen, Franz von 381
Paris 100, 102, 104
   English occupation of 131
   Peace Conference 603, 607–8, 617, 618, 651–2, 736–7
Parker-Bowles, Camilla 572
Parma 422, 423, 426
   Bourbons of 506, 509, 510
Parnell, Charles Stewart 643–4, 659
Pärt, Arvo 719
Parthenopean Republic 508
Pašić, Nikola 598–9, 604, 607
Paternus of the Red Cloak 48
Patrick, St 51–52, 78
'Patriotic Party', Etruria 516
Päts, Konstantin 709, 711, 715
Patten, Chris 329
Patterson, Betsy 523
Paul the Christian 184
Pavia 104, 122
Pays de Vaud see Vaud, Pays de
Peace Conference, Paris 603, 607–8, 617, 618, 651–2, 736–7
Peace People 669
Peasant Party of Konstantin Päts 709
Pedauco, queen 21
Pedro I of Aragon 165, 167
Pedro II of Aragon 180, 186
Pedro III El Grande 191, 193, 195, 197, 198–9
Pedro IV El Ceremonioso 174, 202–5, 206, 207
Pedro V, constable of Portugal 216
Pedro the Cruel of Castile 202

Peipus, Lake 248
Penthelm, 'Leader of the Picts' 63
Pentwine, 'Friend of the Picts' 63
People's Party (Montenegro) 592
Pepe, Guglielmo 413
Pere de Moncada 205
Peremyshl 453
perestroika 721
Peretallada, fortress 184
Perez, Antonio 221–2
Perpignan/Perpinya 153–6, 160, 178, 203, 226
    Palace of the Kings 199
    Treaty of 199
    university 184
Petar I Karadjordjević 590, 601, 603, 606, 607
Petar II Petrović-Njegoš 586–7
Peter the Great of Russia 90, 283, 368, 699
Peter III of Russia 370
Petrograd *see* St Petersburg/Leningrad/Petrograd
Petronilla of Aragon 170, 171, 181
Petrovac 579
Petrović-Njegoš, House of 583, 584, 586–7, 591, 592–3, 601, 612
    Nikola Mirkov *see* Nikola I of Montenegro
Philibert, St 107
Philip II the Prudent 220, 221
Philip III the Pious 220
Philip IV the Great 220
Philip IV, duke of Burgundy (Philip I of Castile) 139
Philip the Bold (Philippe le Hardi/Filips de Stoute) 128, 130, 132, 135–6
Philip the Fair of Burgundy 219
Philip the Good (Philippe le Bon) 132, 137
Philippe III of France 195
Philippe le Bon (Filips de Goede) 132, 137
Philippe de Bourbon, Felipe V 223
Philippe de Bresse 407
Philippe le Hardi *see* Philip the Bold
Philippe de Rouvres 106, 130
Phipps, Sir Eric 568
Phoenix Park, Dublin 647–8, 672
Pictland 58, 60, 61, 63, 65–6
Picts 17, 42, 44, 46, 51, 52, 54, 62, 63–6
    Picto-Gaelic fusion 37n, 63, 65–6
Piedmont 403, 404, 406, 409, 410, 412, 414, 415, 416, 516
    Napoleon and the Piedmontese 501
    Turin *see* Turin (Torino)
Pieracki, Bronisław 477
Pierre II, 'the little Charlemagne' 404–6
pilgrimage 55, 184, 435, 453, 464, 473

Pillars of Hercules (Gibraltar) 20
Pillau 358, 385
Piłsudski, Józef 297, 301, 473–4, 476
Pinerolo, fortress 407
Piombino 214
pirates 37, 110, 260
Pirenne, Henri 136
Pirita 696
Pisa, University of 516
Pisentius Justus, Quintus 48
Pitti Palace, Florence 503, 504, 512, 516, 524, 525, 527, 534, 537
Pius VI 505, 507–8
Pius VII 508, 521, 523–4, 527, 528, 530, 535
Placidia, Galla 18
Plaid Cymru 679–80
Plamenatz, J. S. 611
Plamenatz, John 632
Plantation of Ulster 641
plebiscites 423–8, 435
Płock 342
Plunkett, George 651
Le Plus Grand Crime de la Guerre Mondiale 612
Poblet, abbey of 184
Podgorica 579, 580, 605, 616
Podhale 455
Podkarpatsko 623, 625
    see also Carpatho-Ukraine
Podlasie 272
Podolia 364
    'Podolians' 470
Pogari 714
Poincaré, Raymond 607
Poitiers, Battle of 130
Pol, Wincenty 466
Poland/Poles 281, 284, 335, 413, 618–19, 732
    and Austria 286
    and Carpatho-Ukraine 631
    and France 521
    and Galicia 450–51, 452, 458, 459, 461, 462, 470–71, 472, 476–7
    Holocaust 479, 480
    Lachy 487–8
    Litva and the Kingdom of 253, 254–5, 256, 258–9, 268, 360–61, 734; Act of Union 272; Partitions of Poland 286–9, 287, 732, 734; Polish Lithuanian Commonwealth c. 1635 273; *Rzeczpospolita* 272–84, 286–90; Union of Kreva 254–5, 256, 258, 346
    Małopolska (Lesser Poland) 450, 477
    Napoleon's 'Second Polish War' 293–4
    Poles of Ustrzyki Dolne 479–80

Poland/Poles – *cont.*
  Polish Legions 452, 473, 515
  Polish People's Republic 480, 483, 487
  and Prussia 349, 350–52, 353–4, 355, 362–6
  Russo-Polish war (1791–2) 288
  Solidarity movement 716, 722, 723
  and the Soviet Union 388, 618–19, 716
  and the Teutonic Knights 253, 259, 344–5, 346–8
  World War II 478, 710
Polatsk (Palteskja) 243, 244, 246–7, 248, 249, 268, 286
Polesie 251
Polish Peasant Movement (PSL) 472
Polish Socialist Party (PPS) 297, 472
Pomegasanians 338
Pomerania 338, 345, 349, 370
  see also Danzig/Gdańsk
Pomesania 342
Pommard 137
Pompidou, Georges Jean 583
Ponç de la Guardia 172
Poniatowski, Stanisław-August 285–6, 287, 289–90, 306
Poniatowski, Stanisław (General) 284
Poniatowskis 284
Pontigny, abbey of 108
Poole, R. Lane 113–14n
Portugal 171, 215, 507, 521, 522
Poska, Jaan 706
Possevini 279
Potocki, Andreas 471
Potockis 275, 284, 455
Potsdam 710
  Conference 387–8
Poznań 289
Praga, Battle of 289
Prague 625, 626
  Rudolf II collection 481
  Slav Congress 469
Premyslid dynasty 345
Preti, Mattia 221
Pritsak, Omelian 478
Pronkssödur (*Bronze Soldier*) 696
Prosper of Aquitania, St 20
Prosvita Society 471
Protestant Ascendancy 650, 660, 667, 679
Proudhon, Pierre-Joseph 730
Provence 105, 117, 123, 125, 174, 408
  counts of 118–19
  Kingdom of (*le Royaume de Basse-Bourgogne*) 109, 109–12
Provisional IRA (Provos) 668, 669, 672, 677

Prussia/Borussia and the Prussians 242, 248, 256, 282, 283, 284, 286, 336–92, 337, 349
  13th century 338–44
  14th century 345–6
  15th century 346, 346–9, 349
  16th century 349–55
  17th century 355–66, 360
  18th century 132, 288, 366–7, 368–70, 369; growth of the Kingdom of Prussia, 1701–95 369
  19th century 373–7, 374, 521, 557
  20th century 374, 377–88; abolition of Kingdom of Prussia 380; 'Flight from the East' 384–5; inter-war 382; Potsdam Conference 387–8; termination of Prussia 387–8, 734; World War I 377–80; World War II 382–6, 384
  'Allied Scheme' of 370–72
  Battle of Waterloo 533
  Berlin's memory site of 389–93
  and Brandenburg 355–6, 358; state of Brandenburg-Prussia 358–60, 360, 361–2, 363–6
  and the Commonwealth of Poland-Lithuania 349, 353–4, 355, 362–6; Prussian homage 350–52
  Duchy of Prussia 352–65, 353
  early *Prusai* 336–7
  East Prussia 348, 355, 373, 378, 381, 382, 383–8
  Free State of Prussia (Weimar Prussia) 380–88
  geography of 338
  and Germany 340, 343–4, 345, 351–3, 364, 367–8, 373; and the Nazis 381–8
  Hohenzollern Kingdom of 351–67, 369, 373–80, 374
  Junkers 360, 381
  language (Prusiskan, Old Prussian) 343–4
  Peasants War 354
  'Prussian coup' 381
  Prussian Estates 352, 354, 356, 362
  Prussian League 348
  'Prussian militarism' 370
  Royal Prussia 348–50, 349, 369
  and Russia 368–9, 372, 374; Russo-Prussian treaties (1793) 288
  Schmalkaldic League Wars 354
  and the Soviet Union, World War II and aftermath 382–8
  and the Teutonic Knights/*Ordensstaat* 339–44, 345–8, 346, 350–53
Prussian Blue 367

Prydain 43, 44
Przemyśl 453, 475
Pskov 278–9
Ptolemy 46, 47
Puigcerda 175
Puławy 307, 482–3, 485
Putin, Vladimir 329, 331, 335, 727–8
    and Estonia 696–7
Putina, Lyudmila 329
Pyrenees 156–60, *157*
    Treaty of the 222

Quedlinburg Chronicle 246
Quinctianus of Civitas Rutenorum 23

Racławice, Battle of 289
Radek, Karl 478
Radet, Étienne 526, 528, 529, 535
Radović, Andrija 592, 597, 599, 601, 602, 607
Radziwiłł, Barbara, queen 264, 269–70
Radziwiłł, Jan I 264
Radziwiłł, Janusz 281
Radziwiłł, Karol Stanisław 'Panie Kochanku' 287
Radziwiłł, Michal Kazimierz 'Rybeńko 287
Radziwiłł, Mikołaj 'the Black' 264
Radziwiłł, Mikołaj Krzysztof 'Sierotka' 264
Radziwiłł, Mikołaj 'the Red' 264, 266, 271–2
Radziwiłłs 263–4, *264*, 275, 278, 284–5, 294
RAF (Royal Air Force) 383
Rainald/Renaud III 124, 128
Ramiro I of Aragon 163, 164–5
Ramiro II El Monaco 170
Ramolino, Maria-Letizia 500
Ramón Berenguer I El Vell 168–9, *174*, *175*
Ramón Berenguer IV El Sant 170, 177
Ravenna 24, 97
Raymond de Peñafort, St 181–2
Ražnatović, Željko 614–15
Reagan, Ronald 716
Real IRA 673
Reconquista against the Muslims 115, *164*, 166–9, 173, 181, 183, 184
Red Army 89, 301, 302, 382–7, 446, 478, 479, 618, 631, 702, 705, 710, 712, 713, 714
Red Clydeside 40
Red Cross 421
Red Ruthenia 268, 346
Redemption of Christian Captives, Order for 181
Redl, Alfred 471–2

Refit Site One 40
Reged-ham (Rochdale) 56
Reges Gothorum 23
Řehoř, František 464
René d'Anjou 211, 212, 216–17
Renfrew, Barony of 79
Rennes 102
Rennes-le-Château 27
Renzi, Matteo 498
Republic of Ireland Act 664
Rere/Rear/Rey Cross, Stainmore 72
Restoration of Order in Ireland Act (1920) 653
Retinger, Joseph 478
Reval *see* Tallinn/Reval
Revay, Julian 626, 633
Revolt of the *Barretinas* 222
Rhedae 27
Rheged 49, 53, 56–57, 59–60
Rheinfelden 121
Rhône valley 109, 110, 115, 118, 125, 179
Rhun, son of Urien 60
Rhun map Arthgal 69–70, 77
Rhydderch (Roderick) Hael 55, 57, 61
Ribagorza 159, 162, 163, 164, 221
RIC (Royal Irish Constabulary) 652–3
Riccarton Castle 79
Richard the Justiciar, count of Autun 106, 112
Richelieu, cardinal 407
Richildis, queen 106
Ricimer 96–7, 97
Rieti, Golden Bull of 340
Riga 248, 285, 338, 342
    Treaty of 306
Rimsky-Korsakov, Alexander 294
Riothamus 23
Ripoll 175
    abbey of 184
Risorgimento (Unification of Italy) 413, 416, 419, 437–8, 735
    fall of Rome 429
Rob Roy MacGregor 83
Robert le Vieux 106
Robert of Naples 197
Robinson, Mary 672
Robinson, Peter 677
Rock, Kingdom of the *see* Alt Clud, Kingdom of the Rock
Rodestvedt, Kelly 571
Rodez, counts of 175
Rodrigo Díaz de Vivar (El Cid) 167–9
Roger Deslaur/de Flor (Ruggier Desflors) 196
Rogneda 246
Rogvolod 246

Rogvolodichi 246
Rohatyn 442
Rokossowski, Konstantin 302, 384
Romagna 422, 423, 426, 505
Roman Catholic Church
  in Galicia 462
  in Ireland 644–5, 659–61, 671–2
  in Litva 253, 255, 266, 303
  in Prussia 342–3
  Second Vatican Council 671
Roman Empire 16, 23, 91–3, 321, 336
  and the Byzantine Empire 313–17, 321;
    see also Byzantine Empire/Byzantines
  Holy *see* Holy Roman Empire
  Roman Aquitania 17, 18–20, 24
  Roman Gaul 17
Roman, Pan 446
Romanovs 368–9, 570, 587
Rome
  Charlemagne in 104
  fall, under Risorgimento 429
  Festa della Repubblica 397–400
  French driven out by Neapolitan troops 529
  French occupation (1798) 506, 507
  modern 398
  sacking by Alaric the Visigoth 16
  sacking by the Vandals 22
Roncevalles, Pass of 162
Roosevelt, Franklin D. 10
Rosenau Castle 542–3, 544, 545–6, 557, 558, 562, 567, 570
Rosselló 177–9, 200, 222
Roth, Joseph 478
Rothesay 38
Rousillon/Rosselló 153, 154–5, 157, 158, 162, 177–9, 185, 200, 222
  Languedoc-Roussillon 153, 226
Rousseau, Jean-Jacques 729–30, 734–5
Roxalana/Hurrem 442–3
Royal Academy, London 320
Royal Air Force (RAF) 383
Royal and Parliamentary Titles Act (Ireland, 1927) 661
Royal Irish Constabulary (RIC) 652–3
Royal Navy 40, 41, 505, 506, 507, 663, 679, 705
Royal Ulster Constabulary (RUC) 654, 666, 667, 668, 669
RSFSR (Russian Soviet Federative Socialist Republic) 328, 702n, 703, 721
Ruaidre Ua Chobar 640
RUC *see* Royal Ulster Constabulary
Rudolf I, emperor 132
Rudolf II 113–14
Rudolf III 114, 117, 118, 119

Rudolf of Auxerre 110–12
Ruffo, cardinal 508
Ruggier Desflors (Roger Deslaur/de Flor) 196
Ruggiero di Lauria 193
Runciman, Sir Steven 318
Rurik (Hroerekh) 243, 244
Rurikids 245–7
'Ruritania' 623, 632–4
Rus' 242, 243, 245, 246–8, 247, 249, 267
  Kievan Rus' 244, 245, 265
  Ruthenia *see* Ruthenia/Ruthenians
Rusalka Dnistrovaia 467
ruski 243, 261, 265, 270, 282, 303, 304, 450, 460–61
Ruskin, John 317
Russia/Russians
  Bolsheviks *see* Bolsheviks
  and Estonia *see* Estonia
  and France 505–6
  and Galicia 471–2, 473, 474, 475
  and Germany 377–80, 701–2, 703–4
  Great Northern War 283
  Kaliningrad 327–33, 335–6
  and Litva 283–4, 290, 291–303, 300–301; partitioning of Poland-Lithuania 286, 287–9
  and Montenegro 587–8, 597–8
  nationalism 298
  Ottoman war 287–8
  provisional government under Kerensky 701, 704, 738
  and Prussia 368–9, 372, 374, 382–8; Russo-Prussian treaties (1793) 288
  Russian Civil War 698, 702, 705
  Russian Federation 725, 727–8
  Russian Socialist/Soviet Federative Soviet Republic (RSFSR, Soviet Russia) 328, 702, 703, 717, 721
  Russo-American START Treaty 335
  Russo-Japanese conflict 590
  Russo-Polish war (1791–2) 288
  Soviet Union *see* Soviet Union (CCCP)
  Tartu Treaty 705–6
  and terminology 291
  Tsarist Empire of 'all the Russias' 699–701, 703
  and the Turks 288, 587–8
  and the US 727
  Western Russia in the nineteenth century 292
  White Russia 291
  World War I 377–80, 701–2, 703
  YedRo ('United Russia') Party 335

Russian Orthodoxy 265, 295, 298, 463,
    719
Russian Socialist/Soviet Federative Soviet
    Republic (RSFSR) 328, 702n, 703,
    717, 721
Russophiles 288, 463, 625, 632
Rusticus of Narbonne, St 20
Rusyns 623–34
    see also Ruthenia/Ruthenians
Ruthenia/Ruthenians 248, 249, 251, 265,
    266–7, 267, 275, 277, 298
    Black Ruthenia 249, 289
    Carpathian Ruthenia *see* Carpatho-
        Ukraine
    and Galicia 450, 451, 456, 458, 462,
        463, 470, 471, 477; literary movement
        467; modern Halich 448–9; Ruthenian
        Congress 470; Supreme Ruthenian
        Council 470
    Orthodox Ruthenians 347
    Red Ruthenia 252, 268, 346
    Rusyns 623–34
    White Ruthenia 249, 251, 254, 260,
        265, 267, 284–5, 291, 295; *see also*
        Belarus
Ruthenian Congress 470

Sabaudia *see* Savoy/Sabaudia
Sacher-Masoch, Leopold von 467
Sachsen-Coburg-Kohary, Ferdinand 559
St Andrews Agreement 674
St Bartholomew's Eve massacre 277
St Germain, Treaty of 625
St Gotthard pass 125
St Jean-de Maurienne 435
St John, Bayle 402, 416, 417–19, 434
St Maurice 112
St Petersburg/Leningrad/Petrograd 301,
    335, 383, 699, 703, 704, 710
    Siege of Leningrad 383, 712, 714
Saint-Quentin 407
'The Salmon and the Ring' 56
Salses 158
Salvatico, Odoardo 515
Salza, Hermann von 339–40
Sambia/Sambians 338, 342, 343
Samogitia 248, 275
San Ildefonso, Treaty of 507, 522
San Juan de la Peña, monastery
    184–5
San Miniato 501
San Pedro de la Nava, Zamora 29
San Pedro de Siresa monastery 164
Sancho El Mayor of Navarre 155,
    162–3
Sancho the Populator 171

Sanfedisti 508
Sanguszko 272
Santángel, Luis de 218
Santarosa, Santorre de 414
Sapieha, Lev 275
Sapiehas 455
Saracens 104, 117, 186–7
    corsairs 110
Sardinia 197, 201–2, 206, 220, 501
    Franco-Sardinian Treaty 423–5, 436
    late 18th-century Kingdom of 410, 735
    and Sabaudia 409–10, 411–12, 415–17,
        421, 423–5, 428–9, 735; Treaty of
        Turin 423–5, 436
Sarmatism 284
    Sarmatian Myth 350
Saturnin, St 20
Saunière, Bérenger 27–8
Sava, St 592
Savaric of Auxerre 104
Saville Inquiry 677
Savoy League (*Ligue Savoisienne*) 436
Savoy Manor 406
Savoy/Sabaudia 401–38
    counts of 405
    and England 406
    and France 404–6, 407, 412, 414, 417,
        435, 436; annexation 412, 425–7,
        435, 436, 501; Napoleon III 419–22,
        423, 425; Nice 409, 410, 412, 421,
        423–5, 426; plebiscite 423–8, 435;
        Treaty of Turin 423–5, 436
    and Italy 413–14, 421–3
    nationalism 414–15
    and Piedmont 403, 404, 406, 409, 410,
        412, 414, 415, 416
    and the plebiscite 423–8, 435
    provinces 402; *see also specific*
        provinces
    and Sardinia 409–10, 411–12, 415–17,
        421, 423–5, 428–9, 735; Treaty of
        Turin 423–5, 436
    Savoy province 402, 412
    shield of the House of Savoy 400
    skiing industry 434–5
    and Switzerland 409, 425–6
    Turin Treaty 423–5, 436
    wines 433
    World War II 436
Saxe-Coburg and Gotha
    Albrecht, prince of *see* Albert, prince
    Duchy of 545, 557, 559–70; abolition of
        570
    Saxe-Coburg family 431, 543–73,
        564
Saxe-Coburg soup 559

Saxony 368
  House of (Wettins) 543, 550, 555–6
  Saxon mini-states, c. 1900 544; Duchy
    of Saxe-Coburg and Gotha 545, 557,
    559–70
Schlieffen, Alfred von 378, 379
Schlieffen Plan 378
Schloss Rosenau see Rosenau Castle
Schmalkaldic League Wars 354
Schollenen Gorge 125
Schratt, Katharina 469
Schröder, Gerhard 329, 331
Schulz, Bruno 478
Schwarz, Chris 486
Schwerin, Otto von 362
Scone, abbey of 65
I Scorpioni (The Scorpions) 499
Scotch whiskey 40
Scotland 40–41, 66, 75–6, 81–3, 683–5
Scots 17, 37n, 42, 53, 62, 63, 70, 72, 81
  Alban 74
  Picto-Gaelic fusion 37n, 63, 65–6
  Scotti (Hibernian pirates) 37
Scott, Sir Walter 82–3
Scottish Home Rule Bill 679
Scottish Labour Party 680
Scottish National Party (SNP) 679–80,
    683
Scottish Presbyterians 641, 667
SDLP (Social Democratic Labour Party)
    674, 681
Segura, Isabela 190–91
Selgovae 46, 47
Selim II 442
Senchus (Register) of Dalriada 63
Senlis, Treaty of 139
Serbia/Serbs 580–81, 581, 583, 587,
    589–90, 594–5, 600–610, 614–16,
    619, 733, 736–7
  and Austria 597–9
  'Greater Serbia' 597, 598–9, 604
  see also Montenegro/Tsernagora; Serbs,
    Croats and Slovenes, Kingdom of
Serbia and Montenegro (country) 577
Serbian Orthodox Church 581, 592, 605,
    614
Serbs, Croats and Slovenes, Kingdom of
    597, 604–6, 608, 614
Sergianni (Giovanni) Caracciolo 211
Serra, Orso 423–4
Serristori, Averardo 515
Servanus, St 55
Seton-Watson, Hugh 8
Seton-Watson, R. W. 597
Seven Sleepers, Battle of 76
Seversk 268, 275, 286

Sheptytskyi, Andrei 463
Shevchenko, Taras 467
Shkoder 595
Shroud of Turin 406, 409, 432
Siberia 458, 479, 690, 699, 703, 715
Sibylla of Saxe-Coburg and Gotha 569,
    571
Sich Guard 625, 627, 631
Sich Riflemen 473, 474
Sicily 191
  and Aragon 191–5, 197, 206, 212, 220
  Kingdom of the Two Sicilies 212
  Sicilian Vespers 192–3, 194, 197, 212
  the two medieval Sicilies 193, 194
Siciński 281
Sículo, Lucio Marineo 219
Sidericus, 'king of five days' 18
Sidonius Apollinaris, Gaius Sollius 21–2,
    96
Sidor, Dmitri 631
Siebold, Frau 549n
Sierakowski, Zygmunt 296
Sigebert 102
Sigismund, son of Gundobad 96, 98–9
Sigismund, Johann 355
Sigismund I 353
Sigismund II August 264, 269–74, 353,
    354
Sigismund III Vasa 275, 278, 279–80
Sigismund the Elder 267
Sikorski, Władysław 478
Silesia 248, 281, 346, 373, 458, 463, 479,
    486–7
Simeon Borisov of Saxe-Coburg and
    Gotha, Tsar Simeon II 571
Sinn Féin 640, 650, 651, 654, 660, 672–3,
    674, 678, 680, 681
Siward, Earl of Northumbria 76
Skalić, Paul 354
Skalovians 338
Skarga, Piotr SJ 280–81
Skaryna, Francysk 266
Slaine (Irish king) 640
slavery/slaves 51, 69, 70, 71, 167,
    173, 186–7, 199, 254, 255, 267, 330,
    341, 442, 485, 515, 709
Slavs 242–4, 244, 245, 344
  and 'the gathering of the lands' 699
  Kashubs 338
  Orthodox 260, 267, 277, 463
  in Prussia 374–5
  Rus' see Rus'
  Slav Congress in Prague 469
  see also Ruthenia/Ruthenians; Ukraine/
    Ukrainians
Słomka, Jan 461

Slovakia/Slovaks 476, 625, 626, 627, 631, 736
Slovenes 476, 597
  see also Serbs, Croats and Slovenes, Kingdom of
Sluter, Claus 135
Smalensk 246, 256, 268, 275
Smetona, Antanas 301
Smith, F. E., later earl of Birkenhead 650
Smith, John 680
Smith, Mack: 'The New Feudalism' 206
Smuts, Jan (General) 654
SNP (Scottish National Party) 679–80, 683
Sobelsohn, Karel 478
Sobibór extermination camp 479, 480
Sobieski, Jan 282, 363–4, 459
Sobrarbe 159, 162, 163, 164, 165–6, 185
Social Democratic Labour Party (SDLP) 674, 681
Solferino 421
Solidarity movement 716, 722, 723
Solomon of Montpellier 181
Solsona 181
Solzhenitsyn, Alexander 715
Somalia 731
Somerset, Lord Henry Richard 499
Soviet Communist Party 301, 302, 706, 712, 717, 721, 732–3
  Communist Party of the Soviet Union (KPSS/CPSU) 715
Soviet Russia (RSFSR) 328, 702, 703, 717, 721
Soviet Union (CCCP) 737
  1945–1991 716
  Belarus 231–9, 232
  and the Bolsheviks see Bolsheviks
  and Carpatho-Ukraine 631
  Cold War see Cold War
  collapse and disappearance of 3, 303, 328, 723, 724–5, 727–8, 732–3; dissolution day 699, 723
  concentration camps 382, 479, 706
  creation of 699–703
  détente 716
  economy 706, 725
  and Estonia 689–728
  Five Year Plans 382, 706
  and former Galicia 478, 479–80, 483
  and Germany 301–2, 382–8, 478–9, 710, 712–14, 721; Operation Barbarossa 301–2, 382, 479, 710
  glasnost 721, 722
  and Halich 446, 449
  and Hungary 631
  and the Irish Republic 652

  and Kaliningrad oblast 328
  NKVD 302, 712, 713, 714
  nuclear arsenal 715
  occupation of Lithuania 301–3
  perestroika 721
  and Poland 388, 618–19, 716
  post-war era 715–17
  Red Army 89, 301, 302, 382–7, 446, 478, 479, 618, 631, 702, 705, 710, 712, 713, 714
  resistance to Moscow 722–3
  Stalinism see Stalinism
  Storming of Königsberg 385–7
  as a superpower 3, 710, 724
  takeover of the Baltic States 301–2, 618, 710–12, 737
  transformation under Stalin 706
  and the US 715, 716, 724, 726
  Western former USSR after 1991 726
  World War II 301–2, 382–6, 478, 479–80, 709–15; takeover of the Baltic States 737
Sovietskiy Monument 695–6
Sovyetsk Gvardejsk 334
Spain
  Aragon see Aragon, empire
  and the Bull of Donation 215
  Castile see Castile, relations with Aragon
  Catalonia see Catalonia/Catalans
  and France 506–7, 522–3; Franco-Spanish War 222–3; Treaty of Aranjuez 509
  Valencia see Valencia
Spanish Inquisition 218, 221
Spencer, Lady Diana, princess of Wales 572, 573
Spike Island 663
'Springtime of Nations' 416, 469–70, 560
SSSR/CCCP see Soviet Union (CCCP)
Stalin, Joseph 382, 383, 479, 618, 703, 710, 711, 719–20
  transformation of the USSR 706
Stalingrad 382, 710
Stalinism 233, 301, 382, 477, 478–9, 480, 703, 706–7, 710–15, 717, 719–20
  see also NKVD; Red Army
Stamford Bridge, Battle of 75
Stanford, Sir Charles Villiers 2, 658–9
Stanislas 141
Stanisław-August Poniatowski, king and grand-duke 285–6, 287, 289–90, 305–6
Stanisław, Feast of St 464
Stansgate, William Wedgwood-Benn, viscount 627–8
Stary Sącz 487

statehood 729, 738
  theories of the death of states 729–39
lo Statuto Albertino 416
Stefan Batory, king 278–9
Stefanyk Library, L'viv 487
Stefanyk, Vasyl 467
Steinbach, Erika 392
Stella, Erasmus 349–50
Stockholm 714, 715
Stoye, John 7
Strathclyde 71, 74–5, 76, 77, 78
  Kingdom of see Alt Clud, Kingdom of
    the Rock
Strauss, Johann II, 562
Stuart, Mary 39
Succat 51
Sudan 731
Sudetenland 625
Sudovians 338
Suevi 17, 18, 31
Suleiman the Magnificent 442
Sunningdale Agreement 669
Supreme Ruthenian Council (Holovna
    Ruska Rada) 470
Susi, Arnold 715
Suvorov, Alexander 289, 327, 505
Sveti Stefan 579
Svyatoslav 245
Sweden/Swedes 281–2, 283, 355, 361, 362,
    363, 368
Switzerland 112, 125, 138, 408, 409, 505
  and France 517
  and Sabaudia 409, 425–6
Syagrius 24
Sybel, Heinrich von 367
Szela, Jakub 456
Szeptycki, Andrzej 463

Talleyrand, Charles Maurice de Talleyrand-
    Périgord 506, 511, 515, 517, 536
Tallinn/Reval 339, 691–3, 696, 700–701,
    703, 705, 718, 722, 723
  Museum of Occupations 695
  National (previously Kruetzwald State)
    Library 720
Talorgen 64
Tarnowski, Jan 269
Tarnowski, Stanisław 465
Tarragona 181
Tartars 237, 251, 252, 254, 256, 260, 261,
    265, 268, 269
  Muslim Tartar cavalry 347
Tartu/Dorpat 259, 277, 691, 703, 713
  Tartu Treaty 705–6, 722
Taylor, A. J. P. 4–5, 7
Temperley, H. W. V. 608, 610

Tenew, queen of Lleddiniawn 55
Tennyson, Alfred, Lord 73–4, 589
Teodoricus, Flavius (Theodoric the
    Ostrogoth) 23–4, 25, 26
Teruel 190, 204
Tetmayer, Kazimierz 466
Teudebur map Beli 64
Teutonic Knights 247–8, 252, 253, 256,
    259, 270, 339–42, 350–51
  Teutonic Ordensstaat 340–44, 345–8,
    346, 351–3
Thatcher, Margaret 672
Thatcherism 683
Theodoric I (Theodorid) 18, 20–21
Theodoric II 18, 21–3
Theodoric the Ostrogoth (Flavius
    Teodoricus) 23–4, 25, 26
Theodosius, count 48
Theodosius, St 266
Theodosius I, emperor 46, 314
Theuderic II 102
Thirty Years War 280, 356, 358
Thomas Aquinas, St 730
Thorens, Château de 435
Thorismund 18, 21
Thorn 342, 349
  Treaty of 348, 350
Thun 121
  castle of 122
Thuringia 542
Tiananmen Square massacre 723
Tief, Otto 714
Tigernach, Irish Annals of 64
Tipperary 652
Tiso, Jozef 626
Titan Rain 697
Titles Deprivation Act 566–7
Tito, Josip Broz 614
Titograd 580
  see also Podgorica
Toledo 29
  Visigoth Kingdom of 28
Tolosa, city of Palladia Tolosa 18–20
Tolosa, Kingdom of 19, 18–31, 734
Tõnisson, Jaan 704, 709
Torino see Turin
Torquemada, Tomás de 218
Torrellas, Arbitration of 189
Tortosa 177
Tournus, abbey of 107
Traugutt, Romuald 296
Treason (Felony) Act 682
Trefusis, Violet (née Keppel) 499
Treitschke, Heinrich von 353, 367, 376
Trevor-Roper, Hugh 5
Trimble, David 674

Trinacria, Kingdom of 193, 194, 197
Troki 275
Troki, Isaac ben: *Hizzuq Emunah* 280
Trokiele 266
Trotsky, Leon 300, 702
troubadours 167, 172–3
True People's Party (Montenegro) 592
Trumbić, Ante 598–9, 604, 607
Tsernagora *see* Montenegro/Tsernagora
Tsukanov, Nikolay 335–6
Tully 643
Turbil, M. 426
Turin (Torino) 406, 407, 409, 415, 416, 417, 418–19, 429, 437
   Shroud 406, 409, 432
   Treaty of 423–5, 436
Turkish Ottomans *see* Ottomans
Turkmenistan 725
Tuscany 214, 422, 426, 501–3, 505, 506–8, 509, 515, 529, 534
   Etruria *see* Etruria
   Florence *see* Florence/Florentines
   and France 525, 526
   regiments 525
Tutagual 52, 57
Two Swords, doctrine of 122

Uberti 496
UDA (Ulster Defence Association) 669
UDR (Ulster Defence Regiment) 669
Ujejski, Kornel 462
Ukraine/Ukrainians 244, 251, 252, 260, 265, 267, 281, 282, 288, 368, 703, 706, 738
   Carpatho-Ukraine *see* Carpatho-Ukraine
   Cossacks *see* Cossacks
   'Ukrainian Awakening' 467
   Ukrainian Insurrectionary Army (UPA) 479
   West Ukraine/east Galicia 442, 450–51, 477, 478, 480, 481–3; *see also* Galicia; *Distrikt Galizien* 479; Halich 441–9
Ulcinj 579
Ulster 655, 656, 667–8, 676
   Annals of 52, 61, 69
   and the Northern Ireland 'Troubles' 667–9, 677, 679–80
   Plantation of 641
   Protestants 641, 650, 654, 660, 667–9, 674, 684
   Royal Ulster Constabulary 654, 666, 667, 668, 669
   Volunteers 645, 650, 656; *see also* Ulster Volunteer Force
Ulster Bank 677

Ulster Defence Association (UDA) 669
Ulster Defence Regiment (UDR) 669
Ulster Unionist Party (UUP) 641, 645, 650–51, 665, 666–7, 668, 673, 677, 678, 680, 681, 684
Ulster Volunteer Force (UVF) 668, 669
Uluots, Jüri 714
Umberto I *Il Buono* 429
Umberto II 400–401, 429, 431–2
Una Vincenzo, Lady Troubridge 499
Undaunted 530
Uniate (Greek Catholic) Church 237, 277, 295, 301, 463, 625
United Irishmen 642
United Kingdom 3, 41, 578, 641, 650, 666, 673, 732, 735
   disintegration of 6, 648, 679–85
   and the fate of the monarchy 681–2
   New Labour 680
   see also Britain
United Nations 577, 616
United Sich Riflemen 473, 474
United States of America
   and Albania 601
   and Charles Edward, duke of Saxe-Coburg and Gotha 569–70
   and Montenegro 596, 598, 601, 609, 611
   and the Nazis 569
   and Russia 727
   Russo-American START Treaty 335
   and the Soviet Union 715, 716, 724, 726
   World War II 710
Upper Burgundy 108, 110–15, 113, 118, 138, 147
Urban II 169
Urgell 162, 175, 181
Urien, king of Rheged 56–57
Urraca of Leon 170
Usatges de Barcelona 174
USSR *see* Soviet Union (CCCP)
Ustrzyki Dolne 479–80
Utrecht, Treaty of 223, 409
UVF (Ulster Volunteer Force) 668, 669
Uzbekistan 233, 721, 725
Uzhgorod 623, 624, 625, 627

Vagad, Gualberto Fabricio de 219
Vaino, Karl 717
Valdemar/Volodimir (Vladimir the Great) 245–6
Valdemar the Victorious 89
Valdensians/Vaudois 126, 408, 416
Valdo, Peter 126

Valencia 173, 176, 189–90, 221, 222–3, 225, 736
bishopric 181
Furs de Valencia ('Charters of Valencia') 190
pogrom 182
university 184
Valentinois 118
Vall d'Aran 159
Valladolid 210
Vallia 18
Vandals 17, 18, 22, 23, 31
VAPSI movement 709
Varangians *see* Vikings/Varangians
Varmia/Varmians 338, 342, 349
Vasari, Giorgio 213
Vatican Council II 671
Vaud, Pays de 404, 407
Grandson in the Vaud 138
Venel, General 600, 606
Venice 429, 739
Grimani Collection 481
Verdun, Treaty of 104, 106
Versailles settlement 380, 381, 382
Verulamium 46
Vesontio (Besançon) 95, 118
Vézelay, abbey of 108
Via Aquitania 19–20
Viareggio 534
Vic 173, 181
Victoria, queen 3, 83, 549–51, 554–5, 557, 558–9, 562, 643, 648
Victoria, princess royal, 'Vickie' 558
Victoria Adelaide of Schleswig-Holstein 566, 571
Victoria Maria Louisa of Saxe-Coburg and Gotha 546–7, 549–51, 556
Victoria, Damnonia 46
Victorius 19
Vidal de Besalú, Ramón 172
Vienna/Viennese
Congress of Vienna 294, 369, 412, 415, 420, 451, 533, 534, 536
and Galicia 452–3, 455–6, 470, 471, 734
museums 481
Ottoman Siege of Vienna 282, 364
Palais Coburg 559
Vienna Awards 625
Vienne 108
Colonia Julia Vienna 95, 97
Council of 200–201
counts of 127
Vigilantius 20
Vikings/Varangians 53, 66–9, 70, 72, 242, 738
invasion routes 67

Villiers, George 417
Vilna Martyrs 254
Vilna-Radom Act 256
Vilnius/Vilna//Wilno 238, 251–2, 255, 261, 266–7, 275, 280, 281, 289, 290, 291, 293, 298, 300, 301
Vincent of Saragossa, St 181
Vincent the Deacon, St 181
Vincentius 20
Vincenz, Stanisław 465
Vindogara 46
Visigoths 16–19, 26, 27–31
Kingdom of Toledo 28
Kingdom of Tolosa 18–31, 19
sacred art 29
Viskuli 303
Vistula 285, 344, 345, 349, 453
Vitebsk 249, 275, 277, 286, 291
Vittorio Amadeo II /Victor Amadeus II 409–10
Vittorio Amadeo III 411
Vittorio Emanuele I 415
Vittorio Emanuele II 416–17, 422, 424, 429
Vittorio Emanuele III 429, 430, 431, 593
Vittorio Emanuele IV 432–3
Vivarais 125
VKP (*Vsyesoyuznaya Kommunisticheskaya Partia*) 703
Vladimir the Great (Valdemar/Volodimir) 245–6
Vladimiri, Paulus 347–8
Vojtech of Prague (St Adalbert of Prussia) 337
Vojvodina 605
Volchin (Wolczyn) 306, 307
Volhynia 264, 270, 272
Volodymyr (Lodomeria) 450
and Galicia *see* Galicia: Kingdom of Galicia and Lodomeria
Volodymyr, Pan 441–2, 443, 445, 448
Voloshyn, Avgustyn 625, 626, 631, 633
Voltaire 280, 283, 285, 315, 419, 583
Votadini 46, 47
Vouillé 15, 25, 26
Voulon 26
Vsyesoyuznaya Kommunisticheskaya Partia (VKP) 703
Vyazma, fortress 268
Vytautas the Great 255–6, 260, 262

Wadowice 453
Waldensians *see* Valdensians/Vaudois
Wales/the Welsh 42–3, 684
Walewska, Maria 531, 533

Walewski, Alexander Florian Colonna- 533
Wallace, William 39, 79–80
Wallerstein, Immanuel 632
War of the Reapers 222
War of the Two Peters 207
Warhol, Andy 624
Warsaw 277, 289, 293, 296, 349,
    358, 361
  Battle of Praga 289
  creation of Duchy of 452
Washington, George 641–2
Waterloo, Battle of 533
Wawel Castle 306
Wedgwood-Benn, William 627–8
Wedgwood, Josiah 505
Wehlau, Treaty of 361, 364
Weigl, Rudolf 478
Weimar Republic 380, 567
Weiss, Leopold (Muhammad Asad) 478
Wells, H. G. 308
Welsh Annals 52, 68–9, 70
Wemyss Bay 38
Wessex 68, 72
West Francia 104, 106, 110, 115
Westphalia, Treaty of 132, 409
Weyden, Roger van der 135
Whitby 57
  Synod of 60
White Russia 291
White Ruthenia 249, 251, 254, 260, 265,
    267, 284–5, 291, 295
Whithorn 63
  Candida Casa 52
Widgery Report 677
Widsith 93
Wieniawa-Długoszowski, Bolesław 473
Wiesenthal, Simon 478
Wikileaks scandal 235
Wilde, Oscar 650
Wilfred the Hairy (Guifré El Pilós) 175,
    184, 224
Wilfrid, St 60
Wilhelm I 374, 376
Wilhelm II 377, 378, 379, 561, 562, 566,
    567
Wilhelm Gustloff 385, 386n
Willebad 103
Willets, Harry 8
William, duke of Cambridge 682
William III of Orange 641, 650–51
William IV 549, 551
William of Normandy 75
William of Toulouse 171
Wilno see Vilnius/Vilna//Wilno
Wilson, Woodrow 602, 607, 611, 618
Winch, Michael 628–31

Winckelmann, Johann Joachim 317
Windsors 566–7
  Mountbatten-Windsors 572
Winrich von Kniprode 341
Wiśniowiecki 272
Witos, Wincenty 477
Władysław II Jagiełło 347
Władysław III 256
Władysław IV Waza (Ladislas IV Vasa)
    278, 280
  court of 359
Wolfsschanze ('Wolf's Lair') 383
Wolowicz, Ostafi 271–2
women's rights (Ireland) 671–2
Wordsworth, William 739
World War I 377–80, 599–600
  Galicia 473–6
  and Germany 377–80, 474–5, 701,
    703
  and Italy 430
  and Lithuania 300
  and Russia 377–80, 701–2, 703
World War II
  Estonia 695, 710–15
  and the former Galicia 478–80
  and Germany 301–2, 382–6, 478–9,
    710, 712–14; see also Nazism
  Holocaust 302, 479, 480
  and Ireland 663–4
  and Lithuania 301–2
  Nazism see Nazism
  Operation Barbarossa 301–2, 382, 479,
    710
  and Prussia 382–6, 384
  and Sabaudia 436
  Soviet Union 301–2, 382–6, 478,
    479–80, 709–15
Worms
  Borbetomagus 93
  Concordat of 122
Wrocław 486–7
Wyspiański, Stanisław 466

X-Case 672

Yalta 710
Yantarny 334
Yaroslav the Wise 246, 253
Yeats, William Butler, 'Byzantium' 323–4
Yeltsin, Boris 721
York, Viking Kingdom of 68, 72
Young Poland (Młoda Polska) 466
Yrfai, son of Wulfsten 58, 59
Ystrad Clut 74
  see also Alt Clud, Kingdom of the Rock
Yugoslav Committee 598–9, 604

Yugoslavia 578, 580, 581, 597, 598,
       602–3, 605, 606, 610, 725
    after 1945 615
    Federal Republic of 577, 614, 615, 733
    Montenegro as part of 614–16
    wars of the 1990s 614–16, 619
Ywain map Dynfwal of Strathclyde (Owen
    of Cumbria) 72
Ywain of 'The Rock' 61

Zadowski, Stefan 356–8
Zagreb 604
Zähringen Castle 120
Zähringer 120–22
Zakarpattia see Carpatho-Ukraine
Zalesskaya Zemlya ('The Land beyond the
    Forest') 244
Zamora, San Pedro de la Nava 29

Zamoyski, Jan 279
Zamoyskis 275
Zaragoza 160, 162, 169, 170, 181,
    182, 184, 215, 224
Zebrzydowski Confederation 280
Zeleniogorsk 336
Zeta 588, 611
    see also Montenegro/Tsernagora
Zhdanov, Andrei 711
Zhirovice 266
Zhukov, Georgy 384
Zielence 288
Zionism 299
    'Hatikvah' 462
Zorka (daughter of Nikola I) 590
Zukor, Adolph 624
Zvitomir II, king of Croatia 430
Zygmunt III Waza see Sigismund III Vasa